# Lecture Notes in Computer Science 9363

Commenced Publication in 1973
Founding and Former Series Editors:
Gerhard Goos, Juris Hartmanis, and Jan van Leeuwen

## Advanced Research in Computing and Software Science

Subline of Lecture Notes in Computer Science

Yoram Moses (Ed.)

# Distributed Computing

29th International Symposium, DISC 2015
Tokyo, Japan, October 7–9, 2015
Proceedings

*Editor*
Yoram Moses
Technion
Haifa
Israel

ISSN 0302-9743         ISSN 1611-3349   (electronic)
Lecture Notes in Computer Science
ISBN 978-3-662-48652-8       ISBN 978-3-662-48653-5   (eBook)
DOI 10.1007/978-3-662-48653-5

Library of Congress Control Number: 2015952037

LNCS Sublibrary: SL1 – Theoretical Computer Science and General Issues

Printed on acid-free paper

Springer-Verlag GmbH Berlin Heidelberg is part of Springer Science+Business Media
(www.springer.com)

# Preface

DISC, the International Symposium on Distributed Computing, is an international forum on the theory, design, analysis, implementation, and application of distributed systems and networks. DISC is organized in cooperation with the European Association for Theoretical Computer Science (EATCS).

This volume contains the papers presented at DISC 2015, the 29th International Symposium on Distributed Computing, held during October 7–9, 2015, in Tokyo, Japan. The volume also includes the citation for the 2015 Edsger W. Dijkstra Prize in Distributed Computing, jointly sponsored by DISC and PODC (the ACM Symposium on Principles of Distributed Computing), which was presented at DISC 2015 in Tokyo to Michael Ben-Or and Michael Rabin, for initiating the field of fault-tolerant randomized distributed algorithms.

In total, 136 regular papers and seven brief announcements were submitted. The Program Committee selected 42 contributions out of the 136 submissions for regular presentations at the symposium. Each presentation was accompanied by a paper of up to 15 pages in this volume. Every submission was read and evaluated by at least three members of the Program Committee (PC). The committee was assisted by close to 100 external reviewers. This year preliminary reviews were sent to the authors for rebuttals that were used to inform the PC discussions. Following a two-week discussion period, the PC held a physical meeting in San Sebastian, Spain, on July 19, 2015, with some of the PC members participating electronically. Final consultations were held during the PODC conference, and notifications were sent out as PODC 2015 came to a close. Revised and expanded versions of several selected papers will be considered for publication in a special issue of the journal *Distributed Computing*. Some of the regular submissions that were rejected, but generated substantial interest among the members of the PC, were invited to be published as brief announcements. In total, 14 brief announcements appeared at DISC 2015. Each of the two-page brief announcements summarizes ongoing work or recent results, and it can be expected that these results will appear as full papers in later conferences or journals. Authors of additional papers were invited to present posters at the conference. Eight posters were presented at a special poster session during the conference. A list of the poster titles and authors appears at the end of this volume.

The Best Paper Award for DISC 2015 was presented to Rati Gelashvili for his paper "On the Optimal Space Complexity of Consensus for Anonymous Processes." The Best Student Paper was presented to Yuezhou Lv for his paper "Local Information in Influence Networks" together with Thomas Moscibroda.

The program featured two keynote talks, one presented by Thomas Moscibroda of Microsoft Research, Beijing, and the other by Michael Ben-Or of the Hebrew University (a co-recipient of the 2015 Dijkstra award). An abstract of the first invited lecture is included in these proceedings. Two workshops were co-located with the DISC symposium this year: the Workshop on Distributed Robotic Swarms (WRDS), organized by Paola Flocchini, Fukuhito Ooshita, and Yukiko Yamauchi, and the 4th Workshop on Advances on Distributed Graph Algorithms (ADGA) chaired by Keren Censor Hillel. WRDS was held on October 5 and ADGA on October 6. Two tutorials were presented on October 6: "Communication Complexity in Distributed Computing," by Rotem Oshman, and "Distributed Fault-Tolerant Runtime Verification" by Borzoo Bonakdarpour, Pierre Fraigniaud and Sergio Rajsbaum.

I wish to thank the many contributors to DISC 2015: The authors of the submitted papers, the PC members, who performed a huge and difficult job, the keynote speakers Thomas Moscibroda and Michael Ben-Or, the conference general chairs and local organizers led by the general chairs Toshimitsu Masuzawa and Koichi Wada for the great effort they put in, the publicity chairs Chen Avin and Tal Mizrahi, student fellowship chair Alessia Milani, the workshop organizers and tutorial speakers, the Steering Committee for its guidance, and especially the chair of the DISC Steering Committee Antonio Fernandez Anta.

August 2015                                                              Yoram Moses

# Organization

DISC, the International Symposium on Distributed Computing, is an annual forum for presentation of research on all aspects of distributed computing. It is organized in cooperation with the European Association for Theoretical Computer Science (EATCS). The symposium was established in 1985 as a biannual International Workshop on Distributed Algorithms on Graphs (WDAG). The scope was soon extended to cover all aspects of distributed algorithms and WDAG came to stand for International Workshop on Distributed AlGorithms, becoming an annual symposium in 1989. To reflect the expansion of its area of interest, the name was changed to DISC (International Symposium on Distributed Computing) in 1998, opening the symposium to all aspects of distributed computing. The aim of DISC is to reflect the exciting and rapid developments in this field.

## Program Committee Chair

Yoram Moses            Technion, Israel

## Program Committee

| | |
|---|---|
| Marcos K. Aguilera | VMware Research Group, USA |
| Dan Alistarh | Microsoft Research, UK |
| Lorenzo Alvisi | University of Texas, Austin, USA |
| Francois Bonnet | JAIST, Japan |
| Armando Castañeda | UNAM, Mexico |
| Gregory Chockler | Royal Holloway, University of London, UK |
| Xavier Defago | JAIST, Japan |
| Danny Dolev | The Hebrew University, Israel |
| Michael Elkin | Ben Gurion University, Israel |
| Nate Foster | Cornell University, USA |
| Pierre Fraigniaud | CNRS and University of Paris Diderot, France |
| Juan Garay | Yahoo Labs, USA |
| Cyril Gavoille | Bordeaux University, France |
| Maurice Herlihy | Brown University, USA |
| Taisuke Izumi | Nagoya Institute of Technology, Japan |
| Prasad Jayanti | Dartmouth College, USA |
| Amos Korman | CNRS and University of Paris Diderot, France |
| Petr Kuznetsov | Telecom ParisTech, France |
| Zvi Lotker | Ben-Gurion University, Israel |
| Nancy Lynch | MIT, USA |
| Maged Michael | IBM Research, USA |
| Adam Morrison | Technion, Israel |
| Achour Mostefaoui | University of Nantes, France |

| Danupon Nanongkai | KTH, Sweden |
| Rotem Oshman | Tel Aviv University, Israel |
| Noam Rinetzky | Tel Aviv University, Israel |
| Ulrich Schmid | Vienna University of Technology, Austria |
| Yukiko Yamauchi | Kyushu University, Japan |
| Haifeng Yu | National University of Singapore, Singapore |
| Moti Yung | Google, USA |

## Steering Committee

| Yehuda Afek | Tel Aviv University, Israel |
| Marcos K. Aguilera | VMware Research Group, USA |
| Keren Censor-Hillel | Technion, Israel |
| Shlomi Dolev | Ben-Gurion University, Israel |
| Antonio Fernandez Anta (Chair) | Inst. IMDEA Networks |
| Fabian Kuhn | University of Freiburg, Germany |
| Yoram Moses | Technion, Israel |
| Achour Mostefaoui | University of Nantes, France |

## Local Arrangements

| Chen Avin (Publicity) | Ben-Gurion University, Israel |
| Sayaka Kamei | Hiroshima University, Japan |
| Yoshiaki Katayama | Nagoya Institute of Technology, Japan |
| Yoshifumi Manabe | Kogakuin University, Japan |
| Toshimitsu Masuzawa (General Chair) | Osaka University, Japan |
| Alessia Milani (Student Fellowships) | LaBRI, Bordeaux, France |
| Tal Mizrahi (Publicity) | Technion, Israel |
| Fukuhito Ooshita | Nara Institute of Science and Technology, Japan |
| Yuichi Sudo | NTT Corporation, Japan |
| Koichi Wada (General Chair) | Hosei University, Japan |

## Additional Reviewers

| Manuel Alcantara | Leonid Barenboim | Shiri Chechik |
| Ei Ando | Edward Bortnikov | Sandro Coretti |
| Maya Arbel | Zohir Bouzid | Roberto Cortiñas |
| James Aspnes | Elette Boyle | Bruno Courcelle |
| Hagit Attiya | Viveck Cadambe | Artur Czumaj |
| Evangelos Bampas | Keren Censor-Hillel | Shantanu Das |

Sebastian Daum
Oksana Denysyuk
Aleksandar Dragojevic
Moez Draief
Faith Ellen
Matthias Függer
Leszek Gasieniec
Tingjian Ge
Rati Gelashvili
Konstantinos Georgiou
Mohsen Ghaffari
George Giakkoupis
Alexey Gotsman
Vassos Hadzilacos
Sandeep Hans
Danny Hendler
Kirsten Hildrum
Stephan Holzer
Swen Jacobs
Tomasz Jurdzinski
Christoph Lenzen
Mohsen Lesani
Sayaka Kamei
Yoshiaki Katayama
Shuji Kijima
Aniket Kate
Kishore Kothapalli

Fabian Kuhn
Alptekin Küpçü
Arnaud Labourel
Ori Lahav
Anissa Lamani
William Leiserson
Christoph Lenzen
Sidi Ahmed Mahmoudi
Toshimitsu Masuzawa
Alex Matveev
Moti Medina
Tal Mizrahi
Cameron Musco
Junya Nakamura
Emanuele Natale
Brahim Neggazi
Thomas Nowak
Fukuhito Ooshita
Oded Padon
Konstantinos Panagiotou
Gopal Pandurangan
Merav Parter
Francesco Pasquale
Boaz Patt-Shamir
Ami Paz
Paolo Penna
Matthieu Perrin

Dimitrios Prountzos
Tsvetomira Radeva
Sergio Rajsbaum
Peter Robinson
Liam Roditty
Alexander Spiegelman
Srikanth Sastry
Thomas Sauerwald
Stefan Schmid
Johannes Schneider
Ilya Sergey
Alexander Shraer
Manfred Schwarz
Mark Silberstein
Andreas Steininger
Hsin-Hao Su
Moshe Sulamy
He Sun
Yael Tauman Kalai
Jara Uitto
Viktor Vafeiadis
Marko Vukolic
Koichi Wada
Josef Widder
Kyrill Winkler

## Sponsoring Organizations

European Association
for
Theoretical Computer Science

HOSEI University

Osaka University

  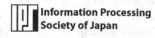

DISC 2015 acknowledges the use of the EasyChair system for handling submissions, managing the review process, and compiling these proceedings.

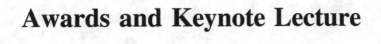

# Awards and Keynote Lecture

# The 2015 Edsger W. Dijkstra Prize in Distributed Computing

The E.W. Dijkstra Prize Committee decided to grant the 2015 Edsger W. Dijkstra Prize in Distributed Computing jointly to the following two papers:

- "Another Advantage of Free Choice: Completely Asynchronous Agreement Protocols," by Michael Ben-Or, published in the Proceedings of the Second ACM PODC conference, 1983.
- "Randomized Byzantine Generals," by Michael O. Rabin, published in the Proceedings of the 24th IEEE FOCS conference, 1983.

The prize is awarded for outstanding papers on the principles of distributed computing, whose significance and impact on the theory and/or practice of distributed computing have been evident for at least a decade. In these seminal papers, published in close succession in 1983, Michael Ben-Or and Michael O. Rabin started the field of fault-tolerant randomized distributed algorithms. In 1983, randomized algorithms, still in their infancy, were starting to make headway in sequential algorithms and complexity theory. The role of randomization at that time was to improve the complexity of solving certain problems. It was shown that problems, such as primality testing, that were deterministically solvable with a given time or space complexity, could be solved in less time or space by allowing the algorithm to make random choices. Ben-Or and Rabin were the first to use randomness to solve to a problem, consensus in an asynchronous distributed system subject to failures, which had provably no deterministic solution. In other words, they were addressing a computability question and not a complexity one, and the answer was far from obvious. Underlying both algorithms is the notion of a shared coin, i.e., a mechanism that enables separate processes to make a common random choice. Ben-Or's solution is fully distributed and relies on no assumptions, but requires a potentially exponential series of independent coin tosses to implement a shared coin. Rabin's solution uses cryptographic techniques to implement the shared coin in constant time. Ben-Or and Rabin's algorithms opened the way to a large body of work on randomized distributed algorithms in asynchronous systems, not only on consensus, but also on both theoretical problems, such as renaming, leader election, and snapshots, as well as applied topics, such as dynamic load balancing, work distribution, contention reduction, and coordination in concurrent data structures.

The E.W. Dijkstra Prize is sponsored jointly by the ACM Symposium on Principles of Distributed Computing (PODC) and the EATCS Symposium on Distributed Computing (DISC). The prize is presented annually, with the presentation taking place alternately at PODC and DISC. This year the prize was presented at DISC, in Tokyo, Japan, on October 8, 2015.

Dijkstra Prize Committee 2015:

| | |
|---|---|
| James Aspnes | Yale |
| Pierre Fraigniaud | University of Paris Diderot |
| Rachid Guerraoui | EPFL |
| Nancy Lynch | MIT |
| Yoram Moses | Technion |
| Paul Spirakis | University of Liverpool and CTI, Chair |

# The 2015 Doctoral Dissertation Award in Distributed Computing

The Doctoral Dissertation Award Committee awarded the Doctoral Dissertation Award in Distributed Computing 2015 to Dr. Leonid Barenboim. Dr. Barenboim completed his thesis on "Efficient Network Utilization in Locality-Sensitive Distributed Algorithms," in December 2013 under the supervision of Prof. Michael Elkin at Ben-Gurion University. Leonid's dissertation considers the LOCAL model, a distributed message passing model in which in $t$ time units, every node can learn the complete network topology up to distance $t$ from it. In this model, the challenge is to compute some global property of the network graph in significantly less time than it takes to propagate full information in the graph, that is, in time significantly less than the size or the diameter of the graph. This classic model captures the essence of graph locality issues in distributed network algorithms, and received much attention in the literature.

The dissertation studies several fundamental problems in this setting, including vertex coloring, edge coloring, maximal independent set, and network decomposition. For all of these problems, novel solutions are devised that significantly improve the best previously known results. In particular, it provides a substantial improvement to the problem of distributed coloring, one of the key problems to study symmetry breaking in networks. The dissertation addresses a challenge that has been open over two decades. In particular, it reduces the number of colors achieved in deterministic logarithmic coloring time from quadratic to essentially linear. It also demonstrates the first constant-time locality-sensitive solution for an NP-complete problem. These and other results advance our knowledge in nontrivial ways. The results are deep, technically challenging, and innovative.

The award is sponsored jointly by the ACM Symposium on Principles of Distributed Computing (PODC) and the EATCS Symposium on Distributed Computing (DISC). This award is presented annually, with the presentation taking place alternately at PODC and DISC. In 2015 it was presented at PODC, in Donostia/San Sebastián, Spain, July 21–23, 2015.

Distributed Computing Doctoral Dissertation Award Committee 2015:

| | |
|---|---|
| Shlomi Dolev | Ben-Gurion University |
| Fabian Kuhn | University of Freiburg |
| Dahlia Malkhi (Chair) | VMware Research |
| Philipp Woelfel | University of Calgary |

# DISC 2015 Invited Lecture:
# System Algorithms for the Cloud and Big Data

Thomas Moscibroda

Microsoft Research, Beijing, China

Cloud computing and big data are two industry-transforming paradigms that are changing the field of computing. Algorithms play a crucial role in both of these areas. Resource allocation, scheduling, and update algorithms are among the most important ingredients that determine how cost-efficiently and reliably cloud offerings can be operated; aggregation and query optimization algorithms largely determine how efficiently big data can be processed; complex distributed and parallel algorithms are used to achieve fault-tolerance and scalability. In all these (and many more) examples, advances in computing are relying on highly sophisticated algorithms and optimizations. At the same time, these algorithms rarely operate in environments that are "clean" and abstract, with easy-to-capture models and optimization functions. Instead, these *system algorithms* are typically characterized by a highly complex interplay between system design, underlying hardware features, and algorithms. In this talk, I discuss two examples of our recent system algorithmic work and show how the algorithms under discussion have impacted Microsoft's production systems, and how in turn the algorithm design has been impacted by the specific needs and constraints of these systems.

Global public cloud providers such as Amazon, Microsoft, or Google invest billions of dollars every year into their cloud infrastructure. Given the scale of these investments, it may be surprising that the actual utilization of many infrastructure resources is often low. At any point in time, the cumulative amount of entire data centers full of resources is wasted. I will discuss how different resource allocation algorithms in Azure address some of these inefficiencies, resulting in major reductions of operating costs.

Large-scale data-intensive computation has become an indispensable part of industrial cloud computing, and building appropriate system support and algorithms for efficiently analyzing massive amounts of data has become a key focus, both in industry and in the research community. For example, data volume within Microsoft nearly doubles every year and there are thousands of business-critical data analytics jobs running on hundreds of thousands of machines every day. Yet, while the amount of data and the number of production pipeline jobs grow exponentially, the number of machines cannot grow equally fast, resulting in new fundamental bottlenecks. IO-efficiency for data processing is one such bottleneck because data IO typically constitutes a significant fraction of the total query latency. In the second part of the talk, I discuss some of our algorithmic efforts to improve IO-efficiency of big data processing.

# Contents

# On the Computational Complexity of MapReduce

Benjamin Fish[1], Jeremy Kun[1(✉)], Ádám D. Lelkes[1], Lev Reyzin[1],
and György Turán[1,2]

[1] Department of Mathematics, Statistics, and Computer Science,
University of Illinois at Chicago, Chicago, IL 60607, USA
{bfish3,jkun2,alelke2,lreyzin,gyt}@uic.edu
[2] MTA-SZTE Research Group on Artificial Intelligence, Szeged, Hungary

**Abstract.** In this paper we study the MapReduce Class (MRC) defined by Karloff et al., which is a formal complexity-theoretic model of MapReduce. We show that constant-round MRC computations can decide regular languages and simulate sublogarithmic space-bounded Turing machines. In addition, we prove hierarchy theorems for MRC under certain complexity-theoretic assumptions. These theorems show that sufficiently increasing the number of rounds or the amount of time per processor strictly increases the computational power of MRC. Our work lays the foundation for further analysis relating MapReduce to established complexity classes. Our results also hold for Valiant's BSP model of parallel computation and the MPC model of Beame et al.

## 1 Introduction

MapReduce is a programming model originally developed to separate algorithm design from the engineering challenges of massively distributed computing. A programmer can separately implement a "map" function and a "reduce" function that satisfy certain constraints, and the underlying MapReduce technology handles all the communication, load balancing, fault tolerance, and scaling. MapReduce frameworks and their variants have been successfully deployed in industry by Google [4], Yahoo! [18], and many others.

MapReduce offers a unique and novel model of parallel computation because it alternates parallel and sequential steps, and imposes sharp constraints on communication and random access to the data. This distinguishes MapReduce from classical theoretical models of parallel computation and this, along with its popularity in industry, is a strong motivation to study the theoretical power of MapReduce. From a theoretical standpoint we ask how MapReduce relates to established complexity classes. From a practical standpoint we ask which problems can be efficiently modeled using MapReduce and which cannot.

In 2010 Karloff et al. [12] initiated a principled theoretical study of MapReduce, providing the definition of the complexity class MRC and comparing it with the classical PRAM models of parallel computing. But to our knowledge,

© Springer-Verlag Berlin Heidelberg 2015
Y. Moses (Ed.): DISC 2015, LNCS 9363, pp. 1–15, 2015.
DOI: 10.1007/978-3-662-48653-5_1

since this initial paper, almost all of the work on MapReduce has focused on algorithmic issues.

Complexity theory studies the classes of problems defined by resource bounds on different models of computation in which they are solved. A central goal of complexity theory is to understand the relationships between different models, i.e. to see if the problems solvable with bounded resources on one computational model can be solved with a related resource bound on a different model. In this paper we prove a result that establishes a connection between MapReduce and space-bounded computation on classical Turing machines. Another traditional question asked by complexity theory is whether increasing the resource bound on a certain computational resource strictly increases the set of solvable problems. Such so-called hierarchy theorems exist for time and space on deterministic and non-deterministic Turing machines, among other settings. In this paper we prove conditional hierarchy theorems for MapReduce rounds and time.

First we lay a more precise theoretical foundation for studying MapReduce computations (Section 3). In particular, we observe that Karloff et al.'s definitions are non-uniform, allowing the complexity class to contain undecidable languages. We reformulate the definition of [12] to make a uniform model and to more finely track the parameters involved (Section 3.2). In addition, we point out that our results hold for other important models of parallel computations, including Valiant's Bulk-Synchronous Processing (BSP) model [20] and the Massively Parallel Communication (MPC) model of Beame et al [2]. (Section 3.3). We then prove two main theorems: $SPACE(o(\log n))$ has constant-round MapReduce computations (Section 4) and, conditioned on a version of the Exponential Time Hypothesis, there are strict hierarchies within MRC. In particular, sufficiently increasing time or number of rounds increases the power of MRC (Section 5).

Our sub-logarithmic space result is achieved by a direct simulation, using a two-round protocol that localizes state-to-state transitions to the section of the input being simulated, combining the sections in the second round. It is a major open problem whether undirected graph connectivity (a canonical logarithmic-space problem) has a constant-round MapReduce algorithm, and our result is the most general that can be proven without a breakthrough on graph connectivity. Our hierarchy theorem involves proving a conditional time hierarchy within linear space achieved by a padding argument, along with proving a time-and-space upper and lower bounds on simulating MRC machines within P. To the best of our knowledge our hierarchy theorem is the first of its kind. We conclude with a discussion and open questions raised by our work (Section 6).

## 2   Background and Previous Work

### 2.1   MapReduce

The MapReduce protocol can be roughly described as follows. The input data is given as a list of key-value pairs, and over a series of rounds two things happen per round: a "mapper" is applied to each key-value pair independently (in parallel), and then for each distinct key a "reducer" is applied to all corresponding values for a group of keys. The canonical example is counting word frequencies with a two-round MapReduce protocol. The inputs are (index, word) pairs, the first mapper maps $(k, v) \mapsto (v, k)$, and the first reducer computes the sum of the word frequencies for the given key. In the second round the mapper sends all data to a single processor via $(k, n_k) \mapsto (1, (k, n_k))$, and the second processor formats the output appropriately.

One of the primary challenges in MapReduce is data locality. MapReduce was designed for processing massive data sets, so MapReduce programs require that every reducer only has access to a substantially sublinear portion of the input, and the strict modularization prohibits reducers from communicating within a round. All communication happens indirectly through mappers, which are limited in power by the independence requirement. Finally, it's understood in practice that a critical quantity to optimize for is the number of rounds [12], so algorithms which cannot avoid a large number of rounds are considered inefficient and unsuitable for MapReduce.

There are a number of MapReduce-like models in the literature, including the MRC model of Karloff et al. [12], the "mud" algorithms of Feldman et al. [6], Valiant's BSP model [20], the MPC model of Beame et al. [2], and extensions or generalizations of these, e.g. [8]. The MRC class of Karloff et al. is the closest to existing MapReduce computations, and is also among the most restrictive in terms of how it handles communication and tracks the computational power of individual processors. In their influential paper [12], Karloff et al. display the algorithmic power of MRC, and prove that MapReduce algorithms can simulate CREW PRAMs which use subquadratic total memory and processors. It is worth noting that the work of Karloff et al. did not include comparisons to the standard (non-parallel) complexity classes, which is the aim of the present work.

Since [12], there has been extensive work in developing efficient algorithms in MapReduce-like frameworks. For example, Kumar et al. [13] analyze a sampling technique allowing them to translate sequential greedy algorithms into log-round MapReduce algorithms with a small loss of quality. Farahat et al. [5] investigate the potential for sparsifying distributed data using random projections. Kamara and Raykova [11] develop a homomorphic encryption scheme for MapReduce. And much work has been done on graph problems such as connectivity, matchings, sorting, and searching [8]. Chu et al. [3] demonstrate the potential to express any statistical-query learning algorithm in MapReduce. Finally, Sarma et al. [16] explore the relationship between communication costs and the degree to which a computation is parallel in one-round MapReduce problems. Many of these papers pose general upper and lower bounds on MapReduce computations as an open problem, and to the best of our knowledge our results are the first to do so with classical complexity classes.

The study of MapReduce has resulted in a wealth of new and novel algorithms, many of which run faster than their counterparts in classical PRAM models. As such, a more detailed study of the theoretical power of MapReduce is warranted. Our paper contributes to this by establishing a more precise definition of the

MapReduce complexity class, proving that it contains sublogarithmic deterministic space, and showing the existence of certain kinds of hierarchies.

## 2.2  Complexity

From a complexity-theory viewpoint, MapReduce is unique in that it combines bounds on time, space and communication. Each of these bounds would be very weak on its own: the total time available to processors is polynomial; the total space and communication are slightly less than quadratic. In particular, even though arranging the communication between processors is one of the most difficult parts of designing MapReduce algorithms, classical results from communication complexity do not apply since the total communication available is more than linear. These innocent-looking bounds lead to serious restrictions when combined, as demonstrated by the fact that it is unknown whether constant-round MRC machines can decide graph connectivity (the best known result achieves a logarithmic number of rounds with high probability [12]), although it is solvable using only logarithmic space on a deterministic Turing machine.

We relate the MRC model to more classical complexity classes by studying simultaneous time-space bounds. $\text{TISP}(T(n), S(n))$ are the problems that can be decided by a Turing machine which on inputs of length $n$ takes at most $O(T(n))$ time and uses at most $O(S(n))$ space. Note that in general it is believed that $\text{TISP}(T(n), S(n)) \neq \text{TIME}(T(n)) \cap \text{SPACE}(S(n))$. The complexity class TISP is studied in the context of time-space tradeoffs (see, for example, [7,22]). Unfortunately much less is known about TISP than about TIME or SPACE; for example there is no known time hierarchy theorem for fixed space. The existence of such a hierarchy is mentioned as an open problem in the monograph of Wagner and Wechsung [21].

To prove the results about TISP that imply the existence of a hierarchy in MRC, we use the Exponential Time Hypothesis (ETH) introduced by Impagliazzo, Paturi, and Zane [9,10], which conjectures that 3-SAT is not in $\text{TIME}(2^{cn})$ for some $c > 0$. This hypothesis and its strong version have been used to prove conditional lower bounds for specific hard problems like vertex cover, and for algorithms in the context of fixed parameter tractability (see, e.g., the survey of Lokshtanov, Marx and Saurabh [14]). The first open problem mentioned in [14] is to relate ETH to some other known complexity theoretic hypotheses.

We show in Lemma 1 that ETH implies directly a time-space trade-off statement involving time-space complexity classes. This statement is not a well-known complexity theoretic hypothesis, although it is related to the existence of a time hierarchy with a fixed space bound. In fact, as detailed in Section 5, a hypothesis weaker than ETH is sufficient for the lemma. The relative strengths of ETH, the weaker hypothesis, and the statement of the lemma seem to be unknown.

## 3  Models

In this section we introduce the model we will use in this paper, a uniform version of Karloff's MapReduce Class (MRC), and contrast MRC to other models of parallel computation, such as Valiant's Bulk-Synchronous Parallel (BSP) model, for which our results also hold.

## 3.1  MapReduce and MRC

The central piece of data in MRC is the key-value pair, which we denote by a pair of strings $\langle k, v \rangle$, where $k$ is the key and $v$ is the value. An input to an MRC machine is a list of key-value pairs $\langle k_i, v_i \rangle_{i=1}^N$ with a total size of $n = \sum_{i=1}^N |k_i| + |v_i|$. The definitions in this subsection are adapted from [12].

**Definition 1.** *A mapper $\mu$ is a Turing machine[1] which accepts as input a single key-value pair $\langle k, v \rangle$ and produces a list of key-value pairs $\langle k'_1, v'_1 \rangle, \ldots, \langle k'_s, v'_s \rangle$.*

**Definition 2.** *A reducer $\rho$ is a Turing machine which accepts as input a key $k$ and a list of values $\langle v_1, \ldots, v_m \rangle$, and produces as output the same key and a new list of values $\langle v'_1, \ldots, v'_M \rangle$.*

**Definition 3.** *For a decision problem, an input string $x \in \{0, 1\}^*$ to an MRC machine is the list of pairs $\langle i, x_i \rangle_{i=1}^n$ describing the index and value of each bit. We will denote by $\langle x \rangle$ the list $\langle i, x_i \rangle$.*

An MRC machine operates in rounds. In each round, a set of mappers running in parallel first process all the key-value pairs. Then the pairs are partitioned (by a mechanism called "shuffle and sort" that is not considered part of the runtime of an MRC machine) so that each reducer only receives key-value pairs for a single key. Then the reducers process their data in parallel, and the results are merged to form the list of key-value pairs for the next round. More formally:

**Definition 4.** *An $R$-round MRC machine is an alternating list of mappers and reducers $M = (\mu_1, \rho_1, \ldots, \mu_R, \rho_R)$. The execution of the machine is as follows. For each $r = 1, \ldots, R$:*

1. *Let $U_{r-1}$ be the list of key-value pairs generated by round $r - 1$ (or the input pairs when $r = 1$). Apply $\mu_r$ to each key-value pair of $U_{r-1}$ to get the multiset $V_r = \bigcup_{\langle k,v \rangle \in U_{r-1}} \mu_r(k, v)$.*
2. *Shuffle-and-sort groups the values by key. Call each of the pieces $V_{k,r} = \{k, (v_{k,1}, \ldots, v_{k,s_k})\}$.*
3. *Assign a different copy of reducer $\rho_r$ to each $V_{k,r}$ (run in parallel) and set $U_r = \bigcup_k \rho_r(V_{k,r})$.*

The output is the final set of key-value pairs. For decision problems, we define $M$ to accept $\langle x \rangle$ if in the final round $U_R = \emptyset$. Equivalently we may give each reducer a special accept state and say the machine accepts if at any time any reducer enters the accept state. We say $M$ *decides* a language $L$ if it accepts $\langle x \rangle$ if and only if $x \in L$.

---

[1] The definitions of [12] were for RAMs. However, because we wish to relate MapReduce to classical complexity classes, we reformulate the definitions here in terms of Turing machines.

The central caveat that makes MRC an interesting class is that the reducers have space constraints that are sublinear in the size of the input string. In other words, no sequential computation may happen that has random access to the entire input. Thinking of the reducers as processors, cooperation between reducers is obtained not by message passing or shared memory, but rather across rounds in which there is a global communication step.

In the MRC model we use in this paper, we require that every mapper and reducer arise as separate runs of the same Turing machine $M$. Our Turing machine $M(m, r, n, y)$ will accept as input the current round number $r$, a bit $m$ denoting whether to run the $r$-th map or reduce function, the total input size $n$, and the corresponding input $y$. Equivalently, we can imagine a list of mappers and reducers in each round $\mu_1, \rho_1, \mu_2, \rho_2, \ldots$, where the descriptions of the $\mu_i, \rho_i$ are computable in polynomial time in $|i|$.

**Definition 5 (Uniform Deterministic MRC).** *A language $L$ is said to be in* $\mathrm{MRC}[f(n), g(n)]$ *if there is a constant $0 < c < 1$, an $O(n^c)$-space and $O(g(n))$-time Turing machine $M(m, r, n, y)$, and an $R = O(f(n))$, such that for all $x \in \{0, 1\}^n$, the following holds.*

1. *Letting $\mu_r = M(1, r, n, -), \rho_r = M(0, r, n, -)$, the MRC machine $M_R = (\mu_1, \rho_1, \ldots, \mu_R, \rho_R)$ accepts $x$ if and only if $x \in L$.*
2. *Each $\mu_r$ outputs $O(n^c)$ distinct keys.*

This definition closely hews to practical MapReduce computations: $f(n)$ represents the number of times global communication has to be performed, $g(n)$ represents the time each processor gets, and sublinear space bounds in terms of $n = |x|$ ensure that the size of the data on each processor is smaller than the full input.

*Remark 1.* By $M(1, r, n, -)$, we mean that the tape of $M$ is initialized by the string $\langle 1, r, n \rangle$. In particular, this prohibits an MRC algorithm from having $2^{\Omega(n)}$ rounds; the space constraints would prohibit it from storing the round number.

*Remark 2.* Note that a polynomial time Turing machine with sufficient time can trivially simulate a uniform MRC machine. All that is required is for the machine to perform the key grouping manually, and run the MRC machine as a subroutine. As such, $\mathrm{MRC}[\mathrm{poly}(n), \mathrm{poly}(n)] \subseteq P$. We give a more precise computation of the amount of overhead required in the proof of Lemma 2.

**Definition 6.** *Define by $\mathrm{MRC}^i$ the union of uniform MRC classes*

$$\mathrm{MRC}^i = \bigcup_{k \in \mathbb{N}} \mathrm{MRC}[\log^i(n), n^k].$$

So in particular $\mathrm{MRC}^0 = \bigcup_{k \in \mathbb{N}} \mathrm{MRC}[1, n^k]$.

## 3.2   Nonuniformity

A complexity class is generally called uniform if the descriptions of the machines solving problems in it do not depend on the input length. Classical complexity classes defined by Turing machines with resource bounds, such as P, NP, and SPACE($\log(n)$), are uniform. On the other hand, circuit complexity classes are naturally nonuniform since a fixed Boolean circuit can only accept inputs of a single length. There is ambiguity about the uniformity of MRC as defined in [12]. Since we wish to relate the MRC model to classical complexity classes such as P and SPACE($\log(n)$), making sure that the model is uniform is crucial. Indeed, innocuous-seeming changes to the definitions above introduce nonuniformity (and in particular this is true of the original MRC definition in [12]). In the appendix we show that the nonuniform MRC model defined in [12] allows MRC machines to solve undecidable problems in a logarithmic number of rounds, including the halting problem. We introduced our uniform version of MRC above to rule out such pathological behavior.

## 3.3   Other Models of Parallel Computation

Several other models of parallel computation have been introduced, including the BSP model of Valiant [20] and the MPC model of Beame et. al. [2]. The main difference between BSP and MapReduce is that in the BSP models the key-value pairs and the shuffling steps needed to redistribute them are replaced with point-to-point messages. Similarly to [12], in Valiant's paper [20] there is also ambiguity about the uniformity of the model. In this paper, when we refer to BSP we mean a uniform deterministic version of the model. We give the exact definition in the appendix.

Goodrich et al. [8] and Pace [15] showed that MapReduce computations can be simulated in the BSP model and vice versa, with only a constant blow-up in the computational resources needed. This implies that our theorems about MapReduce automatically apply to BSP.

Similarly, the MPC model uses point-to-point messages and Beame et. al.'s paper [2] does not discuss the uniformity of the model. The main distinguishing charateristic of the MPC model is that it introduces the number of processors $p$ as an explicit paramter. Setting $p = O(n^c)$, our results will also hold in this model.

There are other variants of these models, including the model that Andoni et. al. [1] uses, which follows the MPC model but also introduces the additional constraint that total space used across each round must be no more than $O(n)$. It is straightforward to check that the proofs of our results never use more than $O(n)$ space, implying that our results hold even under this more restrictive model.

## 4   Space Complexity Classes in MRC$^0$

In this section we prove that small space classes are contained in constant-round MRC. Again, the results in this section also hold for other similar models of parallel computation, including the BSP model and the MPC model. First, we prove that the class REGULAR of regular languages is in $MRC^0$. It is well known that $SPACE(O(1)) = REGULAR$ [17], and so this result can be viewed as a warm-up to the theorem that $SPACE(o(\log n)) \subseteq MRC^0$. Indeed, both proofs share the same flavor, which we sketch before proceeding to the details.

We wish to show that any given DFA can be simulated by an $MRC^0$ machine. The simulation works as follows: in the first round each parallel processor receives a contiguous portion of the input string and constructs a state transition function using the data of the globally known DFA. Though only the processor with the beginning of the string knows the true state of the machine during its portion of the input, all processors can still compute the *entire* table of state-to-state transitions for the given portion of input. In the second round, one processor collects the transition tables and chains together the computations, and this step requires only the first bit of input and the list of tables.

We can count up the space and time requirements to prove the following theorem.

**Theorem 1.** REGULAR $\subsetneq MRC^0$

*Proof.* Let $L$ be a regular language and $D$ a deterministic finite automaton recognizing $L$. Define the first mapper so that the $j^{\text{th}}$ processor has the bits from $j\sqrt{n}$ to $(j + 1)\sqrt{n}$. This means we have $K = O(\sqrt{n})$ processors in the first round. Because the description of $D$ is independent of the size of the input string, we also assume each processor has access to the relevant set of states $S$ and the transition function $t : S \times \{0, 1\} \to S$.

We now define $\rho_1$. Fix a processor $j$ and call its portion of the input $y$. The processor constructs a table $T_j$ of size at most $|S|^2 = O(1)$ by simulating $D$ on $y$ starting from all possible states and recording the state at the end of the simulation. It then passes $T_j$ and the first bit of $y$ to the single processor in the second round.

In the second round the sole processor has $K$ tables $T_j$ and the first bit $x_1$ of the input string $x$ (among others but these are ignored). Treating $T_j$ as a function, this processor computes $q = T_K(\ldots T_2(T_1(x_1)))$ and accepts if and only if $q$ is an accepting state. This requires $O(\sqrt{n})$ space and time and proves containment. To show this is strict, inspect the prototypical problem of deciding whether the majority of bits in the input are 1's.

*Remark 3.* While the definition of $MRC^0$ inclues languages with time complexity $O(n^k)$ for all $k \geq 0$, our Theorem 1 is more efficient than the definition implies: we show that regular languages can be computed in $MRC^0$ in time and space $O(\sqrt{n})$, with the option of a tradeoff between time $n^\varepsilon$ and space $n^{1-\varepsilon}$.

One specific application of this result is that for any given regular expression, a two-round MapReduce computation can decide if a string matches that regular expression, even if the string is so long that any one machine can only store $n^\epsilon$ bits of it.

We now move on to prove SPACE($o(\log n)$) $\subseteq$ MRC$^0$. It is worth noting that this is a strictly stronger statement than Theorem 1. That is, REGULAR = SPACE($O(1)$) $\subsetneq$ SPACE($o(\log n)$). Several non-trivial examples of languages that witness the strictness of this containment are given in [19].

The proof is very similar to the proof of Theorem 1: Instead of the processors computing the entire table of state-to-state transitions of a DFA, the processors now compute the entire table of all transitions possible among the configurations of the work tape of a Turing machine that uses $o(\log n)$ space.

**Theorem 2.** SPACE($o(\log n)$) $\subseteq$ MRC$^0$.

*Proof.* Let $L$ be a language in SPACE($o(\log n)$) and $T$ a Turing machine recognizing $L$ in polynomial time and $o(\log(n))$ space, with a read/write work tape $W$. Define the first mapper so that the $j^{\text{th}}$ processor has the bits from $j\sqrt{n}$ to $(j+1)\sqrt{n}$. Let $\mathcal{C}$ be the set of all possible configurations of $W$ and let $S$ be the states of $T$. Since the size of $S$ is independent of the input, we can assume that each processor has the transition function of $T$ stored on it.

Now we define $\rho_1$ as follows: Each processor $j$ constructs the graph of a function $T_j : \mathcal{C} \times \{L, R\} \times S \rightarrow \mathcal{C} \times \{L, R\} \times S$, which simulates $T$ when the read head starts on either the left or right side of the $j$th $\sqrt{n}$ bits of the input and $W$ is in some configuration from $\mathcal{C}$. It outputs whether the read head leaves the $y$ portion of the read tape on the left side, the right side, or else accepts or rejects. To compute the graph of $T_j$, processor $j$ simulates $T$ using its transition function, which takes polynomial time.

Next we show that the graph of $T_j$ can be stored on processor $j$ by showing it can be stored in $O(\sqrt{n})$ space. Since $W$ is by assumption size $o(\log n)$, each entry of the table is $o(\log n)$, so there are $2^{o(\log n)}$ possible configurations for the tape symbols. There are also $o(\log n)$ possible positions for the read/write head, and a constant number of states $T$ could be in. Hence $|\mathcal{C}| = 2^{o(\log n)}o(\log n) = o(n^{1/3})$. Then processor $j$ can store the graph of $T_j$ as a table of size $O(n^{1/3})$.

The second map function $\mu_2$ sends each $T_j$ (there are $\sqrt{n}$ of them) to a single processor. Each is size $O(n^{1/3})$, and there are $\sqrt{n}$ of them, so a single processor can store all the tables. Using these tables, the final reduce function can now simulate $T$ from starting state to either the accept or reject state by computing $q = T_k^*(\ldots T_2^*(T_1^*(\emptyset, L, initial)))$ for some $k$, where $\emptyset$ denotes the initial configuration of $T$, $initial$ is the initial state of $T$, and $q$ is either in the accept or reject state. Note $T_j^*$ is the modification of $T_j$ such that if $T_j(x)$ outputs $L$, then $T_j^*(x)$ outputs $R$ and vice versa. This is necessary because if the read head leaves the $j^{\text{th}}$ $\sqrt{n}$ bits to the right, it enters the $j+1^{\text{th}}$ $\sqrt{n}$ bits from the left, and vice versa. Finally, the reducer accepts if and only if $q$ is in an accept state.

This algorithm successfully simulates $T$, which decides $L$, and only takes a constant number of rounds, proving containment.

## 5   Hierarchy Theorems

In this section we prove two main results (Theorems 3 and 4) about hierarchies within MRC relating to increases in time and rounds. They imply that allowing MRC machines sufficiently more time or rounds strictly increases the computing power of the machines. The first theorem states that for all $\alpha, \beta$ there are problems $L \notin \mathrm{MRC}[n^\alpha, n^\beta]$ which can be decided by *constant time* MRC machines when given enough extra rounds.

**Theorem 3.** *Suppose the ETH holds with constant c. Then for every $\alpha, \beta \in \mathbb{N}$ there exists a $\gamma = O(\alpha + \beta)$ such that*

$$\mathrm{MRC}[n^\gamma, 1] \not\subseteq \mathrm{MRC}[n^\alpha, n^\beta].$$

The second theorem is analogous for time, and says that there are problems $L \notin \mathrm{MRC}[n^\alpha, n^\beta]$ that can be decided by a *one round* MRC machine given enough extra time.

**Theorem 4.** *Suppose the ETH holds with constant c. Then for every $\alpha, \beta \in \mathbb{N}$ there exists a $\gamma = O(\alpha + \beta)$ such that*

$$\mathrm{MRC}[1, n^\gamma] \not\subseteq \mathrm{MRC}[n^\alpha, n^\beta].$$

As both of these theorems depend on the ETH, we first prove a complexity-theoretic lemma that uses the ETH to give a time-hierarchy within linear space TISP. Recall that TISP is the complexity class defined by simultaneous time and space bounds. The lemma can also be described as a time-space tradeoff. For some $b > a$ we prove the existence of a language that can be decided by a Turing machine with simultaneous $O(n^b)$ time and linear space, but cannot be decided by a Turing machine in time $O(n^a)$ even without any space restrictions. It is widely believed such languages exist for *exponential* time classes (for example, TQBF, the language of true quantified Boolean formulas, is a linear space language which is PSPACE-complete). We ask whether such tradeoffs can be extended to polynomial time classes, and this lemma shows that indeed this is the case.

**Lemma 1.** *Suppose that the ETH holds with constant c. Then for any positive integer a there exists a positive integer $b > a$ such that*

$$\mathrm{TIME}(n^a) \not\subseteq \mathrm{TISP}(n^b, n).$$

*Proof.* By the ETH, 3-SAT $\in \mathrm{TISP}(2^n, n) \setminus \mathrm{TIME}(2^{cn})$. Let $b := \lceil \frac{a}{c} \rceil + 2$, $\delta := \frac{1}{2}(\frac{1}{b} + \frac{c}{a})$. Pad 3-SAT with $2^{\delta n}$ zeros and call this language $L$, i.e. let $L := \{x0^{2^{\delta|x|}} \mid x \in \text{3-SAT}\}$. Let $N := n + 2^{\delta n}$. Then $L \in \mathrm{TISP}(N^b, N)$ since $N^b > 2^n$. On the other hand, assume for contradiction that $L \in \mathrm{TIME}(N^a)$. Then, since $N^a < 2^{cn}$, it follows that 3-SAT $\in \mathrm{TIME}(2^{cn})$, contradicting the ETH.

There are a few interesting complexity-theoretic remarks about the above proof. First, the starting language does not need to be 3-SAT, as the only assumption we needed was its hypothesized time lower bound. We could relax the assumption to the hypothesis that there exists a $c > 0$ such that TQBF, the PSPACE-complete language of true quantified Boolean formulas, requires $2^{cn}$ time, or further still to the following complexity hypothesis.

*Conjecture 1.* There exist $c', c$ satisfying $0 < c' < c < 1$ such that $\mathrm{TISP}(2^n, 2^{c'n}) \setminus \mathrm{TIME}(2^{cn}) \neq \emptyset$.

Second, since $\mathrm{TISP}(n^a, n) \subseteq \mathrm{TIME}(n^a)$, this conditionally proves the existence of a hierarchy within $\mathrm{TISP}(\mathrm{poly}(n), n)$. We note that finding time hierarchies in fixed-space complexity classes was posed as an open question by [21], and so removing the hypothesis or replacing it with a weaker one is an interesting open problem.

Using this lemma we can prove Theorems 3 and 4. The proof of Theorem 3 depends on the following lemma.

**Lemma 2.** *For every $\alpha, \beta \in \mathbb{N}$ the following holds:*

$$\mathrm{TISP}(n^\alpha, n) \subseteq \mathrm{MRC}[n^\alpha, 1] \subseteq \mathrm{MRC}[n^\alpha, n^\beta] \subseteq \mathrm{TISP}(n^{\alpha+\beta+2}, n^2).$$

*Proof.* The first inequality follows from a simulation argument similar to the proof of Theorem 2. The MRC machine will simulate the $\mathrm{TISP}(n^\alpha, n)$ machine by making one step per round, with the tape (including the possible extra space needed on the work tape) distributed among the processors. The position of the tape is passed between the processors from round to round. It takes constant time to simulate one step of the $\mathrm{TISP}(n^\alpha, n)$ machine, thus in $n^\alpha$ rounds we can simulate all steps. Also, since the machine uses only linear space, the simulation can be done with $O(\sqrt{n})$ processors using $O(\sqrt{n})$ space each. The second inequality is trivial.

The third inequality is proven as follows. Let $T(n) = n^{\alpha+\beta+2}$. We first show that any language in $\mathrm{MRC}[n^\alpha, n^\beta]$ can be simulated in time $O(T(n))$, i.e. $\mathrm{MRC}[n^\alpha, n^\beta] \subseteq \mathrm{TIME}(T(n))$. The $r$-th round is simulated by applying $\mu_r$ to each key-value pair in sequence, shuffle-and-sorting the new key-value pairs, and then applying $\rho_r$ to each appropriate group of key-value pairs sequentially. Indeed, $M(m, r, n, -)$ can be simulated naturally by keeping track of $m$ and $r$, and adding $n$ to the tape at the beginning of the simulation. Each application of $\mu_r$ takes $O(n^\beta)$ time, for a total of $O(n^{\beta+1})$ time. Since each mapper outputs no more than $O(n^c)$ keys, and each mapper and reducer is in $\mathrm{SPACE}(O(n^c))$, there are no more than $O(n^2)$ keys to sort. Then shuffle-and-sorting takes $O(n^2 \log n)$ time, and the applications of $\rho_r$ also take $O(n^{\beta+1})$ time. So a round takes $O(n^{\beta+1} + n^2 \log n)$ time. Note that keeping track of $m,r$, and $n$ takes no more than the above time. So over $O(n^\alpha)$ rounds, the simulation takes $O(n^{\alpha+\beta+1} + n^{\alpha+2} \log(n)) = O(T(n))$ time.

Now we prove Theorem 3.

*Proof.* By Lemma 1, there is a language $L$ in $\text{TISP}(n^\gamma, n) \setminus \text{TIME}(n^{\alpha+\beta+2})$ for some $\gamma$. By Lemma 2, $L \in \text{MRC}[n^\gamma, 1]$. On the other hand, because $L \notin \text{TIME}(n^{\alpha+\beta+2})$ and $\text{MRC}[n^\alpha, n^\beta] \subseteq \text{TIME}(n^{\alpha+\beta+2})$, we can conclude that $L \notin \text{MRC}[n^\alpha, n^\beta]$.

Next, we prove Theorem 4 using a padding argument.

*Proof.* Let $T(n) = n^{\alpha+\beta+2}$ as in Lemma 2. By Lemma 1, there is a $\gamma$ such that $\text{TISP}(n^\gamma, n) \setminus \text{TIME}(T(n^2))$ is nonempty. Let $L$ be a language from this set. Pad $L$ with $n^2$ zeros, and call this new language $L'$, i.e. let $L' = \{x0^{|x|^2} \mid x \in L\}$. Let $N = n + n^2$. There is an $\text{MRC}[1, N^\gamma]$ algorithm to decide $L'$: the first mapper discards all the key-value pairs except those in the first $n$, and sends all remaining pairs to a single reducer. The space consumed by all pairs is $O(n) = O(\sqrt{N})$. This reducer decides $L$, which is possible since $L \in \text{TISP}(n^\gamma, n)$. We now claim $L'$ is not in $\text{MRC}[N^\alpha, N^\beta]$. If it were, then $L'$ would be in $\text{TIME}(T(N))$. A Turing machine that decides $L'$ in $T(N)$ time can be modified to decide $L$ in $T(N)$ time: pad the input string with $n^2$ ones and use the decider for $L'$. This shows $L$ is in $\text{TIME}(T(n^2))$, a contradiction.

We conclude by noting explicitly that Theorems 3, 4 give proper hierarchies within MRC, and that proving certain stronger hierarchies imply the separation of L and P.

**Corollary 1.** *Suppose the ETH. For every $\alpha, \beta$ there exist $\mu > \alpha$ and $\nu > \beta$ such that*
$$\text{MRC}[n^\alpha, n^\beta] \subsetneq \text{MRC}[n^\mu, n^\beta]$$
*and*
$$\text{MRC}[n^\alpha, n^\beta] \subsetneq \text{MRC}[n^\alpha, n^\nu].$$

*Proof.* By Theorem 4, there is some $\mu > \alpha$ such that $\text{MRC}[n^\mu, 1] \not\subseteq \text{MRC}[n^\alpha, n^\beta]$. It is immediate that $\text{MRC}[n^\alpha, n^\beta] \subseteq \text{MRC}[n^\mu, n^\beta]$ and also that $\text{MRC}[n^\mu, 1] \subseteq \text{MRC}[n^\mu, n^\beta]$. So $\text{MRC}[n^\alpha, n^\beta] \neq \text{MRC}[n^\mu, n^\beta]$. The proof of the second claim is similar.

**Corollary 2.** *If $\text{MRC}[\text{poly}(n), 1] \subsetneq \text{MRC}[\text{poly}(n), \text{poly}(n)]$, then it follows that $\text{SPACE}(\log(n)) \neq \text{P}$.*

*Proof.*
$$\text{SPACE}(\log(n)) \subseteq \text{TISP}(\text{poly}(n), \log n) \subseteq \text{TISP}(\text{poly}(n), n) \subseteq \text{MRC}[\text{poly}(n), 1]$$
$$\subseteq \text{MRC}[\text{poly}(n), \text{poly}(n)] \subseteq \text{P}.$$

The first containment is well known, the third follows from Lemma 2, and the rest are trivial.

Corollary 2 is interesting because if any of the containments in the proof are shown to be proper, then $\text{SPACE}(\log(n)) \neq \text{P}$. Moreover, if we provide MRC with a polynomial number of rounds, Corollary 2 says that determining whether time provides substantially more power is at least as hard as separating $\text{SPACE}(\log(n))$ from P. On the other hand, it does not rule out the possibility that $\text{MRC}[\text{poly}(n), \text{poly}(n)] = \text{P}$, or even that $\text{MRC}[\text{poly}(n), 1] = \text{P}$.

# 6 Discussion and Open Problems

In this paper we established the first general connections between MapReduce and classical complexity classes, and showed the conditional existence of a hierarchy within MapReduce. Our results also apply to variants of MapReduce, most notably Valiant's BSP model.

Our work suggests some natural open problems. How does MapReduce relate to other complexity classes, such as the circuit class uniform $AC^0$? Can one improve the bounds from Corollary 1 or remove the dependence on Hypothesis 1? Does Lemma 1 imply Hypothesis 1? Can one give explicit hierarchies for space or time alone, e.g. $MRC[n^\alpha, poly(n)] \subsetneq MRC[n^\mu, poly(n)]$?

We also ask whether $MRC[poly(n), poly(n)] = P$. In other words, if a problem has an efficient solution, does it have one with using data locality? A negative answer implies $SPACE(\log(n)) \neq P$ which is a major open problem in complexity theory, and a positive answer would likely provide new and valuable algorithmic insights. Finally, while we have focused on the relationship between rounds and time, there are also implicit parameters for the amount of (sublinear) space per processor, and the (sublinear) number of processors per round. A natural complexity question is to ask what the relationship between all four parameters are.

**Acknowledgments.** We thank Howard Karloff and Benjamin Moseley for helpful discussions.

# References

1. Andoni, A., Nikolov, A., Onak, K., Yaroslavtsev, G.: Parallel algorithms for geometric graph problems. In: STOC, pp. 574–583 (2014)
2. Beame, P., Koutris, P., Suciu, D.: Communication steps for parallel query processing. In: PODS, pp. 273–284 (2013)
3. Chu, C.-T., Kim, S.K., Lin, Y.-A., Yu, Y., Bradski, G.R., Ng, A.Y., Olukotun, K.: Map-reduce for machine learning on multicore. In: NIPS, pp. 281–288 (2006)
4. Dean, J., Ghemawat, S.: Mapreduce: simplified data processing on large clusters. Commun. ACM **51**(1), 107–113 (2008)
5. Farahat, A.K., Elgohary, A., Ghodsi, A., Kamel, M.S.: Distributed column subset selection on mapreduce. In: ICDM, pp. 171–180 (2013)
6. Feldman, J., Muthukrishnan, S., Sidiropoulos, A., Stein, C., Svitkina, Z.: On distributing symmetric streaming computations. ACM Transactions on Algorithms, 6(4) (2010)
7. Fortnow, L.: Time-space tradeoffs for satisfiability. J. Comput. Syst. Sci. **60**(2), 337–353 (2000)
8. Goodrich, M.T., Sitchinava, N., Zhang, Q.: Sorting, searching, and simulation in the mapreduce framework. In: Asano, T., Nakano, S., Okamoto, Y., Watanabe, O. (eds.) ISAAC 2011. LNCS, vol. 7074, pp. 374–383. Springer, Heidelberg (2011)
9. Impagliazzo, R., Paturi, R.: The complexity of k-sat. In: 2012 IEEE 27th Conference on Computational Complexity, p. 237 (1999)
10. Impagliazzo, R., Paturi, R., Zane, F.: Which problems have strongly exponential complexity? J. Comput. Syst. Sci. **63**(4), 512–530 (2001)

11. Kamara, S., Raykova, M.: Parallel homomorphic encryption. In: Financial Cryptography Workshops, pp. 213–225 (2013)
12. Karloff, H., Suri, S., Vassilvitskii, S.: A model of computation for mapreduce. In: SODA 2010, pp. 938–948. Society for Industrial and Applied Mathematics, Philadelphia (2010)
13. Kumar, R., Moseley, B., Vassilvitskii, S., Vattani, A.: Fast greedy algorithms in mapreduce and streaming. In: SPAA 2013, pp. 1–10. ACM, New York (2013)
14. Lokshtanov, D., Marx, D., Saurabh, S.: Lower bounds based on the exponential time hypothesis. Bulletin of the EATCS **105**, 41–72 (2011)
15. Pace, M.F.: BSP vs mapreduce. In: Proceedings of the International Conference on Computational Science, ICCS 2012, Omaha, Nebraska, USA, June 4–6, 2012, pp. 246–255 (2012)
16. Sarma, A.D., Afrati, F.N., Salihoglu, S., Ullman, J.D.: Upper and lower bounds on the cost of a map-reduce computation. In: PVLDB 2013, pp. 277–288. VLDB Endowment (2013)
17. Shepherdson, J.C.: The reduction of two-way automata to one-way automata. IBM J. Res. Dev. **3**(2), 198–200 (1959)
18. Shvachko, K., Kuang, H., Radia, S., Chansler, R.: The hadoop distributed file system. In: Khatib, M.G., He, X., Factor, M. (eds.) MSST, pp. 1–10. IEEE Computer Society (2010)
19. Szepietowski, A.: Turing machines with sublogarithmic space. Ernst Schering Research Foundation Workshops. Springer (1994)
20. Valiant, L.G.: A bridging model for parallel computation. Commun. ACM **33**(8), 103–111 (1990)
21. Wagner, K., Wechsung, G.: Computational Complexity. Mathematics and its Applications. Springer (1986)
22. Williams, R.: Time-space tradeoffs for counting NP solutions modulo integers. Computational Complexity **17**(2), 179–219 (2008)

# Appendix

## A    Nonuniform MRC

In this section we show that the original MRC definition of [12] allows MRC machines to decide undecidable languages. This definition required a polylogarithmic number of rounds, and also allowed completely different MapReduce machines for different input sizes. For simplicity's sake, we will allow a linear number of rounds, and use our notation $\mathrm{MRC}[f(n), g(n)]$ to denote an MRC machine that operates in $O(f(n))$ rounds and each processor gets $O(g(n))$ time per round. In particular, we show that nonuniform $\mathrm{MRC}[n, \sqrt{n}]$ accepts all unary languages, i.e. languages of the form $L \subseteq \{1^n \mid n \in \mathbb{N}\}$.

**Lemma 3.** *Let $L$ be a unary language. Then $L$ is in nonuniform $\mathrm{MRC}[n, \sqrt{n}]$.*

*Proof.* We define the mappers and reducers as follows. Let $\mu_1$ distribute the input as contiguous blocks of $\sqrt{n}$ bits, $\rho_1$ compute the length of its input, $\mu_2$ send the counts to a single processor, and $\rho_2$ add up the counts, i.e. find $n = |x|$

where $x$ is the input. Now the input data is reduced to one key-value pair $\langle \star, n \rangle$. Then let $\rho_i$ for $i \geq 3$ be the reducer that on input $\langle \star, i - 3 \rangle$ accepts if and only if $1^{i-3} \in L$ and otherwise outputs the input. Let $\mu_i$ for $i \geq 3$ send the input to a single processor. Then $\rho_{n+3}$ will accept iff $x$ is in $L$. Note that $\rho_1, \rho_2$ take $O(\sqrt{n})$ time, and all other mappers and reducers take $O(1)$ time. All mappers and reducers are also in SPACE($\sqrt{n}$).

In particular, Lemma 3 implies that nonuniform $\mathrm{MRC}[n, \sqrt{n}]$ contains the unary version of the halting problem. A more careful analysis shows all unary languages are even in $\mathrm{MRC}[\log n, \sqrt{n}]$, by having $\rho_{i+3}$ check $2^i$ strings for membership in $L$.

# B    Uniform BSP

We define the BSP model of Valiant [20] similarly to MRC, where essentially key-value pairs are replaced with point-to-point messages.

A BSP machine with $p$ processors is a list $(M_1, \ldots, M_p)$ of $p$ Turing machines which on any input, output a list $((j_1, y_1), (j_2, y_2), \ldots, (j_m, y_m))$ of messages to be sent to other processors in the next round. Specifically, message $y_k$ is sent to prcessor $j_k$. A BSP machine operates in rounds as follows. In the first round the input is partitioned into equal-sized pieces $x_{1,0}, \ldots, x_{p,0}$ and distributed arbitrarily to the processors. Then for rounds $r = 1, \ldots, R,$

1. Each processor $i$ takes $x_{i,r}$ as input and computes some number $s_i$ of messages $M_i(x_{i,r}) = \{(j_{i,k}, y_{i,k}) : k = 1, \ldots, s_i\}$.
2. Set $x_{i,r+1}$ to be the set of all messages sent to $i$ (as with MRC's shuffle-and-sort, this is not considered part of processor $i$'s runtime).

We say the machine *accepts* a string $x$ if any machine accepts at any point before round $R$ finishes. We now define uniform deterministic BSP analogously to MRC.

**Definition 7 (Uniform Deterministic BSP).** *A language $L$ is said to be in* $\mathrm{BSP}[f(n), g(n)]$ *if there is a constant* $0 < c < 1$, *an $O(n^c)$-space and $O(g(n))$-time Turing machine $M(p, y)$, and an $R = O(f(n))$, such that for all $x \in \{0, 1\}^n$, the following holds: letting $M_i = M(i, -)$, the BSP machine $M = (M_1, M_2, \ldots, M_{n^c})$ accepts $x$ in $R$ rounds if and only if $x \in L$.*

*Remark 4.* As with MRC, we count the size and number of each message as part of the space bound of the machine generating/receiving the messages. Differing slightly from Valiant, we do not provide persistent memory for each processor. Instead we assume that on processor $i$, any memory cell not containing a message will form a message whose destination is $i$. This is without loss of generality since we are not concerned with the cost of sending individual messages.

# Efficient Counting with Optimal Resilience

Christoph Lenzen[1] and Joel Rybicki[1,2]([⊠])

[1] Max Planck Institute for Informatics, Saarbrücken, Germany
clenzen@mpi-inf.mpg.de
[2] Helsinki Institute for Information Technology HIIT,
Department of Computer Science, Aalto University, Espoo, Finland
joel.rybicki@aalto.fi

**Abstract.** In the synchronous $c$-counting problem, we are given a synchronous system of $n$ nodes, where up to $f$ of the nodes may be Byzantine, that is, have arbitrary faulty behaviour. The task is to have all of the correct nodes count modulo $c$ in unison in a self-stabilising manner: regardless of the initial state of the system and the faulty nodes' behavior, eventually rounds are consistently labelled by a counter modulo $c$ at all correct nodes.

We provide a deterministic solution with resilience $f < n/3$ that stabilises in $O(f)$ rounds and every correct node broadcasts $O(\log^2 f)$ bits per round. We build and improve on a recent result offering stabilisation time $O(f)$ and communication complexity $O(\log^2 f / \log \log f)$ but with sub-optimal resilience $f = n^{1-o(1)}$ (PODC 2015). Our new algorithm has optimal resilience, asymptotically optimal stabilisation time, and low communication complexity. Finally, we modify the algorithm to guarantee that after stabilisation very little communication occurs. In particular, for optimal resilience and polynomial counter size $c = n^{O(1)}$, the algorithm broadcasts only $O(1)$ bits per node every $\Theta(n)$ rounds without affecting the other properties of the algorithm; communication-wise this is asymptotically optimal.

## 1 Introduction

In this work, we seek to minimize the amount of communication required for fast self-stabilising, Byzantine fault-tolerant solutions to the *synchronous counting problem*. We are given a complete communication network on $n$ nodes with arbitrary initial states. There are up to $f$ faulty nodes that may behave in an arbitrary manner. The task is to synchronise the correct nodes so that they will count rounds modulo $c$ in agreement. For example, the following is a possible execution for $n = 4$ nodes, $f = 1$ faulty node, and counting modulo $c = 4$; the execution stabilises after $T = 4$ rounds:

| | | Stabilisation | | | | Counting | | | |
|---|---|---|---|---|---|---|---|---|---|
| Node 1 | ◯ | 3 | I | I | 3 | 2 | 3 | 0 | I |
| Node 2 (faulty) | ✖ | * | * | * | * | * | * | * | * |
| Node 3 | ◯ | 0 | 2 | 0 | 0 | 2 | 3 | 0 | I |
| Node 4 | ◯ | 2 | 0 | 2 | 2 | 2 | 3 | 0 | I |

© Springer-Verlag Berlin Heidelberg 2015
Y. Moses (Ed.): DISC 2015, LNCS 9363, pp. 16–30, 2015.
DOI: 10.1007/978-3-662-48653-5_2

In the severe fault-model considered in this work, synchronous counting is an important service for establishing the classic synchronous abstraction: even if a common clock signal is available, local counters may become inconsistent due to transient faults; these in turn induce arbitrary states, which is addressed by the self-stabilisation paradigm. Many, if not most, synchronous algorithms require synchronous round counters to operate correctly.

Synchronous counting is a coordination primitive that can be used e.g. in large integrated circuits to synchronise subsystems to easily implement *mutual exclusion* and *time division multiple access* in a fault-tolerant manner. Note that in this context, it is natural to assume that a synchronous clock signal is available, but the clocking system usually does not provide explicit round numbers. Solving synchronous counting thus yields highly dependable round counters for subcircuits.

If we neglect communication, counting and consensus are essentially equivalent [3–5]. In particular, many lower bounds on (binary) consensus directly apply to the counting problem [6,9,13]. However, the known generic reduction of counting to consensus incurs a factor-$f$ overhead in space and message size. In recent work [12], we presented an approach that reduces the number of bits nodes broadcast in each round to $O(\log^2 f / \log\log f + \log c)$ at the expense of reduced resilience of $f = n^{1-o(1)}$. In this paper, we improve on the technique to achieve optimal resilience with $O(\log^2 f + \log c)$ bits broadcast by each node per round.

## 1.1   Contributions

In this work, we take the following approach. In order to devise *communication-efficient* algorithms, we first design *space-efficient* algorithms, that is, algorithms in which each node stores only a few bits between consecutive rounds. This comes with additional advantages:

- Local computations will (typically) be simple.
- Communication becomes simple, as one can afford to broadcast the entire state.
- This reduces the complexity of implementations.
- In turn, it becomes easier to use reliable components for an implementation, increasing the overall reliability of the system.

The key challenge that needs to be overcome in constructing space-efficient (and fast) solutions to counting appears to be a chicken-and-egg problem: given that the correct nodes agree on a counter, they can jointly run a (single) instance of synchronous consensus; given that they can run consensus, they can agree on a counter. In [12], this obstacle is navigated by making the statement more precise: given that the correct nodes agree on a counter *for a while*, they can run consensus. This is used to facilitate agreement on the output counter, in a way which maintains agreement even if the unreliable counters used for stabilisation fail later on.

The task of constructing counters that "work" only once in a while is easier; in particular, it does not require to solve consensus in the process. The drawback of the recursive solution in [12] is that, in order to be time-efficient, it sacrifices resilience. Our main contribution is to provide an improved construction that preserves optimal resilience.

**Theorem 1.** *For any integers $c, n > 1$ and $f < n/3$, there exists an $f$-resilient synchronous $c$-counter that runs on $n$ nodes, stabilises in $O(f)$ rounds, and requires $O(\log^2 f + \log c)$ bits to encode the state of a node.*

The main hurdle that needs to be taken in order to arrive at this result when building on the techniques of [12] is the following. In both approaches, the nodes are partitioned into blocks, each of which runs a counter of smaller resilience; the construction proceeds inductively on increasing values of $f$, so such a counter exists by the induction hypothesis. In [12], it is assumed that a majority of these blocks contains sufficiently few faulty nodes for the counter to be operational, causing the relative resilience to deteriorate with each level of recursion in the construction. To achieve optimal resilience, we must drop this assumption, in turn necessitating novel ideas on how to establish a joint counter that is once in a while counting correctly at *all* non-faulty nodes. We show how to obtain such a counter based on simple local consistency checks, timeouts, and threshold voting.

Last but not least, we show how to reduce the number of bits broadcast after stabilisation to $\log c / \log \kappa + O(1)$ per node and $\kappa$ rounds for an essentially unconstrained choice of $\kappa$, at the expense of additively increasing the stabilisation time by $O(\kappa)$. In particular, for the special case of optimal resilience and polynomial counter size, we obtain the following result.

**Corollary 1.** *For any $n > 1$ and $c = n^{O(1)}$ that is an integer multiple of $n$, there exists a synchronous $c$-counter that runs on $n$ nodes, has optimal resilience $f = \lfloor (n-1)/3 \rfloor$, stabilises in $O(n)$ rounds, requires $O(\log^2 n)$ bits to encode the state of a node, and for which after stabilisation correct nodes broadcast (asymptotically optimal) $O(1)$ bits every $\Theta(n)$ rounds.*

## 1.2  Prior Work

In terms of lower bounds, several impossibility results for consensus directly yield bounds for the counting problem as well [3]: counting cannot be solved in the presence of at least $n/3$ Byzantine failures [13] and any deterministic algorithm needs to run for at least $f$ rounds [9] and communicate $\Omega(nf)$ bits to stabilise [6].

In contrast, there exist several algorithms to the synchronous counting problem, albeit these solutions exhibit different trade-offs in terms of resilience, stabilisation time, space and/or communication complexity, or whether a source of random bits is required. For a brief summary, see Table 1.

Designing space-efficient *randomised* algorithms for synchronous counting is fairly straightforward [3,7,8]: for example, the nodes can simply choose random states until a clear majority of nodes has the same state, after which they start

**Table 1.** Summary of counting algorithms for the case $c = 2$. For randomised algorithms, we list the expected stabilisation time. The solution from [10] relies on a shared coin. "(*)" indicates that details vary, but all known shared coins with large resilience require large states and messages.

| resilience | stabilisation time | state bits | deterministic | ref. |
|---|---|---|---|---|
| $f < n/3$ (*) | $O(1)$ | $n^{O(1)}$ (*) | no | [1] |
| $f < n/3$ | $O(f)$ | $O(f \log f)$ | yes | [4] |
| $f < n/3$ | $2^{2(n-f)}$ | 2 | no | [7,8] |
| $f < n/3$ | $\min\{2^{2f+2} + 1, 2^{O(f^2/n)}\}$ | 1 | no | [3] |
| $f = 1, n \geq 4$ | 7 | 2 | yes | [3] |
| $f = n^{1-o(1)}$ | $O(f)$ | $O(\log^2 f / \log \log f)$ | yes | [12] |
| $f < n/3$ | $O(f)$ | $O(\log^2 f)$ | yes | **here** |

to follow the majority. Likewise, given a shared coin, one can quickly reach agreement by defaulting to the coin whenever no clear majority is observed [1]; alas, existing shared coins are highly inefficient in terms of communication. Designing quickly stabilising algorithms that are both communication- and space-efficient has turned out to be a challenging task [3–5], and it remains open to what extent randomisation can help in designing such algorithms.

In the case of deterministic algorithms, algorithm synthesis has been used for computer-aided design of optimal algorithms with resilience $f = 1$, but the approach does not scale due to the extremely fast-growing space of possible algorithms [3]. In general, many fast-stabilising algorithms build on a connection between Byzantine consensus and synchronous counting, but require a large number of states per node [4] due to, e.g., running a large number of consensus instances in parallel. In [12], the approach outlined earlier was leveraged to ensure that each node participates in only $O(\log f / \log \log f)$ instances of consensus, resulting in small state and communication complexity, but reducing resilience to $f = n^{1-o(1)}$.

As a side note, the recursive construction presented in this work bears similarity to the recursive variant of the phase king algorithm [2], for which the goal of the recursion was also to control the communication complexity (reducing it from $\Theta(n^3)$ to $\Theta(n^2)$ for optimal resilience). In retrospect, the structural similarity is striking; one may think of our algorithm as a generalization of the approach to the case where there is no initial agreement on round numbers. The initial lack of consistent round labels is what causes a roughly factor $n$ larger communication complexity in our case, which then can be removed after stabilisation leveraging consistent counters.

### 1.3   Structure of the Article

In the next section, we provide formal descriptions of the model and the problem, and introduce some notation. In Section 3, we prove the main technical result on optimal resilience boosting and infer Theorem 1. In Section 4, we describe how to reduce the amount of bits communicated after stabilisation. Finally, in Section 5, we discuss how randomisation can help in further reducing the communication complexity and conclude the paper.

## 2   Preliminaries

In this section, we define the model of computation and the counting problem.

*Model of Computation.* We consider a fully-connected synchronous message-passing network. That is, our distributed system consists of a network of $n$ nodes, where each node is a state machine and has communication links to all other nodes in the network. All nodes have a unique identifier from the set $[n] = \{0, 1, \ldots, n-1\}$. The computation proceeds in synchronous communication rounds. In each round, all processors perform the following in a lock-step fashion: (1) *broadcast* their current state to all nodes, (2) *receive* messages from all nodes, and (3) *update* their local state. We assume that the initial state of each node is arbitrary and there are up to $f$ Byzantine nodes. A Byzantine node may have arbitrary behaviour, that is, it can deviate from the protocol in any manner. In particular, the Byzantine nodes can collude together in an adversarial manner and a single Byzantine node can send *different* messages to different correct nodes.

*Algorithms and Executions.* Formally, we define an algorithm as a tuple $\mathbf{A} = \langle X, g, p \rangle$, where $X$ is the set of all states any node can have, $g \colon [n] \times X^n \to X$ is the *state transition function*, and $p \colon [n] \times X \to [c]$ is the *output function*. That is, at each round when node $v$ receives a vector $\mathbf{x} = \langle x_0, \ldots, x_{n-1} \rangle$ of messages, node $v$ updates it state to $g(v, \mathbf{x})$ and outputs $p(v, x_v)$. As we consider $c$-counting algorithms, the set of output values is the set set $[c]$ of counter values. Note that the tuples passed to $g$ are ordered according to the node identifiers, i.e., nodes can identify the sender of a message (this is frequently referred to as source authentication).

For any set of $\mathcal{F} \subseteq [n]$ of faulty nodes, we define a projection $\pi_{\mathcal{F}}$ that maps any state vector $\mathbf{x} \in X^n$ to a *configuration* $\pi_F(\mathbf{x}) = \mathbf{e}$, where $e_v = *$ if $v \in \mathcal{F}$ and $e_v = x_v$ otherwise. That is, the values given by Byzantine nodes are ignored and a configuration consists of only the states of correct nodes. A configuration $\mathbf{d}$ is *reachable* from configuration $\mathbf{e}$ if for every correct node $v \notin \mathcal{F}$ there exists some $\mathbf{x} \in X^n$ satisfying $\pi_{\mathcal{F}}(\mathbf{x}) = \mathbf{e}$ and $g(v, \mathbf{x}) = d_v$. Essentially, this means that when the system is in configuration $\mathbf{e}$, the Byzantine nodes can send node $v$ messages so that it decides to switch to state $d_v$. An *execution* of an algorithm $\mathbf{A}$ is an infinite sequence of configurations $\xi = \langle \mathbf{e}_0, \mathbf{e}_1 \ldots, \rangle$ where configuration $\mathbf{e}_{r+1}$ is reachable from configuration $\mathbf{e}_r$.

*Synchronous Counters.* We say that an execution $\xi = \langle \mathbf{e}_0, \mathbf{e}_1 \ldots, \rangle$ of algorithm $\mathbf{A}$ stabilises in time $T$ if there is some $x \in [c]$ such that for every correct node $v \notin \mathcal{F}$ it holds that

$$p(v, e_{T+r,v}) = r - x \bmod c \text{ for all } r \geq 0,$$

where $e_{T+r,v}$ is the state of node $v$ on round $T + r$.

An algorithm **A** is said to be a *synchronous c-counter* with *resilience* $f$ that stabilises in time $T$, if for every $\mathcal{F} \subseteq [n]$, $|\mathcal{F}| \leq f$, all executions of algorithm **A** stabilise within $T$ rounds. In this case, we say that the *stabilisation time* $T(\mathbf{A})$ of **A** is the minimal such $T$ that all executions of **A** stabilise in $T$ rounds. The *state complexity* of **A** is $S(\mathbf{A}) = \lceil \log |X| \rceil$, that is, the number of bits required to encode the state of a node between subsequent rounds. For brevity, we will often refer to $\mathcal{A}(n, f, c)$ as the family of synchronous $c$-counters over $n$ nodes with resilience $f$. For example, $\mathbf{A} \in \mathcal{A}(4, 1, 2)$ denotes a synchronous 2-counter over 4 nodes tolerating one failure.

# 3  Optimal Resilience Boosting

In this section, we show how to use existing synchronous counters to construct new counters in larger networks with higher resilience. The construction is similar in spirit to the one given in [12], but somewhat simpler and allows for optimal resilience boosting. We first state the boosting theorem together with a general overview of the approach, then provide our novel construction, and subsequently discuss how to stabilise the output counters using the unreliable "helper" counters. Finally, we prove the main result.

## 3.1  The Road Map

The high-level idea of the resilience boosting method is as follows. We first start with counters that have a low resilience and use these to construct a new "weaker" counter that has a higher resilience but only needs to behave correctly *once in a while* for sufficiently long. Once such a weak counter exists, it can be used to provide consistent round numbers for long enough to execute a *single* instance of a high-resilience consensus protocol. This can be used to reach agreement on the output counter. Once we can boost resilience in the above manner, we can recursively apply this approach to get the desired resilience.

We now focus on a single recursion step of the resilience boosting. As in [12], the basic idea is to use multiple counters that run in parallel to perform a leader election process that is guaranteed to consider each of the counters as leader eventually. Eventually, a stabilised and correctly behaving counter is elected as a leader for some time and can be used to clock the consensus protocol.

The approach in [12] is inefficient in the sense that using many parallel counters scales poorly in terms of how fast the process operates, which in turn results in large stabilisation times. On the other hand, using only a small number of parallel counters yields poor resilience. Here, we introduce an approach that can—and in fact, must—operate with two counters only, resulting in optimal resilience and fast stabilisation. The key idea is that by running only two counters in parallel, we can utilise all the nodes for filtering out "bad counter values" for both counters and have the nodes carefully choose which counter to follow (and for how long).

In each application of the resilience boosting, each of the two counters is run by roughly half of the nodes. For $f = 0$, these counters are trivial: all nodes simply reproduce a local counter of a designated leader node. For $f > 0$, we assume that reliable counters for all $f' < f$ already exist, and combine an $f_0$-resilient and an $f_1$-resilient counter with $f_0, f_1 < f$ so that $f_0 + f_1 + 1 = f$. This implies that, no matter which nodes are faulty, one of the two counters will eventually stabilise.

Our first goal is to construct a $\tau$-counter that counts correctly only once in a while; $\tau$ will roughly be the running time of the consensus protocol we will execute later on. In order to do this, we take two counting algorithms $\mathbf{A}_i$, $i \in \{0, 1\}$ with different counter ranges. We will have these two counters alternatively point to a "leader counter" for $\tau = \Theta(f)$ rounds, simply by dividing the counters by $\tau$, rounding down, and taking the result modulo 2. However, to ensure that each $\mathbf{A}_i$ is eventually considered the leader for $\tau$ rounds by *both* counters, we let the pointer generated by $\mathbf{A}_1$ switch between leaders by factor 2 slower than the one of $\mathbf{A}_0$.

Obviously, employing this approach naively is not good enough: since $f > \max\{f_1, f_2\}$, it may happen that either $\mathbf{A}_0$ or $\mathbf{A}_1$ never stabilises. However, we are satisfied if nodes *behave* as if following an operational counter for $\tau$ rounds. To this end, we apply for each node $v$ executing $\mathbf{A}_i$ the trivial consistency check whether the local output variable of $\mathbf{A}_i$ increases by 1 in each round. If not, it will switch to using $\mathbf{A}_{1-i}$ as reference for a sufficient number, in this case $\Theta(\tau)$, of rounds to ensure that both $v$ and the nodes executing $\mathbf{A}_{1-i}$ will consider $\mathbf{A}_{1-i}$ as the leader for sufficiently long.

This almost cuts it—except that two nodes $w \neq v$ executing $\mathbf{A}_i$ may have a different opinion on the output variable for $\mathbf{A}_i$, as there are more than $f_i$ faulty nodes executing $\mathbf{A}_i$. This final hurdle is passed by enlisting the help of *all* nodes for a majority vote on what the current output of $\mathbf{A}_i$ actually is. Essentially, here we use threshold voting, which in each round $r$ at each node yields either a globally unique counter value $c_i(r)$ for $\mathbf{A}_i$ or $\bot$, indicating that $\mathbf{A}_i$ is not operating correctly. This entails that, eventually,

- There are unique values $c_i(r)$ that increase by 1 in each round and are considered to be the current counter value of $\mathbf{A}_i$ by all nodes executing $\mathbf{A}_i$ that are not currently relying on the counter of $\mathbf{A}_{1-i}$.
- If a node executing $\mathbf{A}_i$ defaults to the counter of $\mathbf{A}_{1-i}$, there are fewer than $f_{1-i}$ faulty nodes executing $\mathbf{A}_{1-i}$.
- Hence, all correct nodes consider $\mathbf{A}_i$ with fewer than $f_i$ faults for $\tau$ rounds as the leader.

We leverage this last property to execute the *phase king algorithm* [2] in the same way as in [12] to stabilise the output counters.

We remark that the stabilisation time on each level is the maximum of that for the used counters plus $O(f)$; by choosing $f_1 \approx f_2 \approx f/2$, we can thus ensure an overall stabilisation time of $O(f)$, irrespectively of the number of recursion levels. Formally, we prove the following theorem:

**Theorem 2.** *Let $c, n > 1$ and $f < n/3$. Define $n_0 = \lfloor n/2 \rfloor$, $n_1 = \lceil n/2 \rceil$, $f_0 = \lfloor (f-1)/2 \rfloor$, $f_1 = \lceil (f-1)/2 \rceil$, and $\tau = 3(f+2)$. If for $i \in \{0, 1\}$ there exist synchronous counters $\mathbf{A}_i \in \mathcal{A}(n_i, f_i, c_i)$ such that $c_i = 3^i \cdot 2\tau$, then there exists a synchronous c-counter $\mathbf{B} \in (n, f, c)$ such that*

- $T(\mathbf{B}) = \max\{T(\mathbf{A}_0), T(\mathbf{A}_1)\} + O(f)$, and
- $S(\mathbf{B}) = \max\{S(\mathbf{A}_0), S(\mathbf{A}_1)\} + O(\log f + \log c)$.

We fix the notation of this theorem for the remainder of this section, as it is dedicated to its proof. Moreover, for notational convenience we abbreviate $T = \max\{T(\mathbf{A}_0), T(\mathbf{A}_1)\}$ and $S = \max\{S(\mathbf{A}_0), S(\mathbf{A}_1)\}$.

### 3.2    Agreeing on a Common Counter (Once in a While)

In this part, we construct a counter that will eventually count consistently at all nodes for $\tau$ rounds. The $\tau$-counter then will be used as a common clock for executing the phase king algorithm.

First, we partition $V = V_0 \cup V_1$ such that $V_0 \cap V_1 = \emptyset$, $|V_0| = n_0$ and $|V_1| = n_1$. We often refer to the set $V_i$ as *block i*. For both $i \in \{0, 1\}$, the nodes in set $V_i$ execute the algorithm $\mathbf{A}_i$. In case block $i$ has more than $f_i$ faults, we call the block $i$ *faulty*. Otherwise, we say that block $i$ is *correct*. By construction, at least one of the blocks is correct. Hence, there is a correct block $i$ for which $\mathbf{A}_i$ stabilises within $T$ rounds, i.e., nodes in block $i$ output a consistent $c_i$-counter in rounds $r \geq T$.

**Lemma 1.** *For some $i \in \{0, 1\}$, block i is correct.*

*Proof.* By choice of $f_i$, we have $f = f_0 + f_1 + 1$. Hence, at least one of the sets $V_i$ will contain at most $f_i$ faults.

Next, we apply the typical threshold voting mechanism employed by most Byzantine tolerant algorithms in order to filter out differing views of counter values that are believed to be consistent. This is achieved by broadcasting candidate counter values and applying a threshold of $n - f$ as a consistency check, which guarantees that only one candidate value (besides the fallback value $\perp$ indicating an inconsistency) can remain. This is applied for each block concurrently, and all nodes participate in the process, so we can be certain that fewer than one third of the voters are faulty.

In addition to passing this voting step, we require that the counters also have behaved consistently over a sufficient number of rounds; this is verified by the obvious mechanism of testing whether the counter increases by 1 each round and counting the number of rounds since the last inconsistency was detected.

In the following, nodes frequently examine a set of values, one broadcast by each node, and determine majority values. Note that Byzantine nodes may send different values to different nodes, that is it may happen that correct nodes output different values from such a vote. We refer to a *strong majority* as at least $n - f$ nodes supporting the same value, which is then called the *majority value*. If a

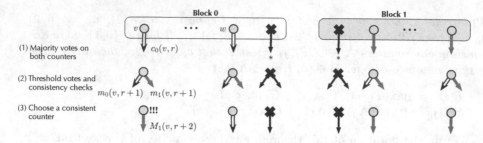

**Fig. 1.** Forming an opinion. The white block depicts nodes in the set $V_0$ running the $c_0$-counter, and the gray block the set $V_1$ running the $c_1$-counter. The white and gray filled arrows indicate the messages output by the white or gray block, respectively. The crosses denote Byzantine nodes with arbitrary output. In the above scenario, the white block is faulty and node $v$ observes that the $c_0$-counter behaves inconsistently, hence it chooses to use the majority output of block 1; node $w$ in the same block still relies on the $c_0$-counter, as it appears consistent from the perspective of node $w$.

node does not see a strong majority, it outputs the symbol $\perp$ instead. Clearly, this procedure is well-defined for $f < n/2$.

We will refer to this procedure as a *majority vote*, and slightly abuse notation by saying "majority vote" when, precisely, we should talk of "the output of the majority vote at node $v$". Since we require that $f < n/3$, the following standard argument shows that for each vote, there is a unique value such that each node either outputs this value or $\perp$.

**Lemma 2.** *If $v, w \in V \setminus \mathcal{F}$ both observe a strong majority, they output the same majority value.*

*Proof.* Fix any set $A$ of $n - f$ correct nodes. As correct nodes broadcast the same value to each node, $v$ and $w$ observing strong majorities for different values would require that for each value $A$ contains $n - 2f$ supporting it. However, this is impossible since $2(n - 2f) = n - f + (n - 3f) > n - f = |A|$.

We now put this principle to use. We introduce the following local variables for each node $v \in V$, block $i \in \{0, 1\}$, and round $r$:

- $m_i(v, r)$ stores the most frequent counter value in block $i$ in round $r$, which is determined from the broadcasted output variables of $\mathbf{A}_i$ with ties broken arbitrarily,
- $M_i(v, r)$ stores the majority vote on $m_i(v, r - 1)$,
- $w_i(v, r)$ is a cooldown counter which is reset to $2c_1$ whenever the node perceives "the" counter of block $i$ behaving inconsistently, that is, $M_i(v, r) \neq M_i(v, r - 1) + 1 \bmod c_i$. Note that this test will automatically fail if either value is $\perp$. Otherwise, if the counter behaves consistently, $w_i(v, r) = \max\{w_i(v, r - 1) - 1, 0\}$.

Figure 1 illustrates how the values of the $m_i$ and $M_i$ are determined. Clearly, these variables can be updated based on the local values from the previous round and the states broadcasted at the beginning of the current round. This requires nodes to store $O(\log c_i) = O(\log f)$ bits.

Furthermore, we define the following derived variables for each $v \in V$, $i \in \{0,1\}$, and round $r$:

- $d_i(v,r) = M_i(v,r)$ if $w_i(v,r) = 0$, otherwise $d_i(v,r) = \perp$,
- $\ell_i(v,r) = \lfloor d_i(v,r)/(3^i \tau) \rfloor$ if $d_i(v,r) \neq \perp$, otherwise $\ell_i(v,r) = \perp$,
- for $v \in V_i$, $\ell(v,r) = \ell_i(v,r)$ if $\ell_i(v,r) \neq \perp$, otherwise $\ell(v,r) = \ell_{1-i}(v,r)$, and
- $d(v,r) = d_{\ell(v,r)}(v,r) \bmod \tau$ if $\ell(v,r) \neq \perp$, otherwise $d(v,r) = 0$.

These can be computed locally, without storing or communicating additional values. The variable $\ell(v,r)$ indicates the block that node $v$ currently considers leader.

We now verify that $\ell_i(v,r)$ has the desired properties. To this end, we analyse $d_i(v,r)$. We start with a lemma showing that eventually a correct block's counter will be consistently observed by all correct nodes.

**Lemma 3.** *Suppose block $i \in \{0,1\}$ is correct. Then for all $v,w \in V \setminus \mathcal{F}$, and rounds $r \geq R = T + O(f)$ it holds that $d_i(v,r) = d_i(w,r)$ and $d_i(v,r) = d_i(v,r-1) + 1 \bmod c_i$.*

*Proof.* Within $T(\mathbf{A}_i)$ rounds, $\mathbf{A}_i$ stabilises. Moreover, any Byzantine tolerant counter must satisfy that $f_i < n_i/3$, implying that $m_i(v,r+1) = m_i(v,r) + 1 \bmod c_i$ for all $r \geq T(\mathbf{A}_i)$. Consequently, $M_i(v,r+1) = M_i(v,r) + 1 \bmod c_i$ for all $r \geq T(\mathbf{A}_i) + 1$. Therefore, $w_i(v,r)$ cannot be reset in rounds $r \geq T(\mathbf{A}_i) + 2$, yielding that $w_i(v,r) = 0$ for all $r \geq T(\mathbf{A}_i) + 2 + 2c_1 = T + O(f)$. The claim follows from the definition of variable $d_i(v,r)$. □

The following lemma states that if a correct node $v$ does not detect an error in a block's counter, then this means that any other correct node considering the block's counter correct *in any of the last $2c_1$ rounds* computed a counter value for that block consistent with the one of $v$.

**Lemma 4.** *Suppose for $i \in \{0,1\}$, $v \in V \setminus \mathcal{F}$, and $r \geq 2c_1 = O(f)$ it holds that $d_i(v,r) \neq \perp$. Then for each $w \in V \setminus \mathcal{F}$ and each $r' \in \{r - 2c_1 + 1, \ldots, r\}$ either $d_i(w,r') = d_i(v,r) - (r - r') \bmod c_i$ or $d_i(w,r') = \perp$.*

*Proof.* Suppose $d_i(w,r') \neq \perp$. Thus, $d_i(w,r') = M_i(w,r') \neq \perp$. By Lemma 2, either $M_i(v,r') = \perp$ or $M_i(v,r') = M_i(w,r')$. However, $M_i(v,r') = \perp$ would imply that $w_i(v,r') = 2c_1$ and thus

$$w_i(v,r) \geq w_i(v,r') + r - r' = 2c_1 + r - r' > 0,$$

contradicting the assumption that $d_i(v,r) \neq \perp$. Thus, $M_i(v,r') = M_i(w,r') = d_i(w,r')$. More generally, we get from $r - r' < 2c_1$ and $w_i(v,r) = 0$ that $w_i(v,r'') \neq 2c_1$ for all $r'' \in \{r', \ldots, r\}$. Therefore, we have that $M_i(v,r''+1) = M_i(v,r'') + 1 \bmod c$ for all $r'' \in \{r', \ldots, r-1\}$, implying

$$d_i(v,r) = M_i(v,r) = M_i(v,r') + r - r' = d_i(w,r') + r - r',$$

proving the claim of the lemma. □

The above properties allow us to prove a key lemma: within $T+O(f)$ rounds, there will be $\tau$ consecutive rounds during which the variable $\ell_i(v,r)$ points to the same correct block for all correct nodes.

**Lemma 5.** *Let $R$ be as in Lemma 3. There is a round $r \leq R+O(f) = T+O(f)$ and a correct block $i$ so that for all $v \in V \setminus \mathcal{F}$ and $r' \in \{r,\ldots,r+\tau-1\}$ it holds that $\ell(v,r') = i$.*

*Proof.* By Lemma 1, there exists a correct block $i$. Thus by Lemma 3, variable $d_i(v,r)$ counts correctly during rounds $r \geq R$. If there is no round $r \in \{R,\ldots,R+c_i-1\}$ such that some $v \in V \setminus \mathcal{F}$ has $\ell_{1-i}(v,r) \neq \bot$, then $\ell(v,r) = \ell_i(v,r)$ for all such $v$ and $r$ and the claim of the lemma holds true by the definition of $\ell_i(v,r)$ and the fact that $d_i(v,r)$ counts correctly and consistently.

Hence, assume that $r_0 \in \{R,\ldots,R+c_i-1\}$ is minimal with the property that there is some $v \in V \setminus \mathcal{F}$ so that $\ell_{1-i}(v,r_0) \neq \bot$. Therefore, $d_{1-i}(v,r_0) \neq \bot$ and, by Lemma 4, this implies for all $w \in V \setminus \mathcal{F}$ and all $r \in \{r_0,\ldots,r_0+2c_1-1\}$ that either $d_{1-i}(w,r) = \bot$ or $d_{1-i}(w,r) = d_{1-i}(v,r_0)+r-r_0$. In other words, there is a "virtual counter" that equals $d_{1-i}(v,r_0)$ in round $r_0$ so that during $\{r_0,\ldots,r_0+2c_1-1\}$ correct nodes' $d_{1-i}$ variable either equals this counter or $\bot$.

Consequently, it remains to show that both $\ell_i$ and the variable $\ell_{1-i}$ derived from this virtual counter equal $i$ for $\tau$ consecutive rounds during the interval $\{r_0,\ldots,r_0+2c_1-1\}$, as then $\ell(v,r) = i$ for $v \in V \setminus \mathcal{F}$ and such a round $r$. Clearly, the $c_1$-counter consecutively counts from $0$ to $c_1-1$ at least once during rounds $\{r_0,\ldots,r_0+2c_1-1\}$. Recalling that $c_1 = 6\tau$, we see that $\ell_1(v,r) = i$ for all $v \in V \setminus \mathcal{F}$ with $\ell_1(v,r) \neq \bot$ for $3\tau$ consecutive rounds during $\{r_0,\ldots,r_0+2c_1-1\}$. As $c_0 = 2\tau$, we have that $\ell_0(v,r) = i$ for all $v \in V \setminus \mathcal{F}$ with $\ell_0(v,r) \neq \bot$ for $\tau$ consecutive rounds during this subinterval. As argued earlier, $\ell_0(v,r) \neq \bot$ or $\ell_1(v,r) \neq \bot$ and hence $\ell(v,r) = i$ for each such node and round. Because $r_0 + 2c_1 - 1 < R + 3c_1 = T + O(f)$, this completes the proof. $\qed$

Using the above lemma, we get a counter where all nodes eventually count correctly and consistently modulo $\tau$ for at least $\tau$ rounds.

**Corollary 2.** *There is a round $r = T + O(f)$ so that (1) for all $v,w \in V \setminus \mathcal{F}$ it holds that $d(v,r) = d(w,r)$ and (2) for all $v \in V \setminus \mathcal{F}$ and $r' \in \{r+1,\ldots,r+\tau-1\}$ we have $d(v,r') = d(v,r'-1)+1 \bmod \tau$.*

*Proof.* By Lemma 5, there is a round $r = T + O(f)$ and a correct block $i$ such that for all $v \in V \setminus \mathcal{F}$ we have $\ell(v,r') = i$ for all $r' \in \{r,\ldots,r+\tau-1\}$. Moreover, $r$ is sufficiently large to apply Lemma 3 to $d_i(v,r') = d(v,r')$ for $r' \in \{r+1,\ldots,r+\tau-1\}$, yielding the claim. $\qed$

### 3.3   Reaching Consensus

For every node $v \in V$, let $a(v,r)$ denote the output variable of the synchronous $c$-counting algorithm **B** we are constructing. Similarly as in a prior work [12], we now apply the phase king consensus algorithm [2] to get all nodes in the network agree on the output value of the $c$-counter. The phase king algorithm has the following properties:

- the algorithm tolerates $f < n/3$ Byzantine failures,
- the running time of the algorithm is $O(f)$ rounds and it uses $O(\log c)$ bits of state,
- if node $v$ is correct, then agreement is reached if all correct nodes execute rounds $3v$, $3v + 1$, and $3v + 2$ consecutively,
- once agreement is reached, then agreement persists even when nodes execute *different* rounds.

More formally, we have the following lemma:

**Lemma 6 (Adapted from [12]).** *Let $v \in [f + 2]$ be a correct node and $r \geq 0$.*

- *If all correct nodes execute the instructions $3v + k$ of the phase king algorithm during round $r + k$ for all $k \in \{0, 1, 2\}$, then for any $r' > r + 2$, we have $a(u, r') = a(w, r')$ and $a(u, r' + 1) = a(u, r') + 1 \bmod c$ for all $u, w \in V \setminus \mathcal{F}$.*
- *If $a(u, r') = a(w, r')$ for all $u, w \in V \setminus \mathcal{F}$, then $a(u, r' + 1) = a(w, r' + 1) = a(w, r') + 1 \bmod c$ no matter which (even if different) instructions nodes $u$ and $w$ execute on round $r'$.*

### 3.4 Proofs of Theorems 1 and 2

We are now ready to prove our main results of this section.

**Theorem 2.** *Let $c, n > 1$ and $f < n/3$. Define $n_0 = \lfloor n/2 \rfloor$, $n_1 = \lceil n/2 \rceil$, $f_0 = \lfloor (f - 1)/2 \rfloor$, $f_1 = \lceil (f - 1)/2 \rceil$, and $\tau = 3(f + 2)$. If for $i \in \{0, 1\}$ there exist synchronous counters $\mathbf{A}_i \in \mathcal{A}(n_i, f_i, c_i)$ such that $c_i = 3^i \cdot 2\tau$, then there exists a synchronous c-counter $\mathbf{B} \in (n, f, c)$ such that*

- $T(\mathbf{B}) = \max\{T(\mathbf{A}_0), T(\mathbf{A}_1)\} + O(f)$, *and*
- $S(\mathbf{B}) = \max\{S(\mathbf{A}_0), S(\mathbf{A}_1)\} + O(\log f + \log c)$.

*Proof.* First, we apply the construction underlying Corollary 2. Then we have every node $v \in V$ in each round $r$ execute the instructions for round $d(v, r)$ of the phase king algorithm discussed in the previous paragraph. It remains to show that this yields a correct algorithm $\mathbf{B}$ with stabilisation time $T(\mathbf{B}) = T + O(f)$ and space complexity $S(\mathbf{B}) = S + O(\log f + \log c)$, where $T = \max\{T(\mathbf{A}_i)\}$ and $S = \max\{S(\mathbf{A}_i)\}$.

By Corollary 2, there exists a round $r = T + O(f)$ so that the variables $d(v, r)$ behave as a consistent $\tau$-counter during rounds $\{r, \ldots, r + \tau - 1\}$ for all $v \in V \setminus \mathcal{F}$. As there are at most $f$ faulty nodes, there exist at least two correct nodes $v \in [f + 2]$. Since $\tau = 3(f + 2)$, for at least one correct node $v \in [f + 2] \setminus \mathcal{F}$, there is a round $r \leq r_v \leq r + \tau - 3$ such that $d(w, r_v + k) = 3v + k$ for all $w \in V \setminus \mathcal{F}$ and $k \in \{0, 1, 2\}$. By Lemma 6, it follows that the output variables $a(w, r')$ count correctly and consistently for all $r' \geq r_v + 3$ and $w \in V \setminus \mathcal{F}$. Thus, the algorithm stabilises in $r_v + 3 \leq r + \tau = r + O(f) = T + O(f)$ rounds.

The bound for the space complexity follows from the facts that, at each node, we need (a) at most $S$ bits to store the state of $\mathbf{A}_i$, (b) $O(\log \tau) = O(\log f)$ bits to store the auxilary variables underlying Corollary 2, (c) $O(\log \tau) = O(\log f)$ bits for the helper variables underlying Lemma 6 [12], and (d) $\lceil \log c \rceil$ bits to store the output variable $a(v, r)$.

**Theorem 1.** *For any integers $c, n > 1$ and $f < n/3$, there exists an $f$-resilient synchronous $c$-counter that runs on $n$ nodes, stabilises in $O(f)$ rounds, and requires $O(\log^2 f + \log c)$ bits to encode the state of a node.*

*Proof.* We show the claim by induction on $f$. The induction hypothesis is that for all $f > f' \geq 0$, $c > 1$, and $n > 3f'$, we can construct $\mathbf{B} \in \mathcal{A}(f', n, c)$ with

$$T(\mathbf{B}) = 1 + \alpha f' \sum_{k=0}^{\lceil \log f' \rceil} (1/2)^k \quad \text{and} \quad S(\mathbf{B}) = \beta(\log^2 f' + \log c),$$

where $\alpha$ and $\beta$ are sufficienlty large constants and for $f' = 0$ the sum is empty, that is, $T(\mathbf{B}) = 1$. As $\sum_{k=0}^{\infty} (1/2)^k = 2$, this will prove the theorem. Note that for $f \geq 0$ it is sufficient to show the claim for $n(f) = 3f + 1$, as we can easily generalise to any $n > n(f)$ by running $\mathbf{B}$ on the first $n(f)$ nodes and letting the remaining nodes follow the majority counter value among the $n(f)$ nodes executing the algorithm; this increases the stabilisation time by one round and induces no memory overhead.

For the base case, observe that a 0-tolerant $c$-counter of $n(0) = 1$ node is trivially given by the node having a local counter. It stabilises in 0 rounds and requires $\lceil \log c \rceil$ state bits. As pointed out above, this implies a 0-tolerant $c$-counter for any $n$ with stabilisation time 1 and $\lceil \log c \rceil$ bits of state.

For the inductive step to $f$, we apply Theorem 2. For $i \in \{0, 1\}$, we have that $f_i \leq f/2$, $n_i > 3f_i$, and $c_i = O(f)$. This implies by the induction hypothesis that there are $\mathbf{A}_i(n_i, f_i, c_i)$ with

$$T(\mathbf{A}_i) = 1 + \frac{\alpha f}{2} \sum_{k=0}^{\lceil \log f/2 \rceil} \left(\frac{1}{2}\right)^k + O(f) = 1 + \alpha f \sum_{k=0}^{\lceil \log f \rceil} \left(\frac{1}{2}\right)^k,$$

where in the last step we use that $\alpha$ is sufficiently large, and

$$S(\mathbf{B}) = \beta \left( \log^2 \frac{f}{2} + \log \frac{f}{2} \right) + O(\log f + \log c) = \beta \left( \log^2 f + \log c \right),$$

where we exploit that $\beta$ is sufficiently large. Hence, the induction step succeeds.

## 4    Less Communication After Stabilisation

We now sketch how to reduce the number of bits broadcast by a node after stabilisation; see [11] for the complete construction. The techniques we use are very similar to the ones we used for deriving Theorem 1. Essentially, we devise a "silencing wrapper" for algorithms given by Theorem 1. Let $\mathbf{A}$ be such a counting algorithm. The high-level idea and the key ingredients are the following:

- The goal is that nodes eventually become *happy*: they assume stabilisation has occured and check for counter consistency only every $\kappa$ rounds (as self-stabilising algorithms always need to verify their output).

- Happy nodes do not execute the underlying algorithm **A** to avoid the involved communication. This necessitates a fall-back stabilisation mechanism covering the case that a subset of the correct nodes is happy, but does not detect a problem.
- Using a cooldown counter with similar effects as shown in Lemma 4, we enforce that all happy nodes output consistent counters.
- We override the phase king instruction of **A** if at least $n - 2f \geq f + 1$ nodes (claim to be) happy and propose a counter value $x$. Instead nodes adjust their counter output accordingly to match $x$. If there is no strong majority of happy nodes a supporting counter value, either all nodes become unhappy or all correct nodes reach agreement and start counting correctly.
- If all correct nodes are unhappy, they execute **A** "as is" reaching agreement eventually.
- The agreed-upon counters are used to make all nodes concurrently switch their state to being happy (once the cooldown counters have expired), in a way that does not interfere with the above stabilisation process.

The final observation is that happy nodes can communicate their counter values very efficiently in a manner that self-stabilises within $\kappa$ rounds. As their counter increases by 1 modulo $c$ in every round (or they become unhappy), they can use $\kappa$ rounds to encode a counter value; the recipient simply counts locally in the meantime.

## 5    Discussion

We presented a deterministic counting algorithm that has low state and communication complexity, optimal resilience, and asymptotically optimal stabilisation time. In addition, we gave a variant of the algorithm that communicates extremely little once stabilisation is achieved. In [12], we consider the so-called pulling model, in which nodes *request* messages from others instead of broadcasting a message to everyone, and use randomisation to reduce the amount of bits communicated (in contrast to broadcasting) by each correct node to $\log^{O(1)} n$ per round. We remark that this approach can also applied to the solution given in this work.

From our point of view, the most thrilling open question is whether similar ideas can be applied to randomised consensus routines in order to achieve sublinear stabilisation time with high resilience and small communication overhead. Another point of note is that this general type of recursion, which we essentially extended from its use for synchronous consensus [2] (where the clock is implicitly given by the synchronous start), might also prove useful for deriving improved pulse synchronisation [4] algorithms. Interestingly, no reduction from consensus to pulse synchronisation is known, so there is hope for efficient deterministic algorithms that stabilise in sublinear time.

**Acknowledgments.** We thank anonymous reviewers for helpful feedback and Jukka Suomela for discussions and comments.

# References

1. Ben-Or, M., Dolev, D., Hoch, E.N.: Fast self-stabilizing Byzantine tolerant digital clock synchronization. In: Proc. 27th Annual ACM Symposium on Principles of Distributed Computing (PODC 2008), pp. 385–394. ACM Press (2008). doi:10.1145/1400751.1400802
2. Berman, P., Garay, J.A., Perry, K.J.: Towards optimal distributed consensus. In: Proc. 30th Annual Symposium on Foundations of Computer Science (FOCS 1989). pp. 410–415. IEEE (1989). doi:10.1109/SFCS.1989.63511
3. Dolev, D., Heljanko, K., Järvisalo, M., Korhonen, J.H., Lenzen, C., Rybicki, J., Suomela, J., Wieringa, S.: Synchronous counting andcomputational algorithm design (2015). http://arxiv.org/abs/1304.5719v2
4. Dolev, D., Hoch, E.N.: On self-stabilizing synchronous actions despite Byzantine attacks. In: Pelc, A. (ed.) DISC 2007. LNCS, vol. 4731, pp. 193–207. Springer, Heidelberg (2007)
5. Dolev, D., Korhonen, J.H., Lenzen, C., Rybicki, J., Suomela, J.: Synchronous counting and computational algorithm design. In: Higashino, T., Katayama, Y., Masuzawa, T., Potop-Butucaru, M., Yamashita, M. (eds.) SSS 2013. LNCS, vol. 8255, pp. 237–250. Springer, Heidelberg (2013)
6. Dolev, D., Reischuk, R.: Bounds on information exchange for Byzantine agreement. Journal of the ACM **32**(1), 191–204 (1985). doi:10.1145/2455.214112
7. Dolev, S.: Self-Stabilization. The MIT Press, Cambridge (2000)
8. Dolev, S., Welch, J.L.: Self-stabilizing clock synchronization in the presence of Byzantine faults. Journal of the ACM **51**(5), 780–799 (2004). doi:10.1145/1017460.1017463
9. Fischer, M.J., Lynch, N.A.: A lower bound for the time to assure interactive consistency. Information Processing Letters **14**(4), 183–186 (1982). doi:10.1016/0020-0190(82)90033-3
10. Hoch, E.N., Dolev, D., Daliot, A.: Self-stabilizing Byzantine digital clock synchronization. In: Datta, A.K., Gradinariu, M. (eds.) SSS 2006. LNCS, vol. 4280, pp. 350–362. Springer, Heidelberg (2006)
11. Lenzen, C., Rybicki, J.: Efficient counting with optimal resilience (2015). http://arxiv.org/abs/1508.02535
12. Lenzen, C., Rybicki, J., Suomela, J.: Towards optimal synchronous counting. In: Proc. 34th Annual ACM Symposium on Principles of Distributed Computing (PODC 2015), pp. 441–450. ACM Press (2015). doi:10.1145/2767386.2767423
13. Pease, M.C., Shostak, R.E., Lamport, L.: Reaching agreement in the presence of faults. Journal of the ACM **27**(2), 228–234 (1980). doi:10.1145/322186.322188

# The Computational Power of Beeps

Seth Gilbert[1] and Calvin Newport[2]([⊠])

[1] National University of Singapore, Singapore, Singapore
seth.gilbert@comp.nus.edu.sg
[2] Georgetown University, Washington, D.C, USA
cnewport@cs.georgetown.edu

**Abstract.** We study the quantity of computational resources (state machine states and/or probabilistic transition precision) needed to solve specific problems in a single hop network where nodes communicate using only beeps. We begin by focusing on randomized leader election. We prove a lower bound on the states required to solve this problem with a given error bound, probability precision, and (when relevant) network size lower bound. We then show the bound tight with a matching upper bound. Noting that our optimal upper bound is slow, we describe two faster algorithms that trade some state optimality to gain efficiency. We then turn our attention to more general classes of problems by proving that once you have enough states to solve leader election with a given error bound, you have (within constant factors) enough states to simulate correctly, with this same error bound, a logspace TM with a constant number of unary input tapes: allowing you to solve a large and expressive set of problems. These results identify a key simplicity threshold beyond which useful distributed computation is possible in the beeping model.

## 1 Introduction

The beeping model of network communication [1–3,10,14,20] assumes a collection of computational *nodes*, connected in a network, that interact by *beeping* in synchronous rounds. If a node decides to beep in a given round, it receives no feedback from the channel. On the other hand, if a node decides to listen, it is able to differentiate between the following two cases: (1) no neighbor in the network topology beeped in this round, and (2) one or more neighbors beeped.

Existing work on this model provide two motivations. The first concerns digital communication networks (e.g., [10,12]). Standard network communication (in which nodes interact using error-corrected packets containing many bits of information) requires substantial time, energy, and computational overhead (at multiple stack layers) to handle the necessary packet encoding, modulation, demodulation, and decoding. Beeps, on the other hand, provide an abstraction capturing the simplest possible communication primitive: a detectable burst of

---

S. Gilbert—Supported in part by NUS FRC T1-251RES1404.
C. Newport—Supported in part by NSF grant CCF 1320279.

Y. Moses (Ed.): DISC 2015, LNCS 9363, pp. 31–46, 2015.
DOI: 10.1007/978-3-662-48653-5_3

energy. In theory, beep layers could be implemented using a fraction of the complexity required by standard packet communication, establishing the possibility of *micro-network* stacks for settings where high speed and low cost are crucial. The second motivation for the beeping model concerns a connection to biological systems (e.g., [3,19,20]). Network communication in nature is often quite simple; e.g., noticing a flash of light from nearby fireflies or detecting a chemical marker diffused by nearby cells. Therefore, understanding how to achieve distributed coordination using such basic primitives can provide insight into how such coordination arises in nature (see [19] for a recent survey of this approach).

*A Key Question.* As detailed below, existing work on the beeping model seeks to solve useful problems as *efficiently* as possible in this primitive network setting. In this paper, by contrast, we focus on solving useful problems as *simply* as possible (e.g., as measured by factors such as the size of the algorithm's state machine representation), asking the key question: is it possible to solve problems with both simple communication *and* simple algorithms? Notice, the answer is not *a priori* obvious. It might be the case, for example, that complexity is conserved, so that simplifying the communication model requires more complex algorithms. Or it might be the case that simple algorithms coordinating with beeps are sufficient for even complex tasks. Given the above motivations for studying beeps, answering this question is crucial, as it will help us probe the feasibility of useful networked systems—whether constructed by engineers or evolution—that are truly simple in both their communication methods and control logic.

*Our Answers.* Consider a collection of $n$ nodes connected in a *single hop* topology (i.e., the network graph is a clique). We model the randomized process executing on each node as a probabilistic state machine. The two parameters describing the complexity of these algorithms are: (1) an upper bound on the number of states (indicated by integer $s \geq 1$); and (2) an upper bound on the precision of the probabilistic transitions (indicated by integer $q \geq 2$, where we allow probabilistic transitions to be labeled with probability 0, 1, or any value in the interval $[\frac{1}{q}, 1 - \frac{1}{q}]$). We ask how large these values must grow to solve specific problems. Our motivating premise is that smaller values imply simpler algorithms. (Notice, by considering both $s$ and $q$, we can capture the trade-off between memory and probabilistic precision, a question of standalone interest; c.f., [16]).

We begin by considering *leader election*, a fundamental primitive in distributed systems. We prove that for a given error bound $\epsilon \in [0, 1/2]$ and probabilistic precision $q$, any algorithm that solves leader election with probability $1 - \epsilon$ requires $s = \Omega(\log_q (1/\epsilon))$ states. Given a lower bound $\widetilde{N}$ on the size of the network, this lower bound *reduces* to $s = \Omega(\log_q (1/\epsilon)/\widetilde{N})$ states. Thus, the more nodes in the network, the fewer states each node needs to solve the problem.

This lower bound leverages a reduction argument. We begin by defining and lower bounding a helper problem called $(1, k)$-*loneliness detection*, which requires an algorithm to differentiate between $n = 1$ and $n \geq k$ (but has no requirements for intermediate network sizes). This bound uses an indistinguishability argument regarding how nodes move through a specified state sequence. We then show how to transform a solution to leader election for size lower bound $\widetilde{N}$, to solve $(1, \widetilde{N})$-loneliness detection—allowing our loneliness bound to carry over to leader election.

We then turn our attention to leader election upper bounds. We begin by proving our lower bound tight by showing, for every network size lower bound $\widetilde{N} \geq 1$, how to solve leader election with $s = O(\log_q (1/\epsilon)/\widetilde{N})$ states. The key idea behind this algorithm is to have nodes work together to implement a distributed timer. The more nodes in the network, the longer the distributed timer runs, and the longer the distributed timer runs, the higher the probability that we succeed at leader election. In this way, increasing the network size reduces the states required to hit a specific error bound. A shortcoming of this new algorithm, however, is that its expected running time is exponential in the network size. With this mind, we then describe two faster algorithms (their time is polylogarithmic in the relevant parameters) that require only the minimum precision of $q = 2$. The cost for their efficiency, however, is a loss of state optimality in some circumstances.

The first algorithm requires $s = O(\log (1/\epsilon))$ states and solves leader election with probability at least $1 - \epsilon$, for any network size $n$. It terminates in $O(\log (n + 1/\epsilon) \log (1/\epsilon))$ rounds, with probability at least $1 - \epsilon$. The key idea behind this algorithm is to test a potentially successful election by having the potential leader(s) broadcast with probability $1/2$ for $\log (1/\epsilon)$ rounds, looking for evidence of company. It is straightforward to see that a single such test fails with probability no more than $(1/2)^{\log (1/\epsilon)} = \epsilon$. The problem, however, is that as the network size grows, the number of such tests performed also increases, making it more likely that one fails. We neutralize this problem in our analysis by showing that the test failure probabilities fall away as a geometric series in the test count—bounding the cumulative error sum as the network grows.

The second algorithm requires only $s = O(1)$ states, and yet, for every network size $n$, it solves leader election with high probability in $n$ when run in a network of that size. It requires only $O(\log^2 n)$ rounds, with high probability. The key idea driving this algorithm is to harness the large amount of total states in the network to implement a distributed timer that requires $\Theta(\log n)$ time to countdown to 0, when executed among $n$ nodes. This duration is sufficient for the nodes to safely reduce contention down to a single leader.

After studying leader election, we turn our attention to more general classes of distributed decision problems. Leveraging our leader election algorithms as a key primitive, we show how to simulate a logspace decider Turing Machine (TM) with a constant number of unary inputs (all defined with respect to the network size $n$). Perhaps surprisingly, this algorithm requires only $O(\log (1/\epsilon))$ states to complete the simulation with probability $1 - \epsilon$, and only $O(1)$ states to achieve high probability in $n$. (Notice that this is not enough states for an individual node to store even a single pointer to the tape of the simulated machine.) Our simulation uses the same general strategy first highlighted in the study of population protocols [4]: simulate a counter machine with a constant number of counters that hold values from 0 to $O(n)$, and then apply a transformation due to Minsky [17] to simulate a logspace TM with this machine. Due to the differences between the beeping and population protocol models, however, our counter machine simulation strategies are distinct from [4].

*Implications.* The results summarized above establish that the $\log(1/\epsilon)$ state threshold for leader election with bounded error is (in some sense) a fundamental simplicity threshold for solving useful problems with beeps. It is striking that if you have *slightly less* than this much memory, even the basic symmetry breaking task of leader election is impossible, but if you instead have *slightly more*, then suddenly you can solve large classes of complicated problems (i.e., everything solvable by a logspace TM). If you are satisfied with high probability solutions (which is often the case), then this treshhold reduces even more all the way down to $O(1)$. Given these results, we tentatively claim a positive answer to the key question posed above: *complexity is not destiny; you can solve hard problems simply in simple network models.*

Before proceeding into the technical details of our paper, we will first take the time to place both our model and our results in the context of the several different areas of relevant related work. Among other questions, we want to understand the relationship of our bounds to existing beep results, and how the beeping model compares and contrasts to similar settings.

*Comparison to Existing Beep Results.* The algorithmic study of beeping networks began with Degesys et al. [12], who introduced a continuous variant of the beeping model, inspired by the pulse-coupled oscillator framework. They studied biologically inspired strategies for solving a *desynchronization* problem. Follow-up work generalized the results to multihop networks [11,18]. Cornejo and Kuhn [10] introduced the discrete (i.e., round-based) beeping model studied in this paper. They motivated this model by noting the continuous model in [11,12,18] was unrealistic and yielded trivial solutions to desynchronization, they then demonstrated how to solve desynchronization without these assumptions. Around this same time, Afek et al. [3] described a maximal independent set (MIS) algorithm in a strong version of the discrete beeping model. They argued that something like this algorithm might play a role in the proper distribution of sensory organ precursor cells in fruit fly nervous system development. Follow-up work [1,2,20] removed some of the stronger assumptions of [3] and improved the time complexity. In recent work, Förster et al. [14] considered deterministic leader election in a multihop beeping network.

To place this paper in this context of the existing work on the beeping model, it is important to note that the above-cited papers focus primarily on two goals: minimizing time complexity and minimizing information provided to nodes (e.g., network size, max degree, global round counter). They do not, however, place restrictions on the amount of states used by their algorithms. Accordingly, these existing results require either: the ability to store values as large as $\Theta(n)$ [1–3, 10,20], or uniques ids [14] (which in our framework would require a machine with

$n$ different initial states, or equivalently, $n$ different machines). In this paper, we prove that the algorithmic complexity threshold for solving many useful problems is actually much lower: $O(1)$ states are sufficient for high probability results and $O(\log(1/\epsilon))$ states are sufficient for fixed error bound results.[1] We argue the direction pursued in this paper (how complex must algorithms become to solve useful problems with beeps) complements the direction pursued in existing papers (how fast can algorithms solve useful problems with beeps). Answers to both types of queries is necessary to continue to understand the important topic of coordination in constrained network environments.

*Comparison to the Radio Network Model.* The standard radio network model allows nodes to send large messages, but assumes concurrent transmissions lead to message loss (that may or may not be detectable). The key difference between the radio network model and the beeping model is that in the former you can recognize the case where exactly one node broadcast (e.g., because you receive a message). This capability, which the beeping model does not offer (a single beeper looks like multiple beepers), is powerful. It allows, for example, algorithms that can solve leader election with deterministic safety using only a constant amount of state, when run in network of size at least 2. If you assume receiver collision detection, these solutions require only polylogarithmic expected time.[2] These results violate our lower bounds for leader election with beeps (where the state size grows toward infinity as you drive the error bound toward 0)— indicating that the communication limitations in the beeping model matter from a computability perspective.

*Comparison to the Stone Age Computing Model.* It is also important to place our results in the context of other simplified communication/computation models. Consider, for example, the stone age distributed computing model introduced by Emek and Wattenhofer [13]. This model assumes state machines of constant size connected in a network and executing asynchronously. The machines communicate with a constant-size message alphabet and when transitioning can distinguish between having received 0, 1, or $\geq b$ messages of each type, for some constant parameter $b \geq 1$. For $b = 1$, this model is essentially an asynchronous version of the beeping model. To this end, nodes in our model can simulate nodes in the stone age model with $b = 1$ indefinitely using a constant number of states.

---

[1] Notice, direct comparisons between many of these results is complicated by the variety of possible assumptions; e.g., synchronous versus asynchronous starts, multihop versus single hop, small versus large probability precision.

[2] For example: divide rounds into pairs of even and odd rounds. In even rounds, nodes broadcast a simple message with constant probability. If a node ever succeeds in broadcasting alone, all other nodes become *heralds*. They stop competing in even rounds and begin competing in odd rounds. When the winner (who is now the only non-herald in the network) eventually hears a message in an odd round, it elects itself leader. If we assume collision detection, we can reduce contention fast in the even rounds with basic knockout protocols; e.g., if you choose to listen and detect a collision you are knocked out and just wait to become a herald.

For $b > 1$, however, any such simulation likely becomes impossible in the beeping model with a constant number of states. As noted in our discussion of the radio network model, the ability to safely recognize the case of exactly one message being sent provides extra power beyond what is achievable (without error) using only beeps.

*Comparison to the Population Protocol Model.* Another relevant simplified communication/computation setting is the well-studied population protocol model [4–9]. This model describes nodes as state machines of constant size that interact in a pairwise manner—transforming both states asymmetrically. In the basic version of the model, a fair scheduler chooses pairs to interact. A version in which the scheduler is randomized adds more power. There are similarities in the goals pursued by the beeping and population protocol models: both seek (among other things) to understand the limits of limited state in distributed computation. The core difference between the two settings is the role of the algorithm in communication scheduling. In the beeping model, algorithms must reduce contention and schedule communication on their own. In the population protocol model the scheduler ensures fair and reliable interactions. Imagine, for example, a continuous leader election problem where every node has a *leader* bit, and the problem requires in an infinite execution that: (1) every node sets *leader* to 1 an infinite number of times; and (2) there is never a time at which two nodes both have *leader* set to 1. This problem is trivial in the population protocol: simply pass a leader token around the network. In the beeping model, by contrast, it is impossible as it essentially requires nodes to solve leader election correctly an infinite number of times—a feat which would require an unachievable error bound of 0. It follows that in some respects these two models are studying the impact of limited state on different aspects of distributed computation.

## 2    Model

We model a collection of $n$ probabilistic computational agents (i.e., "nodes") that are connected in a single hop network and communicate using a unary primitive; i.e., *beeps*. They execute in synchronous rounds in which each node can either beep or receive. Receiving nodes can distinguish between the following two cases: (1) no node beeped; (2) one or more nodes beeped. We characterize these agents by $s$ (a bound on the number of states in their state machine), and $q$ (a bound on the precision allowed in probabilistic transitions, with larger values enabling more accurate transition probabilities). In more detail:

*Node Definition.* We specify the algorithm executing on each node as a probabilistic state machine $M = (Q_r, Q_b, q_s, \delta_\perp, \delta_\top)$, where: $Q_r$ and $Q_b$ are two disjoint sets of states corresponding to receiving and beeping, respectively; $q_s$ is the start state; and $\delta_\perp$ and $\delta_\top$ are the probabilistic transition functions[3] for the cases where the node detects silence and where the node beeps/detects a beep,

---

[3] Transition functions map the current state to a distribution over states to enter next.

respectively. Some problems have all nodes execute the same state machine, while others include multiple machine types, each corresponding to a different initial value.

*Executions.* Executions proceed in synchronous rounds with all nodes in their machine's start state. At the beginning of round $r$, for a node $u$ running a machine $(Q_r, Q_b, q_s, \delta_\perp, \delta_\top)$, if its current state $q_u$ is in $Q_b$, then $u$ emits a beep, otherwise it receives. If at least one node beeps in $r$, then *all* nodes either beep or detect a beep in this round. Therefore, each node $u$ applies the transition function $\delta_\top$ to its current state $q_u$ and selects its next state according to the distribution $\delta_\top(q_u)$. If no node beeps in $r$, then each node $u$ applies the transition function $\delta_\perp$, selecting its next state from the distribution, $\delta_\perp(q_u)$.

*Parameters.* We parameterize state machines with two values. The first, indicated by $s \geq 1$, is an upper bound on the number of states allowed (i.e., $|Q_r| + |Q_b| \leq s$). The second, indicated by $q \geq 2$, bounds the precision of the probabilistic transitions allowed by the $\delta$ functions. In more detail, for a given $q$, the probabilities assigned to states by distributions in the range of $\delta$ must either be 0, 1, or in the interval, $[\frac{1}{q}, 1 - \frac{1}{q}]$. For the minimum value of $q = 2$, probabilistic transitions can occur only with probability $1/2$. As $q$ increases, smaller probabilities, as well as probabilities closer to 1, become possible. Finally, we parameterize an execution with $n$—the number of nodes in the network.

## 3   Leader Election

The first computational task we consider is leader election: eventually, one node designates itself leader. An algorithm state machine that solves leader election must include a final *leader state* $q_\ell$ that is terminal (once a node enters the state, it never leaves). Entering this state indicates a node has elected itself leader. For a given error bound $\epsilon \in [0, 1/2]$, we say an algorithm *solves* leader election with respect to $\epsilon$ if when executed in a network of any size, it satisfies the following two properties: (1) *liveness*: with probability 1, at least one node eventually enters the leader state; and (2) *safety*: with probability at least $1 - \epsilon$, there is never more than 1 node in the leader state. We also consider algorithms for leader election that are designed for networks of some minimal size $\tilde{N}$. In this case, the algorithm must guarantee liveness in every execution, but it needs to guarantee safety only if the network size $n$ is at least $\tilde{N}$. Our goal is to develop algorithms that use a minimum number of states to solve leader election for a given error bound $\epsilon$, probability precision $q$, and, when relevant, network size minimum $\tilde{N}$.

*Roadmap.* In Section 3.1, we present a lower bound for leader election. In Section 3.2, we present a universal algorithm template, followed by three specific instantiations in Sections 3.3, 3.4, and 3.5. Due to space constraints, proofs are deferred to the full version of this extended abstract [15].

## 3.1  Leader Election Lower Bound

Here we analyze the number of states required to solve leader election given a fixed $\epsilon$, $q$, and network size lower bound $\tilde{N}$. Our main result establishes that the number of states, $s$, must be in $\Omega(\lceil \frac{\log_q (1/\epsilon)}{\tilde{N}} \rceil)$.

To prove this result, we begin by defining and bounding a helper problem called $(1,k)$-*loneliness detection*, which requires an algorithm to safely distinguish between $n = 1$ and $n \geq k$. The bound leverages a probabilistic indistinguishability argument concerning a short execution of the state machine in both the $n = 1$ and $n = k$ cases. We then show that loneliness detection captures a core challenge of leader election by demonstrating how to transform a leader election algorithm that works for $n \geq \tilde{N}$ into a solution to $(1, \tilde{N})$-loneliness detection. The bound for the latter then carries over to leader election by reduction.

$(1,k)$-*Loneliness Detection.* The $(1,k)$-loneliness detection problem is defined for some integer $k > 1$ and error bound $\epsilon$. It assumes all nodes run the same state machine with two special terminal final states that we label $q_a$ (indicating "I am alone") and $q_c$ (indicating "I am in a crowd"). The *liveness* property of this problem requires that with probability 1, every node eventually enters a final state. The *safety* property requires that with probability at least $1 - \epsilon$, the following holds: if $n = 1$, then the single node in the system eventually enters $q_a$; and if $n \geq k$ then all nodes eventually enter $q_c$. Crucial to this problem definition is that we do not place any restrictions on the final states nodes enter for the case where $1 < n < k$.

The following bound shows that it becomes easier to break symmetry, i.e., easier to solve loneliness detection, as the threshold for detecting a crowd grows. Put another way: a big crowd is easier to detect than a small crowd.

**Lemma 1.** *Fix some integer $k > 1$. Let $\mathcal{L}$ be an algorithm that solves $(1,k)$-loneliness detection with error bound $\epsilon$ and probability precision $q$ using $s$ states. It follows that $s = \Omega(\frac{\log_q (1/\epsilon)}{k})$.*

*Reducing Loneliness Detection to Leader Election.* We now leverage the above result on $(1,k)$-loneliness detection to prove a lower bound for leader election under the guarantee that the network size $n \geq \tilde{N}$. The proof proceeds by reduction: we show how to transform such a leader election solution into a loneliness detection algorithm of similar state size.

**Theorem 1.** *Fix some network size lower bound $\tilde{N} \geq 1$. Let $\mathcal{A}$ be an algorithm that solves leader election with error bound $\epsilon$ and probability precision $q$ using $s$ states in any network where $n \geq \tilde{N}$. It follows that $s \in \Omega(\frac{\log_q (1/\epsilon)}{\tilde{N}})$.*

## 3.2  The Universal Leader Election Algorithm

We now turn our attention to leader election upper bounds. The three results that follow adopt a template/subroutine approach. In more detail, Figure 3.1 describes what we call the *universal leader election* algorithm. This algorithm, in turn, makes calls to a "termination subroutine." Different versions of this subroutine can be plugged into the universal algorithm, yielding different guarantees. Notice, this universal algorithm is parameterized with probability precision $q$ and error bound $\epsilon$, which it uses to define the useful parameter $\hat{q} = \min\{q, (1/\epsilon)\}$. This algorithm (as well as one of our termination subroutines) uses $1/\hat{q}$, not $1/q$, as its smallest transition probability (intuitively, there is little advantage in using a probability too much smaller than the bound $\epsilon$).

The basic operation of the algorithm is simple. Every node is initially active. Until the termination subroutine determines that it is time to stop, nodes repeatedly execute the knockout loop (lines 7–25). In each iteration of the loop, each active node beeps with probability $1 - 1/\hat{q}$ and listens otherwise. If a node ever hears a beep, it is knocked out, setting $ko = true$ and $active = false$. In any silent iteration where

---

**Algorithm 1.** Universal Leader Election

```
1:  active ← 1
2:  ko ← 1
3:  q̂ ← min{q, (1/ε)}
4:  done ← [Term. Subroutine](active, ko)
5:  ko ← 0
6:
7:  while (not done) do
8:
         ▷ Returns 0 with prob 1/q̂, else 1
9:      participate ← random_bit(1/q̂)
10:     chan ← ⊤
11:
         ▷ Knock Out Logic
12:     if active ∧ participate then
13:        beep()
14:     else
15:        chan ← recv()
16:     end if
17:     if active ∧ not participate then
18:        if chan = ⊤ then
19:           active ← 0
20:           ko ← 1
21:        end if
22:     end if
23:
         ▷ Termination Detection Logic
24:     if chan = ⊥ then
25:        done ← [Term. Subroutine](active, ko)
26:        ko ← 0
27:     end if
28:  end while
29:
         ▷ Become Leader if Still Active
30:  if active then
31:     leader ← 1
32:  else
33:     leader ← 0
34:  end if
35:  return(leader)
```

---

no node beeps, they execute the termination subroutine to decide whether to stop. Once termination is reached, any node that remains active becomes the leader.

*Termination Subroutines.* The goal of the termination subroutine is to decide whether leader election has been solved: it returns *true* if there is a leader and *false* otherwise. The termination subroutine is called simultaneously by all the nodes in the system, and it is passed two parameters: the value of *active*, which indicates whether or not the calling node is still contending to become leader, and *ko*, which indicates whether or not it has been knocked out in the main loop since the last call to the subroutine. We fix $R = 4 \log_{\hat{q}}(\max(n, 1/\epsilon))$: a parameter, which as we will later elaborate, captures a bound on the calls to the subroutine needed before likely termination. We consider the following properties of a termination detection routine, defined with respect to $\epsilon$ and $R$:

1. *Agreement*: Every node always returns the same value.
2. *Safety*: Over the first $R$ invocations, the probability that it returns true in any invocation with more than 1 active node is at most $\epsilon/2$.
3. *Eventual Termination*: If it is called infinitely often with only one active node, then eventually (with probability 1), it returns true.
4. *Fast Termination*: If it is called with only one active node, and with at least one node where $ko = true$, then it returns true.

*Universal Leader Election Analysis.* We now observe that the universal leader election algorithm is correct when combined with a termination subroutine that satisfies the relevant properties from above. To do so, we first determine how many rounds it takes until there is only one active node, and hence one possible leader. We say that an iteration of the knockout loop (lines 7–25) is *silent* if no node beeps during it. (Notice that the termination routine is only executed in silent iterations of the knockout loop.) We first bound how long it takes to reduce the number of active nodes:

**Lemma 2.** *Given probability $\epsilon \le 1/2$ and parameter $R = 4 \log_{\hat{q}}(\max(n, 1/\epsilon))$: after $R$ silent iterations of the knockout loop (lines 7–25), there remains exactly one active node, with probability at least $1 - \epsilon/2$.*

Let $T$ be a termination subroutine that satisfies Agreement and Eventual Termination. In addition, assume that $T$ satisfies safety in networks of size at least $\widetilde{N}$. We can now show that the universal leader election algorithm is correct with termination subroutine $T$:

**Theorem 2.** *If termination subroutine $T$ uses $s$ states and precision $q$, then the universal algorithm solves leader election with error $\epsilon$, $s + O(1)$ states, and $q$ precision (guaranteeing safety only in networks of size $n \ge \widetilde{N}$).*

While the preceding theorem can be used to show the feasibility of solving leader election, it does not bound the performance. For that, we rely on termination subroutines that ensure fast termination:

**Theorem 3.** *If termination subroutine $T$ satisfies Fast Termination instead of Eventual Termination, and if it uses $s$ states and $q$ precision, and if it runs in time $t$, then the universal algorithm solves leader election with error $\epsilon$ with $s + O(1)$ states and $q$ precision (guaranteeing safety only in networks of size $\ge \widetilde{N}$). Furthermore, it terminates in $O(t \log_{\hat{q}}(n + 1/\epsilon))$ rounds, with probability at least $1 - \epsilon$.*

## 3.3   Optimal Leader Election

Here we define a termination subroutine that, when combined with the universal leader election algorithm, matches our lower bound from Theorem 1. In more detail, fix an error bound $\epsilon$ and probability precision $q$. Fix some lower bound $\widetilde{N} \geq 1$ on the network size. We describe a termination detection subroutine that we call $StateOptimal(\widetilde{N})$ that requires $O(\lceil \frac{\log_q (1/\epsilon)}{\widetilde{N}} \rceil)$ states, and guarantees Agreement, Termination, and Safety in any network of size $n \geq \widetilde{N}$.

There are two important points relevant to this leader election strategy. First, for $\widetilde{N} = 1$, it provides a general solution that works in every size network. Second, the state requirements for this algorithm are asymptotically optimal according to Theorem 1. As will be clear from its definition below, the cost of this optimality is inefficiency (its expected time increases exponentially with $n$). We will subsequently identify a pair of more efficient solutions that gain efficiency at the cost of some optimality under some conditions.

*The* StateOptimal($\widetilde{N}$) *Termination Detection Subroutine.* The $StateOptimal(\widetilde{N})$ subroutine, unlike the other subroutines we will consider, ignores the *active* and *ko* parameters. Instead, it runs simple distributed coin flip logic among *all* nodes. In more detail, recall from the definition of the universal algorithm that $\hat{q} = \min\{q, (1/\epsilon)\}$. The subroutine consists of $\delta = \lceil \frac{c \log_{\hat{q}} (1/\epsilon)}{\widetilde{N}} \rceil$ rounds, defined for some constant $c \geq 1$ we will bound in the analysis. In each round, each node beeps with probability $1 - 1/\hat{q}$. At the end of the $\delta$ rounds, each node returns 1 if all $\delta$ rounds were silent, otherwise it returns 0.

*Analysis.* It is straightforward to determine that all nodes return the same value from this subroutine (i.e., if any node beeps or detects a beep, all nodes will return 0). It is also straightforward to verify that implementing this subroutine for a given $\delta$ requires $\Theta(\delta) = \Theta(\lceil \frac{\log_{\hat{q}} (1/\epsilon)}{\widetilde{N}} \rceil) = \Theta(\lceil \frac{\log_q (1/\epsilon)}{\widetilde{N}} \rceil)$ states (we can replace the $\hat{q}$ with $q$ in the final step because once $q$ gets beyond size $1/\epsilon$, the function stabilizes at 1). Eventual termination is also easy to verify, as every call to the subroutine has a probability strictly greater than 0 of terminating.

To show safety, we observe that the routine returns true only if all $n$ nodes are silent for all $\delta$ rounds. The probability of this happening is exponentially small in $(\delta n)$ and hence it is not hard to show that every $R$ invocations, the probability that the subroutine returns true in any invocation with more than one active node is at most $\epsilon/2$.

**Lemma 3 (Safety).** *Over the first $R$ invocations, the probability that the subroutine returns true in any invocation with more than 1 active node is at most $\epsilon/2$.*

Combined with Theorem 2, this yields the following conclusion:

**Theorem 4.** *For any network size lower bound $\widetilde{N}$, error parameter $\epsilon$ and precision $q$, the universal leader election algorithm combined with the*

*StateOptimal($\widetilde{N}$) subroutine, solves leader election with respect to these parameters when run in a network of size $n \geq \widetilde{N}$, and requires only $s = \Theta(\lceil \frac{\log_q (1/\epsilon)}{\widetilde{N}} \rceil)$ states.*

## 3.4   Fast Leader Election with Sub-Optimal State

The leader election algorithm from Section 3.3 can solve the problem with the optimal number of states for any combination of system parameters. It achieves this feat, however, at the expense of time: it is straightforward to determine that this algorithm requires time exponential in the network size. Here we consider a termination subroutine that trades state optimality for a solution that is fast (polylogarthmic in $1/\epsilon$ rounds) and simple to define (it uses the minimal probabilistic precision of $q = 2$). Furthermore, its definition is independent of the network size $n$, yet it still works for every possible $n$. For the purpose of this section, we assume that $q = \hat{q} = 2$. As we show below, this subroutine uses $\Theta(\log (1/\epsilon))$ states. This is suboptimal when high precision (i.e., larger $q$) is available, and when there is a lower bound $\widetilde{N}$ on the size of the network.

*The* Fixed Error *Termination Detection Subroutine.* This termination subroutine consists of a fixed schedule of $\lceil \log (2/\epsilon) \rceil + 2$ rounds. During the first round, any node that calls the subroutine with parameter *ko* equal to 1 beeps while all other nodes receive. If no node beeps, then the subroutine is aborted and all nodes return false.

Assume this does not occur, i.e., at least one node beeps in the first round. For each of the $\lceil \log (2/\epsilon) \rceil$ rounds that follow, every node with parameter *active* = 1, will flip a fair two-sided coin. If it comes up heads, it will beep, otherwise it will receive. Each node with *active* = 1 will start these rounds with a flag *solo* initialized to 1. If such a node ever detects a beep during a round that it receives, it will reset *solo* to 0 (as it just gained evidence that it is not alone).

The final round is used to determine if anyone detected a non-solo execution. To do so, every node with *active* = 1 and *solo* = 0 beeps. If no node beeps in this final round, then all nodes return true. Otherwise, all nodes return false.

*Analysis.* We proceed as before, observing that all nodes return the same value from this subroutine since all observe the same channel activity in the first and last rounds. It is also straightforward to verify that implementing this subroutine requires $O(\log (1/\epsilon))$ states to count the rounds and record *solo*. Fast termination follows directly from a case analysis of the algorithm.

**Lemma 4 (Fast Termination).** *If the* Fixed Error *subroutine is called with only 1 active node and with at least 1 node where ko = true, then it returns true.*

Safety requires a little more care, showing that the failure probabilities over $R$ invocations can be bounded by $\epsilon/2$, since the error probability depends on the number of active nodes.

**Lemma 5 (Safety).** *Over the first $R$ invocations of the subroutine, the probability that it returns true in any invocation with more than one active node is at most $\epsilon/2$.*

Combined with Theorem 3, these properties yield the following conclusion:

**Theorem 5.** *For error parameter $\epsilon$, the universal leader election algorithm combined with the Fixed Error subroutine, solves leader election with respect to $\epsilon$ in every size network, using only $s = \Theta(\log{(1/\epsilon)})$ states and $q = 2$. With probability at least $1 - \epsilon$, it terminates in $O(\log{(n + 1/\epsilon)}\log{(1/\epsilon)})$ rounds.*

### 3.5    Fast Leader Election with $O(1)$ States and High Probability

The final termination detection subroutine we consider requires only a constant number of states, and when executed in a network of size $n$, for any $n > 1$, it solves leader election with high probability in $n$. At first glance, this result may seem to violate the lower bound from Section 3.1, which notes that the state requirement grows with a $\log{(1/\epsilon)}$ factor as $\epsilon$ decreases. The question is why a constant number of states is sufficient here even though this term grows with $n$. The answer lies in the fact that $\epsilon$ is here a function of $n$, such that for any fixed $n$, it is true that $\widetilde{N} \geq n$, and therefore the $\widetilde{N}$ factor in the denominator of our lower bound swamps the growth of the $\log n$ factor in the numerator.

*The* Constant State *Termination Detection Subroutine.* The subroutine here is identical to the *Fixed Error* subroutine, except the length of subroutine is not fixed in advance (no node has enough states to count beyond a constant number of rounds—which is not enough for our purposes). Instead, we dynamically adapt the length of the subroutine to a sufficiently large function of $n$ using a distributed counting strategy.

In more detail, during the first round, any node that called the subroutine with parameter *ko* equal to 1 beeps while all other nodes receive. If no node beeps, then subroutine is aborted and all nodes will return value false (as is true for *Fixed Error*). Assuming the subroutine has not aborted, the nodes then proceed as follows: We partition rounds into even and odd pairs. During the odd numbered rounds, we proceed as in *Fixed Error*: every node with parameter *active* $= 1$, flips a fair coin; if it comes up heads, it will beep, otherwise it will receive; each node with *active* $= 1$ will start these rounds with a flag *solo* initialized to 1; if such a node ever detects a beep during a round that it receives, it will reset *solo* to 0 (as it just gained evidence that it is not alone).

During the even rounds, the nodes run a repeated knockout protocol for $O(1)$ iterations, for some fixed constant bounded in the analysis. In more detail, each node (regardless of whether or not it has *active* equal to true) begins the subroutine with a flag *attack* $= 1$ and a counter *count* $= 0$. In each even round, each node with *attack* $= 1$ flips a fair coin and beeps if it comes up heads; otherwise it listens. Any node that listens in an even round and hears a beep sets *attack* $= 0$. If there is an even round in which no node beeps, then all nodes increment *count* and reset *attack* = 1. This continues until *count* grows larger than the fixed constant mentioned above, When this occurs, all nodes move to the final round, which is identical to the final round in *Fixed Error*. That is: every node with *active* = 1 and *solo* = 0 beeps. If no node beeps in this final round, then all nodes return true. Otherwise, all nodes return false.

*Analysis.* The Liveness and Fast Termination properties follow from the same arguments used in our analysis of *Fixed Error*. The main difficulty in analyzing this subroutine is proving Safety. To do so, we first bound how long the subroutine is likely to run on any given invocation:

**Lemma 6.** *For any constant c, there exists a $c' > c$ and a constant bound for count, such that the main body of the subroutine runs for at least $c \log(n)$ rounds but no more than $c' \log n$ rounds, with high probability.*

**Lemma 7 (Safety).** *Over the first R invocations of the subroutine, the probability that it returns true in any invocation with more than one active node is at most $1/n^c$, for a constant c we can grow with our constant bound on count.*

We can then show that the subroutine guarantees safety. Combined with the Theorem 3, these properties yields the following conclusion:

**Theorem 6.** *For any network size n, the universal leader election algorithm combined with the Constant State termination detection subroutine, solves leader election with high probability in n using $s = O(1)$ states and $q = 2$. Also with high probability in n, it terminates in $O(\log^2 n)$ rounds.*

# 4   Solving General Distributed Decision Problems

In this section, we use a combination of our fast leader election algorithms as a key primitive in constructing an algorithm that simulates a logspace (in $n$) decider Turing Machine (TM) with a constant number of unary input tapes (of size $O(n)$ each). The simulation has error probability at most $\epsilon$, requires only the minimum probabilistic precision ($q = 2$), and uses $s = O(\log(1/\epsilon))$ states. If high probability in $n$ is sufficient, then the state size can be reduced to $s = O(1)$. In other words, once you have enough states to solve leader election, you can also solve a large class of expressive problems. Formally:

**Theorem 7.** *For any problem solvable by a logspace TM with a constant number of unary input tapes, there exist constants $c, d \geq 1$, such that for any error probability $\epsilon \in [0, 1/2]$ and network size $n \geq 1$, we can solve the problem in the beeping model in a network of size n with probability at least $1 - \epsilon$ using $s = c \log(1/\epsilon)$ states, precision $q = 2$, and an expected running time of $O(n^d \log^2(n + 1/\epsilon))$ rounds. For high probability correctness, $s = O(1)$ states are sufficient.*

Our strategy follows the outline originally identified in [4], where it was used to simulate a TM using a population protocol in the randomized interaction model. We first simulate a simple counter machine with a constant number of counters that can take values of size $O(n)$. We then apply a classical computability result due to Minsky [17] which shows how to simulate a logspace TM (with unary input tapes) using a counter machine of this type. The counter machine simulation in the beeping model, combined with Minsky's TM simulation, yields a TM simulation in the beeping model. See the full version of this extended abstract [15] for the details of our simulation, its analysis, and a discussion of its implications.

# References

1. Afek, Y., Alon, N., Bar-Joseph, Z., Cornejo, A., Haeupler, B., Kuhn, F.: Beeping a maximal independent set. In: Peleg, D. (ed.) Distributed Computing. LNCS, vol. 6950, pp. 32–50. Springer, Heidelberg (2011)
2. Afek, Y., Alon, N., Bar-Joseph, Z., Cornejo, A., Haeupler, B., Kuhn, F.: Beeping a maximal independent set. Distributed Computing 26(4), 195–208 (2013)
3. Afek, Y., Alon, N., Barad, O., Hornstein, E., Barkai, N., Bar-Joseph, Z.: A biological solution to a fundamental distributed computing problem. Science 331(6014), 183–185 (2011)
4. Angluin, D., Aspnes, J., Diamadi, Z., Fischer, M.J., Peralta, R.: Computation in networks of passively mobile finite-state sensors. Distributed Computing 18(4), 235–253 (2006)
5. Angluin, D., Aspnes, J., Eisenstat, D.: Stably computable predicates are semilinear. In: Proceedings of the Symposium on Principles of Distributed Computing (PODC), pp. 292–299 (2006)
6. Angluin, D., Aspnes, J., Eisenstat, D.: Fast computation by population protocols with a leader. Distributed Computing 21(3), 183–199 (2008)
7. Angluin, D., Aspnes, J., Eisenstat, D.: A simple population protocol for fast robust approximate majority. Distributed Computing 21(2), 87–102 (2008)
8. Angluin, D., Aspnes, J., Eisenstat, D., Ruppert, E.: The computational power of population protocols. Distributed Computing 20(4), 279–304 (2007)
9. Chatzigiannakis, I., Spirakis, P.G.: The dynamics of probabilistic population protocols. In: Taubenfeld, G. (ed.) DISC 2008. LNCS, vol. 5218, pp. 498–499. Springer, Heidelberg (2008)
10. Cornejo, A., Kuhn, F.: Deploying wireless networks with beeps. In: Lynch, N.A., Shvartsman, A.A. (eds.) DISC 2010. LNCS, vol. 6343, pp. 148–162. Springer, Heidelberg (2010)
11. Degesys, J., Nagpal, R.: Towards desynchronization of multi-hop topologies. In: Proceedings of the International Conference on Self-Adaptive and Self-Organizing Systems (SASO 2008) (2008)
12. Degesys, J., Rose, I., Patel, A., Nagpal, R.: Desync: self-organizing desynchronization and tdma on wireless sensor networks. In: Proceedings of the International Conference on Information Processing in Sensor Networks (2007)
13. Emek, Y., Wattenhofer, R.: Stone age distributed computing. In: Proceedings of the Symposium on Principles of Distributed Computing (PODC) (2013)

14. Förster, K.-T., Seidel, J., Wattenhofer, R.: Deterministic leader election in multi-hop beeping networks - (extended abstract). In: Kuhn, F. (ed.) DISC 2014. LNCS, vol. 8784, pp. 212–226. Springer, Heidelberg (2014)
15. Gilbert, S., Newport, C.: The computational power of beeps. Full version available online at. http://people.cs.georgetown.edu/~cnewport/pubs/Beeps-Full.pdf (arXiv)
16. Lenzen, C., Lynch, N., Newport, C., Radeva, T.: Trade-offs between selection complexity and performance when searching the plane without communication. In: Proceedings of the Symposium on Principles of Distributed Computing (PODC) (2014)
17. Minsky, M.L.: Computation: finite and infinite machines. Prentice-Hall (1967)
18. Motskin, A., Roughgarden, T., Skraba, P., Guibas, L.J.: Lightweight coloring and desynchronization for networks. In: Proceedings of the of the Conference on Computer Communication (INFOCOM) (2009)
19. Navlakha, S., Bar-Joseph, Z.: Distributed information processing in biological and computational systems. Communications of the ACM **58**(1), 94–102 (2014)
20. Scott, A., Jeavons, P., Xu, L.: Feedback from nature: an optimal distributed algorithm for maximal independent set selection. In: Proceedings of the Symposium on Principles of Distributed Computing (PODC) (2013)

# Byzantine Fireflies

Rachid Guerraoui and Alexandre Maurer[(✉)]

EPFL, Lausanne, Switzerland
{rachid.guerraoui,alexandre.maurer}@epfl.ch

**Abstract.** This paper addresses the problem of synchronous beeping, as addressed by swarms of fireflies. We present Byzantine-resilient algorithms ensuring that the correct processes eventually beep synchronously despite a subset of nodes beeping asynchronously. We assume that $n > 2f$ ($n$ is the number of processes and $f$ is the number of Byzantine processes) and that the initial state of the processes can be arbitrary (self-stabilization). We distinguish the cases where the beeping period is known, unknown or approximately known. We also consider the situation where the processes can produce light continuously.

## 1 Introduction

Biologically inspired algorithms have become increasingly popular in the last decades [21]. This field is motivated by fascinating emerging phenomena in nature: swarms of simple individuals (cells [15], ants [3], cuckoos [7], bats [13], ...) that seem to achieve a very consistent and regular behavior without centralized control and with very limited communications. It is appealing to design distributed algorithms reproducing their behavior with minimal communication assumptions.

One of these phenomena is the synchronization of fireflies [18,19]. Fireflies are insect that can produce flashes of light at night. They can do so synchronously and with a regular period. Our interest here is to recreate this phenomena in the field of distributed computing.

At first sight, this problem has similarities with the problem of clock synchronization [4,8,9], which can also be declined for wireless ad hoc networks [16] and simultaneous-action synchronization problems [20]. These problems are however typically studied in message passing systems: the processes can identify each other and send semantically rich messages with timestamps. Such strong communication assumptions do not seem to be available in a fireflies swarm. In this paper, we therefore consider minimal communication primitives.

The fireflies synchronization problem has first been studied from a mathematical point of view [12,14]: the individuals are represented as dynamical oscillators, and the problem is modeled as a system of differential equations. Another model, more related to the field of distributed computing, proposed in [2,11,17], involves processes that can produce discrete *beeps* at arbitrary moments, and must eventually beep synchronously.

© Springer-Verlag Berlin Heidelberg 2015
Y. Moses (Ed.): DISC 2015, LNCS 9363, pp. 47–59, 2015.
DOI: 10.1007/978-3-662-48653-5_4

Solutions to these problems [2,11,17] use averaging methods to achieve synchronous beeping. These solutions are efficient, but are also very sensitive to incorrect processes, which can easily move forward the mean value. Therefore, if there is no limit on the frequency of malicious beeps, one single incorrect process is sufficient to prevent synchronization.

In this paper, we consider that some fireflies may have an incorrect behavior: they can be broken, dead, ill, or trying to eat each other [1]. Our motivation is the intuition that a biological system should be inherently resilient to such malfunctions. We thus consider the problem of synchronous beeping in the presence of malicious (*Byzantine*) processes. A first solution relaxes the requirement to "beeping in a bounded interval" [5]. However, we would like to preserve perfect synchronous beeping here. In order to tolerate malicious beeps, our strategy is not based on averaging methods, but on the number of simultaneous beeps and the delay between two groups of beeps.

*Our Contribution.* We consider a system where each process can produce *discrete* and *anonymous* beeps (flashes of light). Each process can "see" all beeps, and count the number of beeps produced at a given instant. The processes can however not distinguish the authors of the beeps, and no other communication is allowed between the processes. We consider the most general failure model: *Byzantine* failures [10], where the failing processes have a totally arbitrary behavior. Among the $n$ processes, at most $f$ are Byzantine. We assume that $n > 2f$ (we show that this condition is necessary in Section 3).

We consider the context of *self-stabilization* [6]: the initial state is arbitrary – that is, each process has initially memorized an arbitrary sequence of beeps. This assumption encompasses any chaotic sequence of events occurring before the synchronization (for instance, some processes can join and leave the system, which is usually the case in swarms of insects). Then, we show how to achieve synchronous beeping: all correct processes beep simultaneously and with the same period, whatever the behavior of Byzantine processes may be.

We present the model and the problem in Section 2, and show that the condition $n > 2f$ is necessary in Section 3. Then, we present four algorithms for this problem:

- We first give two algorithms for the cases where the desired beeping period is known (Section 4) and unknown (Section 5).
- Then, we give an algorithm for the case where each process has an approximate knowledge of the desired period (Section 6), which may be the case of insects. Thus, the correct processes must agree on a same period, *and* this period must be in the range of the desired one. This problem is more difficult, as correct processes are disorganized while Byzantine processes are perfectly coordinated. In this part, we relax the self-stabilization property (we give an impossibility result) and assume that $n > 3f$.
- Finally, we consider an alternative model where processes can produce light continuously. We give an algorithm with approximate period knowledge that does not relax the two aforementioned properties (Section 7).

These solutions show that synchronous beeping is feasible even in the presence of adversaries with an unbounded power. They could be adapted for clock synchronization with minimal communication assumptions.

## 2 Model and Problem

In this section, we state the distributed system model and the problem.

*Communication Model.* We consider a distributed system of $n$ processes and a continuous time domain. A process can *beep* at any time $t$. A beep is discrete, and is entirely described by its time position $t$ (we will revisit this assumption in Section 7). No other communication than beeping is available, and the beeps are anonymous.

For any time $t$, let $S(t)$ be a multiset containing the time of each previous beep ($\forall t' \in S(t)$, $t' < t$). If $m$ processes beep simultaneously at time $t'$, then $t'$ appears $m$ times in $S(t)$ (for instance, if $S(t) = \{t_1, t_2, t_2, t_2, t_3\}$ with $t_1 < t_2 < t_3$, 3 processes beep simultaneously at time $t_2$). For $S(t) = \{t_1, t_2, t_3, \dots\}$, let $S'(t) = \{t - t_1, t - t_2, t - t_3, \dots\}$.

For any time $t$, each process knows the set $S'(t)$. In other words, each process only knows the position of the previous beeps relatively to the current time: there is no common time origin (otherwise, the problem would be trivial and would not correspond to swarms of fireflies). The processes can count the beeps at a given instant, but cannot distinguish the authors of the beeps. We do not consider any memory restriction that would prevent the processes from knowing $S'(t)$ entirely. No other form of memory (such as internal variables) is available.

We denote by $m(t)$ the number of processes beeping at time $t$. The beeps are strictly discrete: there exists no time interval $[t_1, t_2]$ with $t_1 < t_2$ such that, $\forall t \in [t_1, t_2]$, $m(t) \neq 0$. Therefore, there must always be a time interval between two successive and non-simultaneous beeps.

*Correct and Byzantine Processes.* At most $f$ processes are *Byzantine*, and may exhibit an arbitrary behavior. The other processes are *correct*, and follow the algorithm assigned to them. We assume that $n > 2f$. All correct processes follow the same algorithm.

*Self-stabilization.* Our objective is to achieve synchronization despite any arbitrary initial state. Therefore, we assume the previous model encompasses such an arbitrary initial state.

Let $t_0$ be a given time, unkown to the correct processes. We assume that, before $t_0$, each correct process has memorized an arbitrary sequence of beeps (which may be different for each process). Then, starting from $t_0$, all correct processes register the same beeps.

More precisely, for any process $p$, let $A(p) = \{t_1, t_2, t_3, \dots\}$ be an arbitrary set with repetition such that, $\forall t \in A(p)$, $t < t_0$. $A(p)$ represents the arbitrary sequence of beeps memorized by $p$ before $t_0$. For any time $t$, let

$A'(p, t) = \{t - t_1, t - t_2, t - t_3, \dots\}$. Then, we now assume that for any time $t$, $p$ knows $S'(t) \cup A'(p, t)$.

An algorithm ensuring a given property in such a context (the initial state is arbitrary) is *self-stabilizing* [6]. In particular, it can represent the fact that some processes join and leave the system arbitrarily before $t_0$.

*Problem.* Let $T$ be any time period. We say that the processes achieve *synchronous beeping* at time $t$ if, starting from time $t$, all correct processes beep and only beep at time $t$, $t + T$, $t + 2T$, $t + 3T$, ...

## 3  Lower Bound

Is this section, we show that it is necessary to have a strict majority of correct processes ($n > 2f$) to solve the problem.

**Theorem 1.** *An algorithm can only ensure synchronous beeping if $n > 2f$.*

*Proof.* Suppose the opposite: there exists an algorithm ensuring synchronous beeping with $n \leq 2f$. In particular, let us suppose that $n = 2f$.

We first show that for any initial state, there exists a time period $T'$ and a time $t_1$ such that, $\forall t \geq t_1$, the behavior of the correct processes at time $t$ (that is, their decision to beep or not) only depends of the time interval $]t - T', t[$. Suppose the opposite. Then, there exists an initial state such that $\forall t \geq t_0$, there exists $t' \geq t$ such that two correct processes do not have the same behavior at time $t'$. Therefore, at time $t'$, at least one correct process beeps and at least one correct process does not beep. Thus, as synchronous beeping requires all correct processes to have the same behavior after a time $t \geq t_0$, we do not have synchronous beeping: contradiction. Thus, there exists such a time $t_1$ and such a time period $T'$.

Let $t, t + T, t + 2T \dots$ be the times of synchronous beeping. Let us suppose that the Byzantine processes beep at times $t + T/2, t + 3T/2, t + 5T/2 \dots$ Let $i$ be an integer such that $iT > T'$ and $t + iT \geq t_1$. As we have synchronous beeping, all correct processes must beep at time $t + (i + 1)T$. As $f$ processes beep a time $t, t + T/2, t + T, t + 3T/2 \dots$, the interval $]t' - T', t'[$ contains exactly the same beeps for $t' = t + (i + 1)T$ and for $t' = t + (i + 1)T + T/2$. Thus, all correct processes also beep at time $t + (i + 1)T + T/2$, and we do not have synchronous beeping: contradiction.

## 4  Known Beeping Period

In this section, we assume that all correct processes know the same time period $T$. We give an algorithm ensuring synchronous beeping in this setting.

## 4.1   Algorithm (Known Period Synchronous Beeping - KPSB)

A correct process beeps at time $t$ if at least one of the two following conditions is true:

1. $\forall t' \in ]t - T, t[, \, m(t') = 0$
2. $(m(t - T) \neq 0) \wedge (\forall t' \in ]t - T, t[, m(t') \leq f)$

## 4.2   Informal Description

The KPSB algorithm performs in three steps:

- If no process beeps, then eventually, some correct process beeps (condition 1 of the algorithm).
- Then, $T$ time units after a beep, all correct processes beep (condition 2 of the algorithm).
- Finally, when at least $f + 1$ processes beep at the same time, the correct processes wait $T$ time units and beep (condition 2 of the algorithm). Then, we have synchronous beeping.

## 4.3   Correctness Proof

**Lemma 1.** *There exists $t \geq t_0$ such that $m(t) \neq 0$.*

*Proof.* Suppose the opposite: $\forall t \geq t_0, \, m(t) = 0$. Then, according to condition 1 of the algorithm, a correct process eventually beeps: contradiction.

**Lemma 2.** *There exists $t \geq t_0$ such that $m(t) > f$.*

*Proof.* Suppose the opposite: $\forall t \geq t_0, m(t) \leq f$. According to Lemma 1, there exists a time $t' \geq t_0$ such that $m(t') \neq 0$. Then, according to condition 2 of the algorithm, all correct processes beep at time $t' + T$, and $m(t' + T) > f$: contradiction. Thus, the result.

**Theorem 2.** *Algorithm KPSB ensures synchronous beeping.*

*Proof.* According to Lemma 2, there exists a time $t$ such that $m(t) > f$. Then, according to condition 2 of the algorithm, no correct process can beep in $]t + T[$.

Suppose that a correct process $p$ does not beep at time $t + T$. Consider the point of view of $p$. Then, according to condition 2 of the algorithm, there exists $t' \in ]t, t + T[$ such that $m(t') > f$. Thus, as no correct process beeps in $]t + T[$, at least $f + 1$ Byzantine processes beep at time $t'$: contradiction. Thus, all correct processes beep a time $t + T$, and $m(t + T) > f$.

Therefore, by induction, we achieve synchronous beeping at time $t + T$.

# 5   Unknown Beeping Period

We now assume that no common time period is initially known to the processes. We thus give an algorithm where the correct processes achieve synchronous beeping after agreeing on a same period. Note that, as the processes do no have any common time metric, this can represent the case where the processes have a different perception of time.

## 5.1   Preliminaries

The algorithm makes use of the following predicates.

Let $t$ be any time, let $t_1 < t$, and let $t_2 < t_1$. We define the following predicates:

- $C_1(t, t_1, t_2) \equiv (m(t_1) > f) \wedge (m(t_2) > f) \wedge (\forall t' \in ]t_2, t_1[\cup]t_1, t[, m(t') \leq f)$
- $C_2(t, t_1, t_2) \equiv (m(t_1) \neq 0) \wedge (m(t_2) \neq 0)$

For any time $t$ and $\forall i \in \{1, 2\}$, we also define the following predicates:

- $now_i(t)$: there exists $t_1 < t$ and $t_2 < t_1$ such that $C_i(t, t_1, t_2)$ is true and $t - t_1 = t_1 - t_2$
- $wait_i(t)$: there exists $t_1 < t$ and $t_2 < t_1$ such that $C_i(t, t_1, t_2)$ is true and $t - t_1 < t_1 - t_2$

## 5.2   Algorithm (Unknown Period Synchronous Beeping - UPSB)

Let $p$ be a correct process. Let $T(p)$ be a totally arbitrary time period known by $p$.

Process $p$ beeps if one of the following conditions is satisfied:

1. $now_1(t)$
2. $\neg wait_1(t) \wedge now_2(t)$
3. $\neg wait_1(t) \wedge \neg wait_2(t) \wedge (\forall t' \in ]t - T(p), t[, m(t') = 0)$

## 5.3   Informal Description

The UPSB algorithm performs in three steps:

- If no process beeps, then eventually, some correct process beeps (condition 3 of the algorithm).
- If two processes beep with a time interval $T$, then all correct processes beep $T$ time units after the second beep (condition 2 of the algorithm). This ensures that at least $f + 1$ processes beep at the same time.
- If at least $f + 1$ processes beep at two different times, then all correct processes beep with the same time interval (condition 1 of the algorithm). Thus, we have synchronous beeping.

To avoid collisions between the conditions, we define the algorithm such that condition 1 has priority over condition 2, and condition 2 has priority over condition 3. This is ensured by the conditions $wait_i$ and $now_i$.

## 5.4   Correctness Proof

**Lemma 3.** *Let $t \geq t_0$. There exists $t' \geq t$ such that $m(t) \neq 0$.*

*Proof.* Suppose the opposite: $\forall t' > t, m(t) = 0$.
   Consider the point of view of a given process $p$.

- If there exists $t_1 < t$ and $t_2 < t_1$ such that $C_1(t, t_1, t_2)$ is true and $t - t_1 \leq t_1 - t_2$, then according to condition 1 of the algorithm, $p$ beeps at time $t' = 2t_1 - t_2 \geq t$.
- Otherwise, if there exists $t_1 < t$ and $t_2 < t_1$ such that $C_2(t, t_1, t_2)$ is true and $t - t_1 \leq t_1 - t_2$, then according to condition 2 of the algorithm, $p$ beeps at time $t' = 2t_1 - t_2 \geq t$.
- Otherwise, according to condition 3 of the algorithm, $p$ beeps at time $t' \in [t, t + T(p)]$.

Therefore, in all cases, $p$ beeps at a time $t' \geq t$: contradiction. Thus, the result.

**Lemma 4.** *Let $t \geq t_0$. There exists $t' \geq t$ such that $m(t) > f$.*

*Proof.* Suppose the opposite: $\forall t' \geq t, m(t) \leq f$.
   Consider the point of view of a given correct process $p$. If there exists $t_1 < t$ and $t_2 < t_1$ such that $C_1(t, t_1, t_2)$ is true, then $\forall t' > 2t_1 - t_2$, $now_1(t')$ is false. Otherwise, $\forall t' \geq t$, $now_1(t')$ is false. Thus, there exists a date $t_3(p) \geq t$ such that, $\forall t' \geq t_3(p)$, $now_1(t')$ and $now_2(t')$ are false. Let $t_3$ be such that, for any correct process $p$, $t_3 \geq t_3(p)$.
   According to Lemma 3, there exists $t_4 \geq t_3$ and $t_5 > t_4$ such that $m(t_4) \neq 0$ and $m(t_5) \neq 0$. Thus, at time $t' = 2t_5 - t_4$, $now_3(t')$ is true. As $t_5 > t_4 \geq t_0$, for all correct processes, condition 2 of the algorithm is satisfied at time $t'$. Thus, all correct processes beep at time $t'$, and $m(t') > f$: contradiction. Thus, the result.

**Theorem 3.** *Algorithm UPSB ensures synchronous beeping.*

*Proof.* According to Lemma 4, there exists $t \geq t_0$ and $t_1 > t$ such that $m(t) > f$ and $m(t_1) > f$. Let $t_2$ be the earliest time such that $t_2 > t$ and $m(t_2) > f$. Let $T = t_2 - t$.
   According to the algorithm, no correct process can beep a time $t' \in ]t, t + T[$. Thus, as there is at most $f$ Byzantine processes, $\forall t' \in ]t, t + T[$, $m(t) \leq f$. Thus, as $t \geq 0$, for all correct processes, condition 1 of the algorithm is satisfied at time $t + T$. Thus, all correct process beep at time $t$, and $m(t) > f$.
   Therefore, by induction, we achieve synchronous beeping at date $t$, with a period $T$.

# 6    Average Beeping Period

In the two previous sections, we gave an algorithm for the case where a same period $T$ is initially known to all correct processes, and then one for the case where this period is unknown, and where the correct processes must agree on the same period. However, this can be any period.

We now consider the case where the correct processes have an approximate knowledge of a desired period $T_0$, and must agree on a period close to $T_0$. This is a more difficult problem, as correct processes are disorganized while Byzantine processes keep their perfect coordination capabilities.

For these reasons, we consider a more restrictive setting than the previous section. We now assume that $n > 3f$, and that no process beeps before a time $t_0$. This second assumption is justified in Section 6.1.

We assume that each correct process knows a time period $T(p)$ which is in a certain interval around $T_0$: $T(p) \in [T_0, (1+\epsilon)T_0]$, with $\epsilon \in ]0, 1[$. The parameter $\epsilon$ can be as small as we want, and represents the precision of the knowledge of the period. We give an algorithm that ensures synchronous beeping with a period $T \in [(1-\epsilon)T_0, (1+\epsilon)T_0]$.

## 6.1    Lower Bound

First, let us justify the removal of the self-stabilizing property for this part. We show that, if we require self-stabilization, no algorithm can ensure that the beeping period is in the desired interval.

**Theorem 4.** *There is no self-stabilizing algorithm ensuring synchronous beeping with a period $T \in [(1-\epsilon)T_0, (1+\epsilon)T_0]$.*

*Proof.* Suppose the opposite. Then, for a given initial state, there exists $T'$ and $t_1$ such as described in Theorem 1.

Let $t$ be a time where we have synchronous beeping with a period $T$. Let $i$ be such that $iT \geq T'$. Then, all correct processes beep at time $t_2 = t + (i+1)T$. Let $p$ be a correct process and let $T_1 = T(p)$.

Now, let $q$ be a correct process, and suppose that the content of the interval $]t_2 - T', t_2[$ is the initial state for $q$. Then, if $T(q) = T_1$, $q$ beeps at times $t_0$, $t_0 + T_1$, $t_0 + 2T_1 \ldots$

Let us show that there exists $T_2 > T_1$ such that, if $T(q) = T_2$, $q$ does not beep at all times $t_0, t_0 + T_1, t_0 + 2T_1 \ldots$ Suppose the opposite. Then, the beeping period $T_1$ is independent of $T(q)$, and it is impossible to ensure that $T_1 \in [(1-\epsilon)T_0, (1+\epsilon)T_0]$: contradiction. Let $T_2$ be the smallest period having this property, and let $T_3 = T_2/(1+\epsilon)$.

Now, let us consider the two following situations:

1. For one correct process $q$, $T(q) = T_3$. For each other correct process $p$, $T(p) = T_2$. One Byzantine process $b$ acts like a correct process with $T(b) = T_2$.
2. For each correct process $p$, $T(p) = T_2$. One Byzantine process $b$ acts like a correct process with $T(b) = T_3$.

In situation 2, as the algorithm ensures synchronous beeping, all correct processes beep at date $t_0$, $t_0 + T_1, t_0 + 2T_1 \ldots$ Thus, as the two situations are indistinguishable for the correct processes, each correct process $p$ such that $T(p) = T_2$ beeps at the same times. However, there exists a time $t'$ such that all correct processes but $q$ beep. As the behavior of $q$ at a given time $t$ only depends of the time interval $]t - T', t[$, the same situation repeats each $T'$ time units, and $q$ never beeps synchronously with other correct processes. Thus, we do not have synchronous beeping: contradiction.

## 6.2  Preliminaries

Our algorithm uses the following function $g$ as well as several predicates.

Let $T$ and $T'$ be two time periods. Let $k \in \mathbb{Z}$ be the largest rational integer such that $T(1 + \epsilon)^k \leq T'$. Then, let $g(T, T') = T(1 + \epsilon)^k$.

Let $t$ be any time, let $t_1 < t$, and let $t_2 < t_1$. We define the following predicates:

- $C_1(t, t_1, t_2) \equiv (m(t_1) > f) \wedge (m(t_2) > f) \wedge (\forall t' \in ]t_2, t_1[ \cup ]t_1, t[, m(t') \leq f) \wedge (\exists t' < t_2, m(t')$
- $C_2(t, t_1, t_2) \equiv (m(t_1) > f) \wedge (m(t_2) \neq 0) \wedge (\forall t' \in ]t_2, t_1[, m(t') = 0) \wedge (\forall t' \in ]t_1, t[, m(t') \leq f)$
- $C_3(t, t_1, t_2) \equiv (m(t_1) \neq 0) \wedge (m(t_2) \neq 0)$

Then, for any time $t$ and $\forall i \in \{1, 3\}$, we consider the following predicates:

- $now_i(t)$: there exists $t_1 < t$ and $t_2 < t_1$ such that $C_i(t, t_1, t_2)$ is true and $t - t_1 = t_1 - t_2$
- $wait_i(t)$: there exists $t_1 < t$ and $t_2 < t_1$ such that $C_i(t, t_1, t_2)$ is true and $t - t_1 < t_1 - t_2$

At last, we add the two following predicates:

- $now(t, T)$: there exists $t_1 < t$ and $t_2 < t_1$ such that $C_2(t, t_1, t_2)$ is true and $t - t_1 = g(t_1 - t_2, T)$.
- $wait(t, T)$: there exists $t_1 < t$ and $t_2 < t_1$ such that $C_2(t, t_1, t_2)$ is true and $t - t_1 < g(t_1 - t_2, T)$.

## 6.3  Algorithm (Average Period Synchronous Beeping - APSB)

A correct process $p$ beeps if one of the following conditions is satisfied:

1. $now_1'(t)$
2. $\neg wait_1'(t) \wedge now(t, T(p))$
3. $\neg wait_1'(t) \wedge \neg wait(t, T(p)) \wedge now_3(t)$
4. $\neg wait_1'(t) \wedge \neg wait(t, T(p)) \wedge \neg wait_3(t) \wedge (\forall t' \in ]t - T(p), t[, m(t') = 0)$

## 6.4   Informal Description

The main difficulty is that the correct processes are disorganized. For instance, if each process $p$ beeps $T(p)$ time units after a given beep, the correct processes may never beep at the same time.

To overcome this difficulty, we use a function $g(T, T')$ that uses any time measure $T$ to split the periods $T(p)$ in two groups (see Lemma 5). The two possible output periods are in the interval $[(1 - \epsilon)T_0, (1 + \epsilon)T_0]$ (see Lemma 6). Thus, as $n > 3f$, a majority of correct processes beep with the same period, which is in the desired interval.

The formalism is similar to the previous algorithm. The principle is as follows:

- Condition 4 of the algorithm ensures that a process always eventually beeps.
- Condition 3 ensures that all correct processes eventually beep at the same time.
- Condition 2 computes the aforementioned principle.
- Condition 1 reproduces the same time period and ensures synchronous beeping.

## 6.5   Correctness Proof

**Lemma 5.** *For a given* $T > 0$, *let* $G(T) = \bigcup_{T' \in [T_0, (1+\epsilon)T_0]} g(T, T')$. *Then,* $|G(T)| \leq 2$.

*Proof.* Let $k \in \mathbb{Z}$ be the largest relative integer such that $T(1 + \epsilon)^k \leq T_0$. Thus, $g(T, T_0) = T(1 + \epsilon)^k$ and $T_0 < T(1 + \epsilon)^{k+1}$. Therefore, $(1 + \epsilon)T_0 < T(1 + \epsilon)^{k+2}$ and $g(T, (1 + \epsilon)T_0) \leq T(1 + \epsilon)^{k+1}$. Then, either $G(T) = \{T(1 + \epsilon)^k\}$ or $G(T) = \{T(1 + \epsilon)^k, T(1 + \epsilon)^{k+1}\}$, and $|G(T)| \leq 2$.

**Lemma 6.** $\forall T > 0$ *and* $\forall T' \in [T_0, (1 + \epsilon)T_0]$, $g(T, T') \in [(1 - \epsilon)T_0, (1 + \epsilon)T_0]$.

*Proof.* Let $k$ be largest relative integer such that $T(1 + \epsilon)^k \leq T_0$. Then, $T_0 < T(1 + \epsilon)^{k+1} = g(T, T_0)(1 + \epsilon)$. As $(1 - \epsilon)(1 + \epsilon) = 1 - \epsilon^2 < 1$, $1 - \epsilon < 1/(1 + \epsilon)$, and $g(T, T_0) > T_0/(1 + \epsilon) > (1 - \epsilon)T_0$. Thus, $g(T, T') \geq (1 - \epsilon)T_0$. Besides, as $g(T, T') \leq T'$, $g(T, T') \leq (1 + \epsilon)T_0$. Thus, the result.

**Lemma 7.** *There exists* $t \geq t_0$ *such that* $m(t) \neq 0$.

*Proof.* Suppose the opposite: $\forall t \geq t_0$, $m(t) = 0$. Let $p$ be a correct process. Then, according to condition 4 of the algorithm, $p$ beeps at time $t_0 + T(p)$: contradiction. Thus, the result.

**Lemma 8.** *There exists* $t \geq t_0$ *and* $t' < t$ *such that* $m(t) > f$ *and* $m(t') \neq 0$.

*Proof.* Suppose the opposite: there exists no such $t$ and $t'$. According to Lemma 7, there exists a time $t_1$ such that $m(t_1) \neq 0$. Let $t_1$ be the earliest date such that $m(t_1) \neq 0$. According to Lemma 7, there exists $t' \geq t_0$ such that $t' > t_1$ and $m(t') \neq 0$. Then, according to condition 3 of the algorithm, all correct processes beep at time $2t' - t_1$, and $m(2t' - t_1) > f$: contradiction. Thus, the result.

**Theorem 5.** *Algorithm APSB ensures synchronous beeping with a period* $T \in [(1 - \epsilon)T_0, (1 + \epsilon)T_0]$.

*Proof.* Let $t$ be the earliest time such as described in Lemma 8. Let $t'$ be the latest time such that $t' < t$ and $m(t') \neq 0$. According to condition 2 of the algorithm, each correct process $p$ beeps at time $t + g(t - t', T(p))$.

According to Lemma 5 and Lemma 6, there are only two possible value $T_1$ and $T_2$ of $g(t - t', T(p))$, and $\{T_1, T_2\} \in [(1 - \epsilon)T_0, (1 + \epsilon)T_0]$. Let $P_1$ (resp. $P_2$) be the set of correct processes beeping at time $t + T_1(p)$ (resp. $t + T_2(p)$). As $n > 3f$, then either $|P_1| > f$ or $|P_2| > f$. Thus, there exists $t_1 \in \{t + T_1(p), t + T_2(p)\}$ such that $m(t_1) > f$. Let $t_1$ be the earliest time such that $t_1 > t$ and $m(t_1) > f$.

Let us show that $T = t_1 - t \in [(1 - \epsilon)T_0, (1 + \epsilon)T_0]$. Suppose the opposite. Then, according to condition 2 of the algorithm, no correct process beeps at time $t_1$. Thus, at least $f + 1$ Byzantine nodes beep at time $t_1$: contradiction.

Then, according to condition 1 of the algorithm, all correct processes beep at time $t_1 + T$, and no correct process beeps in the time interval $]t_1, t_1 + T[$. Therefore, by induction, we have synchronous beeping at time $t_1$ with a period $T \in [(1 - \epsilon)T_0, (1 + \epsilon)T_0]$.

# 7  Synchronous Lighting

In the previous sections, we assumed that the processes could produce discrete beeps. In this section, we assume that a process $p$ can continuously increase and decrease a luminosity variable $l(p)$. We define an alternative but similar problem (*synchronous lighting*) and give an algorithm for the case where the desired period is approximately known. In this section, $n > 2f$.

Each correct process $p$ knows a time period $T(p) \in [T_0, (1 + \epsilon)T_0]$, and holds a variable $l(p) \in [0, 1]$. $l(p)$ is a continuous function of time. We assume that the time to increase (resp. decrease) $l(p)$ from 0 to 1 (resp. 1 to 0) is at most $\epsilon T_0$. Let $P$ be the set of processes. Let $L(t)$ be the value of $\Sigma_{p \in P} l(p)$ at time $t$.

## 7.1  Problem

We say that the processes achieve *synchronous lighting* at time $t_1$ if there exists $t_2, t_3, t_4 \ldots$ such that:

1. Each time $t_i$ corresponds to a peak of luminosity: $\forall i \in \{1, 2, 3, \ldots\}$, $L(t_i) \geq n - f$.
2. The delay between two consecutive times $t_i$ is approximately equal to $T_0$: $\forall i \in \{1, 2, 3, \ldots\}$, $t_{i+1} - t_i \in [T_0, (1 + 2\epsilon)T_0]$.
3. The correct processes only produce light around times $t_i$: for a given correct process $p$, if $l(p) \neq 0$ at time $t$, then there exists $i \in \{1, 2, 3, \ldots\}$ such that $|t - t_i| \leq 2\epsilon T_0$.

## 7.2   Algorithm (Average Period Synchronous Lighting - APSL)

Each correct process $p$ has the following behavior:

- If there exists $t' \in ]t - T(p), t[$ such that $L(t') \geq n - f$, decrease $l(p)$.
- Otherwise, increase $l(p)$.

## 7.3   Correctness Proof

**Lemma 9.** *There exists $t \geq t_0$ such that $L(t) \geq n - f$.*

*Proof.* Suppose the opposite: $\forall t \geq t_0$, $L(t) < n - f$. Let $p$ be a correct process. Then, according to the algorithm, starting from time $t_0 + T(p)$, $l(p)$ increases. Therefore, at time $t_0 + (1 + 2\epsilon)T_0$, for each correct process $p$, $l(p) = 1$. Thus, $L(t_0 + (1 + 2\epsilon)T_0) \geq n - f$: contradiction. Thus, the result.

**Theorem 6.** *Algorithm APSL ensures synchronous lighting.*

*Proof.* According to Lemma 9, there exists $t \geq t_0$ such that $L(t) \geq n - f$. Therefore, according to the algorithm, starting from time $t$, each correct process $p$ decreases $l(p)$. Therefore, at time $t + \epsilon T_0$, for each correct process $p$, $l(p) = 0$. Then, as there are at most $f$ Byzantine processes, $\forall t' \in ]t + \epsilon T_0, t + T_0[$, $L(t') \leq f \leq n - f$.

Now, let us show that there exists $t_1 \in [t + T_0, t + (1 + 2\epsilon)T_0]$ such that $L(t_1) \geq n - f$. Suppose the opposite. Let $p$ be a correct process. Then, according to the algorithm, starting from time $t + T(p)$, $l(p)$ increases. Therefore, at time $t + (1 + 2\epsilon)T_0$, for each correct process $p$, $l(p) = 1$. Thus, $L(t + (1 + 2\epsilon)T_0) \geq n - f$: contradiction.

Then, $L(t_1) \geq n - f$, $t_1 - t \in [T_0, (1 + 2\epsilon)T_0]$ and for each correct process $p$, if $t' \in ]t + \epsilon T_0, t + T_0[$, $l(p) = 0$ at time $t'$. Thus, if $l(p) \neq 0$ at time $t' \in [t, t_1]$, then either $|t' - t| \leq 2\epsilon T_0$ or $|t' - t_1| \leq 2\epsilon T_0$.

Therefore, by induction, we have synchronous lighting at time $t$.

# 8   Conclusion

We considered the problem of synchronous beeping. We assumed the presence of Byzantine processes that can beep as often as they want. We gave synchronization algorithms for the cases where the period is known, unknown and approximately known. We also considered an alternative continuous model.

An open question is the tightness of the condition $n > 3f$ for the average beeping knowledge. Also, many extensions could be made on the communication graph and the communication delays.

**Acknowledgement.** This work has been supported in part by the European ERC Grant 339539 - AOC.

# References

1. Facts about fireflies. http://www.firefly.org/facts-about-fireflies.html
2. Alistarh, D., Cornejo, A., Ghaffari, M., Lynch, N.: Firefly synchronization with asynchronous wake-up. In: Workshop on Biological Distributed Algorithms (BDA 2014)
3. Cornejo, A., Dornhaus, A., Lynch, N., Nagpal, R.: Task allocation in ant colonies. In: Kuhn, F. (ed.) DISC 2014. LNCS, vol. 8784, pp. 46–60. Springer, Heidelberg (2014)
4. Cristian, F.: Probabilistic clock synchronization. Distributed Computing **3**, 146–158 (1989)
5. Daliot, A., Dolev, D., Parnas, H.: Self-stabilizing pulse synchronization inspired by biological pacemaker networks. In: Huang, S.-T., Herman, T. (eds.) SSS 2003. LNCS, vol. 2704, pp. 32–48. Springer, Heidelberg (2003)
6. Dolev, S.: Self-Stabilization. MIT Press (2000)
7. Gandomi, A.H., Yang, X.-S., Alavi, A.H.: Cuckoo search algorithm: a meta-heuristic approach to solve structural optimization problems. Engineering with Computers **29**, 17–35 (2013)
8. Kopetz, H.: Clock synchronization in distributed real-time systems. IEEE Transactions on Computers **C–36**, 933–940 (1987)
9. Lamport, L.: Time, clocks, and the ordering of events in a distributed system. Communications of the ACM **21**, 558–565 (1978)
10. Lamport, L., Shostak, R.E., Pease, M.C.: The byzantine generals problem. ACM Trans. Program. Lang. Syst. **4**(3), 382–401 (1982)
11. Lucarelli, D., Wang, I.-J.: Decentralized synchronization protocols with nearest neighbor communication. In: SenSys, pp. 62–68 (2004)
12. Mirollo, R.E., Strogatz, S.H.: Synchronization of pulse-coupled biological oscillators. SIAM J. Appl. Math. **50**, 1645–1662 (1990)
13. Nakamura, R.Y.M., Pereira, L.A.M., Costa, K.A., Rodrigues, D., Papa, J.P., Yang, X.-S.: BBA: a binary bat algorithm for feature selection. In: 25th Conference on Graphics, Patterns and Images (SIBGRAPI 2012) (2012)
14. Peskin, C.S.: Mathematical aspects of heart physiology (1973)
15. Reid, C., MacDonald, H., Latty, T., Mann, R., Garnier, S.: Cellular decision-making: how an amoeboid organism solves the two-armed bandit problem. In: Workshop on Biological Distributed Algorithms (BDA 2014) (2014)
16. Römer, K.: Time synchronization in ad hoc networks. In: Proceedings of the 2nd ACM International Symposium on Mobile ad hoc Networking and Computing, pp. 173–182 (2001)
17. Simeone, O., Spagnolini, U., Bar-Ness, Y., Strogatz, S.: Distributed synchronization in wireless networks. IEEE Signal Processing Magazine **25**(5), 81–97 (2008)
18. Smith, H.M.: Synchronous flashing of fireflies. Science **82**(2120), 151–152 (1935)
19. Strogatz, S.H.: Sync: The emerging science of spontaneous order, 1st edn. Hyperion
20. Weyns, D., Holvoet, T.: Regional Synchronization for simultaneous actions in situated multi-agent systems. In: Mařík, V., Müller, J.P., Pěchouček, M. (eds.) CEEMAS 2003. LNCS (LNAI), vol. 2691, pp. 497–510. Springer, Heidelberg (2003)
21. Yang, X.-S., Cui, Z., Xiao, R., Gandomi, A.H., Karamanoglu, M.: Swarm Intelligence and Bio-Inspired Computation, Theory and Applications. Elsevier Insights (2013)

# Wait-Freedom is Harder Than Lock-Freedom Under Strong Linearizability

Oksana Denysyuk[✉] and Philipp Woelfel

Department of Computer Science, University of Calgary, Calgary, Canada
{oksana.denysyuk,woelfel}@ucalgary.ca

**Abstract.** In randomized algorithms, replacing atomic shared objects with *linearizable* [1] implementations may affect probability distributions over outcomes [2]. To avoid this problem in the adaptive adversary model, it is necessary and sufficient that implemented objects satisfy *strong linearizability* [2]. In this paper we study the existence of strongly linearizable implementations from *multi-writer* registers. We prove the impossibility of *wait-free* strongly linearizable implementations for a number of standard objects, including snapshots, counters, and max-registers, all of which have wait-free linearizable implementations. To do so, we introduce a new notion of *group valency* that is useful to analyze (strongly linearizable) implementations from registers. Furthermore, we show that many objects, including snapshots, do have *lock-free* strongly linearizable implementations. These results separate lock-freedom from wait-freedom under strong linearizability.

## 1 Introduction

Linearizability [1] is the gold standard for correctness conditions of concurrent shared memory algorithms. The main reason for its attractiveness is that replacing atomic objects in a deterministic shared memory algorithm with linearizable ones preserves the worst-case behaviour of the algorithm. This simplifies programming concurrent code significantly, as it allows programmers to assume that the implemented linearizable operations get completed in a single atomic step. Unfortunately, linearizability has anomalies that can cause undesirable effects when used with randomized algorithms [2]: probability distributions over outcomes of an algorithm that uses atomic objects can differ significantly from those of the same algorithm using linearizable objects. As a result, algorithm designers cannot analyze running times or error probabilities of their algorithms under the assumption that linearizable operations complete in a single step.

To address this problem, *strong linearizability* [2] has been introduced. Roughly, strong linearizability requires operations to be linearized based on past and present behavior rather than the future. In a system where processes are scheduled by a strong adaptive adversary (i.e., the future schedule may depend on all past random decisions made by processes), this requirement preserves probability distributions over outcomes of algorithms, if atomic objects are

© Springer-Verlag Berlin Heidelberg 2015
Y. Moses (Ed.): DISC 2015, LNCS 9363, pp. 60–74, 2015.
DOI: 10.1007/978-3-662-48653-5_5

replaced with strongly linearizable ones (see Section 2 for details). Moreover, strong linearizability is necessary to achieve this behaviour [2].

Unfortunately, little is known about whether and how strongly linearizable objects can be implemented. Clearly, using only registers, it is impossible to obtain wait-free or lock-free implementations of any type with consensus number two or greater [3] under linearizability. This implies *a fortiori* impossibilities under strong linearizability.

Many useful shared memory primitives, such as snapshots or counters, have wait-free linearizable implementations even from single-writer registers. Prior to our work it was unclear, however, whether those primitives have also wait-free strongly linearizable implementations. For systems providing only *single-writer* atomic registers, Helmi, Higham, and Woelfel [4] already showed that many objects have no wait-free strongly linearizable implementations, even though they have linearizable ones. In particular, under the stronger correctness condition multi-writer registers cannot be implemented from single-writer ones. But their proof technique does not apply to systems that readily provide atomic multi-writer registers. We present new proof techniques that yield the following result.

**Theorem 1.** *There are no deterministic strongly linearizable wait-free implementations of snapshots, counters, or max-registers for three or more processes, from multi-writer registers.*

We also show that, perhaps surprisingly, these types do have *lock-free* strongly linearizable implementations.

**Theorem 2.** *There exist deterministic strongly linearizable lock-free implementations of (general) counters, snapshots, and logical clock objects for any number of processes, from multi-writer registers.*

Theorems 1 and 2 provide a separation between these two progress conditions under strong linearizability. In fact, to our knowledge, this is the first result to show a separation of wait-free and lock-free implementations for natural types such as snapshots and counters. Prior work [5] claims a separation between wait-freedom and lock-freedom under linearizability for an *ad hoc* object called "iterated approximate agreement".

To prove Theorem 1, we show that a monotonic counter does not have a wait-free strongly linearizable implementation from registers (even though it has a wait-free linearizable implementation [6]). By reduction, this implies the other impossibilities stated in Theorem 1. To facilitate the proof, we introduce two new concepts, *group valency* and *supervalency*, which generalize the traditional notion of valency used in the FLP impossibility result for consensus [7,8]. (In a consensus algorithm, all participating processes have to agree on one of their input values.) In the consensus impossibility proof, a history $H$ is multivalent if it has two different extensions, in which different values are output. Intuitively, that means that the decision has not been determined at the end of $H$. To show our result, we extend the notion of valency in two ways.

First, we consider the ability of a set $G$ of processes to linearize the operation op of another process $p \notin G$. Roughly, $v$ is in the $G$-valency of op, if processes in $G$ executing alone can linearize op, causing op to return $v$. This is closely tied to the notion of *helping* in wait-free implementations, where one or more processes help another process to complete op. In the impossibility proof for strongly linearizable monotonic counters, we apply the notion of group valency to a group $G$ of processes that repeatedly increment the counter while another process $p \notin G$ wishes to execute op to read the counter. Using group valency, we show that if processes in $G$ try to help $p$, they end up causing $p$ to execute forever, thus violating wait-freedom.

Second, we introduce the notion of *supervalent histories*. In the traditional FLP proof, a multivalent (or bivalent) history is one in which the consensus output is undetermined (so both decisions of 0 or 1 are possible). We extend this notion to a history in which, not only the outcome of some operation op by $p \notin GF$ is undetermined, but processes in $G$ can execute an unbounded number of steps alone without fixing the outcome of op (i.e., without linearizing op). This is called a $G$-supervalent history. Intuitively, in executing an unbounded number of steps, processes in $G$ can influence the future return value of op to be any of an unbounded number of possibilities (e.g., as processes in $G$ increment the counter, the future return value of the operation op that reads the counter can be arbitrarily high). We show that a supervalent history may remain supervalent forever, so that op can never return the correct value of the counter. The notion of supervalent histories is more powerful than the notion of multivalent histories for our impossibility result: we found algorithms for which it is impossible to show that a multivalent history can remain multivalent as op continues to execute.

Theorem 2 identifies several common primitives that have lock-free strongly linearizable implementations from registers. To prove this, we first define a class of *versioned types*, which are types that maintain a monotonic version number that increases for each update operation. Many objects of the standard types (snapshots, max-registers, counters, logical clocks) can be easily extended into objects of a versioned type by incorporating a counter as the version number. Moreover, many lock-free linearizable implementations of those types have the additional property that update operations consist of a single atomic step. We then transform such linearizable implementations into *strongly linearizable* lock-free ones. This transformation uses a simple generalization of a max-register, which admits a strongly linearizable lock-free implementation [4].

## 2   Preliminaries

We consider the standard shared memory model, where $n$ asynchronous processes with distinct IDs in $\{0, \ldots, n-1\}$ communicate by accessing shared atomic multi-reader multi-writer registers. Each register $R$ has initially value $\chi$, and supports operations $R$.read(), which returns the value of $R$, and $R$.write(), where $R$.write($x$) changes the value of $R$ to $x$ and returns nothing.

*Atomicity and Linearizability.* A type specifies operations, and the outcome of those operations in any sequential execution. An object is obtained by implementing the operations of type, by providing algorithms for them. A process $p$

executes an operation op by executing the steps of the algorithm beginning with an invocation step and ending with a response step. Other processes can be taking steps during the interval in which $p$ is executing the method for $o$ and these steps may interleave. This sequence of steps that results as processes execute their program is called a *history*. We restrict our attention to histories that *can* arise in an execution. Consider an object $O$ and the histories that can arise as processes execute operations on $O$. A method of $O$ is *atomic*, if it consists of a single shared memory step[1]. In this case, we may assume that the invocation and response step of the method occur at the same time as the shared memory step. An object is atomic, if all its methods are, and the histories that can arise by processes executing operations on such an object are *sequential*.

The behaviour of a type is given by its *sequential specification*, which is a set of sequential histories that are allowed to arise from atomic objects of that type. An *implemented history* on $O$ arises when the operations on $O$ may be non-atomic. The *interpretation* of an implemented history $H$, denoted $\Gamma(H)$, is formed by removing from $H$ all the steps of every method call except the invocation and response steps. Let $H$ be an implemented history arising from an execution of operations on $O$. Operation op completes in $H$ if $H$ contains the invocation and response of op. $Cmp(H)$ denotes the set of operations that complete in $H$. Operation op is pending in $H$ if $H$ contains the invocation but not the response of op. For implemented operations $op_1$ and $op_2$, $op_1$ *happens-before* $op_2$ in $H$, denoted $op_1 \prec op_2$, if the response of $op_1$ precedes the invocation of $op_2$ in $H$. Interpreted history $H$ is *linearizable* if, for some subset $S$ of pending operations in $H$, there is a sequential history $H_{seq}$ that contains each operation in $Cmp(H) \cup S$ exactly once, is in the sequential specification of $O$, and preserves $\prec$. Such $H_{seq}$ is *linearization* of $H$. An implementation of $O$ is linearizable if every history that can arise from the implementation is linearizable. The property that makes linearizability attractive is the following: If $\mathcal{A}$ is a deterministic algorithm that uses objects of some type $T$, then for every history $H$ that can arise from $\mathcal{A}$, the linearization of $\Gamma(H)$ can arise from the same algorithm using atomic objects of type $T$ instead. But linearizability may not preserve probability distributions over outcomes, if $\mathcal{A}$ is a randomized algorithm. Thus, linearizable implementations are less suitable to accurately analyze the expected running times or error probabilities of randomized algorithms.

*Strong Linearizability.* In a randomized algorithm, processes can use local coin flips to decide which steps to execute in their program. The type and object of an operation may influence the speed with which an operation is executed, so the order in which processes take steps is indirectly influenced by their random decisions. Adversary models are used to capture that influence. One of the most common adversaries is the strong adaptive one. Informally, the strong adaptive adversary can look at the entire past execution, including the result of all coin flips made by processes, to decide which process will take the next step.

---

[1] Sometimes, however, in literature atomicity is defined to be the same as linearizability [9].

Let $close(\mathcal{H})$ denote the prefix closure of a set of histories in $\mathcal{H}$. That is, $G \in close(\mathcal{H})$ if and only if there is a sequence $S$ of invocation and response steps such that $G \circ S \in \mathcal{H}$. (Operation $\circ$ denotes concatenation.) A function $f$ that maps a set $\mathcal{H}$ of histories to a set $\mathcal{H}'$ of histories, is *prefix preserving*, if for any two histories $G, H \in \mathcal{H}$, where $G$ is a prefix of $H$, $f(G)$ is a prefix of $f(H)$.

**Definition 3.** *[2]A set of histories $\mathcal{H}$ is strongly linearizable if there exists a function $f$ mapping histories in $close(\mathcal{H})$ to sequential histories, such that for any $H \in close(\mathcal{H})$, $f(H)$ is a linearization of the interpreted history $\Gamma(H)$, and $f$ is prefix preserving. A function satisfying these properties is called a* strong linearization function *for $\mathcal{H}$.*

Intuitively, strong linearizability requires that the linearization points of method calls are determined as the history is created. As soon as a step is taken, whether or not a particular method is linearized at that step is uniquely determined by the history up to this step; it cannot be influenced by future steps.

We say an object is strongly linearizable, if the set of histories that can be obtained by executions of operations on that object is strongly linearizable. Golab et al. [2] showed that strongly linearizable objects can serve the same purpose for randomized algorithms under a strong adaptive adversary model, as linearizable objects do for deterministic algorithms: Consider a randomized algorithms $\mathcal{A}$ and an adversary $Z$. For an infinite vector $c = (c_1, c_2, \dots)$ over $\{0, 1\}$, let $H_{Z,\mathcal{A},c}$ be the unique history obtained if algorithm $\mathcal{A}$ is scheduled by adversary $Z$, and the sequence of coin flips of $H_{Z,\mathcal{A},c}$ is a prefix of $c$ (or equals $c$ if the history is infinite). Now suppose $\mathcal{A}$ is a randomized algorithm using atomic objects of some type, and $\mathcal{A}'$ is obtained by replacing those atomic objects with strongly linearizable ones of the same type. Golab et al. proved that for every strong adversary $Z'$ there exists a strong adversary $Z$, such that for every coin flip vector $c$, $\Gamma(H_{Z,\mathcal{A},c})$ and $\Gamma(H_{Z',\mathcal{A}',c})$ have a common linearization. Moreover, strong linearizability is necessary for this: If for some adversary $Z'$ there exists an adversary $Z$ such that $\Gamma(H_{Z,\mathcal{A},c})$ and $\Gamma(H_{Z',\mathcal{A}',c})$ have a common linearization for every coin flip vector $c$, then the set of all histories $\Gamma(H_{Z',\mathcal{A}',c})$ obtained from all possible coin flip vectors $c$ is strongly linearizable. Hence, atomic objects can be replaced with implemented ones without changing the probability distribution over linearizations only, if the set of possible histories that can be obtained from any possible strong adversary is strongly linearizable.

Thus, strong linearizability is the correctness condition of choice for randomized algorithm against the strong adaptive adversary.

*Configurations, Schedules, and Progress Conditions.* A *configuration* $C$ of a system with $n$ processes and $m$ registers is a tuple $(s_1, \dots, s_n, v_1, \dots, v_m)$, which denotes that process $p_i$, $1 \le 1 \le n$, is in state $s_i$, and register $r_j$, $1 \le j \le m$, has value $v_j$. The initial configuration is denoted by $C_0$. We usually assume without mentioning it explicitly that histories are obtained by processes taking steps starting in $C_0$.

A *schedule* $\sigma$ is a (possibly infinite) sequence of process indices. Let $C$ be a configuration resulting from execution of a finite history $H$. $H \triangleright \sigma$ denotes a history resulting from executing a sequence of steps in $\sigma$ beginning in configuration $C$ and moving through successive configurations one at a time. At each step, next process $p$ indicated in $\sigma$ takes the next step in its deterministic program. If $\sigma$ is a sequence of length one, we say $\sigma=p$. If $\sigma$ and $\pi$ are finite schedules then $\sigma\pi$ denotes the concatenation of $\sigma$ and $\pi$. Let $P$ be a set of processes, and $\sigma$ a schedule. We say $\sigma$ is $P$-only if only indices of processes in $P$ appear in $\sigma$.

Configurations $C_1=(s_1,\ldots,s_n,r_1,\ldots,r_m)$ and $C_2=(s_1',\ldots,s_n',r_1',\ldots,r_m')$ are indistinguishable to process $p_i$, denoted $C_1 \overset{p_i}{\sim} C2$, if $s_i=s_i'$ and $r_j=r_j'$ for $1\leq j\leq m$. If $S$ is a set of processes, and $C_1 \overset{p}{\sim} C_2$ for every process $p \in S$, then we write $C_1 \overset{S}{\sim} C_2$; if $S=\{1,\ldots,n\}$ is the set of all processes, we simply write $C_1 \sim C_2$. If $C_1 \overset{p}{\sim} C_2$, then for any $S$-only schedule $\sigma$, configurations resulting from execution of $\sigma$ from $C_1$ and $C_2$ are indistinguishable to every process in $S$. Two histories $H_1$ and $H_2$ are indistinguishable, denoted $H_1 \sim H_2$, if $H_1$ and $H_2$ generate indistinguishable configurations.

An implementation is *lock-free* if, for any history $H$ and every infinite schedule $\sigma$, there exists a process $p$ with a pending operation op in $H$, and $p$ takes infinitely many steps in $\sigma$, then op completes in a finite number of steps in history $H\triangleright\sigma$. An implementation is *wait-free* [7] if, in any history, any process with a pending operation completes in a finite number of steps, regardless of the steps taken by other processes.

*Some Common Types.* We refer to the types monotonic counters, (general) counters, max-registers, and snapshots, as defined below: A *monotonic counter* has two operations, `increment()` and `read()`, where `increment()` increases the counter value by one, and `read()` returns the counter value. A *(general) counter* is defined similarly, but the `increment()` operations takes an argument, $x$, and increases the value of the counter by $x$. A *max-register* has two operations, `maxWrite(v)` and `read()`, such that `read()` returns the largest value written by any preceding `maxWrite` operation. A snapshot object stores $n$ segments, one for each process. It supports two operations, `update(v)` and `scan()`. Operation `update(v)`, when executed by process $i$, changes the value of the $i$-th segment to $v$, and `scan()` returns a vector of $n$ elements containing the $n$ segments.

## 3 Impossibilities

We show that there is no strongly linearizable wait-free implementation of a monotonic counter from registers. Assume by contradiction that there exists such an implementation. We will consider an execution with three processes: $r$, $w_0$, and $w_1$. We call $r$ the reader and $w_i$ the writers. Initially, $r$ starts executing `read()`, while $w_0$ and $w_1$ start executing `increment()`. If process $w_0$ or $w_1$ finishes executing `increment()`, it invokes the operation again and again in an infinite loop. We will construct an infinite fair schedule, i.e., a schedule in which every process takes infinitely many steps, such that $r$ never finishes its `read()`. This contradicts the assumption that the implementation is wait-free.

### 3.1    Group Valency and Super Valency

We now define the notions *total valency* and *group valency*. In the definitions, op denotes an operation, $S$ a set of processes, and $H$ a finite history.

**Definition 4 (Total Valency).** *The* total valency *of $H$ (w.r.t. op) is the set of values $\nu$ such that, for some finite schedule $\sigma$, op returns $\nu$ in history $H \triangleright \sigma$.*

In the proofs, op is a fixed operation so we often omit references to it. To prove the impossibility, it will be critical to consider the possible values the reader may return if it gets linearized by the writers. To facilitate this we define the notion of *group-valency*.

**Definition 5 (Group Valency).** *The $S$-valency of $H$ (with respect to op) is the set of values $\nu$ for which there exists an $S$-only schedule $\sigma$, such that in $f(H \triangleright \sigma)$ op returns $\nu$.*

Some histories have the property that all sufficiently long $S$-only schedules will linerize op, even if op is not an operation by a process in $S$. These are called $S$-closed. Histories that are not $S$-closed are called $S$-supervalent.

**Definition 6 (Super Valency).** *We say that $H$ is $S$-closed (w.r.t. op) if there exists an integer $K \geq 0$ such that, for every $S$-only schedule $\sigma$ of length at least $K$, op appears in $f(H \triangleright \sigma)$. We say that $H$ is $S$-supervalent (w.r.t. op) if $H$ is not $S$-closed, that is, for every $K$, there is an $S$-only schedule $\sigma$ of length at least $K$ such that op does not appear in $f(H \triangleright \sigma)$.*

The above definitions immediately imply the following:

**Observation 7.** *(1) If $H$ is $S$-closed then the $S$-valency of $H$ is not empty. (2) All $S$-only extensions of an $S$-closed history are $S$-closed. (3) From an $S$-supervalent history $H$, there exists an $S$-only non-empty schedule $\sigma$ such that $H \triangleright \sigma$ is also $S$-supervalent. (4) For any finite schedule $\sigma$, the $S$-valency of $H \triangleright \sigma$ is contained in the $S$-valency of $H$.*

### 3.2    Impossibility Proof

In the proof we analyze the possible outputs of the **read**() operation using the concepts of group valency and supervalency when the group is the set of writers. Specifically, we fix op to be the **read**() operation of $r$, and we fix $S$ to be the set of both writers $\{w_0, w_1\}$. For a finite history $H$, we denote by $V(H)$ the total valency of $H$ (w.r.t. op), and we denote by $\mathcal{W}(H)$ the $S$-valency of $H$ (w.r.t. op). Because $S$ is the set of writers, we often use the terms writers-valency, writers-supervalent, and writers-closed to refer to the concepts of $S$-valency, $S$-supervalent, and $S$-closed defined above, respectively.

By the standard argument we obtain the following.

**Lemma 8.** *Consider some valid histories $H$ and $H'$:*

(a) If $H$ is writers-supervalent then $read()$ is not in $f(H)$.
(b) If $|\mathcal{W}(H)| \geq 2$ then $read()$ is not in $f(H)$.
(c) If $H \sim H'$ then $V(H) = V(H')$ and $\mathcal{W}(H) = \mathcal{W}(H')$.
(d) If $H$ is writers-closed and $H \overset{w_i,r}{\sim} H'$, for some $i \in \{0,1\}$, then $\mathcal{W}(H) \cap \mathcal{W}(H') \neq \emptyset$.

In the following lemma we show that if history $H$ is writers-closed and $|\mathcal{W}(H)| \geq 2$, then there exists a step by a writer $w_i$ such that $|\mathcal{W}(H \triangleright w_i)| \geq 2$.

**Lemma 9.** *If $H$ is writers-closed and $|\mathcal{W}(H)| \geq 2$, then for some $i \in \{0,1\}$, $H \triangleright w_i$ is writers-closed and $|\mathcal{W}(H \triangleright w_i)| \geq 2$.*

*Proof.* By Lemma 8(b), since $|\mathcal{W}(H)| \geq 2$, $read$ is not in $f(H)$. Suppose $H$ is writers-closed. From Observation 7, for all writers-only schedules $\sigma$, $H \triangleright \sigma$ is also writers-closed. By contradiction, suppose that for all $i \in \{0,1\}$, $|\mathcal{W}(H \triangleright w_i)| \leq 1$. By Observation 7, $\mathcal{W}(H \triangleright w_i)$ is not empty. Thus, $\mathcal{W}(H \triangleright w_0) = \{x_0\}$ and $\mathcal{W}(H \triangleright w_1) = \{x_1\}$ for two distinct $x_0, x_1 \in \mathcal{W}(H)$.

**Case 1.** *For some $i \in \{0,1\}$, $w_i$ is poised to read in $H$.* Then $H \triangleright w_i \overset{r,w_{1-i}}{\sim} H$ and so $H \triangleright w_i w_{1-i} \overset{r,w_{1-i}}{\sim} H \triangleright w_{1-i}$. However, $\mathcal{W}(H \triangleright w_i w_{1-i}) \subseteq \mathcal{W}(H \triangleright w_i)$ and $\mathcal{W}(H \triangleright w_{1-i}) \cap \mathcal{W}(H \triangleright w_i) = \emptyset$, and so $\mathcal{W}(H \triangleright w_{1-i}) \cap \mathcal{W}(H \triangleright w_i w_{1-i}) = \emptyset$. This contradicts Lemma 8(d).
**Case 2.** *Both writers are poised to write to different registers.* Then $H \triangleright w_0 w_1 \sim H \triangleright w_1 w_0$. Since $\mathcal{W}(H \triangleright w_0) \cap \mathcal{W}(H \triangleright w_1) = \emptyset$, $\mathcal{W}(H \triangleright w_0 w_1) \cap \mathcal{W}(H \triangleright w_1 w_0) = \emptyset$. This contradicts Lemma 8(d).
**Case 3.** *Both writers are poised to write to the same register.* Then $H \triangleright w_0 w_1 \overset{r,w_1}{\sim} H \triangleright w_1$. Since $\mathcal{W}(H \triangleright w_0) \cap \mathcal{W}(H \triangleright w_1) = \emptyset$, $\mathcal{W}(H \triangleright w_0 w_1) \cap \mathcal{W}(H \triangleright w_1) = \emptyset$. This contradicts Lemma 8(d). □

The above lemma implies that the writers-valency of writers-closed histories contains only one value.

**Lemma 10.** *If history $H$ is writers-closed, then $|\mathcal{W}(H)| = 1$.*

In the following we show that, from a writers-supervalent history $H$, no writers-only schedules can linearize the $read$ operation, i.e. $\mathcal{W}(H) = \emptyset$. To proof is by contradiction, assuming that $\mathcal{W}(H)$ contains an element $x$. In the following lemma, we first show that if such a writers-supervalent history $H$ exists, then we can extend that history to a history $H'$, so that the writers-valencies obtained by a single step of $w_0$ respectively $w_1$ are distinct.

**Lemma 11.** *If there exists a writers-supervalent history $H$ such that $x \in \mathcal{W}(H)$, then there is a finite writers-only schedule $\sigma$ and an index $j \in \{0,1\}$, such that*

(a) $H \triangleright \sigma w_j$ is writers-supervalent and $x \notin \mathcal{W}(H \triangleright \sigma w_j)$; and
(b) $H \triangleright \sigma w_{1-j}$ is writers-closed and $\mathcal{W}(H \triangleright \sigma w_{1-j}) = \{x\}$.

*In particular, $\mathcal{W}(H \triangleright \sigma w_j) \cap \mathcal{W}(H \triangleright \sigma w_{1-j}) = \emptyset$.*

*Proof.* Let $\sigma$ be a longest possible writers-only schedule such that for each prefix $\sigma''$ of $\sigma$, history $H{\triangleright}\sigma''$ is writers-supervalent and $x \in \mathcal{W}(H{\triangleright}\sigma'')$.

First we prove that $\sigma$ is finite. Suppose it is not. Then in $H{\triangleright}\sigma$ at least one of the writers takes infinitely many steps. By wait-freedom that writer completes infinitely many **increment** operations in $H{\triangleright}\sigma$. Let $\sigma'$ be some finite prefix of $\sigma$ such that $H{\triangleright}\sigma'$ contains at least $x{+}1$ complete **increment** operations. By the construction of $\sigma$, $H{\triangleright}\sigma'$ is writers-supervalent and $x \in \mathcal{W}(H{\triangleright}\sigma')$. From writers-supervalency it follows that the **read** cannot appear in $f(H{\triangleright}\sigma')$, while on the other hand this linearization contains at least $x{+}1$ **increment** operations. Since $f$ is prefix preserving, if the **read** appears in $f(H{\triangleright}\sigma'\lambda)$ for any schedule $\lambda$, then it must be preceded by at least $x{+}1$ **increment** operations, and thus return a value of at least $x{+}1$. Hence, $x \notin \mathcal{W}(H{\triangleright}\sigma')$, contradicting the construction of $\sigma$.

We conclude that $\sigma$ is finite. In particular, for every writer $w_i$, $i \in \{0,1\}$, either $H{\triangleright}\sigma w_i$ is writers-closed or $x \notin \mathcal{W}(H{\triangleright}\sigma)$. According to Observation 7, the extensions $H{\triangleright}\sigma w_0$ and $H{\triangleright}\sigma w_1$ cannot be both writers-closed. Hence, there is an index $j \in \{0,1\}$ such that $H{\triangleright}\sigma w_j$ is writers-supervalent and $H{\triangleright}\sigma w_{1-j}$ is writers-closed. Since $H{\triangleright}\sigma w_j$ is writers-supervalent, we know from the definition of $\sigma$ that $x \notin \mathcal{W}(H{\triangleright}\sigma w_j)$. But since $x \in \mathcal{W}(H{\triangleright}\sigma) = \mathcal{W}(H\sigma w_0) \cup \mathcal{W}(H{\triangleright}\sigma w_1)$, it must be in $\mathcal{W}(H{\triangleright}\sigma w_{1-j})$. Because $H{\triangleright}\sigma w_{1-j}$ is writers-closed, we obtain from Lemma 10 that $\mathcal{W}(H{\triangleright}\sigma w_{1-j}) = \{x\}$. Hence, (a)-(b) are satisfied, and thus $\mathcal{W}(H{\triangleright}\sigma w_j) \cap \mathcal{W}(H{\triangleright}\sigma w_{1-j}) = \emptyset$. $\qquad\square$

**Lemma 12.** *If history $H$ is writers-supervalent, then $\mathcal{W}(H) = \emptyset$.*

*Proof.* Suppose that $H$ is writers-supervalent and assume by contradiction that there exists some value $\nu \in \mathcal{W}(H)$. By Lemma 8(a), **read** is not in $f(H)$. By Lemma 11, there is an extension $H'$ of $H$ and an index $i \in \{0,1\}$ such that

$$H'{\triangleright}w_{1-i} \text{ is writers-closed and } \mathcal{W}(H'{\triangleright}w_{1-i}) \cap \mathcal{W}(H'{\triangleright}w_i) = \emptyset. \qquad (1)$$

Let $R_{1-i}$ and $R_i$ be the registers that $w_{1-i}$ and $w_i$ are poised to access in $H'$.

**Case 1.** *There is an index $j \in \{0,1\}$ such that in $H'$, $w_j$ is poised to read $R_j$.* Then $H'{\triangleright}w_j \overset{r,w_{1-j}}{\sim} H'$ and so $H'{\triangleright}w_j w_{1-j} \overset{r,w_{1-j}}{\sim} H'{\triangleright}w_{1-j}$. Now, either $H'{\triangleright}w_j w_{1-j}$ or $H'{\triangleright}w_{1-j}$ is writers-closed (depending on whether $j{=}i$ or $j{=}1{-}i$). Thus, by Lemma 8(d), $\mathcal{W}(H'{\triangleright}w_j w_{1-j}) \cap \mathcal{W}(H'{\triangleright}w_{1-j}) \neq \emptyset$. This contradicts Eq. (1).

**Case 2.** $w_0$ *is poised to write to $R_0$ in $H'$, $w_1$ is poised to write to $R_1$ and $R_0 \neq R_1$.* Then $H'{\triangleright}w_0 w_1 \sim H'{\triangleright}w_1 w_0$. Also, either $H'{\triangleright}w_0 w_1$ or $H'{\triangleright}w_1 w_0$ is writers-closed. By Lemma 8(d), $\mathcal{W}(H'{\triangleright}w_0 w_1) \cap \mathcal{W}(H'{\triangleright}w_1 w_0) \neq \emptyset$, contradicting Eq. (1).

**Case 3.** $w_0$ *is poised to write to $R_0$ in $H'$, $w_1$ is poised to write to $R_1$ and $R_0 = R_1$.* Then $H'{\triangleright}w_0 w_1 \overset{r,w_1}{\sim} H'{\triangleright}w_1$. Now, either $H'{\triangleright}w_0 w_1$ or $H'{\triangleright}w_1$ is writers-closed (depending on whether $i{=}1$ or $i{=}0$). By Lemma 8(d), $\mathcal{W}(H'{\triangleright}w_0 w_1) \cap \mathcal{W}(H'{\triangleright}w_1) \neq \emptyset$. This contradicts Eq. (1).

In all cases the assumption that $\nu \in \mathcal{W}(H)$ is contradicted. Hence, $\mathcal{W}(H) = \emptyset$. $\qquad\square$

**Lemma 13.** *Let $H$ be a writers-supervalent history and $S \subseteq \{w_1, w_2\}$. Then:*

*(a) For any integer $y$ and any infinite $S$-only schedule $\gamma$, there is a prefix $\gamma'$ of $\gamma$ such that for every schedule $\lambda$, either $\mathcal{W}(H \triangleright \gamma' \lambda) = \emptyset$ or $\min(\mathcal{W}(H \triangleright \gamma' \lambda)) > y$.*

*(b) If $x \in \mathcal{W}(H \triangleright r)$, then there exists a finite $S$-only schedule $\sigma$, such that $x \in \mathcal{W}(H \triangleright \sigma r)$ and $x \notin \mathcal{W}(H \triangleright \sigma w_i r)$ for any $w_i \in S$.*

*Proof.* We first prove Part (a). In $H \triangleright \gamma$ at least one of the writers executes infinitely many steps, and thus by wait-freedom infinitely many **increment** operations. Hence, there is a finite prefix $\gamma'$ of $\gamma$ such that in $H \triangleright \gamma'$ at least $y+1$ **increment** operations complete. By Lemma 12, $\mathcal{W}(H) = \emptyset$, and since $\gamma'$ is writers-only, the **read** does not linearize in $H \triangleright \gamma'$. I.e., $f(H \triangleright \gamma')$ does not contain a **read**, while it contains at least $y+1$ **increment** operations. Since $f$ is prefix-preserving it follows that if the **read** appears in $f(H \triangleright \gamma' \lambda)$ for any schedule $\lambda$, then it is preceded by at least $y+1$ **increment** operations and thus returns a value of at least $y+1$. Hence, either $\mathcal{W}(H \triangleright \gamma' \lambda) = \emptyset$ or $\min \mathcal{W}(H \triangleright \gamma' \lambda) \geq y+1$.

For Part (b), we let $\sigma$ be a longest possible $S$-only schedule with $x \in \mathcal{W}(H \triangleright \sigma r)$. From Part (a) (with $\lambda = r$) we obtain that $\sigma$ is finite. Hence, by construction $x \in \mathcal{W}(H \triangleright \sigma r)$ and $x \notin \mathcal{W}(H \triangleright \sigma w_i r)$ for any $w_i \in S$. This completes the proof. $\qquad\square$

Below we state and prove our main lemma. It says that from any writers-supervalent history $H$ we can construct a finite schedule $\sigma$, which includes at least one step by $r$, such that $H \triangleright \sigma$ is writers-supervalent.

**Lemma 14.** *If a history $H$ is writers-supervalent, then there exists a finite writers-only schedule $\sigma$, such that $H \triangleright \sigma r$ is also writers-supervalent.*

*Proof.* Let $H$ be a writers-supervalent history. For the purpose of a contradiction, we suppose that for every finite writers-only schedule $\sigma$, $\mathcal{W}(H \triangleright \sigma r)$ is writers-closed. By Lemma 10, for every such $\sigma$, $|\mathcal{W}(H \triangleright \sigma r)| = 1$.

By Lemma 13 (b) there exists a writers-only schedule yielding an extension $H'$ of $H$ such that $\mathcal{W}(H' \triangleright r) = \{x\}$, and $x \notin \mathcal{W}(H' \triangleright w_0 r) \cup \mathcal{W}(H' \triangleright w_1 r)$. By our assumption $H' \triangleright w_i r$ is writers-closed for any $i \in \{0, 1\}$, and by Lemma 10, $|\mathcal{W}(H' \triangleright w_i r)| = 1$. Thus, there exist values $y_0, y_1$ such that

$$\forall i \in \{0, 1\}: \quad \mathcal{W}(H' \triangleright w_i r) = \{y_i\} \neq \{x\} = \mathcal{W}(H' \triangleright r). \tag{2}$$

In particular, for any schedule $\lambda$, by $\mathcal{W}(H' \triangleright r \lambda) \subseteq \mathcal{W}(H' \triangleright r)$, we have

$$\forall i \in \{0, 1\}: \quad \mathcal{W}(H' \triangleright w_i r) \cap \mathcal{W}(H' \triangleright r \lambda) = \emptyset. \tag{3}$$

We look at the steps that the processes are poised to take in $H'$. Let $R_0$, $R_1$, and $R_2$ be registers accessed by $w_0$, $w_1$, and $r$ respectively. Recall that by assumption all extensions $H' \circ H''$ of $H'$ are writer-closed provided that $r$ takes a step in $H''$.

**Case 1.** *There is an index $i \in \{0, 1\}$ such that in $H'$ process $w_i$ is poised to read $R_i$.* Then, $H' \triangleright r \overset{r, w_{1-i}}{\sim} H' \triangleright w_i r$, and thus by Lemma 8(d), $\mathcal{W}(H' \triangleright r) \cap \mathcal{W}(H' \triangleright w_i r) \neq \emptyset$. This contradicts (3).

**Case 2.** *Both $w_0$ and $w_1$ are poised to write in $H'$:*

**Case 2.1.** *There is an index $i \in \{0,1\}$ such that $R_i \neq R_2$.* This means that $H' \triangleright w_i r \sim H' \triangleright r w_i$ and thus by Lemma 8(d), $\mathcal{W}(H' \triangleright w_i r) \cap \mathcal{W}(H' \triangleright r w_i) \neq \emptyset$, which contradicts (3).

**Case 2.2.** *All three processes access the same register.* I.e., there exists register $R$ such that for any $i \in \{0,1,2\}$, $R = R_i$.

**Case 2.2.1.** *$r$ is poised to write in $H'$.* Then, $H' \triangleright w_0 r w_1 \sim H' \triangleright r w_0 w_1$ and thus by Lemma 8(d), $\mathcal{W}(H' \triangleright w_0 r w_1) \cap \mathcal{W}(H' \triangleright r w_0 w_1) \neq \emptyset$. This contradicts (3).

**Case 2.2.2.** *$r$ is poised to read in $H'$.* We will construct two indistinguishable histories, in which $r$ outputs different values. This establishes a contradiction. Recall that by our assumption, for any writers-only schedule $\sigma$, $H' \sigma r$ is writers-closed and thus by Lemma 10, $|\mathcal{W}(H' \sigma r)|=1$. Then according to Lemma 13(a), there is a $w_1$-solo schedule $w_1^{k_1}$ of length $k_1$ such that for any schedule $\lambda$, the unique value in $\mathcal{W}(H' \triangleright w_1^{k_1} \lambda r)$ is larger than $y_0$. Let $z$ be the value in $\mathcal{W}(H' \triangleright w_1^{k_1} r)$. Applying Lemma 13(b), we obtain a $w_1$-solo schedule $w_1^{k_2}$ of length $k_2$ such that for $k=k_1+k_2$ we have $z \in \mathcal{W}(H' \triangleright w_1^k r)$ and $z \notin \mathcal{W}(H' \triangleright w_1^{k+1} r)$. In particular,

$$\mathcal{W}(H' \triangleright w_1^k r) \cap \mathcal{W}(H' \triangleright w_1^{k+1} r) = \emptyset. \qquad (4)$$

We now consider the histories
$$H_1 = H' \triangleright w_1^k w_0 r w_1 \quad \text{and} \quad H_2 = H' \triangleright w_0 r w_1^{k+1}.$$
Recall that by the construction above, for any schedule $\lambda$, the unique value in $\mathcal{W}(H' \triangleright w_1^{k_1} \lambda r)$ is larger than $y_0$. In particular, this is true for $\lambda = w_1^{k_2} w_0$, and thus $\mathcal{W}(H' \triangleright w_1^k w_0 r) = \mathcal{W}(H_1) = \{z'\}$, for some integer $z' > y_0$. On the other hand, by (2), $\mathcal{W}(H' \cdot w_0 r) = \{y_0\}$, and thus $\mathcal{W}(H_2) = \{y_0\}$. Therefore, $\mathcal{W}(H_1) \neq \mathcal{W}(H_2)$.

We now show that $H_1 \sim H_2$. This contradicts Lemma 8(d) according to which $\mathcal{W}(H_1) = \mathcal{W}(H_2)$.

First, observe that all processes take equally many steps after $H'$. By the assumption of Case 2, the first step by each process $w_0$ and $w_1$ following $H'$ is a write to $R$, while the first step by $r$ is a read of $R$. Hence, in both histories in their single steps following $H'$, process $w_0$ writes some value $\nu$ to $R$ and process $r$ reads that value $\nu$.

Observe that $w_1$ is poised to write to $R$ in $H' \triangleright w_1^k$. Otherwise, the steps $w_1$ and $r$ would be commutative and thus $H' \triangleright w_1^{k+1} r \overset{r, w_1}{\sim} H' \triangleright w_1^k r w_1$. Then Lemma 8(d) would imply $\mathcal{W}(H' \triangleright w_1^{k+1} r) \cap \mathcal{W}(H' \triangleright w_1^k r w_1) \neq \emptyset$, which contradicts (4). Since the first step by $w_1$ is also a write to $R$, in both histories following $H'$, in each single step process $w_1$ either writes to $R$, it reads from $R$ what itself has written to $R$, or it accesses a register other than $R$. In any of those cases, $w_1$ cannot distinguish between $H_1$ and $H_2$. Thus, we conclude that $H_1 \sim H_2$.

Hence, the assumption that from a writers-supervalent history, all finite schedules $\{w_0, w_1\}^* r$ lead to writers-closed histories, leads to contradictions in all cases. This completes the proof of the lemma. $\qquad \square$

**Lemma 15.** *Any history $H$, in which $r$ has taken no steps, is writers-supervalent.*

*Proof.* For the purpose of a contradiction assume that $H$ is writers-closed. By Lemma 10 there is an integer $x \geq 0$ such that $\mathcal{W}(H) = \{x\}$. Then there is a writers-only schedule $\gamma$ such that $f(H \triangleright \gamma)$ contains a **read** operation that returns $x$. By wait-freedom, there is a $w_0$-only schedule $\sigma$ such that in $H \triangleright \gamma \sigma$ process $w_0$ completes at least $x+1$ **increment** operations. Again by wait-freedom, for a long enough $r$-only schedule $\lambda$, the **read** operation returns in history $H \triangleright \gamma \sigma \lambda$. In that history, the **read** is invoked after at least $x+1$ **increment** operations completed, so in $f(H \triangleright \gamma \sigma \lambda)$ the **read** also appears only after at least $x+1$ **increment** operations. But then $f(H \triangleright \gamma \sigma)$, where the **read** appears after only $x$ **increment** operations, cannot be a prefix of $f(H \triangleright \gamma \sigma \lambda)$, contradicting the prefix-preserving property of $f$. □

**Theorem 16.** *There is no (deterministic) strongly linearizable wait-free implementation of a monotonic counter for three processes, from registers.*

*Proof.* Suppose by contradiction that there exists such a wait-free strongly linearizable implementation of a counter. Consider an algorithm, where processes $w_0$ and $w_1$ execute repeated **increment** operations in an infinite loop and process $r$ executes a single **read** operation.

We prove by induction that for any integer $k \geq 0$ there is a writers-supervalent history $H_0 \circ H_1 \ldots \circ H_k$ in which $r$ takes at least $k$ steps. We let $H_0$ be the empty history. By Lemma 15, $H_0$ is writers-supervalent. Now suppose we constructed a writers-supervalent history $H_0 \circ \ldots \circ H_k$ in which $r$ takes at least $k$ steps. By Lemma 14, there is a schedule $\sigma$ such that $r \in \sigma$ and history $H_0 \circ \ldots \circ H_k \circ H_{k+1} := H_0 \circ \ldots \circ H_k \triangleright \sigma$ is also writers-supervalent. In that history $r$ takes at least $k+1$ steps, and the inductive hypothesis follows. Since $H_0 \circ \ldots \circ H_k$ is writers-supervalent, the **read** is pending in this history, as it does not appear in $f(H_0 \circ \ldots \circ H_k)$. Hence, there exists a history in which $r$ takes infinitely many steps but never finishes its **read** operation. This contradicts wait-freedom. □

Strong linearizability is a composable property [2]. Hence, if there is a strongly linearizable implementation of a type $T$ from atomic base objects of types in a set $B$, then $T$ also has a strongly linearizable implementation from strongly linearizable objects of types in $B$. Strongly linearizable monotonic counters can be implemented from atomic (and thus from strongly linearizable) snapshot objects and general counters. Thus, Theorem 1 for snapshots and general counters follows from Theorem 16.

Now suppose there is a wait-free strongly linearizable max-register $R$. In Section 4, we give an algorithm that uses a linearizable object $V$ of a type $T$ from a certain class of types together with $R$, and yields a strongly linearizable object $V_{strong}$ of type $T$. The algorithm itself is wait-free, so if $V$ and $R$ are wait-free, then so is $V_{strong}$. We can apply this algorithm, using for $V$ a standard wait-free implementation of a monotonic counter with atomic **increment** operations. Using that we obtain a wait-free strongly linearizable monotonic counter $V_{strong}$, contradicting Theorem 16. As a consequence, the assumption that there is a wait-free strongly linearizable max-register $R$ is wrong. This completes the proof of Theorem 1.

## 4    Lock-Free Implementations

We now explain how to obtain several lock-free strongly linearizable objects from atomic multi-writer registers. These objects include monotonic counters, snapshot objects, general counters, and logical clocks. We first define the notion of a *versioned* object, which is an object that increases a version number whenever it changes the state of the object. We give several examples of *linearizable* lock-free versioned objects including counters and snapshot objects. All those implementations have in common that update operations are atomic, and only the read operations are non-atomic. Then, we show how to transform any lock-free linearizable versioned object with atomic update operations into a lock-free strongly linearizable object of the same type. This transformation yields many lock-free strongly linearizable implementations from multi-writer registers.

*Versioned Objects.* Many objects are easy to augment with version numbers that increase with every successful update operation. In the following we define such versioned variants of those types formally.

We consider a class $T$ of types that support two operations, read() and update($v$). The sequential specification of each type in the class is uniquely defined by the state space $Q$ of the sequential object of that type, its initial state, $q_0$, and two functions, $f$ and $g$. For the following discussion, the initial state, $q_0$, is not relevant, so we ignore it, and denote such a type as $T_{Q,f,g}$. A read() operation on the sequential object does not change the state of the object, but returns $f(q)$, where $q$ is its current state. The operation update($v$) changes the state of the object from its current state, $s$, to $g(s)$, and does not return anything. It is easy to see that snapshots, counters, and max-registers are all types in $T$. For example, the monotonic counter is the type $T_{Q,f,g}$ with $Q = \mathbb{N} \cup \{0\}$, $f(x) = x$, and $g(x) = x + 1$.

Let $T_{Q,f,g}$ be some type in $T$. A type $T_{Q',f',g'}$ is called a *versioned* variant of type $T$, if $Q' = Q \times \mathbb{N}$, $f'(x,v) = (f(x),v)$, and $g'(x,v) = (g(x),v')$, where $v' > v$. I.e., the versioned variant of type $T$ stores exactly the same information as $T$ in addition to a *version number*, $v$. That version number gets returned by read operations, and increased with every update operation. For example, a versioned variant of the monotonic counter is the type $T_{Q',f',g'}$, where $Q'=\mathbb{N}\times\mathbb{N}$, $f(x,x)=(x,x)$, and $g(x)=(x+1,x+1)$.

It is easy to obtain linearizable versioned variants of some popular types, including snapshots, by embedding in each object an internal counter that gets incremented atomcially with each update operation. The lock-free linearizable snapshot implementation by [6] has the property that update operations are atomic. Hence, for the versioned variants of all types mentioned above, in particular snapshots, (general) counters and logical clocks, we obtain lock-free linearizable implementations from registers, with atomic update operations.

*Making Linearizable Versioned Objects Strongly Linearizable.* We show that any lock-free linearizable implementation of a versioned object can be transformed into a lock-free strongly linearizable one, provided that update operations of the versioned object are atomic. For that we use the lock-free strongly linearizable max-register implementation of Helmi et al. [4]. We augment the integer value stored in a max-register with some additional information.

An *augmented max-register* stores a pair $(x, y)$, where $x \in \mathbb{N} \cup \{0\}$, and $y$ is from some arbitrary domain $D$. It supports the operations maxRead() and maxWrite($x, y$). If the state of the object is $(x, y)$, then a maxRead() returns $(x, y)$, and maxWrite($x', y'$) changes the object's state to $(x', y')$ provided that $x' > x$. Otherwise, the object's state remains unchanged.

Existing linearizable max-register implementations from registers (e.g., [10]) can be easily transformed into linearizable augmented max-register objects. This is also true for the lock-free strongly linearizable max-register implementation of Helmi et al. [4].

We now give an implementation of an object $V_{strong}$ of type $T \in \mathcal{T}$, from an implementation $V$ of a versioned variant of $T$ and an augmented max-register $R$. Object $V_{strong}$ is strongly linearizable, provided that $R$ is strongly linearizable, $V$ is linearizable, and the update operations of $V$ are atomic.

The idea is simple: to execute $V_{strong}$.update($x$), a process first updates $V$ using $V$.update($x$), and then reads $V$ to obtain the pair $(y, vno)$, where $vno$ is the current version number of the object. Finally, it max-writes the pair $(vno, y)$ into the augmented max-register $R$. To read object $V_{strong}$, a process simply returns the augmented value read from the max-register $R$.

**Lemma 17.** *If $R$ is strongly linearizable, $V$ is linearizable, and operations $V$.update are atomic, then $V_{strong}$ is strongly linearizable.*

The implementation of $V_{strong}$ uses only wait-free code in addition to the operations on $V$ and $R$. Hence, if $V$ and $R$ are lock-free, then so is $V_{strong}$. As mentioned, there exists a lock-free implementation of augmented max-registers. Thus, we obtain the following theorem, which immediately implies Theorem 2.

**Theorem 18.** *Let $T$ be a type in $\mathcal{T}$, and $T'$ a versioned variant of $T$. If $T'$ has a lock-free linearizable implemenation with atomic update operations, then $T'$ also has a lock-free strongly linearizable implementation.*

## 5    Discussion

In this paper, we proved that several important types, such as snapshots, counters, and max-registers, have lock-free, but not wait-free, strongly linearizable implementations from registers. The negative results show that in a system with atomic registers, strong linearizability is significantly harder to obtain than linearizability.

On the other hand, recall that strong linearizability is necessary to preserve probability distributions when replacing atomic objects with implemented ones in randomized algorithms scheduled by a strong adaptive adversary [2]. Therefore, it remains an important task to find ways of implementing synchronization primitives that are robust for randomized algorithms. This can be achieved, for example, by using stronger base objects, such as compare-and-swap. However, care needs to be taken to ensure that the system that provides those base objects (e.g., the hardware) ensures that they are at least strongly linearizable. Another way could be to use *randomized* wait-free implementations of objects. Note that strong linearizability has been defined only for deterministic objects (whereas the algorithms that use those objects can be randomized). Additional work is needed to formalize an equivalent notion for randomized objects.

**Acknowledgments.** This research was undertaken, in part, thanks to funding from the Canada Research Chairs program and from the Discovery Grants program of the Natural Sciences and Engineering Research Council of Canada (NSERC).

We thank Hagit Attiya for the useful discussion on wait-freedom versus lock-freedom.

# References

1. Herlihy, M.P., Wing, J.M.: Linearizability: A correctness condition for concurrent objects. ACM Trans. Program. Lang. Syst. **12**, 463–492 (1990)
2. Golab, W., Higham, L., Woelfel, P.: Linearizable implementations do not suffice for randomized distributed computation. In: Proceedings of the Forty-third Annual ACM Symposium on Theory of Computing, STOC 2011, pp. 373–382. ACM, New York (2011)
3. Herlihy, M.: Wait-free synchronization. ACM Trans. Program. Lang. Syst. **13**, 124–149 (1991)
4. Helmi, M., Higham, L., Woelfel, P.: Strongly linearizable implementations: possibilities and impossibilities. In: Proceedings of the 2012 ACM Symposium on Principles of Distributed Computing, PODC 2012, pp. 385–394. ACM, New York (2012)
5. Herlihy, M.: Impossibility results for asynchronous pram (extended abstract). In: Proceedings of the Third Annual ACM Symposium on Parallel Algorithms and Architectures, SPAA 1991, pp. 327–336. ACM, New York (1991)
6. Afek, Y., Dolev, D., Attiya, H., Gafni, E., Merritt, M., Shavit, N.: Atomic snapshots of shared memory. In: Proceedings of the Ninth Annual ACM Symposium on Principles of Distributed Computing, PODC 1990, pp. 1–13. ACM, New York (1990)
7. Fischer, M.J., Lynch, N.A., Paterson, M.S.: Impossibility of distributed consensus with one faulty process. J. ACM **32**, 374–382 (1985)
8. Loui, M.C., Abu-Amara, H.H.: Memory requirements for agreement among unreliable asynchronous processes. Advances in Computing Research, 163–183 (1987)
9. Lynch, N.A.: Distributed Algorithms. Morgan Kaufmann Publishers Inc., San Francisco (1996)
10. Aspnes, J., Attiya, H., Censor, K.: Max registers, counters, and monotone circuits. In: Proceedings of the 28th ACM Symposium on Principles of Distributed Computing, PODC 2009, pp. 36–45. ACM, New York (2009)

# Simulating a Shared Register
# in an Asynchronous System
# that Never Stops Changing
## (Extended Abstract)

Hagit Attiya[1]([✉]), Hyun Chul Chung[2,4], Faith Ellen[3],
Saptaparni Kumar[2], and Jennifer L. Welch[2]

[1] Department of Computer Science, Technion, Haifa, Israel
hagit@cs.technion.ac.il
[2] Department of Computer Science and Engineering,
Texas A&M University, College Station, TX, USA
hcchung76@gmail.com, saptaparni@tamu.edu, welch@cse.tamu.edu
[3] Department of Computer Science, University of Toronto, Toronto, Canada
faith@cs.toronto.edu
[4] Epoch Labs, Inc., Austin, TX, USA

**Abstract.** Simulating a shared register can mask the intricacies of
designing algorithms for asynchronous message-passing systems subject
to crash failures, since it allows them to run algorithms designed for
the simpler shared-memory model. The simulation replicates the value
of the register in multiple servers and requires readers and writers to
communicate with a majority of servers. The success of this approach
for static systems, where the set of nodes (readers, writers, and servers)
is fixed, has motivated several similar simulations for dynamic systems,
where nodes may enter and leave. However, all existing simulations need
to assume that the system eventually stops changing for a long enough
period or that the system size is fixed.

This paper presents the first simulation of an atomic read/write register in a crash-prone asynchronous system that can change size and
withstand nodes continually entering and leaving. The simulation allows
the system to keep changing, provided that the number of nodes entering
and leaving during a fixed time interval is at most a constant fraction of
the current system size.

## 1 Introduction

Simulating a shared read/write register can mask the intricacies of designing
algorithms for asynchronous message-passing systems subject to crash failures,
since it allows them to run algorithms designed for the simpler shared-memory
model. The ABD simulation [5] replicates the value of the register in server nodes.
It assumes that a majority of the server nodes do not fail. Consider the simplified
case of a single writer and a single reader. To write the value $v$, the writer sends

© Springer-Verlag Berlin Heidelberg 2015
Y. Moses (Ed.): DISC 2015, LNCS 9363, pp. 75–91, 2015.
DOI: 10.1007/978-3-662-48653-5_6

$v$, tagged with a sequence number, to all servers and waits for acknowledgements from a majority of them. Similarly, to read, the reader contacts all servers, waits to receive values from a majority of them and then, returns the value with the highest sequence number. This approach can be extended to the case of multiple writers and multiple readers by having each operation consist of a read phase, used by a writer to determine its sequence number and used by a reader to obtain the return value, followed by a write phase, used by a writer to disseminate the value (and sequence number) and used by a reader to announce the sequence number of the value it is about to return [16].

The success of this approach for static systems, where the set of readers, writers, and servers is fixed, has motivated several similar simulations for dynamic systems, where nodes may enter and leave, a phenomenon called *churn*. (See [21] for a survey.) However, existing simulations rely either on the assumption that churn eventually stops for a long enough period (e.g., [2,7]) or on the assumption that the system size never changes (e.g., [6]).

In this paper, we take a different approach: *we allow churn to continue forever, while still ensuring that read and write operations complete and nodes can join the system.* Our churn model puts an upper bound on the number of nodes that can enter or leave during any time interval of a certain length. The upper bound is a constant fraction of the number of nodes that are present in the system at the beginning of the time interval. So, as the system size grows, the allowable number of changes to its composition grows as well. Similarly, as the system size shrinks, the allowable number of changes shrinks.

The time interval with respect to which the churn is bounded is set as the maximum message delay. We assume an *unknown* upper bound $D$ on the delay of any message (between nonfaulty nodes). Our churn model is that, in any time interval of length $D$, the number of nodes that can enter or leave in the interval is at most a constant fraction $\alpha$ of the number of nodes in the system at the beginning of the interval. It is important to note that we set no lower bound on the delay of messages, so consensus cannot be solved in this model even in the static case with no nodes entering or leaving but the possibility of one node crashing.

We believe ours is a reasonable churn model. For instance, if each node has the same probability of leaving in a time interval, then the number of leaves is expected to be a fixed fraction of the total number of nodes. (See [15] for a discussion of churn behavior in practice.)

Our algorithm, called CCREG (for *Continuous Churn Register*), combines the simple static algorithm for multiple readers and multiple writers outlined above with a joining protocol and careful estimations of the number of nodes from which responses should be received for joining, reading, and writing. In order to join, a newly entered node announces its entry and waits to receive sufficiently many acknowledgements. Then it joins as a participating node and announces that it has done so. A node leaves the system by announcing its departure. Each node maintains a set of changes to the composition of the system, based on the announcements of nodes entering, joining and leaving. This information is also propagated through appropriate echo messages and by having each node append its changes set to its messages that echo enter announcements.

A joining node calculates the number of acknowledgements it needs as a fraction (depending on $\alpha$) of the number of nodes it believes are in the system when it first receives an acknowledgement from a node that has already joined. Then it subtracts $f$, the maximum number of crashes. This number must be large enough to ensure that at least one acknowledgement is from a node $p$ that has been in the system sufficiently long, so that $p$ has up-to-date information. This ensures that information about the system composition is propagated properly. The number of necessary acknowledgements must also be small enough to ensure that the node will eventually receive enough of them.

Each reader and writer keeps track of the number of servers that have joined, but not left. We call these *members*. The read and write phases of operations wait for responses from a fixed fraction of the servers believed to be members, plus $f/2$. As in the joining protocol, this number of responses must be small enough so that termination is guaranteed. To prove CCREG is linearizable, we consider two cases: If a read occurs close to a write, then we must ensure that the sets of servers contacted by the two operations are intersecting. This is analogous to the situation in the static, majority algorithm. If operations are farther apart in time, then, as in the join protocol, we ensure that information about writes to the register is propagated properly.

Our churn model has the pleasing property that it is algorithm-independent: It only refers to nodes that enter or leave and ignores whether they complete the join protocol.

**Related Work:** A simple simulation of a single-writer, multi-reader register in a static network was presented in [5]. It was followed by extensions that, for example, reduce complexity [4,10,13,14], support multiple writers [16], or tolerate Byzantine failures [1,3,18,20]. To optimize load and resilience, the simple majority quorums used in these papers can be replaced by other, more complicated, quorum systems (e.g., [19,24]).

RAMBO [17] was the first simulation of a multi-writer, multi-reader register in a dynamic system, where nodes may enter and leave. It includes a dedicated reconfiguration module for handling configuration changes and for installing a new quorum system. This module relies on eventually-terminating consensus. As long as the consensus does not terminate, the protocol communicates with quorums from a possibly large number of different configurations. This assumption is also made in other variants of RAMBO (e.g., [8,9,11,12]). These papers assume that churn eventually stops.

DynaStore [2] simulates a multi-writer, multi-reader register in a dynamic system, by reconfiguring the servers without using consensus. Dynastore and its variant [22] also assume that churn eventually stops.

One simulation whose model has a similar flavor to ours is [6], in that at most a *fixed* fraction of nodes enter and leave periodically and there is an unknown upper bound on message delay. However, in their model, the system size is assumed to be constant (and known to the nodes), i.e., the number of nodes entering is the same as the number of nodes leaving at each point in time. Our model is more general, as we do not require that the system size is always the same. Instead, in our model, the system can grow, shrink, or alternately grow and shrink.

Baldoni et al. [6] also prove that it is impossible to simulate a register when there is no upper bound on message delay. Their proof works by considering scenarios in which at least half of the nodes fail or leave. Then they invoke the lower bound in [5], which shows that simulating a register is impossible unless fewer than half the nodes are faulty. Their proof can be adapted to hold when there is an unknown upper bound, $D$, on message delay and half the nodes can be replaced during any time interval of length $D$, provided that nodes are not required to announce when they leave. This means that *leaves are essentially the same as crashes.*

In the same vein, the discrepancy between our result and those in [23] and a footnote in [2] claiming that a finite number of changes is necessary for liveness can be attributed to differences in the churn models. An important difference between our simulation and those in [2,17] is that they ensure safety even when their churn and synchrony assumptions are violated, whereas ours does not when the churn is very large. One of the contributions of this paper is to point out that by making different, yet still reasonable, assumptions on churn it is possible to get a solution with different, yet still reasonable, properties and, in particular, to overcome the prior constraint that churn must stop to ensure liveness. That is, we are suggesting a different point in the solution space.

## 2  Model

We consider an asynchronous message-passing system, with nodes running *client* (*reader* or *writer*) and *server* threads. Each node runs exactly one server thread, at most one reader thread, and at most one a writer thread. Nodes can enter and leave the system during an execution. A node that leaves the system cannot re-enter the system. (This restriction is easy to remove by giving a new name to a node that wants to re-enter.) We assume that at most $f \geq 0$ nodes can crash during an execution.

We say that a node is *present* at time $t$ if it has entered but has not left by time $t$ and we let $N(t)$ denote the number of servers whose nodes are present at time $t$. We assume that there are always at least $N_{min}$ servers whose nodes are present in the system, i.e., at all times $t$, $N(t) \geq N_{min}$.

Nodes communicate through a broadcast service that provides a mechanism to send the same message to all nodes in the system. If a server wants to send a message to one of the clients, it can do so by broadcasting the message and indicating that it should be ignored by the other clients. A message that is broadcast by a node $p$ at time $t$ is guaranteed to arrive at each node $q \neq p$ within $D$ units of time, provided that $q$ is present throughout the interval $[t, t + D]$. If $q$ is present for some but not all of $[t, t + D]$, then $q$ might or might not receive the message. Nodes that enter after time $t + D$ do not (directly) receive the message.

All messages broadcast by $p$ are received by $q$ in the order in which $p$ sent them. In addition to the maximum transmission delay, $D$ includes the maximum time for handling the message at both the sender and the receiver. There is no lower bound on the actual length of time it takes for a message to be transmitted, nor on the amount of time to perform local computation at a node, i.e., they could take an arbitrarily small amount of time.

Nodes do not have clocks, so they cannot determine the current time nor directly measure how much time has elapsed since some event. They also do not know the value of $D$. The system is essentially asynchronous as there is no bound on the ratio between the fastest and slowest messages. In fact, any problem that can be solved in our model can be solved in the same model, but without the upper bound, $D$, on message delivery time. To see why, consider any execution in an asynchronous message passing model. Suppose that step $i$ of this execution occurs at time $1 - 2^{-i}$. Then every message that is received by a process is received within time $D = 1$. Moreover, if, in the original execution, messages are received along a link in the order they were sent, then the same is true in this timed execution. Hence, consensus cannot be solved in our model.

We assume the set of nodes that are present does not change too quickly: For all times $t$, at most $\alpha \cdot N(t)$ nodes enter or leave during the interval $[t, t+D]$. We call $\alpha$ the *churn rate* and we assume that the value of $\alpha$ is known to all nodes.

Let $S_0$ denote the set of nodes that are present initially, i.e. at time 0, $|S_0| = N(0)$.

## 3   The CCReg Algorithm

The algorithm combines a mechanism for tracking the composition of the system, with a simple algorithm, very similar to [16], for reading and writing the register.

In order to track the composition of the system (Algorithm 1), each node $p$ maintains a set of events, $Changes_p$, concerning the nodes that have entered the system. When a node $q$ enters, it adds $enter(q)$ to $Changes_q$ and broadcasts an enter message requesting information about prior events. When a node $p$ finds out that $q$ has entered the system, either by receiving this message or by learning indirectly from another node, it adds $enter(q)$ to $Changes_p$. When $q$ has received sufficiently many messages in response to its request, it knows relatively accurate information about prior events and the value of the register. (Setting the bound on the number of messages that should be received is a key challenge in the algorithm.) When this happens, $q$ adds $join(q)$ to $Changes_q$, sets its $is\_joined_q$ flag to *true*, and broadcasts a message saying that it has joined. We say that $q$ *joins* when this broadcast is sent. When $p$ finds out that $q$ has joined, either by receiving this message or by learning indirectly from another node, it adds $join(q)$ to $Changes_p$. When $q$ leaves, it simply broadcasts a leave message. When $p$ finds out that $q$ has left the system, either by receiving this message or by learning indirectly from another node, it adds $leave(q)$ to $Changes_p$.

When a node $p$ receives an enter message from a node $q$, it responds with an enter-echo message containing $Changes_p$, its current estimate of the register

---

**Algorithm 1.** CCREG—Common code, for node $p$.

---

**Local Variables:**

*is_joined* // Boolean to check if $p$ has joined the system; initially *false*

*join_counter* // for counting the number of enter-echo messages received by $p$; initially 0

*join_bound* // if non-zero, the number of enter-echo messages $p$ should receive before joining; initially 0

*Changes* // set of $enter(\cdot)$'s, $leave(\cdot)$'s, and $join(\cdot)$'s known by $p$; initially $\{enter(q), join(q) \mid q \in S_0\}$ if $p \in S_0$, and $\emptyset$, otherwise

*val* // latest register value known to $p$; initially $\perp$

*seq* // sequence number of latest value known to $p$; combined with next variable to make a unique timestamp for the write; initially 0

*id* // id of node that wrote latest value known to $p$; initially $\perp$

**Derived Variable:**

$Present = \{q \mid enter(q) \in Changes \wedge leave(q) \notin Changes\}$

---

**When $p$ enters the system:**
1: bcast $\langle$"enter", $p\rangle$
2: Add $enter(p)$ to *Changes*

**When $\langle$"enter", $q\rangle$ is received:**
3: add $enter(q)$ to *Changes*
4: bcast $\langle$"enter-echo", *Changes*, $(val, seq, id)$, *is_joined*, $q\rangle$

**When $\langle$"enter-echo", $C$, $(v, s, i)$, $j$, $q\rangle$ is received:**
5: **if** $(s, i) > (seq, id)$ **then**
6:    $(val, seq, id) := (v, s, i)$
7: $Changes := Changes \cup C$
8: **if** $\neg is\_joined \wedge (p = q)$ **then**
9:    **if** $(j = true) \wedge (join\_bound = 0)$ **then**
10:      $join\_bound := \gamma \cdot |Present| - f$
11:    $join\_counter++$
12:    **if** $join\_counter \geq join\_bound > 0$ **then**
13:      $is\_joined := true$
14:      add $join(p)$ to *Changes*
15:      bcast $\langle$"joined", $p\rangle$

**When $\langle$"joined", $q\rangle$ is received:**
16: add $join(q)$ to *Changes*
17: add $enter(q)$ to *Changes*
18: bcast $\langle$"joined-echo", $q\rangle$

**When $\langle$"joined-echo", $q\rangle$ is received:**
19: add $join(q)$ to *Changes*
20: add $enter(q)$ to *Changes*

**When $p$ leaves the system:**
21: bcast $\langle$"leave", $p\rangle$

**When $\langle$"leave", $q\rangle$ is received:**
22: add $leave(q)$ to *Changes*
23: bcast $\langle$"leave-echo", $q\rangle$

**When $\langle$"leave-echo", $q\rangle$ is received:**
24: add $leave(q)$ to *Changes*

---

value (together with its timestamp), $is\_joined_p$ (indicating whether $p$ has joined yet), and $q$. When $q$ receives an enter-echo in response (i.e., that ends with $q$), it increments its *join-counter*. The first time $q$ receives such an enter-echo from a joined node, it computes *join_bound*, the number of enter-echo messages it needs in response before it can join.

Once a node has joined, its reader and writer threads can handle read and write operations. A node is a *member* at time $t$ if it has joined but not left by time $t$.

Initially, $Changes_p = \{enter(q), join(q) \mid q \in S_0\}$, if $p \in S_0$, and $\emptyset$ otherwise. A node $p$ also maintains the set $Present_p = \{q \mid enter(q) \in Changes_p \wedge leave(q) \notin Changes_p\}$ of nodes that $p$ thinks are present, i.e., nodes that have entered, but have not left, as far as $p$ knows.

The server, reader and writer threads at the node share the variable *Changes* as well as its derived variable *Present*.

The client thread treats read and write operations in a similar manner (Algorithm 2). Both operations start with a read phase, used to obtain the current value of the register, using a query message, followed by a write phase, using an update message. A read operations just broadcasts the value it is about to return, keeping its sequence number. As in [5], write-back is needed to ensure linearizability of read operations. A write operation broadcasts the new value it wishes to write, with a sequence number one larger than the largest sequence number it has seen. Both the read phase and the read phase wait to receive sufficiently many response messages. (Again, setting the bound on the number of messages that should be received is a key challenge in the algorithm.)

A client $p$ maintains a sequence number, *tag*, which it increments at the beginning of each read phase. This is used to identify responses with the right read or write phase.

The server thread is simple (Algorithm 3). The server maintains the latest value of the register it knows about. When it receives an update message with a newer value for the register, it updates the current value. (Note that $(seq, id)$ pairs are compared lexicographically.) When it receives a query, it responds with the current value.

The correctness of CCREG relies on the following relations between the parameters:

$$f/(1 - \alpha)^3 < N_{min} \tag{A}$$

$$\frac{3f/2(1 - \alpha)^2}{(1 - \alpha)^3/(1 + \alpha)^2 - \beta} \leq N_{min} \tag{B}$$

$$[(1 + \gamma)(1 - \alpha)^3 - (1 + \alpha)^3]N_{min} \geq 2f \tag{C}$$

$$(1 - \alpha)^3/(1 + \alpha)^3 \geq \gamma \tag{D}$$

$$\frac{(1 + \alpha)^5 - 1}{(1 - \alpha)^4} < \beta \tag{E}$$

$$(1 + 6\alpha + 2\alpha^3)/(2 - 2\alpha + \alpha^2) < \beta \tag{F}$$

These assumptions hold for $\alpha = 0.04$ and $N_{min} = 10f$, when taking $\beta = 0.65$ and $\gamma = 0.5$. Taking a smaller churn rate $\alpha = 0.02$ reduces the minimal size to $N_{min} = 5f$, with $\beta = 0.58$ and $\gamma = 0.56$. Note that for both these values of $\alpha$,

$$-1/\log_2(1 - \alpha) \geq 4 \tag{G}$$

## Algorithm 2. CCREG—Client code, for node $p$.

**Local Variables:**

$rw\_value$ // temporary storage for the written value or the return value

$tag$ // used to uniquely identify read and write phases of an operation; initially 0

$quorum\_size$ // stores the quorum size for a read or write phase; initially 0

$heard\_from$ // the number of responses/acks received for a read/write phase; initially 0

$rp\_pending$ // Boolean indicating whether a read phase is in progress; initially $false$

$wp\_pending$ // Boolean indicating whether a write phase is in progress; initially $false$

$read\_pending$ // Boolean indicating whether a read is in progress; initially $false$

$write\_pending$ // Boolean indicating whether a write is in progress; initially $false$

---

**When READ is invoked:**

30: $read\_pending := true$
31: call BeginReadPhase()

**When WRITE($v$) is invoked:**

32: $write\_pending := true$
33: $rw\_value := v$
34: call BeginReadPhase()

**Procedure** BeginReadPhase()

35: $tag++$
36: bcast $\langle$"query", $tag, p\rangle$
37: $quorum\_size := \beta|Members| + f/2$
38: $heard\_from := 0$
39: $rp\_pending := true$

**When** $\langle$"response", $(v, s, i), rt\rangle$ **is received:**

40: **if** $rp\_pending \wedge (rt = tag)$ **then**
41:     **if** $(s, i) > (seq, id)$ **then**
42:         $(val, seq, id) := (v, s, i)$
43:     $heard\_from++$
44:     **if** $heard\_from \geq quorum\_size$ **then**
45:         $rp\_pending := false$
46:         call BeginWritePhase($(val, seq, id)$)

**Procedure** BeginWritePhase($(v, s, i)$)

47: **if** $write\_pending$ **then**
48:     $seq++$
49:     bcast $\langle$"update", $(rw\_value, seq, p)$,
              $tag, p\rangle$
50: **if** $read\_pending$ **then**
51:     $rw\_value := v$
52:     bcast $\langle$"update", $(v, s, i), tag, p\rangle$
53: $quorum\_size := \beta|Members| + f/2$
54: $heard\_from := 0$
55: $wp\_pending := true$

**When** $\langle$"ack", $wt\rangle$ **is received:**

56: **if** $wp\_pending \wedge (wt = tag)$ **then**
57:     $heard\_from++$
58:     **if** $heard\_from \geq quorum\_size$ **then**
59:         $wp\_pending := false$
60:         **if** $read\_pending$ **then**
61:             $read\_pending := false$
62:             RETURN $rw\_value$
63:         **if** $write\_pending$ **then**
64:             $write\_pending := false$
65:             ACK

---

## 4    Correctness Proof

Consider any execution. We begin by putting bounds on the number of nodes that enter and leave during an interval of time and the number of nodes that are present at the end of the interval, as compared to the number present at the beginning. Extra work is required in the proof of Lemma 2 as the calculation of the maximum number of nodes that leave during an interval is complicated by

---

**Algorithm 3.** CCREG—Server code, for node $p$.

| | |
|---|---|
| **When** ⟨"update", $(v, s, i), wt, q$⟩ is received: | **When** ⟨"query", $rt, q$⟩ is received: |
| 70: **if** $(s, i) > (seq, id)$ **then** | 75: **if** $is\_joined$ **then** |
| 71:    $(val, seq, id) := (v, s, i)$ | 76:    send ⟨"response", $(val, seq, id), rt$⟩ to (read-phase invoker) $q$ |
| 72: **if** $is\_joined$ **then** | **When** ⟨"update-echo", $(v, s, i)$⟩ is received: |
| 73:    send ⟨"ack", $wt$⟩ to (write-phase invoker) $q$ | 77: **if** $(s, i) > (seq, id)$ **then** |
| 74: bcast ⟨"update-echo", $(val, seq, id)$⟩ | 78:    $(val, seq, id) := (v, s, i)$ |

---

the possibility of nodes entering during an interval and thus allowing additional nodes to leave.

**Lemma 1.** *For all $i \in \mathbb{N}$ and all $t \geq 0$, at most $((1 + \alpha)^i - 1)N(t)$ nodes enter during $(t, t + Di]$ and $(1 - \alpha)^i N(t) \leq N(t + Di) \leq (1 + \alpha)^i N(t)$.*

**Lemma 2.** *For all nonnegative integers $i \leq -1/\log_2(1 - \alpha)$ and all $t \geq 0$, at most $(1 - (1 - \alpha)^i)N(t)$ nodes leave during $(t, t + Di]$.*

We say that a node is *active* at time $t$ if it has entered by time $t$, but has not left or crashed by time $t$. The next lemma shows that some node remains active throughout any interval of length $3D$.

**Lemma 3.** *For every $t > 0$, at least one node is active throughout $[\max\{0, t - 2D\}, t + D]$.*

We define $SysInfo^I = \{enter(q) \mid t_q^e \in I\} \cup \{join(q) \mid t_q^j \in I\} \cup \{leave(q) \mid t_q^\ell \in I\}$ to be the set of all enter, join, and leave events that occur during time interval $I$. In particular, $SysInfo^{[0,0]} = \{enter(q) \mid q \in S_0\} \cup \{join(q) \mid q \in S_0\}$. The next observation holds since a node $p$ that is active throughout $[t_p^e, t + D]$ will directly receive all enter, joined, and leave messages broadcast during $[t_p^e, t]$ within $D$ time.

**Observation 1.** *For every node $p$ and all times $t \geq t_p^e$, if $p$ is active at time $t + D$, then $SysInfo^{[t_p^e, t]} \subseteq Changes_p^{t+D}$.*

Together with the assumption that $SysInfo^{[0,0]} \subseteq Changes_p^0$ for all $p \in S_0$, we get:

**Observation 2.** *For every node $p \in S_0$, if $p$ is active at time $t \geq 0$, then $SysInfo^{[0,\max\{0,t-D\}]} \subseteq Changes_p^t$.*

The purpose of Lemmas 4, 5, and 6 is to show that information about nodes entering, joining, and leaving is propagated properly, via the *Changes* sets.

**Lemma 4.** *Suppose a node $p \notin S_0$ receives an enter-echo message at time $t''$ from a node $q$ that sent it at time $t'$ in response to an enter message from $p$. If $p$ is active at time $t + 2D$ and $q$ is active throughout $[\max\{0, t' - 2D\}, t + D]$, where $\max\{0, t'' - 2D\} \leq t \leq t_p^e$, then $SysInfo^{(\max\{0,t'-2D\},t]} \subseteq Changes_p^{t+2D}$.*

*Proof.* Consider any node $r$ that enters, joins, or leaves at time $\hat{t}$, where $\max\{0, t'-2D\} < \hat{t} \leq t$. If $q$ receives the message about this change from $r$ before the enter message from $p$, then the change is in $Changes_p^{t''} \subseteq Changes_p^{t+2D}$. Otherwise, $q$ receives the message from $r$ after the enter message from $p$ and sends an echo message in response by time $\hat{t} + D$. Since $p$ receives this message from $q$ by time $\hat{t} + 2D \leq t + 2D$, it follows that the change is in $Changes_p^{t+2D}$. Thus, $SysInfo^{(\max\{0,t'-2D\},t]} \subseteq Changes_p^{t+2D}$. □

**Lemma 5.** *For every node $p$, if $p$ is active at time $t \geq t_p^e + 2D$, then $SysInfo^{[0,t-D]} \subseteq Changes_p^t$.*

**Lemma 6.** *For every node $p \notin S_0$, if $p$ joins at time $t_p^j$ and is active at time $t \geq t_p^j$, then $SysInfo^{[0,\max\{0,t-2D\}]} \subseteq Changes_p^t$.*

*Proof.* Let $p \notin S_0$ be a node that joins at time $t_p^j \leq t$ and suppose the claim holds for all nodes that join before $p$. If $t \geq t_p^e + 2D$, then the claim follows by Lemma 5. So, assume that $t < t_p^e + 2D$.

Before $p$ joins, it receives an enter-echo message from a joined node in response to its enter message. Suppose $p$ first receives such an enter-echo message at time $t''$ and this enter-echo was sent by $q$ at time $t'$. Then $t_p^e \leq t' \leq t'' \leq t_p^j$. Since $q$ joined prior to $p$ and is active at time $t' \geq t_q^j$, $SysInfo^{[0,\max\{0,t'-2D\}]} \subseteq Changes_q^{t'} \subseteq Changes_p^{t''} \subseteq Changes_p^t$. If $t \leq 2D$ then $\max\{0, t - 2D\} = 0$ and the claim is true. So, assume that $t > 2D$.

Let $S$ be the set of nodes present at time $\max\{0, t' - 2D\}$, so $|S| = N(\max\{0, t'-2D\})$. By Lemma 2 and Assumption (G), at most $(1-(1-\alpha)^3)|S|$ nodes leave during $(\max\{0, t' - 2D\}, t' + D]$. Since $t'' \leq t' + D$, it follows that $|Present_p^{t''}| \geq |S| - (1 - (1 - \alpha)^3)|S| = (1-\alpha)^3|S|$. Hence, $p$ waits until it has received at least $\gamma|Present_p^{t''}| - f \geq \gamma(1-\alpha)^3|S| - f$ enter-echo messages before joining.

By Lemma 1, the number of nodes that enter during $(\max\{0, t'-2D\}, t'+D]$ is at most $((1+\alpha)^3 - 1)|S|$. The number of nodes that leave during this interval is at most $(1-(1-\alpha)^3)|S|$ and at most $f$ nodes crash. Note that $p$ enters during $[\max\{0, t' - 2D\}, t' + D]$, but does not receive an enter-echo message from itself. Hence, the number enter-echo messages $p$ receives before joining from nodes that were active throughout $[\max\{0, t' - 2D\}, t' + D]$ is at least

$$\gamma(1-\alpha)^3|S| - f - [((1+\alpha)^3 - 1)|S| + (1 - (1-\alpha)^3)|S| + f - 1]$$
$$= [(1+\gamma)(1-\alpha)^3 - (1+\alpha)^3]|S| - 2f + 1$$

This is at least 1, since $\gamma = (1-\alpha)^3/(1+\alpha)^3$ and $f \leq |S|[(1-\alpha)^6 + (1-\alpha)^3(1+\alpha)^3 - (1+\alpha)^6]/2(1+\alpha)^3$. (By Assumption (C).)

Hence $p$ receives an enter-echo message by time $t_p^j$ from a node $q'$ that is active throughout $[\max\{0, t' - 2D\}, t' + D] \supseteq [\max\{0, t' - 2D\}, t - D]$.

Since $\max\{0, t'' - 2D\} \leq t - 2D \leq t_p^e \leq t' < t_p^e + D$, Lemma 4 implies that $SysInfo^{[\max\{0,t'-2D\},t-2D]} \subseteq Changes_p^t$. However, $SysInfo^{[0,\max\{0,t'-2D\}]} \subseteq Changes_p^t$, and hence, $SysInfo^{[0,\max\{0,t-2D\}]} \subseteq Changes_p^t$.      □

Next we prove that every node that remains active sufficiently long after it enters succeeds in joining.

**Theorem 1.** *Every node* $p \notin S_0$ *that is active at time* $t_p^e + 2D$ *joins by time* $t_p^e + 2D$.

*Proof.* Let $p \notin S_0$ be a node that enters at time $t_p^e$ and is active at time $t_p^e + 2D$. Suppose the claim is true for all nodes that enter before $p$.

By Lemma 3, there is a node $q$ that is active throughout $[\max\{t_p^e - 2D, 0\}, t_p^e + D]$. If $q \in S_0$, then $q$ joins at time 0. If not, then $t_q^e < t_p^e$, so, by the induction hypothesis, $q$ joins by $t_q^e + 2D < t_p^e$. Since $q$ is active at time $t_p^e + D$, it receives the enter message from $p$ during $[t_p^e, t_p^e + D]$ and sends an enter-echo message in response. Since $p$ is active at time $t_p^e + 2D$, it receives the enter-echo message from $q$ by time $t_p^e + 2D$. Hence, by time $t_p^e + 2D$, $p$ received at least one enter-echo message from a joined node in response to its enter message.

Suppose the first enter-echo message $p$ received from a joined node in response to its enter message was sent by node $q'$ at time $t'$ and received by $p$ at time $t''$. By Lemma 6, $SysInfo^{[0,\max\{0,t'-2D\}]} \subseteq Changes_{q'}^{t'} \subseteq Changes_p^{t''}$.

Let $S$ be the set of nodes present at time $\max\{0, t' - 2D\}$. Then, by Lemma 1, $N(t' - D) \leq (1+\alpha)|S|$ and $N(t') \leq (1+\alpha)^2|S|$. Since $t'' \leq t' + D$, it follows from the churn assumption that at most $\alpha(1+(1+\alpha)+(1+\alpha)^2)|S|$ nodes entered during $(t' - 2D, t'']$. Thus, $|Present_p^{t''}| \leq (1+\alpha(1+(1+\alpha)+(1+\alpha)^2))|S| = (1+\alpha)^3|S|$ and $join\_bound_p \leq \gamma(1+\alpha)^3|S| - f$.

By Lemma 2 and Assumption (G), at most $(1 - (1-\alpha)^3)|S|$ nodes leave during $(\max\{0, t' - 2D\}, t' + D]$. Since $t_p^e \leq t' \leq t_p^e + D$ and at most $f$ nodes crash, at least $(1-\alpha)^3|S| - f$ nodes in $S$ were active throughout $[t_p^e, t_p^e + D]$ and, hence, sent enter-echo messages in response to $p$'s enter message. By time $t_p^e + 2D$, $p$ receives all these enter-echo messages. Since $(1-\alpha)^3 \geq \gamma(1+\alpha)^3$ (Assumption (D)), node $p$ joins by time $t_p^e + 2D$.      □

We now proceed to show that all read and write operations terminate. The key is to show that the number of responses for which an operation waits is small enough so that it is guaranteed to receive at least that many.

Since $enter(q)$ is added to $Changes_p$ whenever $join(q)$ is, we get:

**Observation 3.** *For every time* $t \geq 0$ *and every node* $p$ *that is active at time* $t$, $Members_p^t \subseteq Present_p^t$.

Lemma 7 relates the number of nodes present in the system $2D$ time in the past to the value of a node's current estimate of the number of nodes present. Lemma 8 relates the number of nodes present in the system $4D$ time in the past to the value of a node's current estimate of the number of nodes that are members. These are useful for showing that a node's calculated quorum size is close to reality.

**Lemma 7.** *For every node $p$ and every time $t \geq t_p^j$ at which $p$ is active,*

$$(1-\alpha)^2 \cdot N(\max\{0, t-2D\}) \leq |Present_p^t| \leq (1+\alpha)^2 \cdot N(\max\{0, t-2D\}).$$

**Lemma 8.** *For every node $p$ and every time $t \geq t_p^j$ at which $p$ is active,*

$$(1-\alpha)^4 \cdot N(\max\{0, t-4D\}) \leq |Members_p^t| \leq (1+\alpha)^4 \cdot N(\max\{0, t-4D\}).$$

The next lemma shows a lower bound on the number of nodes that will reply to an operation's query or update message.

**Lemma 9.** *If node $p$ is active at time $t \geq t_p^j$, then the number of nodes that join by time $t$ and are still active at time $t+D$ is at least $\frac{(1-\alpha)^3}{(1+\alpha)^2}|Present_p^t| - f$.*

**Theorem 2.** *Every read or write operation completes if invoked by a node that remains active for $4D$ time.*

*Proof.* Each operation consists of a read phase and a write phase. Thus, if both the read and write phases of an operation terminate, then the operation itself terminates. We show that each phase terminates within $2D$ time, provided the client remains active for $4D$ time.

Consider a phase of an operation by client $p$ that starts at time $t$. Every node that joins by time $t$ and is still active at time $t+D$ receives $p$'s query or update message and replies with a response or ack message by time $t+D$. By Lemma 9, there are at least $\frac{(1-\alpha)^3}{(1+\alpha)^2}|Present_p^t| - f$ such nodes.

From Lemma 7 and Assumption (B),

$$|Present_p^t| \geq (1-\alpha)^2 N(\max\{0, t-2D\}) \geq (1-\alpha)^2 N_{min}$$

$$\geq \frac{3f/2}{(1-\alpha)^3/(1+\alpha)^2 - \beta},$$

so

$$|Present_p^t| \left( \frac{(1-\alpha)^3}{(1+\alpha)^2} - \beta \right) \geq \frac{3f}{2}.$$

Hence, by Observation 3,

$$\frac{(1-\alpha)^3}{(1+\alpha)^2}|Present_p^t| - f \geq \beta|Present_p^t| + f/2$$

$$\geq \beta|Members_p^t| + f/2 = quorum\_size_p^t.$$

Thus, by time $t+2D$, $p$ receives sufficiently many response or ack messages to complete the phase. $\square$

Now we prove linearizability of the CCREG algorithm.

A write operation $w$ by node $p$ consists of a read phase followed by a write phase. Let $t_w$ denote the time at the beginning of its write phase. At time $t_w$, node $p$ broadcasts an update message (on Line 49 or Line 52 of Algorithm 2) containing a triple $(v, s, i)$, where $value(w) = v$ is the *value written by* $w$ and $ts(w) = (s, i) = (seq_p^{t_w}, id_p^{t_w})$ is the *timestamp* of $w$.

For any node $p$, let $ts_p^t = (seq_p^t, id_p^t)$ denote the *timestamp* of node $p$ at time $t$. Note that timestamps are created by write operations (on Line 48 of Algorithm 2) and are sent via enter-echo, update, and update-echo messages. Initially, $ts_p^0 = (0, \perp)$ for all nodes $p$. For any read or write operation $o$ by node $p$, the *timestamp of its read phase* is $ts^{rp}(o) = ts_p^t$, where $t$ is the time at the end of its read phase (i.e., when the conditional in Line 44 of Algorithm 2 is true). The *timestamp of its write phase* is $ts^{wp}(o) = ts_p^t$, where $t$ is the time at the beginning of its write phase (i.e., when it broadcasts on Line 49 or Line 52 of Algorithm 2). Note that $ts(w) = ts^{wp}(w)$ for every write operation $w$. Likewise, $ts(r) = ts^{rp}(r)$ is the *timestamp of a read operation* $r$.

The next series of lemmas (10 through 13) show that information about writes propagates properly throughout the system, and is analogous to previous results relating to the propagation of information about nodes entering, joining, and leaving (Observation 2 and Lemmas 4 through 6).

**Lemma 10.** *If $o$ is an operation whose write phase starts at $t_w$, node $p$ is active at time $t \geq t_w + D$, and $t_p^e \leq t_w$, then $ts_p^t \geq ts^{wp}(o)$.*

**Lemma 11.** *Suppose a node $p \notin S_0$ receives an enter-echo message at time $t''$ from a node $q$ that sends it at time $t'$ in response to an enter message from $p$. If $o$ is an operation whose write phase starts at $t_w$, $p$ is active at time $t \geq \max\{t'', t_w + 2D\}$, and $q$ is active throughout $[t_w, t_w + D]$, then $ts_p^t \geq ts^{wp}(o)$.*

**Lemma 12.** *If $o$ is an operation whose write phase starts at $t_w$ and node $p$ is active at time $t \geq \max\{t_p^e + 2D, t_w + D\}$, then $ts_p^t \geq ts^{wp}(o)$.*

**Lemma 13.** *If $o$ is an operation whose write phase starts at $t_w$, node $p \notin S_0$ joins at time $t_p^j$, and $p$ is active at time $t \geq \max\{t_p^j, t_w + 2D\}$, then $ts_p^t \geq ts^{wp}(o)$.*

**Theorem 3.** CCREG *ensures linearizability.*

*Proof.* Given an execution, we order all the read and write operations in the execution that perform Line 49 or 52 as follows. First, order the write operations in order of their timestamps. Note that all write operations have different timestamps, since each write operation by node $p$ has a timestamp with second component $p$ and first component larger than any timestamp $p$ has previously seen. Then insert each read operation immediately following the write operation with the same timestamp. Break ties among read operations by their start times. By construction, this total order is legal. It remains to show that if $op_1$ finishes before $op_2$ starts, then the construction orders $op_1$ before $op_2$.

Since each operation consists of a read phase followed by a write phase, it suffices to show that $ts^{wp}(op_1) \leq ts^{rp}(op_2)$. For convenience, we will refer to $ts^{wp}(op_1)$ as $\tau_w$ and $ts^{rp}(op_2)$ as $\tau_r$.

Let $w$ denote the write phase of $op_1$ and let $r$ denote the read phase of $op_2$. Let $p_1$ be the node that invokes $op_1$ and let $p_2$ be the node that invokes $op_2$. Let $t_w$ be the start time of $w$ and $t_r$ be the start time of $r$. Then $t_w < t_r$. Let $Q_w$ be the set of nodes that $p_1$ hears from during $w$ (i.e. that sent messages causing $p_1$ to increment *heard_from* on Line 57 of Algorithm 2) and $Q_r$ be the set of nodes that $p_2$ hears from during $r$ (i.e. that sent messages causing $p_2$ to increment *heard_from* on Line 43 of Algorithm 2). Let $P_w$ and $M_w$ be the sizes of the *Present* and *Members* sets of $p_1$ at time $t_w$, and $P_r$ and $M_r$ be the sizes of the *Present* and *Members* sets of $p_2$ at time $t_r$.

**Case 1:** $t_r > t_w + 2D$.

We start by showing there exists a node $q$ in $Q_r$ such that $t_q^j \leq \max\{0, t_r - 2D\}$. Each node in $Q_r$ receives and responds to $r$'s query, so it joins by time $t_r + D$. By Theorem 1, the number of nodes that can join in $(t_r - 2D, t_r + D]$ is at most the number of nodes that can enter in $(\max\{0, t_r - 4D\}, t_r + D]$. By Lemma 1, the number of nodes that can enter in $(\max\{0, t_r - 4D\}, t_r + D]$ is at most $((1 + \alpha)^5 - 1) \cdot N(\max\{0, t_r - 4D\})$. By Lemma 8, $N(\max\{0, t - 4D\}) \leq M_r/(1 - \alpha)^4$. From the code, $|Q_r| \geq \beta M_r + f/2$, which is larger than $\beta M_r$. By Assumption (E), it follows that $\beta M_r > M_r((1 + \alpha)^5 - 1)/(1 - \alpha)^4$, which is at most the number of nodes that can enter in $(\max\{0, t_r - 4D\}, t_r + D]$. Thus $|Q_r|$ is larger than the number of nodes that join in $(\max\{0, t_r - 2D\}, t_r + D]$.

Suppose $q$ receives $r$'s query message at time $t' \geq t_r$. If $q \in S_0$, then $t_q^j = 0$ and, by Lemma 10, $ts_q^{t'} \geq \tau_w$. So, suppose $q \notin S_0$. Then $0 < t_q^j \leq t_r - 2D < t'$. Since $t_w + 2D < t_r \leq t'$, Lemma 13 implies that $ts_q^{t'} \geq \tau_w$. Thus, $q$ responds to $r$'s query message with a timestamp at least as large as $\tau_w$ and, as a result, $\tau_r \geq \tau_w$.

**Case 2:** $t_r \leq t_w + 2D$.

Let $J$ be the set of nodes that could reply to $r$'s query. Then $J = \{p \mid t_p^j < t_r$ and $p$ is active at time $t_r\} \cup \{p \mid t_r \leq t_p^j \leq t_r + D\}$. By Theorem 1, all nodes that are present at time $\max\{0, t_r - 2D\}$ join by time $t_r$ if they remain active. Therefore all nodes in $J$ are either active at time $\max\{0, t_r - 2D\}$ or enter during $(\max\{0, t_r - 2D\}, t_r + D]$ and, by Lemma 1, $|J| \leq N(\max\{0, t_r - 2D\}) + ((1 + \alpha)^3 - 1)N(\max\{0, t_r - 2D\}) = (1 + \alpha)^3 N(\max\{0, t_r - 2D\})$.

Let $K = \{p \mid t_p^j \leq t_r, p$ is active at $t_r + D$, and $ts_p^{t_r} \geq \tau_w\}$. Note that $K$ contains all the nodes in $Q_w$ that do not leave or fail during $[t_w, t_r + D] \subseteq [\max\{0, t_r - 2D\}, t_r + D]$. By Lemma 2 and Assumption (G), at most $(1 - (1 - \alpha)^3)N(\max\{0, t_r - 2D\})$ nodes leave during this interval and at most $f$ fail. From the code, $|Q_r| \geq \beta M_r + f/2$ and, by Lemma 8, $M_r \geq (1 - \alpha)^4 N(\max\{0, t_r - 4D\})$. Similarly, $|Q_w| \geq \beta(1 - \alpha)^4 N(\max\{0, t_w - 4D\}) + f/2$. Therefore, $|K| \geq (\beta(1 - \alpha)^4 N(\max\{0, t_w - 4D\}) + \frac{f}{2}) - (1 - (1 - \alpha)^3)N(\max\{0, t_r - 2D\}) - f$. Since $t_w < t_r \leq t_w + 2D$, Lemma 1 implies that $N(\max\{0, t_w - 4D\}) \geq$

$(1-\alpha)^{-2}N(\max\{0, t_r - 4D\})$. Also by Lemma 1, $N(\max\{0, t_r - 4D\}) \geq (1-\alpha)^{-2}N(\max\{0, t_r - 2D\})$.

By Assumption (F), $\beta > (1 + 6\alpha + 2\alpha^3)/(2 - 2\alpha + \alpha^2)$. Hence

$$\begin{aligned}
|Q_r| + |K| &\geq \beta(1-\alpha)^4 N(\max\{0, t_r - 4D\}) \\
&\quad + \beta(1-\alpha)^4(1-\alpha)^{-2}N(\max\{0, t_r - 4D\}) \\
&\quad - (1 - (1-\alpha)^3)N(\max\{0, t_r - 2D\}) \\
&= \beta(1-\alpha)^2(2 - 2\alpha + \alpha^2)N(\max\{0, t_r - 4D\}) \\
&\quad - (3\alpha - 3\alpha^2 + \alpha^3)N(\max\{0, t_r - 2D\}) \\
&\geq \beta(2 - 2\alpha + \alpha^2)N(\max\{0, t_r - 2D\}) \\
&\quad - (3\alpha - 3\alpha^2 + \alpha^3)N(\max\{0, t_r - 2D\}).
\end{aligned}$$

Thus $\begin{aligned}[t]
|Q_r| + |K| &> [(1 + 6\alpha + 2\alpha^3) - (3\alpha - 3\alpha^2 + \alpha^3)]N(\max\{0, t_r - 2D\}) \\
&= [1 + 3\alpha + 3\alpha^2 + \alpha^3]N(\max\{0, t_r - 2D\}) \\
&= (1 + \alpha)^3 N(\max\{0, t_r - 2D\}) \\
&\geq |J|.
\end{aligned}$

This implies that $K$ and $Q_r$ intersect, since $K, Q_r \subseteq J$. For each node $p$ in the intersection, $ts_p \geq \tau_w$ when $p$ sends its response to $r$ and, thus, $\tau_r \geq \tau_w$.   □

## 5   Discussion

We have shown how to simulate an atomic read/write register in a crash-prone asynchronous system where nodes can enter and leave, as long as the number of nodes entering and leaving during each time interval of length $D$ is at most a constant fraction of the current system size.

It would be nice to improve the constants for the churn rate and the maximum fraction of faulty nodes, perhaps with a tighter analysis. Proving lower bounds or tradeoffs on these parameters is an interesting avenue for future work. In fact, it might be possible to completely avoid the bound $\alpha$ on the churn rate, by spreading out the handling of node joins and leaves: To ensure a minimal number of nonfaulty nodes, a node might need to obtain permission before leaving, similarly to joins. This will also mean that the algorithm will maintain safety even when the churn bound is exceeded.

CCREG sends increasingly large Changes sets. The amount of information communicated might be reduced by sending only recent events, or by removing very old events. Another interesting research direction is to extend CCREG to tolerate more severe kinds of failures.

**Acknowledgments.** This work is supported by the Israel Science Foundation (grants 1227/10 and 1749/14), by Yad HaNadiv foundation, by the Natural Science and Engineering Research Council of Canada, and by the US National Science Foundation grant 0964696.

# References

1. Abraham, I., Chockler, G., Keidar, I., Malkhi, D.: Byzantine disk paxos: optimal resilience with Byzantine shared memory. Dist. Comp. **18**(5), 387–408 (2006)
2. Aguilera, M.K., Keidar, I., Malkhi, D., Shraer, A.: Dynamic atomic storage without consensus. J. ACM **58**(2), 7 (2011)
3. Aiyer, A.S., Alvisi, L., Bazzi, R.A.: Bounded wait-free implementation of optimally resilient byzantine storage without (unproven) cryptographic assumptions. In: Pelc, A. (ed.) DISC 2007. LNCS, vol. 4731, pp. 7–19. Springer, Heidelberg (2007)
4. Attiya, H.: Efficient and robust sharing of memory in message-passing systems. J. Alg. **34**(1), 109–127 (2000)
5. Attiya, H., Bar-Noy, A., Dolev, D.: Sharing memory robustly in message-passing systems. J. ACM **42**(1), 124–142 (1995)
6. Baldoni, R., Bonomi, S., Kermarrec, A.M., Raynal, M.: Implementing a register in a dynamic distributed system. In: IEEE International Conference on Distributed Computing Systems, pp. 639–647 (2009)
7. Baldoni, R., Bonomi, S., Raynal, M.: Implementing a regular register in an eventually synchronous distributed system prone to continuous churn. IEEE Transactions on Parallel and Distributed Systems **23**(1), 102–109 (2012)
8. Beal, J., Gilbert, S.: RamboNodes for the metropolitan ad hoc network. In: Workshop on Dependability in Wireless Ad Hoc Networks and Sensor Networks (2003)
9. Chockler, G., Gilbert, S., Gramoli, V., Musial, P.M., Shvartsman, A.A.: Reconfigurable distributed storage for dynamic networks. J. Par. Dist. Comp. **69**(1), 100–116 (2009)
10. Dutta, P., Guerraoui, R., Levy, R.R., Chakraborty, A.: How fast can a distributed atomic read be? In: Proceedings of the 23rd Annual ACM Symposium on Principles of Distributed Computing, pp. 236–245 (2004)
11. Georgiou, C., Musial, P.M., Shvartsman, A.A.: Long-lived RAMBO: Trading knowledge for communication. Theo. Comp. Sci. **383**(1), 59–85 (2007)
12. Gilbert, S., Lynch, N.A., Shvartsman, A.A.: Rambo: A robust, reconfigurable atomic memory service for dynamic networks. Dist. Comp. **23**(4), 225–272 (2010)
13. Guerraoui, R., Levy, R.: Robust emulations of shared memory in a crash-recovery model. In: Proceedings of the International Conference on Distributed Computing Systems, pp. 400–407 (2004)
14. Guerraoui, R., Vukolić, M.: Refined quorum systems. In: Proceedings of the 26th Annual ACM Symposium on Principles of Distributed Computing, pp. 119–128 (2007)
15. Ko, S.Y., Hoque, I., Gupta, I.: Using tractable and realistic churn models to analyze quiescence behavior of distributed protocols. In: IEEE Symposium on Reliable Distributed Systems, pp. 259–268 (2008)
16. Lynch, N.A., Shvartsman, A.A.: Robust emulation of shared memory using dynamic quorum-acknowledged broadcasts. In: Proceedings of the 27th International Symposium on Fault-Tolerant Computing, pp. 272–281 (1997)
17. Lynch, N.A., Shvartsman, A.A.: Rambo: A reconfigurable atomic memory service for dynamic networks. In: Proceedings of the 16th International Conference on Distributed Computing, pp. 173–190 (2002)
18. Malkhi, D., Reiter, M.K.: Byzantine quorum systems. Dist. Comp. **11**(4), 203–213 (1998)

19. Malkhi, D., Reiter, M.K., Wool, A., Wright, R.N.: Probabilistic quorum systems. Information and Computation **170**(2), 184–206 (2001)
20. Martin, J.P., Alvisi, L., Dahlin, M.: Minimal byzantine storage. In: Proceedings of the 16th International Conference on Distributed Computing, pp. 311–325 (2002)
21. Musial, P., Nicolaou, N., Shvartsman, A.A.: Implementing distributed shared memory for dynamic networks. Commun. ACM **57**(6), 88–98 (2014)
22. Shraer, A., Martin, J.P., Malkhi, D., Keidar, I.: Data-centric reconfiguration with network-attached disks. In: Proceedings of the 4th International Workshop on Large Scale Distributed Systems and Middleware, pp. 22–26 (2010)
23. Spiegelman, A., Keidar, I.: On liveness of dynamic storage. CoRR abs/1507.07086 (July 2015). http://arxiv.org/abs/1507.07086
24. Vukolic, M.: Quorum Systems: With Applications to Storage and Consensus. Synthesis Lectures on Distributed Computing Theory, Morgan & Claypool Publishers (2012)

# Plane Formation by Synchronous Mobile Robots in the Three Dimensional Euclidean Space

Yukiko Yamauchi$^{(\boxtimes)}$, Taichi Uehara, Shuji Kijima, and Masafumi Yamashita

Kyushu University, 744 Motooka, Nishi-ku, Fukuoka 819-0395, Japan
yamauchi@inf.kyushu-u.ac.jp

**Abstract.** Creating a swarm of mobile computing entities frequently called robots, agents or sensor nodes, with self-organization ability is a contemporary challenge in distributed computing. Motivated by this, this paper investigates the *plane formation problem* that requires a swarm of robots moving in the three dimensional Euclidean space to reside in a common plane. The robots are fully synchronous and endowed with visual perception. But they have neither identifiers, access to the global coordinate system, any means of explicit communication with each other, nor memory of past. Though there are plenty of results on the agreement problem for robots in the two dimensional plane, for example, the point formation problem, the pattern formation problem, and so on, this is the first result for robots in the *three dimensional space*. This paper presents a necessary and sufficient condition to solve the plane formation problem. An implication of the result is somewhat counter-intuitive: The robots *cannot* form a plane from most of the semi-regular polyhedra, while they *can* from every regular polyhedron (except a regular icosahedron), which consists of the same regular polygon faces and the robots on its vertices are "more" symmetric than semi-regular polyhedra.

**Keywords:** Mobile robots in the three dimensional space · Plane formation · Rotation group · Symmetry breaking

## 1 Introduction

Self-organization in a swarm of mobile computing entities frequently called robots, agents or sensor nodes, has gained much attention as sensing and controlling devices are developed and become cheaper. It is expected that mobile robot systems perform patrolling, sensing, and exploring in a harsh environment such as disaster area, deep sea, and space. For robots moving in the *three dimensional* Euclidean space (3D-space), we investigate the *plane formation problem*, which is a fundamental self-organization problem that requires robots to occupy distinct positions on a common plane from initial positions, mainly motivated

This work was supported by a Grant-in-Aid for Scientific Research on Innovative Areas "Molecular Robotics" (No. No. 24104003 and No. 15H00821) of The Ministry of Education, Culture, Sports, Science, and Technology, Japan.

© Springer-Verlag Berlin Heidelberg 2015
Y. Moses (Ed.): DISC 2015, LNCS 9363, pp. 92–106, 2015.
DOI: 10.1007/978-3-662-48653-5_7

by an obvious observation: Robots on a plane would be easier to control than those deployed in 3D-space.

In this paper, a mobile robot system consists of autonomous robots that move in 3D-space and cooperate with each other to accomplish their tasks without any central control. A robot is represented by a point in 3D-space and repeats executing the "Look-Compute-Move" cycle, during which, it observes, in *Look phase*, the positions of all robots by taking a snapshot, which we call a *local observation* in this paper, computes the next position based only on the snapshot just taken and using a given deterministic algorithm in *Compute phase*, and moves to the next position in *Move phase*. This definition of Look-Compute-Move cycle implies that it has *full vision*, i.e., the vision is unrestricted, the algorithm is *oblivious*, i.e., it does not depend on a snapshot of the past, and the move is an atomic action, i.e., each robot does not stop en route to the next position and we do not care which route it takes. A robot has no access to the global *x-y-z* coordinate system, and all actions are done in terms of its local *x-y-z* coordinate system. We assume that it has *chirality*, which means that it has the sense of clockwise and counter-clockwise directions. In particular, we assume that local coordinate systems are right-handed.

The robots can see each other, but do not have direct communication capabilities; communication among robots must take place solely by moving and observing robots' positions, tolerating possible inconsistency among the local coordinate systems. The robots are *anonymous*; they have no unique identifiers and are indistinguishable by their looks, and execute the same algorithm. Finally, they are fully-synchronous (FSYNC); they all start the *i*-th Look-Compute-Move cycle simultaneously, and synchronously execute each of its Look, Compute and Move phases.

The purpose of this paper is to show a necessary and sufficient condition for the solvability of the plane formation problem. The *line formation problem* in the two dimensional Euclidean space (2D-space or plane) is the counter-part of the plane formation problem in 3D-space, and is *unsolvable* from an initial configuration $P$ (i.e., positions of the robots), if $P$ is a regular polygon, intuitively because anonymous robots forming a regular polygon cannot break symmetry among themselves, and lines they propose are also symmetric, so that they cannot agree on one line from them [9]. Hence symmetry breaking among robots would play a crucial role in our study on the plane formation in 3D-space, too.

The *pattern formation problem* requires robots to form a target pattern from an initial configuration, and our plane formation problem is a subproblem of the pattern formation problem in 3D-space. To investigate the pattern formation problem in 2D-space, which contains the line formation problem as a subproblem, Suzuki and Yamashita [9] used the concept of *symmetricity* to measure the degree of symmetry of a configuration consisting of the robots' positions on the plane.[1] Let $P$ be a configuration of robots on a plane, where we regard the configuration as a set of points. Then its symmetricity $\rho(P)$ is the order of the cyclic group of $P$,

---

[1] The symmetricity was originally introduced in [10] for anonymous networks to investigate the solvability of some agreement problems.

where its rotation center $o$ is the center of the smallest enclosing circle of $P$, if $o \notin P$. That is, its rotational symmetry is $\rho(P)$ and $\rho(P)$ is the number of angles such that rotating $P$ by $\theta$ ($\theta \in [0, 2\pi)$) around $o$ produces $P$ itself, which intuitively means that the $\rho(P)$ robots forming a regular $\rho(P)$-gon in $P$ may not be able to break symmetry among themselves. However, when $o \in P$, the symmetricity $\rho(P)$ is defined to be 1, independently of its rotational symmetry. This is the crucial difference between the rotational symmetry and the symmetricity, and reflects the fact that the robot at $o$ *can* break the symmetry in $P$ by leaving $o$. Then the following result has been obtained [7,9,11]: A target pattern $F$ is formable from an initial configuration $P$, if and only if $\rho(P)$ divides $\rho(F)$.

In order to investigate the plane formation problem in 3D-space, we measure the symmetry of a configuration in 3D-space with the rotation group of the configuration. In 3D-space, rotation groups with finite order are classified into the cyclic groups, the dihedral groups, the tetrahedral group, the octahedral group, and the icosahedral group. The cyclic groups and the dihedral groups are said to be *two-dimensional* (2D), in the sense that the plane formation problem is obviously solvable, since there is a single rotation axis or a single principal rotation axis, and all robots can agree on a plane perpendicular to the single (or principal) axis and containing the center of the smallest enclosing ball of themselves. Then FSYNC robots can easily solve the plane formation problem by moving onto the agreed plane.

The other three rotation groups are defined by the rotations of corresponding regular polyhedra, and these rotation groups are called polyhedral groups. A regular polyhedron consists of regular polygon faces and has *vertex-transitivity*, that is, there are rotations that replace any two vertices with keeping the polyhedron unchanged as a whole. For example, we can rotate a cube around any axis containing two opposite vertices, any axis containing the centers of opposite faces, and any axis containing the midpoints of opposite edges. For each regular polyhedron, rotations applicable to the polyhedron form a group, and, in this way, the three rotation groups, i.e., the tetrahedral group, the octahedral group and the icosahedral group, are defined. We call them *three-dimensional* (3D) rotation groups.

When a configuration has a 3D rotation group, the robots are not on any plane. In addition, the vertex-transitivity among the robots may allow corresponding robots to have an identical local observation, and the robots may result in an infinite execution, where they keep symmetric movements and never agree on a plane. A vertex-transitive set of points is in general obtained by specifying a seed point and a set of symmetry operations, which consists of rotations around an axis, reflections for a mirror plane (*bilateral symmetry*), reflections for a point (*central inversion*), and *rotation-reflections* [2]. However, it is sufficient to consider vertex-transitive set of points constructed from transformations that preserve the center of the smallest enclosing ball of robots, and keep Euclidean distance and handedness, in other words, direct congruent transformations, since otherwise, the robots have chirality and can break the symmetry. Such symmetry operations consist of rotations around some axes. (See e.g., [1,2] for more detail.)

Let $P$ and $\gamma(P)$ be a set of points in 3D-space and its rotation group, respectively. Then the points (i.e., the robots) are partitioned into vertex-transitive subsets by the group action of $\gamma(P)$. Hence, for each subset, the robots in it may have the same local observation. We call this decomposition $\gamma(P)$-*decomposition* of $P$. The goal of this paper is to show the following theorem:

**Theorem 1.** *Let $P$ and $\{P_1, P_2, \ldots, P_m\}$ be an initial configuration and the $\gamma(P)$-decomposition of $P$, respectively. Then oblivious FSYNC robots can form a plane from $P$ if and only if (i) $\gamma(P)$ is a 2D rotation group, or (ii) $\gamma(P)$ is a 3D rotation group and there exists a subset $P_i$ such that $|P_i| \notin \{12, 24, 60\}$.*

Theorem 1 implies the following, which is somewhat counter-intuitive: The plane formation problem is *solvable*, even if $P$ is a regular polyhedron (except a regular icosahedron), i.e., even if the robots initially occupy the vertices of such regular polyhedron, while it is *unsolvable* for most of the semi-regular polyhedra.

We can rephrase this theorem as follows: Oblivious FSYNC robots cannot form a plane from $P$ if and only if $\gamma(P)$ is a 3D rotation group and $|P_i| \in \{12, 24, 60\}$ for each $P_i$. The impossibility proof is by a construction based on the decomposition of the robots. Obviously $12, 24$, and $60$ are the orders of 3D rotation groups, and when the cardinality of a vertex-transitive set of points is in $\{12, 24, 60\}$, the corresponding rotation group enables "symmetric" local coordinate systems that imposes an infinite execution, where the robots' positions keep the axes of the rotation group. We will show this fact by constructing the worst-case local coordinate systems.

For the possibility proof, we present a plane formation algorithm that breaks regular polyhedra for solvable cases. In the 2D-space, the symmetricity of a configuration is defined to be 1 when a robot is on the rotation axis of the cyclic group, because the robot on the center can break the symmetry by leaving the center. In the same way, a rotation axis of a 3D rotation group disappears when a robot on it leaves the axis. Fortunately, there is always a robot on a rotation axis, if the cardinality of a vertex-transitive robots is not in $\{12, 24, 60\}$ and we can use it to reduce the number of rotation axes. Although there are multiple rotation axes in a 3D rotation group, the proposed algorithm transforms a configuration whose rotation group is a 3D rotation group into another configuration whose rotation group is a 2D rotation group, by reducing the number of rotation axes.

**Related Works.** We roughly review some of works on robots in 2D-space, since there is few research on robots in 3D-space, although an autonomous mobile robot system in 2D-space has been extensively investigated (see e.g., [3–7,9,11]). Besides fully synchronous (FSYNC) robots, there are two other types of robots, semi-synchronous (SSYNC) and asynchronous (ASYNC) robots. The robots are SSYNC if some robots do not start the $i$-th Look-Compute-Move cycle for some $i$, but all of those who have started the cycle synchronously execute their Look, Compute and Move phases [9], and they are ASYNC if no assumptions are made on the execution of Look-Compute-Move cycles [5]. The book by Flocchini et al. [4] contains almost all results on ASYNC robots up to year 2012.

As for the pattern formation problem in 2D-space, which includes the line formation problem as a subproblem, the solvable cases are determined for each of the FSYNC, SSYNC and ASYNC models [7,9,11], which are summarized as follows: (1) For non-oblivious FSYNC robots, a pattern $F$ is formable from an initial configuration $P$ if and only if $\rho(P)$ divides $\rho(F)$. (2) Pattern $F$ is formable from $P$ by oblivious ASYNC robots if $F$ is formable from $P$ by non-oblivious FSYNC robots, except for $F$ being a point of multiplicity 2.

This exceptional case is called the rendezvous problem. Indeed, it is trivial for two FSYNC robots, but is unsolvable for two SSYNC (and hence ASYNC) robots [9]. Therefore it is a bit surprising to observe that the point formation problem for more than two robots is solvable even for ASYNC robots. The result first appeared in [9] for SSYNC robots and then is extended for ASYNC robots in [3]. As a matter of fact, except the existence of the rendezvous problem, the point formation problem (for more than two robots) is the easiest problem in that it is solvable from any initial configuration $P$, since $\rho(F) = n$ when $F$ is a point of multiplicity $n$, and $\rho(P)$ is always a divisor of $n$ by the definition of the symmetricity, where $n$ is the number of robots.

The other easiest case is a regular $n$-gon (frequently called the circle formation problem), since $\rho(F) = n$. A circle is formable from any initial configuration, like the point formation problem for more than two robots. Recently the circle formation problem for $n$ robots ($n \neq 4$) is solved without chirality [6].

**Organization.** After explaining the model in Section 2, we introduce the rotation group of points in 3D-space and show some properties of vertex-transitive set of points in Section 3. In Section 4, we then prove Theorem 1. Finally, Section 5 concludes this paper by giving some concluding remarks. Because of the page limitation, we omit detailed proofs. Please see the full version [12].

## 2    Robot Model

Let $R = \{r_1, r_2, \ldots, r_n\}$ be a set of $n$ anonymous robots represented by points in 3D-space. We use the index just for description. Without loss of generality, we can assume $n \geq 4$, since all robots are already on a plane when $n \leq 3$. By $Z_0$ we denote the global $x$-$y$-$z$ coordinate system. Let $p_i(t) \in \mathbb{R}^3$ be the position of $r_i$ at time $t$ in $Z_0$, where $\mathbb{R}$ is the set of real numbers. A *configuration* of $R$ at time $t$ is denoted by $P(t) = \{p_1(t), p_2(t), \ldots, p_n(t)\}$. We assume that the robots initially occupy distinct positions, i.e., $p_i(0) \neq p_j(0)$ for all $1 \leq i < j \leq n$. In general, $P(t)$ can be a multiset, but it is always a set throughout this paper since the proposed algorithm avoids any multiplicity.[2] The robots have no access to $Z_0$. Instead, each robot $r_i$ has a local $x$-$y$-$z$ coordinate system $Z_i$, where the origin

---

[2] It is impossible to break up multiple oblivious FSYNC robots (with the same local coordinate system) on a single position as long as they execute the same algorithm, and thus our algorithm avoids any multiplicity. However, we need to take into account any algorithm that may lead $R$ to a configuration with multiplicities, when proving the impossibility result by reduction to the absurd.

is always its current location and the direction of $x$-$y$-$z$ axes and unit distance are arbitrary. However, we assume that $Z_0$ and all $Z_i$ are right-handed. By $Z_i(p)$ we denote the coordinate of a point $p$ in $Z_i$.

We investigate fully synchronous (FSYNC) robots in this paper. They all start the $t$-th Look-Compute-Move cycle simultaneously, and synchronously execute each of its Look, Compute and Move phases. We specifically assume without loss of generality that the $(t + 1)$-th Look-Compute-Move cycle starts at time $t$ and finishes before time $t + 1$. At time $t$, $r_i$ (and all other robots simultaneously) looks and obtains a set $Z_i(P(t)) = \{Z_i(p_1(t)), Z_i(p_2(t)), \ldots, Z_i(p_n(t))\}$.[3] We call $Z_i(P(t))$ the *local observation* of $r_i$ at $t$. Next, $r_i$ computes its next position using an algorithm $\psi$, which is common to all robots. Formally, $\psi$ is a total function from $\mathcal{P}_n^3$ to $\mathbb{R}^3$, where $\mathcal{P}_n^3 = (\mathbb{R}^3)^n$ is the set of all configurations (which may contain multiplicities). Finally, $r_i$ moves to $\psi(Z_i(P(t)))$ in $Z_i$ before time $t + 1$. An infinite sequence of configurations $\mathcal{E} : P(0), P(1), \ldots$ is called an *execution* from an *initial configuration* $P(0)$. Observe that the execution $\mathcal{E}$ is uniquely determined, once initial configuration $P(0)$, local coordinate systems $Z_i$ at time 0, and algorithm $\psi$ are fixed.

We say that an algorithm $\psi$ *forms a plane* from an initial configuration $P(0)$, if, regardless of the choice of initial local coordinate systems $Z_i$ of $r_i \in R$, the execution $P(0), P(1), \ldots$ eventually reaches a configuration $P_f$ that satisfies the following three conditions:

(a) $P_f$ is contained in a plane,
(b) $|P_f| = n$, i.e., all robots occupy distinct positions, and
(c) Once the system reaches $P_f$, the robots do not move anymore.

## 3 Symmetry in 3D-Space

In 3D-space, we consider the smallest enclosing ball and the convex hull of the positions of robots, i.e., robots are vertices of a convex polyhedron. We do not care for non-convex polyhedra. A *uniform polyhedron* is a polyhedron consisting of regular polygons and all its vertices are congruent. The family of uniform polyhedra contains the regular polyhedra (Platonic solids) and the semi-regular polyhedra (Archimedean solids). Any uniform polyhedron is *vertex-transitive*, i.e., for any pair of vertices of the polyhedron, there exists a symmetry operation that moves one vertex to the other with keeping the the polyhedron as a whole.

In general, symmetry operations on a polyhedron consists of rotations around an axis, reflections for a mirror plane (*bilateral symmetry*), reflections for a point (*central inversion*), and *rotation-reflections* [2]. But as briefly argued in Section 1, since all local coordinate systems are right-handed, it is sufficient to consider only direct congruent transformations, and those keeping the center are rotations around some axes that contains the center. We thus concentrate on rotation groups with finite order.

---

[3] Since $Z_i$ changes whenever $r_i$ moves, notation $Z_i(t)$ is more rigid, but we omit parameter $t$ to simplify its notation.

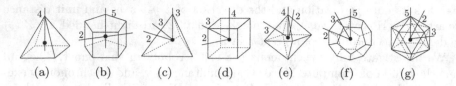

**Fig. 1.** Rotation groups: (a) the cyclic group $C_4$, (b) the dihedral group $D_5$, (c) the tetrahedral group $T$, (d)(e) the octahedral group $O$, and (f)(g) the icosahedral group $I$. Figures show only one axis for each fold of axes.

**Table 1.** Rotation groups $T, O$ and $I$, and their elements.

| Rotation group | 2-fold axes | 3-fold axes | 4-fold axes | 5-fold axes | Order |
|---|---|---|---|---|---|
| $T$ | 3 | 8 | - | - | 12 |
| $O$ | 6 | 8 | 9 | - | 24 |
| $I$ | 15 | 20 | - | 24 | 60 |

A rotation axis is a $k$-*fold axis* if the rotation around it is $2\pi/k, 4\pi/k, \ldots, 2\pi$. There are five kinds of rotation groups of finite order [1,2]: The cyclic group $C_k$ consists of the single $k$-fold rotation axis ($k \geq 1$), the dihedral group $D_\ell$ consists of the single $\ell$-fold principal axis and $\ell$ 2-fold axes ($\ell \geq 2$) perpendicular to the principal axis. The remaining three groups, the tetrahedral group $T$, the octahedral group $O$, and the icosahedral group $I$ are called *polyhedral groups*, because they are defined by the rotations of corresponding polyhedra (Figure 1). Table 1 shows for each of the rotation groups $T$, $O$, and $I$, the number of elements around its $k$-fold rotation axes ($k \in \{2,3,4,5\}$).

In the group theory, we do not distinguish the principal axes of $D_2$ from the other two 2-fold axes. Consider a sphenoid consisting of 4 congruent isosceles triangles (Figure 2). Rotation operations on such a sphenoid are those of $D_2$, however we can recognize, for example, the vertical 2-fold axis from the others by their lengths (between the midpoints connecting). The family of sets of points on which only $D_2$ can act are lines, rectangles, such sphenoids, and their compositions. Actually, we can easily show that a set of points to which $D_2$ can act but we cannot distinguish the principal axis have four 3-fold rotation axes, thus $T$ can also act on the set. Hence, the sets of points to which only $D_2$ can act have the principal axis. Later we will show that the robots can form a plane if they can recognize a single rotation axis or a principal axis. Based on this, we say that the cyclic groups and the dihedral groups are *two-dimensional* (2D), while the polyhedral groups are *three-dimensional* (3D) since polyhedral groups cannot act on a set of points on a plane.

Let $\mathbb{S} = \{C_k, D_\ell, T, O, I \mid k = 1, 2, \ldots, and \ \ell = 2, 3, \ldots\}$ be the set of rotation groups, where $C_1$ is the rotation group with order 1; its unique element is the identity element (i.e., 1-fold rotation). When $G'$ is a subgroup of $G$ ($G, G' \in \mathbb{S}$), we denote it by $G' \preceq G$. If $G'$ is a proper subgroup of $G$ (i.e., $G \neq G'$), we denote

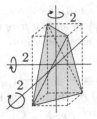

**Fig. 2.** A sphenoid consisting of 4 congruent isosceles triangles. Its rotation group is $D_2$. Since the vertices are not placed equidistant positions from the three axes, we can distinguish an axis as the principal axis from the others.

it by $G' \prec G$. For example, we have $D_2 \prec T, T \prec O, I$, and if $G \in \mathbb{S}$ has a $k$-fold rotation axis, $C_{k'} \preceq G$ if $k'$ divides $k$.

For any $P \in \mathcal{P}_n^3$, by $B(P)$ and $b(P)$, we denote the smallest enclosing ball of $P$ and its center, respectively. We now define the rotation group of a set of points in 3D-space. For a set of points $P \in \mathcal{P}_n^3$, the rotation group that acts on $P$ and no proper supergroup of it acts on $P$ is uniquely determined. We call such group the *rotation group* of $P$ and denote it by $\gamma(P)$. Hence, even when the points of $P$ are on one plane, its rotation group is chosen from cyclic groups and dihedral groups. For example, the rotation group of four points forming a square is $D_4$.[4] It is worth noting that each robot $r_i$ can obviously calculate $\gamma(P)$ from $P$ (more specifically, from its local observation $Z_i(P)$), by checking all rotation axes that keep $P$ unchanged.

A point on the sphere of a ball is said to be *on* the ball, and we assume that the *interior* or the *exterior* of a ball does not include its sphere. For a set of points $P$, when all points of $P$ are on $B(P)$, we say $P$ is *spherical*. We say that a set of points $P$ is *vertex-transitive* regarding a rotation group $G$, if (i) for any two points $p, q \in P$, $g * p = q$ for some $g \in G$, and (ii) $g * p \in P$ for all $g \in G$ and $p \in P$, where $*$ denotes the group action. Note that a vertex-transitive set of points is always spherical.

Given a set of points $P$, $\gamma(P)$ determines the arrangement of its rotation axes. We thus use the name of a rotation group and the arrangement of rotation axes interchangeably. We define an embedding of a rotation group to another rotation group. For two groups $G, G' \in \mathbb{S}$, an *embedding* of $G$ to $G'$ is an embedding of each rotation axis of $G$ to one of the rotation axes of $G'$ so that any $k$-fold axis of $G$ overlaps a $k'$-fold axis of $G'$ satisfying $k|k'$ with keeping the arrangement of the axes of $G$, where $a|b$ denotes that $a$ divides $b$. For example, we can embed $T$ to $O$, and $T$ to $I$, but cannot embed $O$ to $I$. In fact, group $G$ can be embedded to an arrangement of group $G'$ if $G \preceq G'$.

---

[4] This is the major difference between the rotation group of robots in 3D-space and the symmetricity of robots on 2D-plane. In our context, existing works assume that robots agree on the "top" direction against the plane where robots resides and their symmetricity is chosen from cyclic groups [7,9,11].

**Theorem 2.** *Let $P \in \mathcal{P}_n^3$ be any initial configuration. Then $P$ can be decomposed into subsets $\{P_1, P_2, \ldots, P_m\}$ in such a way that each $P_i$ is vertex-transitive regarding $\gamma(P)$. Furthermore, the robots can agree on a total ordering among the subsets.*

*Proof.* (Sketch.) For any point $p \in P$, let $Orb(p) = \{g * p \in P : g \in \gamma(P)\}$ be the orbit of the group action of $\gamma(P)$ through $p$. By definition $Orb(p)$ is vertex-transitive regarding $\gamma(P)$. Let $\{Orb(p) : p \in P\} = \{P_1, P_2, \ldots, P_m\}$ be its orbit space. Then $\{P_1, P_2, \ldots, P_m\}$ is obviously a partition which satisfies the first part of the statement. Such a decomposition is unique as a matter of fact.

Then, we can show that there exists a translation of a local observation of a robot to a "local view" that satisfies the following two properties:

1. All robots in $P_i$ have the same local view for $i = 1, 2, \ldots, m$.
2. Any two robots, one in $P_i$ and the other in $P_j$, have different local views, for all $i \neq j$.

We will show the idea of the translation. Let $L(P)$ be the *largest empty ball* that is centered at $b(P)$, contains no point of $P$ in its interior, and contains at least one point of $P$ on its sphere. Intuitively, the local view of $r_i \in R$ is constructed by considering $L(P)$ as the earth and line $\overline{p_i b(P)}$ as the earth's axis, where $p_i$ is the position of $r_i$. Then, the positions of each robot is represented by its amplitude, longitude, and latitude. This local view does not depend on any local coordinate systems, and each robot can compute the local view of other robots. Then, the robots can agree on the total ordering of the subsets. □

We call $\{P_1, P_2, \ldots, P_m\}$ the $\gamma(P)$-*decomposition* of $P$. The robots can agree on the decomposition and the ordering of the subsets, and each robot can recognize which subset it resides. In the following, we assume that $\{P_1, P_2, \ldots, P_m\}$ is ordered in this ordering, thus $P_1$ is on $L(P)$ and $P_m$ is on $B(P)$.

We go on to the analysis of the structure of a set of points that is vertex-transitive regarding a 3D rotation group. Any vertex-transitive (spherical) set of points $P$ is specified by a rotation group $G$ and a seed point $s$ as the orbit $Orb(s)$ of the group action of $G$ through $s$. Not necessarily $|G| = |Orb(s)|$ holds. For any $p \in P$, we call $\mu(p) = |\{g \in G : g * p = p\}|$ the *multiplicity* of $p$.[5] We of course count the identity element of $G$ for $\mu(p)$, and $\mu(p) \geq 1$ holds for all $p \in P$. We can show that the multiplicity of $p \in P$ is identical, and $\mu(p) > 1$ when it is on the $\mu(p)$-fold rotation axis of $G$.

For a set of points $P \in \mathcal{P}_n^3$ and its $\gamma(P)$-decomposition $\{P_1, P_2, \ldots, P_m\}$, if $\gamma(P)$ is a 3D rotation group, each $P_i$ is one of the polyhedra shown in Table 2.

## 4    Proof of Theorem 1

This section proves Theorem 1. In Subsection 4.1, we show the necessity of Theorem 1 by showing that any algorithm for oblivious FSYNC robots cannot form

---

[5] The word "multiplicity" is also used for a multiset. Here, the multiplicity of a point $p$ is the size of the stabilizer of $G$ respect to $p$ [8]. Readers can identify the meaning clearly from the context.

**Table 2.** Vertex-transitive sets of points generated by 3D rotation groups: rotation group, order, multiplicity, and cardinality.

| Rotation group | Order | Multiplicity | Cardinality | Polyhedron |
|:---:|:---:|:---:|:---:|:---|
| $T$ | 12 | 3 | 4 | Regular tetrahedron |
| | | 2 | 6 | Regular octahedron |
| | | 1 | 12 | Infinitely many polyhedra |
| $O$ | 24 | 4 | 6 | Regular octahedron |
| | | 3 | 8 | Cube |
| | | 2 | 12 | Cuboctahedron |
| | | 1 | 24 | Infinitely many polyhedra |
| $I$ | 60 | 5 | 12 | Regular icosahedron |
| | | 3 | 20 | Regular dodecahedron |
| | | 2 | 30 | Icosidodecahedron |
| | | 1 | 60 | Infinitely many polyhedra |

a plane if an initial configuration does not satisfy the condition in Theorem 1. In Subsection 4.2, we show the sufficiency by presenting a plane formation algorithm for oblivious FSYNC robots.

### 4.1   Necessity

Provided $|P| \in \{12, 24, 60\}$, we first show that when a set of points $P$ is a vertex-transitive set of points regarding a 3D rotation group, there is an arrangement of local coordinate systems of robots forming $P$ such that the execution from $P$ keeps a 3D rotation group forever, no matter which algorithm they obey.

**Lemma 1.** *Assume $n = |R| \in \{12, 24, 60\}$. Then the plane formation problem is unsolvable from an initial configuration $P(0)$ for oblivious FSYNC robots, if $P(0)$ is a vertex-transitive set of points regarding a 3D rotation group.*

*Proof.* (Sketch.) The idea of the proof is to show that we can construct local coordinate systems in $P(0)$ that keep the rotation axes of group $G$ forever in the execution of any algorithm, where $G$ is given as follows:

$$G = \begin{cases} T & \text{if } n = 12, \\ O & \text{if } n = 24, \\ I & \text{if } n = 60. \end{cases}$$

We construct a set of symmetric local coordinate systems based on the fact that $P(0)$ is vertex-transitive regarding $G$. If $G = \gamma(P(0))$, this property clearly holds. The only case where $G \neq \gamma(P(0))$ is when $G = T$ and $\gamma(P(0)) \in \{O, I\}$, but we can show that there exists an embedding of $T$ to $\gamma(P(0))$ such that no robot is on the rotation axes of $T$. With the fact that $|P(0)| = |T|$, $P(0)$ is vertex-transitive regarding $T$.

Let $P(0) = \{p_1, p_2, \ldots, p_n\}$ where $p_i$ is the position of $r_i \in R$. We fix a local coordinate system $Z_1$ arbitrarily for $r_1 \in R$, that is fixed by the origin, the positions of $(1,0,0)$, $(0,1,0)$, and $(0,0,1)$ of $Z_1$ in $Z_0$. Then, because for each $r_i \in R$ there exists a distinct element $g_i \in G$ such that $p_i = g_i * p_1$, we obtain the local coordinate system of $r_i$ by applying $g_i$ to $Z_1$. The local coordinate systems of the robots are symmetric regarding $G$, local observations of the robots are identical, and the output of the algorithm that the robots execute are identical at the robots, i.e., the destination of robots are symmetric regarding $G$. After the movement, the positions and local coordinate systems of the robots are still symmetric regarding $G$. Let $P(1)$ be this new configuration. In the same way, in $P(1)$, the next destinations are symmetric regarding $G$. In this way, robots repeat symmetric movement regarding $G$ forever and any configuration that appears in the execution keeps $G$. □

From Lemma 1, the plane formation problem is unsolvable from each of the semi-regular polyhedra except an icosidodecahedron consisting of 30 robots. Some of the minimum unsolvable instances are a regular icosahedron, a truncated tetrahedron, and a cuboctahedron, each of which consists of 12 robots.

When an initial configuration $P$ is not vertex-transitive, we obtain the following theorem by applying Lemma 1 to each of the subsets of the $\gamma(P)$-decomposition of $P$.

**Theorem 3.** *Let $P$ and $\{P_1, P_2, \ldots, P_m\}$ be an initial configuration and the $\gamma(P)$-decomposition of $P$, respectively. Then the plane formation problem is unsolvable from $P$ for oblivious FSYNC robots, if $\gamma(P)$ is a 3D rotation group, and $|P_i| \in \{12, 24, 60\}$ for $i = 1, 2, \ldots, m$.*

## 4.2   Sufficiency

This subsection proves the following theorem by showing a plane formation algorithm for oblivious FSYNC robots.

**Theorem 4.** *Let $P$ and $\{P_1, P_2, \ldots, P_m\}$ be an initial configuration and the $\gamma(P)$-decomposition of $P$, respectively. Then oblivious FSYNC robots can form a plane from $P$ if either (i) $\gamma(P)$ is a 2D rotation group, or (ii) $\gamma(P)$ is a 3D rotation group and there exists a subset $P_i$ such that $|P_i| \notin \{12, 24, 60\}$.*

A very rough idea behind the plane formation algorithm is the following: Let $P(0)$ and $\{P_1, P_2, \ldots, P_m\}$ be an initial configuration and the $\gamma(P(0))$-decomposition of $P(0)$.

If $\gamma(P(0))$ is a 2D rotation group, since there is a single rotation axis or a principal axis, which is obviously recognizable by the robots, they can agree on the plane perpendicular to this axis and containing $b(P(0))$, and indeed the robots can select distinct landing points on the plane.

Suppose otherwise that $\gamma(P(0))$ is a 3D rotation group. Then there is a subset $P_i$ such that $|P_i| \notin \{12, 24, 60\}$. That is, $|P_i| < |\gamma(P(0))|$ $(\gamma(P(0)) = \gamma(P_i))$, and all robots in $P_i$ are on some rotation axes of $\gamma(P(0))$. The proposed symmetry breaking algorithm moves the robots of $P_i$ so that none of them will be on any rotation axes of $\gamma(P(0))$. This move cannot maintain $\gamma(P(0))$, otherwise

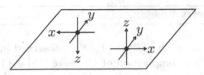

**Fig. 3.** Two robots on a plane do not agree on the clockwise direction even when they have chirality.

these robots form a vertex-transitive set of points with multiplicity one regarding $\gamma(P(0))$, thus $|P_i| = |\gamma(P(0))|$ which is a contradiction. Specifically, such $P_i$ forms a regular tetrahedron, a cube, a regular octahedron, a regular dodecahedron, or an icosidodecahedron from Table 2. Our symmetry breaking algorithm breaks the symmetry of these (semi-)regular polyhedral configurations, and as a result configuration $P(1)$ yields such that $\gamma(P(1))$ is a 2D rotation group.

In the following, we assume that $b(P(0)) \notin P(0)$ because the robots trivially can translate a configuration $P(0)$ with $b(P(0)) \in P(0)$ to another configuration $P(1)$ with $\gamma(P(1)) = C_1$ by the robot on $b(P(0))$ leaving the center.

The proposed plane formation algorithm consists of three phases. The first phase selects $P_s$ with the smallest index among the subsets whose size is not in $\{12, 24, 60\}$, and shrinks $P_s$ so that it becomes the innermost subset in the next configuration $P(1)$, i.e., only the robots that formed $P_s$ is on $L(P(1))$ and these robots form the same (semi-)regular polyhedron as $P_s$. This phase is necessary to keep the center of the smallest enclosing circle of robots.

The second phase breaks the (semi-)regular polyhedron formed by the robots on $L(P(1))$ and configuration $P(2)$ yields whose rotation group $\gamma(P(2))$ is a 2D rotation group. We call this phase "go-to-center" phase. Intuitively, this phase makes the robots on $L(P(1))$ select an adjacent face of polyhedron that they form and approach the center, but stop $\epsilon$ before the center. We will show that the destinations of robots do not have any 3D rotation group, and the robots succeeds in breaking their symmetry.

Finally, in the third phase, the robots agree on the plane $F$ perpendicular to the single rotation axis (or the principal axis) and containing $b(P(2))$. Then, they land distinct positions of $F$. Each robot selects the foot of the perpendicular line from its current position to $F$ as its destination. Let $P_1'', P_2'', \ldots, P_\ell''$ be the $\gamma(P(2))$-decomposition of $P(2)$. For each $P_i''$, at most two robots select the same destination, however, these robots can easily select new different destinations. Because all local coordinate systems are right-handed, if the negative $z$-axis of the two robots points to $F$, the clockwise directions (e.g., rotation from the positive $y$-axis to positive $x$-axis) of the two robots are different (Figure 3). By using this property and $b(P(2))$ as a reference point, the two robots select different points on a small circle centered at their common foot as their destinations.

Because of the page restriction, we focus on the second phase. The proposed symmetry breaking algorithm is shown in Algorithm 4.1.

---

**Algorithm   4.1** Symmetry breaking algorithm for robot $r_i \in R$

**Notation**

  $P$: Current configuration with $\gamma(P) \in \{T, O, I\}$ observed in $Z_i$.

  $\{P_1, P_2, \ldots, P_m\}$: $\gamma(P)$-decomposition of $P$ where $|P_1| \notin \{12, 24, 60\}$.

  $\epsilon$: An arbitrarily small distance compared to the distance between any two
  centers of the faces of $P_1$ and determined by using the radius of $B(P)$.

  $p_i$: Current position of $r_i$ (i.e., the origin).

**Algorithm**

  **If** $p_i \in P_1$ **then**

      **If** $P_1$ forms an icosidodecahedron **then**

          Select an adjacent regular pentagon face.

          Destination $d$ is the point $\epsilon$ before the center of the face
          on the line from $p_i$ to the center.

      **Else**

          // $P_1$ forms a regular tetrahedron, a regular octahedron,
          // a cube or a regular dodecahedron.

          Select an adjacent face of the regular polyhedron.

          Destination $d$ is the point $\epsilon$ before the center of the face
          on the line from $p_i$ to the center.

      **Endif**

      Move to $d$.

  **Endif**

---

**Lemma 2.** *Let $P$ be a configuration such that $\gamma(P)$ is 3D rotation group and $|P_1| \notin \{12, 24, 60\}$ where $\{P_1, P_2, \ldots, P_m\}$ is the $\gamma(P)$-decomposition of $P$. Then the robots execute Algorithm 4.1 at $P$ and suppose that a configuration $P'$ yields as the result. Then $\gamma(P')$ is a 2D rotation group.*

*Proof.* (Sketch.) Let $\{P_1, P_2, \ldots, P_m\}$ be the $\gamma(P)$-decomposition of $P$. Because of the assumption, we have $|P_1| \notin \{12, 24, 60\}$. Thus, $P_1$ is either a regular tetrahedron, a regular octahedron, a cube, a regular dodecahedron or an icosi-dodecahedron by Table 2.

In Algorithm 4.1, only the robots in $P_1$ move. Each robot $p \in P_1$ selects a face $F$ of $P_1$ incident on $p$, and moves to $d$ which is at distance $\epsilon$ from the center $c(F)$ of $F$ on line segment $\overline{pc(F)}$, with a restriction that $p$ needs to select a regular pentagon if $P_1$ is an icosidodecahedron. Note that $\epsilon$ is common to all robots in $P_1$. Then, letting $D$ be the set of points consisting of the candidates for $d$ (for $p \in P_1$), $D$ forms one of the polyhedra shown in Figure 4. Specifically, Figure 4(a) illustrates an $\epsilon$-cantellated tetrahedron, which corresponds to the candidate set $D$ when $P_1$ is a regular tetrahedron. Figure 4(b) illustrates an $\epsilon$-cantellated cube, which corresponds to the candidate set $D$ when $P_1$ is a regular octahedron. Figure 4(c) illustrates an $\epsilon$-cantellated octahedron, which corresponds to the candidate set $D$ when $P_1$ is a cube. Figure 4(d) illustrates an $\epsilon$-cantellated icosahedron, which corresponds to the candidate set $D$ when $P_1$ is a regular dodecahedron. Finally, Figure 4(e) illustrates an $\epsilon$-truncated

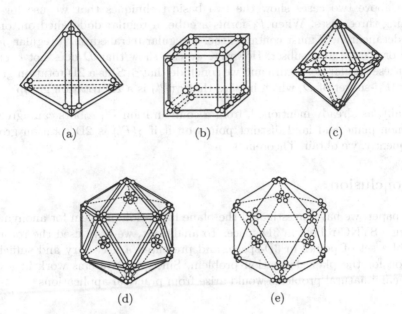

(a)            (b)            (c)

(d)                 (e)

**Fig. 4.** Candidate set $D$. White circles are the points of $D$. (a) $\epsilon$-cantellated tetrahedron, (b) $\epsilon$-cantellated cube, (c) $\epsilon$-cantellated octahedron, (d) $\epsilon$-cantellated icosahedron, and (e) $\epsilon$-truncated icosahedron.

icosahedron, which corresponds to the candidate set $D$ when $P_1$ is an icosidodecahedron. We would like to emphasize the difference between $\epsilon$-cantellated icosahedron and an $\epsilon$-truncated icosahedron.

Let $S \subset D$ be any set such that $|S| = |P_1|$. Then it is sufficient to show that $\gamma(S)$ is a 2D rotation group. To derive a contradiction, suppose that there is an $S$ such that $\gamma(S)$ is a 3D rotation group. We first claim $b(S) = b(D)$, otherwise $\gamma(S)$ is a 2D rotation group because the intersection of two balls is either a point, a circle, or a ball. For each of the polyhedra that $P_1$ can be, we can show that $\gamma(S)$ is a 2D rotation group for each of the five cases by contradiction.

First, when $P_1$ forms a regular tetrahedron, $D$ is an $\epsilon$-cantellated tetrahedron (Figure 4(a)). If $\gamma(S)$ is a 3D rotation group, $S$ must be a regular tetrahedron, since $|S| = |P_1| = 4$. Since $S$ is a regular tetrahedron, one point should be selected from the four faces of $P_1$. Then we can show the non-existence of a desirable $S$ by checking, for each candidates for $S$ in an exhaustive way, its inconsistency.

Second, when $P_1$ forms a regular octahedron, $D$ is an $\epsilon$-cantellated cube (Figure 4(b)). If $\gamma(S)$ is a 3D rotation group, because $|S| = 6$, $S$ must be a regular octahedron, since otherwise $S$ was the union of a regular tetrahedron and a 2-set, and $\gamma(S)$ would be a 2D rotation group. Obviously $S$ cannot be a regular octahedron, since $D$ is an $\epsilon$-cantellated cube and all vertices are around vertices of a cube.

The above two cases show the two basic techniques that we use for the remaining three cases. When $P_1$ forms a cube, a regular dodecahedron, or an icosidodecahedron, $S$ must contain either a regular tetrahedron, a regular octahedron or a cube as a subset. However, we can show that $D$ does not contain any of these regular polyhedra and we conclude that $\gamma(S)$ is a 2D rotation group for any $|P_1|$-subset of $D$, which implies that $\gamma(P')$ is a 2D rotation group. $\quad\square$

Finally, as already mentioned, from a configuration $P'$, robots can agree on a common plane and land distinct points on it if $\gamma(P')$ is 2D rotation group. Consequently, we obtain Theorem 4.

## 5    Conclusion

In this paper, we have investigated the plane formation problem for anonymous oblivious FSYNC robots in 3D-space. To analyze it, we have used the rotation group of a set of points in 3D-space, and presented a necessary and sufficient condition for the plane formation problem. Since real systems work in a 3D-space, many natural problems would arise from practical applications.

## References

1. Coxeter, H.S.M.: Regular polytopes. Dover Publications (1973)
2. Cromwell, P.: Polyhedra. University Press (1997)
3. Cieliebak, M., Flocchini, P., Prencipe, G., Santoro, N.: Distributed computing by mobile robots: gathering. SIAM J. Comput. **41**(4), 829–879 (2012)
4. Flocchini, P., Prencipe, G., Santoro, N.: Distributed computing by oblivious mobile robots. Morgan & Claypool (2012)
5. Flocchini, P., Prencipe, G., Santoro, N., Widmayer, P.: Arbitrary pattern formation by asynchronous, anonymous, oblivious robots. Theor. Comput. Sci. **407**, 412–447 (2008)
6. Flocchini, P., Prencipe, G., Santoro, N., Viglietta, G.: Distributed computing by mobile robots: solving the uniform circle formation problem. In: Aguilera, M.K., Querzoni, L., Shapiro, M. (eds.) OPODIS 2014. LNCS, vol. 8878, pp. 217–232. Springer, Heidelberg (2014)
7. Fujinaga, N., Yamauchi, Y., Ono, H., Kijima, S., Yamashita, M.: Pattern formation by oblivious asynchronous mobile robots. SIAM J. Comput. **44**(3), 740–785 (2015)
8. Rotman, J.J.: An introduction to the theory of groups, 4th edn. Springer-Verlag New York, Inc. (1994)
9. Suzuki, I., Yamashita, M.: Distributed anonymous mobile robots: Formation of geometric patterns. SIAM J. Comput. **28**(4), 1347–1363 (1999)
10. Yamashita, M., Kameda, T.: Computing on anonymous networks: Part I-Characterizing the solvable cases. IEEE Trans. Parallel Distrib. Syst. **7**(1), 69–89 (1996)
11. Yamashita, M., Suzuki, I.: Characterizing geometric patterns formable by oblivious anonymous mobile robots. Theor. Comput. Sci. **411**, 2433–2453 (2010)
12. Yamauchi, Y., Uehara, T., Kijima, S., Yamashita, M.: Plane formation by synchronous mobile robots in the three dimensional Euclidean space (2015). arXiv:1505.04546

# Anonymous Graph Exploration with Binoculars

Jérémie Chalopin, Emmanuel Godard[✉], and Antoine Naudin

LIF, Université Aix-Marseille and CNRS, Marseille, France
emmanuel.godard@lif.univ-mrs.fr

**Abstract.** We investigate the exploration of networks by a mobile agent. It is long known that, without global information about the graph, it is not possible to make the agent halts after the exploration except if the graph is a tree. We therefore endow the agent with *binoculars*, a sensing device that can show the local structure of the environment at a constant distance of the agent current location.

We show that, with binoculars, it is possible to explore and halt in a large class of non-tree networks. We give a complete characterization of the class of networks that can be explored using binoculars using standard notions of discrete topology. This class is much larger than the class of trees: it contains in particular chordal graphs, plane triangulations and triangulations of the projective plane. Our characterization is constructive, we present an Exploration algorithm that is universal; this algorithm explores any network explorable with binoculars, and never halts in non-explorable networks.

## 1 Introduction

Mobile agents are computational units that can progress autonomously from place to place within an environment, interacting with the environment at each node that it is located on. Such software robots (sometimes called bots, or agents) are already prevalent in the Internet, and are used for performing a variety of tasks such as collecting information or negotiating a business deal. More generally, when the data is physically dispersed, it can be sometimes beneficial to move the computation to the data, instead of moving all the data to the entity performing the computation. The paradigm of mobile agent computing / distributed robotics is based on this idea. As underlined in [8], the use of mobile agents has been advocated for numerous reasons such as robustness against network disruptions, improving the latency and reducing network load, providing more autonomy and reducing the design complexity, and so on (see e.g. [17]).

For many distributed problems with mobile agents, exploring, that is visiting every location of the whole environment, is an important prerequisite. In its thorough exposition about Exploration by mobile agents [8], Das presents numerous variations of the problem. In particular, it can be noted that, given some global information about the environment (like its size or a bound on the

---

This work was partially supported by ANR project MACARON (ANR-13-JS02-0002).

Y. Moses (Ed.): DISC 2015, LNCS 9363, pp. 107–122, 2015.
DOI: 10.1007/978-3-662-48653-5_8

diameter), it is always possible to explore, even in environments where there is no local information that enables to know, arriving on a node, whether it has already been visited (e.g. anonymous networks). If no global information is given to the agent, then the only way to perform a network traversal is to use a *unlimited* traversal (e.g. with a classical BFS or Universal Exploration Sequences [1,15,19] with increasing parameters). This infinite process is sometimes called *Perpetual Exploration* when the agent visits infinitely many times every node. Perpetual Exploration has application mainly to security and safety when the mobile agents are a way to regularly check that the environment is safe. But it is important to note that in the case where no global information is available, it is impossible to always detect when the Exploration has been completed. This is problematic when one would like to use the Exploration algorithm composed with another distributed algorithm.

In this note, we focus on Exploration with termination. It is known that in general anonymous networks, the only topology that enables to stop after the exploration is the tree-topology. From standard covering and lifting techniques, it is possible to see that exploring with termination a (small) cycle would lead to halt before a complete exploration in huge cycles. Would it be possible to explore, with full stop, non-tree topologies without global information? We show here that it is possible to explore a larger set of topologies while only providing the agent with some local information.

The information that is provided can be informally described as giving *binoculars* to the agent. This constant range sensor enables the agent to see the relationship between its neighbours. Using binoculars is a quite natural enhancement for mobile robots. In some sense, we are trading some a priori global information (that might be difficult to maintain efficiently) for some local information that the agent can *autonomously* and *dynamically* acquire. We give here a complete characterization of which networks can be explored with binoculars.

## 2    Exploration with Binoculars

### 2.1    The Model

*Mobile Agents.* We use a standard model of mobile agents. A mobile agent is a computational unit evolving in an undirected simple graph $G = (V, E)$ from vertex to vertex along the edges. A vertex can have some labels attached to it. There is no global guarantee on the labels, in particular vertices have no identity (anonymous/homonymous setting), i.e., local labels are not guaranteed to be unique. The vertices are endowed with a port numbering function available to the agent in order to let it navigate within the graph. Let $v$ be a vertex, we denote by $\delta_v : V \rightarrow \mathbb{N}$, the injective port numbering function giving a locally unique identifier to the different adjacent nodes of $v$. We denote by $\delta_v(w)$ the port number of $v$ leading to the vertex $w$, i.e., corresponding to the edge $vw$ at $v$. We denote by $(G, \delta)$ the graph $G$ endowed with a port numbering $\delta = \{\delta_v\}_{v \in V(G)}$.

When exploring a network, we would like to achieve it for any port numbering. So we consider the set of every graph endowed with a port numbering function, called $\mathcal{G}^\delta$. By abuse of notation, since the port numbering is usually fixed, we denote by $G$ a graph $(G, \delta) \in \mathcal{G}^\delta$.

The behaviour of an agent is cyclic: it obtains local information (local label and port numbers), computes some values, and moves to its next location according to its previous computation. We also assume that the agent can backtrack, that is the agent knows via which port number it accessed its current location. We do not assume that the starting point of the agent (that is called the *homebase*) is marked. All nodes are a priori indistinguishable except from the degree and the label. We assume that the mobile agent is a Turing machine (with unbounded local memory). Moreover we assume that an agent accesses its memory and computes instructions instantaneously. An execution $\rho$ of an algorithm $\mathcal{A}$ for a mobile agent is composed by a (possibly infinite) sequence of edge traversals (or *moves*) by the agent. The length $|\rho|$ of an execution $\rho$ is the total number of moves. The complexity measure we are interested in is the number of moves performed by the agent during the execution of the algorithm.

**Binoculars.** Our agent can use "binoculars" of range 1, that is, it can "see" the graph (with the labels and the port numbers) that is induced by its current location and the adjacent nodes. In order to reuse standard techniques and algorithms, we will actually assume that the nodes of the graph we are exploring are labelled by these induced balls. It is straightforward to see that in a graph with such a *binoculars labelling* of the nodes, an agent with binoculars has the same computational power as an agent without binoculars (the "binoculars" primitive gives only access to more information, it does not enable more moves).

## 2.2 The Exploration Problem

We consider the Exploration Problem with Binoculars for a mobile agent. An algorithm $\mathcal{A}$ is an Exploration algorithm if for any graph $G = (V, E)$ with binoculars labelling, for any port numbering $\delta_G$, starting from any arbitrary vertex $v_0 \in V$,

- either the agent visits every vertex at least once and terminates;
- either the agent never halts.[1]

In other words, if the agent halts, then we know that every vertex has been visited. The intuition in this definition is to model the absence of global knowledge while maintaining safety of composition. Since we have no access to global information, we might not be able to visit every node on some networks, but, in this case, we do not allow the algorithm to appear as correct by terminating. This allows to safely compose an Exploration algorithm with another algorithm without additional global information.

We say that a graph $G$ is *explorable* if there exists an Exploration algorithm that halts on $G$ starting from any point. An algorithm $\mathcal{A}$ explores $\mathcal{F}$ if it is an

---

[1] A seemingly stronger definition could require that the agent performs perpetual exploration in this case. It is easy to see that this is actually equivalent for computability considerations since it is always possible to compose in parallel (see below) a perpetual BFS to any never halting algorithm.

Exploration algorithm such that for all $G \in \mathcal{F}$, $\mathcal{A}$ explores and halts. (Note that since $\mathcal{A}$ is an Exploration algorithm, for any $G \notin \mathcal{F}$, $\mathcal{A}$ either never halts, or $\mathcal{A}$ explores $G$.)

In the context of distributed computability, a very natural question is to characterize the maximal sets of explorable networks. It is not immediate that there is a maximum set of explorable networks. Indeed, it could be possible that two graphs are explorable, but not explorable with the same algorithm. However, we note that explorability is monotone. That is if $\mathcal{F}_1$ and $\mathcal{F}_2$ are both explorable then $\mathcal{F}_1 \cup \mathcal{F}_2$ is also explorable. Consider $\mathcal{A}_1$ that explores $\mathcal{F}_1$ and $\mathcal{A}_2$ that explores $\mathcal{F}_2$ then the parallel composition of both algorithms (the agent performs one step of $\mathcal{A}_1$ then backtracks to perform one step of $\mathcal{A}_2$ then backtracks, etc ...; and when one of $\mathcal{A}_1$ or $\mathcal{A}_2$ terminates, the composed algorithm terminates) explores $\mathcal{F}_1 \cup \mathcal{F}_2$ since these two algorithms guarantee to have always explored the full graph when they terminate on any network. So there is actually a maximum set of explorable graphs.

## 2.3  Our Results

We give here a complete characterization of which networks can be explored with binoculars. We first give a necessary condition for a graph to be explorable with binoculars using the standard lifting technique. Using the same technique, we give a lower bound on the move complexity to explore a given explorable graph. Then we show that the Exploration problem admits a universal algorithm, that is, there exists an algorithm that halts after visiting all vertices on all explorable graphs. This algorithm, together with the necessary condition, proves that the explorable graphs are exactly the graphs whose clique complexes admit a finite universal cover (these are standard notions of discrete topology, see Section 3). This class is larger than the class of tree networks that are explorable without binoculars. It contains graphs whose clique complex is simply connected (like chordal graphs or planar triangulations), but also triangulations of the projective plane. Finally, we show that the move complexity of any universal exploration algorithm cannot be upper bounded by any computable function of the size of the network.

**Related Works.** To the best of our knowledge, using binoculars has never been considered for mobile agent on graphs. In the classical "Look-Compute-Move" model [16, Chap.5.6], vision is usually global and only coordination problems, like Rendezvous or Gathering, have been considered, even when the vision is limited to the immediate neighbourhood (e.g. in [10]). When the agent can only see the label and the degree of its current location, it is well-known that any Exploration algorithm can only halts on trees and a standard DFS algorithm enables to explore any tree in $O(n)$ moves. Gasieniec et al. [2] show that an agent can explore any tree and stop on its starting position using only $O(\log n)$ bit of memory matching a lower bound proved in [9]. For general anonymous graphs, Exploration with halt has mostly been investigated assuming some global bounds are known, in the goal of optimizing the move complexity. It can be done in $O(\Delta^n)$ moves using a DFS traversal while knowing the size $n$ when the maximum degree is $\Delta$. This can be reduced to $O(n^3 \Delta^2 \log n)$ using Universal Exploration Sequences [1,15] that are sequences of port numbers that an agent can follow and be assured to visit any vertex of any graph of size at most $n$ and maximum degree at most $\Delta$. Reingold [19] showed that universal exploration sequences can be constructed in logarithmic space.

Trading global knowledge for structural local information by designing specific port numberings, or specific node labels that enable easy or fast exploration of anonymous graphs have been proposed in [7,11,14]. Note that using binoculars is a local information that can be locally maintained contrary to the schemes proposed by these papers where the local labels are dependent of the full graph structure. See also [8] for a detailed discussion about Exploration using other mobile agent models (with pebbles for examples).

## 3 Definitions and Notations

### 3.1 Graphs

We always assume simple and connected graphs. Let $G$ be a graph, we denote $V(G)$ (resp. $E(G)$) the set of vertices (resp. edges). If two vertices $u, v \in V(G)$ are adjacent in $G$, the edge between $u$ and $v$ is denoted by $uv$.

A *path* $p$ of *length* $k$ in a graph $G$ is a sequence of vertices $(v_0, \ldots, v_k)$ such that $v_i v_{i+1} \in E(G)$ for every $0 \le i < k$. A path is *simple* if for any $i \ne j$, $v_i \ne v_j$. A *cycle* $c$ of length $k$ is a path $(v_0, \ldots, v_k)$ such that $v_0 = v_k$. A cycle $(v_0, \ldots, v_k)$ is simple if it is the empty path (i.e., $k = 0$) or if the path $(v_0, \ldots, v_{k-1})$ is simple. A *loop* $c$ of length $k$ is a sequence of vertices $(v_0, \ldots, v_k)$ such that $v_0 = v_k$ and $v_i = v_{i+1}$ or $v_i v_{i+1} \in E(G)$, for every $0 \le i < k$; the length of a loop is denoted by $|c|$. On a graph endowed with a port numbering, a path $p = (v_0, \ldots, v_k)$ is labelled by $\lambda(p) = (\delta_{v_0}(v_1), \delta_{v_1}(v_2), \ldots, \delta_{v_{k-1}}(v_k))$.

The distance between two vertices $v$ and $v'$ in a graph $G$ is denoted by $d_G(v, v')$. It is the length of a shortest path between $v$ and $v'$ in $G$. Let $N_G(v, k)$ be the set of vertices at distance at most $k$ from $v$ in $G$. We denote by $N_G(v)$, the vertices at distance at most 1 from $v$. We define $B_G(v, k)$ to be the subgraph of $G$ induced by the set of vertices $N_G(v, k)$.

**Binoculars labelling.** In the following, we always assume that every vertex $v$ of $G$ has a label $\nu(v)$ corresponding to the *binoculars labelling* of $v$. This binoculars label $\nu(v)$ is a graph isomorphic to $B_G(v, 1)$ with its port numbering.

**Coverings.** We now present the formal definition of graph homomorphisms that capture the relation between graphs that locally look the same in our model. A map $\varphi : V(G) \to V(H)$ from a graph $G$ to a graph $H$ is a *homomorphism* from $G$ to $H$ if for every edge $uv \in E(G)$, $\varphi(u)\varphi(v) \in E(H)$. A homomorphism $\varphi$ from $G$ to $H$ is a *graph covering* if for every $v \in V(G)$, $\varphi_{|N_G(v)}$ is a bijection between $N_G(v)$ and $N_H(\varphi(v))$.

These standard definitions extend naturally to labelled graphs: for any functions *label* defined on $V(G)$ and *label'* defined on $V(H)$ and for any port numberings $\delta$ of $G$ and $\delta'$ of $H$, $\varphi : V(G) \to V(H)$ is a homomorphism (resp. a graph covering) from $(G, \delta, label)$ to $(H, \delta', label')$ if $\varphi : G \to H$ is a homomorphism (resp. a graph covering) such that $label'(\varphi(u)) = label(u)$ for every $u \in V(G)$ and $\delta_u(v) = \delta'_{\varphi(u)}(\varphi(v))$ for every edge $uv \in E(G)$.

## 3.2  Simplicial Complexes

Definitions in this section are standard notions from discrete topology [18]. Given a set $V$, a *simplex* $s$ of dimension $n \in \mathbb{N}$ is a subset of $V$ of size $n+1$. A *simplicial complex* $K$ is a collection of simplices such that for every simplex $s \in K$, $s' \subseteq s$ implies $s' \in K$. A simplicial complex $K$ is $k$-dimensional if the largest dimension of a simplex of $K$ is $k$.

A graph $G$ can be seen as a 1-dimensional simplicial complex where $V(G)$ is the set of 0-dimensional simplices and $E(G)$ is the set of 1-dimensional simplices.

Given a simplicial complex $K$, the 0-dimensional simplices of $K$ are the *vertices* of $K$ and the 1-dimensional simplices of $K$ are the *edges* of $K$. For a simplicial complex $K$, we denote by $V(K)$ (resp. $E(K)$) the set of vertices (resp. of edges) of $K$, and the *1-skeleton* of $K$ is the graph $G(K) = (V(K), E(K))$. A simplicial complex is said to be connected if its 1-skeleton is connected. We consider only connected complexes.

The *star* $St(v, K)$ of a vertex $v$ in a simplicial complex $K$ is the subcomplex defined by taking the collection of simplices of $K$ containing $v$ and their subsimplices.

It also possible to have a notion of covering for simplicial complexes. A *simplicial map* $\varphi : K \to K'$ is a map $\varphi : V(K) \to V(K')$ such that for any simplex $s = \{v_1, \ldots, v_k\}$ in $K$, $\varphi(s) = \{\varphi(v_1), \ldots, \varphi(v_k)\}$ is a simplex in $K'$.

**Definition 1.** *A simplicial map $\varphi : K \to K'$ is a simplicial covering if for every vertex $v \in V(K)$, $\varphi|_{St(v,K)}$ is a bijection between $St(v, K)$ and $St(\varphi(v), K')$.*

Examples of simplicial coverings are presented at the end of this section. For any simplicial complex $K$, the following proposition shows that there always exists a "maximal" cover of $K$ that is called *the universal cover* of $K$.

**Proposition 1 (Universal Cover).** *For any simplicial complex $K$, there exists a possibly infinite complex (unique up to isomorphism) denoted $\widehat{K}$ and a simplicial covering $\mu : \widehat{K} \to K$ such that, for any complex $K'$, for any simplicial covering $\varphi : K' \to K$, there exists a simplicial covering $\gamma : \widehat{K} \to K'$ and $\varphi \circ \gamma = \mu$.*

Given a graph $G = (V, E)$, the *clique complex* of $G$, denoted $\mathcal{K}(G)$ is the simplicial complex formed by the cliques of $G$. Note that for any graph $G$, the 1-skeleton of $\mathcal{K}(G)$ is $G$. Examples of simplicial coverings and clique complexes are presented in Figure 1.

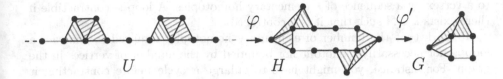

**Fig. 1.** $\mathcal{K}(H)$ is a (simplicial) cover of $\mathcal{K}(G)$. $\mathcal{K}(U)$ is an infinite graph that is a simplicial cover of both $\mathcal{K}(H)$ and $\mathcal{K}(G)$.

Given two graphs $G, G'$, a map $\varphi : V(G) \to V(G')$ is a simplicial map from $\mathcal{K}(G)$ to $\mathcal{K}(G')$ if and only if for each edge $uv \in E(G)$, either $\varphi(u) = \varphi(v)$ or $\varphi(u)\varphi(v) \in E(G')$. Note that if $\varphi : \mathcal{K}(G) \to \mathcal{K}(G')$ is a simplicial covering, then $\varphi$ is also a graph covering from $G$ to $G'$. Note however that the converse does not hold. Indeed, let $C_3$ and $C_6$ be two cycles of respective lengths 3 and 6. There is a graph covering from $C_6$ to $C_3$ but there is no simplicial covering from $C_6$ to $C_3$ since every vertex of $\mathcal{K}(C_3)$ belongs to a 2-dimensional simplex while no vertex of $\mathcal{K}(C_6)$ does.

However, when we consider graphs labelled with their binoculars labelling, the two notions are equivalent. Note that in the previous example with $C_6$ and $C_3$, there is no graph covering from $C_6$ to $C_3$ that preserves the binoculars labels.

**Proposition 2.** *Let $G$ and $H$ be two graphs labelled with their binoculars labelling and consider a homomorphism $\varphi : G \to H$. The map $\varphi$ is a graph covering from $G$ to $H$ if and only if $\varphi$ is a simplicial covering from $\mathcal{K}(G)$ to $\mathcal{K}(H)$.*

From standard distributed computability results [3,4,5,20], it is known that the structure of graph coverings explains what can be computed or not. So in order to investigate the structure induced by coverings of graphs with binoculars labelling, we will investigate the structure of simplicial coverings of simplicial complexes.

In the following, we will only consider simplicial coverings, and for sake of simplicity, we will name them "coverings".

*Homotopy.* We say that two loops $c = (v_0, v_1, \ldots, v_{i-1}, v_i, v_{i+1}, \ldots, v_k)$ and $c' = (v_0, v_1, \ldots, v_{i-1}, v_{i+1}, \ldots, v_k)$ in a complex $K$ are related by an *elementary homotopy* if one of the following conditions holds: $v_i = v_{i+1}$, $v_{i-1} = v_{i+1}$, or $v_{i-1}v_iv_{i+1}$ is a triangle of $K$ (i.e., $v_{i-1}v_{i+1}$ is an edge of $K$ when $K$ is a clique complex).

Note that being related by an elementary homotopy is a reflexive relation (we can either increase or decrease the length of the loop). We say that two loops $c$ and $c'$ are homotopic equivalent if there is a sequence of loops $c_1, \ldots, c_k$ such that $c_1 = c$, $c_k = c'$, and for every $1 \le i < k$, $c_i$ is related to $c_{i+1}$ by an elementary homotopy. A loop is $k$-contractible (for $k \in \mathbb{N}$) if it can be reduced to a vertex by a sequence of $k$ elementary homotopies. A loop is contractible if there exists $k \in \mathbb{N}$ such that it is $k$-contractible.

Remark that the number of elementary homotopies required to contract a loop is not necessarily monotone nor bounded by the number of vertices in the graph. For instance, you might have to enlarge a cycle before contracting it (think about the top cycle of a "sockwind-like surface").

**Simple Connectivity.** A *simply connected* complex is a complex where every loop can be reduced to a vertex by a sequence of elementary homotopies. These complexes have lots of interesting combinatorial and topological properties.

**Proposition 3 ([18]).** *Let $K$ be a connected complex, then $K$ is isomorphic to its universal cover $\widehat{K}$ if and only if it is simply connected.*

In fact, in order to check the simple connectivity of a simplex $K$, it is enough to check that all its simple cycles are contractible. The proof is straightforward.

**Proposition 4.** *A complex $K$ is simply connected if and only if every simple cycle is contractible.*

**Complexes with Finite Universal Cover.** We define $\mathcal{FC} = \{G \mid$ the universal cover of $\mathcal{K}(G)$ is finite $\}$ and $\mathcal{IC} = \{G \mid G$ is finite and the universal cover of $\mathcal{K}(G)$ is infinite $\}$. Note that $\mathcal{FC}$ admits one interesting sub-class $\mathcal{SC} = \{G \mid G$ is finite and $\mathcal{K}(G)$ is simply connected$\}$.

## 4    First Impossibility Result and Lower Bound

First, in Lemma 1, we propose a Lifting Lemma for coverings of clique complexes. This lemma shows that every execution on a graph $G$ can be lifted up to every graph $G'$ such that $\mathcal{K}(G')$ is a cover of $\mathcal{K}(G)$, and in particular, to the 1-skeleton $\widehat{G}$ of the universal cover of $\mathcal{K}(G)$.

Consider an algorithm $\mathcal{A}$ and an execution of $\mathcal{A}$ performed by a mobile agent with binoculars starting on a vertex $v$ in a network $G$. For any $i \in \mathbb{N}$, we denote respectively the position of the agent and its state (i.e., the content of its memory) at step $i$ by $\mathrm{pos}_i(\mathcal{A}, G, v)$ and $\mathrm{mem}_i(\mathcal{A}, G, v)$. By standard techniques ([3,4,5,20]), we have the following lemma.

**Lemma 1 (Lifting Lemma).** *Consider two graphs $G$ and $G'$ such that there exists a covering $\varphi : \mathcal{K}(G') \to \mathcal{K}(G)$. For any algorithm $\mathcal{A}$ and for any vertices $v \in V(G)$ and $v' \in V(G')$ such that $\varphi(v') = v$, for any step $i \in \mathbb{N}$, $\mathrm{mem}_i(\mathcal{A}, G', v') = \mathrm{mem}_i(\mathcal{A}, G, v)$ and $\varphi(\mathrm{pos}_i(\mathcal{A}, G', v')) = \mathrm{pos}_i(\mathcal{A}, G, v)$.*

Using the Lifting Lemma above, we are now able to prove a first result about explorable graphs and the move complexity of their exploration.

**Proposition 5.** *Any explorable graph $G$ belongs to $\mathcal{FC}$, and any Exploration algorithm exploring $G$ performs at least $|V(\widehat{G})| - 1$ moves, where $\widehat{G}$ is the 1-skeleton of the universal cover of the clique complex $\mathcal{K}(G)$.*

*Proof.* Suppose it is not the case and assume there exists an exploration algorithm $\mathcal{A}$ that explores a graph $G \in \mathcal{IC}$ when it starts from a vertex $v_0 \in V(G)$. Let $r$ be the number of steps performed by $\mathcal{A}$ on $G$ when it starts on $v_0$.

Let $\widehat{G}$ be the 1-skeleton of the universal cover of $\mathcal{K}(G)$. Consider a covering $\varphi : \mathcal{K}(\widehat{G}) \to \mathcal{K}(G)$ and consider a vertex $\widehat{v}_0 \in V(\widehat{G})$ such that $\varphi(\widehat{v}_0) = v_0$. By Lemma 1, when executed on $\widehat{G}$, $\mathcal{A}$ stops after $r$ steps. Consider the graph $H = B_{\widehat{G}}(\widehat{v}_0, r + 1)$. Since $G \in \mathcal{IC}$, $\widehat{G}$ is infinite and $|V(H)| > r + 1$. When executed on $H$ starting in $\widehat{v}_0$, $\mathcal{A}$ behaves as in $\widehat{G}$ during at least $r$ steps since the $r$ first moves can only depend of $B_H(\widehat{v}, r) = B_{\widehat{G}}(\widehat{v}, r)$. Consequently $\mathcal{A}$ stops after $r$ steps when executed on $H$ starting in $\widehat{v}_0$. Since $|V(H)| > r + 1$, $\mathcal{A}$ stops before it has visited all nodes of $H$ and thus $\mathcal{A}$ is not an Exploration algorithm, a contradiction.

The move complexity bound is obtained from the Lifting Lemma applied to any covering $\varphi : \mathcal{K}(\widehat{G}) \to \mathcal{K}(G)$. Assume we have an Exploration algorithm $\mathcal{A}$ halting on $G$ at some step $q$. If $|V(\widehat{G})| > q + 1$ then $\mathcal{A}$ halts on $\widehat{G}$ and has not visited all vertices of $\widehat{G}$ since at most one vertex can be visited in a step (plus the homebase). A contradiction.    □

Note that this is the same lifting technique that shows that, without binoculars, tree networks are the only explorable networks without global knowledge.

## 5    Exploration of $\mathcal{FC}$

We propose in this section an Exploration algorithm for the family $\mathcal{FC}$ in order to prove that this family is the maximum set of explorable networks.

The goal of Algorithm 1 is to visit, in a BFS fashion, a ball centered on the homebase of the agent until the radius of the ball is sufficiently large to ensure that $G$ is explored. Once such a radius is reached, the agent stops. To detect when the radius is sufficiently large, we use the view of the homebase (more details below) to search for a simply connected graph which locally looks like the explored ball.

The view of a vertex is a standard notion in anonymous networks [4,20]. The *view* of a vertex $v$ in a labelled graph $(G, label)$ is a possibly infinite tree composed by paths starting from $v$ in $G$. From [20], the view $\mathcal{T}_G(v)$ of a vertex $v$ in $G$ is the labelled rooted tree built recursively as follows. The root of $\mathcal{T}_G(v)$, denoted by $x_0$, corresponds to $v$ and is labelled by $label(x_0) = label(v)$. For every vertex $v_i$ adjacent to $v$, we add a node $x_i$ in $V(\mathcal{T}_G(v))$ with $label(x_i) = label(v_i)$ and we add an edge $x_0 x_1$ in $E(\mathcal{T}_G(v))$ with $\delta_{x_0}(x_i) = \delta_v(v_i)$ and $\delta_{x_i}(x_0) = \delta_{v_i}(v)$. To finish the construction, every node $x_i$ adjacent to $x_0$ is identified with the root of the tree $\mathcal{T}_G(v_i)$. We denote by $\mathcal{T}_G(v, k)$, the view $\mathcal{T}_G(v)$ truncated at depth $k$. If the context permits it, we denote it by $\mathcal{T}(v, k)$. Given an integer $k \in \mathbb{N}$, we define an equivalence relation on vertices using the views truncated at depth $k$: $v \sim_k w$ if $\mathcal{T}_G(v, k) = \mathcal{T}_G(w, k)$.

Note that in the following, we will consider the case where for each node $v$, $label(v)$ is equal to $\nu(v)$, the graph that is obtained using binoculars from $v$.

---

**Algorithm 1.** $\mathcal{FC}$-Exploration algorithm

---

$k := 0$;
**repeat**
  Increment $k$ ;
  Compute $\mathcal{T}(v_0, 2k)$;
  Find a complex $H$ (if it exists) such that:
    – $|V(H)| < k$, and
    – $\exists \widetilde{v}_0 \in V(H)$ such that $\widetilde{v}_0 \sim_{2k} v_0$, and
    – every simple cycle of $\mathcal{K}(H)$ is $k$-contractible;
  **until** $H$ *is defined*;
  Stop the exploration;

---

## 5.1  Presentation of the Algorithm

Consider a graph $G$ and let $v_0 \in V(G)$ be the homebase of the agent in $G$. Let $k$ be an integer initialized to 1. Algorithm 1 is divided in phases. At the beginning of a phase, the agent follows all paths of length at most $2k$ originating from $v_0$ in order to compute the view $\mathcal{T}(v_0, 2k)$ of $v_0$.

At the end of the phase, the agent backtracks to its homebase, and enumerates all graphs of size at most $k$ until it finds a graph $H$ such that all simple cycles of $\mathcal{K}(H)$ are $k$-contractible and such that there exists a vertex $\widetilde{v}_0 \in V(H)$ that has the same view at distance $2k$ as $v_0$, i.e., $\mathcal{T}_H(\widetilde{v}_0, 2k) = \mathcal{T}_G(v_0, 2k)$.

If such an $H$ exists then the algorithm stops. Otherwise, $k$ is incremented and the agent starts another phase.

Deciding the $k$-contractibility of a given cycle is computable (by considering all possible sequences of elementary homotopies of length at most $k$). Since the total number of simple cycles of a graph is finite, Algorithm 1 can be implemented on a Turing machine.

## 5.2  Correction of the Algorithm

In order to prove the correction of this algorithm, we prove that when the first graph $H$ satisfying every condition of Algorithm 1 is found, then $\mathcal{K}(H)$ is actually the universal cover of $\mathcal{K}(G)$ (Corollary 1). Intuitively, this is because it is not possible to find a *simply connected* complex that looks locally the same as a *strict subpart* of another complex.

Remember that given a path $p$ in a complex $G$, $\lambda(p)$ denotes the sequence of outgoing port numbers followed by $p$ in $G$. We denote by $\text{DEST}_G(v_0, \lambda(p))$, the vertex in $G$ reached by the path starting in $v_0$ and labelled by $\lambda(p)$. We show (Proposition 6) that if we fix a vertex $\widetilde{v}_0 \in V(H)$ such that $\widetilde{v}_0 \sim_{2k} v_0$, we can define unambiguously a map $\varphi$ from $V(H)$ to $V(G)$ as follows: for any $\widetilde{u} \in V(H)$, let $p$ be any path from $\widetilde{v}_0$ to $\widetilde{u}$ in $H$ and let $u = \varphi(\widetilde{u})$ be the vertex reached from $v_0$ in $G$ by the path labelled by $\lambda(p)$.

**Proposition 6.** *Consider a graph $G$ such that Algorithm 1 stops on $G$ when it starts in $v_0$. Let $k \in \mathbb{N}$ and let $H$ be the graph computed by the algorithm before it stops. Consider any vertex $\tilde{v}_0 \in V(H)$ such that $v_0 \sim_{2k} \tilde{v}_0$.*

*For any vertex $\tilde{u} \in V(H)$, for any two paths $\tilde{q}, \tilde{q}'$ from $\tilde{v}_0$ to $\tilde{u}$ in $H$,*
$\mathrm{DEST}_G(v_0, \lambda(\tilde{q})) = \mathrm{DEST}_G(v_0, \lambda(\tilde{q}'))$.

The proof is rather technical and involves careful inductions inside the space of homotopies. It is omitted here for lack of space, the complete proof is presented in the full version [6]. Showing that $\varphi$ is a covering, we get the following corollary.

**Corollary 1.** *Consider a graph $G$ such that Algorithm 1 stops on $G$ when it starts in $v_0 \in V(G)$ and let $H$ be the graph computed by the algorithm before it stops. The clique complex $\mathcal{K}(H)$ is the universal cover of $\mathcal{K}(G)$.*

*Proof.* By the definition of Algorithm 1, the complex $\mathcal{K}(H)$ is simply connected. Consequently, we just have to show that $\mathcal{K}(H)$ is a cover of $\mathcal{K}(G)$.

Consider any vertex $\tilde{v}_0 \in V(H)$ such that $v_0 \sim_{2k} \tilde{v}_0$. For any vertex $\tilde{u} \in V(H)$, consider any path $\tilde{p}_{\tilde{u}}$ from $\tilde{v}_0$ to $\tilde{u}$ and let $\varphi(\tilde{u}) = \mathrm{DEST}_G(v_0, \lambda(\tilde{p}_{\tilde{u}}))$. From Proposition 6, $\varphi(\tilde{u})$ is independent from our choice of $\tilde{p}_{\tilde{u}}$. Since $v_0 \sim_{2k} \tilde{v}_0$ and since $|V(H)| \leq k$, for any $\tilde{u} \in V(H)$, $\nu(\varphi(\tilde{u})) = \nu(\tilde{u})$. Consequently, for any $\tilde{u} \in V(H)$ and for any neighbour $\tilde{w} \in N_H(\tilde{u})$, there exists a unique $w \in N_G(\varphi(\tilde{u}))$ such that $\lambda(\tilde{u}, \tilde{w}) = \lambda(\varphi(\tilde{u}), w)$. Conversely, for any $w \in N_G(\varphi(\tilde{u}))$, there exists a unique $\tilde{w} \in N_H(\tilde{u})$ such that $\lambda(\tilde{u}, \tilde{w}) = \lambda(\varphi(\tilde{u}), w)$. In both cases, let $\tilde{p}_{\tilde{w}} = \tilde{p}_{\tilde{u}} \cdot (\tilde{u}, \tilde{w})$; this is a path from $\tilde{v}_0$ to $\tilde{w}$. From Proposition 6, $\varphi(\tilde{w}) = \mathrm{DEST}_G(v_0, \lambda(\tilde{p}_{\tilde{w}})) = \mathrm{DEST}_G(u, \lambda(\tilde{u}, \tilde{w})) = w$. Consequently, $\varphi$ is a graph covering from $H$ to $G$, and by definition of $H$, $\varphi$ also preserves the binoculars labelling. Therefore, the complex $\mathcal{K}(H)$ is a cover of the complex $\mathcal{K}(G)$. $\square$

To finish to prove that Algorithm 1 is an Exploration algorithm for $\mathcal{FC}$, we remark that, when considering connected complexes (or graphs), coverings are always surjective. Consequently, $G$ has been explored when the algorithm stops.

**Theorem 1.** *Algorithm 1 is an Exploration algorithm for $\mathcal{FC}$.*

*Proof.* From Corollary 1, we know that if Algorithm 1 stops, then the clique complex $\mathcal{K}(H)$ of the graph $H$ computed by the algorithm is a cover of $\mathcal{K}(G)$. Moreover, since $|V(G)| \leq |V(H)| \leq k$ and since the agent has constructed $T_G(v, 2k)$, it has visited all vertices of $G$.

We just have to prove that Algorithm 1 always halts on any graph $G \in \mathcal{FC}$. Consider any graph $G \in \mathcal{FC}$ and let $\widehat{G}$ be the 1-skeleton of the universal cover of $\mathcal{K}(G)$. Since $G \in \mathcal{FC}$, $\widehat{G}$ is finite and there exists $k' \in \mathbb{N}$ such that every simple cycle of $\widehat{G}$ is $k'$-contractible. Let $k = \max(|V(\widehat{G})|, k')$. At phase $k$, since $\mathcal{K}(\widehat{G})$ is the universal cover of $\mathcal{K}(G)$, there exists $\tilde{v}_0 \in V(\widehat{G})$ such that $T_G(v_0) = T_{\widehat{G}}(\tilde{v}_0)$. Consequently, $T_G(v_0, 2k) = T_{\widehat{G}}(\tilde{v}_0, 2k)$, $|V(\widehat{G})| \leq k$, and every simple cycle of $\mathcal{K}(\widehat{G})$ is $k$-contractible. Therefore, at iteration $k$, the halting condition of Algorithm 1 is satisfied. $\square$

From Proposition 5 and Theorem 1 above, we get the following corollary.

**Corollary 2.** *The family $\mathcal{FC}$ is the maximum set of Explorable networks.*

# 6  Complexity of the Exploration Problem

In the previous section, we did not provide any bound on the number of moves performed by an agent executing our universal exploration algorithm. In this section, we study the complexity of the problem and we show that there does not exist any exploration algorithm for all graphs in $\mathcal{FC}$ such that one can bound the number of moves performed by the agent by a computable function.

The first reason that such a bound cannot exist is rather simple: if the 1-skeleton $\widehat{G}$ of the universal cover of the clique complex of $G$ is finite, then by Lemma 1, when executed on $G$, any exploration algorithm has to perform at least $|V(\widehat{G})| - 1$ steps before it halts. In other words, one can only hope to bound the number of moves performed by an exploration algorithm on a graph $G$ by a function of the size of $\widehat{G}$.

However, in the following theorem, we show that even if we consider only graphs with simply connected clique complexes (i.e., they are isomorphic to their universal covers), there is no Exploration algorithm for this class of graph such that one can bound its complexity by a computable function. Our proof relies on a result of Haken [12] that show that it is undecidable to detect whether a finite simplicial complex is simply connected or not.

**Theorem 2.** *Consider any algorithm $\mathcal{A}$ that explores every finite graph $G \in \mathcal{SC}$. For any computable function $t : \mathbb{N} \to \mathbb{N}$, there exists a graph $G \in \mathcal{SC}$ such that when executed on $G$, $\mathcal{A}$ executes strictly more than $t(|V(G)|)$ steps.*

*Proof.* Suppose this is not true and consider an algorithm $\mathcal{A}$ and a computable function $t : \mathbb{N} \to \mathbb{N}$ such that for any graph $G \in \mathcal{SC}$, $\mathcal{A}$ visits all the vertices of $G$ and stops in at most $t(|V(G)|)$ steps. We show that in this case, it is possible to algorithmically decide whether the clique complex of any given graph $G$ is simply connected or not. However, this problem is undecidable [12] and thus we get a contradiction[2].

Algorithm 2 is an algorithm that takes as an input a graph $G$ and then simulates $\mathcal{A}$ on $G$ for $t(|V(G)|)$ steps. If $\mathcal{A}$ does not stop within these $t(|V(G)|)$ steps, then by our assumption on $\mathcal{A}$, we know that $G \notin \mathcal{SC}$ and the algorithm returns NO. If $\mathcal{A}$ stops within these $t(|V(G)|)$ steps, then we check whether there exists a graph $H$ such that $|V(G)| < |V(H)| \leq t(|V(G)|)$ and such that the clique complex $\mathcal{K}(H)$ is a cover of $\mathcal{K}(G)$. If such an $H$ exists, then $G \notin \mathcal{SC}$ and the algorithms returns NO. If we do not find such an $H$, the algorithm returns YES.

In order to show Algorithm 2 decides simple connectivity, it is sufficient to show that when the algorithm returns YES on a graph $G$, the clique complex $\mathcal{K}(G)$ is simply connected. Suppose it is not the case and let $\widehat{G}$ be the 1-skeleton of the universal cover of the clique complex $\mathcal{K}(G)$. Consider a covering $\varphi$ from

---

[2] Note that the original result of Haken [12] does not assume that the simplicial complexes are clique complexes. However, for any simplicial complex $K$, the barycentric subdivision $K'$ of $K$ is a clique complex that is simply connected if and only if $K$ is simply connected (see [13]).

---

**Algorithm 2.** An algorithm to check simple connectivity

---

**Input**: a graph $G$

Simulate $\mathcal{A}$ starting from an arbitrary starting vertex $v_0$ during $\mathsf{t}(|V(G)|)$ steps ;
**if** $\mathcal{A}$ *halts within* $\mathsf{t}(|V(G)|)$ *steps* **then**
    **if** *there exists a graph $H$ such that $|V(G)| < |V(H)| \leq \mathsf{t}(|V(G)|)$ and such*
    *that the clique complex $\mathcal{K}(H)$ is a cover of the clique complex $\mathcal{K}(G)$* **then**
       | **return** NO; // $\mathcal{K}(G)$ is not simply connected
    **else**
       | **return** YES; // $\mathcal{K}(G)$ is simply connected
**else return** NO; // $\mathcal{K}(G)$ is not simply connected;

---

$\mathcal{K}(\widehat{G})$ to $\mathcal{K}(G)$ and let $\widehat{v}_0 \in V(\widehat{G})$ be any vertex such that $\varphi(\widehat{v}_0) = v_0$. By Lemma 1, when executed on $\widehat{G}$ starting in $\widehat{v}_0$, $\mathcal{A}$ stops after at most $\mathsf{t}(|V(G)|)$ steps.

If $\widehat{G}$ is finite, then $\widehat{G} \in \mathcal{SC}$ and by our assumption on $\mathcal{A}$, when executed on $\widehat{G}$, $\mathcal{A}$ must explore all vertices of $\widehat{G}$ before it halts. Consequently, $\mathcal{K}(\widehat{G})$ is a covering of $\mathcal{K}(G)$ with at most $\mathsf{t}(|V(G)|)$ vertices. Since $\mathcal{K}(G)$ is not simply connected, necessarily $|V(G)| < |V(\widehat{G})|$ and in this case, the algorithm returns NO and we are done.

Assume now that $\widehat{G}$ is infinite. Let $r = \mathsf{t}(|V(G)|)$ and let $B = B_{\widehat{G}}(\widehat{v}_0, r)$. Note that when $\mathcal{A}$ is executed on $\widehat{G}$ starting in $\widehat{v}_0$, any node visited by $\mathcal{A}$ belongs to $B$. Given two vertices, $\widehat{u}, \widehat{v} \in V(\widehat{G})$, we say that $\widehat{u} \equiv_B \widehat{v}$ if there exists a path from $\widehat{u}$ to $\widehat{v}$ in $\widehat{G} \setminus B$. It is easy to see that $\equiv_B$ is an equivalence relation, and that every vertex of $B$ is the only vertex in its equivalence class. For a vertex $\widehat{u} \in V(\widehat{G})$, we denote its equivalence class by $[\widehat{u}]$. Let $H$ be the graph defined by $V(H) = \{[\widehat{u}] \mid \widehat{u} \in V(\widehat{G})\}$ and $E(H) = \{[\widehat{u}][\widehat{v}] \mid \exists \widehat{u}' \in [\widehat{u}], \widehat{v}' \in [\widehat{v}], \widehat{u}'\widehat{v}' \in E(\widehat{G})\}$.

We now show that the clique complex $\mathcal{K}(H)$ is simply connected. Let $\varphi : V(\widehat{G}) \to V(H)$ be the map defined by $\varphi(\widehat{u}) = [\widehat{u}]$. By the definition of $H$, for any edge $\widehat{u}\widehat{v} \in E(\widehat{G})$, either $[\widehat{u}] = [\widehat{v}]$, or $[\widehat{u}][\widehat{v}] \in E(H)$. Consequently, $\varphi$ is a simplicial map. Consider a loop $c_0 = (u_1, u_2, \ldots, u_p)$ in $H$. By the definition of $H$, there exists a loop $\widehat{c}_0 = (\widehat{u}_{1,1}, \ldots, \widehat{u}_{1,\ell_1}, \widehat{u}_{2,1}, \ldots, \widehat{u}_{2,\ell_2}, \ldots, \widehat{u}_{p,1}, \ldots, \widehat{u}_{p,\ell_p})$ in $G$ such that for each $1 \leq i \leq p$ and each $1 \leq j \leq \ell_i$, $\varphi(\widehat{u}_{i,j}) = u_i$. Note that $\varphi(\widehat{c}_0) = (\varphi(\widehat{u}_{1,1}) = u_1, \ldots, \varphi(\widehat{u}_{1,\ell_1}) = u_1, \varphi(\widehat{u}_{2,1}) = u_2, \ldots, \varphi(\widehat{u}_{2,\ell_2}) = u_2, \ldots, \varphi(\widehat{u}_{p,1}) = u_p, \ldots, \varphi(\widehat{u}_{p,\ell_p}) = u_p)$ is homotopic to $c_0$.

Since $\mathcal{K}(\widehat{G})$ is simply connected, $\widehat{c}_0$ is contractible and thus there exists a sequence $\widehat{c}_0, \widehat{c}_1, \ldots, \widehat{c}_p$ such that $|\widehat{c}_p| = 1$ and there is an elementary homotopy between $\widehat{c}_{i-1}$ and $\widehat{c}_i$ for every $1 \leq i \leq p$. Since $\varphi$ is a simplicial map, for every $1 \leq i \leq p$, there is an elementary homotopy between $\varphi(\widehat{c}_{i-1})$ and $\varphi(\widehat{c}_i)$. Consequently, $\varphi(\widehat{c}_0)$ is contractible and thus $c_0$ is also a contractible loop of $H$. Therefore, $H$ is simply connected.

Since $G$ is finite, the degree of every vertex of $\widehat{G}$ is bounded by $|V(G)|$ and consequently, the number of equivalence classes for the relation $\equiv_B$ is finite. Consequently, the graph $H$ is finite and thus $H \in \mathcal{SC}$. Moreover, since for every

$\widehat{u} \in B$, $[\widehat{u}] = \{\widehat{u}\}$, the ball $B_H([\widehat{v_0}], r)$ is isomorphic to $B$. Consequently, when $\mathcal{A}$ is executed on $H$ starting in $[\widehat{v_0}]$, $\mathcal{A}$ stops after at most $r$ steps before it has visited all vertices of $H$, contradicting our assumption on $\mathcal{A}$.    □

## 7  Conclusion

Enhancing a mobile agent with binoculars, we have shown that, even without any global information it is possible to explore and halt in the class of graphs whose clique complex have a finite universal cover. This class is maximal and is the counterpart of tree networks in the classical case without binoculars. Note that, contrary to the classical case, where the detection of unvisited nodes is somehow trivial (any node that is visited while not backtracking is new, and the end of discovery of new nodes is immediate at leaves), here we had to introduced tools from discrete topology in order to be able to detect when it is no more possible to encounter "new" nodes.

The class where we are able to explore is fairly large and has been proved maximal when using binoculars of range 1. When considering binoculars of range $k$, clique complexes are no longer the right tool to use, but we believe we can obtain a similar characterization of explorable graphs by considering other cell complexes associated with the graph. Note that for triangle-free networks, enhancing the agent with binoculars of range 1 does not change the class of explorable networks. More generally, from the proof techniques in Section 4, it can also be shown that providing only local information (e.g. using binoculars of range $k$) cannot be enough to explore all graphs (e.g. graphs with large girth).

While providing binoculars is a natural enhancement, it appears here that explorability increases at the cost of a huge increase in complexity: the number of moves, as a function of the size of the graph, increase faster that any computable function. This cannot be expected to be reduced for all explorable graphs for fundamental Turing computability reasons. But preliminary results show that it is possible to explore with binoculars with a linear move complexity in a class that is way larger that the tree networks. So the fact that the full class of explorable networks is not explorable efficiently should not hide the fact that the improvement is real for large classes of graphs. One of the interesting open problem is to describe the class of networks for which explorability is increased while still having reasonable move complexity, like networks that are explorable in linear time.

Note that our Exploration algorithm can actually compute the universal cover of the graph, and therefore yields a Map Construction algorithm if we know that the underlying graph has a simply connected clique complex. However, note that there is no algorithm that can construct the map for all graphs of $\mathcal{FC}$. Indeed, there exist graphs in $\mathcal{FC}$ that are not simply connected (e.g. triangulations of the projective plane) and by the Lifting Lemma, they are indistinguishable from their universal cover. Note that without binoculars, the class of trees is not only the class of graphs that are explorable without information, but also the class of graphs where we can reconstruct the map without information.

Here, adding binoculars, not only enables to explore more networks but also give a model with a richer computability structure : some problems (like Exploration and Map Construction) are no longer equivalent.

# References

1. Aleliunas, R., Karp, R.M., Lipton, R., Lovász, L., Rackoff, C.: Random walks, universal traversal sequences, and the complexity of maze problems. In: FOCS 1979, pp. 218–223 (1979)
2. Ambühl, C., Gąsieniec, L., Pelc, A., Radzik, T., Zhang, X.: Tree exploration with logarithmic memory. ACM Transactions on Algorithms 7(2), 17:1–17:21 (2011)
3. Angluin, D.: Local and global properties in networks of processors. In: STOC 1980, pp. 82–93 (1980)
4. Boldi, P., Vigna, S.: An effective characterization of computability in anonymous networks. In: Welch, J.L. (ed.) DISC 2001. LNCS, vol. 2180, pp. 33–47. Springer, Heidelberg (2001)
5. Chalopin, J., Godard, E., Métivier, Y.: Election in partially anonymous networks with arbitrary knowledge in message passing systems. Distributed Computing 25(4), 297–311 (2012)
6. Chalopin, J., Godard, E., Naudin, A.: Anonymous graph exploration with binoculars. Tech. rep. (2015). http://arxiv.org/abs/1505.00599
7. Cohen, R., Fraigniaud, P., Ilcinkas, D., Korman, A., Peleg, D.: Label-guided graph exploration by a finite automaton. In: Caires, L., Italiano, G.F., Monteiro, L., Palamidessi, C., Yung, M. (eds.) ICALP 2005. LNCS, vol. 3580, pp. 335–346. Springer, Heidelberg (2005)
8. Das, S.: Mobile agents in distributed computing: Network exploration. Bulletin of the EATCS 109, 54–69 (2013)
9. Diks, K., Fraigniaud, P., Kranakis, E., Pelc, A.: Tree exploration with little memory. J. Algorithms 51(1), 38–63 (2004)
10. Guilbault, S., Pelc, A.: Gathering asynchronous oblivious agents with local vision in regular bipartite graphs. Theor. Comput. Sci. 509, 86–96 (2013)
11. Gąsieniec, L., Radzik, T.: Memory efficient anonymous graph exploration. In: Broersma, H., Erlebach, T., Friedetzky, T., Paulusma, D. (eds.) WG 2008. LNCS, vol. 5344, pp. 14–29. Springer, Heidelberg (2008)
12. Haken, W.: Connections between topological and group theoretical decision problems. In: Word Problems Decision Problems and the Burnside Problem in Group Theory, Studies in Logic and the Foundations of Mathematics, vol. 71, pp. 427–441. North-Holland (1973)
13. Hatcher, A.: Algebraic topology. Cambridge University Press (2002)
14. Ilcinkas, D.: Setting port numbers for fast graph exploration. Theor. Comput. Sci. 401(1–3), 236–242 (2008)
15. Koucký, M.: Universal traversal sequences with backtracking. J. Comput. Syst. Sci. 65(4), 717–726 (2002)
16. Kranakis, E., Krizanc, D., Markou, E.: The Mobile Agent Rendezvous Problem in the Ring. Synthesis lectures on distributed computing theory. Morgan & Claypool Publishers (2010)
17. Lange, D.B., Oshima, M.: Seven good reasons for mobile agents. Commun. ACM 42(3), 88–89 (1999)

18. Lyndon, R., Schupp, P.: Combinatorial Group Theory. Ergebnisse der Mathematik und ihrer Grenzgebiete. Springer-Verlag (1977)
19. Reingold, O.: Undirected connectivity in log-space. J. ACM **55**(4) (2008)
20. Yamashita, M., Kameda, T.: Computing on anonymous networks: Part I - Characterizing the solvable cases. IEEE Trans. Parallel Distrib. Syst. **7**(1), 69–89 (1996)

# Limit Behavior of the Multi-agent Rotor-Router System

Jérémie Chalopin[1], Shantanu Das[1], Paweł Gawrychowski[2], Adrian Kosowski[3], Arnaud Labourel[1], and Przemysław Uznański[4(✉)]

[1] LIF, CNRS and Aix-Marseille University, Marseille, France
[2] Institute of Informatics, University of Warsaw, Warsaw, Poland
[3] Inria Paris and LIAFA, Paris Diderot University, Paris, France
[4] Department of Computer Science, Helsinki Institute for Information Technology HIIT, Aalto University, Espoo, Finland
przemyslaw.uznanski@aalto.fi

**Abstract.** The *rotor-router* model, also called the *Propp machine*, was introduced as a deterministic alternative to the random walk. In this model, a group of identical tokens are initially placed at nodes of the graph. Each node maintains a cyclic ordering of the outgoing arcs, and during consecutive turns the tokens are propagated along arcs chosen according to this ordering in round-robin fashion. The behavior of the model is fully deterministic. Yanovski *et al.* (2003) proved that a single rotor-router walk on any graph with $m$ edges and diameter $D$ stabilizes to a traversal of an Eulerian circuit on the set of all $2m$ directed arcs on the edge set of the graph, and that such periodic behaviour of the system is achieved after an initial transient phase of at most $2mD$ steps.

The case of multiple parallel rotor-routers was studied experimentally, leading Yanovski *et al.* to the experimental observation that a system of $k > 1$ parallel walks also stabilizes with a period of length at most $2m$ steps. In this work we disprove this observation, showing that the period of parallel rotor-router walks can in fact, be superpolynomial in the size of graph. On the positive side, we provide a characterization of the periodic behavior of parallel router walks, in terms of a structural property of stable states called a *subcycle decomposition*. This property provides us the tools to efficiently detect whether a given system configuration corresponds to the transient or to the limit behavior of the system. Moreover, we provide polynomial upper bounds of $\mathcal{O}(m^4 D^2 + mD \log k)$ and $\mathcal{O}(m^5 k^2)$ on the number of steps it takes for the system to stabilize. Thus, we are able to predict any future behavior of the system using an algorithm that takes polynomial time and space. In addition, we show that there exists a separation between the stabilization time of the single-walk and multiple-walk rotor-router systems, and that for some graphs the latter can be asymptotically larger even for the case of $k = 2$ walks.

Research supported by the ANR projects DISPLEXITY (ANR-11-BS02-0014) and MACARON (ANR-13-JS02-0002). Part of the work was done while PU was affiliated with LIF, CNRS and Aix-Marseille University, supported by the Labex Archiméde and by the ANR project MACARON. A full version of the paper is available online at http://arxiv.org/abs/1407.3200.

© Springer-Verlag Berlin Heidelberg 2015
Y. Moses (Ed.): DISC 2015, LNCS 9363, pp. 123–139, 2015.
DOI: 10.1007/978-3-662-48653-5_9

# 1   Introduction

Dynamical processes occurring in nature provide inspiration for simple, yet powerful distributed algorithms. For example, the *heat equation*, which describes real-world processes such as heat and particle diffusion, also proves useful when designing schemes for load-balancing and token rearrangement in a discrete graph scenario. In the diffusive model of load-balancing on a network, each node of the network is initially endowed with a certain load value, and in each step it distributes a fixed proportion of its load evenly among its neighbors. Given that such a balancing operation is performed for load which is infinitely divisible (so-called *continuous diffusion*), in the long term the distribution of load converges on a degree-regular network to uniform over all nodes. When load is composed of indivisible unit tokens, the continuous diffusion process is no longer practicable. It is, however, possible to design randomized schemes in which the *expected* value of load of each node at each moment of time corresponds precisely to the value of its load in the corresponding continuous diffusion process. This may be achieved, for instance, by allowing each token of load to follow an independent random walk on the network, as well as by applying more refined techniques admitting stronger concentration of the load distribution, cf. [19]. Such methods are stochastic in their very nature, and it is natural to ask whether there exist *deterministic* methods which mimic this type of stochastic load balancing behavior? The answer is affirmative, with the natural candidate process being the so-called *rotor-router* model.

Formally, the rotor-router mechanism is represented by an undirected anonymous graph $G = (V, E)$. Initially, a set of identical tokens is released on vertices of the graph. At discrete, synchronous steps, the tokens are propagated according to the deterministic round robin rule, where after sending each token, the pointer is advanced to the next exit port in the fixed cyclic ordering. Such a mechanism has been proposed as a viable alternative to stochastic and random-walk-based processes in the context of load balancing problems [5,7,9], exploration of graphs [1,8,10,12,15], and stabilization of distributed processes [3,6,17,22].

The resemblance between the rotor-router token distribution mechanism and stochastic balancing processes based on continuous diffusion is at least twofold, in that: (1) the number of tokens on each node for the rotor-router process has a bounded discrepancy with respect to that in the continuous diffusion process [5,20], and (2) when performing time-averaging of load over sufficiently long time intervals, the observed load averages for all nodes in the rotor-router process converge precisely to their corresponding value for the continuous diffusion process.

By contrast to time-averaged load, for any *fixed* moment of time, the deterministic rotor-router process and the stochastic approaches exhibit important differences. A stochastic load balancing process based on tokens following random walks leads the system towards a "heat death" stochastic state, which is completely independent of the starting configuration. For a rotor-router system, the number of possible configurations is finite, hence, after a transient initial phase, the process must stabilize to a cyclic sequence of states which will be repeated ever after. Natural questions arise, concerning the eventual structural behavior observed in this limit cycle of the rotor-router system, the length of the limit cycle, and the duration of the stabilization phase leading to it. So far, the only known answer concerned the case when only a single token is operating in the entire system. Yanovski et al. [22] showed that such a single token stabilizes within a polynomial number of steps to periodic behavior, in which it performs a traversal of some Eulerian cycle on the directed version of the network graph.

In this work, we provide a complete structural characterization of the limit behavior of the rotor-router for an *arbitrary* number $k > 1$ of tokens. The obtained characterization shows that the rotor-router mechanism provides a way of self-organizing tokens, initially spread out arbitrarily over a graph, into balanced groups, each of which follows a well-defined walk in some part of the network graph. The practical implications of our result may be seen as twofold. On the one hand, when viewing the rotor-router as a load-balancing process, we obtain a better understanding of its limit behavior. On the other hand, when considering each of the tokens as a walker in the graph, we show that the rotor-router may prove to be a viable strategy for perpetual graph exploration, with possible applications in so-called network patrolling problems.

## 1.1 Related Work

*Load Balancing.* The rotor-router mechanism of token distribution has been considered in problems of balancing workload among network nodes for specific network topologies. In this context, each token is considered as a unit-length task to be performed by one of the processors in a network of computers. Cooper and Spencer [7] studied load balancing with parallel rotor walks in $d$-dimensional grid graphs and showed a constant bound on the discrepancy between the number of tokens at a given node $v$ in the rotor-router model and the expected number of tokens at $v$ in the random-walk model. The structural properties of the distribution of tokens for a rotor-router system on the 2-dimensional grid were considered by Doerr and Friedrich [9]. Akbari and Berenbrink [2] proved an upper bound of $\mathcal{O}(\log^{3/2} n)$ on the load-balancing discrepancy for hypercubes, and for tori of constant dimensions, they showed that the discrepancy is bounded by a constant. For general $d$-regular graphs, a bound of $O(d \log n / \mu)$ on the discrepancy of the rotor-router mechanism with respect to continuous diffusion follows from the general framework of [18], where $\mu$ is the eigenvalue gap of the graph, under the assumption that a sufficient number of self-loops are present at each node of the graph. This discrepancy bound has recently been improved to $O(d\sqrt{\log n / \mu})$ in [5].

*Graph Exploration.* The rotor-router mechanism has also been studied in the context of graph exploration, sometimes under the name of *Edge Ant Walks* [21,22], and in the context of traversing a maze and marking edges with pebbles, *e.g.* in [6]. Cover times of rotor-router systems have been investigated by Wagner et al. [21] who showed that starting from an arbitrary initial configuration[1], a single token following the rotor-router rule explores all nodes of a graph on $n$ nodes and $m$ edges within $\mathcal{O}(nm)$ steps. Later, Bhatt *et al.* [6] showed that after at most $\mathcal{O}(nm)$ steps, the token continues to move periodically along an Eulerian cycle of the (directed symmetric version of the) graph. Yanovski *et al.* [22] and Bampas *et al.* [3] studied the stabilization time and showed that the token starts circulating in the Eulerian cycle within $\Theta(mD)$ steps, in the worst case, for a graph of diameter $D$. Studies of the rotor router system for specific classes of graphs were performed in [11]. While all these studies were restricted to static graphs, Bampas *et al.* [4] considered the time required for the rotor-router to stabilize to a new Eulerian cycle after an edge is added or removed from the graph.

Studies of the parallel (*i.e.*, multiple token) rotor-router were performed by Yanovski *et al.* [22] and Klasing *et al.* [14], and the speedup of the system due to parallelization was considered for both worst-case and best-case scenarios. In [8], Dereniowski *et al.* establish bounds on the minimum and maximum possible cover time for a worst-case initialization of a $k$-rotor-router system in a graph $G$ with $m$ edges and diameter $D$, as $\Omega(mD/k)$ and $\mathcal{O}(mD/\log k)$ respectively. In [15], Kosowski and Pajak provided a more detailed analysis of the speedup for specific classes of graphs, providing tight bounds of cover-time speed-up for all values of $k$ for degree-restricted expanders, random graphs, and constant-dimensional tori. For hypercubes, they resolve the question precisely, except for values of $k$ much larger than $n$.

## 1.2  Our Results

In this work we provide a structural characterization of the limit behavior of the rotor-router model with multiple tokens. Yanovski *et al.* [22] experimentally observed that the rotor-router system enters a short sequence of states (of length at most $2m$), which repeats cyclically ever after. We start this work by disproving this observation. In fact, we display an example of a starting configuration which admits a limit cycle with a period of superpolynomial length ($\exp(\Omega(\sqrt{n \log n}))$) with respect to the size of the graph. Our example is similar to the construction presented by Kiwi *et al.* [13] to prove the existence of super-polynomial periods for chip firing games on graphs (although the rules of chip firing games are only very loosely related to those of the rotor-router).

By contrast, it turns out the fact that the rotor-router admits long limit cycles does not signify that the limit behavior of the rotor-router should be perceived as a "disordered" discrete dynamical system. The long period in our counterexample comes from the system being composed from many smaller parts, each of which exhibits a small (but different) period length. We show that for any limit sequence of states in the rotor-router model, the graph can be partitioned into arc-disjoint directed Eulerian cycles, with each token in the limit periodically traversing arcs of one particular cycle. We name such behavior a *subcycle*

---

[1] A configuration is defined by: the cyclic order of outgoing arcs, the initial pointers at the nodes, and the current location of the token.

*decomposition*, the exact properties of which are described in Section 3. To complement the lower bound, we provide an upper bound of $\exp(\mathcal{O}(\sqrt{m \log m}))$ on the period of parallel rotor walks in its limit behavior. This upper bound asymptotically almost matches the lower bound from our example.

There are several consequences of our structural characterization of the limit behavior of the rotor-router. First, we show that it is possible to determine efficiently whether the system has already stabilized (*i.e.*, reached a configuration that will repeat itself) or not. This detection is based on the analysis of the properties of stable states, that is, of how the tokens arriving at a node are distributed into groups leaving on different outgoing arcs. The main point of this analysis is the observation that the cumulative number of tokens entering a vertex $v$ (over the time period $\{t, (t+1), \ldots, (t+\Delta t)\}$) is equal to the cumulative number of tokens leaving vertex $v$ (over time $\{(t+1), (t+2), \ldots, (t+\Delta t+1)\}$), for arbitrary $\Delta t$.

Next, by defining an appropriate potential of a system and showing its monotonicity, we can give a polynomial bound on a number of steps necessary for a system with an arbitrary initialization to reach a periodic configuration. We provide an upper bound of $\mathcal{O}(m^4 D^2 + mD \log k)$, together with examples of graphs with initial configuration having just 2 tokens that require $\Omega(m^2 \log n)$ steps. This analysis is presented in Section 4. The obtained polynomial upper bound means that the rotor-router is an efficient means of self-organizing tokens so as to perform a periodic traversal of the edges of the graph.

Finally, Section 5 is dedicated to showing how the previous results can be applied in a constructive way with regard to efficient simulation of a rotor-router system. We show how the properties of subcycle decomposition can be applied to provide a way to preprocess any starting configuration in a way that makes it possible to answer queries of certain type in a polynomial time. This shows that a structural characterization of the rotor-router system is not only important as a theoretical tool for understanding the limit behavior of the system, but also as a practical tool for solving certain problems related to the rotor-router system.

As a complementary result, we show for the single-token rotor-router how to efficiently compute the Eulerian traversal cycle on which the token would be locked-in, faster than by running the process directly. A naive simulation would take $\mathcal{O}(mD)$ time, but by using the structural properties of a single token walk together with application of efficient data structures we show how to preprocess the input graph in time $\mathcal{O}(n+m)$ such that we can answer queries about token position at any given time $T$, in $\mathcal{O}(\log \log m)$ time per query.

## 2   Model and Preliminaries

Let $G = (V, E)$ be an undirected connected graph with $n$ nodes, $m$ edges and *diameter* $D$. Let $k$ be the number of tokens. The digraph $\vec{G} = (V, \vec{E})$ is the directed version of $G$ created by replacing every edge $(u, v)$ with two directed arcs $\vec{uv}$ and $\vec{vu}$. We will refer to the undirected links in graph $G$ as *edges* and to the directed links in the graph $\vec{G}$ as *arcs*. Given a vertex $v$, we will denote its set of incoming arcs by $in(v)$ and outgoing arcs by $out(v)$. Each vertex $v$ of $G$ is equipped with a fixed ordering of all its outgoing arcs $\rho_v = (e_1, e_2, \ldots, e_{\deg(v)})$.

The precise definition of the rotor-router model on the system $(\vec{G}, (\rho_v)_{v \in V})$ is as follows:

A *state* at the current time step $t$ is a tuple: $\mathcal{S}_t = ((pointer_v)_{v \in V}, (tokens_v)_{v \in V})$, where $pointer_v$ is an arc outgoing from node $v$, which is referred to as *the current port pointer at node* $v$, and $tokens_v$ is the number of tokens at any given node. For an arc $(\vec{vu})$, let $next(\vec{vu})$ denote the arc after the arc $(\vec{vu})$ in the cyclic order $\rho_v$. During each step, each node $v$ distributes in round-robin fashion all of its tokens, using the following algorithm:

While there is a token at node $v$, do

1. Send token to $pointer_v$,
2. Set $pointer_v = next(pointer_v)$.

Note that during a single time step all tokens at a node $v$ are sent out and at exactly the next time step all those tokens arrive at their respective destination nodes.

For a given state $\mathcal{S}_t$, we say that it is *stable* iff there exists $t' > t$ such that $\mathcal{S}_{t'} = \mathcal{S}_t$. The *stabilization time* of state $\mathcal{S}_0$, denoted $t_s$, is the smallest value such that $\mathcal{S}_{t_s}$ is stable. We call *the periodicity* of state $\mathcal{S}_0$ the smallest $t_p > 0$ such that $\mathcal{S}_{t_s} = \mathcal{S}_{t_s + t_p}$.

Throughout the paper, we denote multisets using $\{\{\}\}$ notation, while for integer ranges, we write $[a \mathbin{..} b] \stackrel{\text{def}}{=} \{a, a+1, \ldots, b\}$, $[a \mathbin{..} b) \stackrel{\text{def}}{=} \{a, a+1, \ldots, b-1\}$.

## 3  Periodicity of the Rotor-Router System

We begin with the observation that knowledge of the first $t_s + t_p$ states of the system, that is $\mathcal{S}_0, \ldots, \mathcal{S}_{t_s + t_p - 1}$, gives us full knowledge of any future state for arbitrarily large time $t \geq t_s$: $\mathcal{S}_t = \mathcal{S}_{t_s + ((t - t_s) \bmod t_p)}$.

So as to be able to efficiently predict the future evolution of any rotor-router state, it would be useful to put a polynomial bound on $t_p$ and $t_s$ (with respect to $n, m$ and $k$). If $k = 1$, due to results from Yanovski *et al.* [22], we know that $t_p = 2m$ and $t_s = O(mD)$. For arbitrary $k$, Yanovski *et al.* [22] experimentally observed that $t_p \leq 2m$ for any graph $G$ regardless of the initial state. However, the following negative result disproves their observation and shows that the periodicity cannot be polynomially bounded for parallel rotor-routers.

**Theorem 1.** *There exists a family of graphs and initial states, with $k = 2m$ tokens, having the periodicity $t_p = 2^{\Omega(\sqrt{n \log n})}$.*

*Proof.* We will construct such a family of graphs $\mathcal{G}_r$ for any sufficiently large integer $r$, and an appropriate initial configuration of tokens. First consider a balloon graph $G_x$ consisting of a cycle of $x > 3$ vertices $\{v_0, v_1, \ldots v_{x-1}\}$ and an additional vertex $v_x$ (called the *base vertex*) that is joined by an edge to vertex $v_{x-1}$ of the cycle (see Figure 1(a)). Let the initial token distribution at vertices $(v_0, \ldots, v_x)$ be $(1, 2, 2, \ldots 2, 4, 1)$. Further let the exit pointers at vertex $v_i$, $0 \leq i \leq x - 2$ be oriented towards $v_{i-1 \bmod x}$ (in the counter-clockwise direction, in the figure), while at the vertex $v_{x-1}$ the exit pointer is oriented towards $v_0$ (i.e. in the opposite direction). At the base vertex $v_x$ there is only one outgoing arc and so, the exit pointer at $v_x$ will always point towards this arc.

Observe that for a vertex of out-degree two, the exit pointer remains unchanged if an even number of tokens exit this vertex in the current round, while the exit pointer is rotated if an odd number of tokens exit in the current round.

We will now analyze the movement of tokens along the arcs of the graph in each round. During the first round, the number of tokens moving on the arcs $(v_0, v_1)$, $(v_1, v_2)$, $\ldots (v_{x-1}, v_0)$ of the cycle in the clockwise direction is given by the sequence $S_0 = (0, 1, 1, \ldots, 1, 2)$. During the same round, the number of tokens moving on the arcs in the counter-clockwise direction on the cycle is given by $(1, 1, \ldots 1)$. On the branch edge $(v_{x-1}, v_x)$ there is exactly one token moving in each direction.

During the second round, the number of tokens moving on the arcs $(v_0, v_1)$, $(v_1, v_2)$, $\ldots (v_{x-1}, v_0)$ of the cycle (in the clockwise direction) is given by the sequence $S_1 = (1, 1, \ldots, 1, 2, 0)$ which is a cyclic rotation of the sequence $S_0$. The number of tokens moving on the arcs in the counter-clockwise direction on the cycle is still given by $(1, 1, \ldots 1)$. Again, the branch edge $(v_{x-1}, v_x)$ has exactly one token moving in each direction.

Continuing with the above analysis, it is easy to see that in subsequent rounds, the number of tokens moving on the arcs of the cycle (in the clockwise direction) is given by cyclic rotations of $S_0$, i.e., by the sequences $(1, \ldots, 1, 2, 0, 1)$, $(1, \ldots, 1, 2, 0, 1, 1)$, $(1, \ldots, 1, 2, 0, 1, 1, 1)$ and so on. The number of tokens moving along the cycle in the counterclockwise direction is always one token per arc of the cycle. On the branch edge $(v_0, v_x)$ there is exactly one token moving in each direction in each round. Since the length of the sequence $S_0$ is $|S_0| = x$, after every $x$ steps the configuration of tokens moving on the arcs of the cycle is the same. In other words, the periodicity of this rotor-router system is $x$. Notice that the graph $G_x$ has $x + 1$ vertices and $2(x + 1)$ arcs, and there are exactly $2(x + 1)$ tokens in the system.

We will now construct the family of graphs $\mathcal{G}_r$. For any given $r$, let $p_1, p_2, \ldots p_r$ be the first $r$ prime numbers starting from $p_1 = 3$. We take $r$ balloon graphs of sizes $(1 + p_1), (1 + p_2), \ldots, (1 + p_r)$ respectively and join them by merging all the base vertices into one vertex, with arbitrary port ordering (see Figure 1(b)). In each balloon graph we place the tokens as before, such that the merged base vertex now contains $r$ tokens. During each step, $r$ tokens will exit the base vertex through the $r$ outgoing arcs and $r$ other tokens will enter the base vertex through the $r$ incoming arcs. Thus, irrespective of the initial state of the exit pointer at the base vertex, the system will behave in the same manner. The behavior of the system in the distinct balloons would be independent of each other and for each balloon of size $(1 + p_i)$ the configuration of the balloon

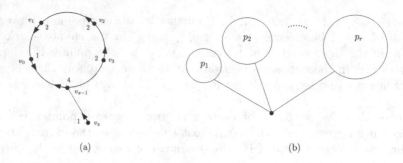

**Fig. 1.** (a) The balloon graph and the initial token distribution. (b) The family of graphs $\mathcal{G}_r$ consisting of $r$ balloons.

would repeat itself in exactly $p_i$ steps as before. Thus, the global state of the system would repeat in $\text{lcm}(p_1, \ldots p_r) = \prod_{i=1}^{r} p_i$ steps. Note that the size of the graph, $\mathcal{G}_r$, is given by $n = 1 + \sum_{i=1}^{r} p_i = \Theta(r^2 \log r)$. In general, for any given integer $n$, we can construct a similar example graph by partitioning the $n-1$ vertices into balloons of appropriate sizes joined to the $n$th vertex, such that the period of the system is equal to the *Landau function* [16] $g(n-1) = 2^{\Omega(\sqrt{n \log n})}$.

We remark that a similar result exists for parallel chip-firing games [13].

We now present an upper bound on the periodicity of $k$ parallel rotor walks, for arbitrary values of $k$. First, we will show that even though a stable state can exhibit very long (super-polynomial) periodicity, the underlying graph $G$ can be partitioned into parts, such that each part separately exhibits small (linear) periodicity.

We will use calligraphic large letters (*e.g.* $\mathcal{L} : \vec{E} \cup V \rightarrow \mathbb{Z}$) to denote *token distributions*. Thus:

- $\mathcal{L}_t(v)$ (*load of node* $v$) is number of tokens located at node $v$ in time step $t$,
- $\mathcal{L}_t(e)$ (*load of arc* $e$) is number of tokens sent out on arc $e$ at time step $t$.

Thus, although tokens cannot be located on edges in our model, we can view the tokens in vertex as located already on the outgoing ports that they will be distributed to.

We will use specifically $\mathcal{L}_t$ to denote token distribution associated with state $\mathcal{S}_t$. (It is important to note, that it is possible for two states to satisfy $\forall_e \mathcal{L}_t(e) = \mathcal{L}_{t'}(e)$ and yet $\mathcal{S}_t \neq \mathcal{S}_{t'}$, as we also require that pointers be in the same positions in identical states.)

We begin with a series of observations on the token distribution process in a rotor-router system.

**Observation 1.** *Since every token is pushed onto some outgoing arc, we have:*
$\sum_{e \in \text{out}(v)} \mathcal{L}_t(e) = \mathcal{L}_t(v); \sum_{e \in \text{in}(v)} \mathcal{L}_t(e) = \mathcal{L}_{t+1}(v).$

We also generalize token distribution into the *cumulative token distribution*. Given two time steps $t_1 \leq t_2$, we define $\mathcal{C}_{t_1}^{t_2} \stackrel{\text{def}}{=} \sum_{t \in [t_1 \,..\, t_2)} \mathcal{L}_t$, in particular, for a vertex $v$ and arc $e$:

$$\mathcal{C}_{t_1}^{t_2}(v) \stackrel{\text{def}}{=} \sum_{t \in [t_1 \,..\, t_2)} \mathcal{L}_t(v), \quad \mathcal{C}_{t_1}^{t_2}(e) \stackrel{\text{def}}{=} \sum_{t \in [t_1 \,..\, t_2)} \mathcal{L}_t(e).$$

Consequently, a natural generalization of Observation 1 from load to cumulative load is as follow:

**Observation 2.** $\sum_{e \in \text{out}(v)} \mathcal{C}_{t_1}^{t_2}(e) = \mathcal{C}_{t_1}^{t_2}(v); \sum_{e \in \text{in}(v)} \mathcal{C}_{t_1}^{t_2}(e) = \mathcal{C}_{t_1+1}^{t_2+1}(v).$

The next observation follows from the fact that rotor-router distributes tokens in a round-robin fashion among all outgoing arcs of a vertex:

**Observation 3.** $\forall_{e_1,e_2 \in \text{out}(v)} |\mathcal{C}_{t_1}^{t_2}(e_1) - \mathcal{C}_{t_1}^{t_2}(e_2)| \leq 1.$

Since arbitrarily large discrepancies (between two incoming edges) of incoming number of tokens are smoothed discretely, we can see the process of token propagation as a load-balancing scheme.

We now define the concept of *potential* of a token distribution system, which will be helpful to derive the necessary and sufficient conditions for a system state to be stable.

**Definition 1.** *Given a token distribution $\mathcal{A}$ over edges, we define its potential as:* $\Phi(\mathcal{A}) \stackrel{\text{def}}{=} \sum_{e \in \bar{E}} (\mathcal{A}(e))^2.$
*We also introduce a shorthand notation for the i-th potential of a given rotor-router state $\mathcal{S}_t$ as:* $\Phi_i(\mathcal{S}_t) \stackrel{\text{def}}{=} \Phi(\mathcal{C}_t^{t+i}) = \sum_{e \in \bar{E}} (\mathcal{C}_t^{t+i}(e))^2.$

Note that $\Phi_1 \equiv \Phi$. It is important to note that while arbitrary convex function can be used in the potential definition, usage of quadratic function will prove advantageous when analyzing the speed of convergence to a stable state, not only its properties.

The following folklore lemma provides us with a characterization of the minimum of the potential sums.

**Lemma 1.** *Over all partitions of integer $S$ into $d$ integers, the partition $\{\{\lfloor \frac{S}{d} \rfloor, \ldots, \lfloor \frac{S}{d} \rfloor, \lceil \frac{S}{d} \rceil, \ldots, \lceil \frac{S}{d} \rceil\}\}$ uniquely minimizes the value of sum of squares of elements.*

**Lemma 2.** *For arbitrary $i$ and $t$, the i-th potential is non-increasing: $\Phi_i(\mathcal{S}_{t+1}) \leq \Phi_i(\mathcal{S}_t)$.*

*Proof.* To prove the lemma we have to observe how the round-robin property of the rotor-router acts locally on the groups of tokens (cumulative over the time interval $[t, t+i)$). From Observation 2 we know, that:

$$\sum_{e \in \text{out}(v)} \mathcal{C}_{t+1}^{t+i+1}(e) = \mathcal{C}_{t+1}^{t+i+1}(v) = \sum_{e \in \text{in}(v)} \mathcal{C}_t^{t+i}(e).$$

However, from Observation 3 and Lemma 1 we get that the multiset of values over outgoing arcs *minimizes* the sum of squares. Thus:

$$\sum_{e \in \text{out}(v)} (\mathcal{C}_{t+1}^{t+i+1}(e))^2 \le \sum_{e \in \text{in}(v)} (\mathcal{C}_t^{t+i}(e))^2,$$

which leads to:

$$\Phi_i(\mathcal{S}_{t+1}) = \sum_v \sum_{e \in \text{out}(v)} (\mathcal{C}_{t+1}^{t+i+1}(e))^2 \le \sum_v \sum_{e \in \text{in}(v)} (\mathcal{C}_t^{t+i}(e))^2 = \Phi_i(\mathcal{S}_t).$$

Observe that Lemma 2 implies that if the system is stable, all of the potentials are preserved at every (future) time step. This observation is powerful enough to derive strong characterization of stable states (see Theorem 2, equivalence of (i) and (ii)). However, in order to be able to reason about bounds on stabilization time, we need a more powerful notion of being able to characterize even the temporary regularities in token trajectories (for not necessarily stable states).

**Definition 2.** *We say that a state $\mathcal{S}_T$ admits a $\Delta t$-step subcycle decomposition, if in every vertex $v$ we can define a one-to-one mapping between incoming and outgoing arcs of $v$ $M_v : \text{in}(v) \rightarrow \text{out}(v)$, such that:*

$$\forall_{e \in \text{in}(v)} \forall_{t \in [T \,.. \, T+\Delta t]} \mathcal{L}_t(e) = \mathcal{L}_{t+1}(M_v(e)). \tag{1}$$

The subcycle decomposition has the following equivalent interpretation. We partition $\vec{E} = \vec{E}_1 \cup \ldots \cup \vec{E}_c$, such that each $\vec{E}_i$ induces a strongly-connected subgraph of $G$, and for each $\vec{E}_i$ there exists an Eulerian cycle covering it such that each token traversing arcs of $\vec{E}_i$ follows this particular Eulerian cycle during time steps $T, T+1, \ldots, T+\Delta t - 1$.

Observe that the mapping $M$ in Definition 2 does not need to be necessarily unique. We will call any such mapping $M$ *a valid mapping with respect to $\Delta t$ subcycle decomposition* if (1) holds for it.

The following lemma gives a series of equivalent characterizations of subcycle decomposition, connecting the existence of such a decomposition during any time interval with lack of potential drop during the time interval, as well as a load-balancing discrepancy criterion over all shorter sub-intervals of time.

**Lemma 3.** *The following statements are equivalent:*

(i) $\mathcal{S}_T$ *admits a $\Delta t$-step subcycle decomposition,*

(ii) $\forall_v \forall_{t,t':[t\,..\,t') \subseteq [T\,..\,T+\Delta t)}, \{\{\mathcal{C}_t^{t'}(e)\}\}_{e \in \text{in}(v)} = \{\{\mathcal{C}_{t+1}^{t'+1}(e)\}\}_{e \in \text{out}(v)}$ *(multisets of cumulative loads are preserved locally),*

(iii) $\forall_{t,t':[t\,..\,t') \subseteq [T\,..\,T+\Delta t)} \{\{\mathcal{C}_t^{t'}(e)\}\}_{e \in \vec{E}} = \{\{\mathcal{C}_{t+1}^{t'+1}(e)\}\}_{e \in \vec{E}}$ *(multisets of cumulative loads are preserved globally),*

(iv) $\forall_{0 \le i \le \Delta t} \Phi_i(\mathcal{S}_T) = \Phi_i(\mathcal{S}_{T+1}) = \ldots = \Phi_i(\mathcal{S}_{T+\Delta t-i+1})$ *(potential is constant),*

(v) $\forall_v \forall_{e_1,e_2 \in \text{in}(v)} \forall_{t,t':[t\,..\,t') \subseteq [T\,..\,T+\Delta t)} |\mathcal{C}_t^{t'}(e_1) - \mathcal{C}_t^{t'}(e_2)| \le 1$ *(incoming discrepancy is at most one).*

For a fixed value of $\Delta t = 1$, Lemma 3 captures the property that as long as $\Phi(\mathcal{S}_T)$ remains constant, the loads on edges are only permuted between any two consecutive timesteps. Coupled with Lemma 2 it immediately implies aforementioned property. Unfortunately, this property is not strong enough for our purposes. However, for arbitrary values of $\Delta t$, we can still employ the notion of higher order potentials $\Phi_{\Delta t}$ (as defined previously), and observe the load balancing properties from Observation 2. The fact that stable state, by Lemma 2 and Lemma 3 admits load balancing properties even when collapsing multiple timesteps into a single frame, is our lever which will be used to derive strong properties of such states in the rest of this section.

**Definition 3.** *We say that a state $\mathcal{S}_t$ admits a $\infty$-subcycle decomposition if it admits $i$-steps subcycle decomposition for arbitrarily large $i$.*

Now we proceed to obtain a more algorithmic characterization of stable states. First, we show that if we do not experience a potential drop during $2m^2$ time steps, then the rotor-router system has reached its limit configuration.

**Theorem 2.** *The following conditions are equivalent:*

*(i) $\mathcal{S}_T$ is stable,*
*(ii) $\mathcal{S}_T$ admits a $\infty$-subcycle decomposition,*
*(iii) $\mathcal{S}_T$ admits a $(2m^2)$-subcycle decomposition.*

As a direct consequence of the proof of Theorem 2, we have:

**Corollary 1.** *For a stable state $\mathcal{S}_T$, any mapping between incoming and outgoing arcs of $v$ denoted $M_v : \mathrm{in}(v) \to \mathrm{out}(v)$ that is valid with respect to $2m^2$-subcycle decomposition, is also valid with respect to $\infty$-subcycle decomposition.*

We are now ready to provide a stronger characterization of a stable state in Theorem 3 (compared to Theorem 2), based on refined analysis of the potential behavior.

**Theorem 3.** *State $\mathcal{S}_T$ is stable iff: $\sum_{i=1}^{3m} \Phi_i(\mathcal{S}_T) = \sum_{i=1}^{3m} \Phi_i(\mathcal{S}_{T+2m^2})$.*

Finally, we provide an upper bound on the length of the period for any rotor-router state. It is interesting to see that the upper bound is not far from the period of the example graph given in Theorem 1.

**Theorem 4.** *For any stable state $\mathcal{S}_T$, the period length of the limit cycle is bounded by $t_p = \mathcal{O}(\exp(\sqrt{(m \log m)}))$.*

*Proof.* Observe, that any arc in $G$ can be part of exactly one cycle in any given subcycle decomposition. As the period length of any stable state is upperbounded by the least common multiple of the length of the cycles, we get the desired upper bound as the value of the *Landau's function* on the total number of arcs in $G$.

# 4    Stabilization Time of the Rotor-Router System

In this section we provide upper and lower bounds on the stabilization time of parallel rotor-router systems. Since the values of potentials are discrete and non-increasing, in Theorem 3 we have a very powerful tool to reason about the stabilization of a state — if the sum of potentials remains unchanged for more than $3m$ time steps, the system has reached a stable state. Thus, we can naively bound each of the potentials by $\mathcal{O}((mk)^2)$, and so also bound the sum of potentials by $\mathcal{O}(m \cdot (mk)^2)$. This gives the following corollary.

**Corollary 2.** *For any initial state $\mathcal{S}_0$, there exists $T = O(m^5k^2)$ such that $\mathcal{S}_T$ is stable.*

We will now show how to obtain an even stronger bound (in terms of dependence on $k$), but for this we need a refined upper bound on initial potential. To achieve this, we need to treat the rotor-router system as a load balancing process.

*Round-Fair Processes.* As we intend to provide bounds on the values of the $i$-th potential for rotor-router process (given sufficiently long initialization time), we need to analyze the behavior of the cumulative rotor-router processes, *i.e.*, for a fixed $\Delta t$, to observe how the distribution of tokens $\mathcal{C}_t^{t+\Delta t}$ evolves with time. Thus, in the following, we will use the broader concept of *round-fair processes* denoted by $\mathcal{W}$, as introduced in [18]. Specifically, we will call an algorithm *strictly fair* if, in every step, the number of tokens that are sent out over any two edges incident to a node differs by at most one.

**Definition 4.** *A process of token distribution (denoted by $\mathcal{W}$) is round-fair, if:*

$$\forall_{e\in\text{out}(v)}\mathcal{W}_t(e) \in \left\{ \left\lfloor \frac{\mathcal{W}_t(v)}{\deg(v)} \right\rfloor, \left\lceil \frac{\mathcal{W}_t(v)}{\deg(v)} \right\rceil \right\} \tag{2}$$

*and no tokens are left in nodes:* $\mathcal{W}_t(v) = \sum_{e\in\text{out}(v)} \mathcal{W}_t(e)$.

We observe that any rotor-router process is round-fair. Also, by Observations 1, 2 and 3, for any fixed $\Delta t$, cumulative rotor-router in the sense of $\mathcal{W}_t = \mathcal{C}_t^{t+\Delta t}$ is also round-fair.

The round-fairness condition can be strengthened into algorithms which are *cumulatively fair*. We will call an algorithm *cumulatively fair* if for every interval of consecutive time steps, the total number of tokens sent out by a node differs by at most a small constant for any two adjacent edges. It is easy to see that cumulative fair algorithms under the constraint that every token is propagated, are performing the rotor-router distribution (and vice versa, rotor-router distribution is cumulative fair with every token propagated).

In the rest of this section, in order to simplify notation, we will assume that $G$ is not bipartite. For the full formulation of subsequent definitions and lemmas, we refer the reader to the full version of the paper.

**Definition 5.** *A sequence of arcs $e_1, e_2, \ldots, e_p$ is called an* alternating path *(of length $p-1$), if either every pair of arcs $e_{2i}, e_{2i+1}$ shares starting vertex and every pair of arcs $e_{2i-1}, e_{2i}$ shares ending vertex, or vice-versa: every pair of arcs $e_{2i}, e_{2i+1}$ shares ending vertex and every pair of arcs $e_{2i-1}, e_{2i}$ shares starting vertex.*

**Definition 6.** *We define the notion of* distance *between two arcs $e, e'$, denoted by $d(e, e')$, as a length of shortest alternating path having $e$ and $e'$ as first and last arcs.*

In other words, a distance can be treated as a transitive closure of a relation where we define any pair of arcs sharing starting or ending vertex as at distance one.

**Lemma 4.** *For any two arcs $e, e'$ in non-bipartite graph $G$: $d(e, e') \leq 4D + 1$ moreover there exists an alternating path connecting $e$ and $e'$ containing at most $2D$ pairs of arcs sharing ending vertices and at most $2D+1$ pairs of arcs sharing starting vertices.*

Now we will proceed to analyze the behavior of the potential defined as in Definition 1, with respect to a round-fair processes.

Recall that $\Phi(\mathcal{W}_t) \stackrel{\text{def}}{=} \sum_{e \in \vec{E}} (\mathcal{W}_t(e))^2$. We will denote the smallest value of the potential achieved by distribution of tokens that preserves sums of loads over load balancing sets of arcs (ignoring the restriction that loads are integers) by:

$$\mathcal{B}(\mathcal{W}_t) \stackrel{\text{def}}{=} 2m \cdot \left( \underset{e \in \vec{E}}{\mathbf{avg}}\, \mathcal{W}_t(e) \right)^2, \tag{3}$$

For non-bipartite graphs, (3) reduces to the following form: $\mathcal{B}(\mathcal{W}_t) = \frac{k^2}{2m} = $ const. The following lemma follows directly from the convexity of quadratic functions.

**Lemma 5.** $\Phi(\mathcal{W}_t) \geq \mathcal{B}(\mathcal{W}_t)$.

**Definition 7.** *We say that a configuration of tokens $\mathcal{W}_t$ in non-bipartite graph $G$ has* discrepancy over arcs *equal to $\max_{e, e' \in \vec{E}}(\mathcal{W}_t(e) - \mathcal{W}_t(e'))$.*

The next observation follows directly from (2).

**Observation 4.** *The discrepancy over arcs is non-increasing in time, that is:*

$$\max_{e, e' \in \vec{E}} (\mathcal{W}_t(e) - \mathcal{W}_t(e')) \geq \max_{e, e' \in \vec{E}} (\mathcal{W}_{t+1}(e) - \mathcal{W}_{t+1}(e')).$$

We also put the following bound on the potential drop with respect to the discrepancy of number of tokens over arcs.

**Lemma 6.** *Consider a timestep $t$ such that $\mathcal{W}_t$ has discrepancy over arcs $x > 4D + 1$. Then: $\Phi(\mathcal{W}_t) - \Phi(\mathcal{W}_{t+1}) \geq \frac{(x-4D-1)(x-1)}{4D}$.*

**Lemma 7.** *If $\mathcal{W}_t$ has discrepancy $x$, then $\Phi(\mathcal{W}_t) \leq \mathcal{B}(\mathcal{W}_0) + \frac{1}{2}mx^2$.*

**Theorem 5.** *If $T \geq 16mD \ln k$, then $\mathcal{W}_T$ has discrepancy over arcs at most $10D$.*

*Proof.* Observe that for discrepancies $x \geq 10D$ we have, by Lemma 6:

$$\Phi(\mathcal{W}_t) - \Phi(\mathcal{W}_{t+1}) \geq \frac{(x - 4D - 1)(x - 1)}{4D} \geq \frac{x^2}{16D}.$$

However, by Lemma 7: $x^2 \geq 2\frac{(\Phi(\mathcal{W}_t) - \mathcal{B}(\mathcal{W}_0))}{m}$. Thus:

$$\Phi(\mathcal{W}_{t+1}) - \mathcal{B}(\mathcal{W}_0) \leq (\Phi(\mathcal{W}_t) - \mathcal{B}(\mathcal{W}_0))\left(1 - \frac{1}{8mD}\right).$$

Let us assume that after $T \geq 16mD \ln k$ steps the discrepancy is larger than $10D$. Since $\Phi(\mathcal{W}_0) - \mathcal{B}(\mathcal{W}_0) \leq \Phi(\mathcal{W}_0) \leq k^2$, we have:

$$\Phi(\mathcal{W}_T) - \mathcal{B}(\mathcal{W}_0) \leq k^2 \cdot \left(1 - \frac{1}{8mD}\right)^{16mD \ln k} < k^2(1/e)^{2\ln k} = 1,$$

implying that $\Phi(\mathcal{W}_T) = \lceil \mathcal{B}(\mathcal{W}_0) \rceil$, which implies that $\Phi(\mathcal{W}_T)$ minimizes potential among integer load distribution. Thus $\mathcal{W}_T$ has discrepancy at most 1, a contradiction.

We are now ready to prove our main result on the time of stabilization of any rotor-router initial state.

**Theorem 6.** *For any initial state $\mathcal{S}_0$, there exists $T = O(m^4D^2 + mD\log k)$ such that $\mathcal{S}_T$ is stable.*

*Proof.* Let $t_0 = \lceil 16mD \ln(3km) \rceil$. We observe that the cumulative rotor-router process (taken over $\Delta t$ rounds) is round-fair, with the number of tokens equal to $\Delta t \cdot k$. For $t \geq t_0$, $\Delta t \leq 3m$, by Theorem 5 the token distribution of $\mathcal{C}_t^{t+\Delta t}$ has discrepancy over arcs at most $10D$, thus: $\mathcal{B}(\mathcal{C}_0^{\Delta t}) \leq \Phi_{\Delta t}(\mathcal{S}_t) = \Phi(\mathcal{C}_t^{t+\Delta t}) \overset{(7)}{\leq} \mathcal{B}(\mathcal{C}_0^{\Delta t}) + 50mD^2$. We next obtain:

$$\sum_{i=1}^{3m} \mathcal{B}(\mathcal{C}_0^i) \leq \sum_{i=1}^{3m} \Phi_i(\mathcal{S}_t) \leq 150m^2D^2 + \sum_{i=1}^{3m} \mathcal{B}(\mathcal{C}_0^i). \tag{4}$$

Let $T > 300m^4D^2 + \lceil 16mD \ln(3km) \rceil$. Let us assume that $\mathcal{S}_T$ is not stable. Thus, for all $t \in [t_0 .. T]$, $\sum_{i=1}^{3m} \Phi_i(\mathcal{S}_t) - \sum_{i=1}^{3m} \Phi_i(\mathcal{S}_{t+2m^2}) \geq 1$, and in particular: $\sum_{i=1}^{3m} \Phi_i(\mathcal{S}_{t_0}) - \sum_{i=1}^{3m} \Phi_i(\mathcal{S}_T) \geq \lceil \frac{(T-t_0)}{2m^2} \rceil > 150m^2D^2$, which contradicts with (4).

We now give a lower bound on the stabilization time of parallel rotor-router walks.

**Theorem 7.** *For any $N, M > 0$, $N \leq M \leq N^2$, there exists an initialization of the rotor router system in some graph with $\Theta(N)$ nodes and $\Theta(M)$ edges such that the stabilization time is $\Omega(M^2 \log N)$.*

# 5   Simulation of the Rotor-Router

In this section, we answer the question of how to efficiently query for the state of a parallel rotor-router system after a given number of steps. The result below is for an arbitrary number of tokens ($k \geq 1$). For a single token ($k = 1$) rotor-router mechanism we provide a faster simulation algorithm in the full version of the paper.

**Theorem 8.** *We can preprocess any $\mathcal{S}_0$, in polynomial time and space (with respect to $n, m, \log k$) so that we can answer queries of state $\mathcal{S}_\tau$ or queries of $\mathcal{C}_0^\tau(e)$ (the total number of visits until time step $\tau$) both in time $\mathcal{O}(n + m)$.*

*Proof.* Our first step is to find $T$ such that $\mathcal{S}_T$ is stable. By Theorem 6 it is enough to take any $T > 300m^4D^2 + \lceil 16mD \ln(3km) \rceil$. We compute and maintain states $\mathcal{S}_0, \mathcal{S}_1, \ldots, \mathcal{S}_T$, thus answering any queries of $\mathcal{S}_\tau$ with $\tau < T$ in $\mathcal{O}(n + m)$ time. We store preprocessed $\mathcal{C}_0^\tau(e)$ for any $\tau \in [0 .. T]$.

By Corollary 1, we can find any valid $\infty$-subcycle decomposition of $\mathcal{S}_T$ in polynomial time. By the properties of the subcycle decomposition, we can then find the values of $\mathcal{S}_{T+\tau}(e)$ by finding $e'$ being shifted by $\tau$ along the cycle $e$ belongs to. In a similar fashion we find $\mathcal{C}_T^{T+\tau}(e)$ for each arc $e$, giving us $\mathcal{C}_T^{T+\tau}(v)$ for each vertex $v$, thus we know the new pointer location for $v$. Each cycle can be preprocessed with prefix sums such that queries of this type can be answered in $\mathcal{O}(1)$ time, thus giving $\mathcal{O}(n + m)$ time for full $\mathcal{S}_{T+\tau}$ query.

We can preprocess each cycle with prefix sums, thus giving us the access to $\mathcal{C}_T^\tau(e)$ for $\tau \in [T .. \infty)$. By adding the value of $\mathcal{C}_0^T(e)$ we get desired $\mathcal{C}_0^\tau(e)$.

# 6   Conclusion

The rotor-router process has, in previous work, been identified as an efficient deterministic technique for a number of distributed graph processes, such as graph exploration and load balancing. In these settings, it rivals or outperforms the random walk, in some cases (such as parallel exploration of graphs) providing provable guarantees on performance, the counterparts of which need yet to be shown for the random walk. In this paper, we provide a complete characterization of the long-term behavior of the rotor-router, showing an inherent order in the limit state to which the system rapidly converges. This provides us with a better understanding of, e.g., the long-term load balancing properties of rotor-router-based algorithms, while at the same time opening the area for completely new applications. For instance, in view of our work, the rotor-router becomes a natural candidate for a self-organizing locally coordinated algorithm for the *team patrolling problem* — a task in which the goal is to periodically and regularly traverse all edges of the graph with $k$ agents. This topic, and related questions, such as bounding the maximum distance between tokens on their respective Eulerian cycles in the limit state of the rotor-router, are deserving of future attention.

# References

1. Afek, Y., Gafni, E.: Distributed algorithms for unidirectional networks. SIAM J. Comput. **23**(6), 1152–1178 (1994)
2. Akbari, H., Berenbrink, P.: Parallel rotor walks on finite graphs and applications in discrete load balancing. In: SPAA, pp. 186–195. ACM (2013)
3. Bampas, E., Gąsieniec, L., Hanusse, N., Ilcinkas, D., Klasing, R., Kosowski, A.: Euler tour lock-in problem in the rotor-router model. In: Keidar, I. (ed.) DISC 2009. LNCS, vol. 5805, pp. 423–435. Springer, Heidelberg (2009)
4. Bampas, E., Gąsieniec, L., Klasing, R., Kosowski, A., Radzik, T.: Robustness of the rotor-router mechanism. In: Abdelzaher, T., Raynal, M., Santoro, N. (eds.) OPODIS 2009. LNCS, vol. 5923, pp. 345–358. Springer, Heidelberg (2009)
5. Berenbrink, P., Klasing, R., Kosowski, A., Mallmann-Trenn, F., Uznański, P.: Improved analysis of deterministic load-balancing schemes. In: PODC, pp. 301–310 (2015)
6. Bhatt, S.N., Even, S., Greenberg, D.S., Tayar, R.: Traversing directed eulerian mazes. J. Graph Algorithms Appl. **6**(2), 157–173 (2002)
7. Cooper, J.N., Spencer, J.: Simulating a random walk with constant error. Combinatorics, Probability & Computing **15**(6), 815–822 (2006)
8. Dereniowski, D., Kosowski, A., Pająk, D., Uznański, P.: Bounds on the cover time of parallel rotor walks. In: STACS. LIPIcs, vol. 25, pp. 263–275 (2014)
9. Doerr, B., Friedrich, T.: Deterministic random walks on the two-dimensional grid. Combinatorics, Probability & Computing **18**(1–2), 123–144 (2009)
10. Fraenkel, A.S.: Economic traversal of labyrinths. Mathematics Magazine **43**, 125–130 (1970)
11. Friedrich, T., Sauerwald, T.: The cover time of deterministic random walks. In: Thai, M.T., Sahni, S. (eds.) COCOON 2010. LNCS, vol. 6196, pp. 130–139. Springer, Heidelberg (2010)
12. Gąsieniec, L., Radzik, T.: Memory efficient anonymous graph exploration. In: Broersma, H., Erlebach, T., Friedetzky, T., Paulusma, D. (eds.) WG 2008. LNCS, vol. 5344, pp. 14–29. Springer, Heidelberg (2008)
13. Kiwi, M., Ndoundam, R., Tchuente, M., Goles, E.: No polynomial bound for the period of the parallel chip firing game on graphs. Theoretical Computer Science **136**, 527–532 (1994)
14. Klasing, R., Kosowski, A., Pająk, D., Sauerwald, T.: The multi-agent rotor-router on the ring: a deterministic alternative to parallel random walks. In: PODC, pp. 365–374 (2013)
15. Kosowski, A., Pająk, D.: Does adding more agents make a difference? A case study of cover time for the rotor-router. In: Esparza, J., Fraigniaud, P., Husfeldt, T., Koutsoupias, E. (eds.) ICALP 2014, Part II. LNCS, vol. 8573, pp. 544–555. Springer, Heidelberg (2014)
16. Landau, E.: Uber die maximalordnung der permutationen gegebenen grades. Arch. Math. Phys. **5**, 92–103 (1903)
17. Priezzhev, V., Dhar, D., Dhar, A., Krishnamurthy, S.: Eulerian walkers as a model of self-organized criticality. Phys. Rev. Lett. **77**(25), 5079–5082 (1996)
18. Rabani, Y., Sinclair, A., Wanka, R.: Local divergence of Markov chains and the analysis of iterative load-balancing schemes. In: FOCS, pp. 694–703, November 1998
19. Sauerwald, T., Sun, H.: Tight bounds for randomized load balancing on arbitrary network topologies. In: FOCS, pp. 341–350 (2012)

20. Shiraga, T., Yamauchi, Y., Kijima, S., Yamashita, M.: $L_\infty$-discrepancy analysis of polynomial-time deterministic samplers emulating rapidly mixing chains. In: Cai, Z., Zelikovsky, A., Bourgeois, A. (eds.) COCOON 2014. LNCS, vol. 8591, pp. 25–36. Springer, Heidelberg (2014)
21. Wagner, I.A., Lindenbaum, M., Bruckstein, A.M.: Distributed covering by ant-robots using evaporating traces. IEEE Trans. Robotics and Automation **15**, 918–933 (1999)
22. Yanovski, V., Wagner, I.A., Bruckstein, A.M.: A distributed ant algorithm for efficiently patrolling a network. Algorithmica **37**(3), 165–186 (2003)

# Elastic Configuration Maintenance via a Parsimonious Speculating Snapshot Solution

Eli Gafni[1]([⊠]) and Dahlia Malkhi[2]

[1] UCLA, Los Angles, USA
eli@cs.ucla.edu
[2] VMware Research, Palo Alto, USA
dmalkhi@vmware.com

## 1 Introduction

In order to provide dynamic reconfiguration of a distributed service, we extract a fundamental new task SpSn. This new task facilitates a consensus-free coordination among *clients* on incorporating changes to the set of *servers* they all access, and through which they negotiate the changes. The danger is of course that when transitioning from one configuration to the other, the system might break up isolating the clients into several groups that cannot communicate with each other.

*SpSn.* We start with a formal definition of the new task in a generic from. A processor $p_i$ invokes the task with input $I_i$, and returns a pair $(Q_i, Y_i)$, where for some contextual value-space $U$, $I_i, Q_i \subseteq U$, and $Y_i \subseteq 2^U$, and such that:

1. $Q_i \subseteq \cup_{j \in players} I_j$, where *players* $\subseteq$ *clients* is the set of participating clients, $I_i \subseteq Q_i$, and the $Q_j$'s returned are related by containment, and
2. For all $i, j$ if $Q_j \subseteq Q_i$, then $Q_j \in Y_i$.

Since the outputs are snapshots of the inputs, as well as a "speculation" of any output that earlier processors might have obtained, we name the task *Speculating Snapshot*, in short SpSn.

In our context the input for the task per client is a *configuration change* proposal from a set $P = \{+s, -s\}_{s \in servers}$[1].

*Parsimonious Solution to SpSn.* A possible solution to SpSn is for $Q$ to be a snapshot of the inputs, and for $Y$ to be the power-set of $Q$, i.e. the set of all subset of $Q$. However, this is inefficient in the number of configurations which clients observe in our use of SpSn to affect a configuration change. We later show why existing solutions to the dynamic configuration problem contain a solution to SpSn, and how the complexity of a reconfiguration scheme is related to the various solutions to SpSn. Here, we will be concerned with the most parsimonious solution in terms of the cardinality of $Y_i$. If we solve SpSn by consensus on a

---

[1] We assume that each server is added and removed at most once, so to be reintroduced into the system it bears a new identity.

© Springer-Verlag Berlin Heidelberg 2015
Y. Moses (Ed.): DISC 2015, LNCS 9363, pp. 140–153, 2015.
DOI: 10.1007/978-3-662-48653-5_10

total order of configuration-changes, we can get $Y_i$ to be precisely the number of previously output snapshots. The number of configurations here is linear in the number of proposals. However, the worst-case cost here is an infinite execution, as mandated by the FLP impossibility theorem [5].

We want to be as parsimonious as consensus-based solutions without relying on consensus. Briefly, a parsimonious solution to SpSn wait-free SWMR Read-Write is to go through a sequence of phases. Each phase is built around a two-step protocol which posts a proposal and collects all other proposals. In the second step, if the first collect was uniform, a processor marks it as a *commit proposal*. This structure borrows from the Commit-Adopt building block of Gafni [6]. At the end of the second step, if a commit value is unanimous, processor $p_i$ returns it as $Q_i$. Otherwise, it accumulates all commit values in $Y_i$ and continues to another phase. The body of the paper contains a precise description of this solution.

Wheras so far, we expressed the solution in a shared-memory model, it may be implemented distributed and fault tolerant using the Read-Write register emulation due to Attiya et al. [3]. In the body of the paper, we first describe our solution to SpSn using shared registers for abstraction (Section 3). This requires pre-allocating registers per client, hence the solution is not adaptive. We then "open" the shared register emulation and derive an *adaptive* solution (Section 4).

*The Dynamic Reconfiguration Problem.* We now discuss how we use the above solution SpSn in solving the *Dynamic Reconfiguration* problem. In this problem there is an initial configuration of *servers* known to all clients. We say that clients are initially *subscribed* to this initial configuration. In a one-shot Dynamic Reconfiguration problem, every client process in a subset *players* $\subseteq$ *clients* proposes one configuration-change from $P$. (We will later discuss the long-lived Dynamic Reconfiguration problem.) The goal is for all *players* to eventually subscribe to a common, final configuration encompassing all the proposals. Recall that a set of proposals uniquely defines a set of *servers*, hence we focus on converging on the set of proposals.

It should be understood that although there is no a priori bound on the number of steps taken until convergence, any solution must, at some point, allow a client to subscribe to a new configuration. However, this may not necessarily be a final subscription, because the set *players* is not a priori known, and proposals may continue arriving. Hence, even after it subscribes to a new configuration, a client must continue observing other proposals written into its latest subscribed configuration, and potentially subscribe to a newer configurations. Our problem definition mandates that after all proposals have arrived, all *players*, provided they take enough steps, will subscribe to a final configuration that will not change. The clients themselves may not know that this is the final configuration (namely, the set *players* of participating clients is unknown to clients).

We now return to discuss long-lived Dynamic Reconfiguration. In this problem, clients, over time, are not restricted to request just one change. We can reduce Dynamic Reconfiguration into the problem of one shot by conceptualizing a new change request by a client as a new client. Obviously, that new virtual client can start at the configuration that the old virtual client ended.

If clients were able to access the initial configuration forever, the Dynamic Reconfiguration problem would not be hard to solve. Clients would simply repeatedly collect proposals written to the initial configuration and output their union. In our problem, once a client subscribes to some configuration $S$, it 'expires' previous configurations in the following sense: Every configuration $S'$, where $S' \subseteq S$, may stop receiving new change proposals. (How they might "know" that they expired is of no concern here.) This is what makes the problem useful: Clients better not diverge into disjoint configurations, because there would be no way for them to find out about each other and converge back.

Having stated the problem, we can easily see how to solve it using SpSn. Every client participates in implementing SpSn using the set of servers in the initial configuration. The client provides its input proposal to SpSn. While solving SpSn in the initial configuration it accumulates sets into its $Y$. These sets might have been subscribed to by other processors. Hence it now solves SpSn in each one of them. There are two ways to do it, one akin to depth first, and one to breadth first. We comment on the latter in the conclusions. In the former, the client solves SpSn in each of the speculated configurations in its $Y$ set, one by one. The output from one SpSn is the input to the next. It does this until its input to SpSn is the same as the output from it. Only then it subscribes to that configuration.

*Garbage Collection.* We intentionally formulated our dynamic problem without modeling failures, focusing only on the necessary ingredients to guarantee that information can be passed from one configuration to the next. As a practical matter, it is worth noting that since we expire old configurations, we may garbage collect their resources and not have to rely on their availability. What will a client do if it cannot perform SpSn in a configuration $S$ which it is subscribed to? We stipulate that the client can be notified by an auxiliary mechanism that a new configuration subscription caused $S$ to expire. Note that this is a very weak assumption, it only provides a client with eventual expiration notification on a configuration $S$ which it already subscribed to. Relying on an external 'oracle' notifications after old configurations are garbage collected is inherent in dynamic systems, see e.g., [2, 9].

*Application.* We demonstrate a use-case of consensus-free Dynamic Reconfiguration, a dynamically reconfigurable store. A single-register store is built by interjecting reads and writes of the register during Dynamic Reconfiguration, and likewise observing configuration information during normal Read/Write operation. During reconfiguration, a client reads the register within every configuration in $Y$ and writes it into to the output configuration $S$. Within a Write operation, a client starts at the latest subscribed configuration and performs write–then–SpSn. It repeats this for every speculated configuration in $Y$. A Read starts with the latest subscribed configuration, calls SpSn and then iterates within every configuration in $Y$ doing SpSn–then–read. Correctness intuitively stems from the fact that in every configuration in which a Write is performed, either a Read observes the value, or the written value is first copied to a newer configuration. Section 6 contains a brief description of dynamic store algorithm and a correctness sketch.

*Organization.* The remainder of the paper is organized as follows. We comment on related works in Section 1.1. A formal execution model is provided in Section 2. The solution is laid out in two parts. First, in Section 3 we solve SpSn Read-Write. Then we provide a distributed SpSn protocol in Section 4. We use SpSn as building block to solve the Dynamic Reconfiguration problem in Section 5. We briefly outline the design of an elastic Read-Write store utilizing SpSn in Section 6. We conclude and discuss future work in Section 7.

## 1.1   Related Work

Much of our modularity owes to two prior celebrated results, the Read-Write register emulation of Attiyah, Bar-Noy and Dolev (ABD) [3], and the COMMIT-ADOPT protocol of Gafni et al. [6].

Our story begins with the ABD emulation which provides an atomic Read-Write service over a fixed collection of $2F + 1$ servers, $F$ of which may become unavailable. In a nutshell, the emulation is built of two communication phases. One is used for querying about the currently stored value and its timestamp. The second one is used for updating the stored value and its timestamp. Each phase employs a majority-exchange, guaranteeing intersection with past phases in at least one server. Our SpSn emulation is first presented using Read-Write registers within each configuration as building block for modularity. We then leverage the ABD fault-tolerant emulation within each fixed configuration to derive a message-passing protocol.

To make the ABD emulation *elastic*, the pioneering work of RAMBO integrated a configuration consensus service to facilitate reconfiguration; the first RAMBO works operated the configuration service separately from the emulation [7,9], and later, it became intertwined with the register emulation itself [4]. That work opened the formal treatment and definition of elastic problems.

SpSn identifies the crux of a reconfiguration task which is embedded in such elastic solutions. Indeed, a degenerate form of SpSn occurs in any dynamic system which employs consensus for configuration such as RAMBO [9]. Here, every client is handed a global sequence of configurations. Each prefix of the sequence could be reduced to an SpSn output by "speculating" every prefix of the sequence. Consensus-based reconfiguration is parsimonious in the number of configuration-changes, but relies on the strength of consensus. Our interest is in consensus-less elasticity.

The most relevant prior work is DynaStore [2,11], a previously known consensus-free dynamic store. The complexity of DynaStore's SpSn is an exponential number of configurations. This can be easily seen as follows. A client in DynaStore starts with the last known configuration and participates in implementing with the servers in this configuration a new primitive named *Weak Snapshot*. Weak Snapshot returns to every client a collection of proposals, with one common proposal included in all collections, which are otherwise otherwise unconstrained. With $n$ proposals, there are $2^{(n-1)}$ possible such collections, which DynaStore clients traverse in order to converge on a final configuration.

There are other differences between SpSn and DynaStore along several dimensions.

- Relying on the strong foundations of atomic Read-Write registers and COMMIT-ADOPT, we provide a fairly succinct and modular solution, which is described in less than 20 LOC. Although elegance is an elusive property, we feel that a deductive re-visit is warranted given the importance of the DynaStore contribution.
- DynaStore provides reconfigurable atomic Read-Write storage. We provide a modular approach which separates reconfiguration as a building block by itself.

More generally, dynamic storage is a fundamental service which received tremendous attention in both theory and practice, beyond the scope we can cover here. We refer the reader to two recent surveys which may shed light into this arena: A tutorial on foundations is given in [1], and a more broad survey which covers both theory and practice is provided in [10].

## 2    Problem Model

The introduction already introduces the participants: A set *clients* of client-processes and a set *servers* of server-processes, and a subset *players* ⊆ *clients* participating in solving the SpSn tasks and in Dynamic Reconfiguration. We proceed to formally indicate the execution paradigm and the interaction model among participants.

We consider two coordination models. In one, processes use shared atomic single-writer multi-reader (SWMR) Read-Write registers. Each register $r$ provides two operations, $r$.read and $r$.write. Each process may invoke one operation on any register and wait for it to return. There is no a priori bound on operation execution times nor on processing speeds of processes. That is, the system is asynchronous. An execution may interleave operations by different clients on registers. For every execution, there exists an equivalent sequential execution in which read and write operations return the same results as the real execution, and furthermore, the sequential execution respects real-time ordering between non-overlapping operations in the real execution. That is, every execution is *linearizable*. For a formal treatment of atomic registers, executions, execution equivalence and linearizability, we refer the reader to the classic literature [12].

Our second coordination model uses messages for communication between client-processes and server-processes. There is no a priori bound on message transfer times between clients, but it is guaranteed that message origins are authentic and that messages between live processes arrive in tact. That is, the system employs the standard asynchronous message-passing model [12].

*Configurations.* A *configuration* is expressed in one of two interchangeable forms. One is simply as a subset $S \subseteq servers$. The other is as a *change-set* $S \subseteq \{+s, -s\}_{s \in servers}$. The latter form reduces to a subset by subtracting all the servers $s$ included in $-s$ form, from those in $+s$ form.

*Availability and Garbage Collection.* In order to capture system elasticity, we model configurations as being either *Active* or *Expired*. In the shared-memory model, an Active configuration provides clients with access to atomic Read-Write registers belonging to the configuration. When a client tries to write a register of an expired configuration, the environment throws an exception indicating that the configuration is expired, and provides the cause of its expiration. In the message-passing model, an Active configuration has a majority of servers available and responsive to client messages. An Expired configuration in the message-passing model is the same as a shared-memory one, and notifies clients that attempt to access it about its expiration through an exception.

The set of Active configurations is determined as follows. Initially, the system starts with an a priori fixed Active configuration $C_0$. Whenever SpSn returns $Y$ to some client, every configuration $C \in Y$ becomes Active.

At any moment, every participating client has a single configuration which it is *subscribed* to. Clients start by default subscribed to $C_0$. During an execution, a client may adopt a configuration and subscribe to it. This may occur an unbounded number of times. If a client crashes, we proforma regard it as if the client remains subscribed to the last configuration is was subscribed to before the crash; this has no effect on our problem specification or solution.

To allow garbage collection, when a client subscribes to a configuration $S$, the subscription to $S$ causes every configuration $S'$ such that $S' \subseteq S$ to become *Expired*.

## 3   SpSn Read-Write Solution

This section provides a solution for the SpSn problem defined in the Introduction. The procedure C.SpSn($I_i$) in Algorithm 1 captures the actions of a client-process $p_i$ whose input is $I_i$.

The solution builds around a two-*step* protocol which is repeatedly invoked. The protocol bears similarity to the COMMIT-ADOPT procedure of Gafni [6]. For each client $p_i$ and for each internal *phase* counter $k = 1, 2, ...$, the implementation uses two SWMR shared atomic registers, $I_i(k, 1)$ and $I_i(k, 2)$. In phase $k$, at the first step, a client $p_i$ first writes its proposal to $I_i(k, 1)$ and then collects all written $I_j(k, 1)$ values. If all the values it observes are identical, in the second step it writes to $I_i(k, 2)$ a *commit-proposal* (with a commit-bit set) with this value. Otherwise, it proposes as non-commit a union of all values it observed in the first step. It then collects all written $I_j(k, 2)$ values. Every commit-proposal is kept in $Y_i$.

If any non-commit proposal $I_j(k, 2)$ was collected, then another phase is started. In the next phase, the initial proposal is the union of all the $I_j(k, 2)$ values. Otherwise, if all the $I_j(k, 2)$ values are commit proposals (a fortiori, they are all identical), then SpSn returns this value as $Q_i$, along with the set $Y_i$. At this point, $Y_i$ contains all commit values which were accumulated in preceding phases.

We remind that the formulation of SpSn in shared-memory is for pedagogical purposes. Section 4 gives a message passing implementation which is also *adaptive* and does not require prior knowledge of the client-set.

---

**Algorithm 1.** $C.SpSn$ protocol at process $p_i$

```
 1: local variables:
 2:      proposal, collect, commit, w
 3:      Y_i, initially ∅
 4:
 5: procedure C.SpSn(I_i)
 6:
 7:      proposal ← I_i
 8:      for k = 1, 2, 3, ... do
 9:                                                        ▷ first phase
10:          commit ← true, collect ← ∅
11:          I_i(k, 1).write(proposal)
12:          for every client p_j do
13:              w ← I_j(k, 1).read
14:              if w ≠ ∅ and w ≠ proposal then
15:                  collect ← collect ∪ w, commit ← false
16:                                                        ▷ second phase
17:          I_i(k, 2).write(⟨commit, collect⟩)
18:          for every client p_j do
19:              ⟨w.commit, w.set⟩ ← I_j(k, 2).read
20:              if w.commit ≠ true then
21:                  commit ← false
22:              if w.commit == true then
23:                  Y_i ← Y_i ∪ w.set
24:              proposal ← proposal ∪ w.set
25:
26:          if commit == true then
27:              return proposal, Y_i
```

---

## Correctness of SpSn RW Solution

**Lemma 1.** *In each phase $k$ of the SpSn procedure, if any two commit values are written to $I_i(k, 2)$, $I_j(k, 2)$ (i.e., both have the commit bit set), then they are the same. Furthermore, the value must be the first value whose write in the first step of phase $k$ has completed.*

*Proof.* Fix some $k$, and let $p_f$ be the client whose write into $I_f(k, 1)$ is the first to complete. Let $p_i$ be any client writing a commit value to $I_i(k, 2)$. Therefore, the collect of all $I_j(k, 1)$ by $p_i$ returned identical values. Furthermore, by assumption, $p_i$'s read of $I_f(k, 1)$ must have returned the value written by $p_f$. Therefore, $p_i$'s unanimous collect value must be $I_f(k, 1)$, and the lemma is proved.

**Lemma 2.** *Procedure SpSn in Algorithm 1 maintains the properties listed under the SpSn problem definition in the Introduction.*

*Proof.* Property 1 of SpSn in the Introduction has two components, Validity and Containment. The Validity property that $I_i \subseteq Q_i$ immediately follows from the fact that a process $p_i$ first writes its own proposal into $I_i(k, 1)$ and then collects all $I_j(k, 1)$.

To prove Containment, note that by Lemma 1, every phase inside SpSn has a unique commit value (if any). Denote the phase $k$ commit-value by $C_k$. By Lemma 1, every collect of $I_j(k, 1)$ in phase $k$ must see $C_k$. Consequently, all values proposed in all higher phases must contain $C_k$. It follows that for $k' > k$, if there exist a commit value $C_{k'}$ at phase $k'$, then $C_{k'} \supseteq C_k$, and Containment follows.

We now prove property 2, the Speculation component of SpSn. We consider two clients $p_i$ and $p_{i'}$, and assume that $p_i$ returns at phase $k$ from SpSn with return value $Q_i$, and $p_{i'}$ returns $Q_{i'}$ at a higher phase $k' > k$. By Containment, $Q_i \subseteq Q_{i'}$. We want to prove that $Q_i \in Y_{i'}$. Indeed, at the second step of phase $k$, both $p_i$ and $p_{i'}$ collect the first value whose write into $I_j(k, 2)$ completed. By assumption, $p_i$ collects only the $(commit, Q_i)$ value, hence, $p_{i'}$ must see this commit-value and insert it to $Y_{i'}$ as needed.

## Complexity of SpSn RW Solution

Our implementation of SpSn guarantees a return value $Y$ with a **linear** number of configurations. This stems from the fact that only commit configurations are inserted into $Y$, and by Lemma 2, these configurations are related by containment, hence at most linear in the size of the set of proposals.

In terms of the number of primitive operations, $C.SpSn()$ contains multiple rounds of write-collect. More specifically, within a single invocation of $C.SpSn()$, the number of phases may be $n$, where $n$ is the number of proposals. The number of individual write/read operations is $O(m * n)$, where $m$ is the number of participating processes. In the message-passing implementation below ( Section 4), the factor $m$ is absorbed into the size of messages.

## 4   SpSn Message-Passing Solution

There exists a straight-forward message-passing emulation of the $C.SpSn$ RW solution above (Algorithm 1): Use an ABD SWMR emulation [3] by the servers-set $C$ per each abstract register $I_i(k, step)$. Naively implemented, every write to each SWMR register incurs one exchange between the single-writer, the client $p_i$, and servers in $C$, and every read incurs two exchanges. Each phase in the RW solution performs two steps, each does one write and $m$ reads. Hence, the naive message-passing emulation takes $2 \times (2m + 1)$ majority-exchanges with $C$.

If we "open" the ABD emulation, we can easily see that there is no reason to iterate through the $m$ registers one at a time. Instead, we can utilize two exchanges to bulk-read all registers. The message size will be proportional to the actual number of participants, which is $m$ at worst, but in any real execution it may be much smaller than $m$. We can further optimize and coalesce some exchanges from different SpSn steps. Specifically, as evident from the proof of Lemma 1, it suffices for the registers to maintain regular semantics [8], not necessarily atomic. Therefore, we can omit the second exchange, the 'write-back', from read operations. The SpSn message-passing protocol resulting from all these improvements is depicted in Algorithm 2. It has a total of four exchanges between a client $p_i$ and servers in $C$. More importantly, this protocol is *adaptive*, i.e., it removes the requirement to a priori know $m$.

With respect to correctness, because this message passing protocol simply "opens" the high-level shared-object abstractions, its correctness follows directly from the correctness of Algorithm 1.

## 5   Dynamic Reconfiguration Using SpSn

In this section, we use SpSn to manage configuration changes, which are expressed as a set of changes.

The core of procedure Propose($I_i$) is very simple: Client process $p_i$ invokes it with input $I_i$. It starts at the latest subscribed configuration. Propose() invokes SpSn, adopts the new configuration change $Q_i$, and repeats in every speculated configuration[1] $Y_i$. This continues until the proposed configuration is the same as the output from SpSn. Then the client subscribes to it.

The only issue that somewhat compounds the treatment is a possible expiration of configurations. There are two ways in which a client may learn that its configuration subscription has been expired. The first is if an attempted SpSn fails. Recall that in our probem model (Section 2), we model this case as an exception raised during execution, indicating as cause a subscription of a new configuration that affected the expiration (line 4, Algorithm 3).

The second way is when a client $p_i$ encounters a proposal by a client $p_j$ which started Propose() with a newer configuration subscription. We model this case by annotating each proposal $I_i$ at the beginning of Propose (line 8, Algorithm 3) with the starting configuration subscription, and denote it $I_i.start$. If $p_i$ ever collects a proposal $I_j$ whose $I_j.start$ indicates a later configuration subscription than $I_i.start$, then $p_i$ starts over at $I_j.start$.

### Correctness of Dynamic Reconfiguration Protocol

The key insight driving the Dynamic Reconfiguration solution to convergence is that every configuration $C$ has a unique successor that is guaranteed to appear in the output of every C.SpSn. We name the configuration *seed*, and define it formally as follows. Define $seed(C)$ as the commit configuration $I_j(k, 2)$ returned from C.SpSn as $Q_j$, whose phase $k$ is the lowest for all returned $Q_j$. Inductively, define $seed^1(C) := seed(C)$, and $seed^{(i+1)}(C) := seed(seed^i(C))$. Intuitively, all that matters are seed configurations, since clients cannot skip them. The rest are

---

**Algorithm 2.** $C.SpSn$ message-passing protocol for client $p_i$ and server $q \in C$

1: server $q \in C$ local variables:
2:    | $I(process, phase, step) \rightarrow value$, relation-map, initially empty
3:
4: client $p_i$ local variables:
5:    | $proposal, collect, commit, w$
6:    | $Y_i$, initially $\emptyset$
7:
8: **procedure** SPSN($I_i$)
9:    | client $p_i$:
10:    |                                                                     ▷ initialization
11:    |      $proposal \leftarrow I_i$
12:    |      **for** $k = 1, 2, 3, \ldots$ **do**
13:    |                                                          ▷ first phase
14:    |          $commit \leftarrow true$, $collect \leftarrow \emptyset$
15:    |          send $(C, write, p_i, k, 1, proposal)$ to all servers in $C$
16:    |          wait for acknowledgments from a majority of $C$
17:    |          send $(C, read, p_i, k, 1)$ to all servers in $C$
18:    |          **for** each reply $w$ **do**
19:    |              **if** $w \neq \emptyset$ and $w \neq proposal$ **then**
20:    |                 $collect \leftarrow collect \cup w$, $commit \leftarrow false$
21:    |                                           ▷ second phase
22:    |          send $(C, write, p_i, k, 2, \langle commit, collect \rangle)$ to all servers in $C$
23:    |          wait for acknowledgments from a majority of $C$
24:    |          send $(C, read, p_i, k, 2)$ to all servers in $C$
25:    |          **for** each reply $\langle w.commit, w.set \rangle$ **do**
26:    |              **if** $w.commit \neq true$ **then**
27:    |                 $commit \leftarrow false$
28:    |              **if** $w.commit == true$ **then**
29:    |                 $Y_i \leftarrow Y_i \cup w.set$
30:    |              $proposal \leftarrow proposal \cup w.set$
31:
32:    |          **if** $commit == true$ **then**
33:    |              return $proposal, Y_i$
34:
35:    | server $q$, on receipt of $(C, write, p_j, k, step, value)$:
36:    |      insert a relation $(p_i, k, step) \rightarrow value$ into $I$
37:    |      send back acknowledgment to $p_j$
38:
39:    | server, on receipt of $(C, read, p_j, k, step)$:
40:    |      send back all non-empty $(\cdot, k, step)$ values of $I$
41:

---

mere inefficiencies, namely, speculated configurations traversed unnecessarily by clients due to the lack of consensus. This is the price of asynchrony.

**Algorithm 3.** Reconfiguration protocol at client $p_i$

1: local variables:
2: | *speculated, done, proposal*
3:
4: on exception "*current configuration subscription expired by new configuration $C$*":
5: | subscribe to $C$ and start Propose over
6:
7: **procedure** Propose($I_i$)
8: | $I_i.start \leftarrow$ current configuration subscription
9: | *speculated* $\leftarrow \{I_i.start\}$, *done* $\leftarrow \emptyset$, *proposal* $\leftarrow I_i$
10: | **for** $U \in speculated \setminus done$), in increasing containment order **do**
11: | | $(Q_i, Y_i) \leftarrow U.SpSn(proposal)$
12: | | *done* $\leftarrow done \cup \{U\}$
13: | | *proposal* $\leftarrow Q_i$
14: | | **if** $\max_{I_j \in proposal} I_j.start$ is later than current subscription **then**
15: | | | subscribe to $\max_{I_j \in proposal} I_j.start$ and start Propose over
16: | | *speculated* $\leftarrow speculated \cup Y_i$
17: | subscribe to *proposal* and return it

**Theorem 1.** *If every live client $p_i$ proposes one change in $Propose(I_i)$, and then forever invokes Propose with an empty change, then eventually there is a time at which all living clients subscribe to the same configuration.*

*Proof.* Let $U$ be a seed-configuration, and let $p_i$ invoke $U.SpSn$ inside Propose() and return $(Q_i, Y_i)$. It follows immediately from property 2 of SpSn (see Introduction) that $seed(U) \in Y_i$. Therefore, $p_i$ invokes SpSn in $seed(U)$, and inductively in every $seed^i(U)$. Once new proposals cease to arrive, then starting from any seed configuration a client is subscribed to, the client will traverse all the seed configurations to the end of the succession.

## Complexity of Dynamic Reconfiguration Solution

The number of speculated configurations in $Y_i$ output from C.SpSn to all clients is linear in the number of proposals, since they are related by Containment. Things are not so simple when we consider the $Y_j$ sets returned by SpSn's in different configurations. Invoking SpSn in two different configurations, say $C.SpSn$ and $C'.SpSn$, might return $C.Y_j$ and $C'.Y_j$ containing items which are not related by containment. However, by negation, for every pair of speculations which are not related by containment, one must contain an input injected in a later subscription than the other. Hence, when a client encounters the later speculation (say $D$), it causes the client to subscribe to $D$ and restart Propose in it. Therefore, the configurations actually traversed by clients (not the total ones ever held inside *speculated*) are ordered by containment. It follows that clients traverse in total a linear number of configurations in the number of different proposed changed.

# 6    Application: Read-Write Store

In this section we outline the design of a dynamic service, an elastic Read-Write store, built using Dynamic Reconfiguration. This service emulates a single, atomic multiple-writer multi-reader (MWMR) Read-Write register in our dynamic execution model. That is, in a dynamic store, our set *client* of client processes access a shared store service through the set *servers* of servers. The availability of servers for responding to Write and Read requests is governed by the client subscriptions to configurations. As in the Dynamic Reconfiguration problem, Propose() requests may occur independently and concurrently with Read and Write requests. The solution consists of three components:

- Inside Propose(), following every $U.SpSn$ a client needs to read the value stored at configuration $U$. At the end of Propose, the client writes the latest value with its original timestamp to the final configuration before it subscribes to it.
- To write a new value, a client first writes it into its current subscription configuration, and then invokes an empty Propose() in order to transfer the value into any new configuration subscription.
- To read the latest value, a client first invokes an empty Propose() and then returns the value it finishes with.

We now give the key insight for correctness. The key idea is that writing new information into subscription-configurations is done write-then-SpSn, while information gets transferred from one seed-configuration to the next by doing SpSn-then-read in each configuration. Consider a client $p_i$ traversing through configuration $C$. If there is any write done in $C$, either the writer finished before the read, hence the read will see it. Or the writer's SpSn starts after the the reader's SpSn, hence see any reconfiguration proposal by the client. Finally, for any client not traversing through configuration $C$, there must exist some client which transferred information from $C$ to a later configuration.

# 7    Conclusions

The germination of this paper is instructive. Being deeply invested in the idea that "behind any non-trivial distributed question there is a simple task," we asked ourselves what is the simple task behind the question in [2,11]. We identified the task Speculating Snapshots (SpSn), and showed how previous solutions to the problem of reconfiguration solved the task, how we can solve the task in various models, and how to build a dynamic reconfiguration around it. Our parsimonious solution to the SpSn task in read-write wait-free drives a reconfiguration scheme linear in the number of intermediate configurations used, which is optimal. The number of operations may be subject to further optimization, in particular, using a BFS-like intermingling of SpSn's; this is left open for future work.

The problem tackled in this paper is fundamental to the dynamic nature of distributed systems. In distributed, mission critical settings, it is reasonable to assume that these dynamic changes occur slowly and allow to carefully migrate information in a changing system. This is the model assumed here. We already showed utility with a straw-man dynamic store design, and we envision that other dynamic services can be built equally easily.

More generally, in our solution to Speculating Snapshots (SpSn), we introduced a slight modification of Commit-Adopt. We expect that this new technique may become useful in other contexts.

Our work leaves open the question of operation complexity. Likewise, quantifying the relationship between real world scenarios and our slowly-changing fault model may be an interesting, practical challenge. Finally, we hope to employ this approach (identifying what is the **task** behind a problem) in other problems, as this experience shows promise.

**Acknowledgments.** We are thankful to Idit Keidar, Leslie Lamport and Alex Speigelman for helpful discussions. Part of this work was done when the first author visited MIT supported by National Science Foundation: CCF-1217921,CCF-1301926, and U.S. Department of Energy: DE-SC0008923.

# References

1. Aguilera, M., Keidar, I., Martin, J.-P., Shraer, A.: Reconfiguring replicated atomic storage: A tutorial. Bulletin of the EATCS **102**, 84–108 (2010)
2. Aguilera, M.K., Keidar, I., Malkhi, D., Shraer, A.: Dynamic atomic storage without consensus. J. ACM **58**(2), 7:1–7:32 (2011)
3. Attiya, H., Bar-Noy, A., Dolev, D.: Sharing memory robustly in message-passing systems. J. ACM **42**(1), 124–142 (1995)
4. Chockler, G., Gilbert, S., Gramoli, V., Musial, P.M., Shvartsman, A.A.: Reconfigurable distributed storage for dynamic networks. J. Parallel Distrib. Comput. **69**(1), 100–116 (2009)
5. Fischer, M.J., Lynch, N.A., Paterson, M.S.: Impossibility of distributed consensus with one faulty process. J. ACM **32**(2), 374–382 (1985)
6. Gafni, E.: Round-by-round fault detectors (extended abstract): unifying synchrony and asynchrony. In: Proceedings of the Seventeenth Annual ACM Symposium on Principles of Distributed Computing. PODC 1998, pp. 143–152. ACM, New York (1998)
7. Gilbert, S., Lynch, N., Shvartsman, A.: RAMBO II: Rapidly reconfigurable atomic memory for dynamic networks. In: Proceedings of International Conference on Dependable Systems and Networks, pp. 259–268 (2003)
8. Lamport, L.: How to make a multiprocessor computer that correctly executes multiprocess programs. IEEE Trans. Comput. **28**(9), 690–691 (1979)
9. Lynch, N.A., Shvartsman, A.A.: RAMBO: a reconfigurable atomic memory service for dynamic networks. In: Proceedings of the 16th International Conference on Distributed Computing. DISC 2002, pp. 173–190. Springer-Verlag, London (2002)

10. Musial, P., Nicolaou, N., Shvartsman, A.A.: Implementing distributed shared memory for dynamic networks. Commun. ACM **57**(6), 88–98 (2014)
11. Shraer, A., Martin, J.-P., Malkhi, D., Keidar, I.: Data-centric reconfiguration with network-attached disks. In: Proceedings of the 4th International Workshop on Large Scale Distributed Systems and Middleware. LADIS 2010, pp. 22–26. ACM, New York (2010)
12. Welch, J.L., Attiya, H.: Distributed Computing: Fundamentals, Simulations and Advanced Topics. McGraw-Hill Inc., Hightstown (1998)

# SmartMerge: A New Approach to Reconfiguration for Atomic Storage

Leander Jehl[1][(✉)], Roman Vitenberg[2], and Hein Meling[1]

[1] Department of Electrical Engineering and Computer Science,
University of Stavanger, Stavanger, Norway
`leander.jehl@uis.no`
[2] Department of Informatics, University of Oslo, Oslo, Norway

**Abstract.** In this paper, we study reconfiguration mechanisms for atomic storage systems. We observe that the state of the art approach for reconfiguration in an asynchronous environment has several disadvantages compared to the classical consensus-based approach, which requires eventual synchrony. For example, an unfortunate combination of remove operations may lead to a configuration with too few or even no processes. We present SmartMerge, a novel approach that provides most of the benefits of consensus-based reconfiguration, yet can be implemented in a fully asynchronous system. SmartMerge utilizes a merge function to aptly combine concurrently issued changes to both the set of processes and the quorum system of the storage. The approach is general and can use any suitable function.

In addition to the expressive reconfiguration policies enabled by SmartMerge, our atomic storage also has improved efficiency: Every reconfiguration imposes only a constant overhead on concurrent read and write operations.

**Keywords:** Atomic storage · Reconfiguration · Asynchronous system

## 1 Introduction

In the age of cloud computing, an abundance of compute resources with different capabilities are available at data centers across the globe. These data centers deploy a variety of services replicated for fault-tolerance. It is typical for the administrators of the data center to update both the composition of machines in the data center and the composition of replicas running a service, because of the need to regularly upgrade the machines, replace failed components, and accommodate for changes in the service load. Such reconfiguration operations are rather frequent in practice as evident, e.g., from the traces of a Google data center [1].

One of the main challenges of supporting reconfiguration is to ensure consistency when multiple users submit concurrent requests. A monitoring component can be tracking software and hardware failures, upgrades, and load of queries and updates to the replicas. Acting upon this information, it may be issuing requests

© Springer-Verlag Berlin Heidelberg 2015
Y. Moses (Ed.): DISC 2015, LNCS 9363, pp. 154–169, 2015.
DOI: 10.1007/978-3-662-48653-5_11

autonomously, without human intervention [2]. It is envisioned that many such components may be deployed in a large-scale data center at the same time, which may result in multiple concurrent uncoordinated and even conflicting requests for reconfiguration.

The traditional approach to resolve this situation is to use consensus to choose one of the proposed configurations, see e.g. [3]. The proposal for a new configuration in this scheme would include a desired set of replicas along with a quorum system to use. The main disadvantage of this consensus-based approach is that its liveness is impossible to guarantee in asynchronous systems characteristic of large-scale data centers.

In order to address this issue, an alternative conceptual approach proposed in the DynaStore system [4] is to provide the users with an interface to request incremental additions or removal of processes. In case of commutative concurrent requests, the system directly combines the changes instead of choosing just one of them. Furthermore, since changes commute, they do not need to be ordered. This allows the approach to be implemented in a fully asynchronous system, without relying on eventual synchrony or leader election to solve consensus. Henceforward we refer to this conceptual approach as *DirectCombine*.

Another advantage of DirectCombine over the consensus-based approach is that non-conflicting changes can be proposed concurrently. For example, two changes, one removing replica $a$ and one replacing replica $b$ with $e$, can be issued concurrently by different processes and are both realized in the resulting configuration. Using the consensus-based approach, only one of these requests would be chosen and applied.

However, the fact that all proposed changes are applied can also lead to problems. If two proposed reconfigurations are trying to remove a different replica each, applying both removals may incidentally result in a configuration with a small number of replicas and thus, low fault-tolerance. In the extreme case, a combination of several removals may result in an empty configuration, in which no further operations can be performed.

It might be preferable for a system to abort the reconfiguration process than to switch to such a configuration. In general, configurations with too few or too many processes, or with an unfavorable distribution of processes across data centers can be *unacceptable* in practice, because of low fault tolerance, high network latencies, or administrative restrictions. Using the consensus-based approach, the system can only be reconfigured to an unacceptable configuration, if such a configuration was proposed. Thus it is easy to avoid these configurations.

Another disadvantage of the automatic combination of different reconfiguration requests in DirectCombine is the need to autonomously recompute the quorum system on the fly. While such dynamic computation is simple for majority quorums, it may not be feasible in the general case or in real-world situations. In heterogeneous systems spanning over multiple data centers and a complex network topology, quorum systems may have topology-induced structure. Furthermore, adjusting weights and the balance between read and write quorums

**Table 1.** Comparison of reconfiguration approaches

|  | Avoids unacceptable configurations? | Can combine multiple proposals? | Can easily switch quorum system? | Asynchronous system |
|---|---|---|---|---|
| Consensus-based | yes | no | yes | no |
| DirectCombine | no | yes | no | yes |
| SmartMerge | yes | yes | yes | yes |

can be the key to meeting service level agreements under dynamic load patterns. It is therefore undesirable to limit these systems to majority quorums.

In this paper we present a novel approach called SmartMerge. In the core of the approach lies a SmartMerge function that intelligently combines different, concurrently issued reconfiguration requests. The approach based on such a function has several advantages:

**Generalized interface for the reconfiguration operation,** that instead of just adding and removing one specific process can operate with rules and policies to change the number of replicas, add several replicas as a group, set weights or priorities to individual potential replicas, or introduce any correlation between replicas. Such policies allow the SmartMerge function to produce meaningful resulting configurations in the case of concurrent divergent requests, or to configure the set of replicas automatically in presence of failures.

**Easy switching between different quorum systems:** For example, a replication scheme can employ write-all read-one quorums, to minimize the latency of parallel reads, while switching to majority quorums before upgrades are performed, or whenever failures and temporary outages are expected.

**Definition and avoidance of unacceptable configurations** as part of the policy: In the simplest case, it is possible to define the minimum number of replicas and maintain it across all reconfigurations and failures.

Similarly to DirectCombine, SmartMerge can be implemented in an asynchronous system. We summarize the pros and cons of the three approaches in Table 1.

The SmartMerge function can be tailored to the specifics of the service, replication scheme, data center and its topology, and many additional factors. We show a concrete example of such a function in Section 2, in order to illustrate the aforementioned features of the approach.

We apply our approach to reconfiguration of atomic storage. Atomic storage is a key problem in distributed systems that can be implemented in an asynchronous system [5]. Both the consensus-based approach [3] and DirectCombine [4] have been applied to this problem.

The main contribution of this work is that we show how SmartMerge can be implemented for atomic storage in an asynchronous system. This is done in a generic way parametrized by an externally defined SmartMerge function, such as the one presented in Section 2.

The key idea behind our implementation is as follows: Under the assumption that the SmartMerge function is commutative, associative, and idempotent, it induces a lattice of all possible reconfiguration requests. If finitely manyconcurrent requests are proposed, we ensure that eventually every process will adopt the merge (i.e., a lattice join) of all these competing requests as its configuration.

To implement wait-free reads and writes, these operations cannot wait until a reconfiguration has completed. A common solution to this problem is to read from or write to the old, the new and all possible intermediate configurations, while reconfigurations are ongoing. However, before reaching the lattice element that is the join of all concurrent requests, the service can intermediately adopt a join of any subset of these requests. The number of such joins in the lattice is exponential with the number of competing requests. To avoid contacting processes in all these configurations during read and write operations, we submit proposed requests to lattice agreement, which returns elements from a totally ordered subset of the lattice, including the greatest element. We use only elements, that were returned by lattice agreement as intermediate configurations. The number of different configurations returned by lattice agreement during an execution is at most the number of changes proposed during this execution, making it feasible to read from or write to all intermediate configurations. Additionally, if one of these configurations is adopted by the service, operations need no longer read from or write to elements smaller than this configuration.

To read a value from the register while changes are applied to the configuration, we read the register values stored in all configurations returned by lattice agreement and return the most recent one. Similarly, to write a value, we write to all these configurations. Read and write operations do not participate in lattice agreement, but only contact processes in configurations returned by lattice agreement. We show that in an execution where at most $r$ changes are proposed, all read and write operations cumulatively contact processes in at most $r + 1$ different configurations. A single read or write operation contacts the processes in any configuration at most twice. This gives a bound on the latency of read and write operations that is the same as for the consensus-based approach in [3], but a significant improvement compared to DynaStore [4].

## 2    System Model

We assume a possibly infinite set of processes $\Pi$, communicating via asynchronous channels. Each process $\mathbf{p} \in \Pi$ has a unique identifier $\mathbf{p}.id$.

Processes can fail at any time during an execution by stopping to take any actions. We assume that messages are not corrupted and that, if two processes do not fail during an execution, all messages sent between these processes are eventually delivered.

Not all processes in $\Pi$ need to be known a priori. We therefore maintain a finite set of available processes $\mathcal{A} \subset \Pi$. Newly discovered processes are added to

$\mathcal{A}$ by a reconfiguration operation. We also maintain a set $\mathcal{A}_{rm}$ which contains processes that are no longer available and have been removed from $\mathcal{A}$. If two processes disagree whether $\mathbf{p}$ is available, they can use $\mathcal{A}_{rm}$ to determine if one process missed to add $\mathbf{p}$ or the other missed out on removing $\mathbf{p}$. Thus two processes using $\mathcal{A}^1, \mathcal{A}_{rm}^1$ and $\mathcal{A}^2, \mathcal{A}_{rm}^2$ respectively, can combine their knowledge and both switch to using $\mathcal{A} = (\mathcal{A}^1 \backslash \mathcal{A}_{rm}^2) \cup (\mathcal{A}^2 \backslash \mathcal{A}_{rm}^1)$ and $\mathcal{A}_{rm} = \mathcal{A}_{rm}^1 \cup \mathcal{A}_{rm}^2$ instead. While it is impossible to distinguish a faulty process from a slow process in an asynchronous system, recent works have proposed failure detectors that reliably detect all [6] or at least some failures [7], without relying on timing assumptions. The possibility to remove processes from $\mathcal{A}$ allows our service to be used together with a reliable, unreliable or no failure detector.

Only a subset $\mathcal{P} \subset \mathcal{A}$ of the available processes is actually running the service. These are organized in a *service configuration*. A service configuration $c$ is a tuple $(\mathcal{P}_c, \mathcal{WQ}_c, \mathcal{RQ}_c)$, where $\mathcal{P}_c \subset \Pi$ is a finite set of processes, and $\mathcal{WQ}_c$ and $\mathcal{RQ}_c$ are collections of subsets of $\mathcal{P}_c$, called read and write quorums, such that any read quorum from $\mathcal{RQ}_c$ intersects with every write quorum from $\mathcal{WQ}_c$. We write $\mathfrak{C}$ for the domain of all such configurations.

Given the set $\mathcal{A}$ of available processes, the choice of a service configuration is determined by a policy. We model such a policy as a tuple $(srvConf(), info)$, where $srvConf$ is a function $\mathcal{P}_f(\Pi) \to \mathfrak{C}$ that maps any finite subset of $\Pi$ to a service configuration. $info$ is auxiliary information describing how the policy is combined with other policies. We write $\mathcal{PL}$ for the set of all policies $(srvConf(), info)$ that can appear in an execution.

A reconfiguration can both add and remove available processes and propose a new policy. We say that a reconfiguration proposes a *Blueprint* for a service configuration. We express a Blueprint as a tuple $(\mathcal{A}, \mathcal{A}_{rm}, policy)$, with finite sets $\mathcal{A}, \mathcal{A}_{rm} \subset \Pi$ and $policy \in \mathcal{PL}$. We write $\mathfrak{R}$ for all such tuples. Applying $policy.srvConf(\mathcal{A})$ results in a service configuration that includes only available processes and satisfies the rules expressed by $policy$. We say that a Blueprint $r = (\mathcal{A}, \mathcal{A}_{rm}, policy)$ determines the service configuration $c = policy.srvConf(\mathcal{A})$.

*Lattice and Order of Blueprints.* For SmartMerge, we require that the system manager provides a commutative, associative and idempotent function, *join*, to merge policies. These properties are quite intuitive in practice, as it can be seen in the example later in this section. We merge Blueprints by combining $\mathcal{A}$ and $\mathcal{A}_{rm}$ as described above and use *join* to combine the policies. Collectively, this defines a function $merge(\mathfrak{R}, \mathfrak{R}) \to \mathfrak{R}$ that combines Blueprints. We assume an initial element $r_I \in \mathfrak{R}$, such that $\forall r \in \mathfrak{R} : merge(r, r_I) = r$ holds.

Since *join* is commutative, associative and idempotent, these properties also hold for *merge*. A set $\mathfrak{R}$, together with the *merge* function, thus is an algebraic semi-lattice [8]. Again, due to these properties we can write $merge(\{r_1, r_2, ...\})$ instead of $merge(r_1, merge(r_2, ...))$.

This lattice $(\mathfrak{R}, merge)$ is bounded by the initial element $r_I$. In the remainder of this work, we simply write *lattice* instead of bounded semi-lattice. Due to its properties, *merge* defines a partial ordering $\sqsubseteq$ on $\mathfrak{R}$ by the relation $\forall r_1, r_2 \in \mathfrak{R} :$ $r_1 \sqsubseteq r_2 \Leftrightarrow merge(r_1, r_2) = r_2$. We write $r_1 \sqsubset r_2$ for $(r_1 \sqsubseteq r_2 \wedge r_1 \neq r_2)$ and say that $r_2$ is a *greater Blueprint* (as lattice element) than $r_1$ and that $r_1$ is a *smaller Blueprint*. We write $r_1 \not\sqsubseteq r_2$ for the negation of $r_1 \sqsubseteq r_2$. Note that $r_1 \not\sqsubseteq r_2$ is not equivalent to $r_2 \sqsubset r_1$, since $\sqsubseteq$ is only a partial order.

The properties of *merge* imply that for any $r_1, r_2 \in \mathfrak{R}$, $r_1 \sqsubseteq merge(r_1, r_2)$ holds. A process can test whether $r_1 \sqsubseteq r_2$ holds by comparing $r_2$ and $merge(r_1, r_2)$. In our algorithm in Section 4, we use this to compute the minimal or maximal element in a set of comparable Blueprints.

*Lattice Agreement Service GLA.* As mentioned in the introduction, if reconfigurations propose different Blueprints we want to reconfigure to the merge of all proposed Blueprints. We use an external generalized lattice agreement service (GLA) for this. GLA offers an operation **la-propose**$(r)$, that takes a Blueprint $r \in \mathfrak{R}$ as argument and returns another Blueprint $r'$, such that the following properties hold. These properties imply that the merge of all input values is among the returned values.

*Validity.* A returned value is the merge of inputs to **la-propose** operations.
*Monotonicity.* An operation **la-propose**$(r)$ returns $r'$ such that $r \sqsubseteq r'$.
*Comparability.* Any two values returned by **la-propose** are comparable with respect to $\sqsubseteq$.

GLA can be easily implemented using the algorithm specified in [9]. In generalized lattice agreement on a lattice $(\mathfrak{R}, merge, \sqsubseteq)$, processes can receive values $v_i \in \mathfrak{R}$ from clients. The processes then learn a sequence of values $w_0 \sqsubseteq w_1 \sqsubseteq \ldots$ such that validity and comparability hold for learned values. Further, if a value $v_i$ is received at a correct process, every correct process eventually learns a value $w_j$, such that $v_i \sqsubseteq w_j$ holds. The **la-propose**$(r)$ operation can be easily implemented by sending $r$ to all processes running generalized lattice agreement and returning some value $r'$ learned by any of these processes, for which $r \sqsubseteq r'$ holds. The complexity of the algorithm, as presented in [9] adapts to the number of values actually proposed. Thus, if **la-propose** is invoked only $r$ times during an execution, every invocation will return after at most $\mathcal{O}(r)$ steps.

Some works using the consensus-based approach assume an external configuration manager that receives reconfiguration requests and chooses a sequence of configurations (e.g. [3]). Different from these works our GLA can be implemented in an asynchronous system and does not need consensus. However GLA only returns comparable elements without sequence numbers. Thus, if $r$ and $r'$ have been returned by two **la-propose** invocations to process $p$, and $r \sqsubset r'$ holds, it is impossible for $p$ to determine if some other value $\hat{r}$ for which $r \sqsubset \hat{r} \sqsubset r'$ holds, has been returned by another **la-propose** invocation to a different process. We show in this paper that the weaker guarantees of GLA are still sufficient to implement a reconfigurable atomic register.

*Example.* We now give a more detailed example of a merge function, that illustrates the use of policies, easy switching between different quorum systems, and avoidance of unacceptable configurations, which are defined as configurations

**Table 2.** Rules for building a configuration, supported by our example

| Rule | Effect | Rule | Effect |
|------|--------|------|--------|
| $addMan(p)$ | mark $p$ as mandatory | $setSize(n)$ | specify desired size $n$ for $\mathcal{P}$ |
| $remMan(p)$ | mark $p$ as optional | $majority()$ | use majority quorums |
| | | $waro()$ | use write-all-read-one quorums |

with fewer than $k$ processes. In this example, policies are determined by a set of rules, shown in Table 2. One reconfiguration can change several of these rules.

We can use $addMan(p)$ to mark a specific process $p$ as mandatory element of $\mathcal{P}$. Similarly, we can specify a process $p$ as optional using $remMan(p)$. Once marked as optional, a process can no longer be marked as mandatory. The reason for this is explained in Section 3. Additionally, we can specify a desired size for $\mathcal{P}$ using $setSize(n)$. If the number of mandatory processes is fewer than the desired size, the policy function adds additional processes from $\mathcal{A}$. Finally we can use $majority()$ and $waro()$ to specify whether the quorum system should use majority or write-all-read-one (WARO) quorums. For WARO quorums we simply set $\mathcal{WQ}_c = \{\mathcal{P}_c\}$ and $\mathcal{RQ}_c = \{\{\mathbf{p}\}|\mathbf{p} \in \mathcal{P}_c\}$. For majority quorums any subset containing at least a majority of the processes in $\mathcal{P}_c$ forms a write quorum ($\mathcal{WQ}$), while any subset containing at least half the processes is a read quorum ($\mathcal{RQ}$). When the size or quorum system is changed, using $setSize(n)$, or $majority()$ and $waro()$, the policy info has to specify an epoch number that is used in the combination function.

When combining policies, we differentiate between processes explicitly marked as optional, and unmarked processes. Combining two policies, a process explicitly marked as optional in one of the policies retains this marking. Processes marked as mandatory in one of the policies and not explicitly marked as optional remain mandatory. When two policies include different $setSize$ rules or specify different quorum systems we adopt the size and quorum system from the policy with the higher epoch number. If epoch numbers are equal, we choose the larger $size$ and majority quorums, if present, since these choices provide higher fault tolerance.

Using the rules from this example, $|\mathcal{P}| \geq k$ holds as long as $setSize(n)$ with $n < k$ is invoked and there are at least $k$ processes available.

## 3   Problem: Atomic Storage Using Smart Merge

In this section we specify our reconfigurable multi-reader multi-writer atomic register. We assume a set of possible register values $\mathcal{V}$, and a lattice of Blueprints $(\mathfrak{R}, \sqsubseteq, merge)$ with minimal element $r_I$. We provide three operations, **read**, **write** and **reconf**. A **read**() operation returns either a value $v \in \mathcal{V}$ or $\perp \notin \mathcal{V}$. A **write**($v$) operation takes an input $v \in \mathcal{V}$.

We require that **read** and **write** operations are linearizable [10], and that in a sequential execution, every **read** returns the value of the last **write**, or $\perp$ if no **write** occurred before the **read**. This is the standard safety property of atomic registers. The liveness of **read** and **write** depends on the reconfigurations invoked. A reconfiguration changes which processes may fail, but also which processes should invoke operations. We therefore discuss the **reconf** operation, before presenting a common liveness property for all operations.

A **reconf**($r$) operation proposes a Blueprint $r \in \mathfrak{R}$, and returns a value $r' \in \mathfrak{R}$ that determines the service configuration of the register. We say that a Blueprint $r$ is *chosen* before time $t$ in an execution, if $r$ was returned by a **reconf** operation before $t$ in that execution. We say that $r_I$ is chosen by an implicit **reconf** operation, at the beginning of any execution. The following safety properties govern which values may be chosen. These properties and other concepts introduced in this section are defined in the context of a single execution:

*Validity.* A chosen value $r'$ is the merge of input values to **reconf** operations.
*Monotonicity.* If $r'$ is chosen by **reconf**($r$), then $r \sqsubseteq r'$ holds.
*Comparability.* Any two chosen values are comparable, with respect to $\sqsubseteq$.
*Stability.* If $r$ was chosen before the invocation of **reconf**, which returns $r'$, then $r \sqsubseteq r'$ holds.

Validity, monotonicity and comparability are standard requirements for values returned from a lattice (e.g. in lattice agreement [9], [11]). However, to our knowledge we are the first to require these properties in the context of reconfiguration. Validity ensures that no arbitrary value is chosen. Monotonicity implies that $r'$ is the merge of $r$ with another Blueprint, e.g. $r' = merge(r, r')$. This implies that rules introduced in $r$ are also applied in $r'$. For example, a process mandatory in $r$ will also be mandatory in $r'$, unless it was explicitly removed by another **reconf** operation.

Our goal is for our service to eventually use a single service configuration. This can be accomplished since comparability implies that at any time $t$, there exists a Blueprint among those chosen before $t$, that is maximal with respect to $\sqsubseteq$. We call this the *current Blueprint* at time $t$, and the service configuration, determined by this Blueprint is called the *current configuration*.

To change the current Blueprint, a **reconf** operation has to choose a Blueprint that is a greater lattice element than all previously chosen Blueprints. Thus the service can only replace $r_1$ with $r_2$ if $r_1 \sqsubseteq r_2$ holds. It is therefore not possible to add a process to $\mathcal{A}$ after it has been removed, since it will be listed in $\mathcal{A}_{rm}$. Similarly for our example above, adding $addMan(p)$ after $remMan(p)$ will not result in any changes. In practice however, a process can be re-added with a different identifier.

Stability allows us to use the **reconf** operation to read the current Blueprint. In our example in Section 2, this can be used to determine the current epoch number. Stability also implies that a new Blueprint will always be merged with a previously chosen Blueprint. Thus, the input to a **reconf** operation does not need to specify all desired rules and available processes. It is enough to include all new rules and processes relative to some previously chosen Blueprint.

We now specify which processes need to be correct to guarantee liveness. We say that a process is *correct* at time $t$, if it did not fail before $t$. A service configuration is *available* at time $t$, if there exists a read and write quorum of this service configuration, such that all processes in these quorums are correct at $t$. We require that the current configuration is available. To allow state transfer during a reconfiguration, we also require that the service configurations of any new Blueprints are available. This is a common requirement for reconfigurations [3]. For SmartMerge, we define that $r$ is a *candidate Blueprint* at time $t$, if it is a possible return value for some outstanding **reconf** operation at time $t$, and it is greater than the current Blueprint ($cur \sqsubseteq r$). A service configuration determined by a candidate Blueprint, is called a *candidate configuration*.

We only require liveness for operations invoked by a process currently running the register. These processes are called active: A process **p** is *active* if it is correct at all times and after some time $t$, $\mathbf{p} \in \mathcal{P}_{cur}$ always hold for the current configuration $cur$. This definition is similar to [4]. We could also include a larger set of clients, which can invoke operations, similar to [3] or [12]. This adds no significant challenges to the problem and we omit it due to space constraints.

The following property summarizes under which conditions an operation is required to return:

*Liveness.* Suppose that only finitely many **reconf** operations are invoked during an execution, and at any time the current and all candidate configurations are available. Then a **read**, **write** or **reconf** operation, invoked by an active process will return.

It was established in [13] that even a regular register is impossible to implement, if the configuration changes infinitely often. Thus, we assume that only finitely many reconfigurations are invoked.

Once $cur \not\sqsubseteq r$ holds for a Blueprint $r$ and the current Blueprint $cur$, then $r$ can no longer become the new current Blueprint. Thus $r$ can be discarded. We say that $r$ is *outdated*. According to the definition of the current Blueprint, $r$ is outdated, when some **reconf** operation returned $r'$, such that $r' \not\sqsubseteq r$ holds. A process can easily test the condition $r' \not\sqsubseteq r$ by computing $merge(r', r) \neq r$.

According to liveness, a process **p** can stop once it can no longer become part of the current configuration. In our example, this is the case once $\mathbf{p} \in \mathcal{A}_{rm}$ holds for the current Blueprint.

To our knowledge we are the first to propose a scheme that determines which Blueprints are outdated and which processes can stop, based on return values of reconfigurations. RAMBO [3] uses a garbage collection mechanism to find outdated configurations. Thus it potentially takes longer to detect outdated configurations. Furthermore, it is not possible to determine which configurations are outdated, based on return values of reconfiguration operations. The specification of DynaStore [4] does not use configurations, thus no outdated configurations or Blueprints are defined. Instead, a process can stop as soon as its removal is proposed. To guarantee liveness DynaStore has to restrict the number of concurrent removals. This poses a significant restriction on reconfigurations, e.g. it disallows concurrent replacement of all processes with new ones.

# 4    Algorithm: Atomic Storage Using Smart Merge

We now present our implementation of a reconfigurable atomic register. The implementation consists of a support for **reconf** operations (Algorithm 2) and two functions **get** and **set** (Algorithm 3) that access the state of the register. Algorithm 2 and Algorithm 3 internally use a configuration object to contact the processes and access the state stored in a service configuration. We present the implementation of a configuration object in Algorithm 1. The **set** and **get** functions mask concurrent reconfigurations, so that we can use them to implement regular or atomic registers, using standard algorithms designed for a single configuration (e.g. [5], [14]). For completeness, we show an implementation of such atomic reads and writes in Algorithm 4.

The highlights and new techniques of our implementation include the use of the lattice agreement abstraction in Algorithm 2 and handling of the returned values. It makes the algorithm significantly more efficient, since the use of generalized lattice agreement reduces the number of configurations that have to be processed. Furthermore, we implement **set** and **get** without relying on a sequence of chosen configurations, using only the weaker guarantees provided by GLA. Finally, in our implementation, the removal of outdated Blueprints and their configuration objects is gracefully and efficiently integrated with concurrent operations.

Our reconfigurable register relies on a configuration object $C$ (Algorithm 1), which includes the service configuration $c$, the register state $S$, and a set $next \subset \mathfrak{R}$. A *register state* $S \in \mathcal{V} \times \mathcal{T}$ is a pair, consisting of a register value $v \in \mathcal{V} \cup \{\bot\}$ and a timestamp $ts = (n, id) \in \mathcal{T}$. A timestamp consists of a sequence number $n \in \mathbb{N}$ and a process identifier $id$. Timestamps are ordered lexicographically. $next$ holds a set of Blueprints whose purpose we explain below.

The configuration object $C$ also abstracts communication between the processes in $\mathcal{P}_c$ through a set of regular registers. For every process $\mathbf{p} \in \mathcal{P}_c$, $C$ contains registers $\mathbf{p}.S$ and $\mathbf{p}.next$ with the state of $\mathbf{p}$'s local variables. Only $\mathbf{p}_i$ can write to $\mathbf{p}_i.S$ and $\mathbf{p}_i.next$, but they can be read by all processes in $\mathcal{P}_c$. To read the register state of $C$, a process invokes $C.readS()$, which reads all registers $\mathbf{p}.S : \mathbf{p} \in \mathcal{P}_c$ and returns the state with the highest timestamp. To read the set of next Blueprints, a process reads all registers $\mathbf{p}.next$ and returns the union of these values. Finally, we use reliable broadcast $(rb)$, to notify members of a new configuration when it becomes the current configuration. If some process completes $C.rb.broadcast(m)$, and a quorum of processes in $\mathcal{P}_c$ do not fail, all correct processes in $\mathcal{P}_c$ will eventually invoke $C.rb.deliver(m)$.

Regular registers and reliable broadcast can be implemented using textbook algorithms [15], designed for an asynchronous message passing system with a known finite set of processes and a fixed quorum system. Our configuration object encapsulates the processes and quorums of a static configuration, which forms the system on which these algorithms operate. To use a different configuration, we create a new object. If a configuration becomes outdated, its processes might stop and the static algorithms that operate on this configuration might never return. We therefore abort any method in an outdated configuration.

**Algorithm 1.** Configuration object $C$ at process $\mathbf{p}_i$

1: **State** :
2:    $c : (\mathcal{P}_c, \mathcal{RQ}_c, \mathcal{WQ}_c)$                                 {Service configuration}
3:    $S : (S.v, S.ts) \leftarrow s_0$             {Register state $S \in \mathcal{V} \times \mathcal{T}$, $s_0 = (\bot, \mathbf{p}_i.id)$}
4:    $next \leftarrow \emptyset$                              {Next Blueprints, $next \subset \mathfrak{R}$}
5: **Communication Abstractions:**
6:    Regular SWMR registers
7:        **for each** $\mathbf{p} \in \mathcal{P}_c : \mathbf{p}.S : (S.v, S.ts)$     {storing $S \in \mathcal{V} \times \mathcal{T}$, initially $s_0$}
8:        **for each** $\mathbf{p} \in \mathcal{P}_c : \mathbf{p}.next$          {storing $next \subset \mathfrak{R}$, initially $\emptyset$}
9:    $rb$                                         {Reliable broadcast}

10: $readS()$
11:    **for** $\mathbf{p} \in \mathcal{P}_c$
12:        $s_\mathbf{p} \leftarrow \mathbf{p}.S.read()$
13:    $t \leftarrow \max\{s_\mathbf{p}.ts | \mathbf{p} \in \mathcal{P}_c\}$
14:    **return** $s_\mathbf{p}$: **s.t.** $\mathbf{p} \in \mathcal{P}_c \wedge s_\mathbf{p}.ts = t$

15: $writeNext(target)$     {invoked by $\mathbf{p}_i$}
16:    $next \leftarrow next \cup \{target\}$
17:    $\mathbf{p}_i.next.write(next)$

18: $readNext()$
19:    **for** $\mathbf{p} \in \mathcal{P}_c$ **do**
20:        $C_\mathbf{p} \leftarrow \mathbf{p}.next.read()$
21:    **return** $\bigcup\{C_\mathbf{p} | \mathbf{p} \in \mathcal{P}_c\}$

22: $writeS(s)$              {invoked by $\mathbf{p}_i$}
23:    **if** $s.ts > S.ts$ **then**
24:        $\mathbf{p}_i.S.write(s)$
25:        $S \leftarrow s$

In our algorithm, we use the **la-propose** primitive specified in Section 2. We say that a value returned by **la-propose** is *learned*. Every process maintains a set $L$, that contains the current and some candidate Blueprints (Algorithm 2). All elements in $L$ were learned from **la-propose**. Comparability for **la-propose** implies that $L$ is totally ordered by $\sqsubseteq$. For every Blueprint $r \in L$, we also store a configuration object $C[r]$ determined by $r$. $C[r]$ is created or deleted, when $r$ is added or removed from $L$. $C[r]$ can also be created, when it is accessed remotely though its communication abstractions. However, accesses to objects, that belong to outdated Blueprints are ignored.

We now discuss the **reconf** operation shown in Algorithm 2. The operation starts by passing the Blueprint $rr$ to **la-propose**. We add the value learned from **la-propose** to $L$. Since $L$ is totally ordered by $\sqsubseteq$, we can choose the maximum in $L$, as *target* blueprint for our reconfiguration. To ensure that other processes know that *target* was learned, we write *target* to all configurations that were created using elements of $L$ (Line 11). We also read the register state in all these configurations to collect an up-to-date state (Line 12). On Line 14 we invoke $C[fr].readNext()$, to find other learned Blueprints and add them to $L$. Since we assign elements from $L$ to $fr$ in order (Line 16), and $C[fr].readNext()$ only returns Blueprints larger than $fr$, these new Blueprints will be processed later.

Validity and comparability already hold for *target* on Line 6. To ensure stability, we replace *target* with a larger learned value on Line 8, if possible. After processing all elements from $L$, we transfer the register state with the highest timestamp, that was read, to $C[target]$ (Line 18).

Before returning, and thus choosing *target*, we broadcast a $\langle\text{CHOSEN}, target\rangle$ message to all processes in $C[target].\mathcal{P}_c$ using the reliable broadcast (Line 19).

The processing of a $\langle$CHOSEN, $target\rangle$ message is shown in Algorithm 5. We ignore a CHOSEN message for a Blueprint smaller than $cur$. If $\langle$CHOSEN, $target\rangle$ was sent, some process completed state transfer to $target$. We can therefore remove all elements smaller than $target$ from $L$. Finally, if $target$ was returned by a **reconf** operation, smaller Blueprints $r \sqsubset target$ are outdated, according to our definition in Section 3. Thus $C[r]$ might no longer be available. In this case, it may become impossible to read from or write to the registers in $C[r]$. We therefore abort all current and future methods on $C[r]$. On abort, the write methods $writeNext$, $writeS$ and $rb.broadcast$ simply return, while $readNext$ and $readS$ return the default values ($\emptyset$ and $s_0$).

We next present our **set** and **get** functions used to read and write the register state (value, timestamp) from the current configuration. They are shown in Algorithm 3. **set** writes a register state to all configuration objects $C[r]$ that were created using $r \in L$, while **get** reads the register state in all these configurations, and returns the one with the highest timestamp. Note that when using $writeS(s)$, the register state is only overwritten if its timestamp is smaller than $s.ts$. **set** and **get** also invoke $readNext$ to add new learned values to $L$.

Algorithm 4 shows a possible implementation of atomic reads and writes using **set** and **get**. Note that on Line 7, we create a unique timestamp by increasing the sequence number returned by **get**, and adding the writer's identifier $p_i.id$.

*Discussion.* We say that a Blueprint $r$ is *used* in an operation if the operation invokes methods on $C[r]$. To analyze the overhead concurrent **reconf** operations impose on **read** and **write** operations, we first establish the maximum number of Blueprints and configuration objects used in one operation. An operation only uses Blueprints from $L$, which only holds the initial element $r_I$ and values learned from GLA (Algorithm 2, Lines 6, 7). In an execution with $r$ **reconf** operations, at most $r$ different values are learned. Thus all operations use at most $r + 1$ different Blueprints.

In DynaStore [4], the only other reconfigurable atomic register using a purely asynchronous system, a single operation may have to contact processes in many different configurations. Reconfigurations in DynaStore do not invoke lattice agreement. Instead a configuration uses a weak snapshot object to store the set of next configurations $next$. Without lattice agreement, non-comparable values can be written to $next$. Therefore a process in DynaStore adopts the merge of all configurations, returned by $readNext$ as new target configuration. If three reconfigurations, with target configurations $c_x$, $c_y$ and $c_z$ are started concurrently, they can all be written to $r_I.next$. A concurrent **read** operation might not only have to contact $c_x$, $merge(c_x, c_y)$ and $merge(c_x, c_y, c_z)$, but also $c_y$ and $c_z$. Additionally, **read** operations in DynaStore also write to $next$. Thus, a **read** operation concurrent with the three reconfigurations above might read $\{c_x, c_z\}$ from $r_I.next$, and thus write $c_{xz} = merge(c_x, c_z)$ to $c_x.next$. This creates another configuration that other **read** operations have to contact. If $2^{r-1} - r$ **read** operations and $r$ reconfigurations are invoked concurrently, each by a different process, one of these reads might have to contact as many as $2^{r-1} + r$ configurations.

We now analyze the number of communication steps for **read** and **write** operations. Note that, the different registers that read in a *readS* or *readNext* method, can be read concurrently (see Algorithm 1). It is even possible to perform the methods $C[gt].readS$ and $C[gt].readNext$ on Lines 4 and 6 of

---

**Algorithm 2.** Register Reconfiguration

```
 1: State :
 2:     L ← {r_I}                        {Ordered set of learned, not outdated Blueprints}
 3:     ∀r ∈ L : C[r] = CO(c : r.policy.srvConf(r.A))  {Conf. object, determined by r}
 4:     cur ← r_I                         {Current Blueprint}
 5: reconf(r)
 6:     target ← la-propose(r)                           {See Section 2}
 7:     L ← L ∪ {target}
 8:     fr ← cur ; s ← s_0
 9:     repeat
10:         target ← max(L)           {Maximum wrt. ⊑; target for reconfiguration}
11:         C[fr].writeNext(target)                  {Record: target was learned}
12:         s_r ← C[fr].readS()
13:         if s.ts < s_r.ts then s ← s_r     {Remember most up-to-date register state}
14:         L ← L ∪ C[fr].readNext()               {Check for learned Blueprints}
15:         if ∃r ∈ L : fr ⊑ r then
16:             fr ← min({r ∈ L|fr ⊑ r})                    {Minimum wrt. ⊑}
17:         else break
18:     C[target].writeS(s)                         {Transfer state to target}
19:     C[target].rb.broadcast(⟨CHOSEN, target⟩)    {Inform about new configuration}
20:     return target
```

---

**Algorithm 3.** Get and Set Register State

```
 1: get()                               10: set(s)   {s a (timestamp,value) pair}
 2:     gt ← cur ; s ← s_0              11:     st ← cur
 3:     repeat                          12:     repeat
 4:         s_r ← C[gt].readS()         13:         C[st].writeS(s)
 5:         if s.ts < s_r.ts then s ← s_r   14:         L ← L ∪ C[st].readNext()
 6:         L ← L ∪ C[gt].readNext()    15:         if ∃r ∈ L : st ⊑ r then
 7:         if ∃r ∈ L : gt ⊑ r then     16:             st ← min({r ∈ L|st ⊏ r})
 8:             gt ← min({r ∈ L|gt ⊏ r})   17:         else return
 9:         else return s
```

---

**Algorithm 4.** Atomic read/write at $p_i$     **Algorithm 5.** Processing ⟨CHOSEN⟩

```
 1: read()          5: write(v)         1: on    C.rb.deliver(⟨CHOSEN, target⟩)
 2:     s ← get()    6:     (v',t') ← get()   with cur ⊏ target
 3:     set(s)       7:     t ← (t'.n+1, p_i.id)  2:     L ← L ∪ {target}
 4:     return       8:     s ← (v,t)      3:     cur ← target
     s.v             9:     set(s)         4:     for r ∈ L : r ⊏ target do
                                           5:         abort any method on C[r]
                                           6:         L ← L\{r}
```

Algorithm 3 concurrently, reading $\mathbf{p}.S$ and $\mathbf{p}.next$ at the same time. Thus a **get** function only requires one communication step per used Blueprint. Similarly, we can perform the methods $C[st].writeS$ and $C[st].readNext$ invoked in the **set** function concurrently. Since both **set** and **get** use at most $r + 1$ Blueprints, a **read** or **write** operation requires at most $2r + 2$ communication steps. This bound is the same as for the consensus-based approach in RAMBO [3].

## 5   Related Work

Previous work on reconfiguration of registers mainly use either the consensus-based approach or DirectCombine, as introduced in Section 1. Early work [16, 17] assumed reconfigurations were issued by a single process. Thus avoiding the problem of concurrent reconfigurations, but failure of this process prevents further reconfigurations.

Several works use the consensus-based approach to handle concurrent reconfigurations. They either implement consensus [18,19], or assume an external, replicated configuration manager [3], [20]. All these systems establish a sequence of configurations. Since consensus is impossible in the face of asynchrony [21], these systems require additional assumptions, such as a failure detector or eventual synchrony. To guarantee liveness they assume, as we do, that an old configuration remains available until a newer configuration has started.

In [22] a group communication system is used to implement reconfiguration of an atomic register. This approach is similar to the consensus-based approach.

To our knowledge, DirectCombine has only been used in a few systems [4], [12,13]. These systems do not establish a sequence of configurations. Instead, processes can be added to or removed from the service at any time. To guarantee liveness they assume that only a bounded fraction of processes is removed concurrently [4], [12], or during a specific time interval [13]. Different from our work, [13] assumes an infinite sequence of reconfigurations. They also show this is impossible in an asynchronous system.

A replicated state machine (RSM) [23] is a general approach to replicate a service. An RSM can be used to implement atomic storage, where read and write operations are chosen using consensus. Consensus-based reconfiguration of an RSM was proposed in both [23,24] and has also been deployed in production systems [25]. In our previous work, we showed that an RSM can be reconfigured without relying on consensus [26]. In retrospect this work can be viewed as an application of SmartMerge. It uses a trivial combination function, that always chooses the configuration with the highest timestamp.

## 6   Conclusion

We presented an atomic register that uses a novel approach to combine concurrently issued reconfigurations in an asynchronous system. Our approach allows reconfigurations to specify a policy, that determines how to form a service configuration from the available processes. Different policies are aptly combined by a merge function.

# References

1. Reiss, C., Tumanov, A., Ganger, G.R., Katz, R.H., Kozuch, M.A.: Heterogeneity and dynamicity of clouds at scale: Google trace analysis. In: SOCC (2012)
2. Ardekani, M.S., Terry, D.B.: A self-configurable geo-replicated cloud storage system. In: OSDI (2014)
3. Gilbert, S., Lynch, N.A., Shvartsman, A.A.: Rambo: a robust, reconfigurable atomic memory service for dynamic networks. Distr. Comp. **23**(4) (2010)
4. Aguilera, M.K., Keidar, I., Malkhi, D., Shraer, A.: Dynamic atomic storage without consensus. J. ACM **58**(2), 7 (2011)
5. Attiya, H., Bar-Noy, A., Dolev, D.: Sharing memory robustly in message-passing systems. J. ACM **42**(1), 124–142 (1995)
6. Leners, J.B., Wu, H., Hung, W.L., Aguilera, M.K., Walfish, M.: Detecting failures in distributed systems with the falcon spy network. In: SOSP (2011)
7. Leners, J.B., Gupta, T., Aguilera, M.K., Walfish, M.: Improving availability in distributed systems with failure informers. In: OSDI (2013)
8. Vickers, S.: Topology Via Logic. Cambridge University Press (1989)
9. Faleiro, J.M., Rajamani, S., Rajan, K., Ramalingam, G., Vaswani, K.: Generalized lattice agreement. In: PODC (2012)
10. Herlihy, M.P., Wing, J.M.: Linearizability: A correctness condition for concurrent objects. ACM Trans. Program. Lang. Syst. **12**(3), 463–492 (1990)
11. Attiya, H., Herlihy, M., Rachman, O.: Atomic snapshots using lattice agreement. Distrib. Comput. **8**(3), 121–132 (1995)
12. Shraer, A., Martin, J.P., Malkhi, D., Keidar, I.: Data-centric reconfiguration with network-attached disks. In: LADIS (2010)
13. Baldoni, R., Bonomi, S., Kermarrec, A.M., Raynal, M.: Implementing a register in a dynamic distributed system. In: ICDCS (2009)
14. Shao, C., Pierce, E., Welch, J.L.: Multi-writer consistency conditions for shared memory objects. In: Fich, F.E. (ed.) DISC 2003. LNCS, vol. 2848, pp. 106–120. Springer, Heidelberg (2003)
15. Cachin, C., Guerraoui, R., Rodrigues, L.: Introduction to Reliable and Secure Distributed Programming, 2nd edn. Springer Publishing Company (2011)
16. Lynch, N.A., Shvartsman, A.A.: Robust emulation of shared memory using dynamic quorum-acknowledged broadcasts. In: FTCS (1997)
17. Englert, B., Shvartsman, A.A.: Graceful quorum reconfiguration in a robust emulation of shared memory. In: ICDCS (2000)
18. Rodrigues, R., Liskov, B., Chen, K., Liskov, M., Schultz, D.: Automatic reconfiguration for large-scale reliable storage systems. IEEE Trans. Dependable Secur. Comput. **9**(2), 145–158 (2012)
19. Chockler, G., Gilbert, S., Gramoli, V., Musial, P.M., Shvartsman, A.A.: Reconfigurable distributed storage for dynamic networks. Journal of Parallel and Distributed Computing **69**(1), 100–116 (2009)
20. Martin, J.P., Alvisi, L.: A framework for dynamic byzantine storage. In: DSN (2004)
21. Fischer, M.J., Lynch, N.A., Paterson, M.S.: Impossibility of distributed consensus with one faulty process. J. ACM **32**(2), 374–382 (1985)
22. De Prisco, R., Fekete, A., Lynch, N.A., Shvartsman, A.: A dynamic primary configuration group communication service. In: Jayanti, P. (ed.) DISC 1999. LNCS, vol. 1693, pp. 64–78. Springer, Heidelberg (1999)

23. Schneider, F.B.: Implementing fault-tolerant services using the state machine approach: A tutorial. ACM Comput. Surv. **22**(4), 299–319 (1990)
24. Lamport, L.: The part-time parliament. ACM Trans. Comput. Syst. **16**(2), 133–169 (1998)
25. Shraer, A., Reed, B., Malkhi, D., Junqueira, F.: Dynamic reconfiguration of primary/backup clusters. In: USENIX ATC (2012)
26. Jehl, L., Meling, H.: Asynchronous reconfiguration for paxos state achines. In: ICDCN (2014)

# Towards Automatic Lock Removal
# for Scalable Synchronization

Maya Arbel[1,2], Guy Golan-Gueta[1], Eshcar Hillel[1(✉)], and Idit Keidar[1,2]

[1] Yahoo Labs, Haifa, Israel
mayaarl@cs.technion.ac.il, {ggolan,eshcar}@yahoo-inc.com,
idish@ee.technion.ac.il
[2] The Technion, Haifa, Israel

**Abstract.** We present a *code transformation* for concurrent data structures, which increases their scalability without sacrificing correctness. Our transformation takes lock-based code and replaces some of the locking steps therein with optimistic synchronization in order to reduce contention. The main idea is to have each operation perform an optimistic traversal of the data structure as long as no shared memory locations are updated, and then proceed with pessimistic code. The transformed code inherits essential properties of the original one, including linearizability, serializability, and deadlock freedom.

Our work complements existing pessimistic transformations that make sequential code thread-safe by adding locks. In essence, we provide a way to optimize such transformations by reducing synchronization bottlenecks (for example, locking the root of a tree). The resulting code scales well and significantly outperforms pessimistic approaches. We further compare our synthesized code to state-of-the-art data structures implemented by experts. We find that its performance is comparable to that achieved by the custom-tailored implementations. Our work thus shows the promise that automated approaches bear for overcoming the difficulty involved in manually hand-crafting concurrent data structures.

## 1 Introduction

The steady increase in the number of cores in today's computers is driving software developers to allow more and more parallelism. An important focal point for such efforts is scaling the concurrency of shared data structures, which are often a principal friction point among threads. Many recent works have been dedicated to developing scalable concurrent data structures (e.g., [5,8,10–12,15, 20,22,25,32,38,40]), some of which are widely used in real-world systems [44].

Each of these projects generally focuses on a single data structure (e.g., a binary search tree [11] or a queue [38]) and manually optimizes its implementation. These data structures are developed by concurrency experts, typically PhDs or PhD candidates, and proving their correctness is painstaking; for example,

Maya Arbel is supported in part by the Technion Hasso Platner Institute (HPI) Research School.

Y. Moses (Ed.): DISC 2015, LNCS 9363, pp. 170–184, 2015.
DOI: 10.1007/978-3-662-48653-5_12

the proofs of [10,22] are 31 and 20 pages long, respectively. The rationale behind dedicating so much effort to one data structure is that it is generic and can be used by many applications. Nevertheless, systems often use data structures in unique ways that necessitate changing or extending their code (e.g., [2,3,43,46]), in which cases custom-tailored implementations may not meet the requirements. Here, we propose an approach to facilitate this labor-intensive process, making scalable synchronization more readily available.

Specifically, we present in Section 2 an algorithm for a source-to-source code transformation that takes a lock-based concurrent data structure implementation as its input and generates more scalable code for the same data structure via judicious use of optimism. Our approach combines optimism and pessimism in a practical way. Like some previous hand-crafted solutions [31], we exploit the common access pattern in data structure operations, (e.g., tree insertion or deletion), which typically begin by traversing the data structure (to the insertion or deletion point), and then perform local updates at that location. Our solution replaces locks in the initial read-only traversal with optimistic synchronization, and performs updates using the original lock-based code. It may thus be seen as a form of software lock elision for read-only prefixes of operations (transactions). Combining optimism and pessimism allows us to achieve "the best of both worlds" – while the optimistic traversal increases concurrency and eliminates bottlenecks, the use of pessimistic updates saves the overhead associated with speculative or deferred shared memory updates, (as occurs in *software transactional memory (STM)* [30]).

In the full version of the paper [9] we show that our transformation preserves the external behavior (e.g., linearizability, serializability, and deadlock-freedom) of the original lock-based code; Moreover, our transformation preserves *disjoint access parallelism* [34], (the property that threads that access disjoint data objects do not contend on low level shared memory locations), as it refrains from introducing a shared global clock (as some STM systems do [45]) or other sources of contention.

One important use case for our transformation is to apply it in conjunction with automatic lock-based parallelization mechanisms [26,36]. The latter instrument sequential code and add fine-grained locks that ensure its safety in concurrent executions. Our evaluation shows that, by themselves, solutions of this sort may scale poorly. This is due to synchronization bottlenecks, e.g., the root of a tree, which is locked by all operations. By subsequently applying our transformation, one can optimize the lock-based code they produce, yielding an end-to-end approach to scalable parallelization of sequential code.

In Section 3 we evaluate our transformation by generating an unbalanced search tree and a treap (randomized balanced search tree). We synthesize these data structures from *sequential implementations* by applying first the algorithm of [26] (*domination locking*) to create lock-based code, and then our transformation. We evaluate the scalability of the resulting code in a range of workload scenarios on a 32-core machine. In all cases, the lock-based implementations do not scale – their throughput remains flat as the number of running threads increases. In contrast, the code generated by our transformation is scalable, and its throughput continues to grow with the number of threads. We further use the Synchrobench framework [27] to compare our synthesized code to data structures that were recently hand-crafted by experts in the field [1,11,15,20,22], as well as a state-of-the-art STM [45]. Our results show that the implementations we have generated perform comparably to custom-tailored solutions.

The advantage of our approach is in its *generic* nature, which allows us to parallelize existing code without requiring experts to perform manual optimizations. Other generic approaches we are familiar with are domination locking [26] and STM [45], both of which perform worse than our transformed code in our experiments. Further discussion of related work appears in Section 4.

To conclude, this paper demonstrates that generic synchronization, based on a careful combination of optimism and pessimism, is a promising approach for bringing legacy code to emerging computer architectures. While this paper illustrates the method for tree data structures, we believe that the general direction is more broadly applicable, and maybe used with a variety of locking schemes, such as two phase locking. Section 5 concludes the paper and touches on some directions for future work.

## 2  Transformation

We present an algorithm for a source-to-source transformation, whose goal is to optimize the code of a given data structure implemented using lock-based concurrency control. In Section 2.1, we detail our assumptions about the given code and the locks it uses. Section 2.2 overviews our general approach to combining optimism and pessimism, while Section 2.3 details how the code is instrumented.

### 2.1  Lock-Based Data Structures

A *data structure* defines a set of *operations* that may be invoked by clients of the data structure, potentially concurrently. Operations have parameters and local (private) variables. The operations interact via *shared memory variables*, which are also called *shared objects*. Each shared object supports atomic *read* (load) and *write* (store) instructions. More formal definitions appear in the full version [9].

In addition, each shared object is associated with a lock, which can be unique to the object or common to several (or even all) objects. The object supports atomic *lock* and *unlock* instructions. Locks are exclusive (i.e., a lock can be held by at most one thread at a time), and blocking. We assume that in the given code every (read or write) access by an operation to a shared object is performed when the executing thread holds the lock associated with that object.

The given code only uses the *lock* and *unlock* instructions, while the transformed code can apply in addition atomic non-blocking *tryLock* and *isLockedByAnother* instructions: *tryLock* returns *false* if the lock is currently held by another thread, otherwise it acquires the lock and returns *true*; *isLockedByAnother* returns *true* if and only if the lock is currently held by another thread.

## 2.2   Combining Optimism and Pessimism

Optimistic concurrency control is a form of synchronization, which accesses shared variables without using locks in the hope that they will not be modified by others before the end of the operation (or more generally, the transaction). To verify the latter, optimistic concurrency control relies on *validation*, which is typically implemented using *version numbers*. If validation fails, the operation restarts. Optimistic execution of update operations requires either performing roll-back (reverting variables to their old values) upon validation failure, or deferring writes to commit time; both approaches induce significant overhead [13]. We therefore refrain from speculative shared memory updates.

The main idea behind our approach is to judiciously use optimistic synchronization only as long as an operation does not update shared state; we use a standard approach based on version numbers to allow validation of optimistic reads. Once an operation writes to shared memory, we revert to pessimistic (lock-based) synchronization. In other words, we rely on validation in order to render redundant locks that would have been acquired and freed before the first update. This scheme is particularly suitable for data structures, since the common behavior of their operations is to first traverse the data structure, and then perform modifications. Since the read only prefix has no side effects we can sandbox it by catching exceptions and infinite loops, and defer validation to the end of the traversal.

Conceptually, our approach thus divides an operation into three phases: an optimistic *read-only phase*, a pessimistic *update phase* and a *validation phase* that conjoins them. The read-only phase traverses the data structure without taking any locks, while maintaining in thread-local variables sufficient information to later ensure the correctness of the traversal. The read phase is *invisible* to other threads, as it updates no shared variables. The update phase uses the original pessimistic (lock-based) synchronization, with the addition of updating version numbers. The validation phase bridges between the optimistic and pessimistic ones. It first locks the objects for which a lock would have been held at this point by the original locking code, and then validates the correctness of the read-only phase. This allows the update phase to run as if an execution of the original pessimistic synchronization took place. If the validation fails, the operation restarts. In order to avoid livelock, we set a threshold on the number of restarts. If the threshold is exceeded, the code falls back on pessimistic execution. We show below that it is safe to do so, since our semi-optimistic code is compatible with the fully pessimistic one.

*Phase Transition.* In many cases, the transition from the read-only phase to the update phase occurs at a statically-defined code location. For example, many data structure operations begin with a read-only traversal to locate the key of interest, and when it is found, proceed to execute code that modifies the data structure. This is the case in all the examples we consider in Section 3 below.

More generally, it is possible to switch from the optimistic read-only execution (via the validation phase) to pessimistic execution at any point before the first update. Moreover, the phase transition point can be determined dynamically at run time.

One possible way to dynamically track the execution mode is using a flag **opt**, initialized to true, indicating the optimistic phase. Every shared memory update operation is then instrumented with code that checks **opt**, and if it is true, executes the validation phase followed by setting **opt** to false and continuing the execution from the same location.

## 2.3    Transforming the Code Phases

We now describe how we synthesize the code for each of the phases. We first describe the regular three-phase flow, and then continue with describing the exceptional cases.

**Normal Flow.** We illustrate the transformation for a simple code snippet that adds a new element as the third node in a linked list. Each node is associated with a lock. The original and transformed code are provided in Figure 1. The latter uses the tracking and validation functions in Figures 2 and 3, resp. For clarity of exposition, we present a statically instrumented version, without tracking the phases using **opt**.

Our transformation instruments each lock with an additional field *version*. We assume each object supports *getVersion* and *incVersion* instruction to read and increment the version number of the lock associated with the object. We invoke *incVersion* when holding the lock, and are therefore are not concerned about contention. Note that each lock has its own version, i.e., version numbers of different locks are independent of each other.

*Read-Only Phase.* In this phase the executing thread is invisible to other threads, i.e., avoids contention on shared memory both in terms of writing and in terms of locking. During this phase, our synchronization maintains two thread-local multi-sets: *lockedSet* and *readSet*. The *lockedSet* tracks the objects that were supposed to be locked by the original synchronization. The *readSet* tracks versions of all objects read by the operation, in order to allow us to later validate that the operation has observed a consistent view of shared memory.

At the beginning of the read-only phase, we insert code that initializes *lockedSet* and *readSet* to be empty (see lines 2-3 of Figure 1b). Throughout the read-only phase, (i.e., when **opt** is true with dynamic phase transitions), we replace every lock and unlock instruction with the corresponding code in Table 1. A lock instruction on object *o* is replaced with code that tracks the object and the version of its lock in *lockedSet* and *readSet* (see Figure 2). An unlock instruction on object *o* is replaced with code that removes *o* from *lockedSet* (see lines 2-13 of Figure 1b).

In Figure 2 (lines 5-6), we use an eager validation scheme[1]: If the object already exists in *readSet*, we check that the current version of its lock is equal

---

[1] Eager validation is not required for correctness.

```
 1: FUNCTION addThird(List          1: FUNCTION addThird(List list,
    list, Node new)                    Node new)
    ----------  ▷ read-only phase      ----------       ▷ read-only phase
 2:                                 2:   lockedSet.init()
 3:                                 3:   readSet.init()
 4:   list.lock()                   4:   if !track(list) then goto 1
 5:   Node prev = list.head         5:   Node prev = list.head
 6:   prev.lock()                   6:   if !track(prev) then goto 1
 7:   list.unlock()                 7:   lockedSet.remove(list)
 8:   Node succ = prev.next         8:   Node succ = prev.next
 9:   succ.lock()                   9:   if !track(succ) then goto 1
10:   prev.unlock()                10:   lockedSet.remove(prev)
11:   prev = succ                  11:   prev = succ
12:   succ = succ.next             12:   succ = succ.next
13:   succ.lock()                  13:   if !track(succ) then goto 1
    ----------                         ----------        ▷ validation phase
14:                                14:   read fence
15:                                15:   for all obj in lockedSet do
16:                                16:     if !obj.tryLock() then
17:                                17:       unlockAll()
18:                                18:       goto 1
19:                                19:   if !validateReadSet() then
20:                                20:     unlockAll()
21:                                21:     goto 1
    ----------  ▷ update phase         ----------        ▷ update phase
22:   prev.next = new             22:   prev.next = new
23:   new.lock()                  23:   new.lock()
24:   new.next = succ            24:   new.next = succ
25:                               25:   prev.incVersion
26:   prev.unlock()              26:   prev.unlock()
27:                               27:   new.incVersion
28:   new.unlock()               28:   new.unlock()
29:                               29:   succ.incVersion
30:   succ.unlock()              30:   succ.unlock()
```

(a) Code with original locking     (b) The code produced by our transformation

**Fig. 1.** Code transformation example. The synchronization code is in bold.

```
1: FUNCTION track(obj)
2:   lockedSet.add(obj)
3:   long ver = obj.getVersion()
4:   readSet.add(⟨obj,ver⟩)
5:   if ⟨obj,v⟩ ∈readSet and v!=ver then return false
6:   if obj.isLockedByAnother() then return false
7:   return true
```

**Fig. 2.** In read-only phase, locking is replaced by tracking locks and read objects' versions.

```
1: FUNCTION validateReadSet()
2:     for all ⟨obj,ver⟩ in readSet do
3:         if obj.isLockedByAnother() then
4:             return false                    ▷ validation failed (locked object)
5:         if obj.getVersion() != ver then
6:             return false                    ▷ validation failed (different version)
7:     retrun true                             ▷ validation succeed
```

**Fig. 3.** Read set validation: verify that objects are unlocked and their versions are unchanged.

**Table 1.** Transformation for read-only phase: each locking instruction (left column) is replaced with the corresponding code on the right; $S$ denotes the beginning of the operation.

| Original code | Transformed Code |
|---|---|
| x.lock() | if !track(x) then goto S |
| x.unlock() | lockedSet.remove(x) |

to the version in *readSet*; and if the versions are different the operation restarts (line 5). Similarly, it is checked to be unlocked, and the operation restarts if it is locked (line 6).

Although it only accesses thread-local data structures, lock tracking induces a certain overhead due to the need to search a lock in the *lockedSet* in order to unlock it. (In our experiments presented below, in large data structures, this overhead slows operations down by up to 40%). We suggest some optimizations to mitigate this cost. First, we observe that the *lockedSet* does not need to be tracked in read-only operations, which a compiler can easily detect. We can further avoid this overhead in update operations in certain cases by relying on the structure of the transformed code. For example, if the lock-based code is created from sequential code using domination locking [26], then at any given time in the read phase, it holds locks on a well-defined set of objects – the ones currently pointed by the operation's local variables. When applying our transformation to code generated by this scheme, we can optimize it to remove lock-tracking, and instead populate the *lockedSet* with the appropriate locks immediately before executing the validation phase.

*Validation Phase.* The code of the validation phase is invoked between the read-only phase and the update phase (lines 14-21 of Figure 1b). It locks the objects that are left in *lockedSet* and validates the objects in *readSet*. To avoid deadlocks, the locks are acquired using a *tryLock* instruction. If any *tryLock* fails, the code unlocks all previously acquired locks and restarts from the beginning (lines 15-18).

The function *validateReadSet* in Figure 3 verifies that the objects in the read set have not been updated. The function checks that each object in the read set is not locked by another thread, and that the current version of the lock associated with the object matches the version saved in the *readSet*. This check guarantees that the object was not locked from the time it was read until the time it was validated. Since operations write only to locked objects, it follows that the object was not changed. This *readSet* validation can be viewed as a double collect [4] of all objects accessed by the read-only phase. The operation is restarted if the validation fails (lines 19-21).

We assume that, following standard practice in lock implementations, the function *isLockedByAnother* imposes a *memory fence* (barrier). This ensures that the lock and version are read during *track* before the object's value is read optimistically during the read-only phase. To ensure that the second read of the lock and version, during the validation phase, succeeds the optimistic read of the object's value, we precede the validation phase with a memory fence as well (line 14). Note that it suffices to impose a *read fence* (sometimes called acquire or load fence) prior to the validation as well as during *isLockedByAnother*, because this part of the code does not include writes to shared memory.

*Update Phase.* In this phase our transformation preserves the original locking while maintaining the versions of the objects, i.e., the version of an object $o$ is incremented every time $o$ is unlocked. Here, (i.e., in case **opt** is false with dynamic phase transitions), before each unlock instruction $x.unlock()$ we insert the code $x.incVersion()$ . An example is shown in lines 22-30 of Figure 1b.

**Exceptions from Regular Flow.** The read phase does not validate past reads during its executions (other than when re-reading the same variable). As a result, it may observe an inconsistent state of shared memory, which may lead to infinite loops or spurious exceptions (as explained, e.g., in [30]). We avoid such infinite loops using a timeout. If the timeout expires before the read-only phase completes, read set validation takes place (via the function *validateReadSet*). If the validation fails, the operation is restarted. This is realized by inserting code that examines the timeout in every loop iteration in the original code. Similarly, we avoid spurious exceptions by catching all exceptions and performing validation. Here too, if the validation fails, the operation is restarted. Otherwise, the exception is handled as in the original code.

Our sandboxing relies on properties of managed languages like Java or C#:

1. We can identify all instructions that may update shared memory and end the read phase before they occur.
2. The ability to capture all exits from a block via the try-finally mechanism ensures that we never exit the read phase without performing validation.
3. The code is not self-modifying and hence the tracking and validation code is executed as intended.
4. The speculative execution does not alter the references to the thread-local variables we introduce (readSet, lockedSet) since they are constant references to well-typed objects.

Hence, our tracking and validation code executes correctly.

While recent work [17] has shown that differing validation to the end of a transaction can be unsafe, this problem does not occur in our solution. The key problem shown there is that access to the object on which the conflict is checked (namely the lock) is deferred until after other unchecked shared accesses, which could potentially be inconsistent and cause the lock not to be accessed. In our case, on the other hand, all accesses to shared data are recorded for validation purposes. If an object that should be accessed (like the lock in the lock elision case) is not accessed because of earlier conflicts, these earlier conflicts will be detected and the transaction will abort.

Note that, using our transformation, the shared state at the end of the validation phase is identical to the state that would have been reached had the code been executed pessimistically from the outset. Hence, the three-phase version of the code is compatible with the instrumented pessimistic version. This means that if the optimistic phase is unsuccessful for any reason, we can always fall back on the pessimistic version. Moreover, we can switch from optimistic to pessimistic synchronization *at any point* during the read phase. We use this property in two ways. First, we avoid livelocks by limiting the number of restarts due to conflicts: The validation phase tracks the number of restarts in a thread-local variable. If this number exceeds a certain threshold, we perform the entire operation optimistically.

Second, this property offers the optimistic implementation the liberty of failing spuriously, even in the absence of conflicts, because it can always fall back on the safe pessimistic version of the code. One can take advantage of this liberty, and implement the *readSet* using a constant size array. In case the array becomes full, the optimistic version cannot proceed, but there is no need to start the operation anew. Instead, one can immediately perform the validation phase, which, if successful, switches to a pessimistic modus operandi, after having acquired all the needed locks.

## 3    Evaluation

We evaluate the performance of our approach on search trees supporting insert, delete, and get operations. We compare the throughput of our approach to fully pessimistic solutions applying fine-grain locking, solutions based on software transactional memory, and hand-crafted state-of-the-art data structure implementations.

*Methodology.* We use the micro-benchmark suite *Synchrobench* [27], configured as follows. Each experiment consists of 5 trials. A trial is a five second run in which each thread continuously executes randomly chosen operations drawn from the workload distribution, with keys selected uniformly at random from the range $[0, 2 \cdot 10^6]$. Each trial is preceded by initiating a new data structure with $10^6$ keys and a warm-up of five seconds. Our graphs present the average throughput over all trials. We consider three representative workloads distributions: a *read-only* workload comprised of 100% lookup operations, a *write-dominated* workload consisting of insert and delete operations (50% each), and a *mixed workload* with 50% lookups, 25% inserts, and 25% deletes.

*Platform.* All implementations are in Java. We ran the experiments on a dedicated machine with four Intel Xeon E5-4650 processors, each with 8 cores, for a total of 32 threads (with hyper-threading disabled). We used Ubuntu 12.04.4 LTS and Java Runtime Environment (build 1.7.0_51-b13) using the 64-Bit Server VM (build 24.51-b03, mixed mode).

*Implementations.* We start from textbook sequential implementations of an unbalanced internal binary tree and a treap [7]. We next synthesize concurrent lock-based code by (manually) applying the domination locking technique [26] to the sequential data structures. The resulting algorithms are denoted Lock-Tree and Lock-Treap. Then, we manually apply our lock-removal transformation to the reference implementations by following the algorithm line-by-line (requiring no understanding of the base code) to get our semi-optimistic versions of the code, which we call LR-Tree and LR-Treap, respectively. Note that this solution does not track the *lockedSet* for read-only operations and does not use eager validation of version numbers. Finally, we apply the optimization described in Section 2.3, which eliminates explicit tracking of the *lockedSet* in update operations, and instead locks all objects the thread holds a pointer to in the validation phase; this optimization is applicable since our parallel implementation is synthesized using domination locking. The resulting algorithms are denoted Opt-LR-Tree and Opt-LR-Treap.

For the competition, we parallelize the sequential implementations also using Deuce [24], a Java implementation of TL2 [18]. The resulting algorithms are denoted STM-Tree and STM-Treap. We further compare our implementations to their hand-crafted state-of-the-art counterparts listed in Table 2.

**Table 2.** Hand-crafted state-of-the-art data structures. The code of LO-Tree was provided by the authors, all other implementations provided by Synchrobench.

| Unbalanced | | Balanced | |
|---|---|---|---|
| **LO-Tree** | Locked-based [20] | **LO-AVL** | Lock-based relaxed AVL   [20] |
| **LF-Tree** | Lock-free [22] | **Snap-Tree** | Lock-based relaxed AVL [11] |
| | | **CF-Tree** | Contention-friendly tree [15] |
| | | **Skiplist** | Java lock-free skiplist |

We also measured the performance of global lock-based implementations. In all workloads, the results were identical or inferior to those achieved by pessimistic fine-grain locking. We hence omitted these results to avoid obscuring the presentation.

*Results.* Figures 4 and 5 show the throughput of unbalanced and balanced data structures, resp. We see that our semi-optimistic solution, both optimized and unoptimized, is far superior to the fully-pessimistic automated approach; it successfully overcomes the bottlenecks associated with lock contention in Lock-Tree and Lock-Treap.

Our approach also outperforms STM by 1.5x to 2.5x. The additional overhead of STM most likely stems from two reasons: deferring writes to commit time, and using a global clock to ensure a consistent view of the read set. The latter is done in order to satisfy opacity [29], which we avoid by "sandboxing". In our experiments, the code *never* incurred a spurious exception or timeout due to inconsistent reads, and so the sandboxing was not associated with a performance penalty.

Our solution comes close to custom-tailored implementations, and the optimized version is even superior to some of them. The throughput of our read-only operations is up to 1.5x lower than that achieved by the best-in-class. By profiling the code, we learned that the bulk of this overhead stems from the need to track all read objects, which is inherent to our transformation. This is in contrast with the hand-crafted implementations, which have small overhead on reads that complete without any retries. In workloads that include update operations, our solution is up to 2.2x slower. This stems from tracking read and locked sets and not from retries as the percentage of retries is less than 1%.

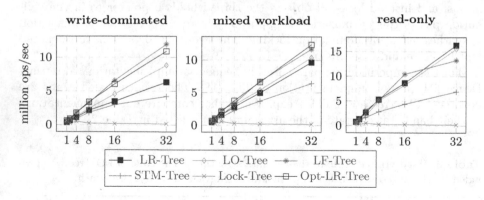

**Fig. 4.** Throughput of unbalanced data structures.

## 4    Related Work

*Concurrent Data Structures.* Many sophisticated concurrent data structures (e.g., [5, 8, 10–12, 15, 20, 22, 25, 32, 38, 40]) were developed and used in concurrent software systems [44]. Implementing efficient synchronization for such data structures is considered a challenging and error-prone task [19, 35, 44]. As a result, concurrent data structures are manually implemented by concurrency experts. This paper shows that (in some cases) an automatic algorithm can produce synchronization that is comparable to synchronization implemented by experts.

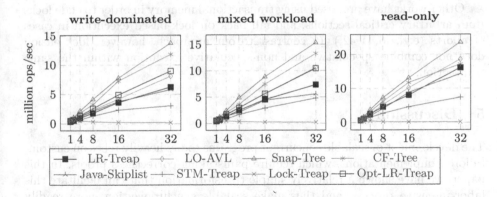

**Fig. 5.** Throughput of balanced data structures.

*Lock Inference Algorithms.* There has been a lot of work on automatically inferring locks for transactions. Most algorithms in the literature infer locks that follow the two-phase locking protocol [14,16,23,28,33,36]. Our approach can potentially be used to optimize the synchronization produced by these algorithms. For example, for algorithms that employ a two-phase variant in which all locks are acquired at the beginning of a transaction (e.g., [14,28]), our approach may be used to defer the locking (e.g., to just before the first write operation) and even to eliminate some of the locking steps. We demonstrate the benefit of combining our transformation with such algorithms by using the domination locking protocol [26] to produce efficient concurrency control for dynamic data structures.

*Transactional Memory.* Transactional memory approaches (TMs) dynamically resolve inconsistencies and deadlocks by rolling back partially completed transactions. Unfortunately, in spite of a lot of effort and many TM implementations (see [30]), existing TMs have not been widely adopted due to various concerns [13, 21,37], including high runtime overhead, poor performance and limited ability to handle irreversible operations. Modern concurrent programs and data structures are typically based on hand-crafted synchronization, rather than on a TM approach [44].

*Lock Elision.* Our transformation is inspired by the idea of *sequential locks* [37] and the approach presented in [39], which replace locks with optimistic concurrency control in read-only transactions. But in contrast to these works, we handle read-only prefixes of transactions (operations) that do update the shared memory. In fact, as shown in Section 3, our approach is best suited for update-dominated workloads. Moreover, using these approaches for a highly-contended data structure (as in Section 3) is likely to provide limited performance, because each update transaction causes many read-only transactions to abort.

Other works have proposed using transactional memory in order to elide locks from arbitrary critical sections, and fall back on lock-based execution in cases of aborts (e.g., [6,41,42]). In contrast to our approach, however, lock elision does not combine speculative and non-speculative execution within the same transaction.

## 5    Discussion

The development of scalable concurrent programs today heavily relies on custom-tailored implementations, which require painstaking correctness proofs. In this paper, we have shown a relatively simple transformation that can facilitate this labor-intensive process, and thus make scalable synchronization more readily available. The input for our transformation is a conventional lock-based concurrent program, which may be either constructed manually or synthesized from sequential code. Our source-to-source transformation then makes judicious use of optimism in order to eliminate principal concurrency bottlenecks in the given program and improve its scalability.

We have illustrated our method for unbalanced and balanced search trees. The transformed code performed significantly better than the original lock-based one, and scaled comparably to hand-crafted implementations that had taken considerably more effort to produce. In these examples, we have applied our transformation manually. An interesting direction for future work would be to create a tool that automatically applies our transformation at compile time.

Our approach makes use of a common pattern in data structures, where an operation typically begins with a long read-only traversal, followed by a handful of (usually local) modifications. A promising direction for future work is to try and exploit similar patterns in order to parallelize or remove locks in other types of code (not data structures), for example, programs that rely on two-phase locking. Furthermore, for programs that follow different patterns, other combinations of optimism and pessimism may prove effective.

Finally, there still remains a gap between the performance achievable by manually optimized solutions and what we could achieve automatically. Our algorithm induces inherent overhead for tracking all operations in the read-only phase for later verification. In specific data structures, these checks might be redundant, but it is difficult to detect this automatically. We believe that it may well be possible to bridge the remaining performance gap using computer-assisted optimizations. For example, a programmer may provide hints regarding certain invariants that are always preserved in the code, in order to eliminate the need for tracking some values for later validation.

## References

1. Concurrentskiplistmap from java.util.concurrent. http://docs.oracle.com/javase/7/docs/api/java/util/concurrent/ConcurrentSkipListMap.html

2. A fast and lightweight key/value database library by google. http://code.google.com/p/leveldb
3. jmonkeyengine: a 3d game engine for java developers. http://jmonkeyengine.org/
4. Afek, Y., Attiya, H., Dolev, D., Gafni, E., Merritt, M., Shavit, N.: Atomic snapshots of shared memory. J. ACM **40**(4), 873–890 (1993)
5. Afek, Y., Kaplan, H., Korenfeld, B., Morrison, A., Tarjan, R.E.: CBTree: a practical concurrent self-adjusting search tree. In: Aguilera, M.K. (ed.) DISC 2012. LNCS, vol. 7611, pp. 1–15. Springer, Heidelberg (2012)
6. Afek, Y., Levy, A., Morrison, A.: Software-improved hardware lock elision. In: PODC (2014)
7. Aragon, C.R., Seidel, R.: Randomized search trees. In: FOCS, pp. 540–545 (1989)
8. Arbel, M., Attiya, H.: Concurrent updates with RCU: search tree as an example. In: PODC, pp. 196–205 (2014)
9. Arbel, M., Golan-Gueta, G., Hillel, E., Keidar, I.: Towards automatic lock removal for scalable synchronization (full version). https://labs.yahoo.com/publications/8476/towards-automatic-lock-removal-scalable-synchronization-full-version
10. Braginsky, A., Petrank, E.: A lock-free B+tree. In: SPAA, pp. 58–67 (2012)
11. Bronson, N.G., Casper, J., Chafi, H., Olukotun, K.: A practical concurrent binary search tree. In: PPOPP, pp. 257–268 (2010)
12. Brown, T., Ellen, F., Ruppert, E.: A general technique for non-blocking trees. In: PPoPP, pp. 329–342 (2014)
13. Cascaval, C., Blundell, C., Michael, M., Cain, H.W., Wu, P., Chiras, S., Chatterjee, S.: Software transactional memory: Why is it only a research toy? Queue **6**(5), 46–58 (2008)
14. Cherem, S., Chilimbi, T., Gulwani, S.: Inferring locks for atomic sections. In: PLDI (2008)
15. Crain, T., Gramoli, V., Raynal, M.: A contention-friendly binary search tree. In: Wolf, F., Mohr, B., an Mey, D. (eds.) Euro-Par 2013. LNCS, vol. 8097, pp. 229–240. Springer, Heidelberg (2013)
16. Cunningham, D., Gudka, K., Eisenbach, S.: Keep off the grass: locking the right path for atomicity. In: Hendren, L. (ed.) CC 2008. LNCS, vol. 4959, pp. 276–290. Springer, Heidelberg (2008)
17. Dice, D., Harris, T.L., Kogan, A., Lev, Y., Moir, M.: Hardware extensions to make lazy subscription safe (2014). CoRR, abs/1407.6968
18. Dice, D., Shalev, O., Shavit, N.: Transactional locking II. In: Dolev, S. (ed.) DISC 2006. LNCS, vol. 4167, pp. 194–208. Springer, Heidelberg (2006)
19. Doherty, S., Detlefs, D.L., Groves, L., Flood, C.H., Luchangco, V., Martin, P.A., Moir, M., Shavit, N., Steele Jr, G.L.: Dcas is not a silver bullet for nonblocking algorithm design. In: SPAA (2004)
20. Drachsler, D., Vechev, M.T., Yahav, E.: Practical concurrent binary search trees via logical ordering. In: PPoPP, pp. 343–356 (2014)
21. Duffy, J.: A (brief) retrospective on transactional memory (2010). http://joeduffyblog.com/2010/01/03/a-brief-retrospective-on-transactional-memory
22. Ellen, F., Fatourou, P., Ruppert, E., van Breugel, F.: Non-blocking binary search trees. In: PODC, pp. 131–140 (2010)
23. Emmi, M., Fischer, J.S., Jhala, R., Majumdar, R.: Lock allocation. In: POPL, pp. 291–296 (2007)
24. Felber, G.K., Shavit, P.N.: Deuce: noninvasive concurrency with a Java STM. In: MULTIPROG (2010)
25. Fraser, K.: Practical lock-freedom. Ph.D thesis, University of Cambridge (2004)

26. Golan-Gueta, G., Bronson, N.G., Aiken, A., Ramalingam, G., Sagiv, M., Yahav, E.: Automatic fine-grain locking using shape properties. In: OOPSLA, pp. 225–242 (2011)
27. Gramoli, V.: More than you ever wanted to know about synchronization: synchrobench, measuring the impact of the synchronization on concurrent algorithms. In: PPoPP (2015)
28. Gudka, K., Harris, T., Eisenbach, S.: Lock inference in the presence of large libraries. In: Noble, J. (ed.) ECOOP 2012. LNCS, vol. 7313, pp. 308–332. Springer, Heidelberg (2012)
29. Guerraoui, R., Kapalka, M.: On the correctness of transactional memory. In: PPOPP, pp. 175–184 (2008)
30. Harris, T., Larus, J., Rajwar, R.: Transactional memory, 2nd edn. Synthesis Lectures on Computer Architecture, vol. 5(1) (2010)
31. Heller, S., Herlihy, M., Luchangco, V., Moir, M., Scherer III, W.N., Shavit, N.: A lazy concurrent list-based set algorithm. In: Anderson, J.H., Prencipe, G., Wattenhofer, R. (eds.) OPODIS 2005. LNCS, vol. 3974, pp. 3–16. Springer, Heidelberg (2006)
32. Herlihy, M., Lev, Y., Luchangco, V., Shavit, N.: A simple optimistic skiplist algorithm. In: Prencipe, G., Zaks, S. (eds.) SIROCCO 2007. LNCS, vol. 4474, pp. 124–138. Springer, Heidelberg (2007)
33. Hicks, M., Foster, J.S., Prattikakis, P.: Lock inference for atomic sections. In: Proceedings of the First ACM SIGPLAN Workshop on Languages Compilers, and Hardware Support for Transactional Computing, June 2006
34. Israeli, A., Rappoport, L.: Disjoint-access-parallel implementations of strong shared memory primitives. In: PODC, pp. 151–160 (1994)
35. Jin, G., Zhang, W., Deng, D., Liblit, B., Lu, S.: Automated concurrency-bug fixing. In: OSDI (2012)
36. McCloskey, B., Zhou, F., Gay, D., Brewer, E.: Autolocker: synchronization inference for atomic sections. In: POPL, pp. 346–358 (2006)
37. McKenney, P.E.: Is parallel programming hard, and if so, what can you do about it?. Linux Technology Center. IBM Beaverton, August 2012
38. Michael, M.M., Scott, M.L.: Simple, fast, and practical non-blocking and blocking concurrent queue algorithms. In: PODC (1996)
39. Nakaike, T., Michael, M.M.: Lock elision for read-only critical sections in java. In: PLDI, pp. 269–278 (2010)
40. Natarajan, A., Mittal, N.: Fast concurrent lock-free binary search trees. In: PPoPP, pp. 317–328 (2014)
41. Rajwar, R., Goodman, J.R.: Transactional lock-free execution of lock-based programs. SIGOPS Oper. Syst. Rev. 36(5), 5–17 (2002)
42. Roy, A., Hand, S., Harris, T.: A runtime system for software lock elision. In: EuroSys (2009)
43. Shacham, O.: Verifying Atomicity of Composed Concurrent Operations. Ph.D thesis, Tel Aviv University (2012)
44. Shacham, O., Bronson, N., Aiken, A., Sagiv, M., Vechev, M., Yahav, E.: Testing atomicity of composed concurrent operations. In: OOPSLA (2011)
45. Shalev, O., Shavit, N.: Predictive log-synchronization. In: Berbers, Y., Zwaenepoel, W. (eds.) EuroSys, pp. 305–315. ACM (2006)
46. Zyulkyarov, F., Gajinov, V., Unsal, O.S., Cristal, A., Ayguadé, E., Harris, T., Valero, M.: Atomic quake: using transactional memory in an interactive multiplayer game server. In: ACM Sigplan Notices, vol. 44, pp. 25–34. ACM (2009)

# Inherent Limitations of Hybrid Transactional Memory

Dan Alistarh[1], Justin Kopinsky[2], Petr Kuznetsov[3], Srivatsan Ravi[4(✉)], and Nir Shavit[2,5]

[1] Microsoft Research, Cambridge, UK
[2] Massachuseets University of Technology, Cambridge, USA
[3] Télécom ParisTech, Paris, France
[4] TU Berlin, Berlin, Germany
Srivatsan.ravi@inet.tu-berlin.de
[5] Tel Aviv University, Tel Aviv, Israel

**Abstract.** Several Hybrid Transactional Memory (HyTM) schemes have recently been proposed to complement the fast, but best-effort nature of Hardware Transactional Memory (HTM) with a slow, reliable software backup. However, the costs of providing concurrency between hardware and software transactions in HyTM are still not well understood.

In this paper, we propose a general model for HyTM implementations, which captures the ability of hardware transactions to buffer memory accesses. The model allows us to formally quantify and analyze the amount of overhead (instrumentation) caused by the potential presence of software transactions. We prove that (1) it is impossible to build a strictly serializable HyTM implementation that has both uninstrumented reads and writes, even for very weak progress guarantees, and (2) the instrumentation cost incurred by a hardware transaction in any progressive opaque HyTM is linear in the size of the transaction's data set. We further describe two implementations which exhibit optimal instrumentation costs for two different progress conditions. In sum, this paper proposes the first formal HyTM model and captures for the first time the trade-off between the degree of hardware-software TM concurrency and the amount of instrumentation overhead.

## 1 Introduction

*Hybrid Transactional Memory.* Since its introduction by Herlihy and Moss [17], *Transactional Memory (TM)* has been a tool with tremendous promise. It is therefore not surprising that the recently introduced Hardware Transactional Memory (HTM) implementations [1,21,22] have been eagerly anticipated and scrutinized by the community.

P. Kuznetsov—The author is supported by the Agence Nationale de la Recherche, ANR-14-CE35-0010-01, project DISCMAT.

N. Shavit—Support is gratefully acknowledged from the National Science Foundation under grants CCF-1217921, CCF-1301926, and IIS-1447786, the Department of Energy under grant ER26116/DE-SC0008923, and the Oracle and Intel corporations.

© Springer-Verlag Berlin Heidelberg 2015
Y. Moses (Ed.): DISC 2015, LNCS 9363, pp. 185–199, 2015.
DOI: 10.1007/978-3-662-48653-5_13

Early experience with programming HTM, e.g. [3,11,12], paints an interesting picture: if used carefully, HTM can significantly speed up and simplify concurrent implementations. At the same time, it is not without its limitations: since HTMs are usually implemented on top of the cache coherence mechanism, hardware transactions have inherent *capacity constraints* on the number of distinct memory locations that can be accessed inside a single transaction. Moreover, all current proposals are *best-effort*, as they may abort under imprecisely specified conditions. In brief, the programmer should not solely rely on HTMs.

Several *Hybrid Transactional Memory (HyTM)* schemes [9,10,18,19] have been proposed to complement the fast, but best-effort nature of HTM with a slow, reliable software transactional memory (STM) backup. These proposals have explored a wide range of trade-offs between the overhead on hardware transactions, concurrent execution of hardware and software, and the provided progress guarantees.

Early HyTM proposals [10,18] share interesting features. First, transactions that do not conflict on the *data items* they access are expected to run concurrently, regardless of their type (software or hardware). This property is referred to as *progressiveness* [14] and is believed to allow for higher parallelism. Second, hardware transactions usually employ *code instrumentation* techniques. Intuitively, instrumentation is used by hardware transactions to detect concurrency scenarios and abort in the case of data conflicts.

Reducing instrumentation in the frequently executed hardware fast-path is key to efficiency. In particular, recent work by Riegel *et al.* [24] surveys a series of techniques to reduce instrumentation. Despite considerable algorithmic work on HyTM, there is currently no formal basis for specifying and understanding the cost of building HyTMs with non-trivial concurrency. In particular, what are the inherent instrumentation costs of building a HyTM? What are the trade-offs between these costs and the ability of the HyTM system to run software and hardware transactions in parallel?

*Modelling HyTM.* To address these questions, we propose the first model for hybrid TM systems which formally captures the notion of *cached* accesses provided by hardware transactions, and defines instrumentation costs in a precise, quantifiable way.

Specifically, we model a hardware transaction as a series of memory accesses that operate on locally cached copies of the memory locations, followed by a *cache-commit* operation. In case a concurrent (hardware or software) transaction performs a (read-write or write-write) conflicting access to a cached base object, the cached copy is invalidated and the hardware transaction aborts. Thus, detecting contention on memory locations is provided "automatically" to code running inside hardware transactions.

Further, we notice that a HyTM implementation imposes a logical partitioning of shared memory into *data* and *metadata* locations. Intuitively, metadata is used by transactions to exchange information about contention and conflicts, while data locations only store the *values* of data items read and updated within transactions. Recent experimental evidence [20] suggests that the overhead imposed by accessing metadata, and in particular code to detect concurrent software transactions, is a significant performance bottleneck. Therefore, we quantify instrumentation cost by measuring the number of accesses to *metadata* memory locations which transactions perform. Our framework captures all known HyTM proposals which combine HTMs with an STM fallback [9,10,18,19,23].

*The Cost of Concurrency.* We then explore the implications of our model. The first, immediate application is an impossibility result showing that instrumentation *is necessary* in a HyTM implementation, even if we only provide *sequential* progress, *i.e.*, if a transaction is only guaranteed to commit if it runs in isolation.

The second application concerns the *instrumentation overhead* of progressive HyTM schemes, which constitutes our main technical contribution. We prove that any progressive HyTM, satisfying reasonable livenesss guarantees, must, in certain executions, force read-only transactions to access a *linear* (in the size of their data sets) number of metadata memory locations, even in the absence of contention.

Our proof technique is interesting in its own right. Inductively, we start with a sequential execution in which a "large" set $S_m$ of read-only hardware transactions, each accessing $m$ distinct data items and $m$ distinct metadata memory locations, run after an execution $E_m$. We then construct execution $E_{m+1}$, an extension of $E_m$, which forces at least half of the transactions in $S_m$ to access a *new* metadata base object when reading a new $(m+1)^{th}$ data item, running after $E_{m+1}$. The technical challenge, and the key departure from prior work on STM lower bounds, *e.g.* [7,13,14], is that hardware transactions practically possess "automatic" conflict detection, aborting on contention. This is in contrast to STMs, which must take steps to detect contention on memory locations.

This linear lower bound is tight. We match it with an algorithm which, additionally, allows for uninstrumented writes, *invisible reads* and is provably *opaque* [14]. To the best of our knowledge, this is the first formal proof of correctness of a HyTM algorithm.

*Low-Instrumentation HyTM.* Our main lower bound result shows that there are high inherent instrumentation costs to progressive HyTM designs [10,18]. Interestingly, some recent HyTM schemes [9,19,20,24] sacrifice progressiveness for *constant* instrumentation cost (*i.e.*, not depending on the size of the data set). Instead, only sequential progress is ensured. (Despite this fact, these schemes perform well due to the limited instrumentation in hardware transactions.)

We extend these schemes to provide an upper bound for non-progressive *low-instrumentation* HyTMs. We present a HyTM with invisible reads *and* uninstrumented hardware writes which guarantees that a hardware transaction accesses at most *one* metadata object in the course of its execution. Software transactions are mutually progressive, while hardware transactions are guaranteed to commit only if they do not run concurrently with an updating software transaction. This algorithm shows that, by abandoning progressiveness, the instrumentation costs of HyTM can be reduced to the bare minimum required by our first impossibility result. In other words, the cost of avoiding the linear instrumentation lower bound is that hardware transactions may be aborted by non-conflicting software ones.

*Roadmap.* Section 2 introduces the basic TM model and definitions. Section 3 presents our first contribution: a formal model for HyTM implementations. Section 4 formally defines instrumentation and proves the impossibility of implementing uninstrumented HyTMs. Section 5 establishes a linear lower bound on metadata accesses for progressive HyTMs while Section 6 describes our instrumentation-optimal opaque HyTM implementations. Section 7 presents the related work and Section 8 concludes the paper. The tech report contains the formal proofs of the lower bounds, algorithm pseudo-code and their correctness proofs [4].

## 2    Preliminaries

**Transactional Memory (TM).** A *transaction* is a sequence of *transactional operations* (or *t-operations*), reads and writes, performed on a set of *transactional objects* (*t-objects*). A TM *implementation* provides a set of concurrent *processes* with deterministic algorithms that implement reads and writes on t-objects using a set of *base objects*. More precisely, for each transaction $T_k$, a TM implementation must support the following t-operations: $read_k(X)$, where $X$ is a t-object, that returns a value in a domain $V$ or a special value $A_k \notin V$ (*abort*), $write_k(X, v)$, for a value $v \in V$, that returns $ok$ or $A_k$, and $tryC_k$ that returns $C_k \notin V$ (*commit*) or $A_k$.

**Configurations and Executions.** A *configuration* of a TM implementation specifies the state of each base object and each process. In the *initial* configuration, each base object has its initial value and each process is in its initial state. An *event* (or *step*) of a transaction invoked by some process is an invocation of a t-operation, a response of a t-operation, or an atomic *primitive* operation applied to base object along with its response. An *execution fragment* is a (finite or infinite) sequence of events $E = e_1, e_2, \ldots$. An *execution* of a TM implementation $\mathcal{M}$ is an execution fragment where, informally, each event respects the specification of base objects and the algorithms specified by $\mathcal{M}$. In the next section, we define precisely how base objects should behave in a hybrid model combining direct memory accesses with *cached* accesses (hardware transactions).

The *read set* (resp., the *write set*) of a transaction $T_k$ in an execution $E$, enoted $Rset_E(T_k)$ (and resp. $Wset_E(T_k)$), is the set of t-objects that $T_k$ attempts to read (and resp. write) by issuing a t-read (and resp. t-write) invocation in $E$ (for brevity, we sometimes omit the subscript $E$ from the notation). The *data set* of $T_k$ is $Dset(T_k) = Rset(T_k) \cup Wset(T_k)$. $T_k$ is called *read-only* if $Wset(T_k) = \emptyset$; *write-only* if $Rset(T_k) = \emptyset$ and *updating* if $Wset(T_k) \neq \emptyset$.

For any finite execution $E$ and execution fragment $E'$, $E \cdot E'$ denotes the concatenation of $E$ and $E'$ and we say that $E \cdot E'$ is an *extension* of $E$. For every transaction identifier $k$, $E|k$ denotes the subsequence of $E$ restricted to events of transaction $T_k$. If $E|k$ is non-empty, we say that $T_k$ *participates* in $E$, and let $txns(E)$ denote the set of transactions that participate in $E$. Two executions $E$ and $E'$ are *indistinguishable* to a set $\mathcal{T}$ of transactions, if for each transaction $T_k \in \mathcal{T}$, $E|k = E'|k$.

**Complete and Incomplete Transactions.** A transaction $T_k \in txns(E)$ is *complete in* $E$ if $E|k$ ends with a response event. The execution $E$ is *complete* if all transactions in $txns(E)$ are complete in $E$. A transaction $T_k \in txns(E)$ is *t-complete* if $E|k$ ends with $A_k$ or $C_k$; otherwise, $T_k$ is *t-incomplete*. $T_k$ is *committed* (resp. *aborted*) in $E$ if the last event of $T_k$ is $C_k$ (resp. $A_k$). The execution $E$ is *t-complete* if all transactions in $txns(E)$ are t-complete. A configuration $C$ after an execution $E$ is *quiescent* (resp. *t-quiescent*) if every transaction $T_k \in txns(E)$ is complete (resp. t-complete) in $E$.

**Contention.** We assume that base objects are accessed with *read-modify-write* (rmw) primitives. A rmw primitive $\langle g, h \rangle$ applied to a base object atomically updates the value of the object with a new value, which is a function $g(v)$ of the old value $v$, and returns a response $h(v)$. A rmw primitive event on a base object is *trivial* if, in any configuration, its application does not change the state of the object. Otherwise, it is called *nontrivial*.

Events $e$ and $e'$ of an execution $E$ *contend* on a base object $b$ if they are both primitives on $b$ in $E$ and at least one of them is nontrivial. In a configuration $C$ after an execution $E$, every incomplete transaction $T$ has exactly one *enabled* event in $C$, which is the next event $T$ will perform according to the TM implementation. We say that a transaction $T$ is *poised to apply an event $e$ after* $E$ if $e$ is the next enabled event for $T$ in $E$. We say that transactions $T$ and $T'$ *concurrently contend* on $b$ in $E$ if they are each poised to apply contending events on $b$ after $E$. We say that an execution fragment $E$ is *step contention-free* for t-operation $op_k$ if the events of $E|op_k$ are contiguous in $E$. An execution fragment $E$ is *step contention-free for* $T_k$ if the events of $E|k$ are contiguous in $E$, and $E$ is *step contention-free* if $E$ is step contention-free for all transactions that participate in $E$.

**TM Correctness.** A *history exported* by an execution fragment $E$ is the subsequence of $E$ consisting of only the invocation and response events of t-operations. Let $H_E$ denote the history exported by an execution $E$. Two histories $H$ and $H'$ are *equivalent* if $txns(H) = txns(H')$ and for every transaction $T_k \in txns(H)$, $H|k = H'|k$. For any two transactions $T_k, T_m \in txns(E)$, we say that $T_k$ precedes $T_m$ in the *real-time order* of $E$ $(T_k \prec_E^{RT} T_m)$ if $T_k$ is t-complete in $E$ and the last event of $T_k$ precedes the first event of $T_m$ in $E$. If neither $T_k$ precedes $T_m$ nor $T_m$ precedes $T_k$ in real-time order, then $T_k$ and $T_m$ are *concurrent* in $E$. An execution $E$ is *sequential* if every invocation of a t-operation is either the last event in $H_E$ or is immediately followed by a matching response. An execution $E$ is *t-sequential* if there are no concurrent transactions in $E$.

Informally, a t-sequential history $S$ is *legal* if every t-read of a t-object returns the *latest written value* of this t-object in $S$. A history $H$ is *opaque* if there exists a legal t-sequential history $S$ equivalent to $H$ such that $S$ respects the real-time order of transactions in $H$ [14].

# 3   Hybrid Transactional Memory (HyTM)

**Direct Accesses and Cached Accesses.** We now describe the execution model of a *Hybrid Transactional Memory (HyTM)* implementation. In our HyTM model, every base object can be accessed with two kinds of primitives, *direct* and *cached*.

In a direct access, the rmw primitive operates on the memory state: the direct-access event atomically reads the value of the object in the shared memory and, if necessary, modifies it.

In a cached access performed by a process $i$, the rmw primitive operates on the *cached* state recorded in process $i$'s *tracking set* $\tau_i$. One can think of $\tau_i$ as the *L1 cache* of process $i$. A *hardware transaction* is a series of cached rmw primitives performed on $\tau_i$ followed by a *cache-commit* primitive.

More precisely, $\tau_i$ is a set of triples $(b, v, m)$ where $b$ is a base object identifier, $v$ is a value, and $m \in \{shared, exclusive\}$ is an access *mode*. The triple $(b, v, m)$ is added to the tracking set when $i$ performs a cached rmw access of $b$, where $m$ is set to *exclusive* if the access is nontrivial, and to *shared* otherwise. We assume that there exists some constant $TS$ (representing the size of the L1 cache) such that the condition $|\tau_i| \leq TS$ must always hold; this condition will be enforced by our model. A base object $b$ is *present* in $\tau_i$ with mode $m$ if $\exists v, (b, v, m) \in \tau_i$.

A trivial (resp. nontrivial) cached primitive $\langle g, h \rangle$ applied to $b$ by process $i$ first checks the condition $|\tau_i| = TS$ and if so, it sets $\tau_i = \emptyset$ and immediately returns $\perp$ (we call this event a *capacity abort*). We assume that $TS$ is large enough so that no transaction with data set of size 1 can incur a capacity abort. If the transaction does not incur a capacity abort, the process checks whether $b$ is present in exclusive (resp. any) mode in $\tau_j$ for any $j \neq i$. If so, $\tau_i$ is set to $\emptyset$ and the primitive returns $\perp$. Otherwise, the triple $(b, v, shared)$ (resp. $(b, g(v), exclusive)$) is added to $\tau_i$, where $v$ is the most recent cached value of $b$ in $\tau_i$ (in case $b$ was previously accessed by $i$ within the current hardware transaction) or the value of $b$ in the current memory configuration, and finally $h(v)$ is returned.

A tracking set can be *invalidated* by a concurrent process: if, in a configuration $C$ where $(b, v, exclusive) \in \tau_i$ (resp. $(b, v, shared) \in \tau_i$), a process $j \neq i$ applies any primitive (resp. any *nontrivial* primitive) to $b$, then $\tau_i$ becomes *invalid* and any subsequent cached primitive invoked by $i$ sets $\tau_i$ to $\emptyset$ and returns $\perp$. We refer to this event as a *tracking set abort*.

Finally, the *cache-commit* primitive issued by process $i$ with a valid $\tau_i$ does the following: for each base object $b$ such that $(b, v, exclusive) \in \tau_i$, the value of $b$ in $C$ is updated to $v$. Finally, $\tau_i$ is set to $\emptyset$ and the primitive returns *commit*.

Note that HTM may also abort spuriously, or because of unsupported operations [22]. The first cause can be modelled probabilistically in the above framework, which would not however significantly affect our claims and proofs, except

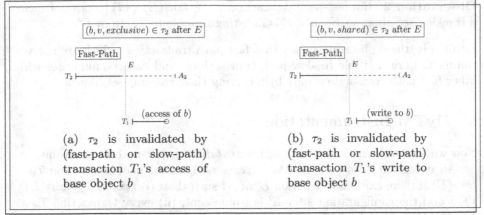

**Fig. 1.** Tracking set aborts in fast-path transactions

for a more cumbersome presentation. Also, our lower bounds are based exclusively on executions containing t-reads and t-writes. Therefore, in the following, we only consider tracking set and capacity aborts.

**Slow-Path and Fast-Path Transactions.** In the following, we partition HyTM transactions into *fast-path transactions* and *slow-path transactions*. Practically, two separate algorithms (fast-path one and slow-path one) are provided for each t-operation.

A slow-path transaction models a regular software transaction. An event of a slow-path transaction is either an invocation or response of a t-operation, or a rmw primitive on a base object.

A fast-path transaction essentially encapsulates a hardware transaction. An event of a fast-path transaction is either an invocation or response of a t-operation, a cached primitive on a base object, or a *cache-commit*: *t-read* and *t-write* are only allowed to contain cached primitives, and *tryC* consists of invoking *cache-commit*. Furthermore, we assume that a fast-path transaction $T_k$ returns $A_k$ as soon an underlying cached primitive or *cache-commit* returns $\perp$. Figure 1 depicts such a scenario illustrating a tracking set abort: fast-path transaction $T_2$ executed by process $p_2$ accesses a base object $b$ in shared (and resp. exclusive) mode and it is added to its tracking set $\tau_2$. Immediately after the access of $b$ by $T_2$, a concurrent transaction $T_1$ applies a nontrivial primitive to $b$ (and resp. accesses $b$). Thus, the tracking of $p_2$ is invalidated and $T_2$ must be aborted in any extension of this execution.

We provide two key observations on this model regarding the interactions of non-committed fast path transactions with other transactions. Let $E$ be any execution of a HyTM implementation $\mathcal{M}$ in which a fast-path transaction $T_k$ is either t-incomplete or aborted. Then the sequence of events $E'$ derived by removing all events of $E|k$ from $E$ is an execution $\mathcal{M}$. Moreover:

**Observation 1.** To every slow-path transaction $T_m \in txns(E)$, $E$ is indistinguishable from $E'$.

**Observation 2.** If a fast-path transaction $T_m \in txns(E) \setminus \{T_k\}$ does not incur a tracking set abort in $E$, then $E$ is indistinguishable to $T_m$ from $E'$.

Intuitively, these observations say that fast-path transactions which are not yet committed are invisible to slow-path transactions, and can communicate with other fast-path transactions only by incurring their tracking-set aborts.

## 4    HyTM Instrumentation

Now we define the notion of *code instrumentation* in fast-path transactions.

An execution $E$ of a HyTM $\mathcal{M}$ *appears t-sequential* to a transaction $T_k \in txns(E)$ if there exists an execution $E'$ of $\mathcal{M}$ such that: (i) $txns(E') \subseteq txns(E) \setminus \{T_k\}$ and the configuration after $E'$ is t-quiescent, (ii) every transaction $T_m \in txns(E)$ that precedes $T_k$ in real-time order is included in $E'$ such that $E|m = E'|m$, (iii) for every transaction $T_m \in txns(E')$, $Rset_{E'}(T_m) \subseteq Rset_E(T_m)$ and $Wset_{E'}(T_m) \subseteq Wset_E(T_m)$, and (iv) $E' \cdot E|k$ is an execution of $\mathcal{M}$.

**Definition 1 (Data and metadata base objects).** *Let $\mathcal{X}$ be the set of t-objects operated by a HyTM implementation $\mathcal{M}$. Now we partition the set of base objects used by $\mathcal{M}$ into a set $\mathbb{D}$ of data objects and a set $\mathbb{M}$ of metadata objects $(\mathbb{D} \cap \mathbb{M} = \emptyset)$. We further partition $\mathbb{D}$ into sets $\mathbb{D}_X$ associated with each t-object $X \in \mathcal{X}$: $\mathbb{D} = \bigcup_{X \in \mathcal{X}} \mathbb{D}_X$, for all $X \neq Y$ in $\mathcal{X}$, $\mathbb{D}_X \cap \mathbb{D}_Y = \emptyset$, such that:*

1. *In every execution $E$, each fast-path transaction $T_k \in txns(E)$ only accesses base objects in $\bigcup_{X \in DSet(T_k)} \mathbb{D}_X$ or $\mathbb{M}$.*
2. *Let $E \cdot \rho$ and $E \cdot E' \cdot \rho'$ be two t-complete executions, such that $E$ and $E \cdot E'$ are t-complete, $\rho$ and $\rho'$ are complete executions of a transaction $T_k \notin txns(E \cdot E')$, $H_\rho = H_{\rho'}$, and $\forall T_m \in txns(E')$, $Dset(T_m) \cap Dset(T_k) = \emptyset$. Then the states of the base objects $\bigcup_{X \in DSet(T_k)} \mathbb{D}_X$ in the configuration after $E \cdot \rho$ and $E \cdot E' \cdot \rho'$ are the same.*
3. *Let execution $E$ appear t-sequential to a transaction $T_k$ and let the enabled event $e$ of $T_k$ after $E$ be a primitive on a base object $b \in \mathbb{D}$. Then, unless $e$ returns $\perp$, $E \cdot e$ also appears t-sequential to $T_k$.*

Intuitively, the first condition says that a transaction is only allowed to access data objects based on its data set. The second condition says that transactions with disjoint data sets can communicate only via metadata objects. Finally, the last condition means that base objects in $\mathbb{D}$ may only contain the "values" of t-objects, and cannot be used to detect concurrent transactions. Note that our results will lower bound the number of metadata objects that must be accessed under particular assumptions, thus from a cost perspective, $\mathbb{D}$ should be made as large as possible.

All HyTM proposals we aware of, such as *HybridNOrec* [9,23], *PhTM* [19] and others [10,18], conform to our definition of instrumentation in fast-path transactions. For instance, HybridNOrec [9,23] employs a distinct base object in

$\mathbb{D}$ for each t-object and a global *sequence lock* as the metadata that is accessed by fast-path transactions to detect concurrency with slow-path transactions. Similarly, the HyTM implementation by *Damron et al.* [10] also associates a distinct base object in $\mathbb{D}$ for each t-object and additionally, a *transaction header* and *ownership record* as metadata base objects.

**Definition 2 (Uninstrumented HyTMs).** *A HyTM implementation $\mathcal{M}$ provides* uninstrumented writes (resp. reads) *if in every execution $E$ of $\mathcal{M}$, for every write-only (resp. read-only) fast-path transaction $T_k$, all primitives in $E|k$ are performed on base objects in $\mathbb{D}$. A HyTM is uninstrumented if both its reads and writes are uninstrumented.*

**Observation 3.** Consider any execution $E$ of a HyTM implementation $\mathcal{M}$ which provides uninstrumented reads (resp. writes). For any fast-path read-only (resp. write-only) transaction $T_k \notin txns(E)$, that runs step-contention free after $E$, the execution $E$ appears t-sequential to $T_k$.

**Impossibility of Uninstrumented HyTMs.** We can now show that any strictly serializable HyTM must be instrumented, even under a very weak liveness and progress assumptions of *sequential TM-liveness* and *sequential TM-progress*. *sequential* TM-liveness Sequential TM-liveness guarantees that t-operations running in the absence of concurrent transactions return in a finite number of its steps. Sequential TM-progress stipulates that a transaction can only be aborted only if it is concurrent with another transaction. Note that sequential TM-liveness and TM-progress allow a transaction not running t-sequentially to abort or block indefinitely.

**Theorem 1.** *There does not exist a strictly serializable uninstrumented HyTM implementation that ensures sequential TM-progress and TM-liveness.*

Due to space constraints, we defer the proof the technical report [4], and provide an outline below. Suppose by contradiction that such a HyTM exists and let $E$ be a t-sequential execution of it in which a slow-path transaction $T_0$ reads t-object $Z$ (returning the initial value), then writes a new value $nv$ to t-objects $X$ and $Y$, and commits. Since the HyTM is uninstrumented, Observation 3 implies that a fast-path transaction running step contention-free cannot detect the presence of a concurrent transaction and, by sequential TM-liveness and TM-progress, the transaction must eventually commit. Thus, there exists $E'$, the longest prefix of $E$ that cannot be extended with the t-complete step-contention-free execution neither of a fast-path transaction $T_x$ reading $X$ and returning $nv$ nor of a fast-path transaction $T_y$ reading $Y$ and returning $nv$. Without loss of generality, suppose that if $T_0$ takes one more step $e$ after $E'$, then $T_y$ running step contention-free after $E \cdot e$ would find the new value in $Y$.

Next, we show the following execution exists: starting from $E'$, a fast-path $T_z$ writes a new value to $Z$ and commits, then a fast-path $T_x$ reads the old value of $X$ and commits, then $T_0$ takes one more step (setting $Y$ to the new value), and a fast-path $T_y$ reads the new value of $Y$.

However, such an execution is not strictly serializable. Indeed, as the value written by $T_0$ is returned by transaction $T_y$, $T_0$ must be committed and precede $T_y$ in any serialization. Since $T_x$ returns the initial value of $X$, $T_x$ must precede $T_0$. Since $T_0$ reads the initial value of $Z$, $T_0$ must precede $T_z$, implying a cycle, which creates the contradiction.

## 5    Linear Instrumentation Lower Bound

In this section, we focus on a natural progress condition called progressiveness [14] by which a transaction can only abort under read-write or write-write conflict with a concurrent transaction:

**Definition 3 (Progressiveness).** *Transactions $T_i$ and $T_j$ conflict in an execution $E$ on a t-object $X$ if $X \in Dset(T_i) \cap Dset(T_j)$ and $X \in Wset(T_i) \cup Wset(T_j)$. A HyTM implementation $\mathcal{M}$ is* fast-path *(resp.* slow-path*) progressive if in every execution $E$ of $\mathcal{M}$ and for every fast-path (and resp. slow-path) transaction $T_i$ that aborts in $E$, either $A_i$ is a capacity abort or $T_i$ conflicts with some transaction $T_j$ that is concurrent to $T_i$ in $E$. We say $\mathcal{M}$ is* progressive *if it is both fast-path and slow-path progressive.*

We first prove the following auxiliary lemma concerning progressive HyTMs. It shows that a fast path transaction in a progressive HyTM can contend on a base object only with a conflicting transaction. Intuitively, the proof is based on the observation that, if two non-conflicting transactions, of which one is fast-path, concurrently contend on a base object in some execution, the fast-path transaction may incur a tracking set abort. However, this contradicts the fact that in a progressive HyTM, a transaction may be aborted only due to a conflict.

**Lemma 1.** *Let $\mathcal{M}$ be any fast-path progressive HyTM implementation. Let $E \cdot E_1 \cdot E_2$ be an execution of $\mathcal{M}$ where $E_1$ (and resp. $E_2$) is the step contention-free execution fragment of transaction $T_1 \notin txns(E)$ (and resp. $T_2 \notin txns(E)$), $T_1$ (and resp. $T_2$) does not conflict with any transaction in $E \cdot E_1 \cdot E_2$, and at least one of $T_1$ or $T_2$ is a fast-path transaction. Then, $T_1$ and $T_2$ do not contend on any base object in $E \cdot E_1 \cdot E_2$.*

We then notice that Lemma 1 can be extended to prove the following key auxiliary result: If a t-operation of a fast-path transaction does not access any *metadata* base object, then the process executing the transaction cannot distinguish two executions that each export identical histories, *i.e.*, the process cannot tell the difference by only looking at the invocation and responses of the t-operations.

After establishing these auxiliary lemmas, we are ready to prove our main result. We show that read-only fast-path transactions in a progressive opaque HyTM providing *obstruction-free (OF) TM-liveness* (every t-operation running step contention-free returns in a finite number of its own steps) may have to access a *linear* (in the size of their data sets) number of distinct metadata memory locations, even in the absence of concurrency. The complete proof can be found in the technical report [4]; here, we provide a high-level overview of the technique.

**Theorem 2.** *Let $\mathcal{M}$ be any progressive, opaque HyTM implementation that provides OF TM-liveness. For every $m \in \mathbb{N}$, there exists an execution $E$ in which some fast-path read-only transaction $T_k \in txns(E)$ satisfies either (1) $Dset(T_k) \leq m$ and $T_k$ incurs a capacity abort in $E$ or (2) $Dset(T_k) = m$ and $T_k$ accesses $\Omega(m)$ distinct metadata base objects in $E$.*

*Proof (Outline).* Let $\kappa$ be the smallest integer such that some fast-path transaction running step contention-free after a t-complete execution performs $\kappa$ t-reads and incurs a *capacity* abort. In other words, if a fast-path transaction reads less than $\kappa$ t-objects, it cannot incur a capacity abort.

We prove that, for all $m \leq \kappa - 1$, there exists a t-complete execution $E_m$ and a set $S_m$ ($|S_m| = 2^{\kappa-m}$) of read-only fast-path transactions such that (1) each transaction in $S_m$ reads $m$ t-objects, (2) the data sets of any two transactions in $S_m$ are disjoint, (3) in the step contention-free execution of any transaction in $S_m$ extending $E_m$, every t-read accesses at least one distinct metadata base object.

By induction, we assume that the induction statement holds for all $m < \kappa - 1$ (the base case $m = 0$ is trivial) and build $E_{m+1}$ and $S_{m+1}$ satisfying the above condition. Pick any two transactions from the set $S_m$. We construct $E'_m$, a t-complete extension of $E_m$ by the execution of a slow-path transaction writing to two distinct t-objects $X$ and $Y$, such that the two picked transactions, running step contention-free after that, cannot distinguish $E_m$ and $E'_m$.

Next, we let each of the transactions read one of the two t-objects $X$ and $Y$. Specifically, we construct the execution $E'_m$ as follows. We first extend $E_m$ with the t-incomplete execution of a slow-path transaction writing to $X$ and $Y$ such that this extension cannot be further extended with the step contention-free executions of either of the picked fast-path transactions performing their $m$ t-reads, followed by the $(m+1)^{th}$ t-read of $X$ or $Y$ that returns the respective "new value."

We show that at least one of the two transactions must access a new metadata base object in this $(m+1)^{th}$ t-read when running step contention-free after this slow-path transaction. Otherwise, the resulting execution would not be opaque. Indeed, without accessing a new metadata base object, such an execution appears t-sequential to the fast-path transactions. This allows us to construct the t-complete execution $E'_m$ such that at least one of the fast-path transactions, running step contention-free after this execution is poised to access a distinct new metadata base object during the $(m+1)^{th}$ t-read.

By repeating this argument for each pair of transactions, we derive that there exists $E_{m+1}$, a t-complete extension of $E_m$, such that *at least half* of the transactions in $S_m$ must access a new distinct metadata base object in its $(m+1)^{th}$ t-read when it runs t-sequentially after $E_{m+1}$. Intuitively, we construct $E_{m+1}$ by "gluing" all these executions $E'_m$ together, which is possible thanks to Lemma 1 and its extensions. These transactions constitute $S_{m+1} \subset S_m$, $|S_{m+1}| = |S_m|/2 = 2^{\kappa-(m+1)}$.

# 6    Instrumentation-Optimal HyTM Algorithms

In this section, we describe two "instrumentation-optimal" progressive HyTMs. We show that these implementations are provably opaque in our HyTM model where a fast-path transaction is not "visible" to a concurrent (slow-path or fast-path) transaction until it has committed (Observations 1 and 2).

**A Linear Upper Bound on Instrumentation.** We prove that the lower bound in Theorem 2 is tight by describing a progressive opaque HyTM implementation that provides *wait-free TM-liveness* (every t-operation returns in a finite number of its steps) and uses *invisible reads* (read-only transactions do not apply any nontrivial primitives). The algorithm works as follows.

*(Base objects)* For every t-object $X_j$, our implementation maintains a base object $v_j \in \mathbb{D}$ that stores the value of $X_j$ and a metadata base object $r_j$, which is a *lock bit* that stores 0 or 1.

*(Fast-path transactions)* For a fast-path transaction $T_k$, the $read_k(X_j)$ implementation first reads $r_j$ to check if $X_j$ is locked by a concurrent updating transaction. If so, it returns $A_k$, else it returns the value of $X_j$. Updating fast-path transactions use uninstrumented writes: $write(X_j, v)$ simply stores the cached state of $X_j$ along with its value $v$ and if the cache has not been invalidated, updates the shared memory during $tryC_k$ by invoking the *commit-cache* primitive.

*(Slow-path transactions)* Any $read_k(X_j)$ invoked by a slow-path transaction first reads the value of the object from $v_j$, checks if $r_j$ is set and then performs *value-based validation* on its entire read set to check if any of them have been modified. If either of these conditions is true, the transaction returns $A_k$. Otherwise, it returns the value of $X_j$. A read-only transaction simply returns $C_k$ during the tryCommit. An updating slow-path transaction $T_k$ attempts to obtain exclusive write access to its entire write set by performing *compare-and-set* (*cas*) primitive that checks if the value of $r_j$, for each $X_j \in Wset(T_k)$, is not 1 and, if so, replaces it with 1. If all the locks on the write set were acquired successfully, $T_k$ checks if any t-object in $Rset(T_k)$ is concurrently being updated by another transaction and $T_k$ is aborted if so. Otherwise, $T_k$ attempts to write the values of the t-objects via *cas* operations. If any *cas* on the individual base objects fails, there must be a concurrent fast-path writer, and so $T_k$ rolls back the state of the base objects that were updated, releases locks on its write set and returns $A_k$.

**Theorem 3.** *There exists an opaque HyTM implementation that provides uninstrumented writes, invisible reads, progressiveness and wait-free TM-liveness such that in its every execution $E$, every read-only fast-path transaction $T \in txns(E)$ accesses $O(|Rset(T)|)$ distinct metadata base objects.*

**Providing Partial Concurrency at Low Cost.** Allowing fast-path transactions to run concurrently in HyTM results in an instrumentation cost that is proportional to the read-set size of a fast-path transaction. But can we run *some* transactions concurrently with constant instrumentation cost, while still keeping invisible reads?

We describe a *slow-path progressive* opaque HyTM with invisible reads and wait-free TM-liveness. To fast-path transactions, it only provides *sequential* TM-progress (they are only guaranteed to commit in the absence of concurrency), but in return the algorithm is only using a single metadata base object *Count* that is read once by a fast-path transaction and accessed twice with a *fetch-and-add* primitive by an updating slow-path transaction. Thus, the instrumentation cost of the algorithm is constant.

Intuitively, *Count* allows fast-path transactions to detect the existence of concurrent updating slow-path transactions. Each time an updating slow-path updating transaction tries to commit, it increments *Count* and once all writes to data base objects are completed (this part of the algorithm is identical to the implementation above) or the transaction is aborted, it decrements *Count*. Therefore, $Count \neq 0$ means that at least one slow-path updating transaction is incomplete. A fast-path transaction simply checks if $Count \neq 0$ in the beginning and aborts if so, otherwise, its code is identical to the one above. Note that this way, any update of *Count* automatically causes a tracking set abort of any incomplete fast-path transaction.

# 7   Related Work

The term *instrumentation* was originally used in the context of HyTMs [9,19,23] to indicate the overhead a hardware transaction induces in order to detect pending software transactions. The impossibility of designing HyTMs without any code instrumentation was informally suggested in [9]. We prove this formally in this paper.

In [6], Attiya and Hillel considered the instrumentation cost of *privatization*, *i.e.*, allowing transactions to isolate data items by making them private to a process so that no other process is allowed to modify the privatized item. The model we consider is fundamentally different, in that we model hardware transactions at the level of cache coherence, and do not consider non-transactional accesses. The proof techniques we employ are also different.

Uninstrumented HTMs may be viewed as being *disjoint-access parallel (DAP)* [7]. As such, some of the techniques used in the proof of Theorem 1 extend those used in [7,13,14]. However, proving lower bounds on the instrumentation costs of the HyTM fast-path is challenging, since such t-operations can automatically abort due to any contending concurrent step.

Circa 2005, several papers introduced HyTM implementations [5,10,18] that integrated HTMs with variants of *DSTM* [16]. These implementations provide nontrivial concurrency between hardware and software transactions (progressiveness), by imposing instrumentation on hardware transactions: every t-read operation incurs at least one extra access to a metadata base object. Our Theorem 2 shows that this overhead is unavoidable. Of note, write operations of these HyTMs are also instrumented, but our result shows that it is not necessary. References [15,23] provide detailed overviews on HyTM implementations.

# 8  Concluding Remarks

We have introduced an analytical model for HyTM that captures the notion of cached accesses as performed by hardware transactions. We then derived lower and upper bounds in this model that capture the inherent tradeoff between the degree of concurrency between hardware and software transactions, and the metadata-access overhead introduced on the hardware.

To precisely characterize the costs incurred by hardware transactions, we made a distinction between the set of memory locations which store the data values of the t-objects, and the locations that store the metadata information. To the best of our knowledge, all known HyTM proposals, such as *HybridNOrec* [9,23], *PhTM* [19] and others [10,18] avoid co-locating the data and metadata within a single base object.

Recent work has investigated alternatives to the STM fallback, such as *sand-boxing* [2,8] and the use of both direct *and* cached accesses within the same hardware transaction to reduce instrumentation overhead [23,24]. Another recent approach proposed *reduced hardware transactions* [20], where a part of the slow-path is executed using a short fast-path transaction, which allows to partially eliminate instrumentation from the hardware fast-path. We plan to extend our model to incorporate such schemes in future work.

Our HyTM model is a natural extension of previous frameworks developed for STM, and has the advantage of being relatively simple. We hope that our model and techniques will enable more research on the limitations and power of HyTM systems, and that our results will prove useful for practitioners.

# References

1. Advanced Synchronization Facility Proposed Architectural Specification, March 2009. http://developer.amd.com/wordpress/media/2013/09/45432-ASF_Spec_2.1.pdf
2. Afek, Y., Levy, A., Morrison, A.: Software-improved hardware lock elision. In: PODC. ACM (2014)
3. Alistarh, D., Eugster, P., Herlihy, M., Matveev, A., Shavit, N.: Stacktrack: an automated transactional approach to concurrent memory reclamation. In: Proceedings of the Ninth European Conference on Computer Systems. EuroSys 2014, pp. 25:1–25:14. ACM, New York (2014)
4. Alistarh, D., Kopinsky, J., Kuznetsov, P., Ravi, S., Shavit, N.: Inherent limitations of hybrid transactional memory (2014). CoRR, abs/1405.5689. http://arxiv.org/abs/1405.5689
5. Ananian, C.S., Asanovic, K., Kuszmaul, B.C., Leiserson, C.E., Lie, S.: Unbounded transactional memory. In: Proceedings of the 11th International Symposium on High-Performance Computer Architecture. HPCA 2005, pp. 316–327. IEEE Computer Society, Washington (2005)
6. Attiya, H., Hillel, E.: The cost of privatization in software transactional memory. IEEE Trans. Computers **62**(12), 2531–2543 (2013)
7. Attiya, H., Hillel, E., Milani, A.: Inherent limitations on disjoint-access parallel implementations of transactional memory. Theory of Computing Systems **49**(4), 698–719 (2011)

8. Calciu, I., Shpeisman, T., Pokam, G., Herlihy, M.: Improved single global lock fall-back for best-effort hardware transactional memory. In: Transact 2014 Workshop. ACM (2014)

9. Dalessandro, L., Carouge, F., White, S., Lev, Y., Moir, M., Scott, M.L., Spear, M.F.: Hybrid NOrec: a case study in the effectiveness of best effort hardware transactional memory. In: Gupta, R., Mowry, T.C. (eds.) ASPLOS, pp. 39–52. ACM (2011)

10. Damron, P., Fedorova, A., Lev, Y., Luchangco, V., Moir, M., Nussbaum, D.: Hybrid transactional memory. SIGPLAN Not. **41**(11), 336–346 (2006)

11. Dice, D., Lev, Y., Moir, M., Nussbaum, D.: Early experience with a commercial hardware transactional memory implementation. In: Proceedings of the 14th International Conference on Architectural Support for Programming Languages and Operating Systems. ASPLOS XIV, pp. 157–168. ACM, New York (2009)

12. Dragojević, A., Herlihy, M., Lev, Y., Moir, M.: On the power of hardware transactional memory to simplify memory management. In: Proceedings of the 30th Annual ACM SIGACT-SIGOPS Symposium on Principles of Distributed Computing. PODC 2011, pp. 99–108. ACM, New York (2011)

13. Guerraoui, R., Kapalka, M.: On obstruction-free transactions. In: Proceedings of the Twentieth Annual Symposium on Parallelism in Algorithms and Architectures. SPAA 2008, pp. 304–313. ACM, New York (2008)

14. Guerraoui, R., Kapalka, M.: Principles of Transactional Memory. Synthesis Lectures on Distributed Computing Theory. Morgan and Claypool (2010)

15. Harris, T., Larus, J.R., Rajwar, R.: Transactional Memory, 2nd edn. Synthesis Lectures on Computer Architecture. Morgan & Claypool Publishers (2010)

16. Herlihy, M., Luchangco, V., Moir, M., Scherer III, W.N.: Software transactional memory for dynamic-sized data structures. In: Proceedings of the Twenty-Second Annual Symposium on Principles of Distributed Computing. PODC 2003, pp. 92–101. ACM, New York (2003)

17. Herlihy, M., Moss, J.E.B.: Transactional memory: architectural support for lock-free data structures. In: ISCA, pp. 289–300 (1993)

18. Kumar, S., Chu, M., Hughes, C.J., Kundu, P., Nguyen, A.: Hybrid transactional memory. In: Proceedings of the Eleventh ACM SIGPLAN Symposium on Principles and Practice of Parallel Programming. PPoPP 2006, pp. 209–220. ACM, New York (2006)

19. Lev, Y., Moir, M., Nussbaum, D.: Phtm: phased transactional memory. In: Workshop on Transactional Computing (Transact) (2007). http://research.sun.com/scalable/pubs/TRANSACT2007PhTM.pdf

20. Matveev, A., Shavit, N.: Reduced hardware transactions: a new approach to hybrid transactional memory. In: Proceedings of the 25th ACM Symposium on Parallelism in Algorithms and Architectures, pp. 11–22. ACM (2013)

21. Ohmacht, M.: Memory Speculation of the Blue Gene/Q Compute Chip (2011). http://wands.cse.lehigh.edu/IBM_BQC_PACT2011.ppt

22. Reinders, J.: (2012). http://software.intel.com/en-us/blogs/2012/02/07/transactional-synchronization-in-haswell/

23. Riegel, T.: Software Transactional Memory Building Blocks (2013)

24. Riegel, T., Marlier, P., Nowack, M., Felber, P., Fetzer, C.: Optimizing hybrid transactional memory: the importance of nonspeculative operations. In: Proceedings of the 23rd ACM Symposium on Parallelism in Algorithms and Architectures, pp. 53–64. ACM (2011)

# Why Non-blocking Operations
# Should be Selfish

Joel Gibson[1] and Vincent Gramoli[1,2]($\boxtimes$)

[1] University of Sydney, Sydney, Australia
[2] NICTA, Sydney, Australia
jgib4447@uni.sydney.edu.au, vincent.gramoli@sydney.edu.au

**Abstract.** Non-blocking data structures are often analysed by giving an upper *amortised* running time bound in terms of the size of the data structure and a measure of contention. The two most commonly used measures are the point contention $c_P$, the maximum number of processes active at any one time during an operation, and the interval contention $c_I$, the number of operations overlapping with a given operation. In this paper, we show that when summed across every operation in an execution, the interval contention $c_I$ is within a factor of 2 of the point contention $c_P$. Our proof relies on properties of interval graphs where at least one simplicial vertex exists, and uses it to construct a lower bound on the overall point contention. We show that this bound is tight.

This result contradicts the folklore belief that point contention leads to a tighter bound on complexity in an amortised context, and provides some theoretical grounds for recent observations that using less helping in non-blocking data structures can lead to better performance. We also propose a linked list algorithm based on Fomitchev and Ruppert's algorithm but with *selfish* operations: read-only operations that do not help others but rather execute wait-free. The higher performance of our approach compared to the original list confirms that reducing helping can increase performance, with the same asymptotic amortised complexity.

**Keywords:** Helping · Lock-freedom · Wait-freedom · Point contention · Process contention · Interval contention · Overlapping-interval contention

## 1  Introduction

*Non-blocking* algorithms guarantee that some process completes an operation in every sufficiently long execution[1]. They are appealing because they (i) do not suffer from the preemption imposed by the scheduler, and (ii) do not require the high cost of helping needed by common *wait-free* algorithms to make all operations complete in a finite number of steps [2]. As an example, existing non-blocking data structures that make use exclusively of compare-and-swaps

---

[1] Note that non-blocking is sometimes used to refer to a larger class of progress conditions, instead we use the less general definition from [1].

© Springer-Verlag Berlin Heidelberg 2015
Y. Moses (Ed.): DISC 2015, LNCS 9363, pp. 200–214, 2015.
DOI: 10.1007/978-3-662-48653-5_14

(CASes) for synchronisation have recently been shown to outperform other state-of-the-art data structures [3]. A non-blocking update typically reads a memory location, then takes steps before executing a CAS that compares the previously seen value to the current value. A difference in these values indicates an *inconsistency* due to a concurrent modification: the CAS fails and the steps are typically re-executed. In a lock-free algorithm the *step complexity* (i.e., the worst-case number of steps taken in an execution) of a single operation cannot be bounded because it can fail and retry arbitrarily many times. Instead we consider the step complexity across every operation in the execution, usually stated as the *amortised* cost of an operation in terms of the size of the data structure and some contention parameter $c$.

Two notions of contention have attracted lots of interest in the recent years [4–8]. First, the *interval contention* $c_I$ is the number of operations overlapping with a given operation. An amortised bound on the step complexity in terms of the interval contention is relatively easy to obtain by making operations charge each other for steps that would usually be unnecessary in a sequential execution. Provided an operation charges any other overlapping operation a constant amount and at most a constant number of times, this leads naturally to an amortised additive $O(c_I)$ term. Unfortunately, the interval contention of an operation can be arbitrarily large in a system involving as few as two processes. Second, the *point contention* $c_P$ is the maximum number of processes active at any time during the operation [4]. An amortised bound on the step complexity in terms of point contention is usually harder to achieve, for example the proofs in [5,8] rely on reasoning about the relative ordering of individual CAS steps inside operations. Some authors [6,7] have provided modifications of their algorithms which perform extra helping so that they can tighten what would otherwise be a bound in terms of the interval contention to a bound in terms of the point contention. Since the point contention is bounded above by the maximum number of concurrent processes, it appears to be a tighter and more realistic bound than the interval contention.

In this paper, we show that when summed across every operation in an execution, $c_I$ is within a factor of 2 of $c_P$. Our proof relies on properties of interval graphs where the point (resp. interval) contention of an operation $op$ is the size of one of the largest cliques containing $op$ (resp. $op$'s degree + 1). The presence of at least one special vertex called simplicial, in any interval graph, allows us then to construct a lower bound on the overall point contention. In other words, we show that point contention and interval contention are interchangeable additive factors of the amortised complexity of concurrent algorithms. We show that this bound is tight, in the sense that given any $0 < \epsilon < 1/2$, there are executions in which the ratio of the overall interval contention to the overall point contention is arbitrarily close to $2 - \epsilon$. Finally, we also compare these contention definitions to two other definitions, the original interval contention definition [9] that we call *process contention*, and the *overlapping-interval contention* [6]. We believe our result to be important as it shows that point contention does not give a tighter amortised complexity bound than interval contention.

Our result challenges a popular belief that increasing the amount of helping done by operations can reduce the asymptotic step complexity of data structures. For example, in [6], the amortised complexity of a skip list operation is given as $O(c_I)$, as an inconsistency caused by an update may be encountered by every traversal concurrent with that update, and so the update may be charged $O(c_I)$ times. The authors argue that by making the traversals perform extra helping so as to resolve this inconsistency, the update will be charged at most $O(c_P)$ times. So it seems that by introducing more helping into the algorithm, an additive term of $O(c_I)$ can be reduced to $O(c_P)$. The authors of [7] argue similarly for their lock-free binary search tree.

To illustrate how helping seemingly reduces the cost due to contention, consider the execution of an algorithm depicted in Figure 1 representing the intervals of seven operations, $A$, $B$, $C$, $D$, $E$, $F$, $G$, where time increases from left to right. Operation $A$ updates shared data, as indicated by the vertical bar. Before operation $A$ completes, other operations observe a transient inconsistent state produced by $A$ that incurs a cost. We say that operations, whose interval overlaps $A$'s interval, charge $A$ for the cost of observing this inconsistency. Since the inconsistency was introduced by $A$, and must be resolved for $A$ to finish, at most $c_I$ operations can charge $A$ for this. If, however, the first operation that observes this inconsistency, namely $B$, *helps* the update by resolving it, then subsequent operations $E$, $F$, $G$ will no longer observe this inconsistency. As long as every operation eagerly attempts to remove this inconsistency, at most $c_P$ operations can charge $A$ for observing the inconsistency. Since $c_P \leq c_I$ for each operation, up until now it was believed to lead to a tighter bound on complexity, even in an amortised context.

By contrast, extra helping could intuitively lower the performance of a data structure, especially by forcing an operation, which would otherwise be read-

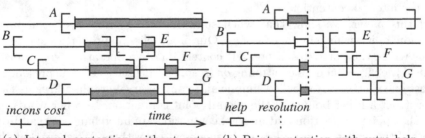

(a) Interval contention without extra help

(b) Point contention with extra help

**Fig. 1.** It was recently noted [6,7] that if an update $A$ creates a transient inconsistent state, *incons*, that is encountered by concurrent traversals $B, C, D, E, F, G$ then making the other operations *help* another when encountering an inconsistency can reduce the interval contention $O(c_I)$ to the point contention $O(c_P)$ by simply resolving the inconsistency as early as the first operation, say $B$, encounters the inconsistency

only, to write. Such a behaviour was recently observed on the Harris' list-based set [10] and led researchers to prevent read-only operations from writing: they implemented what they called an "optimised" variant of Harris' with a contains operation that traverses logically deleted nodes without physically unlinking them. The authors compared these two implementations on up to 40 hardware threads and observed that their optimised version increases performance. Former implementation variants of Harris' algorithm also suggested the appeal of a wait-free contains [11,12].

In the light of our result, we designed a new non-blocking list-based set algorithm based on Fomitchev and Ruppert's [5], but with a wait-free contains operation which performs no writes. Their original list has amortised complexity $O(n + c_P)$ per operation, whereas the modification is easily seen as $O(n + c_I)$, which our result tells us is equivalent. We implemented Fomitchev and Ruppert's linked list in C. We compared the performance of our linked list against the performance of Fomitchev and Ruppert's linked list on a 64-core machine with various sizes and update ratios. The results show that our linked list is more efficient in all tested settings than Fomitchev and Ruppert's. While we do not claim that helping is always detrimental to the performance, these results confirm empirically that limiting helping *can* lead to better performance, at no increase of the amortised cost of an operation.

To conclude, we believe our result is not only insightful for theoreticians but also for practitioners. First, an amoritised complexity with an additive $O(c_I)$ term is equivalent to having an $O(c_P)$ term instead, without the burden of modifying the algorithm or complicating the analysis required to measure the point contention. Second, as modern chip multiprocessors offer more and more cores, it is likely that enough processes (or threads) accessing a concurrent data structures can proceed without being preempted by the operating system. In this case, it seems that an implementation with *selfish* operations, which are wait-free read-only operations that do not help other operations, could lead to higher performance, simply because (i) read-only operations would avoid writing, hence limiting cache invalidations and (ii) update operations would fix any inconsistency they introduce without being arbitrarily delayed via preemption. Our result gives theoretical grounds to support favouring selfish operations over helpful operations when all that distinguishes them is an additive $O(c_P)$ or $O(c_I)$ term.

In Section 2 we define existing contention measures and explain how to reason about them in terms of interval graphs. In Section 3, we show that in any finite execution the overall point contention cannot be twice as large as the point contention and that this bound is tight, and briefly show related results for the process contention and the overlapping-interval contention. In Section 4 we show empirically that replacing a helpful contains operation by a selfish one increases the performance of Fomitchev and Ruppert's linked list. We list directions to explore new contention metrics in Section 5. We present the related work in Section 6 and we conclude in Section 7.

## 2    Preliminaries

Let a finite execution $\alpha$ involving $P$ processes be a finite set $\mathcal{O}$ of *operations* with two mappings $I$ and $\pi$. $I : \mathcal{O} \to \mathbb{R} \times \mathbb{R}$ maps operations to compact real intervals, and $\pi : \mathcal{O} \to \{1, \dots, P\}$ maps operations to the processes that executed them. If for two operations $op, op' \in \mathcal{O}$ we have $I(op) \cap I(op') \neq \emptyset$, we say that $op$ and $op'$ *overlap*. Furthermore, $I$ should be injective[2], and the execution should be *well-formed*: any two operations mapping to the same process should not overlap. Figure 2 shows an example of a finite execution.

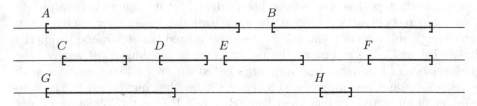

**Fig. 2.** An example execution involving 3 processes and 8 operations. The point contentions of $A$, $C$, $D$, and $G$ are 3, while $E$, $B$, $H$, and $F$ are 2. The process contention of $E$ is 2, and of $B$ is 3. The interval contentions of $A$, $B$, and $C$ are 5, 4, and 3 respectively. The overlapping-interval contention of $E$ is 5.

**Definition 1.** *In a finite execution* $\alpha = (\mathcal{O}, P, I, \pi)$, *the point contention* $c_P$, *process contention* $c_K$, *interval contention* $c_I$, *and overlapping-interval contention* $c_{OI}$ *are functions* $\mathcal{O} \to \mathbb{Z}_+$ *defined by:*

$$c_P(op) = \max_{x \in I(op)} |\{op' \in \mathcal{O} : x \in I(op')\}|$$

$$c_K(op) = |\{\pi(op') : op' \in \mathcal{O} \wedge op' \text{ overlaps } op\}|$$

$$c_I(op) = |\{op' \in \mathcal{O} : op' \text{ overlaps } op\}|$$

$$c_{OI}(op) = \max_{\substack{op' \in \mathcal{O} \\ op' \text{ overlaps } op}} c_I(op')$$

**Proposition 1.** *For any operation* $op$, $1 \leq c_P(op) \leq c_K(op) \leq c_I(op) \leq c_{OI}(op)$, *and* $c_K(op) \leq P$.

*Proof.* Let $S = \{op' \in \mathcal{O} : op' \text{ overlaps } op\}$, and for any $x \in I(op)$, let $S_x = \{op' \in \mathcal{O} : x \in I(op')\}$. The definitions of contention for the operation $op$ now become:

$$c_P(op) = \max_{x \in I(op)} |S_x| \qquad\qquad c_I(op) = |S|$$

$$c_K(op) = |\pi(S)| \qquad\qquad c_{OI}(op) = \max_{op' \in S} c_I(op')$$

---

[2] This is not restrictive: any finite execution in which two intervals are identical may be perturbed slightly such that they are not, without affecting contention.

By these characterisations we find $c_{OI}(op) \geq c_I(op)$ because $op \in S$, and $c_I(op) \geq c_K(op)$ because a set is at least as large as its image under a map. Note that since the execution is well-formed, $|S_x| = |\pi(S_x)|$, and since we have $S_x \subseteq S$ for all $x \in I$, it follows that $c_P(op) \leq c_K(op)$. Finally, all of these bounds are tight by considering an execution containing one operation and one process.

All that is needed to calculate $c_I$ and $c_{OI}$ is information about which pairs of operations overlap. In fact, this is the case for $c_P$ as well. Hence a natural setting to analyse these measures of contention is an *interval graph*, which retains the information of which operations overlap, while hiding the complications of processes and exact points in time. First we introduce some terminology.

Any graphs $G = (V, E)$ considered here are finite, undirected, and without multiple edges or loops. $V$ denotes the vertex set and $E$ denotes the edge set. For any vertex subset $U \subseteq V$, $G[U] = (U, E \cap (U \times U))$ is called the *subgraph induced by* $U$. A vertex subset $U \subseteq V$ forms a *clique* if the subgraph $G[U]$ is complete. For any vertex $v$, its *neighbourhood* $N(v)$ consists of all vertices incident to $v$. A vertex $v$ is called *simplicial* if the subgraph induced by its neighbours and itself $G[\{v\} \cup N(v)]$ is complete.

**Definition 2.** *The interval graph of a finite set of real intervals $S$ is the graph with vertex set $S$, with an edge between two intervals $I, J \in S$ if $I \neq J$ and $I \cap J \neq \emptyset$.*

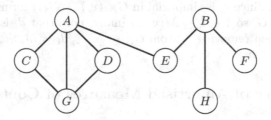

**Fig. 3.** The interval graph corresponding to the execution in Figure 2. The vertices $C$, $D$, $H$ and $F$ are simplicial in this graph.

**Definition 3.** *A perfect elimination order is an ordering $\{v_i\}_{i=1}^n$ of vertices in a graph such that for all $1 \leq i \leq n$, $v_i$ is simplicial in $G[v_1, \ldots, v_i]$.*

Interval graphs belong to a larger class of graphs called *chordal* graphs, which are graphs in which any cycle of length 4 or more always contains a *chord*, an edge connecting two non-adjacent vertices of the cycle. It is a well-known fact that chordal graphs are characterised completely by the existence of a perfect elimination order. In the case of interval graphs the existence of such an order is easy to see, and so a short proof is given below.

**Lemma 1.** *Every interval graph on $n$ vertices admits a perfect elimination order.*

*Proof.* The case for $n = 1$ is clear. We proceed by induction: assume that the claim holds for interval graphs with $n-1$ vertices. Take the vertex $v$ corresponding to the interval with earliest finishing time: this vertex is simplicial since the finishing time intersects every interval which overlaps $v$. We already have a perfect elimination order $\{v_i\}_{i=1}^{n-1}$ of $G - v$ by assumption, and so setting $v_n = v$ gives a perfect elimination order $\{v_i\}_{i=1}^{n}$ of $G$.

Finally, in the interval graph of an execution, the point contention of an interval is equal to the size of the largest clique containing the vertex corresponding to that interval. This can be seen by considering the mapping $\mathbb{R} \to 2^{\mathcal{O}}$, $x \mapsto \{op \in \mathcal{O} \mid x \in I(op)\}$ which maps points to the operations active at that point in time: it will always map a point to an empty set, or a maximal clique. For this reason we consider the following lemma, which will allow us to put a lower bound on the overall point contention in terms of the number of vertices $n$ and the number of edges $m$.

**Lemma 2.** *In an interval graph $G$, let $M(v)$ be the size of a maximum clique containing the vertex $v$. Then $\sum_{v \in V} M(v) \geq n + m$.*

*Proof.* Take a perfect elimination order $\{v_i\}_{i=1}^{n}$ of the vertices of $G$, and define $G_i = G[v_1, \ldots, v_i]$. This gives a family of graphs $G_n, \ldots, G_1$, such that $G_n = G$, $G_1$ is a single vertex, and $G_j = G_{j+1} - v_{j+1}$ for all $1 \leq j < n$. Let $d_i$ be the degree of $v_i$ in $G_i$. Since $v_i$ is simplicial in $G_i$, $\{v_i\} \cup N(v_i)$ forms a clique in $G_i$ and hence also in $G$, so $1 + d_i \leq M(v_i)$. Finally, note that $d_i$ is the number of edges removed when removing $v_i$ from $G_i$, so $\sum_{i=1}^{n} d_i = m$. So $\sum_{v \in V} M(v) \geq \sum_{i=1}^{n} (1 + d_i) = n + m$.

## 3    Equivalence of Amortised Measures of Contention

For any finite execution $\alpha$, let $c_P(\alpha) = \sum_{op \in \mathcal{O}} c_P(op)$, and likewise for the other measures of contention.

**Theorem 1.** *In any finite execution $\alpha$, $c_P(\alpha) \leq c_I(\alpha) < 2c_P(\alpha)$.*

*Proof.* Form the interval graph using the intervals $I(op)$ for each $op \in \alpha$. By the definitions of contention given in Section 2, we can see that the interval contention of a single operation $op$ is $c_I(op) = 1 + \deg op$, where $\deg$ denotes the degree of the operation's interval in the interval graph. Summing across all operations, $c_I(\alpha) = n + 2m$, where $n$ is the number of vertices and $m$ the number of edges in the interval graph. As discussed previously, the point contention $c_P(op)$ is the size of the largest clique containing $op$ in the interval graph. So by Lemma 2 we have $n + m \leq c_P(\alpha)$.

Putting these together with the inequality in Proposition 1, we find that

$$n + m \leq c_P(\alpha) \leq c_I(\alpha) \leq n + 2m$$

and so by taking the ratio of $c_I(\alpha)$ to $c_P(\alpha)$,

$$1 \le \frac{c_I(\alpha)}{c_P(\alpha)} \le \frac{n + 2m}{n + m} = 1 + \frac{m}{n + m} < 2$$

Although this fact alone tells us that in amortised terms, $c_P = \Theta(c_I)$ and so the point contention and interval contention are equivalent, it is interesting to examine what a "worst-case" execution is. Intuitively, we want to keep the point contention small, while making intervals overlap as many times as possible. Such a construction is given in the proof of Theorem 2 and illustrated in Figure 4, and shows that the bound given above is tight.

**Theorem 2.** *For any $0 < \epsilon < 1/2$, there exists a family of executions $\{\alpha_n\}_{n \ge 1}$ where each $\alpha_n$ has n operations and $\epsilon n$ processes, such that*

$$\lim_{n \to \infty} \frac{c_I(\alpha_n)}{c_P(\alpha_n)} = 2 - \epsilon.$$

*Proof.* Let $\alpha_n$ be an execution containing $n$ operations labelled $op_i$ for $0 \le i < n$, and let $1 \le k \le n/2$. We define the mappings $\pi(op_i) = i \pmod{k}$ and $I(op_i) = [i, i + k - \frac{1}{2}]$ for all $0 \le i < n$. It is easy to check that at the start or end point of each operation there are $k$ operations active at that point in time and so $c_P(op) \ge k$ for all operations. Since there are only $k$ processes, $c_P(op) = k$ for all operations, so $c_P(\alpha_n) = nk$.

By the length and placement of operations, for every operation $op$ the set of operations intersecting its left endpoint is disjoint to the set of operations intersecting its right endpoint, and the union of these is every operation concurrent with $op$. Hence every operation but the first $k - 1$ and the last $k - 1$ operations have interval contention $2k - 1$. The first operation has interval contention $k$, the next $k + 1$, and so on until the $k$th operation has interval contention $2k - 1$, and similarly for the last $k$ operations. By overcounting the interval contention overall and subtracting off the start and end deficits, we find that $c_I(\alpha_n) = n(2k - 1) - 2(0 + 1 + \ldots + (k - 1)) = 2nk - n - k(k - 1)$. Letting $k = \epsilon n$ and taking the ratio of interval to point contention, we get $c_I(\alpha_n)/c_P(\alpha_n) = 2 - \epsilon - \frac{1 - \epsilon}{\epsilon n}$.

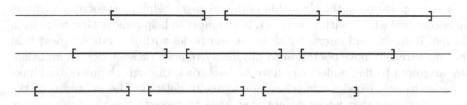

**Fig. 4.** An example worst-case construction with $n = 9$ and $k = 3$.

Finally, Theorem 1 and Proposition 1 give the chain of inequalities $c_P(\alpha) \le c_K(\alpha) \le c_I(\alpha) < 2c_P(\alpha)$ and so the process contention is also amortised equivalent to the point contention. The overlapping-interval contention, on the other hand, cannot be bounded within a constant factor of the point contention. Consider an execution of two processes, where the first process has one long-running operation, and the second process runs $n - 1$ short operations, all of which execute inside the interval of the long-running operation. In this execution $\alpha$, we have $c_P(op) = 2$ and $c_{OI}(op) = n$ for every operation, so $c_P(\alpha) = 2n$ and $c_{OI}(\alpha) = n^2$.

# 4    Evaluation of the Selfish Linked List

A key application of Theorem 1 is that algorithms which had very strict helping requirements in order to attain a $O(c_P)$ amortised additive complexity term may be able to be modified to have weaker helping requirements, without any change in asymptotic complexity. It has been observed in practice [10] that having wait-free read-only operations on concurrent data structures often gives an increase in performance, regardless of asymptotic complexity. Here we modify an existing non-blocking linked-list algorithm by Fomitchev and Ruppert [5] to have a wait-free contains operation and show that the resulting algorithm, namely the *Selfish linked list*, gives better performance.

## 4.1    The Selfish Linked List Algorithm

First, we recall Fomitchev and Ruppert's construction of the list. Each node stores three fields: a *key* field, indicating the value represented by that node in the set, a *backlink* field, used when traversal is interrupted by a concurrent modification, and a *successor* field. The *successor* field stores a *right* pointer to the next node in the list and two booleans *flag* and *mark*. The list contains two dummy *head* and *tail* nodes, with keys $-\infty$ and $\infty$ respectively.

When a node is to be deleted, its predecessor's *flag* bit is set, indicating that the predecessor's successor field may not be modified until the node has been removed. Following this, the node's *mark* bit is set, indicating its successor field may not be modified from now on, and the node's *backlink* field is set to point to the predecessor. Finally, the predecessor's *successor* field is modified to remove the *flag* bit and swing the *right* pointer over the node being deleted.

Every operation in the algorithm performs eager helping: as soon as a traversal encounters a node with a *mark* set, it attempts to help remove that node from the list. Removes and inserts which encounter nodes with *flag* bits set must help the concurrent remove operation to physically remove those nodes. In addition, any attempts to flag nodes may have to backtrack through chains of backlinks in order to reach nodes which are not logically deleted. The existence of the backlinks means that nodes do not ever have to restart from the beginning of the list and is key to an amortised $O(n + c_P)$ time per operation.

Our modification is very similar to the modification of the Harris list presented in [11,12] to replace the contains operation, which would usually attempt to help remove marked nodes from the list, with a read-only operation which makes a single pass through the list. The pseudocode of the contains operation is

---

**Algorithm 1.** The wait-free Contains operation

```
1: procedure CONTAINS(k)
2:     current ← head
3:     marked ← false
4:     while current.key < k do
5:         succ ← current.succ
6:         marked ← succ.mark
7:         current ← succ.right
8:     end while
9:     return (current.key = k) ∧ (marked = false)
10: end procedure
```

---

depicted in Algorithm 1. The operation is linearisable and wait-free, and replaces the original lock-free contains operation: all other operations of the list remain as in the original. Since the operations in the original list had an amortised complexity of $O(n + c_P)$ and we change only the read-only operation, we conclude our new list has an amortised complexity of $O(n + c_I)$ for each operation: in the presence of only updates, the complexity is $O(n + c_P)$ as originally shown by Fomitchev and Ruppert, and introducing contains operations means that at most $c_I$ more is billed to each concurrent update by a contains operation that traverses a logically deleted node. We implemented both the original algorithm and our modification in C and we did not include any memory reclamation technique. Implementing a memory reclamation technique is not straightforward and can substantially impact performance [13].

## 4.2 Experimental Evaluation

We performed the experiment with Synchrobench [3] on a 4 socket AMD Opteron 6378 2.4 GHz 16 cores (64 cores in total) machine running Fedora Linux 18. GCC 4.9.2 was used to compile the C code. The benchmarking program initialises the data structures with $N$ elements randomly selected from $\{1, \ldots, 2N\}$, and spawns from 1 to 78 threads. Each test runs for 10 seconds. Each thread chooses of the three operations contains, insert, or remove based on the *update ratio*. In the data shown here, the update ratio is always 10%, meaning that 10% of operations are contains operations, 45% are insert, and 45% are remove. Each datapoint shown is an average of 20 runs, and the error bars are the sample standard deviation of those runs.

As shown in Figure 5, the list with our modification has much higher throughput than the original algorithm, especially in the small case of a 128 element list, where there is a 20% throughput improvement. We conclude that limiting helping can increase performance in concurrent data structures, and our result in Theorem 1 gives a guarantee that our new $O(n + c_I)$ algorithm is asympotically equivalent to the old $O(n + c_P)$ algorithm.

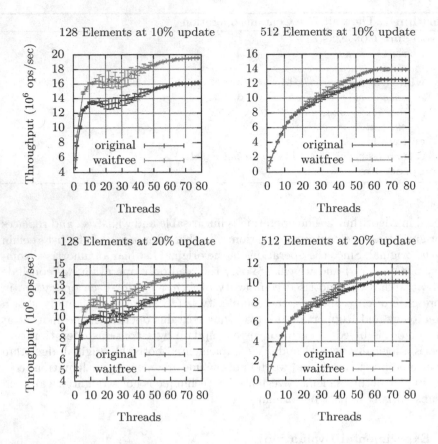

**Fig. 5.** A comparison of Fomitchev and Ruppert's original algorithm to our modified version with a wait-free contains implementation. Both algorithms have the same asymptotic worst-case complexity. Each datapoint shown is an average of 20 runs of 10 seconds each. The vertical bars represent the sample standard deviation.

## 5   Towards a More Refined Notion of Contention

As discussed previously, there has been a view that by introducing more helping into an algorithm, the amortised step complexity can be "tightened" from an additive term of $O(c_I)$ to $O(c_P)$. By Theorem 1, we know these two quantities to be amortised equivalent, so clearly this cannot be distinguished by the point or interval contention. However, this does not rule out the existence of a more refined measure of contention that does separate these cases.

Consider an execution of one long-running process $Q$ and $m$ short-running processes $P_1, \ldots, P_m$. Suppose we have a structure featuring logical deletions, and the first step in a removal is to mark a node logically deleted. The long-running process $Q$ marks an element as logically deleted before being suspended for a long time, while the short-running processes repeatedly access the data

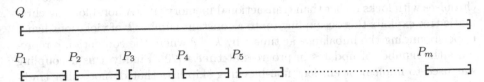

**Fig. 6.** Suppose $Q$ causes an inconsistency in the data structure and then gets suspended for a long time. If every operation performs eager helping, an inconsistency caused by $Q$ will only be observed once. If no operations perform helping, it will be observed $m$ times.

structure. This is illustrated in Figure 6. If the short running processes $P_i$ perform no helping to try to physically remove the node, each will spend extra time traversing a node not present in the set, and incur a constant cost. The total cost of these extra steps is $\Theta(m)$. On the other hand, if every operation eagerly tries to help finish any partially completed delete operation it comes across, the first short operation $P_1$ will suffer this (constant) cost, and the rest will traverse with no extra cost. So without helping, there are $\Theta(m)$ extra steps that need to be carried out, and with helping there is only $O(1)$.

The current measures we have of contention, the point and interval contention, will not separate these cases. Some finer measure of contention is needed to capture this case and show when helping can really benefit an algorithm in an asymptotic sense. We believe that some of the theory developed here could be useful in determining and analysing a new measure of contention that separates these two cases.

## 6   Related Work

For more than two decades, contention has been known to be an important complexity factor of concurrent algorithms [14]. This observation motivated the definitions of various contention measures: hot-spot contention [14], process contention (originally called interval contention) [9], interval and point contentions [4], step contention [15] and overlapping-interval contention [6]. An overview of some of these properties was given in [16].

To diminish contention several techniques were adopted. Adaptive algorithms [4] were designed to implement applications that could adapt to the point contention during the execution of an operation. Contention-sensitive data structures [17] propose to reduce the cost of lock-based data structures in the absence of contention.

A pragmatic way of reducing contention in data structures is to split operations into abstract updates and structural updates. The speculation-friendly binary search tree was the first algorithm to generalize this decoupling by both keeping logically deleted nodes and relaxing the balance constraints [18].

The contention-friendly binary search tree adopts the same decoupling but synchronises with locks rather than transactional memory [19]. A non-blocking chromatic tree exploits this decoupling up to a constant number $k$ of violations hence upper-bounding the imbalance at time $t$ by $k + c$ where the contention $c$ represents the number of updates in progress at time $t$ [20]. Finally, this decoupling was used to implement efficient non-blocking skip lists that do not suffer traditional contention hotspots [21,22].

Many linked list algorithms have been proposed over the last two decades [5, 11,23–25]. Although potentially very efficient, lock-based linked lists [11,25] generally do not perform as well as non-blocking ones [5,24] when the number of processes exceeds the number of available computing resources. This is typically due to the contention induced on locks. Non-blocking linked lists are thus particularly interesting. Harris' linked list [24] is still one of the fastest [3] but its cost per operation can be $\Omega(nc_P)$ in some execution. Fomitchev and Ruppert provide a linked list with an amortized complexity of $O(n+c_P)$ per operation [5]. Our Selfish list, of asymptotically equivalent complexity $O(n + c_I)$, shows better performance.

Both wait-free and non-blocking properties guarantee progress regardless of the way the operating system schedules threads [26]. Our algorithm is non-blocking but not wait-free as it guarantees wait-freedom only of the contains operation. Recent results showed that under a stochastic scheduler, some non-blocking algorithms, also called single CAS universal, are wait-free with probability 1 [27], however, our algorithm does not fall in this category. There exist both methodologies [28] and simulation techniques [29] to obtain wait-freedom with a slight performance loss: one can run a lock-free fast path and start a wait-free slow path if the fast path was unsuccessful.

# 7   Conclusion

When summed across every operation in an execution, the point contention cannot be twice larger than interval contention. Our proof is interesting in its own right as it draws a natural relation between the theory of contention and the theory of interval graphs, where the point contention of an operation is its degree plus one in the graph and the interval contention is the size of one of the largest cliques the operation belongs to in the graph.

The execution $\alpha$ of several non-blocking data structure algorithms [5–8] is known to have an asymptotic amortised complexity with an additive contention term of either $c_I(\alpha)$ or $c_P(\alpha)$. Our result shows that these terms are equivalent, hence contradicting the folklore knowledge that operations should necessarily help each other to achieve a tighter complexity bound even in an amortised context.

We evaluated the performance of a non-blocking list and a new variant of it that consists of the same algorithm but with a selfish contains operation. Their complexities $O(n + c_P)$ and $O(n + c_I)$, respectively, are known now to be equivalent. Our results on a 64-core machine show that selfishness increases performance in all settings we tested, confirming the practical relevance of our bound.

We believe that our result will be useful to simplify the analysis of non-blocking data structures in terms of amortised complexity as deriving the complexity based on interval contention seems easier than point contention. As part of future work, we would like to analyse existing algorithms in the light of our new result.

**Availability.** The source code used in this paper is available in Synchrobench: https://sites.google.com/site/synchrobench.

**Acknowledgments.** NICTA is funded by the Australian Government through the Department of Communications and the Australian Research Council through the ICT Centre of Excellence Program.

# References

1. Herlihy, M.: Wait-free synchronization. ACM Trans. Program. Lang. Syst. **13**(1), 124–149 (1991)
2. Censor-Hillel, K., Petrank, E., Timnat, S.: Help! In: PODC, pp. 241–250 (2015)
3. Gramoli, V.: More than you ever wanted to know about synchronization: Synchrobench, measuring the impact of the synchronization on concurrent algorithms. In: PPoPP, pp. 1–10 (2015)
4. Attiya, H., Fouren, A.: Algorithms adapting to point contention. J. ACM **50**(4), 444–468 (2003)
5. Fomitchev, M., Ruppert, E.: Lock-free linked lists and skip lists. In: PODC, pp. 50–59 (2004)
6. Oshman, R., Shavit, N.: The SkipTrie: low-depth concurrent search without rebalancing. In: PODC, pp. 23–32 (2013)
7. Chatterjee, B., Nguyen, N., Tsigas, P.: Efficient lock-free binary search trees. In: PODC, pp. 322–331 (2014)
8. Ellen, F., Fatourou, P., Helga, J., Ruppert, E.: The amortized complexity of non-blocking binary search trees. In: PODC, pp. 332–340 (2014)
9. Afek, Y., Stupp, G., Touitou, D.: Long lived adaptive splitter and applications. Distributed Computing **15**(2), 67–86 (2002)
10. David, T., Guerraoui, R., Trigonakis, V.: Asynchronized concurrency: the secret to scaling concurrent search data structures. In: ASPLOS, pp. 631–644 (2015)
11. Heller, S., Herlihy, M.P., Luchangco, V., Moir, M., Scherer III, W.N., Shavit, N.N.: A lazy concurrent list-based set algorithm. In: Anderson, J.H., Prencipe, G., Wattenhofer, R. (eds.) OPODIS 2005. LNCS, vol. 3974, pp. 3–16. Springer, Heidelberg (2006)
12. Herlihy, M., Shavit, N.: The Art of Multiprocessor Programming. Morgan Kaufmann Publishers Inc., San Francisco (2008)
13. Michael, M.M.: High performance dynamic lock-free hash tables and list-based sets. In: SPAA, pp. 73–82 (2002)
14. Dwork, C., Herlihy, M., Waarts, O.: Contention in shared memory algorithms. J. ACM **44**(6), 779–805 (1997)

15. Attiya, H., Guerraoui, R., Kouznetsov, P.: Computing with reads and writes in the absence of step contention. In: Fraigniaud, P. (ed.) DISC 2005. LNCS, vol. 3724, pp. 122–136. Springer, Heidelberg (2005)
16. Hendler, D.: Non-blocking algorithms. In: Encyclopedia of Parallel Computing. Springer, pp. 1321–1329 (2011)
17. Taubenfeld, G.: Contention-sensitive data structures and algorithms. In: Keidar, I. (ed.) DISC 2009. LNCS, vol. 5805, pp. 157–171. Springer, Heidelberg (2009)
18. Crain, T., Gramoli, V., Raynal, M.: A speculation-friendly binary search tree. In: PPoPP, pp. 161–170 (2012)
19. Crain, T., Gramoli, V., Raynal, M.: A contention-friendly binary search tree. In: Wolf, F., Mohr, B., an Mey, D. (eds.) Euro-Par 2013. LNCS, vol. 8097, pp. 229–240. Springer, Heidelberg (2013)
20. Brown, T., Ellen, F., Ruppert, E.: A general technique for non-blocking trees. In: PPoPP, pp. 329–342 (2014)
21. Crain, T., Gramoli, V., Raynal, M.: No hot spot non-blocking skip list. In: ICDCS, pp. 196–205 (2013)
22. Dick, I., Fekete, A., Gramoli, V.: Logarithmic data structures for multicores. Technical Report 697, University of Sydney (2014)
23. Valois, J.D.: Lock-free linked lists using compare-and-swap. In: PODC, pp. 214–222 (1995)
24. Harris, T.L.: A pragmatic implementation of non-blocking linked-lists. In: Welch, J.L. (ed.) DISC 2001. LNCS, vol. 2180, pp. 300–314. Springer, Heidelberg (2001)
25. Gramoli, V., Kuznetsov, P., Ravi, S., Shang, D.: Brief announcement: a concurrency-optimal list-based set. In: DISC. LNCS (2015)
26. Herlihy, M., Shavit, N.: On the nature of progress. In: Fernàndez Anta, A., Lipari, G., Roy, M. (eds.) OPODIS 2011. LNCS, vol. 7109, pp. 313–328. Springer, Heidelberg (2011)
27. Alistarh, D., Censor-Hillel, K., Shavit, N.: Are lock-free concurrent algorithms practically wait-free? In: STOC, pp. 714–723 (2014)
28. Kogan, A., Petrank, E.: A methodology for creating fast wait-free data structures. In: PPoPP, pp. 141–150 (2012)
29. Timnat, S., Petrank, E.: A practical wait-free simulation for lock-free data structures. In: PPoPP, pp. 357–368 (2014)

# Hybrid Transactional Memory Revisited

Wenjia Ruan and Michael Spear[✉]

Department of Computer Science and Engineering,
Lehigh University, Bethlehem, USA
{wer210,spear}@cse.lehigh.edu

**Abstract.** Hybrid Transactional Memory (TM) uses available hardware TM resources to execute language-level transactions, and falls back to a software TM implementation for those transactions that cannot complete in hardware. Ideally, a hybrid TM would allow hardware and software transactions to run concurrently, but would not waste hardware TM resources on coordination between the two classes of transactions. In addition, it should scale well, incur little latency, offer strong safety guarantees, and provide some degree of fairness.

We introduce a new hybrid TM algorithm, "Hybrid Cohorts", in which hardware transactions do not modify global metadata, and software transactions have extremely low per-access overhead. The tradeoff is that hardware transactions cannot commit while software transactions are in flight. Evaluation on an 8-thread Intel Haswell CPU shows competitive performance with the current state-of-the-art. Furthermore, it does so while providing acceptable levels of fairness and safety, and offering opportunities for hardware acceleration.

## 1 Introduction

Since the time when Hybrid Transactional Memory (TM) was first proposed [6], hardware TM (HTM) support has become available in microprocessors from IBM [11,21] and Intel [10]. These HTM systems are "best effort", meaning that they do not guarantee that they will successfully commit *any* transaction attempt. Failure may arise for many reasons, to include conflicts with other transactions, memory footprints that exceed the HTM capacity, system calls, and timer interrupts. The goal of Hybrid TM (HyTM) is to exploit best-effort HTM whenever possible, and fall back to software TM (STM) when a transaction cannot complete in hardware [6]. This approach promises to scale well and incur low latency when most transactions complete in hardware, with worst-case overhead and scalability comparable to the underlying STM.

The traditional approach to implementing HyTM is to begin with an STM, and try to accelerate it using HTM. Early STM algorithms required interaction with per-location metadata, and hybrid versions of these algorithms wasted limited hardware capacity on this metadata [6,12,16]. Worse yet, false sharing of cache lines that held metadata could result in additional HTM aborts, and increased fallback to the STM path. The use of NOrec STM [5] as a baseline enabled HyTM algorithms to avoid per-access overheads. In NOrec-based HyTM [4,14,16], a sequence lock serializes the commit of the STM, and

© Springer-Verlag Berlin Heidelberg 2015
Y. Moses (Ed.): DISC 2015, LNCS 9363, pp. 215–231, 2015.
DOI: 10.1007/978-3-662-48653-5_15

all conflicts are detected by comparing the values read by transactions. However, NOrec-based HyTM algorithms suffer from a scalability bottleneck, since hardware transactions must read, and often write, the sequence lock. Aborts from these accesses could be avoided if the hardware allowed nontransactional accesses [4], but the accesses themselves are necessary. Furthermore, if these accesses are delayed until the end of the transaction [2,3], the TM ceases to provide the minimum safety requirement of opacity [9], and it can admit erroneous behavior [7]. However, "eager subscription" to the metadata for coordinating hardware and software transactions causes all hardware transactions to abort on any software commit.

The most recent innovation in HyTM is to add hardware acceleration to the STM path, as in Reduced Hardware NOrec (RHNOrec) [14]. The resulting "reduced transaction" technique transforms certain software transactions into hardware transactions, thereby avoiding fallback to a slow STM. The current state of the art achieves performance comparable to Hybrid NOrec, but does not require nontransactional loads.

A common assumption among HyTM algorithms is that STM and HTM transactions should coexist at any time, with neither favored over the other. In contrast, PhaseTM [13], required all transactions to use same mode, whether HTM, STM, or serialized on a single lock. Mode switches were expensive, but in return the HTM mode had no overhead for interacting with STM. The most popular HyTM in practice today is a PhaseTM that switches between HTM mode and a single global lock [24]. If we accept that HTM capacities are more likely to increase than to decrease, then we may assume that STM fall-back will grow increasingly rare. However, as core counts rise, fall-back to a single lock becomes increasingly untenable. These observations motivate our approach. We seek to make the common case (HTM) as fast as possible, by avoiding interaction with (unlikely) concurrent software transactions. When a software transaction is needed, we want it to finish as quickly as possible, to limit its impact on current and future hardware transactions. We also require the HyTM to be opaque.

The innovation we propose is to prioritize software transactions while they are running, by augmenting the Cohorts algorithm [18]. In Cohorts, transactions block at their commit point, until such time as all threads are either (a) ready to commit a transaction, or (b) not executing a transaction. This allows software transactions to avoid any high-latency global metadata accesses during execution. In Hybrid Cohorts (HyCo), we prevent hardware transactions from committing when software transactions are in-flight. We also apply the reduced transaction technique to the Cohorts commit phase, which prevents blocking and eliminates a bottleneck from Cohorts STM. The net effect is an opaque HyTM that scales well and avoids bottlenecks for hardware transactions.

The remainder of this paper is organized as follows. In Section 2, we discuss the overall approach of the Hybrid Cohorts algorithm, with a focus on the state machine that governs transaction behavior. Section 3 presents the pseudocode for one implementation of the state machine, which aims to limit the impact on transactions that use HTM resources throughout their execution. In Section 4, we present the results of performance experiments. Section 5 concludes and discusses future research directions.

## 2 The Hybrid Cohorts Approach

HyTM algorithms that descend from NOrec share two key properties: First, the opacity of each software transaction (STx) is preserved by requiring every hardware transaction (HTx) increment a global counter on hardware transaction commit; the counter is checked by every STx on every read of shared data. (Note that the increment may be elided if it can be proven that no STx exist.) Second, to prevent an HTx from observing inconsistent state, it must not perform reads or commit during the interval when an STx is committing its writes. In Hybrid NOrec, the second property was kept performant via a set of per-thread counters, or via special instrumentation on every load by an HTx.[1] In RHNOrec, the overhead of second property is avoided by executing the suffix of all but the largest STx (the interval between its first write through the completion of their commit) as a hardware transaction.

HyCo takes a different approach to these challenges. First, to ensure the opacity of STx, HTx are not allowed to commit whenever any STx is between its begin and commit points. In the absence of nontransactional loads, this necessitates that HTx abort if they reach their commit point and then observe an active STx. However, it also means that HTx do not need to modify shared variables at commit time in order to notify concurrent STx of the need to validate. Second, to ensure that HTx do not observe inconsistent state, the commit-time validation and writeback of STx is first attempted as a "reduced" hardware transaction. If the reduced transaction cannot commit, the STx waits until all concurrent HTx complete, and then performs serialized writeback. Note that by also blocking STx commits when there are concurrent in-flight STx, validation by in-flight STx is no longer necessary: during any STx execution, memory is immutable. Less instrumentation is required within STx, which reduces STx execution time and should limit the impact of HTx blocking or aborting at their commit point due to concurrent STx execution.

To make the behavior of transactions in HyCo more clear, Figure 1 presents a state machine to describe the behavior of transactions. There are 6 states:

- No STx (NS): This is the default state of the system. In this state, HTx may begin, commit, and abort.
- One Serial Transaction (S): Only one transaction is running, and it cannot be aborted. This allows a transaction to perform I/O [20,23].
- STx Active (SA): At least one STx has started but has not yet reached its commit point. No transaction is allowed to commit changes to shared state.
- STx Commit Pending (CP): A proper, nonempty subset of STx have reached their commit points. No transaction is allowed to commit changes to shared

---

[1] This instrumentation requires nontransactional loads from within the transaction, which are not supported by TSX.

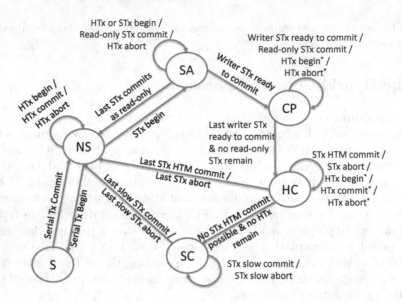

**Fig. 1.** State transitions of the Hybrid Cohorts algorithm.

state. To prevent extended blocking of ready-to-commit STx, new STx may not begin.

– STx Hardware Commit (HC): All STx have reached their commit point, and are attempting to commit via reduced hardware transactions. STx cannot begin, since shared memory may be changed.

– STx Software Commit (SC): A proper, nonempty subset of STx cannot commit via reduced hardware transactions, and are in the process of committing sequentially. No new transactions may begin.

State transitions are triggered by the following transaction events. With the exception of HTx Abort, these events occur on the boundaries of transactions:

– HTx Begin: A thread attempts to begin a transaction in HTx mode.
– HTx Commit: An HTx commits its changes to shared memory.
– HTx Abort: An HTx fails due to conflicts with other transactions.
– Serial Begin: A thread begins a serial transaction.
– Serial Commit: A serial transaction commits.
– STx Begin: A thread attempts to begin a transaction in STx mode.
– STx Commit (read-only): When an STx reaches its commit point, if it determines that it is read-only, it does not need to block in order to commit, since its commit cannot affect concurrent STx.
– STx Ready to Commit: An STx reaches its commit point, and is not read-only.
– STx Abort: An STx, during its commit operation, validates and determines that it conflicts with a committed transaction.
– STx HC Commit: An STx commits using a reduced hardware transaction.

- STx HC Fail: An STx cannot commit via a reduced hardware transaction (e.g., because it has accessed too many locations).
- STx Slow Commit: An STx commits via the serialized commit protocol.

In Figure 1, the lack of a label on an arc indicates that a transaction behavior is either impossible or not allowed. For example, an HTx is not allowed to commit in the SA or CP states, and it is not possible for an STx to abort in these states. Labels marked with an asterisk(*) are optional, and provide more opportunities for HTx to make progress. The order in which transactions are scheduled in the HC and SC modes can be governed by arbitrary contention management policies. For this discussion, we assume that the contention manager randomly chooses the order in which transactions attempt to commit in SC, and transactions attempt to commit immediately upon transition to HC.

Following Dalessandro et al. [4], the underlying STM uses value-based validation. STx do not update memory directly, but instead buffer their writes in a private log, and then replay them at commit time. These decisions ensure that HTx do not observe uncommitted state during their execution, and need not check per-location metadata on each load and store. The only global metadata for HyCo is related to the state machine, and it is only accessed at transaction boundaries. This results in a constant amount of global metadata, and a constant overhead for HTx to access that metadata.

Section 3 discusses mechanisms for achieving those transitions that are not obvious. For example, the transition from NS to S can be achieved by either (a) forcibly aborting any in-flight hardware transactions, or (b) setting a flag to prevent subsequent HTx and STx from beginning, and then waiting for the system to be in the NS state with no HTx running. Our goal is to achieve each transition without causing HTx conflicts on state machine metadata. As an example, an HTx can start as long as the system is not in S or SC state, but it need not know the exact system state until it reaches its commit point. If the state changes during HTx execution (e.g., from NS to SA, or even from HC to NS), the HTx should not immediately abort. At commit time, the HTx should be able to quickly check the precise state, and then self abort if necessary (e.g., if the state is CP).

HyCo provides opacity [9] for STx by ensuring that when an STx is in-flight, no concurrent HTx or STx may perform an operation that modifies locations that have been, or may be, read by the in-flight STx. A concurrent STx may reach its commit point, but may not transition to the HC or SC state, and since its writes are buffered, it cannot modify memory. (Note that a read-only STx may commit during this time, but by definition it does not modify shared memory.) Thus no concurrent STx can perform an operation that changes the memory visible to the in-flight STx. Similarly, a concurrent HTx may not transition from SA to HC, where it can complete its transaction. In this case, the HTM provides write buffering for the not-yet-committed HTx.

When the underlying HTM is opaque, Dalessandro et al. established that in a lazy HyTM, an HTx transaction can only experience an opacity violation if it overlaps with an STx commit [4]. Specifically, the STx might perform a

**Listing 1.** Hybrid Cohorts metadata. Global variables are clustered according to whether they assist in (a) coordinating all transactions, (b) coordinating HTx transactions, or (c) coordinating STx transactions.

```
Thread Variable Type:
tx_state   : Enum{NO, S, HW, SW} // state of thread's transaction
writes     : Map<addr,val>       // write set if this transaction is in STx mode
reads      : Set<addr,val>       // read set if this transaction is in STx mode
my_order   : Integer             // commit order if STx in SC mode
cp         : Checkpoint          // checkpoint of thread state, for STx aborts

Global Variables:
threads    : Set<Thread> // For reaching each thread's per-thread variables

started    : Integer     // Count of current active STx transactions
ser_kill   : Boolean     // Allow a Serial transaction to force immediate HTx aborts
stx_kill   : Boolean     // Allow an STx in SC mode to force immediate HTx aborts
stx_comm   : Boolean     // Indicate that all STx are ready to commit

cpending   : Integer     // Count of STx that are in the CP state
order      : Integer     // Counter to order STx in SC mode
time       : Integer     // Second counter for STx in SC mode
serial     : Boolean     // Token for transitions to Serial mode
```

partial write-back concurrent with the HTx, so that the HTx reads some of the STx's committed state, but not all of it. A sufficient condition is to prevent incomplete STx write-back from being visible to an HTx execution. In HyCo, this is achieved by (a) forbidding an STx from reaching the SC state until there are no concurrent HTx, and (b) attempting to commit STx in a reduced hardware transaction. In the HC state, the reduced transaction validates and performs write-back; consequently the STx cannot expose its partial state: the entire set of updates becomes visible when the hardware transaction commits.

HyCo supports a variety of approaches to ensuring fairness and progress. A few properties are relatively obvious: Any transaction can be guaranteed to complete if it executes in Serial mode, every read-only transaction will complete on its first attempt in STx mode, and an STx will not abort unless some other HTx or STx commits. Our implementation exposes two knobs for tuning progress. The first is a count of the number of HTx aborts before falling back to STx mode. The second is a count of the number of STx aborts before falling back to Serial mode. When combined with optional contention management at the beginning of the HC and SC states, there is ample opportunity to ensure that the most advantageous transactions are given priority. Additional scheduling decisions can be made when transitioning out of the CP state (i.e., by allowing a high priority transaction to abort all HTx, transition directly to SC, and commit first).

## 3   Implementation

The primary challenge in implementing HyCo is to achieve a low-latency implementation of the state machine from Figure 1. Our solution employs the metadata in Listing 1 to split the state machine into three parts. First, there is a list

**Algorithm 1.** The HyCo Algorithm. The parameter to `xbegin` (overridden by `xabort`) indicates the location to jump to when a hardware transaction aborts.

```
function TxBEGINHTx()
1    tx_state ← HW        // Announce active HTx
2    _xbegin(5)
     // Detect Serial and SC modes
3    if ser_kill ∨ stx_kill then  xabort(5)
4    return
     // Unannounce, wait if Serial or SC mode
5    tx_state ← NO
6    while ser_kill ∨ stx_kill do spin
     // Execute as STx or switch to Serial?
7    if switch_mode() then return
8    goto line 1

function TxCOMMITHTx()
     // Commit if all STx in HC mode or no STx
1    if stx_comm ∨ started = 0 then
2        _xend
3        tx_state ← NO
4        return
     // Cannot commit: SA or CP mode
5    xabort(TxBEGINHTx() line 5)

function TxBEGINSTx()
1    cp ← make_checkpoint()
     // Increment started only if NS or SA mode
2    while serial ∨ cpending > 0 do spin
3    atomic_incr(started)
     // Double-check NS or SA mode
4    if cpending > 0 ∨ serial then
5        atomic_decr(started)
6        goto line 2
7    tx_state ← SW
     // Lazy cleanup of STx-HC flag
8    if stx_comm then stx_comm ← false

function TxBEGINSERIAL()
     // Acquire serial lock, wait for STx to finish
1    while ¬cas(serial, false, true) do  spin
2    tx_state ← S
3    while started > 0 do spin
     // Optional: allow HTx to complete
4    for tx ∈ {threads − this_thread} do
5        wait_until(tx.tx_state = NO)
6    ser_kill ← true      // Abort remaining HTx

function TxCOMMITSERIAL()
     // Re-enable HTx, then release serial lock
1    ser_kill ← false
2    serial ← false
3    tx_state ← NO

function TxREAD(addr)
     // Serial and HTM fast-path
1    if tx_state ∈ {S, HW} then  return *addr
     // Handle read-after-write
2    if addr ∈ writes then  return writes[addr]
     // Read the value, and log it for commit-time
     validation
3    v ← *addr
4    reads ← reads ∪ {⟨addr, v⟩}
5    return v
```

```
function TxWRITE(addr, val)
     // Serial and HTM fast-path
1    if tx_state ∈ {S, HW} then  *addr = val
     // Buffer the write until commit time
2    else  writes ← writes ∪ {⟨addr, v⟩}

function TxCOMMITSTx()
     // Read-only fast path
1    if writes = ∅ then
2        atomic_decr(started)
3        reads ← ∅
4        return
     // Wait until all STx ready to commit
5    atomic_incr(cpending)
6    while cpending < started do spin
     // Move to HC mode, commit STx via HTM
7    if ¬stx_comm then stx_comm ← true;
8    _xbegin(18)
9    if reads.validate() then
10       writes.redo()
11       _xend
12       atomic_decr(started)
13       atomic_decr(cpending)
14       reads ← writes ← ∅
15       tx_state ← NO
16       return
17   else xabort(37)
     // Serialized commit
18   my_order ← atomic_incr(order)
     // Lead thread waits for HC to end
19   if order = 0 then
20       while order < started do spin
         // Optional: allow HTx to complete
21       for tx ∈ {threads − this_thread} do
22           wait_until(tx.tx_state ≠ HW)
23       stx_kill ← true   // Abort remaining HTx
     // Other threads wait their turn
24   else while time ≠ my_order do spin
     // Writeback only if validation succeeds
25   if reads.validate() then writes.redo()
26   else failed ← true
27   time ← time + 1   // Let next STx commit
     // Last thread moves metadata back to NS
28   old ← atomic_decr(started)
29   if old = 1 then
30       stx_kill ← false
31       time ← order ← 0
32   atomic_decr(cpending);
33   tx_state ← NO
34   reads ← writes ← ∅
35   if failed then cp.restore()
36   else return
     // Reachable only on HC validation failure
37   atomic_decr(started);
38   atomic_decr(cpending);
39   reads ← writes ← ∅
40   tx_state ← NO
41   cp.restore()
```

of Thread objects, through which per-thread states for non-transactional (NO), Serial, HTM, and STM modes can be discerned. Second, we use an Integer and three Booleans to control when HTx can begin, and when they must immediately abort. Finally, three Integers and one Boolean are used to manage the states of STx and Serial transactions. The code in Algorithm 1 uses these variables in flag-based and Dekker-style coordination.

The default system state is NS, in which HTx may begin and commit. Departing from this state requires an STx or Serial transaction to begin. To keep overheads low for HTx, we subscribe to the *ser_kill* flag when an HTx begins. After becoming serial, but before accessing shared memory, a Serial transaction sets this flag to immediately abort all HTx. By optionally using the *threads* set first (TxBeginSerial lines 4-5), we can opt to prioritize running HTx over new Serial transactions.

Since HTx can execute concurrently with STx, we do not repeat this behavior when STx begin. Instead, we must ensure that HTx do not commit when either (a) STx are between their begin and end, or (b) STx are performing serial commit. The *stx_kill* flag expresses condition (b). To handle condition (a), we use the *started* and *cpending* counters. When they are equal, every STx transaction has reached its commit point, and is trying to commit using HTM. In this case, HTx can commit, since the HTM will mediate conflicts. However, if they differ, then the HTx must abort.

STx are expected to be less frequent than HTx, and also to be longer-running. Thus we tolerate some contention over metadata, since it reduces the number of locations that HTx must check. Specifically, we use the *started* counter to track the number of STx that are not yet committed, and *cpending* to track the number of STx that have reached their commit point. The *order* and *time* counters are used only for SC commits, to enforce one-at-a-time commit of large STx. To maximize HTx concurrency with STx, we do not eagerly inform HTx of transitions between NS, SA, CP, and HC. Instead, we use the *stx_comm* flag, which indicates that STx have moved to HC state. This reduces the frequency of reads of the *started* and *cpending* counters by HTx. To avoid additional synchronization on STx commit, we defer resetting *stx_comm* to TxBeginSTx. Doing so is immaterial to HTx behavior, since HTx can progress in full from both the NS and HC modes.

The additional transition to SC for serialized commit of STx is expected to be rarest. We employ the same technique as Serial transactions, where a flag (*stx_kill*) is coupled with a traversal of the *threads* set (TxCommitSTx lines 21-22) to allow HTx to complete before serial STx. A final complication is that, for the sake of fairness, we do not allow new STx to begin once any STx is ready to commit writes. This necessitates care in TxBeginSTx, since we must double-check *cpending* after incrementing *started*.

Serial transactions are least common, justifying more overhead whenever one begins. After acquiring the *serial* token, a transaction will wait for all active STx and HTx to complete. Setting the *serial* flag first effectively prevents new STx. After allowing some HTx to complete, it sets *ser_kill* to prevent additional

HTx, at which point it can begin. Both flags are cleared when the transaction completes.

For completeness, Algorithm 1 also presents the read and write instrumentation for the HyCo algorithm. Per-access instrumentation is minimal, entailing neither metadata access nor memory fences. This is because (a) memory is immutable during STx execution, (b) Serial transactions execute in the absence of concurrency, and (c) HTx conflicts are mediated through the HTM, not through metadata.

## 4    Evaluation

We now evaluate the performance of HyCo using microbenchmarks, the STAMP benchmarks [15,17] and Memcached [19]. Experiments were conducted on a machine with single-chip 3.40GHz Intel Core i7-4770 with 4 cores / 8 threads, running Ubuntu Linux 13.04, kernel 3.8.0-21, and a 4.9 GCC compiler with O3 and m64 flags. Results are the average of 5 trials. We compare the following TM implementations:

- **STM_Eager** is the default STM provided with GCC. It is based on write-through TinySTM [8], using per-location ownership records, undo logging, encounter-time locking, and read set validation. The algorithm is opaque, and uses commit-time quiescence [22] to achieve privatization safety.
- **STM_Lazy** is a commit-time locking version of STM_Eager. Writes are stored in a redo log, implemented as a hash table of 64-byte blocks. Ownership records are acquired at commit time. STM_Lazy exposes overheads related to redo logs.
- **HTM** is the default HTM implementation provided with GCC. It is a PhaseTM that falls back to serial mode after two consecutive HTM aborts. HTM_20 does not fall back to serial until 20 consecutive aborts.
- **HyNOrec** is the "P-counter" version of Hybrid NOrec, which does not require nontransactional loads [4]. For Memcached, we also report the "2-counter" version.
- **HyNOrec_RH** is the most recent reduced hardware Hybrid NOrec implementation [14]. We did not apply complier static analysis to reduce the instrumentation of read-only hardware transactions, for fair comparison with other TM implementations, which could all benefit from such analysis.

In the interest of fairness, we observe the following differences among systems:

- **Privatization:** STM_Eager and STM_Lazy require quiescence-based privatization, whereas the HTM and hybrid algorithms do not. This can result in better scalability at high thread counts for hybrids, since they do not require blocking at commit time.
- **Mode Switching:** The Serial modes of our HyTMs are achieved via spin waiting, whereas the GCC-based algorithms use a more heavyweight blocking mechanism.
- **Un-instrumented HTM Loads and Stores:** GCC creates two code paths for transactions: an STM path, in which loads and stores of shared memory are instrumented, and an HTM path in which they are not. HyNOrec_RH and HyCo HTx benefit from this lower-latency code path.

We set HyCo thresholds as follows: An HTx transaction will switch to STx mode after 20 failed attempts to commit. An STx transaction will switch from committing in HC mode to committing in SC mode after 2 failed attempts. Fall-back to Serial mode occurs after 5 failed commit-time validations by an STx transaction. We also present HyCo-Turbo, which eagerly transitions STx to a mode where they run in isolation and perform all updates in-place. An STx can invoke turbo mode by a) confirming it is the only STx, (b) blocking new STx from starting, and (c) aborting all concurrent HTx. A turbo mode STx effectively executes as a Serial transaction.

## 4.1  Microbenchmark Performance

Figure 2 presents four red-black tree microbenchmarks. The experiments differ in terms of the range of keys present in the tree and the ratio of lookups to inserts and removes (inserts and removes are always performed in equal amount). All trees are pre-populated to 50% full. At one thread, HTM and HyCo performance are identical, and uniformly better than STM. This is expected, since most transactions are small enough to complete without exceeding hardware capacity. As we increase the thread count, and contention increases, we see a significant shift: the rapid fall-back to serial mode hurts HTM, both because it is too early, and because it limits concurrency. Even HTM_20, our version of the GCC HTM that retries 20 times before falling back to serial mode, cannot keep up with HyCo: the opportunity cost of serialization, even after 20 failed attempts, is simply too high. This is especially true for the highest contention configuration (8-bit keys, 33% lookup), where HTM_20 performance degrades beyond 4 threads.

Eager and Lazy STM scale well, and their use of validation affords for fewer aborts than HTM. However, latency is high: they incur a function call on every load and store, and Lazy pays even more due to accesses to the write log on many loads (these costs are only incurred in HyCo's STx mode). Furthermore, STM scales worse than HyCo, due to the overhead of quiescence, and the cost to support irrevocability via mode switching.

To gain a better understanding of the importance of HyTM versus PhaseTM, we measured the frequency of each type of commit for the HyCo execution of the benchmarks. While the majority of transactions can commit using HTM (NS state), up to 9% of HTx commit in HC mode. Thus while fallback to serial (for GCC) or STx (for HyCo) is rare, the impact on concurrent HTx can be significant. In HTM and HTM_20, every fallback to STx becomes a fallback to Serial, and all concurrency is lost.

## 4.2  STAMP Performance

STAMP performance is shown in Figure 3. Unlike microbenchmark experiments, STAMP performance is shown as total time. The expectation is that more threads will result in a decreased execution time. We do not report Bayes performance, since it exhibits nondeterministic behavior. We also note that since Labyrinth was rewritten to match the Draft C++ TM Specification [17], it shows

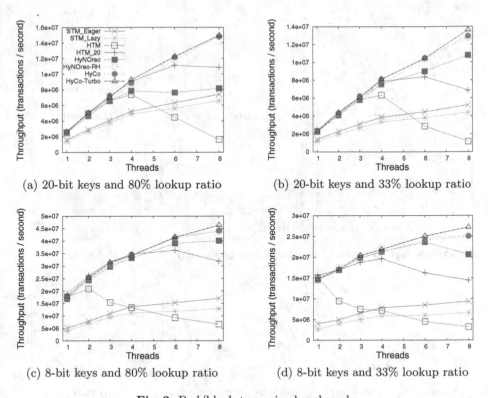

(a) 20-bit keys and 80% lookup ratio

(b) 20-bit keys and 33% lookup ratio

(c) 8-bit keys and 80% lookup ratio

(d) 8-bit keys and 33% lookup ratio

**Fig. 2.** Red/black tree microbenchmarks

little variation among algorithms because transactions no longer comprise a significant portion of execution time.

Among the remaining 8 benchmark configurations, we see two trends emerge. First, on workloads with high contention, such as KMeans and Vacation, HTM performs best at one thread, but its performance degrades as the thread count increases, due to its reliance on serialization to ensure progress after repeated aborts. In contrast, HyCo manages to maintain its performance as contention increases, by falling back to STx. This trend peters out to some degree at 8 threads for Vacation-HC, due hardware multithreading effects: with four cores and 8 hardware threads, transaction write capacities are effectively halved at 8 threads. The low-contention variants of KMeans and Vacation show that as contention decreases, HTM is able to perform on-par with HyCo, but HyCo remains a superior choice overall. The same is true for SSCA2, where small transactions run bottleneck-free in HyCo and HTM.

The second trend is shown by Genome, Intruder, and Yada, where HyCo incurs higher latency than HTM in order to interact with its write set. Recall that for STx transactions, HyCo must perform a lookup on each read, and must buffer its writes in a manner compatible with lookup. This necessitates a more

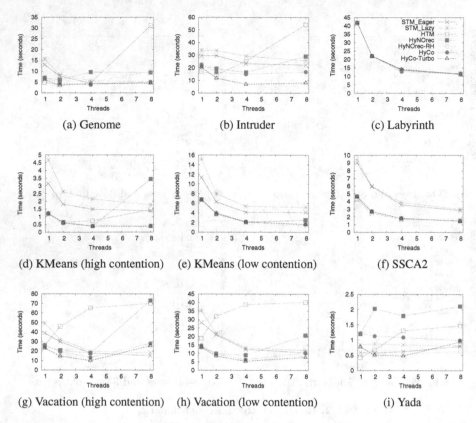

(a) Genome    (b) Intruder    (c) Labyrinth

(d) KMeans (high contention)    (e) KMeans (low contention)    (f) SSCA2

(g) Vacation (high contention)    (h) Vacation (low contention)    (i) Yada

**Fig. 3.** STAMP performance

complex data structure (hash of blocks with masks) than the undo log used by
eager STM and the HTM fall-back. Consequently, we see that STM_Lazy is a
constant factor slower than STM_Eager, and that HyCo similarly incurs higher
overhead. The problem is most extreme in Yada, where HTx abort late in their
execution, fall back to STx, and then incur write set overhead. Similarly, in
Genome and Intruder, the frequency of lookups creates overhead.

On this last point, we conducted experiments with two different write set
implementations: a hash table and an unbalanced BST. These tests showed that
the data structure itself was not the slowdown. Rather, the cost came from
manipulating bit masks in order to handle the case where a byte is accessed as
part of multiple accesses of varying granularity (e.g., the byte is written, and
then the enclosing word is read). These costs are shared by all of our Hybrid
TM implementations.

## 4.3    Memcached Performance

Lastly, we evaluate all TM implementations on memcached. We followed the
experiment configuration of Ruan et.al [19]. The configuration results in a num-

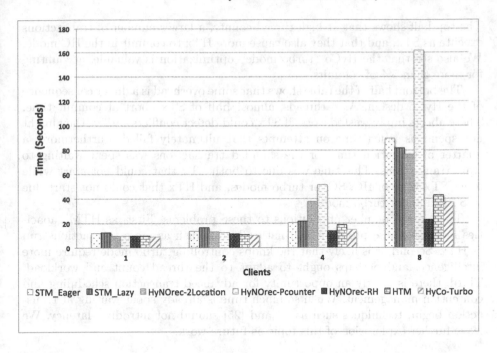

**Fig. 4.** Memcached Performance

**Table 1.** Frequency of each type of commit for Memcached at different client counts with HyCo-Turbo. Values were reported by a randomly chosen thread.

| Client Count | NS | HTx:HC | STx:RO | STx:HC | STx:SC | STx:Turbo | Serial |
|---|---|---|---|---|---|---|---|
| 2 | 7.48M | 65 | 0 | 85 | 10 | 4.4k | 0 |
| 8 | 5.44M | 544.3K | 0 | 195.7k | 72.2k | 295.9k | 0 |

| Client Count | STx aborts in HC/SC mode | Time spent spinning in TxBegin |
|---|---|---|
| 2 | 3.04% | 1.55% |
| 8 | 42.64% | 25.97% |

ber of operations proportional to the number of threads: flat curves indicate perfect scaling, higher values represent slowdown. The results are presented in Figure 4. Note that the number of transactions per thread is not constant, due to the use of transactions to read shared memory when spin waiting.

Memcached presents a number of interesting behaviors. First, we observed that Hybrid NOrec with P counters, where P is the number of threads, performed worse than the two-counter version. In our prior experiments, P-counter was superior. Second, HTM and HyCo performance were close, and HyNOrec-RH performed best at 8 threads. This was the first instance in which HyCo did not match or outperform HyNOrec-RH. Table 1 provides more detail. The data was collected by sampling one thread's behavior during a multithreaded execution.

The top half shows that at high thread counts, a larger number of transactions execute as STx, and that they also cause more HTx to commit in the HC mode. We also see that the HyCo "turbo mode" optimization is valuable, accounting for more than 5% of commits.

The bottom half of the table shows that some overhead is a direct consequence of the HyCo design. At 8 threads, almost half of STx abort at commit time. These aborts imply wasted work: if STx could detect conflicts earlier, they might not spend as much time on attempts that ultimately failed. Furthermore, a quarter of execution time for the sampled transactions was spent waiting to start transactions. This time was due to both STx that could not start while other STx were in HC, SC, or turbo modes, and HTx that could not start due to STx in SC or turbo modes.

There are a number of solutions to these problems. First, as HTM capacities increase, these problems will naturally diminish as more transactions run as HTx. Second, it is likely that the knobs controlling turbo mode require more intelligence, and perhaps ought to adapt to the thread count and workload. Third, there is clearly an opportunity for advanced transaction scheduling and contention management. When so much time is already spent waiting at transaction begin, techniques such as [1] and [25] should not introduce latency. We leave further exploration of this topic as future work.

## 5   Conclusions and Future Work

This paper presented the Hybrid Cohorts (HyCo) algorithm. HyCo prioritizes software-mode transactions over hardware-mode transactions, and then employs HTM resources to accelerate the commit phase of software transactions. Hardware transactions do not write to global metadata, and in-flight software transactions do not even read global metadata. Performance is on par with the current state-of-the-art, RHNOrec.

HyCo and RHNOrec represent distinct points in the HyTM design space. Both are informed by Riegel et al. [16] and Dalessandro et al. [4]: they use value-based validation to avoid wasting HTM capacity on per-location metadata, and they avoid serialization when transactions cannot complete in HTM. HyCo adapts the "reduced hardware transaction" innovation from RHNOrec: rather than execute the postfix of transactions in HTM, HyCo commits (validation and writeback) via HTM. Another significant difference is how the algorithms handle the worst case: in HyCo, many transactions can run in the slowest mode simultaneously, but they must validate; in RHNOrec, one transaction can use the slowest mode at a time, but fewer transactions require the slowest mode. Additionally, when a slow transaction runs, HyCo can still allow hardware transactions to commit, whereas RHNOrec does not. HyCo also appears to offer more opportunity for contention management, though we did not evaluate that possibility in this paper.

Which algorithm is "better" is likely to depend on how HTM evolves. Clearly, both systems can benefit from increased HTM capacity, which will allow more transactions to execute fully in hardware. As multi-chip HTM becomes more prevalent, HyCo may benefit more: RHNOrec inherits NOrec's requirement that some committing writers increment a global shared counter, which is known to scale poorly on multi-chip machines; HyCo has no such bottleneck. Another open question is how nontransactional loads might improve the algorithms: HyCo could employ nontransactional reads to allow hardware transactions to spin, rather than abort, when software transactions block their commit. No such opportunity is apparent for RHNOrec.

Unfortunately, we cannot draw stronger conclusions without better TM benchmarks. On microbenchmarks, and on STAMP, RHNOrec and HyCo perform similarly despite significant differences in design (especially in the fall-back path). On the only realistic workload available, Memcached, RHNOrec performs better at high core counts, where symmetric multithreading reduces HTM capacity. We are hopeful that as more programmers use TM, there will be new opportunities to contrast HyTM implementations and draw conclusions about what costs are most important to avoid.

**Acknowledgments.** We thank our reviewers, and the TRANSACT community, for their excellent advice. This material is based upon work supported by the National Science Foundation under Grants CAREER-1253362 and CCF-1218530. Any opinions, findings, and conclusions or recommendations expressed in this material are those of the authors and do not necessarily reflect the views of the National Science Foundation.

# References

1. Attiya, H., Epstein, L., Shachnai, H., Tamir, T.: Transactional contention management as a non-clairvoyant scheduling problem. In: Proceedings of the 25th ACM Symposium on Principles of Distributed Computing, Denver, CO, August 2006
2. Calciu, I., Gottschlich, J., Shpeisman, T., Pokam, G., Herlihy, M.: Invyswell: A hybrid transactional memory for haswell's restricted transactional memory. In: Proceedings of the 23rd International Conference on Parallel Architectures and Compilation Techniques, Edmonton, AB, Canada, August 2014
3. Calciu, I., Shpeisman, T., Pokam, G., Herlihy, M.: Improved single global lock fallback for best-effort hardware transactional memory. In: Proceedings of the 9th ACM SIGPLAN Workshop on Transactional Computing, Salt Lake City, UT, March 2014
4. Dalessandro, L., Carouge, F., White, S., Lev, Y., Moir, M., Scott, M., Spear, M.: Hybrid NOrec: A case study in the effectiveness of best effort hardware transactional memory. In: Proceedings of the 16th International Conference on Architectural Support for Programming Languages and Operating Systems Newport Beach, CA, March 2011
5. Dalessandro, L., Spear, M., Scott, M.L.: NOrec: streamlining stm by abolishing ownership records. In: Proceedings of the 15th ACM Symposium on Principles and Practice of Parallel Programming, Bangalore, India, January 2010
6. Damron, P., Fedorova, A., Lev, Y., Luchangco, V., Moir, M., Nussbaum, D.: Hybrid transactional memory. In: Proceedings of the 12th International Conference on Architectural Support for Programming Languages and Operating Systems, San Jose, CA, October 2006

7. Dice, D., Harris, T., Kogan, A., Lev, Y., Moir, M.: Pitfalls of lazy subscription. In: Proceedings of the 6th Workshop on the Theory of Transactional Memory, Paris, France, July 2014
8. Felber, P., Fetzer, C., Riegel, T.: dynamic performance tuning of word-based software transactional memory. In: Proceedings of the 13th ACM Symposium on Principles and Practice of Parallel Programming, Salt Lake City, UT, February 2008
9. Guerraoui, R., Kapalka, M.: on the correctness of transactional memory. In: Proceedings of the 13th ACM Symposium on Principles and Practice of Parallel Programming, Salt Lake City, UT, February 2008
10. Intel Corporation. Intel Architecture Instruction Set Extensions Programming (Chapter 8: Transactional Synchronization Extensions), February 2012
11. Jacobi, C., Slegel, T., Greiner, D.: Transactional memory architecture and implementation for IBM system Z. In: Proceedings of the 45th International Symposium On Microarchitecture, Vancouver, BC, Canada, December 2012
12. Kumar, S., Chu, M., Hughes, C.J., Kundu, P., Nguyen, A.: Hybrid transactional memory. In: Proceedings of the 11th ACM Symposium on Principles and Practice of Parallel Programming, New York, NY, March 2006
13. Lev, Y., Moir, M., Nussbaum, D.: PhTM: Phased transactional memory. In: Proceedings of the 2nd ACM SIGPLAN Workshop on Transactional Computing, Portland, OR, August 2007
14. Matveev, A., Shavit, N.: Reduced hardware NOrec: A safe and scalable hybrid transactional memory. In: Proceedings of the 20th International Conference on Architectural Support for Programming Languages and Operating Systems, Istanbul, Turkey, March 2015
15. Minh, C.C., Chung, J., Kozyrakis, C., Olukotun, K.: STAMP: Stanford transactional applications for multi-processing. In: Proceedings of the IEEE International Symposium on Workload Characterization, Seattle, WA, September 2008
16. Riegel, T., Marlier, P., Nowack, M., Felber, P., Fetzer, C.: Optimizing hybrid transactional memory: the importance of nonspeculative operations. In: Proceedings of the 23rd ACM Symposium on Parallelism in Algorithms and Architectures, June 2011
17. Ruan, W., Liu, Y., Spear, M.: STAMP need not be considered harmful. In: Proceedings of the 9th ACM SIGPLAN Workshop on Transactional Computing, Salt Lake City, UT, March 2014
18. Ruan, W., Liu, Y., Wang, C., Spear, M.: On the platform specificity of stm instrumentation mechanisms. In: Proceedings of the 2013 International Symposium on Code Generation and Optimization, Shenzhen, China, February 2013
19. Ruan, W., Vyas, T., Liu, Y., Spear, M.: Transactionalizing legacy code: an experience report using GCC and memcached. In: Proceedings of the 19th International Conference on Architectural Support for Programming Languages and Operating Systems, Salt Lake City, UT, March 2014
20. Spear, M., Silverman, M., Dalessandro, L., Michael, M.M., Scott, M.L.: Implementing and exploiting inevitability in software transactional memory. In: Proceedings of the 37th International Conference on Parallel Processing, Portland, OR, September 2008
21. Wang, A., Gaudet, M., Wu, P., Amaral, J.N., Ohmacht, M., Barton, C., Silvera, R., Michael, M.: Evaluation of blue gene/q hardware support for transactional memories. In: Proceedings of the 21st International Conference on Parallel Architectures and Compilation Techniques, Minneapolis, MN, September 2012

22. Wang, C., Chen, W.-Y., Wu, Y., Saha, B., Adl-Tabatabai, A.-R.: Code generation and optimization for transactional memory constructs in an unmanaged language. In: Proceedings of the 2007 International Symposium on Code Generation and Optimization, San Jose, CA, March 2007

23. Welc, A., Saha, B., Adl-Tabatabai, A.-R.: Irrevocable transactions and their applications. In: Proceedings of the 20th ACM Symposium on Parallelism in Algorithms and Architectures, Munich, Germany, June 2008

24. Yoo, R., Hughes, C., Lai, K., Rajwar, R.: Performance evaluation of intel transactional synchronization extensions for high performance computing. In: Proceedings of the International Conference for High Performance Computing, Networking, Storage and Analysis, Denver, CO, November 2013

25. Yoo, R., Lee, H.-H.: adaptive transaction scheduling for transactional memory systems. In: Proceedings of the 20th ACM Symposium on Parallelism in Algorithms and Architectures, Munich, Germany, June 2008

# Grasping the Gap Between Blocking and Non-Blocking Transactional Memories

Petr Kuznetsov[1] and Srivatsan Ravi[2]([⊠])

[1] Télécom ParisTech, Paris, France
petr.kuznetsov@telecom-paristech.fr
[2] TU Berlin, Berlin, Germany
srivatsan.ravi@inet.tu-berlin.de

**Abstract.** Transactional memory (TM) is an inherently optimistic synchronization abstraction: it allows concurrent processes to execute sequences of shared-data accesses (transactions) speculatively, with an option of aborting them in the future. Early TM designs avoided using locks and relied on non-blocking synchronization to ensure *obstruction-freedom*: a transaction that encounters no step contention is not allowed to abort. However, it was later observed that obstruction-free TMs perform poorly and, as a result, state-of-the-art TM implementations are nowadays *blocking*, allowing aborts because of data *conflicts* rather than step contention.

In this paper, we explain this shift in the TM practice theoretically, via complexity bounds. We prove a few important lower bounds on obstruction-free TMs. Then we present a *lock-based* TM implementation that beats all of these lower bounds. In sum, our results exhibit a considerable complexity gap between non-blocking and blocking TM implementations.

## 1 Introduction

Transactional memory (TM) allows concurrent processes to organize sequences of operations on shared *data items* into *transactions*. A transaction may commit, in which case its updates of data items "take effect" or it may *abort*, in which case no data item is modified. Typically, it is required that all committed transactions appear to execute sequentially, respecting the timing of non-overlapping transactions (*strict serializability*).

As a *synchronization abstraction*, TM came as an alternative to conventional lock-based synchronization, and it therefore appears natural that early TM *implementations* [12,18,23,26], *i.e.*, algorithms for implementing operations on data items using shared *base objects*, avoided using locks. Instead, early TM designs relied on *non-blocking* (sometimes also called *lock-free*) synchronization, where a prematurely halted transaction cannot prevent all other transactions from committing. Possibly the weakest non-blocking progress condition

P. Kuznetsov—The author is supported by the Agence Nationale de la Recherche, ANR-14-CE35-0010-01, project DISCMAT.

Y. Moses (Ed.): DISC 2015, LNCS 9363, pp. 232–247, 2015.
DOI: 10.1007/978-3-662-48653-5_16

is *obstruction-freedom* [17,19] stipulating that every transaction running in the absence of *step contention*, *i.e.*, not encountering steps of concurrent transactions, must commit.

In 2005, Ennals [11] argued that obstruction-free TMs inherently yield poor performance, because they require transactions to forcefully abort each other. Ennals further described a *lock-based* TM implementation [10] that he claimed to outperform *DSTM* [18], the most referenced obstruction-free TM implementation at the time. Inspired by [11], more recent lock-based TMs, such as *TL* [7], *TL2* [6] and *NOrec* [5], demonstrate better performance than obstruction-free TMs on most workloads. These TMs typically ensure *progressiveness*: a transaction may be aborted only if it encounters a read-write or a write-write conflict on a data item with a concurrent transaction [14].

There is a considerable amount of empirical evidence on the performance gap between non-blocking (obstruction-free) and blocking (progressive) TM implementations but, to the best of our knowledge, no analytical result explains it. Complexity lower and upper bounds presented in this paper provide such an explanation.

**Lower Bounds for Non-blocking TMs.** Our first result focuses on strictly serializable TM implementations that satisfy two important properties: *weak disjoint-access-parallelism* (weak DAP) and *read invisibility*. Informally, weak DAP [4] is believed to improve TM performance by ensuring that two transactions concurrently contend on the same base object only if their data sets are connected in the *conflict graph*, capturing data-set overlaps among all concurrent transactions [4]. The requirement of invisible reads [3,8], believed to be important for most commonly observed read-dominated workloads, ensures that a transaction cannot reveal any information about its read set to other transactions.

There exist weak DAP lock-based TM implementations that use invisible reads [7,10]. In contrast, we establish that it is impossible to implement an obstruction-free TM that provides both weak DAP and read invisibility. Indeed, DSTM [18] and FSTM [12] are weak DAP, but use *visible* reads for aborting pending writing transactions.

We then derive lower bounds on the *stall complexity* [9] of obstruction-free TM implementations. Intuitively, the metric captures the fact that the time a process might have to spend before it applies a primitive on a base object can be proportional to the number of processes that try to update the object concurrently. We show that a read operation in an $n$-process obstruction-free TM implementation may incur $\Omega(n)$ stalls.

Finally, we prove that any *read-write (RW) DAP opaque* obstruction-free TM implementation has an execution in which a read-only transaction incurs $\Omega(n)$ non-overlapping *RAWs* or *AWARs*. Intuitively, RAW (read-after-write) or AWAR (atomic-write-after-read) patterns [2] capture the amount of "expensive synchronization", *i.e.*, the number of costly conditional primitives or memory barriers [24] incurred by the implementation. The metric appears to be more practically relevant than simple step complexity, as it accounts for expensive cache-coherence operations or conditional instructions. RW DAP, a restriction

|  | Obstruction-free | Progressive $LP$ (Sec. 4) |
|---|---|---|
| strict DAP | No [13] | Yes |
| invisible reads+weak DAP | No (Sec. 3.1) | Yes |
| stall complexity of reads | $\Omega(n)$ (Sec. 3.2) | $O(1)$ |
| RAW/AWAR complexity | $\Omega(n)$ (Sec. 3.3) | $O(1)$ |
| read-write base objects, wait-free termination | No [15] | Yes |

**Fig. 1.** Complexity gap between blocking and non-blocking TMs; $n$ is the number of processes

of weak DAP, defines the conflict graph based on the *write-set overlaps* among concurrent transactions and is satisfied by several popular obstruction-free implementations [12,18,26]. For this lower bound, probably the most interesting and technically challenging, we assume opacity [15], a restriction of strict serializability that ensures safety of incomplete and aborted transactions.

**An Upper Bound for Blocking TMs.** We describe a progressive opaque TM implementation that uses invisible reads and beats *all* the lower bounds we established for obstruction-free TMs.

Our implementation, denoted $LP$, (1) uses only read-write base objects and ensures that every transactional operation terminates in a wait-free manner, (2) ensures *strict DAP* [15] (a restriction of RW DAP), (3) has invisible reads, (4) performs $O(1)$ non-overlapping RAWs/AWARs per transaction, and (5) incurs $O(1)$ memory stalls per read operation. In contrast, from prior work and our lower bounds we know that (i) no OF TM that provides wait-free transactional operations can be implemented using only read-write base objects [15]; (ii) no OF TM can provide strict DAP [13]; (iii) no weak DAP OF TM has invisible reads (Section 3.1) and (iv) no OF TM ensures a constant number of stalls incurred by a read operation (Section 3.2). Finally, (v) no RW DAP *opaque* OF TM has constant RAW/AWAR complexity (Section 3.3). Thus, (iv) and (v) exhibit a linear separation between blocking and non-blocking TMs w.r.t expensive synchronization and memory stall complexity, respectively.

Our results are summarized and put in perspective in Figure 1. Altogether, we grasp a considerable complexity gap between blocking and non-blocking TM implementations, justifying theoretically the shift in TM practice we observed during the past decade.

Overcoming our lower bounds for obstruction-free TMs individually is comparatively easy. Say, TL [7] combines strict DAP with invisible reads, but it is not read-write, and it does not provide constant RAW/AWAR and stall complexities.

Coming out with a single algorithm that beats all these lower bounds is quite nontrivial. Our algorithm $LP$ incurs the cost of *incremental validation*, *i.e.*, checking that the current read set has not changed per every new read operation. This is, however, unavoidable for invisible read algorithms [15,21], and is, in fact, believed to yield better performance in practice than "visible" reads [5,7,10], and we show that it enables constant stall and RAW/AWAR complexity.

**Roadmap.** Sections 2 defines our model and the classes of TMs considered in this paper. Section 3 contains lower bounds for obstruction-free TMs. Section 4 describes our progressive TM implementation $LP$. Sections 5 and 6 present related work and concluding remarks respectively. Due to space constraints, formal proofs are delegated to the technical report [22].

## 2    TM Model and Properties

**TM Interface.** *Transactional memory* (in short, *TM*) allows a set of data items (called *t-objects*) to be accessed via atomic *transactions*. A transaction $T_k$ may contain the following *t-operations*: $read_k(X)$ returns a value in some domain $V$ (denoted $read_k(X) \to v$) or a special value $A_k \notin V$ (*abort*); $write_k(X, v)$, for a value $v \in V$, returns $ok$ or $A_k$; $tryC_k$ returns $C_k \notin V$ (*commit*) or $A_k$.

**TM Implementations.** We consider an asynchronous shared-memory system in which a set of $n$ processes, communicate by applying *primitives* on shared *base objects*. We assume that processes issue transactions sequentially, *i.e.*, a process starts a new transaction only after its previous transaction has *completed* (committed or aborted). A TM *implementation* provides processes with algorithms for implementing $read_k$, $write_k$ and $tryC_k()$ of a transaction $T_k$ by *applying primitives* from a set of shared *base objects*, each of which is assigned an *initial value*. A primitive is a generic *read-modify-write* (*rmw*) procedure applied to a base object [9,16]. It is characterized by a pair of functions $\langle g, h \rangle$: given the current state of the base object, $g$ is an *update function* that computes its state after the primitive is applied, while $h$ is a *response function* that specifies the outcome of the primitive returned to the process. A rmw primitive is *trivial* if it never changes the value of the base object to which it is applied. Otherwise, it is *nontrivial*.

**Executions and Configurations.** An *event* of a transaction $T_k$ (sometimes we say a *step* of $T_k$) is a rmw primitive $\langle g, h \rangle$ applied by $T_k$ to a base object $b$ along with its response $r$ (we call it a *rmw event* and write $(b, \langle g, h \rangle, r, k)$), or the invocation or the response of a t-operation performed by $T_k$.

A *configuration* (of a TM implementation) specifies the value of each base object and the state of each process. The *initial configuration* is the configuration in which all base objects have their initial values and all processes are in their initial states.

An *execution fragment* is a (finite or infinite) sequence of events. An *execution* of a TM implementation $M$ is an execution fragment where, starting from the initial configuration, each event is issued according to $M$ and each response of a RMW event $(b, \langle g, h \rangle, r, k)$ matches the state of $b$ resulting from the preceding events. If an execution can be represented as $E \cdot E'$ (concatenation of execution fragments $E$ and $E'$), then we say that $E \cdot E'$ is an *extension* of $E$ or $E'$ extends $E$.

Let $E$ be an execution fragment. For a transaction $T_k$ (and resp. process $p_k$), $E|k$ denotes the subsequence of $E$ restricted to events of $T_k$ (and resp. $p_k$). If $E|k$ is non-empty, we say that $T_k$ (resp. $p_k$) *participates* in $E$, else we say $E$ is $T_k$-*free* (resp. $p_k$-*free*). Two executions $E$ and $E'$ are *indistinguishable* to a set $T$ of transactions, if for each transaction $T_k \in T$, $E|k = E'|k$. A TM *history* is the subsequence of an execution consisting of the invocation and response events of t-operations. Two histories $H$ and $H'$ are *equivalent* if $txns(H) = txns(H')$ and for every transaction $T_k \in txns(H)$, $H|k = H'|k$.

The *read set* (resp., the *write set*) of a transaction $T_k$ in an execution $E$, denoted $Rset_E(T_k)$ (and resp. $Wset_E(T_k)$), is the set of t-objects that $T_k$ attempts to read (and resp. write) by issuing a t-read (and resp. t-write) invocation in $E$ (for brevity, we sometimes omit the subscript $E$ from the notation). The *data set* of $T_k$ is $Dset(T_k) = Rset(T_k) \cup Wset(T_k)$. $T_k$ is called *read-only* if $Wset(T_k) = \emptyset$; *write-only* if $Rset(T_k) = \emptyset$ and *updating* if $Wset(T_k) \neq \emptyset$. Note that we consider the conventional dynamic TM model: the data set of a transaction is identifiable only by the set of t-objects the transaction has invoked a read or write in the given execution.

**Orders on Transactions.** Let $txns(E)$ denote the set of transactions that participate in $E$. An execution $E$ is *sequential* if every invocation of a t-operation is either the last event in the history $H$ exported by $E$ or is immediately followed by a matching response. We assume that executions are *well-formed*, *i.e.*, for all $T_k$, $E|k$ begins with the invocation of a t-operation, is sequential and has no events after $A_k$ or $C_k$. A transaction $T_k \in txns(E)$ is *complete in* $E$ if $E|k$ ends with a response event. The execution $E$ is *complete* if all transactions in $txns(E)$ are complete in $E$. A transaction $T_k \in txns(E)$ is *t-complete* if $E|k$ ends with $A_k$ or $C_k$; otherwise, $T_k$ is *t-incomplete*. $T_k$ is *committed* (resp., *aborted*) in $E$ if the last event of $T_k$ is $C_k$ (resp., $A_k$). The execution $E$ is *t-complete* if all transactions in $txns(E)$ are t-complete.

For transactions $\{T_k, T_m\} \in txns(E)$, we say that $T_k$ *precedes* $T_m$ in the *real-time order* of $E$, denoted $T_k \prec_E^{RT} T_m$, if $T_k$ is t-complete in $E$ and the last event of $T_k$ precedes the first event of $T_m$ in $E$. If neither $T_k \prec_E^{RT} T_m$ nor $T_m \prec_E^{RT} T_k$, then $T_k$ and $T_m$ are *concurrent* in $E$. An execution $E$ is *t-sequential* if there are no concurrent transactions in $E$.

**Contention.** If a transaction $T$ is incomplete in an execution $E$, it has exactly one *enabled* event, which is the next event the transaction will perform according to the TM implementation. Events $e$ and $e'$ of an execution $E$ *contend* on a base object $b$ if they are both events on $b$ in $E$ and at least one of them is nontrivial (the event is trivial (resp., nontrivial) if it is the application of a trivial (resp., nontrivial) primitive).

We say that $T$ is *poised to apply an event* $e$ after $E$ if $e$ is the next enabled event for $T$ in $E$. We say that transactions $T$ and $T'$ *concurrently contend* on $b$ in $E$ if they are poised to apply contending events on $b$ after $E$.

We say that an execution fragment $E$ is *step contention-free for t-operation* $op_k$ if the events of $E|op_k$ are contiguous in $E$. We say that an execution fragment $E$ is *step contention-free for* $T_k$ if the events of $E|k$ are contiguous in $E$. We say that $E$ is *step contention-free* if $E$ is step contention-free for all transactions that participate in $E$.

**TM-correctness.** Informally, a t-sequential history $S$ is *legal* if every t-read of a t-object returns the *latest written value* of this t-object in $S$. A history $H$ is *opaque* if there exists a legal t-sequential history $S$ equivalent to $H$ such that $S$ respects the real-time order of transactions in $H$ [15]. A weaker condition called *strict serializability* ensures opacity only with respect to committed transactions.

**TM-liveness.** We say that a TM implementation $M$ provides *obstruction-free (OF) TM-liveness* if for every finite execution $E$ of $M$, and every transaction $T_k$ that applies the invocation of a t-operation $op_k$ immediately after $E$, the finite step contention-free extension for $op_k$ contains a matching response. A TM implementation $M$ provides *wait-free TM-liveness* if in every execution of $M$, every t-operation returns a matching response in a finite number of its steps.

**TM-progress.** Progress for TMs specifies the conditions under which a transaction is allowed to abort. We say that a TM implementation $M$ provides *obstruction-free (OF) TM-progress* if for every execution $E$ of $M$, if any transaction $T_k \in txns(E)$ returns $A_k$ in $E$, then $E$ is not step contention-free for $T_k$.

We say that transactions $T_i, T_j$ *conflict* in an execution $E$ on a t-object $X$ if $T_i$ and $T_j$ are concurrent in $E$ and $X \in Dset(T_i) \cap Dset(T_j)$, and $X \in Wset(T_i) \cup Wset(T_j)$. A TM implementation $M$ provides *progressive* TM-progress (or *progressiveness*) if for every execution $E$ of $M$ and every transaction $T_i \in txns(E)$ that returns $A_i$ in $E$, there exists prefix $E'$ of $E$ and a transaction $T_k \in txns(E')$ such that $T_k$ and $T_i$ conflict in $E$.

**Read Invisibility.** Informally, in a TM using invisible reads, a transaction cannot reveal any information about its read set to other transactions. Thus, given an execution $E$ and some transaction $T_k$ with a non-empty read set, transactions other than $T_k$ cannot distinguish $E$ from an execution in which $T_k$'s read set is empty. This prevents TMs from applying nontrivial primitives during t-read operations and from announcing read sets of transactions during tryCommit. Most popular TM implementations like *TL2* [6] and *NOrec* [5] satisfy this property (the formal definition can be found in the technical report [22]).

**Disjoint-Access Parallelism (DAP).** A TM implementation $M$ is *strictly disjoint-access parallel (strict DAP)* if, for all executions $E$ of $M$, and for all transactions $T_i$ and $T_j$ that participate in $E$, $T_i$ and $T_j$ contend on a base object in $E$ only if $Dset(T_i) \cap Dset(T_j) \neq \emptyset$ [15].

We now describe two relaxations of strict DAP. For the definitions, we introduce the notion of a *conflict graph* which captures the dependency relation among t-objects accessed by transactions.

We denote by $\tau_E(T_i, T_j)$, the set of transactions ($T_i$ and $T_j$ included) that are concurrent to at least one of $T_i$ and $T_j$ in an execution $E$.

Let $G(T_i, T_j, E)$ be an undirected graph whose vertex set is $\bigcup_{T \in \tau_E(T_i, T_j)} Dset(T)$ and there is an edge between t-objects $X$ and $Y$ *iff* there exists $T \in \tau_E(T_i, T_j)$ such that $\{X, Y\} \in Dset(T)$. We say that $T_i$ and $T_j$

are *disjoint-access* in $E$ if there is no path between a t-object in $Dset(T_i)$ and a t-object in $Dset(T_j)$ in $G(T_i, T_j, E)$ [4,25].

Let $\tilde{G}(T_i, T_j, E)$ be a subgraph of $G(T_i, T_j, E)$ where t-objects $X$ and $Y$ are connected with an edge *iff* there exists $T \in \tau_E(T_i, T_j)$ such that $\{X, Y\} \in Wset(T)$. Respectively, $T_i$ and $T_j$ are *read-write disjoint-access* in $E$ if there is no path between a t-object in $Dset(T_i)$ and a t-object in $Dset(T_j)$ in $\tilde{G}(T_i, T_j, E)$.

A TM implementation $M$ is *read-write disjoint-access parallel (RW DAP)* (and resp. weak DAP) if, for all executions $E$ of $M$, transactions $T_i$ and $T_j$ contend (and resp. concurrently contend) on the same base object in $E$ only if $T_i$ and $T_j$ are not read-write disjoint-access (and resp. disjoint-access) in $E$ or there exists a t-object $X \in Dset(T_i) \cap Dset(T_j)$. The technical report [22] provides further details and examples on the DAP definitions.

# 3 Lower Bounds for Obstruction-Free TMs

Let $\mathcal{OF}$ denote the class of TMs that provide OF TM-progress and OF TM-liveness. In Section 3.1, we show that no strict serializable TM in $\mathcal{OF}$ can be weak DAP and have invisible reads. In Section 3.2, we determine stall complexity bounds for strict serializable TMs in $\mathcal{OF}$, and in Section 3.3, we present a linear (in $n$) lower bound on the RAW/AWAR complexity for RW DAP opaque TMs in $\mathcal{OF}$.

## 3.1 Impossibility of Invisible Reads

In this section, we prove that it is impossible to derive TM implementations in $\mathcal{OF}$ that combine weak DAP and invisible reads. The formal proof is given in the technical report [22], we present an intuition below.

**Theorem 1.** *There does not exist a weak DAP strictly serializable TM implementation in $\mathcal{OF}$ that uses invisible reads.*

*Proof (Outline).* Suppose, by contradiction, that such a TM implementation $M$ exists. Consider an execution $E$ of $M$ in which a transaction $T_0$ performs a t-read of t-object $Z$ (returning the initial value $v$), writes $nv$ (new value) to t-object $X$, and commits. Let $E'$ denote the longest prefix of $E$ that cannot be extended with the t-complete step contention-free execution of any transaction that reads $nv$ in $X$ and commits.

Thus if $T_0$ takes one more step after $E'$, then the resulting execution $E' \cdot e$ can be extended with the t-complete step contention-free execution of a transaction $T_1$ that reads $nv$ in $X$ and commits (Figure 2a).

Since $M$ uses invisible reads, the following execution exists: $E'$ can be extended with the t-complete step contention-free execution of a transaction $T_2$ that reads the initial value $v$ in $X$ and commits, followed by the step $e$ of $T_0$ after which transaction $T_1$ running step contention-free reads $nv$ in $X$ and commits (Figure 2b). Moreover, this execution is indistinguishable to $T_1$ and $T_2$ from an execution in which the read set of $T_0$ is empty. Thus, we can modify this

$$T_0 \xmapsto{\quad R_0(Z) \to v \quad} \xmapsto{\quad W_0(X,nv) \quad} \xmapsto{\quad tryC_0 \quad} \cdots \qquad \overset{\circ}{e}^{\text{(event of } T_0\text{)}} \qquad T_1 \xmapsto[\text{new value}]{\quad R_1(X) \to nv \quad}$$

(a) $T_1$ must read the base object updated in $e$ and return the new value $nv$ of $X$

$$T_0 \xmapsto{\; R_0(Z) \to v \;} \xmapsto{\; W_0(X,nv) \;} \xmapsto{\; tryC_0 \;} \cdots \quad T_2 \xmapsto[\text{initial value}]{\; R_2(X) \to v \;} \overset{\circ}{e}^{\text{(event of } T_0\text{)}} \; T_1 \xmapsto[\text{new value}]{\; R_1(X) \to nv \;}$$

(b) $T_1$ returns new value of $X$ since $T_2$ is invisible

$$T_0 \xmapsto{R_0(Z) \to v} \xmapsto{W_0(X,nv)} \xmapsto{tryC_0} \cdots \; T_3 \xmapsto[\text{write new value}]{W_3(Z,nv)} T_2 \xmapsto[\text{initial value}]{R_2(X) \to v} \overset{\circ}{e}^{\text{(event of } T_0\text{)}} T_1 \xmapsto[\text{new value}]{R_1(X) \to nv}$$

(c) By weak DAP and invisible reads, $T_1$ and $T_2$ do not observe the presence of $T_3$

**Fig. 2.** Executions describing the proof sketch of Theorem 1; execution in 2c is not strictly serializable

execution by inserting the step contention-free execution of a committed transaction $T_3$ that writes a new value to $Z$ after $E'$, but preceding $T_2$ in real-time order. Intuitively, by weak DAP, transactions $T_1$ and $T_2$ cannot distinguish this execution from the original one in which $T_3$ does not participate.

Thus, we can show that the following execution exists: $E'$ is extended with the t-complete step contention-free execution of $T_3$ that writes $nv$ to $Z$ and commits, followed by the t-complete step contention-free execution of $T_2$ that reads the initial value $v$ in $X$ and commits, followed by the step $e$ of $T_0$, after which $T_1$ reads $nv$ in $X$ and commits (Figure 2c).

This execution is, however, not strictly serializable: $T_0$ must appear in any serialization ($T_1$ reads a value written by $T_0$). Transaction $T_2$ must precede $T_0$, since the t-read of $X$ by $T_2$ returns the initial value of $X$. To respect real-time order, $T_3$ must precede $T_2$. Finally, $T_0$ must precede $T_3$ since the t-read of $Z$ returns the initial value of $Z$. The cycle $T_0 \to T_3 \to T_2 \to T_0$ implies a contradiction.

## 3.2   Stall Complexity

We prove a linear (in $n$) lower bound for strictly serializable TM implementations in $\mathcal{OF}$ on the total number of *memory stalls* incurred by a single t-read operation.

Let $E = \alpha \cdot e_1 \cdots e_m \cdot e \cdot \beta$ be an execution of $M$, where $\alpha$ and $\beta$ are execution fragments, $e$ is a primitive applied by a process $p$ on a base object $b$ within a t-operation $op$, and $e_1 \cdots e_m$ is a maximal sequence of $m \geq 1$ consecutive nontrivial events by distinct processes other than $p$ that access $b$. Then, we say that $op$ incurs $m$ *memory stalls in $E$ on account of $e$*. The *number of memory stalls incurred by $op$ in $E$* is the sum of memory stalls incurred by all events of $op$ in $E$ [1,9].

**Theorem 2.** *Every strictly serializable TM implementation $M \in \mathcal{OF}$ has an execution in which some t-read operation incurs $\Omega(n)$ stalls.*

We give an intuitive sketch below, but the full proof can be found in [22]. Inductively, for each $k \leq n - 1$, we construct a specific $k$-*stall execution* [9] in which some t-read operation by a process $p$ incurs $k$ stalls. In the $k$-stall execution, $k$ processes are partitioned into disjoint subsets $S_1, \ldots, S_i$. The execution can be represented as $\alpha \cdot \sigma_1 \cdots \sigma_i$; $\alpha$ is $p$-free, where in each $\sigma_j$, $j = 1, \ldots, i$, $p$ first runs by itself, then each process in $S_j$ applies a *nontrivial* event on a base object $b_j$, and then $p$ applies an event on $b_j$. Moreover, $p$ does not detect step contention in this execution and, thus, must return a non-abort value in its t-read and commit in the solo extension of it. Additionally, it is guaranteed that in any extension of $\alpha$ by the processes other than $\{p\} \cup S_1 \cup S_2 \cup \ldots \cup S_i$, no nontrivial primitive is applied on a base object accessed in $\sigma_1 \cdots \sigma_i$.

Assuming a $k$-stall execution $\alpha \cdot \sigma_1 \cdots \sigma_i$ for process $p$ executing a t-read operation where $k \leq n - 2$, we introduce a not previously used process executing an updating transaction immediately after $\alpha$, so that the subsequent t-read operation executed by $p$ is "perturbed" (must return another value). This will help us to construct a $(k + k')$-stall execution $\alpha \cdot \alpha' \cdot \sigma_1 \cdots \sigma_i \cdot \sigma_{i+1}$, where $k' > 0$. Thus, the TM has a $(n - 1)$-stall execution for some t-read operation.

### 3.3   RAW/AWAR Complexity

In this section, we characterize the complexity of implementations in $\mathcal{OF}$ by measuring the amount of expensive synchronization patterns like $RAW$ (read-after-write) or $AWAR$ (atomic-write-after-read) that read-only transactions may need to perform.

A RAW pattern performed by a transaction $T_k$ in an execution $\pi$ is a pair of its events $e$ and $e'$, such that: (1) $e$ is a write to a base object $b$ by $T_k$, (2) $e'$ is a subsequent read of a base object $b' \neq b$ by $T_k$, and (3) no event on $b$ by $T_k$ takes place between $e$ and $e'$. In this paper, we are concerned only with *non-overlapping* RAWs, *i.e.*, the read performed by one RAW precedes the write performed by the other RAW. An AWAR pattern $e$ in an execution $\pi \cdot e$ is a nontrivial rmw event on an object $b$ which atomically returns the value of $b$ (resulting after $\pi$) and updates $b$ with a new value, *e.g.*, a successful *compare-and-swap*.

We prove that opaque, RW DAP TM implementations in $\mathcal{OF}$ have executions in which some read-only transaction performs a linear (in $n$) number of non-overlapping RAWs or AWARs. Our result illustrates why individual t-read operations of RW DAP obstruction-free TMs like DSTM [18] must forcefully abort pending conflicting transactions using compare-and-swap in some executions.

**Theorem 3.** *Every RW DAP opaque TM implementation $M \in \mathcal{OF}$ has an execution $E$ in which some read-only transaction $T \in txns(E)$ performs $\Omega(n)$ non-overlapping RAW/AWARs.*

*Proof (Outline).* We first construct an execution of the form $\bar{\rho}_1 \cdots \bar{\rho}_m$, where for all $j \in \{1, \ldots, m\}$; $m = n - 3$, $\bar{\rho}_j$ denotes the t-complete step contention-free execution of transaction $T_j$ that reads the initial value $v$ in a distinct t-object $Z_j$, writes a new value $nv$ to a distinct t-object $X_j$ and commits. Observe that since any two transactions that participate in this execution are mutually read-write disjoint-access, they cannot contend on the same base object and, thus, the execution appears solo to each of them.

Let each of two new transactions $T_{n-1}$ and $T_n$ perform $m$ t-reads on objects $X_1, \ldots, X_m$. For $j \in \{1, \ldots, m\}$, we now define $\rho_j$ to be the longest prefix of $\bar{\rho}_j$ such that $\rho_1 \cdots \rho_j$ cannot be extended the complete step contention-free execution fragment of $T_{n-1}$ or $T_n$ where the t-read of $X_j$ returns $nv$. Let $e_j$ be the event by $T_j$ enabled after $\rho_1 \cdots \rho_j$. Let us count the number of indices $j \in \{1, \ldots, m\}$ such that $T_{n-1}$ (resp., $T_n$) reads the new value $nv$ in $X_j$ when it runs after $\rho_1 \cdots \rho_j \cdot e_j$. Without loss of generality, assume that $T_{n-1}$ has more such indices $j$ than $T_n$. We are going to show that, in the worst-case, $T_n$ must perform $\lceil \frac{m}{2} \rceil$ non-overlapping RAW/AWARs in the course of performing $m$ t-reads of $X_1, \ldots, X_m$ immediately after $\rho_1 \cdots \rho_m$.

Consider any $j \in \{1, \ldots, m\}$ such that $T_{n-1}$, when it runs step contention-free after $\rho_1 \cdots \rho_j \cdot e_j$, reads $nv$ in $X_j$. We claim that, in $\rho_1 \cdots \rho_m$ extended with the step contention-free execution of $T_n$ performing $j$ t-reads $read_n(X_1) \cdots read_n(X_j)$, the t-read of $X_j$ must contain a RAW or an AWAR.

Suppose not. Then we are going to schedule a specific execution of $T_j$ and $T_{n-1}$ concurrently with $read_n(X_j)$ so that $T_n$ cannot detect the concurrency. By the definition of $\rho_j$ and the fact that the TM is RW DAP, $T_n$, when it runs step contention-free after $\rho_1 \cdots \rho_m$, must read $v$ (the initial value) in $X_j$. Then the following execution exists: $\rho_1 \cdots \rho_m$ is extended with the t-complete step contention-free execution of $T_{n-2}$ writing $nv$ to $Z_j$ and committing, after which $T_n$ runs step contention-free and reads $v$ in $X_j$. Since, by the assumption, $read_n(X_j)$ contains no RAWs or AWARs, we show that we can run $T_{n-1}$ performing $j$ t-reads concurrently with the execution of $read_n(X_j)$ so that $T_n$ and $T_{n-1}$ are unaware of step contention and $read_{n-1}(X_j)$ still reads the value $nv$ in $X_j$.

To understand why this is possible, consider the following: we take the execution constructed above, but without the execution of $read_n(X_j)$, *i.e,* $\rho_1 \cdots \rho_m$ is extended with the step contention-free execution of committed transaction $T_{n-2}$ writing $nv$ to $Z_j$, after which $T_n$ runs step contention-free performing $j - 1$ t-reads. This execution can be extended with the step $e_j$ by $T_j$, followed by the step contention-free execution of transaction $T_{n-1}$ in which it reads $nv$ in $X_j$. Indeed, by RW DAP and the definition of $\rho_j \cdot e_j$, there exists such an execution.

Since $read_n(X_j)$ contains no RAWs or AWARs, we can reschedule the execution fragment $e_j$ followed by the execution of $T_{n-1}$ so that it is concurrent with the execution of $read_n(X_j)$ and neither $T_n$ nor $T_{n-1}$ see a difference. Therefore, in this execution, $read_n(X_j)$ still returns $v$, while $read_{n-1}(X_j)$ returns $nv$.

However, the resulting execution is not opaque. In any serialization the following must hold. Since $T_{n-1}$ reads the value written by $T_j$ in $X_j$, $T_j$ must be committed. Since $read_n(X_j)$ returns the initial value $v$, $T_n$ must precede $T_j$. The committed transaction $T_{n-2}$, which writes a new value to $Z_j$, must precede $T_n$ to respect the real-time order on transactions. However, $T_j$ must precede $T_{n-2}$ since $read_j(Z_j)$ returns the initial value and the implementation is opaque. The cycle $T_j \rightarrow T_{n-2} \rightarrow T_n \rightarrow T_j$ implies a contradiction.

Thus, we can show that transaction $T_n$ must perform $\Omega(n)$ RAW/AWARs during the execution of $m$ t-reads immediately after $\rho_1 \cdots \rho_m$.

# 4    Upper Bound for Opaque Progressive TMs

In this section, we describe a *progressive*, opaque TM implementation $LP$ (Algorithm 1) that is not subject to any of the lower bounds we derived so far for $\mathcal{OF}$ (cf. Figure 1). In our TM $LP$, every transaction performs at most a single RAW, every t-read operation incurs $O(1)$ memory stalls and maintains exactly one version of every t-object in every execution. Moreover, the implementation is strict DAP and uses only read-write base objects.

**Base Objects.** For every t-object $X_j$, $LP$ maintains a base object $v_j$ that stores the *value* of $X_j$. Additionally, for each $X_j$, we maintain a bit $L_j$, which if set, indicates the presence of an updating transaction writing to $X_j$. Also, for every process $p_i$ and t-object $X_j$, $LP$ maintains a *single-writer bit* $r_{ij}$ to which only $p_i$ is allowed to write. Each of these base objects may be accessed only via read and write primitives.

**Read Operations.** The implementation first reads the value of t-object $X_j$ from base object $v_j$ and then reads the bit $L_j$ to detect contention with an updating transaction. If $L_j$ is set, the transaction is aborted; if not, read validation is performed on the entire read set. If the validation fails, the transaction is aborted. Otherwise, the implementation returns the value of $X_j$. For a read-only transaction $T_k$, $tryC_k$ simply returns the commit response.

**Updating Transactions.** The $write_k(X, v)$ implementation by process $p_i$ simply stores the value $v$ locally, deferring the actual updates to $tryC_k$. During $tryC_k$, process $p_i$ attempts to obtain exclusive write access to every $X_j \in Wset(T_k)$. This is realized through the single-writer bits, which ensure that no other transaction may write to base objects $v_j$ and $L_j$ until $T_k$ relinquishes its exclusive write access to $Wset(T_k)$. Specifically, process $p_i$ writes 1 to each $r_{ij}$, then checks that no other process $p_t$ has written 1 to any $r_{tj}$ by executing a series of reads (incurring a single RAW). If there exists such a process that concurrently contends on write set of $T_k$, for each $X_j \in Wset(T_k)$, $p_i$ writes 0 to $r_{ij}$ and aborts $T_k$. If successful in obtaining exclusive write access to $Wset(T_k)$, $p_i$ sets the bit $L_j$ for each $X_j$ in its write set. Implementation of $tryC_k$ now checks if any t-object in its read set is concurrently contended by another transaction and then validates its read set. If there is contention on the read set or validation fails (indicating the presence of a conflicting transaction), the transaction is aborted. If not, $p_i$ writes the values of the t-objects to shared memory and relinquishes exclusive

**Algorithm 1.** Strict DAP progressive opaque TM implementation $LP$; code for $T_k$ executed by process $p_i$

```
1:  Shared base objects:
2:    v_j, for each t-object X_j
         allows reads and writes
3:    r_ij, for every p_i and t-object X_j
         single-writer bit
         allows reads and writes
4:    L_j, for every t-object X_j
         allows reads and writes

5:  Local variables:
6:    Rset_k, Wset_k for every T_k;
         dictionaries storing {X_m, v_m}

7:  read_k(X_j):
8:    if X_j ∉ Rset(T_k) then
9:        [ov_j, k_j] := read(v_j)
10:       Rset(T_k).add({X_j, [ov_j, k_j]})
11:       if read(L_j) ≠ 0 then
12:           Return A_k
13:       if validate() then
14:           Return A_k
15:       Return ov_j
16:   else
17:       [ov_j, ⊥] := Rset(T_k).locate(X_j)
18:       Return ov_j

19: write_k(X_j, v):
20:   nv_j := v
21:   Wset(T_k).add({X_j})
22:   Return ok

23: tryC_k():
24:   if |Wset(T_k)| = ∅ then
25:       Return C_k
26:   locked := acquire(Wset(T_k))
27:   if ¬ locked then
28:       Return A_k
29:   if isAbortable() then
30:       release(Wset(T_k))
31:       Return A_k
      // Exclusive write access to each v_j
32:   for all X_j ∈ Wset(T_k) do
33:       write(v_j, [nv_j, k])
34:   release(Wset(T_k))
35:   Return C_k

36: Function: release(Q):
37:   for all X_j ∈ Q do
38:       write(L_j, 0)
39:   for all X_j ∈ Q do
40:       write(r_ij, 0)
41:   Return ok

42: Function: acquire(Q):
43:   for all X_j ∈ Q do
44:       write(r_ij, 1)
45:   if ∃X_j ∈ Q; t ≠ i : read(r_tj) = 1 then
46:       for all X_j ∈ Q do
47:           write(r_ij, 0)
48:       Return false
      // Exclusive write access to each L_j
49:   for all X_j ∈ Q do
50:       write(L_j, 1)
51:   Return true

52: Function: isAbortable() :
53:   if ∃X_j ∈ Rset(T_k) : X_j ∉ Wset(T_k) ∧
         read(L_j) ≠ 0 then
54:       Return true
55:   if validate() then
56:       Return true
57:   Return false

58: Function: validate() :
      // Read validation
59:   if ∃X_j ∈ Rset(T_k):[ov_j, k_j] ≠
         read(v_j) then
60:       Return true
61:   Return false
```

write access to each $X_j \in Wset(T_k)$ by writing 0 to each of the base objects $L_j$ and $r_{ij}$.

**Complexity.** Read-only transactions do not apply any nontrivial primitives. Any updating transaction performs at most a single RAW in the course of acquiring exclusive write access to the transaction's write set. Thus, every transaction performs $O(1)$ non-overlapping RAWs in any execution. However, just as state-of-the-art progressive opaque TM implementations like TL [7] and NOrec [5] that use invisible reads, $LP$ must incur the inherent incremental validation cost that is linear in the size of the read set [15, 21].

Recall that a transaction may write to base objects $v_j$ and $L_j$ only after obtaining exclusive write access to t-object $X_j$, which in turn is realized via single-writer base objects. Thus, no transaction performs a write to any base object $b$ immediately after a write to $b$ by another transaction, *i.e.*, every transaction incurs only $O(1)$ memory stalls on account of any event it performs. The $read_k(X_j)$ implementation reads base objects $v_j$ and $L_j$, followed by the validation phase in which it reads $v_k$ for each $X_k$ in its current read set. Note that if the first read in the validation phase incurs a stall, then $read_k(X_j)$ aborts. It follows that each t-read incurs $O(1)$ stalls in every execution.

Thus, we can prove the following theorem:

**Theorem 4.** *Algorithm 1 describes a progressive, opaque and strict DAP TM implementation LP that provides wait-free TM-liveness, uses invisible reads, uses only read-write base objects, and for every execution E and transaction $T_k \in txns(E)$: (i) $T_k$ performs at most a single RAW, and (ii) every t-read operation performed by $T_k$ incurs $O(1)$ memory stalls in E.*

## 5   Related Work

Attiya *et al.* [4] were the first to formally define DAP for TMs. They proved the impossibility of implementing weak DAP strictly serializable TMs that use invisible reads and guarantee that read-only transactions eventually commit, while updating transactions are guaranteed to commit only when they run sequentially [4]. This class is orthogonal to the class of obstruction-free TMs, as is the proof technique used to establish the impossibility arguments (Section 3.1).

Perelman *et al.* [25] showed that *mv-permissive* weak DAP TMs cannot be implemented. In mv-permissive TMs, only updating transactions may be aborted, and only when they conflict with other updating transactions. In particular, read-only transactions cannot be aborted and updating transactions may sometimes be aborted even in the absence of step contention, which makes the impossibility result in [25] unrelated to ours (Section 3.1).

Guerraoui and Kapalka [15] proved that it is impossible to implement strict DAP obstruction-free TMs. They also proved that a strict serializable TM that provides OF TM-progress and wait-free TM-liveness cannot be implemented using only read and write primitives. We show in Section 4 that progressive TMs are not subject to either of these lower bounds.

Attiya *et al.* [2] proved that it is impossible to derive RAW/AWAR-free implementations of data types like *stacks*, *queues* and *deadlock-free mutual exclusion*. The metric was previously used in [20] to measure the complexity of read-only transactions in a strictly stronger (than $\mathcal{OF}$) class of *permissive* TMs (assuming wait-free TM-liveness) which ensure that a transaction may be aborted only if committing it would violate opacity. This lower bound in [20] is unrelated to Theorem 3 on RW DAP obstruction-free TMs. Detailed coverage on memory fences and the RAW/AWAR metric can be found in [24].

To derive the linear lower bound on the memory stall complexity of obstruction-free TMs (Section 3.2), we adopted the definition of a *k-stall execution* and certain proof steps from [1,9].

Our upper bound $LP$ that theoretically demonstrates the advantages of adapting TMs to data conflicts rather than step contention is inspired by the progressive TM of [20]. Complexity optimizations for progressive TMs like reducing the cost of read-validation by slightly relaxing strict DAP, as achieved in TL2 [6], can also be applied to $LP$.

The technical report [22] provides details on the DAP definitions as well as opaque implementations in $\mathcal{OF}$ that satisfy weak and RW DAP. The definition of invisible reads used in this paper is adopted from [3].

# 6   Concluding Remarks

As highlighted in [7,11], obstruction-free TMs require an *indirection* from the t-object *metadata* in order to find the current version of the t-object. This suggests that obstruction-free TMs must forcefully abort pending conflicting transactions in order to return the correct t-object version. This observation inspires the impossibility of invisible reads (Theorem 1). Typically, to detect the presence of a conflicting transaction and abort it, the reading transaction must employ a RAW or read-modify-write primitives like compare-and-swap, motivating the linear lower bound on expensive synchronization (Theorem 3). Also, in obstruction-free TMs, a transaction may not wait for a concurrent inactive transaction to complete and, as a result, we may have an execution in which a transaction incurs a distinct stall due to a transaction run by each other process (Theorem 2). Intuitively, since transactions in progressive TMs may abort themselves in case of conflicts, they can employ invisible reads and maintain constant stall and RAW/AWAR complexities.

Some benefits of obstruction-free TMs, namely their ability to make progress even if some transactions prematurely fail, are not provided by progressive TMs. However, several papers [6,7,11] argued that lock-based TMs tend to outperform obstruction-free ones by allowing for simpler algorithms with lower overhead, and their inherent progress issues may be resolved using timeouts and contention-managers. This paper explains the empirically observed performance gap between blocking and non-blocking TMs via a series of lower bounds on obstruction-free TMs and a progressive TM algorithm that beats all of them.

# References

1. Attiya, H., Guerraoui, R., Hendler, D., Kuznetsov, P.: The complexity of obstruction-free implementations. J. ACM **56**(4) (2009)
2. Attiya, H., Guerraoui, R., Hendler, D., Kuznetsov, P., Michael, M., Vechev, M.: Laws of order: Expensive synchronization in concurrent algorithms cannot be eliminated. In: POPL, pp. 487–498 (2011)
3. Attiya, H., Hillel, E.: The cost of privatization in software transactional memory. IEEE Trans. Computers **62**(12), 2531–2543 (2013)
4. Attiya, H., Hillel, E., Milani, A.: Inherent limitations on disjoint-access parallel implementations of transactional memory. Theory of Computing Systems **49**(4), 698–719 (2011)
5. Dalessandro, L., Spear, M.F., Scott, M.L.: NOrec: streamlining STM by abolishing ownership records. In: PPOPP, pp. 67–78 (2010)
6. Dice, D., Shalev, O., Shavit, N.N.: Transactional locking II. In: Dolev, S. (ed.) DISC 2006. LNCS, vol. 4167, pp. 194–208. Springer, Heidelberg (2006)
7. Dice, D., Shavit, N.: What really makes transactions fast? In: Transact (2006)
8. Dice, D., Shavit, N.: TLRW: return of the read-write lock. In: SPAA, pp. 284–293 (2010)
9. Ellen, F., Hendler, D., Shavit, N.: On the inherent sequentiality of concurrent objects. SIAM J. Comput. **41**(3), 519–536 (2012)
10. Ennals, R.: The lightweight transaction library. http://sourceforge.net/projects/libltx/files/
11. Ennals, R.: Software transactional memory should not be obstruction-free (2005)
12. Fraser, K.: Practical lock-freedom. Technical report, Cambridge University Computer Laborotory (2003)
13. Guerraoui, R., Kapalka, M.: On obstruction-free transactions. In: Proceedings of the Twentieth Annual Symposium on Parallelism in Algorithms and Architectures, SPAA 2008, pp. 304–313. ACM, New York (2008)
14. Guerraoui, R., Kapalka, M.: The semantics of progress in lock-based transactional memory. In: POPL, pp. 404–415 (2009)
15. Guerraoui, R., Kapalka, M.: Principles of transactional memory. In: Synthesis Lectures on Distributed Computing Theory. Morgan and Claypool (2010)
16. Herlihy, M.: Wait-free synchronization. ACM Trans. Prog. Lang. Syst. **13**(1), 123–149 (1991)
17. Herlihy, M., Luchangco, V., Moir, M.: Obstruction-free synchronization: double-ended queues as an example. In: ICDCS, pp. 522–529 (2003)
18. Herlihy, M., Luchangco, V., Moir, M., Scherer III, W.N.: Software transactional memory for dynamic-sized data structures. In: PODC, pp. 92–101 (2003)
19. Herlihy, M., Shavit, N.: On the nature of progress. In: Fernàndez Anta, A., Lipari, G., Roy, M. (eds.) OPODIS 2011. LNCS, vol. 7109, pp. 313–328. Springer, Heidelberg (2011)
20. Kuznetsov, P., Ravi, S.: On the cost of concurrency in transactional memory. In: Fernàndez Anta, A., Lipari, G., Roy, M. (eds.) OPODIS 2011. LNCS, vol. 7109, pp. 112–127. Springer, Heidelberg (2011)
21. Kuznetsov, P., Ravi, S.: Progressive transactional memory in time and space. In: Malyshkin, V. (ed.) PaCT 2015. LNCS, vol. 9251, pp. 410–425. Springer, Heidelberg (2015)
22. Kuznetsov, P., Ravi, S.: Why transactional memory should not be obstruction-free (2015). http://arxiv.org/abs/1502.02725

23. Marathe, V.J., Scherer III, W.N., Scott, M.L.: Adaptive software transactional memory. In: Fraigniaud, P. (ed.) DISC 2005. LNCS, vol. 3724, pp. 354–368. Springer, Heidelberg (2005)
24. McKenney, P.E.: Memory barriers: a hardware view for software hackers. Linux Technology Center, IBM Beaverton, June 2010
25. Perelman, D., Fan, R., Keidar, I.: On maintaining multiple versions in STM. In: PODC, pp. 16–25 (2010)
26. Tabba, F., Moir, M., Goodman, J.R., Hay, A.W., Wang, C.: Nztm: Nonblocking zero-indirection transactional memory. In: SPAA 2009, pp. 204–213. ACM, New York (2009)

# Fast Consensus for Voting
# on General Expander Graphs

Colin Cooper[1], Robert Elsässer[2], Tomasz Radzik[1(✉)], Nicolás Rivera[1],
and Takeharu Shiraga[3]

[1] Department of Informatics, King's College London, London, UK
{colin.cooper,tomasz.radzik,nicolas.rivera}@kcl.ac.uk
[2] Department of Computer Sciences, University of Salzburg, Salzburg, Austria
elsa@cosy.sbg.ac.at
[3] Theoretical Computer Science Group, Department of Informatics, Kyushu
University, Fukuoka, Japan
shiraga@tcslab.csce.kyushu-u.ac.jp

**Abstract.** Distributed voting is a fundamental topic in distributed computing. In the standard model of pull voting, at each step every vertex chooses a neighbour uniformly at random and adopts its opinion. The voting is completed when all vertices hold the same opinion. In the simplest case, each vertex initially holds one of two different opinions. This partitions the vertices into arbitrary sets $A$ and $B$. For many graphs, including regular graphs and irrespective of their expansion properties, if both $A$ and $B$ are sufficiently large sets, then pull voting requires $\Omega(n)$ expected steps, where $n$ is the number of vertices of the graph.

In this paper we consider a related class of voting processes based on sampling two opinions. In the simplest case, every vertex $v$ chooses two random neighbours at each step. If both these neighbours have the same opinion, then $v$ adopts this opinion. Otherwise, $v$ keeps its own opinion. Let $G$ be a connected graph with $n$ vertices and $m$ edges. Let $P$ be the transition matrix of a simple random walk on $G$ with second largest eigenvalue $\lambda < 1/\sqrt{2}$. We show that if the initial imbalance in degree between the two opinions satisfies $|d(A) - d(B)|/2m \geq 2\lambda^2$, then with high probability voting completes in $O(\log n)$ steps, and the opinion with the larger initial degree wins.

The condition that $\lambda < 1/\sqrt{2}$ includes many classes of expanders, for example random $d$-regular graphs where $d \geq 10$. If however $1/\sqrt{2} \leq \lambda(P) \leq 1 - \epsilon$ for a constant $\epsilon > 0$, or only a bound on the conductance of the graph is known, the sampling process can be modified so that voting still provably completes in $O(\log n)$ steps with high probability. The modification uses two sampling based on probing to a fixed depth $O(1/\epsilon)$ from any vertex.

In its most general form our voting process allows vertices to bias their sampling of opinions among their neighbours to achieve a desired outcome. This is done by allocating weights to edges.

This work was supported in part by EPSRC grant EP/M005038/1, "Randomized algorithms for computer networks". N. Rivera was supported by funding from Becas CHILE.

Y. Moses (Ed.): DISC 2015, LNCS 9363, pp. 248–262, 2015.
DOI: 10.1007/978-3-662-48653-5_17

# 1   Introduction

## 1.1   Background on Distributed Pull Voting

Distributed voting has applications in various fields including consensus and leader election in large networks [3,14], serialisation of read-write in replicated databases [13] and the analysis of social behaviour in game theory [11]. Voting algorithms are usually simple, fault-tolerant, and easy to implement [14,16].

One simple form of distributed voting is *pull voting*. In the beginning each vertex of a connected undirected graph has an initial opinion. The voting process proceeds synchronously in discrete time steps called rounds. During each round, each vertex independently contacts a random neighbour and adopts the opinion of that neighbour.

In the *two-opinion voter model*, all vertices initially hold one of two opinions. Hassin and Peleg [14] and Nakata *et al.* [20] considered the two-opinion voter model and its application to consensus problems in distributed systems. Let $G = (V, E)$ be an undirected connected graph with $n$ vertices and $m$ edges. Let the opinions be labeled 0 and 1, and let $A$ be the set of vertices with opinion 0 and $B$ the set of vertices with opinion 1; where $A \cup B = V$. Let $d(v)$ be the degree of a vertex $v$ and $d(S) = \sum_{v \in S} d(v)$ the degree of a set $S$. Thus $d(A)$ is the initial degree of opinion 0 and $d(A) + d(B) = 2m$. We say that $A$ wins (equiv. opinion 0 wins), if all vertices eventually adopt the opinion held initially by the set $A$. Let $P_A$ be the probability that opinion $A$ wins the vote in the two-opinion model. The central result of [14] and [20] is that

$$P_A = \frac{d(A)}{2m}. \tag{1}$$

Thus in the case of connected regular graphs, the probability that $A$ wins is proportional to the original size of $A$, irrespective of the graph structure.

Apart from the probability of winning the vote, another quantity of interest is the time taken for voting to complete. The completion time $T$ of a voting process is the number of rounds needed for a single opinion to emerge. This is normally measured in terms of its expectation $\mathbf{E}T$. It is proven in [14] that $\mathbf{E}T = O(n^3 \log n)$ for general graphs.

It was shown in [8] that the completion time on any connected graph $G$ is upper bounded with high probability (w.h.p.) by $O(n/(\nu(1 - \lambda))$, where $\lambda$ is the second largest eigenvalue of the transition matrix of random walk on $G$ and $\nu = n \sum_{v \in V} d^2(v)/(2m)^2$ indicates the regularity of $G$ ($1 \leq \nu \leq n^2/(2m)$, with $\nu = 1$ for regular graphs). Tighter bounds can be derived for some specific classes of graphs. For example, it is proven in [7] that in the case of random $d$-regular graphs, w.h.p. $\mathbf{E}T \sim 2n(d - 1)/(d - 2)$. This means that two-opinion voting (almost always) needs $\Theta(n)$ time to complete on random $d$-regular graphs.

Thus the performance of the two-opinion pull-voting seems unsatisfactory in two ways. Firstly, it is reasonable to require that a clear majority opinion should win with high probability. From (1), even if initially only a single vertex $v$ holds opinion $A$, then this opinion wins with probability $P_A = d(v)/2m$. Secondly, the expected completion time is $\Omega(n)$ on many classes of graphs, including regular expanders and complete graphs. This seems a long time to wait to resolve a dispute between two opinions in the context of distributed systems. A more reasonable waiting time would depend on the graph diameter, which is $O(\log n)$ for many classes of expanders.

To address these issues, we consider a modified version of pull voting in which each vertex $v$ randomly queries two neighbours at each step. On the basis of the sample taken, vertex $v$ revises its opinion as follows. If both neighbours have the same opinion, the calling vertex $v$ adopts this opinion. If the two opinions differ, the calling vertex $v$ retains its current opinion in this round. To distinguish this process from the conventional pull voting, we refer to it as *two-sample voting*. The aim of two-sample voting is to ensure that voting finishes quickly and the initial majority wins. Two-sample voting is intrinsically attractive, as it seems to mirror the way people behave. If you hear it twice it must be true.

## 1.2    Main Results

Two-sample voting is used in [9] to speed up time to consensus for pull voting on $d$-regular expander graphs. It was shown that synchronous two-sample-voting completed in $O(\log n)$ time w.h.p. even under adversarial conditions, and also that the initial majority opinion wins, provided sufficient initial imbalance between the sizes of the two opinions. In related work, in a non-adversarial context, Abdullah and Draief [1] obtained a $O(\log_d \log_d n)$ bound for the majority multi-sample-voting on $d$-regular graphs where at least five neighbours are consulted (hence requiring $d \geq 5$). They also proved that this bound is asymptotically best possible for a wide class of voting protocols. For the case of the complete graph, Cruise and Ganesh [10] made a more general analysis of multi-sample-voting strategies.

In this paper we extend the analysis of two-sample voting from [9] to general (inhomogeneous) expander graphs, with no regularity restriction on the vertex degrees, and prove that the speed of this protocol remains $O(\log n)$ (Theorem 1). However, the property that the initial majority opinion wins is found to be restricted to regular graphs. For inhomogeneous graphs, the party with the largest initial degree wins, provided sufficient initial imbalance between the degrees of the two opinions. As a special case, we get a stronger result for two sample-voting on regular expander graphs than in [9] by significantly reducing the required initial imbalance between the sizes of the two opinions.

Our analysis uses a different approach from previous work on two sample voting. The main technical theorem (Theorem 3) is based on the connection between the voting and the related random walk process. Using this theorem, we can obtain results for a wide range of protocols in which vertices sample neighbours at random according to predetermined edge weights. We refer to this generalization of two-sample-voting as *best-of-two voting*, and reserve two-sample-voting for the special case where neighbours are chosen uniformly at random (equiv. the edges weights are uniform). We show that the speed of best-of-two voting is $O(\log n)$ for general weighted expanders (Theorem 2).

Additionally, we consider an extension of the best-of-two voting, which we refer to as *k-extended best-of-two voting*. In this process in each round every vertex $v$ performs two independent $k$ step random walks. If the vertices visited by the walks at the $k$-th step have the same opinion, vertex $v$ adopts this opinion; otherwise $v$ keeps its current opinion in this round. The case $k = 1$ is best-of-two voting, and $k \geq 2$ extends the model by allowing vertices to obtain opinions beyond their immediate neighbourhood. Once again the protocol takes $O(\log n)$ rounds for general expanders (Corollary 1). It will emerge that $k$-extended best-of-two voting can be seen as best-of-two voting in a different weighted graph. A major advantage is that by increasing the value of $k$, Corollary 1 can be applied to graphs with poor expansion, which are not covered by Theorems 1 and 2.

**Voting in Weighted Graphs.** For an undirected connected weighted graph $G = (V, E)$, let $w(u, v)$ denote the positive weight assigned to an edge $(u, v) \in E$. We use $N(v)$ for the set of neighbours of $v$ and define $w(v) = \sum_{x \in N(v)} w(v, x)$ the weight of $v$, $w(S) = \sum_{u \in S} w(u)$ the weight of a set $S \subseteq V$, and $w(G) = \sum_{v \in V} w(v)$ the (total) weight of the graph. Best-of-two voting is a synchronous process in which during each step, every vertex $v \in V$ independently queries two neighbours $u'$ and $u''$, not necessary distinct, which are chosen randomly using the selection probabilities proportional to the edge weights. If $u'$ and $u''$ have at the beginning of the step the same opinion $X$, then at the end of this step $v$ also has opinion $X$. If $u'$ and $u''$ have different opinions, then at the end of the step $v$ has the same opinion as it had at the beginning of this step. Using the selection probabilities proportional to the edge weights means that $v$ selects an ordered pair of its neighbours $\langle u', u'' \rangle$ (not necessarily distinct) with probability $P(v, u')P(v, u'')$, where $P(v, u) = w(v, u)/w(v)$. The probability that a vertex $v$ in $A$ moves to $B$ at a given step is equal to

$$\mathbf{Pr}(v \text{ chooses twice in } B) = \left( \sum_{u \in B \cap N(v)} \frac{w(v, u)}{w(v)} \right)^2 = \left( \sum_{u \in B \cap N(v)} P(v, u) \right)^2.$$

Two-sample voting can be viewed as the special case of best-of-two voting when the edge weights are uniform: $w(e) = 1$ for each $e \in E$, $w(v) = d(v)$, $w(S) = d(S)$, $w(G) = 2m$ and $P(v, u) = 1/d(v)$.

Observe that $P$ is the transition matrix of a reversible random walk on $G$. We assume that $G$ is not bipartite so that this random walk is aperiodic and has a well defined stationary distribution $\pi$: $\pi(u) = w(u)/w(G)$. (For a bipartite graph $G = (V_1 \cup V_2, E)$, the voting would never converge, if one opinion resided on $V_1$ and the other on $V_2$.) Conversely, if $P$ is the transition matrix of a reversible random walk on $G$ with the stationary distribution $\pi$ (that is, $P(u, v) > 0$ iff $(u, v) \in E$, $\sum_{u \in N(v)} P(v, u) = 1$ for each $v \in V$, and $\pi(u)P(u, v) = \pi(v)P(v, u)$ for each $(u, v) \in E$), then we can associate positive edge weights $\boldsymbol{w} = (w(e), e \in E)$ with $P$ so that the transition probabilities of $P$ are proportional to these weights (set $w(u, v) = \pi(u)P(u, v)$ to have $P(u, v) = w(v, u)/w(v)$). For a set $S \subseteq V$, we have $\pi(S) = \sum_{u \in S} \pi(u) = w(S)/w(G)$, so $\pi$ and $w$ are the same measures of the subsets of vertices up to the scaling factor $w(G)$. For the transition matrix $P$ of simple (uniform) random walk, which corresponds to two-sample voting, $\pi(v) = d(v)/(2m)$ for each $v \in V$, and $\pi(S) = d(S)/(2m)$ for a subset $S \subseteq V$.

Thus best-of-two voting can be defined equivalently either by specifying edge weights or a transition matrix $P$ of a reversible aperiodic random walk. The transition matrix of simple (uniform) random walk gives two-sample voting. We stress that we do not establish a relation between the best-of-two voting process based on matrix $P$ of selection probabilities and the random walk process based on matrix $P$ of transition probabilities other than that both processes use the same matrix $P$ (but for somewhat different purposes). Some properties of such matrices, which have been developed largely in the context of analysing random walks, turn out to be useful for studying the best-of-two voting.

Let the eigenvalues of matrix $P$ be ordered in decreasing value $1 = \lambda_1(P) > \lambda_2(P) \geq \cdots \geq \lambda_n(P) > -1$, and let $\lambda = \lambda(P) = \max(|\lambda_2(P)|, |\lambda_n(P)|)$. An expander graph $G$ (or simply, an expander) is commonly defined as a graph with $\lambda(P)$ bounded away from 1, where $P$ is the transition matrix of the simple random walk $G$. Generalising this, a weighted expander is a weighted graph with $\lambda(P)$ bounded away from 1, where $P$ is the transition matrix of the random walk $G$ with transition probabilities proportional to the edge weights (see, e.g. [2]).

In the formal statements of our results, "with high probability" (w.h.p.) means with probability at least $1 - 1/n^\alpha$ for some constant $\alpha$. Before discussing our results in their most general form, we give the findings for two-sample-voting, and also some specific examples.

**Theorem 1. (Two-sample Voting)** *Let $G$ be a connected non-bipartite graph with $n$ vertices and $m$ edges, let $P$ be the transition matrix of a simple random walk on $G$, and let $\nu = n \left( \sum_{vV} d^2(v) \right) / (2m)^2$. Let $A$ and $B$ denote the sets of vertices of $G$ with initial opinions of the two types, and let $\epsilon_0 = |d(A) - d(B)|/2m$ denote the initial degree imbalance between these sets.*

*Provided $\lambda = \lambda(P) \leq 1/\sqrt{2} - \delta$ for arbitrarily small constant $\delta > 0$, $\epsilon_0 \geq 2\lambda^2$ and $n\epsilon_0^2/\nu \geq K \log n$ for sufficiently large constant $K$, then*

(a) *w.h.p. two-sample voting is completed in $O(\log n)$ rounds and the winner is the opinion with the larger initial degree;*

(b) *if $\lambda = o(1)$ and $n\lambda^\xi/\nu \geq K \log n$, for arbitrarily small constant $\xi > 0$ and sufficiently large constant $K$, then w.h.p. two-sample voting is completed in $O(\log 1/\epsilon_0) + O(\log \log(1/\lambda)) + O(\log_{1/\lambda} n)$ rounds and the winner is the opinion with the larger initial degree.*

Examples of graphs with $\lambda < 1/\sqrt{2}$ include random $d$-regular graphs with $d \geq 10$. The analysis of two-sample-voting on such graphs given in [9] required the initial imbalance between the opinions $\epsilon_0 \geq K\lambda$, for a large constant $K$, while the above theorem requires a weaker bound $\epsilon_0 \geq \max\{2\lambda^2, (K \log n)/n\}$ (as $\nu = 1$ for regular graphs). Examples of graphs with $\lambda(P) = o(1)$ include random $d$-regular graphs $d \to \infty$, pseudo-regular graphs of high degree, random graphs $G(n, p)$ when $np = \Omega(\log n)$, and Chung-Lu random graphs [4] satisfying certain conditions on minimum, average and maximum degree. The Chung-Lu graphs include many classes of inhomogeneous random graphs with wide variation in vertex degree. A more complete description of these classes of graphs, and proofs or descriptions of the results are given in Section 4.

**Theorem 2. (Best-of-two Voting)** *Let $G = (V, E)$ be a connected non-bipartite graph, let $P$ be the transition matrix of a reversible random walk on $G$ with stationary distribution $\pi$, let $\boldsymbol{w} = (w(e), e \in E)$ be positive edge weights associated with $P$, and let $\nu = \nu(\boldsymbol{w}) = n \left( \sum_{v \in V} w^2(v) \right) / w^2(G)$. Let $A$ and $B$ denote the sets of vertices of $G$ with initial opinions of the two types, and let $\epsilon_0 = |w(A) - w(B)| / w(G)$ denote the initial weight imbalance between these sets.*

*Provided $\lambda = \lambda(P) \leq 1/\sqrt{2} - \delta$ for an arbitrarily small constant $\delta$, $\epsilon_0 \geq 2\lambda^2$ and $n\epsilon_0^2 / \nu \geq K \log n$ for a sufficiently large constant $K$, then*

*(a) w.h.p. best-of-two voting is completed in $O(\log n)$ rounds and the winner is the opinion with the larger initial weight;*

*(b) if $\lambda = o(1)$ and $n\lambda^\xi / \nu \geq K \log n$ for arbitrarily small constant $\xi > 0$ and sufficiently large constant $K$, then w.h.p. best-of-two voting is completed in $O(\log 1/\epsilon_0) + O(\log \log(1/\lambda)) + O(\log_{1/\lambda} n)$ rounds and the winner is the opinion with the larger initial weight.*

Regarding the conditions of Theorems 1 and 2, we need the lower bound on the initial imbalance of the opinions $\epsilon_0 \geq 2\lambda^2$ to show that in each step the majority opinion is expected to increase. We need the additional bound $\epsilon_0 \geq \sqrt{(K\nu \log n)/n}$ (and the condition $n\lambda^\xi / \nu \geq K \log n$ for the part (b) of the theorems) to argue that this increase happens w.h.p.

The advantage of best-of-two voting is that by choosing neighbours in the voting process based on assigning suitable weights to the edges we can tailor the outcome to our needs. In the simplest case that all edges are weighted equally we have the ordinary two-sample voting. The set with the largest initial degree wins w.h.p. The weights $w(u, v) = d(u) + d(v)$ biass voting towards the opinions of high degree vertices. The weights $w(u, v) = \max\{1/d(u), 1/d(v)\}$ biass voting towards the opinions of low degree vertices. To completely remove the effect of vertex degree on the voting process, we can use the following Metropolis process. Let $M = \max_{v \in V} d(v)$ be the maximum degree of $G$. Let each edge of $G$ have weight one, and each vertex $v$ introduce a self-loop of weight $M - d(v)$. Then $\pi(v) = 1/n$, so $w(A)/w(B) = \pi(A)/\pi(B) = |A|/|B|$ and the majority wins.

Theorems 1 and 2 both require the upper bound $1/\sqrt{2}$ on $\lambda$ and the lower bound $2\lambda^2$ on the initial imbalance of the two opinions. We introduce the *k-extended best-of-two voting*, which can deal with cases when one or both of these conditions are not satisfied. This voting is a synchronous process in which during each round, every vertex $v$ performs $k$ steps of two independent weighted random walks starting at $v$. If the two vertices visited at step $k$ of these two random walks have the same opinion, then vertex $v$ adopts such opinion. This voting can be viewed as the best-of-two voting which uses $P^k$ as the matrix of the sampling probabilities, where $P$ is the transition matrix of the weighted random walk. Since $P^k$ is reversible and $\lambda(P^k) = (\lambda(P))^k$, Theorem 2 implies the following corollary. Note that one round of the *k-extended best-of-two voting* involves $k$ random-walk steps. This is the price to pay, if $\lambda$ is poor and/or the initial imbalance of the two opinions is small.

**Corollary 1. (Extended best-of-two voting)** *Assume the same conditions as in Theorem 2 but $\lambda = \lambda(P) \geq 1/\sqrt{2}$ or $\epsilon_0 < 2\lambda^2$. Let an integer $k \geq 1$ be such that $\lambda^k < 1/\sqrt{2} - \delta$ for an arbitrarily small constant $\delta$ and $\epsilon_0 \geq 2\lambda^2$. Then*

(a) *w.h.p. $k$-extended best-of-two voting is completed in $O(\log n)$ rounds and the winner is the opinion with the larger edge weight;*

(b) *if $\lambda^k = o(1)$ and $n\lambda^{\xi k}/\nu \geq K \log n$, for arbitrarily small constant $\xi > 0$ and sufficiently large constant $K$, then with high probability $k$-extended best-of-two voting is completed in $O(\log 1/\epsilon_0) + O(\log \log(1/\lambda)) + O(\log_{1/\lambda} n)$ rounds and the winner is the opinion with the larger weight.*

An example where Corollary 1 can be applied is preferential attachment graphs generated by a scale-free process model in which each new vertex attaches $d$ edges to the existing graph. The endpoints of the edges are chosen proportional to their current degree. For large $d$, $k = 7$ steps of random walks are enough for the corollary to hold. The details are given in Section 4.

## 2    Expected Change in Weight after One Step of Voting

In this section we derive a lower bound on the expected increase in the weight of the larger of the two sets $A$ and $B$ after one step of the voting process. The bound is very general and requires only the following two assumptions. $(i)$ Each vertex $v$ makes two choices at each step, and the choices are made independently among the vertices $u$ of the graph with a fixed probability $P(v, u)$. $(ii)$ The matrix $P$ of probabilities $P(v, u)$ is the transition matrix of an irreducible aperiodic reversible random walk, and thus has a unique stationary distribution $\pi = (\pi(v), v \in V)$. We assume that there are always weights associated with the edges of the underlying graph, as explained in the previous section.

As an example of our approach, consider the transition matrix of a simple random walk. To make a transition from vertex $v$, the walk chooses a random neighbour $u \in N(v)$ with probability $P(v, u) = 1/d(v)$. Using this transition matrix $P$ in the voting process corresponds to $v$ choosing two neighbours uniformly at random with replacement. If $v \in A$ and the chosen neighbours are in $B$, then $v$ changes its opinion to $B$. The degree $d(B)$ of $B$ and the stationary probability (in the context of random walks) of $B$ thus increase by $d(v)$ and $\pi(v) = d(v)/2m$, respectively.

Scaling the edge weights does not change the matrix $P$ (hence does not change the random walk or the voting processes), so in our analysis we can use either the weights of sets $w(S)$ or the "normalised weights" $\pi(S)$, whichever is more convenient. Bearing this in mind, let for $x \in A$,

$$X_x^B = \begin{cases} \pi(x), & \text{if } x \text{ chooses twice in } B, \\ 0, & \text{otherwise.} \end{cases} \tag{2}$$

Thus $X_x^B$ is the contribution of the vertex $x \in A$ to the increase of the (normalised) weight of $B$ at the end of the step. Similarly, for $x \in B$ define $X_x^A = \pi(x)$, if $x$ chooses twice in $A$, and zero otherwise. Adopting the notation $P(x, B) = \sum_{y \in B} P(x, y)$, we have for $x \in A$,

$$\mathbf{E}(X_x^B) = \pi(x)\mathbf{Pr}(X_x^B = \pi(x)) = \pi(x)\left(\sum_{y \in B} P(x, y)\right)^2 = \pi(x)(P(x, B))^2.$$

Let $X_A^B = \sum_{x \in A} X_x^B$, and let $R(A, B) = \mathbf{E}(X_A^B)$ be the expected increase of the weight of $B$ in the current step (which is equal to the expected decrease of the weight of $A$) due to vertices moving from $A$ to $B$. Then

$$R(A, B) = \mathbf{E}(X_A^B) = \sum_{x \in A} \mathbf{E}(X_x^B) = \sum_{x \in A} \pi(x)(P(x, B))^2. \qquad (3)$$

Similarly, $R(B, A) = \sum_{x \in B} \pi(x)(P(x, A))^2$ is the expected increase of the weight of $A$ due to vertices moving from $B$ to $A$. If $P$ is the transition matrix of simple random walk on $G$, then (3) can be written as

$$R(A, B) = \sum_{x \in A} \frac{d(x)}{2m}\left(\sum_{y \in B \cap N(x)} \frac{1}{d(x)}\right)^2 = \frac{1}{2m} \sum_{x \in A} \frac{(d^B(x))^2}{d(x)},$$

where $d^S(x) = |N(x) \cap S|$.

The next theorem and its corollary are the fundamental observations of this paper. They give lower bounds on $R(B, A) - R(A, B)$, which is the expected increase of the weight of set $A$ in the current step. We use the notation $Q(A, B)$, which can be viewed as the normalised weight of the cut between $A$ and $B$:

$$Q(A, B) = \sum_{x \in A} \sum_{y \in B} \pi(x)P(x, y) = \sum_{x \in A} \pi(x)P(x, B). \qquad (4)$$

Note that for a reversible matrix $P$, $\pi(x)P(x, y) = \pi(y)P(y, x)$ implies $Q(A, B) = Q(B, A)$, and from the point of view of edge weights,

$$Q(A, B) = \sum_{x \in A} \sum_{y \in B \cap N(x)} w(x, y)/w(G) = \frac{w(A, B)}{w(G)}.$$

The proof of Theorem 3 refers to the inner product $\langle f, g \rangle_\pi$ of two vectors $f, g$ of length $n$, defined by

$$\langle f, g \rangle_\pi = \sum_{x \in V} \pi(x)f(x)g(x).$$

Let $f_1, f_2, \ldots, f_n$ be (right) eigenvectors of $P$ associated with the eigenvalues $1 = \lambda_1 > \lambda_2 \geq \cdots \geq \lambda_n > -1$. As we suppose $P$ is reversible, we can assume that the eigenvectors $\{f_j\}_{j=1}^n$ are orthonormal with respect to the inner product $\langle \cdot, \cdot \rangle_\pi$ (see [17], Lemma 12.2); in particular, $f_1 = 1$. Thus $\langle f_i, f_j \rangle_\pi = 0$, if $i \neq j$, $\langle f_i, f_i \rangle_\pi = 1$ and for any $h \in \mathbb{R}^n$,

$$h = \sum_{j=1}^n \langle h, f_j \rangle_\pi f_j, \quad \text{and} \quad P^t h = \sum_{j=1}^n \lambda_j^t \langle h, f_j \rangle_\pi f_j. \tag{5}$$

**Theorem 3.** *Let $P$ be a reversible transition matrix on $G$ with stationary distribution $\pi$, $A \subseteq V$, $B = V \setminus A$ and let $\phi = Q(A, B)/\pi(B)$. Then*

$$R(B, A) - R(A, B) \geq \pi(B) \left( (1 - \lambda^2)\pi(A) - 2\phi(1 - \phi) \right). \tag{6}$$

Since $0 < \phi < 1$, Theorem 3 gives immediately the following corollary.

**Corollary 2.** *Let $P$ be a reversible transition matrix on $G$ with stationary distribution $\pi$, $A \subseteq V$ and $B = V \setminus A$. Then*

$$R(B, A) - R(A, B) \geq \pi(B) \left( (1 - \lambda^2)\pi(A) - 1/2 \right). \tag{7}$$

*Proof of Theorem 3.* Let

$$g(x) = \begin{cases} \pi(A), & \text{if } x \in B, \\ -\pi(B), & \text{if } x \in A; \end{cases} \tag{8}$$

The $x$-coordinate of the vector $Pg$ is equal to

$$(Pg)(x) = P(x,.) \cdot g = \sum_{y \in V} P(x,y)g(y) = \sum_{y \in A} P(x,y)g(y) + \sum_{y \in B} P(x,y)g(y)$$

$$= \sum_{y \in A} P(x,y)(-\pi(B)) + \sum_{y \in B} P(x,y)\pi(A)$$

$$= -\pi(B)P(x,A) + \pi(A)P(x,B)$$

$$= \pi(A) - P(x,A) = P(x,B) - \pi(B). \tag{9}$$

Using (9) in (10) and (3) and (4) in (11), we have

$$\langle Pg, Pg \rangle_\pi = \sum_{x \in V} \pi(x)((Pg)(x))^2 = \sum_{x \in A} \pi(x)((Pg)(x))^2 + \sum_{x \in B} \pi(x)((Pg)(x))^2$$

$$= \sum_{x \in A} \pi(x)\Big(P(x,B) - \pi(B)\Big)^2 + \sum_{x \in B} \pi(x)\Big(\pi(A) - P(x,A)\Big)^2 \tag{10}$$

$$= \sum_{x \in A} \pi(x)P(x,B)^2 + \sum_{x \in A} \pi(x)\pi(B)^2 + \sum_{x \in A} \pi(x)\Big(-2P(x,B)\pi(B)\Big)$$

$$+ \sum_{x \in B} \pi(x)P(x,A)^2 + \sum_{x \in B} \pi(x)\pi(A)^2 + \sum_{x \in B} \pi(x)\Big(-2P(x,A)\pi(A)\Big)$$

$$= R(A,B) + R(B,A) + \pi(A)\pi(B)\Big(\pi(B) + \pi(A)\Big)$$

$$\quad - 2Q(B,A)\Big(\pi(B) + \pi(A)\Big) \tag{11}$$

$$= R(A,B) + R(B,A) + \pi(A)\pi(B) - 2Q(B,A). \tag{12}$$

Equation (12) is equivalent to:

$$R(B, A) - R(A, B) = \pi(A)\pi(B) - \langle Pg, Pg\rangle_\pi - 2\Big(Q(B, A) - R(B, A)\Big). \quad (13)$$

We find that

$$Q(B, A) - R(B, A) =$$

$$= \sum_{x \in B} \pi(x) P(x, A) - \sum_{x \in B} \pi(x) \left(P(x, A)\right)^2$$

$$= \pi(B) \sum_{x \in B} \frac{\pi(x)}{\pi(B)} P(x, A)(1 - P(x, A))$$

$$\leq \pi(B) \left(\sum_{x \in B} \frac{\pi(x)}{\pi(B)} P(x, A)\right) \left(1 - \sum_{x \in B} \frac{\pi(x)}{\pi(B)} P(x, A)\right) \quad (14)$$

$$= \pi(B) \frac{Q(B, A)}{\pi(B)} \left(1 - \frac{Q(B, A)}{\pi(B}\right) = \pi(B)\phi(1 - \phi), \quad (15)$$

where (14) follows from the fact that the function $z(z-1)$ is concave. The claimed bound (6) follows from (13), (15) and the following result:

$$\langle Pg, Pg\rangle_\pi \leq \lambda^2 \pi(A)\pi(B). \quad (16)$$

To verify (16), check first that $\langle Pg, Pg\rangle_\pi = \langle P^2 g, g\rangle_\pi$, using reversibility of $P$, and $\langle g, g\rangle_\pi = \pi(A)\pi(B)$, using the definition of $g$. Then using (5) and $\langle g, f_1\rangle_\pi = 0$ (since $f_1 = 1$), derive $\langle g, g\rangle_\pi = \sum_{j=2}^n \langle g, f_j\rangle_\pi^2$ and finally

$$\langle P^2 g, g\rangle_\pi = \sum_{j=2}^n \lambda_j^2 \langle g, f_j\rangle_\pi^2 \leq \lambda^2 \sum_{j=2}^n \langle g, f_j\rangle_\pi^2 = \lambda^2 \langle g, g\rangle_\pi = \lambda^2 \pi(A)\pi(B).$$

$$\square$$

The following known result generalizes the Expander Mixing Lemma for undirected graphs to weighted graphs. While bound (7) given in Corollary 2 will be sufficient in the proofs of part (a) of Theorems 1 and 2, the tighter bound (6) given in Theorem 3 together with Lemma 1 will be needed to prove part (b).

**Lemma 1.** *Let $P$ be the transition matrix of the weighted random walk on a connected undirected graph $G = (V, E)$ with edge weights $\boldsymbol{w} = (w(e), e \in E)$, and let $\lambda = \max(|\lambda_2(P)|, |\lambda_n(P)|)$. Then*

$$|w(A, B) - w(A)w(B)/w(G)| \leq \lambda \, w(A)w(B)/w(G). \quad (17)$$

## 3   Proof of Theorem 1

In this section we give the proof of Theorem 1. The proof of Theorem 2 is very similar. Assume $\lambda^2 \leq 1/2 - \delta$ for small constant $\delta > 0$, $2\lambda^2 \leq \epsilon_0 < 1$

and $\epsilon_0^2 \geq (K\nu \log n)/n$, for some large constant $K$. We first prove the part (a) of Theorem 1. We assume that $B$ is the minority set with the initial degree $d(B) = m(1 - \epsilon_0)$. The proof is in two phases. Phase I reduces $d(B)$ to $cm$ in $T_{\mathrm{I}} = O(\log 1/\epsilon_0)$ steps, w.h.p., where $c > 0$ is an arbitrarily small constant. Then Phase II reduces $d(B)$ to zero in $T_{\mathrm{II}} = O(\log n)$ steps, w.h.p.

**Proof of Theorem 1(a), Phase I.**    Let $\Delta_{AB}$ be the increase in degree of the vertices of $A$ at a given step of the voting. Then by Corollary 2,

$$\mathbf{E}\Delta_{AB} = 2m(R(B, A) - R(A, B)) \geq d(B) \left((1 - \lambda^2)d(A)/(2m) - 1/2\right). \quad (18)$$

Let $\epsilon = (d(A) - d(B))/2m$. Thus $d(A) = m(1+\epsilon)$ and $d(B) = m(1-\epsilon) > cm$. We assume $\epsilon \geq \epsilon_0$ (by induction, the imbalance $\epsilon$ increases in each step in Phase I w.h.p.). Thus $\epsilon \geq 2\lambda^2$, which together with $\delta \leq 1/2 - \lambda^2$ gives

$$\mathbf{E}\Delta_{AB} \geq \frac{d(B)}{2} \left((1 - \lambda^2)(1 + \epsilon) - 1\right) = \frac{d(B)}{2}(\epsilon - \lambda^2(1 + \epsilon)) \geq d(B)\frac{\epsilon\delta}{2}. \quad (19)$$

The following version of the Hoeffding Lemma can be found in e.g. [18]. Let $X_k$, $k = 1, ..., N$ be independent random variables, where for each $k$, $a_k \leq X_k \leq b_k$. Let $X = \sum_{k=1}^{N} X_k$ and let $\mu = \mathbf{E}X$. Then for any $t > 0$

$$\mathbf{Pr}(|X - \mu| \geq Nt) \leq 2\exp\left(-2N^2t^2/\sum_{k=1}^{N}(b_k - a_k)^2\right). \quad (20)$$

Let $C$ be the vertices which have a neighbour in the other vote set, that is, the wertices which have positive probability of changing their vote. Let $A_C = C \cap A$ and $B_C = C \cap B$. We use (20) with $N = |C|$ and take $X_v$, for $v \in C$, as the signed degree of $v$ based on (2). For $v \in A_C$, $X_v = -X_v^B \cdot 2m$, which is either $-d^B(v)$ or 0, and for $v \in B_C$, $X_v = X_v^A \cdot 2m$, which is either $d^A(v)$ or 0. Thus $\sum_{v \in C} X_v = \Delta_{AB}$ and the sum $\sum_{v \in C}(b_v - a_v)^2$ in (20) is

$$\sum_{v \in C}(b_v - a_v)^2 = \sum_{v \in A_C}(d^B(v))^2 + \sum_{v \in B_C}(d^A(v))^2 \leq \sum_{v \in V} d^2(v) = (2m)^2\nu/n.$$

From (19), (20), $d(B) \geq cm$ and $n\epsilon^2/\nu \geq K\log n$, we find

$$\mathbf{Pr}(\Delta_{AB} \leq \mathbf{E}\Delta_{AB}/2) \leq \mathbf{Pr}(|\Delta_{AB} - \mathbf{E}\Delta_{AB}| \geq \mathbf{E}\Delta_{AB}/2)$$

$$\leq 2\exp\left(\frac{-2(\mathbf{E}\Delta_{AB}/2)^2}{(2m)^2\nu/n}\right) \leq 2\exp\left(-\frac{n(d(B)\epsilon\delta)^2}{32m^2\nu}\right)$$

$$\leq 2\exp\left(-\frac{n\epsilon^2}{\nu}\frac{(c\delta)^2}{32}\right) \leq \frac{1}{n^\alpha}, \quad (21)$$

for constant $\alpha = K(c\delta)^2/32$.

Let $B$ and $B'$ be the set of vertices with the $B$ vote at the beginning of the current and next step, respectively. If $\Delta_{AB} \geq \mathbf{E}\Delta_{AB}/2$, then it follows from (19) that the size of $d(B')$ is

$$d(B') = d(B) - \Delta_{AB} \leq d(B) - \mathbf{E}\Delta_{AB}/2 \leq d(B)(1 - \epsilon\delta/4). \quad (22)$$

Suppose firstly that $\epsilon \leq 1/2$, then in one step $d(B)$ decreases w.h.p. from $m(1-\epsilon)$ to at most $m(1 - \epsilon(1 + \delta/8))$. Starting from $d(B_0) = m(1 - \epsilon_0)$, after $j$ steps we have that $d(B_j) \leq m(1 - (1 + \delta/4)^j \epsilon_0)$. On the other hand, if $\epsilon > 1/2$, that is, $d(B) \leq m/2$, then (22) implies that $d(B)$ reduces to size $cm$ in a constant number of steps. Thus after $T_{\mathrm{I}} = O(\log 1/\epsilon_0)$ steps, w.h.p. $d(B_{T_{\mathrm{I}}}) \leq cm$.

**Proof of Theorem 1(a), Phase II.** Let $B$ and $B'$ denote the set of vertices with the $B$ vote at the beginning of the current and the next step, respectively. At the end of Phase I, $d(B) \leq cm$, so $\pi(B) \leq c/2$ for some small constant $c > 0$. Firstly, using (21), we observe that $d(B)$ remains below $cm$ w.h.p. for polylogarithmic number of steps:

$$\mathbf{Pr}(d(B') \geq cm \,|\, d(B) \leq cm) \leq \mathbf{Pr}(d(B') \geq cm \,|\, d(B) = cm) \leq \frac{1}{n^\alpha}. \tag{23}$$

Using (19) (which, as (18), applies to $A$ and $B = V \setminus A$ of any sizes) and noting that $d(B) \leq cm$ implies $\epsilon \geq 1 - c \geq 2/3$, we have for any $0 \leq q \leq cm$,

$$\mathbf{E}(d(B')|d(B) = q) \leq (1 - \delta/3)q. \tag{24}$$

Let $B_0$ be the $B$-set at the beginning of Phase II and let $B_i$ be the $B$-set after $i$ steps. We assume that $d(B_0) \leq cm$, and generally $0 \leq d(B_i) \leq 2m$, for each $i \geq 1$. We now bound $\mathbf{E}(d(B_i))$, for $i \geq 1$. Denoting $\mathcal{B}_i \equiv \{d(B_i) \leq cm\}$, for $i \geq 0$, we have

$$\mathbf{E}(d(B_i)) \leq \mathbf{E}(d(B_i)|\mathcal{B}_{i-1}) \cdot \mathbf{Pr}(\mathcal{B}_{i-1}) + (2m) \cdot \mathbf{Pr}(\neg \mathcal{B}_{i-1}). \tag{25}$$

Further,

$$\mathbf{E}(d(B_i)|\mathcal{B}_{i-1}) \cdot \mathbf{Pr}(\mathcal{B}_{i-1})$$
$$= \sum_{0 \leq q \leq cm} \mathbf{E}(d(B_i)|d(B_{i-1}) = q) \cdot \mathbf{Pr}(d(B_{i-1}) = q|\mathcal{B}_{i-1}) \cdot \mathbf{Pr}(\mathcal{B}_{i-1})$$
$$= \sum_{0 \leq q \leq cm} \mathbf{E}(d(B_i)|d(B_{i-1}) = q) \cdot \mathbf{Pr}(d(B_{i-1}) = q)$$
$$\leq \sum_{0 \leq q \leq cm} (1 - \delta/3) \cdot q \cdot \mathbf{Pr}(d(B_{i-1}) = q) \leq (1 - \delta/3)\,\mathbf{E}(d(B_{i-1})), \tag{26}$$

and, using (23),

$$\mathbf{Pr}(\neg \mathcal{B}_{i-1}) \leq \sum_{j=1}^{i-1} \mathbf{Pr}(\mathcal{B}_{j-1} \text{ and } \neg \mathcal{B}_j) \leq \sum_{j=1}^{i-1} \mathbf{Pr}(\neg \mathcal{B}_j \,|\, \mathcal{B}_{j-1}) \leq \frac{i}{n^\alpha}. \tag{27}$$

Putting (26) and (27) in (25), we get

$$\mathbf{E}(d(B_i)) \leq (1 - \delta/3)\,\mathbf{E}(d(B_{i-1})) + 2mi/n^\alpha, \quad \text{and}$$
$$\mathbf{E}(d(B_i)) \leq (1 - \delta/3)^i\, d(B_0) + (3/\delta)2mi/n^\alpha.$$

Thus for $T = T_{II} = (3/\delta)(2 + \alpha) \ln n$,

$$\mathbf{E}(d(B_T)) \leq (1 - \delta/3)^T cm + (3/\delta)2mT/n^\alpha \leq 1/n^{\alpha/2},$$

so

$$\mathbf{Pr}(d(B_T) = 0) = 1 - \mathbf{Pr}(d(B_T) \geq 1) \geq 1 - \mathbf{E}(d(B_T)) \geq 1 - n^{-\alpha/2}.$$

This means that w.h.p. Phase II completes in $T = T_{II} = O(\log n)$ steps and the winner is vote $A$.

**Proof of Theorem 1(b).** For a simple random walk, all edges have weight one, so in Lemma 1, $w(A)$ and $w(B)$ are $d(A)$ and $d(B)$, $w(G) = 2m$ and $w(A, B) = d(A, B)$, the number of edges between sets $A$ and $B$. Thus (17) gives the following inequality for any sets $A$ and $B = V \setminus A$.

$$\left| \frac{d(A, B)}{d(B)} - \frac{d(A)}{2m} \right| \leq \lambda \frac{d(A)}{2m}. \tag{28}$$

In Theorem 3, $\phi = Q(A, B)/\pi(B) = d(A, B)/d(B)$ and $\pi(A) = d(A)/(2m)$, so (28) implies that $\pi(A)(1 - \lambda) \leq \phi \leq \pi(A)(1 + \lambda)$. For this range of $\phi$, if $\pi(A) \geq 1/2$, then $\phi(1 - \phi)$ in (6) is maximised at $\phi = \pi(A)(1 - \lambda)$, so (6) implies

$$R(B, A) - R(A, B) \geq \pi(B)\pi(A)(1 - \lambda)^2(1 - 2\pi(B)).$$

Hence after one step, the set $B$ is replaced by a set $B'$ of expected degree

$$\begin{aligned}
\mathbf{E}(d(B') \mid d(B)) &= d(B) - 2m(R(B, A) - R(A, B)) \\
&\leq d(B) \left( 1 - (1 - \pi(B))(1 - \lambda)^2(1 - 2\pi(B)) \right) \\
&\leq d(B)(2\lambda + 3\pi(B)).
\end{aligned} \tag{29}$$

In the analysis of Phase II, we use now the bound (29) on $\mathbf{E}(d(B')|d(B))$ instead of the bound (24). We split Phase II into two parts. First $d(B)$ keeps decreasing from $cm$ to $\lambda^{\xi/4}m$. For this range of $d(B)$, $\pi(B) \geq \lambda$, so (29) implies that $\mathbf{E}(\pi(B')) \leq 5(\pi(B))^2$. If $\pi(B') \geq \mathbf{E}(\pi(B')) + (\pi(B))^2$, then $\Delta_{AB} \leq \mathbf{E}(\Delta_{AB}) - 2m(\pi(B))^2$, so we have, in a similarly way as in (21) and using $\pi(B) \geq \lambda^{\xi/4}/2$ and the assumption that $n\lambda^\xi/\nu \geq K \log n$,

$$\begin{aligned}
\mathbf{Pr}\left( \pi(B') \geq 6(\pi(B))^2 \right) &\leq \mathbf{Pr}\left( |\Delta_{AB} - \mathbf{E}\Delta_{AB}| \geq 2m(\pi(B))^2 \right) \\
&\leq 2\exp\left( -2(2m(\pi(B))^2)^2/((2m)^2\nu/n) \right) \\
&\leq 2\exp\left( -\frac{n\lambda^\xi}{8\nu} \right) \leq \frac{1}{n^{K/8}}.
\end{aligned}$$

Thus w.h.p. in each step of the first part of Phase II, $\pi(B') \geq 6(\pi(B))^2$, giving $O(\log \log(1/\lambda))$ steps. Then $d(B)$ decreases from $\lambda^{\xi/4}m$ to zero and for this part of Phase II, (29) implies that $d(B') \leq 5\lambda^{\xi/4}d(B)$, leading to the $O(\log_{1/\lambda} n)$ bound on the number of rounds.

# 4   Specific Examples and Notes on Eigenvalue Gaps

We give various examples of graphs which satisfy our theorems. In some cases, additional work, not discussed here, is required to relate known results to the second eigenvalue $\lambda(P)$ of the transition matrix $P$.

**Random Graphs $G(n,p)$.** From Coja-Oghlan [6], Theorem 1.2, if $2(1 + o(1)) \log n \leq np \leq 0.99n$, then w.h.p. $\max_{j \geq 2} |\lambda_j(P)| \leq (1 + o(1)) \frac{2}{\sqrt{np}}$.

**Chung-Lu Model.** This model generalizes random graphs $G(n,p)$ to the space of random graphs $G(w)$ where $w$ is a sequence of positive weights $w = (w_1, w_2, ..., w_n)$. Edges are included independently, and edge $\{i,j\}$ has probability $p_{ij} = w_i w_j / \rho$ where $\rho = \sum_i w_i$. There is a further constraint that $\max_i w_i^2 < \rho$ to ensure $p_{ij} \leq 1$. The average degree is $\overline{w} = \sum_{i=1}^n w_i / n = \rho/n$. The expected degree of vertex $i$ is $w_i$, and the minimum expected degree $w_{\min} = \min_i w_i$.

The following result is from [5], where $\omega$ is any slowly growing function.

$$\max_{j \geq 2} |\lambda_j(P)| \leq (1 + o(1)) \frac{4}{\sqrt{\overline{w}}} + \frac{\omega \log^2 n}{w_{\min}}.$$

Thus provided $w_{\min} \gg \omega \log^2 \sqrt{\overline{w}}$, the generated graphs have small $\lambda(P)$.

**Pseudo-regular Graphs.** Take a random $d$-regular graph $G$ and add extra edges, at most $c$ at any vertex, where $c \leq \epsilon d$ for some small constant $\epsilon$. This gives $\lambda(P) \leq (3\sqrt{d} + 2c)/(d + c)$.

**Metropolis Walks.** Let $G$ have degree bounded between $d$ and $M = (1 + a)d$. The transition matrix $\widetilde{P}$ of the Metropolis process has transition probabilities $\widetilde{P}_{ij} = 1/M$ if $\{i,j\}$ is an edge of $G$ and loop probability $\widetilde{P}_{ii} = 1 - d(i)/M$. If $P$ is the transition matrix of a simple random walk on $G$, then $|\lambda_k(\widetilde{P}) - \lambda_k(P)| \leq 2a/(1 + a)$.

**Preferential Attachment Model.** The model $G_{m,t}$ generates a preferential attachment graph as follows. At any step $t \geq 1$ a new vertex $v_t$ with $m$ edges is attached to the existing graph $G_{m,t-1}$. The edges from $v_t$ are attached to existing vertices chosen with probability proportional to their degree. The following result is given in [19]. For any $m \geq 2$, if positive constants $a$ and $c$ satisfy $c < 2(m - 1) - 4a - 1$, then the conductance $\Phi$ of $G_{m,n}$ satisfies

$$\mathbf{Pr}(\Phi \leq a/(m + a)) = o(n^{-c}).$$

Taking constants $a$ and $c$ such that $2c = 2(m - 1) - 4a - 1$, we have w.h.p.

$$\Phi \geq \frac{2m - 3 - 2c}{6m - 3 - 2c}.$$

Choosing $c$ small and using the relationship that $\lambda_2 \leq 1 - \Phi^2/2$, we have that $\lambda_2(m)$ satisfies $\lambda_2(2) \leq 199/200$ and for $m$ large $\lambda_2(m) < 19/20$. In both cases, two-sample voting cannot provably guarantee the outcome. If we use $k$-extended best-of-two voting algorithm with $k = 70$ for the first case and $k = 7$ for the second, then we obtain $\lambda^k < 1/\sqrt{2}$ and thus Corollary 1 applies.

# References

1. Abdullah, M., Draief, M.: Consensus on the Initial Global Majority by Local Majority Polling for a Class of Sparse Graphs (2013). http://www.arXiv.org
2. Bolla, M.: Beyond the Expanders. International Journal of Combinatorics **2011**, Article ID 787596, 11 (2011)
3. Brahma, S., Macharla, S., Pal, S.P., Singh, S.K.: Fair leader election by randomized voting. In: Ghosh, R.K., Mohanty, H. (eds.) ICDCIT 2004. LNCS, vol. 3347, pp. 22–31. Springer, Heidelberg (2004)
4. Chung, F.R.K., Lu, L.: Connected components in random graphs with given expected degree sequences. Annals of Combinatorics **6**, 125–145 (2002)
5. Chung, F.R.K., Lu, L., Vu, V.: The spectra of random graphs with given expected degrees. Internet Mathematics **1**, 257–275 (2003)
6. Coja-Oghlan, A.: On the Laplacian Eigenvalues of $G_{n,p}$. Combinatorics, Probability and Computing **16**, 923–946 (2007)
7. Cooper, C., Frieze, A., Radzik, B.: Multiple Random Walks in Random Regular Graphs. SIAM J. on Discrete Math. **23**, 1738–1761 (2009)
8. Cooper, C., Elsässer, R., Ono, H., Radzik, T.: Coalescing Random Walks and Voting on Connected Graphs. SIAM J. on Discrete Math. **27**, 1748–1758 (2013)
9. Cooper, C., Elsässer, R., Radzik, T.: The power of two choices in distributed voting. In: Esparza, J., Fraigniaud, P., Husfeldt, T., Koutsoupias, E. (eds.) ICALP 2014, Part II. LNCS, vol. 8573, pp. 435–446. Springer, Heidelberg (2014)
10. Cruise, J., Ganesh, A.: Probabilistic consensus via polling and majority rules. Queueing Systems: Theory and Applications. **78**, 99–120 (2014)
11. Deng, X., Papadimitriou, C.: On the Complexity of Cooperative Solution Concepts. Mathematics of Operations Research **19**, 257–266 (1994)
12. Friedman, J.: A proof of Alon's second eigenvalue conjecture. In: STOC 2003: Proc. 35th Annual ACM Symposium on Theory of Computing, pp. 720–724 (2003)
13. Gifford, D.: Weighted voting for replicated data. In: SOSP 1979: Proceedings of the 7th ACM Symposium on Operating Systems Principles, pp. 150–162 (1979)
14. Hassin, Y., Peleg, D.: Distributed probabilistic polling and applications to proportionate agreement. Information & Computation **171**, 248–268 (2001)
15. Horn, R.A., Johnson, C.R.: Matrix analysis. In: CUP (2006)
16. Johnson, B.: Design and Analysis of Fault Tolerant Digital Systems. Addison-Wesley (1989)
17. Levine, D.A., Peres, Y., Wilmer, E.L.: Markov Chain and Mixing Times. American Mathematical Society (2008)
18. McDiarmid, C.: On the method of bounded differences. In: Siemons, J. (ed.) Surveys in Combinatorics, pp. 148–188. CUP (1989)
19. Mihail, M., Papadimitriou, C., Sabieri, A.: On certain connectivity properties of the internet topology. In: Proceedings of Foundations of Computer Science, FOCS 2003, pp. 28–35 (2003)
20. Nakata, T., Imahayashi, H., Yamashita, M.: Probabilistic local majority voting for the agreement problem on finite graphs. In: Asano, T., Imai, H., Lee, D.T., Nakano, S., Tokuyama, T. (eds.) COCOON 1999. LNCS, vol. 1627, pp. 330–338. Springer, Heidelberg (1999)

# Randomness vs. Time in Anonymous Networks

Jochen Seidel[✉], Jara Uitto, and Roger Wattenhofer

ETH Zurich, Zurich, Switzerland
{seidelj,juitto,wattenhofer}@ethz.ch

**Abstract.** In an anonymous network, symmetry breaking tasks can only be solved if randomization is available. But how many random bits are required to solve any such task? As it turns out, the answer to this question depends on the desired runtime of the algorithm.

Since any randomized anonymous network algorithm can be decomposed into a randomized 2-hop coloring stage and a deterministic stage, we tackle the question by focusing on the randomized stage. We establish that for any reasonable target function $f$, there is a randomized 2-hop coloring scheme running in $\mathcal{O}(f(n))$ time. Our coloring scheme allows to trade an increase in runtime by a factor of $d$ for a decrease by the $d^{\text{th}}$ root in the random bit complexity.

To show that the achieved trade-off is asymptotically optimal for any choice of $f$, we establish a trade-off lower bound. Our bounds yield that it is sufficient to consider the cases when $f$ is between $\Omega(\log^* n)$ and $\mathcal{O}(\log \log n)$. We obtain that for the two extreme cases, i.e., where $f \in \Theta(\log^* n)$ and $f \in \Theta(\log \log n)$, the random bit complexity is $\Theta(\sqrt[d]{n})$ and $\Theta(\log n)$, respectively, for any constant $d$. The trade-off achieved by our scheme is asymptotically optimal for any $f$, i.e., reducing the runtime must lead to an increase in the random bit complexity.

## 1 Introduction

We consider randomized algorithms running in a network of $n$ communicating nodes. The network is *anonymous*, as opposed to identified networks in which nodes can be distinguished by their unique identifiers (IDs). The computational power of deterministic anonymous network algorithms has been found to be rather limited [31]. When nodes have access to random bits however, many interesting tasks become solvable. But what is the amount of random bits, i.e., the *random bit complexity*, required to solve any such task?

Consider, for example, the fundamental symmetry breaking problem of graph coloring, where the goal is to assign colors to nodes so that every two neighbors get a different color. In a complete network, i.e., when every node is connected to all other nodes, a unique color must be used for every node. Therefore, for complete networks the answer is at least $\log n$ random bits. One result of our

---

Due to space constraints, in this extended abstract all proofs had to be omitted. The full version of this paper is available at http://disco.ethz.ch/publications/DISC2015-coloring.pdf.

© Springer-Verlag Berlin Heidelberg 2015
Y. Moses (Ed.): DISC 2015, LNCS 9363, pp. 263–275, 2015.
DOI: 10.1007/978-3-662-48653-5_18

work is that in expectation $\Omega(\log n)$ random bits are required even if every node in the network has at most 3 neighbors. Moreover, we establish that $\mathcal{O}(\log n)$ random bits in expectation are also sufficient to solve all tasks in any network.

Alongside the random bit complexity, as a second efficiency measure, we consider the *runtime* required to solve such tasks. Increasing the runtime allows one to draw the random bits more carefully, thus reducing the number of unnecessarily drawn random bits. Conversely, it is true that drawing random bits more generously enables faster runtime. We study how exactly the random bit complexity relates to the runtime.

More precisely, we show that there is an *efficiency trade-off* between the runtime and the random bit complexity required to solve any task. Our contribution is to establish asymptotically tight lower and upper bounds on the achievable trade-off. Those bounds imply that using more than $\mathcal{O}(\log \log n)$ rounds to solve a task does not result in a better random bit complexity. Linial's local symmetry breaking lower bound, showing that one requires roughly $\log^* n$ rounds [27] to 3-color a ring, already hints that the interesting cases occur when the asymptotic runtime is between $\log^* n$ and $\log \log n$. In the respective extreme cases, i.e., when the runtime is $\log^* n$ or $\log \log n$, our lower bound states that the random bit complexity is $\Omega(\sqrt[d]{n})$ and $\Omega(\log n)$, correspondingly, where $d$ is a constant that depends on the runtime.

For the upper bound we devise a randomized scheme that produces sufficiently many random bits for any anonymous network algorithm. To this end we introduce the notion of a *target function* $f$ which specifies the desired runtime of our scheme, and consider the cases where $f(n)$ is asymptotically between $\log^* n$ and $\log \log n$. The trade-off achieved by our scheme asymptotically matches the lower bound with high probability[1] and in expectation, also for all runtimes $f$ that lie between the two extremes.

Our scheme is *uniform*: The algorithm does not require any knowledge about the network topology, such as its size or diameter. Note that this rules out the trivial approach of drawing a unique identifier with $O(\log n)$ bits, which would succeed with high probability. Being uniform, our scheme can be used to devise new uniform algorithms for classic symmetry breaking problems by utilizing existing deterministic algorithms. This is due to the fact that those algorithms often assume IDs, but function correctly even if those IDs are only *locally* unique. As one example, consider the deterministic coloring algorithm from [35] which runs in $\mathcal{O}(\log^* n)$ time on graphs with bounded growth. By applying our scheme, we obtain a uniform coloring algorithm for anonymous networks with the same runtime. Our lower bounds imply that an $\mathcal{O}(\log^* n)$ runtime is the best possible. This speed comes at the cost of a relatively high random bit complexity, which is $\Theta(\sqrt[d]{n})$. Note, however, that $d$ is a freely selectable parameter of our scheme (a constant) that is hidden in the big-$\mathcal{O}$ notation. If one is willing to sacrifice the asymptotic runtime, on the other end of the spectrum, our approach allows to solve the same task in $\mathcal{O}(\log \log n)$ time using as little as $\mathcal{O}(\log n)$ random

---

[1] We say an event occurs *with high probability* (w.h.p.) if it occurs with probability $1 - n^{-c}$ for any constant $c$.

bits. By tuning the $f$ parameter, any trade-off between the two extremes can be achieved.

So how can we possibly bound the random bit complexity for any computable task? The answer to this *complexity* question can be based on a recent *computability* result by Emek et al. [14], where they showed that a 2-hop coloring[2] is necessary and sufficient to replace access to random bits in any anonymous network algorithm. We therefore establish our upper bound by devising a 2-hop coloring algorithm whose runtime and random bit complexity are tuneable by a target function $f$ and a constant $d$.

## 1.1 Related Work

The theory of distributed computability began with Angluin's insight that leader election is impossible in anonymous rings [3]. A similar impossibility argument can be made for deterministic algorithms that solve local symmetry breaking tasks, e.g., coloring or MIS, and literally hundreds of more impossibilities are known [6]. In short, the computational power of deterministic anonymous network algorithms is limited [31].

Under the assumption of uniform algorithms, the leader election impossibility result from [3] extends to the case where randomization is available. In contrast to that, when randomization is available, there are well known algorithms that solve the local symmetry breaking problems coloring [27] and MIS [1,28] also in anonymous networks. It is interesting to note that both randomized MIS algorithms are used to construct completely derandomized (deterministic) variants under the assumption that unique identifiers are available. How much randomization an anonymous network will ever need from a *computability* perspective can be characterized in terms of a 2-hop coloring [15]. In this paper, based on that observation, we tackle the *complexity* question, i.e., the random bits and runtime necessary to obtain a 2-hop coloring. When unique IDs are available, runtime and messages (size and quantity) can be traded, e.g., in MIS and coloring algorithms [22]. Focusing on anonymous algorithms, we trade runtime with a fourth complexity measure, namely the random bit complexity. Also outside of anonymous algorithms, randomization has many applications in distributed computing (cf. [7]), e.g., in agreement [4,5], self stabilization [14], and non-uniform leader election [1].

Still, one of the most basic tasks to solve in a distributed setting remains coloring, and often coloring and MIS algorithms go hand in hand. As such, they were studied thoroughly (please refer to [10] for an extensive overview), usually aiming to use at most $\Delta + 1$ (or at least some small function of $\Delta$) many colors. Perhaps surprisingly, when identifiers are available, deterministic coloring algorithms are among the fastest. A recent series of results by Barenboim, Elkin, and Kuhn [8,25,11] yields a $\Delta + 1$ coloring in $\mathcal{O}(\Delta + \log^* n)$ runtime by utilizing a new defective coloring technique. The picture is completed by the observation

---

[2] A 2-hop coloring is a coloring of the network in which every node's color is different from the colors used by any other node within distance 2 (see Section 2).

that colors can be traded for runtime [9], i.e., one can get $\mathcal{O}(\Delta^\varepsilon + \log^* n)$ for $\mathcal{O}(\Delta)$ colors or $\mathcal{O}(\log \Delta \cdot \log^* n)$ for $\mathcal{O}(\Delta^{1+\varepsilon})$ colors. These deterministic coloring algorithms have in common that they need to assume IDs. Also randomized algorithms (e.g. [35,34]) often assume IDs and are not uniform, i.e., they assume knowledge about $n$ or some other global network parameter. Relieving the algorithm from that knowledge, we focus on achieving a good random bit complexity instead of a low number of used colors, and refer to standard methods (e.g., the deterministic approach in [19]) to reduce this number. On the other hand, the $\mathcal{O}(\log n)$ algorithms for MIS [1,28] and coloring [27] are uniform, and can be formulated even in very restricted models [36]. We improve on the runtime at the lowest possible price one needs to pay for that in terms of random bit complexity.

It is worth mentioning that in the context of self-stabilization [13], uniform MIS and (2-hop) coloring protocols were studied also for anonymous networks. For instance, [37] considers deterministic and randomized protocols that color paths and rings, and later [21] obtain randomized protocols for MIS and coloring in arbitrary networks. The recent work [12] presents a 2-hop coloring protocol for graphs of bounded degree. In the self-stabilization context, the difficulty lies in dealing with faults. The random bit complexity is of no concern in the protocols mentioned above, and the runtime of [12] is necessarily much higher than in our non-faulty environment.

Sequential probabilistic computability was pioneered by Gill [18], showing that, e.g., ZPP = RP ∩ co-RP, and Rabin [33], who reduced certain probabilistic automata to deterministic ones. Reducing the error probability using few additional random bits was studied, e.g., for the classes RP ([23], cf. [38]) and BPP (e.g., [2]), and [26] relates BPP to the polynomial hierarchy. Derandomization [29] is closely related to extracting randomness from low entropy sources [32,38]. The field of randomized computability and complexity is covered in great detail in [30]. A distributed version of BPP, so called $(p, q)$-deciders, and derandomization in this setting were studied in [16]. We characterize how many random bits are necessary to solve any anonymous network task with probability 1 depending on the desired runtime.

A concept related to that of randomization is non-determinism. Study of this concept's distributed notion, where often IDs are assumed, was initiated by Naor and Stockmeyer [31], who studied what could be *checked* by deterministic constant-time algorithms if some labeling (non-determinism) is known in advance. Subsequently, the number of non-deterministic choices required to solve decision problems in this distributed manner was investigated [24]. A hierarchy of decidable problems depending on the necessary amount of non-determinism arises [20], also when the network is anonymous. Recently, it was found that in fact the *combination* of non-determinism with randomization allows distributed algorithms to decide any language in constant time [17].

## 2    Preliminaries

We model the network as a simple, undirected graph $G = (V, E)$, where $V$ and $E$ denote the set of nodes and edges, respectively. The *network size*, i.e., the cardinality of $V$, is denoted by $n$. Furthermore, the *exclusive neighborhood* of a node $u \in V$ in $G$ is the set $\Gamma(u) = \{v : (u,v) \in E\}$. Similarly, we denote by $\Gamma^2(u) = \Gamma(u) \cup_{v \in \Gamma(u)} \{w : w \neq u, (v,w) \in E\}$ the *exclusive 2-hop neighborhood* of $u$. Note that throughout this paper, we assume that all logarithms are taken to base 2.

*Uniform Randomized Algorithms.* We consider randomized algorithms that always return a correct output and have finite expected runtime (Las Vegas algorithms). Our algorithms run under the synchronous broadcast model, i.e., the execution of an algorithm can be divided into discrete *rounds* starting from round 1. Furthermore, the execution of any round $r + 1$ for any node $u$ begins only when every other node has finished executing round $r$. Round $r$ executed by a node $u$ is divided into 4 parts in the following manner.

1. **Receive.** Node $u$ receives the messages sent by nodes in $\Gamma(u)$ in round $r-1$.
2. **Randomized Computation.** Node $u$ can perform arbitrary computations. During the computation $u$ can draw a finite amount of random bits. The source of random bits for node $u$ is independent from the source of random bits for any other node $v \in V$, and for the sake of simplicity we assume that each source is uniformly distributed.
3. **Output.** Node $u$ can decide on an output value. An output is irrevocable, i.e., once $u$ has decided on an output value, it cannot be changed.
4. **Send.** Node $u$ sends a finite length broadcast message to all nodes in $\Gamma(u)$.

An algorithm $\mathcal{A}$ is called *deterministic* if $\mathcal{A}$ does not draw any random bits. When all nodes in the network have decided on an output value we say that $\mathcal{A}$ *has terminated.* We restrict ourselves to *uniform* algorithms, i.e., the nodes are unaware of any network parameter, e.g., the network size $n$, nor do they have unique identifiers (the network is *anonymous*).

We consider two complexity measures of an algorithm $\mathcal{A}$. (1) The *runtime* of $\mathcal{A}$ in some graph $G$ is the number of rounds that are executed until all nodes terminate, and (2) the *random bit complexity* of $\mathcal{A}$ is the maximum number of random bits drawn by any node during the execution of $\mathcal{A}$.

*2-Hop Colorings.* Throughout the paper, we study algorithms that aim to color the input graph. For a graph $G$, a *k-coloring* is a function $\gamma : V \to \{1, \ldots k\}$ such that $\gamma(v) \neq \gamma(u)$ for any $(u,v) \in E$, where $k$ is the number of colors. When the number of colors is not of concern, $\gamma$ is called simply a coloring. In other words, the color of $u$ is different from the color of all $v \in \Gamma(u)$. This definition naturally extends to multiple hops and in this paper, we are especially interested in the 2-hop version of coloring, where $\gamma(u) \neq \gamma(w)$ for any $u, v, w \in V$ such that $w \neq u$, $(u,v) \in E$ and $(v,w) \in E$, i.e., the color of $u$ is different from the color of any node $w \in \Gamma^2(u)$.

*The Target Function $f(n)$.* A function $f$ is called a *target function* if $f$ is positive, strictly increasing, and continuous. Note that the properties of a target function $f$ ensure that the *inverse target function* $f^{-1}(n)$ of $f(n)$ is well-defined. For easier readability, we denote the inverse function by $g_f(n) = f^{-1}(n)$, or $g(n)$ if $f$ is clear from the context.

The purpose of a target function is to capture the runtime of some deterministic algorithm $\mathcal{A}$. The runtime $f_*(n)$ of $\mathcal{A}$ is positive, but not necessarily strictly increasing in the input size $n$, nor continuous. However, for any $\xi > 0$, there is a target function $f$ such that $f_*(n) \leq f(n) \leq f_*(n) + \xi$, i.e., $f$ "captures" $f_*$ at all integer values $n \geq 1$.

# 3   Tailor-Made 2-Hop Coloring

Our technical contribution starts by presenting a 2-hop coloring algorithm, called TAILOR-2-HOP-COLORING, with a customizable runtime. Specifically, our algorithm is parametrized by a target function $f$ and two integers $a > 2, d \geq 2$. As discussed before, we assume that $f(n)$ is between $\log^* n$ and $\log \log n$ (see Section 4). Then, the algorithm finds a 2-hop coloring in $3d \cdot f(n)$ rounds in expectation and with probability $1 - n^{2-a}$.

The main difficulty is to choose how quickly random bits should be drawn, without knowledge of $n$. From the discussion above we know that in some round $3d \cdot f(n)$, we should have drawn at least $\Omega(\log n)$ bits. If we draw the bits too quickly, however, we might draw too many bits in the last round before the algorithm finishes. To deal with that, we design our *bit drawing function* $b(i)$ for the target function $f$ and the integer parameters $a$ and $d$ as follows. Let $i$ be some positive integer, and write $i = dp + s$ with $0 \leq s \leq d - 1$, i.e., $p = \lfloor i/d \rfloor$ and $s = i \pmod d$. The bit drawing function for $i$ is defined as

$$b(i) = b(dp + s) = a \cdot \lceil \log g(p) \rceil^{(d-s)/d} \cdot \lceil \log g(p+1) \rceil^{s/d}.$$

We describe TAILOR-2-HOP-COLORING from the perspective of node $u \in V$ (please refer to Algorithm 1 for a pseudo-code description). The algorithm progresses in phases $p$, starting from phase 1, and every phase consists of $d$ sub-phases, which in turn consist of 3 rounds each.

Node $u$ maintains a variable $x$ storing all random bits drawn in the course of the execution. In the first sub-phase of each phase, $u$ appends bits to $x$ until the length of $x$ is $b(dp)$. In the remaining $d - 1$ sub-phases $s = 1, \ldots, d - 1$ of phase $p$, by appending bits to $x$, the number of used random bits is increased to $b(dp + s)$. This process takes place in the first round of each sub-phase. After drawing bits in round 1 of sub-phase $i$, $u$ sends its (preliminary) color $x$ to all nodes $v \in \Gamma(u)$.

In the beginning of the second round of sub-phase $i$, node $u$ receives the colors chosen by all nodes in $\Gamma(u)$. The list consisting of $u$'s own color $x$ and all the received colors is then sent to all neighbors of $u$. In the beginning of the third round of sub-phase $i$ node $u$ receives such a list from each neighbor. If $x$ occurs only once in each list, then $u$ selects color $x$ and terminates. Otherwise, if $x$ was used by multiple nodes, the process continues.

The idea behind TAILOR-2-HOP-COLORING is as follows. In the first sub-phase of each phase, every node $u$ draws a random color $x$ from the set

---

**Algorithm 1.** TAILOR-2-HOP-COLORING$(f, a, d)$ as executed by node $u$.

---

**Initialization:**
- $g(n) \leftarrow f^{-1}(n)$
- $x \leftarrow \varepsilon$         ▷ *the empty bit string*

**Phase** $p = 1, 2, \ldots$:
- **For sub-phase** $s = 0, 1, 2, \ldots, d - 1$:

  ▷ *Round 1 of sub-phase $s$:*
  Append random bits to $x$ until $|x| = b(pd + s)$
  **Send** $x$ to all neighbors

  ▷ *Round 2 of sub-phase $s$:*
  **Receive** $x_1, \ldots, x_\delta$ from each non-terminated neighbor $v_1, \ldots, v_\delta \in \Gamma(u)$
  **Send** list $\langle x, x_1, \ldots, x_\delta \rangle$ to all neighbors

  ▷ *Round 3 of sub-phase $s$:*
  **Receive** lists $L_1, \ldots, L_\delta$ from each neighbor
  **if** $x$ *appears exactly once in every list* **then**
      Choose color $x$ and terminate

---

$\{1, \ldots, g(p)^a\}$. Our choice of $b$ ensures that the remaining sub-phases of phase $p$ are used to interpolate between $g(p)^a$ and $g(p+1)^a$ if the chosen colors are not a valid 2-hop coloring. The interpolation is performed so that within each phase $p$, the multiplicative increase in the number of random bits used in each sub-phase is fixed. If, for instance, TAILOR-2-HOP-COLORING is in the first sub-phase of some phase $p = \lceil f(n) \rceil$, then the number of bits used by $u$ is at least $a \log n$.

Please note that in round 3 of each sub-phase, a node chooses a color only if it does not violate the 2-hop coloring constraint. Thus, the output of TAILOR-2-HOP-COLORING is always a valid 2-hop coloring. The remainder of this section is dedicated to establishing the following theorem.

**Theorem 1.** *The runtime of* TAILOR-2-HOP-COLORING *with high probability and in expectation is* $\mathcal{O}(f(n))$ *rounds. The random bit complexity of* TAILOR-2-HOP-COLORING *with high probability and in expectation is* $\mathcal{O}(h(f(n)) \cdot \log n)$ *bits, where*

$$h(i) = \sqrt[d]{\frac{\lceil \log g(i+1) \rceil}{\lceil \log g(i) \rceil}}.$$

It will sometimes be convenient to express the bit drawing function in terms of $h$:

$$b(pd + s) = b(dp) \cdot h(p)^s, \qquad \text{for } 0 \leq s \leq d, \text{ and} \tag{1}$$
$$b(pd + s + 1) = b(dp + s) \cdot h(p), \quad \text{for } 0 \leq s \leq d. \tag{2}$$

Consider the last phase $p$ and sub-phase $s$ for which $b(pd + s) < a \log n$. In that case, $b(pd + s + 1) \geq a \log n$ bits are drawn in the next step. Thus, due to the second expression, the essence of Theorem 1 is that TAILOR-2-HOP-COLORING "overshoots" the necessary $a \log n$ bits by at most a factor of $h(p)$.

Recall that the target function $f$ can be thought of as the runtime function of any deterministic algorithm that relies on a 2-hop coloring. Before getting into the details of the analysis, let us briefly put Theorem 1 into perspective by considering the corner cases where $f \in \Theta(\log \log n)$ or $f \in \Theta(\log^* n)$. In the former case $h(f(n))$ is in $\mathcal{O}(1)$, whereas in the latter case $h(f(n))$ is in $\mathcal{O}(\sqrt[d]{n})$. Thus, we obtain the following corollary from Theorem 1.

**Corollary 1.** *Consider a target function $f$, and let $R$ denote the random bit complexity of* TAILOR-2-HOP-COLORING.

1. *If $f(n) \in \Theta(\log^* n)$, then $R$ is $\mathcal{O}(\sqrt[d]{n} \cdot \log n) \subseteq \mathcal{O}(\sqrt[d-1]{n})$ w.h.p. and in expectation.*
2. *If $f(n) \in \Theta(\log \log n)$, then $R$ is $\mathcal{O}(\log n)$ w.h.p. and in expectation.*

The analysis of TAILOR-2-HOP-COLORING's runtime and random bit complexity are done separately. We first establish the high-probability results, beginning with the runtime.

**Lemma 1.** TAILOR-2-HOP-COLORING *terminates after at most $\mathcal{O}(f(n))$ rounds w.h.p.*

We validate the claim by showing that all nodes terminate in phase $f(n)$ with probability $1 - n^{2-a}$. This is sufficient, since each phase consists of exactly $3d$ rounds. The next lemma ensures the desired high probability result for the random bit complexity, and can be shown in a similar manner. However, this time our analysis takes the exact sub-phase in which TAILOR-2-HOP-COLORING terminates (w.h.p.) into account.

**Lemma 2.** *The random bit complexity of* TAILOR-2-HOP-COLORING *is at most $h(f(n)) \cdot a \log n$ with high probability.*

Next, we establish the results for the expected values.

**Lemma 3.** *The runtime of* TAILOR-2-HOP-COLORING *is at most $\mathcal{O}(f(n))$ in expectation.*

Our proof of the above lemma again considers the phase in which TAILOR-2-HOP-COLORING terminates. The idea is to split the summation of the expected value into two parts, namely before and including phase $f(n)$, and after phase $f(n)$. Both terms can then be bounded individually.

**Lemma 4.** *If $f(n)$ is at least $\log^* n$, then the random bit complexity of* TAILOR-2-HOP-COLORING *is $\mathcal{O}(h(f(n)) \cdot \log n)$ in expectation.*

The proof of Lemma 4, similar to that of Lemma 3, relies on carefully inspecting the round in which TAILOR-2-HOP-COLORING terminates. However, due to the possibly large growth of $g$ (which directly affects the growth of the bit drawing function), the analysis requires more attention. Instead of considering only

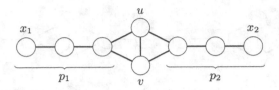

**Fig. 1.** A $(u, v)$-gadget of length $i = 4$, consisting of $2i$ nodes: The two special nodes $u$ and $v$, and the two paths $p_1$ and $p_2$ of length $i-1$ with endpoints $x_1$ and $x_2$, respectively. Since the gadget is symmetric, symmetry between $u$ and $v$ can only be broken by their individual random coin tosses.

the phase in which TAILOR-2-HOP-COLORING terminates, we take the exact step in that phase into account. This yields a division of the expected value into 5 (instead of the previous 2) terms. Bounding each term individually leads to a rather lengthy proof. Theorem 1 is then established by combining Lemmas 1 to 4.

## 4 Trade-off Lower Bound

Our goal in this section is to show that the trade-off achieved by TAILOR-2-HOP-COLORING's bit drawing function is asymptotically optimal. For this effort, it is sufficient to study lower bounds for the 1-hop variant of the coloring problem, since every 2-hop coloring is also a 1-hop coloring. More precisely, we are going to establish the following:

**Theorem 2.** *Let $\mathcal{A}$ be any randomized uniform anonymous coloring algorithm. If the expected runtime of $\mathcal{A}$ is asymptotically smaller than that of TAILOR-2-HOP-COLORING, then $\mathcal{A}$'s expected random bit complexity is asymptotically larger than that of TAILOR-2-HOP-COLORING.*

The rough idea is that in order to break symmetry, the nodes have to draw random bits according to some (possibly randomized) scheme. We distinguish two cases: In the first case, $\mathcal{A}$ may try to break symmetry quickly by using many random bits. We show that then, the expected random bit complexity of $\mathcal{A}$ needs to be large. For the second case, where $\mathcal{A}$ prevents this behavior, we show that the expected runtime of $\mathcal{A}$ is asymptotically as large as that of TAILOR-2-HOP-COLORING.

Our proof relies on a graph construction consisting of several so-called $(u, v)$-gadgets. A $(u, v)$-gadget of length $i$ (depicted in Figure 1) consists of $2i$ nodes, namely two paths $p_1, p_2$ of length $i - 1$ and two special nodes $u$ and $v$, connected by an edge. Furthermore, nodes $u$ and $v$ are connected to one endpoint of both $p_1$ and $p_2$. The other endpoints of $p_1$ and $p_2$ are referred to as $x_1$ and $x_2$, respectively. We obtain the graph $G(m, i)$ utilized in our lower bound proofs by connecting $m$ $(u, v)$-gadgets of length $i$ in a ring-like topology. This is done by

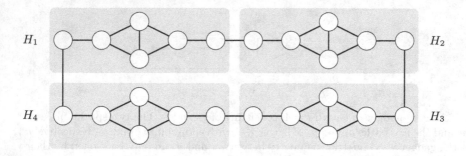

**Fig. 2.** The graph $G(4,3)$, consisting of 4 $(u,v)$-gadgets $H_1, H_2, H_3$, and $H_4$, each of length 3.

simply chaining the $m$ gadgets together by their endpoint nodes $x_1$ and $x_2$—please refer to Figure 2 for an illustration. We note that $G(m,i)$ consists of $2im$ nodes.

Consider, for example, the graph $G = G(2^k, 3)$ for some arbitrarily large $k$. Since the graph $G$ is symmetric from the perspective of each $(u,v)$-pair in any of the gadgets, every such pair can break symmetry only by their individual random coin tosses. Assume now for the sake of contradiction, that there is a coloring algorithm $\mathcal{A}$ with an expected bit complexity $\beta \in o(\log n)$. In that case, with arbitrarily large probability, at least one of the $(u,v)$-pairs tosses exactly the same sequence of random bits. This contradicts the claim that $\beta \in o(\log n)$, and thus we obtain the following result from our graph construction.

**Corollary 2.** *Any coloring algorithm must have an expected random bit complexity in $\Omega(\log n)$.*

In our effort to prove the trade-off lower bound we would like to have a better grip than that on the random coin tosses made by the nodes. Specifically, for any algorithm $\mathcal{A}$ and $(u,v)$-gadget $H$, we denote by $B_{\mathcal{A}}(i, H)$ the random variable taking on the maximum number of random bits drawn by nodes $u$ and $v$ in $H$ until and including round $i$. Whenever $\mathcal{A}$ is clear from the context, we omit it in the notation and write $B(i, H)$ instead. The following insight about those random variables in the graph $G(m,i)$ is based on the observation that the length of the paths in the $(u,v)$-gadgets guarantee independence. We formally note this in the following Lemma 5, which will be helpful in our proof of Theorem 2.

**Lemma 5.** *Consider any algorithm $\mathcal{A}$, and let $H$ be a single $(u,v)$-gadget of length $i$. Let $m \geq 2$ be an integer, and denote by $H_1, \ldots, H_m$ the $m$ $(u,v)$-gadgets in the graph $G(m,i)$. For any $j \leq i$, all the random variables $B(j, H_k)$, obtained from an execution of $\mathcal{A}$ in $G(m,i)$, are independent and distributed like $B(j, H)$.*

As noted before, the proof for Theorem 2 is divided into two parts, depending on how $\mathcal{A}$ chooses to draw random bits (in expectation). For that, based on the bit drawing function $b$ used by TAILOR-2-HOP-COLORING (for fixed parameters $f, a$, and $d$), we introduce a threshold for the number of random bits drawn by some algorithm as follows.

**Definition 1 (Drawing few/a lot of random bits).** *Fix a bit drawing function $b$, parametrized by a target function $f$ and two constants $a > 2$ and $d \geq 2$. Let $H$ be a $(u, v)$-gadget of length $i$, and let $\mathcal{A}$ be a randomized algorithm. We say that $\mathcal{A}$ draws* a lot of random bits *if*

$$\exists i_0 \forall i \geq i_0 \quad \mathbf{E}[B(i, H)] \geq b(3i)/4.$$

*If $\mathcal{A}$ does not draw a lot of random bits, then we say that $\mathcal{A}$ draws* few *random bits.*

Due to Lemma 5, properties of single $(u, v)$-gadgets can be lifted to instances of $G(m, i)$. One such property we will use is encapsulated in the following technical lemma, which can be established using induction.

**Lemma 6.** *Let $\mathcal{A}$ be any coloring algorithm. If $\mathcal{A}$ draws a lot of random bits, then*

$$\exists i_0 \forall i \geq i_0 \exists j \leq i \quad \mathbf{E}[B(j, H)] \leq b(i)/4, \text{ and } \mathbf{E}[B(j+1, H)] \geq b(i+2)/4,$$

*where $H$ is a $(u, v)$-gadget of length $i$.*

We now have the essential tools to prove Theorem 2, and first consider the case where $\mathcal{A}$ draws a lot of random bits. In that case, for sure, the runtime of $\mathcal{A}$ can be better than that of TAILOR-2-HOP-COLORING. Imagine for example a process that draws infinitely many random bits in the first round—one would immediately obtain a 2-hop coloring within a single round with probability 1, albeit at the cost of an infinite random bit complexity. The essential insight of the following Lemma 7 is that no matter how "smartly" one tries to draw a lot of random bits in hopes to get a better runtime, the expected bit complexity will be asymptotically worse than that of TAILOR-2-HOP-COLORING.

**Lemma 7.** *Let $\mathcal{A}$ be any coloring algorithm. If $\mathcal{A}$ draws a lot of random bits, then $\mathcal{A}$'s expected random bit complexity is $\Omega(h(f(n))^2 \cdot \log n)$.*

In our proof, we carefully choose a gadget graph of a certain size. We then utilize Lemma 5 to "copy" the property obtained from Lemma 6 for a single $(u, v)$-gadget to all gadgets in the graph. Applying Markov's inequality twice, the choice of the gadget graph then allows us to derive the desired lower bound. With the next lemma we consider the opposite case where $\mathcal{A}$ draws only few random bits.

**Lemma 8.** *Let $\mathcal{A}$ be any coloring algorithm. If $\mathcal{A}$ draws few random bits, then the expected runtime of $\mathcal{A}$ is $\Omega(df(n))$.*

Our proof follows similar lines as that for Lemma 7. The key difference is how the size of the gadget graph is chosen. We obtain the desired optimality of TAILOR-2-HOP-COLORING from Lemma 7 only if $h(f(n))^2 \in \omega(h(f(n)))$. In the case where $f \in \mathcal{O}(\log \log n)$, however, $h(f(n))$ is bounded from above by a constant. It may thus appear that such an $f$ is not covered by our lemmas.

To see that this is not an issue, observe that the constant 3 in the definition of drawing a lot of random bits was chosen arbitrarily. In other words, when $h(f(n))$ is bounded by some constant $\rho$, one may replace 3 in the above definition with $\rho + 3$. This way, we obtain that the coloring algorithm $\mathcal{A}$ draws "$\rho$-few" random bits. We can now apply the same reasoning as in the proof of Lemma 8 to obtain that the runtime of $\mathcal{A}$ is in the same order as that of TAILOR-2-HOP-COLORING. This concludes our effort to establish Lemma Theorem 2.

# References

1. Alon, N., Babai, L., Itai, A.: A fast and simple randomized parallel algorithm for the maximal independent set problem. Journal of Algorithms **7**, 567–583 (1986)
2. Andreev, A.E., Clementi, A.E.F., Rolim, J.D.P., Trevisan, L.: Weak random sources, hitting sets, and BPP simulations. SIAM J. Comput. **28**, 2103–2116 (1999)
3. Angluin, D.: Local and global properties in networks of processors (extended abstract). In: STOC (1980)
4. Aspnes, J., Waarts, O.: Randomized consensus in expected o(n log$^2$ n) operations per processor. SIAM J. Comput. **25**, 1024–1044 (1996)
5. Attiya, H., Censor, K.: Tight bounds for asynchronous randomized consensus. J. ACM **55** (2008)
6. Attiya, H., Ellen, F.: Impossibility Results for Distributed Computing. Morgan & Claypool Publishers (2014)
7. Attiya, H., Welch, J.: Distributed Computing: Fundamentals, Simulations and Advanced Topics. John Wiley & Sons (2004)
8. Barenboim, L., Elkin, M.: Distributed (delta+1)-coloring in linear (in delta) time. In: STOC (2009)
9. Barenboim, L., Elkin, M.: Deterministic distributed vertex coloring in polylogarithmic time. J. ACM **58**, 23 (2011)
10. Barenboim, L., Elkin, M.: Distributed Graph Coloring: Fundamentals and Recent Developments. Morgan & Claypool Publishers (2013)
11. Barenboim, L., Elkin, M., Kuhn, F.: Distributed (delta+1)-coloring in linear (in delta) time. SIAM J. Comput. **43**, 72–95 (2014)
12. Blair, J.R.S., Manne, F.: An efficient self-stabilizing distance-2 coloring algorithm. Theor. Comput. Sci. **444**, 28–39 (2012)
13. Dolev, S.: Self-Stabilization. Mit Press (2000)
14. Dolev, S., Tzachar, N.: Randomization adaptive self-stabilization. Acta Inf. **47**, 313–323 (2010)
15. Emek, Y., Pfister, C., Seidel, J., Wattenhofer, R.: Anonymous networks: randomization = 2-hop coloring. In: PODC (2014)
16. Fraigniaud, P., Göös, M., Korman, A., Parter, M., Peleg, D.: Randomized distributed decision. Distributed Computing **27**(6), 419–434 (2014)
17. Fraigniaud, P., Korman, A., Peleg, D.: Towards a complexity theory for local distributed computing. J. ACM **60**, 35 (2013)

18. Gill, J.: Computational complexity of probabilistic turing machines. SIAM J. Comput. **6**, 675–695 (1977)
19. Goldberg, A.V., Plotkin, S.A., Shannon, G.E.: Parallel symmetry-breaking in sparse graphs. SIAM J. Discrete Math. **1**, 434–446 (1988)
20. Göös, M., Suomela, J.: Locally checkable proofs. In: PODC (2011)
21. Gradinariu, M., Tixeuil, S.: Self-stabilizing vertex coloration and arbitrary graphs. In: OPODIS (2000)
22. Schneider, J., Wattenhofer, R.: Trading bit, message, and time complexity of distributed algorithms. In: Peleg, D. (ed.) Distributed Computing. LNCS, vol. 6950, pp. 51–65. Springer, Heidelberg (2011)
23. Karp, R., Pippenger, N., Sipser, M.: A time-randomness tradeoff. In: AMS Conference on Probabilistic Computational Complexity (1985)
24. Korman, A., Kutten, S., Peleg, D.: Proof labeling schemes. In: PODC (2005)
25. Kuhn, F.: Weak graph colorings: distributed algorithms and applications. In: SPAA (2009)
26. Lautemann, C.: BPP and the polynomial hierarchy. Inf. Process. Lett. **17**, 215–217 (1983)
27. Linial, N.: Locality in Distributed Graph Algorithms. SIAM Journal on Computing (1992)
28. Luby, M.: A simple parallel algorithm for the maximal independent set problem. In: STOC (1985)
29. Luby, M., Wigderson, A.: Pairwise independence and derandomization. Foundations and Trends in Theoretical Computer Science **1** (2005)
30. Motwani, R., Raghavan, P.: Randomized Algorithms. Cambridge University Press (1995)
31. Naor, M., Stockmeyer, L.: What can be computed locally? SIAM Journal on Computing **24**, 1259–1277 (1995)
32. Nisan, N., Ta-Shma, A.: Extracting randomness: A survey and new constructions. J. Comput. Syst. Sci. **58**, 148–173 (1999)
33. Rabin, M.O.: Probabilistic automata. Information and Control **6**, 230–245 (1963)
34. Schneider, J., Elkin, M., Wattenhofer, R.: Symmetry breaking depending on the chromatic number or the neighborhood growth. Theor. Comput. Sci. **509**, 40–50 (2013)
35. Schneider, J., Wattenhofer, R.: A log-star distributed maximal independent set algorithm for growth-bounded graphs. In: PODC (2008)
36. Scott, A., Jeavons, P., Xu, L.: Feedback from nature: an optimal distributed algorithm for maximal independent set selection. In: PODC (2013)
37. Shukla, S.K., Rosenkrantz, D.J., Ravi, S.S.: Developing self-stabilizing coloring algorithms via systematic randomization. In: Proceedings of the International Workshop on Parallel Processing (1994)
38. Vadhan, S.P.: Pseudorandomness. Foundations and Trends in Theoretical Computer Science **7**, 1–336 (2012)

# Fast Byzantine Leader Election
# in Dynamic Networks

John Augustine[1], Gopal Pandurangan[2]([✉]), and Peter Robinson[3]

[1] Indian Institute of Technology Madras, Chennai, TN, India
[2] Department of Computer Science, University of Houston, Houston, TX, USA
gopalpandurangan@gmail.com
[3] Queen's University Belfast, Belfast, UK

**Abstract.** We study the fundamental Byzantine leader election problem in dynamic networks where the topology can change from round to round and nodes can also experience heavy *churn* (i.e., nodes can join and leave the network continuously over time). We assume the full information model where the Byzantine nodes have complete knowledge about the entire state of the network at every round (including random choices made by all the nodes), have unbounded computational power and can deviate arbitrarily from the protocol. The churn is controlled by an adversary that has complete knowledge and control over which nodes join and leave and at what times and also may rewire the topology in every round and has unlimited computational power, but is oblivious to the random choices made by the algorithm.

Our main contribution is an $O(\log^3 n)$ round algorithm that achieves Byzantine leader election under the presence of up to $O(n^{1/2-\varepsilon})$ Byzantine nodes (for a small constant $\varepsilon > 0$) and a churn of up to $O(\sqrt{n}/\operatorname{polylog}(n))$ nodes per round (where $n$ is the stable network size). The algorithm elects a leader with probability at least $1 - n^{-\Omega(1)}$ and guarantees that it is an honest node with probability at least $1 - n^{-\Omega(1)}$; assuming the algorithm succeeds, the leader's identity will be known to a $1 - o(1)$ fraction of the honest nodes. Our algorithm is fully-distributed, lightweight, and is simple to implement. It is also scalable, as it runs in polylogarithmic (in $n$) time and requires nodes to send and receive messages of only polylogarithmic size per round. To the best of our knowledge, our algorithm is the first scalable solution for Byzantine leader election in a dynamic network with a high rate of churn; our protocol can also be used to solve Byzantine agreement in a straightforward way. We also show how to implement an (almost-everywhere) public coin with constant bias in a dynamic network with Byzantine nodes and provide a mechanism for enabling honest nodes to store information reliably in the network, which might be of independent interest.

John Augustine was supported by IIT Madras New Faculty Seed Grant, IIT Madras Exploratory Research Project, and Indo-German Max Planck Center for Computer Science (IMPECS).

Gopal Pandurangan was supported in part by NSF grant CCF-1527867.

Peter Robinson was partly supported by the European Community's Seventh Framework Programme (FP7/2007-2013) under the ASAP project, grant agreement no. 619706.

Y. Moses (Ed.): DISC 2015, LNCS 9363, pp. 276–291, 2015.
DOI: 10.1007/978-3-662-48653-5_19

# 1    Introduction

Motivated by the need for robust and secure distributed computation in large-scale (sparse) networks such as peer-to-peer (P2P) and overlay networks, we study the fundamental *Byzantine leader election* problem in *dynamic* networks, where a large number of nodes can join and leave the network continuously and the topology can also change continuously. The Byzantine leader election problem in dynamic networks is challenging because the goal is to guarantee that an honest (i.e., non-Byzantine) node is elected as a leader with probability at least $1 - o(1)$ and whose identity is known to *most* honest nodes[1] despite the adversarial network dynamism and the presence of Byzantine nodes. Byzantine leader election is related to another fundamental and central problem in distributed computing, namely, *Byzantine agreement*. In fact, in our setting, Byzantine leader election is a harder problem, since it can be used to solve *almost-everywhere* Byzantine agreement in a straightforward way.

Byzantine agreement and leader election have been challenging problems even in static networks. Indeed, until recently, almost all the work known in the literature (see e.g., [14,19,20,22,31]) have addressed the Byzantine almost-everywhere agreement problem only in static networks. Unfortunately, these approaches fail in dynamic networks where both nodes *and* edges can change by a large amount in *every* round. For example, Upfal [31] showed how one can achieve almost-everywhere agreement under up to a linear number — up to $\varepsilon n$, for a sufficiently small $\varepsilon > 0$ — of Byzantine faults in a bounded-degree expander network ($n$ is the network size). However, the algorithm requires knowledge of the global topology, since at the start, nodes need to have this information hardcoded. The work of King et al. [23] is important in the context of P2P networks, as it was the first to study scalable (polylogarithmic communication and number of rounds) algorithms for Byzantine leader election and agreement. However, as pointed out by the authors, their algorithm works only for static networks. Similar to Upfal's algorithm, the nodes require hardcoded information on the network topology to begin with and thus the algorithm does not work when the topology changes (in particular, when the edges are also changing in every round). In fact, this work ([23]) raised the open question of whether one can design Byzantine leader election and agreement protocols that can work in highly dynamic networks with a large churn rate.

The work of [4] was the first to study the Byzantine agreement problem in a dynamic network with a large churn rate. However, this algorithm does not directly solve the *leader election* problem, since the value that (most of) the honest nodes agree may be a value that was generated by a Byzantine node; using the agreement algorithm in a straightforward way does not give any guarantee that an honest node will be elected as leader. Hence, a more involved approach is needed for Byzantine leader election.

---

[1] In sparse, bounded-degree networks, an adversary can always isolate some number of honest nodes, hence "almost-everywhere" is the best one can hope for in such networks (cf. [14]).

**Our Main Result.** We study Byzantine leader election in dynamic networks where the topology can change from round to round and nodes can also experience heavy *churn* (i.e., nodes can join and leave the network continuously over time). Our goal is to design a fast distributed algorithm (running in a small number of rounds) that guarantees, despite a relatively large number of Byzantine nodes and high node churn, that an honest node is elected as leader and almost all honest nodes know the identity of this leader.

Before we state our results, we briefly describe the key ingredients of our model here. (Our model is described in detail in Section 1.1, it is similar to the model considered in prior work, e.g., [4,5,6].) We consider a dynamic network as a sparse bounded degree *expander* graph whose topology — *both nodes and edges* — can change arbitrarily from round to round and is controlled by an adversary. However, we assume that the total number of nodes in the network is stable. Note that our model is quite general in the sense that we only assume that the topology is an expander[2] at every step; no other special properties are assumed. Indeed, expanders have been used extensively to model dynamic P2P networks in which the expander property is preserved under insertions and deletions of nodes (e.g., [26,29]). Since we do not make assumptions on how the topology is preserved, our model is applicable to all such expander-based networks. (We note that various prior work on dynamic network models make similar assumptions on preservation of topological properties — such as connectivity, expansion etc. — at every step under dynamic *edge* insertions/deletions — cf. Section 1. The issue of how such properties are preserved are abstracted away from the model, which allows one to focus on the dynamism. Indeed, this abstraction has been a feature of most dynamic models e.g., see the survey of [10].) Furthermore, our results are applicable to dynamic network models with good expansion where only edges change (and no churn) —such models have been studied extensively in recent years (cf. Section 1).

The number of node changes *per round* is called the *churn rate* or *churn limit*. We consider a churn rate of up to $O(\sqrt{n}/\text{polylog}(n))$, where $n$ is the stable network size. Furthermore, we assume that a large number of nodes can be *Byzantine*. We allow up to $O(n^{\frac{1}{2}-\varepsilon})$ Byzantine nodes in any round, where $\varepsilon > 0$ is a small constant. Byzantine nodes (who have unbounded computational power) are "adaptive", in the sense that they know the entire states of all nodes at the beginning of every round and thus can take the current state of the network into account when determining their next action. In each round, an *oblivious adversary* chooses some $O(\sqrt{n}/\text{polylog}(n))$ nodes that are replaced by new nodes. The oblivious adversary has complete control over what nodes join and leave and at what time and also may rewire the edges in every round and has unlimited computational power but is oblivious to the random choices of the nodes. (Note that an adaptive churn adversary that knows the current state of all the nodes is not very interesting in the context of leader election, since it can churn out the leader as soon as it is elected.)

---

[2] In principle, our results can potentially be extended to graphs with weaker expansion guarantees as well; however the amount of churn and Byzantine nodes that can be tolerated will be reduced correspondingly.

Our main contribution is a randomized distributed algorithm that achieves leader election with high probability[3] even under a large number of Byzantine nodes and continuous adversarial churn in a number of rounds that is polylogarithmic in $n$ (where $n$ is the stable network size). In particular, we show the following theorem:

**Theorem 1 (Main Theorem).** *Let $\varepsilon > 0$ be any fixed constant. Consider a synchronous dynamic $n$-node ($n$ is the stable network size) expander network where up to $O(n^{\frac{1}{2}-\varepsilon})$ nodes are Byzantine (who can behave arbitrarily and who have full knowledge of the current network state including past random choices made by other nodes), and suppose that up to $O(\sqrt{n}/\operatorname{polylog}(n))$ nodes are subjected to churn per round determined by an oblivious adversary. There exists an algorithm that elects a leader with probability $1 - n^{-\Omega(1)}$ who is known by all except $o(n)$ nodes, and the leader is an honest node with probability $1 - n^{-\Omega(1)}$. The algorithm runs in $O(\log^3 n)$ rounds and uses messages of $O(\operatorname{polylog}(n))$ size.*

Our algorithm is the first-known, decentralized Byzantine leader election algorithm in highly dynamic networks. Our algorithm is localized (does not require any global topological knowledge), simple, and easy to implement. It can serve as a building block for implementing other non-trivial distributed coordination tasks in highly dynamic networks with churn.

**Technical Overview.** The main technical challenge that we have to overcome is designing and analyzing distributed algorithms with the presence of Byzantine nodes in networks where both nodes *and* edges can change by a large amount continuously in *each round*. The same challenge was present in solving the Byzantine agreement problem in such networks which was addressed in [4]. However, this does not directly solve the *leader election* problem, since the value that (most of) the honest nodes agree may be a value that was generated by a Byzantine node; using the agreement algorithm in a straightforward way does not give any guarantee that an honest node will be elected as leader. Hence, a more involved approach is needed for Byzantine leader election. We outline key ingredients of our approach here (Sections 2.1 and 2.2 give a more detailed overview).

While Byzantine agreement itself does not directly help, it can be used to generate an almost-everywhere public coin, i.e., an almost fair public coin that is known to most honest nodes. This is the first key ingredient. To the best of our knowledge, we present the first solution to such an almost everywhere (AE) common coin in a highly dynamic network.

Our protocol requires nodes to independently generate "lottery tickets" which are bit strings of certain length. Essentially, a node that has the winning lottery ticket becomes part of the small set of finalists from which a leader will be chosen eventually. However, there is a problem in naively implementing this approach. The Byzantine nodes, who know the current network state *including* random choices of other nodes, can change location and might lie about their lottery ticket number, thus claiming to be the winner. To overcome this, we implement

---

[3] In this paper, with high probability refers to a probability of $\geqslant 1 - n^{-\Omega(1)}$.

a *verification* mechanism that allows the honest nodes to check whether the Byzantine nodes are lying. This mechanism is as follows. Once a node generates its lottery ticket it "stores" it in about $\sqrt{n}$ (randomly chosen) nodes (exceeding the number of Byzantine nodes by an $n^\varepsilon$ factor). To verify whether a node is indeed the owner of the lottery ticket that it claims, honest nodes will check with these $\sqrt{n}$ nodes. This prevents a Byzantine node from falsely claiming a lottery ticket that it did not generate in the first place. We show how such a storage and verification mechanism can be implemented efficiently despite the presence of Byzantine nodes in a dynamic network. The last ingredient of the protocol is an efficient and fault-tolerant mechanism to disseminate the identity of the leader to almost all the honest nodes.

We use random walks as the main tool for communication in our protocol. Previously, flooding techniques proved useful in solving the agreement problem under high churn but without Byzantine nodes [6]. In the presence of Byzantine nodes, however, flooding is less useful as it enables Byzantine nodes to disseminate lots of (corrupting) information along with those sent by honest nodes. On the other hand, if honest nodes use random walks (which are lightweight and local) in their information spreading protocol, the Byzantine nodes are no longer able to congest the network without bound. This proves crucial for getting a scalable protocol that uses only polylogarithmic message sizes per round and finishes in polylogarithmic rounds. We use a key technical result on random walks in a dynamic network with Byzantine nodes and adversarial churn called the "*dynamic random sampling* theorem" (cf. Theorem 2) that shows mixing properties of random walks (despite Byzantine nodes and large adversarial churn) and enables us to communicate efficiently among honest nodes.

Our protocol can tolerate up to $O(n^{\frac{1}{2}-\varepsilon})$ Byzantine nodes (for a small constant $\varepsilon > 0$) and up to $O(\sqrt{n}/\operatorname{polylog}(n))$ churn. This is essentially the best that our protocol can handle for two reasons. Our storage and verification mechanism needs to store each lottery ticket in about $\sqrt{n}$ nodes, and to be scalable in terms of the number of messages generated, it can handle only about $\sqrt{n}$ nodes (each such node generates a ticket, thus overall there will be about $n \operatorname{polylog}(n)$ messages — anything significantly more than this will cause much more congestion). The second reason is that for solving Byzantine agreement, we use a majority rule to progress towards agreement [12,4]. This majority rule algorithm works as long as the number of Byzantine nodes are bounded by $O(\sqrt{n})$.

**Related Work.** There has been a lot of recent work on distributed agreement, byzantine agreement, and fault-tolerant protocols in dynamic networks. We refer to [17,6,4,3] and the references therein for details on these works. Here we restrict ourselves to those works that are most closely related.

There has been significant work in designing peer-to-peer networks that are provably robust to a large number of Byzantine faults [15,18,27,30]. These focus only on robustly enabling storage and retrieval of data items. The problem of achieving almost-everywhere agreement among nodes in P2P networks (modeled as an expander graph) is considered by King et al. in [23] in the context of the leader election problem; essentially, [23] is a sparse (expander) network implementation of the full information protocol of [22]. More specifically, [23] assumes that the adversary corrupts a constant fraction $b < 1/3$ of the processes that are under its control throughout the run of the algorithm. The protocol of [23] guarantees that with constant probability an uncorrupted leader will be elected and that a $1 - O(\frac{1}{\log n})$ fraction of the uncorrupted processes know this leader. We note that the algorithm of [23] does not work for dynamic networks, in particular, when just the edges are rewired from round to round (while still preserving expander topology). In another recent work [21], the authors use a spectral technique to "blacklist" malicious nodes leading to faster and more efficient Byzantine agreement in static networks. The idea of blacklisting, unfortunately, won't work in our dynamic network model, since the adversary can change the identities of Byzantine nodes by churning out old ones and introducing new ones (cf. Section 2).

The work of [6] addresses the agreement problem in a dynamic P2P network under an adversarial churn model where the churn rates can be very large, up to linear in the number of nodes in the network. (It also crucially makes use of expander graphs.) This introduced the dynamic model with churn that is used subsequently in other papers ([3,4]), including this paper. However, the algorithms and techniques of [6] will not work under the presence of Byzantine nodes; even one malicious node can foil their algorithms. The work of [3] presented storage and search algorithms for a highly dynamic network that can have churn rate up to $n/$ polylog $n$. However, these algorithms do not work in the presence of Byzantine nodes. The random walk approach to dynamic sampling was introduced in this paper and subsequently extended to Byzantine nodes in [4]. [17] presents a solution for maintaining a clustering of the network where each cluster contains more than two thirds honest nodes with high probability in a setting where the size of the network can vary polynomially over time.

The work of [4] presents Byzantine almost-everywhere agreement algorithms that can tolerate the same amount of churn as the present paper, i.e., $\sqrt{n}/$ polylog $n$, but it works even under adaptive churn. For this algorithm, only the "rewiring" adversary, which controls the edges between the adaptively churned nodes, needs to be oblivious — this is needed for the random walk approach to work. We use this algorithm as a key building block for implementing our almost-everywhere common coin. [4] also presented an almost tight (up to polylog $n$ factor) lower bound of $\Omega(\sqrt{n}/$ polylog $n)$ for the amount of churn that can be tolerated if one requires polylogarithmic round algorithms. This lower bound crucially makes use of the adaptive nature of the churn adversary. It is not clear if the same lower bound holds for the oblivious adversary as considered in this paper.

Expander graphs and spectral properties have been applied extensively to improve the network design and fault-tolerance in distributed computing (cf. [31,14,9]). The work of [26] provides a distributed algorithm for maintaining an expander in the presence of churn with high probability by using Hamiltonian cycles.

In recent years, adversarial models for dynamic networks have been studied extensively by [7,11,28,25] and others; see the recent survey of [10] and the references therein. Unlike many early works on dynamic networks (e.g., [1,13,16,2,8]) these recent works do not assume that the network will eventually stabilize and stop changing. On the other hand, we would prefer distributed algorithms to work correctly even if the network is *changing continuously over time* (as assumed in our paper). The works of [25,7,11] study a model in which the communication graph can change completely from one round to another, with the only constraint being that the network is *connected at each round* ([25] and [11] also consider a stronger model where the constraint is that the network should be an expander or should have some specific expansion in each round). The model has also been applied to agreement problems in dynamic networks; various versions of coordinated consensus (where all nodes must agree) have been considered in [25]. We note that the model of [24] allows only edge changes from round to round while the nodes remain fixed. The model considered here is more general than the model of [24], as it captures dynamic settings where edges change *and* nodes are subjected to churn. It is impossible to solve Byzantine agreement when only assuming the (oblivious) adversary of [24] that keeps the graph connected in each round; for example, a Byzantine node placed at a bottleneck point of the network can forever prevent any reasonable information flow between the two separated parts of the network. For the case where the "edge adversary" of [24] adheres to our expansion and regularity assumption, we can apply our results to this model as well.

## 1.1 Computing Model and Problem Definition

We consider a synchronous dynamic network with Byzantine nodes represented by a graph with a dynamically changing topology (both nodes and edges change) whose nodes execute a distributed algorithm and whose edges represent connectivity in the network. The computation is structured into synchronous rounds, i.e., we assume that nodes run at the same processing speed (and have access to a synchronized clock) and any message that is sent by some node $u$ to its neighbors in some round $r \geq 1$ will be received by the end of $r$. The dynamic network is represented by a sequence of graphs $\mathcal{G} = (G^0, G^1, \ldots)$ where each $G^r = (V^r, E^r)$. Nodes might be subjected to churn, which means that in each round, up to $C(n)$ nodes ($C(n) \in O(\sqrt{n}/\log^k n)$) can be replaced by new nodes; the constant $k$ will be fixed in the analysis. We require that, for all $r \geq 0$, $|V^r \setminus V^{r+1}| = |V^{r+1} \setminus V^r| \leq C(n)$. Furthermore, we allow the edges to change from round to round, but we assume that each $G^r$ is a $d$-regular expander graph with constant spectral gap. The churn and the evolution of the edges are under the control of an *oblivious adversary* who has to choose the entire sequence of $(G^0, G^1, \ldots)$ in advance.

Up to $B(n) \in O(n^{\alpha/2})$ nodes can be *Byzantine* and deviate arbitrarily from the given protocol, where $\alpha > 0$ is a constant adhering to Equation(1) on Page 283. We say that a node $u$ is *honest* if $u$ is not a Byzantine node and use $V_{\text{corr}}$ to denote the set of honest nodes in the network. Byzantine nodes are "adaptive", in the sense that they know the entire states of all nodes at the beginning of every round and thus can take the current state of the computation into account when determining their next action. This setting is commonly referred to as the *full information model*. We consider the usual assumption that Byzantine nodes cannot fake their identity, i.e., if a Byzantine node $w$ sends a message to nodes $u$ and $v$, then both $u$ and $v$ can identify $w$ as the same sender of the message. Note that this does not stop Byzantine nodes from forwarding fake messages on behalf of other nodes as we do not assume any authentication service. We assume, without loss of generality, that the adversary only subjects honest nodes to churn, i.e., Byzantine nodes remain in the network permanently. (The analysis of our algorithms can be extended easily to the case where Byzantine nodes are subject to churn as well).

We assume that if a node $u$ enters the network at some later round $r$, then $u$ knows the number of rounds that have passed since the start of the computation. Any information about the network at large is only learned through the messages that node $u$ receives and $u$ has no a priori knowledge about who its neighbors will be in the future.

We now describe the sequence of events that occur in each round $r \geqslant 1$. Firstly, we modify the network $G^{r-1} = (V^{r-1}, E^{r-1})$ by subjecting up to $C(n)$ nodes to churn (yielding $V^r$) and then changing the edge connectivity; recall that these changes are predetermined by the oblivious adversary. At this point, we emphasize that Byzantine nodes are always adaptive in the sense that they can observe the current network state including all past random choices. After the adversary has made its moves, the algorithm operates on the graph $G^r = (V^r, E^r)$ in round $r$. Each honest node $u$ becomes aware of its current neighbors in $G^r$, can perform local computation and is able to reliably exchange messages with its neighbors according to the edges in $E^r$.

As stated above, our algorithm tolerates $O(n^{\alpha/2})$ Byzantine nodes and churn per round. Let $c_1 > 2$ be any fixed constant. Our algorithm requires the following condition on $\alpha$:

$$\alpha \leqslant -\log(1 - 1/c_1)/\log c_1 - 8\log\log n/\log n - 1/c_1^2 \qquad (1)$$

We now present the formal definition of the Byzantine leader election problem. Note that since we assume a dynamic network which is a *sparse* expander in each round, we cannot hope to obtain an algorithm where every honest node eventually knows the leader; for example, the adversary could simply keep churning out all neighbors of a node $u$, effectively isolating $u$ throughout the run. This motivates us to consider the following "almost everywhere" variant of leader election:

**Byzantine Leader Election (BLE).** Suppose that there are $B(n)$ Byzantine nodes in the network. We say that an *algorithm A solves Byzantine Leader Election in T rounds* if, in any run of $A$, there is exactly 1 node $u_\ell$ such that
(a) all honest nodes terminate in $T$ rounds whp,
(b) all except $B(n) + o(n)$ honest nodes accept $u_\ell$ as the leader, and
(c) node $u_\ell$ is honest with probability $\geqslant 1 - \frac{B(n)}{n} - o(1)$.

## 2   The Byzantine Leader Election Algorithm

In this section we present an algorithm for electing a leader in the presence of $O(n^{\alpha/2}/\operatorname{polylog}(n))$ Byzantine nodes and churn. Before presenting the details of our algorithm, we first discuss why more straightforward approaches do not work: At a first glance, it appears as if we might be able to simply use the Byzantine almost everywhere agreement (BAE) algorithm of [4] to elect a leader. For example, running bitwise BAE agreement on the node ids will inevitably yield almost everywhere agreement on some specific node id. (After agreeing on the $i$-th bit $v$, we only consider nodes as candidates whose id has $v$ as the $i$-th bit.) This, however, is poised to fail, since the adversary will simply choose the initial node ids in a way such that the BAE algorithm yields a decision on an id of a Byzantine node.

An immediate but insufficient improvement of the above approach is to initially instruct each honest node to generate a random id, and then run bitwise BAE agreement on these random ids to elect a leader. In this case, the oblivious adversary, who has to choose the churn and the initial nodes in advance, has no advantage in making an initial guess on the elected id. Byzantine nodes, on the other hand, have full knowledge of the current network state including past random choices in the full-information model. Thus, a Byzantine node $u$ that announces an initially chosen value $id_u$, can adaptively lie about the actual value of $id_u$ as soon as the outcome of the agreement algorithm becomes apparent, and subsequently claim leadership. Of course, if the network topology was static, the neighbors of $u$ will notice that $u$ has changed its initial value and could simply inform the remaining network to blacklist $u$ as being malicious. In our model, however, the adversary has the power to rewire the topology over time and to subject nodes to churn, possibly causing all initial neighbors of $u$ to be several hops away from $u$ (or even churned out) during later rounds. This makes it difficult for an honest node $v$ to conclude whether $u$ has deviated from its initial choice, if $u$ and $v$ were not neighbors initially. In fact, any information that $v$ has learned about $u$ while not being a neighbor of $u$ was learned indirectly via other nodes. As we neither assume an authentication service nor make any assumptions on how Byzantine nodes are distributed in the network, an easy indistinguishability argument shows that $v$ has no way of knowing if the learned information was injected by other Byzantine nodes.

## 2.1  Preliminaries and Technical Tools

*Random Walk Implementation.* To ensure lightweight communication costs, our algorithm relies on random walks as a means of communication. We now describe a simple token-passing implementation of random walks in our model (cf. [3,4]): When an honest node $u$ initiates a random walk, it generates a token with its id, a counter initialized to the length of the walk, and possibly attaches some piece of information of $O(\log n)$ size. This token is then forwarded to a (current) neighbor of $u$ chosen uniformly at random, which in turn forwards the token and so forth. The counter is decreased by 1 each time the token is forwarded, until it reaches 0, which marks the final destination of this walk. Since Byzantine nodes can deviate arbitrarily from this protocol, honest nodes only forward tokens that are *legit*, which means that they adhere to above described data format. Our algorithm requires nodes to initiate $h \log n$ random walks simultaneously, for a sufficiently large constant $h$. During the run of the algorithm, an honest node $u$ might receive a large number of tokens (possibly generated by Byzantine nodes). More precisely, the random walks that arrive at a node $u$ are placed in a FIFO buffer according to the order of their arrival. To prevent Byzantine nodes from congesting the entire network with fake tokens, node $u$ forwards up to $h \log n$ of the tokens from its buffer in each step. This ensures (whp) passage of random walks that matter to us.

Our algorithm employs a technical result that shows almost uniform mixing for most random walks in our dynamic network. Its proof relies on a combination of several technical results and is related to Theorem 1 of [4]; we defer the details to the full paper and will focus on the new aspects of our leader election algorithm here. Intuitively speaking, Theorem 2 says that there is a large set Core of honest nodes such that, after walking for $\Theta(\log n)$ steps, tokens originating from these nodes have probability of $\approx 1/n$ to be at any node in Core. It is important to keep in mind that, since the size of Core is only guaranteed to be $\geqslant n - o(n)$, there is a nonzero probability for such a token to end up at nodes that are not in Core; for example, by being forwarded to a Byzantine node.

**Theorem 2 (Dynamic Random Sampling).** *Let $T = \Theta(\log^2 n)$ and consider a dynamic $n$-node expander network $\mathcal{G}$ under an oblivious adversary, and suppose that at most $O(n^{\alpha/2})$ nodes are Byzantine and at most $O(\sqrt{n}/\log^k n)$ nodes are subjected to churn in each round, where $k$ is a sufficiently large constant and for any fixed constant $\alpha < 1$. Then, there exists a set of honest nodes Core of size $\geqslant n - O(\sqrt{n}/\log^{k-6} n)$ such that, in every time interval $[iT + 1, (i+1)T]$ for $0 \leqslant i \leqslant \Theta(\log n)$ the following hold:*

1. *A random walk token originating from a node in Core has probability in $[\frac{1}{n} - \frac{1}{n^3}, \frac{1}{n} + \frac{1}{n^3}]$ to terminate at any particular node in Core.*
2. *At most $O(\sqrt{n}/\log^{k-8} n)$ nodes in Core receive tokens that did not originate in Core, and $\geqslant n - O(\sqrt{n}/\log^{k-9} n)$ nodes in Core only receive tokens that took all their steps among nodes in Core.*

*Byzantine Almost-Everywhere Agreement.* The following BAE agreement algorithm is given in [4]: Each honest node initially starts with an input bit (either 0 or 1) and instances of the random walk implementation by generating tokens that contain its input bit. Once such an instance is complete (after $\Theta(\log^2 n)$ rounds), each honest node tries to update its current input value with the majority value of the triple consisting of its input value and 2 of its received tokens. In particular, it follows from the analysis in [4] that $\Theta(\log n)$ repetitions suffice to converge to almost-everywhere agreement among all except $O(\sqrt{n}/\log^{k-6} n)$ nodes with high probability.

The following result lower bounds the number of nodes that agree in all instances when we run $\Theta(\log n)$ instances of this BAE agreement algorithm in parallel. (This is what we do when flipping the common coin in Phase 3 of our algorithm for choosing the winning lottery ticket.)

**Corollary 1 (Parallel BAE Agreement, Follows from [4]).** *Let $T = \Theta(\log^3 n)$ and suppose that at most $O(n^{\alpha/2})$ nodes are Byzantine, while up to*

$O(\sqrt{n}/\log^k n)$ nodes are subjected to churn in any round, for any constant $\alpha < 1$. Suppose that the honest nodes execute $\ell \leqslant \Theta(\log n)$ parallel instances of the BAE algorithm of [4]. Then, with high probability, there is a set $\mathsf{Agr} \subseteq \bigcap_{0\leqslant r\leqslant T} V^r$ of honest nodes such that in each BAE agreement instance $i$ $(1 \leqslant i \leqslant \ell)$, all nodes in $\mathsf{Agr}$ decide on a common bit $b_i$ within $T = \Theta(\log^3 n)$ rounds, and $|\mathsf{Agr}| = n - O(\sqrt{n}/\log^{k-7} n)$.

**Good and Bad Nodes.** For convenience, we define $\mathsf{Bad}^r = V^r \setminus (\mathsf{Agr} \cup \mathsf{Core})$; that is, $\mathsf{Bad}^r$ is of size $O(\sqrt{n}/\log^{k-7} n)$, contains all Byzantine nodes, and all honest nodes that are in the network in round $r$ and that are either not part of our $\mathsf{Core}$ set given by Theorem 2 or decided wrongly in at least one of the parallel BAE agreement algorithm instances. We also define the set $\mathsf{Good} = \mathsf{Agr} \cap \mathsf{Core}$.

## 2.2    A Byzantine Leader Election Algorithm

We now describe the details of our leader election algorithm and provide some intuition for its correctness.

**Phase 1. Determining Candidates:** To keep the overall message complexity per node polylogarithmic, we first subsample a set of candidates $\mathsf{Cand}$, by instructing each node to randomly choose to become a candidate with probability $8 \log n/\sqrt{n}$. Our algorithm heavily depends on the sampling capabilities provided by Theorem 2. Recall that the churn and the changes of the communication links are chosen obliviously (cf. Section 1.1), while Byzantine nodes can adapt their behavior by taking into account the current network state. Intuitively speaking, the following lemma shows that the Byzantine nodes have no influence over which honest nodes end up in the set $\mathsf{Core}$, as the $\mathsf{Core}$ set is solely determined by the churn and the topology changes, both of which are chosen in advance by the *oblivious* adversary (cf. Section 1.1):

**Lemma 1 (Independence of Core).** *The membership of nodes in the set $\mathsf{Core}$ (as defined in Theorem 2) is independent of the behaviour of the Byzantine nodes.*

Observing that each node chooses to become a candidate uniformly at random, it follows by a simple Chernoff bound that $|\mathsf{Cand}| \geqslant 4\sqrt{n} \log n$ whp. According to Lemma 1, the number of candidates that are in $\mathsf{Core}$ cannot be biased by the Byzantine nodes, but depend only on the churn and the topology changes, which are chosen in advance by an oblivious adversary. This motivates us to restrict ourselves to *core candidates* defined as $\mathsf{CCand} = \mathsf{Core} \cap \mathsf{Cand} \cap \mathsf{Agr}$, which are the candidates that agree in all instances of the BAE agreement algorithm (cf. Corollary 1) and are part of the $\mathsf{Core}$ set. From Corollary 1, it follows that $|\mathsf{Agr}| \geqslant n - o(\sqrt{n})$ and from Theorem 2 we know that $|\mathsf{Core}| \geqslant n - O(\sqrt{n}/\log^{k-6} n) \geqslant n - o(\sqrt{n})$. Therefore, the independence of $\mathsf{Core}$ from the behaviour of Byzantine nodes implies the following:

**Corollary 2 (Number of Agreeing Core Candidates).** *With high probability, we have $|\mathsf{CCand}| \geqslant 2\sqrt{n} \log n$.*

**Phase 2. Obtaining and Storing Lottery Tickets:** In this phase, we first instruct the candidate nodes to participate in the "leader lottery" by generating tickets. To this end, each candidate generates a lottery ticket represented as a private random bit string of length $\lceil \frac{\log n}{2 \log c_1} \rceil$, where $c_1 > 0$ is a constant depending on the bias of the "almost everywhere common coin" introduced in Phase 3. Note that all Byzantine nodes can pretend to be candidates and can collude to generate lottery tickets that maximize their chances. Next, we implement a storage mechanism to ensure that this information persists in the network despite the high churn rate and the dynamic topology changes.

Recall that we allow nodes to attach additional information onto their random walk tokens that they generate. Therefore, when referring to some information $I$ communicated by a node $v$, we mean the additional information (of size $O(\log n)$) that $v$ has piggybacked onto a random walk token message, as described in the random walk implementation (cf. Section 2.1). We say that *node $u$ has stored information $I$ in the network*, if $u$ has generated $I$ and there exist at least $\Theta(\sqrt{n} \log n)$ honest nodes that are witnesses regarding $I$. Keep in mind that Byzantine nodes are omniscient regarding the current network state, enabling them to claim to be witnesses for some arbitrary (possibly fake) information.

Since we assume a sparse network with a dynamically changing topology and only allow messages of polylogarithmic size, we cannot leverage techniques commonly used in static networks; in particular, we cannot bind Byzantine nodes to their initial choice by broadcasting this information to all nodes or requiring neighbors to keep track of each other's choices. Instead, we invoke a storage mechanism, which allows us to keep track of the initial choice of Byzantine nodes.

In more detail, we initiate the following branching process: When an (honest) candidate $u$ invokes STORE($z$), for some ticket $z$, it generates a random walk of sufficient length and piggybacks $z$ onto the random walk token message. Suppose that the walk has reached only honest nodes and terminated at some honest node $v$. Node $v$ in turn starts $\Theta(\log n)$ new random walks, each of which contains $z$. Each of these walks that reaches only honest nodes will in turn spawn $\Theta(\log n)$ new random walks and so forth; we repeat this branching process $\Theta(\log n)$ times. We can think of the branching process as creating a tree having $\Omega(\sqrt{n} \log n)$ leafs. Every honest node that corresponds to a leaf of this tree, locally stores $z$ and becomes a *witness* of ticket $z$ of node $u$. In the following, we say that $u$ *plays ticket $z$* if $z$ has been stored successfully.

**Lemma 2.** *Suppose that all candidates execute Procedure* STORE($I$) *in parallel. Then, with high probability, each of the core candidate (i.e. set* CCand $\subset$ Good) *is able to play its tickets.*

To ensure that nodes in Bad (which includes all Byzantine nodes) have a small chance to guess the winning ticket, we upper bound the number of distinct tickets that Byzantine nodes can play:

**Lemma 3.** *Let $\mathcal{I}$ be the set of distinct tickets generated by nodes in Bad such that each $I \in \mathcal{I}$ is stored in the network, i.e., $I$ has $\Omega(\sqrt{n}\log n)$ (fake or honest) witnesses. Then $|\mathcal{I}| \in O(n^{\alpha/2}\log^4 n)$.*

**Phase 3. Running the Lottery to Determine the Winning Ticket:** While we cannot directly use Byzantine almost everywhere (BAE) agreement to obtain an honest leader with good probability, we will use the time-tested method of employing such an BAE agreement algorithm as a subroutine to obtain an almost-everywhere common coin (cf. Definition 1 below), which is one of the tools used by our algorithm. The goal of this phase is to determine the *finalists*, i.e., the nodes who generated the winning lottery ticket. To this end, we generate the winning ticket by flipping an almost-everywhere common coin:

**Definition 1 (Almost Everywhere (AE) Common Coin).** *Consider an algorithm $P$ where every honest node outputs a bit and let $Comm_Q$ be the event that all nodes in a set $Q$ output the same bit value $b$. If there exist a constant $c_1 \geqslant 2$ and a set $Q$ of size $n - o(n)$ such that (A) $\mathbb{P}[Comm_Q] \geqslant 1 - n^{-\Omega(1)}$, and (B) $\frac{1}{c_1} \leqslant \mathbb{P}[b = 0 \mid Comm_Q] \leqslant 1 - \frac{1}{c_1}$, then we say that $P$ implements an almost everywhere common coin (AE common coin) on set $Q$ and we say that $P$ has* bias *at most $1/2 - 1/c_1$.*

We will now show that the BAE agreement algorithm given by Corollary 1 can be modified to yield such an AE common coin.

**Theorem 3 (AE Common Coin).** *Consider a synchronous dynamic $n$-node expander network under the control of an oblivious adversary where up to $B(n) = O(n^{\alpha/2})$ nodes are Byzantine, and suppose that up to $C(n) = O(\sqrt{n}/\operatorname{polylog}(n))$ nodes are subjected to churn per round. There exists a polylogarithmic messages and time algorithm that implements an almost everywhere coin on a set of $n - O(B(n) + C(n))$ nodes with a bias bounded by a constant $c < 1/2$.*

The honest nodes jointly perform $\lceil \log n/2\log c_1 \rceil$ flips of this AE common coin to yield the winning ticket that will be known to almost all nodes.

**Lemma 4.** *We partition the set of stored tickets into the set CoreTickets of tickets generated by nodes in Good and the set BadTickets, which contains the tickets played by (honest and Byzantine) nodes in Bad. Consider the winning lottery ticket $s$ yielded by the $\lceil \frac{\log n}{2\log c_1} \rceil$ invocations of the AE common coin algorithm. Then, it holds that (a) $\mathbb{P}[\forall x \in BadTickets: x \neq s] \geqslant 1 - n^{-\Omega(1)}$. (b) $\mathbb{P}[\exists y \in CoreTickets: y = s] \geqslant 1 - n^{-\Omega(1)}$.*

Recalling that the bits of the winning ticket comprises exactly the common decision values of the parallel BAE agreement instances, it follows that all nodes in set Agr know the winning ticket. Thus, each $u \in$ Agr knows whether it is itself a winner (and thus becomes a *finalist*) or if it is among one of the $\Theta(\sqrt{n}\log n)$ witnesses of the finalist nodes. If so, $u$ adds itself to the set of *propagators* $P_v$, for finalist $v$.

**Phase 4. The Final Competition and Leader Election:** In the final phase, one of the finalists must be chosen as the leader despite the fact that Byzantine nodes can behave like finalists and/or witnesses. In particular, we wish to reach a consensus on the finalist $f$ with the smallest id.

We subdivide Phase 4 into $\frac{\log n}{2 \log \log n} + \Theta(1)$ sub-phases, each of $O(\log^2 n)$ rounds. Each honest node $u$ samples $O(\log n)$ nodes per sub-phase via random walks. During this sampling process, $u$ tries to discover the finalist $f$ with the smallest id. Node $u$ maintains a variable MIN-ID initialised to $\infty$. During phase 4, the honest nodes will only pass $O(\log n)$ random walk tokens per time step. At the start of each sub-phase, every honest node $u$ initiates $\Theta(\log n)$ random walk tokens: if $u$ is a witness for a ticket, then that ticket and the MIN-ID value are included in the token; the token is blank otherwise[4]. Each random walk must take $\Theta(\log n)$ random walk steps in order to mix; this can be achieved in $O(\log^2 n)$ rounds (cf. Theorem 2). At the end of the sub-phase, each node looks at all the tokens that terminated on it and checks to see if $v$ has an id smaller than its current MIN-ID and, if needed, updates MIN-ID with the smaller id. We now argue that at the end of $\frac{\log n}{2 \log \log n} + \Theta(1)$ sampling sub-phases, $n - o(n)$ nodes will have their MIN-ID set to $f$. This completes the proof of Theorem 1.

**Lemma 5.** *Let Finalists be the set of all candidates in CCand that played the winning ticket $z$ and assume that $z$ was stored among $\Omega(\sqrt{n} \log n)$ honest witnesses. Suppose that $f \in$ Finalists is the node with the smallest id in Finalists. Then, by the end of Phase 4, $n - o(n)$ nodes accept $f$ as the leader with probability at least $1 - o(1)$.*

## 3    Conclusion

In this paper, we take a step towards designing secure, robust, and scalable algorithms for large-scale dynamic networks. We presented a scalable and lightweight distributed protocol for the fundamental Byzantine leader election in dynamic networks, tolerating near $O(\sqrt{n}/\operatorname{polylog}(n))$ Byzantine nodes and churn per round while using only polylogarithmic amount of messages per node. A key open problem is to show a lower bound that is essentially tight with respect to the amount of Byzantine nodes that can be tolerated, or show a leader election algorithm that can tolerate significantly more Byzantine nodes and churn. The latter might be possible, since we are dealing with an oblivious churn adversary (unlike the adaptive churn adversary of [4]).

## References

1. Afek, Y., Awerbuch, B., Gafni, E.: Applying static network protocols to dynamic networks. In: FOCS 1987, pp. 358–370 (1987)
2. Afek, Y., Gafni, E., Rosen, A.: The slide mechanism with applications in dynamic networks. In: ACM PODC, pp. 35–46 (1992)

---

[4] The blank tokens cannot be discarded because they provide the congestion required to ensure that the number of tokens injected by Byzantine nodes are kept in check.

3. Augustine, J., Molla, A.R., Morsy, E., Pandurangan, G., Robinson, P., Upfal, E.: Storage and search in dynamic peer-to-peer networks. In: SPAA, pp. 53–62 (2013)
4. Augustine, J., Pandurangan, G., Robinson, P.: Fast byzantine agreement in dynamic networks. In: PODC, pp. 74–83 (2013)
5. Augustine, J., Pandurangan, G., Robinson, P., Roche, S., Upfal, E.: Enabling efficient and robust distributed computation in highly dynamic networks. In: FOCS (to appear, 2015)
6. Augustine, J., Pandurangan, G., Robinson, P., Upfal, E.: Towards robust and efficient computation in dynamic peer-to-peer networks. In: SODA, pp. 551–569 (2012)
7. Avin, C., Koucký, M., Lotker, Z.: How to explore a fast-changing world (cover time of a simple random walk on evolving graphs). In: Aceto, L., Damgård, I., Goldberg, L.A., Halldórsson, M.M., Ingólfsdóttir, A., Walukiewicz, I. (eds.) ICALP 2008, Part I. LNCS, vol. 5125, pp. 121–132. Springer, Heidelberg (2008)
8. Awerbuch, B., Patt-Shamir, B., Peleg, D., Saks, M.E.: Adapting to asynchronous dynamic networks. In: STOC 1992, pp. 557–570 (1992)
9. Bagchi, A., Bhargava, A., Chaudhary, A., Eppstein, D., Scheideler, C.: The effect of faults on network expansion. Theory Comput. Syst. **39**(6), 903–928 (2006)
10. Casteigts, A., Flocchini, P., Quattrociocchi, W., Santoro, N.: Time-varying graphs and dynamic networks. CoRR, abs/1012.0009 (2010). Short version in ADHOC-NOW 2011
11. Das Sarma, A., Molla, A.R., Pandurangan, G.: Fast distributed computation in dynamic networks via random walks. In: Aguilera, M.K. (ed.) DISC 2012. LNCS, vol. 7611, pp. 136–150. Springer, Heidelberg (2012)
12. Doerr, B., Goldberg, L.A., Minder, L., Sauerwald, T., Scheideler, C.: Stabilizing consensus with the power of two choices. In: SPAA, pp. 149–158 (2011)
13. Dolev, S.: Self-stabilization. MIT Press, Cambridge (2000)
14. Dwork, C., Peleg, D., Pippenger, N., Upfal, E.: Fault tolerance in networks of bounded degree. SIAM J. Comput. **17**(5), 975–988 (1988)
15. Fiat, A., Saia, J.: Censorship resistant peer-to-peer content addressable networks. In: SODA, pp. 94–103 (2002)
16. Gafni, E., Bertsekas, B.: Distributed algorithms for generating loop-free routes in networks with frequently changing topology. IEEE Trans. Comm. **29**(1), 11–18 (1981)
17. Guerraoui, R., Huc, F., Kermarrec, A.-M.: Highly dynamic distributed computing with byzantine failures. In: PODC, pp. 176–183 (2013)
18. Hildrum, K., Kubiatowicz, J.D.: Asymptotically efficient approaches to fault-tolerance in peer-to-peer networks. In: Fich, F.E. (ed.) DISC 2003. LNCS, vol. 2848, pp. 321–336. Springer, Heidelberg (2003)
19. Kapron, B.M., Kempe, D., King, V., Saia, J., Sanwalani, V.: Fast asynchronous byzantine agreement and leader election with full information. ACM Transactions on Algorithms **6**(4) (2010)
20. King, V., Saia, J.: Breaking the $O(n^2)$ bit barrier: scalable Byzantine agreement with an adaptive adversary. In: PODC, pp. 420–429 (2010)
21. King, V., Saia, J.: Faster agreement via a spectral method for detecting malicious behavior. In: SODA, pp. 785–800 (2014)
22. King, V., Saia, J., Sanwalani, V., Vee, E.: Scalable leader election. In: SODA, pp. 990–999 (2006)
23. King, V., Saia, J., Sanwalani, V., Vee, E.: Towards secure and scalable computation in peer-to-peer networks. In: FOCS, pp. 87–98 (2006)
24. Kuhn, F., Lynch, N., Oshman, R.: Distributed computation in dynamic networks. In: ACM STOC, pp. 513–522 (2010)

25. Kuhn, F., Oshman, R., Moses, Y.: Coordinated consensus in dynamic networks. In: PODC, pp. 1–10 (2011)
26. Law, C., Siu, K.-Y.: Distributed construction of random expander networks. In: Twenty-Second Annual Joint Conference of the IEEE Computer and Communications. INFOCOM 2003, vol. 3, pp. 2133–2143. IEEE Societies, March–April 2003
27. Naor, M., Wieder, U.: A simple fault tolerant distributed hash table. In: IPTPS, pp. 88–97 (2003)
28. O'Dell, R., Wattenhofer, R.: Information dissemination in highly dynamic graphs. In: DIALM-POMC, pp. 104–110 (2005)
29. Pandurangan, G., Raghavan, P., Upfal, E.: Building low-diameter p2p networks. In: FOCS, pp. 492–499 (2001)
30. Scheideler, C.: How to spread adversarial nodes?: rotate! In: STOC, pp. 704–713 (2005)
31. Upfal, E.: Tolerating a linear number of faults in networks of bounded degree. Inf. Comput. 115(2), 312–320 (1994)

# Local Information in Influence Networks

Yuezhou Lv and Thomas Moscibroda$^{(\boxtimes)}$

Microsoft Research, Tsinghua University, Beijing, China
totolv@126.com, moscitho@microsoft.com

**Abstract.** We study how multi-hop information impacts convergence in social influence networks. In influence networks, nodes have a choice between two options $A$ and $B$, and each node prefers to end up choosing the option that a majority of its neighbors choose. We consider the case of innovation adoption in which nodes can only change from $A$ to $B$, but not backwards. For this model, we ask the question, when is it safe for a node to switch from $A$ to $B$? If nodes have multi-hop information about the network, rather than knowing only the state of their immediate neighbors, the answer to this question becomes complex. The reason is that a node needs to recursively reason about what its neighbors know, and whether given their knowledge they will also upgrade to $B$.

In this paper, we assume that each node has complete knowledge about its $k$-hop neighborhood, but does not know anything about the network beyond $k$-hops. We study how different local decision algorithms achieve different properties in terms of *safety* and *conversion ratio* (how many nodes ultimately upgrade to $B$). We characterize the possible algorithms by classifying them into a *hierarchy of algorithms*. Each class of algorithms in this hierarchy is distinguished by a natural safety property that it guarantees. For each class, we give an optimal algorithm in terms of conversion ratio, and we show that each class is fully contained in the class of lower safety level. Conversely, each lower-safety class can achieve strictly higher conversion ratio than any algorithm in the safer class. Thus, our hierarchy reveals a strict trade-off between safety and conversion ratio. Finally, we show that each class of algorithms satisfies two natural closure properties.

**Keywords:** Influence networks · Multi-hop information · Hierarchy of algorithms · Distributed algorithms

## 1 Introduction

Influence networks in all their variants are important in the study of many natural phenomena. In an influence network, each node is an agent and its action in some round $T$, depends on the state of its neighbors. Influence network models

This work was supported in part by the National Basic Research Program of China Grant 2011CBA00300, 2011CBA00301, the National Natural Science Foundation of China Grant 61033001, 61361136003.

Y. Moses (Ed.): DISC 2015, LNCS 9363, pp. 292–308, 2015.
DOI: 10.1007/978-3-662-48653-5_20

have been used in the study of diffusion of innovation, social networks, belief propagation, spring embedders, cellular automata, traffic networks, biological cell systems, etc.

In studies on influence networks, it has been implicitly assumed that not only does the *utility* of a node depend on the state of its neighbors, but – importantly – that each node *only knows the state of its immediate neighbors*. That is, it is assumed that nodes only have information about their neighborhood, or that they do not make sophisticated use of any additional information about the state of nodes outside their 1-hop neighborhood. However, having such additional non-local information can be of critical importance both in terms of convergence speed (i.e., how fast the system converges to its final equilibrium) as well as in terms of convergence ratio (i.e., the overall utility or social welfare achieved by the system in the equilibrium). Consider the following scenario, which we will use as a baseline for our model in this paper: Assume that each node in a network represents a participant that has a choice between staying with a current, older operating system, or upgrading to a newer version of the operating system. Some participants may be early adopters and decide to upgrade regardless of the actions of its neighbors; while others may be wary of change and never want to upgrade. For most participants, however, the utility is such that they will upgrade if the majority of their neighbors also upgrade; and they will stay if the majority of their neighbors stay.

The question is, for such a regular participant – when is it safe to upgrade to the new operating system? If every node only knows its neighbors, (i.e., without any knowledge about its neighbors' neighbors), then it is possible that all nodes will "wait" until a majority of its neighbors have decided to upgrade, and since every node behaves in this same way, no node will ever upgrade. That is, the system is stuck in a suboptimal configuration, simply due to the constraint of having only local information. If, however, each node knows about the state of nodes in its 2-hop or 3-hop neighborhood, then a node could compute locally that it is safe to upgrade, because it can be sure that a majority of its neighbors will ultimately benefit from upgrading, and thus they *will* upgrade. Thus, simply by increasing the amount of local information, the entire system ends up in a better global equilibrium.

To make the example concrete, suppose each node has two states **original** and **upgraded**, and each node is better off by changing from **original** to **upgraded** if and only if *all* its neighbors are upgraded. Consider a line with 5 nodes, $x_1, \ldots, x_5$, in which $x_1$ and $x_5$ are upgraded while the others are original. If each node has only 1-hop information, $x_2, x_3, x_4$ will never upgrade. But, if $x_3$ has 2-hop information, $x_3$ can upgrade first, because $x_2, x_4$ will then also upgrade which finally makes $x_3$ better off. The same happens in a system with 3 nodes that form a triangle. If every node *knows* that the three nodes form a triangle, all of them can upgrade in one step. However, if the nodes do not know whether their neighbors are mutually connected (they may have an independent neighbor each), then none of the nodes will upgrade.

More generally, the study of how multi-hop information impacts the dynamics and convergence of influence networks and leads to fascinating questions. These questions are of the following nature: A node $x$ would like to upgrade, but doing so is only "safe" (i.e., guaranteed to lead to a higher utility), if its neighbors also upgrade. However, in order for $x$ to know whether its neighbors will upgrade, it must determine whether it is "safe" for them to do so. Thus, the problem is recursive: In order for $x$ to determine whether it is "safe" for its neighbor $y$ to upgrade, it must determine what $y$ knows about its neighbors, i.e., including what $y$ knows about what $x$ knows about $y$, etc.

Thus, the extent to which a node knows more than simply its immediate neighborhood fundamentally changes how the system behaves. In this paper, we study how multi-hop local information impacts the convergence of influence networks. We provide a theory of local decision algorithms based on an analysis of the kind of decisions that nodes can safely take, if they are given multi-hop information. Naturally, the answer to the question of "when is it safe to upgrade" fundamentally depends on what each node assumes about the behavior of the other nodes within its vicinity. In other words, whether an action is safe for a node $x$ depends i) on what $x$ knows about its local neighborhood (and recursively , what the nodes in $x$'s neighborhood know about their respective neighborhood, etc), and ii) on the extent to which $x$ can rely on the nodes in its vicinity to behave rationally, trustworthily, conservatively, etc.

We show that these assumptions about the neighbors' behavior imply a natural hierarchy of safety-properties. Each stronger safety property ensures a stronger guarantee that the node's action will be the right choice in the equilibrium. Intriguingly, this hierarchy of safety properties also implies a *hierarchy of local decision algorithms*, and every local decision algorithm can be categorized into one of the classes of the hierarchy.

What is fascinating about this hierarchy of local decision algorithm is that each of its classes is defined along a natural safety concept, satisfies closure properties, and is strictly separated from both the next higher (=safer) class and the next lower (=less safe) class. Specifically, we prove the following results:

- The class of algorithms $C_i$ is a proper superset of every safer class $C_j$, $i > j$.
- For every class $C_i$, we derive the optimal algorithm $OPT(C_i)$ among all local decision algorithms contained in this class. Here, optimal is with regard to the social welfare (conversion ratio) achieved in the final equilibrium.
- We prove that for every class $C_i$, its optimal algorithm $OPT(C_i)$ can achieve a strictly better conversion ratio than any local decision algorithm contained in any safer class $C_j$, $i > j$. That is, each class in the hierarchy is strictly more efficient in terms of conversion ratio. Thus, the hierarchy captures the trade-off between safety and resulting social welfare.
- Finally, we prove that three of the classes ($C_{Byz}, C_{Rat}, C_{Pos}$) satisfy two natural closure properties: i) *subset-closure* (every subset of an algorithm in the class is included in the class), and ii) *union-closure* (the union of two algorithms in the class is included in the class). For the fourth class, $C_{Pro}$, the properties do not hold in general, but only for an important subclass of $C_{Pro}$.

In some classes of the hierarchy, the optimal algorithm is simple and natural, while for others (e.g., $\mathcal{C}_{Pro}$), the optimal algorithm exhibits a complicated recursive structure that may be of independent interest.

## 1.1 Related Work

There is vast literature on graph-based problems in which a node's decision depends on its neighbors' state, including famous examples such as the "game-of-life" simulations [4]; the classic "democrats-vs-republicans" problem [21]; influence maximization problems [2] [8][9][10], or spread (diffusion) of innovation problems[1][16][19]. The process of local majority voting in graphs, and its basic properties has been reviewed in [14]. In economics, this class of problems can be regarded generically as binary decisions with externalities [17]. It has been widely used in sociology and economics[11][12][18][22]. Models in which nodes can only change from "inactive" to "active" have been studied in [7][13][19][20]. The linear threshold model proposed in [8][9] is more closely related to ours. In contrast, an alternative setting allows nodes to change states freely, leading to problems such as stability, periodicity [5][6][15] or convergence time [3]. In all these works, the information used by nodes for decision making is restricted to the nodes' immediate neighborhood, i.e., no multi-hop information.

## 2    Model and Definition

### 2.1    Influence Network Model

We model an Influence Network as a graph $G = (V, E, \Phi)$. Two nodes connected by an edge are *neighbors* – their utility determines each other. A node $x \in V$ is in one of two possible states: the "original" state $A$ or the "upgraded" state $B$. A node has a type $\Phi(x)$: stubborn (unchangeable) or changeable. A *stubborn node* always remains in state $A$. A *changeable node* can change to $B$. Once a node has upgraded to $B$, it cannot switch back to $A$. A special case among the changeable nodes are *early-adopters*, i.e., nodes that start in state $B$ at the beginning. All other (regular) changeable nodes start in state $A$ and switch to $B$ under certain conditions as described below. We denote a changeable node initially in state $A$ as a *regular node*.

The network evolves over a series of rounds. We write $\gamma_T(x)$, $\gamma_T(S)$, and $\gamma_T(G)$ to denote the state of a node $x$, a set of nodes $S$, and the state of the network $G$ in round $T$. At the beginning, the network can include nodes in both state $A$ and $B$ (early-adopters). The evolving *process* on network $G$ is the sequence of network states $\gamma_0(G), \gamma_1(G), \ldots$. The network is in an equilibrium, if there is no further change happening in the process, i.e., no node changes its state.

**Definition 1.** *A network $G$ is in an* equilibrium *in round $T$ iff $\gamma_T(G) = \gamma_{T+1}(G)$.*

The next definition captures whether a regular node is *stable*, i.e., whether it is satisfied with its current state. Let $N(x)$ be the set of neighbors of $x$, and $N_T^B(x)$ be the set of neighbors in state $B$. For a given threshold $q \in [0,1]$, if at least a $q$-fraction of a node $x$'s neighbors are in state $B$, then $x$ is stable if it is also in state $B$, otherwise it is stable if it is in state $A$.

**Definition 2.** *A regular node $x$ is stable in round $T$ if $\gamma_T(x) = B$ and $|N_T^B(x)|/|N(x)| \geq q$, or if $\gamma_T(x) = A$ and $|N_T^B(x)|/|N(x)| < q$.*

## 2.2   $k$-Hop Influence Network and Local Decision Algorithm

In this paper, we extend the basic 1-hop influence network setting to a multi-hop setting. In a *k-hop influence network*, each node has complete information about the topology, and the state and type of all nodes up to a distance of $k$ in the network. Let $V_k(x), E_k(x)$ be the set of nodes and edges within the $k$-hop neighborhood of node $x$. The *view* of a node $x$ is defined as follows:

**Definition 3.** *In a k-hop network, the view $\Gamma(x)$ of node $x$ is a 4-tuple $\Gamma(x) = (V_k(x), E_k(x), \Phi(V_k(x)), \gamma(V_k(x)))$.*

**Local Decision Algorithm:** The only information available to a node is its view. Therefore, the decision of whether a regular node upgrades from state $A$ to state $B$ in a round $T$ depends entirely on its current view. Therefore, we can define a *Local Decision Algorithm* (or short, algorithm) as a mapping of a node's view to a binary decision, whether or not the node changes its state from $A$ to $B$. That is, an algorithm can be seen as defining for which views a regular node decides to upgrade. With this in mind, we characterize a Local Decision Algorithm as *the set of views that lead the node to upgrade*. That is, an algorithm is equivalent to a set of views, called the *Changing View Set $S_{ALG}$*, which cause a regular node $x$ in state $A$ to upgrade to state $B$. Thus, in this paper, we reason about changing view sets when defining properties of algorithms.

Every node's decisions are based on its Local Decision Algorithm. We denote by $\Pi = (S_1, \ldots, S_n)$ the set of algorithms of all regular nodes $x_1, \ldots, x_n$. Let $\Pi_{x_i} = S_i$, and $\Pi_{-x_i} = (S_1, \ldots, S_{i-1}, S_{i+1}, \ldots, S_n)$. We use upper script to indicate that every regular node executes the same algorithm, e.g., $\Pi^{ALG} = (S_{ALG}, \ldots, S_{ALG})$. Since a process depends only on the initial state $\gamma(G)$ and the algorithms of each regular node, we can use the notation $P[\gamma(G), \Pi]$ to characterize a process.

We use the natural notion of social welfare to evaluate the performance of algorithms: How many nodes end up upgrading to state $B$ in the equilibrium. We call this metric the *conversion ratio $|\Omega|$*, where the conversion set $\Omega$ is the set of all nodes in state $B$ in the equilibrium. When comparing algorithms in terms of their conversion ratio, we use the following three definitions.

**Definition 4.** *An algorithm $S_\alpha$ is (strictly) more efficient than an algorithm $S_\beta$ in some network setting $\gamma(G)$ if in $P_\alpha[\gamma(G), \Pi^{S_\alpha}]$ and $P_\beta[\gamma(G), \Pi^{S_\beta}]$, it holds that $|\Omega^{P_\alpha}| \geq |\Omega^{P_\beta}|$ $(|\Omega^{P_\alpha}| > |\Omega^{P_\beta}|)$.*

**Definition 5.** *We define $S_\alpha \succeq S_\beta$ ($S_\alpha \succ S_\beta$) if $S_\alpha$ is more efficient than $S_\beta$ in **any** network setting (and is strictly more efficient than $S_\beta$ in at least one network setting).*

**Definition 6.** *$S$ is optimal within a class of algorithms $\mathcal{C}$, denoted $S = OPT(\mathcal{C})$, if $S \in \mathcal{C}$ and for any algorithm $S_\alpha \in \mathcal{C}$, it holds that $S \succeq S_\alpha$.*

# 3 Hierarchy of Algorithms

In this section, we construct a hierarchy of local decision algorithms. In a $k$-hop influence network, two key factors that determine a node's decision making are i) what it can assume about its neighbor's behavior (i.e., its neighbors' algorithms); and ii) how much "risk" the node is willing to take; how surely the node expects to end up in a stable configuration in the equilibrium (i.e., a node's safety guarantee). There is a fundamental tradeoff between these two factors. The more likely a node upgrades to $B$ based on a belief that some of its neighbors will also upgrade to $B$ in subsequent rounds, the more opportunity the node itself has to take the plunge and upgrade itself, and thus the higher the global conversion ratio will be. Consider two extreme local decision algorithms: In the first algorithm, each regular node in $G$ directly upgrades to $B$ in the very first round. This algorithm clearly leads to the highest possible conversion ratio, but many nodes may end up being unstable in the equilibrium, i.e., they upgrade even though they should not have. At the other extreme end of the spectrum is the standard local 1-hop decision algorithm studied in the existing literature: A node upgrades to $B$ only if a $q$-fraction of its neighbors are $B$. This algorithm guarantees stability for every node, but it is inefficient in terms of conversion ratio. In many situations, few nodes will upgrade, even though all nodes would collectively benefit from doing so. Our hierarchy of local decision algorithms captures this trade-off, showing how different classes of algorithms achieve different natural safety-properties and conversion ratios, depending on the nodes' beliefs about other nodes' algorithms.

Since a local decision algorithm is equivalent to a set of changing views, *any property for an algorithm is entirely a function of its changing view set.* The first property we introduce defines the set of *rational algorithms*. A local decision algorithm is *rational* if it lets a node upgrade when there are a sufficient number of upgraded nodes in its 1-hop neighborhood. That is, an algorithm is rational if it includes all views $\Gamma(x)$ in its changing view set in which $|N^B(x)|/|N(x)| \geq q$ holds.

**Definition 7 (Rational).** *An algorithm $S$ is rational if $S_r \subseteq S$, where*
$$S_r = \{\Gamma(x) || N^B(x)|/|N(x)| \geq q \text{ holds in } \Gamma(x)\}.$$

Any natural algorithm should be rational as for a regular node, if a $q$-fraction of its neighbors have upgraded to $B$, it is sure to be stable by also upgrading. We call the set of all algorithms (including rational and non-rational) *arbitrary*. Our hierarchy includes arbitrary algorithms, but for simplicity we often implicitly assume algorithm to be rational unless we explicitly state that it is arbitrary.

**Safety Properties:** Local decision algorithms can be characterized according to the safety guarantees they achieve. We define an algorithm to be *safe* if when executing this algorithm, a node ends up being stable in the equilibrium. As a weaker version of safety, we consider the concept of *possible-safety*. A local decision algorithm is *possible-safe* if a node–when executing this algorithm–has a chance to end up being stable in the equilibrium. Following these ideas, we classify safety properties for local decision algorithms in sequence from safest to least safe.

The highest level of safety guarantee is *Byzantine-safety*. An algorithm is *Byzantine-safe* if in any network, when executing this algorithm, a node is guaranteed to end up being stable in the equilibrium, regardless of what arbitrary algorithms the other nodes in the network run. While Byzantine-safe algorithms ensure safety even in the presence of irrationally operating neighbors, nodes running a Byzantine-safe algorithm have few opportunities to upgrade to state $B$ and often get stuck unnecessarily in state $A$.

**Definition 8 (Byzantine-safe).** *An algorithm $S$ is* Byzantine-safe *if for any $\gamma(G)$, $x \in G$ and arbitrary $\Pi_{-x}$, in process $P[\gamma(G), (\Pi_{-x}, \Pi_x = S)]$, $x$ is stable in the equilibrium.*

The next lower degree of safety is called *Rational-safety*. It is defined similarly, except that each node assumes that the other nodes in the network execute at least a *rational* (instead of arbitrary) algorithm.

**Definition 9 (Rational-safe).** *An algorithm $S$ is* rational-safe *if for any $\gamma(G)$, $x \in G$ and rational $\Pi_{-x}$, in process $P[\gamma(G), (\Pi_{-x}, \Pi_x = S)]$, $x$ is stable in the equilibrium.*

The third level of safety is *Protocol-safety*. A node $x$ executing a protocol-safe local decision algorithm is guaranteed to end up being stable in the equilibrium, under the assumption that all other nodes will execute *the same algorithm* as $x$ does. In other words, protocol-safety captures the safety guarantee we can achieve if every node in the network follows a given distributed protocol designed by some global algorithm designer, and every node faithfully executes this common protocol.

**Definition 10 (Protocol-safe).** *An algorithm $S$ is* protocol-safe *if for any $\gamma(G)$, $x \in G$, in process $P[\gamma(G), \Pi^S]$, $x$ is stable in the equilibrium.*

Finally, the lowest level of safety is *Possible-safety*. If a node executes a possible-safe algorithm, then there exists a set of specific algorithms for the other nodes such that if each node executes this specific algorithm, every regular node in the graph ends up being stable in the equilibrium. In other words, an algorithm is possible-safe, if there at least *exists a possibility that it leads to all nodes becoming stable in the equilibrium*. Another way to interpret possible-safe local decision algorithms is that these are set of algorithms for "optimists". A node will decide to upgrade, if there is a chance that upgrading will lead to a stable outcome for everyone.

**Definition 11 (Possible-safe).** *An algorithm $S$ is* possible-safe *if for any* $\gamma(G)$, $x \in G$, *there exists a* $\Pi_{-x}$ *such that in process* $P[\gamma(G), (\Pi_{-x}, \Pi_x = S)]$, *each regular node is stable in the equilibrium.*

Notice that the definition of Possible-safety rules out trivial algorithms such as the algorithm in which every node always upgrades to $B$. Indeed, such an algorithm is not possible-safe the neighbors of a node executing such algorithm could all be stubborn.

Thus, we have four classes of algorithms, denoted by $\mathcal{C}_{Byz}, \mathcal{C}_{Rat}, \mathcal{C}_{Pro}$, and $\mathcal{C}_{Pos}$, each of which corresponds to a particular safety-guarantee the algorithm ensures. The following theorem shows that each class of algorithms is entirely contained in the next lower class. A class contains all algorithms that are contained in the next safer class.

**Theorem 1.** $\mathcal{C}_{Byz} \subseteq \mathcal{C}_{Rat} \subseteq \mathcal{C}_{Pro} \subseteq \mathcal{C}_{Pos}$.

We also study closure properties of the different classes. Specifically, a class of algorithms is *union-closed* if the union of any two algorithms in such class is included in it. A class of algorithms is *subset-closed* if the subset of any algorithm in such class is included in the class.

**Definition 12.** *A class of algorithms $\mathcal{C}$ is*
  *1. union-closed if for any $S_\alpha, S_\beta \in \mathcal{C}$, it holds that $(S_\alpha \cup S_\beta) \in \mathcal{C}$.*
  *2. subset-closed if for any $S_\beta \in \mathcal{C}$ and any $S_\alpha \subseteq S_\beta$, it holds that $S_\alpha \in \mathcal{C}$.*

## 4  Algorithms

In the section, we study each class of algorithms. For each class, we derive an algorithm that is optimal among all algorithms within this class. Also, for each class, we verify whether it is subset- and union-closed. Finally, we compare the optimal algorithm in each class in terms of its conversion ratio to all algorithms in the next safer class. Our results imply that the hierarchy is "complete" in the sense that the algorithms in each less safe hierarchy class are strictly more efficient than the algorithms in the safer class.

### 4.1  Preliminaries

We begin with two concepts that are useful across all classes. The first one, *eligible*, describes a set of nodes that can make each other stable by collectively changing to $B$.

**Definition 13.** *A set of nodes $W$ is eligible if,*
  *1. $W$ is a non-empty set including only changeable nodes in state $A$;*
  *2. when upgrading each node in $W$ to state $B$, each node in $W$ is stable.*

Secondly, we derive an important structural characterization of algorithms. We say an algorithm is INCREMENTAL if it is more efficient than any of its own subsets.

**Definition 14.** *$S_\beta$ is INCREMENTAL if $S_\beta \succeq S_\alpha$ for any $S_\alpha \subseteq S_\beta$.*

Intuitively, we would assume that every algorithm is INCREMENTAL. Surprisingly, it turns out that even rational algorithms may not be INCREMENTAL, i.e., an algorithm with fewer changing views that are a proper subset of another algorithm can be more efficient. As a simple example, consider a line network consisting of 5 nodes, with $k = 5$ and $q = 1$. Consider two algorithms $S_\alpha$ and $S_\beta$. Both algorithms include all views in which all neighbors are in state $B$ (which is rational for $q = 1$), and in addition they contain a set of additional changing views $\Gamma^1(x), \ldots, \Gamma^4(x)$ as shown in Figure 1. Let $S_\alpha = S_r \cup \{\Gamma^1(x), \Gamma^2(x), \Gamma^3(x)\}$ and $S_\beta = S_r \cup \{\Gamma^1(x), \Gamma^2(x), \Gamma^3(x), \Gamma^4(x)\}$, i.e., the two algorithms are identical except that $S_\beta$ includes one more changing view $\Gamma^4(x)$. However, in spite of this extra changing view, $S_\beta$ is actually strictly worse than $S_\alpha$ on the 5-node chain. Assume that initially, only the left-most node is in state $B$; the others are regular nodes in state $A$. It can be verified that with $S_\alpha$, all nodes will upgrade to $B$ in the equilibrium; while with $S_\beta$, Nodes 2 and 5 upgrade to $B$ in the first round, but Nodes 3 and 4 are then stuck – they have no chance to upgrade to $B$. Thus, even though $S_\beta$ is rational and a strict superset of $S_\alpha$, $S_\alpha$ is more efficient. Thus, the rational algorithm $S_\beta$ is not INCREMENTAL.

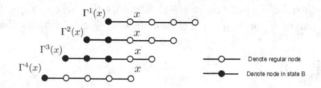

**Fig. 1.** Views $\Gamma^1(x), \Gamma^2(x), \Gamma^3(x), \Gamma^4(x)$.

The reason $S_\beta$ is not INCREMENTAL is that it violates a natural property we call *Augmentation-Completeness*. For a view $\Gamma(x)$, we say a view $\Gamma'(x)$ *augments* $\Gamma(x)$ if $\Gamma'(x)$ is identical to $\Gamma(x)$ except that i) some stubborn nodes in $\Gamma(x)$ are changeable nodes in $\Gamma'(x)$, and ii) some regular nodes in $\Gamma(x)$ are in state $B$ in $\Gamma'(x)$. Clearly, it should always be easier for a node to upgrade to $B$ in a view $\Gamma'(x)$ that augments $\Gamma(x)$ than in $\Gamma(x)$. The augments relationship thus implies a partial order of views in terms of the extent to which nodes are willing to change. Denote by $F^+(.)$ a mapping from an algorithm $S$ to the set of all views that augment at least one view in $S$. I.e., for a set $S$ and any view $\Gamma(x) \in S$, $F^+(S)$ includes all views that augment $\Gamma(x)$. Using this definition, we can show that for two algorithms $S_\alpha$ and $S_\beta$ such that $S_\beta$ is a superset of $F^+(S_\alpha)$, it holds for any $G$ and any initial state, the set of regular nodes changing to state $B$ in $P_\alpha$ is a subset of that in $P_\beta$.

We say an algorithm $S$ is Augmentation-Complete, AUG-COMPLETE, if for any of its views $\Gamma(x) \in S$, $S$ contains all the views that augment $\Gamma(x)$. Formally, $S$ is AUG-COMPLETE if $S = F^+(S)$. Augmentation-Completeness is a powerful tool that enables us to compare the efficiency among different algorithms, and we will use it extensively when constructing the optimal protocol-safe algorithm. With this definition, we can prove the following theorem.

**Theorem 2.** *Any AUG-COMPLETE algorithm is INCREMENTAL.*

### 4.2 Byzantine-Safe Algorithm

It is trivial to see that the only Byzantine-safe algorithm is the simple 1-hop algorithm; nodes upgrade to $B$ is a sufficient number of neighbors have upgraded to $B$. It is the only algorithm that ensure stability even in the presence of irrational neighbors. Since $\mathcal{C}_{Byz}$ contains only a single algorithm, the class is clearly subset-closed and union-closed.

**Theorem 3.** $\mathcal{C}_{Byz} = \{S_{1-hop}\}$.

---

**Algorithm 1.** $S_{1-hop}$

$S_{1-hop} := \{\Gamma(x) | |N^B(x)|/|N(x)| \geq q\}$.

---

### 4.3 Rational-Safe Algorithms

In this subsection, we devise an optimal rational-safe algorithm $S_{fore}$, called *foresee*. $S_{fore}$ works as follows: In order to check whether it should upgrade given its current view, a node $x$ temporarily "assumes" its state to be $B$, and under this assumption repeatedly finds eligible nodes in its view and "upgrades" these node to $B$. If the outcome of this local simulation is such that at least a $q$-fraction of $x$'s neighbors are in state $B$, $x$ upgrades to $B$. The key of $S_{fore}$ is that $x$ assumes itself to be in state $B$ at the outset.

---

**Algorithm 2.** $S_{fore}$

Given a view $\Gamma(x)$. Set the state of $x$ to $B$;
**while** *There exists a node $y \in V_{k-1}(x)$ such that $\{y\}$ is eligible* **do**
  ⌊ Set the state of $y$ to $B$.
**if** $|N^B(x)|/|N(x)| \geq q$ **then**
  ⌊ $\Gamma(x)$ is a changing view. ( i.e., add $\Gamma(x)$ into $S_{fore}$)

---

Algorithm $S_{fore}$ can be much more efficient than the 1-hop algorithm $S_{1-hop}$. Consider a graph $G$ with only regular nodes and threshold $q$ $q < 1/d_{max}$, where $d_{max}$ is the maximum degree of graph $G$. If each node uses $S_{1-hop}$, no node changes to $B$. In contrast, if every regular node uses $S_{fore}$, every node will assume itself to be in state $B$ and execute the while loop. For each of its neighbors $y$, as $q < \frac{1}{d_{max}}$, it holds that $N^B(y)/N(y) = 1/N(y) > 1/d_{max} > q$, i.e., $y$ is eligible and can upgrade to $B$. That is, $x$ knows that each of its neighbors will upgrade to $B$ and it can safely upgrade itself. Therefore, with $S_{fore}$, all nodes simultaneously upgrade to $B$ in the very first round.

Studying $S_{fore}$, we find that each subset of $S_{fore}$ is a rational-safe algorithm and each rational-safe algorithm is a subset of $S_{fore}$.

**Lemma 1.** $S \subseteq S_{fore} \Longleftrightarrow S \in \mathcal{C}_{Rat}$.

Thus, $S_{fore}$ is the rational-safe algorithm with the maximum set of views and it is the superset of each algorithm in $\mathcal{C}_{Rat}$. Therefore, we can infer that $\mathcal{C}_{Rat}$ is subset-closed and union-closed by definition. Furthermore, as $S_{fore}$ is AUG-COMPLETE (we can check any view in $S_{fore}$ according to the definition of AUG-COMPLETE), from Theorem 2, we can infer that $S_{fore}$ is more efficient than any of its subset. Therefore, $S_{fore}$ is optimal within the class of rational-safe algorithms.

**Theorem 4.** *The class of rational-safe algorithms $\mathcal{C}_{Rat}$ is subset-closed and union-closed. Furthermore, $S_{fore} = OPT(\mathcal{C}_{Rat})$.*

## 4.4  Protocol-Safe Algorithms

In many cases, $S_{fore}$ is still very inefficient. Protocol-safe algorithms can be more aggressive and efficient, because they can consider *eligible sets* rather than only eligible individual nodes. We begin with a simple algorithm $S_{trust}$, which is intuitive but not optimal. Let $D(W)$ be the diameter of a node set $W$ in $G$. We can easily infer that $S_{trust}$ is protocol-safe because it only considers eligible sets $W$ with diameter less than $k - 1$. The small diameter ensures that each node in $W$ can see $W$ as an eligible set in its own view. Thus, each node in $W$ can simultaneously upgrade to $B$ together.

---

**Algorithm 3.** $S_{trust}$–Finding eligible sets in view $\Gamma(x)$ with restricted diameter

---

$S_{trust} :=$
$\{\Gamma(x) | \exists W \subseteq V_{k-1}(x)$ such that $W$ is eligible, $D(W) \leq k - 1$ and $x \in W\}$.

---

To see that $S_{trust}$ can be much more efficient than any rational-safe algorithm including $S_{fore}$, consider a network with diameter less than $k$ and threshold $q > 1/d_{min}$ ($d_{min}$ is the minimum degree in $G$), e.g., a complete graph $G$ and $q = 1$. It is easy to see that if each node executes $S_{fore}$, no node changes to $B$. On the other hand, if each node executes $S_{trust}$, every node will find the entire graph as an eligible set and thus all nodes simultaneously upgrade to $B$ in round 1.

However, $S_{trust}$ is not optimal. To see why $S_{trust}$ is not optimal, we show that another protocol-safe algorithm $S_{trust}^{+}$ which is the union of $S_{trust}$ plus a special changing view $\Gamma^{*}(x)$ is more efficient than $S_{trust}$. Consider a 5-node chain of regular nodes, and assume $k = 3$ and $q = 0.1$. In this example, $S_{trust}$ cannot find any eligible set with diameter at most than 3, thus each regular node is stuck in $A$. On the other hand, if the extra changing view $\Gamma^{*}(x)$ is the 5-node chain of regular nodes, then the middle node can upgrade to $B$ in Round 1; and all other nodes will also upgrade in subsequent rounds. We now derive two optimal protocol-safe algorithms - one non-constructive and one constructive with an additional assumption.

**Non-constructive Optimal Protocol-Safe Algorithm:** We give an optimal protocol-safe algorithm $S^*$. To describe $S^*$, we introduce a class of algorithms $\mathcal{C}_{Pro}^+ = \{S | S \in \mathcal{C}_{Pro}$ and $S$ is AUG-COMPLETE$\}$ with all AUG-COMPLETE algorithms in $\mathcal{C}_{Pro}$. Using the definition of $\mathcal{C}_{Pro}^+$, we define $S^* := \bigcup_{S \in \mathcal{C}_{Pro}^+} S$. We show that $S^*$ is optimal within the class of protocol-safe algorithms.

**Theorem 5.** $S^* = OPT(\mathcal{C}_{Pro})$.

The proof is mainly based on three structural lemmas describing protocol-safe algorithms. The first one states that $\mathcal{C}_{Pro}^+$ is union-closed (Intriguingly, we later show that $\mathcal{C}_{Pro}$ itself is not union-closed).

**Lemma 2.** $\mathcal{C}_{Pro}^+$ is union closed.

Since $S^*$ is defined as a union of all algorithms in $\mathcal{C}_{Pro}^+$, from Lemma 2, we can infer that $S^* \in \mathcal{C}_{Pro}^+$. i.e., $S^*$ is protocol-safe and AUG-COMPLETE, and it is trivial to see that $S^*$ is the superset of any algorithm in $\mathcal{C}_{Pro}^+$. Since we want to show $S^*$ is optimal in $\mathcal{C}_{Pro}$, we need to build a connection between $\mathcal{C}_{Pro}$ and $\mathcal{C}_{Pro}^+$. In the following lemma, we find that for any protocol-safe algorithm $S$, $F^+(S) \in \mathcal{C}_{Pro}^+$.

**Lemma 3.** For any $S \in \mathcal{C}_{Pro}$, $F^+(S) \in \mathcal{C}_{Pro}^+$.

As $S^*$ is the superset of any algorithm in $\mathcal{C}_{Pro}^+$, from Lemma 3, we can get that for any protocol-safe algorithm $S$, $F^+(S)$ is a subset of $S^*$. For any algorithm $S$, it holds $S \subseteq F^+(S)$ (from the definition of $F^+(\cdot)$). We conclude in the next lemma that any protocol-safe algorithm $S$ is a subset of $S^*$. (Interestingly, the reverse does not hold, i.e., there exists $S \subseteq S^*$ such that $S \notin \mathcal{C}_{Pro}$. )

**Lemma 4.** If $S \in \mathcal{C}_{Pro}$, then $S \subseteq S^*$.

On the other hand, we know that $S^*$ is AUG-COMPLETE and every AUG-COMPLETE algorithm is INCREMENTAL (Theorem 2). That is, $S^*$ is more efficient than any subset of itself. We can infer that $S^*$ is optimal within the class of protocol-safe algorithms.

Finally, we show that the class of protocol-safe algorithms is not union-closed and subset-closed. It is different from the other three classes of the hierarchy.

**Theorem 6.** *The class of protocol-safe algorithms $\mathcal{C}_{Pro}$ is not union-closed and subset-closed.*

**Constructive Optimal Protocol-safe Algorithm:** Algorithm $S^*$ is optimal, but it is non-constructive and it is entirely unclear how to apply this algorithm in a real network setting. In this section, we give a constructive optimal algorithm $S_\Delta$. The algorithm is based on techniques similar to dynamic programming: we inductively construct a maximal AUG-COMPLETE set of changing views by enumeration in a systematic manner that additionally satisfy a so-called UNIFORM constraint. To do so, a node checks all possible views, according to the total number of nodes and the total number of regular nodes in each view in an increasing order, and adds the valid ones into $S_\Delta$'s changing view set. Ultimately, we can prove that $S_\Delta$ is optimal, but only under the assumption that $S^*$ satisfies the UNIFORM property. We conjecture that this is true, but we do not currently have a formal proof. Therefore, we only claim the weaker theorem that $S_\Delta$ is optimal among all UNIFORM AUG-COMPLETE protocol-safe algorithms.

## 4.5    Possible-Safe Algorithms

For the class of possible-safe algorithms, we show that $S_{hope}$ is optimal. The algorithm includes the finding of an eligible set $W$.

---

**Algorithm 4.** $S_{hope}$

$S_{hope} := \{\Gamma(x) | \exists W \subseteq V_{k-1}(x) \text{ such that } W \text{ is eligible and } x \in W\}.$

---

Again, we show that $S_{hope}$ can be much more efficient than an optimal protocol-safe algorithm $S^*$. Specifically, consider a network of 5 nodes, four of which form a square, and one node is in the middle linking to the other 4 nodes. Suppose $k = 2$ and $q = 1$. With $S^*$, no node will upgrade. With $S_{hope}$, the center node will can see all four neighbors and it knows that the set of all neighbors plus itself is eligible. Thus, the center node upgrades to $B$, which is more efficient albeit unstable, because the corner nodes do not know the topology of the opposite corner node and will remain in $A$.

An defining structural property of the class of possible-safe algorithms (and $S_{hope}$) is that each subset of $S_{hope}$ is a possible-safe algorithm and each possible-safe algorithm is a subset of $S_{hope}$.

**Lemma 5.** $S \subseteq S_{hope} \iff S \in \mathcal{C}_{Pos}$.

Thus, $S_{hope}$ plays the same central role for $\mathcal{C}_{Pos}$ as $S_{fore}$ played for $\mathcal{C}_{Rat}$. Indeed, the rest of the argument follows along the same lines. According to Lemma 5, we know that $S_{hope}$ is the possible-safe algorithm with the maximum set of views and it is the superset of each algorithm in $\mathcal{C}_{Pos}$. Therefore, we can infer that $\mathcal{C}_{Pos}$ is subset-closed and union-closed by definition. Furthermore, as $S_{hope}$ is AUG-COMPLETE, from Theorem 2, we can infer that $S_{hope}$ is more efficient than any of its subset. Therefore, we can conclude that $S_{hope}$ is optimal within the class of possible-safe algorithms.

**Theorem 7.** *The class of possible-safe algorithms $\mathcal{C}_{Pos}$ is subset-closed and union-closed. Furthermore, $S_{hope} = OPT(\mathcal{C}_{Pos})$.*

## 4.6    Putting Everything Together

Combining all the above results, we now show a strict order in terms of conversion ratio among all the optimal algorithms in the four classes of local decision algorithms. The optimal algorithm of a safer class is strictly less efficient than the optimal algorithm in the less safe class. That is, *the achievable safety guarantee of these algorithms precisely corresponds to their performance efficiency in terms of conversion ratio*: A beautiful finding. We construct a family of graphs in which the respectively safer optimal algorithm will have fewer nodes upgrade to $B$, than the respective less safe optimal algorithm.

**Theorem 8.** *It holds* $OPT(\mathcal{C}_{Pos}) \succ OPT(\mathcal{C}_{Pro}) \succ OPT(\mathcal{C}_{Rat}) \succ OPT(\mathcal{C}_{Byz})$, *for any* $k \geq 2, q > 0$.

*Proof.* We first show that the order of efficiency holds. As $\mathcal{C}_{Byz} \subseteq \mathcal{C}_{Rat} \subseteq \mathcal{C}_{Pro} \subseteq \mathcal{C}_{Pos}$ (Theorem 1), we can infer that $OPT(\mathcal{C}_{Pos}) \succeq OPT(\mathcal{C}_{Pro}) \succeq OPT(\mathcal{C}_{Rat}) \succeq OPT(\mathcal{C}_{Byz})$. We know that $S_{1-hop} = OPT(\mathcal{C}_{Byz})$, $S_{fore} = OPT(\mathcal{C}_{Rat})$, $S^* = OPT(\mathcal{C}_{Pro})$ and $S_{hope} = OPT(\mathcal{C}_{Pos})$. Thus, it holds $S_{hope} \succeq S^* \succeq S_{fore} \succeq S_{1-hop}$.

Next, we need to show that the strict order of efficiency holds for any $k \geq 2, q > 0$. In the following context, consider any $k \geq 2, q > 0$.

To show that $OPT(\mathcal{C}_{Rat}) \succ OPT(\mathcal{C}_{Byz})$, we show $S_{fore} \succ S_{1-hop}$. Consider a graph $G$ with 2 regular nodes connected. If each regular node executes $S_{1-hop}$, neither changes to state $B$. If each regular node executes $S_{fore}$, both change to state $B$. Therefore, $S_{fore} \succ S_{1-hop}$.

To show that $OPT(\mathcal{C}_{Pro}) \succ OPT(\mathcal{C}_{Rat})$, as $S^* \succ S_{trust}$, we only need to show that $S_{trust} \succ S_{fore}$. Consider a complete graph $G$ with $n$ regular nodes such that $(n-1) > 1/q$. If each regular node executes $S_{fore}$, no regular node changes to state $B$. If each regular node executes $S_{trust}$, each regular node changes to state $B$. Therefore, $S_{trust} \succ S_{fore}$.

To show that $OPT(\mathcal{C}_{Pos}) \succ OPT(\mathcal{C}_{Pro})$, we show that $S_{hope} \succ S^*$. As we do not know the explicit form of $S^*$, our idea is to construct a graph in which there is one regular node $x$ that can see all the nodes in the graph and only when all nodes change to state $B$, all regular nodes are stable in the equilibrium; then only $x$ changes to state $B$ by running $S_{hope}$ and other nodes will keep state $A$ since they cannot find an eligible set in their view. Moreover, if each regular node executes $S^*$, since every regular node should be stable in the equilibrium, we can infer that no regular node changes to $B$.

We build the construction step by step. Recall that we have shown in Section 4.5 an example in which $S_{hope}$ is more efficient than $S^*$ for $k = 2, q = 1$. Using a similar technique, we extend the case $k = 2, q = 1$ to the general case. In the following example, we show that for any $k \geq 2$ and $q = 1$, it holds that $S_{hope} \succ S^*$.

Suppose $q = 1$ and any $k \geq 2$. Construct graph $G = (V, E)$ as follows: Construct $2k + 2$ chains, where the $i$th chain ($i = 1, 2, ..., 2k + 2$) includes regular nodes $x_{1i}, x_{2i}, ..., x_{(k-1)i}$. In the $i$th chain, $x_{ji}$ links to $x_{(j+1)i}$ ($j = 1, 2, ..., k-2$). There is a regular node $x_{00}$ linking to $x_{11}, x_{12}, ..., x_{1(2k+2)}$. For each $i$ ($i = 1, 2, ..., 2k + 1$), $x_{(k-1)i}$ links to $x_{(k-1)(i+1)}$ and $x_{(k-1)(2k+2)}$ links to $x_{(k-1)1}$. See Figure 2. We call such $G$ a "cage".

In process $P_1$, suppose each regular node in $G$ executes $S^*$. As $S^*$ is protocol-safe, we can infer that each node is stable in the equilibrium. As $q = 1$, we can infer all nodes in the equilibrium in $P_1$ are in the same state, namely either all nodes are in state $A$ or all nodes are in state $B$. Otherwise, a node in state $B$ that has any neighbor in state $A$ is not stable. We then show by contradiction that in $P_1$, all nodes are in state $A$. Suppose all nodes are in state $B$. By symmetry, $x_{(k-1)1}, S_{(k-1)2}, ..., S_{(k-1)(2k+2)}$ should change to $B$ in the same round $T^*$. Thus we know that in $T^* - 1$, nodes $x_{(k-1)1}, S_{(k-1)2}, ..., S_{(k-1)(2k+2)}$

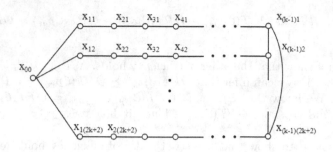

**Fig. 2.** The "Cage" Graph

are all in state $A$. Denote by $\Gamma^*(x_{(k-1)1})$ the view of $x_{(k-1)1}$ in $T^* - 1$. We can infer that $\Gamma^*(x_{(k-1)1}) \in S^*$. Consider another graph $G'$ that has the same topology and type as $G$ and the initial state of $G'$ is the same as $G$ in $T^* - 1$ except that $x_{(k-1)(k+2)}$ is a stubborn node. We still consider that each node in $G'$ executes $S^*$. As $x_{(k-1)1}$ cannot see the state or type of $x_{(k-1)(k+2)}$ (due to $k$-hop information restriction), we can infer that the initial view of $x_{(k-1)1}$ in $G'$ is the same as $\Gamma^*(x_{(k-1)1})$ which means $x_{(k-1)1}$ changes to state $B$ in round 1 in $G'$. Then in $G'$, we get that $x_{(k-1)1}$ is in state $B$ and $x_{(k-1)(k+2)}$ is a stubborn node. It is easy to see that at least one regular node in $\{x_{(k-1)1}, x_{(k-1)2}, ..., x_{(k-1)(k+1)}, x_{(k-1)(k+3)}, ..., x_{(k-1)(2k+2)}\}$ is not stable. This contradicts our assumption that $S^*$ is protocol-safe. Therefore, we know that in $P_1$ in which each regular node executes $S^*$, each regular node is in $A$.

In process $P_2$, suppose each regular node in $G$ executes $S_{hope}$. Denote by $S_0 = \{\text{each view}\}$. As $x_{00}$ knows the whole graph $G$, the entire set of nodes $V$ is an eligible set. Therefore, according to the definition of $S_{hope}$, $x_{00}$ changes to state $B$ in round 1. We can see that at least one node in $P_2$ changes to state $B$. Thus, $S_{hope}$ is more efficient than $S^*$.

Using the "cage" graph, we can extend the specific threshold $q$ to the general case. Suppose $q > 0$ and each node has $(k + 1)$-hop information $k \geq 1$. We construct a "cage" graph $G''$ like above and additionally link $c_{ij}$ stubborn nodes to $x_{ij}$ ($c_{ij}$ will be assigned in the following context). We can get the similar proof of the general case in $G''$ to that above in $G$ with $q = 1$ by achieving the following two rules: 1) only $x_{00}$ can see the whole graph (This can be done since $x_{00}$ in $G'$ has $(k + 1)$-hop information with which it can see all the stubborn nodes and each regular node can not see the whole graph.) and 2) all regular nodes are stable in the equilibrium if and only if all of them are in state $A$ or state $B$. In order to achieve the second rule, for a regular node $x_{ij}$ with $b_{ij}$ regular neighboring nodes, the following two equalities should hold, i) $b_{ij}/(b_{ij} + c_{ij}) \geq q$ and ii) $(b_{ij} - 1)/(b_{ij} + c_{ij}) < q$. Rearranging these equations, we can derive

$$b_{ij}\frac{1-q}{q} - \frac{1}{q} < c_{ij} \leq b_{ij}\frac{1-q}{q}.$$

Since $1/q > 1$, we know that there must be an integer in the range $(b_{ij}\frac{1-q}{q} - \frac{1}{q}, b_{ij}\frac{1-q}{q})$, and hence, $S_{hope}$ is more efficient than $S^*$ for any $k \geq 2, q > 0$.

Thus, we have shown $OPT(\mathcal{C}_{Pos}) \succ OPT(\mathcal{C}_{Pro}) \succ OPT(\mathcal{C}_{Rat}) \succ OPT(\mathcal{C}_{Byz})$.

Also, note again that $\mathcal{C}_{Pro}$ differs from $\mathcal{C}_{Rat}$ with regard to the union-closed and subset-closed property (Thm 6 vs Thm 4). The reason for this difference is that in a rational-safe algorithm, each node assumes every other node being rational, where such assumption is static since all the rational algorithms are known in advance. But in protocol-safe, it is no longer true. In contrast, for a protocol-safe algorithm, it cannot do the same because a node needs to recursively consider what its neighboring algorithm might do. The class of protocol-safe algorithm is in this sense "dynamic".

**Local vs Global Decision Algorithms.** All algorithms in this paper are *local* decision algorithms based on $k$-hop of multi-hop information. This means that all of these algorithms are non-optimal compared to a global optimal decision algorithm that has complete information of the network. Thus, even the most efficient of our local decision algorithms, $S_{hope}$ is not globally optimal. Indeed, a globally optimal algorithm can be regarded as $S_{hope}$ with $k$ being infinitely large. To see that $S_{hope}$ with $k$-hop information can be suboptimal, consider a ring network $G$ with $2k + 2$ regular nodes, and $q > 0.5$. With global view, all nodes should upgrade to $B$, rendering all nodes stable. However, if each node uses algorithm $S_{hope}$ with local view, no node upgrades to $B$.

## 5    Conclusion

In this paper, we have derived a hierarchy of local decision algorithms in a basic influence network setting with multi-hop information. Giving nodes multi-hop information renders the problem more complex since nodes now need to reason about other nodes' behaviors and views. We have shown that the classes of algorithms that achieve different safety properties are strictly separated from each other in terms of efficiency, thus capturing the underlying trade-off between safety-guarantee and ability to "take action". The hierarchy thus disentangles and categorizes the questions raised by the typical recursive distributed problems such as, "I will take action, if my neighbor takes action; and to determine whether he will take action, I need to know whether my neighbor thinks I take action, etc." It is intriguing that such complicated recursive multi-hop patterns give raise to a natural hierarchy of classes of local decision algorithms.

## References

1. Arthur, W.B., Lane, D.A.: Information contagion. Structural Change and Economic Dynamics 4(1), 81–104 (1993)
2. Chen, W., Wang, C., Wang, Y.: Scalable influence maximization for prevalent viral marketing in large-scale social networks. In: Proceedings of the 16th ACM SIGKDD International Conference on Knowledge Discovery and Data Mining, pp. 1029–1038. ACM (2010)

3. Frischknecht, S., Keller, B., Wattenhofer, R.: Convergence in (Social) influence networks. In: Afek, Y. (ed.) DISC 2013. LNCS, vol. 8205, pp. 433–446. Springer, Heidelberg (2013)
4. Gardner, M.: Mathematical games: The fantastic combinations of john conways new solitaire game life. Scientific American **223**(4), 120–123 (1970)
5. Goles, E., Olivos, J.: Periodic behaviour of generalized threshold functions. Discrete Mathematics **30**(2), 187–189 (1980)
6. Goles, E., Tchuente, M.: Iterative behaviour of generalized majority functions. Mathematical Social Sciences **4**(3), 197–204 (1983)
7. Granovetter, M.: Threshold models of collective behavior. American Journal of Sociology **83**(6), 1420 (1978)
8. Kempe, D., Kleinberg, J., Tardos, É.: Maximizing the spread of influence through a social network. In: Proceedings of the ninth ACM SIGKDD International Conference on Knowledge Discovery and Data Mining, pp. 137–146. ACM (2003)
9. Kempe, D., Kleinberg, J.M., Tardos, É.: Influential nodes in a diffusion model for social networks. In: Caires, L., Italiano, G.F., Monteiro, L., Palamidessi, C., Yung, M. (eds.) ICALP 2005. LNCS, vol. 3580, pp. 1127–1138. Springer, Heidelberg (2005)
10. Leskovec, J., Krause, A., Guestrin, C., Faloutsos, C., VanBriesen, J., Glance, N.: Cost-effective outbreak detection in networks. In: Proceedings of the 13th ACM SIGKDD International Conference on Knowledge Discovery and Data Mining, pp. 420–429. ACM (2007)
11. Macy, M.W.: Chains of cooperation: Threshold effects in collective action. American Sociological Review, pp. 730–747 (1991)
12. Macy, M.W., Willer, R.: From factors to actors: Computational sociology and agent-based modeling. Annual review of sociology, pp. 143–166 (2002)
13. Morris, S.: Contagion. The Review of Economic Studies **67**(1), 57–78 (2000)
14. Peleg, D.: Local majorities, coalitions and monopolies in graphs: a review. Theoretical Computer Science **282**(2), 231–257 (2002)
15. Poljak, S., Sra, M.: On periodical behaviour in societies with symmetric influences. Combinatorica **3**(1), 119–121 (1983)
16. Rogers Everett, M.: Diffusion of innovations. New York (1995)
17. Schelling, T.C.: Hockey helmets, concealed weapons, and daylight saving: A study of binary choices with externalities. Journal of Conflict Resolution, 381–428 (1973)
18. Schelling, T.C.: Micromotives and macrobehavior. WW Norton & Company (2006)
19. Valente, T.W.: Network models of the diffusion of innovations. Computational & Mathematical Organization Theory **2**(2), 163–164 (1996)
20. Wasserman, S.: Social network analysis: Methods and applications, vol. 8. Cambridge University Press (1994)
21. Winkler, P.: Puzzled delightful graph theory. Communications of the ACM **51**(8), 104–104 (2008)
22. Young, H.P.: Individual strategy and social structure: An evolutionary theory of institutions. Princeton University Press (2001)

# Amalgamated Lock-Elision

Yehuda Afek[1], Alexander Matveev[2][✉], Oscar R. Moll[2], and Nir Shavit[3]

[1] Tel-Aviv University, Tel-aviv, Israel
afek@post.tau.ac.il
[2] MIT, Cambridge, MA, USA
amatveev@csail.mit.edu, orm@mit.edu
[3] MIT and Tel-Aviv University, Tel-aviv, Israel
shanir@csail.mit.edu

**Abstract.** Hardware lock-elision (HLE) introduces concurrency into legacy lock-based code by optimistically executing critical sections in a *fast-path* as hardware transactions. Its main limitation is that in case of repeated aborts, it reverts to a *fallback-path* that acquires a serial lock. This fallback-path lacks hardware-software concurrency, because all fast-path hardware transactions abort and wait for the completion of the fallback. Software lock elision has no such limitation, but the overheads incurred are simply too high.

We propose *amalgamated lock-elision* (ALE), a novel lock-elision algorithm that provides hardware-software concurrency and efficiency: the fallback-path executes concurrently with fast-path hardware transactions, while the common-path fast-path reads incur no overheads and proceed without any instrumentation. The key idea in ALE is to use a sequence of fine-grained locks in the fallback-path to detect conflicts with the fast-path, and at the same time reduce the costs of these locks by executing the fallback-path as a series segments, where each segment is a dynamic length short hardware transaction.

We implemented ALE into GCC and tested the new system on Intel Haswell 16-way chip that provides hardware transactions. We benchmarked linked-lists, hash-tables and red-black trees, as well as converting KyotoCacheDB to use ALE in GCC, and all show that ALE significantly outperforms HLE.

**Keywords:** Multicore · Hardware lock elision · Hardware transactional memory · Algorithms

## 1 Introduction

Hardware lock-elision (HLE) [30] introduces concurrency into lock-based critical sections by executing these sections in a *fast-path* as hardware transactions. However, hardware transactions are *best-effort* in current Intel Haswell [31] and IBM Power8 [8] processors, which means that they have no progress guarantee: a hardware transaction may always fail due to a hardware-related reason such as an L1 cache capacity limitation, an unsupported instruction, or a page protection

© Springer-Verlag Berlin Heidelberg 2015
Y. Moses (Ed.): DISC 2015, LNCS 9363, pp. 309–324, 2015.
DOI: 10.1007/978-3-662-48653-5_21

or scheduler interrupt; in all such cases it may never commit [17]. Therefore, to ensure progress in HLE, a critical section that repeatedly fails to commit in the hardware fast-path, reverts to execute in a fallback-path that acquires the original serial lock. This fallback-path is expensive because it aborts all current fast-path hardware transactions and executes serially.

Recent work by Afek et al. [32] and Calciu et al. [24] introduced the *lock-removal* (or lazy subscription) lock elision scheme. Lock-removal sacrifices safety guarantees in favor of limited concurrency: the fast-path can execute concurrently with the fallback-path, however, the fast-path cannot commit as long as there is a fallback in process, and can observe inconsistent memory states. These inconsistent states can lead to executing illegal instructions or to memory corruption. It was claimed that HTM sandboxing significantly minimizes chances of unsafe executions, since any inconsistent hardware transaction should simply abort itself, and therefore, one can provide an efficient software-based compiler and the necessary runtime support to detect and handle the unsafe cases that "escape" the HTM sandboxing mechanism. Unfortunately, recent work by Dice et al. [12] shows that this is not the case: there are new cases of unsafe executions, ones not identified in the original lock-removal HLE papers, and require complex compiler and runtime support that would slow lock-removal HLE to a point that eliminates the advantages of using it in the first place. Instead, Dice et al. [12] propose new hardware extensions that can provide a fully safe HTM sandboxing capability.

Roy, Hand, and Harris [2] proposed an all software implementation of HLE in which transactions are executed speculatively in software, and when they fail, or if they cannot be executed due to system calls, the system defaults to the original lock. Their system instruments all object accesses, both memory reads and writes, and employs a special kernel-based thread signaling mechanism. This software based system provides better concurrency than HLE but introduces *software-software concurrency* that complicates the required compiler and runtime support and results in a slow scheme. As an example of a possible software concurrency complication, consider the execution shown in Figure 1(B), where thread P removes a node from a linked-list, and thread Q concurrently reads the removed node. In this case, thread P also modifies the removed node outside the critical section, which results in a divide by zero exception in thread Q. In the original code that uses a lock instead of atomic blocks (software transactions), this erroneous behavior is impossible. This problem is also known as privatization-safety [1, 2, 10, 25, 28]. Fixing this problem in software is expensive, and Attiya et al. [6] show that there is no way to avoid these costs. Afek, Matveev and Shavit [4] proposed PLE, an all-software version of HLE for read-write locks that uses a fully pessimistic STM, but still has software-software concurrency that results in using the expensive quiescence mechanism [10, 21, 22]. A recent paper by Dice et al. [13] proposes to integrate both hardware and software into an adaptive scheme, but has a software mode that has software-software concurrency as well, and proposes manual code modifications to avoid software costs.

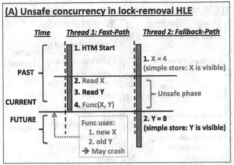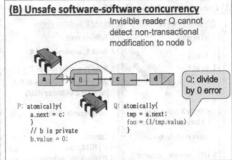

**Fig. 1.** (A) An example of unsafe hardware-software concurrency in lock-removal HLE. (B) An example of unsafe privatization due to software-software concurrency.

In this paper we propose *amalgamated lock-elision* (ALE), a novel lock-elision algorithm that provides both hardware-software concurrency and efficiency: the fallback-path executes concurrently with fast-path hardware transactions, while the common-path fast-path reads incur no overheads and proceed without any instrumentation. The problem is that instrumenting all reads and writes in hardware simply makes it as slow as the software path, so why use hardware in the first place. The key idea in ALE is to use a sequence of fine-grained locks in the fallback-path to detect conflicts with the fast-path, and at the same time, reduce the costs of these locks by executing the fallback-path as a series segments, where each segment is a dynamic length short hardware transaction. Also, ALE forbids software-software concurrency, so that there is no need for complex and expensive software support that it would otherwise require. Instead, the focus in ALE is on making hardware-software concurrency efficient.

The new ALE protocol combines several ideas. First, it uses a "mixed" fallback-path that uses both software and hardware, in the style of [26,27], to preserve full safety guarantees while the fallback-path executes concurrently with fast-path hardware transactions. To understand the problem in doing so, Figure 1(A) presents a simple unsafe scenario of lock-removal HLE [24,32], that may occur when the fallback-path of Thread 2 executes concurrently with a fast-path hardware transaction of Thread 1. As can be seen in the figure, first the fallback updates X, and then the hardware transaction reads both X and Y. But, since the fallback has not yet updated Y, the hardware transaction has read a new X and an old Y relative to the fallback. As a result, at this point in time, the hardware transaction executes on an inconsistent memory state and may perform random operations that may corrupt memory or even crash the system [12]. In ALE, the mixed fallback-path defers the writes to the commit, and executes all of the writes in a "one shot" short hardware transaction, so that intermediate states (some mix of old and new values) are never visible.

ALE combines the mixed fallback-path with fine-grained locks to provide concurrency between fast-path hardware transactions and the fallback-path. More specifically, a lock ownership array, in the style of [11,14,20,29], coordinates the

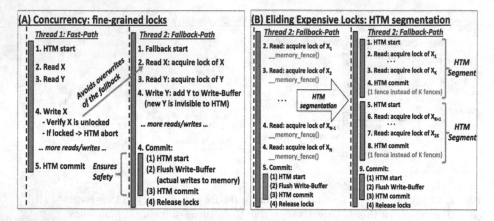

**Fig. 2.** (A) The mixed fallback-path of ALE uses fine-grained locks for conflict detection, and a write-buffer that defers actual writes to the commit, where all writes execute in a short "one-shot" hardware transaction. (B) The fallback-path executes as a series of segments, where each segment is a short hardware transaction that reduces the cost of lock barriers it includes to one barrier (the HTM commit).

reads of the fallback-path with the writes of the fast-path. Figure 2(A) depicts this coordination, where Thread 1 executes a fast-path hardware transaction and Thread 2 a fallback-path. On start, both read X and Y, and the fallback-path also locks the associated locks of X and Y. Then, the fast-path writes to X, but before actually committing it first verifies that X is unlocked. In this way, the fast-path cannot overwrite the fallback-path reads. In Figure 2(A), X is locked, so the fast-path of Thread 1 detects this conflict and aborts. However, if there were no real conflict, the fast-path would be able to commit concurrently.

Figure 2(A) also shows the use of a write-buffer in the fallback-path. The write-buffer is necessary to delay the actual writes to the commit-phase, where the ALE protocol will execute all of the writes as a "one shot" short hardware transaction. In the unlikely case this short hardware transaction fails, ALE acquires the critical section lock, that aborts all hardware transactions, and executes the writeback as is (in software). Notice that this aspect of ALE is similar to HLE, however, hardware transactions in ALE abort and block only for the short duration of the writeback and not for the whole fallback-path execution.

The downside of having a lock for each read of the fallback-path is the expensive memory barriers: a lock acquire must execute a memory barrier to become visible immediately, which forces the processor to drain the store buffer on each lock acquire, before proceeding to the next instruction. To overcome this overhead, ALE elides most of the memory barriers of lock acquires, by executing the fallback-path as a series of segments, where each segment executes as a short hardware transaction. A lock acquire that executes inside a hardware transaction does not need to become visible immediately, and therefore, does not require a memory barrier. As a result, multiple lock acquires that execute in a hardware segment, involve using only one barrier (instead of many) that executes as part of the hardware commit. Figure 2(B) depicts this idea: on the left, the fallback-path executes without segmentation, which involves executing a memory barrier for each read, while on the right, the hardware segmentation allows to reduce the number of barriers from the number of reads to the number of segments.

What if a hardware segment fails to commit? For this purpose, ALE implements a dynamic segmentation [5] policy that adjusts the length of each segment based on hardware aborts. In particular, the protocol counts the number of reads and writes that execute in the hardware segment, and when this count reaches a predefined limit, it commits the hardware segment and starts a new one. The predefined limit is dynamic: it gets reduced on excessive aborts, and gets increased on successive commits. In the extreme case, when a segment cannot commit (unsupported instruction or some interrupt), it reverts to execute in the standard software mode, where each read involves a memory barrier. It is important to notice that subsequent segments may still commit in the hardware, so the fallback is local for the specific segments that repeatedly fail.

We implemented ALE in GCC using the recent transactional memory support [3] and tested it on an Intel Haswell 16-way chip. We executed micro-benchmarks including linked-lists, hash-tables and red-black trees, which all show that ALE is significantly more performant than HLE due to the additional concurrency it provides. In addition, we tested ALE by converting KyotoCacheDB [18], a commercially used database management library, from read-write locks to the GCC based ALE. Our results are encouraging and show that the ALE implementation is two times faster than an HLE one.

## 2    Amalgamated Lock-Elision

### 2.1    Algorithm Overview

The key challenge in the design of ALE is efficiency: it is hard to provide (1) fallback-path that can execute concurrently with fast-path hardware transactions and preserve (2) full safety guarantees. This is why researchers propose to sacrifice safety [24,32] or introduce new hardware extensions [12]. In contrast, ALE provides these properties on commodity multicore architectures of Intel and IBM.

In a nutshell, the ALE protocol works as follows. The fallback mechanism of ALE is similar to HLE: a critical section first starts as a fast-path hardware transaction, and only when it fails multiple times to commit in the hardware, it reverts to execute in the fallback-path.

*Safe concurrency.* ALE mixes fine-grained locks and short hardware transactions in the fallback-path to detect all possible conflicts between fast-path hardware transactions and the fallback-path. First, the fallback-path locks each read location at encounter-time, while fast-path hardware transactions verify the locks of locations they want to write at commit-time. In this way, the fast-path writes detect fine-grained conflicts with the fallback-path reads. Second, the fallback-path writes are buffered and delayed to the commit-phase, where they execute in a "one shot" short hardware transaction. As a result, the hardware detects all conflicts involving fallback-path writes. Put together, both techniques ensure that all conflicts between fast-path hardware transactions and the fallback-path are detected, which allows safe concurrency between the two. Notice, that in the case when there is a conflict, the one that aborts is the fast-path and not the fallback-path. Finally, ALE executes fallbacks one at a time, so there are no possible fallback-to-fallback conflicts.

*Efficiency.* A lock acquire involves executing an expensive memory barrier, and therefore, a fallback-path that involves many reads, will result in many lock acquires that introduce an unacceptable performance penalty. To reduce locking costs, the fallback-path executes as a series of segments, where each segment executes as a short hardware transaction. All lock acquires that execute within a single hardware segment become visible atomically when the hardware segment commits, and therefore have no need to execute individual barriers. This allows multiple lock acquires to share the cost of a single barrier (of the hardware commit). Because hardware transactions may abort, ALE splits the fallback-path dynamically: it adapts each segment length to the specific abort behavior of the code, and falls back to execute the standard locking barriers of the segment, when the segment repeatedly fails to commit.

Naturally, the benefit of ALE depends on the success ratio of the short hardware transactions that execute in the fallback-path. In particular, a high success ratio of the fallback-path writeback is necessary to avoid excessive fast-path aborts. Our empirical results show that this is usually the case, because most operations follow the 80:20 rule (80% reads and 20% writes [23]). In general, other read-write distributions are possible, but we believe that our benchmarks that present a set of popular data-structures and a real-world application are encouraging. In addition, besides the writeback, the fallback-path segments may repeatedly fail to commit in hardware. For example, a segment will always fail when it will try to execute an unsupported instruction or encounter a page fault interrupt. In our experiments, most of the segments succeed to adapt to the specific code behaviors, and only in rare cases, segments must revert to software and execute one barrier per lock.

## 2.2 Algorithm Details

Algorithm 1 and Algorithm 2 present the pseudo-code for ALE fast-path and fallback-path: each critical section first tries to execute in the fast-path as a hardware transaction, and when it repeatedly fails to commit it reverts to execute in the fallback-path. The pseudo-code assumes an elision process for a critical section that is protected by a lock named section-lock, and presents a simplified version of the code that omits the code that handles nested locks and hardware segmentation (similar to [5]).

**Global Structures.** The ALE protocol is based on the following global structures:

- locks-array : An ownership array, in the style of [11,29], that uses a hash function to assign a 64bit lock for each memory location (all initially 0). In our implementation we allocate an array with $2^{19}$ locks and use a "striping" hash function that maps each consecutive $2^8$ bytes of memory to the same lock.
- fallback-lock : A 64bit lock that is also used as a counter by the fallback-path to lock locations. A zero value represents that there is no fallback executing (initially 0).
- acquire-counter/release-counter : 64bit counters that the fallback-paths use to execute one at a time (both initially 1).

In ALE all locks and counters only increase, except for the fallback-lock that alternates between 0 and ever increasing number. This is why ALE uses 64bit counters to avoid overflows.

---

**Algorithm 1.** ALE: fast-path

---

```
 1: function FAST_PATH_START(ctx)              14:     lock-id ← HASH(addr)
 2:     ctx.lock-id-log ← ∅                     15:     ctx.lock-id-log ∪ = {lock-id}
 3:     while HTM_START() = htm-failed do       16:     store(addr, v)           ▷ Direct write
              ▷ Outside HTM                     17:
 4:         ... some fast-path retry policy ... 18: function FAST_PATH_COMMIT(ctx)
 5:         if no retry then                    19:     if ctx.lock-id-log = ∅ then
 6:             ... switch to fallback-path ... 20:         HTM_COMMIT()              ▷ read-only
              ▷ Inside HTM                       21:         return
 7:     if section-lock ≠ 0 then                22:     if fallback-lock = 0 then
 8:         HTM_ABORT()                         23:         HTM_COMMIT()          ▷ no fallback
 9:                                             24:         return
10: function FAST_PATH_READ(ctx, addr)         25:     for id ∈ ctx.lock-id-log do
11:     return load(addr)        ▷ Direct read  26:         if lock-array[id] = fallback-lock then
12:                                             27:             HTM_ABORT()      ▷ conflict found
13: function FAST_PATH_WRITE(ctx, addr, v)     28:     HTM_COMMIT()              ▷ no conflicts
```

---

**Fast-Path.** Algorithm 1 presents the pseudo-code for the fast-path. On start, it resets a local lock-id-log to an empty set, and then initiates a hardware transaction (lines 2 - 3). Then, inside the hardware, it first puts the section-lock into hardware monitoring, by verifying that this lock is free (lines 7 - 8). This step provides the fallback-path with an ability to abort all hardware transactions (for the case when the fallback writeback short hardware transaction fails). Next, during the execution, the reads proceed directly without any instrumentation (line 11), while the lock ids of writes are logged to the lock-id-log (lines 14 - 15).

---

**Algorithm 2.** ALE: fallback-path

```
 1: function FALLBACK_START(ctx)
 2:    ctx.write-log ← ∅
 3:    ACQUIRE_FALLBACK_LOCK(ctx)
 4:    HTM_SEGMENT_START()

 5: function FALLBACK_READ(ctx, addr)
 6:    HTM_SEGMENT_CHECKPOINT()
 7:    if (addr, val) ∈ ctx.write-log then
 8:       return val
 9:    lock-id ← HASH(addr)
10:    lock-array[lock-id] ← fallback-lock
11:    if HTM_ACTIVE() then
12:       return load(addr)        ▷ Elide barrier
13:    else
14:       MEMORY_BARRIER()         ▷ no HTM
15:       return load(addr)

16: function FALLBACK_WRITE(ctx, addr, v)
17:    HTM_SEGMENT_CHECKPOINT()
18:    ctx.write-log ∪ = {addr, v}

19: function FALLBACK_COMMIT(ctx)
20:    HTM_SEGMENT_COMMIT()
21:    WRITE_BACK(ctx)
22:    RELEASE_ALL_LOCKS(ctx)
```

```
23: function WRITE_BACK(ctx)
24:    while HTM_START() = htm-failed do
25:       ... some write-back retry policy ...
26:       if no retry then
27:          section-lock ← 1      ▷ aborts HTM
28:          FLUSH(ctx.write-log)
29:          section-lock ← 0      ▷ resumes HTM
30:          return
31:    FLUSH(ctx.write-log)
32:    HTM_COMMIT()

33: function ACQUIRE_FALLBACK_LOCK(ctx)
34:    turn ← FETCH&ADD(acquire-counter)
35:    while release-counter ≠ turn do
36:       spin-wait           ▷ wait for my turn
37:    fallback-lock ← turn
38:    MEMORY_BARRIER()

39: function RELEASE_ALL_LOCKS(ctx)
40:    fallback-lock ← 0 ▷ releases all locks
41:    FETCH&ADD(release-counter)
```

---

On commit, if the fast-path transaction has been read-only or detects that there is no fallback (lines 19 - 24), then it can simply commit. Otherwise, the fast-path traverses each logged lock-id and verifies that it is free (lines 25 - 27). If some lock is not free, then there is a conflict with a fallback read, and the fast-path aborts, else the fast-path commits safely and concurrently.

**Fallback-Path.** Algorithm 2 presents the pseudo-code for the fallback-path. On start, it resets a local write-log to an empty set, and then acquires the fallback-lock (lines 2 - 3). Next, it initiates the process of hardware segmentation (line 4) that elides the expensive per lock barriers. During the execution, both read and write first execute the segmentation checkpoint function (lines 6 , 17), that controls the dynamic split of hardware segments (increments a local counter of reads/writes and splits the segment when it reaches a limit). Then, on write, it simply buffers the write into the write-log (line 18), and on read, it first checks if the read location is in the write-log (lines 7 - 8). If this is the case, then it returns the value from the write-log, else it proceeds to locking the location and reading its value from the memory (lines 9 - 15).

As can be seen in the read procedure, to lock a read location, the ALE writes the fallback-lock into the lock, and only executes the actual barrier of the lock if the current segment reverted to the software. Notice that only a single fallback can execute at a time, and therefore, the fallback-lock is actually specific to the fallback that currently executes. This allows a fast-path hardware transaction to identify that a lock in the locks-array is taken, by checking that the lock value equals to the current value of the fallback-lock. As a result, the fallback-path can release all locks at once, by a single write that resets the fallback-lock. The next fallback-path will use a subsequent value of the acquire-counter, and therefore, all previous locks will not be seen as taken (lines 34 - 41).

The segmentation process of ALE is dynamic: it adjusts the length of each segment based on hardware aborts it encounters. More specifically, it counts the number of reads and writes in each segment checkpoint call, and when this count reaches a predefined limit, then it initiates a split procedure: commits the current segment and starts a new one. On start, the predefined limit is set to a large value (100 shared accesses), and during the execution gets reduced by 1 on a hardware abort, and gets increased by 1 on 4 successive hardware commits. This simple algorithm could be tuned and made more adaptive.

The success ratio of segmentation also depends on the implementation of the write-set buffer lookup function. If the lookup traverses the whole buffer on each read, then potentially it may introduce excessive HTM capacity aborts into the segments. To avoid this negative effect, ALE implements the write-set buffer as a hash table with 64 buckets, and uses a bloom filter [7,11] to minimize lookups.

**HTM Retry Policy.** Our empirical evaluation shows that the HTM retry policy is performance critical (also shown in [16,32]). We implement a simple policy that we found to perform well. When a fast-path hardware transaction fails, ALE checks the abort code, and if the *IS_RETRY* flag is set, then it retries the fast-path. Else, it reverts to the fallback-path. The limit of retries is set to 10. The short hardware transaction of the fallback-path gets retried in a similar way, while the fallback-path hardware segments retry based on the adaptive segmentation [5].

## 3    Performance Evaluation

We benchmarked using an Intel Core i7-5960X Haswell processor with 8-cores and support for HyperThreading of two hardware threads per core. This chip provides support for hardware transactions that can fit into the capacity of the L1 cache. It is important to notice that the HyperThreading reduces the L1 cache capacity for HTM by a factor of 2, since it executes two hardware threads on the same core (same L1 cache). As a result, in some benchmarks there is a significant penalty above the limit of 8 threads, where the HyperThreading executes and generates an increased amount of HTM capacity aborts.

The operating system is a Debian OS 3.14 x86_64 with GCC 4.8. We added the new ALE scheme into GCC 4.8 that provides compiler and runtime support for instrumenting shared reads and writes and generated two execution paths (the fast-path and the fallback-path), as part of the GCC TM draft specification for C++ [3]. Our results show that the malloc/free library provided with the system is not scalable and imposes significant overheads and false aborts on the HTM mechanism. As a result, we used the scalable *tc-malloc* [19] memory allocator, which maintains local per thread pools.

We compared the following lock elision schemes:

1. *HLE:* This is the state-of-the-art hardware lock elision scheme of Rajwar et al. [30], in which we also implement the advanced fallback mechanism (as described in 2.2 and also noted in [16]). This scheme provides full safety guarantees, but has no concurrency between fast-path hardware transactions and the fallback-path. More specifically, a lock-based critical section starts in the fast-path as a hardware transaction, and then immediately verifies that the lock of this section is free. In this way, when the fast-path repeatedly fails to commit, it reverts to execute in serial mode, in which it acquires the section lock that triggers an abort of all fast-path hardware transactions.

2. *HLE-SCM:* This scheme combines HLE with software-assisted contention management [32]: it introduces an auxiliary lock to serialize fast-path hardware transactions that repeatedly abort due to conflicts. In this way, it reduces unnecessary hardware conflicts under high contention, and increases the success probability of the fast-path.

3. *Unsafe-LR:* The unsafe lock-removal (lazy subscription) lock elision scheme [24,32] that provides improved concurrency: the fallback-path can proceed concurrently with hardware transactions, however, hardware transactions cannot commit as long as there is a concurrent fallback. This improves over HLE, but unfortunately has no safety guarantees. As was shown in the work by Dice et al. [12], lock-removal may result in reading inconsistent memory states, executing illegal instructions, corrupting memory and more. However, we still provide results for lock-removal, as a reference that shows the potential of making this scheme work by providing the new hardware extensions proposed by Dice et al. [12].

4. *ALE:* Our new ALE scheme as described in Section 2 implemented into GCC.

## 3.1   Micro-benchmarks

We executed a set of micro-benchmarks on a red-black tree, hash-table and linked-list. The red-black tree is derived from the *java.util.TreeMap* implementation found in the Java 6.0 JDK. That implementation was written by Doug Lea and Josh Bloch. In turn, parts of the Java TreeMap were derived from Cormen et al. [9]. We implemented a standard linked-list, and use this list to implement a hash table, that is simply an array of lists. In addition, we introduce node padding to avoid false-sharing. We measured various padding lengths for small and large data-structure sizes, and found out that the overall best padding size is 16 longs (each long is 64bit).

All data-structures expose a key-value pair interface of *put*, *delete*, and *get* operations. If the key is not present in the data structure, put will put a new element describing the key-value pair. If the key is already present in the data structure, put will simply insert the value associated with the existing key. The get operation queries the value for a given key, returning an indication if the key was present in the data structure. Finally, delete removes a key from the data

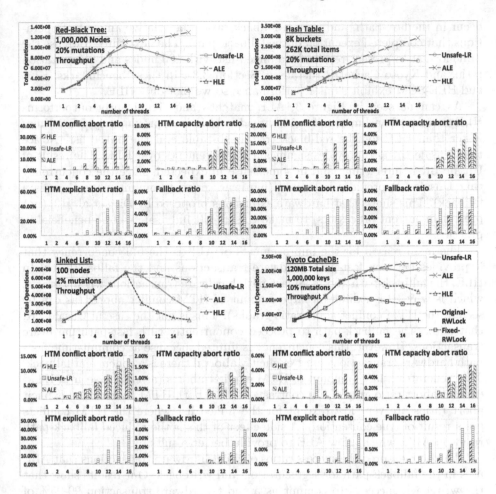

**Fig. 3.** Results for micro-benchmarks and Kyoto CacheDB

structure, returning an indication if the key was found to be present in the data structure.

Our benchmark first populates each data-structure to a predefined *initial-size*, and then executes put() and delete() with equal probability. For example, a *mutation ratio* of 10%, means that there is 5% put() and 5% delete(). We choose a random key for each operation from a *key-range* that is twice the size of the initial-size, so that mutations will actually mutate the data-structure. We report the average *throughput* of 3 runs, where each run executes for 10 seconds.

In top row of Figure 3, we present throughput results for a red-black tree with 1,000,000 nodes, and a hash-table with 262,144 nodes equally distributed over 8,192 buckets (approximately 32 nodes per bucket). We use a 20% mutation ratio for both data-structures. In the next two rows, we present an execution analysis, that reveals HTM (1) conflict, (2) capacity and (3) explicit abort ratios that occur in the fast-path, and the (4) fallback ratio, the relative amount of operations that completed execution in the fallback-path. The next three rows use the same format to present results for a linked-list with 100 nodes and 2% mutation ratio, and Kyoto CacheDB (details in Section 3.3). In these benchmarks, HLE and HLE-SCM exhibit similar performance so we plot only HLE.

As can be seen in Figure 3, ALE matches and significantly outperforms HLE in micro-benchmarks: for 16 threads, ALE is approximately 5.5-7 times faster than HLE for the red-black tree, hash-table and the linked-list. Notice that Unsafe-LR also provides significant improvements over HLE. The result of Unsafe-LR is interesting, and in some sense unexpected, since the concurrency that Unsafe-LR provides is limited (hardware cannot commit when there is a fallback). This shows that hardware extensions proposed by Dice et al. [12] (not present in current processors) to make Unsafe-LR fully safe will be beneficial in practice.

The main reason for the improvements of ALE is the full concurrency that it provides between fast-path hardware transactions and the fallback-path. In HLE, the fallback-path aborts all fast-path hardware transactions when it starts, which is why HLE exhibits a large amount of HTM conflict aborts (as can be seen in the HTM conflict abort ratio graphs). This is not the case in Unsafe-LR, that allows the fallback-path to proceed concurrently with fast-path hardware transactions. However, this concurrency is limited, because at commit-time fast-path hardware transactions must explicitly abort if there is a concurrent fallback. This generates a large amount of HTM explicit aborts (as can be seen in HTM explicit abort ratio graphs). In contrast, in ALE both HTM conflict and explicit abort ratios are very low (except for the linked list where the HTM conflicts are a result of true contention). A side-effect of this is the reduced fallback-path ratios in ALE, which allow ALE to provide better results.

We also measured the success ratios of short hardware transactions that ALE uses in the fallback-path for segmentation and writeback. Our results show that the writeback succeeds to commit as a short hardware transaction 90-95% of the time. Also, the segmentation process works best for segment limits in the range of 20-40 shared reads/writes (per segment), so it reduces the lock barrier overheads by at least an order of magnitude.

## 3.2    Various Red-Black Tree Sizes

Figure 4 shows speedups of HLE, HLE-SCM, Unsafe-LR and ALE for 8 and 16 threads (from left to right) for various sizes of red-black tree. The baseline in these executions is 1-thread HLE.

We can see that ALE and Unsafe-LR are significantly faster than HLE and HLE-SCM for 16 threads. However, for 8 threads, these differences become smaller since less operations revert to execute in the fallback-path. This means that in order to see the advantages of ALE over HLE there should be a sufficient amount of fallbacks.

Notice that HLE-SCM is only beneficial over the standard HLE for small 100 nodes red-black tree on 8 threads. HLE-SCM reduces conflicts by serializing

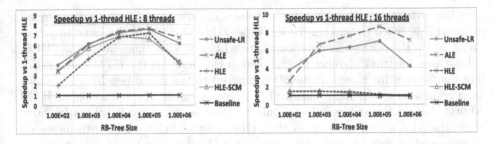

**Fig. 4.** Speedup results for 8 and 16 threads for various red-black tree sizes.

conflicting operations via an auxiliary lock, and since this case (of a small tree) is highly contended, it helps to reduce unnecessary conflicts and improve the overall performance.

### 3.3  KyotoCabinet

KyotoCabinet [18] is a suite of DBM data stores written in C++. In this benchmark, we focused on the in-memory component of the suite, called Kyoto CacheDB, that implements a bounded in-memory cache of key-value pairs where both the keys and values are opaque byte arrays. Internally, Kyoto CacheDB splits the database into slots, where each slot is a hash table of binary search trees. As a result, for each key, it first hashes the key into a slot, and then hashes again into a hash table of the slot. Next, it traverses the binary tree of the slot. The database ensures that the tree is bounded in size, by evicting entries that are least recently used (LRU policy). For synchronization, Kyoto CacheDB uses a single coarse-grained read-write lock to start a database operation, and a per slot mutex lock to access a specific slot.

We replaced all locks of Kyoto CacheDB with ALE. Since our implementation of ALE uses GCC TM, the transformation is automated by the GCC that generates the necessary code paths and instrumentations. Our first comparisons of ALE to the original Kyoto CacheDB showed that the original read-write lock is a performance bottleneck, which concurs with the results of [13]. We also found that Kyoto performs an excessive amount of explicit thread context switches due to the specific implementation of reader-writer spin locks in the Linux pthreads library. Therefore, we replaced the original read-write lock of Kyoto CacheDB with an ingress-egress reader-writer lock implementation [14] that has no explicit context-switches. To the best of our knowledge, the ingress-egress reader-writer locks perform the best on Intel machines (ingress/enter counter and egress/exit counter for read-lock/read-unlock) [4]. We note that one could use hierarchical cohort-based reader-writer locks [15] in our benchmark to reduce the inter-thread cache traffic in Kyoto. However, this would not have a significant effect since the performance analysis reveals that the cache miss ratio is already low (4%-5%).

The benchmark for Kyoto CacheDB works in a similar way to our microbenchmarks: it fills the database to a fixed initial size, and then executes gets/puts/deletes with random keys. Results are shown in Figure 3. We can see that ALE is twice faster than HLE. Notice, that this is not the same improvement like in the micro-benchmarks, where ALE was 5.5-7 times faster than HLE. The reason for this difference can be seen in the analysis: the HTM abort ratios are much lower for Kyoto CacheDB compared to the micro-benchmarks, which also results in low fallback ratios (1-2%). As a result, the reduction in HTM aborts that ALE provides is less dominant than in the micro-benchmarks, however, the ALE is still twice faster than HLE, and we believe that with increased concurrency it will become even more faster. Notice that Unsafe-LR is similar to ALE also due to low HTM aborts. However, in Unsafe-LR there is no safety guarantees and the program may crash, while ALE provides full safety.

## 4   Conclusion

We proposed *amalgamated lock-elision* (ALE), a new lock-elision scheme that provides concurrency between fast-path hardware transactions and the fallback-path, while preserving full safety guarantees. The key idea is to split the fallback-path into dynamic sections that fuse hardware and software with fine-grained locks in a way that provides efficiency. Our empirical results show that ALE is significantly faster than hardware lock elision (HLE) on both micro-benchmarks and a real use-case application, the Kyoto CacheDB. We believe that our results are encouraging, and show that hardware and software may be mixed in new and unexpected ways that were not originally intended by hardware and software designers.

**Acknowledgments.** We thank anonymous DISC referees for helpful and practical suggestions. This helped us to improve the paper and speed-up the algorithm. This work was supported by Israel Science Foundation under grant number 1386/11, National Science Foundation under grants CCF-1217921, CCF-1301926, and IIS-1447786, the Department of Energy under grant ER26116/DE-SC0008923, and the Intel Science and Technology Center in Big Data, Oracle and Intel corporations.

## References

1. Dice, D., Matveev, A., Shavit, N.: Implicit privatization using private transactions. In: Transact 2010, Paris, France (2010)
2. Harris, T., Roy, A., Hand, S.: A runtime system for software lock elision. In: Proceedings of the 4th ACM European conference on Computer systems, EuroSys 2009, pp. 261–274. ACM, New York (2009)
3. Adl-Tabatabai, A.-R., Shpeisman, T., Gottschlich, J.: Draft specification of transactional language constructs for c++ (2012)
4. Afek, Y., Matveev, A., Shavit, N.: Pessimistic software lock-elision. In: Aguilera, M.K. (ed.) DISC 2012. LNCS, vol. 7611, pp. 297–311. Springer, Heidelberg (2012)
5. Alistarh, D., Eugster, P., Herlihy, M., Matveev, A., Shavit, N.: Stacktrack: an automated transactional approach to concurrent memory reclamation. In: Proceedings of the Ninth European Conference on Computer Systems, EuroSys 2014, pp. 25:1–25:14. ACM, New York (2014)

6. Attiya, H., Hillel, E.: The cost of privatization. In: Lynch, N.A., Shvartsman, A.A. (eds.) DISC 2010. LNCS, vol. 6343, pp. 35–49. Springer, Heidelberg (2010)
7. Bloom, B.H.: Space/time trade-offs in hash coding with allowable errors. Commun. ACM **13**(7), 422–426 (1970)
8. Cain, H.W., Michael, M.M., Frey, B., May, C., Williams, D., Le, H.: Robust architectural support for transactional memory in the power architecture. SIGARCH Comput. Archit. News **41**(3), 225–236 (2013)
9. Cormen, T., Leiserson, C., Rivest, R., Stein, C.: Introduction to Algorithms, 2nd edn. MIT Press, Cambridge (2001)
10. Desnoyers, M., Stern, A., McKenney, P., Walpole, J.: User-level implementations of read-copy update. In: IEEE Transactions on Parallel and Distributed Systems (2009)
11. Dice, D., Shalev, O., Shavit, N.N.: Transactional locking II. In: Dolev, S. (ed.) DISC 2006. LNCS, vol. 4167, pp. 194–208. Springer, Heidelberg (2006)
12. Dice, D., Harris, T.L., Kogan, A., Lev, Y., Moir, M.: Hardware extensions to make lazy subscription safe. CoRR, abs/1407.6968 (2014)
13. Dice, D., Kogan, A., Lev, Y., Merrifield, T., Moir, M.: Adaptive integration of hardware and software lock elision techniques. In: Proceedings of the 26th ACM Symposium on Parallelism in Algorithms and Architectures, SPAA 2014, pp. 188–197. ACM, New York (2014)
14. Dice, D., Shavit, N.: Tlrw: return of the read-write lock. In Proceedings of the Twenty-second Annual ACM Symposium on Parallelism in Algorithms and Architectures, SPAA 2010, pp. 284–293. ACM (2010)
15. Dice, D., Marathe, V.J., Shavit, N.: Lock cohorting: A general technique for designing numa locks. ACM Trans. Parallel Comput. **1**(2), 1–42 (2015)
16. Diegues, N., Romano, P.: Self-tuning intel transactional synchronization extensions. In: 11th International Conference on Autonomic Computing (ICAC 2014), pp. 209–219. USENIX Association, Philadelphia, June 2014
17. Diegues, N., Romano, P., Rodrigues, L.: Virtues and limitations of commodity hardware transactional memory. In: Proceedings of the 23rd International Conference on Parallel Architectures and Compilation, PACT 2014, pp. 3–14, ACM, New York (2014)
18. FAL Labs. Kyoto cabinet: A straightforward implementation of dbm (2011)
19. Google (2014). https://sites.google.com/site/tmforcplusplus
20. Harris, T., Fraser, K.: Language support for lightweight transactions. In: Proceedings of the 18th ACM SIGPLAN conference on Object-oriented programing, systems, languages, and applications, pp. 388–402. ACM Press (2003)
21. Harris, T., Fraser, K.: Concurrent programming without locks
22. Hart, T.E., McKenney, P.E., Brown, A.D., Walpole, J.: Performance of memory reclamation for lockless synchronization. J. Parallel Distrib. Comput. **67**(12), 1270–1285 (2007)
23. Herlihy, M., Shavit, N.: The art of multiprocessor programming. Morgan Kaufmann (2008)
24. Irina, C., Tatiana, S., Gilles, P., Maurice, H.: Improved single global lock fallback for best-effort hardware transactional memory. In: Transact 2014 Workshop (2014)
25. Marathe, V., Spear, M., Scott, M.: Scalable techniques for transparent privatization in software transactional memory. In: International Conference on Parallel Processing, pp. 67–74 (2008)
26. Matveev, A., Shavit, N.: Reduced hardware transactions: a new approach to hybrid transactional memory. In: SPAA, pp. 11–22 (2013)

27. Matveev, A., Shavit, N.: Reduced hardware norec: a safe and scalable hybrid transactional memory. In: 20th International Conference on Architectural Support for Programming Languages and Operating Systems, ASPLOS 2015, Istanbul, Turkey. ACM (2015)
28. Menon, V., Balensiefer, S., Shpeisman, T., Adl-Tabatabai, A.-R., Hudson, R.L., Saha, B., Welc, A.: Single global lock semantics in a weakly atomic STM. In: Transact 2008 Workshop (2008)
29. Fetzer, C., Felber, P., Riegel, T.: Dynamic performance tuning of word-based software transactional memory. In: Proceedings of the 13th ACM SIGPLAN Symposium on Principles and practice of parallel programming, PPoPP 2008, pp. 237–246. ACM, New York (2008)
30. Rajwar, R., Goodman, J.: Speculative lock elision: enabling highly concurrent multithreaded execution. In: MICRO, pp. 294–305. ACM/IEEE (2001)
31. Web. Intel tsx (2012). http://software.intel.com/en-us/blogs/2012/02/07/transactional-synchronization-in-haswell
32. Yehuda, A., Amir, L., Adam, M.: Software-improved hardware lock elision. In: PODC 2014, Paris, France. ACM Press (2014)

# Transactional Interference-Less Balanced Tree

Ahmed Hassan, Roberto Palmieri[✉], and Binoy Ravindran

Virginia Tech, Blacksburg, VA, USA
robertop@vt.edu

**Abstract.** In this paper, we present *TxCF-Tree*, a balanced tree whose design is optimized to support transactional accesses. The core optimizations of TxCF-Tree's operations are: providing a traversal phase that does not use any lock and/or speculation, and deferring the lock acquisition or physical modification to the transaction's commit phase; isolating the structural operations (such as re-balancing) in an interference-less housekeeping thread; and minimizing the interference between structural operations and the critical path of semantic operations (i.e., additions and removals on the tree). We evaluated TxCF-Tree against the state-of-the-art general methodologies for designing transactional trees and we show that TxCF-Tree's design pays off in most of workloads.

**Keywords:** Balanced trees · Transactional memory · Semantic synchronization · Concurrent data structures

## 1 Introduction

With the growing adoption of multi-core processors, the design of efficient data structures that allow concurrent accesses without sacrificing performance and scalability becomes more critical than before. In the last decade, different designs of the concurrent version of well-known data structures (e.g., lists, queues, hash tables) have been proposed [20]. Balanced binary search trees, such as AVL and Red-Black trees are data structures whose self-balancing guarantees an appealing logarithmic-time complexity for their operations.

One of the main issues in balanced trees is the need for *rotations*, which are complex housekeeping operations that re-balance the data structure to ensure its logarithmic-time complexity. Although rotations complicate the design of concurrent balanced trees, many solutions have already been proposed: some of them are lock-based [2,3,5,8,9,12], while others are non-blocking [7,13,21,23].

One of the main limitations of concurrent data structures is that they do not compose. For example, atomically inserting two elements in a tree is difficult: if the method internally uses locks, issues like managing the dependency between operations executed in the same transaction, and the deadlock that may occur because of the chain of lock acquisitions, may arise. Similarly, composing non-blocking operations is challenging because of the need to atomically modify different places in the tree using only basic primitives, such as a CAS operation. Lack of composability is a serious limitation of the current designs, especially for

© Springer-Verlag Berlin Heidelberg 2015
Y. Moses (Ed.): DISC 2015, LNCS 9363, pp. 325–340, 2015.
DOI: 10.1007/978-3-662-48653-5_22

legacy systems, as it makes their integration with third-party software difficult. In this paper we focus on composable (transactional) balanced trees.

Although the research has reached an advanced point in designing concurrent trees, transactional trees have not reached this point yet. There are two practical approaches, to the best of our knowledge, that enable transactional accesses on a tree: *1)* The first approach is Transactional Memory (TM) [19] which natively allows composability as it speculates every memory access inside an *atomic* block; *2)* The second approach is Transactional Boosting [18] (TB), which protects the transactional access to a concurrent data structure with a set of *semantic* locks, eagerly acquired before executing the operation on the concurrent data structure. Both TM and TB have serious limitations when used for designing transactional trees. Those limitations originate from the same reason: they are both generic, and they do not consider the specific characteristics of balanced trees, which instead are heavily investigated in literature. For example, TM considers every step in the operation, including the rotations, as low-level memory reads/writes, which clearly increases the number of false conflicts. On the other hand, TB uses the underlying concurrent tree as a black-box, which prevents any further customization, and may nullify the internal optimizations of the concurrent tree due to the eagerly acquired semantic locks.

Recently, a third trend, which we name *Optimistic Semantic Synchronization* (OSS), has emerged to overcome the limitations of the above approaches. Examples of this new approach include methodologies like [1,4,6,15,16,25]. We used the word *optimistic* because all of these solutions share a fundamental optimism. In fact, the common idea behind the aforementioned methodologies is to split data structures' operations into a *traversal* phase and a *commit* phase. A transaction *optimistically* executes the traversal phase without any locking and/or speculation, and it defers the commit phase to the commit time of the enclosing transaction. Unlike TM and TB, OSS only provides guidelines to design transactional data structures, and it leaves all the development details to the data structure designer, thus enabling the possibility of adding further (data structure-specific) optimizations.

OSS is clearly less programmable than TM and TB, but it has the potential to provide better performance and scalability, especially when applied to complex data structures, like the case of balanced trees. Due to their high abstraction level, none of the methodologies listed above discusses in detail how they can be applied to balanced trees without nullifying the body of work related to highly optimized concurrent (non-transactional) balanced trees.

Inspired by OSS, in this paper we present TxCF-Tree, the first balanced tree that is accessible in a *transactional*, rather than just a *concurrent*, manner without monitoring (speculating) the whole traversal path (like in TM) or nullifying the benefits of the efficient concurrent designs (like in TB). TxCF-Tree offers a set of design and low-level innovations, but roughly it can be seen as the transactional version of the recently introduced *Contention Friendly Tree* (CF-Tree) [9]. The main idea of CF-Tree is to decouple the *structural operations* (e.g. rotations and physical deletions) from the *semantic operations* (e.g. queries, logical removals, and insertions), and to execute those structural operations in a dedicated *helper* thread. This separation makes the semantic operations (that need to be transactional in TxCF-Tree) simple: each operation traverses the tree non-speculatively (i.e., without instrumenting any accessed memory location); then, if it is a write operation, it locks and modifies only one node. In an abstract way, the TxCF-Tree's semantic operations can be seen as composed of a *traversal* and *commit* phases, which makes CF-Tree a good candidate for being transactionally boosted using OSS.

In addition to the new transactional capabilities, TxCF-Tree claims one major innovation with respect to CF-Tree, which is fundamental for targeting high performance in a transactional (not only concurrent) data structure. Although CF-Tree decouples the structural operations, those operations are executed in the *helper* thread with the same priority as the semantic operations, and without any control on their interference. With TxCF-Tree, we make the structural operations *interference-less* (when possible) with respect to semantic operations. This property is highly desirable because structural operations do not alter the abstract (or semantic) state of the tree, thus they should not force any transaction to abort. To reduce this interference, one operation should behave differently if it conflicts with a structural operation rather than with a semantic operation.

TxCF-Tree uses two new terms, which help to identify those *false-interleaving* cases and alleviate their effect: *structural lock*, which is a type of lock acquired if the needed modifications on the node do not change its abstract (semantic) state; and *structural invalidation*, which is a transactional invalidation raised only because of a structural modification on the tree rather than having actual conflicts at the abstract level. In TxCF-Tree, transactions do not abort if they face structural locks or false-invalidations during the execution of their operations. We further reduce the interference of the *helper* thread by adopting a simple heuristic to detect if the tree is *almost balanced*. If so, we increase the back-off time between two *helper* thread's iterations.

We assessed the effectiveness of TxCF-Tree[1] through an evaluation study. Our experiments show that TxCF-Tree performs better than the other transactional approaches (TB and STM) in almost all of the cases.

## 2   Background

**Optimistic Semantic Synchronization.** We use the term *Optimistic Semantic Synchronization* (OSS) to represent a set of recent methodologies that leverage the idea of dividing the transaction execution into phases and optimistically executing some of them without any instrumentation (also called *unmonitored* phases). In this section, we overview some of those approaches.

Optimistic Transactional Boosting (OTB) methodology [15, 16] is the optimistic version of TB. It lists three guidelines to convert any optimistic concurrent data structure into a transactional one. According to OTB's first guideline,

---

[1] The implementation of TxCF-Tree is available at www.hyflow.org.

every data structure's operation is split into three phases: *traversal*, which is executed without any instrumentation and/or locking until reaching the position of interest in the data structure; *validation*, which checks the validity of the unmonitored traversal's outcome; and *commit*, which acquires the necessary locks and performs the actual modifications. OTB provides transactional capabilities by *i)* saving the outcome of the *traversal* phase into local *semantic* read/write-sets to be used during the *validation* and *commit* phases; and *ii)* deferring operation's commit phase until the commit of the whole transaction. The unmonitored traversal phase is the actual source of OTB's performance gains as it clearly reduces false conflicts. The second guideline of OTB discusses the necessary and sufficient steps to make this transactional version *semantically opaque* [14], which means that if the data structure is only accessed using its defined APIs, then all of its operations are semantically consistent at any time of the transaction execution, even though opacity may not be ensured at the memory level (e.g., due to the unmonitored traversal phase). The third guideline of OTB is to optimize the data structure internally.

Consistency Oblivious Programming (COP) [1,4] splits the operations into the same three phases as OTB (but under different names). We observe two main differences between COP and OTB. First, COP is introduced mainly to design concurrent data structures and it does not natively provide composability unless changes are made at the hardware level [4]. Second, COP does not use locks at commit. Instead, it enforces atomicity and isolation by executing both the *validation* and *commit* phases using TM transactions.

Partitioned Transactions (ParT) [25] also uses the same trend of splitting the operations into a *traversal* (called *planning*) phase and a *commit* (called *update*) phase, but it gives more general guidelines than OTB. Specifically, ParT does not restrict the planning phase to be a traversal of a data structure and it allows this phase to be any generic block of code. Also, ParT does not obligate the planning phase to be necessarily unmonitored, as in OTB and COP. Instead, it allows both the planning and update phases to be transactions.

Transactional Predication (TP) [6] applies a similar methodology to the aforementioned approaches. However, it solves the specific problem of boosting concurrent sets and maps to be transactional.

Although TxCF-Tree complies with OSS, it is closer to OTB because it uses a well-defined concurrent tree as a base for its design (which fits the terminology of transactional boosting), and it follows the second guideline of OTB to guarantee that the transaction execution is *semantically opaque*.

**Contention Friendly Tree.** Contention Friendly Tree (CF-Tree) [9] is an efficient concurrent lock-based (internal) tree, which finds its main innovation on decoupling the semantic operations (i.e., search, logical deletion, and insertion) from the structural operations (i.e., rotation and physical deletion). The semantic operations are eagerly executed in the original process, whereas the structural operations are deferred to a helper thread. More in details:

*Semantic Operations:* each semantic operation starts by traversing the tree until it reaches a node that matches the requested key or it reaches a leaf node (indicating that the searched node does not exist). After that, a search operation returns immediately with the appropriate result without any locking. For a deletion, if the node exists and it is not marked as deleted, the node is locked and then the *deleted* flag is set (only a logical deletion), otherwise the operation returns false. For a successful insertion, the *deleted* flag is cleared (if the node already exists but marked as *deleted*) or a new node is created and linked to the leaf node (if the node does not exist). An unsuccessful insertion simply returns false. In all cases, each operation locks at most one node.

*Rotations:* re-balancing operations are isolated in a *helper* thread that scans the tree seeking for any node that needs either a rotation or a physical removal. Rotation in this case is relaxed, namely it uses local heights. Although other threads may concurrently modify these heights (resulting in a temporarily unbalanced tree), past work has shown that a sequence of localized operations on the tree eventually results in a strictly balanced tree [5,22]. A rotation locks: the node to be rotated down; its parent node; and its left or right child (depending on the type of rotation). Also, rotations are designed so that any concurrent semantic operation can traverse the tree without any locking and/or instrumentation. To achieve that, the rotated-down node is cloned and the cloned node is linked to the tree instead of the original node.

*Physical Deletion:* The physical deletion is also decoupled and executed separately in the *helper* thread. In addition, a node's deletion is relaxed by leaving a "routing" node in the tree when the deleted node has two children (it is known that deleting a node with two children requires modifying nodes that are far away from each other, which complicates the operation). The physical deletion is done as follows: both the deleted node and its parent are locked, then the node's left and right children links are modified to be pointing at its parent, and finally the node is marked as *physically removed*. This way, concurrent semantic operations can traverse the tree non-speculatively without being lost.

Among the concurrent trees presented in literature, we select CF-Tree as a candidate to be transactionally boosted because it provides the following two properties that fit the OSS principles. First, it uses a lock-based technique for synchronizing the operations, which simplifies the applicability of the OSS methodology. Second, CF-Tree is traversed without any locking and/or speculation, allowing the separation of an unmonitored traversal phase. Also, the semantic operations (`add`, `remove`, and `contains`) are decoupled from the complex structural operations (although they can interfere with each other), like rotations and physical removals, allowing a simple commit phase.

## 3 Reducing the Interference of Structural Operations

Balanced trees store data according to a specific balanced topology so that their operations can take advantage of the efficient logarithmic-time complexity. More specifically, operations are split into two parts: a "semantic" part, which modifies the abstract state of the tree, and a structural part, which maintains the efficient organization of the tree. For example, consider the balanced tree in Figure $1^2$. The tree initially represents the abstract set $\{1, 2\}$ (Figure 1(a)). If we want to insert 3, we first create a new node and link it to the tree in the proper place (Figure 1(b)). Subsequently, the tree is re-balanced because this insertion unbalanced a part of it (Figure 1(c)). Semantically, we can observe the new abstract set, $\{1, 2, 3\}$, right after the first step and before the re-balancing step. However, without the re-balancing step, the tree structure itself may become eventually skewed, and any traversal operation on the tree would take linear time rather than logarithmic time.

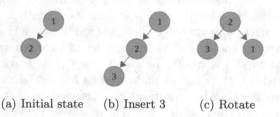

(a) Initial state    (b) Insert 3    (c) Rotate

**Fig. 1.** An insertion followed by a right rotation in a balanced tree.

Although the structural operations are important, like the aforementioned rotations in our case, they represent the main source of conflicts when concurrent accesses on the tree occur. Two independent operations (like inserting two nodes in two different parts of the tree) may conflict only because one of them needs to re-balance the tree. This additional conflict generated by structural operations can significantly slow down the performance of transactional data structures more than their concurrent versions due to two reasons. First, in long transactions, the time period between the tree traversal and the actual modification during commit may be long enough to generate more conflicts because of the concurrent re-balancing. Second, in transactional data structures, any conflict can result in the abort and re-execution of the whole transaction, which possibly includes several non-conflicting operations, unlike concurrent operations that just re-traverse the tree if a conflict occurs.

Although CF-Tree decouples the structural operations in a dedicated *helper* thread, which forms an important step towards shortening the critical path of the processing (i.e., the semantic operations), it does not prevent the structural operations running in the *helper* thread from interfering with the semantic operations and delaying/aborting them. To minimize such a interference, we propose the following simple guideline (named *G-Pr*):

"*Semantic operations should have higher priority than structural operations.*"

This guideline allows semantic operations to proceed if a conflict with structural modifications occurs. Our rationale is that, delaying (or aborting) semantic operations affects the performance, whereas delaying (or aborting) structural operations only defers the step of optimizing the tree to the near future.

---

$^2$ We assume that higher keys are in the left sub-tree to match CF-Tree's design.

# 4    TxCF-Tree

In this section, we discuss how to boost CF-Tree to be transactional using the OSS principles. The key additions of TxCF-Tree over CF-Tree are: *i)* supporting transactional accesses; and *ii)* minimizing the interference between semantic and structural operations. to simplify the presentation, we focus on the changes made on CF-Tree to achieve those two goals, and we briefly mention the unchanged parts whose details can be found in [9].

Each node in TxCF-Tree contains the same fields as CF-Tree: a key (with no duplication allowed), two pointers to its left and right children, a boolean *deleted* flag to indicate the logical state of the node, and an integer *removed* flag to indicate the physical state of the node (a value from the following: NOT-REMOVED, REMOVED, or REMOVED-BY-LEFT-ROTATION). The node structure in TxCF-Tree is only different in the locking fields. In CF-Tree, each node contains only one lock that is acquired by any operation modifying the node. In TxCF-Tree, each node has two different locks: a *semantic-lock*, which is acquired by the operations that modify its semantic state (either the *deleted* or the *removed* flag); and a *structural-lock*, which is a acquired by the operations that modify the structure of the tree without affecting the node itself (i.e. modifying the right or left pointers). Each lock is associated with a *lock-holder* field that saves the ID of the thread that currently holds the lock, which is important to avoid deadlocks.

TxCF-Tree implements a *set* interface with the semantic operations: add, remove, and contains. Extending TxCF-Tree to have key-value pairs is simple, but for clarity we assume that the value of the node is the same as its key.

## 4.1    Structural Operations

The *helper* thread repeatedly calls a recursive depth-first procedure to traverse the entire tree. During this procedure, any unbalanced node is rotated and any logically removed node is physically unlinked from the tree. To minimize the interference of this *housekeeping* procedure, we use an adaptive back-off delay after each traversal iteration. We use a simple hill-climbing mechanism that increases (decreases) the back-off time if the number of housekeeping operations in the current iteration is less (greater) than the most recent iteration. While acknowledging the simplicity of the adopted heuristic, it showed effectiveness in our evaluation study.

**Physical Deletions.** We start by summarizing how the *helper* thread in CF-Tree physically deletes a node $N_n$ ( marked as *deleted* and at least one of its children is null). First, both $N_n$ and its parent $N_p$ are locked. Then, the node's left and right children fields are modified to point back to the parent (so that the concurrent operations currently visiting $N_n$ can still traverse the tree, without experiencing any interruption) and then $N_n$ is marked as REMOVED and unlinked by changing $N_p$ child to be $N_n$'s child instead of $N_n$.

TxCF-Tree modifies this mechanism by providing *less-interfering* locking. Specifically, we only acquire the *structural-lock* of $N_p$ because its semantic state will not change. On the other hand, both the *semantic-lock* and the *structural-lock* have to be acquired on $N_n$ because $N_n$'s *removed* flag, which is part of its semantic state, should be set as REMOVED. To further minimize the interference, the locking mechanism uses only one CAS trial. If it fails, then the whole structural operation is aborted and the *helper* thread resumes scanning the tree.

**Rotations.** In CF-Tree, a right rotation (without losing generality) locks three nodes: the parent node $N_p$, the node to be rotated down $N_n$, and its left child $N_l$. Then, rotation is done by cloning $N_n$ and linking the cloned node at the tree instead of $N_n$ (similar to physical deletion, this cloning protects operations whose "unmonitored" traversal phase is concurrently visiting the same nodes. More details are in [9]). Subsequently $N_n$ is marked as REMOVED (in case of left-rotation it is marked as REMOVED-BY-LEFT-ROTATION) and nodes are unlocked.

In TxCF-Tree, rotations also use a less intrusive locking mechanism. Both $N_p$ and $N_l$ acquire only the *structural-lock* because the rotated-down node $N_n$ is the only node that will change its semantic state (and thus needs to acquire the *semantic-lock*). Also, we found that there is no need to lock the parent node (i.e., $N_p$) at all. This is because the only change to $N_p$ is to make its left (or right) child pointing to $N_l$ rather than $N_n$. This means that $N_p$'s child remains not null before and after the rotation. Only the *helper* thread can change it to null in a later operation by rotating the node down or physically deleting its children. On the other hand, semantic operations only concern about reading/changing the *deleted* flag of a node, if the searched node exists in the tree, or reading/changing a (null) link of a node, if the searched node does not exist in the tree. Thus, modifying the child link of $N_p$ cannot conflict with any concurrent semantic operation, thus it is safe to make this modification without locking. Similarly, if all the sub-trees of $N_n$ and $N_l$ are not null, then no structural locks are acquired, and the only lock acquired is the *semantic-lock* on $N_n$.

## 4.2  Semantic Operations

According to OSS, each operation is divided into the *traversal, validation*, and *commit* phases. We follow this division in our presentation.

**Traversal.** The tree is traversed by following the classical rules of the sequential binary search tree. Traversal ends if we reach the searched node or a null pointer. To be able to execute the operation transactionally, the outcome of the traversal phase is not immediately returned. Instead it is saved in a local semantic read/write sets. Each entry of those sets consists of the following three fields. *Op-key*: the searched key that needs to be inserted, removed, or looked up. *Node*: the last node of the traversal phase. This node is either a node whose key matches op-key (no matter if it is marked as *deleted* or not) or a node whose right (left) child is null and its item is greater (less) than op-key. *Op-type*: an integer that indicates the type of the operation (add, remove, or contains) and its result (successful or unsuccessful).

Those fields are sufficient to verify (by the transaction validation) that the result of the operation is not changed since the execution of the operation, and to modify the tree at commit time. All the operations add an entry to the read-set, but only successful **add** and **remove** operations add entries to the write-set.

Before traversal, the local write-set is scanned for detecting read-after-write hazards. If the key exists in the write-set, the operation returns immediately without traversing the shared tree. Moreover, if a successful **add** operation is followed by a successful **remove** operation of the same item (or vice versa), they locally eliminate each other, in order to save the useless access to the shared tree. The elimination is done only on the write-set, and the entries are kept in the read-set so that the eliminated operations are guaranteed to be consistent.

**Validation.** The second phase of TxCF-Tree's operation is the *validation* phase. To have a comprehensive presentation, we show first the validation procedure in CF-Tree, and then we show how it is modified in TxCF-Tree.

---

**Algorithm 1.** Operation's validation in CF-Tree.

---

```
1: procedure VALIDATE(node, k)        8:    else
2:   if node.removed ≠ NOT-REMOVED then 9:      next = node.left
3:     return false                   10:   if next = null then
4:   else if node.k = k then          11:      return true
5:     return true                    12:   return false
6:   else if node.k > k then
7:     next = node.right              13: end procedure
```

---

In Algorithm 1, the validation in CF-Tree succeeds if the node's key is not physically removed and either the node's key matches the searched key (line 5) or its child (right or left according to the key) is still **null** (line 11). Otherwise, the validation fails (lines 3 and 12). This validation is used during **add/remove** operations as follows (details are in [9]): each operation traverses the tree until it reaches the involved node, then it locks and validates it (using Algorithm 1). If the validation succeeds, the operation stops its traversal loop and starts the actual insertion/deletion. If the validation fails, the node is unlocked and the operation continues the traversal. In [9], it has been proven that continuing the traversal is safe even if the node is physically deleted or rotated by the *helper* thread, due to the mechanism used in the deletion/rotation, as discussed in Section 4.1 (e.g., modifying the left and right links of the deleted node to be pointing to its parent before unlinking it).

---

**Algorithm 2.** Example of semantic opacity.

---

```
1: @Atomic          ▷ initially the tree is empty
2: procedure T1                        7: @Atomic
3:   if tree.contains(x) = false then  8: procedure T2
4:     if tree.contains(y) = true then 9:   tree.add(x)
5:       ...          ▷ hazardous action 10:  tree.add(y)
6: end procedure                       11: end procedure
```

---

In TxCF-Tree, this validation procedure is modified to achieve two goals. **The first goal regards the correctness:** since TxCF-Tree is a transactional tree, validation has also to ensure that the operation's result is not changed until transaction commits; otherwise, the transaction consistency is compromised. As an example, in Algorithm 2 let us assume the following invariant: $y$ exists in the tree if and only if $x$ also exists. If we use the same validation as Algorithm 1, $T1$ may execute line 3 first and return false. Then, let us assume that $T2$ is entirely executed and committed. In this case, $T1$ should abort right after executing line 4 because it breaks the invariant. Aborting the doomed transaction $T1$ should be immediate and it cannot be delayed until the commit phase because it may go into an infinite loop or raise an exception (line 5). To prevent those cases, all of the read-set's entries have to be validated (using Algorithm 3 instead of Algorithm 1) after each operation as well as during commit.

---

**Algorithm 3.** Operation's validation in TxCF-Tree.

```
 1: procedure VALIDATE(read-set-entry)
 2:   if entry.op-type ∈ (unsuccessful add,
 3: successful remove/contains) then
 4:     item-existed = true
 5:   else
 6:     item-existed = false
 7:   if entry.node.removed ≠
 8: NOT-REMOVED then
 9:     return STRUCTURALLY-INVALID
10:   else if entry.node.k = entry.op-key then
11:     if entry.node.deleted xor
12: item-existed then
13:       return VALID

14:   else
15:     return SEMANTICALLY-INVALID
16:   else if entry.node.k > entry.op-key then
17:     next = node.right
18:   else
19:     next = node.left
20:   if next = null then
21:     if item-existed then
22:       return SEMANTICALLY-INVALID
23:     else
24:       return VALID
25:   return STRUCTURALLY-INVALID
26: end procedure
```

---

**The Second Goal Regards Performance:** if the node is physically removed or its child becomes no longer `null` (which are the invalidation cases of CF-Tree), that does not mean that the transaction is not consistent anymore. It only means that the traversal phase has to continue and reach a new node to be validated. It is worth noting that aborting the transaction in those cases does not impact the tree's correctness, while its performance will be affected. In fact, this conservative approach increases the probability of structural operations' interference. For this reason we distinguish between those types of invalidations and the actual *semantic* invalidations, such as those depicted in Algorithm 2. The modified version of the validation is shown in Algorithm 3. The cases covered in CF-Tree are considered *structural-invalidations* (lines 9 and 25), and the actual invalidation cases are considered *semantic-invalidations* (lines 15 and 22).

Algorithm 4 shows how to validate the read-set. For each entry, we firstly check if the entry's node is not locked (lines 4-9). In this step we exploit our lock separation by checking only one of the two locks because each operation validates either the *deleted* flag or the child link. Specifically, if the node's key matches op-key, node's *semantic-lock* is checked, otherwise the *structural-lock* is checked. Moreover, if the entry's node is locked by the *helper* thread, we consider it as unlocked because the helper thread cannot change the abstract state of the tree. The only effect of the *helper* thread is to make the operation structurally invalid, which can be detected in the next steps.

---

**Algorithm 4.** Read-set validation in TxCF-Tree.

---

```
 1: procedure VALIDATE-READSET(read-set)      13:    entry.node = newNode
 2:   for all entries in the read-set do       14:    write-entry = write-set.get(entry.op-key)
 3:     while true do                          15:    if write-entry ≠ null then
 4:       if entry.op-item = entry.node.item then 16:      write-entry.node = newNode
 5:         lock = semantic-lock              17:    else if r = SEMANTICALLY-INVALID
 6:       else                                then
 7:         lock = struct-lock                 18:      return false
 8:       if lockedNotByMeOrHelper(lock) then  19:    else
 9:         return false                       20:      break;
10:       r = VALIDATE(entry)                  21:  return true
11:       if r = STRUCTURALLY-INVALID then     22: end procedure
12:         newNode = CONT-TRAVERSE(entry)
```

---

The next step is to validate the entry itself (line 10). If it is *semantically-invalidated*, then the transaction aborts (line 18). If it is *structurally-invalidated*, the traversal continues as in CF-Tree and the entry is updated with the new node (lines 12-16), then the node is re-validated. If the operation is a successful *add/remove*, the related write-set entry is also updated (line 16).

**Commit.** The *commit* phase (pseudo code in [17]) is similar to the classical two-phase locking mechanism. The nodes in the read/write sets are locked and/or validated first, then the tree is modified, and finally locks are released.

From the commit procedure of TxCF-Tree it is worth mention the following points. The first point is how TxCF-Tree solves the issue of having two dependent operations in the same transaction. For example, if two *add* operations are using the same node (e.g. assume a transaction that adds both 3 and 4 to the tree shown in Figure 1). The effect of the first operation (add 3) should be propagated to the second one (add 4). To achieve that, the add operation uses the node in the write-set only as a starting point and keeps traversing the tree from this node until reaching the new node. Also, the operations lock the added nodes (3 and 4 in our case) before linking them to the tree. Those nodes are unlocked together with the other nodes at the end of the commit phase. Any interleaving transaction or structural operation running in the *helper* thread cannot force the transaction to abort because all the involved nodes are already locked. Also, the other cases of having dependent operations, such as adding (or removing) the same key twice and adding a key and then removing it, are solved earlier during the operation itself (as mentioned in the traversal phase).

The second point is how TxCF-Tree preserves the reduced interferences between the structural and the semantic operations without hampering the two-phase locking mechanism. The main issue in this regard is that *structural invalidations* may not abort the transaction. Thus, a transaction cannot lock the nodes in the write-set and then validate the nodes in the read-set because, if so, in case of a *structural invalidation*, the invalidated operation (which can be a write operation) would continue traversing the tree and reach a new node (which is not yet locked). To solve this problem, we use an *inline* validation of the entries in the write-set. The write-set entries are both locked and validated at the same time. If the write operation fails in its validation: *1)* it unlocks the node; *2)* re-traverses the tree; *3)* locks the new node; and *4)* re-validates the entry.

# 5   Correctness

In this section we briefly discuss the correctness of TxCF-Tree (a detailed proof is in [17]). Since we use the OTB methodology to make CF-Tree transactional, the operations of TxCF-Tree are serialized as described in [15]. The serialization point of a read-write transaction is the point right after acquiring the locks and before the (successful) validation during commit. For a read-only transaction, the serialization point is the return of its last read operation. Both those points are immediately followed by a validation procedure (Algorithm 4). If this validation succeeds, then all the transaction operations are guaranteed to be consistent.

The correctness of the mechanisms used to achieve *interference-less* structural operations can be inferred as follows. *i)* Splitting locks into *structural* and *semantic* locks does not affect correctness by any mean, because any two conflicting operations (e.g., two operations that attempt to delete the same node, or two operations that attempt to insert new nodes on the same link) acquire the same type of lock. *ii) Structural invalidations* are raised and handled in the same way as CF-Tree (as we show in Algorithms 1 and 3). Since we use the same approach for rotation and physical deletion (e.g., cloning the rotated down node and linking the physically deleted node to its parent), re-traversing the tree after a *structural invalidation* is guaranteed to be safe as in CF-Tree itself (see [9] for the complete proof of validation in CF-Tree). *iii) Semantic invalidations* preserve the consistency among the operations within the same transaction. Unlike *structural invalidations*, in those cases, the whole transaction is aborted. *iv)* The *inline* validation during commit does not affect the correctness (although it violates two-phase locking) because every *inline-validated* node is locked before being validated and cannot be invalidated anymore if the validation succeeds. *v)* Validating the whole read-set after each operation and before committing preserves consistency in the presence of concurrent structural operations. For example, assuming the scenario where a structural operation physically removes a node that is used by a running transaction T1, which can be followed by a semantic operation (executed in another transaction T2) that adds this node in a different place of the tree. Although this new addition will not be detected by T1's validation, the expected race condition will be solved because T1 will detect during the validation (after the next operation or at commit) that the *removed* flag of the node has been changed (line 8 in Algorithm 3) and will continue traversing the tree. At this point, T1 will reach the same new node as T2, and they will be serialized independently from the structural operation.

# 6   Evaluation

In our experiments we compared the performance of TxCF-Tree with the performance of TB and some STM approaches. Our implementation of TB uses

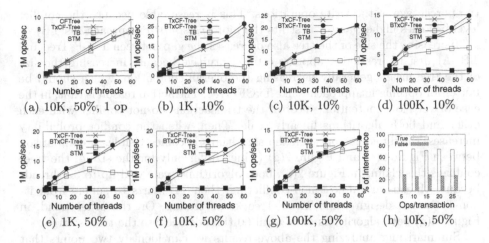

(a) 10K, 50%, 1 op     (b) 1K, 10%     (c) 10K, 10%     (d) 100K, 10%

(e) 1K, 50%     (f) 10K, 50%     (g) 100K, 50%     (h) 10K, 50%

**Fig. 2.** Throughput with one operation (2(a)), and five operations (2(b)-2(g)) per transaction (labels indicate the size of the tree and the % of the add/remove operations). Figure 2(h) shows the percentage of the two interference types using 32 threads.

CF-Tree as the underlying (black-box) tree, which makes a fair comparison. Regarding STM, we tested three different algorithms: LSA [24]; TL2 [11]; and NOrec [10], and, to make plots clear, we reported the best performance collected.

All experiments were conducted on a 64-core machine, which has 4 AMD Opteron (TM) Processors, each with 16 cores running at 1.4 GHz, 32 GB of RAM, and 16KB L1 data cache. Throughput is measured as the number of semantic operations (not transactions) per second to have consistent data points. However, since the benchmark executes 256 no-op instructions in between two transactions, this may result in different throughput ranges for different sizes of transactions. Each data point is the average of five runs.

In Figure 2(a) we show the results for a scenario that mimics the concurrent (non-transactional) case (i.e., each transaction executes only one operation on the tree). We leverage this plot to show the cost of adopting a transactional solution over a pure concurrent tree. Clearly STM does not scale because it "blindly" speculates on all the memory reads and writes. This poor scalability of STM is confirmed in all the experiments we made. On the other hand, both TB and TxCF-Tree scale better than STM and close to CF-Tree (TxCF-Tree is slightly closer). This behavior shows an overhead that is affordable in case one wants to use the TxCF-Tree library even for just handling the concurrency of atomic semantic operations without transactions.

Figures 2(b)-2(g) show the transactional case, in which we deployed five operations per transaction for different sizes of the tree (1K, 10K, and 100K) and different read/write workloads (10% and 50% of add/remove operations). We do not include CF-Tree because it only supports concurrent operations and thus it cannot handle the execution of transactions. TxCF-Tree performs generally better than TB. The gap between the two algorithms decreases when we increase the percentage of the write operations. This is reasonable because the conflict level becomes higher, and it best fits the more *pessimistic* approach (as TB).

Increasing the size of the tree also decreases the gap between TxCF-Tree and TB. At first impression it appears counterintuitive because increasing the size of the tree means generally decreasing the overall contention, which should be better for optimistic approaches like TxCF-Tree. The actual reason is that, in the case of very low contention, most of the transactions do not conflict with each other and both algorithms linearly scale. Then, when the conflict probability increases, the difference between the algorithms becomes visible. A comparison between Figure 2(e) and Figure 2(g) (which differ only for the size of the tree) confirms this claim. In Figure 2(e), both algorithms scale well up to 32 threads because threads are almost non-conflicting, then TB starts to suffers from its non-optimized design while TxCF-Tree keeps scaling. On the other hand, in Figure 2(g) both algorithms scale until 60 threads because the tree is large.

Summarizing, analyzing the above results we can identify two points that allow TxCF-Tree to outperform competitors: *i)* having an optimized unmonitored traversal phase that reduces false conflicts, and *ii)* having optimized validation/commit procedures that minimize the interferences between structural and semantic operations. Both TB and TxCF-Tree gain performance by exploiting the first point, in fact TB itself performs (up to an order of magnitude) better than STM. However, only TxCF-Tree uses an *optimized* design for a balanced tree data structure, and it makes its performance generally (much) better than TB. In the aforementioned experiments we use two versions of TxCF-Tree, one with the adaptive back-off time in between two *helper* thread iterations (named BTxCF-Tree), and one without. The results show that this optimization further enhances the performance, especially in the small tree (the cases of 10% add/remove operations). This gain may increase with a more effective heuristic.

The last experiment we report regards the capability of TxCF-Tree to reduce interferences with structural operations. Although breaking down TxCF-Tree's operations to measure this gain is not straightforward, we roughly estimated the gain by quantifying two metrics: the *true* interferences count, which is simply the actual transactional aborts count; and the *false* interferences count, which is the count of the cases in which the transaction does not abort because the tree is re-traversed instead or because the operations in TxCF-Tree acquire only one (structural or semantic) lock. In Figure 2(h) the false-interferences are 25%-30% of the total interferences for different sizes of the transactions.

## 7   Conclusions

We presented TxCF-Tree, the first interference-less transactional balanced tree. Unlike the former general approaches, it uses an optimized conflict management mechanism that reacts differently according to the type of the operation. Our experiments confirm that TxCF-Tree performs better than the general approaches.

**Acknowledgments.** Authors would thank Vincent Gramoli and anonymous reviewers for the invaluable comments. This work is partially supported by Air Force Office of Scientific Research (AFOSR) under grant FA9550-14-1-0187.

# References

1. Afek, Y., Avni, H., Shavit, N.: Towards consistency oblivious programming. In: Fernàndez Anta, A., Lipari, G., Roy, M. (eds.) OPODIS 2011. LNCS, vol. 7109, pp. 65–79. Springer, Heidelberg (2011)
2. Afek, Y., Kaplan, H., Korenfeld, B., Morrison, A., Tarjan, R.E.: The CB tree: a practical concurrent self-adjusting search tree. DISC **27**(6), 393–417 (2014)
3. Arbel, M., Attiya, H.: Concurrent updates with RCU: search tree as an example. In: PODC, pp. 196–205 (2014)
4. Avni, H., Suissa-Peleg, A.: Brief announcement: cop composition using transaction suspension in the compiler. In: DISC, pp. 550–552 (2014)
5. Bronson, N.G., Casper, J., Chafi, H., Olukotun, K.: A practical concurrent binary search tree. In: PPoPP, pp. 257–268 (2010)
6. Bronson, N.G., Casper, J., Chafi, H., Olukotun, K.: Transactional predication: high-performance concurrent sets and maps for STM. In: PODC, pp. 6–15 (2010)
7. Brown, T., Ellen, F., Ruppert, E.: A general technique for non-blocking trees. In: PPoPP, pp. 329–342 (2014)
8. Crain, T., Gramoli, V., Raynal, M.: A speculation-friendly binary search tree. In: PPoPP, pp. 161–170 (2012)
9. Crain, T., Gramoli, V., Raynal, M.: A contention-friendly binary search tree. In: Wolf, F., Mohr, B., an Mey, D. (eds.) Euro-Par 2013. LNCS, vol. 8097, pp. 229–240. Springer, Heidelberg (2013)
10. Dalessandro, L., Spear, M.F., Scott, M.L.: NOrec: streamlining STM by abolishing ownership records. In: PPoPP, pp. 67–78 (2010)
11. Dice, D., Shalev, O., Shavit, N.N.: Transactional locking II. In: Dolev, S. (ed.) DISC 2006. LNCS, vol. 4167, pp. 194–208. Springer, Heidelberg (2006)
12. Drachsler, D., Vechev, M.T., Yahav, E.: Practical concurrent binary search trees via logical ordering. In: PPoPP, pp. 343–356 (2014)
13. Ellen, F., Fatourou, P., Ruppert, E., van Breugel, F.: Non-blocking binary search trees. In: PODC, pp. 131–140 (2010)
14. Guerraoui, R., Kapalka, M.: On the correctness of transactional memory. In: PPoPP, pp. 175–184 (2008)
15. Hassan, A., Palmieri, R., Ravindran, B.: On developing optimistic transactional lazy set. In: Aguilera, M.K., Querzoni, L., Shapiro, M. (eds.) OPODIS 2014. LNCS, vol. 8878, pp. 437–452. Springer, Heidelberg (2014)
16. Hassan, A., Palmieri, R., Ravindran, B.: Optimistic transactional boosting. In: PPoPP, pp. 387–388 (2014)
17. Hassan, A., Palmieri, R., Ravindran, B.: Transactional interference-less balanced tree. Technical report, ECE Dept., Virginia Tech, August 2015. www.hyflow.org/pubs/disc15-hassan-TR.pdf
18. Herlihy, M., Koskinen, E.: Transactional boosting: a methodology for highly-concurrent transactional objects. In: PPoPP, pp. 207–216 (2008)
19. Herlihy, M., Moss, J.E.B.: Transactional memory: architectural support for lock-free data structures. In: ISCA, pp. 289–300 (1993)
20. Herlihy, M., Shavit, N.: The Art of Multiprocessor Programming, Revised Reprint. Elsevier (2012)

21. Howley, S.V., Jones, J.: A non-blocking internal binary search tree. In: SPAA, pp. 161–171 (2012)
22. Larsen, K.S.: AVL trees with relaxed balance. In: IPPS, pp. 888–893 (1994)
23. Natarajan, A., Mittal, N.: Fast concurrent lock-free binary search trees. In: PPoPP, pp. 317–328 (2014)
24. Riegel, T., Felber, P., Fetzer, C.: A lazy snapshot algorithm with eager validation. In: Dolev, S. (ed.) DISC 2006. LNCS, vol. 4167, pp. 284–298. Springer, Heidelberg (2006)
25. Xiang, L., Scott, M.L.: Software partitioning of hardware transactions. In: PPoPP, pp. 76–86 (2015)

# Analyzing the Performance of Lock-Free Data Structures: A Conflict-Based Model

Aras Atalar[✉], Paul Renaud-Goud, and Philippas Tsigas

Chalmers University of Technology, Gothenburg, Sweden
{aaras,goud,tsigas}@chalmers.se

**Abstract.** This paper considers the modeling and the analysis of the performance of lock-free concurrent data structures that can be represented as linear combinations of fixed size retry loops.

Our main contribution is a new way of modeling and analyzing a general class of lock-free algorithms, achieving predictions of throughput that are close to what we observe in practice. We emphasize two kinds of conflicts that shape the performance: (i) hardware conflicts, due to concurrent calls to atomic primitives; (ii) logical conflicts, caused by concurrent operations on the shared data structure.

We propose also a common framework that enables a fair comparison between lock-free implementations by covering the whole contention domain, and comes with a method for calculating a good back-off strategy.

Our experimental results, based on a set of widely used concurrent data structures and on abstract lock-free designs, show that our analysis follows closely the actual code behavior.[1]

## 1 Introduction

Lock-free programming provides highly concurrent access to data and has been increasing its footprint in industrial settings. Providing a modeling and an analysis framework capable of describing the practical performance of lock-free algorithms is an essential, missing resource necessary to the parallel programming and algorithmic research communities in their effort to build on previous intellectual efforts. The definition of lock-freedom mainly guarantees that at least one concurrent operation on the data structure finishes in a finite number of its own steps, regardless of the state of the operations. On the individual operation level, lock-freedom cannot guarantee that an operation will not starve.

The goal of this paper is to provide a way to model and analyze the practically observed performance of lock-free data structures. In the literature, the common performance measure of a lock-free data structure is the throughput, *i.e.* the number of successful operations per unit of time. It is obtained while threads are accessing the data structure according to an access pattern that interleaves local

---

[1] The research leading to these results has received funding from the European Union Seventh Framework Programme (FP7/2013-2016) under grant agreement 611183 (EXCESS Project, www.excess-project.eu).

© Springer-Verlag Berlin Heidelberg 2015
Y. Moses (Ed.): DISC 2015, LNCS 9363, pp. 341–355, 2015.
DOI: 10.1007/978-3-662-48653-5_23

work between calls to consecutive operations on the data structure. Although this access pattern to the data structure is significant, there is no consensus in the literature on what access to be used when comparing two data structures. So, the amount of local work (that we will refer as parallel work for the rest of the paper) could be constant ([14,15]), uniformly distributed ([10], [7]), exponentially distributed ([17], [8]), null ([12,13]), *etc.* More questionably, the average amount is rarely scanned, which leads to a partial covering of the contention domain.

We propose here a common framework enabling a fair comparison between lock-free data structures, while exhibiting the main phenomena that drive performance, and particularly the contention, which leads to different kinds of conflicts. As this is the first step in this direction, we want to deeply analyze the core of the problem, without impacting factors being diluted within a probabilistic smoothing. Therefore, we choose a constant local work, hence constant access rate to the data structures. In addition to the prediction of the data structure performance, our model provides a good back-off strategy, that achieves the peak performance of a lock-free algorithm.

Two kinds of conflict appear during the execution of a lock-free algorithm, leading to additional work. Hardware conflicts occur when concurrent operations call atomic primitives on the same memory location: these calls collide and conduct to stall time, that we name here *expansion*. Logical conflicts take place if concurrent operations overlap: because of the lock-free nature of the algorithm, several concurrent operations can run simultaneously, but usually only one retry can logically succeed. We show that the additional work produced by the failures is not necessarily harmful for the system-wise performance.

We then show how throughput can be computed by connecting these two key factors in an iterative way. We start by estimating the expansion probabilistically, and emulate the effect of stall time introduced by the hardware conflicts as extra work added to each thread. Then we estimate the number of failed operations, that in turn lead to additional extra work, by computing again the expansion on a system setting where those two new amounts of work have been incorporated, and reiterate the process; the convergence is ensured by a fixed-point search.

We consider the class of lock-free algorithms that can be modeled as a linear composition of fixed size retry loops. This class covers numerous extensively used lock-free designs such as stacks [16] (`Pop`, `Push`), queues [14] (`Enqueue`, `Dequeue`), counters [7] (`Increment`, `Decrement`) and priority queues [13] (`DeleteMin`).

To evaluate the accuracy of our model and analysis framework, we performed experiments both on synthetic tests, that capture a wide range of possible abstract algorithmic designs, and on several reference implementations of extensively studied lock-free data structures. Our evaluation results reveal that our model is able to capture the behavior of all the synthetic and real designs for all different numbers of threads and sizes of parallel work (consequently also contention). We also evaluate the use of our analysis as a tool for tuning the performance of lock-free code by selecting the appropriate back-off strategy that will maximize throughput by comparing our method against widely known back-off policies, namely linear and exponential.

The rest of the paper is organized as follows. We discuss related work in Section 2, then the problem is formally described in Section 3. We consider the logical conflicts in the absence of hardware conflicts in Section 4. In Section 5, we firstly show how to compute the expansion, then combine hardware and logical conflicts to obtain the final throughput estimate. We describe the experimental results in Section 6.

## 2 Related Work

Anderson *et al.* [3] evaluated the performance of lock-free objects in a single processor real-time system by emphasizing the impact of retry loop interference. Tasks can be preempted during the retry loop execution, which can lead to interference, and consequently to an inflation in retry loop execution due to retries. They obtained upper bounds for the number of interferences under various scheduling schemes for periodic real-time tasks.

Intel [11] conducted an empirical study to illustrate performance and scalability of locks. They showed that the critical section size, the time interval between releasing and re-acquiring the lock (that is similar to our parallel section size) and number of threads contending the lock are vital parameters.

Failed retries do not only lead to useless effort but also degrade the performance of successful ones by contending the shared resources. Alemany *et al.* [1] have pointed out this fact, that is in accordance with our two key factors, and, without trying to model it, have mitigated those effects by designing non-blocking algorithms with operating system support.

Alistarh *et al.* [2] have studied the same class of lock-free structures that we consider in this paper. The analysis is done in terms of scheduler steps, in a system where only one thread can be scheduled (and can then run) at each step. If compared with execution time, this is particularly appropriate to a system with a single processor and several threads, or to a system where the instructions of the threads cannot be done in parallel (*e.g.* multi-threaded program on a multi-core processor with only read and write on the same cache line of the shared memory). In our paper, the execution is evaluated in terms of processor cycles, strongly related to the execution time. In addition, the "parallel work" and the "critical work" can be done in parallel, and we only consider retry-loops with one Read and one CAS, which are serialized. In addition, they bound the asymptotic expected system latency (with a big O, when the number of threads tends to infinity), while in our paper we estimate the throughput (close to the inverse of system latency) for any number of threads.

## 3 Problem Statement

### 3.1 Running Program and Targeted Platform

In this paper, we aim at evaluating the throughput of a multi-threaded algorithm that is based on the utilization of a shared lock-free data structure. Such a

**Procedure.** AbstractAlgorithm

```
1  Initialization();
2  while ! done do
3      Parallel_Work();
4      while ! success do
5          current ← Read(AP);
6          new ← Critical_Work(current);
7          success ← CAS(AP, current, new);
```

**Fig. 1.** Thread procedure

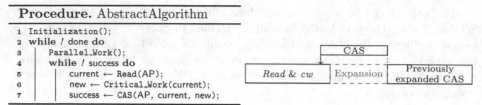

**Fig. 2.** Expansion

program can be abstracted by the Procedure AbstractAlgorithm (see Figure 1) that represents the skeleton of the function which is called by each spawned thread. It is decomposed in two main phases: the *parallel section*, represented on line 3, and the *retry loop*, from line 4 to line 7. A *retry* starts at line 5 and ends at line 7.

As for line 1, the function `Initialization` shall be seen as an abstraction of the delay between the spawns of the threads, that is expected not to be null, even when a barrier is used. We then consider that the threads begin at the exact same time, but have different initialization times.

The parallel section is the part of the code where the thread does not access the shared data structure; the work that is performed inside this parallel section can possibly depend on the value that has been read from the data structure, *e.g.* in the case of processing an element that has been dequeued from a FIFO (First-In-First-Out) queue.

In each retry, a thread tries to modify the data structure, and does not exit the retry loop until it has successfully modified the data structure. It does that by firstly reading the access point AP of the data structure, then according to the value that has been read, and possibly to other previous computations that occurred in the past, the thread prepares the new desired value as an access point of the data structure. Finally, it atomically tries to perform the change through a call to the *Compare-And-Swap (CAS)* primitive. If it succeeds, *i.e.* if the access point has not been changed by another thread between the first *Read* and the *CAS*, then it goes to the next parallel section, otherwise it repeats the process. The retry loop is composed of at least one retry, and we number the retries starting from 0, since the first iteration of the retry loop is actually not a retry, but a try.

The throughput of the lock-free algorithm, *i.e.* the number of successful data structure operations per unit of time, that we denote by $T$, is impacted by several parameters.

- *Algorithm parameters*: the amount of work inside a call to `Parallel_Work` (resp. `Critical_Work`) denoted by $pw$ (resp. $cw$).
- *Platform parameters*: *Read* and *CAS* latencies ($rc$ and $cc$ respectively), and the number $P$ of processing units (cores). We assume homogeneity for the latencies, *i.e.* every thread experiences the same latency when accessing an uncontended shared data, which is achieved in practice by pinning threads to the same socket.

## 3.2   Examples and Issues

We first present two straightforward upper bounds on the throughput, and describe the two kinds of conflict that keep the actual throughput away from those upper bounds.

### 3.2.1   Immediate Upper Bounds

Trivially, the minimum amount of work $rlw^{(-)}$ in a given retry is $rlw^{(-)} = rc + cw + cc$, as we should pay at least the memory accesses and the critical work $cw$ in between.

**Thread-wise:** A given thread can at most perform one successful retry every $pw + rlw^{(-)}$ units of time. In the best case, $P$ threads can then lead to a throughput of $P/(pw + rlw^{(-)})$.

**System-wise:** By definition, two successful retries cannot overlap, hence we have at most 1 successful retry every $rlw^{(-)}$ units of time.

Altogether, the throughput $T$ is upper bounded by the minimum of $1/(rc + cw + cc)$ and $P/(pw + rc + cw + cc)$, i.e.

$$T \leq \begin{cases} \frac{1}{rc + cw + cc} & \text{if } pw \leq (P-1)(rc + cw + cc) \\ \frac{P}{pw + rc + cw + cc} & \text{otherwise.} \end{cases} \tag{1}$$

### 3.2.2   Conflicts

*Logical conflicts:* Equation 1 expresses the fact that when $pw$ is small enough, i.e. when $pw \leq (P-1)rlw^{(-)}$, we cannot expect that every thread performs a successful retry every $pw + rlw^{(-)}$ units of time, since it is more than what the retry loop can afford. As a result, some logical conflicts, hence unsuccessful retries, will be inevitable, while the others, if any, are called *wasted*.

Figure 3 depicts an execution, where the black parts are the calls to Initialization, the blue parts are the parallel sections, and the retries can be either unsuccessful — in red — or successful — in green. After the initial transient state, the execution contains actually, for each thread, one inevitable unsuccessful retry, and one wasted retry, because there exists a set of initialization times that lead to a cyclic execution with a single failure per thread and per period.

We can see on this example that a cyclic execution is reached after the transient behavior; actually, we show in Section 4 that, in the absence of hardware

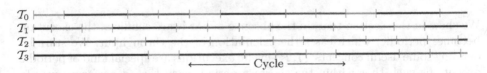

**Fig. 3.** Execution with one wasted retry, and one inevitable failure

conflicts, every execution will become periodic, if the initialization times are spaced enough. In addition, we prove that the shortest period is such that, during this period, every thread succeeds exactly once. This finally leads us to define the additional failures as wasted, since we can directly link the throughput with this number of wasted retries: a higher number of wasted retries implying a lower throughput.

*Hardware conflicts:* The requirement of atomicity compels the ownership of the data in an exclusive manner by the executing core. Therefore, overlapping parts of atomic instructions are serialized by the hardware, leading to stalls in subsequently issued ones. For our target lock-free algorithm, these stalls that we refer to as expansion become an important slowdown factor in case threads interfere in the retry loop. As illustrated in Figure 2, the latency for $CAS$ can expand and cause remarkable decreases in throughput since the $CAS$ of a successful thread is then expanded by others; for this reason, the amount of work inside a retry is not constant, but is, generally speaking, a function depending on the number of threads that are inside the retry loop.

### 3.2.3  Process

We deal with the two kinds of conflicts separately and connect them together through the fixed-point iterative convergence.

In Section 5.1, we compute the expansion in execution time of a retry, noted $e$, by following a probabilistic approach. The estimation takes as input the expected number of threads inside the retry loop at any time, and returns the expected increase in the execution time of a retry due to the serialization of atomic primitives.

In Section 4, we are given a program without hardware conflicts described by the size of the parallel section $pw^{(+)}$ and the size of a retry $rlw^{(+)}$. We compute upper and lower bounds on the throughput $T$, the number of wasted retries $w$, and the average number of threads inside the retry loop $P_{rl}$. Without loss of generality, we can normalize those execution times by the execution time of a retry, and define the parallel section size as $pw^{(+)} = q + r$, where $q$ is a nonnegative integer and $r$ is such that $0 \leq r < 1$. This pair (together with the number of threads $P$) constitutes the actual input of the estimation.

Finally, we combine those two outcomes in Section 5.2 by emulating expansion through work not prone to hardware conflicts and obtain the full estimation of the throughput.

## 4  Execution without Hardware Conflicts

We show in this section that, in the absence of hardware conflicts, the execution becomes periodic, which eases the calculation of the throughput. We start by defining some useful concepts: $(f, P)$-cyclic executions are special kind of periodic executions such that within the shortest period, each thread performs exactly $f$ unsuccessful retries and 1 successful retry. The *well-formed seed* is a set of events that allows us to detect an $(f, P)$-*cyclic execution* early, and the *gaps* are a measure of the quality of the synchronization between threads. The idea is to iteratively add threads into the game and show that the periodicity is maintained. Theorem 1 establishes a fundamental relation between gaps and well-formed seeds, while Theorem 2 proves the periodicity, relying on the disjoint cases depicted on Figures 4a, 4b and 4c. We recall that the complete version of the proofs can be found in [5], together with additional Lemmas. Finally, we exhibit upper and lower bounds on throughput and number of failures, along with the average number of threads inside the retry loop.

## 4.1  Setting

In preamble, note that the events are strictly ordered (according to their instant of occurrence, with the thread id as a tie-breaker). As for correctness, *i.e.* to decide for the success or the failure of a retry, we need instants of occurrence for *Read* and *CAS*; we consider that the entrance (resp. exit) time of a retry is the instant of occurrence of the *Read* (resp. *CAS*).

### 4.1.1  Notations and Definitions

We recall that $P$ threads are executing the pseudo-code described in Procedure AbstractAlgorithm, one retry is of unit-size, and the parallel section is of size $pw^{(+)} = q + r$, where $q$ is a non-negative integer and $r$ is such that $0 \le r < 1$. Considering a thread $T_n$ which succeeds at time $S_n$; this thread completes a whole retry in 1 unit of time, then executes the parallel section of size $pw^{(+)}$, and attempts to perform again the operation every unit of time, until one of the attempt is successful.

**Definition 1.** *An execution with $P$ threads is called $(C, P)$-cyclic execution if and only if (i) the execution is periodic, i.e. at every time, every thread is in the same state as one period before, (ii) the shortest period contains exactly one successful attempt per thread, (iii) the shortest period is $1 + q + r + C$.*

**Definition 2.** *Let $S = (T_i, S_i)_{i \in 0, P-1}$, where $T_i$ are threads and $S_i$ ordered times, i.e. such that $S_0 < \cdots < S_{P-1}$. $S$ is a seed if and only if for all $i \in 0, P - 1$, $T_i$ does not succeed between $S_0$ and $S_i$, and starts a retry at $S_i$.*

*We define $f(S)$ as the smallest non-negative integer such that $S_0 + 1 + q + r + f(S) > S_{P-1} + 1$, i.e. $f(S) = \max(0, \lceil S_{P-1} - S_0 - q - r \rceil)$. When $S$ is clear from the context, we denote $f(S)$ by $f$.*

**Definition 3.** *$S$ is a well-formed seed if and only if for each $i \in 0, P - 1$, the execution of thread $T_i$ contains the following sequence: a successful retry starting at $S_i$, the parallel section, $f$ unsuccessful retries, then a successful retry.*

Those definitions are coupled through the two natural following properties:

*Property 1.* Given a $(C, P)$-cyclic execution, any seed $S$ including $P$ consecutive successes is a well-formed seed, with $f(S) = C$.

*Property 2.* If there exists a well-formed seed in an execution, then after each thread succeeded once, the execution coincides with an $(f, P)$-cyclic execution.

Together with the seed concept, we define the notion of *gap*. The general idea of those gaps is that within an $(f, P)$-cyclic execution, the period is higher than $P \times 1$, which is the total execution time of all the successful retries within the period. The difference between the period (that lasts $1 + q + r + f$) and $P$, reduced by $r$ (so that we obtain an integer), is referred as *lagging time* in the following. If the threads are numbered according to their order of success (modulo $P$), as the time elapsed between the successes of two given consecutive threads is constant (during the next period, this time will remain the same), this lagging time can be seen in a circular manner: the threads are represented on a circle whose length is the lagging time increased by $r$, and the length between two consecutive threads is the time between the end of the successful retry of the first thread and the start of the successful retry of the second one. More formally, for all $(n, k) \in 0, P - 1^2$, we define the gap $G_n^{(k)}$ between $T_n$ and its $k^{\text{th}}$ predecessor based on the gap with the first predecessor:

$$\begin{cases} \forall n \in 1, P - 1 \quad ; \quad G_n^{(1)} = S_n - S_{n-1} - 1 \\ G_0^{(1)} = S_0 + q + r + f - S_{P-1} \end{cases},$$

which leads to the definition of higher order gaps: $\forall n \in 0, P - 1 ; \forall k > 0; G_n^{(k)} = \sum_{j=n-k+1}^{n} G_{j \bmod P}^{(1)}$.

For consistency, for all $n \in 0, P - 1$, $G_n^{(0)} = 0$.

Equally, the gaps can be obtained from the successes: for all $k \in 1, P - 1$,

$$G_n^{(k)} = \begin{cases} S_n - S_{n-k} - k & \text{if } n > k \\ S_n - S_{P+n-k} + 1 + q + r + f - k & \text{otherwise} \end{cases} \tag{2}$$

Note that, in an $(f, P)$-cyclic execution, the lagging time is the sum of all first order gaps, reduced by $r$.

## 4.2   Cyclic Executions

We only give the two main theorems used to show the existence of cyclic executions. The details can be found in the companion research report [5].

**Theorem 1.** *Given a seed $S = (T_i, S_i)_{i \in 0, P-1}$, $S$ is a well-formed seed if and only if for all $n \in 0, P - 1$, $0 \leq G_n^{(f)} < 1$.*

**Theorem 2.** *Assuming $r \neq 0$, if a new thread is added to an $(f, P - 1)$-cyclic execution, then all the threads will eventually form either an $(f, P)$-cyclic execution, or an $(f + 1, P)$-cyclic execution.*

*Proof.* We decompose the Theorem into three Lemmas which we describe here graphically:

- If all gaps of $(f+1)^{\text{th}}$ order are less than 1, then every existing thread will fail once more, and the new steady-state is reached immediately. See Figure 4a.
- Otherwise:
  - Either: everyone succeeds once, whereupon a new $(f, P)$-cyclic execution is formed. See Figure 4b.
  - Or: before everyone succeeds again, a new $(f, P')$-cyclic execution, where $P' \leq P$, is formed, which finally leads to an $(f, P)$-cyclic execution. See Figure 4c.                                                                                  □

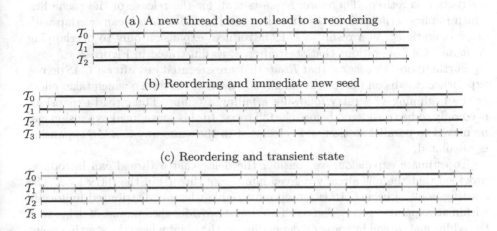

(a) A new thread does not lead to a reordering

$T_0$
$T_1$
$T_2$

(b) Reordering and immediate new seed

$T_0$
$T_1$
$T_2$
$T_3$

(c) Reordering and transient state

$T_0$
$T_1$
$T_2$
$T_3$

**Fig. 4.** Illustration of Theorem 2

### 4.3   Throughput Bounds

The periodicity offers an easy way to compute the expected number of threads inside the retry loop, and to bound the number of failures and the throughput.

**Lemma 1.** *In an $(f, P)$-cyclic execution, the throughput is $T = \frac{P}{q+r+1+f}$, and the average number of threads in the retry loop $P_{rl} = P \times \frac{f+1}{q+r+f+1}$.*

**Lemma 2.** *The number of failures is tighly bounded by $f^{(-)} \leq f \leq f^{(+)}$, and throughput by $T^{(-)} \leq T \leq T^{(+)}$, where*

$$f^{(-)} = \begin{cases} P-q-1 & \text{if } q \leq P-1 \\ 0 & \text{otherwise} \end{cases}, \qquad T^{(-)} = \begin{cases} \frac{P}{P+r} & \text{if } q \leq P-1 \\ \frac{P}{q+r+1} & \text{otherwise.} \end{cases}$$

$$f^{(+)} = \left\lfloor \frac{1}{2}\left((P-1-q-r) + \sqrt{(P-1-q-r)^2 + 4P}\right) \right\rfloor, \quad T^{(+)} = \frac{P}{q+r+1+f^{(+)}}.$$

# 5    Expansion and Complete Throughput Estimation

## 5.1    Expansion

Interference of threads does not only lead to logical conflicts but also to hardware conflicts which impact the performance significantly. We model the behavior of the cache coherency protocols which determine the interaction of overlapping *Read*s and *CAS*s. By taking MESIF [9] as basis, we come up with the following assumptions. When executing an atomic *CAS*, the core gets the cache line in exclusive state and does not forward it to any other requesting core until the instruction is retired. Therefore, requests stall for the release of the cache line which implies serialization. On the other hand, ongoing *Read*s can overlap with other operations. As a result, a *CAS* introduces expansion only to overlapping *Read* and *CAS* operations that start after it, as illustrated in Figure 2.

Furthermore, we assume that *Read*s that are executed just after a *CAS* do not experience expansion (as the thread already owns of the data), which takes effect at the beginning of a retry following a failing attempt. Thus, read expansions need only to be considered before the $0^{\text{th}}$ retry. In this sense, read expansion can be moved to parallel section and calculated in the same way as *CAS* expansion is calculated.

To estimate expansion, we consider the delay that a thread can introduce, provided that there is already a given number of threads in the retry loop. The starting point of each *CAS* is a random variable which is distributed uniformly within an expanded retry. The cost function $d$ provides the amount of delay that the additional thread introduces, depending on the point where the starting point of its *CAS* hits. By using this cost function we can formulate the expansion increase that each new thread introduces and derive the differential equation below to calculate the expansion of a *CAS*.

**Lemma 3.** *The expansion of a CAS operation is the solution of the following system of equations:*

$$\begin{cases} e'(P_{rl}) = cc \times \dfrac{\frac{cc}{2} + e(P_{rl})}{rc + cw + cc + e(P_{rl})}, & \text{where } P_{rl}^{(0)} \text{ is the point where} \\ e\left(P_{rl}^{(0)}\right) = 0 & \text{expansion begins.} \end{cases}$$

*Proof.* To prove the theorem, we compute $e(P_{rl} + h)$, where $h \leq 1$, by assuming that there are already $P_{rl}$ threads in the retry loop, and that a new thread attempts to *CAS* during the retry, within a probability $h$: $e(P_{rl} + h) = e(P_{rl}) + h \times \int_0^{rlw^{(+)}} \frac{d(t)}{rlw^{(+)}} dt$. The complete proof appears in the companion research report [5].

## 5.2    Throughput Estimate

It remains to combine hardware and logical conflicts in order to obtain the final upper and lower bounds on throughput. We are given as an input the expected number of threads $P_{rl}$ inside the retry loop. We firstly compute the expansion accordingly, by solving numerically the differential equation of Lemma 3. As explained in the previous subsection, we have $pw^{(+)} = pw + e$, and $rlw^{(+)} = rc + cw + e + cc$. We can then compute $q$ and $r$, that is the input set (together with the total number of threads $P$) of the method described in Section 4. Assuming that the initialization times of the threads are spaced enough, the execution will superimpose an $(f, P)$-cyclic execution. Thanks to Lemma 1, we can compute the average number of threads inside the retry loop, that we note by $h_f(P_{rl})$. A posteriori, the solution is consistent if this average number of threads inside the retry loop $h_f(P_{rl})$ is equal to the expected number of threads $P_{rl}$ that has been given as an input.

Several $(f, P)$-cyclic executions belong to the domain of the possible outcomes, but we are interested in upper and lower bounds on the number of failures $f$. We can compute them through Lemma 2, along with their corresponding throughput and average number of threads inside the retry loop. We note by $h^{(+)}(P_{rl})$ and $h^{(-)}(P_{rl})$ the average number of threads for the lowest number of failures and highest one, respectively. Our aim is finally to find $P_{rl}^{(-)}$ and $P_{rl}^{(+)}$, such that $h^{(+)}(P_{rl}^{(+)}) = P_{rl}^{(+)}$ and $h^{(-)}(P_{rl}^{(-)}) = P_{rl}^{(-)}$. If several solutions exist, then we want to keep the smallest, since the retry loop stops to expand when a stable state is reached.

Note that we also need to provide the point where the expansion begins. It begins when we start to have failures, while reducing the parallel section. Thus this point is $(2P-1)rlw^{(-)}$ (resp. $(P-1)rlw^{(-)}$) for the lower (resp. upper) bound on the throughput.

**Theorem 3.** *Let* $(x_n)$ *be the sequence defined recursively by* $x_0 = 0$ *and* $x_{n+1} = h^{(+)}(x_n)$. *If* $pw \geq rc + cw + cc$, *then* $P_{rl}^{(+)} = \lim_{n \to +\infty} x_n$.

*Proof.* In [5], we prove that $h^{(+)}$ is non-decreasing when $pw \geq rc + cw + cc$, and obtain the above theorem by applying the Theorem of Knaster-Tarski.

The same line of reasoning holds for $h^{(-)}$. We point out that when $pw < rlw^{(-)}$, we scan the interval of solution, and have no guarantees about the fact that the solution is the smallest one; still this corresponds to very extreme cases.

## 6   Experimental Evaluation

We validate our model and analysis framework through successive steps, from synthetic tests, capturing a wide range of possible abstract algorithmic designs, to several reference implementations of extensively studied lock-free data structure designs that include cases with non-constant parallel section and retry loop. The complete results can be found in [5] and the numerical simulation code in [4].

### 6.1   Setting

We have conducted experiments on an Intel ccNUMA workstation system. The system is composed of two sockets, that is equipped with Intel Xeon E5-2687W v2 CPUs. In a socket, the ring interconnect provides L3 cache accesses and core-to-core communication. Threads are pinned to a single socket to minimize non-uniformity in *Read* and *CAS* latencies. Due to the bi-directionality of the ring that interconnects L3 caches, uncontended latencies for intra-socket communication between cores do not show significant variability. The methodology in [6] is used to measure the *CAS* and *Read* latencies, while the work inside the parallel section is implemented by a for-loop of *Pause* instructions.

In all figures, y-axis provides the throughput, while the parallel work is represented in x-axis in cycles. The graphs contain the high and low estimates (see Section 4), corresponding to the lower and upper bound on the wasted retries, respectively, and an additional curve that shows the average of them.

## 6.2  Synthetic Tests

For the evaluation of our model, we first create synthetic tests that emulate different design patterns of lock-free data structures (value of $cw$) and different application contexts (value of $pw$).

Generally speaking, in Figure 5, we observe two main behaviors: when $pw$ is high, the data structure is not contended, and threads can operate without failure (unsuccessful retries). When $pw$ is low, the data structure is contended, and depending on the size of $cw$ (that drives the expansion) a steep decrease in throughput or just a roughly constant bound on the performance is observed.

An interesting fact is the waves appearing on the experimental curve, especially when the number of threads is low or the critical work big. This behavior is originating because of the variation of $r$ with the change of parallel work, a fact that is captured by our analysis.

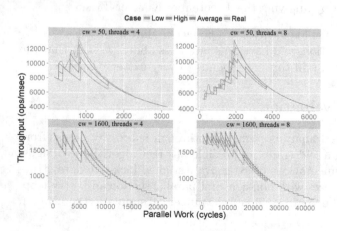

**Fig. 5.** Synthetic program

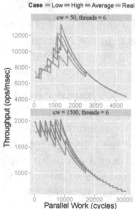

**Fig. 6.** Pop on stack

## 6.3   Treiber's Stack

The lock-free stack by Treiber [16] is typically the first example that is used to validate a freshly-built model on lock-free data structures. A Pop contains a retry loop that first reads the top pointer and gets the next pointer of the element to obtain the address of the second element in the stack, before attempting to *CAS* with the address of the second element. The access to the next pointer of the first element occurs between the *Read* and the *CAS*. Thus, it represents the work in *cw*. By varying the number of elements that are popped at the same time, and the cache misses implied by the reads, we vary the work in *cw* and obtain the results depicted in Figure 6.

## 6.4   Discussion

In this subsection we discuss the adequacy of our model, specifically the cyclic argument, to capture the behavior that we observe in practice. Figure 7 illustrates the frequency of occurrence of a given number of consecutive fails, together with average fails per success values and the throughput values, normalized by a constant factor so that they can be seen on the graph. In the background, the frequency of occurrence of a given number of consecutive fails before success is presented. As a remark, the frequency of 6+ fails is plotted together with 6. We expect to see a frequency distribution concentrated around the average fails per success value, within the bounds computed by our model.

While comparing the distribution of failures with the throughput, we could conjecture that the bumps come from the fact that the failures spread out. However, our model captures correctly the throughput variations and thus strips down the right impacting factor. The spread of the distribution of failures indicates the violation of a stable cyclic execution (that takes place in our model),

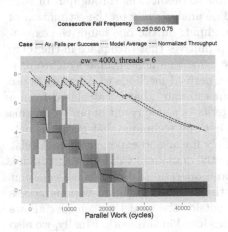

**Fig. 7.** Consecutive Fails Frequency

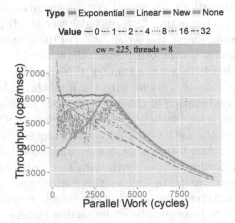

**Fig. 8.** Comparison of back-off schemes

but in these regions, $r$ actually gets close to 0, as well as the minimum of all gaps. The scattering in failures shows that, during the execution, a thread is overtaken by another one. Still, as gaps are close to 0, the imaginary execution, in which we switch the two thread IDs, would create almost the same performance effect. This reasoning is strengthened by the fact that the actual average number of failures follows the step behavior, predicted by our model. This shows that even when the real execution is not cyclic and the distribution of failures is not concentrated, our model that results in a cyclic execution remains a close approximation of the actual execution.

## 6.5  Back-Off Tuning

Together with our analysis comes a natural back-off strategy: we estimate the $pw$ corresponding to the peak point of the average curve, and when the parallel section is smaller than the corresponding $pw$, we add a back-off in the parallel section, so that the new parallel section is at the peak point.

We have applied exponential, linear and our back-off strategy to the Enqueue/Dequeue experiment specified in [5] (sequence of Enqueue and Dequeue interleaved with parallel sections). Our back-off estimate provides good results for both types of distribution. In Figure 8 (where the values of back-off are steps of 115 cycles), the comparison is plotted for the Poisson distribution, which is likely to be the worst for our back-off. Our back-off strategy is better than the other, except for very small parallel sections, but the other back-off strategies should be tuned for each value of $pw$.

## 7  Conclusion

In this paper, we have modeled and analyzed the performance of a general class of lock-free algorithms, and have so been able to predict the throughput of such algorithms, on actual system executions. The analysis rely on the estimation of two impacting factors that lower the throughput: on the one hand, the expansion, due to the serialization of the atomic primitives that take place in the retry loops; on the other hand, the wasted retries, due to a non-optimal synchronization between the running threads. We have derived methods to calculate those parameters, along with the final throughput estimate, that is calculated from a combination of these two previous parameters. As a side result of our work, this accurate prediction enables the design of a back-off technique that performs better than other well-known techniques, namely linear and exponential back-offs.

As a future work, we envision to enlarge the domain of validity of the model, in order to cope with data structures whose operations do not have constant retry loop, as well as the framework, so that it includes more various access patterns. The fact that our results extend outside the model we consider allows us to be optimistic on impacting factors introduced in this work. Finally, we also foresee studying back-off techniques that would combine a back-off in the parallel section (for lower contention) and in the retry loops (for higher robustness).

# References

1. Alemany, J., Felten, E.W.: Performance issues in non-blocking synchronization on shared-memory multiprocessors. In: Hutchinson, N.C. (ed.) Proceedings of the ACM Symposium on Principles of Distributed Computing (PoDC), pp. 125–134. ACM (1992)
2. Alistarh, D., Censor-Hillel, K., Shavit, N.: Are lock-free concurrent algorithms practically wait-free? In: Shmoys, D.B. (ed.) Symposium on Theory of Computing (STOC), pp. 714–723. ACM, June 2014
3. Anderson, J.H., Ramamurthy, S., Jeffay, K.: Real-time computing with lock-free shared objects. ACM Transactions on Computer Systems (TOCS) **15**(2), 134–165 (1997)
4. Atalar, A., Renaud-Goud, P.: Numerical simulation code. http://graal.ens-lyon.fr/prenaud/disc15/
5. Atalar, A., Renaud-Goud, P., Tsigas, P.: Analyzing the performance of lock-free data structures: A conflict-based model. Tech. Rep. 2014:15, Chalmers University of Technology, January 2015. http://arxiv.org/abs/1508.03566
6. David, T., Guerraoui, R., Trigonakis, V.: Everything you always wanted to know about synchronization but were afraid to ask. In: Kaminsky, M., Dahlin, M. (eds.) Proceedings of the ACM Symposium on Operating Systems Principles (SOSP), pp. 33–48. ACM, November 2013
7. Dice, D., Lev, Y., Moir, M.: Scalable statistics counters. In: Blelloch, G.E., Vöcking, B. (eds.) Proceedings of the ACM Symposium on Parallelism in Algorithms and Architectures (SPAA), pp. 43–52. ACM, July 2013
8. Dragicevic, K., Bauer, D.: A survey of concurrent priority queue algorithms. In: Proceedings of the International Parallel and Distributed Processing Symposium (IPDPS), pp. 1–6, April 2008
9. Goodman, J.R., Hum, H.H.J.: Mesif: A two-hop cache coherency protocol for point-to-point interconnects. Tech. rep., University of Auckland, November 2009. http://hdl.handle.net/2292/11594
10. Hendler, D., Shavit, N., Yerushalmi, L.: A scalable lock-free stack algorithm. Journal of Parallel and Distributed Computing (JPDC) **70**(1), 1–12 (2010)
11. Intel: Lock scaling analysis on Intel® Xeon® processors. Tech. Rep. 328878–001, Intel, April 2013
12. Kogan, A., Herlihy, M.: The future(s) of shared data structures. In: Halldórsson, M.M., Dolev, S. (eds.) Proceedings of the ACM Symposium on Principles of Distributed Computing (PoDC), pp. 30–39. ACM, July 2014
13. Lindén, J., Jonsson, B.: A skiplist-based concurrent priority queue with minimal memory contention. In: Baldoni, R., Nisse, N., van Steen, M. (eds.) OPODIS 2013. LNCS, vol. 8304, pp. 206–220. Springer, Heidelberg (2013)
14. Michael, M.M., Scott, M.L.: Simple, fast, and practical non-blocking and blocking concurrent queue algorithms. In: Burns, J.E., Moses, Y. (eds.) Proceedings of the ACM Symposium on Principles of Distributed Computing (PoDC), pp. 267–275. ACM, May 1996
15. Shavit, N., Lotan, I.: Skiplist-based concurrent priority queues. In: Proceedings of the International Parallel and Distributed Processing Symposium (IPDPS), pp. 263–268, May 2000
16. Treiber, R.K.: Systems programming: Coping with parallelism. Thomas J. Watson Research Center, International Business Machines Incorporated (1986)
17. Valois, J.D.: Implementing lock-free queues. In: Proceedings of International Conference on Parallel and Distributed Systems (ICPADS), pp. 64–69, December 1994

# A Constructive Approach for Proving Data Structures' Linearizability

Kfir Lev-Ari[1]([✉]), Gregory Chockler[2], and Idit Keidar[1]

[1] EE Department, Technion – Israel Institute of Technology, Haifa, Israel
kfirla@campus.technion.ac.il
[2] CS Department, Royal Holloway University of London, Egham, UK

**Abstract.** We present a comprehensive methodology for proving correctness of concurrent data structures. We exemplify our methodology by using it to give a roadmap for proving linearizability of the popular Lazy List implementation of the concurrent set abstraction. Correctness is based on our key theorem, which captures sufficient conditions for linearizability. In contrast to prior work, our conditions are derived directly from the properties of the data structure in sequential runs, without requiring the linearization points to be explicitly identified.

## 1 Introduction

While writing an efficient concurrent data structure is challenging, proving its correctness properties is usually even more challenging. Our goal is to simplify the task of proving correctness. We present a methodology that offers algorithm designers a constructive way to analyze their data structures, using the same principles that were used to design them in the first place. It is a generic approach for proving handcrafted concurrent data structures' correctness, which can be used for presenting intuitive proofs.

The methodology we present here generalizes our previous work on reads-write concurrency [10], and deals also with concurrency among write operations as well as with any number of update steps per operation (rather than a single update step per operation as in [10]). To do so, we define the new notions of *base point preserving steps*, *commutative steps*, and *critical sequence*. We demonstrate the methodology by proving linearizability of Lazy List [8], as opposed to toy examples in [10].

Our analysis consists of three stages. In the first stage we identify conditions, called *base conditions* [10], which are derived *entirely* by analysis of sequential behavior, i.e., we analyze the algorithm as if it is designed to implement the data structure correctly only in sequential executions. These conditions link states of the data structure with outcomes of operations running on the data structure

This work was partially supported by the Israeli Science Foundation (ISF), the Intel Collaborative Research Institute for Computational Intelligence (ICRI-CI), by a Royal Society International Exchanges Grant IE130802, and by the Randy L. and Melvin R. Berlin Fellowship in the Cyber Security Research Program.

© Springer-Verlag Berlin Heidelberg 2015
Y. Moses (Ed.): DISC 2015, LNCS 9363, pp. 356–370, 2015.
DOI: 10.1007/978-3-662-48653-5_24

from these states. More precisely, base conditions tell us what needs to be satisfied by a state of the data structure in order for a sequential execution to reach a specific point in an operation from that state. For example, Lazy List's *contains(31)* operation returns *true* if 31 appears in the list. A possible base condition for returning *true* is "there is an element that is reachable from the head of the list and its value is 31". Every state of Lazy List that satisfies this base condition causes *contains(31)* to return *true*.

In the second stage of our analysis we prove the linearization of update operations, (i.e., operations that might modify shared memory). We state two conditions on update operations that together suffice for linearizability. The first is *commutativity* of steps taken by *concurrent updates*. The idea here is that if two operations' writes to shared memory are interleaved, then these operations must be independent. Such behavior is enforced by standard synchronization approaches, e.g., two-phase locking. The second condition requires that some state reached during the execution of the update operation satisfy base conditions of all the update operation's writes. For example, the update steps of an *add(7)* operation in Lazy List depend on the predecessor and successor of 7 in the list. Indeed, Lazy List's *add(7)* operation writes to shared memory only after locking these nodes, which prevent concurrent operations from changing the two nodes that satisfy the base conditions of *add(7)*'s steps.

In the third stage we consider the relationship between update operations and read-only operations. We first require each update operation to have at most one point in which it changes the state of the data structure in a way that "affects" read-only operations. We capture the meaning of "affecting" read-only operations using base conditions. Intuitively, if an update operation has a point in which it changes something that causes the state to satisfy a base condition of a read-only operation, then we know that this point defines the outcome of the read-only operation. For example, Lazy List's *remove(3)* operation first *marks* the node holding 3, and then detaches it from its predecessor. Since *contains* treats marked nodes as deleted, the second update step does not affect *contains*.

In addition, we require that each read-only operation has a state in the course of its execution that satisfies its base condition. In order to show that such a state exists, we need to examine how the steps that we have identified in the update operations affect the base conditions of the read-only operations. For example, in Lazy List, *contains(9)* relies on the fact that if a node holding 9 is reachable from the head of the list, then there was some concurrent state in which a node holding 9 was part of the list. We need to make sure that the update operations support this assumption.

The remainder of this paper is organized as follows: Section 2 provides formal preliminaries. We formally present and illustrate the analysis approach in Section 3. We state and prove our main theorem in Section 4. Then, we demonstrate how base point analysis can be used as a roadmap for proving linearizability of Lazy List in Section 5. Section 6 concludes the paper.

## 2   Preliminaries

We extend here the model and notions we defined in [10]. Generally speaking, we consider a standard shared memory model [1] with one refinement, which is differentiating between local and shared state, as needed for our discussion.

Each process performs a sequence of operations on shared data structures implemented using a set $X = \{x_1, x_2, ...\}$ of shared variables. The shared variables support atomic operations, such as read, write, CAS, etc. A *data structure implementation* (algorithm) is defined as follows:

– A set $\mathcal{S}$ of *shared states*, some of which are *initial*, where $\underline{s} \in \mathcal{S}$ is a mapping assigning a value to each shared variable.
– A set of operations representing methods and their parameters (e.g., $add(7)$ is an operation). Each *operation op* is a state machine defined by: A set of local states $\mathcal{L}_{op}$, which are given as mappings $l$ of values to local variables; and a deterministic transition function $\tau_{op}(\mathcal{L}_{op} \times \mathcal{S}) \rightarrow Steps \times \mathcal{L}_{op} \times \mathcal{S}$ where *Steps* are transition labels, such as *invoke*, *return(v)*, $a \leftarrow read(x_i)$, $write(x_i, v)$, $CAS(x_i, v_{old}, v_{new})$, etc.

Invoke and return steps interact with the application, while read and write steps interact with the shared memory and are defined for every shared state. In addition, the implementation may use synchronization primitives (locks, barriers), which constrain the scheduling of ensuing steps, i.e., they restrict the possible *executions*, as we shortly define.

For a transition $\tau(l, \underline{s}) = \langle step, l', \underline{s}' \rangle$, $l$ determines the step. If *step* is an invoke or return, then $l'$ is uniquely defined by $l$. Otherwise, $l'$ is defined by $l$ and potentially $\underline{s}$. For invoke, return, read and synchronization steps, $\underline{s} = \underline{s}'$. If any of the variables is assigned a different value in $\underline{s}$ than in $\underline{s}'$, then the step is called an *update step*.

A state consists of a local state $l$ and a shared state $\underline{s}$. We omit either the shared or the local component of the state if its content is immaterial to the discussion. A *sequential execution of an operation* from a shared state $\underline{s_i} \in \mathcal{S}$ is a sequence of transitions of the form:

$$\frac{\bot}{\underline{s_i}}, \ invoke, \ \frac{l_1}{\underline{s_i}}, \ step_1, \ \frac{l_2}{\underline{s_{i+1}}}, \ step_2, \ ... \ , \ \frac{l_k}{\underline{s_j}}, \ return_k, \ \frac{\bot}{\underline{s_j}},$$

where $\bot$ is the operation's initial local sate and $\tau(l_m, \underline{s_n}) = \langle step_m, l_{m+1}, \underline{s_{n+1}} \rangle$. The first step is invoke and the last step is a return step.

A *sequential execution of a data structure* is a (finite or infinite) sequence $\mu$:

$$\mu = \frac{\bot}{\underline{s_1}}, \ O_1, \ \frac{\bot}{\underline{s_2}}, \ O_2, \ ... \ ,$$

where $\underline{s_1} \in \mathcal{S}_0$ and every $\frac{\bot}{\underline{s_j}}, O_j, \frac{\bot}{\underline{s_{j+1}}}$ in $\mu$ is a sequential execution of some operation. If $\mu$ is finite, it can end after an operation or during an operation.

In the latter case, we say that the last operation is *pending* in $\mu$. Note that in a sequential execution there can be at most one pending operation.

A *concurrent execution fragment of a data structure* is a sequence of interleaved states and steps of different operations, where each state consists of a set of local states $\{l_i, ..., l_j\}$ and a shared state $\underline{s_k}$, where every $l_i$ is a local state of a *pending* operation, which is an operation that has not returned yet. A *concurrent execution of a data structure* is a concurrent execution fragment that starts from an initial shared state and an empty set of local states. In order to simplify the discussion of initialization, we assume that every execution begins with a dummy (initializing) update operation that does not overlap any other operation. A state $\underline{s}'$ is *reachable from a state* $\underline{s}$ if there exists an execution fragment that starts at $\underline{s}$ and ends at $\underline{s}'$. A state is *reachable* if it is reachable from an initial state.

An operation for which there exists an execution in which it perform update steps is called *update operation*. Otherwise, it is called a *read-only operation*.

A data structure's correctness in sequential executions is defined using a *sequential specification*, which is a set of its allowed sequential executions. A *linearization* of execution $\mu$ is a sequential execution $\mu_l$, such that:

- Every operation that is not invoked in $\mu$ is not invoked in $\mu_l$.
- Every operation that returns in $\mu$ returns also in $\mu_l$ and with the same return value.
- $\mu_l$ belongs to the data structure's sequential specification.
- The order between non-interleaved operations in $\mu$ and $\mu_l$ is identical.

A data structure is *linearizable* [9] if each of its executions has a linearization.

## 3   Base Point Analysis

In this section we present key definitions for analyzing and proving correctness using what we call *base point analysis*. We illustrate the notions we define using Lazy List [8], whose pseudo code appears in Algorithm 1.

We start by defining *base conditions* [10]. A *base condition* establishes some link between the local state that an operation reaches and the shared variables the operation has read before reaching this state. It is given as a predicate $\Phi$ over shared variable assignments. Formally:

**Definition 1 (Base Condition).** Let $l$ be a local state of an operation $op$. A predicate $\Phi$ over shared variables is a *base condition* for $l$ if every sequential execution of $op$ starting from a shared state $\underline{s}$ such that $\Phi(\underline{s})$ is true, reaches $l$.

For completeness, we define a base condition for $step_i$ in an execution $\mu$ to be a base condition of the local state that precedes $step_i$ in $\mu$. For example, consider an execution of Lazy List's *contains(31)* operation that returns *true*. A possible base condition for that return step is $\phi$ : "there is an unmarked node in which $key = 31$, and that node is reachable from the head of the list". Every sequential

▷ $\Phi_{loc}(\underline{s}, n_1, n_2, e)$ : (Head $\xrightarrow{*} n_1$) ∧ ($n_1.next = n_2$) ∧ $\neg n_1.marked$ ∧
$\neg n_2.marked$ ∧ ($n_1.val < e$) ∧ ($e \leq n_2.val$)

| | |
|---|---|
| 1 **Function** *contains(e)* | 27 **Function** *locate(e)* |
| 2 $\quad$ c ← **read**(Head) | 28 $\quad$ **while** *true* |
| 3 $\quad$ **while read**(c.val) < e | 29 $\quad\quad$ $n_1$ ← **read**(Head) |
| 4 $\quad\quad$ c ← **read**(c.next) | 30 $\quad\quad$ $n_2$ ← **read**($n_1.next$) |
| 5 $\quad$ ▷ $\Phi_c$ (Head $\xrightarrow{*}$ c) ∧ (c.val ≥ e) | 31 $\quad\quad$ **while read**($n_2.val$) < e |
| $\quad\quad$ ∧ ($\nexists n$ : (Head $\xrightarrow{*} n$) ∧ | 32 $\quad\quad\quad$ $n_1$ ← $n_2$ |
| $\quad\quad$ (e ≤ n.val < c.val)) | 33 $\quad\quad\quad$ $n_2$ ← **read**($n_2.next$) |
| 6 $\quad$ **if read**(c.marked)∨**read**(c.val) ≠ e | 34 $\quad\quad$ **lock**($n_1$) |
| 7 $\quad$ ▷ $\Phi_c$∧(c.marked ∨ c.val ≠ e) | 35 $\quad\quad$ **lock**($n_2$) |
| 8 $\quad\quad$ **return** *false* | 36 $\quad\quad$ **if read**($n_1.marked$) = *false* ∧ |
| 9 $\quad$ **else** | 37 $\quad\quad$ **read**($n_2.marked$) = *false* ∧ |
| 10 $\quad$ ▷ $\Phi_c$ ∧ (c.val = e) | 38 $\quad\quad$ **read**($n_1.next$) = $n_2$ |
| 11 $\quad\quad$ **return** *true* | 39 $\quad\quad\quad$ **return** $\langle n_1, n_2 \rangle$ |
| | 40 $\quad\quad$ **else** |
| | 41 $\quad\quad\quad$ **unlock**($n_1, n_2$) |
| 12 **Function** *add(e)* | 42 **Function** *remove(e)* |
| 13 $\quad$ $\langle n_1, n_2 \rangle$ ← *locate(e)* | 43 $\quad$ $\langle n_1, n_2 \rangle$ ← *locate(e)* |
| 14 $\quad$ ▷ $\Phi_{loc}(\underline{s}, n_1, n_2, e)$ | 44 $\quad$ ▷ $\Phi_{loc}(\underline{s}, n_1, n_2, e)$ |
| 15 $\quad$ **if read**($n_2.val$) ≠ e | 45 $\quad$ **if read**($n_2.val$) = e |
| 16 $\quad$ ▷ $\Phi_{loc}(\underline{s}, n_1, n_2, e)$ ∧ ($n_2.val ≠ e$) | 46 $\quad$ ▷ $\Phi_{loc}(\underline{s}, n_1, n_2, e)$ ∧ ($n_2.val = e$) |
| 17 $\quad\quad$ **write**($n_3$, **new** Node(e, $n_2$)) | 47 $\quad\quad$ **write**($n_2.marked$, *true*) |
| 18 $\quad\quad$ **write**($n_1.next$, $n_3$) | 48 $\quad\quad$ **write**($n_1.next$, $n_2.next$) |
| 19 $\quad\quad$ **unlock**($n_1$) | 49 $\quad\quad$ **unlock**($n_1$) |
| 20 $\quad\quad$ **unlock**($n_2$) | 50 $\quad\quad$ **unlock**($n_2$) |
| 21 $\quad\quad$ **return** *true* | 51 $\quad\quad$ **return** *true* |
| 22 $\quad$ **else** | 52 $\quad$ **else** |
| 23 $\quad$ ▷ $\Phi_{loc}(\underline{s}, n_1, n_2, e)$ ∧ ($n_2.val = e$) | 53 $\quad$ ▷ $\Phi_{loc}(\underline{s}, n_1, n_2, e)$ ∧ ($n_2.val ≠ e$) |
| 24 $\quad\quad$ **unlock**($n_1$) | 54 $\quad\quad$ **unlock**($n_1$) |
| 25 $\quad\quad$ **unlock**($n_2$) | 55 $\quad\quad$ **unlock**($n_2$) |
| 26 $\quad\quad$ **return** *false* | 56 $\quad\quad$ **return** *false* |

**Algorithm 1.** Lazy List. Base conditions are listed as comments, using $\Phi_{loc}$ defined above the functions.

execution of *contains(31)* from a shared state that satisfied $\phi$ reaches the same *return true* step. Base conditions for all of Lazy List's update and return steps are annotated in Algorithm 1, and are discussed in detail in Section 5.1 below.

For a given base condition, the notion of *base point* [10] links the local state that has base condition $\Phi$ to a shared state $\underline{s}$ where $\Phi(\underline{s})$ holds.

**Definition 2 (Base Point).** Let *op* be an operation in an execution $\mu$, and let $\Phi_t$ be a base condition for the local state at point $t$ in $\mu$. An execution prefix of *op* in $\mu$ has a *base point* for point $t$ with $\Phi_t$, if there exists a shared state $\underline{s}$ in $\mu$, called a *base point of* $t$, such that $\Phi_t(\underline{s})$ holds.

Note that together with Definition 1, the existence of a base point $\underline{s}$ for point $t$ implies that the step or local state at point $t$ in operation $op$ is reachable from $\underline{s}$ in a sequential run of $op$ starting from $\underline{s}$. In Figure 1 we depict two states of Lazy List: $\underline{s_1}$ is a base point for a *return true* step of *contains(7)*, whereas $\underline{s_2}$ is not.

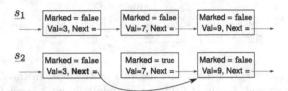

**Fig. 1.** Two states of Lazy List (Algorithm 1): $\underline{s_1}$ is a base point for *contains(7)*'s *return true* step, as it satisfies the base condition "there is a node that is reachable from the head of the list, and its value is 7". The shared state $\underline{s_2}$ is not a base point of this step, since there is no sequential execution of *contains(7)* from $\underline{s_2}$ in which this step is reached.

Let $\underline{s_0}$ and $\underline{s_1}$ be two shared states, and let $\underline{s_0}$, $st$, $\underline{s_1}$ be an execution fragment. We call $\underline{s_0}$ the *pre-state* of step $st$, and $\underline{s_1}$ the *post-state* of $st$.

We now define *base point preserving* steps, which are steps under which base conditions are invariant.

**Definition 3 (Base Point Preserving Step).** A step $st$ is base point preserving with respect to an operation $op$ if for any update or return step $b$ of $op$, for any concurrently reachable pre-state of $st$, $st$'s pre-state is a base point of $b$ if and only if $st$'s post-state is a base point of $b$.

An example of a base point preserving step is illustrated in Figure 2. In this example, the second write step in Lazy List's *remove* operation is base point preserving for *contains*. Intuitively, since *contains* treats marked nodes as removed, the same return step is reached regardless whether the marked node is detached from the list or reachable from the head of the list.

# 4    Linearizability Using Base Point Analysis

We use the notions introduced in Section 3 to define sufficient conditions for linearizability. In Section 4.1 we define conditions for update operations, and in Section 4.2 we define an additional condition on read-only operations, and show that together, our conditions imply linearizability.

## 4.1    Update Operations

We begin by defining the *commutativity* of steps.

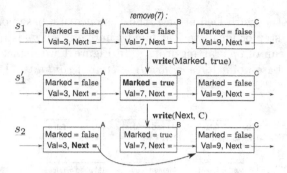

**Fig. 2.** Operation *remove(7)* of Lazy List has two write steps. In the first, *marked* is set to *true*. In the second, the *next* field of the node holding 3 is set to point to the node holding 9. If a concurrent *contains(7)* operation sequentially executes from state $s_1$, it returns true. If we execute *contains(7)* from $s'_1$, i.e., after *remove(7)*'s first write, *contains* sees that 7 is marked, and therefore returns false. If we execute *contains* from state $s_2$, after *remove(7)*'s second write, *contains* does not see B because it is no longer reachable from the head of the list, and also returns false. The second write does not affect the return step, since in both cases it returns false.

**Definition 4 (Commutative Steps).** Consider an execution $\mu$ of a data structure $ds$ that includes the fragment $a, s_1, b, s_2$. We say that steps $a$ and $b$ *commute* if $a, s_1, b, s_2$ in $\mu$ can be replaced with $b, s'_1, a, s_2$, so that the resulting sequence $\mu'$ is a valid execution of $ds$.

We now observe that if two update steps commute, then their resulting shared state is identical for any ordering of these steps along with interleaved read steps.

**Observation 1.** *Let $s_0, a, s_1, b, s_2$ be an execution fragment of two update steps $a$ and $b$ that commute, then $s_2$ is the final shared state in any execution fragment that starts from $s_0$ and consists of a, b and any number of read steps (for any possible ordering of steps).*

We are not interested in commutativity of all steps, but rather of "critical" steps that modify shared memory or determine return values. This is captured by the following notion:

**Definition 5 (Critical Sequence).** The *critical sequence* of an update operation *op* in execution $\mu$ is the subsequence of *op*'s steps from its first to its last update step; if *op* takes no update steps in $\mu$, then the critical sequence consists solely of its last read.

For example, if in Lazy List $op_1 = add(2)$ and $op_2 = add(47)$ concurrently add items in disjoint parts of the list, then all steps in $op_1$'s critical sequence commute with all those in $op_2$'s critical sequence. The same is not true for list traversal steps taken before the critical sequence, since $op_2$ may or may not traverse a node holding 2, depending on the interleaving of $op_1$ and $op_2$'s steps. In general, Lazy List uses locks to ensure that the critical steps of two operations overlap only if these operations' respective steps commute. This is our first condition for linearizability of update operations.

Our second requirement from update operations is that each critical sequence begin its execution from a base point of all the operation's update and return steps. Together, we have:

**Definition 6 (Linearizable Update Operations).** A data structure $ds$ has linearizable update operations if for every execution $\mu$, for every update operation $uo_i \in \mu$:

1. $\forall uo_j \in \mu, i \neq j$, if the critical sequence of $uo_j$ interleaves with the critical sequence of $uo_i$ in $\mu$, then all of $uo_i$'s steps in its critical sequence commute with all of the steps in $uo_j$'s critical sequence, and all the update steps of $uo_i$ and $uo_j$ are base point preserving for $uo_j$ and $uo_i$ respectively.
2. The pre-state of $uo_i$'s critical sequence is a base point for all of $uo_i$'s update and return steps, and moreover, if $uo_i$ is complete in $\mu$, then this state is not a base point for any other possible update step of $uo_i$.

To satisfy these conditions, before its critical sequence, an update operation takes actions to guarantee that the pre-state of its first update will be a base point for the operation's update and return steps, as depicted in Figure 3. For example, any algorithm that follows the two-phase locking protocol [2] satisfies these conditions: operations perform concurrent modifications only if they gain disjoint locks, which means that their steps commute. And in addition, once all locks are obtained by an operation, the shared state is a base point for all of its ensuing steps, i.e., for its critical sequence.

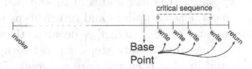

**Fig. 3.** The structure of update operations. The steps before the critical sequence ensure that the pre-state of the first update step is a base point for all of the update and return steps.

We now show that every execution that has linearizable update operations and no read-only operations is linearizable.

**Lemma 1.** *Let $\mu$ be an execution consisting of update operations of some data structure that has linearizable update operations. Let $\mu'$ be a sequential execution of all the operations in $\mu$ starting from the same initial state as $\mu$ such that if some operation $op_1$'s critical sequence ends before the critical sequence of another operation $op_2$ begins in $\mu$, then $op_1$ precedes $op_2$ in $\mu'$. Then $\mu'$ is a linearization of $\mu$.*

**Proof.** By construction, $\mu'$ includes only invoke steps from $\mu$, and every two operations that are not interleaved in $\mu$ occur in the same order in $\mu$ and $\mu'$. It remains to show that every operation has the same return step in $\mu$ and $\mu'$.

Denote by $\mu'_i$ the prefix of $\mu'$ consisting of $i$ operations, and by $\mu_i$ the subsequence of $\mu$ consisting of the steps of the same $i$ operations. Denote by $op_i$ the $i^{\text{th}}$ operation in $\mu'$.

We prove by induction on $i$ that $\mu'_i$ is a linearization of $\mu_i$ and both executions end in the same final state. As noted above, for linearizability, it suffices to show that all operations that return in both $\mu'_i$ and $\mu_i$ return the same value.

The first operation in both $\mu$ and $\mu'$ is a dummy initialization, which returns before all other operations are invoked. Hence, $\mu_1 = \mu'_1$, and their final states are identical.

Assume now that $\mu'_i$ is a linearization of $\mu_i$ and their final states are the same. The critical sequence of $op_{i+1}$ in $\mu_{i+1}$ overlaps the critical sequences of the last zero or more operations in $\mu_i$. We need to show that (1) the execution of $op_{i+1}$ that overlaps these steps in $\mu_{i+1}$ yields the same return value and the same final state as a sequential execution of $op_{i+1}$ from the final state of $\mu_i$; and (2) the return values of the operations that $op_{i+1}$ is interleaved with in $\mu_{i+1}$ are unaffected by the addition of $op_{i+1}$'s steps.

(1) By definition 6, the pre-state $\underline{p}$ of $op_{i+1}$'s critical sequence in $\mu_{i+1}$ is a base point for $op_{i+1}$'s update and return steps. Note that $\underline{p}$ occurs in $\mu_{i+1}$ before any update step of $op_{i+1}$, and thus it also occurs in $\mu_i$. Thus, the same $\underline{p}$ occurs also in $\mu_i$. All the update steps after $\underline{p}$ in $\mu_{i+1}$ belong to operations that have interleaved critical sequences with $op_{i+1}$ in $\mu_{i+1}$, and therefore by definition 6 their update steps are base point preserving for $op_{i+1}$. These are the update steps that occur after $\underline{p}$ in $\mu_i$, and so the final state of $\mu_i$ is a base point for the update and return steps that $op_{i+1}$ takes in $\mu_{i+1}$.

By the induction hypothesis, the last states of $\mu_i$ and $\mu'_i$ are identical, and we conclude that $op_{i+1}$ has the same update and return steps in $\mu_{i+1}$ and $\mu'_{i+1}$.

In addition, the final states of $\mu_{i+1}$ and $\mu'_{i+1}$ occur at the end of execution fragments that consist of the same update steps, s.t. if two update steps have different orders in $\mu_{i+1}$ and in $\mu'_{i+1}$ then they are commute. By Observation 1 we conclude that the last states of $\mu_{i+1}$ and $\mu'_{i+1}$ are identical.

(2) If an update step of $op_{i+1}$ occurs in $\mu_{i+1}$ before operation $op_j$'s return step, then $op_{i+1}$ has an interleaved critical sequence with $op_j$. This means that all of $op_{i+1}$'s update steps are base point preserving for $op_j$. Thus, the same base points are reached before $op_j$'s critical sequences in $\mu_i$ and in $\mu_{i+1}$. By definition 6, $op_j$ takes the same update and return steps in $\mu_i$ and $\mu_{i+1}$.    □

## 4.2    Read-Only Operations

We state two conditions that together ensure linearizability of read-only operations. First, each read-only operation $ro$ should have a base point for its return step, which can be either a post-state of some step of operation that is concurrent to $ro$, or the pre-state of $ro$'s invoke step. Second, update operations should have at most one step that is not base point preserving for read-only operations.

In Theorem 2 we present a sufficient condition for linearizability. Intuitively, we want the linearizable update operations to satisfy two conditions: (1) the read-only operations should see the update operations as a sequence of single steps that mutate the shared state. To express this relation we use the base point preserving property; and (2) the update operations should guarantee the correctness of the returned values of the read-only operation, as expressed by the return steps' base conditions.

**Theorem 2.** *Let ds be a data structure that has linearizable update operations. If ds satisfies the following conditions, it is linearizable:*

1. *Every update operation of ds has at most one step that is not base point preserving with respect to all read-only operations.*
2. *For every execution $\mu$, for every complete read-only operation $ro \in \mu$, there exists in $\mu$ a shared state $\underline{s}$ between the pre-state of $ro$'s invoke step and the pre-state of $ro$'s return step (both inclusive) that is a base-point for $ro$'s return step.*

**Proof.** For a given execution $\mu^-$, let $\mu$ be an execution that is identical to $\mu^-$ with the addition that all pending operations in $\mu^-$ are allowed to complete. Note that $\mu$ also has linearizable update operations. We now show that $\mu$ has a linearization, and therefore $\mu^-$ has a linearization.

We build a sequential execution $\mu_{seq}$ as follows:

1. $\mu_{seq}$ starts from the same shared state as $\mu$.
2. We sequentially execute all the update operations that takes steps of their critical sequence in $\mu$ in the order of their steps that are not base point preserving for read-only operations, (or the last read step in case all steps are base point preserving). We denote this sequence of steps by $\{ord_i\}$. The update operation that performs $ord_i$ in $\mu$ is denoted $uo_i$.
3. Each read-only operation $ro$ of $\mu$ is executed in $\mu_{seq}$ after an update operation $uo_i$ such that the post-state of $ord_i$ in $\mu$ is a base point for $ro$, and is either concurrent to $ro$ or the latest step in $\{ord_i\}$ that precedes $ro$'s invoke step. Such a step exists since (1) by our assumption, $ro$ has a base point between its invoke step's pre-state and its return step's pre-state; and (2) every step that is not in $\{ord_i\}$ is base point preserving for $ro$.
4. The order in $\mu_{seq}$ between non-interleaved read-only operations that share the same base point follows their order in $\mu$. The order between interleaved read-only operations that are executed in $\mu_{seq}$ from the same base point is arbitrary.

Now, by Lemma 1, the sequence of update operations in $\mu_{seq}$ is a linearization of the sequence of update operations in $\mu$.

Therefore we only need to prove that the order between the read-only operations and other operations that are not interleaved in $\mu$ is identical in $\mu_{seq}$ and $\mu$, and that each read-only operation has the same return step in both executions. We observe that:

1. In $\mu$ and $\mu_{seq}$ the steps of $\{ord_i\}$ appear in the same order, and in both executions each read-only operation is either executed after the same $ord_i$ in both, or is executed concurrently to $ord_i$ in $\mu$ and immediately after $uo_i$ in $\mu_{seq}$.
2. Each shared state satisfies the same base conditions since the update steps that appear in a different order in $\mu$ and $\mu_{seq}$ commute.

Therefore each post-state of $ord_i$ remains a base point in $\mu_{seq}$ for the same read-only operations that it was in $\mu$, and thus each read-only operation reaches the same return step as in $\mu$.

Assume towards contradiction that two read-only operations $ro_1$ and $ro_2$ have a different order in $\mu$ and $\mu_{seq}$, and w.l.o.g. $ro_1$ precedes $ro_2$ in $\mu$, and $ro_2$ precedes $ro_1$ in $\mu_{seq}$.

Let $uo_1$ be the update operation that precedes $ro_1$ in $\mu_{seq}$, and $uo_2$ be the update operation that precedes $ro_2$ in $\mu_{seq}$. $uo_2 \neq uo_1$, otherwise $ro_1$ and $ro_2$ had the same base point and their execution order was identical to their order in $\mu$. Since $ro_2$ precedes $ro_1$ in $\mu_{seq}$, we conclude that $ord_2$ occurs before $ord_1$ in $\mu$. $ord_1$ takes place in $\mu$ as last as one step before $uo_1$'s return step. Therefore $ord_2$ must appear somewhere before $ro_1$'s return step. But $ro_1$ precedes $ro_2$ in $\mu$, meaning that $ord_2$ is not the latest steps of $ord$ that precedes $ro_2$'s invoke step, in contradiction.                                     □

# 5    Roadmap for Proving Linearizability

We now prove that Lazy List (Algorithm 1) satisfies the requirements of Theorem 2, implying that it is linearizable. We demonstrate the three stages of our roadmap for proofing linearizability using base point analysis.

## 5.1    Stage I: Base Conditions

We begin by identifying base conditions for the operations' update and return steps. The base conditions are annotated in comments in Algorithm 1. To do so, we examine the possible sequential executions of each operation.

*Add & Remove.* Let $Head \overset{*}{\Rightarrow} n$ denote that there is a set of shared variables $\{Head, x_1, ..., x_k\}$ such that $Head.next = x_1 \wedge x_1.next = x_2 \wedge ... \wedge x_k = n$, i.e., that there exists some path from the shared variable $Head$ to $n$. Let $\Phi_{loc}(\underline{s}, n_1, n_2, e)$ be the predicate indicating that in the shared state $\underline{s}$, the place of the key $e$ in the list is immediately after the node $n_1$, and at or just before the node $n_2$:

$\Phi_{loc}(\underline{s}, n_1, n_2, e) : Head \overset{*}{\Rightarrow} n_1 \wedge n_1.next = n_2 \wedge \neg n_1.marked \wedge \neg n_2.marked \wedge n_1.val < e \wedge e \leq n_2.val.$

**Observation 2.** $\Phi_{loc}(\underline{s}, n_1, n_2, e)$ *is a base condition for the local state of add(e) (remove(e)) after line 14 (resp., 44).*

Now, $\Phi_{loc}(\underline{s}, n_1, n_2, e) \wedge n_2.val \neq e$ is a base condition for *add*'s write and *return true* steps and *removes*'s *return false* step. And a base condition for *add*'s *return false* step and *remove*'s write and *return true* steps is $\Phi_{loc}(\underline{s}, n_1, n_2, e) \wedge n_2.val = e$.

*Contains.* First, we define the following predicate:

$$\Phi_c : \ Head \overset{*}{\Rightarrow} c \wedge \ c.val \ \geq \ e \ \wedge (\not\exists \, n \ : \ Head \overset{*}{\Rightarrow} n \ \wedge e \leq n.val < c.val) \ .$$

In a shared state satisfying $\Phi_c$, $c$ is the node with the smallest value greater than or equal to $e$ in the list. The base condition for *contains*'s *return true* step is $\Phi_c \wedge c.val = e$, and the base condition for *return false* is the predicate $\Phi_c \wedge (c.marked \vee c.val \neq e)$.

These predicates are base conditions since every sequential execution from a shared state satisfying them reaches the same return step, i.e., if $c$ is the node in the list with the smallest value that is greater than or equal to $e$ and is reachable from the head of the list, then after traversing the list and reaching it, the return step is determined according to its value.

## 5.2  Stage II: Linearizability of Update Operations

We next prove that Lazy List has linearizable update operations. Using Definition 6, it suffices to show the following: (1) each update operation has a base point for its update and return steps, (2) each critical sequence commutes with interleaved critical sequences, and (3) the update steps are base point preserving for operations with interleaved critical sequences.

*Base Points for Update and Return Steps*

*Proof Sketch.* First we claim that in every execution of an *add* (*remove*) operation, line 10 (37, respectively), is a base point for all the operation's update and return steps.

**Claim 1.** *Consider the shared state $\underline{s}$ immediately after line 14 (44) of an execution of add(e) (remove(e)). Then $\Phi(\underline{s}, n_1, n_2, e)$ is true.*

Claim 1 can be proven by induction on the steps of an execution. Intuitively, the idea is to show by induction that the list is sorted, and that in each *add* (*remove*) operation, *locate* locks the two nodes and verifies that they are unmarked, and so no other operation can change them and they remain reachable from the head of the list and connected to each other. Formal proofs of this claim were given in [11,13].

Based on Claim 1 and the observation that after line 14 (44) of an execution of *add(e)* (*remove(e)*) the value of $n_2.val$ persists until $n_2$ is unlocked, we conclude that the shared state after *locate* returns is a base point for update operations' update and return steps. Since the locked nodes cannot be modified by concurrent operations, the pre-state of the first update step is also a base point for the same steps. In case the update operation has no update steps, the same holds for the last read step.

*Commutative and Base Point Preserving Steps*

*Proof Sketch.* We now show that the steps of update operations that have interleaved updates are commutative, and that the update steps are base point preserving. Specifically, we examine the steps between the first update step and the last one (or just the last read step in case of an update operation that does no have update steps).

In order to add a key to the list, an update operation locks the predecessor and successor of the new node. For removing a node from the list, the update operation locks the node and it predecessor. This means that every update operation locks the nodes that it changes and the nodes that it relies upon before it verifies its steps' base point. Thus, update operations have concurrent critical sequence only if they access different nodes. Therefore their steps commute, and are base point preserving for one another.

## 5.3    Stage III: Linearizability of Read-Only Operations

The final stage in our proof is to show the conditions stated in Theorem 2 hold for each read-only operation.

*Single Non-Preserving Step per Update Operation.* First we show that every update operation of Lazy List has at most one step that is not base point preserving for all read-only operations.

*Proof Sketch.* We only need to consider update steps, since every other step in *add* and *remove* does not modify the shared memory, and therefore does not affect any base condition of *contains*. There are two update steps in an operation. In *add*, the first update step allocates a new (unreachable) node. Nodes that are not reachable from the head of the list do not affect any base condition. Therefore, only the second step, the one that changes the list, is not base point preserving for *contains*.

In *remove*, the first update step marks the removed node, and the second makes the node unreachable from the head of the list. Since marked nodes are treated in every base condition of *contains* as if they are already detached from the list, the second update step does not change the truth value of the base condition of contains. More precisely, if we compare the second update step's prestate to its post-state, they both satisfy the same base conditions of *contains*'s return steps.

*Concurrent Base Points.* Last, we show that in every execution of *contains*, the return step of *contains* has a base point, and that base point occurs between the pre-state of *contains*'s invoke step and the pre-state of *contains*'s return step.

*Proof Sketch.* When *add* inserts a new value to the list, it locks the predecessor node $n$ and the successor $m$, and verifies that $n$ and $m$ are not marked and that $n.next = m$.

Since $n$ or $m$ cannot be removed as long as they are locked, and since nodes are removed only when their predecessor is also locked, new nodes are not added to detached parts of the list. This means that every node encountered during a traversal of the list was reachable from the head at some point.

In addition, if *add* inserts a value $e$, it satisfies $n.val < e < m.val$, since $n$ and $m$ are locked, and no value other than $e$ is inserted between them before $e$ is added (this can be proven by induction on executions).

The execution of *contains(e)* reaches line 6 only after it traverses the list from its head and reaches the first node $c$ whose value $v$ satisfies $e \leq v$. Thus, there is some concurrent shared state $\underline{s}$ that occurs after the invocation of *contains(e)* in which $c$ is unmarked and reachable from the head of the list. State $\underline{s}$ is a base-point of *contains(e)*'s return step.

# 6 Discussion

We introduced a constructive methodology for proving correctness of concurrent data structures and exemplified it with a popular data structure. Our methodology outlines a roadmap for proving correctness. While we have exemplified its use for writing semi-formal proofs, we believe it can be used at any level of formalism, from informal correctness arguments to formal verification. In particular, our framework has the potential to simplify the proof structure employed by existing formal methodologies for proving linearizability [3–7,11,12], thus making them more accessible to practitioners.

Currently, using our methodology involves manually identifying base conditions, commuting steps, and base point preserving steps. It would be interesting to create tools for suggesting a base condition for each local state, and identifying the interesting steps in update operations using either static or dynamic analysis.

**Acknowledgments.** We thank Naama Kraus, Noam Rinetzky and the anonymous reviewers for helpful comments and suggestions.

# References

1. Attiya, H., Welch, J.: Distributed Computing: Fundamentals, Simulations and Advanced Topics. John Wiley & Sons (2004)
2. Bernstein, P.A., Hadzilacos, V., Goodman, N.: Concurrency Control and Recovery in Database Systems. Addison-Wesley Longman Publishing Co., Inc., Boston (1987)
3. Chockler, G.V., Lynch, N.A., Mitra, S., Tauber, J.: Proving atomicity: an assertional approach. In: Fraigniaud, P. (ed.) DISC 2005. LNCS, vol. 3724, pp. 152–168. Springer, Heidelberg (2005)

4. Colvin, R., Groves, L., Luchangco, V., Moir, M.: Formal verification of a lazy concurrent list-based set algorithm. In: Ball, T., Jones, R.B. (eds.) CAV 2006. LNCS, vol. 4144, pp. 475–488. Springer, Heidelberg (2006)

5. Derrick, J., Schellhorn, G., Wehrheim, H.: Verifying linearisability with potential linearisation points. In: Butler, M., Schulte, W. (eds.) FM 2011. LNCS, vol. 6664, pp. 323–337. Springer, Heidelberg (2011)

6. Dongol, B., Derrick, J.: Proving linearisability via coarse-grained abstraction (2012). CoRR abs/1212.5116

7. Guerraoui, R., Vukolić, M.: A scalable and oblivious atomicity assertion. In: van Breugel, F., Chechik, M. (eds.) CONCUR 2008. LNCS, vol. 5201, pp. 52–66. Springer, Heidelberg (2008)

8. Heller, S., Herlihy, M.P., Luchangco, V., Moir, M., Scherer III, W.N., Shavit, N.N.: A lazy concurrent list-based set algorithm. In: Anderson, J.H., Prencipe, G., Wattenhofer, R. (eds.) OPODIS 2005. LNCS, vol. 3974, pp. 3–16. Springer, Heidelberg (2006)

9. Herlihy, M.P., Wing, J.M.: Linearizability: A correctness condition for concurrent objects. ACM Trans. Program. Lang. Syst. **12**(3), 463–492 (1990)

10. Lev-Ari, K., Chockler, G., Keidar, I.: On correctness of data structures under reads-write concurrency. In: Kuhn, F. (ed.) DISC 2014. LNCS, vol. 8784, pp. 273–287. Springer, Heidelberg (2014)

11. O'Hearn, P.W., Rinetzky, N., Vechev, M.T., Yahav, E., Yorsh, G.: Verifying linearizability with hindsight. In: Proceedings of the 29th ACM SIGACT-SIGOPS Symposium on Principles of Distributed Computing, PODC 2010, pp. 85–94. ACM, New York (2010)

12. Vafeiadis, V., Herlihy, M., Hoare, T., Shapiro, M.: Proving correctness of highly-concurrent linearisable objects. In: Proceedings of the Eleventh ACM SIGPLAN Symposium on Principles and Practice of Parallel Programming, PPoPP 2006, pp. 129–136. ACM, New York (2006)

13. Vafeiadis, V., Herlihy, M., Hoare, T., Shapiro, M.: A safety proof of a lazy concurrent list-based set implementation. Tech. Rep. UCAM-CL-TR-659, University of Cambridge, Computer Laboratory, January 2006

# Modular Verification of Concurrency-Aware Linearizability

Nir Hemed[1], Noam Rinetzky[1(✉)], and Viktor Vafeiadis[2]

[1] Tel Aviv University, Tel Aviv, Israel
maon@cs.tau.ac.il
[2] MPI-SWS, Kaiserslautern, Germany

**Abstract.** Linearizability is the de facto correctness condition for concurrent objects. Informally, linearizable objects provide the illusion that each operation takes effect *instantaneously at a unique point in time* between its invocation and response. Hence, *by design*, linearizability cannot describe behaviors of *concurrency-aware concurrent objects* (CA-objects), objects in which several overlapping operations "seem to take effect *simultaneously*". In this paper, we introduce *concurrency-aware linearizability* (CAL), a generalized notion of linearizability which allows to formally describe the behavior of CA-objects. Based on CAL, we develop a thread- and procedure-modular verification technique for reasoning about CA-objects and their clients. Using our new technique, we present the first proof of linearizability of the elimination stack of Hendler *et al.* [10] in which the stack's elimination subcomponent, which is a general-purpose CA-object, is specified and verified independently of its particular usage by the stack.

## 1 Introduction

Linearizability [12] is a property of the externally observable behavior of concurrent objects and is considered the de facto standard for specifying concurrent objects. Intuitively, a concurrent object is linearizable if in every execution each operation seems to take effect instantaneously between its invocation and response, and the resulting sequence of (seemingly instantaneous) operations respects a given sequential specification. For certain concurrent objects, however, it is *impossible* to provide a useful sequential specification: their behavior in the presence of concurrent (overlapping) operations is, and should be, *observably different* from their behavior in the sequential setting. We refer to such objects as *Concurrency-Aware Concurrent Objects (CA-objects)*. We show that the traditional notion of linearizability is not expressive enough to allow for describing all the desired behaviors of certain important CA-objects without introducing unacceptable ones, i.e., ones which their clients would find to be too lax.

Providing clear and precise specifications for concurrent objects is an important goal and is a necessary step towards developing *thread-modular compositional* verification techniques, i.e., ones which allow to reason about each thread

© Springer-Verlag Berlin Heidelberg 2015
Y. Moses (Ed.): DISC 2015, LNCS 9363, pp. 371–387, 2015.
DOI: 10.1007/978-3-662-48653-5_25

separately (thread-modular verification) and to *compose* the proofs of concurrent objects from the proofs of their subcomponents (compositional verification). Designing such techniques is challenging because they have to take into account the possible *interference* by other threads on the shared subcomponents without exposing the internal structure of the latter.

We continue to describe the notions of CA-objects and CA-linearizability via examples. A prominent example of a CA-object is the *exchanger* object (see, e.g., `java.util. concurrent.Exchanger`). Exchangers allow threads to pair up and *atomically* swap elements so that either both threads manage to swap their elements or none of them does. Although exchangers are widely used in practice in genetic algorithms, pipeline designs, and implementations of thread pools and highly concurrent data structures such as channels, queues, and stacks [10,21, 22,24], they do not have a formal specification, which precludes modular proofs of their clients. This is perhaps not so surprising: exchangers are CA-objects, and as we show, they cannot be given a *useful* sequential specification (see §3). In order to specify CA-objects, we extend the notion of linearizability: we relax the requirement that specifications should be sequential, and allow them to be "*concurrency-aware*" as in the following informal exchanger specification.

$$\{\mathsf{true}\}\ t_1 : x = \mathsf{exchange}(v_1)\ ||\ t_2 : y = \mathsf{exchange}(v_2)\ \{x = (\mathsf{true}, v_2) \wedge y = (\mathsf{true}, v_1)\}$$
$$\{\mathsf{true}\}\qquad\qquad t : x = \mathsf{exchange}(v)\qquad\qquad\qquad \{x = (\mathsf{false}, v)\}$$

where the notation $t : r = \mathsf{exchange(v)}$ indicates that `exchange` is invoked by thread $t$. This specification says that two concurrent threads $t_1$ and $t_2$ can succeed in exchanging their values but that a thread can also fail to find a partner and return back its argument.

We next consider a client of the exchanger, the *elimination stack* of Hendler et al. [10]. The elimination stack is comprised of a lock-free stack and an *elimination module* (an array of exchangers). It achieves high performance under high workloads by allowing concurrent pairs of `push` and `pop` operations to eliminate each other and thus reduce contention on the main stack. To verify the correctness of the elimination stack, one needs to ensure that every `push` operation can be eliminated by exactly one `pop` operation, and vice versa, and that the paired operations agree on the effect of the successful exchange to the observable behavior of the elimination stack as a whole. We present a reasoning technique which allows to provide natural specifications for such intricate interactions, and modularly verify their correct implementation. Intuitively, we instrument the program with an auxiliary variable that logs the sets of "*seemingly simultaneous*" operations on objects (*CA-trace*), e.g., pairs of matching successful exchange operations and singletons of failed ones.

The contributions of this paper can be summarized as follows:

- We identify the class of concurrency-aware objects in which certain operations should "seem to take effect *simultaneously*" and provide formal means to specify them using *concurrency-aware linearizability* (CAL), a generalized notion of linearizability built on top of as restricted form of concurrent specifications.

- We present a simple and effective method for verifying CAL. The unique aspects of our approach are: (i) The ability to treat a *single* atomic action as a *sequence of operations* by *different* threads which must execute completely and without interruptions, thus providing the illusion of simultaneity, and (ii) Allowing CA-objects built over other CA-objects to define their CA-trace as a function over the traces of their encapsulated objects, which makes reasoning about clients straightforward.
- We present the first *modular* proof of linearizability of the elimination stack [10] in which (i) the elimination subcomponent is verified independently of its particular usage by the stack, and (ii) the stack is verified using an implementation-independent *concurrency-aware specification* of the elimination module.

## 2    Motivating Examples

In this section, we describe an implementation of an exchanger object, which we use as our running example, and of one of its clients, an elimination stack. In [9], we describe another client of the exchanger, a synchronous queue [22].

We assume an imperative programming language which allows to implement *concurrent objects* using object-local variables, dynamically (heap) allocated memory and a static (i.e., a priori fixed) number of concurrent subobjects. A program is comprised of a parallel composition of sequential commands (threads), where each thread has its own local variables. Threads share access to the dynamically allocated memory and to a static number of concurrent objects. We assume that concurrent objects follow a strict ownership discipline: (1) objects can be manipulated only by invoking their methods; (2) subobjects contained in an object $o$ can be used only by $o$, the (unique) concurrent object that contains them; and (3) there is a strict separation between the parts of the memory used for the implementation of different objects. The operational semantics of our language is standard and can be found in [9]. We denote the object-local variables of an object $o$ by Vars($o$). For readability, we write our examples in a Java-like syntax.

### 2.1    Exchanger

Figure 1 shows a simplified implementation of the (wait-free) exchanger object in the `java.util.concurrent` library. A client thread uses the exchanger by invoking the `exchange` method with a value that it offers to swap. The `exchange` method attempts to find a partner thread and, if successful, instantaneously exchanges the offered value with the one offered by the partner. It then returns a pair (`true,data`), where `data` is the partner's value of type `int`. If a partner thread is not found, `exchange` returns (`false,v`), communicating to the client that the operation has failed. In more detail, an exchange is performed using `Offer` objects, consisting of the `data` offered for exchange and a `hole` pointer. A

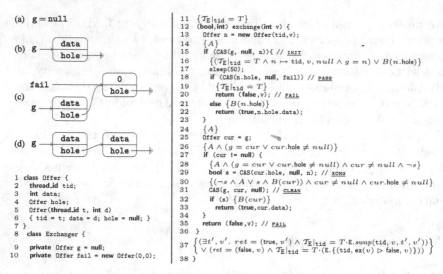

```
(a)  g = null
(b)  g →[ data ]
         [ hole ]→┤├

     fail ──────────────[   0   ]
(c)                     [ hole ]→┤├
     g →[ data ]
         [ hole ]←

(d)  g →[ data ]──[ data ]
         [ hole ]  [ hole ]→┤├

1   class Offer {
2     thread_id tid;
3     int data;
4     Offer hole;
5     Offer(thread_id t, int d)
6     { tid = t; data = d; hole = null; }
7   }
8   class Exchanger {

9     private Offer g = null;
10    private Offer fail = new Offer(0,0);
```

```
11  {𝒯_E|tid = T}
12  (bool,int) exchange(int v) {
13    Offer n = new Offer(tid,v);
14    {A}
15    if (CAS(g, null, n)){ // INIT
16      {(𝒯_E|tid = T ∧ n ↦ tid, v, null ∧ g = n) ∨ B(n.hole)}
17      sleep(50);
18      if (CAS(n.hole, null, fail)) // PASS
19        {𝒯_E|tid = T}
20        return (false,v); // FAIL
21      else {B(n.hole)}
22        return (true,n.hole.data);
23    }
24    {A}
25    Offer cur = g;
26    {A ∧ (g = cur ∨ cur.hole ≠ null)}
27    if (cur != null) {
28      {A ∧ (g = cur ∨ cur.hole ≠ null) ∧ cur ≠ null ∧ ¬s}
29      bool s = CAS(cur.hole, null, n); // XCHG
30      {(¬s ∧ A ∨ s ∧ B(cur)) ∧ cur ≠ null ∧ cur.hole ≠ null}
31      CAS(g, cur, null); // CLEAN
32      if (s) {B(cur)}
33        return (true,cur.data);
34    }
35    return (false,v); // FAIL
36  }
37  {(∃t', v'. ret = (true, v') ∧ 𝒯_E|tid = T·E.swap(tid, v, t', v'))
     ∨ (ret = (false, v) ∧ 𝒯_E|tid = T·(E.{(tid, ex(v) ▷ false, v)}))}
38  }
```

**Fig. 1.** Implementation of the exchanger CA-object annotated with its proof outline.

successful swap occurs when the `hole` pointer in the `Offer` of one thread points to the `Offer` of another thread, as depicted in Figure 1(d).

A thread can participate in a swap in two ways. The first way happens when the thread finds that the value of `g` is null, as in the state depicted in Figure 1(a). In this case, the thread attempts to set `g` to its `Offer` (line 15) resulting in a state like the one shown in Figure 1(b). It then waits for a partner thread to match with (line 17). Upon awakening, it checks whether it was paired with another thread by executing a `CAS` on its own `hole` (line 18). If the `CAS` succeeds, then a match did not occur, and setting the `hole` pointer to point to the `fail` sentinel signals that the thread is no longer interested in the exchange. (The resulting state is depicted in Figure 1(c).) A failed `CAS` means that another thread has already matched the `Offer` and the exchange can complete successfully.

The second way happens when the thread finds at line 15 that `g` is not null. In this case, the thread attempts to update the `hole` field of the `Offer` pointed to by `g` from its initial null value to its own `Offer` (CAS at line 29). An additional `CAS` (line 31) sets `g` back to null. By doing so, the thread helps to remove an already-matched offer from the global pointer; hence, the CAS at line 31 is unconditional. Moreover, this cleanup prevents having to wait for the thread that set `g` to its offer; such a wait would compromise the wait-free property of the exchanger.

## 2.2　Elimination Stack

The *elimination stack* [10] is a scalable concurrent stack implemented using two subobjects: a concurrent stack, S, which implements the internal stack data structure, and an elimination layer, AR. The concurrent stack, S, exposes `push()` and `pop()` methods that perform CAS operations to modify the top of the stack, and fail if there is any contention on the head of the stack. The elimination layer,

```
1  class ElimArray {                      25  class EliminationStack {
2    Exchanger[] E = new Exchanger[K];    26    final int POP_SENTINAL = INFINITY;
3    (bool, int) exchange(int data) {     27    Stack S = new Stack();
4      int slot = random(0,K-1);          28    ElimArray AR = new ElimArray();
5      return E[slot].exchange(data);
6  } }                                    29    bool push(int v) {
                                          30      int d;
7  class Stack {                          31      while(true) {
8    class Cell {int data; Cell next;}    32        bool b = S.push(v);
9    Cell top = null;                     33        if (b) return true;
                                          34        (b,d) = AR.exchange(v);
10   bool push(int data) {                35        if (d == POP_SENTINAL)
11     Cell h = top;                      36          return true;
12     Cell n = new Cell(data, h);        37    } }
13     return CAS(&top, h, n);
14   }                                    38    (bool, int) pop() {
                                          39      bool b;
15   (bool, int) pop() {                  40      int v;
16     Cell h = top;                      41      while(true) {
17     if (h == null)                     42        (b,v) = S.pop();
18       return (false, 0); // EMPTY      43        if (b) return (true,v);
19     Cell n = h.next;                   44        (b,v) = AR.exchange(POP_SENTINAL);
20     if (CAS(&top, h, n))               45        if (v != POP_SENTINAL)
21       return (true, h.data);           46          return (true,v);
22     else                               47    } }
23       return (false, 0);              48  }
24 } }
```

**Fig. 2.** An implementation of the elimination stack of Hendler *et al.* [10].

AR, essentially acts as an exchanger object, but is implemented as an array of exchangers to reduce contention.

Figure 2 shows a simplified version of the elimination stack. A pushing, respectively, popping, thread first tries to perform its operation on the main stack (lines 32 and 42). If it fails due to contention, it uses the elimination layer to directly exchange a value with a concurrently executing thread: A pushing thread invokes AR.exchange (line 34) with its input value as argument, and a popping thread offers the special value POP_SENTINAL (line 44). When push calls AR.exchange, it randomly selects an array entry within the elimination array's range and attempts to exchange a value with another thread. The pushing thread checks if the return value matches the POP_SENTINAL. Symmetrically, a popping thread that calls AR.exchange checks if the return value is not POP_SENTINAL. Note that the exchange operation might fail. This might happen either because no exchange took place (the call to exchange returned (false, 0)) or because the exchange was performed between two threads executing the same operation. A thread deals with such a failure by simply retrying its operation.

## 3  Concurrency-Aware Linearizability (CAL)

Linearizability [12] relates (the observable behavior of) an implementation of a concurrent object with a sequential specification. Both the implementation and the specification are formalized as *prefix-closed sets of histories*. A history $H = \psi_1 \psi_2 \ldots$ is a sequence of method *invocation* (call) and *response* (return) actions. Specifications are given using *sequential histories*, histories in which

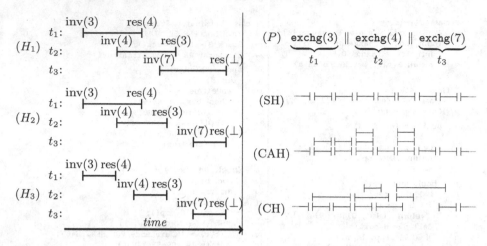

**Fig. 3.** A client program $P$ together with a concurrent history ($H_1$), a CA-history ($H_2$), and an undesired sequential history ($H_3$). We also show schematic depictions of a sequential history (SH), a CA-history (CAH), and an arbitrary concurrent history (CH).

every response is immediately preceded by its matching invocation. Implementations, on the other hand, allow arbitrary interleaving of actions by different threads, as long as the subsequence of actions of every thread is sequential. Informally, a concurrent object $OS_C$ is linearizable with respect to a specification $OS_A$ if every history $H$ in $OS_C$ can be *explained* by a history $S$ in $OS_A$ that "looks similar" to $H$. The similarity is formalized by a real-time relation $H \sqsubseteq_{RT} S$, which requires $S$ to be a permutation of $H$ preserving the per-thread order of actions and the order of non-overlapping operations (execution of methods) on objects.

We claim that it is *impossible* to provide a useful sequential specification for the exchanger. Figure 3 shows a program $P$ which uses an exchanger object and three histories, where an `exchange`(n) operation returning value $n'$ is depicted using an interval bounded by an "inv($n$)" and a "res($n'$)" actions. Note that histories $H_1$ and $H_2$ might occur when $P$ executes, but $H_3$ cannot. Histories $H_1$ and $H_2$ correspond to the case where threads $t_1$ and $t_2$ exchange items 3 and 4, respectively, and $t_3$ fails to pair up. History $H_3$ is one possible sequential explanation of $H_1$. Using $H_3$ to explain $H_1$ raises the following problem: if $H_3$ is allowed by the specification then every prefix of $H_3$ must be allowed as well. In particular, history $H_3'$ in which only $t_1$ performs its operation should be allowed. Note that in $H_3'$, a thread exchanges an item without finding a partner. Clearly, $H_3'$ is an *undesired* behavior. In fact, any sequential history that attempts to explain $H_1$ would allow for similar undesired behaviors. Indeed, sequential histories can explain only executions in which all `exchange` operations fail. We conclude that any sequential specification of the exchanger is either too restrictive or too loose.

## 3.1   A Formal Definition of Concurrency-Aware Linearizability

We now formalize the notion of *concurrency-aware linearizability*. We assume infinite sets of object names $o \in \mathsf{O}$, method names $f \in \mathsf{F}$, and threads identifiers $t \in \mathsf{T}$.

**Definition 1.** *An **object action** is either an **invocation** $\psi = (t, \mathrm{inv}\, o.f(n))$ or a **response** $\psi = (t, \mathrm{res}\, o.f \vartriangleright n)$. We denote the thread, object, and method of $\psi$ by $tid(\psi) = t$, $oid(\psi) = o$, and $fid(\psi) = f$, respectively.*

Intuitively, an invocation $\psi = (t, \mathrm{inv}\, o.f(n))$ means that thread $t$ started executing method $f$ on object $o$ passing $n$ as a parameter, and a *response* $\psi = (t, \mathrm{res}\, o.f' \vartriangleright n)$ means that the execution of method $f'$ terminated with a return value $n$.

**Definition 2.** *A **history** $H$ is a finite sequence of invocations and responses. A history is **sequential** if it comprised of an alternation of invocations and responses starting with an invocation. A history $H$ is **well-formed** if for every thread $t$, $H|_t$ is sequential, where $H|_t$ is the subsequence of $H$ comprised of actions of thread $t$. A history is **complete** if it is well-formed and every invocation has a matching response. History $H^c$ is a **completion** of a well-formed history $H$ if it is complete and can be obtained from $H$ by (possibly) extending $H$ with some response actions and (possibly) removing some invocation actions. We denote by $complete(H)$ the set of all completions of $H$. An **object system** is a prefix-closed set of well-formed histories.*

**Definition 3.** *The **real-time order** between actions of a well-formed history $H$ is an irreflexive partial order $\prec_H$ on (indices of) object actions: $i \prec_H j$ if there exists $i \leq i' < j' \leq j$ such that $tid(H_i) = tid(H_{i'})$, $tid(H_j) = tid(H_{j'})$, $H_{i'} = (\_, \mathrm{res}\, \_)$ and $H_{j'} = (\_, \mathrm{inv}\, \_)$).*

Essentially, a history records the interaction between the the client program and the object system. The interaction is recorded at the interface level of the latter at the point where control passes from the program to the object system and vice versa. Given two operations, the real-time order determines whether one operation precedes the other or whether the two are concurrent, i.e., their executions overlap.

**Definition 4 (CA-traces).** *An **operation** of a concurrent object $o$, denoted by $(t, f(n) \vartriangleright n')$, is a pair of an invocation $(t, \mathrm{inv}\, o.f(n))$ and its matching response$(t, \mathrm{res}\, o.f \vartriangleright n')$. A **concurrency-aware trace** $T$ is a sequence of **CA-elements** where each CA-element is a pair $o.S$ of an object $o$ and a non-empty set $S$ of operations of $o$.*

Roughly speaking, every CA-element represents a set of overlapping operations on one object and a CA-trace is a sequence of such sets. CA-traces provide a uniform representation of complete histories where operations may only overlap in a pairwise manner. For example, the CA-element

$o.\{(t_1, f_1(n_1) \rhd r_1), \ldots, (t_k, f_k(n_k) \rhd r_k)\}$ represents, among others, the history $((t_1, \mathrm{inv}\, o.f_1(n_1)) \cdot \ldots \cdot (t_k, \mathrm{inv}\, o.f_k(n_k)) \cdot (t_1, \mathrm{res}\, o.f_1 \rhd r_1) \cdot \ldots \cdot (t_k, \mathrm{res}\, o.f_k \rhd r_k))$.

Given a CA-trace $T$, the projection of $T$ to a thread $t$, denoted by $T|_t$, is the subsequence of CA-elements of $T$ mentioning $t$. Note that the projection of a trace $T$ to thread $t$ returns not only the operations of $t$ but also all operations of other threads that are concurrent with some operation of thread $t$. Similarly, $T|_o$ denotes the subsequence of CA-elements of $T$ mentioning $o$.

Let $H$ be a complete history, and $i$ and $j$ indices of an invoke action $H_i = (t, \mathrm{inv}\, o.f(n))$ and of its matching response $H_j = (t, \mathrm{res}\, o.f \rhd n')$. The *operation* pertaining to $H_i$, denoted by $OP(H, i)$, is $(t, f(n) \rhd n')$. Let $J \subseteq \{1..H\}$ be a set of indices of actions in $H$ which operate on the same object $o$, i.e., $\forall j \in J.\, oid(H_j) = o$. The *operation set* corresponding to $J$ in $H$, denoted by $OPSet(H, J)$, is $o.\{OP(H, j) \mid j \in J\}$.

**Definition 5.** *A complete history $H$ **agrees** with a CA-trace $T$, denoted by $H \sqsubseteq_{CAL} T$, if there is a surjective function $\pi : \{i \mid 1 \leq i \leq |H| \wedge H_i = (\_, inv\_)\} \to \{1..|T|\}$ such that*

$$\forall i, j.\, (i \prec_H j \implies \pi(i) < \pi(j)) \wedge \forall k \in \{1, \cdots, |T|\}.\, T_k = OPSet(H, \{m \mid \pi(m) = k\}).$$

Intuitively, a complete history $H$ agrees with a CA-trace $T$ if every operation in $H$ appears in one CA-element of $T$, and vice versa. Furthermore, the real-time order between the operations in $H$ must be included in the order of the CA-elements of $T$ that they appear in (i.e., $T$ must preserve the order of any operations ordered according to $H$).

Formally, concurrency-aware linearizability of an object system is described by relating each of its histories to a corresponding CA-trace:

**Definition 6 (Concurrency-Aware Linearizability).** *We say that an object system, $OS$, is **concurrency-aware linearizable (CAL)** with respect to a set of CA-traces, $\mathcal{T}$, if $\forall H \in OS. \exists H^c \in complete(H). \exists T \in \mathcal{T}.\, H^c \sqsubseteq_{\mathsf{CAL}} T$.*

Thus, a *CA-linearizable object* is one that every interaction with it can be "explained" by a CA-trace adhering to its specification.

**Note.** In [8], we formalized the notion of *concurrency-aware linearizability* in terms of a relation between sets of histories. The novelty there was that the specification was comprised of *concurrency-aware* histories (CA-histories) instead of sequential ones. Informally, a CA-history allows for operations of different threads to overlap, as long as they overlap in a pairwise manner: An invoke action can follow a response action only if the latter appears at the end a complete history. As a result, a CA-histories can be seen as a sequence of sets of concurrent operations where each set is an equivalence class with respect to the real-time order. In this paper, we found that it is more convenient to work with CA-traces, which provide an equivalent alternative presentation of complete CA-histories that is insensitive to the order of actions of overlapping operations.

## 4  Specifying Concurrency-Aware Concurrent Objects

In this section, we gradually develop our approach for providing logical (symbolic) specifications of CA-objects by applying it to the exchanger. An accurate specification of the exchanger is one where every successful exchange corresponds to the overlapping of exactly the two operations that participated in the exchange, while an unsuccessful exchange, i.e., one that returns (false, _), does not overlap with any other operation. Formally, the specification of an exchanger object E can be given as the set of CA-traces $S^1 S^2 S^3 \cdots$ where each CA-element $S^i$ is either

- $E.\{(t, \mathsf{ex}(v) \triangleright \mathsf{true}, v'), (t', \mathsf{ex}(v') \triangleright \mathsf{true}, v)\}$ for some $t, t', v, v'$ such that $t \neq t'$ (which in the following we will abbreviate as $E.swap(t, v, t', v')$), or
- $E.\{(t, \mathsf{ex}(v) \triangleright \mathsf{false}, v)\}$ for some thread $t$ and value $v$.

This specification, however, has a very global nature and is therefore cumbersome to use when reasoning about a particular exchange.

What we would like is a *local* way to specify CA-objects that is amenable to logical (syntactic) treatment. Our idea is to specify the effect of individual operations using Hoare triples [13], as is common in the sequential setting. Indeed, Herlihy and Wing [12] have also adopted this approach to describe the set of histories in the sequential specification of linearizable concurrent objects. Can we provide such a specification to the exchanger?

As a first attempt, consider the *concurrent* specification shown in §1. This specification states that *only* two threads that execute exchange() concurrently can match and successfully swap elements, while a thread that failed to find a partner fails to swap.

This specification may appear intuitive, but it is difficult to give it a formal meaning. The standard interpretation of Hoare triples is insufficient, because it precludes thread-modular compositional reasoning. The most obvious problem is that it is not possible to reason about the body of one thread in a sequential manner because the specification explicitly contains the parallel composition operator. A second problem is that it is difficult to adapt the concurrent specification of the exchange operations to an *agreed asymmetric view* in the context in which it is used. For example, when verifying the elimination stack, we would like to pretend that the exchange operation of the pushing thread happens right before that of the popping thread. This would allow to correctly interpret the simultaneous exchange operations as an elimination of a push($n$) operation by a pop() which returns $n$.

To overcome the first problem, we extend the specification with an auxiliary variable $\mathcal{T}_E$ recording the CA-trace witnessing that the exchanger is CAL. The specification of the exchange operation says that if initially the recorded trace was $T$, then after the exchange operation, it contains one more CA-element, corresponding either to the successful exchange if exchange() returns true or to the unsuccessful exchange otherwise.

$$\{\mathcal{T}_E|_{\mathtt{tid}} = T\} \quad \mathtt{tid} : ret = E.\mathtt{exchange}(v)$$
$$\left\{ \begin{array}{l} (\exists t', v'. \; ret = (\mathsf{true}, v') \land \mathcal{T}_E|_{\mathtt{tid}} = T \cdot E.swap(\mathtt{tid}, v, t', v') \land t' \neq \mathtt{tid}) \\ \lor \; (ret = (\mathsf{false}, v) \land \mathcal{T}_E|_{\mathtt{tid}} = T \cdot (E.\{(\mathtt{tid}, \mathsf{ex}(v) \triangleright \mathsf{false}, v)\})) \end{array} \right\}$$

Note that in the precondition and the postcondition, we do not describe the contents of the entire trace, but rather only of its projection to the current thread. We do so because there may be other exchanges running concurrently to the specified exchange, which may also append CA-elements to the recorded trace. To ensure that our specification is usable in a concurrent setting, we thus ensure that the precondition and postcondition are *stable* under interference from other threads, i.e., that concurrent operations cannot invalidate these assertions.

To address the second problem, we only need to perform a minor change. We do not change the specification as such, only the understanding of the auxiliary variable $\mathcal{T}_E$. Instead of having for each object one auxiliary variable that records its CA-trace, we have one global auxiliary variable $\mathcal{T}$ that records the CA-traces for all the objects, and define $\mathcal{T}_E$ to be the view of $\mathcal{T}$ according to object E. Our key idea is to let the exchanger module define $\mathcal{T}_E$ as a function of $\mathcal{T}$. For the exchanger, we simply define $\mathcal{T}_E$ to be the projection of $\mathcal{T}$ to the CA-elements of the exchanger (*i.e.*, $\mathcal{T}_E = \mathcal{T}|_E$).

**Logging the Object Interaction Using an Auxiliary History Variable.** To specify and verify CAL, we instrument the program with an auxiliary variable $\mathcal{T}$ that records the CA-trace that is equivalent to a given concurrent history. Our idea is to add auxiliary assignments to the programs that append CA-elements to $\mathcal{T}$ at the appropriate points.

Since multiple objects can manipulate $\mathcal{T}$, the specification of an object $o$ should not directly mention $o$, but rather its view on $\mathcal{T}$, which we denote as $\mathcal{T}_o$. A simple choice would be to define this view to be $\mathcal{T}|_o$, the projection of the trace to the CA-elements of object $o$. While this works for objects that do not depend on subobjects, it does not enable compositional verification of higher-level objects. The reason is that the desired equivalent CA-trace of a higher-level object is typically determined by the CA-traces of its subobjects. If, however, we want to verify an object compositionally, we are not allowed to peek into the implementations of its subobjects in order to add auxiliary assignments to $\mathcal{T}$.

Instead, we require for each object $o$ to provide a function $F_o$ from the CA-elements of its immediate subobjects to CA-traces containing only operations for $o$. Given such a function $F_o$, we define its total extension $\hat{F}_o$ as the function that given an element $a$ returns $F_o(a)$ if this is defined or $a$ otherwise. Note that $\hat{F}_o$ is idempotent and that for disjoint objects $o$ and $o'$, $\hat{F}_o \circ \hat{F}_{o'} = \hat{F}_{o'} \circ \hat{F}_o$. Next, we define $\overline{F_o}$ to recursively apply $\hat{F}_{o_i}$ for all objects $o_i$ encapsulated by $o$. This is defined by induction on the object nesting depth. At each level, if $o$ depends on objects $o_1, \ldots, o_n$, we define $\overline{F_o} \triangleq \hat{F}_o \circ (\overline{F_{o_1}} \circ \ldots \circ \overline{F_{o_n}})$. Again, because of encapsulation, the order in which $\overline{F_{o_1}}$ to $\overline{F_{o_n}}$ are composed does not matter. Finally, define $\mathcal{T}_o \triangleq \overline{F_o}(\mathcal{T})$.

**Encoding Interference and Cooperation Using Rely-Guarantee Conditions.** Next, since the exchange operations are concurrent, we cannot merely give a sequential specification in Hoare logic, but instead use rely/guarantee reasoning [15], a more expressive formalism that allows expressing concurrent specifications. In rely/guarantee, each program $C$ is specified not only by a precondition $P$ and a postcondition $Q$, but also by a rely condition $R$ and a guarantee condition $G$, which we have written as $R, G \Vdash \{P\}\ C\ \{Q\}$. These rely/guarantee conditions are parameterized by thread identifiers and describe the interaction between threads. For a thread $t$, the rely condition $R^t$ records the interference that $t$ might incur from the other threads, while the guarantee $G^t$ records the effect $t$ is allowed to have on other threads. Rely/guarantee gives thread-modular reasoning as it exposes the interaction between threads without referring to the code of other threads.

Internally, in the verification of the exchanger, these conditions will correlate the concrete state manipulated by the algorithm and the recorded history. For example, they require that when a thread successfully modifies the g.hole to point to its own offer, it also logs in $\mathcal{T}$ a CA-element which records the successful exchange (see §5).

From the client's perspective, however, the internal definitions of $R^{\text{tid}}$ and $G^{\text{tid}}$ are irrelevant. For them to be usable, however, they should adhere to a few minimal constraints, which are common for any object $o$:

- For every two distinct threads $t \neq t'$, we should have $G^t \Rightarrow R^{t'}$. This is the standard requirement in rely/guarantee reasoning ensuring that multiple methods of $o$ may be invoked in parallel.
- The methods of $o$ may only modify the auxiliary history variable, $\mathcal{T}$, the parts of the memory used in its own representation, and (via method calls) the state of its concurrent subobjects. Moreover, they may only append onto $\mathcal{T}$ entries corresponding to $o$ and its encapsulated objects, and pertaining only to threads currently executing one of its methods. Formally, this is
$$G^t \Rightarrow (\exists T.\ \mathcal{T} = \overleftarrow{\mathcal{T}} \cdot T \wedge T = T|_o = T|_t \wedge \forall x \notin \{h\} \cup \mathsf{Vars}(o).\ x = \overleftarrow{x}),\text{ where}$$
we use the hook arrow notation to represent the value of a program variable in prior state.
- The object $o$ does not assume anything about the private state of other objects, and allows them to extend the auxiliary history variable, $\mathcal{T}$. Formally, we require that $\textsc{irrelevant}^t_o \Rightarrow R^t$ where $\textsc{irrelevant}^t_o \triangleq \exists T.\ \mathcal{T}_o =$
$$\overleftarrow{\mathcal{T}_o} \cdot T \wedge T|_t = T|_o = \epsilon \wedge (\forall x \in \mathsf{Vars}(o).\ x = \overleftarrow{x}).$$

Finally, since there are may be multiple threads running concurrently, the precondition and postcondition of the exchange method, we take the projection of $\mathcal{T}_E$ to the thread of interest (i.e., $\mathcal{T}_E|_{\text{tid}}$). As is standard in Hoare logic, we use the logical variable $T$ to record the initial value of $\mathcal{T}_E|_{\text{tid}}$.

**Stack Specification.** The specification of the elimination stack as well as the ordinary concurrent stack it contains is expressed in a similar style. Technically, we say that a sequential history of stack operations is *well-defined* over an initial stack, if executing the (successful) operations in order is possible and yields the same results for the *pop* operations. A history is *well-formed* with respect to the stack object, denoted $\mathrm{WF_S}(H)$, if $H|_S$ is a sequential well-defined history over the empty initial stack. The specifications for the stack methods $f \in \{push, pop\}$

are:

$$R^t, G^t \Vdash \{\mathrm{WF_S}(\mathcal{T_S}) \wedge \mathcal{T_S}|_t = H\} \ t: r := \mathrm{S}.f(n) \ \{\mathrm{WF_S}(\mathcal{T_S}) \wedge \mathcal{T_S}|_t = H \cdot (\mathrm{S}.\{(t, f(n) \rhd r)\})\}$$

The abstract value of a concurrent object, if needed (e.g., to determine the result of a *pop()* operation), can be "computed" by replaying the logged actions.

## 5  Verifying the Exchanger and the Elimination Stack

In this section, we prove that the elimination stack is linearizable by verifying each of objects—the exchanger, the elimination array, the central stack, and the elimination stack—modularly. For space reasons, we only present the key ingredients of the proof. The full proofs can be found in [9].

We start with the elimination array, whose correctness is the simplest to demonstrate. The elimination array, AR, encapsulates an array of exchanger objects E[0],...,E[K-1] and exposes the same specification as a single exchanger. To verify that it conforms to its specification, we define the $F_{AR}$ function as $F_{AR}(\mathrm{E}[i].\mathcal{S}) \triangleq (\mathrm{AR}.\mathcal{S})$, i.e., an exchange done by any of AR's exchanger subobjects is converted to look like an exchange on the elimination array. This hides the implementation of the elimination array from its clients, in our case, the elimination stack. To verify the implementation of the elimination array, we pick the rely condition to be the conjunction of all the rely conditions of the encapsulated objects, $R_{AR}^t \triangleq \bigwedge_i R_{\mathrm{E}[i]}$, and the guarantee condition to be the disjunction of the corresponding guarantee conditions, $G_{AR}^t \triangleq \bigvee_i G_{\mathrm{E}[i]}^t$. The postcondition of AR.exchange follows directly from the postcondition of E[slot].exchange by observing that $h_{AR} = \overline{F_{AR}}(h_{\mathrm{E[slot]}})$.

Verifying that the central stack is a straightforward proof of linearizability, and we omit it for brevity. Next, we consider the elimination stack assuming that the central stack, S, and the elimination array, AR, satisfy their specifications. Given our setup, this proof is also straightforward. The key step is to define the function $F_{ES}$ correctly:

$$F_{ES}((\mathrm{S}.(t, \mathsf{push}(n) \rhd \mathsf{true}))) \triangleq ((\mathrm{ES}.(t, \mathsf{push}(n) \rhd \mathsf{true})))$$

$$F_{ES}((\mathrm{S}.(t, \mathsf{pop}() \rhd \mathsf{true}, n))) \triangleq ((\mathrm{ES}.(t, \mathsf{pop}() \rhd \mathsf{true}, n)))$$

$$F_{ES}\left(\mathrm{AR}. \begin{Bmatrix} (t, ex(n) \rhd \mathsf{true}, \infty), \\ (t', ex(\infty) \rhd \mathsf{true}, n) \end{Bmatrix}\right) \triangleq \frac{(\mathrm{ES}.(t, \mathsf{push}(n) \rhd \mathsf{true})) \cdot}{(\mathrm{ES}.(t', \mathsf{pop}() \rhd \mathsf{true}, n))} \quad \text{provided } n \neq \infty$$

$$F_{ES}(\mathrm{S}._{-}) \triangleq \epsilon \qquad F_{ES}(\mathrm{AR}._{-}) \triangleq \epsilon$$

This function picks as linearization points the successful pushes and pops of S, as well as a successful exchange where the exchanged values are $\infty$ and $n \neq \infty$. In the latter case, the push is linearized before the pop. All other operations are ignored.

$$\text{INIT}^t \triangleq [\exists n.\ \overleftarrow{g} = null \wedge n.\text{tid} = t \wedge n.\text{hole} = null \wedge g = n]_g$$

$$\text{CLEAN}^t \triangleq [\overleftarrow{g}.\text{hole} \neq null \wedge g' = null]_g$$

$$\text{PASS}^t \triangleq [g.\text{hole} = null \wedge g.\text{tid} = t \wedge g.\text{hole} = fail]_{g.\text{hole}}$$

$$\text{XCHG}^t \triangleq \begin{bmatrix} \exists n \neq fail.\ n.\text{tid} = t \wedge \overleftarrow{g}.\text{hole} = null \wedge g.\text{tid} \neq t \wedge g.\text{hole} = n\ \wedge \\ T = \overleftarrow{T} \cdot \text{E}.swap(g.\text{tid}, g.\text{data}, t, n.\text{data}) \end{bmatrix}_{g.\text{hole}, T}$$

$$\text{FAIL}^t \triangleq \begin{bmatrix} \exists d.\ T = \overleftarrow{T} \cdot (\text{E}.\{(t, \text{ex}(d) \triangleright \text{false}, d)\}) \end{bmatrix}_T$$

$$G_E^t \triangleq (\text{INIT}^t \vee \text{CLEAN}^t \vee \text{PASS}^t \vee \text{XCHG}^t \vee \text{FAIL}^t) \qquad R_E^t \triangleq (\text{IRRELEVANT}_E^t \vee \exists t' \neq t.\ G_{\text{ex}}^{t'})$$

$$J \triangleq \forall t.\ g \neq null \wedge g.\text{hole} = null \implies \text{In}_E(g.\text{tid})$$

$$A \triangleq \mathcal{T}_E|_{\text{tid}} = T \wedge (g = null \vee g.\text{hole} \neq null \vee g.\text{tid} \neq \text{tid}) \wedge n \mapsto \text{tid}, p, null$$

$$B(k) \triangleq (k \neq null \wedge k.\text{tid} \neq \text{tid} \wedge \mathcal{T}_E|_{\text{tid}} = T \cdot \text{E}.swap(\text{tid}, p, k.\text{tid}, k.\text{data}))$$

**Fig. 4.** Rely/guarantee conditions and assertions used for the exchanger proof.

## 5.1 Verifying the Exchanger

We move on to the verification of the exchanger, which is more challenging than that of its clients. As the exchanger does not encapsulate other objects besides memory cells, we take $F_E$ to be the completely undefined function, which means that $\mathcal{T}_E = \mathcal{T}|_E$. The proof outline is shown in Figure 1. The proof uses two forms of auxiliary state. First, we instrument the code with assignments to the history variable, $\mathcal{T}$, which appears in the specification of the exchanger. We instrument the code with assignments to $\mathcal{T}$ at the successful CAS on line 29 and at the return statements on line 35. (The exact assignments we add can be read from the corresponding actions in Figure 4.) Second, we extend the `Offer` class with an auxiliary field `tid` to record the identifier of the thread that allocated the offer object. This field is used to ensure that the auxiliary assignment to $\mathcal{T}$ in the XCHG action records the correct thread identifiers.

Figure 4 defines the rely/guarantee conditions that are used in the proof. Following the trend in modern program logics [5,26], the rely/guarantee conditions are defined in terms of actions corresponding to the individual shared state updates performed. Here, actions are parametrized by the thread $t$ performing the action. The first four actions describe the effects of the algorithm's CAS operations to the shared state, when they succeed. They modify $g$ or $g$.hole and in the case of XCHG also the auxiliary history variable $h$. The FAIL action records the auxiliary assignments to $h$ for failed exchanges, while IRR is a 'frame' action allowing other objects to append their events to $h$. Discarding the effects to the memory cells encapsulated by the exchanger (i.e., restricting attention to the variable $h$), the actions match those in the exchanger specification.

Figure 4 also defines the global invariant $J$ saying that $g$ cannot contain an unsatisfied offer of a thread not currently participating in the exchange, and two assertions $A$ and $B$ that will be used in the proof outline. We write $n \mapsto t, d, m$ as an abbreviation for $n.\text{tid} = t \wedge n.\text{data} = d \wedge n.\text{hole} = m$. We note that $J$ is stable both under the rely and guarantee conditions and we implicitly assume it to hold throughout execution.

We now proceed to the proof outline in Figure 1. Thanks to the encapsulated nature of concurrent objects in our programming language, we may assume that just before the start of the function $\neg In_E(\text{tid})$ holds, i.e., that thread tid is not executing a function of E. Hence, from invariant $J$, we can deduce that $g = null \vee g.\text{hole} = null \vee g.\text{tid} \neq \text{tid}$. Then after allocating the offer object, we have the assertion $A$. The assertion states that the thread has not performed its operation yet, which is implied by $\mathcal{T}_E|_{\text{tid}} = T$, and that no other thread can access the newly allocated offer.

If the initialization CAS succeeds at line 15, we know that $g = n \wedge g.\text{hole} = null \wedge \mathcal{T}_E|_{\text{tid}} = T$. This assertion, however, is not stable because another thread can come along and modify $g.\text{hole}$, i.e., performs the XCHG action. If this happens, then it would have made $n.\text{hole}$ non-null and extend the history appropriately (i.e., $B(n.\text{hole})$ will hold). Therefore, at line 16, the disjunction of these two assertions holds: Either an exchange has not happened, and then $n.\text{hole} = null$, or that it was done by some other thread, and then $B(b.\text{hole})$ holds.

The CAS at line 18 checks which of the above cases hold: If it succeeds, it means that waiting passively for a partner thread did not pan out. This failure, indicated by the ability to set $n.\text{hole}$ to $fail$, is manifested in the history by extending it with the failed operation (action $\text{PASS}^t$). If the CAS failed than the wait did work out. Specifically, because a thread can modify the hole field of an offer of anther thread only when it can justify it using the XCHG action, which implies that the partner thread has also logged the successful exchange in the history variable.

Otherwise, if the initialization CAS fails, the algorithm reads $g$ into the local variable $cur$ at line 25. After this, we cannot assert that $g = cur$ because another thread may have modified $g$ in the meantime. For this to happen, however, we know that $cur.\text{hole}$ must be non-null; thus the disjunction $g = cur \vee g.\text{hole} \neq null$ is stable. Then, if $cur$ is non-null, the algorithm performs a CAS at line 29 trying to satisfy the exchange offer made by $cur.\text{tid}$. If the CAS succeeds, we know that $cur = g$ at the point that the CAS succeeded, and thus we can perform action XCHG and get the postcondition $B(cur)$. Whether the CAS succeeds or not, afterwards at line 30, we know that $cur.\text{hole} \neq null$, which allows us to satisfy the precondition of the CLEAN action corresponding to the final CAS operation.

# 6    Related Work

Neiger [18] proposed *set-linearlizability* as a means to unify specification of concurrent objects with task solutions. The main idea is to linearize concurrent operations against (a sequence of) *sets* of simultaneous operations. Neiger showed that set-linearizability is expressive enough to provide a specification for certain important tasks e.g., for Borowsky and Gafni's immediate atomic snapshot objects [2]. The notion of concurrency-aware linereraizabiity is similar to set-linearizability. Neiger, however, neither provides a formal definition of set-linearizability nor a syntactic approach to define concurrent specifications. Also, Neiger does not provide a proof technique that takes advantage of set-linearizability. In contrast, we develop a modualr proof the more general specification. In contrast, we develop all a formal proof technique for verifying concurrency-aware linearizability and employ it to produce the first compositional proof of a CA-object and of its client, namely the exchanger and the elimination stack [10]. Castaneda et al. [3] showed that set-linearizability cannot express certain tasks, e.g., write snapshot, and extended it to *interval-linearizability* which allows for arbitrary concurrent specification.

Linearizability is shown to be equivalent to observational refinement [7]. The equivalence was shown to hold even when the specification is not sequential. Thus, a direct implication of their result is that concurrency-aware linearizability also ensures observational refinement.

The idea of elimination was introduced in [24], where it was used to construct pools and queues using trees. Example for other CA-linearizable concurrent objects can be found in [1,11,17,22].

Scherer et al. present a family of *dual-data structures* [14] which support "operations that must wait for some other thread to establish a precondition". Linearizability of dual-data structures is established by explicitly specifying a "request" and "follow-up" *observable* checkpoints within the object's purview, each with its own linearization point. Dual-data structures are in fact CA-objects. We believe that using CA-histories to describe the behavior of dual data structure would help streamline their specification as it would obviate the need to specify two linearization points.

Vafeiadis [26] gives a thread modular proof for a variant of the HSY stack using RGSep [26], an extension of separation logic [19] to reason about fine-grained concurrency. His proof is not compositional as the reasoning about the elimination module is coupled with the reasoning about the stack. In particular, the elimination module is not given a context-independent specification. Dragoi et al. [6] present a technique for automatically verifying linearizability for concurrent objects are where the linearization points may be is in the body of another thread. Their technique rewrites the program to introduce combined methods whose linearization points are easy to find. They verified the elimination stack by introducing a new method push+pop, which simulates the elimination. As a result, their proof is inherently non compositional. In contrast, we allow for compositional proofs by (i) providing usage-context specifications for CA-object objects, (ii) allowing clients to interpret operations that seem to happen in the same point in time as an imaginary sequence of abstract operations, (iii) hiding operations on subobjects from clients of their containing object.

Sergey et al. [23] present a framework for verifying linearizability of highly concurrent data structures using time-stamped histories and subjective states, and used it to verify Hendler et al.'s flat combining algorithm. Their approach allows to hide the inter-thread interaction in the algorithm, but does not allow, at least by its current instantiations, to verify CA-linearizability. Schellhorn et al. [20] proved that backward simulation is complete for verification linearizability; it would be interesting to see if their result extends to CAL.

A novel feature of our proof technique is that it allows to relate a single concrete atomic step done by *one thread* with a sequence of abstract steps done by *multiple threads*. Our approach stands in contrast with the standard technique of using *atomicity abstraction* [4,16,23,25], which allows to relate several concrete atomic actions with a single abstract step executed by *one thread*.

**Acknowledgments.** This research was sponsored by the EC FP7 FET project ADVENT (308830) and by Broadcom Foundation and Tel Aviv University Authentication Initiative.

# References

1. Afek, Y., Hakimi, M., Morrison, A.: Fast and scalable rendezvousing. Distributed Computing **26**(4), 243–269 (2013)
2. Borowsky, E., Gafni, E.: Immediate atomic snapshots and fast renaming. In: Anderson, J., Toueg, S. (eds.) PODC (1993)
3. Castaneda, A., Rajsbaum, S., Raynal, M.: Specifying concurrent problems: beyond linearizability and up to tasks. In: DISC (2015)
4. da Rocha Pinto, P., Dinsdale-Young, T., Gardner, P.: TaDA: a logic for time and data abstraction. In: Jones, R. (ed.) ECOOP 2014. LNCS, vol. 8586, pp. 207–231. Springer, Heidelberg (2014)
5. Dinsdale-Young, T., Dodds, M., Gardner, P., Parkinson, M.J., Vafeiadis, V.: Concurrent abstract predicates. In: D'Hondt, T. (ed.) ECOOP 2010. LNCS, vol. 6183, pp. 504–528. Springer, Heidelberg (2010)
6. Drăgoi, C., Gupta, A., Henzinger, T.A.: Automatic linearizability proofs of concurrent objects with cooperating updates. In: Sharygina, N., Veith, H. (eds.) CAV 2013. LNCS, vol. 8044, pp. 174–190. Springer, Heidelberg (2013)
7. Filipovic, I., O'Hearn, P., Rinetzky, N., Yang, H.: Abstraction for concurrent objects. Theor. Comput. Sci. **411**(51–52) (2010)
8. Hemed, N., Rinetzky, N.: Brief announcement: concurrency-aware linearizability. In: Halldórsson, M.M., Dolev, S. (eds.) PODC, pp. 209–211. ACM (2014)
9. Hemed, N., Rinetzky, N., Vafeiadis, V.: Modular verification of concurrency-aware linearizability (2015). http://www.cs.tau.ac.il/nirh/disc15-ext.pdf
10. Hendler, D., Shavit, N., Yerushalmi, L.: A scalable lock-free stack algorithm. In: SPAA (2004)
11. Hendler, D., Incze, I., Shavit, N., Tzafrir, M.: Scalable flat-combining based synchronous queues. In: Lynch, N.A., Shvartsman, A.A. (eds.) DISC 2010. LNCS, vol. 6343, pp. 79–93. Springer, Heidelberg (2010)
12. Herlihy, M., Wing, J.M.: Linearizability: A correctness condition for concurrent objects. Trans. Program. Lang. Syst. **12**(3), 463–492 (1990)
13. Hoare, C.A.R.: An axiomatic basis for computer programming. Commun. ACM **12**(10), 576–580 (1969)
14. Scherer III, W.N., Scott, M.L.: Nonblocking concurrent data structures with condition synchronization. In: Guerraoui, R. (ed.) DISC 2004. LNCS, vol. 3274, pp. 174–187. Springer, Heidelberg (2004)
15. Jones, C.B.: Specification and design of (parallel) programs. In: IFIP Congress (1983)

16. Jung, R., Swasey, D., Sieczkowski, F., Svendsen, K., Turon, A., Birkedal, L., Dreyer, D.: Iris: monoids and invariants as an orthogonal basis for concurrent reasoning. In: POPL (2015)
17. Moir, M., Nussbaum, D., Shalev, O., Shavit, N.: Using elimination to implement scalable and lock-free fifo queues. In: SPAA, pp. 253–262. ACM (2005)
18. Neiger, G.: Set-linearizability. In: Anderson, J.H., Peleg, D., Borowsky, E. (eds.) PODC 1994, pp. 396–396. ACM (1994)
19. O'Hearn, P.W., Reynolds, J.C., Yang, H.: Local reasoning about programs that alter data structures. In: Fribourg, L. (ed.) CSL 2001 and EACSL 2001. LNCS, vol. 2142, p. 1. Springer, Heidelberg (2001)
20. Schellhorn, G., Derrick, J., Wehrheim, H.: A sound and complete proof technique for linearizability of concurrent data structures. ACM Trans. Comput. Logic 15(4) (2014)
21. Scherer III, W.N., Lea, D., Scott, M.L.: A scalable elimination-based exchange channel. SCOOL (2005)
22. Scherer III, W.N., Lea, D., Scott, M.L.: Scalable synchronous queues. In: Torrellas, J., Chatterjee, S. (eds.) PPoPP 2006, pp. 147–156. ACM (2006)
23. Sergey, I., Nanevski, A., Banerjee, A.: Specifying and verifying concurrent algorithms with histories and subjectivity. In: Vitek, J. (ed.) ESOP 2015. LNCS, vol. 9032, pp. 333–358. Springer, Heidelberg (2015)
24. Shavit, N., Touitou, D.: Elimination trees and the construction of pools and stacks. Theory Comput. Syst. 30(6), 645–670 (1997)
25. Svendsen, K., Birkedal, L.: Impredicative concurrent abstract predicates. In: Shao, Z. (ed.) ESOP 2014 (ETAPS). LNCS, vol. 8410, pp. 149–168. Springer, Heidelberg (2014)
26. Vafeiadis, V.: Modular fine-grained concurrency verification. Ph.D. thesis, University of Cambridge (2008)

# Transaction Chopping for Parallel Snapshot Isolation

Andrea Cerone[1], Alexey Gotsman[1]([✉]), and Hongseok Yang[2]

[1] IMDEA Software Institute, Madrid, Spain
{andrea.cerone,alexey.gotsman}@imdea.org
[2] University of Oxford, Oxford, UK
Hongseok.Yang@cs.ox.ac.uk

**Abstract.** Modern Internet services often achieve scalability and availability by relying on large-scale distributed databases that provide consistency models for transactions weaker than serialisability. We investigate the classical problem of transaction chopping for a promising consistency model in this class—parallel snapshot isolation (PSI), which weakens the classical snapshot isolation to allow more efficient large-scale implementations. Namely, we propose a criterion for checking when a set of transactions executing on PSI can be chopped into smaller pieces without introducing new behaviours, thus improving efficiency. We find that our criterion is more permissive than the existing one for chopping serialisable transactions. To establish our criterion, we propose a novel declarative specification of PSI that does not refer to implementation-level concepts and, thus, allows reasoning about the behaviour of PSI databases more easily. Our results contribute to building a theory of consistency models for modern large-scale databases.

## 1 Introduction

Modern Internet services often achieve scalability and availability by relying on databases that replicate data across a large number of nodes and/or a wide geographical span [18,22,25]. The database clients can execute transactions on the data at any of the replicas, which communicate changes to each other using message passing. Ideally, we want this distributed system to provide strong guarantees about transaction processing, such as serialisability [9]. Unfortunately, achieving this requires excessive synchronisation among replicas, which increases latency and limits scalability [1,15]. For this reason, modern large-scale databases often provide weaker consistency models that allow non-serialisable behaviours, called *anomalies*. Recent years have seen a plethora of consistency model proposals that make different trade-offs between consistency and performance [6,7,20,22]. Unfortunately, whereas transactional consistency models have been well-studied in the settings of smaller-scale databases [2,13,21] and transactional memory [5,12,14,16], models for large-scale distributed databases are poorly understood. In particular, we currently lack a rich theory that would guide programmers in using such models correctly and efficiently.

© Springer-Verlag Berlin Heidelberg 2015
Y. Moses (Ed.): DISC 2015, LNCS 9363, pp. 388–404, 2015.
DOI: 10.1007/978-3-662-48653-5_26

| (a) Original transactions. | (b) A chopping of `transfer` (`lookup` is left as is). |
|---|---|
| `txn lookup(acct) {`<br>`  return acct.balance; }`<br><br>`txn transfer(acct1,acct2,amnt) {`<br>`  acct1.balance -= amnt;`<br>`  acct2.balance += amnt; }` | `txn withdraw(acct,amnt) {`<br>`  acct.balance -= amnt; }`<br><br>`txn deposit(acct,amnt) {`<br>`  acct.balance += amnt; }` |
| (c) An additional transaction making the chopping incorrect.<br><br>`txn lookup2(acct1,acct2) {`<br>`  return acct1.balance+acct2.balance }` | `chain transfer(acct1,acct2,amnt)`<br>`{ withdraw(acct1,amnt);`<br>`  deposit(acct2,amnt); }` |

**Fig. 1.** Example of chopping transactions.

In this paper we make a step towards building such a theory by investigating the classical problem of transaction chopping [21] for a promising consistency model of *parallel snapshot isolation (PSI)* [22]. PSI weakens the classical *snapshot isolation (SI)* [8] in a way that allows more efficient large-scale implementations. Like in SI, a transaction in PSI reads values of objects in the database from a snapshot taken at its start. Like SI, PSI precludes *write conflicts*: when two concurrent transactions write to the same object, one of them must abort. A PSI transaction initially commits at a single replica, after which its effects are propagated asynchronously to other replicas. Unlike SI, PSI does not enforce a global ordering on committed transactions: these are propagated between replicas in *causal* order. This ensures that, if Alice posts a message that is seen by Bob, and Bob posts a response, no user can see Bob's response without also seeing Alice's original post. However, causal propagation allows two clients to see concurrent events as occurring in different orders: if Alice and Bob concurrently post messages, then Carol may initially see Alice's message, but not Bob's, and Dave may see Bob's message, but not Alice's.

A common guideline for programmers using relational databases and transactional memory is to keep transactions as short as possible to maximise performance; long transactions should be *chopped* into smaller pieces [3,21,24]. This advice is also applicable to PSI databases: the longer a transaction, the higher the chances that it will abort due to a write conflict. Unfortunately, the subtle semantics of PSI makes it non-trivial to see when a transaction can be chopped without introducing undesirable behaviours. In this paper, we determine conditions that ensure this. In more detail, we assume that the code of all transactions operating on the database is known. As a toy example, consider the transactions in Figure 1(a), which allow looking up the balance of an account `acct` and transferring an amount `amnt` from an account `acct1` to an account `acct2` (with a possibility of an overdraft). To improve the efficiency of `transfer`, we may chop this transaction into a *chain* [25] of smaller transactions in Figure 1(b), which the database will execute in the order given: a `withdraw` transaction on the account `acct1` and a `deposit` transaction on the account `acct2`. This chopping is *correct* in that any client-observable behaviour of the resulting chains could be produced by the original unchopped transactions. Intuitively, even though the chopping in Figure 1(b) allows a database state where `amnt` is missing from both accounts, a client cannot notice this, because it can only query the balance of a single account. If we added the transaction `lookup2` in Figure 1(c), which returns the sum of the accounts `acct1` and `acct2`, then the chopping of `transfer` would become incorrect: by executing `lookup2` a client could observe the state with `amnt` missing from both accounts.

We propose a criterion that ensures the correctness of a given chopping of transactions executing on PSI (§5). Our criterion is weaker than the existing criterion for chopping serialisable transactions by Shasha et al. [21]: weakening consistency allows more flexibility in optimising transactions. Recent work has shown that transactions arising in web applications can be chopped in a way that drastically improves their performance when executed in serialisable databases [19,25]. Our result enables bringing these benefits to databases providing PSI.

A challenge we have to deal with in proposing a criterion for transaction chopping is that the specification of PSI [22] is given in a low-level *operational* way, by an idealised algorithm formulated in terms of implementation-level concepts (§2). This complicates reasoning about the behaviour of an application using a PSI database and, in particular, the correctness of a transaction chopping. To deal with this problem, we propose an alternative *axiomatic* specification of PSI that defines the consistency model declaratively by a set of axioms constraining client-visible events (§3). We prove that our axiomatic specification of PSI is equivalent to the existing operational one (§4). The axiomatic specification is instrumental in formulating and proving our transaction chopping criterion.

## 2    Operational Specification of PSI

We first present an operational specification of PSI, which is a simplification of the one originally proposed in [22]. It is given as an idealised algorithm that is formulated in terms of implementation-level concepts, such as replicas and messages, but nevertheless abstracts from many of the features that a realistic PSI implementation would have.

We consider a database storing *objects* $\mathsf{Obj} = \{x, y, \ldots\}$, which for simplicity we assume to be integer-valued. Clients interact with the database by issuing `read` and `write` operations on the objects, grouped into *transactions*. We identify transactions by elements of $\mathsf{Tid} = \{t_0, t_1, \ldots\}$. The database system consists of a set of *replicas*, identified by $\mathsf{Rid} = \{r_0, r_1, \ldots\}$, each maintaining a copy of all objects. Replicas may fail by crashing.

All client operations within a given transaction are initially executed at a single replica (though operations in *different* transactions can be executed at different replicas). When a client terminates the transaction, the replica decides

| operation start: | operation receive($l$): | operation abort: |
|---|---|---|
| requires Current$[r] = \varepsilon$ | requires Current$[r] = \varepsilon$ | requires |
| $t :=$ (unique identifier from TId) | requires $l = (t, \mathtt{start}) \cdot \_$ | Current$[r] =$ |
| Current$[r] := (t, \mathtt{start})$ | Committed$[r] =$ Committed$[r] \cdot l$ | $(t, \mathtt{start}) \cdot \_$ |
| | | Current$[r] := \varepsilon$ |

| operation write($x, n$): | operation commit: |
|---|---|
| requires Current$[r] = (t, \mathtt{start}) \cdot \_$ | requires Current$[r] = (t, \mathtt{start}) \cdot \_$ |
| Current$[r] :=$ Current$[r] \cdot (t, \mathtt{write}(x, n))$ | requires $\neg\exists x, r', t'. ((t, \mathtt{write}(x, \_)) \in$ Current$[r]) \wedge$ |
| | $(r \neq r') \wedge ((t', \mathtt{write}(x, \_)) \in$ Committed$[r']) \wedge$ |
| operation read($x, n$): | $((t', \mathtt{start}) \not\in$ Committed$[r])$ |
| requires Current$[r] = (t, \mathtt{start}) \cdot \_$ | send Current$[r]$ to all other replicas |
| requires $\mathtt{write}(x, n)$ is the last write to $x$ | Committed$[r] :=$ Committed$[r] \cdot$ Current$[r]$ |
| in Committed$[r] \cdot$ Current$[r]$ or | Current$[r] := \varepsilon$ |
| there is no such write and $n = 0$ | |

**Fig. 2.** Pseudocode of the idealised PSI algorithm at replica $r$.

whether to commit or abort it. To simplify the formal development, we assume that every transaction eventually terminates. If the replica decides to commit a transaction, it sends a message to all other replicas containing the **transaction log**, which describes the updates done by the transaction. The replicas incorporate the updates into their state upon receiving the message. A transaction log has the form $(t, \mathtt{start}) (t, \mathtt{write}(x_1, n_1)) \dots (t, \mathtt{write}(x_k, n_k))$, which gives the sequence of values $n_i \in \mathbb{N}$ written to objects $x_i \in$ Obj by the transaction $t \in$ TId; the record $(t, \mathtt{start})$ is added for convenience of future definitions. Transaction logs are ranged over by $l$, and we denote their set by Log.

We assume that every replica executes transactions locally without interleaving (this is a simplification in comparison to the original PSI specification [22] that makes the algorithm cleaner). This assumption allows us to maintain the state of a replica $r$ in the algorithm by:

- Current$[r] \in$ Log$\cup \{\varepsilon\}$—the log of the (single) transaction currently executing at $r$ or an empty sequence $\varepsilon$, signifying that no transaction is currently executing; and
- Committed$[r] \in$ Log$^*$—the sequence of logs of transactions that committed at $r$.

Initially Current$[r] =$ Committed$[r] = \varepsilon$.

We give the pseudocode of the algorithm executing at a replica $r$ in Figure 2. This describes the effects of **operations** executed at the replica, which come from the set

$$\text{Op} = \{\mathtt{start}, \mathtt{receive}(l), \mathtt{write}(x, n), \mathtt{read}(x, n), \mathtt{abort}, \mathtt{commit} \mid$$
$$l \in \text{Log}, x \in \text{Obj}, n \in \mathbb{N}\}$$

and are ranged over by $o$. The execution of the operations is atomic and is triggered by client requests or internal database events, such as messages arriving to the replica. The **requires** clauses give conditions under which an operation can be executed. For convenience of future definitions, operations do not return values. Instead, the value fetched by a read is recorded as its parameter; as we explain below, the **requires** clause for $read(x, n)$ ensures that the operation may only be executed when the value it fetches is indeed $n$. We use · for sequence concatenation, $\in$ to express that a given record belongs to a given sequence, and _ for irrelevant expressions.

When a client starts a transaction at the replica $r$ (operation start), the database assigns it a unique identifier $t$ and initialises Current$[r]$ to signify that $t$ is in progress. Since we assume that the replica processes transactions serially, in the idealised algorithm the transaction can start only if $r$ is not already executing a transaction, as expressed by the **requires** clause. The operation $receive(l)$ executes when the replica receives a message $l$ with the log of some transaction $t$, at which point it appends $l$ to its log of committed transactions. A replica can receive a message only when it is not executing a transaction. When a client issues a write of $n$ to an object $x$ inside a transaction $t$, the corresponding record $(t, write(x, n))$ is appended to the log of the current transaction (operation $write(x, n)$). The **requires** clause ensures that a write operation can only be called inside a transaction. A client can read $n$ as the value of an object $x$ (operation $read(x, n)$) if it is the most recent value written to $x$ at the replica according to the log of committed transactions concatenated with the log of the current one; if there is no such value, the client reads 0 (to simplify examples, in the following we sometimes assume different initial values).

If the current transaction aborts (operation abort), the Current$[r]$ log is reset to be empty. Finally, if the current transaction commits (operation commit), its log is sent to all other replicas, as well as added to the log of committed transactions of the replica $r$. Crucially, as expressed by the second **requires** clause of commit, the database may commit a transaction $t$ only if it passes the ***write-conflict detection*** check: there is no object $x$ written by $t$ that is also written by a concurrent transaction $t'$, i.e., a transaction that has been committed at another replica $r'$, but whose updates have not yet been received by $r$. If this check fails, the only option left for the database is to abort $t$ using the operation abort.

In the algorithm we make certain assumptions about message delivery between replicas. First, every message is delivered to every replica at most once. Second, message delivery is ***causal***: if a replica sends a message $l_2$ after it sends or receives a message $l_1$, then every other replica will receive $l_2$ only after it receives or sends $l_1$; in this case we say that the transaction generating $l_2$ causally depends on the one generating $l_1$. This is illustrated by the execution of the algorithm depicted in Figure 3: due to causal delivery, the transaction $t_3$ that reads *reply* from $y$ is also guaranteed to read *post* from $x$.

The operational specification of PSI is given by all sets of client-database interactions that can arise when executing the implementations of the operations in Figure 2 at each replica in the system. Due to the asynchronous propagation of updates between replicas, the specification of PSI allows non-serialisable behaviours, called ***anomalies***. We introduce structures to describe

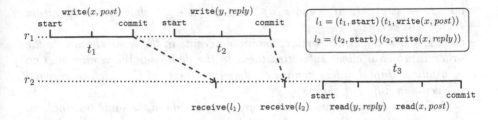

**Fig. 3.** An example execution of the operational PSI specification.

client-database interactions allowed by PSI and discuss its anomalies while presenting our declarative PSI specification, which is the subject of the next section.

# 3  Axiomatic Specification of PSI

Reasoning about PSI database behaviour using the operational specification may get unwieldy. It requires us to keep track of low-level information about the system state, such as the logs at all replicas and the set of messages in transit. We then need to reason about how the system state is affected by a large number of possible interleavings of operations at different replicas. We now present a specification of PSI that is more declarative than the operational one and, in particular, does not refer to implementation-level details, such as message exchanges between replicas. It thus makes it easier to establish results about PSI, such as criteria for transaction chopping.

Our PSI specification is given by a set of *histories*, which describe all client-database interactions that this consistency model allows. To simplify presentation, our specification does not constrain the behaviour of aborted or ongoing transactions, so that histories only record operations inside committed transactions. Our specification also assumes that the database interface allows a client to group a finite number of transactions into a **chain** [25], which establishes an ordering on the transactions, similarly to a *session* [23]. Chains are needed for transaction chopping (§1) and can be implemented, e.g., by executing all transactions from a chain at the same replica.

To define histories and similar structures, we need to introduce some set-theoretic concepts. We assume a countably infinite set of **events** Event = $\{e, f, g, \ldots\}$. A relation $R \subseteq E \times E$ on a set $E$ is a **strict partial order** if it is transitive and irreflexive; it is an **equivalence relation** if it is reflexive, transitive and symmetric. For an equivalence relation $R \subseteq E \times E$ and $e \in E$, we let $[e]_R = \{f \mid (f, e) \in R\}$ be the **equivalence class** of $e$. A **total order** is a strict partial order such that for every two distinct elements $e$ and $f$, the order relates $e$ to $f$ or $f$ to $e$. We write $(e, f) \in R$ and $e \xrightarrow{R} f$ interchangeably.

**Definition 1.** *A **history** is a tuple* $\mathcal{H} = (E, \mathsf{op}, \mathsf{co}, \sim)$, *where:*

- $E \subseteq$ Event *is a finite set of events, denoting reads and writes performed inside committed transactions.*

- op : $E \rightarrow \{\texttt{write}(x,n), \texttt{read}(x,n) \mid x \in \texttt{obj}, n \in \mathbb{N}\}$ *defines the operation each event denotes.*
- co $\subseteq E \times E$ *is the **chain order**, arranging events in the same chain into the order in which a client submitted them to the database. We require that* co *be a union of total orders defined on disjoint subsets of $E$, which correspond to events in different chains.*
- $\sim \subseteq E \times E$ *is an equivalence relation grouping events in the same transaction. Since every transaction is performed by a single chain, we require that* co *totally order events within each transaction, i.e., those from $[e]_\sim$ for each $e \in E$. We also require that a transaction be contiguous in* co*:*

$$\forall e, f, g. \, e \xrightarrow{\text{co}} f \xrightarrow{\text{co}} g \wedge e \sim g \implies e \sim f \sim g.$$

Let Hist be the set of all histories. We denote components of a history $\mathcal{H}$ as in $E_\mathcal{H}$, and use the same notation for similar structures introduced in this paper. Our specification of PSI is given as a particular set of histories allowed by this consistency model. To define this set, we enrich histories with a *happens-before* relation, capturing causal relationships between events. In terms of the operational PSI specification, an event $e$ happens before an event $f$ if the information about $e$ has been delivered to the replica performing $f$, and hence, can affect $f$'s behaviour. The resulting notion of an *abstract execution* is similar to those used to specify weak shared-memory models [4].

**Definition 2.** *An **abstract execution** is a pair $\mathcal{A} = (\mathcal{H}, \text{hb})$ of a history $\mathcal{H}$ and the **happens-before** relation* hb $\subseteq E \times E$, *which is a strict partial order.*

For example, Figure 5(a) shows an abstract execution, which corresponds to the execution of the operational specification in Figure 3 (as we formalise in §4). Our PSI specification is defined by *consistency axioms* (Figure 4), which constrain happens-before and other execution components and thereby describe the guarantees that a PSI database provides about transaction processing. We thus call this specification *axiomatic*.

**Definition 3.** *An abstract execution $\mathcal{A}$ is **valid** if it satisfies the **consistency axioms** in Figure 4. We denote the set of all valid executions by* AbsPSI *and let the set of PSI histories be* HistPSI $= \{\mathcal{H} \in \text{Hist} \mid \exists \text{hb}. \, (\mathcal{H}, \text{hb}) \in \text{AbsPSI}\}$.

The axiom (Reads) constrains the values fetched by a read using the happens-before relation: a read $e$ from an object $x$ has to return the value written by a hb-preceding write $f$ on $x$ that is most recent according to hb, i.e., not shadowed by another write $g$ to $x$. If there is no hb-preceding write to $x$, then the read fetches the default value 0 (we sometimes use other values in examples). The axiom (Chains) establishes a causal dependency between events in the same chain (thus subsuming *session guarantees* [23]), and the transitivity of happens-before required in Definition 2 ensures that the database respects causality. For example, in the abstract execution in Figure 5(a), the chain order between the two writes induces an hb edge according to (Chains). Then, since hb is transitive, we must have an hb edge between the two operations on $x$ and, hence, by (Reads),

$$op(e) = \mathtt{read}(x,n) \implies (\exists f.\, op(f) = \mathtt{write}(x,n) \wedge f \xrightarrow{hb} e \wedge \neg \exists g.\, f \xrightarrow{hb} g \xrightarrow{hb} e \wedge$$

$$op(g) = \mathtt{write}(x,\_)) \vee (n = 0 \wedge \neg \exists f.\, f \xrightarrow{hb} e \wedge op(f) = \mathtt{write}(x,\_)) \qquad \text{(Reads)}$$

| $co \subseteq hb$ | (Chains) | $\{(e',f') \mid e \xrightarrow{hb} f \wedge e \not\sim f \wedge e' \sim e \wedge f \sim f'\} \subseteq hb$ (Atomic) |
|---|---|---|

$$(e \neq f \wedge \{op(e), op(f)\} \subseteq \{\mathtt{write}(x,n) \mid n \in \mathbb{N}\}) \implies (e \xrightarrow{hb} f \vee f \xrightarrow{hb} e) \text{ (Wconflict)}$$

**Fig. 4.** Consistency axioms of PSI, stated for an execution $\mathcal{A} = ((E, op, co, \sim), hb)$. All free variables are universally quantified.

the read from $x$ has to fetch *post*. There is no valid execution with a history where the read from $y$ fetches *reply*, but the read from $x$ fetches the default value. The operational specification ensures this because of causal message delivery.

The axiom (Atomic) ensures the ***atomic visibility*** of transactions: all writes by a transaction become visible to other transactions together. It requires that, if an event $e$ happens before an event $f$ in a different transaction, then all events $e'$ in the transaction of $e$ happen before all the events $f'$ in the transaction of $f$. For example, (Atomic) disallows the execution in Figure 5(b), which is a variant of Figure 5(a) where the two writes are done in a single transaction and the order of the reads is reversed.

The axiom (Wconflict) states that the happens-before relation is total over write operations on a given object. Hence, the same object cannot be written by concurrent transactions, whose events are not related by happens-before. This disallows the ***lost update*** anomaly, illustrated by the execution in Figure 5(c). This execution could arise from the code, also shown in the figure, that uses transactions to make deposits into an account; in this case, one deposit is lost. The execution violates (Wconflict): one of the transactions would have to hb-precede the other and, hence, read 50 instead of 0 from $x$. In the operational specification this anomaly is disallowed by the write-conflict detection, which would allow only one of the two concurrent transactions to commit.

Despite PSI disallowing many anomalies, it is weaker than serialisability. In particular, PSI allows the ***write skew*** anomaly, also allowed by the classical snapshot isolation [8]. We illustrate how our consistency axioms capture this by the valid execution in Figure 5(d), which could arise from the code also shown in the figure. Here each transaction checks that the combined balance of two accounts exceeds 100 and, if so, withdraws 100 from one of them. Both transactions pass the checks and make the withdrawals from different accounts, resulting in the combined balance going negative. The operational specification allows this anomaly because the two transactions can be executed at different replicas and allowed to commit by the write-conflict detection check.

PSI also allows so-called ***long fork*** anomaly in Figure 5(e) [22], which we in fact already mentioned in §1. We have two concurrent transactions writing to $x$ and $y$, respectively. A third transaction sees the write to $x$, but not $y$, and a fourth one sees the write to $y$, but not $x$. Thus, from the perspective of the

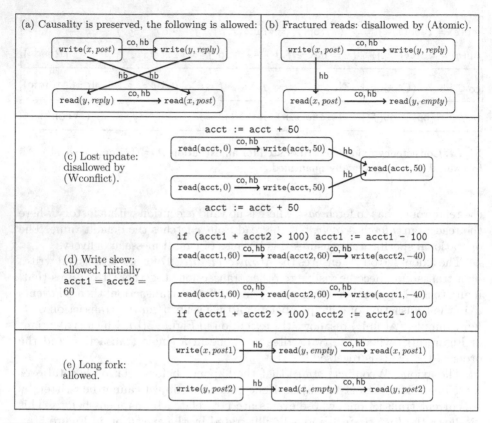

**Fig. 5.** Abstract executions illustrating PSI guarantees and anomalies. The boxes group events into transactions. We omit the transitive consequences of the co and hb edges shown.

latter two transactions, the two writes happen in different orders. It is easy to check that this outcome is not serialisable; in fact, it is also disallowed by the classical snapshot isolation. In the operational specification this anomaly can happen when each transaction executes at a separate replica, and the messages about the writes to $x$ and $y$ are delivered to the replicas executing the reading transactions in different orders.

## 4     Equivalence of the Specifications

We now show that the operational (§2) and axiomatic specifications (§3) are equivalent, i.e., the sets of histories they allow coincide. We start by introducing a notion of *concrete executions* of the operational PSI specification and using it to define the set of histories the specification allows. Concrete executions are similar to abstract ones of Definition 2, but describe *all* operations occurring at replicas as per Figure 2, including both client-visible and database-internal ones. We use the set-theoretic notions introduced before Definition 1.

**Definition 4.** *A **concrete execution** is a tuple* $C = (E, \mathsf{op}, \mathsf{repl}, \mathsf{trans}, \prec)$, *where:*

- *$E \subseteq \mathsf{Event}$ is a finite set of events, denoting executions of operations in Figure 2.*
- $\mathsf{op} : E \to \mathsf{Op}$ *defines which of the operations in Figure 2 a given event denotes.*
- $\mathsf{repl} : E \to \mathsf{Rld}$ *defines the replica on which the event occurs.*
- $\mathsf{trans} : E \to \mathsf{Tld}$ *defines the transaction to which the event pertains.*
- $\prec \subseteq E \times E$ *is a total order, called **execution order**, in which events take place in the system.*

The set $\mathsf{ConcPSI}$ of concrete executions that can be produced by the algorithm in Figure 2 is defined as expected. Due to space constraints, we defer its formal definition to [11, §C]. Informally, the definition considers the execution of any sequence of operations in Figure 2 at arbitrary replicas, subject to the **requires** clauses and the constraints on message delivery mentioned in §2; the values of $\mathsf{repl}$ and $\mathsf{trans}$ are determined by the variables $r$ and $t$ in the code of operations in Figure 2. For example, Figure 3 can be viewed as a graphical depiction of a concrete execution from $\mathsf{ConcPSI}$, with the execution order given by the horizontal placement of events. For a $C \in \mathsf{ConcPSI}$ and $e \in E_C$, we write $e \rhd_C t : o @ r$ if $\mathsf{trans}_C(e) = t$, $\mathsf{op}_C(e) = o$ and $\mathsf{repl}_C(e) = r$.

**Definition 5.** *The history of a concrete execution $C$ is*

$$\mathsf{history}(C) = (E_{\mathcal{H}}, \mathsf{op}_{\mathcal{H}}, \mathsf{co}_{\mathcal{H}}, \sim_{\mathcal{H}}), \; where$$
$$E_{\mathcal{H}} = \{e \in E_C \mid \exists f \in E_C, t \in \mathsf{Tld}.\,(f \rhd_C t : \mathtt{commit} @ \_) \wedge$$
$$((e \rhd_C t : \mathtt{write}(\_,\_) @ \_) \vee (e \rhd_C t : \mathtt{read}(\_,\_) @ \_))\};$$
$$\mathsf{op}_{\mathcal{H}} = (the \; restriction \; of \; \mathsf{op}_C \; to \; E_{\mathcal{H}});$$
$$\mathsf{co}_{\mathcal{H}} = \{(e, f) \in E_{\mathcal{H}} \times E_{\mathcal{H}} \mid \mathsf{repl}_C(e) = \mathsf{repl}_C(f) \wedge e \prec_C f\}.$$
$$\sim_{\mathcal{H}} = \{(e, f) \in E_{\mathcal{H}} \times E_{\mathcal{H}} \mid \mathsf{trans}_C(e) = \mathsf{trans}_C(f)\};$$

For example, the concrete execution in Figure 3 has the history shown in Figure 5(a). The history $\mathsf{history}(C)$ contains only the events describing reads and writes by the committed transactions in $C$. To establish a correspondence between the operational and axiomatic specifications, we assume that chains are implemented by executing every one of them at a dedicated replica. Thus, we define the chain order $\mathsf{co}_{\mathcal{H}}$ as the order of events on each replica according to $\prec_C$. This is, of course, an idealisation acceptable only in a specification. In a realistic implementation, multiple chains would be multiplexed over a single replica, or different transactions in a chain would be allowed to access different replicas [23]. We define the set of histories allowed by the operational PSI specification as $\mathsf{history}(\mathsf{ConcPSI})$, where we use the expected lifting of $\mathsf{history}$ to sets of executions. The following theorem (proved in [11, §D]) shows that this set coincides with the one defined by the axiomatic specification (Definition 3).

**Theorem 1.** $\mathsf{history}(\mathsf{ConcPSI}) = \mathsf{HistPSI}$.

# 5   Chopping PSI Transactions

In this section, we exploit the axiomatic specification of §3 to establish a criterion for checking the correctness of a *chopping* [21] of transactions executing on PSI. Namely, we assume that we are given a set of *chain programs* $\mathcal{P} = \{P_1, P_2, \ldots\}$, each defining the code of chains resulting from chopping the code of a single transaction. We leave the precise syntax of the programs unspecified, but assume that each $P_i$ consists of $k_i$ *program pieces*, defining the code of the transactions in the chain. For example, for given acct1, acct2 and amnt, Figure 1(b) defines a chain program resulting from chopping transfer in Figure 1(a). For a given acct, we can also create a chain program consisting of a single piece lookup(acct) in Figure 1(a). Let $\mathcal{P}^1$ consist of the programs for lookup(acct1), lookup(acct2) and transfer(acct1,acct2,amnt), and $\mathcal{P}^2$ of those for transfer(acct1,acct2,amnt) and lookup2(acct1,acct2).

Following Shasha et al. [21], we make certain assumptions about the way clients execute chain programs. We assume that, if the transaction initiated by a program piece aborts, it will be resubmitted repeatedly until it commits, and, if a piece is aborted due to system failure, it will be restarted. We also assume that the client does not abort transactions explicitly.

In general, executing the chains $\mathcal{P}$ may produce more client-observable behaviours than if we executed every chain as a single PSI transaction. We propose a condition for checking that no new behaviours can be produced. To this end, we check that every valid abstract execution consisting of *fine-grained* transactions produced by the chains $\mathcal{P}$ can be *spliced* into another valid execution that has the same operations as the original one, but where all operations from each chain are executed inside a single *coarse-grained* transaction.

**Definition 6.** *Consider a valid abstract execution* $\mathcal{A} = ((E, \mathsf{op}, \mathsf{co}, \sim), \mathsf{hb}) \in$ AbsPSI *and let* $\approx_\mathcal{A} = \mathsf{co} \cup \mathsf{co}^{-1} \cup \{(e, e) \mid e \in E\}$. *The execution* $\mathcal{A}$ *is* **spliceable** *if there exists* $\mathsf{hb}'$ *such that* $((E, \mathsf{op}, \mathsf{co}, \approx_\mathcal{A}), \mathsf{hb}') \in$ AbsPSI.

The definition groups fine-grained transactions in $\mathcal{A}$, identified by $\sim_\mathcal{A}$, into coarse-grained transactions, identified by $\approx_\mathcal{A}$, which consist of events in the same chain.

We now establish the core technical result of this section—a criterion for checking that an execution $\mathcal{A}$ is spliceable. From this *dynamic* criterion on executions we then obtain a *static* criterion for the correctness of chopping transaction code, by checking that all executions produced by the chain programs $\mathcal{P}$ are spliceable. We first need to define some auxiliary relations, derived from the happens-before relation in an abstract execution [2,4].

**Definition 7.** *Given* $\mathcal{A} \in$ AbsPSI, *we define the* **reads-from** $\mathsf{rf}_\mathcal{A}$, *version-order* $\mathsf{vo}_\mathcal{A}$ *and* **anti-dependency** $\mathsf{ad}_\mathcal{A}$ *relations on* $E_\mathcal{A}$ *as follows:*

$$e \xrightarrow{\text{rf}_\mathcal{A}} f \iff \exists x, n.\, e \xrightarrow{\text{hb}_\mathcal{A}} f \wedge \text{op}_\mathcal{A}(e) = \text{write}(x, n) \wedge \text{op}_\mathcal{A}(f) = \text{read}(x, n) \wedge$$
$$\neg \exists g.\, e \xrightarrow{\text{hb}_\mathcal{A}} g \xrightarrow{\text{hb}_\mathcal{A}} f \wedge \text{op}_\mathcal{A}(g) = \text{write}(x, \_);$$

$$e \xrightarrow{\text{vo}_\mathcal{A}} f \iff \exists x.\, e \xrightarrow{\text{hb}_\mathcal{A}} f \wedge \text{op}_\mathcal{A}(e) = \text{write}(x, \_) \wedge \text{op}_\mathcal{A}(f) = \text{write}(x, \_);$$

$$e \xrightarrow{\text{ad}_\mathcal{A}} f \iff \exists x.\, \text{op}_\mathcal{A}(e) = \text{read}(x, \_) \wedge \text{op}_\mathcal{A}(f) = \text{write}(x, \_) \wedge$$
$$((\exists g.\, g \xrightarrow{\text{rf}_\mathcal{A}} e \wedge g \xrightarrow{\text{vo}_\mathcal{A}} f) \vee (\neg \exists g.\, g \xrightarrow{\text{rf}_\mathcal{A}} e)).$$

The reads-from relation determines the write $e$ that a read $f$ fetches its value from (uniquely, due to the axiom (Wconflict)). The version order totally orders all writes to a given object and corresponds to the order in which replicas find out about them in the operational specification. The anti-dependency relation [2] is more complicated. We have $e \xrightarrow{\text{ad}_\mathcal{A}} f$ if the read $e$ fetches a value that is overwritten by the write $f$ according to $\text{vo}_\mathcal{A}$ (the initial value of an object is overwritten by any write to this object).

Our criterion for checking that $\mathcal{A}$ is spliceable requires the absence of certain cycles in a graph with nodes given by the fine-grained transactions in $\mathcal{A}$ and edges generated using the above relations. The transactions are defined as equivalence classes $[e]_\sim$ of events $e \in E_\mathcal{A}$ (§3).

**Definition 8.** *Given $\mathcal{A} \in \mathsf{AbsPSI}$, its **dynamic chopping graph** $\mathsf{DCG}(\mathcal{A})$ is a directed graph whose set of nodes is $\{[e]_{\sim_\mathcal{A}} \mid e \in E_\mathcal{A}\}$, and we have an edge $([e]_{\sim_\mathcal{A}}, [f]_{\sim_\mathcal{A}})$ if and only if $[e]_{\sim_\mathcal{A}} \neq [f]_{\sim_\mathcal{A}}$ and one of the following holds: $e \xrightarrow{\text{co}_\mathcal{A}} f$ (a **successor** edge); $f \xrightarrow{\text{co}_\mathcal{A}} e$ (a **predecessor** edge); $e \xrightarrow{\text{ad}_\mathcal{A} \setminus \approx_\mathcal{A}} f$ (an **anti-dependency** edge); or $e \xrightarrow{(\text{rf}_\mathcal{A} \cup \text{vo}_\mathcal{A}) \setminus \approx_\mathcal{A}} f$ (a **dependency** edge).*

*A **conflict** edge is one that is either a dependency or an anti-dependency. A directed cycle in the dynamic chopping graph is **critical** if it does not contain two occurrences of the same vertex, contains at most one anti-dependency edge, and contains a fragment of three consecutive edges of the form "conflict, predecessor, conflict".*

**Theorem 2 (Dynamic Chopping Criterion).** *An execution $\mathcal{A} \in \mathsf{AbsPSI}$ is spliceable if its dynamic chopping graph $\mathsf{DCG}(\mathcal{A})$ does not have critical cycles.*

We give a (non-trivial) proof of the theorem in [11, §E]. For example, the execution in Figure 6 satisfies the criterion in Theorem 2 and, indeed, we obtain a valid execution by grouping `withdraw` and `deposit` into a single transaction and adding the dotted happens-before edges.

We now use Theorem 2 to derive a static criterion for checking the correctness of code chopping given by $\mathcal{P}$. As is standard [13,21], we formulate the criterion in terms of the sets of objects read or written by program pieces. Namely, for each chain program $P_i \in \mathcal{P}$ we assume a sequence

$$(R_1^i, W_1^i)\,(R_2^i, W_2^i) \,\cdots\, (R_{k_i}^i, W_{k_i}^i), \tag{1}$$

of **read and write sets** $R_j^i, W_j^i \subseteq \mathsf{Obj}$, i.e., the sets of all objects that can be, respectively, read and written by the $j$-th piece of $P_i$. For example,

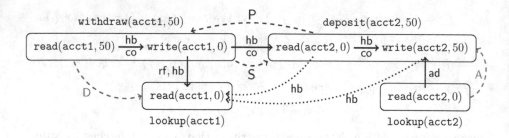

**Fig. 6.** An execution produced by the programs $\mathcal{P}^1$ and its derived relations. Initially acct1 = 50 and acct2 = 0. We omit the transitive consequences of the hb edges shown. The dashed edges show the dynamic chopping graph, with S, P, A, D denoting edge types. The dotted edges show additional happens-before edges that define a splicing of the execution (Definition 6).

the transfer(acct1,acct2,amnt) chain in Figure 1(b) is associated with the sequence ({acct1}, {acct1}) ({acct2}, {acct2}).

We consider a chopping defined by the programs $\mathcal{P}$ correct if all executions that they produce are spliceable. To formalise this, we first define when an execution can be produced by programs with read and write sets given by (1). Due to space constraints, we give the definition only informally.

**Definition 9.** *An abstract execution $\mathcal{A}$ **conforms** to a set of programs $\mathcal{P}$, if there is a one-to-one correspondence between every chain of transactions in $\mathcal{A}$ and a chain program $P_i \in \mathcal{P}$ whose read and write sets (1) cover the sets of objects read or written by the corresponding transactions in the chain.*

For example, the execution in Figures 6 conforms to the programs $\mathcal{P}^1$. Due to the assumptions about the way clients execute $\mathcal{P}$ that we made at the beginning of this section, the definition requires that every chain in an execution $\mathcal{A}$ conforming to $\mathcal{P}$ executes completely, and that all transactions in it commit. Also, for simplicity (and following [21]), we assume that every chain in $\mathcal{A}$ results from a distinct program in $\mathcal{P}$.

**Definition 10.** *Chain programs $\mathcal{P}$ are **chopped correctly** if every valid execution conforming to $\mathcal{P}$ is spliceable.*

We check the correctness of $\mathcal{P}$ by defining an analogue of the dynamic chopping graph from Definition 8 whose nodes are pieces of $\mathcal{P}$, rather than transactions in a given execution. Each piece is identified by a pair $(i, j)$ of the number of a chain $P_i$ and the piece's position in the chain.

**Definition 11.** *Given chain programs $\mathcal{P} = \{P_1, P_2, \ldots\}$ with read and write sets (1), the **static chopping graph** SCG($\mathcal{P}$) is a directed graph whose set of nodes is $\{(i, j) \mid i = 1..|\mathcal{P}|, j = 1..k_i\}$, and we have an edge $((i_1, j_1), (i_2, j_2))$ if and only if one of the following holds: $i_1 = i_2$ and $j_1 < j_2$ (a **successor** edge);*

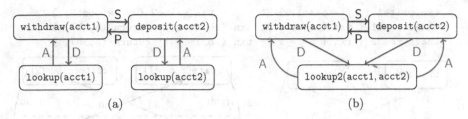

**Fig. 7.** Static chopping graphs for the programs (a) $\mathcal{P}^1$ and (b) $\mathcal{P}^2$.

$i_1 = i_2$ and $j_1 > j_2$ (a **predecessor** edge); $i_1 \neq i_2$, and $R_{j_1}^{i_1} \cap W_{j_2}^{i_2} \neq \emptyset$ (an **anti-dependency** edge); or $i_1 \neq i_2$, and $W_{j_1}^{i_1} \cap (R_{j_2}^{i_2} \cup W_{j_2}^{i_2}) \neq \emptyset$ (a **dependency** edge).

For example, Figures 7(a) and 7(b) show the static chopping graph for the programs $\mathcal{P}^1$ and $\mathcal{P}^2$ respectively. There is a straightforward correspondence between $\mathsf{SCG}(\mathcal{P})$ and $\mathsf{DCG}(\mathcal{A})$ for an execution $\mathcal{A}$ conforming to $\mathcal{P}$: we have an (anti-)dependency edge between two pieces in $\mathsf{SCG}(\mathcal{P})$ if there *may* exist a corresponding edge in $\mathsf{DCG}(\mathcal{A})$ between two transactions resulting from executing the pieces, as determined by the read and write sets. Using this correspondence, from Theorem 2 we easily get a criterion for checking chopping correctness statically.

**Corollary 1 (Static Chopping Criterion).** $\mathcal{P}$ *is chopped correctly if* $\mathsf{SCG}(\mathcal{P})$ *does not contain any critical cycles.*

The graph in Figure 7(a) satisfies the condition of the corollary, whereas the one in Figure 7(b) does not. Hence, the corresponding chopping of `transfer` is correct, but becomes incorrect if we add `lookup2` (we provide an example execution illustrating the latter case in [11, §A]).

The criterion in Corollary 1 is more permissive than the one for chopping serialisable transactions previously proposed by Shasha et al. [21]. The latter does not distinguish between dependency and anti-dependency edges (representing them by a single type of a conflict edge) and between predecessor and successor edges (representing them by *sibling* edges). The criterion then requires the absence of any cycles containing both a conflict and a sibling edge. We illustrate the difference in Figure 8. The static chopping graph for the programs shown in the figure does not have critical cycles, but has a cycle with both a conflict and a sibling edge, and thus does not satisfy Shasha's criterion. We also show an execution produced by the programs: splicing the chains in it into single transactions (denoted by the dashed boxes) yields the execution in Figure 5(e) with a long fork anomaly. We provide a similar example for write skew (Figure 5(d)) in [11, §A]. Thus, the chopping criterion for PSI can be more permissive than the one for serialisability because of the anomalies allowed by the former consistency model.

Finally, we note that Theorem 2 and Corollary 1 do not make any assumptions about the structure of transactions, such as their commutativity properties,

```
txn write1 { x := post1; }              txn write2 { y := post2; }
chain read1 { txn { a := y }; txn { b := x }; return (a, b); }
chain read2 { txn { a := x }; txn { b := y }; return (a, b); }
```

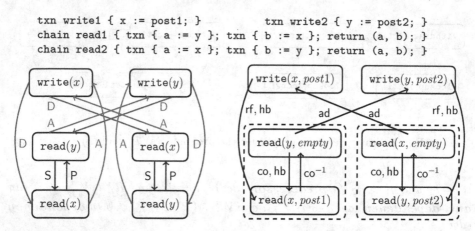

**Fig. 8.** An illustration of the difference between the chopping criteria for PSI and serialisability: programs, their static chopping graph and an example execution. The variables a and b are local.

which may result in an excessive number of conflict edges in chopping graphs. These results can be strengthened to eliminate conflict edges between transactions whose effects commute, as done in [21,25].

# 6  Related Work

Our criterion for the correctness of chopping PSI transactions was inspired by the criterion of Shasha et al. [21] for serialisable transactions. However, establishing a criterion for PSI is much more difficult than for serialisability. Due to the weakly consistent nature of PSI, reasoning about chopping correctness cannot be reduced to reasoning about a total serialisation order of events and requires considering intricate relationships between them, as Theorem 2 illustrates.

Our declarative specification of PSI uses a representation of executions more complex than the one in notions of strong consistency, such as serialisability [9] or linearizability [17]. This is motivated by the need to capture PSI anomalies. In proposing our specification, we built on the axiomatic approach to specifying consistency models, previously applied to eventual consistency [10] and weak shared-memory models [4]. In comparison to prior work, we handle a more sophisticated consistency model, including transactions with write-conflict detection. Our specification is also similar in spirit to the specifications of weak consistency models of relational databases of Adya's [2], which are based on the relations in Definition 7. While PSI could be specified in Adya's framework, we found that the specification based on the happens-before relation (Definition 2) results in simpler axioms and greatly eases proving the correspondence to the operational specification (Theorem 1) and the chopping criterion (Theorem 2).

**Acknowledgements.** We thank Hagit Attiya and Giovanni Bernardi for helpful discussions. This work was supported by EPSRC and an EU FET project ADVENT.

# References

1. Abadi, D.: Consistency tradeoffs in modern distributed database system design: CAP is only part of the story. IEEE Computer **45**(2) (2012)
2. Adya, A.: Weak consistency: A generalized theory and optimistic implementations for distributed transactions: PhD thesis, MIT (1999)
3. Afek, Y., Avni, H., Shavit, N.: Towards consistency oblivious programming. In: Fernàndez Anta, A., Lipari, G., Roy, M. (eds.) OPODIS 2011. LNCS, vol. 7109, pp. 65–79. Springer, Heidelberg (2011)
4. Alglave, J.: A formal hierarchy of weak memory models. Formal Methods in System Design **41**(2) (2012)
5. Attiya, H., Gotsman, A., Hans, S., Rinetzky, N.: A programming language perspective on transactional memory consistency. In: PODC (2013)
6. Bailis, P., Davidson, A., Fekete, A., Ghodsi, A., Hellerstein, J.M., Stoica, I.: Highly available transactions: virtues and limitations. In: VLDB (2014)
7. Bailis, P., Fekete, A., Ghodsi, A., Hellerstein, J.M., Stoica, I.: Scalable atomic visibility with RAMP transactions. In: SIGMOD (2014)
8. Berenson, H., Bernstein, P., Gray, J., Melton, J., O'Neil, E., O'Neil, P.: A critique of ANSI SQL isolation levels. In: SIGMOD (1995)
9. Bernstein, P.A., Hadzilacos, V., Goodman, N.: Concurrency Control and Recovery in Database Systems. Addison-Wesley (1987)
10. Burckhardt, S., Gotsman, A., Yang, H., Zawirski, M.: Replicated data types: specification, verification, optimality. In: POPL (2014)
11. Cerone, A., Gotsman, A., Yang, H.: Transaction chopping for parallel snapshot isolation (extended version). http://software.imdea.org/~gotsman/
12. Doherty, S., Groves, L., Luchangco, V., Moir, M.: Towards formally specifying and verifying transactional memory. Formal Aspects of Computing **25**(5) (2013)
13. Fekete, A., Liarokapis, D., O'Neil, E., O'Neil, P., Shasha, D.: Making snapshot isolation serializable. ACM Trans. Database Syst. **30**(2) (2005)
14. Felber, P., Gramoli, V., Guerraoui, R.: Elastic transactions. In: Keidar, I. (ed.) DISC 2009. LNCS, vol. 5805, pp. 93–107. Springer, Heidelberg (2009)
15. Gilbert, S., Lynch, N.: Brewer's conjecture and the feasibility of consistent, available, partition-tolerant web services. ACM SIGACT News **33**(2) (2002)
16. Guerraoui, R., Kapalka, M.: On the correctness of transactional memory. In: PPoPP (2008)
17. Herlihy, M.P., Wing, J.M.: Linearizability: A correctness condition for concurrent objects. ACM Trans. Program. Lang. Syst. **12**(3) (1990)
18. Lakshman, A., Malik, P.: Cassandra: A decentralized structured storage system. SIGOPS Oper. Syst. Rev. **44**(2) (2010)
19. Mu, S., Cui, Y., Zhang, Y., Lloyd, W., Li, J.: Extracting more concurrency from distributed transactions. In: OSDI (2014)
20. Ardekani, M.S., Sutra, P., Shapiro, M.: Non-monotonic snapshot isolation: scalable and strong consistency for geo-replicated transactional systems. In: SRDS (2013)
21. Shasha, D., Llirbat, F., Simon, E., Valduriez, P.: Transaction chopping: Algorithms and performance studies. ACM Trans. Database Syst. **20**(3) (1995)

22. Sovran, Y., Power, R., Aguilera, M.K., Li, J.: Transactional storage for geo-replicated systems. In: SOSP (2011)
23. Terry, D.B., Demers, A.J., Petersen, K., Spreitzer, M., Theimer, M., Welch, B.W.: Session guarantees for weakly consistent replicated data. In: PDIS (1994)
24. Xiang, L., Scott, M.L.: Software partitioning of hardware transactions. In: PPoPP (2015)
25. Zhang, Y., Power, R., Zhou, S., Sovran, Y., Aguilera, M., Li, J.: Transaction chains: achieving serializability with low latency in geo-distributed storage systems. In: SOSP (2013)

# Computing in Additive Networks
# with Bounded-Information Codes

Keren Censor-Hillel[1], Erez Kantor[2]($\boxtimes$), Nancy Lynch[2], and Merav Parter[2]

[1] Department of Computer Science, Technion, 32000 Haifa, Israel
[2] CSAIL, Massachusetts Institute of Technology, Cambridge, MA 01239, USA
erezk@csail.mit.edu

**Abstract.** This paper studies the theory of the additive wireless network model, in which the received signal is abstracted as an addition of the transmitted signals. Our central observation is that the crucial challenge for computing in this model is not high contention, as assumed previously, but rather guaranteeing a bounded amount of *information* in each neighborhood per round, a property that we show is achievable using a new random coding technique. Technically, we provide efficient algorithms for fundamental distributed tasks in additive networks, such as solving various symmetry breaking problems, approximating network parameters, and solving an *asymmetry revealing* problem such as computing a maximal input. The key method used is a novel random coding technique that allows a node to successfully decode the received information, as long as it does not contain too many distinct values. We then design our algorithms to produce a limited amount of information in each neighborhood in order to leverage our enriched toolbox for computing in additive networks.

## 1 Introduction

The main challenge in wireless communication is the possibility of collisions, occurring when two nearby stations transmit at the same time. In general, collisions provide no information on the data, and in some cases may not even be distinguishable from the case of no transmission at all. Indeed, the ability to merely detect collisions (a.k.a., the collision detection model) gives additional power to wireless networks, and separation results are known (e.g., [26]).

Traditional approaches for dealing with interference (e.g., FDMA, TDMA) treat collisions as something that should be avoided or at least minimized [12,21, 23]. However, modern coding techniques suggest the ability to *retrieve information* from collisions. These techniques significantly change the notion of collisions,

The first author is supported in part by the Israel Science Foundation (grant 1696/14). The last three authors are supported in a part by NSF Award Numbers CCF-1217506, CCF-AF-0937274, 0939370-CCF, and AFOSR Contract Numbers FA9550-14-1-0403 and FA9550-13-1-0042. Merav Parter is also supported by Rothschild and Fulbright Fellowships.

© Springer-Verlag Berlin Heidelberg 2015
Y. Moses (Ed.): DISC 2015, LNCS 9363, pp. 405–419, 2015.
DOI: 10.1007/978-3-662-48653-5_27

which now depends on the model or coding technique used. For example, in *interference cancellation* [2], the receivers may decode interfering signals that are sufficiently strong and *cancel* them from the received signal in order to decode their intended message. Hence, from this viewpoint, collision occurs only when neither the desired signal nor the the interfering signal are relatively strong enough.

In this paper, we consider the *additive network model*, in which colliding signals add up at the receiver and are hence *informative* in some cases. It has been shown that such models approximate the capacity of networks with high signal-to-noise ratio [3], and that they can be useful in these settings for various coding techniques, such as ZigZag decoding [11,22], and bounded-contention coding [6]. While in practice there are limitations for implementing such networks to the full extent of the model, the above previous research shows the importance of understanding the fundamental strength of models that allow the possibility of extracting information out of collisions. In a recent theoretical work [6], the problems of local and global broadcast have been addressed in additive networks, under the assumption that the contention in the system is *bounded*.

The central observation of this paper is that in order to leverage the additive behavior of the system, what needs to be bounded is not necessarily the contention, but rather the total amount of *information* a node has to process at a given round. This observation allows us to extend the quantification of the computational power of the additive network model in solving distributed tasks way beyond local and global broadcast. Our key approach in this paper is *not to assume* a bound on the initial number of pieces of information in the system, but rather *guarantee* a bound on the number of *distinct* pieces of information in a neighborhood of every vertex. We then use a new random coding technique, which we refer to as *Bounded-Information Codes (BIC)*, in order to extract the information out of the received signals. This allows us to efficiently solve various cornerstone distributed tasks.

## 1.1   Contributions and Methods

On the technical side, we provide efficient algorithms for fundamental *symmetry breaking* tasks, such as leader election, and computing a BFS tree and a maximal independent set (MIS), as well as algorithms for *revealing asymmetry* in the inputs, such as computing the maximum. We also provide efficient algorithms for approximating network parameters by a constant factor. Our key methods are based on enriching the toolbox for computing in additive networks with various primitives that leverage the additive behavior of received information and our coding technique.

*Main Techniques:* The work in [6] introduced Bounded-Contention Codes (BCC) as the main technique. BCC allows the decoding of the XOR of any collection of at most $a$ codewords, where $a$ is the bound on the contention. As mentioned, our key approach in this paper is not to assume a bound on the contention, but rather to make sure that the amount of distinct information colliding at a node at a given round is limited. Our main ingredient is augmenting the deterministic

BCC codes with randomization, resulting in Bounded-Information Codes. BIC allows successful decoding of any transmission of $n$ nodes sending at most $O(a)$ distinct values altogether, with high probability.

Randomization plays a key role in the presented scheme in two different aspects. First, the drawback of the standard BCC code is that the transmission of the *same* message by an even number of neighbors is cancelled out. By increasing the message size by factor of $O(\log n)$ and using randomization, BIC codes add random "noise" to the original BCC codeword so that the probability that two BIC messages cause cancellation becomes negligible.

Another useful aspect of randomization is intimately related to the fact that our information bounds are logarithmic in $n$. This allows for a win-win situation: if the number of distinct pieces of information (in a given neighborhood) is small (i.e., $O(\log n)$), the decoding is successful thanks to the BIC codes. On the other hand, if the number of distinct pieces of information is large (i.e., $\Omega(\log n)$), there are sufficiently many transmitting vertices in the neighborhood which allows one to obtain good concentration bounds by, e.g., using Chernoff bounds (for example, in estimating various network parameters). It is noteworthy that our estimation technique bares some similarity to the well-known *decay strategy* [4] which is widely used in radio-networks. The key distinction between the long line of works that apply this scheme and this paper is the dimension to which this strategy in applied. Whereas so-far, the strategy was applied to the *time* axis (e.g., in round $i$, vertex $u$ transmits with probability $2^{-i}$), here it is applied to the *information* (or message) axis (e.g., vertex $u$ writes the specific information in the $i$'th block of its message with probability $2^{-i}$). This highly improves the time bounds compared to the basic radio model (i.e., the statistics are collected over the multiple blocks of the message instead of over multiple slots).

An immediate application of BIC is a simple logarithmic simulation of algorithms for networks that employ full-duplex radios (where a node can transmit and receive concurrently) by nodes who have only half-duplex radios (where a node either transmits or receives in a given round). This allows us to consider algorithms for the stronger model of full-duplex radios and obtain a translation to half-duplex radios, and also allows us to compare our algorithms to a message-passing setting. To make justice with such comparisons, we note that a message-passing setting not only does not suffer from collisions, but also is in some sense similar to having full duplex, as a node receives and sends information in the same round.

Note that in the standard radio model, collision detection is not an integral part of the model but rather an external capability that can be chosen to be added. In BIC, collision detection is an integral part of the model, where *collision* now refers to the situation where the number of distinct pieces of information exceeds the allowed bound. To avoid confusion, the collision detection in the context of BIC, is hereafter referred to as *information-overflow detection*. We show that information-overflow can be detected while inspecting the received codeword, without the need for any additional mechanisms.

*Symmetry Breaking:* The first type of algorithms we devise are for various symmetry breaking tasks. The main tool in this context is the *select-level* function, $\mathcal{SL}$, that outputs two random values according to a predefined distribution. Every vertex $v$ computes the $\mathcal{SL}$ function locally, without any communication. The power of this function lies in its ability to assign random *levels* to nodes, such that with high probability[1] the maximal level contains at most a logarithmic number of nodes (i.e., below the information bound of the BIC code), and the nodes in the maximal level have different values for their second random variable.

The $\mathcal{SL}$ function allows us to elect a leader in $O(D)$ rounds, w.h.p., where $D$ is the diameter of the network. The elected leader is the node with the maximal pair of values chosen by the $\mathcal{SL}$ function. A by-product of this algorithm is a 2-approximation of the diameter, and the analysis is done over a BFS tree rooted at the leader. We also show how to construct a BFS tree rooted at an arbitrary given node in $O(D)$ rounds, w.h.p, by employing both the $\mathcal{SL}$ function and BIC.

Apart from the above new algorithms, our framework allows relatively simple translations of known algorithms for solving various tasks in message passing systems into additive networks. This includes Luby's MIS algorithm [18], Schneider and Wattenhofer's coloring algorithm [24], and approximating the minimum dominating set of Wattenhofer and Kuhn [15], improving significantly over the known bounds for standard radio-model. We give a flavor of these translations by providing the full MIS algorithm and analysis in [7], and sketch the results for coloring and approximating the minimum dominating set.

*Approximations:* We design algorithms for approximating various network parameters. We show how to compute a constant approximation of the degree of a node, as well as a constant approximation of the size and diameter of the network. (Our coding scheme only requires nodes to know a polynomial bound $N$ on the network size $n$.) Our algorithms naturally extend to solve the more general tasks of local-sum and global-sum approximations[2] that have been recently considered in [17]. Yet, the additive setting allows us to obtain much better bounds than those of [17].

*Asymmetry Revealing:* In addition to the above symmetry breaking algorithms, we show that additive networks also allow for fast solutions for tasks which do not require symmetry breaking, but rather already begin with inputs whose asymmetry needs to be revealed: we give an algorithm that computes the *exact* maximal value of all inputs in the network in $O(D \cdot \log n / \log \log n)$ rounds, w.h.p. (in contrast, a 2-approximation for the maximal value can be computed within $\Theta(D)$ rounds). We obtain this because our coding scheme allows us to perform a tournament at a high rate. For example, for single-hop networks, in each round

---

[1] We use the term *with high probability* (w.h.p.) to denote a probability of at least $1 - 1/n^c$ for a constant $c \geq 1$.

[2] These are generalizations of degree-approximation and network-size approximation, respectively.

only a $O(\log n)$ fraction of the remaining competing vertices survive for the next round.

In some sense, asymmetry revealing can be viewed as the counterpart of symmetry breaking. Clearly, if we compute the maximal input in the system then we can obtain a leader as a by-product. However, the opposite does not hold, and indeed in our leader-election algorithm mentioned above we significantly exploit the fact that the leader need not be predetermined, and use our new toolbox to obtain a leader within only $O(D)$ rounds.

## 1.2 Comparison with Related Work

First, we compare our results with previous theoretical work on the additive network model. The work of [6] assumes a bound $a$ on the contention in the system, i.e., there are at most $a$ initial inputs in total in the network. The main method for obtaining global broadcast in the above work is random linear network coding, which can be shown to allow an efficient flow of information in the system. However, this is what requires the bound on the contention. Our BIC coding method bares some technical similarity to the approach of random linear network coding, but allows us to refrain from making assumptions on the total information present in the network.

The aforementioned global broadcast algorithm requires $O(D + a + \log n)$ rounds. While this algorithm can be used to solve many of the problems that we address in this paper, such as electing a leader and computing the maximal input, it would require $O(n)$ rounds, as for these problems it holds that $a$ can be as large as the total number of nodes in the network. In comparison, our $O(D)$-round leader election algorithm is optimal, and our $O(D \log n / \log \log n)$-round algorithm for computing the maximal input is nearly-optimal, as $O(D)$ is a natural lower bound for both problems, even in the message-passing model.

It is important to mention that our algorithms use messages of size $O(\log^3 n)$. While a standard assumption might be that the message size is $O(\log n)$ bits, this difference is far from rendering our results easy. In comparison, the global broadcast algorithm of [6] requires a message size of $O(a \log n + \ell)$ bits for inputs of size $\ell$ and contention bounded by $a$. In our setting, we assume $\ell$ fits the message size (say, is logarithmic in $n$), but since $a$ can be as large as $n$, such a message size would be unacceptable. In addition, if we compare our results to algorithms for the much less restricted message-passing setting, it is crucial to note that even unbounded message sizes do not make distributed tasks trivial. For example, it is possible to compute an MIS in general graphs in $O(\log n)$ rounds even with messages of size $O(1)$ [19], but the best known lower bound is $\Omega(\log \Delta + \sqrt{\log n})$ even with unbounded messages [14]. Recently, Barenboim at el. [5] showed a randomized MIS algorithm with $O(\log \Delta \cdot \sqrt{\log n})$ rounds using unbounded messages.

In [7], we overview results that address the same tasks as this paper in the standard radio network model and in the message-passing model. An additive network can be viewed as lying somewhere in between these two models, as it does suffer from collisions, but to a smaller extent. Nevertheless, while our coding methods assist us in overcoming collisions, the additive network model is still subject to the broadcast nature of the transmissions, and therefore it is highly non-trivial to translate algorithms for the message-passing setting that make use of the ability to send different messages on different links concurrently. The related work overviewed in [7], include algorithms and lower bounds for various problems in radio networks, such as the wake-up problem [9], MIS with and without collision detection [20,26] or with multiple channels [8], leader election [10], and approximation of local parameters [17], as well as MIS algorithms for message passing systems [1,18,25] and lower bounds [14,16].

## 2    Background: Additive Networks and BCC

*The Additive Network Model:* A *radio network* consists of stations that can transmit and receive information. We address a synchronous system, in which in each round of communication each station can either transmit or listen to other transmissions. This is called the half-duplex mode of operation. Mainly due to theoretical interest, we also consider the full-duplex mode of operation which is considered harder to implement. We follow the standard abstraction in which stations are modeled as nodes of a graph $G = (V, E)$, with edges connecting nodes that can receive each other's transmissions.

In the standard radio network model, a node $v \in V$ receives a message $m$ in a given round if and only if in that round exactly one of its neighbors transmits, and its transmitted message is $m$. In the half-duplex mode, it also needs to hold that $v$ is listening in that round, and not transmitting. If none of $v$'s neighbors transmit then $v$ hears silence, and if at least two of $v$'s neighbors transmit simultaneously then a *collision* occurs at $v$. In both cases, $v$ does not receive any message.

Some networks allow for *collision detection*, where the effect at node $v$ of a collision is different from that of no message being transmitted, i.e., $v$ can distinguish a collision from silence (despite receiving no message in both). Other networks operate without a collision detection mechanism, i.e., a node cannot distinguish a collision from silence. It is known that the ability to detect collisions has a significant impact on the computational power of the network [26].

In contrast, in this paper, we study the *additive network model*, in which a collision of transmissions is not completely lost, but rather is modeled as receiving the XOR of the bit representation of all transmissions. More specifically, we model a transmission of a message $m$ by node $v$ as a string of bits. A node $v$ that receives a collision of transmissions of messages $\{m_u \mid u \in \Gamma(v)\}$, receives their bitwise XOR, i.e., receives the message $y = \bigoplus_{u \in \Gamma(v)} m_u$. Here $\Gamma(v)$ is the set of neighbors of $v$. Note that the above notation does not distinguish between the case where a node $u$ transmits to that where it does not, because we model the string of a node that does not transmit as all-zero.

The network topology is unknown, and only a polynomial upper bound $N = n^{O(1)}$ is known for the number of nodes $n$. Throughout, we assume that each vertex $v$ has a unique identifier $\mathrm{id}_v$ in the range $[1, \ldots, n^c]$ for some constant $c \geq 1$. The bandwidth is $O(\mathrm{poly} \log n)$ bits per message.

*Bounded-Contention Coding (BCC):* Bounded-Contention Codes were introduced in [6] for the purpose of obtaining fast local and global broadcast in additive networks. Given parameters $M$ and $a$, a BCC code is a set of $M$ codewords such that the XOR of any subset of size at most $a$ is uniquely decodable. As such, BCC codes can leverage situations where the number of initial messages is bounded by some number $a$, and can be used (along with additional mechanisms) for global broadcast in additive networks. Formally, Bounded-Contention Codes are defined as follows.

**Definition 1.** *An $[M, m, a]$-BCC-code is a set $C \subseteq \{0,1\}^m$ of size $|C| = M$ such that for any two subsets $S_1, S_2 \subseteq C$ (with $S_1 \neq S_2$) of sizes $|S_1|, |S_2| \leq a$ it holds that $\bigoplus S_1 \neq \bigoplus S_2$.*

Simple BCC codes can be constructed using the dual of linear codes. We refer the reader to [6] for additional details and a construction of an $[M, a \log M, a]$-BCC code for given values of $M$ and $a$.

## 3    New Tools

In this section we enrich the toolbox for computing in additive networks with the following three techniques. The first is a method for encoding information such that it can be successfully decoded not when the number of transmitters in limited, but rather when the amount of distinct pieces of information is limited (even if sent by multiple transmitters concurrently). The second technique is a general simulation of any algorithm for full-duplex radios in a setting of half-duplex radios within a logarithmic number of rounds. Finally, we show that we can detect whether the number of distinct messages exceeds the given threshold.

*Bounded-Information Codes (BIC).* Using BCC and randomization allows one to control the number of distinct pieces of information in the neighborhood. Let $G = (V, E)$ be an $n$-vertex network and assume that all the messages are integers in the range $[0, n]$. We show that for a bandwidth of size $O(\log^3 n)$, one can use randomization and BCC codes to guarantee that every vertex $v$, whose neighbors transmit $O(\log n)$ *distinct* messages (i.e., hence bounded pieces of information) in a given round, can decode *all* messages correctly with high probability (i.e., regardless of the number of transmitting neighbors).[3] Let $C$ be an $[n, \log^2 n, \log n]$-BCC code and $x \in [0, n]$. By the definition of $C$, the codeword $C(x) = [b_1, \ldots, b_k] \in \{0,1\}^k$ contains $k = O(\log^2 n)$ bits. Due to the XOR operation, co-transmissions of the same value even number of times are cancelled out. To prevent this, we use a randomized code, named hereafter as a *BIC* code (or BIC for short) as defined next.

---

[3] The definition of the BIC code can be given for any bound $a$ on the number of distinct values. Since we care for messages of polylogarithmic size, we provide the definition for specific bound $a = O(\log n)$.

**Definition 2.** *Let $C$ be an $[n, \log^2 n, \log n]$-BCC code. An $[n, c\log^3 n, \log n]$-BIC code for $C$ is a random code $C^I$ defined as follows. The codeword $C^I(x)$ consists of $k' = \lceil c \cdot \log n \rceil$ blocks, for some constant $c \geq 4$, each block is of size $k = O(\log^2 n)$ (the maximal length of a BCC codeword), and the $i$'th block contains $C(x)$ with probability $1/2$ and the zero word otherwise, for every $i \in \{1, \ldots, k'\}$.*

In other words, for vertex $v$ with value $x$, let $m(v) = C^I(x)$ be the message containing the BIC codeword of $x$ and let $m_i(v)$ denote the $i$'th block of $v$'s message. Then, $m_i(v) = C(x)$ with probability $1/2$ and $m_i(v) = 0^k$ otherwise. Let $m'(v) = \bigoplus_{u \in \Gamma(v)} m(u)$ be the received message obtained by adding the BIC codewords of $v$'s neighbors. Then the decoding is performed by using BCC to decode each block $m_i'(v)$ separately for every $i \in \{1, \ldots, k'\}$, and taking a union over all decoded blocks.

**Lemma 1.** *Let $V' \subseteq V$ be a set of transmitting vertices with values $X' = \bigcup_{v \in V'} \text{VAL}(v)$ where $|X'| = O(\log n)$. For every $v \in V'$, let $C_v^I$ be an $[n, c \cdot \log^3 n, \log n]$-BIC code, for constant $c \geq 4$. Let $m(v)$ be the $C_v^I$ codeword of $\text{VAL}(v)$. Then, the decoding of $\bigoplus_{v \in V'} m(v)$ is successful with probability at least $1 - 1/n^{c-1}$.*

*Proof.* For every $x \in X'$, let $V_x = \{v \in V' \mid \text{VAL}(v) = x\}$ be the set of transmitting vertices in $V'$ with the value $x$. For $x \in X'$ and $i \in \{1, \ldots, k'\}$, let $V_x^i = \{v \in V_x \mid m_i(v) = C(x)\}$ be the set of vertices $v$ whose $i$'th block $m_i(v)$ contains the codeword $C(x)$. We say that block $i$ is *successful* for value $x \in X'$, if $|V_x^i|$ is odd (hence, the messages of $V_x$ are not cancelled out in this block). Let $M_i \subseteq X'$ be the set of values for which the $i$'th block is successful, and let $V_i'$ contain one representative vertex with a value in $M_i$. We first claim that with high probability, every value $x \in X'$ has at least one successful block $i_x \in \{1, \ldots, k'\}$. We then show that the decoding of this $i_x$'th block is successful. The probability that the $i$'th block is successful for $x$ is $1/2$ for every $i \in \{1, \ldots, k'\}$. By the independence between blocks, the probability that $x$ has no successful block is at most $1/n^c$. By applying the union bound over all $m \leq n$ distinct messages, we get that with probability at least $1 - 1/n^{c-1}$, every value $x \in X$ has at least one successful block $i_x$ in the message. Let $m' = \bigoplus_{v \in V'} m(v)$ be the received message and let $m_i'$ be the $i$'th block of the received message. It then holds that $m_i' = \bigoplus_{v \in V'} m_i(v) = \bigoplus_{v \in V_i'} m_i(v)$. To see this, observe that the values with even parity in the $i$'th block are cancelled out and the XOR of an odd number of messages with the same value $C(x)$ is simply $C(x)$. Since $m_i'$ corresponds to the XOR of $|V_i'| = O(\log n)$ distinct messages, the claim follows by the properties of the BCC code. $\qquad\square$

In our algorithms, the messages may contain several fields (mostly a constant) each containing a value in $[0, n^c]$ for some constant $c \geq 1$. To guarantee a proper decoding on each field, the messages are required to be aligned correctly. For example, a message containing $\ell$ fields where the $i$'th field contains $x_i \in [0, n]$ is split evenly into $\ell$ blocks and all bits are initialized to zero. The BIC codeword of $x_i$, denoted by $C^I(x_i)$, is written at the beginning of the $i$'th block. Hence, when the messages are added up, all codewords of a given block are added up separately. To avoid cumbersome notation, a multiple-field message is denoted by concatenation of the BIC codewords of each field, e.g., the content of a two-field message containing $x_1$ and $x_2$ is referred as $C^I(x_1) \circ C^I(x_2)$, where formally the message is divided into two equi-length blocks and $C^I(x_1)$ (resp., $C^I(x_2)$) is written at the beginning of the first (resp., second) block.

*From full-Duplex to Half-Duplex.* The algorithms provided in this paper are mostly concerned with the full-duplex setting. However, in the additive network model, one can easily simulate a full-duplex protocol $P_f$ by half-duplex protocol $P_h$ with a multiplicative overhead of $O(\log n)$ rounds with high probability, as explain in more details in [7].

*Information-Overflow Detection.* In the standard radio model, a collision corresponds to the scenario where multiple vertices transmit in the same round to a given mutual neighbor. In an additive network, this may not be a problem, since with BIC codes, the decoding is successful as long as there are $O(\log n)$ *distinct* pieces of information in a given neighborhood. In this section, we describe a scheme for detecting an event of information-overflow. Our scheme is adapted from the contention estimation scheme of [6], designed for the setting of detecting whether there are more than a certain number of initial messages throughout the network. In our setting, the nodes generate values by themselves, and we will later wish to use the fact that we can detect whether too many different values were generated. The key observation within this context, is that using a BIC code with a doubled information-limit allows one to detect failings with high probability. To see this, assume an information bound $K = c \log n$ for constant $c \geq 1$ and consider an $[n, 2K \log n, 2K]$-BCC code $C$. The BIC code $C^I$ based on $C$ supports $2K$ distinct messages. Throughout, because of space considerations, some of the proofs are omitted. However, all the proofs are given in the full version [7].

**Lemma 2.** *With high probability, either it is detected that the number of distinct values exceeds $K$, or each value $w$ is decoded successfully.*

## 4    Symmetry Breaking Tasks

In this section we show how to solve symmetry breaking tasks efficiently in additive networks. As a key example, we focus on the problem of leader election. In [7], we consider additional tasks that involve symmetry breaking such as computing a BFS tree, computing an MIS and finding a proper vertex coloring. A key ingredient in many of our algorithms is having the vertices choose random variables according to some carefully chosen probabilities, which, at a high level, are used to reduce the amount of information that is sent throughout the network. We refer to this as the $\mathcal{SL}$ (Select Level) function and describe it as follows.

The $\mathcal{SL}$ function does not require communication, and only produces two local random values, an $r$-value and an $z$-value, that can be considered as primary and secondary values for breaking the symmetry between the vertices.

The $r$-value is defined by letting $r = j$ with probability of $2^{-j}$, and the $z$-value, $z$, is sampled uniformly at random from the set $\{1, ..., 2^{8r}\}$.

Note that $\mathcal{SL}$ does not require the knowledge of the number of vertices $n$. We next show that the maximum value of $r(v)$ is concentrated around $O(\log n)$ and that not to many vertices collide on the maximum value. Let $j_{max}^{\mathcal{SL}} = \max\{r(v) \mid v \in V\}$ and $S_{max}^{\mathcal{SL}} = \{v \in V \mid r(v) = j_{max}^{\mathcal{SL}}\}$.

**Lemma 3.** *With high probability, it holds that (a)* $j_{max}^{\mathcal{SL}} \leq 3\log n + 1$; *(b)* $|S_{max}^{\mathcal{SL}}| \leq 2\log n$; *and (c)* $z(v) \neq z(v')$ *for every* $v, v' \in S_{max}^{\mathcal{SL}}$.

*Proof.* Let $P_v = \mathbb{P}(r(v) \geq 3\log n+1)$. Then, by definition, $P_v = \sum_{i=3\log n+1}^{\infty} 2^{-i}$ $= 1/n^3$. By applying the union bound over all vertices in $S$, we get that with probability at least $1 - 1/n^2$, $r(v) \leq 3\log n + 1$, for every $v \in S$, as needed for Part (a). We now turn to bound the cardinality of $S_{max}^{\mathcal{SL}}$. The random choice of $r(v)$ can be viewed as a random process in which each vertex flips a coin with probability $1/2$ and proceeds as long as it gets "head". The value of $r(v)$ corresponds to the first time when it gets a "tail". We now claim that the probability that $|S_{max}^{\mathcal{SL}}| > 2\log n$ is very small. This holds since the probability that all of $2\log n$ coin flips are "tails" is exactly $2^{-2\log n}$ which is less than the probability that $|S_{max}^{\mathcal{SL}}| > 2\log n$ and none of the vertices in $S_{max}^{\mathcal{SL}}$ succeeded in getting another head (and hence in having a larger $r$-value). Hence, the probability that $|S_{max}^{\mathcal{SL}}| \leq 2\log n$ is at least $1 - 2^{-2\log n} = 1 - 1/n^2$, as needed for Part (b).

Finally, consider Part (c). It is sufficient to show that the $z$-values (of vertices of $S_{max}^{\mathcal{SL}}$) are sampled from a sufficient large range. Note that, the size of this range is $2^{8 \cdot j_{max}^{\mathcal{SL}}}$. We later show that $j_{max}^{\mathcal{SL}} \geq \log n/2$ with high probability. This implies that the range size (of the $z$-values) is at least $n^4$ with high probability. Assume that $j_{max}^{\mathcal{SL}} \geq \log n/2$, then the probability that $z(v) = z(v')$, for any pair $v, v' \in S_{max}^{\mathcal{SL}}$ is at most $1/n^4$. Applying the union bound over all pairs in $S_{max}^{\mathcal{SL}}$ gives the claim, since $|S_{max}^{\mathcal{SL}}| \leq n$.

In the remaining, we show that indeed, $j_{max}^{\mathcal{SL}} \geq \log n/2$ with high probability. For every $v \in V$, let $x_v$ be an indicator variable for the event that $r(v) \geq \log n/2$, i.e., $x_v = 1$, if $r(v) \geq \log n/2$ and $x_v = 0$, otherwise. Let $X = \sum_{v \in V} x_v$. Note that, the probability that $X \geq 1$ is the same as the probability that $j_{max}^{\mathcal{SL}} \geq \log n/2$. In addition, $\Pr[x_v = 1] = 2^{-(\log n/2)+1} \geq 2^{-\log n/2}$ and hence (by the linearity of expectation) $\mathbb{E}[X] = \sum_{v \in V} \Pr[x_v = 1] = \sqrt{n}$. By Chernoff bound, the probability that $X = 0$ is exponentially small. Hence, $X \geq 1$ and so $j_{max}^{\mathcal{SL}} \geq \log n/2$ with the high probability. Part (c) holds. □

## 4.1   Leader Election

A Leader-Election protocol is a distributed algorithm run by any vertex such that each node eventually decides whether it is a leader or not, subject to the constraint that there is exactly one leader. Moreover, at the end of the algorithm all vertices know the $\mathcal{SL}$ function values of the leader.

We first describe a two-round leader election protocol for single-hop networks. Let $C^I$ be an $[N, O(\log^3 N), O(\log N)]$-BIC code sampled uniformly at random from the distribution of all random codes that are based on a particular $[N, O(\log^2 N), O(\log N)]$-BCC code $C$ (which is used by all vertices). First, the vertices apply the $\mathcal{SL}$ function to compute $r(v), z(v)$. To do that, in the first communication round, every vertex $v$ transmits $C^I(r(v))$. Since with high probability, by Lemma 3(a), $j^{\mathcal{SL}}_{max} \leq 2\log n$, the information is bounded and by Claim 2, each vertex can compute $S^{\mathcal{SL}}_{max}$ w.h.p. In the second communication round, every vertex $v$ with $r(v) = j^{\mathcal{SL}}_{max}$, transmits $C^I(z(v))$. That is, in the second phase only the vertices of $S^{\mathcal{SL}}_{max}$ transmit the codeword of their $z$'s value. Since by Lemma 3(b), with high probability, $|S^{\mathcal{SL}}_{max}| = O(\log n)$, and by Claim 2 again, the $z$-values of all vertices in $S^{\mathcal{SL}}_{max}$ are known to every vertex in the network w.h.p. Finally, the leader is the vertex $v^* \in S^{\mathcal{SL}}_{max}$ with the largest $z$-value, i.e., $z(v^*) = \max_{v' \in S^{\mathcal{SL}}_{max}} z(v')$. In [7], we consider the general case of electing a leader in a network $G$ with diameter $D$, and also show how it implies a 2-approximation of the diameter as a byproduct.

# 5   Approximation Tasks: Degree Approximation

In this section we consider approximation tasks. As a key example, we focus on the task of approximating the degree, i.e., each vertex $v$ is required to compute an approximation for its degree in the graph $G$. We refer the reader to [7] for additional approximation schemes such as (1) an approximation for the network size; (2) an approximation for the network diameter; and (3) a 2-approximation for the maximum (or minimum).

We describe Algorithm AppDegree that computes with high probability a constant approximation for the degree of the vertices within $O(1)$ rounds. For vertex $v$ and graph $G$, let $\deg(v, G) = |\Gamma(v, G)|$ be the degree of $v$ in $G$. When the graph $G$ is clear from the context, we may omit it and simply write $\deg(v)$. Recall that we assume that each vertex $v$ has a unique identifier $\mathrm{id}_v$ in the range of $[1, \ldots, n^c]$ for some constant $c \geq 1$.

The algorithm consists of two communication rounds (which can be unified into a single round). The first round is devoted for computing the exact degree for low-degree vertices $v$ with degree $\deg(v) \leq c \cdot \log n$. The second round computes a constant approximation for high-degree vertices $v$ with $\deg(v) > c \cdot \log n$. In the first communication round, every vertex $v$ uses a random instance $C^I_v$ of an $[N, c \cdot \log^3 N, c \cdot \log N]$-BIC code to encode its ID and transmits $C^I_v(\mathrm{id}_v)$ as part of $m_1(v)$. In addition, the vertices use the Information-Overflow Detection scheme of Section 3 to verify if their BIC decoding is successful (that is, the message $m_1(v)$ consists of two fields, the first encodes the ID and the second is devoted for overflow detection). Upon receiving $m'_1(v) = \bigoplus_{u \in \Gamma(v)} m_1(u)$, the vertex applies BIC decoding to the first field of the message and applies Information-Overflow Detection to the second field to verify the correctness of the decoding. Note that by the properties of the BIC code, in this round, the low-degree vertices compute their exact degree in $G$.

The second round aims at computing a constant factor approximation for the remaining vertices with high-degree. Set $a = 40 \cdot \log N$ and $b = 2\log N$. Every vertex $v$ sends an $(a \cdot b)$-bit message $m_2(v)$ defined by a collection of $a$ random numbers in the range of $\{1, \ldots, b\}$ sampled independently by each vertex $v$. Specifically, for every $v$ and $i \in \{1, \ldots, a\}$, $r_i(v)$ is sampled according to the geometric distribution, letting $r_i(v) = j$ for $j \in \{1, \ldots, b-1\}$ with probability $2^{-j}$, and $r_i(v) = b$ with probability $2^{-b+1}$ (the remaining probability). For every $i \in \{1, \ldots, a\}$ and every $j \in \{1, \ldots, b\}$, let $x_{i,j}(v) = 1$ if $j < r_i(v)$ and $x_{i,j}(v) = 0$ otherwise. Let $X_i(v) = x_{i,b}(v) \cdots x_{i,2}(v) \cdot x_{i,1}(v)$ and let $m_2(v) = X(v) = X_a(v) \cdots X_2(v) \cdot X_1(v)$ be the transmitted message of $v$. Let $Y(v) = \bigoplus_{u \in \Gamma(v)} X(u)$ be the received message of $v$. The decoding is applied to each of the $a$ blocks of $Y(v)$ separately, i.e., treating $Y(v)$ as $Y(v) = Y_a(v) \cdots Y_2(v) \cdot Y_1(v)$, where $Y_i(v) = y_{i,b}(v) \cdots y_{i,2}(v) \cdot y_{i,1}(v)$, such that $y_{i,j}(v) = \bigoplus_{u \in \Gamma(v)} x_{i,j}(u)$. For every $j \in \{1, \ldots, b\}$ and every $v \in V$, define $\mathrm{SUM}(j, v) = \sum_{i=1}^{a} y_{i,j}(v)$. Finally, define $j^*(v) = \min\{j \mid \mathrm{SUM}(j, v) \leq 0.2 \cdot a\}$, if there exists an index $j$ such that $\mathrm{SUM}(j, v) \leq 0.2 \cdot a$ (we later show that such index do exists with high probability) and $j^*(v) = 0$, otherwise as a default value. The approximation $\delta(v)$ is then given by $2^{j^*(v)-1}$. This completes the description of the algorithm.

As mentioned earlier, the correctness for low-degree vertices follows immediately by the properties of the BIC code and the information-overflow detection (Lemma 1 and Lemma 2). We then show that in the second round, for high-degree vertices $v$, we have $\delta(v)/\deg(v) = O(1)$, with high probability. We thus have the following.

**Theorem 1.** *There exists an $O(1)$-round algorithm that computes w.h.p. the exact degree $\deg(v)$ for vertices with $\deg(v) = O(\log n)$ and a constant approximation if $\deg(v) = \Omega(\log n)$.*

## 6   Revealing Asymmetry – Distributed Tournament

Consider the setting where every vertex is given an input value (corresponding to its rank, for example) and the goal is to find the vertex with the maximum value. We will show that BCC codes with message size of $O(\log^3 n)$ allow one to perform many simultaneous competitions between $\Omega(\log n)$ candidates, which result in a tournament process of $O(D \cdot \log n / \log \log n)$ rounds for a network of diameter $D$. Specifically, the fact that the BCC code provides successful decoding when there are $O(\log^2 n)$ concurrent transmitting neighbors, allows us to reduce the number of competitors by a factor of $\Omega(\log n)$ in every round, and hence the winner is found within $O(D \cdot \log n / \log \log n)$ rounds. Because of space considerations, we presenting here only the protocol for single-hop networks. The protocol for any network of diameter $D > 1$, which requires some subtle modifications is presented in the full version [7].

*Single-Hop Network.* Let $V = \{v_1, \ldots, v_n\}$ be the vertices of the network and let $X = \{x_1, \ldots, x_n\}$, where $x_i \in \{1, \ldots n^2\}$ for all $i$, be the set of integral inputs such that vertex $v_i$ holds the input $x_i$. Let $\max(X) = \max_{i=1}^{n} x_i$ be the maximum value in $X$. Note that by Section 5, a 2-approximation for the maximum can be computed within a single round, w.h.p. The main contribution of this section is the *exact* computation of the maximum value.

**Theorem 2.** *The maximum value* $\max(X)$ *can be computed within* $O\left(\frac{\log n}{\log \log n}\right)$ *rounds, with high probability.*

Algorithm CompMaxSH consists of $O(\log n / \log \log n)$ communication rounds. For simplicity, assume that the input values are distinct. This can be obtained by appending to every input value $\lceil \log n \rceil$ least significant bits corresponding to the ID of the vertex. Let $c \geq 2$ be an upper bound on the approximation ratio of Algorithm ApproxNetSize and set $\tau = \lceil c \cdot \log n / \log \log n \rceil$. Initially, all vertices are active. In round $t = \{1, \ldots, \tau\}$, let $n_t$ be a constant approximation for the number of active vertices at the beginning of round $t$, and let $C$ be an $[n_1, 32c \cdot \log^3 n_1, 32c \cdot \log^2 n_1]$-BCC code[4]. After computing $n_t$, every active vertex $v_j$ transmits $C(x_j)$ with probability $p_t = 4c \cdot \log^2 n_1 / n_t$. If a vertex $v_i$ receives an input $x_j > x_i$ in round $t$, it becomes inactive. The final result $\max(v_i)$ of every vertex $v_i$ corresponds to the maximum input value $x_j$ it received throughout the algorithm. This completes the description of the algorithm.

We now analyze the algorithm and begin with correctness. Let $A_t$ be the active vertex set at the beginning of round $t$. Note that $A_\tau \subseteq \ldots \subseteq A_1 = V$. Let $v_m$ be a vertex with maximum input, i.e., $x_m = \max(X)$.

**Lemma 4.** *For each round* $t \in \{1, \ldots, \tau\}$, *with high probability it holds that* $|A_t| = O(n_1 / \log^{t-1} n_1)$ *and* $x_m \in A_t$.

*Proof.* The claim is shown by induction. For the base of the induction $t = 1$, we have that $A_1 = V$, and $n_1 \leq c \cdot n$ since by the properties of Algorithm ApproxNetSize it holds that with high probability $n_1 \in [n/2, c \cdot n]$ for some constant $c \geq 2$. Assume that the claim holds up to step $t - 1 \geq 1$ and consider step $t$. Order the values of the vertices in $A_{t-1}$ in increasing order of their inputs and consider the subset $H_{t-1} \subset A_{t-1}$ of the $\lceil |A_{t-1}| / \log n_1 \rceil$ vertices with the highest input values in $A_{t-1}$. We first claim that with high probability, at least one of the vertices in $H_{t-1}$ transmits in round $t-1$. Since every vertex in $A_{t-1}$ transmits with probability of $p_{t-1} = 4c \log^2 n_1 / n_{t-1}$ and $n_{t-1} \leq c \cdot |A_{t-1}|$, in expectation there are at least $4 \log n_1$ transmitting vertices in $H_{t-1}$ and hence, by a Chernoff bound, w.h.p there is at least one transmitter in $H_{t-1}$.

We proceed by showing that the number of transmitting vertices in round $t - 1$ is $O(\log^2 n)$. In expectation, the number of transmitting vertices in $A_{t-1}$ is at most $8c \cdot \log^2 n_1$, and hence by Chernoff bound, with high probability there are less than $32c \log^2 n_1$ transmitters. By the properties of the BCC code, all messages received in round $t - 1$ are decodable. This implies that all vertices know the value of at least one vertex in $H_{t-1}$ and as a result all vertices in $V \setminus H_{t-1}$ become inactive. In other words, $A_t \subseteq H_{t-1}$ and hence $n_t \leq |H_{t-1}| = |A_{t-1}| / \log n_1 = O(n_1 / \log^t n_1)$, where the last equality holds w.h.p by the induction assumption. Finally, by the induction assumption for $t - 1$, $v_m \in A_{t-1}$, since all messages were decoded successfully in round $t - 1$ w.h.p, it holds that $v_m$ remains in $A_t$ as well. The claim follows. $\square$

---

[4] This approximation for the size of the network can be obtained by applying Algorithm ApproxNetSize or simply Algorithm AppDegree in the case of single-hop networks (where only the active vertices participate in these algorithms).

We thus have the following, which proves Theorem 2.

**Lemma 5.** *With high probability* $\max(v_i) = \max(X)$ *for every vertex* $v_i \in V$.

## 7   Discussion

It is clear that computing in the additive network model should be doable faster than in the standard radio network model. In this paper we quantify this intuition, by providing efficient algorithms for various cornerstone distributed tasks. Our work leaves open several important open questions for further research. First, it is natural to ask whether our algorithms can be improved. Specifically, most of our algorithms apply for the full-duplex model and translate into half-duplex by paying an extra factor of $O(\log n)$. It would be interesting to obtain better bounds for half-duplex radios without using the full-duplex protocol as a black box. An additional axis that requires investigation is the multiple channels model. It would be interesting to study the tradeoff between running time, message size and the number of channels. Note, that whereas most of our algorithms are optimal for full-duplex radios (up to constant factors), some leave room for improvements. For example, in the problem of computing the maximum input, we believe that some pipelining of the simulation of phases should be able to give a round complexity of $O(D + \log n/\log \log n)$, instead of the current $O(D \cdot \log n/\log \log n)$. However, this is not immediate. Designing lower bounds for this model is another important future goal. It seems that the problem of computing the maximum input in a single-hop network, should be a good starting point, as we believe that this task requires $\Omega(\log n/\log \log n)$ rounds. Another interesting future direction involves the implementation of an abstract MAC layer over *additive* radio network model. Such an implementation was provided recently [13] for the standard radio network model. Finally, we note that all our algorithms are randomized, as opposed to the original definition of BCC codes. Is randomization necessary? What is the computational power of the additive network model without randomization?

## References

1. Alon, N., Babai, L., Itai, A.: A fast and simple randomized parallel algorithm for the maximal independent set problem. J. Algorithms **7**(4), 567–583 (1986)
2. Andrews, J.: Interference cancellation for cellular systems: a contemporary. SIAM Journal on Computing **12**(1), 19–2 (2005)
3. Avestimehr, A.S., Diggavi, S.N., Tse, D.: Wireless network information flow: A deterministic approach. IEEE Trans. on Info. Theory **57**(4), 1872–1905 (2011)
4. Bar-Yehuda, R., Goldreichh, O., Itai, A.: On the time-complexity of broadcast in multi-hop radio networks: An exponential gap between determinism and randomization. J. of Compt. Syst. Sciences **45**, 104–126 (1992)
5. Barenboim, L., Elkin, M., Pettie, S., Schneider, J.: The locality of distributed symmetry breaking. In: FOCS, pp. 321–330 (2012)

6. Censor-Hillel, K., Haeupler, B., Lynch, N., Médard, M.: Bounded-contention coding for wireless networks in the high SNR regime. In: Aguilera, M.K. (ed.) DISC 2012. LNCS, vol. 7611, pp. 91–105. Springer, Heidelberg (2012)
7. Censor-Hillel, K., Kantor, E., Lynch, N.A., Parter, M.: Computing in additive networks with bounded-information codes. arxiv.org/abs/1508.03660 (2015)
8. Daum, S., Ghaffari, M., Gilbert, S., Kuhn, F., Newport, C.: Maximal independent sets in multichannel radio networks. In: PODC, pp. 335–344 (2013)
9. Farach-Colton, M., Fernandes, R.J., Mosteiro, M.A.: Lower bounds for clear transmissions in radio networks. In: Correa, J.R., Hevia, A., Kiwi, M. (eds.) LATIN 2006. LNCS, vol. 3887, pp. 447–454. Springer, Heidelberg (2006)
10. Ghaffari, M., Haeupler, B.: Near optimal leader election in multi-hop radio networks. In: SODA, pp. 748–766 (2013)
11. Gollakota, S., Katabi, D.: Zigzag decoding: combating hidden terminals in wireless networks. In: SIGCOMM, pp. 159–170 (2008)
12. Gupta, P., Kumar, P.: The capacity of wireless networks. IEEE Trans. on Info. Theory, 388–404 (2000)
13. Kuhn, F., Lynch, N., Newport, C.: The abstract MAC layer. Distributed Computing 24, 187–206 (2011)
14. Kuhn, F., Moscibroda, T., Wattenhofer, R.: What cannot be computed locally! In: Proc. PODC, pp. 300–309 (2004)
15. Kuhn, F., Wattenhofer, R.: Constant-time distributed dominating set approximation. Distributed Computing 17(4), 303–310 (2005)
16. Linial, N.: Locality in distributed graph algorithms. SIAM Journal on Computing 21(1), 193–201 (1992)
17. Liu, Z., Herlihy, M.: Approximate local sums and their applications in radio networks. In: Kuhn, F. (ed.) DISC 2014. LNCS, vol. 8784, pp. 243–257. Springer, Heidelberg (2014)
18. Luby, M.: A simple parallel algorithm for the maximal independent set problem. SIAM Journal on Computing 15, 1036–1053 (1986)
19. Métivier, Y., Robson, J., Saheb-Djahromi, N., Zemmari, A.: An optimal bit complexity randomized distributed MIS algorithm. Distributed Computing 23(5–6), 331–340 (2011)
20. Moscibroda, T., Wattenhofer, R.: Maximal independent sets in radio networks. In: PODC, pp. 148–157 (2005)
21. Ozgur, A., Leveque, O., Tse, D.: Hierarchical cooperation achieves optimal capacity scaling in ad hoc networks. IEEE Trans. on Info. Theory, 3549–3572 (2007)
22. ParandehGheibi, A., Sundararajan, J.-K., Médard, M.: Collision helps - algebraic collision recovery for wireless erasure networks. In: WiNC (2010)
23. Ramachandran, K.N., Belding-Royer, E.M., Almeroth, K.C., Buddhikot, M.M.: Interference-aware channel assignment in multi-radio wireless mesh networks. In: INFOCOM, pp. 1–12 (2006)
24. Schneider, J., Wattenhofer, R.: Coloring unstructured wireless multi-hop networks. In: PODC, pp. 210–219 (2009)
25. Schneider, J., Wattenhofer, R.: An optimal maximal independent set algorithm for bounded-independence graphs. Distributed Computing 22(5–6), 349–361 (2010)
26. Schneider, J., Wattenhofer, R.: What is the use of collision detection (in Wireless Networks)? In: Lynch, N.A., Shvartsman, A.A. (eds.) DISC 2010. LNCS, vol. 6343, pp. 133–147. Springer, Heidelberg (2010)

# Specifying Concurrent Problems: Beyond Linearizability and up to Tasks

## (Extended Abstract)

Armando Castañeda[1], Sergio Rajsbaum[1]([✉]), and Michel Raynal[2]

[1] Instituto de Matemáticas, UNAM, 04510 México D.F, México
{armando.castaneda,rajsbaum}@im.unam.mx
[2] IUF & IRISA (Université de Rennes), 35042 Rennes, France
raynal@irisa.fr

**Abstract.** Tasks and objects are two predominant ways of specifying distributed problems. A *task* specifies for each set of processes (which may run concurrently) the valid outputs of the processes. An *object* specifies the outputs the object may produce when it is accessed sequentially. Each one requires its own *implementation* notion, to tell when an execution satisfies the specification. For objects *linearizability* is commonly used, while for tasks implementation notions are less explored.

Sequential specifications are very convenient, especially important is the *locality* property of linearizability, which states that linearizable objects compose for free into a linearizable object. However, most well-known tasks have no sequential specification. Also, tasks have no clear locality property.

The paper introduces the notion of *interval-sequential* object. The corresponding implementation notion of *interval-linearizability* generalizes linearizability. Interval-linearizability allows to specify any task. However, there are sequential one-shot objects that cannot be expressed as tasks, under the simplest interpretation of a task. The paper also shows that a natural extension of the notion of a task is expressive enough to specify any interval-sequential object.

**Keywords:** Concurrent object · Task · Linearizability · Sequential specification

## 1 Introduction

*Concurrent Objects.* Distributed computer scientists excel at thinking concurrently, and building large distributed programs that work under difficult conditions where processes experience asynchrony and failures. Yet, they evade

Full version in http://arxiv.org/abs/1507.00073.
A. Castañeda—Partially supported by UNAM-PAPIIT.
S. Rajsbaum—Partially supported by LAISLA-CONACYT and UNAM-PAPIIT.
R. Raynal—Partially supported by the French ANR project DISPLEXITY, and the Franco-German ANR project DISCMAT

© Springer-Verlag Berlin Heidelberg 2015
Y. Moses (Ed.): DISC 2015, LNCS 9363, pp. 420–435, 2015.
DOI: 10.1007/978-3-662-48653-5_28

thinking about *concurrent* problem specifications. A central paradigm is that of a shared object that processes may access concurrently [19,22], but the object is specified in terms of a sequential specification, i.e., an automaton describing the outputs the object produces only when it is accessed sequentially. Thus, a concurrent algorithm seeks to emulate an allowed sequential behavior.

There are various ways of defining what it means for an algorithm to *implement* an object, namely, that it satisfies its sequential specification. One of the most popular consistency conditions is *linearizability* [20]. An implementation is *linearizable* if each of its executions is *linearizable*: intuitively, for each operation call, it is possible to find a unique point in the interval of real-time defined by the invocation and response of the operation, and these *linearization points* induce a valid sequential execution. Linearizability is very popular to design components of large systems because it is *local*, namely, one can consider linearizable object implementations in isolation and *compose* them for free, without sacrificing linearizability of the whole system [11]. Also, linearizability is a *non-blocking* property, which means that a pending invocation (of a total operation) is never required to wait for another pending invocation to complete.

Linearizability has various desirable properties, additionally to being local and non-blocking: it allows talking about the state of an object, interactions among operations is captured by side-effects on object states; documentation size of an object is linear in the number of operations; new operations can be added without changing descriptions of old operations. However, as we argue here, linearizability is sometimes too restrictive. First, there are problems which have no sequential specifications (more on this below). Second, some problems are more naturally and succinctly defined in term of concurrent behaviors. Third, as it is well known, the specification of a problem should be as general as possible, to allow maximum flexibility to both programmers and program executions.

*Distributed Tasks.* Another predominant way of specifying a one-shot distributed problem, especially in distributed computability, is through the notion of a *task*. Several tasks have been intensively studied in distributed computability, leading to an understanding of their relative power [18], to the design of simulations between models [5], and to the development of a deep connection between distributed computing and topology [17]. Formally, a task is specified by an input/output relation, defining for each set of processes that may run concurrently, and each assignment of inputs to the processes in the set, the valid outputs of the processes. Implementation notions for tasks are less explored, and they are not as elegant as linearizability. In practice, task and implementation are usually described operationally, somewhat informally. One of the versions widely used is that an algorithm *implements* a task if, in every execution where a set of processes participate (run to completion, and the other crash from the beginning), input and outputs satisfy the task specification.

Tasks and objects model in a very different way the concurrency that naturally arises in distributed systems: while tasks explicitly state what might happen when a set of processes run concurrently, objects only specify what happens when processes access the object sequentially.

It is remarkable that these two approaches have largely remained independent, while the main distributed computing paradigm, *consensus*, is central to both. Neiger [21] noticed this and proposed a generalization of linearizability called *set-linearizability*. He discussed that there are tasks, like *immediate snapshot* [4], with no natural specification as sequential objects. An object modeling the immediate snapshot task is necessarily stronger than the immediate snapshot task, because such an object implements test-and-set. In contrast there are read/write algorithms solving the immediate snapshot task and it is well-known that there are no read/write linearizable implementations of test-and-set. Therefore, Neiger proposed the notion of a *set-sequential* object, that allows a set of processes to access an object simultaneously. Then, one can define an immediate snapshot set-sequential object, and there are *set-linearizable* implementations.

*Contributions.* We propose the notion of an *interval-sequential* concurrent object, a framework in which an object is specified by an automaton that can express any concurrency pattern of overlapping invocations of operations, that might occur in an execution (although one is not forced to describe all of them). The automaton is a direct generalization of the automaton of a sequential object, except that transitions are labeled with sets of invocations and responses, allowing operations to span several consecutive transitions. The corresponding implementation notion of *interval-linearizability* generalizes linearizability and set-linearizability, and allows to associate states along the interval of execution of an operation. While linearizing an execution requires finding linearization *points*, in interval-linearizability one needs to identify a linearization *interval* for each operation (the intervals might overlap). Remarkably, this general notion remains local and non-blocking. We show that important tasks have no specification neither as a sequential object nor as a set-sequential object, but they can be naturally expressed as interval-sequential objects.

Establishing the relationship between tasks and (sequential, set-sequential and interval-sequential) automaton-based specifications is subtle, because tasks admit several natural interpretations. Interval-linearizability is a framework that allows to specify any task, however, there are sequential one-shot objects that cannot be expressed as tasks, under the simplest interpretation of what it means to solve a task. However, a natural extension of

**Fig. 1.** Equivalence between *refined* tasks and one-shot interval-sequential objects.

the notion of solving a task, which we call *refined tasks*, has the same expressive power to specify one-shot concurrent problems, hence strictly more than sequential and set-sequential objects. See Figure 1. Interval-linearizability goes beyond unifying sequentially specified objects and tasks, it sheds new light on both of them. On the one hand, interval-sequential linearizability provides an explicit operational semantics for a task (whose semantics, as we argue here, is not well understood), gives a more precise implementation notion, and brings a locality property to tasks. On the other hand, tasks provide a static specification for automaton-based formalisms such as sequential, set-sequential and interval-sequential objects.

Finally, Shavit [24] summarizes beautifully the common knowledge state that "it is infinitely easier and more intuitive for us humans to specify how abstract data structures behave in a sequential setting." We hope interval-linearizability opens the possibility of facilitating reasoning about concurrent specifications, when no sequential specifications are possible.

All proofs and additional examples can be found in [7].

*Related Work.* Neiger proposed unifying sequential objects and tasks, using set-linearizability [21]. Later on, it was again observed that for some concurrent objects it is impossible to provide a sequential specification, and *concurrency-aware* linearizability was defined [16] (still, no locality properties were proved). Set linearizability and concurrency-aware linearizability are closely related and both are strictly less powerful than interval linearizability to model tasks. Transforming the question of wait-free read/write solvability of a one-shot sequential object, into the question of solvability of a task was suggested in [13]. The refined tasks we propose here is reminiscent to the construction in [13] Linearizability can be used in an operation that must wait for some other thread to establish a precondition, by defining two linearization points, representing a request and a follow-up [23]. These points are reminiscent of the interval used to define an interval-linearization. *Higher dimensional automata* are used to model execution of concurrent operations, and are the most expressive model among other common operations [14]. They model transitions which consist of sets of operations, and hence are related to set-linearizability, but do not naturally model interval-linearizability. There is work on partial order semantics of programs, including more flexible notions of linearizability, relating two arbitrary sets of histories [10], although no compositionality result is proved, and concurrent executions are not explicitly studied. It is worth exploring this direction further, as the properties hold for concurrent executions, and it establishes that linearizability implies observational refinement, which usually entails compositionality (see, e.g., [15]).

## 2    Limitations of Linearizability and Set-Linearizability

Sometimes we work with objects with two operations, but that are intended to be used as one. For instance, a snapshot object [1] has operations write() and snapshot(). This object has a sequential specification and there are linearizable read/write algorithms implementing it (see, e.g., [19,22]). But many times, a snapshot object is used in a canonical way, namely, each time a process invokes write(), immediately after it always invokes snapshot(). Indeed, one would like to think of such an object as providing a single operation, write_snapshot(), invoked with a value $x$ to be deposited in the object, and when the operation returns, it gives back to the invoking process a snapshot of the contents of the object.

It turns out that this write-snapshot object has neither a natural sequential nor a set-sequential specification. However, it can be specified as a task and actually is implementable from read/write registers.

As observed in [21], in a sequential specification of write-snapshot any of its executions can be seen as if all invocations occurred one after the other, in some order. Thus, always there is a first invocation, which must output the set containing only its input value, and hence could solve test-and-set, contradicting the fact that test-and-set cannot be implemented from read/write registers. Neiger noted this problem in the context of the immediate snapshot task. He proposed in [21] the idea that a specification should allow to express that sets of operations that can be concurrent. He called this notion *set-linearizability*. In set-linearizability, an execution accepted by a *set-sequential* automaton is a sequence of non-empty sets with operations, and each set denotes operations that are executed concurrently. While set-linearizability is sufficient to model the immediate-snapshot task, it is not enough for specifying the write-snapshot task, and most other tasks.

In set-linearizability, in the execution in Figure 2, one has to decide if the operation of $q$ goes together with the one of $p$ or $r$. In either case, in the resulting execution a process seems to predict a future operation. The problem is that there are operations that are affected by several operations that are not concurrent. This cannot be expressed as a set-sequential execution. Hence, to succinctly express this type of behavior, we need a more flexible framework in which it is possible to express that an operation happens in an interval of time that can be affected by several operations.

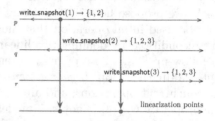

**Fig. 2.** A write-snapshot execution that is not set-linearizable.

To deal with these problematic tasks, one is tempted to separate an operation into two operations, set() and get(). The first communicates the input value of a process, while the second produces an output value to a process. For instance, $k$-set agreement is easily transformed into an object with a sequential specification, by accessing it through set() to deposit a value into the object and get() to obtain one of the values in the object. In fact, every task can be represented as a sequential object by splitting the operation of the task in two operations.

Separating an operation into a proposal operation and a returning operation has several problems (although it is useful in other contexts [23]). First, the program is forced to produce two operations, and wait for two responses. There is a consequent loss of clarity in the code of the program, in addition to a loss in performance, incurred by a two-round trip delay. Also, the intended meaning of linearization points is lost; an operation is now linearized at *two* linearization points. Furthermore, the resulting object may be more powerful; a phenomenon that has been observed several times in the context of iterated models e.g. [9].

*Additional Examples of Problematic Tasks.* Several tasks are problematic for dealing with them through linearizability, and have no deterministic sequential specifications. Some have been studied in the past, such as the following.

- *adopt-commit* [12] is useful to implement round-based protocols for set-agreement and consensus. Given an input $u$ to the object, the result is an output of the form $(commit, v)$ or $(adopt, v)$, where $commit/adopt$ is a decision that indicates whether the process should decide value $v$ immediately or adopt it as its preferred value in later rounds of the protocol.
- *conflict detection* [3] has been shown to be equivalent to the adopt-commit. Roughly, if at least two different values are proposed concurrently at least one process outputs true.
- *safe-consensus* [2], a weakening of consensus, where the agreement condition of consensus is retained, but the validity condition becomes: if the first process to invoke it returns before any other process invokes it, then it outputs its input; otherwise the consensus output can be arbitrary, not even the input of any process.
- *immediate snapshot* [4], which plays an important role in distributed computability [17]. A process can write a value to the shared memory using this operation, and gets back a snapshot of the shared memory, such that the snapshot occurs immediately after the write.
- *k-set agreement* [8], where processes agree on at most $k$ input values.
- *Exchanger* [16], is a Java object that serves as a synchronization point at which threads can pair up and atomically swap elements.

# 3   Concurrent Objects

## 3.1   System Model

The presentation follows [6,20,22]. The *system* consists of $n$ asynchronous sequential processes, $P = \{p_1, \ldots, p_n\}$, which communicate through a set of concurrent objects, $OBS$. Given a set $OP$ of operations offered by the objects of the system to the processes $P$, let $Inv$ be the set of all invocations to operations that can be issued by a process in a system, and $Res$ be the set of all responses to the invocations in $Inv$. There are functions: (1) $id : Inv \to P$, (2) $Inv \to OP$, (3) $Res \to OP$, (4) $Res \to Inv$ and (5) $obj : OP \to OBS$, where $id(in)$ tells which process invoked $in \in Inv$, $op(in)$ tells which operation was invoked, $op(r)$ tells which operation was responded, $res(r)$ tells which invocation corresponds to $r \in Res$, and $obj(oper)$ indicates the object that offers operation $oper$. There is an induced function $id : Res \to P$ defined by $id(r) = id(res(r))$. Also, induced functions $obj : Inv \to OBS$ defined by $obj(in) = obj(op(in))$, and $obj : Res \to OBS$ defined by $obj(r) = obj(op(r))$. The set of operations of an object $X$, $OP(X)$, consists of all operations $oper$, with $obj(oper) = X$. Similarly, $Inv(X)$ and $Res(X)$ are resp. the set of invocations and responses of $X$.

A *process* is a deterministic automaton that interacts with the objects in $OBS$. It produces a sequence of steps, where a *step* is an invocation of an object's operation, or reacting to an object's response (including local processing). Consider the set of all operations $OP$ of objects in $OBS$, and all the corresponding possible invocations $Inv$ and responses $Res$. A process $p$ is an automaton $(\Sigma, \nu, \tau)$, with states $\Sigma$ and functions $\nu, \tau$ that describe the interaction of the process with the objects. Often there is also a set of initial states $\Sigma_0 \subseteq \Sigma$. Intuitively, if $p$ is in state $\sigma$ and $\nu(\sigma) = (op, X)$ then in its next step $p$ will apply operation $op$ to object $X$. Based on its current state, $X$ will return a response $r$ to $p$ and will enter a new state, in accordance to its transition relation. Finally, $p$ will enter state $\tau(\sigma, r)$ as a result of the response it received from $X$.

A *system* consists of a set of processes, $P$, a set of objects $OBS$ so that each $p \in P$ uses a subset of $OBS$, together with an initial state for each of the objects.

A *configuration* is a tuple consisting of the state of each process and each object, and a configuration is *initial* if each process and each object is in an initial state. An *execution* of the system is modeled by a sequence of events $H$ arranged in a total order $\widehat{H} = (H, <_H)$, where each event is an invocation $in \in Inv$ or a response $r \in Res$, that can be produced following the process automata, interacting with the objects. Namely, an execution starts, given any initial configuration, by having any process invoke an operation, according to its transition relation. In general, once a configuration is reached, the next event can be a response from an object to an operation of a process or an invocation of an operation by a process whose last invocation has been responded. Thus, an execution is well-formed, in the sense that it consists of an interleaving of invocations and responses to operations, where a processes invokes an operation only when its last invocation has been responded.

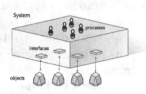

## 3.2  The Notion of an *Interval-Sequential* Object

To generalize the usual notion of a sequential object e.g. [6,20] instead of considering sequences of invocations and responses, we consider sequences of *sets* of invocations and responses. An *invoking concurrency class* $C \subseteq 2^{Inv}$, is a nonempty subset of $Inv$ such that $C$ contains at most one invocation by the same process. A *responding concurrency class* $C$, $C \subseteq 2^{Res}$, is defined similarly.

*Interval-Sequential Execution.* An *interval-sequential execution* $h$ is an alternating sequence of invoking and responding concurrency classes, starting in an invoking class, $h = I_0, R_0, I_1, R_1, \ldots, I_m, R_m$, where the following conditions are satisfied

1. For each $I_i \in h$, any two invocations $in_1, in_2 \in I_i$ are by different processes, $id(in_1) \neq id(in_2)$. Similarly, for $R_i \in h$ if $r_1, r_2 \in R_i$ then $id(r_1) \neq id(r_2)$,
2. Let $r \in R_i$ for some $R_i \in h$. There is $in \in I_j$ for some $j \leq i$, such that $res(r) = in$ and there is no other $in'$ with $id(in) = id(in')$ and $in' \in I_{j'}$, $j < j' \leq i$.

It follows that an execution $h$ consists of matching invocations and responses, perhaps with some pending invocations with no response.

*Interval-Sequential Object.* An *interval-sequential* object $X$ is a (not necessarily finite) Mealy state machine $(Q, 2^{Inv(X)}, 2^{Res(X)}, \delta)$ whose output values $R$ are responding concurrency classes $R$ of $X$, $R \subseteq 2^{Res(X)}$, are determined both by its current state $s \in Q$ and the current input $I \in 2^{Inv(X)}$, where $I$ is an invoking concurrency class of $X$. There is a set of *initial states* $Q_0$ of $X$, $Q_0 \subseteq Q$. The transition relation $\delta \subseteq Q \times 2^{inv(X)} \times 2^{Res(X)} \times Q$ specifies both, the output of the automaton and its next state. If $X$ is in state $q$ and it receives as input a set of invocations $I$, then, if $(R, q') \in \delta(q, I)$, the meaning is that $X$ may return the non-empty set of responses $R$ and move to state $q'$. We stress that always both $I$ and $R$ are non-empty sets.

*Interval-Sequential Execution of an Object.* Consider an initial state $q_0 \in Q_0$ of $X$ and a sequence of inputs $I_0, I_1, \ldots I_m$. Then a sequence of outputs that $X$ may produce is $R_0, R_1, \ldots R_m$, where $(R_i, q_{i+1}) \in \delta(q_i, I_i)$. Then the *interval-sequential execution* of $X$ starting in $q_0$ is $q_0, I_0, R_0, q_1, I_1, R_1, \ldots, q_m, I_m, R_m$. However, we require that the object's response at a state uniquely determines the new state, i.e. we assume if $\delta(q, I_i)$ contains $(R_i, q_{i+1})$ and $(R_i, q'_{i+1})$ then $q_{i+1} = q'_{i+1}$. Then we may denote the interval-sequential execution of $X$, starting in $q_0$ by $h = I_0, R_0, I_1, R_1, \ldots, I_m, R_m$, because the sequence of states $q_0, q_1, \ldots, q_m$ is uniquely determined by $q_0$, and by the sequences of inputs and responses. When we omit mentioning $q_0$ we assume there is some initial state in $Q_0$ that can produce $h$.

Note that $X$ may be non-deterministic, in a given state $q_i$ with input $I_i$ it may move to more than one state and return more than one response. Sometimes it is convenient to require that the object is *total*, meaning that, for every singleton set $I \in 2^{Inv}$ and every state $q$ in which the invocation $inv$ in $I$ is not pending, there is an $(R, q') \in \delta(q, I)$ in which there is a response to $inv$ in $R$.

Our definition of interval-sequential execution is motivated by the fact that we are interested in *well-formed* executions $h = I_0, R_0, I_1, R_1, \ldots, I_m, R_m$. Informally, the processes should behave well, in the sense that a process does not invoke a new operation before its last invocation received a response. Also, the object should behave well, in the sense that it should not return a response to an operation that is not pending.

The *interval-sequential specification* of $X$, $ISSpec(X)$, is the set of all its interval-sequential executions.

*Representation of Interval-Sequential Executions.* In general, we will be thinking of an interval-sequential execution $h$ as an alternating sequence of invoking and responding concurrency classes starting with an invoking class, $h = I_0, R_0, I_1, R_1, \ldots, I_m, R_m$. However, it is sometimes convenient to think of an execution as a a total order $\widehat{S} = (S, \xrightarrow{S})$ on a subset $S \subseteq CC(X)$, where $CC(X)$, is the set with all invoking and responding concurrency classes of $X$; namely, $h = I_0 \xrightarrow{S} R_0 \xrightarrow{S} I_1 \xrightarrow{S} R_1 \xrightarrow{S} \cdots \xrightarrow{S} I_m \xrightarrow{S} R_m$.

In addition, the execution $h = I_0, R_0, I_1, R_1, \ldots, I_m, R_m$ can be represented by a table, with a column for each element in the sequence $h$, and a row for each process. A member $in \in I_j$ invoked by $p_k$ (resp. a response $r \in R_j$ to $p_k$) is placed in the $k$'th row, at the $2j$-th column (resp. $2j + 1$-th column). Thus, a transition of the automaton will correspond to two consecutive columns, $I_j, R_j$. See Figure 3, and several more examples in the figures below.

*Remark 1.* Let $X$ be an interval-sequential object. Suppose for all states $q$ and all $I$, if $\delta(q, I) = (R, q')$, then $|R| = |I|$, and additionally each $r \in R$ is a response to one $in \in I$. Then $X$ is a *set-sequential* object. If in addition, $|I| = |R| = 1$, then $X$ is a sequential object in the usual sense (see Figure 1).

### 3.3   An Example: The Validity Task

Consider an object $X$ with a single operation validity$(x)$, that can be invoked by each process, with a *proposed* input parameter $x$, and a very simple specification: an operation returns a value that has been proposed. This problem is easily specified as a task. Indeed, many tasks include this property, such as consensus, set-agreement, write-snapshot, etc. As an interval-sequential object, it is formally specified by an automaton, where each state $q$ is labeled with two values, $q.vals$ is the set of values that have been proposed so far, and $q.pend$ is the set of processes with pending invocations. The initial state $q_0$ has $q_0.vals = \emptyset$ and $q_0.pend = \emptyset$. If $in$ is an invocation to the object, let $val(in)$ be the proposed value, and if $r$ is a response from the object, let $val(r)$ be the responded value. For a set of invocations $I$ (resp. responses $R$) $vals(I)$ denotes the proposed values in $I$ (resp. $vals(R)$). The transition relation $\delta(q, I)$ contains all pairs $(R, q')$ such that:

- If $r \in R$ then $id(r) \in q.pend$ or there is an $in \in I$ with $id(in) = id(r)$,
- If $r \in R$ then $val(r) \in q.vals$ or there is an $in \in I$ with $val(in) = val(r)$,
- $q'.vals = q.val \cup vals(I)$ and $q'.pend = (q.pend \cup ids(I)) \setminus ids(R)$.

On the right of Figure 3 there is part of a validity object automaton. On the left of Figure 3 it is illustrated an interval-sequential execution with the vertical red double-dot lines: $I_0, R_0, I_1, R_1$, where $I_0 = \{p.\text{validity}(1), q.\text{validity}(2)\}$, $R_0 = \{p.\text{resp}(2)\}$, $I_1 = \{r.\text{validity}(3)\}$, $R_1 = \{q.sfresp(3), r.\text{resp}(1)\}$.

The interval-linearizability consistency notion described in Section 4 will formally define how a general execution (blue double-arrows in the figure) can be represented by an interval-sequential execution (red double-dot lines), and hence tell if it satisfies the validity object specification. Notice that the execution in Figure 3 shows that the validity object has no specification neither as a sequential nor as a set-sequential object.

## 4   Interval-Linearizability

*Interval-Sequential Execution of the System.* Consider a subset $S \subseteq CC$ of the concurrency classes of the objects $OBS$ in the system and an interval-

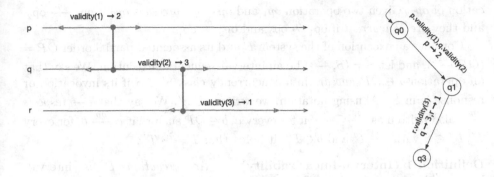

**Fig. 3.** An execution of a validity object, and the corresponding part of its interval-sequential automaton

sequential execution $\widehat{S} = (S, \xrightarrow{S})$, defining an alternating sequence of invoking and responding concurrency classes, starting with an invoking class. For an object $X$, the *projection of* $\widehat{S}$ *at* $X$, $\widehat{S}|_X = (S_X, \xrightarrow{S_X})$, is defined as follows: (1) for every $C \in S$ with at least one invocation or response on $X$, $S_X$ contains a concurrency class $C'$, consisting of the (non-empty) subset of $C$ of all invocations or responses of $X$, and (2) for every $C', C'' \in S_X$, $C' \xrightarrow{S_X} C''$ if and only if there are $T', T'' \in S$ such that $C' \subseteq T'$, $C'' \subseteq T''$ and $T' \xrightarrow{S} T''$.

We say that $\widehat{S} = (S, \xrightarrow{S})$ is an *interval-sequential execution of the system* if $\widehat{S}|_X$ is an interval-sequential execution of $X$ for every $X \in OBS$. That is, if $\widehat{S}|_X \in ISSpec(X)$, the interval-sequential specification of $X$, for every $X \in OBS$. Let $\widehat{S} = (S, \xrightarrow{S})$ be an interval-sequential execution. For a process $p$, the *projection of* $\widehat{S}$ *at* $p$, $\widehat{S}|_p = (S_p, \xrightarrow{S_p})$, is defined as follows: (1) for every $C \in S$ with an invocation or response by $p$, $S_p$ contains contains a class $C$ with the invocation or response by $p$ (there is at most one event by $p$ in $C$), and (2) for every $a, b \in S_p$, $a \xrightarrow{S_p} b$ if and only if there are $T', T'' \in S$ such that $a \in T'$, $b \in T''$ and $T' \xrightarrow{S} T''$.

*Interval-Linearizability.* Recall that an execution of the system is a sequence of invocations and responses (Section 3.1). An invocation in an execution $E$ is *pending* if it has no matching response, otherwise it is *complete*. An *extension* of an execution $E$ is obtained by appending zero or more responses to pending invocations.

An *operation call* in $E$ is a pair consisting of an invocation and its matching response. Let $comp(E)$ be the sequence obtained from $E$ by removing its pending invocations. The order in which invocation and responses in $E$ happened, induces the following partial order: $\widehat{OP} = (OP, \xrightarrow{op})$ where $OP$ is the set with all operation calls in $E$, and for each pair $op_1, op_2 \in OP$, $op_1 \xrightarrow{op} op_2$ if and only if $term(op_1) < init(op_2)$ in $E$, namely, the response of $op_1$ appears before the invocation of $op_2$. Given two operation $op_1$ and $op_2$, $op_1$ *precedes* $op_2$ if $op_1 \xrightarrow{op} op_2$, and they are *concurrent* if $op_1 \xrightarrow{op}\!\!\!\!\!\!/\;\; op_2$ and $op_2 \xrightarrow{op}\!\!\!\!\!\!/\;\; op_1$.

Consider an execution of the system $E$ and its associated partial order $\widehat{OP} = (OP, \xrightarrow{op})$, and let $\widehat{S} = (S, \xrightarrow{S})$ be an interval-sequential execution. We say that an operation $a \in OP$ *appears* in a concurrency class $S' \in S$ if its invocation or response is in $S'$. Abusing notation, we write $a \in S'$. We say that $\xrightarrow{S}$ *respects* $\xrightarrow{op}$, also written as $\xrightarrow{op} \subseteq \xrightarrow{S}$, if for every $a, b \in OP$ such that $a \xrightarrow{op} b$, for every $T', T'' \in S$ with $a \in T'$ and $b \in T''$, it holds that $T' \xrightarrow{S} T''$.

**Definition 1 (Interval-linearizability).** *An execution $E$ is interval-linearizable if there is an extension $\overline{E}$ of $E$ and an interval-sequential execution $\widehat{S} = (S, \xrightarrow{S})$ such that*

1. *for every process $p$, $comp(\overline{E})|_p = \widehat{S}|_p$,*
2. *for every object $X$, $\widehat{S}|_X \in ISS(X)$ and*
3. *$\xrightarrow{S}$ respects $\xrightarrow{op}$, where $\widehat{OP} = (OP, \xrightarrow{op})$ is the partial order associated to $comp(\overline{E})$.*

*We say that $\widehat{S} = (S, \xrightarrow{S})$ is an interval-linearization of $E$.*

*Remark 2.* When we restrict to interval-sequential executions in which for every invocation there is a response to it in the very next concurrency class, then interval-linearizability boils down to set-linearizability. If in addition we demand that every concurrency class contains only one element, then we have linearizability. See Figure 1.

We can now complete the example of the validity object. In Figure 4 there is an interval linearization of the execution in Figure 3.

| | init | term | init | term |
|---|---|---|---|---|
| $p$ | validity(1) | resp(2) | | |
| $q$ | validity(2) | | | resp(3) |
| $r$ | | | validity(3) | resp(1) |

**Fig. 4.** An execution of a Validity object

Even though interval-linearizability is much more general than linearizability it retains some of its benefits.

**Theorem 1 (Locality of Interval-Linearizability).** *An execution $E$ is interval-linearizable if and only if $E|_X$ is interval-linearizable, for every object $X$.*

**Theorem 2 (Set-Linearizability is Non-Blocking).** *Let $E$ be an interval-linearizable execution in which there is a pending invocation $inv(op)$ of a total operation. Then, there is a response $res(op)$ such that $E \cdot res(op)$ is interval-linearizable.*

# 5    Tasks and Interval-Sequential Objects

A task is a static way of specifying a *one-shot* concurrent problem, namely, a problem with one operation that can be invoked only once by each process. Here we study the relationship between tasks and the automata-based ways of specifying a concurrent problem that we have been considering.

A task is usually specified informally, in the style of Section 2. E.g., for the $k$-set agreement task one would say that each process proposes a value, and decides a value, such that (validity) a decided value has been proposed, and (agreement) at most $k$ different values are decided.

Formally, a task $(\mathcal{I}, \mathcal{O}, \Delta)$ consists of an *input complex* $\mathcal{I}$, an *output complex* $\mathcal{O}$, and an input/output relation $\Delta$. Each complex consists of a set of *simplexes*, of the form $s = \{(\mathrm{id}_1, x_1), \ldots, (\mathrm{id}_k, x_k)\}$, and closed under containment. An input (resp. output) simplex specifies an assignment of input (resp. output) values, $x_i$ to process $\mathrm{id}_i$. A singleton simplex is a *vertex*. The relation $\Delta$ specifies for each input simplex $s \in \mathcal{I}$, a sub-complex $\Delta(s) \subseteq \mathcal{O}$, such that if $s, s'$ are two simplexes in $\mathcal{I}$ with $s' \subset s$, then $\Delta(s') \subset \Delta(s)$.

A task has only one operation, task(), which process $\mathrm{id}_i$ may call with value $x_i$, if $(\mathrm{id}_i, x_i)$ is a vertex of $\mathcal{I}$. The operation task($x_i$) may return $y_i$ to the process, if $(\mathrm{id}_i, y_i)$ is a vertex of $\mathcal{O}$. Let $E$ be an execution where each process calls task() once. Then, $\sigma_E$ is the input simplex defined as follows: $(\mathrm{id}_i, x_i)$ is in $\sigma_E$ iff in $E$ there is an invocation of task($x_i$) by process $\mathrm{id}_i$. The output simplex $\tau_E$ is defined similarly: $(\mathrm{id}_i, y_i)$ is in $\tau_E$ iff there is a response $y_i$ to a process $\mathrm{id}_i$ in $E$. We say that $E$ *satisfies* $\langle I, O, \Delta \rangle$ if for every prefix $E'$ of $E$, it holds that $\tau_{E'} \in \Delta(\sigma_{E'})$. The prefix requirement prevents executions that globally seem correct, but in a prefix a process predicts future invocations.[1]

*From Tasks to Interval-Sequential Objects.* A task is a very compact way of specifying a distributed problem that is capable of describing allowed behaviors for certain concurrency patterns, and indeed it is hard to understand what exactly is the problem being specified. The following theorem (with its proof) provides an automata-based representation of a task, explaining which outputs may be produced in each execution, as permitted by $\Delta$.

**Theorem 3.** *For every task $T$, there is an interval-sequential object $O_T$ such that an execution $E$ satisfies $T$ if and only if it is interval-linearizable with respect to $O_T$.*

To give an intuition of this theorem, consider the immediate snapshot task for three processes in Figure 5 with two additional output simplexes, $\sigma_1$ and $\sigma_2$. A simple case is the output simplex in the center of the output complex, where the three processes output $\{p, q, r\}$. The case is simple because this simplex does not intersect the boundary, hence, it can be produced as output only when all

---

[1] This requirement has been implicitly considered in the past by stating that an algorithm solves a task if any of its executions agree with the task specification.

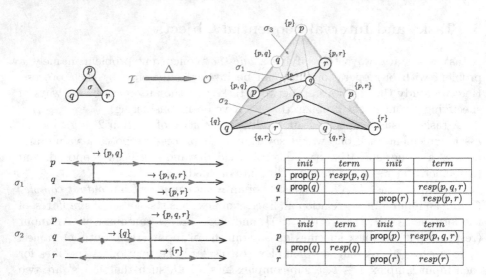

**Fig. 5.** Two special output simplexes $\sigma_1, \sigma_2$, and interval-linearizations of two executions with corresponding outputs

three operations are concurrent and then the corresponding interval-sequential object models this simplex with a single interval-sequential execution in which the three processes run concurrently. More interesting is the output simplex $\sigma_3$, where the processes also may run concurrently, but in addition, the same outputs may be returned in a fully sequential execution, because $\sigma_3$ intersects both the 0-dimensional (the corners) and the 1-dimensional boundary of the output complex. In fact $\sigma_3$ can also be produced if $p, q$ are concurrent, and later comes $r$, because 2 vertices of $\sigma_3$ are in $\Delta(p, q)$ (such an execution is set-sequential).

Now, consider the two more awkward output simplexes $\sigma_1, \sigma_2$ in $\Delta(\sigma)$ added to the immediate-snapshot output complex, where $\sigma_1 = \{(p, \{p, q\}), (q, \{p, q, r\}), (r, \{p, r\})\}$, and $\sigma_2 = \{(p, \{p, q, r\}), (q, \{q\}), (r, \{r\})\}$. At the bottom of the figure, two executions and their interval-linearizations are shown, though there are more executions that are interval-linearizable and can produce $\sigma_1$ and $\sigma_2$. Consider $\sigma_2$. It has a face, $\{(q, \{q\})\}$, in $\Delta(\{q\})$, and another face, $\{(r, \{r\})\}$ in $\Delta(\{r\})$. This specifies a different behavior from the output simplex in the center, that does not intersect with the boundary. Since $\{(q, \{q\})\} \in \Delta(\{q\})$, it is OK for $q$ to return $\{q\}$ when it invokes and returns before the others invoke. But also it is OK for $q$ to return $\{q\}$ when it invokes and runs concurrently with $p$ and $r$ because $\{(q, \{q\})\} \in \Delta(\{p, q, r\})$. It similarly happens to $r$. Additionally since $\{(p, \{p, q, r\})\}$ is not in the boundary, $p$ can return $\{p, q, r\}$ only if it runs concurrently with the others. The main observation here is that the structure of the mapping $\Delta$ encodes the interval-sequential executions that can produce the outputs in a given output simplex. In the example, $\Delta$ precludes the possibility that in a sequential execution the processes outputs the values in $\sigma_1$, since $\Delta$ specifies no process can decide without seeing anyone else.

*From One-Shot Interval-Sequential Objects to Tasks.* The converse of Theorem 3 is not true. Lemma 1 shows that even some sequential objects, such as one-shot queues, cannot be represented as a task. Also, recall that there are tasks with no set-sequential specification. Thus, both tasks and set-sequential objects are interval-sequential objects, but they are incomparable.

**Lemma 1.** *There is a sequential one-shot object $O$ such that there is no task $T_O$, satisfying that an execution $E$ is linearizable with respect to $O$ if and only if $E$ satisfies $T_O$ (for every $E$).*

While this version of tasks have strictly less expressive power than interval-sequential one-shot objects, a slightly different version has the same power for specifying distributed one-shot problems. Roughly, tasks cannot model interval-sequential objects because they do not have a mechanism to encode the state of an object. The extension below allows to model states.

In a *refined* task $T = \langle \mathcal{I}, \mathcal{O}, \Delta \rangle$, $\mathcal{I}$ is defined as usual and each output vertex of $\mathcal{O}$ has the form $(id_i.y_i, \sigma_i')$ where $id_i$ and $y_i$ are, as usual, the ID of a process and an output value, and $\sigma_i'$ is an input simplex called the *set-view* of $id_i$. The properties of $\Delta$ are maintained and in addition it satisfies the following: for every $\sigma \in \mathcal{I}$, for every $(id_i, y_i, \sigma_i') \in \Delta(\sigma)$, it holds that $\sigma_i' \subseteq \sigma$. An execution $E$ *satisfies* a refined task $T$ if for every prefix $E'$ of $E$, it holds that $\Delta(\sigma_{E'})$ contains the simplex $\{(id_i, y_i, \sigma_{i\,E''}) : (id_i, y_i) \in \tau_{E'} \wedge E''$ (which defines $\sigma_{i E''}$) is the shortest prefix of $E'$ containing $(id_i, y_i)\}$.

We stress that, for each input simplex $\sigma$, for each output vertex $(id_i, y_i, \sigma_i) \in \Delta(\sigma)$, $\sigma_i$ is a way to model distinct output vertexes in $\Delta(\sigma)$ whose output values (in $(id_i, y_i)$) are the same, then a process that outputs that vertex does not actually output $\sigma_i$. In fact, the set-view of a process $id_i$ corresponds to the set of invocations that precede the response $(id_i, y_i)$ to its invocation in a given execution (intuitively, the invocations that a process "sees" while computing its output value ). Set-views are the tool to encode the state of an object. Also observe that if $E$ satisfies a refined task $T$, then the set-views behave like snapshots: (1) a process itself (formally, its invocation) appears in its set-view and (2) all set-view are ordered by containment (since we assume $E$ is well-formed).

**Theorem 4.** *For every one-shot interval-sequential object $O$ with a single total operation, there is a refined task $T_O$ such that any execution $E$ is interval-linearizable with respect to $O$ if and only if $E$ satisfies $T_O$.*

**Theorem 5.** *For every refined task $T$, there is an interval-sequential object $O_T$ such that an execution $E$ satisfies $T$ if and only if it is interval-linearizable with respect to $O_T$.*

# References

1. Afek, Y., Attiya, H., Dolev, D., Gafni, E., Merritt, M., Shavit, N.: Atomic snapshots of shared memory. Journal of the ACM **40**(4), 873–890 (1993)
2. Afek, Y., Gafni, E., Lieber, O.: Tight group renaming on groups of size g is equivalent to g-consensus. In: Keidar, I. (ed.) DISC 2009. LNCS, vol. 5805, pp. 111–126. Springer, Heidelberg (2009)
3. Aspnes, J., Ellen, F.: Tight bounds for adopt-commit objects. Theory Computing Systems **55**(3), 451–474 (2014)
4. Borowsky, E., Gafni, E.: Immediate atomic snapshots and fast renaming. In: Proc. 12th ACM Symposium on Principles of Distributed Computing (PODC 1993). ACM Press, pp. 41–51 (1993)
5. Borowsky, E., Gafni, E., Lynch, N., Rajsbaum, S.: The BG distributed simulation algorithm. Distributed Computing **14**(3), 127–146 (2001)
6. Chandra, T.D., Hadzilacos, V., Jayanti, P., Toueg, S.: Generalized irreducibility of consensus and the equivalence of $t$-resilient and wait-free implementations of consensus. SIAM Journal of Computing **34**(2), 333–357 (2004)
7. Castañeda, A., Rajsbaum, S., Raynal, M.: Specifying Concurrent Problems: Beyond Linearizability. http://arxiv.org/abs/1507.00073
8. Chaudhuri, S.: More choices allow more faults: set consensus problems in totally asynchronous systems. Information and Computation **105**(1), 132–158 (1993)
9. Conde, R., Rajsbaum, S.: The complexity gap between consensus and safe-consensus. In: Halldórsson, M.M. (ed.) SIROCCO 2014. LNCS, vol. 8576, pp. 68–82. Springer, Heidelberg (2014)
10. Filipović, I., O'Hearn, P., Rinetky, N., Yang, H.: Abstraction for concurrent objects. Theoretical Computer Science **411**(51–52), 4379–4398 (2010)
11. Friedman, R., Vitenberg, R., Chokler, G.: On the composability of consistency conditions. Information Processing Letters **86**(4), 169–176 (2003)
12. Gafni, E.: Round-by-round fault detectors: unifying synchrony and asynchrony. In: Proc. 17th ACM Symposium on Principles of Distributed Computing (PODC 1998). ACM Press, pp. 143–152 (1998)
13. Gafni, E., Snapshot for time: the one-shot case. arXiv:1408.3432v1, p. 10 (2014)
14. van Glabbeek, R.J.: On the expressiveness of higher dimensional automata. Theoretical Computer Science **356**(3), 265–290 (2006)
15. Gotsman, A., Musuvathi, M., Yang, H.: Show no weakness: sequentially consistent specifications of TSO libraries. In: Aguilera, M.K. (ed.) DISC 2012. LNCS, vol. 7611, pp. 31–45. Springer, Heidelberg (2012)
16. Hemed, N., Rinetzky, N.: Brief announcement: concurrency-aware linearizability. In: Proc. 33th ACM Symposium on Principles of Distributed Computing (PODC 2014), pp. 209–211. ACM Press (2014). Full version to appear in these proceedings
17. Herlihy, M., Kozlov, D., Rajsbaum, S.: Distributed computing through ombinatorial topology. Morgan Kaufmann (2014)
18. Herlihy, M., Rajsbaum, S., Raynal, M.: Power and limits of distributed computing shared memory models. Theoretical Computer Science **509**, 3–24 (2013)
19. Herlihy, M., Shavit, N.: The art of multiprocessor programming. Morgan Kaufmann (2008)
20. Herlihy, M., Wing, J.: Linearizability: a correctness condition for concurrent objects. ACM Transactions on Progr. Lang. and Systems **12**(3), 463–492 (1990)

21. Neiger, G.: Set-linearizability. brief announcement. In: Proc. 13th ACM Symposium on Principles of Distributed Computing (PODC 1994). ACM Press, p. 396 (1994)
22. Raynal, M.: Concurrent programming: algorithms, principles, and foundations. Springer (2013)
23. Scherer III, W.N., Scott, M.L.: Nonblocking concurrent data structures with condition synchronization. In: Guerraoui, R. (ed.) DISC 2004. LNCS, vol. 3274, pp. 174–187. Springer, Heidelberg (2004)
24. Shavit, N.: Data structures in the multicore age. Comm. ACM **54**(3), 76–84 (2011)

# From Geometric Semantics to Asynchronous Computability

Éric Goubault[1]([✉]), Samuel Mimram[1], and Christine Tasson[2]

[1] LIX, École Polytechnique, Palaiseau, France
Eric.Goubault@polytechnique.edu
[2] PPS, Université Paris 7, Paris, France

**Abstract.** We show that the protocol complex formalization of fault-tolerant protocols can be directly derived from a suitable semantics of the underlying synchronization and communication primitives, based on a geometrization of the state space. By constructing a one-to-one relationship between simplices of the protocol complex and dihomotopy classes of dipaths in the latter semantics, we describe a connection between these two geometric approaches : protocol complexes and directed algebraic topology. This is exemplified on atomic snapshot, iterated snapshot and layered immediate snapshot protocols, where a well-known combinatorial structure, interval orders, plays a key role. We believe that this correspondence between models will extend to proving impossibility results for much more intricate fault-tolerant distributed architectures.

## 1 Introduction

Fault-tolerant distributed computing is concerned with designing algorithms, and, when possible, solving so-called *decision tasks* on a given distributed architecture, in the presence of faults. The seminal result in this field was established by Fisher, Lynch and Paterson in 1985, who proved the existence of a simple task that cannot be solved in a message-passing system (or in shared memory [27]) with at most one potential crash [11]. In particular, there is no way in such a distributed system to solve the very fundamental consensus problem: each processor starts with an initial value in local memory, typically an integer, and should end up with a common value, which is one of the initial values.

Later on, Biran, Moran and Zaks developed a characterization of the decision tasks that can be solved by a (simple) message-passing system in the presence of one failure [3]. The argument uses a "similarity chain", which can be seen as a connectedness result of a representation of the space of all reachable states, called the *view complex* [25] or the *protocol complex* [24]. Of course, this argument turned out to be difficult to extend to models with more failures, as higher-connectedness properties of the protocol complex matter in these cases. This technical difficulty was first tackled, using homological considerations, by Herlihy and Shavit [23] (and independently [5,31]): there are simple decision tasks, such as $k$-set agreement, a weaker form of consensus, that cannot be solved for $k < n$ in the wait-free asynchronous model, i.e. shared-memory distributed protocols on $n$

Y. Moses (Ed.): DISC 2015, LNCS 9363, pp. 436–451, 2015.
DOI: 10.1007/978-3-662-48653-5_29

processors, with up to $n-1$ crash failures. Then, the full characterization of wait-free asynchronous decision tasks with atomic reads and writes (or equivalently, with atomic snapshots) was described by Herlihy and Shavit [24]: this relies on the central notion of chromatic (or colored) simplicial complexes, and their subdivisions. All these results stem from the contractibility of the "standard" chromatic subdivision, which was completely formalized in [25,26] (and even for *iterated* models [19]) and corresponds to the *protocol complex* of distributed algorithms solving layered immediate snapshot protocols.

Over the years, the geometric approach to problems in fault-tolerant distributed computing has been very successful, see [22] for a fairly complete up-to-date treatment. One potential limitation however is that for some intricate models, it is extremely difficult to produce their corresponding protocol complex. In this paper, we are exploring the links between the semantics of the synchronization and communication primitives we are considering on a given distributed architecture, and the protocol complex. The interest is that the semantics of such synchronization primitives is much simpler to write down than the protocol complex, which is very error-prone to describe, as we will see in Section 3.2. We advocate in this paper the calculation of protocol complexes directly from the formal semantics of the underlying synchronization primitives.

The other aim of this article is to make the link between two geometric theories of concurrent and distributed computations: one based on protocols complexes, and the other, based on *directed algebraic topology*. Actually, the semantics of concurrent and distributed systems can be given by topological models, as pushed forward in a series of seminal papers in concurrency, in the early 1990s. These papers have explored the use of precubical sets and *Higher-Dimensional Automata* (which are labeled precubical sets equipped with a distinguished beginning vertex) [30,32], begun to suggest possible homology theories [17,18,6] and pushed the development of a specific homotopy theory, part of a general *directed algebraic topology* [20]. On the practical side, directed topological models have found applications to deadlock and unreachable state detection [9], validation and static analysis [15,4,7], state-space reduction (as in e.g. model-checking) [16], serializability and correctness of databases [21] (see also [14,10] for a panorama of applications).

In order to instantiate this link, we will be considering the simple model of shared-memory concurrent machines with crash failures, where processors compute and communicate through shared locations, and where reads and writes are supposed to be atomic. This model can also be presented [28] as *atomic snapshot protocols* [1,2], where processors are executing the following instructions: scanning the entire shared memory (and copying it into their local memory), computing in its local memory, and updating its "own value", i.e. writing the outcome of its computation in a specific location in global memory, assigned to him only. The methodology we are describing here is by no means limited to this simple model: we have provided in this paper a general framework that builds protocol complexes from the semantics of communication primitives. However, what is more difficult is determining the set of *directed homotopy classes* of directed paths in this semantics. This is one of the reasons why we chose to exemplify the method on a well-known and simple case in fault-tolerant distributed computing. In general, this step is by no means trivial, reinforcing the need for formally deriving protocol complexes from semantics. The other reason is that the reader will be more familiar with the model and the expected result, and will be able to focus on the new technical (directed algebraic topological) aspects of the paper.

**Contents of the Paper and Main Contributions.** Section 2.1 begins by defining the *standard semantics* (or interleaving semantics) of atomic read/write protocols, and more precisely of atomic snapshot protocols where read and write primitives are replaced by update and (global) scan ones. In Section 2.2, we give an alternative *geometric* semantics, which encodes also independence of actions, as a form of *homotopy* in a geometric model. The very basics of *directed algebraic topology* have been introduced for this purpose, but we refer the reader to [20,8] for more details. Yet, for the wider picture, we prove the fact that (directed) homotopy encodes commutation of actions, in the form of an equivalence between the standard semantics and the geometric semantics. It is shown in Section 2.3, Proposition 4 that two traces in the interleaving semantics modulo commutation of actions induce dihomotopic (directed) paths in the geometric model. The converse is shown in Section 2.3, Proposition 9, using the combinatorial notion of *interval order* [12]. We then combine these results with the semantic equivalence of Proposition 6, Section 2.3; this is the first main contribution of the paper.

In Section 3, we turn to the other geometric model of distributed systems: protocol complexes. The second main contribution of the paper is developed in Section 3.2: the protocol complex for atomic snapshot protocols (possibly iterated) is derived from the geometric semantics of Section 2.2, through interval orders. We specify this construction in Section 3.3 to the case of *layered immediate snapshot* which is generally studied by most authors, since it is much simpler to study, and is enough to prove the classical impossibility theorems, as e.g. [23]. Our explicit description of the protocol complex in the latter case is the same as the one of [19] (linked as well to the equivalent presentation of [25]), see Theorem 19. Combined with the result of [19] it proves that the layered immediate snapshot protocols produce collapsible protocol complexes, for any number of rounds. It then implies the asynchronous computability theorem of [23] all the way from the semantics of the communication primitives.

# 2 Concurrent Semantics of Asynchronous Read/Write Protocols

## 2.1 Interleaving Semantics of Atomic Read/Write Protocols

In *atomic snapshot* protocols, $n$ processes communicate through shared memory using two primitives: update and scan. Informally, the shared memory is partitioned in $n$ parts, each one corresponding to one of the $n$ processes. The part of the memory associated with process $P_i$, with $i \in \{0, \ldots, n-1\}$, is the one on which process $P_i$ can write, by calling update. This primitive writes onto that part of memory, a value computed from the value stored in a local register of $P_i$. Note that as the memory is partitioned, there are never any write conflicts on memory. Conversely, all processes can read the entire memory through the scan primitive. Note also that there are never any read conflicts on memory. Still, it is well known that atomic snapshot protocols are equivalent [28] with respect to their expressiveness in terms of fault-tolerant decision tasks they can solve, to the protocols based on atomic registers with atomic reads and writes. Generic snapshot protocols are such that all processes loop, any number of times, on the three successive actions: locally compute a *decision value*, update then scan. It is also known [23,24] that, as far as fault-tolerant properties are concerned, an equivalent model of computation can be considered: the full-information protocol where, for each process, decisions are only taken at the end of the protocol, i.e. after rounds of update then scan, only remembering the history of communications.

**Interleaving Semantics and Trace Equivalence.** Formally, we consider a fixed set $\mathcal{V}$ of *values*, together with two distinguished subsets $\mathcal{I}$ and $\mathcal{O}$ of *input* and *output values*, the elements of $\mathcal{V} \setminus (\mathcal{I} \cup \mathcal{O})$ being called *intermediate values*, and an element $\perp \in \mathcal{I} \cap \mathcal{O}$ standing for an *unknown value*. We suppose that the sets of values and intermediate values are infinite countable, so that pairs $\langle x, y \rangle$ of values $x, y \in \mathcal{V}$ can be encoded as intermediate values, and similarly for tuples. We suppose fixed a number $n \in \mathbb{N}$ of processes. We also write $[n]$ as a shortcut for the set $\{0, \dots, n-1\}$, and $\mathcal{V}^n$ for the set of $n$-tuples of elements of $\mathcal{V}$, whose elements are called *memories*. Given $v \in \mathcal{V}^n$ and $i \in [n]$, we write $v_i$ for the $i$-th component of $v$. We write $\perp^n$ for the memory $l$ such that $l_i = \perp$ for any $u \in [n]$.

There are two families of memories, each one containing one memory cell for each process $P_i$: the *local memories* $l = (l_i)_{i \in [n]} \in \mathcal{V}^n$, and the *global (shared) memory*: $m = (m_i)_{i \in [n]} \in \mathcal{V}^n$. A *state* of a program is a pair $(l, m) \in \mathcal{V}^n \times \mathcal{V}^n$ of such memories. Processes can communicate by performing actions which consist in updating and scanning the global memory, using their local memory: we denote by $u_i$ any update by the $i$-th process and $s_i$ any of its scan. We write $\mathcal{A}_i = \{u_i, s_i\}$ and $\mathcal{A} = \bigcup_{i \in [n]} \mathcal{A}_i$ for the set of *actions*.

Formally, the effect of the actions on the state is defined by a *protocol* $\pi$ which consists of two families of functions $\pi_{u_i} : \mathcal{V} \to \mathcal{V}$ and $\pi_{s_i} : \mathcal{V} \times \mathcal{V}^n \to \mathcal{V}$ indexed by $i \in [n]$ such that $\pi_{s_i}(x, m) = x$ for $x \in \mathcal{O}$. Starting from a state $(l, m)$, the effect of actions is as follows: $u_i$ means "replace the contents of $m_i$ by $\pi_{u_i}(l_i)$", and $s_i$ means "replace the contents of $l_i$ by $\pi_{s_i}(l_i, m)$".

A protocol is *full-information* when $\pi_{u_i}(x) = x$ for every $x \in \mathcal{V}$, i.e. each process fully discloses its local state in the global memory. A sequence of actions $T \in \mathcal{A}^*$ is called an *interleaving trace*, and we write $[\![T]\!]_\pi(l, m)$ for the state reached by the protocol $\pi$ after executing the actions in $T$, starting from the state $(l, m)$. A sequence of actions $T \in \mathcal{A}^*$ is *well-bracketed* or *well-formed* (giving some form of generic protocol) when for every $i \in [n]$ we have $\text{proj}_i(T) \in (u_i s_i)^*$, where $\text{proj}_i : \mathcal{A}^* \to \mathcal{A}_i^*$ is the obvious projection which only keeps the letters in $\mathcal{A}_i$ in a word over $\mathcal{A}$. We denote by $\mathcal{A}^\omega$ the set of countably infinite sequences of actions; such a sequence is well-bracketed when every finite prefix is.

It can be noticed that different interleaving traces may induce the same final local view for any process. Indeed, if $i \neq j$, then $u_i$ and $u_j$ modify different parts of the global memory, as we already noted informally, and thus $u_i u_j$ and $u_j u_i$ induce the same action on a given state. Similarly, $s_i$ and $s_j$ change different parts of the local memory, and thus $s_i s_j$ and $s_j s_i$ induce the same action on a given state. On the contrary, $u_i s_j$ and $s_j u_i$ may induce different traces as $u_i$ may modify the global memory that is scanned by $s_j$. We thus define an *equivalence* $\approx$ on interleaving traces, as the smallest congruence such that $u_j u_i \approx u_i u_j$ and $s_j s_i \approx s_i s_j$ for every indices $i$ and $j$. Therefore :

**Proposition 1.** *The equivalence $\approx$ of traces induces an operational equivalence: two equivalent interleaving traces starting from the same initial state lead to the same final state.*

This justifies that we consider traces *up to equivalence* in the following. We use the usual notions on such operational semantics: *execution traces*, *interleaving traces* will denote any finite sequences of actions $u_i$ and $s_i$ in $\mathcal{A}^*$, *maximal execution traces* are traces that cannot be further extended. We also use the classical notions of *length* and *concatenation* of execution traces.

**Decision Tasks.** We are going to consider the possibility of solving a particular task with an asynchronous protocol. Formally, those tasks are specified as follows:

**Definition 2.** *A* wait-free task specification $\Theta$ *is a relation* $\Theta \subseteq \mathcal{I}^n \times \mathcal{O}^n$ *such that for all* $(l, l') \in \Theta$, $i \in [n]$ *s.t.* $l_i = \bot$, *and* $x \in \mathcal{I}$, *we also have* $(l_i^x, l') \in \Theta$ *where* $l_i^x$ *is the memory obtained from $l$ by replacing the $i$-th value by $x$. We note* $\mathrm{dom}\,\Theta = \{l \in \mathcal{I}^n \mid \exists l' \in \mathcal{O}^n, (l, l') \in \Theta\}$ *for the* domain *of a wait-free task specification* $\Theta$ *and* $\mathrm{codom}\,\Theta = \{l' \in \mathcal{O}^n \mid \exists l \in \mathcal{I}^n, (l, l') \in \Theta\}$ *for its* codomain.

Notice that $\mathrm{dom}\,\Theta$ induces a simplicial complex, with $[n] \times (\mathcal{I} \setminus \{\bot\})$ as vertices, and simplices are of the form $\{(i, x) \in [n] \times \mathcal{V} \mid l_i = x \neq \bot\}$, for any $l \in \mathrm{dom}\,\Theta$. This simplicial complex is called the *input complex*; the *output complex* is defined similarly from $\mathrm{codom}\,\Theta$. We say that a protocol $\pi$ *solves* a task specification $\Theta$ when for every $l \in \mathrm{dom}\,\Theta$, and well-bracketed infinite sequence of actions $T \in \mathcal{A}^\omega$, there exists a finite prefix $T'$ of $T$ such that $(l, l') \in \Theta$ where $l'$ is the local memory after executing $T'$, i.e. $(l', m') = [\![T']\!]_\pi (l, \bot^n)$. It can be shown [24] that, w.r.t. task solvability, we can assume that $\mathrm{dom}\,\Theta$ contains only the memory $l$ such that $l_i = i$, for all $i$, and its faces; for simplicity we will do so in Section 3.

Of particular interest is the *view protocol* (sometimes identified with the full-information protocol in the literature) $\pi^\lhd$ such that $\pi_{u_i}^\lhd(x) = x$ for $x \in \mathcal{V}$, i.e. the protocol is full-information, and $\pi_{s_i}^\lhd(x, m) = \langle x, \langle m \rangle \rangle$ for $x \in \mathcal{V}$ and $m \in \mathcal{V}^n$: when reading the global memory, the protocol stores (an encoding of) the pair constituted of its current local memory $x$ and (an encoding as a value of) the global memory $m$ it has read. This is akin to the use of *generic protocols in normal form* [24], where protocols only exchange their full history of communication for a fixed given number of rounds, and then apply a local decision function. It can be shown that the view protocol is the "most general one" (i.e. initial in a suitable category). Thus, we will be satisfied with describing the potential sets of histories of communication between processes, without having to encode the decision values: this is the basis of the geometric semantics of Section 2.2. As a direct consequence, we recover the usual definition of the solvability of a task as a simplicial map from some iterated protocol complex to the output complex [24,22].

## 2.2  Directed Geometric Semantics

In this section, we give an alternative semantics to atomic snapshot protocols, using a geometric encoding of the state space, together with a notion of "time direction". One of the most simple settings in which this can be performed is the one of pospaces [29,13]: a *pospace* is a topological space $\mathbb{X}$ endowed with a partial order $\leq$ such that the graph of the partial order is closed in $\mathbb{X} \times \mathbb{X}$ with the product topology. The intuition is that, given two points $x, y \in \mathbb{X}$ such that $x \leq y$, $y$ cannot be reached before $x$. The encoding, or semantics of a concurrent or distributed protocol in terms of directed topological spaces of some sort can be done in a more general manner [7,8]. Here, we simply define, directly, the pospace that gives the semantics we are looking for. It is rather intuitive and we will check this is correct with respect to the interleaving semantics, in Section 2.3.

Consider the pospace $\mathbb{X}_{(r)}^n$ below, indexed by the number $n$ of processes and the vector of number of rounds $(r) = (r_0, \ldots, r_{n-1})$ (each $r_i \in \mathbb{N}$, with $i \in [n]$, is the number of times process $P_i$ performs update followed by scan). Here, we use a vector to represent the number of rounds : this is because we do not want to treat only the layered immediate snapshot protocols, but more general atomic snapshot protocols. We claim now that the geometric semantics of the generic protocol, for $n$ processes and $(r)$ rounds, is represented by the pospace

$$\mathbb{X}_{(r)}^n = \prod_{i \in [n]} [0, r_i] \setminus \bigcup_{i,j \in [n], k \in [r_i], \, l \in [r_j]} U_i^k \cap S_j^l \tag{1}$$

endowed with the product topology and product order induced by $\mathbb{R}^n$, where

- $n, r_i \in \mathbb{N}$ and $u, s$ are any reals such that $0 < u < s < 1$ : $u$ (resp. $v$) is representing the local time at which an update (resp. scan) takes place in a round, and their precise values will not matter,
- $U_i^k = \left\{ x \in \prod_{i \in [n]} [0, r_i] \mid x_i = k + u \right\}$ stands for the region where the $i$-th process updates the global memory with its local memory for the $k$-th time,
- $S_j^l = \left\{ x \in \prod_{i \in [n]} [0, r_i] \mid x_j = l + s \right\}$ stands for the region where the $j$-th process scans the global memory into its local memory for the $l$-th time.

The meaning of (1) is that a state $(x_0, \ldots, x_{n-1}) \in \prod_{i \in [n]}[0, r_i]$, i.e. a state in which each process $P_i$ is at local time $x_i$, is allowed except when it is in $U_i^k \cap S_j^l$ (for $i, j \in [n]$ and $k \in [r_i]$, $l \in [r_j]$): these forbidden states are precisely the states for which there is a scan and update conflict. Namely, states in $U_i^k \cap S_j^l$ are states for which process $P_i$ updates (for the $k$-th time) while process $P_j$ scans (for the $l$-th time), which is forbidden in the semantics. Indeed, the memory has to serialize the accesses since shared locations are concurrently read and written, and either the scan operation will come before the update one, or the contrary, but the two operations cannot occur at the same time. This is

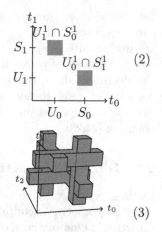

$$(2)$$

$$(3)$$

reflected in the geometric semantics by a hole in the state space, as pictured on (2) for two processes with one round each, and in (4) for two processes with several rounds each. Notice that the holes are depicted as squares instead of points to improve the visibility on the diagram. In higher-dimensions, the holes exhibit a complicated combinatorics.

For instance, for three processes, and one round each, as in (3) shows forbidden regions that intersect one another. What happens in dimension 3 is that for all 3 pairs of processes $(P, Q)$, we have to produce a forbidden region which has a projection, on the two axes corresponding to $P$ and $Q$, similar to the one on (2). Hence for all three pairs of processes, we have two cylinders with square section punching entirely the set of global states of the system. Each of these 6 cylinders correspond to a pair $(P, Q)$ of processes, and a hole created either by a scan of $P$ and an update of $Q$, or a scan of $Q$ and an update of $P$. Consider the cylinder created by the conflict between the scan of $P$ with the update of $Q$: it intersects exactly two cylinders (parallel to the other axes), the one created by the scan of the third processor $R$ and the update of $Q$, and the one created by the update of $R$ and the scan of $P$, see (3).

## 2.3   Equivalence of the Standard and Geometric Semantics

In the geometric semantics of Section 2.2, we can define notions analogous to equivalence of traces as for the standard interleaving semantics of Section 2.1 (Proposition 1). A *dipath* (or *directed path*) in a pospace $(\mathbb{X}, \leq)$ is a continuous map $\alpha : [0, 1] \to \mathbb{X}$ which is continuous and non decreasing when $[0, 1]$ is endowed with the order and topology induced by the real line. A dipath is the continuous counterpart (as we will make clear later) of a trace in the interleaving semantics, or an execution. A dipath $\alpha : [0, 1] \to \mathbb{X}$ is called *inextendible*, if there is no dipath $\beta : [0, 1] \to \mathbb{X}$ such that $\alpha([0, 1]) \subsetneq \beta([0, 1])$. This is the analogous, in our geometric setting, to maximal execution traces. The *concatenation* of two dipaths $\alpha, \alpha' : [0, 1] \to \mathbb{X}$ with compatible ends, i.e. $\alpha(1) = \alpha'(0)$ is the dipath $\alpha \cdot \alpha'$ such that $\alpha \cdot \alpha'(x)$ is $\alpha(x)$ (resp. $\alpha'(2x - 1)$) when $x \leq 0.5$ (resp. $x \geq 0.5$).

The continuous setting allows us to use the classical concepts of (di)homotopy, which is the natural notion of equivalence between paths, and to use some tools from algebraic topology to derive properties of protocols (and more generally programs [14]). A *dihomotopy* is a continuous map $H : [0,1] \times [0,1] \rightarrow$
$\mathbb{X}$ such that for all $t \in [0,1]$, the map $H(-,t)$ is a dipath. Two dipaths $\alpha, \beta$ such that $\alpha(0) = \beta(0)$ and $\alpha(1) = \beta(1)$ are *dihomotopic*, if there is a dihomotopy $H :$ $[0,1] \times [0,1] \rightarrow \mathbb{X}$ with

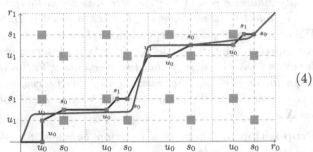

(4)

$H(-,0) = \alpha$ and $H(-,1) = \beta$. We denote by $[\alpha]$ the set of inextendible dipaths dihomotopic to $\alpha$ and $\mathbf{dPath}(\mathbb{X})$ the set of dipaths up to dihomotopy. For instance, two dipaths that are dihomotopic in the geometric semantics $X^2_{(4,2)}$ can be pictured as in Figure (4).

### From Equivalence Classes of Interleaving Traces to Dipaths Modulo Dihomotopy.

To any interleaving trace $T$ with $n$ processes and $(r)$ rounds, we associate a dipath $\alpha_T$ in $\mathbb{X}^n_{(r)}$. This dipath accurately reflects the whole computation of $T$, e.g. if $T'$ extends $T$, then $\alpha_{T'}$ also extends $\alpha_T$. For example, the black path of (4) is the dipath associated to the trace $u_0 u_1 s_0 u_0 s_1 s_0 u_1 u_0 s_0 u_0 s_1 s_0$: the points along it correspond to actions and the path consists of a linear interpolation between those. The dipath $\alpha_T$ is built by induction on the length of trace $T$: when $T$ is of length 0, $\alpha_T$ is the constant dipath staying at the origin; when $T$ is the concatenation of a trace $T_1$ with an action $A$, we concatenate the dipath $\alpha_{T_1}$ and a dipath $\beta$ which is defined according to the previous actions in $T_1$ :

**Lemma 3.** *There exists a (not necessarily inextendible) dipath $\alpha_T$ in $\mathbb{X}^n_{(r)}$ such that $\alpha_T(0)_i = 0$, for every $i \in [n]$, and satisfying the following. For any $i \in [n]$, if the last action of process $i$ in $T$ is its $k$-th update, then $\alpha_T(1)_i \in \{k + u, k + \frac{u+s}{2}\}$. If it is its $k$-th scan, then $\alpha_T(1)_i \in \{k + s, k + 1\}$. If the last action in $T$ is the $k$-th update of process $i$, then $\alpha_T(1)_i = k + u$. If it is the $k$-th scan of process $i$, then $\alpha_T(1)_i = k + s$.*

To a maximal interleaving trace $T$, we associate an inextendible dipath $\alpha'_T$ by further extending $\alpha_T$ to reach $(r_i)_{i \in [n]}$, the end of all inextendible dipaths in $\mathbb{X}^n_{(r)}$. Now,

**Proposition 4.** *Two equivalent interleaving traces induce dihomotopic dipaths.*

### Equivalence Between Equivalence Classes of Interleaving Traces and (Colored) Interval Orders.

In order to prove that dipaths modulo dihomotopy are in bijection with interleaving traces modulo equivalence, we introduce a combinatorial tool encoding the history of events observable on both an equivalence class of interleaving traces, and a dihomotopy class of dipaths in our continuous models.

**Definition 5.** *Let* $(I_x)_{x \in X}$ *be a family of intervals on the real line* $(\mathbb{R}, \leq)$. *This family induces a poset* $(X, \preceq)$, *where* $\prec$ *is defined as* $x \prec y$ *if and only if for every* $s \in I_x$ *and* $t \in I_y$ *we have* $s < t$. *Such a poset is called an* interval order *[12]. We denote as* $x \| y$ *the independence* relation.

*An* $[n]$-*colored interval order is given by an interval order* $(X, \preceq)$ *and a labeling function* $\ell : X \to [n]$ *such that two elements with the same label are comparable. Then for any* $i \in [n]$, *the restriction of the interval order to intervals labeled by* $i$ *is a total order. We denote as* $\mathbf{cIO}(X)$ *the set of colored interval orders on a set* $X$.

**Proposition 6.** *There is a bijection between* $[n]$-*colored interval orders and traces up to equivalence.*

From Propositions 4 and 6, we can associate to any interval order a class of dipaths modulo dihomotopy. Let $i : \mathbf{cIO}(X_n) \to \mathbf{dPath}(\mathbb{X}^n_{(r)})$ be mapping an interval order to a dipath up to dihomotopy.

**From Dipaths Modulo Dihomotopy to Equivalence Classes of Interleaving Traces.** As already mentioned, dipaths geometrically represent execution traces, keeping in mind that dipaths which can be deformed through a continuous family of executions are operationally equivalent. This argument can be made concrete for the asynchronous model we are working on, by giving the explicit relation between dipaths and colored interval orders (Definition 5), because of Proposition 6.

To any inextendible dipath $\alpha : [0,1] \to \mathbb{X}^n_{(r)}$, we associate an interval order $\preceq_\alpha$ on the set $X^n_{(r)} = \{(i, k) \mid i \in [n], k \in [r_i]\}$ through the interval collection for $i \in [n]$, $I_{(i,k)} = [u^k_i, s^k_i]$ colored by $i$ where $u^k_i$ or $s^k_i$ respectively correspond to the event "$\alpha$ enters an update or scan hyperplane":

$$u^k_i = \inf \left\{ t \in [0,1] \mid \alpha(t)_i \in U^k_i \right\}, \qquad s^k_i = \inf \left\{ t \in [0,1] \mid \alpha(t)_i \in S^k_i \right\}.$$
(5)

For any $i \in [n]$, the restriction of this order to the intervals labeled by $i$ is a total order. Indeed, dipaths $\alpha$ are non decreasing, $u < s$ and $\alpha(u^k_i)_i = k + u$, $\alpha(s^k_i)_i = k + s$, hence for all $k \in [r_i]$, $u^k_i < s^k_i$ and if $k \neq 0$, $s^{k-1}_i < u^k_i$.

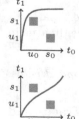

Let us give simple examples of this in dimension 2 and 3. In dimension 2, and for one round, consider the three inextendible dipaths in $\mathbb{X}^2_{(1,1)}$ pictured on the left (we are not writing the round number as upper index since we are considering here only one round). Those are representatives of the three dihomotopy classes of dipaths in this pospace. The dipath $\alpha_0$, on the above figure, corresponds to an execution in which process 1 does its update and scan before process 0 even starts updating. Hence, the interval of local times at which process 1 updates and scans is less than the interval of local times at which process 0 updates and scans: this is reflected by the corresponding interval order $[u_1, s_1] \prec_{\alpha_0} [u_0, s_0]$. The one on the figure below, $\alpha_Z$ is symmetric: the corresponding interval order is $[u_0, s_0] \prec_{\alpha_2} [u_1, s_1]$. The dipath on the middle corresponds to an execution in which the two processes are running synchronously, updating at the same time, and scanning at the same time: the corresponding interval order is $[u_0, s_0] \| [u_1, s_1]$.

In dimension 3, there are more dipaths that one can draw. Consider, for instance, the synchronous execution of the three processes (i.e. the pospace $\mathbb{X}^3_{(1,1,1)}$), shown on the right. It corresponds to the interval order where the intervals $[u_0, s_0]$, $[u_1, s_1]$ and $[u_2, s_2]$ are not comparable. The path figured corresponds to a synchronous execution.

We then have the following simple facts first :

**Lemma 7.** *Two inextendible dipaths $\alpha$ and $\beta$, which intersect the update and scan hyperplanes in the same order, are dihomotopic.*

We write $\alpha \leftrightsquigarrow \beta$ when the two dipaths are dihomotopic.

**Proposition 8.** *A dipath $\alpha$ is dihomotopic to the dipath associated to the interval order induced by $\alpha$, that is, $i \circ r(\alpha) \leftrightsquigarrow \alpha$.*

This implies the following, among the main results of this article:

**Proposition 9.** *Two dihomotopic inextendible dipaths on $\mathbb{X}^n_{(r)}$ induce the same interval order.*

**Theorem 10.** *There is a bijective correspondence between traces up to equivalence and dipaths up to dihomotopy over $\mathbb{X}^n_{(r)}$, that is, $r : \mathbf{dPath}(\mathbb{X}^n_{(r)}) \to \mathbf{cIO}(X_n)$ which maps a dipath up to dihomotopy to an interval order, satisfies $r \circ i = \mathrm{id}_{\mathbf{cIO}(X_n)}$.*

# 3    Protocol Complexes, Derived from the Concurrent Semantics

We will see that two executions modulo dihomotopy correspond to higher-dimensional simplices in protocol complexes (Proposition 13). In the case of update/scan protocols, these executions modulo dihomotopy are characterized by the nice combinatorial notion of interval order, which makes the construction of the protocol complex (Definition 17) from the geometric semantics immediate.

## 3.1    Protocol Complex

The protocol complex has been designed [24] to represent the possible reachable states, at some given round, of the generic protocol in normal form, i.e. it is going to encode all possible histories of communication between processes, and as we will prove later on, all interleaving traces up to equivalence (or equivalently the dipaths up to dihomotopy), by maximal simplices :

**Definition 11.** *The* protocol complex *for atomic snapshot protocols is the abstract simplicial complex constructed from the generic protocol in normal form, and whose vertices are pairs $(i, l_i)$ where $i \in [n]$ represents the name of a process and $l_i$ its local memory, and whose maximal simplices are $\{(0, l_0), \dots, (n, l_n)\}$ where $l_i$ is the local view by process $i$ at the end of the execution represented by this simplex.*

*Example 12.* The local views in each vertex are determined by the operational semantics of Section 2.1, as in the following example:

$$\text{Global} \quad \boxed{\perp}\ \boxed{\perp} \xrightarrow{u_0} \boxed{0}\ \boxed{\perp} \xrightarrow{u_1} \boxed{0}\ \boxed{1} \xrightarrow{s_1} \boxed{0}\ \boxed{1} \xrightarrow{s_0} \boxed{0}\ \boxed{1}$$
$$\text{Local} \quad \boxed{0}\ \boxed{1} \qquad \boxed{0}\ \boxed{1} \qquad \boxed{0}\ \boxed{1} \qquad \boxed{0}\ \boxed{01} \qquad \boxed{01}\ \boxed{01}$$

leading to the local view $l = \langle\langle 0, \langle 0, 1\rangle\rangle, \langle 1, \langle 0, 1\rangle\rangle\rangle$. Similarly, the trace $u_0 s_0 u_1 s_1$ leads to the local view $l = \langle\langle 0, \langle 0, \perp\rangle\rangle, \langle 1, \langle 0, 1\rangle\rangle\rangle$, and there is a third potential outcome of the computation, symmetric to this last case, in which process 1 updates and scans before process 0 does. Putting this together, according to Definition 11, we get the protocol complex for one round and two processes [24]:

$$0, (0\perp) \text{------} 1, (01) \text{------} 0, (01) \text{------} 1, (\perp 1)$$

The encoding of the local states, i.e. vertices in the graph above, is as follows. The identifier of the process whose local view is the number before the comma, e.g. the state $0, (0\perp)$ above is the local view of processor 0. The group of numbers or $\perp$ within parentheses, e.g. $(0\perp)$ in the state above, is a condensed notation for the local state where $l_0 = \langle 0, \langle 0, \perp\rangle\rangle$, see Section 2.1. Similarly, state $1, (01)$ denotes the local view of processor 1, with local state such that $l_1 = \langle 1, \langle 0, 1\rangle\rangle$.

## 3.2 Construction of the Protocol Complex from the Directed Geometric Semantics

We can now link protocol complexes with interval orders, i.e. traces up to equivalence or dipaths up to dihomotopy: a colored interval order represents indeed an execution and we can deduce the local view of the $i$-th process by restricting the interval order to the last scan of $i$. We encode local views restricting to the full information generic protocol in normal form with initial local state $l_i = i$ for $i \in [n]$ (this only changes the naming of local states, and not the structure of the protocol complex).

**Proposition 13.** *Let $(X^n_{(r)}, \preceq)$ be an $[n]$-colored interval order. Then the local memory of the $i$-th process at round $k$ of its corresponding execution[1]. is given*

---

[1] In the full-information generic protocol in normal form, i.e. its view, see Proposition 6 and the following example.

*by its restriction $V_i^k$ to the $k$-th scan $S_i^k$ of the $i$-th process, i.e.*

$$V_i^k \;=\; \{(j,l) \mid (i,k)\|(j,l) \text{ or } (j,l) \prec (i,k)\}$$

*meaning that it is the value of the local state $l_i$ under the semantics of Section 2.1 for the interleaving path corresponding to the interval order $V_i^k$ under the equivalence of Proposition 6.*

*Example 14.* Consider again the one round, two processes case. We have represented below the protocol complex already depicted in Example 12, and decorated its maximal simplices, i.e. edges, with the corresponding dipaths modulo dihomotopy above, and the corresponding interval order, below:

$$0,(0\!\perp) \xrightarrow[0\prec 1]{\boxed{\,^{\textbf{.}}\square}} 1,(01) \xrightarrow[0\;\;1]{\boxed{\,^{\textbf{/}}}} 0,(01) \xrightarrow[0\succ 1]{\boxed{\,^{\textbf{.}}\square}} 1,(\perp\!1)$$

The local view of process 0 which is $0,(0\!\perp)$ comes from the restriction of the interval order $0\!\prec\!1$, subscript of the leftmost edge in the graph above, to 0: an interleaving trace corresponding to this interval order, under Proposition 6 is $u_0 s_0$ leading to local state $(0\!\perp)$ on process 0. Similarly, $1,(01)$ corresponds to the local state $l_1 = (01)$ for process 1, both for the restriction $0\!\prec\!1$ of $0\!\prec\!1$ to $V_1^1$ (corresponding to a trace $u_0 s_0 u_1 s_1$, as in the trace $\boxed{\,^{\textbf{.}}}$ superscript of the edge on the left of the graph above) and for the restriction $0\;1$ of $0\;1$ to $V_1^1$ (corresponding to a trace $u_0 u_1 s_0 s_1$ for instance, as in the trace $\boxed{\,^{\textbf{/}}}$ superscript of the middle edge of the graph above).

We are now in a position to give a combinatorial description of the protocol complex of Definition 11, using interval orders. We call the resulting equivalent complex, the *interval order complex*:

**Definition 15.** *The* interval order complex *is the simplicial complex whose*

- *vertices are $((i,k),V_i^k)$ where $i$ stands for the $i$-th process, $k$ for the round number and $V_i^k$ for an interval order such that for all $(j,l) \in V_i^k$, either $(i,k)\|(j,l)$ or $(j,l) \prec (i,k)$,*
- *maximal simplices are $\{((0,r_0),V_0^{r_0}),\ldots,((n,r_n),V_n^{r_n})\}$ such that there is an interval order $(X_{(r)}^n, \prec)$ whose restriction to $(i,r_i)$ is $V_i^{r_i}$.*

*In that case we say that it is the interval order complex on $(r)$ rounds and for $n+1$ processes.*

*Example 16.* An example of interval order complex with the traces corresponding to the execution for 2 processes, 2 rounds is depicted at Figure 1. Note that this is not the classical iterated subdivision in three parts at each round, i.e. a 9 edges complex, that is depicted for atomic snapshot protocols [22]. This is because we are considering more executions than the classical *layered immediate snapshot protocols* [22]: we allow round 2 of process 0 to begin while process 1 is still in round 1 for instance. Consider the interval order $\overset{0 \to 1}{\underset{0 \to 1}{\uparrow\!\!\!\diagup\!\!\!\!\diagdown\,\uparrow}}$ labeling the

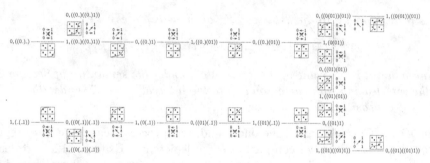

**Fig. 1.** Interval order complex, together with corresponding traces, of 2 processes, 2 rounds.

upper left edge of the protocol complex in Figure 1, where an arrow $x \rightarrow y$ means $x \prec y$. As shown in the same figure, it corresponds to the execution ▦ precisely where process 0 is executing its 2 rounds before process 1 even starts its first round. The local view of process 0 at (its) round 2 corresponds to the interval order $\overset{0}{\underset{0}{\wedge}}$, restriction of $\overset{0 \rightarrow 1}{\underset{0 \rightarrow 1}{\wedge\times\wedge}}$ to $\mathcal{V}_0^{(2,0)}$. An interleaving trace corresponding to this is e.g. $u_0 s_0 u_0 s_0$, which, by the semantics of Section 2.1, leads to the local state of process 0: $\langle 0, \langle 0, \langle 0, \perp \rangle\rangle\perp\rangle$ written in condensed form as the upper left local state $0, ((0_-)_-)$ in Figure 1.

In Figure 2, we show the interval order complex for 3 processes and 1 round. Note again that we do not have exactly the same picture as in [22]: to the 13 triangles of [22], we have to add the 6 extra blue triangles that make the complex not faithfully representable as a planar shape and which correspond to non immediate snapshot executions. For instance, the upper left blue triangle is labeled with the interval order where 0 is not comparable to both 1 and 2, and 2 is less than 1. An interleaving trace (up to equivalence) corresponding to this interval order is given on the same figure: $u_0 u_2 s_2 u_1 s_1 s_0$.

### 3.3  Particular Case of 1-Round Immediate Snapshot Protocols

We have not quite finished with describing the connections between directed algebraic topology and the protocol complex approach : the combinatorial description of the protocol complex in the case of layered immediate snapshot protocols seems, at first glance, of a different nature than the one using interval order complexes of Definition 15. We recall that an (layered, for multi-round protocols) *immediate snapshot* protocol [22] is a protocol where the snapshot of a given process comes "right after" its update, meaning that the allowed traces (within one round), up to equivalence, should be, of the form $u_{i_1} \ldots u_{i_k} s_{i_1} \ldots s_{i_k}$. Of course, there is some difference in that interval order complexes account for non necessarily layered nor "immediate" protocols. It is the aim of this section to make the connection between the subcomplex of interval order complexes describing layered immediate snapshot protocols, and the equivalent two definitions

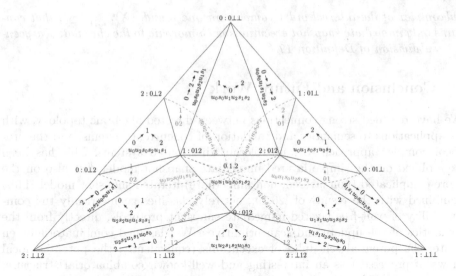

**Fig. 2.** Interval order complex with traces of 3 processes, 1 round.

of chromatic barycentric subdivision [25,19] that describe combinatorially the protocol complex in that case.

The standard chromatic subdivision $\chi(\Delta^{[n]})$ of the standard $[n]$-colored simplicial complex $\Delta^{[n]}$ is defined as follows (see [19], where an equivalence with the Definition in [25] is also shown):

**Definition 17.** *The* standard chromatic subdivision $\chi(\Delta^{[n]})$ *of* $\Delta^{[n]}$ *is the* $[n]$*-colored simplicial complex whose vertices are pairs* $(V, i)$ *with* $V \subseteq [n]$ *and* $i \in V$ *and simplices are sets of the form* $\sigma = \{(V_0, i_0), \dots, (V_d, i_d)\}$ *with* $d \geq -1$ *(* $\sigma = \emptyset$ *when* $d = -1$ *) which are*

1. *well-colored: for every* $k, l \in [d]$, $i_k = i_l$ *implies* $k = l$,
2. *ordered: for every* $k, l \in [d]$, $V_k \subseteq V_l$ *or* $V_l \subseteq V_k$,
3. *transitive: for every* $k, l \in [d]$, $i_l \in V_k$ *implies* $V_l \subseteq V_k$.

*This complex is colored via the second projection:* $\ell(V, i) = i$.

*Remark 18.* The transitivity (property 3) of Definition 17 is equivalent to looking only at immediate snapshot executions. Observe the left upper blue triangle of Figure 1, which is composed of vertices $(0 : 012)$, $(1 : 012)$ and $(2 : 0\bot2)$ (respectively meaning $(\{0, 1, 2\}, 0)$, $(\{0, 1, 2\}, 1)$ and $(\{0, 2\}, 2)$ in the notations of Definition 17). It does not correspond to a layered execution: it corresponds to the equivalence class of traces $u_0u_2s_2u_1s_1s_0$. Transitivity does not hold either: $0 \in \{0, 2\}$ but $\{0, 1, 2\} \not\subseteq \{0, 2\}$. This leads us to the last main result of our article.

**Theorem 19.** *Layered immediate snapshot executions correspond to the interval orders such that:* $J \prec K$ *and* $I$ *is not comparable with* $J$ *implies* $I \prec K$*. The* *subcomplex of the interval order complex on one round, $(X^n_{(1,...,1)}, \preceq)$, that contains only immediate snapshot executions is isomorphic to the chromatic barycentric subdivision of Definition 17.*

## 4   Conclusion and Future Work

We have revealed strong connections between directed algebraic topology, with its applications to semantics and validation of concurrent systems, and the protocol complex approach to fault-tolerant distributed systems. This has been exemplified on the simple layered immediate snapshot model, but also on the more complicated (non layered, non immediate) iterated snapshot model. This, combined with the results of [26,19], entirely classifies geometrically the computability of wait-free layered immediate snapshot protocols, directly from the semantics of the update and scan primitives. We classified combinatorially, en route, the potential schedules of executions (equivalently, the potential local views of processes) as an interesting and well-known combinatorial structure: interval orders.This is a first step towards a more ambitious program. Fault-tolerant distributed models, whose protocol complex are more complex to guess combinatorially, may be handled by going through the very same steps we went through, starting with the geometric semantics of the communication primitives, and classifying dipaths modulo dihomotopy. We shall apply this to atomic read/write protocols with extra synchronization primitives such as test&set, compare&swap and others. In the long run, we would like to derive impossibility results directly by observing some obstructions in the semantics, in the form of suitable directed algebraic topological invariants.

**Acknowledgments.** The first two authors were partially supported by by the academic chair "Complex Systems Engineering" of École polytechnique-ENSTA-Télécom-Thalès-Dassault Aviation-DCNS-DGA-FX-Fondation ParisTech-FDO ENSTA. We also gratefully acknowledge Maurice Herlihy, Sergio Rajsbaum and Dmitry Kozlov for numerous discussions, and the referees for helping us improve this paper.

## References

1. Afek, Y., Attiya, H., Dolev, D., Gafni, E., Merritt, M., Shavit, N.: Atomic snapshots of shared memory. J. ACM **40**(4), September 1993
2. Anderson, J.H.: Composite registers. In: Conference on Principles of Distributed Computing. ACM, New York (1993)
3. Biran, O., Moran, S., Zaks, S.: A combinatorial characterization of the distributed tasks which are solvable in the presence of one faulty processor. In: PoDC. ACM (1988)
4. Bonichon, R., Canet, G., Correnson, L., Goubault, E., Haucourt, E., Hirschowitz, M., Labbé, S., Mimram, S.: Rigorous evidence of freedom from concurrency faults in industrial control software. In: Flammini, F., Bologna, S., Vittorini, V. (eds.) SAFECOMP 2011. LNCS, vol. 6894, pp. 85–98. Springer, Heidelberg (2011)
5. Borowsky, E., Gafni, E.: Generalized FLP impossibility result for $t$-resilient synchronous computations. In: STOC (1993)

6. Dubut, J., Goubault, É., Goubault-Larrecq, J.: Natural homology. In: Halldórsson, M.M., Iwama, K., Kobayashi, N., Speckmann, B. (eds.) ICALP 2015. LNCS, vol. 9135, pp. 171–183. Springer, Heidelberg (2015)
7. Fajstrup, L., Goubault, É., Haucourt, E., Mimram, S., Raussen, M.: Trace spaces: an efficient new technique for state-space reduction. In: Seidl, H. (ed.) Programming Languages and Systems. LNCS, vol. 7211, pp. 274–294. Springer, Heidelberg (2012)
8. Fajstrup, L., Goubault, É., Haucourt, E., Mimram, S., Raussen, M.: Directed Algebraic Topology and Concurrency. Springer (to be published) (2015)
9. Fajstrup, L., Goubault, É., Raußen, M.: Detecting deadlocks in concurrent systems. In: Sangiorgi, D., de Simone, R. (eds.) CONCUR 1998. LNCS, vol. 1466, pp. 332–347. Springer, Heidelberg (1998)
10. Fajstrup, L., Raussen, M., Goubault, É.: Algebraic topology and concurrency. TCS **357**(1) (2006)
11. Fischer, M.J., Lynch, N.A., Paterson, M.S.: Impossibility of distributed consensus with one faulty process. Journal of the ACM (JACM) **32**(2), 374–382 (1985)
12. Fishburn, P.C.: Intransitive indifference with unequal indifference intervals. Journal of Mathematical Psychology **7**(1), 144–149 (1970)
13. Gierz, G.: A Compendium of continuous lattices. Springer (1980)
14. Goubault, É.: Some geometric perspectives in concurrency theory. Homology, Homotopy and Appl. (2003)
15. Goubault, É., Haucourt, E.: A practical application of geometric semantics to static analysis of concurrent programs. In: Abadi, M., de Alfaro, L. (eds.) CONCUR 2005. LNCS, vol. 3653, pp. 503–517. Springer, Heidelberg (2005)
16. Goubault, É., Heindel, T., Mimram, S.: A geometric view of partial order reduction. MFPS, Electr. Notes. Theor. Comput. Sci. **298**, (2013)
17. Goubault, É., Jensen, T.P.: Homology of higher-dimensional. In: Cleaveland, W.R. (ed.) CONCUR 1992. LNCS, vol. 630, pp. 254–268. Springer, Heidelberg (1992)
18. Goubault, É: The Geometry of Concurrency. Ph.D. dissertation, ENS (1995)
19. Goubault, É., Mimram, S., Tasson, C.: Iterated chromatic subdivisions are collapsible. Applied Categorical Structures (2014)
20. Grandis, M.: Directed Algebraic Topology: Models of Non-Reversible Worlds. New Mathematical Monographs, vol. 13. Cambridge University Press (2009)
21. Gunawardena, J.: Homotopy and concurrency. Bulletin of the EATCS **54**, 184–193 (1994)
22. Herlihy, M., Kozlov, D., Rajsbaum, S.: Distributed Computing Through Combinatorial Topology. Elsevier (2014)
23. Herlihy, M., Shavit, N.: The asynchronous computability theorem for $t$-resilient tasks. In: Proceedings of the Twenty-Fifth Annual ACM Aymposium on Theory of Computing, pp. 111–120. ACM (1993)
24. Herlihy, M., Shavit, N.: The topological structure of asynchronous computability. Journal of the ACM (JACM) **46**(6), 858–923 (1999)
25. Kozlov, D.: Chromatic subdivision of a simplicial complex. Homology, Homotopy and Appl. **14** (2012)
26. Kozlov, D.: Topology of the view complex. arXiv preprint arXiv:1311.7283 (2013)
27. Loui, M.C., Abu-Amara, H.H.: Memory requirements for agreement among unreliable asynchronous processes. Advances in Computing Research **4** (1987)
28. Lynch, N.A.: Distributed algorithms. Morgan Kaufmann (1996)
29. Nachbin, L.: Topology and order. Van Nostrand, Van Nostrand mathematical studies (1965)
30. Pratt, V.: Modeling concurrency with geometry. In: POPL. ACM Press (1991)
31. Saks, M.E., Zaharoglou, F.: Wait-free $k$-set agreement is impossible: the topology of public knowledge. In: STOC (1993)
32. van Glabbeek, R.: Bisimulation semantics for higher dimensional automata. Technical report, Stanford (1991)

# On the Optimal Space Complexity
# of Consensus for Anonymous Processes

Rati Gelashvili[✉]

MIT, Cambridge, USA
gelash@mit.edu

**Abstract.** The optimal space complexity of consensus in shared memory is a decades-old open problem. For a system of $n$ processes, no algorithm is known that uses a sublinear number of registers. However, the best known lower bound due to Fich, Herlihy, and Shavit requires $\Omega(\sqrt{n})$ registers.

The special symmetric case of the problem where processes are anonymous (run the same algorithm) has also attracted attention. Even in this case, the best lower and upper bounds are still $\Omega(\sqrt{n})$ and $O(n)$. Moreover, Fich, Herlihy, and Shavit first proved their lower bound for anonymous processes, and then extended it to the general case. As such, resolving the anonymous case might be a significant step towards understanding and solving the general problem.

In this work, we show that in a system of anonymous processes, any consensus algorithm satisfying nondeterministic solo termination has to use $\Omega(n)$ read-write registers in some execution. This implies an $\Omega(n)$ lower bound on the space complexity of deterministic obstruction-free and randomized wait-free consensus, matching the upper bound and closing the symmetric case of the open problem.

## 1   Introduction

The celebrated Fischer, Lynch and Paterson (FLP) [FLP85] result proved that fundamental synchronization tasks including consensus and test-and-set are not solvable in a wait-free manner using read-write registers. However, the work of Ben-Or [BO83] shows that it is possible to circumvent FLP and obtain efficient distributed algorithms, if we relax the problem specification to allow probabilistic termination. It is also possible to solve these tasks deterministically, but obstruction-free instead of wait-free; it is known how to convert any deterministic obstruction-free algorithm into a randomized wait-free algorithm against an oblivious adversary (see [GHHW13]).

The space complexity of an algorithm is the maximum number of registers used in any execution. A lot of research has been dedicated to improving the upper and lower bounds on the space complexity for canonical tasks. For test-and-set, an $\Omega(\log n)$ lower bound was shown in [SP89] and independently in [GW12]. On the other hand, an $O(\sqrt{n})$ deterministic obstruction-free upper bound was given in [GHHW13]. The final breakthrough was the

© Springer-Verlag Berlin Heidelberg 2015
Y. Moses (Ed.): DISC 2015, LNCS 9363, pp. 452–466, 2015.
DOI: 10.1007/978-3-662-48653-5_30

recent obstruction-free algorithm designed by Giakkoupis et al. [GHHW14], with $O(\log n)$ space complexity, essentially closing the problem[1].

For consensus, an upper bound with $n$ registers was long known from [AH90]. A lower bound of $\Omega(\sqrt{n})$ by Fich et al. [FHS98] first appeared in 1993. The proof is notorious for its technicality and utilizes a neat inductive combination of covering and valency arguments. Another version of the proof appeared in a textbook [AE14]. However, a linear lower bound or a sublinear space algorithm has remained elusive to date.

The authors of [FHS98] conjectured a tight lower bound of $\Omega(n)$. But the linear lower bound has not been proven even in a restricted, symmetric case, where all processes are anonymous. In such a system processes can be thought of as running the same code: all processes with the same input start in the same initial state and behave identically. The same linear upper bound holds for anonymous processes, since a deterministic obstruction free consensus algorithm that uses $O(n)$ registers is known [GR05]. Interestingly, the proof in [FHS98] starts by showing the $\Omega(\sqrt{n})$ lower bound for anonymous processes, which is then extended to a much more complex argument for the general case. Therefore, a linear lower bound in the anonymous setting might prove to be a meaningful step in better understanding and solving the general case of the open problem.

**Contribution:** In this paper we prove the $\Omega(n)$ lower bound in the symmetric (anonymous) case for consensus algorithms satisfying the standard *nondeterministic solo termination* property. Any lower bound for algorithms satisfying the nondeterministic solo termination implies a lower bound for deterministic obstruction-free and randomized wait-free algorithms. As in [FHS98, AE14], the bound is for the worst-case space complexity of the algorithm, i.e. for the number of registers used in some execution, regardless of its actual probability.

Our argument relies on a specific class of executions which we call *reserving*, and on the ability to define valency, corresponding to possible return values, for these executions. This definition of valency and the ability to cover registers with modified contents by reserved processes greatly simplifies the task of performing an inductive argument. We hope these techniques will be useful for future work.

We also show how the lower bound can be extended to a non-anonymous, adaptive, setting where processes come from a very large namespace and the bound depends on the size of the subset of processes that actually participate in the execution. However, this extension requires additional restrictions on register size and termination, and is provided mainly to illustrate an approach.

**Definitions and Notation:** We use the standard shared-memory model and similar notation to [FHS98, AE14]. We consider anonymous processes and atomic read-write registers. A process is *covering* a register $R$, if the next step of $p$ can be a write to $R$. A *block write* of a set of processes $P$ to a set of covered registers $V$ is a sequence of write steps by processes in $P$, where each step is a write to a different register and all registers get written to.

---

[1] The space complexity of randomized test-and-set against a strong (adaptive) adversary remains open.

In a system of anonymous processes, if a process $p$ in state $s$ performs a particular operation, for any configuration with any process $q$ in the same state $s$, $q$ can also perform the exact same operation. Finally, if $p$ and $q$ perform the same operation from the same state with the same outcome (i.e. read the same value), then both $p$ and $q$ end up in the same state after the operation. In randomized algorithms, anonymous processes always perform the same operation from the same state (including flipping coins with the same random distribution), and end up in identical state if they observe the same results.

A *clone* of a process $p$, exactly as in [FHS98, AE14], is defined as another process with the same input as $p$, that shadows $p$ by performing the same operations as $p$ in lockstep, reading and writing the same values immediately after $p$, and remaining in the same state, all the way until some write of $p$. Because the system consists of anonymous processes, in any execution with sufficiently many processes, for any write operation of $p$, there always exists an alternative execution with a clone $q$ that shadowed $p$ all the way until the write. In particular, in the alternative execution, process $q$ *covers* the register and is about to write the value that $p$ last wrote there. Moreover, the two executions with or without the clone covering the register are completely indistinguishable to all processes other than the clone itself.

An execution is a sequence of steps by processes and a *solo* execution is an execution where all steps are taken by a single process. An execution interval is a subsequence of consecutive steps from some execution. In the binary consensus problem each participating process starts with a binary input 0 or 1, and must return a binary output. The correctness criterium is that all outputs must be the same and equal to the input of some process. We say that an execution interval *decides* 0 (or 1) if some process returns 0 (or 1, respectively) during this execution interval.

A wait-free termination requirement means that each participating process must eventually return an output within a finite number of own steps, regardless of how the other processes are scheduled. The FLP result shows that in the asynchronous shared memory model with read-write registers, no deterministic algorithm can solve binary consensus in a wait-free way. However, it is possible to deterministically solve obstruction-free consensus, i.e. when processes are only required to return an output if they run solo from some configuration. It is also possible to solve consensus in a randomized wait-free way, when processes are allowed to flip random coins and decide their next steps accordingly. A *nondeterministic solo termination* property of an algorithm means that from each reachable configuration, for each process, there exists a finite solo execution by the process where it terminates and returns an output. We prove our lower bounds for binary consensus algorithms that satisfy this *nondeterministic solo termination* property, because both deterministic obstruction-free algorithms and randomized wait-free algorithms fall into this category.

# 2   Space Complexity Lower Bound

In order to demonstrate our approach, we start by presenting a different proof of the $\Omega(\sqrt{n})$ space lower bound in the anonymous setting. It uses induction on the number of registers written during an execution, as opposed to induction on the tuple of sizes of pending block writes in [FHS98]. The proof also has an additional benefit that the use of covering and valency arguments is decoupled. As usual, we use covering to enforce writing to a new register, while a valency argument reminiscent of [FLP85] ensures that both decision values remain reachable by solo executions.

Next, building upon this new argument, we prove an $\Omega(n)$ space lower bound for consensus with nondeterministic solo termination in a system of anonymous processes. There are some significant differences, for instance, the execution is constructed in such a way that after a register is written to, it always remains covered. Moreover, valency is redefined to account for this specific class of executions. The rest is induction.

## 2.1   A Square-Root Lower Bound

In this section, we define *valency* as follows. If there is a solo execution of some process returning 0 from a configuration, then we call this configuration *0-valent* (and *1-valent* if there is a solo execution of a process that returns 1). Solo termination implies that every configuration is 0-valent or 1-valent. Note that unlike the standard definition of valency, our definition allows the same configuration to be simultaneously 0-valent and 1-valent. We call such configurations that are both 0-valent and 1-valent *bivalent*, and *univalent* otherwise. Notice that a configuration is bivalent if two solo executions of the same process return different values. If a configuration is 0-valent, but not 1-valent (i.e. no solo execution from this configuration decides 1), then we call it 0-univalent, meaning that the configuration is univalent with valency 0. Analogously, a configuration is 1-univalent if it is 1-valent but not 0-valent.

Observe that if we have at least two processes, then in every bivalent configuration we can always find two distinct processes $p$ and $q$, such that there is a solo execution of $p$ returning 0 and a solo execution of $q$ returning 1. This is because either the configuration is bivalent because of solo executions of distinct processes, in which case we are done, or two solo executions of some process return different values, in which case it suffices to consider any terminating solo execution of another process.

For the system of anonymous processes, and a consensus algorithm that uses atomic read-write registers and satisfies the nondeterministic solo termination property, we prove the following statement by induction:

**Lemma 1.** *For $r \geq 0$, there exists a system of $\frac{(r-1)r}{2} + 2$ anonymous processes, such that for any consensus algorithm, a configuration $C_r$ is reachable by an execution $E_r$ with the following properties:*

- *There is a set $R$ of $r$ registers, each of which has been written to during $E_r$, and*
- *the configuration $C_r$ is bivalent.*

*Proof.* The proof is by induction, with the base case $r = 0$. Our system consists of two processes $p$ and $q$, $p$ starts with input 0, $q$ starts with input 1, and $C_0$ is the initial state. Clearly, no registers have been written to in $C_0$ and bivalency follows by nondeterministic solo termination.

Now, let us assume the induction hypothesis for some $r$ and prove it for $r+1$. By the induction hypothesis, we can reach a configuration $C_r$ using $\frac{(r-1)r}{2} + 2$ processes. The goal is to use another $r$ processes and extend $C_r$ to $C_{r+1}$, completing the proof since $r + \frac{(r-1)r}{2} + 2 = \frac{r(r+1)}{2} + 2$.

As discussed above, because we have at least 2 processes and $C_r$ is bivalent, there exists a process $p$ and its solo execution $\alpha$ from $C_r$ after which $p$ returns 0 and a process $q \neq p$ and its solo execution $\beta$ from $C_r$ after which $q$ returns 1.[2] Recall that $R$ is the set of $r$ registers that were written to in execution $E_r$. For each register in $R$, let a new process clone the process that last wrote to it all the way to covering the register poised to write the same value as present in the register in configuration $C_r$.

Let us now apply the covering argument utilizing the clones. Consider execution $E_r\alpha\gamma\beta$, where $\gamma$ is a block write to $R$ by the new clones. We know that process $p$ returns 0 after $E_r\alpha$. During its solo execution $\alpha$, process $p$ has to write to a register outside of $R$. Otherwise, the configuration after $E_r\alpha\gamma$ is indistinguishable from $C_r$ to process $q$ as the values in all registers are the same, and $q$ is still in the same state as in $C_r$. Hence, $q$ will return 1 after $E_r\alpha\gamma\beta$ as it would after $E_r\beta$, contradicting the correctness of the consensus algorithm. Analogously, process $q$ has to write outside of $R$ during $\beta$. Let $\alpha = \alpha'w_p\alpha''$, where $w_p$ is the first write of $p$ outside the set of registers $R$, and let $\beta = \beta'w_q\beta''$, with $w_q$ being the first write outside of $R$. Let $\ell$ be the length of $\gamma\beta'w_q$ and $B_i$ be a prefix of $\gamma\beta'w_q$ of length $i$, for all possible $0 \leq i \leq \ell$.

Next, we use a valency argument to reach $C_{r+1}$. We show that either the configuration reached after $\mathsf{E}_r\alpha'\gamma\beta'w_q$, or one of the configurations reached after $\mathsf{E}_r\alpha'B_iw_p$ for some $i$, satisfies the properties necessary to be $C_{r+1}$. Clearly, we have used the right number of processes to reach any of these configurations and $r + 1$ registers have been written to while doing so, including $R$ and the register written by $w_p$ or $w_q$. Thus, we only need to show that one of these configurations is *bivalent*.

Assume the contrary. The configuration for $i = 0$ must be 0-univalent, since $p$ returns 0 only throughout $\alpha''$, and we assumed that the configuration is not bivalent. Similarly, the configuration reached after $\mathsf{E}_r\alpha'\gamma\beta'w_q = E_r\alpha'B_\ell$ is 1-univalent. It is univalent by our assumption and 1-valent as $q$ running solo returns 1 through $\beta''$ ($\alpha'$ does not involve a write outside of $R$ and $q$ cannot distinguish from $E_r\beta'w_q\beta''$). Because the configuration reached after $E_r\alpha'B_\ell$ is

---

[2] Alternatively one can say execution $E_r\alpha$ ends with $p$ returning 0 and $E_r\beta$ ends with $q$ returning 1.

1-univalent, any terminating solo execution of process $p$ from that configuration must also return 1. In particular, every terminating solo execution that starts by $p$ performing its next step $w_p$ returns 1. So the configuration reached after $E_r \alpha' B_\ell w_p$ must be 1-univalent: solo executions of $p$ return 1 (some solo execution terminates due to nondeterministic solo execution), and it is univalent by our assumption (it is the same as configuration for $i = \ell$). Therefore, the configuration reached after $E_r \alpha' B_i w_p$ is 0-univalent for $i = 0$ and 1-univalent for $i = \ell$. Hence, we can find a switching point for some $i$ and $i + 1$, where the configuration $X$ reached by $E_r \alpha' B_i w_p$ is 0-univalent, while the configuration $Y$ reached by $E_r \alpha' B_{i+1} w_p$ is 1-univalent. Let $o$ be the extra operation in $B_{i+1}$.

Operation $o$ is not by $p$ and may not be a read or a write to the same register as $w_p$ writes to since $p$ would not distinguish between $X$ and $Y$ and would return the same output from both configurations through the same solo execution, contradicting the existence of the different univalencies. Otherwise, operations $w_p$ and $o$ commute. Let $\sigma$ be a terminating solo execution from $Y$ by the process that performed operation $o$, where it returns 1 due to the univalency of $Y$. Also consider this process performing its next operation $o$ from $X$. Since $w_p$ and $o$ commute, and $o$ is not a read, the process cannot distinguish between the resulting configuration and $Y$ and returns 1 through $\sigma$ as from $Y$. However, $o\sigma$ is a solo execution from $X$ that returns 1, contradicting the 0-univalency of $X$. The contradiction proves the induction step, completing our induction.

Notice that for $n$ processes, Lemma 1 directly implies the existence of an execution where $\Omega(\sqrt{n})$ registers are written to, proving the desired lower bound.

## 2.2  Linear Lower Bound

Consider systems with $n$ anonymous processes and an arbitrary correct consensus algorithm satisfying the nondeterministic solo termination property. We will assume that no execution of the algorithm uses more than $n/20$ registers (otherwise, we are trivially done), and prove that such an algorithm has to use $\Omega(n)$ registers, which completes the proof. For notational convenience, let us define $m$ to be $n/20$.

The argument in Lemma 1 relies on a new set of clones in each iteration to overwrite the changes to the contents of the registers made during the inductive step. This is the primary reason why we only get an $\Omega(\sqrt{n})$ lower bound. As the authors of [FHS98] also mention, to get a stronger lower bound we would instead have to reuse existing processes. In order to do so, these existing processes need to cover the registers in our inductive configurations (we must also ensure proper valency conditions on what they are about to write, but let us focus on the covering). Now, even if we reach such a configuration, during a solo execution interval of some process in the subsequent induction step, all the registers may get written to, and we would have to use all the covering existing processes to overwrite the changes. Therefore, in the next configuration, there is no way to guarantee that the existing processes would still cover various registers.

This is the primary reason why we have to replace solo executions in the proof with a different class of executions that we call *reserving*. Intuitively, reserving executions ensure that for the registers that are written to, some processes are reserved to cover them. This way, we can have reserved processes cover the registers in subsequent inductive configurations. Notice that the definition of valency used in the proof of Lemma 1 was based on solo executions. Thus, we also redefine valency based on reserving executions.

**Reserving Executions.** The following is a formal definition of a reserving execution interval.

**Definition 1.** *Let $C$ be some configuration reachable by the algorithm, and let $P$ be a set of at least $m+1$ processes. We call an execution interval $\gamma$ that starts from configuration $C$ reserving from $C$ by $P$ if:*
- *Every step in $\gamma$ is by a process in $P$.*
- *At any time during the execution of $\gamma$: if we let $R_w$ be the set of registers written to so far during $\gamma$, then, for each register in $R_w$, there is a reserved process $p \in P$ covering that register, one per register.*
- *If a process $p \in P$ returns during $\gamma$ then it does so in the last step of $\gamma$.*

Notice that by definition any prefix of a reserving execution interval is also a reserving execution interval. Let $\mathsf{Res}(C, P)$ be the set of all reserving execution intervals from $C$ by processes in $P$ that end with a process $p \in P$ returning. We first show that given sufficiently many processes, such an execution interval exists. This is essential for defining the valency later. Recall that we assumed a strict upper bound of $m$ on the number of registers that can ever be written.

**Lemma 2.** *For any reachable configuration $C$ and a set of at least $m + 1$ processes $P$, none of which have returned yet, we have that $\mathsf{Res}(C, P) \neq \varnothing$.*

*Proof.* For a given $C$ and $P$, we will prove the lemma by constructing a particular reserving execution interval $\gamma$ that ends when some process $p \in P$ returns. We start with an empty $\gamma$ and continuously extend it. In the first stage, one by one, for each process $p \in P$:
- Due to the nondeterministic solo termination, there exists a solo execution of $p$ where $p$ returns.
  - If $p$ ever writes to any register during this solo execution, extend $\gamma$ by the prefix of the execution before this write, and move to the next process in $P$.
  - Otherwise, complete $\gamma$ by extending it with the whole solo execution of $p$.

We have finitely many processes and the first stage described above consists of extending the execution interval at most $|P|$ times. Each time, because of the nondeterministic solo termination for some process $p \in P$, we extend $\gamma$ by a prefix of a finite solo execution of $p$. Moreover, all operations are reads by processes in $P$, and therefore the prefix of $\gamma$ constructed so far is reserving.

If some process returns in the first stage, the construction of $\gamma$ is complete. Otherwise, since the first stage is finite, we move on to the second stage described below. In the configuration after the first stage each of the at least $m+1$ processes in $P$ is covering a register (by their next write operation after the first stage). From that configuration, the execution interval $\gamma$ is extended by repeatedly doing the following:

1. Let $R$ be the set of covered registers by processes of $P$. Since $|R| \leq m < |P|$, we can find two processes $p, q \in P$ covering the same register in $R$.
2. Due to the nondeterministic solo termination, there exists a solo execution of $p$ where $p$ returns.
   - If $p$ ever writes to a register outside of $R$ during this solo execution, extend $\gamma$ by the prefix of the execution before this write, and continue from the first step. Notice that at the beginning of the next iteration, process $p$ still covers a register as required.
   - Otherwise, complete $\gamma$ by extending it with the whole solo execution of $p$.

In the second stage, each iteration terminates, since for any process $p \in P$, we can extend by at most the terminating solo execution of $p$, which exists and is finite. After each iteration, if the construction is not complete, the size of $R$ increases by one. But there are at most $m$ registers in the system and $|R| \leq m$. Thus, after at most $m$ finite extensions, we will complete the construction of $\gamma$ when some process returns.

The execution is reserving because at all times, the registers that were written-to are in $R$. Moreover, for each register in $R$, there is always a process covering it starting from the time it was first covered by some process $p$ in the second step of some iteration all the way until the end of $\gamma$.

The next lemma follows immediately from the definition of reserving executions.

**Lemma 3.** *Consider a reachable configuration $C$, a set of at least $m+1$ processes $P'$ none of which have returned yet, and another configuration $C'$ reached after some process $p \notin P'$ performs a write operation $w_p$ in $C$. Moreover, assume that another process $q \neq p$ with $q \notin P'$ is covering the same register that $w_p$ writes to. Then if $\gamma \in \mathsf{Res}(C', P')$, then $w_p\gamma$ is in $\mathsf{Res}(C, P)$ where $P = P' \cup \{p\} \cup \{q\}$.*

**New Definition of Valency.** We say that a configuration $C$ is 0-valent$_U$ with respect to the set of processes $U$, if there exists a subset of at least $m + 1$ processes $P \subseteq U$ and a reserving execution in $\mathsf{Res}(C, P)$ that finishes when some process in $P$ returns 0. We call $C$ 0-valent$_U^{m+1}$ w.r.t. $U$, if there exists a subset of *exactly* $m + 1$ processes $P \subseteq U$ ($|P| = m+1$), and a reserving execution interval in $\mathsf{Res}(C, P)$ returning 0. We define 1-valent$_U$ and 1-valent$_U^{m+1}$ analogously. If $U$ contains at least $m + 1$ processes that have not returned, Lemma 2 implies that every configuration is 0-valent$_U^{m+1}$ or 1-valent$_U^{m+1}$ (and thus 0-valent$_U$ or 1-valent$_U$).

As in our earlier definition in Section 2.1, but unlike the standard definition, a configuration that is 0-valent$_U^{m+1}$ can still also be 1-valent$_U^{m+1}$ in which case we call it bivalent$_U^{m+1}$. Basically, a configuration is bivalent$_U^{m+1}$ if it is both 0-valent$_U^{m+1}$ due to some $P \subseteq U$ and 1-valent$_U^{m+1}$ due to some $Q \subseteq U$. A configuration that is not bivalent$_U^{m+1}$ is called univalent$_U^{m+1}$. Finally, similar to our earlier convention, we define a configuration to be 0-univalent$_U^{m+1}$ if it is 0-valent$_U^{m+1}$ but not 1-valent$_U^{m+1}$. On the other hand, a configuration that is 1-valent$_U^{m+1}$ but not 0-valent$_U^{m+1}$ is called 1-univalent$_U^{m+1}$. Terms bivalent$_U$, univalent$_U$, 0-univalent$_U$ and 1-univalent$_U$ are defined analogously.

Next we prove a lemma that lets us find reserving executions consisting of disjoint processes.

**Lemma 4.** *Consider a configuration $C$ which is bivalent$_U$ w.r.t. $U$. Assume that there are (possibly intersecting) sets of at least $m + 1$ processes each $P \subseteq U$ and $Q \subseteq U$ such that $|U| \geq |P| + |Q| + m$, and some reserving execution in $\mathsf{Res}(C, P)$ ends when $p \in P$ returns 0, while some reserving execution in $\mathsf{Res}(C, Q)$ ends when $q \in Q$ returns 1. Then there are also disjoint sets of processes $P' \subseteq U$ and $Q' \subseteq U$ ($P' \cap Q' = \varnothing$), such that an execution in $\mathsf{Res}(C, P')$ returns 0 and an execution in $\mathsf{Res}(C, Q')$ returns 1. Moreover, $m + 1 \leq \min(|P'|, |Q'|) \leq \min(|P|, |Q|)$ and $\max(|P'|, |Q'|) \leq \max(|P|, |Q|)$.*

*Proof.* None of the processes in $U$ may have already returned in configuration $C$, as that would contradict the existence of a reserving execution returning the other output. If $P$ and $Q$ do not intersect then we set $P' = P$ and $Q' = Q$. Otherwise, we can find a set $H \subseteq U - P - Q$ of $m+1$ processes. By Lemma 2, $\mathsf{Res}(C, H)$ is non-empty, and without loss of generality, some execution in $\mathsf{Res}(C, H)$ returns 0. Then, we set $P' = H$ and $Q' = Q$ (if all executions in $\mathsf{Res}(C, H)$ return 1, we would set $P' = P$ and $Q' = H$).

**The Process-Clone Pairs and the Proof.** As mentioned earlier, it is obviously not sufficient to simply cover registers with existing processes without any knowledge of what they are about to write. In the proof of Lemma 1 we used new clones that covered registers to block-overwrite these registers back to the contents whose valency we knew. In order to do something similar with existing processes, we associate a dedicated clone to each process. The process and its clone remain in the same states and perform the same operations during the whole execution.

Usually, when we schedule a process to perform an operation, its clone performs the same operation immediately after the process. Thus the pair of the process and the clone remain in the same state. Under these circumstances, we can treat the pair of the process and its clone as a single process, because no process can distinguish the execution from when the clone would not take steps. However, sometimes we will *split* the pair by having only the process perform a write operation and let the clone cover the register. We will explicitly say when this is the case. After we split the pair of process and clone in such a way, we will not schedule the process to take any more steps and thus the clone will remain poised to write to the covered register. After some delay, we will schedule the clone of the process to write, effectively resetting the register to the value it had when the process wrote. Moreover, because meanwhile the process did not take any steps, after the write the clone will again be in the same state as its associated process. Hence the pair of the process and clone will no longer be split, and will continue taking steps in sync like a single process.

This is different from the way clones were used in the proof of Lemma 1, because after the pair of the process and its clone is united, it can be split again. Therefore, the same clone can reset the contents of registers written by its associated process multiple times, instead of requiring a new clone every time.

We call a split pair of a process and a clone *fresh* as long as the register that the process wrote to, and its clone is covering, has not been overwritten. After the register is overwritten, we call the split pair *stale*.

In addition, we also use cloning in a way similar to the proof of Lemma 1, except that we do this at most constantly many times, as opposed to $r$ times, to reach the next configuration $C_{r+1}$. Moreover, each time when we do this, we create duplicates of both the process and its corresponding clone. This new process-clone pair is in the same state as the original pair, and from there on behaves like a single new process similar to all other pairs. We will always consider valency with respect to sets of processes whose pairs are not split. Therefore, the definition of valency does not need to change when the clones keep taking steps immediately after their processes.

Sometimes, when considering process-clone pairs, none of which are split, we may refer to them as processes, i.e. we may talk about a process taking steps or returning a value. As mentioned earlier, it is assumed that as long as the pair is not split, the clone always follows and takes the same steps right after the process. Hence, in this context, a process taking a step means a pair taking a step.

Now we are ready to prove the main result.

**Theorem 1.** *In the system of anonymous processes, consider any correct consensus algorithm satisfying nondeterministic solo termination, with the property that every execution uses at most $m$ registers. For each $r$ with $0 \leq r \leq m$, there exists a set $U$ containing $5m+6+2r$ process-clone pairs such that a configuration $C_r$ is reachable through an execution $E_r$ by processes and clones in $U$ with the following properties:*

1. *There exists a set $R$ of $r$ registers, that can be partitioned in two disjoint subsets $R = R_s \cup R_c$, where:*
   - *$R_s$ consists of all registers in the system that each have one fresh split pair on them, last written by some process whose clone has not yet performed the write and is covering the register.*
   - *$R_c = R - R_s$. Each register in $R_c$ is covered by an unique pair of both a process and its clone.*

   *Thus, each fresh pair is split on a different register in $R_s$, and an additional $|R_c|$ pairs are covering the registers in $R_c$. Let $V$ be the set of these $|R_s| + |R_c| = r$ pairs.*

2. *There are at most $r$ stale split pairs in the system, that are all split on pairwise different registers from $R$. Let $L$ be the set of these at most $r$ stale split pairs.*

3. *There exist disjoint sets of process-clone pairs that are not split $P, Q \subseteq U - V - L$ with $|P| + |Q| \leq 2m + 4$, such that an execution in $\mathsf{Res}(C_r, P)$ returns $0$ and an execution in $\mathsf{Res}(C_r, Q)$ returns $1$.[3]*

*Proof.* The proof is by induction on $r$, with the base case $r = 0$. Out of the $5m + 6$ processes-clone pairs, half of them start with an input $0$ and half start with an input $1$. We let $C_0$ be the initial state, $P$ be a set of some $m + 1$ pairs with input $0$, and $Q$ be a set of some $m + 1$ pairs with input $1$. The first two properties are trivially satisfied; also $P \cap Q = \varnothing$ and $|P| + |Q| = 2m + 2$. By Lemma 2 and correctness of consensus, there is a reserving execution in $\mathsf{Res}(C_0, P)$ that decides $0$, and a reserving execution in $\mathsf{Res}(C_0, Q)$ that decides $1$ ($C_0$ is bivalent$_U$). Observe that the pairs are not split and for the purposes of valency we can just consider the steps of processes.

Now, let us assume induction hypothesis for some $r$, i.e. the existence of $E_r$ and $C_r$ with the required three properties, and prove the step for $r + 1$ by extending $E_r$ to $E_{r+1}$, resulting in the configuration $C_{r+1}$. Let $U$, $P$, $Q$, $V$, $L$ and $R = R_s \cup R_c$ all be defined as in the theorem statement for $r$. Our goal is to construct sets $U'$, $P'$, $Q'$, $V'$, $L'$ and $R' = R'_s \cup R'_c$ for $r + 1$. In $U' - U$ we have two more process-clone pairs available that have not taken steps and can be used to clone an existing process-clone pair. Let $T$ denote $U - V - L - P - Q$. Since $|V| = r$, $L \leq r$ and $|P| + |Q| \leq 2m + 4$, we have $|T| \geq 3m + 2$.

For all but $|R_s| + |L|$ split pairs both processes and clones are in the same states, about to perform the same operations. By definition, each stale pair in $L$ is split on a different register from $R$. In the following argument, we extend the execution from $E_r$ to $E_{r+1}$ by steps of processes and clones not in $L$. This can introduce new stale split pairs and the resulting configuration $C_{r+1}$ may not immediately satisfy the second property. We will then show how to modify the extension and unite some stale split pairs, such that the resulting configuration satisfies all properties, including the second property with the new $L'$.

Let $\alpha \in \mathsf{Res}(C_r, P)$ be the reserving execution interval that returns $0$, and let $\beta \in \mathsf{Res}(C_r, Q)$ be the reserving execution interval that returns $1$. Notice that each time a process in $P$ or $Q$ takes a step in $\alpha$ or $\beta$, its clone performs an identical step immediately after. The execution $E_r\alpha$ ends with a process-clone pair $p \in P$ returning $0$ and the execution $E_r\beta$ ends with a process-clone pair $q \in Q$ returning $1$.

Each register in $R_c$ was covered by some pair of both a process and its clone in $V$. Let $\gamma_c$ be a block write to all registers in $R_c$ by only the processes but not the clones of these respective covering pairs: i.e. after each write we get a new fresh split pair. Consider a configuration $D$ reached from $C_r$ by executing this block write, i.e. a configuration reached after $E_r\gamma_c$. Assume that $D$ is 1-valent$_T^{m+1}$,

---

[3] The pairs of processes in $P$ and $Q$ are not split, because all split pairs belong to $V \cup L$ (fresh to $V$ and stale to $L$). Also, the third condition implies that the configuration $C_r$ is bivalent$_{U-V-L}$.

without loss of generality, because it has a valency. For any execution interval $e$, let us denote by $W(e)$ the set of registers written to during $e$. Hence, $R_s \cap W(e)$ is the set of registers in $R_s$ that are written-to during $e$. Each register in $R_s$ is covered by a clone of a split pair whose process has already performed the write and is stopped. Define $\gamma_s(e)$ as a block write to all registers in $R_s \cap W(e)$ by these trailing clones of the split pairs in $V$: i.e. after each write another clone catches up with its process and a previously split pair is united. Basically, if we run an execution interval $e$ from $C_r$ that changes contents of some registers in $R_s$, we can then clean these changes up by executing $\gamma_s(e)$, which leads to all registers in $R_s$ having the same contents as in $C_r$.

Using a crude covering argument we can first show that

**Lemma 5.** *The execution interval $\alpha$ must contain a write operation outside $R$.*

The proof of this lemma is provided later.

Based on this we can write $\alpha = \alpha' w_p \alpha''$, where $w_p$ is the write operation to a register $\mathsf{reg} \notin R$, performed by some process-clone pair $p \in P$.

Looking ahead, when we reach $C_{r+1}$, the new set of registers $R'$ will be $R \cup \{\mathsf{reg}\}$. Next, we prove the following lemma using an FLP-like case analysis:

**Lemma 6.** *We can extend execution $E_r$ (i.e. from $C_r$) with an execution interval $e$ and reach a configuration satisfying the first and the third inductive requirements to be $C_{r+1}$ with a properly defined $U'$, $P'$, $Q'$, $V'$ and $R' = R'_s \cup R'_c$, and with all process-clone pairs that are not split being in sync. But the second property is not immediately satisfied. All stale split pairs from $L$ remain stale and split, but some pairs that were fresh and split on registers in $R_s \cap W(e)$ may have become stale in $C_{r+1}$ (because neither the process nor the clone in the split pair has taken steps while the register was overwritten in $e$). However, these are the only possible new stale split pairs in $C_{r+1}$, and they do not belong to the new sets $V' \cup P' \cup Q'$.*

The proof of this lemma can be found in the full version.[4]

In order to finish the proof of the theorem, we need to show how to construct $L'$. According to the above Lemma 6 we can extend the execution to reach the next configuration $C_{r+1}$ satisfying first and third but not the second property about the stale split pairs $L'$. In $C_r$ we had at most $r$ stale pairs in the system, each split on a different register, and $L$ was the set of these pairs. But on the way to reaching $C_{r+1}$, we may have introduced new stale pairs in the system. According to Lemma 6 these must be the pairs that were fresh and split on registers in $R_s \cap W(e)$ in $C_r$, and whose associated register in $R_s$ has been overwritten during $e$, making them stale in $C_{r+1}$.

The set of all stale pairs in $C_{r+1}$ may not satisfy the requirements imposed for $L'$, since there could already have been a stale pair split on a register in $R_s \cap W(e)$ in $L$ (in $C_r$). Then two stale pairs would be split on this register in $C_{r+1}$, violating the second property. However, for each such register in $R_s \cap W(e)$, we know a stale pair $\rho \in L$ was split on it in $C_r$, and that this register was

---

[4] Available at http://arxiv.org/abs/1506.06817.

written-to during extension $W(e)$. We now modify the extension $e$; we add a single write by the clone of the stale split pair $\rho$ immediately before a write operation to the same register that was already in $e$. This way, no pair other than the clone of $\rho$ observes a difference between the two executions, and we will use the configuration reached by the modified execution as $C_{r+1}$. Because of this indistinguishability, the new $C_{r+1}$ still satisfies other required properties. Moreover, the pair $\rho$ is not split anymore; it is united since the clone has caught up with its process.

We can do the above modification to the execution for each register in $R_s \cap W(e)$ that previously ended up with two stale split processes in $C_{r+1}$. Let the modified execution extension be $e'$. In $e'$, some stale split pairs from $L$ are united, indistinguishably to all other processes and clones, leading to a configuration $C_{r+1}$, that still satisfies the first and third properties, and has at most one stale pair split on any register. We take $L'$ to be the set of stale split pairs. By construction, all stale pairs are split on registers in $R'$ and no two on the same register, so we do have $|L'| \leq r + 1$ as desired. Hence, we have reached configuration $C_{r+1}$ satisfying all properties and completing the proof.

**Corollary 1.** *In a system of $n$ anonymous processes, any consensus algorithm satisfying non-deterministic solo termination must use $\Omega(n)$ registers.*

*Proof.* Theorem 1 directly implies the $\Omega(n)$ lower bound on the number of registers used in some execution. If $n$ is the number of anonymous processes and no execution uses more than $m = n/20$ registers, by Theorem 1 we can reach $C_m$ for large enough $n$, and we have enough processes $n \geq 10m + 12 + 4m$. In $C_m$ there are $m$ registers in $R$, each of which has either already been written-to ($R_s$) or are covered by unique processes ($R_c$). We could perform a block write to $R_c$ by covering processes from $V$ in $C_m$, after which in the resulting execution $m = n/20 = \Omega(n)$ different registers would have been written to.

We now provide the delayed proof of Lemma 5.

*Proof.* Assume the contrary. We know that the execution $E_r \alpha$ decides 0. No process or clone that takes a step in $\gamma_c$ or $\gamma_s(\alpha)$ appears in $\alpha$ (they belong to $V$, disjoint from $P$ and $Q$), and by definition, no process or clone from $T$ takes a step in $\alpha$, $\gamma_c$ or $\gamma_s(\alpha)$. Thus, to all processes (and clones) in $T$, the configurations after $E_r \alpha \gamma_s(\alpha) \gamma_c$ and after $E_r \gamma_c$, which is configuration $D$, are indistinguishable. This is because no process (or clone) in $T$ has taken steps, the registers in $R$ contain the same values, and other registers were not touched during $\alpha$, $\gamma_s(\alpha)$ or $\gamma_c$. Configuration $D$ is 1-valent$_T^{m+1}$, so some extension from $E_r \alpha \gamma_s(\alpha) \gamma_c$ by an execution interval from $\mathsf{Res}(D, T)$ decides 1. This contradicts the correctness of the algorithm.

# 3    Extensions

**Adaptive Lower Bound:** Let us sketch a proof for an adaptive linear lower bound on the space complexity of consensus for non-anonymous processes but under extra restrictions on register size and solo termination. In this setting, processes are no longer anonymous, but we assume they come from a very large namespace. Each of these huge number of processes executes its own code, however, we get to choose which subset of processes participates in the execution. We show that there is a linear space lower bound that depends on the number of participating processes, that is, for large enough namespace, we can find an execution of $n$ processes (out of all processes) where $\Omega(n)$ registers get written.

The restrictions are that the registers have a bounded size and that the consensus algorithm satisfies bounded nondeterministic solo termination property, meaning that there always is a terminating solo execution of a process consisting of less than certain number of steps. If we had bounded nondeterministic solo termination, the lower bound execution for anonymous processes constructed in Theorem 1 would always contain less than $B$ steps, where $B$ is a finite bound that only depends on $n$ and the solo termination bound. As registers have a bounded size, for both input values, a process can exhibit only finitely many different behaviors during its first $B$ steps, because in each step it can either read or write a fixed number of different values. For a sufficiently large namespace (depending on $B$, $n$ and register size), by pigeon-hole principle, we can find $n$ processes such that half of them start with input 1, half start with 0 and all processes with the same input behave as anonymous for the first $B$ steps of an execution. Hence, we can use Theorem 1 and get an execution where $n/20$ registers are written to, as described at the end of Section 2.2.

**Future Work:** We believe that is should be possible to derive the above adaptive lower bound without the bounded solo termination assumption, and to get good estimate on the required size of the namespace. However, the major open problem is still to resolve the general, non-anonymous and non-adaptive case, i.e. to get tight bounds on the space required to solve consensus with exactly $n$ asymmetric processes.

**Acknowledgments.** Support is gratefully acknowledged from the National Science Foundation under grants CCF-1217921, CCF-1301926, and IIS-1447786, the Department of Energy under grant ER26116/DE-SC0008923, and the Oracle and Intel corporations.

The author would like to thank Nir Shavit, Michael Coulombe and Dan Alistarh for helpful conversations and feedback, and the anonymous reviewers for their excellent comments.

# References

[AE14]  Attiya, H., Ellen, F.: Impossibility results for distributed computing. Synthesis Lectures on Distributed Computing Theory **5**(1), 1–162 (2014)

[AH90]  Aspnes, J., Herlihy, M.: Fast randomized consensus using shared memory. Journal of Algorithms **11**(3), 441–461 (1990)

[BO83]  Ben-Or, M.: Another advantage of free choice (extended abstract): Completely asynchronous agreement protocols. In: Proceedings of the Second Annual ACM Symposium on Principles of Distributed Computing, PODC 1983, pp. 27–30. ACM, New York (1983)

[FHS98]  Fich, F., Herlihy, M., Shavit, N.: On the space complexity of randomized synchronization. Journal of the ACM (JACM) **45**(5), 843–862 (1998)

[FLP85]  Fischer, M.J., Lynch, N.A., Paterson, M.S.: Impossibility of distributed consensus with one faulty process. Journal of the ACM (JACM) **32**(2), 374–382 (1985)

[GHHW13]  Giakkoupis, G., Helmi, M., Higham, L., Woelfel, P.: An $O(\sqrt{n})$ space bound for obstruction-free leader election. In: Afek, Y. (ed.) DISC 2013. LNCS, vol. 8205, pp. 46–60. Springer, Heidelberg (2013)

[GHHW14]  Giakkoupis, G., Helmi, M., Higham, L., Woelfel, P.: Test-and-set in optimal space. In: Accepted to STOC 2015 (2014–2015)

[GR05]  Guerraoui, R., Ruppert, E.: What can be implemented anonymously? In: Fraigniaud, P. (ed.) DISC 2005. LNCS, vol. 3724, pp. 244–259. Springer, Heidelberg (2005)

[GW12]  Giakkoupis, G., Woelfel, P.: On the time and space complexity of randomized test-and-set. In: Proceedings of the 2012 ACM Symposium on Principles of Distributed Computing, pp. 19–28. ACM (2012)

[SP89]  Styer, E., Peterson, G.L.: Tight bounds for shared memory symmetric mutual exclusion problems. In: Proceedings of the Eighth Annual ACM Symposium on Principles of Distributed Computing, pp. 177–191. ACM (1989)

# Compressing Communication in Distributed Protocols

Yael Tauman Kalai[1]  and Ilan Komargodski[2]([⊠])

[1] Microsoft Research, Cambridge, USA
yael@microsoft.com
[2] Weizmann Institute of Science, 76100 Rehovot, Israel
ilan.komargodski@weizmann.ac.il

**Abstract.** We show how to compress communication in distributed protocols in which parties do not have private inputs. More specifically, we present a generic method for converting any protocol in which parties do not have private inputs, into another protocol where each message is *"short"* while preserving the same number of rounds, the same communication pattern, the same output distribution, and the same resilience to error. Assuming that the output lies in some universe of size $M$, in our resulting protocol each message consists of only $\mathsf{polylog}(M, n, d)$ many bits, where $n$ is the number of parties and $d$ is the number of rounds. Our transformation works in the full information model, in the presence of either static or adaptive Byzantine faults.

In particular, our result implies that for any such $\mathsf{poly}(n)$-round distributed protocol which generates outputs in a universe of size $\mathsf{poly}(n)$, long messages are not needed, and messages of length $\mathsf{polylog}(n)$ suffice. In other words, in this regime, any distributed task that can be solved in the $\mathcal{LOCAL}$ model, can also be solved in the $\mathcal{CONGEST}$ model with the *same* round complexity and security guarantees.

As a corollary, we conclude that for any $\mathsf{poly}(n)$-round collective coin-flipping protocol, leader election protocol, or selection protocols, messages of length $\mathsf{polylog}(n)$ suffice (in the presence of either static or adaptive Byzantine faults).

## 1  Introduction

In classical algorithmic design the goal is to design efficient algorithms, where the common complexity measures are time and space. In distributed algorithms, where a set of parties tries to perform a predefined task, there are more parameters of interest,, such as round complexity, message complexity, fault-tolerance, and more.

---

I. Komargodski—Part of this work done while an internat MSR New England. Supported in part by a grant from the I-CORE Program of the Planning and Budgeting Committee, the Israel Science Foundation, BSF and the Israeli Ministry of Science and Technology.

© Springer-Verlag Berlin Heidelberg 2015
Y. Moses (Ed.): DISC 2015, LNCS 9363, pp. 467–479, 2015.
DOI: 10.1007/978-3-662-48653-5_31

These measures have been studied in the literature under two main models: $\mathcal{LOCAL}$ and $\mathcal{CONGEST}$ [11]. The $\mathcal{LOCAL}$ model is aimed at studying "localized" executions of distributed protocols, and thus, messages of unlimited size are allowed. The $\mathcal{CONGEST}$ model is geared towards understanding the effect of congestion in the network, and thus, messages of poly-logarithmic size (in the number of parties) are allowed.[1]

Most of the work in distributed computing assumes one of the models above and focuses on optimizing resources such as round complexity, message complexity and fault-tolerance. We initiate the study of the following question:

*Is there a generic way to transform protocols in the $\mathcal{LOCAL}$ model to protocols in the $\mathcal{CONGEST}$ model, without negatively affecting the round complexity, fault-tolerance and other resources?*

We give a positive answer to this question for protocols in which parties do not have private inputs, without incurring *any* cost to the round complexity or the resilience to errors. More details follow.

**Our Model.** In this work, our focus is on the synchronous, full information model. Namely, we consider a distributed model in which $n$ parties are trying to perform a predefined task. Each party is equipped with a source of private randomness and a unique ID. We assume the existence of a global counter which synchronizes parties in between rounds, but the parties are asynchronous within each round. The goal is to fulfill the task even in the presence of Byzantine faults. In the full information model no restrictions are made on the computational power of the faulty parties or the information available to them. Namely, the faulty parties may be infinitely powerful, and we do not assume the existence of private channels connecting pairs of honest parties.

We model faulty parties by a computationally unbounded adversary who controls a subset of parties and whose aim is to bias the output of the protocol. We assume that the adversary has access to the entire transcript of the protocol, and once a party is corrupted, the adversary gains complete control over the party and can send any messages on its behalf, and the messages can depend on the entire transcript so far. In addition, we allow our adversary to be "rushing", i.e., it can schedule the delivery of the messages within each round. We consider two classes of adversaries: *static* and *adaptive*. A static adversary is an adversary that chooses which parties to corrupt ahead of time, before the protocol begins. An adaptive adversary, on the other hand, is allowed to choose which parties to corrupt *adaptively* in the course of the protocol as a function of the messages seen so far.

---

[1] We note that often the term $\mathcal{CONGEST}$ is a short-hand writing for $\mathcal{CONGEST}(B)$, where $B$ is a bandwidth constraint. In many cases, the convention is to set $B$ to be bounded by $O(\log n)$, where $n$ is the number of parties. Here, we take a more liberal interpretation, which allows for messages of size bounded by $\mathsf{polylog}(n)$ (see e.g., [14]).

The focus of this work, is on protocols in which parties do not have private inputs. Many classical distributed tasks fall in this category, including collective coin-flipping, leader election, selection and more.

**A Concrete Motivation: Adaptively-Secure Coin-Flipping.** An important distributed task that was extensively studied in the full information model, is that of *collective coin-flipping*. In this problem, a set of $n$ parties use private randomness and are required to generate a common random bit. The goal of the parties is to jointly output a somewhat uniform bit even in the case that some of the parties are faulty and controlled by a static (resp. adaptive) adversary whose goal is to bias the output of the protocol in some direction.

This problem was first formulated and studied by Ben-Or and Linial [1]. In the case of static adversaries, collective coin-flipping is well studied and almost matching upper and lower bounds are known [2,13], whereas the case of adaptive adversaries has received much less attention. Ben-Or and Linial [1] showed that the majority protocol (in which each party sends a uniformly random bit and the output of the protocol is the majority of the bits sent) is resilient to $\Theta(\sqrt{n})$ adaptive corruptions. Furthermore, they conjectured that this protocol is optimal, that is, they conjectured that any coin-flipping protocol is resilient to at most $O(\sqrt{n})$ adaptive corruptions. Shortly afterwards, Lichtenstein, Linial and Saks [8] proved the conjecture for protocols in which each party is allowed to send only *one* bit. Very recently, Goldwasser, Kalai and Park [4] proved a different special-case of the aforementioned conjecture: any *symmetric* (many-bit) one-round collective coin-flipping protocol[2] is resilient to at most $\widetilde{O}(\sqrt{n})$ adaptive corruptions. Despite all this effort, proving a general lower bound, or constructing a collective coin-flipping protocol that is resilient to at least $\omega(\sqrt{n})$ adaptive corruptions, remains an intriguing open problem.

The result of [8] suggests that when seeking for a collective coin-flipping protocol that is resilient to at least $\omega(\sqrt{n})$ adaptive corruptions, to focus on protocols that consist of many communication rounds, or protocols in which parties send long messages. Our main result (Theorem 1) is that long messages are not needed in adaptively secure coin-flipping protocols with $\mathsf{poly}(n)$ rounds, and messages of length $\mathsf{polylog}(n)$ suffice. This is true more generally for leader election protocols, and for selection protocols where the output comes from a universe of size at most quasi-polynomial in $n$.

## 1.1 Our Results

Our main result is that "long" messages are not needed for distributed tasks in which parties do not have private inputs. More specifically, we show how to convert any $n$-party $d$-round protocol, where parties do not have private inputs, and whose output comes from a universe of size $M$, into a $d$-round protocol, with the same communication pattern, the same output distribution, the same

---

[2] A symmetric protocol $\Pi$ is one that is oblivious to the order of its inputs: namely, for any permutation $\pi\colon [n] \to [n]$ of the parties, it holds that $\Pi(r_1,\ldots,r_n) = \Pi(r_{\pi(1)},\ldots,r_{\pi(n)})$.

security guarantees, and where each message is of length $\mathsf{polylog}(M, n, d)$. Note that for many well studied distributed tasks, such as coin-flipping, leader election, and more, the output is from a universe of size at most $\mathsf{poly}(n)$, in which case our result says that if we consider $\mathsf{poly}(n)$-round protocols, then messages of length $\mathsf{polylog}(n)$ suffice.

**Our Results in More Detail.** Formally, we say that a protocol $\Pi$, in which parties do not have private inputs, is $(t, \delta, s)$-*statically (resp., adaptively) secure* if for any adversary $\mathcal{A}$ that *statically (resp., adaptively)* corrupts at most $t = t(n)$ parties, and any subset $S$ of the output universe such that $|S| = s$, it holds that

$$\Big| \Pr\left[\text{Output of } \mathcal{A}(\Pi) \in S\right] - \Pr\left[\text{Output of } \Pi \in S\right]\Big| \leq \delta,$$

where "Output of $\mathcal{A}(\Pi)$" means the output of the protocol when executed in the presence of the adversary $\mathcal{A}$, "Output of $\Pi$" means the output of the protocol when executed honestly, and the probabilities are taken over the internal randomness of the parties. In addition, we say that a protocol $\Pi$ *simulates* a protocol $\Pi'$ if the outcomes of the protocols are statistically close (when executed honestly) and their communication patterns are the same.

Our main result is a generic communication compression theorem which, roughly speaking, states that $(t, \delta, s)$-statically (resp., adaptively) secure protocols in the above model *do not* need "long" messages. Namely, we show that any secure protocol which sends arbitrary long messages can be simulated by a protocol which is almost as secure and sends short messages.

**Theorem 1 (Main theorem – informal).** *Any $(t, \delta, s)$-statically (resp., adaptively) secure d-round protocol that outputs m bits (or more generally, has an output universe of size $2^m$), can be simulated by a d-round $(t, \delta', s)$-statically (resp., adaptively) secure protocol, where $\delta' = \delta + \mathsf{negl}(n)$, and in which parties send random messages of length at most $m \cdot \mathsf{polylog}(n, d)$.*

Our results can also be seen as a transformation of protocols (in which parties do not have private inputs) in the $\mathcal{LOCAL}$ model to protocols in the $\mathcal{CONGEST}$ model, as discussed above. Our main theorem (Theorem 1) implies that any task, whose output consists of at most $\mathsf{polylog}(n)$ bits, and in which parties do not have private inputs, that can be solved in the $\mathcal{LOCAL}$ model with $d \leq \mathsf{poly}(n)$ rounds, can also be solved in the $\mathcal{CONGEST}$ model with $d$ rounds.

**Corollary 1.** *Any n-party $(t, \delta, s)$-statically (resp., adaptively) secure $\mathsf{poly}(n)$-round protocol that outputs $\mathsf{polylog}(n)$ bits in the $\mathcal{LOCAL}$ model, can be simulated by a $(t, \delta', s)$-statically (resp., adaptively) secure protocol in the $\mathcal{CONGEST}$ model, where $\delta' = \delta + \mathsf{negl}(n)$.*

We emphasize that our results holds for any underlying communication pattern including the broadcast channel or the message-passing model with any underlying communication graph.

Finally, we note that the transformation in Theorem 1 preserves the computational efficiency of the honest parties, but the resulting protocol is *non-uniform*, even if the protocol we started with is uniform. We elaborate on this in Section 1.3.

## 1.2 Related Work

The resource of communication is central in several fields of computer science. The field of communication complexity is devoted to the study of which problems can be solved with as little communication as possible. We refer to the book of Kushilevitz and Nisan [6] for an introduction to the field. In cryptography, minimizing communication has been the focus of several works in several contexts, including private information retrieval [7], random access memory machines [9], and more.

Interestingly, in the setting of distributed computing most of the work focuses on optimizing other resources such as round complexity, fault-tolerance, and the quality of the outcome. Very few works focus on optimizing the maximal message length being sent during the protocols. Moreover, most of the work in the literature focuses on *static* adversaries, and very few papers study distributed protocols with respect to *adaptive* adversaries. Our results hold in both settings.

Finally, we mention that separations between the $\mathcal{LOCAL}$ and $\mathcal{CONG}\text{-}\mathcal{EST}$ models are known for general tasks. For example, for network graphs of diameter $D = \Omega(\log n)$, computing the minimum spanning tree (MST) in the $\mathcal{LOCAL}$ model requires $\Theta(D)$ rounds, whereas in the $\mathcal{CONG}\mathcal{EST}$ model every distributed MST algorithm has round complexity $\Omega(D + \sqrt{n}/\log^2 n)$ [12].

## 1.3 Overview of Our Techniques

In this section we provide a high-level overview of our main ideas and techniques. First, we observe that one can assume, without loss of generality, that any protocol in which parties do not have private inputs, can be transformed into a public-coin protocol, in which honest parties' messages consist only of random bits. This fact is a folklore, and for the sake of completeness we include a proof sketch of it in Section 4.

Our main result is a generic transformation that converts any public-coin protocol, in which parties send arbitrarily long messages, into a protocol in which parties send messages of length $m \cdot \mathsf{polylog}(n \cdot d)$, where $m$ is the number of bits the protocol outputs, $n$ is the number of parties participating in the protocol, and $d$ is the number of communication rounds. The resulting protocol simulates the original protocol, has the same round complexity and satisfies the same security guarantees. Next, we elaborate on how this transformation works.

Suppose for simplicity that in our underlying protocol each message sent is of length $L = L(n)$ (and thus the messages come from a universe of size $2^L$), and think of $L$ as being very large. We convert any such protocol into a new protocol where each message consists of only $\ell$ bits, where think of $\ell$ as being significantly smaller than $L$. This is done by a priori choosing $2^\ell$ messages within the $2^L$-size universe, and restricting the parties to send messages from this restricted universe. Thus, now each message is of length $\ell$, which is supposedly significantly smaller than $L$. We note that a similar approach was taken in [10] in the context of transforming public randomness into private randomness in communication complexity, in [3] to reduce the number of random bits needed for property testers, and most recently in [4] to prove a lower bound for coin-flipping protocols in the setting of strong adaptive adversaries.

A priori, it may seem that such an approach is doomed to fail, since by restricting the honest parties to send messages from a small universe within the large $2^L$-size universe, we give the adversary a significant amount of information about future messages (especially in the multi-round case). Intuitively, the reason security is not compromised is that there are *many* possible restrictions, and it suffices to prove that a few (or only one) of these restrictions is secure. In other words, very loosely speaking, since we believe that most of the bits sent by honest parties are not "sensitive", we believe that it is safe to post some information about each message ahead of time.

For the sake of simplicity, in this overview we focus on static adversaries, and to simplify matters even further, we assume the adversary always corrupts the first $t$ parties. This simplified setting already captures the high-level intuition behind our security proof in Section 3.

Let us first consider one-round protocols. Note that for one-round protocols restricting the message space of honest parties does not affect security at all since we consider rushing adversaries, who may choose which messages to send based on the content of the messages sent by all honest parties in that round. Thus, reducing the length of messages is trivial in this case, assuming the set of parties that the adversary corrupts is predetermined. We mention that even in this extremely simplified setting, we need $\ell$ to be linear in $m$ for correctness ("simulation"), i.e., in order to ensure that the output is distributed correctly.

Next, consider a multi-round protocol $\Pi$. We denote by $H$ the restricted message space, i.e., $H$ is a subset of the message universe of size $2^\ell$, and denote by $\Pi_H$ the protocol $\Pi$, where the messages are restricted to the set $H$. Suppose that for any set $H$ there exists an adversary $\mathcal{A}^H$ that biases the outcome of $\Pi_H$, say towards 0.[3] We show that in this case there exists an adversary $\mathcal{A}$ in the underlying protocol that biases the outcome towards 0. Loosely speaking, at each step the adversary $\mathcal{A}$ will simulate one of the adversaries $\mathcal{A}^H$. More specifically, at any point in the underlying protocol, the adversary will randomly choose a set $H$ such that the transcript so far is consistent with a run of protocol $\Pi_H$ with the adversary $\mathcal{A}^H$, and will simulate the adversary $\mathcal{A}^H$. The main difficulty is to show that with high probability there exists such $H$ (i.e., the remaining set of consistent $H$'s is non-empty). This follows from a counting argument and basic probability analysis.

In our actual construction, we have a distinct set $H$ of size $2^\ell$ corresponding to *each* message of the protocol. Thus, if the underlying protocol $\Pi$ has $d$ rounds, and all the parties send a message in each round, then the resulting (short-message) protocol is associated with $d \cdot n$ sets $H_1, \ldots, H_{d \cdot n}$ each of size $2^\ell$, where the message of the $j^{\text{th}}$ party in the $i^{\text{th}}$ round is restricted to be in the set $H_{i,j}$. We denote all these sets by a matrix $H \in \left( \{0,1\}^L \right)^{d \cdot n \times 2^\ell}$, where the row $(i,j)$

---

[3] Of course, it may be that for different sets $H$, the adversary $\mathcal{A}^H$ biases the outcome to a different value. For simplicity we assume here that all the adversaries bias the outcome towards a fixed message, which we denote by 0.

of $H$ corresponds to the set of messages that the $j^{\text{th}}$ party can send during the $i^{\text{th}}$ round.

Note that there are $2^{L \cdot 2^\ell \cdot d \cdot n}$ such matrices. Each time an honest party sends a uniformly random message in $\Pi$ it reduces the set of consistent matrices by approximately a $2^L$-factor (with high probability). Any time the adversary $\mathcal{A}$ sends a message, it also reduces the set of consistent matrices $H$, since his message is consistent only with some of the adversaries $\mathcal{A}^H$, but again a probabilistic argument can be used to claim that it does not reduce the set of matrices by too much, and hence, with high probability there always exist matrices $H$ that are consistent with the transcript so far.

We briefly mention that the analysis in the case of adaptive corruptions follows the same outline presented above. One complication is that the mere decision of whether to corrupt or not reduces the set of consistent matrices $H$. Nevertheless, we argue that many consistent matrices remain.

We emphasize that the above is an over-simplification of our ideas, and the actual proof is more complex. We refer to Section 3 for more details.

## 2   Preliminaries

In this section we present the notation and basic definitions that are used in this work. For an integer $n \in \mathbb{N}$ we denote by $[n]$ the set $\{1, \ldots, n\}$. For a distribution $X$ we denote by $x \leftarrow X$ the process of sampling a value $x$ from the distribution $X$. Similarly, for a set $X$ we denote by $x \leftarrow X$ the process of sampling a value $x$ from the uniform distribution over $X$. Unless explicitly stated, we assume that the underlying probability distribution in our equations is the uniform distribution over the appropriate set. We let $\mathbf{U}_L$ denote the uniform distribution over $\{0,1\}^L$. We use $\log x$ to denote a logarithm in base 2.

A function $\mathsf{negl} \colon \mathbb{N} \to \mathbb{R}$ is said to be *negligible* if for every constant $c > 0$ there exists an integer $N_c$ such that $\mathsf{negl}(n) < n^{-c}$ for all $n > N_c$.

The *statistical distance* between two random variables $X$ and $Y$ over a finite domain $\Omega$ is defined as

$$\mathsf{SD}(X, Y) \triangleq \frac{1}{2} \sum_{\omega \in \Omega} |\Pr[X = \omega] - \Pr[Y = \omega]|. \tag{1}$$

### The Model

**The Communication Model and Distributed Tasks.** We consider the *synchronous model* where a set of $n$ parties $\mathsf{P}_1, \ldots, \mathsf{P}_n$ run protocols. Each protocol consists of *rounds* in which parties send messages. We assume the existence of a global counter which synchronizes parties in between rounds (but they are asynchronous within a round).

The focus of this work is on tasks where parties do not have any private inputs. Examples of such tasks are coin-flipping protocols, leader election protocols, Byzantine agreement protocols, etc.

Throughout this paper, we restrict ourselves to public-coin protocols.

**Definition 1 (Public-coin protocols).** *A protocol is* public-coin *if all honest parties' messages consist only of uniform random bits.*

Jumping ahead, we consider adversaries in the full information model. In Section 4 we argue that the restriction to public-coin protocols is without loss of generality since in the full information model any protocol (in which parties do not have private inputs) can be converted into a public-coin one, without increasing the round complexity and without degrading security (though this transformation may significantly increase the communication complexity).

**The Adversarial Model.** We consider the *full information model* where it is assumed the adversary is all powerful, and may see the entire transcript of the protocol. The most common adversarial model considered in the literature is the Byzantine model, where a bound $t = t(n) \leq n$ is specified, and the adversary is allowed to corrupt up to $t$ parties. The adversary can see the entire transcript, has full control over all the corrupted parties, and can send any messages on their behalf. Moreover, the adversary has control over the order of the messages sent within each round of the protocol.[4] We focus on the Byzantine model throughout this work.

Within this model, two types of adversaries were considered in the literature: *static* adversaries, who need to specify the parties they corrupt *before* the protocol begins, and *adaptive* adversaries, who can corrupt the parties *adaptively* based on the transcript so far. Our results hold for both types of adversaries. Throughout this work, we focus on the adaptive setting, since the proof is more complicated in this setting. In Subsection 3.1 we mention how to modify (and simplify) the proof for the static setting.

**Correctness and Security.** For any protocol $\Pi$ and any adversary $\mathcal{A}$, we denote by

$$\mathsf{out}(\mathcal{A}_\Pi \mid \mathsf{r}_1, \ldots, \mathsf{r}_n)$$

the output of the protocol $\Pi$ when executed with the adversary $\mathcal{A}$, and where each honest party $\mathsf{P}_i$ uses randomness $\mathsf{r}_i$.

Let $\Pi$ be a protocol whose output is a string in $\{0,1\}^m$ for some $m \in \mathbb{N}$. Loosely speaking, we say that an adversary is "successful" if he manages to bias the output of the protocol to his advantage. More specifically, we say that an adversary is "successful" if he chooses a predetermined subset $M \subseteq \{0,1\}^m$ of some size $s$, and succeeds in biasing the outcome towards the set $M$. To this end, for any set size $s$, we define

$$\mathsf{succ}_s(\mathcal{A}_\Pi) \overset{\mathrm{def}}{=} \max_{M \subseteq \{0,1\}^m \text{ s.t. } |M|=s} \mathsf{succ}_M(\mathcal{A}_\Pi)$$

$$\overset{\mathrm{def}}{=} \max_{M \subseteq \{0,1\}^m \text{ s.t. } |M|=s} \left( \Pr_{\mathsf{r}_1,\ldots,\mathsf{r}_n} [\mathsf{out}(\mathcal{A}_\Pi \mid \mathsf{r}_1, \ldots, \mathsf{r}_n) \in M] - \right.$$

$$\left. \Pr_{\mathsf{r}_1,\ldots,\mathsf{r}_n} [\mathsf{out}_\Pi(\mathsf{r}_1, \ldots, \mathsf{r}_n) \in M] \right),$$

---

[4] Such an adversary is often referred to as "rushing".

where $\mathsf{out}_\Pi(r_1, \ldots, r_n)$ denotes the outcome of the protocol $\Pi$ if all the parties are honest, and use randomness $r_1, \ldots, r_n$.

Intuitively, the reason we parameterize over the set size $s$ is that we may hope for different values of $\mathsf{succ}_M(\mathcal{A}_\Pi)$ for sets $M$ of different sizes, since for a large set $M$ it is often the case that $\Pr_{r_1, \ldots, r_n}[\mathsf{out}_\Pi(r_1, \ldots, r_n) \in M]$ is large, and hence $\mathsf{succ}_M(\mathcal{A}_\Pi)$ is inevitably small, whereas for small sets $M$ the value $\mathsf{succ}_M(\mathcal{A}_\Pi)$ may be large.

For example, for coin-flipping protocols (where $m = 1$ and the outcome is a uniformly random bit in the case that all parties are honest), often an adversary is considered successful if it biases the outcome to his preferred bit with probability close to 1, and hence an adversary is considered successful if $\mathsf{succ}_M(\mathcal{A}_\Pi) \geq \frac{1}{2} - o(1)$ for either $M = \{0\}$ or $M = \{1\}$, whereas for general selection protocols (where $m$ is a parameter) one often considers subsets $M \subseteq \{0,1\}^m$ of size $\gamma \cdot 2^m$ for some constant $\gamma > 0$, and an adversary is considered successful if there exists a constant $\delta > 0$ such that $\mathsf{succ}_M(\mathcal{A}_\Pi) \geq \delta$.

**Definition 2 (Security).** *Fix any constant $\delta > 0$, any $t = t(n) \leq n$, and any $n$-party protocol $\Pi$ whose output is an element in $\{0,1\}^m$. Fix any $s = s(m)$. We say that $\Pi$ is $(t, \delta, s)$-adaptively secure if for any adversary $\mathcal{A}$ that adaptively corrupts up to $t = t(n)$ parties, it holds that*

$$\mathsf{succ}_s(\mathcal{A}_\Pi) \leq \delta.$$

We note that this definition generalizes the standard security definition for coin-flipping protocols and selection protocols. We emphasize that our results are quite robust to the specific security definition that we consider, and we could have used alternative definitions as well. Intuitively, the reason is that we show how to transform any $d$-round protocol $\Pi$ into another $d$-round protocol with short messages, that simulates $\Pi$ (see Definition 3 below), where this transformation is *independent* of the security definition. Then, in order to prove that the resulting protocol is as secure as the original protocol $\Pi$, we show that if there exists an adversary for the short protocol that manages to break security according to some definition, then there exists an adversary for $\Pi$ that "simulates" the adversary of the short protocol and breaches security in the same way. (See Section 1.3 for more details, and Section 3 for the formal argument).

Finally, we mention that an analogous definition to Definition 2 can be given for static adversaries. Our results hold for the static definition as well.

**Definition 3 (Simulation).** *Let $\Pi$ be an $n$-party protocol with outputs in $\{0,1\}^m$. We say that an $n$-party protocol $\Pi'$ simulates $\Pi$ if*

$$\mathsf{SD}\left(\mathsf{out}_\Pi, \mathsf{out}_{\Pi'}\right) = \mathsf{negl}(n),$$

*where $\mathsf{out}_\Pi$ is a random variable that corresponds to the output of protocol $\Pi$ assuming all parties are honest, and $\mathsf{out}_{\Pi'}$ is a random variable that corresponds to the output of protocol $\Pi'$ assuming all parties are honest.*

# 3  Compressing Communication in Distributed Protocols

In this section we show how to transform any $n$-party $d$-round $t$-adaptively secure public-coin protocol, that outputs messages of length $m$ and sends messages of length $L$, into an $n$-party $d$-round $t$-adaptively secure public-coin protocol in which every party sends messages of length $\ell = m \cdot \mathsf{polylog}(n, d)$.

Throughout this section, we fix $\mu^*$ to be the negligible function defined by

$$\mu^* = \mu^*(n, d) = \left(\sqrt{\varepsilon} + 1 - (1 - \varepsilon)^{dn}\right) \cdot 2dn, \tag{2}$$

and where $\varepsilon = 2^{-\log^2(dn)}$.

**Theorem 2.** *Fix any $m = m(n)$, $d = d(n)$, $L = L(n)$, and any $n$-party $d$-round public-coin protocol $\Pi$ that outputs messages in $\{0, 1\}^m$ and in which all parties send messages of length $L = L(n)$. Then, for any constant $\delta > 0$, any $t = t(n) < n$, and any $s = s(m)$, if $\Pi$ is $(t, \delta, s)$-adaptively secure then there exists an $n$-party $d$-round $(t, \delta', s)$-adaptively secure public-coin protocol, that simulates $\Pi$, where all parties send messages of length $\ell = m \cdot \log^4(n \cdot d)$, and where $\delta' \leq \delta + \mu^*$ (and $\mu^* = \mu^*(n, d)$ is the negligible function defined in Equation (2)).*

*Proof.* Fix any $m = m(n)$, $d = d(n)$, $L = L(n)$, and any $n$-party $d$-round public-coin protocol $\Pi$ that outputs messages in $\{0, 1\}^m$ and in which all parties send messages of length $L = L(n)$. Fix any constant $\delta > 0$, any $t = t(n) < n$, and any $s = s(m)$ such that $\Pi$ is $(t, \delta, s)$-adaptively secure. We start by describing the construction of the (short message) protocol. Let

$$N = 2^{\ell} = 2^{m \cdot \log^4(n \cdot d)}. \tag{3}$$

Let

$$\mathcal{H} = \{H : [d \cdot n] \times \{0, 1\}^{\ell} \to \{0, 1\}^{L}\}$$

be the set all possible $[d \cdot n] \times \{0, 1\}^{\ell} \equiv [d \cdot n] \times [N]$ matrices, whose elements are from $\{0, 1\}^L$. Note that $|\mathcal{H}| = 2^{d \cdot n \cdot N \cdot L}$. We often interpret $H : [d \cdot n] \times \{0, 1\}^{\ell} \to \{0, 1\}^L$ as a function

$$H : [d] \times [n] \times \{0, 1\}^{\ell} \to \{0, 1\}^{L},$$

or as a matrix where each row is described by a pair from $[d] \times [n]$. We abuse notation and denote by

$$H(i, j, \mathsf{r}) \triangleq H((i - 1)n + j, \mathsf{r}).$$

As a convention, we denote by R a message from $\{0, 1\}^L$ and by r and a message from $\{0, 1\}^{\ell}$.

From now on, we assume for the sake of simplicity of notation, that in protocol $\Pi$, in each round, all the parties send a message. Recall that we also assume for the sake of simplicity (and without loss of generality) that $\Pi$ is a public-coin protocol (see Definition 1). For any $H \in \mathcal{H}$ we define a protocol $\Pi_H$ that simulates the execution of the protocol $\Pi$, as follows.

**The Protocol $\Pi_H$.** In the protocol $\Pi_H$, for every $i \in [d]$ and $j \in [n]$, in the $i^{\text{th}}$ round, party $\mathsf{P}_j$ sends a random string $\mathsf{r}_{i,j} \leftarrow \{0,1\}^\ell$. We denote the resulting transcript in round $i$ by

$$\mathsf{Trans}_{H,i} = (\mathsf{r}_{i,1}, \ldots, \mathsf{r}_{i,n}) \in \left(\{0,1\}^\ell\right)^n,$$

and denote the entire transcript by

$$\mathsf{Trans}_H = (\mathsf{Trans}_{H,1} \ldots, \mathsf{Trans}_{H,d}).$$

We abuse notation, and define for every round $i \in [d]$,

$$H(\mathsf{Trans}_{H,i}) = (H(i,1,\mathsf{r}_{i,1}), \ldots, H(i,n,\mathsf{r}_{i,n})).$$

Similarly, we define

$$H(\mathsf{Trans}_H) = (H(\mathsf{Trans}_{H,1}) \ldots, H(\mathsf{Trans}_{H,d})).$$

The outcome of protocol $\Pi_H$ with transcript $\mathsf{Trans}_H$ is defined to be the outcome of protocol $\Pi$ with transcript $H(\mathsf{Trans}_H)$.

It is easy to see that the round complexity of $\Pi_H$ (for every $H \in \mathcal{H}$) is the same as that of $\Pi$. Moreover, we note that with some complication in notation we could have also preserved the exact communication pattern (instead of assuming that in each round all parties send a message).

In order to prove Theorem 1 it suffices to prove the following two lemmas.

**Lemma 1.** *There exists a subset $\mathcal{H}_0 \subseteq \mathcal{H}$ of size $\frac{|\mathcal{H}|}{2}$, such that for every matrix $H \in \mathcal{H}_0$ it holds that $\Pi_H$ is $(t,\delta',s)$-adaptively secure for $\delta' = \delta + \mu^*$, where $\mu^*$ is the negligible function defined in Equation (2).*

**Lemma 2.** *There exists a negligible function $\mu = \mu(n,d)$ such that,*

$$\Pr_{H \leftarrow \mathcal{H}}[\mathsf{SD}(\mathsf{out}_{\Pi_H}, \mathsf{out}_\Pi) \leq \mu] \geq \frac{2}{3}.$$

Indeed, given Lemmas 1 and 2, we obtain that there exists an $H \in \mathcal{H}$ such that $\Pi_H$ is $(t,\delta',s)$-adaptively secure and it simulates $\Pi$.

The proofs of Lemmas 1 and 2 can be found in the full version [5].

## 3.1   Static Adversaries

We note that Theorem 2 holds also for static adversary. For completeness, we restate the theorem for static adversaries.

**Theorem 3.** *Fix any $m = m(n)$, $d = d(n)$, $L = L(n)$, and any $n$-party $d$-round public-coin protocol $\Pi$ that outputs messages in $\{0,1\}^m$ and in which all parties send messages of length $L = L(n)$. Then, for any constant $\delta > 0$, any $t = t(n) < n$, and any $s = s(m)$, if $\Pi$ is $(t, \delta, s)$-statically secure then there exists an $n$-party $d$-round $(t, \delta', s)$-statically secure public-coin protocol that simulates $\Pi$, where all parties send messages of length $\ell = m \cdot \log^4(n \cdot d)$, and where $\delta' \leq \delta + \mu^*$ (where $\mu^* = \mu^*(n, d)$ is the negligible function defined in Equation (2)).*

The proof of Theorem 3 is almost identical to the proof of Theorem 2. An outline is given in the full version [5].

# 4    Public-Coin Protocols

In this section we show how to convert any distributed protocol in which parties do not have private inputs into a public-coin protocol.

**Theorem 4.** *Every protocol $\Pi$ in which parties do not have private inputs can be transformed into a protocol $\Pi'$ which simulates $\Pi$ and such that the messages sent in $\Pi'$ are uniformly random. Moreover, the protocol $\Pi'$ preserves the security of $\Pi$ and its round complexity.*

The proof sketch of this theorem can be found in the full version [5].

**Acknowledgments.** We thank Nancy Lynch, Merav Parter and David Peleg for helpful remarks and pointers. The second author thanks his advisor Moni Naor for his continuous support.

# References

1. Ben-Or, M., Linial, N.: Collective coin flipping, robust voting schemes and minima of banzhaf values. In: 26th Annual Symposium on Foundations of Computer Science, FOCS, pp. 408–416 (1985)
2. Feige, U.: Noncryptographic selection protocols. In: 40th Annual Symposium on Foundations of Computer Science, FOCS, pp. 142–153 (1999)
3. Goldreich, O., Sheffet, O.: On the randomness complexity of property testing. Computational Complexity **19**(1), 99–133 (2010)
4. Goldwasser, S., Kalai, Y.T., Park, S.: Adaptively secure coin-flipping, revisited. In: Halldórsson, M.M., Iwama, K., Kobayashi, N., Speckmann, B. (eds.) ICALP 2015. LNCS, vol. 9135, pp. 663–674. Springer, Heidelberg (2015)
5. Kalai, Y.T., Komargodski, I.: Compressing communication in distributed protocols. In: Electronic Colloquium on Computational Complexity (ECCC), vol. 22, p. 92 (2015)
6. Kushilevitz, E., Nisan, N.: Communication complexity. Cambridge University Press (1997)
7. Kushilevitz, E., Ostrovsky, R.: Replication is NOT needed: SINGLE database, computationally-private information retrieval. In: 38th Annual Symposium on Foundations of Computer Science, FOCS, pp. 364–373 (1997)

8. Lichtenstein, D., Linial, N., Saks, M.E.: Some extremal problems arising form discrete control processes. Combinatorica **9**(3), 269–287 (1989)
9. Naor, M., Nissim, K.: Communication preserving protocols for secure function evaluation. In: 33rd Annual ACM Symposium on Theory of Computing, STOC, pp. 590–599 (2001)
10. Newman, I.: Private vs. common random bits in communication complexity. Inf. Process. Lett. **39**(2), 67–71 (1991)
11. Peleg, D.: Distributed Computing: A Locality-sensitive Approach. Society for Industrial and Applied Mathematics (2000)
12. Peleg, D., Rubinovich, V.: A near-tight lower bound on the time complexity of distributed minimum-weight spanning tree construction. SIAM J. Comput. **30**(5), 1427–1442 (2000)
13. Russell, A., Saks, M.E., Zuckerman, D.: Lower bounds for leader election and collective coin-flipping in the perfect information model. SIAM J. Comput. **31**(6), 1645–1662 (2002)
14. Sarma, A.D., Molla, A.R., Pandurangan, G., Upfal, E.: Fast distributed pagerank computation. Theor. Comput. Sci. **561**, 113–121 (2015)

# Privacy-Conscious Information Diffusion in Social Networks

George Giakkoupis[1], Rachid Guerraoui[2], Arnaud Jégou[1],
Anne-Marie Kermarrec[1], and Nupur Mittal[1]([✉])

[1] INRIA, Rennes, France
{george.giakkoupis,arnaud.jegou,anne-marie.kermarrec,
nupur.mittal}@inria.fr
[2] EPFL, Lausanne, Switzerland
rachid.guerraoui@eplf.ch

**Abstract.** We present RIPOSTE, a distributed algorithm for disseminating information (ideas, news, opinions, or trends) in a social network. RIPOSTE ensures that information spreads widely if and only if a large fraction of users find it interesting, and this is done in a "privacy-conscious" manner, namely without revealing the opinion of any individual user. Whenever an information item is received by a user, RIPOSTE decides to either forward the item to all the user's neighbors, or not to forward it to anyone. The decision is randomized and is based on the user's (private) opinion on the item, as well as on an upper bound $s$ on the number of user's neighbors that have not received the item yet. In short, if the user likes the item, RIPOSTE forwards it with probability slightly larger than $1/s$, and if not, the item is forwarded with probability slightly smaller than $1/s$. Using a comparison to branching processes, we show for a general family of random directed graphs with arbitrary out-degree sequences, that if the information item appeals to a sufficiently large (constant) fraction of users, then the item spreads to a constant fraction of the network; while if fewer users like it, the dissemination process dies out quickly. In addition, we provide extensive experimental evaluation of RIPOSTE on topologies taken from online social networks, including Twitter and Facebook.

## 1 Introduction

Social networking websites have become an important medium for communicating and disseminating news, ideas, political opinions, trends, and behaviors. Such online networks typically provide a *reposting* functionality, e.g., *sharing* in Facebook or *retweeting* in Twitter, which allows users to share other's posts with their own friends and followers. As information is reposted from user to user, large cascades of reposts can develop, and an information item can potentially reach a large number of people, much larger than the number of users exposed to the information initially (e.g., the users who witness a news event, or learned about it from some local media). Since people tend to propagate

© Springer-Verlag Berlin Heidelberg 2015
Y. Moses (Ed.): DISC 2015, LNCS 9363, pp. 480–496, 2015.
DOI: 10.1007/978-3-662-48653-5_32

information which they find interesting and worth sharing (rather than random content) [21], an information item may spread widely only if sufficiently many users find it interesting. Ideally, the opposite direction should also hold: content that a sufficiently large fraction of users would find interesting and would propagate (if they knew about it), should be likely to spread widely. This is, however, not always the case.

In countries with authoritarian regimes, users may not propagate anti-government ideas for the fear of being prosecuted. There are in fact several examples of political activists (and others) that have been convicted for posting or just reposting anti-government opinions on social media [24, 26]. But even in democratic regimes, users may refrain from openly supporting their opinion on certain sensitive issues, from politics and religion to sexuality and criminal activity. For example, a user may not propagate a post supporting recreational drug use for the fear that it may have a negative impact on his career—as it is a common practice of employers to use social media for screening prospective employees [14]. Or more generally, users may refrain from reposting a (political or other) opinion when they believe it is not widely shared by their cycle—a well known principle in sociology known as the "spiral of silence" [23]. In all these cases, the dissemination of an idea in the social network is impeded by privacy considerations; even if many users support the idea, they may choose not to contribute to its propagation because they do not wish to reveal their own opinion (as reposting the idea would suggest the user is in favor of it).

**Our Contribution: Privacy-Conscious Diffusion.** We investigate a dissemination algorithm that has, roughly speaking, the following properties: (1) information that a sufficiently large fraction of the population finds interesting is likely to spread widely; (2) information that not sufficiently many people find interesting does not spread far beyond the set of users exposed to it initially; and (3) by observing the spreading process (in particular, the users' reposts), one cannot determine (with sufficient confidence) the opinion of any single user on the information that is disseminated.

More specifically, we propose the following simple, local dissemination algorithm, which we call RIPOSTE. Let $G$ denote the (directed) graph modeling the social network, and $n$ be the total number of users, and suppose that some (small) initial set of users learn an information item $t$. For each user $u$ that learns $t$, RIPOSTE decides to either repost $t$, to all $u$'s outgoing neighbors in $G$, or to not repost $t$, to anyone. The decision is randomized and depends on the user's (private) opinion on the information, and the number of the user's neighbors that have not received the information yet. Precisely, if $u$ likes $t$, then $t$ is reposted with probability $\lambda/s_u$, and if $u$ does not like $t$, then $t$ is reposted with a (smaller) probability $\delta/s_u$, where $0 < \delta < 1 < \lambda$ are global parameters of the dissemination mechanism, and $s_u$ is an *upper bound* on the number of $u$'s outgoing neighbors that have not received $t$ yet. If the algorithm cannot have access to information about whether $u$'s neighbors already know the information, then the *total* number of $u$'s outgoing neighbors can be used as the upper bound $s_u$.[1]

We argue that RIPOSTE achieves the property of *plausible deniability*: A user $u$ can claim that, with reasonable probability, the act of reposting (or not) some information, does not reflect $u$'s truthful opinion on the information, and is a result of the randomness in the decision mechanism. Intuitively, the closer the parameters $\lambda$ and $\delta$ are to each other, the better the privacy. In the extreme case of $\lambda = \delta$, we have perfect privacy, but then the dissemination is independent of $u$'s opinion (and thus of how interesting the information is). In the other extreme, if $\lambda$ is the maximum degree and $\delta = 0$ (i.e., the user reposts the information iff it likes it), the act of reposting (or not) the information reveals with certainty $u$'s opinion. We formally quantify the privacy properties of RIPOSTE in terms of $\epsilon$-*differential privacy*. In particular, we argue that RIPOSTE is $\ln(\lambda/\delta)$-differentially private.

For the dissemination of information, we prove the following threshold behavior. Suppose that each user likes a given item $t$ with probability $p_t$, independently of the other users ($p_t$ is the same for all users and depends only on $t$). Thus $p_t$ is a measure of how interesting item $t$ is, and is equal to the expected fraction of users that like $t$. Let $S$ denote the set of users who receive item $t$ initially (e.g., these users receive the information from a news channel). We show that if $p_t < p^*$, for $p^* = (1-\delta)/(\lambda-\delta)$, then the expected number of users that learn the information is $O(|S|)$, i.e., at most a constant factor larger than the users exposed to the information initially. This is true for any graph $G$. On the other hand, we show that the following statement holds for a $G$ from a family of random directed graphs with arbitrary out-degree distribution [6]. (Such a graph could, for example, model the Twitter network). If $p_t > p^*$, then for a random initial set $S$, information $t$ spreads to $\Theta(n)$ users (i.e., at least some constant fraction of the network), with probability $1 - e^{\Omega(|S|/d)}$, where $d$ denotes the average degree of $G$. In particular, this result says that information spreads to $\Theta(n)$ users with constant probability when $|S|$ is close to the average degree, and with high probability if $|S|$ is $\log n$ times larger than the average degree. The analysis draws from the theory of branching processes [3], and the intuition is simple: Basic computations yield that the expected number of users that a given user passes the information to, is less than 1 when $p_t < p^*$, and greater than 1 if $p_t > p^*$. The threshold phenomenon we observe follows then from a similar phenomenon in branching processes. We note that the result for $p_t > p^*$ does not hold for arbitrary graphs. However, we expect that it should hold for many graph families, of sufficiently high *expansion*.

We complement our analysis with extensive experimental results. We use a complete snapshot of the Twitter graph of roughly 40 million users from 2009, and smaller samples from other social networks, including Facebook and LiveJournal. The experiments demonstrate clearly the predicted threshold phenomenon, with

---

[1] RIPOSTE can be viewed as a set of distributed pieces of software running at each user's machine connected to the social network. It is not the user who has the control of whether the item will be eventually reposted or not but this piece of software. It solicits the user's opinion on the item, and then flips a coin to determine whether the information will be reposted.

very limited spread below the $p^*$ threshold, and substantial spread above $p^*$. The latter suggests that our result for $p_t > p^*$ should qualitatively hold for a larger family of networks than the stylized model analysed formally. We also experiment with non-uniform distributions of user opinions, where users closer to the source users are more likely to like the information, obtaining qualitatively similar results. Experiments suggest that reasonable values for RIPOSTE's parameters in the networks considered are $\delta = 0.75$ and $\lambda = 3$. For these values, the plausible deniability achieved ensures that, for example, if the prior probability for a user to like the information is 0.01 or 0.1, and the user reposts the information, then the probability increases to 0.04 and 0.3 respectively (see Sect. 2.1 for details).

We view the results of this paper as potentially useful for addressing some of the increasing concerns about users' privacy in social networking services. In particular, we think that RIPOSTE could be of interest as a tool for spreading information and petitions in Internet-based activism, a topic of considerable current interest [10,12]. More generally, it is a tool that could be used for widespread dissemination of sensitive information, which people would care to be exposed to, but are not willing to disseminate themselves for the fear of being charged, stigmatized, or isolated. We believe that such a tool could be incorporated in existing social network services. Also our technique could find applications to other distributed problems, such as distributed polling algorithms.

**Related Work.** RIPOSTE uses a technique that is conceptually similar to the *randomized response technique (RRT)*. RRT was first introduced in 1965 [27] for survey interviews, to increase the validity of responses to sensitive questions. Roughly, the idea is to tell responder to *lie* with some fixed, predetermined, probability $p_{lie}$ (e.g., roll a die and lie whenever the die shows one or two, in which case $p_{lie} = 1/3$).[2] Since $p_{lie}$ is known to the interviewer, the distribution of responders' truthful answer can be easily estimated, and thus, accurate estimations of aggregate results can be extracted—but an individual's answer is always plausibly deniable. (See [5] for other variations of RRT, and [2] for a variant using cryptography to guarantee that the responder follows the RRT.) In our diffusion mechanism, the same probability of reposting could be achieved using the following RRT-like approach: User $u$ is asked if she likes the post, but is instructed to lie with probability $p_{lie} = \delta/(\delta + \lambda)$; and if the answer is 'yes' then the post is reposted with probability $(\delta + \lambda)/s_u$.

We are not aware of other works that use randomized responses in a way similar to ours: to achieve dissemination that reflects user's aggregate opinion, while preserving the privacy of individual users' opinion. In a more standard use of RRT, Quercia et al. [25] proposed a method to aggregate location data of mobile phone users by having each user report several erroneous locations in addition to the correct one. Recently, Erlingsson et al. [11] presented an RRT-based algorithm for crowdsourcing of population statistics from end-user client software, deployed on Google's Chrome Web browser.

---

[2] The closer is $p_{lie}$ to $1/2$ the better the privacy.

Another mechanism provided by social networking services, besides reposting, which has the potential to make interesting posts widely visible is that of *liking*. This mechanism has similar privacy issues as reposting. In [1], Alves et al. proposed a scheme to anonymize user's likes, which keeps the actual like count of a post without revealing the names of the users who like it. Unlike our approach, the scheme employs cryptographic techniques to achieve privacy, and requires a centralized server (but the server does not know the users' opinion).

We have said that our diffusion scheme could provide a tool for Internet-based activism [10,12]. The use of pseudonyms, combined with methods for hiding the user's IP, has also been a common practice used by activists to hide their identity while spreading sensitive information [29]. Our scheme protects the users who contribute to the dissemination of information, but not the sources of the information. This is not a problem in some settings, for example, if we assume that anti-government information originates from a news channel (say, WikiLeaks) located in a different country. If this is not the case, then pseudonyms could be used to protect the privacy of the source.

We measure the privacy properties of our diffusion scheme in terms of *differential privacy* [8,9]. Differential privacy was introduced in the context of privacy-preserving analysis of statistical databases. Roughly speaking, differential privacy ensures that (almost, and quantifiably) no risk is incurred by joining a statistical database. More relevant to our setting is the *local model* of differential privacy [17], also known as *fully distributed model*. In this model, there is no central database administrator of private data; each individual maintains their own data element (a database of size 1), and answers questions about it only in a differentially private manner. The local privacy model was first introduced in the context of learning, where it was shown that private learning in the local model is equivalent to non-private learning in the statistical query model [15,17].

## 2    The Diffusion Algorithm

In this section, we describe our diffusion mechanism for disseminating information in an online social network, and provide an analysis of its properties.

We model the social network as a directed graph $G = (V, E)$ with $|V| = n$ nodes. Each node $u \in V$ represents a user (from now on we will use the terms node and user interchangeably), and a directed edge from node $u$ to $v$ denotes that user $u$ can send information to $v$. For example, for the case of the Twitter social network, an edge $(u, v) \in E$ in the underlying graph $G$ denotes that user $v$ is "following" $u$. Borrowing Twitter's parlance, in this paper, we will say that $v$ is a *follower* of $u$ if $(u, v) \in E$. The number of $u$'s followers is thus the same as $u$'s out-degree.

We assume that initially a set of users $S \subseteq V$ learns an information item (from a source external to the network). From each user that learns the information, this information can be *reposted* to all its followers. (So, information can either be sent to all followers of the user, or to none.) We propose a randomized distributed algorithm, running locally at each user (i.e., at the user's device connected to the social network service), which decides whether or not to repost the received information; we call this algorithm RIPOSTE.

RIPOSTE takes as input the opinion of the user on the information item, i.e., if the user *likes* or *does not like* the information, and the algorithm's effect is to either repost the information or not. RIPOSTE' decision depends on: (1) the user's opinion, (2) an upper bound on the number of the user's followers that have not received the information yet, and (3) two global parameters of the protocol (the same for all users), denoted $\delta$ and $\lambda$; both parameters are non-negative real numbers satisfying $\delta < 1$ and $\lambda > 1$. As explained later, these parameters control the privacy properties of the protocol, and influence the dissemination.

**Riposte Algorithm:** For each new information item received by user $u$, if $u$ has $k$ followers and $s \leq k$ is an estimate bounding from above the number of $u$'s followers that have not received the item yet, then:
if $u$ likes the item, the algorithm reposts the item with probability

$$r_{\text{like}}(s) := \begin{cases} \lambda/s, & \text{if } s \geq \lambda + \delta, \\ 1 - \frac{\delta(s-\delta)}{\lambda s}, & \text{if } 0 < s < \lambda + \delta; \end{cases}$$

if $u$ does not like the item, it is reposted with probability $r_{\text{dis}}(s) := \delta/s$ (if $s > 0$).

It is easy to verify that $r_{\text{dis}}(s) \leq r_{\text{like}}(s)$, for all $s$, i.e., the probability of reposting is larger when $u$ likes the item. Also, the closer are $\delta$ and $\lambda$ to each other, the closer are the two probabilities $r_{\text{dis}}$ and $r_{\text{like}}$.

The definition of $r_{\text{like}}(s)$ for the case of $s < \lambda + \delta$ will be justified when we analyse the privacy of the protocol. Until then we can assume the following simpler definition for *all* $s > 0$: $r_{\text{like}}(s) := \min\{\lambda/s, 1\}$.

RIPOSTE needs to know an upper bound on the number of the user's followers who have not yet received the item. This information is readily available in some existing social network services, including Twitter, where the default setting is that a user can access the list of items each of its followers has received. If this information is not available, then the total number of followers $k$ of the user can be used as the upper bound $s$. For the analysis and the experimental evaluation, we will make use also of that special variant of RIPOSTE, where $s = k$.

**DB-Riposte Algorithm (Degree-Based-Riposte):** This algorithm is a special instance of RIPOSTE, where the total number of followers $k$ of user $u$ is used as the upper bound $s$ on the number of $u$'s followers who have not already received the information.

An attractive analytical property of DB-RIPOSTE is that the outcome of the dissemination does not depend on the order in which the algorithm is executed at different users, unlike in the general RIPOSTE algorithm. For our analysis of RIPOSTE we assume that the order can be arbitrary.

We stress that RIPOSTE does not reveal any information on the value of its input (the user's private opinion), other than the statistical information inferred by the outcome of the algorithm, to repost or not. Also, the user cannot *prevent* the algorithm from reposting the information, even if she does not like the information. In particular, if the user refuses to answer whether she likes an item or not, this is interpreted as a negative answer by the algorithm (the user has an incentive to answer positively if she likes the item, as this would potentially result in larger spread).

We now analyze the properties of RIPOSTE, regarding privacy and the spread of information.

## 2.1  Privacy

RIPOSTE achieves the property of *plausible deniability*: A user can claim that, with reasonable probability, the act of reposting (or not) an information, does not reflect the user's truthful opinion on the information, and is a result of the randomness in the algorithm.

The standard notion used to quantify plausible deniability is that of *differential privacy* [9]. We recall now the definition of an $\varepsilon$-differentially private algorithm. Let $A$ be a randomized algorithm with input a collection of values, $x_1, \ldots, x_m$, that returns a value from some domain $R$. Since the algorithm is randomized, for a fixed input $x_1, \ldots, x_m$, its output $A(x_1, \ldots, x_m)$ is a random variable, with some distribution over $R$. Suppose that the input to $A$ is not known to us (is private), and by observing the output of $A$ we want to find out the value of some of the inputs. More generally, we may have some information about the input, i.e., a distribution over the possible combinations of input values, and we want, by observing $A$'s output, to improve this information, i.e., obtain a distribution closer to the true input values. We can quantify the extent to which this is possible in terms of $\varepsilon$-differential privacy: algorithm $A$ is $\varepsilon$-differentially private if changing exactly one of it inputs $x_1, \ldots, x_m$ changes the distribution of the output by at most an $e^\varepsilon$ factor.

**Definition 1 ($\varepsilon$-differential privacy).** *A randomized algorithm $A$ with inputs $x_1, \ldots, x_m$ from some finite domain and output $A(x_1, \ldots, x_m)$ on some domain $R$, is $\varepsilon$-differentially private if for any two sets of inputs $x_1, \ldots, x_m$ and $x'_1, \ldots, x'_m$ that differ in exactly one value, and for any set of outputs $Q \subseteq R$,*

$$\Pr\left(A(x_1, \ldots, x_m) \in Q\right) \le e^\varepsilon \cdot \Pr\left(A(x'_1, \ldots x'_m) \in Q\right).$$

In our setting, algorithm $A$ is RIPOSTE, which takes a single binary input: the opinion of the user, and has a binary output: repost or not-repost.

**Theorem 2.** RIPOSTE *is $\varepsilon$-differentially private for $\varepsilon = \ln(\lambda/\delta)$.*

The proof is a straightforward application of the definitions, and can be found in the full version of the paper [13].

Theorem 2 implies that the closer is the ratio $\lambda/\delta$ to 1, the better the achieved privacy. In particular, if $\delta = \lambda$ we have perfect privacy, as the probability of reposting does not depend on the user's opinion—but this is not desirable from a dissemination point of view.

We discuss now what Theorem 2 implies about the information one can gain for the opinion of a user on some information item it receives, by observing whether or not the item was reposted from that user.

Let $q$ be the (prior) probability that the user likes the information, capturing the knowledge of an observer about the user's opinion *before* the observer sees whether or not this information is reposted from the user. Then from Theorem 2 it follows that the probability $\hat{q}$ with which the observer believes that the user likes the information, after the observer learns whether or not there was a repost, satisfies the inequalities

$$\frac{q}{q + (1-q)(\lambda/\delta)} \leq \hat{q} \leq \frac{q}{q + (1-q)(\delta/\lambda)}. \tag{1}$$

(The proof is by Bayes' Rule.) For the typical parameter values $\delta = 3/4$ and $\lambda = 3$ we use later in the experimental evaluation, Ineq. (1) yield, e.g., that if $q = 0.01$ then $0.0025 < \hat{q} < 0.039$; if $q = 0.1$ then $0.027 < \hat{q} < 0.31$; and if $q = 0.9$ then $0.69 < \hat{q} < 0.97$.

Above we have considered the amount of information leaked when observing the cascade of a single information item. However, if one can observe the cascades of a *sufficiently large* number of *sufficiently similar* items, possibly over a long period, then more information can potentially be leaked about the opinion of a user on this type of information. We leave as a future work the study of such correlation attacks.

## 2.2  Dissemination

In terms of dissemination, the goal of RIPOSTE is that the fraction of users receiving an information item should reflect the users' overall opinion on the item. In particular, information that a large fraction of users like should, typically, be received by a lot of users, while less interesting information should not be received by many users. In the following, we quantify the notions of interesting/not-interesting information by defining a *popularity* threshold, and we provide bounds on the spread of *popular* items (with popularity above this threshold) and *unpopular* items (with popularity below the threshold).

For the analysis, we make the assumption that all users are equally likely to like a given item, independently of their position in the network and the opinion of other users.

**Definition 3 (Uniform opinion model & popularity).** *Each item $t$ is associated with a probability $p_t$, called the* popularity *of $t$, and for each user $u$, the probability that $u$ likes $t$ is equal to $p_t$ and independent of the other users' opinion about $t$.*

We note that popularity $p_t$ is also equal to the expected fraction of users that like $t$. An item's popularity is not known in advance by the diffusion protocol.

We define the popularity threshold $p^*$ as follows. Suppose that user $u$ receives an item with popularity $p$. Since $u$ has probability $p$ of liking the item in the uniform model, the probability that RIPOSTE reposts the item, if $s > 0$, is $p \cdot r_{\text{like}}(s) + (1-p) \cdot r_{\text{dis}}(s)$. If $s \geq \lambda + \delta$, this probability is $p \cdot (\lambda/s) + (1-p) \cdot (\delta/s)$. Moreover, if $s$ is the exact number of $u$'s followers that have not received the item yet, then the expected number of new users that learn the item from $u$ is $s$ times that, i.e., $p\lambda + (1-p)\delta$. The popularity threshold $p^*$ is then the probability $p$ for which this expectation is equal to 1.

**Definition 4 (Popular/Unpopular items).** *For given $\lambda$ and $\delta$, we define the popularity threshold $p^* := \frac{1-\delta}{\lambda-\delta}$, and we call an information item $t$ popular if its popularity is $p_t > p^*$, and unpopular if $p_t < p^*$.*[3]

Next we establish an upper bound on the spread of unpopular items, and a lower bound on the spread of popular items.

We first argue that the expected number of users who receive a given unpopular item is by at most a constant factor larger that the number of user $|S|$ who receive the item initially (e.g., from a source external to the network). The constant factor depends on the popularity of the item and parameters $\delta$ and $\lambda$. This bound holds for any network $G$, assuming the uniform opinion model. Recall that an item is unpopular if its popularity is smaller than $p^* = (1-\delta)/(\lambda-\delta)$.

**Theorem 5 (Spread of unpopular items).** *For any $G$, and under the uniform opinion model, RIPOSTE guarantees that an item with popularity $p < p^*$ starting from any set $S$ of users is received by an expected total number of at most $|S|/\beta$ users, where $\beta = (p^* - p)(\lambda - \delta)$.*

The proof of Theorem 5, which can be found in the full version of the paper [13], is based on the fact that the expected number of new users that learn the item from a given user that knows the item is smaller than one.

Observe that as $p$ approaches the popularity threshold $p^*$, factor $\beta$ decreases, and thus the bound on the expected spread increases. Further, substituting the definition of $p^*$ gives $\beta = 1 - \delta - p(\lambda - \delta)$, which implies that increasing either $\lambda$ or $\delta$ increases the expected spread. These observations are consistent with the intuition.

Next we consider the spread of popular items. We focus on a particular family of random directed graphs which is convenient for our analysis, but is also a reasonable model of some social network graphs, such as the Twitter graph, characterized by large variation in the nodes' out-degree (i.e., the number of followers) and small variation in the nodes' in-degree. This model is a simplification of one considered in [6], and has a single parameter, a distribution $\phi$ on the nodes' out-degree.

---

[3] For the asymptotic bounds we show later, we assume for a popular item $t$ that $p_t > p^* + \epsilon$, and for an unpopular item $t$ that $p_t < p^* - \epsilon$, for some arbitrary small constant $\epsilon > 0$.

**Definition 6 (Random graph $G_\phi$).** *For any probability distribution $\phi$ on the set $\{0,\ldots,n-1\}$, $G_\phi$ is an $n$-node random directed graph such that the out-degrees of nodes are independent random variables with the same distribution $\phi$, and for each node $u$, if $u$ has out-degree $k$, then the set of $u$'s outgoing neighbors is a uniformly random set among all $k$-sets of nodes not containing $u$.*

We establish a lower bound on the probability of a popular item to be received by a constant fraction of users in $G_\phi$, for an arbitrary distribution $\phi$ (under a mild constraint on the min out-degree). The above probability and the fraction size grow respectively with the number $\sigma = |S|$ of source nodes, and the popularity $p$ of the item. In particular, the probability converges to 1 for $\sigma$ larger than the average node degree $\mu$.

**Theorem 7 (Spread of popular items).** *Let $\phi$ be any probability distribution on the set $\{\lceil \lambda + \delta \rceil,\ldots,n-1\}$, let $\epsilon,\epsilon' > 0$ be arbitrary small constants, and $1 \leq \sigma \leq n$ be an integer. Any information item with popularity $p \geq p^* + \epsilon$, that starts from a random initial set of $\sigma$ nodes and spreads in $G_\phi$ using RIPOSTE, is received by at least $(1 - \epsilon') \cdot \frac{\beta n}{\beta+1}$ users, with probability at least $1 - e^{-\Omega(\sigma/\mu)}$, where $\beta = (p - p^*)(\lambda - \delta)$ and $\mu$ is the mean of distribution $\phi$.*

Observe that the same constant $\beta = |p - p^*| \cdot (\lambda - \delta)$ appears in both Theorems 5 and 7. Unlike the bound of Theorem 5, the bound of $(1 - \epsilon') \cdot \frac{\beta n}{\beta+1}$ in Theorem 7 is independent of the number $\sigma = |S|$ of source nodes; substituting the definitions of $\beta$ and $p^*$, yields $\frac{\beta}{\beta+1} = 1 - \frac{1}{p\lambda+(1-p)\delta}$, thus the bound above increases when any of $\lambda$, $\delta$, or $p$ increases. The independence from $\sigma$ is intuitively justified, because as long as the item reaches a "critical mass" of users, it will almost surely spread to a constant fraction of the network. However, the probability with which such a critical mass will be reached does depend on $\sigma$. For $\sigma$ close to the average degree $\mu$, this probability is at least a constant, and quickly converges to 1 as $\sigma/\mu$ increases above 1.

The proof of Theorem 7 uses a coupling between the dissemination process and an appropriate branching process, to show that the probability of the event we are interested in, that at least a certain fraction of users receive the item, is lower-bounded by the survival probability of the branching process. Then we bound this survival probability using a basic result for branching processes.

**Proof of Theorem 7.** It suffices to prove the claim for DB-RIPOSTE. The reasons is that the reposting probabilities $r_{\text{like}}(s)$ and $r_{\text{dis}}(s)$ are minimized when $s$ equals the number $k$ of the user's followers, and thus a standard coupling argument shows that the number of users that receive the item if DB-RIPOSTE is used is dominated stochastically by the same quantity when RIPOSTE is used.

We couple the diffusion process in $G_\phi$ with an appropriate branching process. Recall that a (Galton-Watson) branching process is a random process starting with one or more individuals, and in each step of the process a single individual produces zero of more offsprings and then dies. The number of offsprings of an individual follows a fixed probability distribution, the same for all individuals.

The process either finishes after a finite number of steps, when no individuals are left, or continues forever. The probabilities of these two complementary events are called *extinction* and *survival probability*, respectively.

First we compute the distribution of the number of new users that learn the item from a user $u$, at a point in time when *fewer than $\ell$ users in total have received the item*—we will fix the value of $\ell$ later. The probability that $u$ has exactly $i$ followers is $\phi(i)$, for $i \in \{\lceil \lambda + \delta \rceil, \ldots, n - 1\}$ (and 0 for other $i$). Given that $u$ has $i$ followers, the probability that DB-RIPOSTE reposts the item from $u$ is $(p\lambda + (1 - p)\delta)/i = (\beta + 1)/i$. Further, by the principle of deferred decision, we can assume that if the item is reposted from $u$, only then are $u$'s $i$ followers chosen. We can also assume that they are chosen sequentially, one after the other, and the item is sent to a follower before the next follower is chosen (this does not change the overall outcome of the dissemination). Then the probability that the $j$-th follower of $u$ has not already received the item is at least $1 - \ell/n$, provided that at most $\ell$ users already know the item (including the first $j - 1$ followers of $u$).

Consider now the branching process in which $\sigma$ individuals exist initially, and the number $X$ of offsprings of an individual is determined as follows. First an integer $i$ is drawn from distribution $\phi$; then with probability $1 - (\beta + 1)/i$ we have $X = 0$ offspring, and with the remaining probability, $(\beta + 1)/i$, we draw $X$'s value from the binomial distribution $B(i, q)$, for $q := 1 - \ell/n$ (this is the distribution of the number of successes among $i$ independent identical trials with success probability $q$).

We use a simple coupling of the diffusion process with the branching process above, until the point when $\ell$ users have received the item or the dissemination has finished (whichever occurs first). We assume that the diffusion process evolves in steps, and each step involves the execution of the DB-RIPOSTE algorithm at a single node. Similarly a step in the branching process is that a single individual reproduces and then dies. Let $N_t$ denote the number of new users that learn the item in step $t$ of the diffusion process, and let $X_t$ be the number of offsprings born in step $t$ of the branching process. From our discussion above on the distribution of $N_t$ and from the definition of the distribution of $X_t \sim X$, it follows that we can couple $N_t$ and $X_t$ such that $N_t \geq X_t$ if no more than $\ell$ users in total have received the item in the first $t$ steps.

From this coupling, it is immediate that the probability at least $\ell$ users receive the item in total, is lower-bounded by the probability that the total progeny of the branching process (i.e., the total number of individuals that ever existed) is at least $\ell$. Further, the latter probability is lower bounded by the *survival probability* of the branching process; we denote this survival probability by $\zeta_\sigma$. Thus to prove the theorem it suffices to show

$$\zeta_\sigma = 1 - e^{-\Omega(\sigma/\mu)},$$

for $\ell := (1 - \epsilon') \cdot \beta n/(\beta + 1)$. The remainder of the proof is devoted to that.

By the definition of the branching process, the expected number of offsprings of an individual is

$$\mathbf{E}[X] = \sum_i \phi(i) \cdot \frac{\beta + 1}{i} \cdot \mathbf{E}[B(i, q)]$$

$$= \sum_i \phi(i) \cdot \frac{\beta + 1}{i} \cdot iq = \sum_i \phi(i) \cdot (\beta + 1) \cdot q = (\beta + 1) \cdot q.$$

We observe that $\mathbf{E}[X] > 1$, as

$$(\beta + 1) \cdot q = (\beta + 1) \cdot \left(1 - \frac{(1 - \epsilon')\beta}{\beta + 1}\right) = 1 + \epsilon'\beta. \tag{2}$$

Further,

$$\mathbf{E}[X^2] = \sum_i \phi(i) \cdot \frac{\beta + 1}{i} \cdot \mathbf{E}[(B(i, q))^2] = \sum_i \phi(i) \cdot \frac{\beta + 1}{i} \cdot (i^2 q^2 + iq(1 - q))$$

$$= \sum_i \phi(i) \cdot (\beta + 1) \cdot (iq^2 + q(1 - q)) = (\beta + 1) \cdot (\mu q^2 + q(1 - q)),$$

where $\mu = \sum_i \phi(i) \cdot i$ is the mean of $\phi$. We will use the following standard lower bound on the survival probability $\zeta_1$, when there is just one individual initially (see, e.g., [16, Sect. 5.6.1]),

$$\zeta_1 \geq \frac{2(\mathbf{E}[X] - 1)}{\mathbf{E}[X^2] - \mathbf{E}[X]}.$$

Substituting the values for $\mathbf{E}[X]$ and $\mathbf{E}[X^2]$ computed above yields

$$\zeta_1 \geq \frac{2(q(\beta + 1) - 1)}{(\beta + 1)(\mu q^2 + q(1 - q)) - q(\beta + 1)} = \frac{2(q(\beta + 1) - 1)}{q^2(\beta + 1)(\mu - 1)}$$

$$= \frac{2(q(\beta + 1) - 1)(\beta + 1)}{q^2(\beta + 1)^2(\mu - 1)} \overset{(2)}{=} \frac{2\epsilon'\beta(\beta + 1)}{(1 + \epsilon'\beta)^2(\mu - 1)} = \Omega(1/\mu),$$

where the final equation holds because $\beta = (p - p^*)(\lambda - \delta) \geq \epsilon(\lambda - \delta) = \Omega(1)$.

We can now express $\zeta_\sigma$ in terms of $\zeta_1$, by observing that a branching process starting with $\sigma$ individuals can be viewed as $\sigma$ independent copies of the branching process starting with a single individual each.[4] The former branching process survives if and only if at least one of the latter ones survives, thus,

$$\zeta_\sigma = 1 - (1 - \zeta_1)^\sigma \geq 1 - e^{-\zeta_1\sigma} = 1 - e^{-\Omega(\sigma/\mu)}.$$

This completes the proof of Theorem 7. □

---

[4] This is true for any branching process, and does not relate to the original diffusion process.

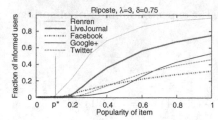

**Fig. 1.** Dissemination for RIPOSTE as a function of the item popularity.

**Table 1.** Network topologies used in the experiments. By avg-deg we denote the average degree of the network.

| Network | Nodes | Edges | Avg-deg | Source |
|---|---|---|---|---|
| Twitter | 41.65M | 1468M | 35.2 | [18] |
| LiveJournal | 4.847M | 68.99M | 14.2 | [4,19] |
| Facebook | 3.097M | 23.66M | 15.3 | [28] |
| Renren | 965.3K | 57.56M | 59.6 | [7] |
| Google+ | 107.6K | 13.67M | 127 | [20] |

## 3    Experiments

In this section we provide experimental evaluation of the dissemination achieved by RIPOSTE on some real topologies of online social networks. The results are surprisingly consistent with our analysis, even though some of the analytical results were proven only for an ideal random graph model.

**Datasets.** We use the network topologies listed in Table 1. The Twitter dataset is a complete snapshot of the network from 2009 [18], while the other datasets are partial network samples. Twitter is a micro-blogging network service, LiveJournal is a blogging network site, while Facebook, Renren, and Google+ are online social networking sites. In each of these networks, every user maintains a list of friends, and/or a list of users she follows. The friendship relation is typically reciprocal, whereas the follower relation is not; the former is represented as an undirected edge, and the latter as a directed. In Twitter, LiveJournal and Google+ edges are directed, while in Renren and Facebook undirected.

**Setup.** We consider the following protocols: (1) RIPOSTE, with exact information on the number of non-informed followers, i.e., $s$ is the *actual* number of the user's followers that do not know the item yet—not just an upper bound; (2) DB-RIPOSTE, where no information about the followers status is available, and thus $s$ is the total number of followers; (3) the basic non privacy-conscious protocol where a user reposts an item if she likes it and does not repost it if she does not like it; we refer to this as the STANDARD protocol.

While datasets on social network topologies are publicly available, access to user's activity, including the list of items they post, receive, like or repost, is severely restricted. Therefore, for our evaluation we rely on two synthetic models to generate users' opinions: (i) the *uniform opinion model*, where every item is assigned a popularity $p \in [0, 1]$, and each user likes the item independently with probability $p$—this is the same model used in the analysis (see Definition 3); and (ii) the *distance-threshold opinion model*, where a user likes the item precisely if the (shortest-path) distance from a source to the user is at most some threshold $h$. The latter model is motivated by the principle that users close to each other tend to have similar opinions [22].

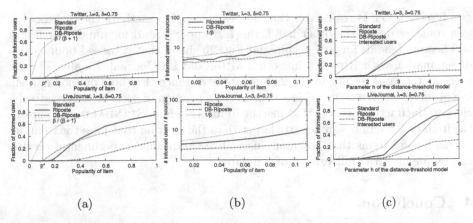

(a)                           (b)                           (c)

**Fig. 2.** Dissemination in Twitter (top) and LiveJournal (bottom). (a) Comparison with STANDARD and the $\beta/(\beta+1)$ lower bound of Theorem 7. (b) Comparison with the $1/\beta$ upper bound of Theorem 5 for unpopular items. (c) Distance-threshold model (all users within distance $h$ from the source, and only them, like the item).

In all experiments, we choose the set $S$ of users who know the item initially to be the followers of a random user, among all users with at least $\mu$ followers, where $\mu$ is the average degree. We think that this is more realistic than choosing an arbitrary or random set $S$: It is often the case that the source of the information (e.g., a news channel) is itself a node in the online social network; then the followers of that node constitute the set $S$ of nodes exposed to the information initially. For each point in the plots we present, we average the results over 10,000 random independent experiments, with a new random set $S$ each time. For the RIPOSTE algorithm, where the dissemination may depend on the order in which the protocol is executed at different users, we experimented with both breadth-first and depth-first orders, obtaining very similar results.

**Results.** Fig. 1 shows the average number of users that receive the item when using RIPOSTE, as a function of the item popularity, for all networks (for parameters $\lambda = 3$ and $\delta = 0.75$). In all cases, unpopular items (with popularity $p$ below the threshold $p^*$ identified by our analysis) have very limited spread, while popular items (with $p > p^*$) spread to a fraction of the networks that grows quickly with $p$. Due to space limitations, in the following we present results only for Twitter and LiveJournal; the results for the other three datasets are qualitatively similar and can be found in the full version [13].

Fig. 2a compares the dissemination using RIPOSTE to that of DB-RIPOSTE and STANDARD, and also to the lower bound for the spread of popular items predicted by Theorem 7. As expected, DB-RIPOSTE informs fewer users than RIPOSTE but has overall qualitatively similar behaviour. STANDARD achieves significantly wider dissemination, even for items with very low popularity, which may be undesirable. The $\beta/(1-\beta)$ bound of Theorem 7 is relatively close to the curve for RIPOSTE (slightly above it in the case of Twitter and intersecting it in the case of LiveJournal). This lower bound was derived for an idealized random graph model, so it is reasonable that it does not apply exactly to the real topologies considered. On the other hand, the $1/\beta$ upper bound for unpopular items of Theorem 5 holds for *any* graph, and Fig. 2b shows that it indeed bounds the dissemination with RIPOSTE in both Twitter and LiveJournal. Finally, Fig. 2c presents the same results as Fig. 2a but for the distance-threshold opinion model. We observe that RIPOSTE achieves spread to a fraction of users that is relatively close to the fraction of users that like the item. As before, STANDARD may spread the item to a fraction significantly larger than the fraction that likes the item, in particular, for items that not many users like. Additional experimental results can be found in the full version of the paper [13].

## 4   Conclusion

We have presented a simple and local diffusion mechanism for social networks, which guarantees widespread dissemination of interesting but possibly sensitive information, in a privacy-conscious manner. The mechanism randomizes the user's action of reposting (or not) the information, in a way reminiscent of the randomized response technique, and chooses the probabilities so that a branching-process-like phenomenon takes place: if more than a certain fraction of people like the information then a large cascade of reposts is formed, and if fewer people like it then the diffusion process dies quickly. We believe this mechanism to be relevant as a tool for internet-based activism, and more generally for promoting free speech. We also think that our techniques could find applications to other distributed problems, such as distributed polling.

## References

1. Alves, P., Ferreira, P.: AnonyLikes: anonymous quantitative feedback on social networks. In: Eyers, D., Schwan, K. (eds.) Middleware 2013. LNCS, vol. 8275, pp. 466–484. Springer, Heidelberg (2013)
2. Ambainis, A., Jakobsson, M., Lipmaa, H.: Cryptographic randomized response techniques. In: 7th International Workshop on Theory and Practice in Public Key Cryptography (PKC), pp. 425–438 (2004)
3. Athreya, K.B., Ney, P.E.: Branching processes. Springer (1972)
4. Backstrom, L., Huttenlocher, D., Kleinberg, J., Lan, X.: Group formation in large social networks: Membership, growth, and evolution. In: 12th ACM SIGKDD International Conference on Knowledge Discovery and Data Mining (KDD), pp. 44–54 (2006)
5. Chaudhuri, A.: Randomized response and indirect questioning techniques in surveys. CRC Press (2010)
6. Chen, N., Olvera-Cravioto, M.: Directed random graphs with given degree distributions. Stochastic Systems **3**(1), 147–186 (2013)
7. Ding, C., Chen, Y., Fu, X.: Crowd crawling: Towards collaborative data collection for large-scale online social networks. In: 1st ACM Conference on Online Social Networks (COSN), pp. 183–188 (2013)

8. Dwork, C., McSherry, F., Nissim, K., Smith, A.: Calibrating noise to sensitivity in private data analysis. In: Halevi, S., Rabin, T. (eds.) TCC 2006. LNCS, vol. 3876, pp. 265–284. Springer, Heidelberg (2006)
9. Dwork, C., Roth, A.: The algorithmic foundations of differential privacy. Foundations and Trends in Theoretical Computer Science **9**(3–4), 211–407 (2014)
10. Earl, J.: The dynamics of protest-related diffusion on the web. Information, Communication & Society **13**(2), 209–225 (2010)
11. Erlingsson, Ú., Pihur, V., Korolova, A.: RAPPOR: Randomized aggregatable privacy-preserving ordinal response. In: ACM Conference on Computer and Communications Security (CCS), pp. 1054–1067 (2014)
12. Garrett, K.: Protest in an information society: A review of literature on social movements and new icts. Information, Communication & Society **9**(02), 202–224 (2006)
13. Giakkoupis, G., Guerraoui, R., Jégou, A., Kermarrec, A.-M., Mittal, N.: Privacy-conscious information diffusion in social networks. Technical report, INRIA Rennes - Bretagne Atlantique, August 2015. https://hal.archives-ouvertes.fr/hal-01184246
14. Grasz, J.: Forty-five percent of employers use social networking sites to research job candidates, CareerBuilder survey finds. CareerBuilder Press Releases, August 2009.       http://www.careerbuilder.com/share/aboutus/pressreleasesdetail.aspx?id=pr519&sd=8%2f19%2f2009&ed=12%2f31%2f2009&siteid=cbpr&sc_cmp1=cb_pr519_
15. Gupta, A., Hardt, M., Roth, A., Ullman, J.: Privately releasing conjunctions and the statistical query barrier. SIAM Journal on Computing **42**(4), 1494–1520 (2013)
16. Haccou, P., Jagers, P., Vatutin, V.A.: Branching processes: Variation, growth, and extinction of populations. Cambridge Univ. Press (2005)
17. Kasiviswanathan, S.P., Lee, H.K., Nissim, K., Raskhodnikova, S., Smith, A.: What can we learn privately? SIAM Journal of Computing **40**(3), 793–826 (2011)
18. Kwak, H., Lee, C., Park, H., Moon, S.: What is Twitter, a social network or a news media? In: 19th International Conference on World Wide Web (WWW), pp. 591–600 (2010)
19. Leskovec, J., Lang, K.J., Dasgupta, A., Mahoney, M.W.: Community structure in large networks: Natural cluster sizes and the absence of large well-defined clusters. Internet Mathematics **6**(1), 29–123 (2009)
20. Leskovec, J., Mcauley, J.J.: Learning to discover social circles in ego networks. In: Advances in Neural Information Processing Systems (NIPS), pp. 539–547 (2012)
21. Macskassy, S.A., Michelson, M.: Why do people retweet? Anti-homophily wins the day! In: 5th International Conference on Weblogs and Social Media (ICWSM) (2011)
22. McPherson, M., Smith-Lovin, L., Cook, J.M.: Birds of a feather: Homophily in social networks. Annual Review of Sociology **27**, 415–444 (2001)
23. Noelle-Neumann, E.: The spiral of silence a theory of public opinion. Journal of Communication **24**(2), 43–51 (1974)
24. NPR news In South Korea, old law leads to new crackdown, December 2011. http://www.npr.org/2011/12/01/142998183/in-south-korea-old-law-leads-to-new-crackdown
25. Quercia, D., Leontiadis, I., McNamara, L., Mascolo, C., Crowcroft, J.: SpotME if you can: Randomized responses for location obfuscation on mobile phones. In: 31st IEEE International Conference on Distributed Computing Systems (ICDCS), pp. 363–372 (2011)

26. TIME magazine. Indian women arrested over facebook post, November 2012. http://newsfeed.time.com/2012/11/19/indian-woman-arrested-over-facebook-like/
27. Warner, S.L.: Randomized response: A survey technique for eliminating evasive answer bias. Journal of the American Statistical Association **60**(309), 63–69 (1965)
28. Wilson, C., Boe, B., Sala, A., Puttaswamy, K.P., Zhao, B.Y.: User interactions in social networks and their implications. In: EuroSys, pp. 205–218 (2009)
29. Wulf, V., Misaki, K., Atam, M., Randall, D., Rohde, M.: 'On the ground' in Sidi Bouzid: Investigating social media use during the tunisian revolution. In: 16th ACM Conference on Computer Supported Cooperative Work (CSCW), pp. 1409–1418 (2013)

# Fair Distributed Computation
# of Reactive Functions

Juan Garay[1], Björn Tackmann[2(⊠)], and Vassilis Zikas[3]

[1] Yahoo Labs, Sunnyvale, CA, USA
garay@yahoo-inc.com
[2] Computer Science and Engineering, UC San Diego, San Diego, CA, USA
btackmann@eng.ucsd.edu
[3] Department of Computer Science, ETH Zurich, Zurich, Switzerland
vzikas@inf.ethz.ch

**Abstract.** A *fair* distributed protocol ensures that dishonest parties
have no advantage over honest parties in learning their protocol's output.
What makes fairness a particularly intriguing research topic is Cleve's
seminal result [STOC'86], which proved that fairness is impossible to
achieve in the presence of dishonest majorities and ignited a quest for
more relaxed, yet meaningful definitions of fairness. A common pattern
in existing works, however, is that they only treat the case of *non-
reactive* computation—i.e., distributed computation of "one-shot" (state-
less) functions, in which parties give all inputs strictly before any output
is computed. Yet, many natural cryptographic tasks are of a *reactive*
(stateful) nature.

In this work, we introduce the first notion of fairness tailored to
reactive distributed computation, which can be realized in the presence
of dishonest majorities. Our definition builds on the recently suggested
utility-based fairness notion (for non-reactive functions) by Garay *et
al.* [PODC'15], which, informally, measures the protocol's fairness by
means of the utility of an adversary who aims to break it As in the
[PODC'15] work, our approach enjoys the advantage of offering a comparative notion, inducing a partial order on protocols with respect to
fairness.

We investigate protocols that restrict the adversary's utility and provide, for each choice of parameters specifying this utility, a protocol for
fair and reactive two-party computation, which is optimal for a (natural)
range of parameters. Our study shows that achieving fairness in the reactive setting is more complex than in the much-studied case of one-shot
functions, as increasing the number of rounds used for reconstructing the
output can lead to improved fairness, and the minimal required number
of rounds depends on the *exact values* of the adversary's utility.

The full version of this paper can be found in [13].

B. Tackmann—Research done in part while at ETH Zurich, and partly supported by
the SNF through Fellowship no. P2EZP2-155566 and by NSF grant CNS-1228890.
V. Zikas—Research supported in part by the SNF through Ambizione grant
PZ00P-2142549

Y. Moses (Ed.): DISC 2015, LNCS 9363, pp. 497–512, 2015.
DOI: 10.1007/978-3-662-48653-5_33

**Keywords:** Cryptographic protocols · Secure multi-party computation ·
Fairness · Game theory

# 1  Introduction

In secure multi-party computation (MPC) [14,19], a set of $n$ parties wish to
perform some joint computation on their inputs in a secure manner, despite the
arbitrary behavior of some of them. The basic security requirements are *privacy*
(cheating parties learn only their output of the computation) and *correctness*
(cheaters cannot distort the outcome of the computation). An additional desired
property is *fairness*, which, roughly speaking, requires that the protocol does not
give a cheating party any advantage in learning the output of the computation
over the honest parties.

In traditional cryptographic definitions, the worst-case scenario of collaborative cheating is captured by the notion of a (central) adversary. Informally, the
adversary is an entity which takes control of ("corrupts") parties and then uses
them to attack the computation. Unfortunately, an early impossibility result by
Cleve [8] established that with such an adversary it is impossible to achieve all
three properties—correctness, privacy and fairness—simultaneously, unless there
is a majority of *honest* (i.e., uncorrupted) parties.

Following Cleve's impossibility, much work has focused on achieving meaningful weaker notions of fairness. One main example of this are *gradual release*-
type approaches [2,4,5,9,12,18], in which parties take turns in releasing bits of
information. More recently, Asharov *et al.* [1] suggested a definition of fairness
for the case of two parties using ideas from so-called "rational cryptography,"
where all the protocol participants are modeled as rational players aiming to
maximize a given utility function, and presented a gradual-release-based protocol satisfying their definition. This rational model for fairness was later enhanced
and extended in various ways (e.g., arbitrary instead of fail-stop misbehavior,
ideal-world/real-world definition) by Groce and Katz [16].

All of these weaker notions of fairness, however, are formalized in an "all-
or-nothing" manner, in the sense that either a protocol achieves the respective
security definition, or the notion renders the protocol unfair and makes no further statement about it. For example, this is the case for *resource fairness* [12],
which formalizes the intuition of the *gradual release* paradigm [2,4,5,9,18] in a
simulation-based framework. Indeed, a resource-fair protocol should ensure that,
upon abort by the adversary, the amount of computation that the honest party
needs for producing the output is comparable to the adversary's for the same
task; yet, a protocol that achieves a worse ratio between the amount of work
required by the honest party and the adversary is not distinguished from a fully
unfair one. The same holds for the above fairness definitions in rational cryptography, which require the protocol to be an equilibrium strategy with respect to
a preference/utility function for *curious-but-exclusive* agents, where each agent
prefers learning the output to not learning it, but would rather be the only
one that learns it. We remark, though, that some of these frameworks do offer

completeness results, in the sense that they show that one *can* construct protocols that are fair in the respective notions; nevertheless, none of them provides a comparative statement for protocols which do not fully satisfy their property.

Recent work by Garay *et al.* [11] introduced a *quantitative* approach to fairness, based on the idea that one can use an appropriate utility function to express the preferences of an adversary who wants to break fairness.[1] The approach allows for comparing protocols with respect to how fair they are, placing them in a partial order according to a relative-fairness relation. Previously, the only other notion providing any sort of comparative statement was that of $1/p$-*security* (aka. "partial fairness") [3,15], where security is given up with probability $1/p$ for some polynomial $p$, but which does not always guarantee privacy and correctness (see [11] for a detailed comparison).

Technically, the approach of [11] builds on machinery developed in the recently proposed *Rational Protocol Design* (RPD) framework of Garay *et al.* [10]. In more detail, the framework describes how to design protocols which keep the utility of an attacker aiming at provoking certain security breaches as low as possible. At a high level, this is then used as follows: first, one specifies the class of utility functions that naturally capture an adversary attacking a protocol's fairness, and then one interprets the actual utility that the best attacker (i.e., the one maximizing its utility) obtains against a given protocol as a measure of the protocol's success in satisfying the property. The more a protocol limits its best attacker with respect to the fairness-specific utility function, the fairer the protocol is. We remark that, in addition, this quantitative fairness approach preserves the composability of the underlying security model (such as when using, e.g., [6,7]) with respect to standard secure protocols, in the sense that it allows the replacement of an ideal component (a "hybrid" or ideal functionality in the language of [7]) in a fair/optimal protocol by a protocol which securely implements it without affecting its fairness/optimality.

**Our Contributions.** We present the first notion of fairness tailored to *reactive* distributed computation, where parties provide inputs and receive outputs multiple times during the course of the computation; the notion can be realized in the presence of dishonest majorities.

We specify the utility function characterizing the incentives of an attacker who aims at breaking fairness of a two-party MPC protocol, deriving the natural quantitative notions of fairness and of protocol optimality. However, and as expected, formulation and analysis are quite more complex here than in the non-reactive case [11], where for example the honest parties can simply restart the protocol after an "early abort" where no party received outputs, using default inputs for the parties that caused the abort. In contrast, in the reactive case earlier rounds in the computation may already have leaked information to the adversary, which makes a restart potentially unsafe. As a result, the protocol we present bounds the adversary's utility by the maximum of two terms, one of which is the same as in the non-reactive case and corresponds to the adversary's

---

[1] This approach is incomparable to the one in rational cryptography, as the honest parties are *not* rational and follow whichever protocol is designed for them.

strategy of aborting right after obtaining its output, and the other one stems from the potential "early aborts" and depends on the number of rounds used in the reconstruction of the protocol output as well as the exact values of the adversary's utility.

We then derive lower bounds, showing the protocol optimally fair for a natural class of parameter values—at a high level, those expressing that the adversary prefers that the honest party does not get the output, to the extent that he is willing to have negative utility when all parties receive the output (otherwise previous results apply), but only up to a point, after which the adversary's aversion toward giving the output to the honest parties is so large that he will abort any protocol prematurely. Besides being optimally fair, the protocol is also optimal with respect to the number of *reconstruction rounds*. For the remaining values, the lower bound we derive is close to the bound achieved by our protocol but not tight; we leave the closing of this gap as an open problem.

**Organization of the Paper.** The remainder of the paper is organized as follows. In Section 2 we describe notation and the very basics of the RPD framework [10] that are needed for understanding and evaluating our results. In Section 3 we define the utility function of attackers who aim at violating fairness, which enables the relative assessment of protocols as well as the notions of "optimal" fairness which we use in this work. This section is a generalization of the approach in [11] to the reactive computation case. Section 4 is dedicated to the fair reactive protocol, starting with a general outline in Section 4.1, and Section 4.2 explaining the protocol in detail; lower bounds are shown in Section 4.3.

## 2    Preliminaries and Model

We first establish some notational conventions. For an integer $m \in \mathbb{N}$, the set of positive numbers smaller or equal to $m$ is $[m] := \{1, \ldots, m\}$. In the context of two-party protocols, we will always refer to the parties as $p_1$ and $p_2$, and for $i \in \{1, 2\}$ the symbol $\neg i$ refers to the value $3 - i$ (so $p_{\neg i} \neq p_i$). Most statements in this paper are actually asymptotic with respect to an (often implicit) security parameter $k \in \mathbb{N}$. Hence, $f \leq g$ means that $\exists k_0 \, \forall k \geq k_0 : f(k) \leq g(k)$, and a function $\mu : \mathbb{N} \to \mathbb{R}$ is *negligible* if for all polynomials $p$, $\mu \leq 1/p$, and *noticeable* if there exists a polynomial $p$ with $\mu \geq 1/p$. We further introduce the symbol $f \stackrel{\text{negl}}{\approx} g$ to denote that $\exists$ negligible $\mu : \; |f - g| \leq \mu$, and $f \stackrel{\text{negl}}{\geq} g$ to denote $\exists$ negligible $\mu : f \geq g - \mu$, with $\stackrel{\text{negl}}{\leq}$ defined analogously.

For the model of computation and protocol composition, we follow Canetti's adaptive simulation-based model for multi-party computation [6]. The protocol execution is formalized by collections of interactive Turing machines (ITMs); the set of all *efficient* ITMs is denoted by ITM. We generally denote our protocols by $\Pi$ and our (ideal) functionalities (which are also referred to as *the trusted party* [6]) by $\mathcal{F}$ both with descriptive super- or subscripts, the adversary by $\mathcal{A}$, the simulator (aka the ideal-world adversary) by $\mathcal{S}$, and the environment by $\mathcal{Z}$.

The random variable ensemble $\{\text{EXEC}_{\Pi,\mathcal{A},\mathcal{Z}}(k,z)\}_{k\in\mathbb{N},z\in\{0,1\}^*}$, which is more compactly often written as $\text{EXEC}_{\Pi,\mathcal{A},\mathcal{Z}}$, describes the contents of $\mathcal{Z}$'s output tape after an execution with $\Pi$, $\mathcal{F}$, and $\mathcal{A}$, on auxiliary input $z \in \{0,1\}^*$.

**Secure Computation of Reactive Functions.** The framework in [6] considers synchronous protocols with guaranteed termination and allows for sequential and modular composition, but lacks a formal definition of computation of reactive functions.[2] We describe here the real-world/ideal-world experiments for reactive functions based on the model with adaptive adversaries [6, Sect. 5]. Although we will be designing protocols only for two-party computation (2PC), since this is the first formal treatment of the reactive setting with respect to fairness, we provide definitions for the more general case of $n$ parties. The resulting model allows for modular composition in a similar sense as in [6]: in each round of a protocol, the parties can make use of a sub-protocol computing another functionality. For the reduction to work, it is important that the higher-level protocol does not continue—apart from interacting with the sub-protocol—until the sub-protocol has terminated.

As discussed in [17], reactive computation can be seen as an ordered sequence of computations of non-reactive functions that can maintain a joint (private) state. More concretely, reactive computation is specified by a vector of (probabilistic) functions $\boldsymbol{f} = (f_1,\ldots,f_m)$, where each $f_\lambda \in \boldsymbol{f}$ takes as input a vector of values from $\{0,1\}^* \cup \{\bot\}$ (corresponding to the parties inputs to $f_\lambda$), a uniformly random value $r$ from a known domain $R$ (corresponding to the random coins used for evaluating $f_\lambda$), and a *state vector* $\boldsymbol{S}_\lambda \in ((\{0,1\}^*\cup\{\bot\})^n \times R)^{(\lambda-1)}$, which includes the inputs and random coins used for the evaluation of functions $f_1,\ldots,f_{\lambda-1}$. Each $f_\lambda \in \boldsymbol{f}$ outputs a vector of strings $\boldsymbol{y}_\lambda = (y_{1,\lambda},\ldots,y_{n,\lambda}) \in \{0,1\}^n$, where $y_{i,\lambda}$ is $p_i$'s output.

*The Ideal Process.* At a high level, execution in the ideal world is similar to the corresponding experiment in [6], but instead of a single function, the trusted third party (TTP, or "functionality") $\mathcal{F}_{\text{RC}}^{\boldsymbol{f}}$ is parameterized by the vector $\boldsymbol{f} = (f_1,\ldots,f_m)$ of functions to be sequentially evaluated, with each of these functions receiving as input the state vector (consisting of all inputs received so far as well as the used randomness) along with parties' inputs to the function which is currently computed. The output of the computation is taken to be the vector of outputs of all functions in $\boldsymbol{f}$.

The ability to maintain a joint state, however, is not the only difference between reactive and non-reactive computation. Rather, we need to ensure that parties be able to choose their input for any $f_\lambda, \lambda \in [m]$, depending on inputs and outputs from the evaluation of $f_1,\ldots,f_{\lambda-1}$. Thus, we cannot fix the input sequence of the parties at the beginning of the protocol execution as is the case with the ideal-evaluation experiment of non-reactive functions. Instead, we assume that every party $p_i \in \mathcal{P}$ gives as input to the trusted party a sequence

---

[2] Our definitions can be extended to Universally Composable (UC) security [7] using the approach of Katz *et al.* [17] to model terminating synchronous (reactive) computation in UC.

of $m$ *input-deciding functions* $\mathrm{Inp}_i^1, \ldots, \mathrm{Inp}_i^m$, where for each $\lambda \in [m]$, $\mathrm{Inp}_i^\lambda$ : $(((\{0,1\}^*)^{\lambda-1})^2 \to \{0,1\}^*$ is a function that on input the inputs and outputs from the evaluation of functions $f_1, \ldots, f_{\lambda-1}$ computes the input for the evaluation of $f_\lambda$. (Without loss of generality, assume that $p_i$'s input to $f_1$ is $\mathrm{Inp}_i^1(0,0)$.) Unlike the parties, the simulator is allowed to to choose his inputs during his ongoing interaction with the TTP.

*The Real-World Execution.* The real-world experiment in analogous to the corresponding experiment in [6], where the input of each party $p_i$ is his input-deciding function vector $\mathrm{Inp}_i^1, \ldots, \mathrm{Inp}_i^m$.

**Rational Protocol Design.** Our results utilize the *Rational Protocol Design* (RPD) framework [10]. Here we review the basic elements that are needed to motivate and express our definitions and results; we refer to the framework paper [10] for further details. In RPD, security is defined via a two-party sequential zero-sum game with perfect information, called the *attack game*, between a protocol *designer* D and an *attacker* A. The designer D plays first by specifying a protocol $\Pi$ for the (honest) participants to run; subsequently, the attacker A, who is informed about D's move (i.e., learns the protocol) plays by specifying a polynomial-time attack strategy $\mathcal{A}$ by which it may corrupt parties and try to subvert the execution of the protocol (uncorrupted parties follow $\Pi$ as prescribed). It suffices to define the utility $u_A$ of the adversary as the game is zero-sum; the utility $u_D$ of the designer is then $-u_A$.

In RPD, the definition of utilities relies on the simulation paradigm[3], with the caveat that the real-world execution is compared to an ideal process in which $\mathcal{S}$ gets to interact with a *relaxed* version of the functionality which, in addition to implementing the task as $\mathcal{F}$ would, also allows the simulator to perform the attacks we are interested in capturing. For example, an attack to the protocol's correctness is modeled by the functionality allowing the simulator to modify the outputs (even of honest parties). Given such a functionality, the utility of any given adversary is defined as the expected utility of the best simulator for this adversary, where the simulator's utility is defined according to which weaknesses of the ideal functionality the simulator is forced to exploit.

# 3   Utility-Based Fairness and Protocol Optimality

In this section, we utilize the RPD machinery to introduce a natural fairness relation (partial order) to the space of efficient protocols for secure reactive two-party computation (2PC) and define maximal elements in this order to be optimal protocols with respect to fairness. Towards that goal, we follow the three-step process described in [10,11] for specifying an adversary's utility, instantiating this process with parameters that capture a fairness-targeted attacker.

---

[3] In RPD the statements are formalized in Canetti's Universal Composition (UC) framework [7]; however, one can use any other simulation-based model, in particular the one in [6] described above.

**Step 1: Relaxing the Ideal Experiment to Allow Attacks on Fairness.**
First, we relax the ideal world to allow the simulator to perform fairness-related attacks. In particular, we consider the ideal-world experiment for reactive MPC described in Sect. 2 but modify it to allow the simulator $\mathcal{S}$ to (1) refuse receiving his inputs from the functionality and/or (2) refuse the functionality to deliver outputs to the parties (i.e., instruct it to abort); analogously to [11], the simulator is allowed to choose when to abort, i.e., before or after receiving his inputs if he chooses to. The reactive MPC ideal functionality is parameterized by the (sequence of) functions $f = (f_1, \ldots, f_m)$ as described in Sect. 2 and is denoted $\mathcal{F}_{RC}^{f,\perp}$ (or simply $\mathcal{F}_{RC}^{\perp}$ if the function sequence is clear from the context). We point out that when $\mathcal{F}_{RC}^{\cdot,\perp}$ is parameterized with a single function (as in $\mathcal{F}_{RC}^{f,\perp}$) then it corresponds to the standard SFE functionality $\mathcal{F}_{SFE}^{f,\perp}$ (i.e., computation of non-reactive functions) with unfair abort as in [11].

**Step 2: Events and Payoffs.** Next, we specify a set of events in the experiment corresponding to the ideal evaluation of $\mathcal{F}_{RC}^{\perp}$ which capture whether or not a fairness breach occurs, and assign to each such event a "payoff" value capturing the severity of provoking the event. The relevant questions to ask with respect to fairness are:

1. Does the adversary learn "noticeable" information about the output of the corrupted parties?
2. Do honest parties learn their output?

In comparison to the non-reactive case, there are *a priori* different ways to define the events, based on whether one asks for the adversary to receive *any* output or *all* the outputs. Since the reactive computation proceeds round by round, a natural choice is to ask for the honest parties to receive *all* outputs, or otherwise to ask for the adversary to also not receive information about *some* output. The corresponding events (which we use to describe fairness) correspond to the four possible combinations of answers to the above questions. In particular, we define the events indexed by a string $ij \in \{0,1\}^2$, where $i$ (resp., $j$) equals 1 if the answer to the first (resp., second) question is yes and 0 otherwise. The events are then as follows:

$E_{00}^R$: The simulator does not ask $\mathcal{F}_{RC}^{f,\perp}$ for the all of the corrupted party's outputs and instructs $\mathcal{F}_{RC}^{f,\perp}$ to abort. This corresponds to neither the honest party nor the adversary receiving all their outputs.

$E_{01}^R$: The simulator does not ask $\mathcal{F}_{RC}^{f,\perp}$ for all of the corrupted party's outputs and does not instruct it to abort. This corresponds to the honest party receiving all its outputs and the adversary not receiving some of its outputs. This accounts also for the case where no party is corrupted.

$E_{10}^R$: The simulator asks $\mathcal{F}_{RC}^{f,\perp}$ for all his outputs and instructs it to abort before the honest party receives all its outputs. This corresponds to the adversary receiving all its outputs and the honest party not receiving some of its outputs.

$E_{11}^{R}$: The simulator asks the functionality for all his outputs, and allows the honest party to receive all its outputs (i.e., it does not abort). This accounts also for the case where all parties are corrupted.

We remark that our definition does not give full advantage to an adversary corrupting both parties. This is consistent with the intuitive notion of fairness, as when there is no honest party, the adversary has nobody to gain an unfair advantage over.

To each of the events $E_{ij}^{R}$ we associate a real-valued *payoff* $\gamma_{ij}$ which captures the adversary's utility when provoking this event. Thus, the adversary's payoff is specified by vector $\gamma = (\gamma_{00}, \gamma_{01}, \gamma_{10}, \gamma_{11}) \in \mathbb{R}^4$, corresponding to events $\boldsymbol{E}^R = (E_{00}^{R}, E_{01}^{R}, E_{10}^{R}, E_{11}^{R})$.

Finally, we define the expected payoff of a given simulator $\mathcal{S}$ (for an environment $\mathcal{Z}$) to be[4]:

$$U_I^{\mathcal{F}_{RC}^{\perp}, \gamma}(\mathcal{S}, \mathcal{Z}) \quad := \quad \sum_{i,j \in \{0,1\}} \gamma_{ij} \Pr[E_{ij}^{R}]. \tag{1}$$

**Step 3: Defining the Attacker's Utility.** Given $U_I^{\mathcal{F}_{RC}^{\perp}, \gamma}(\mathcal{S}, \mathcal{Z})$, the utility $u_A(\Pi, \mathcal{A})$ for a pair $(\Pi, \mathcal{A})$ of a protocol $\Pi$ and an adversary $\mathcal{A}$ is defined following the methodology in [10] as the expected payoff of the *best* simulator[5] that simulates $\mathcal{A}$ in the $\mathcal{F}_{RC}^{\perp}$-ideal world in presence of the least favorable environment—i.e., the one that is *most* favorable to the attacker. To make the payoff vector $\gamma$ explicit, we sometimes denote the above utility as $\hat{U}^{\Pi, \mathcal{F}_{RC}^{\perp}, \gamma}(\mathcal{A})$ and refer to it as the *payoff of strategy* $\mathcal{A}$ (for attacking $\Pi$).

More formally, for a protocol $\Pi$, denote by $\text{SIM}_{\mathcal{A}}$ the class of simulators for $\mathcal{A}$, i.e, $\text{SIM}_{\mathcal{A}} = \{\mathcal{S} \in \text{ITM} \mid \forall \mathcal{Z} : \text{EXEC}_{\Pi, \mathcal{A}, \mathcal{Z}} \approx \text{EXEC}_{\mathcal{F}_{RC}^{\perp}, \mathcal{S}, \mathcal{Z}}\}$. The payoff of strategy $\mathcal{A}$ (for attacking $\Pi$) is then defined as:

$$u_A(\Pi, \mathcal{A}) \quad := \quad \hat{U}^{\Pi, \mathcal{F}_{RC}^{\perp}, \gamma}(\mathcal{A}) \quad := \quad \sup_{\mathcal{Z} \in \text{ITM}} \inf_{\mathcal{S} \in \text{SIM}_{\mathcal{A}}} \{U_I^{\mathcal{F}_{RC}^{\perp}, \gamma}(\mathcal{S}, \mathcal{Z})\}. \tag{2}$$

To complete our formulation, we now describe a natural relation among the values in $\gamma$ which is both intuitive and consistent with existing approaches to fairness, and which we will assume to hold for the remainder of the paper. Specifically, we will consider attackers whose least preferred event is that the honest parties receive their output while the attacker does not, i.e., we assume that $\gamma_{01} = \min_{\gamma \in \gamma}\{\gamma\}$. Furthermore, we will assume that the attacker's favorite choice is that he receives the output and the honest parties do not, i.e., $\gamma_{10} = \max_{ij \in \{0,1\}^2}\{\gamma_{ij}\}$. Lastly, we point out that for an arbitrary payoff vector $\gamma$, one can assume without loss of generality that any one of its values equals zero, and, therefore, we can set $\gamma_{00} = 0$. This can be seen immediately by setting $\gamma_{ij}' = \gamma_{ij} - \gamma_{01}$. We denote the set of all payoff vectors adhering to the above

---

[4] Refer to [10, Sect. 2] for the rationale behind this formulation.

[5] The best simulator is taken to be the one that minimizes his payoff [10].

restrictions by $\Gamma_{\text{fair}} \subseteq \mathbb{R}^4$. Summarizing, our fairness-specific payoff ("preference") vector $\gamma$ satisfies

$$0 = \gamma_{01} \leq \min\{\gamma_{00}, \gamma_{11}\} \quad \text{and} \quad \max\{\gamma_{00}, \gamma_{11}\} < \gamma_{10}.$$

**Optimally Fair Protocols.** We are now ready to define our partial order relation for protocols with respect to fairness. Informally, a protocol $\Pi$ will be *at least as fair* as another protocol $\Pi'$ if the utility of the best adversary $\mathcal{A}$ attacking $\Pi$ (i.e, the adversary which maximizes $u_{\mathcal{A}}(\Pi, \mathcal{A})$) is no larger than the utility of the best adversary attacking $\Pi'$ (except for some negligible quantity).

**Definition 1.** *Let $\Pi$ and $\Pi'$ be protocols, and $\gamma \in \Gamma_{\text{fair}}$ be a preference vector. We say that $\Pi$ is* at least as fair as $\Pi'$ *with respect to $\gamma$ (i.e., it is at least as $\gamma$-fair), denoted $\Pi \overset{\gamma}{\succeq} \Pi'$, if*

$$\sup_{\mathcal{A} \in \text{ITM}} u_{\mathcal{A}}(\Pi, \mathcal{A}) \overset{\text{negl}}{\leq} \sup_{\mathcal{A} \in \text{ITM}} u_{\mathcal{A}}(\Pi', \mathcal{A}). \tag{3}$$

We will refer to a protocol which is a maximal element according to the above fairness relation as an *optimally fair* protocol.

**Definition 2.** *Let $\gamma \in \Gamma_{\text{fair}}$. A protocol $\Pi$ is* optimally $\gamma$-fair *if it is at least as $\gamma$-fair as any other protocol $\Pi'$.*

## 4 Fair and Reactive 2PC

The optimally fair two-party computation (2PC) protocol in the non-reactive case [11] can be described as follows: the protocol chooses one party uniformly at random, and the output is reconstructed toward this party first. If one party aborts the protocol early (that is, before the reconstruction phase), the other party can restart the protocol with a default input for the (corrupted) party that aborted. Intuitively, this means that the only way for a corrupted party to prevent the honest party from receiving output is to run the protocol until the reconstruction phase, hope to be the one that is chosen to receive the output first, and then abort the protocol. The result is that the adversary's expected payoff is bounded by $(\gamma_{10} + \gamma_{11})/2$, where $\gamma_{10}$ is the payoff for an unfair abort, and $\gamma_{11}$ is the payoff for a fair execution.

The most intuitive idea for solving the same problem for reactive computation is to apply the same reconstruction protocol for distributing the outputs in each round of the reactive computation. Unfortunately, the resulting protocol is not optimal: if the adversary aborts prior to the reconstruction phase in *some* round of the reactive computation, but it already achieved outputs in previous rounds, the honest party *cannot* safely restart the protocol with a default input for the corrupted party. Hence, adversaries with a utility satisfying $\gamma_{00} > \gamma_{11}$ may be better off by aborting the protocol early and thus definitely preventing the honest party from obtaining output—the simple adversarial strategy of choosing one party to corrupt at random and aborting as soon as an output is received is, in contrast to the non-reactive case, no longer optimal. In fact, even in the reactive case, if $\gamma_{11} \geq \gamma_{00} = 0$, then the adversary has no incentive to stop the protocol before obtaining output, so we can use the same protocol as in [11].

## 4.1  Better Fairness Through More Rounds

In case the adversary's utility satisfies $\gamma_{00} > \gamma_{11}$, one can improve fairness guarantees by adding more rounds to a protocol's reconstruction phase. The reason is that if the adversary puts more emphasis on keeping the honest party from learning the output than on him learning the output himself, he might be tempted to abort the protocol even without obtaining output. We use the assumption that $E_{01}^{R}$ is the adversary's least preferred event to threaten him with potentially only obtaining payoff $\gamma_{01}$ in case of an early abort—and $\gamma_{01} < \gamma_{11}$. By carefully adapting the probabilities with which we output the value in a certain round of a reconstruction protocol, we can consistently keep the adversary in the dilemma between continuing the execution of the protocol or aborting it, maximizing the honest party's probability of obtaining the output.

We describe a protocol with $r$ rounds, where one party—chosen at random— obtains the output during the first $r - 1$ rounds, and the other party obtains it only in the last round. In more detail, for each round $l = 1, \ldots, r - 1$ there is a probability $p_l \in [0, 1]$ for a party to obtain the output in that round. The probabilities are the same for both parties since the setting is symmetric. In each of the rounds, the adversary has the advantage to receive his output before the honest party; this corresponds to the adversary in each round delaying his message until receiving the honest party's message, which is possible unless the timing guarantees given by the network are extremely strong. Consequently, in each round $l = 1, \ldots, r - 1$, the adversary can trade giving the probability $p_l$ corresponding to the current $i$th round to the honest party, obtaining the probability $p_{l+1}$ of the next $(l+1)$st round in exchange. We now have to determine the values $p_1, \ldots, p_{r-1}$ such as to keep the adversary in a constant dilemma.

The payoff for the adversary aborting in round $l \in [1, \ldots, r - 1]$ can be computed by the probabilities for the honest party $(p_1 + \cdots + p_{l-1})$ and the adversary $(p_1 + \cdots + p_l)$ to have received the value and the respective payoff values $\gamma_{01}$ and $\gamma_{10}$. The condition is then described by the equation

$$\left( \sum_{u=1}^{l+1} p_u \right) \gamma_{10} + \left( \sum_{u=1}^{l} p_u \right) \gamma_{01} = \left( \sum_{u=1}^{l} p_u \right) \gamma_{10} + \left( \sum_{u=1}^{l-1} p_u \right) \gamma_{01},$$

which corresponds to, for all $l = 1, \ldots, r - 2$,

$$p_{l+1} = p_l \left( \frac{-\gamma_{01}}{\gamma_{10}} \right).$$

With $\varrho := -\frac{\gamma_{01}}{\gamma_{10}}$, we obtain by induction that $p_l = \varrho^{l-1}p_1$. Providing the output to the other party only in the last round means that

$$\sum_{l=1}^{r-1} p_l = \sum_{l=1}^{r-1}(\varrho^{l-1}p_1) = \left(\sum_{l=1}^{r-1}\varrho^{l-1}\right) \cdot p_1 = 1/2,$$

or $p_1 = 1/2\left(\sum_{l=1}^{r-1}\varrho^{l-1}\right)^{-1}$. In fact, we show in the remaining of the paper that the protocol achieving this distribution of probabilities is optimal.

As only the rounds of the reconstruction phase are relevant for the achieved fairness, we call a protocol an *r-round-reconstruction protocol* if it requires only $r$ rounds of interaction to reconstruct the outputs after the computation has taken place. For simplicity, we only consider functionalities in which all parties receive the same output; the extension to the general case can be achieved using standard techniques. We now turn to a more detailed description of a fair reactive 2PC protocol, which is optimal when $\gamma_{11} > -\gamma_{10}$, as it follows from our lower bound results (Sect. 4.3).

## 4.2 The Fair Reactive Protocol

At a high level, the protocol works as follows: The functionality is sequentially evaluating the functions $f_1, \ldots, f_m$; the invariant of the computation is that at any point, the state of the computation (i.e., the inputs and randomness used so far) is shared according to a two-out-of-two authenticated secret sharing. Each function $f_\lambda$, for $1 \leq \lambda \leq m$, is evaluated by having the two parties evaluate the function $f_{\mathrm{sh},f_\lambda,\mathcal{D}}$ (formally specified in Figure 2) which on input a sharing $\langle S_{\lambda-1}\rangle$ of the current state along with the parties' inputs $x_{1,\lambda}$ and $x_{2,\lambda}$, outputs a sharing $\langle S_\lambda \rangle$ of the updated state $S_\lambda$ along with a sharing $\langle f_\lambda \rangle$ of the outputs of $f_\lambda$ evaluated on $S_{\lambda-1}$, $x_{1\lambda}$ and $x_{2,\lambda}$. Next, the sharing $\langle f_\lambda \rangle$ is reconstructed in an *r-round-reconstruction* protocol as follows:

- The index of some party $i \in_R \{0,1\}$ is chosen uniformly at random (this will be the party that will receive the output during some *early output round*, i.e., before the last round $r$);
- for this party $p_i$, a round $l^* \in [r-1]$ is chosen according to the probability distribution described in Section 4.1;
- in each round $l \in [r-1] \setminus \{l^*\}$ of the reconstruction protocol, party $p_i$ learns only that this round was not chosen;
- in round $l^*$, $p_i$ learns the complete output;
- in the last round $r$, the sharing is reconstructed to both parties.

The idea behind the above construction is to have the adversary, in each round, face the following conundrum: To increase the expected payoff, that is, the probability of obtaining the output, it has to proceed to the next round. This means, however, that it first has to finish the current round by sending a message to the honest party, which will of course increase the honest party's probability of receiving the value (and hence reduce the adversary's payoff).

For this technique to work, however, we need to make sure that no information about the chosen party and round leaks before the actually chosen party obtains the message in the chosen round.

To achieve the above properties, we use the function $f_{\mathrm{sh},f_\lambda,\mathcal{D}}$ to compute (and output) $r$ pairs of sharings $(\langle y_{11}\rangle, \langle y_{21}\rangle), \ldots, (\langle y_{1r}\rangle, \langle y_{2r}\rangle)$ as follows: for each round $l \in [r-1] \setminus \{l_i\}$, $y_{1l} = y_{2l} = \mathtt{DummyRound}$, where $\mathtt{DummyRound}$ is a default value signifying that this is not the output; for round $l_i$, $y_{il_i}$ is set to the output of the function, whereas $y_{\neg i l_i}$ is $\mathtt{DummyRound}$ as before. Finally, for the last round $l = r$, both $y_{0r}$ and $y_{1r}$ are set to the output of the function.

We are now ready to describe our reactive computation protocol, $\Pi_{\mathrm{RC}}^{\mathrm{fair}}$, for evaluating the two-party functionality described by $\boldsymbol{f} = (f_1, \ldots, f_m)$. The protocol is parametrized by the function vector $\boldsymbol{f}$, the number $r$ of reconstruction rounds used for each output, and the probability distribution $\mathcal{D}$ on $[r-1]$ of the early output round $l^*$.

---

### Protocol $\Pi_{\mathrm{RC}}^{\mathrm{fair}}$ $(p_1, p_2, \mathcal{D}, r, f_1, \ldots, f_m)$

Initialize $S_0 := (\bot, \bot, 0)$; the parties compute a default sharing of $S_0$, denoted $\langle S_0 \rangle$. For $\lambda = 1, \ldots, m$, evaluate $f_\lambda$ *sequentially* as follows:

1. Use an (unfair MPC) sub-protocol to compute $f_{\mathrm{sh},f_\lambda,\mathcal{D}}$ on input the sharing $\langle S_{\lambda-1} \rangle$ of the current state and the $f_\lambda$-inputs $x_1^{(\lambda)}$ and $x_2^{(\lambda)}$ of parties $p_1$ and $p_2$, respectively; if the protocol aborts then abort the execution of $\Pi_{\mathrm{RC}}^{\mathrm{fair}}$, otherwise denote by $\langle S_\lambda \rangle, (\langle y_{1,1}^{(\lambda)}\rangle, \langle y_{2,1}^{(\lambda)}\rangle), \ldots, (\langle y_{1,r}^{(\lambda)}\rangle, \langle y_{2,r}^{(\lambda)}\rangle)$ the output of the evaluation.
2. For $l = 1, \ldots, r$ do the following *sequentially*: have $\langle y_{1,l}^{(\lambda)}\rangle$ and $\langle y_{2,l}^{(\lambda)}\rangle$ reconstructed towards $p_1$ and $p_2$, respectively (by having $p_i$ send his share to $p_{\neg i}$).
3. For each $p_i \in \{p_1, p_2\}$, if any of the reconstructions yields a value $y \notin \{\bot, \mathtt{DummyRound}\}$ then output $y$; otherwise abort.

---

**Fig. 1.** The protocol for fair reactive 2PC.

We give a complete description of the function $f_{\mathrm{sh},\lambda,\mathcal{D}}$ used by $\Pi_{\mathrm{RC}}^{\mathrm{fair}}$ in Fig. 2. The function is parameterized by the function $f$ whose output is to be computed, and further by a probability distribution $\mathcal{D}$ on the set $[r-1]$ according to which the round $l^*$ is chosen.

We now analyze the degree of fairness achieved by $\Pi_{\mathrm{RC}}^{\mathrm{fair}}$, which we later (Sect. 4.3 show optimal for certain parameters by proving a lower bound on the adversary's payoff. The proof of the theorem appears in the full version.

**Theorem 1.** *Let* $\boldsymbol{\gamma} = (\gamma_{00}, \gamma_{01}, \gamma_{10}, \gamma_{11}) \in \Gamma_{\mathrm{fair}}$. *Then*

$$\bar{u}_{\mathsf{A}}(\Pi_{\mathrm{RC}}^{\mathrm{fair}}, \mathcal{A}) \overset{\mathrm{negl}}{\leq} \max\left\{\frac{\gamma_{10}}{2\sum_{l=1}^{r-1}\varrho^{l-1}}, \frac{\gamma_{10} + \gamma_{11}}{2}\right\},$$

*with* $\varrho = \left|\frac{\gamma_{01}}{\gamma_{10}}\right|$. *In particular, if* $\gamma_{11} > -\gamma_{10}$, *then* $\bar{u}_{\mathsf{A}}(\Pi_{\mathrm{RC}}^{\mathrm{fair}}, \mathcal{A}) \overset{\mathrm{negl}}{\leq} \frac{\gamma_{10}+\gamma_{11}}{2}$.

---

**Function** $f_{\mathrm{sh},f,\mathcal{D}}(\langle S \rangle, x_1, x_2)$

- Upon receiving inputs $(x_1, \langle S \rangle_1)$ and $(x_2, \langle S \rangle_2)$ from $p_1$ and $p_2$, do:
  1.  If the shares $\langle S \rangle_1$ and $\langle S \rangle_2$ are inconsistent or the reconstructed state is the abort vector $S = (\mathbf{abt}, \mathbf{abt})$, then set the output to $y := \perp$; otherwise, choose $r \in_R \{0,1\}^*$, set $y = f(x_1, x_2, S, r)$, and update $S$ by appending $x_1, x_2$ and $r$ to $S$; denote by $S'$ the updated state.

  2.  Compute an authenticated sharing $\langle S' \rangle$ of $S'$.

  3.  Choose a party index $i \in_R \{1, 2\}$ uniformly at random and choose a round index $l^* \xleftarrow{\mathcal{D}} [r-1]$ according to $\mathcal{D}$.

  4.  For $l = 1, \ldots, r - 1$, compute the authenticated-sharing pair $(\langle y_{1,l} \rangle, \langle y_{2,l} \rangle)$, where $y_{jl}$ is computed as follows:
      - If $l < r$, $y_{\neg i,l} := \mathrm{DummyRound}$, whereas $y_{i,l} := \begin{cases} y & \text{if } l = l^*; \\ \mathrm{DummyRound} & \text{otherwise.} \end{cases}$
      - If $l = r$, $y_{1,l} = y_{2,l} = y$.

- Output $\langle S' \rangle, (\langle y_{1,1} \rangle, \langle y_{2,1} \rangle), \ldots, (\langle y_{1,r} \rangle, \langle y_{2,r} \rangle)$.

---

**Fig. 2.** The function computing the authenticated sharings used in protocol $\Pi_{\mathrm{RC}}^{\mathrm{fair}}$.

The adversary's payoff depends on the number of rounds used in the reconstruction, and the optimal number of rounds depends on the exact values of the adversary's utility. As long as $\gamma_{11} > -\gamma_{10}$, we can adapt the probabilities such that the adversary is incentivized to continue with the protocol, if $\gamma_{11} \le -\gamma_{10}$, then an abort during the first (non-trivial) reconstruction round is always preferable. We provide more details on this relation in the full version.

### 4.3   Lower Bounds

In this section, we prove lower bounds on the adversary's payoff that hold with respect to arbitrary protocols. In the case $\gamma_{11} > -\gamma_{10}$, this actually shows that protocol $\Pi_{\mathrm{RC}}^{\mathrm{fair}}$ is optimally fair, as the lower bound tightly matches the upper bound from Theorem 1. In the other case, i.e., $\gamma_{11} \le -\gamma_{10}$, we still give a lower bound which is close to the upper bound we proved.

We show the lower bounds on the adversary's expected payoff using a specific "two-phase exchange" functionality $f_{2\mathrm{Ex}}^{\perp}$ that works as follows: Both parties input a $2k$-bit string, and in the first phase, both obtain the first $k$ bits of the other party's input. In the second phase, they both obtain the remaining $k$ bits of the other party's input. (See Fig. 3.)

There are simple and generic adversarial strategies $\mathcal{A}_i$ that corrupt party $p_i$ in the beginning but follow the protocol honestly until the last output phase of the protocol. Then, it aborts as soon as it obtained the output—that is, in each round $\mathcal{A}_i$ checks whether the protocol *would* already provide the output if the other (honest) party *would* abort; in this case, $\mathcal{A}_i$ aborts the protocol without

---

**Function $f_{2Ex}^{\perp}$**

The functionality $f_{2Ex}^{\perp}$ is a two-party functionality that proceeds in two rounds:

- Obtain from each $p_i$ an input $x_i \in \{0,1\}^{2k}$, and split $x_i$ into $x_i = y_i | z_i$ with $y_i, z_i \in \{0,1\}^k$. Output $y_1$ to $p_2$ and $y_2$ to $p_1$.
- No inputs: output $z_1$ to $p_2$ and $z_2$ to $p_1$.

---

**Fig. 3.** The two-phase exchange functionality.

sending the messages for that round.[6] The bound proven in the following lemma comes from the fact that if one of the parties gets the output first, then the adversary $\mathcal{A}_{gen}$ corrupting one party at random has a $1/2$ chance to corrupt this party and be the only one to get the output. The payoff of this strategy is the same as for the SFE (non-reactive) case, and the proof of the lemma also resembles the proof of the simpler case.

**Lemma 1.** *Let* $\gamma = (\gamma_{00}, \gamma_{01}, \gamma_{10}, \gamma_{11}) \in \Gamma_{fair}$. *For every protocol* $\Pi$ *which securely implements the functionality* $f_{2Ex}^{\perp}$, *there exists an adversary* $\mathcal{A}$ *with*

$$\bar{u}_{\mathsf{A}}(\Pi, \mathcal{A}) \overset{negl}{\geq} \frac{\gamma_{10} + \gamma_{11}}{2}. \tag{4}$$

The lemma shows the optimality of the protocol described in Sect. 4.2 for all cases where $\gamma_{11} > -\gamma_{10}$. The next lemma provides a lower bound that is relevant in the more general case without this restriction, and is also interesting for protocols for which the bound from Equation (4) is not tight because, e.g., they use too few rounds. In fact, in the case of reactive MPC, the maximum utility of the adversary generally depends on the number of protocol rounds, and in particular we show a trade-off between the payoff of the generic adversary and the payoff of adversaries that potentially abort during the protocol without receiving their output. The proof is in the full version.

**Lemma 2.** *Let* $\gamma = (\gamma_{00}, \gamma_{01}, \gamma_{10}, \gamma_{11}) \in \Gamma_{fair}$, *and* $\Pi$ *be an* $r$-*round-reconstruction protocol that securely implements the functionality* $f_{2Ex}^{\perp}$, *such that*

$$\bar{u}_{\mathsf{A}}(\Pi, \mathcal{A}_{gen}) \leq \frac{\gamma_{10} + \gamma_{11}}{2} + \omega.$$

*Then, there exists an adversary* $\mathcal{A}$ *with*

$$\bar{u}_{\mathsf{A}}(\Pi, \mathcal{A}) \overset{negl}{\geq} \frac{\left(\frac{1}{2} - \frac{\omega}{\gamma_{10} - \gamma_{11}}\right) \gamma_{10}}{\sum_{\ell=1}^{r-1} \varrho^{\ell-1}},$$

*where* $\varrho = -\gamma_{01}/\gamma_{10}$.

---

[6] In the case of (reactive) MPC the protocol may output only either the correct value or an "abort" symbol, as an honest party cannot restart the protocol with a default input because the adversary already obtained output in the previous rounds.

By increasing the number of rounds in the reconstruction phase and choosing a suitable distribution of probabilities over the rounds, we can decrease the payoff of the "aborting" adversaries below the bound of the generic adversary, thus establishing that protocol $\Pi_{RC}^{fair}$ is optimally fair. The necessary number of rounds for the optimal result depends on the exact values of the adversary's utility, and can be computed as in Sect. 4.1; details appear in the full version.

**Corollary 1.** *Let* $\gamma = (\gamma_{00}, \gamma_{01}, \gamma_{10}, \gamma_{11}) \in \Gamma_{fair}$ *and* $\gamma_{11} > -\gamma_{01}$. *Then protocol* $\Pi_{RC}^{fair}$ *from Fig. 1 is optimally* $\gamma$-*fair*.

# References

1. Asharov, G., Canetti, R., Hazay, C.: Towards a game theoretic view of secure computation. In: Paterson, K.G. (ed.) EUROCRYPT 2011. LNCS, vol. 6632, pp. 426–445. Springer, Heidelberg (2011)
2. Beaver, D., Goldwasser, S.: Multiparty computation with faulty majority. In: FOCS 1989, pp. 468–473. IEEE (1989)
3. Beimel, A., Lindell, Y., Omri, E., Orlov, I.: $1/p$-Secure multiparty computation without honest majority and the best of both worlds. In: Rogaway, P. (ed.) CRYPTO 2011. LNCS, vol. 6841, pp. 277–296. Springer, Heidelberg (2011)
4. Blum, M.: How to exchange (secret) keys. ACM Transactions on Computer Science **1**, 175–193 (1984)
5. Boneh, D., Naor, M.: Timed commitments. In: Bellare, M. (ed.) CRYPTO 2000. LNCS, vol. 1880, pp. 236–254. Springer, Heidelberg (2000)
6. Canetti, R.: Security and composition of multiparty cryptographic protocols. Journal of Cryptology **13**, 143–202 (2000)
7. Canetti, R.: Universally composable security: A new paradigm for cryptographic protocols. In: FOCS 2001, pp. 136–145. IEEE (2001)
8. Cleve, R.E.: Limits on the security of coin flips when half the processors are faulty. In: STOC 1986, pp. 364–369. ACM, Berkeley (1986)
9. Damgård, I.: Practical and provably secure release of a secret and exchange of signatures. Journal of Cryptology **8**(4), 201–222 (1995)
10. Garay, J.A., Katz, J., Maurer, U., Tackmann, B., Zikas, V.: Rational protocol design: Cryptography against incentive-driven adversaries. In: FOCS 2013. IEEE (2013)
11. Garay, J.A., Katz, J., Tackmann, B., Zikas, V.: How fair is your protocol? A utility-based approach to protocol optimality. In: Spirakis, P. (ed.) PODC 2015. ACM Press (2015)
12. Garay, J.A., MacKenzie, P.D., Prabhakaran, M., Yang, K.: Resource fairness and composability of cryptographic protocols. In: Halevi, S., Rabin, T. (eds.) TCC 2006. LNCS, vol. 3876, pp. 404–428. Springer, Heidelberg (2006)
13. Garay, J.A., Tackmann, B., Zikas, V.: Fair distributed computation of reactive functions. Cryptology ePrint Archive, Report 2015/807, August 2015
14. Goldreich, O., Micali, S., Wigderson, A.: How to play any mental game–A completeness theorem for protocols with honest majority. In: STOC 1987, pp. 218–229. ACM (1987)
15. Gordon, S.D., Katz, J.: Partial fairness in secure two-party computation. In: Gilbert, H. (ed.) EUROCRYPT 2010. LNCS, vol. 6110, pp. 157–176. Springer, Heidelberg (2010)

16. Groce, A., Katz, J.: Fair computation with rational players. In: Pointcheval, D., Johansson, T. (eds.) EUROCRYPT 2012. LNCS, vol. 7237, pp. 81–98. Springer, Heidelberg (2012)
17. Katz, J., Maurer, U., Tackmann, B., Zikas, V.: Universally composable synchronous computation. In: Sahai, A. (ed.) TCC 2013. LNCS, vol. 7785, pp. 477–498. Springer, Heidelberg (2013)
18. Pinkas, B.: Fair secure two-party computation. In: Biham, E. (ed.) EUROCRYPT 2003. LNCS, vol. 2656, pp. 87–105. Springer, Heidelberg (2003)
19. Yao, A.C.: Theory and applications of trapdoor functions. In: FOCS 1982, pp. 80–91. IEEE (1982)

# Smoothed Analysis of Dynamic Networks

Michael Dinitz[1], Jeremy Fineman[2], Seth Gilbert[3], and Calvin Newport[4(✉)]

[1] Johns Hopkins University, Baltimore, USA
mdinitz@cs.jhu.edu
[2] Georgetown University, Washington, DC, USA
jfineman@cs.georgetown.edu
[3] National University of Singapore, Singapore, Singapore
seth.gilbert@comp.nus.edu.sg
[4] Georgetown University, Washington, DC, USA
cnewport@cs.georgetown.edu

**Abstract.** We generalize the technique of *smoothed analysis* to distributed algorithms in dynamic networks. Whereas standard smoothed analysis studies the impact of small random perturbations of input values on algorithm performance metrics, dynamic graph smoothed analysis studies the impact of random perturbations of the underlying changing network graph topologies. Similar to the original application of smoothed analysis, our goal is to study whether known strong lower bounds in dynamic network models are *robust* or *fragile*: do they withstand small (random) perturbations, or do such deviations push the graphs far enough from a precise pathological instance to enable much better performance? Fragile lower bounds are likely not relevant for real-world deployment, while robust lower bounds represent a true difficulty caused by dynamic behavior. We apply this technique to three standard dynamic network problems with known strong worst-case lower bounds: random walks, flooding, and aggregation. We prove that these bounds provide a spectrum of robustness when subjected to smoothing—some are extremely fragile (random walks), some are moderately fragile / robust (flooding), and some are extremely robust (aggregation).

## 1 Introduction

Dynamic network models describe networks with topologies that change over time (c.f., [10]). They are used to capture the unpredictable link behavior that characterize challenging networking scenarios; e.g., connecting and coordinating moving vehicles, nearby smartphones, or nodes in a widespread and fragile overlay. Because fine-grained descriptions of link behavior in such networks are hard to specify, most analyses of dynamic networks rely instead on a worst-case

M. Dinitz—Supported in part by NSF grant #1464239.
J. Fineman—Supported in part by NSF grants CCF-1218188 and CCF-1314633.
S. Gilbert—Supported in part by Singapore MOE Tier 2 ARC project 2014-T2-1-157.
C. Newport—Supported in part by NSF grant CCF 1320279.

Y. Moses (Ed.): DISC 2015, LNCS 9363, pp. 513–527, 2015.
DOI: 10.1007/978-3-662-48653-5_34

selection of graph changes. This property is crucial to the usefulness of these analyses, as it helps ensure the results persist in real deployment.

A problem with this worst case perspective is that it often leads to extremely strong lower bounds. These strong results motivate a key question: *Is this bound* robust *in the sense that it captures a fundamental difficulty introduced by dynamism, or is the bound* fragile *in the sense that the poor performance it describes depends on an exact sequence of adversarial changes?* Fragile lower bounds leave open the possibility of algorithms that might still perform well in practice. By separating fragile from robust results, we can expand the algorithmic tools available to those seeking useful guarantees in these challenging environments.

In the study of traditional algorithms, an important technique for explaining why algorithms work well in practice, despite disappointing worst case performance, is *smoothed analysis* [16,17]. This approach studies the expected performance of an algorithm when the inputs are slightly perturbed. If a strong lower bound dissipates after a small amount of smoothing, it is considered fragile—as it depends on a carefully constructed degenerate case. Note that this is different from an "average-case" analysis, which looks at instances drawn from some distribution. In a smoothed analysis, you still begin with an adversarially chosen input, but then slightly perturb this choice. Of course, as the perturbation grows larger, the input converges to something entirely random. (Indeed, in the original smoothed analysis papers [16,17], the technique is described as interpolating between worst and average case analysis.)

In this paper, we take the natural step of adapting smoothed analysis to the study of distributed algorithms in dynamic networks. Whereas in the traditional setting smoothing typically perturbs numerical input values, in our setting we define smoothing to perturb the network graph through the random addition and deletion of edges. We claim that a lower bound for a dynamic network model that improves with just a small amount of graph smoothing of this type is fragile, as it depends on the topology evolving in an exact manner. On the other hand, a lower bound that persists even after substantial smoothing is robust, as this reveals a large number of similar graphs for which the bound holds.

*Results.*    We begin by providing a general definition of a dynamic network model that captures many of the existing models already studied in the distributed algorithms literature. At the core of a dynamic network model is a dynamic graph that describes the evolving network topology. We provide a natural definition of *smoothing* for a dynamic graph that is parameterized with a *smoothing factor* $k \in \{0, 1, ..., \binom{n}{2}\}$. In more detail, to $k$-smooth a dynamic graph $\mathcal{H}$ is to replace each static graph $G$ in $\mathcal{H}$ with a smoothed graph $G'$ sampled uniformly from the space of graphs that are: (1) within edit distance[1] $k$ of $G$, and (2) are allowed by the relevant dynamic network model. (E.g., if the model requires the graph to be connected in every round, smoothing cannot generate a disconnected graph.)

---

[1] Edit distance, in this paper, is the number of edge additions/deletions needed to transform one graph to another, assuming they share the same node set.

**Table 1.** A summary of our main results. The columns labelled "$k$-smoothed" assume $k > 0$. Different results assume different upper bounds on $k$.

| | Graph | $k$-Smoothed Algorithm | $k$-Smoothed Lower Bound | 0-Smoothed Lower Bound |
|---|---|---|---|---|
| Flooding | Connected | $O(n^{2/3} \log n/k^{1/3})$ | $\Omega(n^{2/3}/k^{1/3})$ | $\Omega(n)$ |
| Hitting Time | Connected | $O(n^3/k)$ | $\Omega(n^{5/2}/(\sqrt{k} \log n))$ | $\Omega(2^n)$ |
| Aggregation | Paired | $O(n)$-competitive | $\Omega(n)$-competitive | $\Omega(n)$-competitive |

We next argue that these definitions allow for useful discernment between different dynamic network lower bounds. To this end, we use as case studies three well known problems with strong lower bounds in dynamic network models: flooding, random walks, and aggregation. For each problem, we explore the robustness/fragility of the existing bound by studying how it improves under increasing amounts of smoothing. Our results are summarized in Table 1. We emphasize the surprising variety in outcomes: these results capture a wide spectrum of possible responses to smoothing, from quite fragile to quite robust.

For the minimal amount of smoothing ($k = 1$), for example, the $\Omega(2^n)$ lower bound for the hitting time of a random walk in connected dynamic networks (established in [2]) decreases by an *exponential* factor to $O(n^3)$; the $\Omega(n)$ lower bound for flooding time in these same networks (well-known in folklore) decreases by a *polynomial* factor to $O(n^{2/3} \log n)$; and the $\Omega(n)$ lower bound on the achievable competitive ratio for token aggregation in pairing dynamic graphs (established in [4]) decreases by only a *constant* factor.

As we increase the smoothing factor $k$, our upper bound on random walk hitting time decreases as $O(n^3/k)$, while our flooding upper bound reduces more slowly as $O(n^{2/3} \log n/k^{1/3})$, and our aggregation bound remains in $\Omega(n)$ for $k$ values as large as $\Theta(n/\log^2 n)$. In all three cases we also prove tight or near tight lower bounds for all studied values of $k$.

Among other insights, these results indicate that the exponential hitting time lower bound for dynamic walks is extremely fragile, while the impossibility of obtaining a good competitive ratio for dynamic aggregation is quite robust. Flooding provides an interesting intermediate case. While it is clear that an $\Omega(n)$ bound is fragile, the claim that flooding can take a polynomial amount of time (say, in the range $n^{1/3}$ to $n^{2/3}$) seems well-supported.

*Full Version.* Due to space constraints, we omit proofs from this extended abstract. Full details for our results can be found in the full version [6].

*Next Steps.* The definitions and results that follow represent a first (but far from final) step toward the goal of adapting smoothed analysis to dynamic networks. There are many additional interesting dynamic network bounds that could be subjected to a smoothed analysis. Moreover, there are many other reasonable definitions of smoothing beyond the ones herein. While our definition is natural and our results suggestive, for other problems or models other definitions might be more appropriate. Rather than claiming that our approach here is the "right" way to study the fragility of dynamic network lower bounds, we instead claim that smoothed analysis generally speaking (in all its various possible formulations) is an important and promising tool when trying to understand the fundamental limits of distributed behavior in dynamic network settings.

*Related Work.* Smoothed analysis was introduced by Spielman and Teng [16,17], who used the technique to explain why the simplex algorithm works well in practice despite strong worst-case lower bounds. It has been widely applied to traditional algorithm problems (see [18] for a good introduction and survey). Recent interest in studying distributed algorithms in dynamic networks was sparked by Kuhn et al. [11]. Many different problems and dynamic network models have since been proposed; e.g., [1,3,5,7–9,12,14] (see [10] for a survey). The dynamic random walk lower bound we study was first proposed by Avin et al. [2], while the dynamic aggregation lower bound we study was first proposed by Cornejo et al. [4]. We note other techniques have been proposed for exploring the fragility of dynamic network lower bounds. In recent work, for example, Denysyuk et al. [5] thwart the exponential random walk lower bound due to [2] by requiring the dynamic graph to include a certain number of static graphs from a well-defined set, while work by Ghaffari et al. [8] studies the impact of adversary strength, and Newport [14] studies the impact of graph properties, on lower bounds in the dynamic radio network model.

## 2    Dynamic Graphs, Networks, and Types

There is no single dynamic network model. There are, instead, many different models that share the same basic behavior: nodes executing synchronous algorithms are connected by a network graph that can change from round to round. Details on how the graphs can change and how communication behaves given a graph differ between model types.

In this section we provide a general definition for a dynamic network models that captures many existing models in the relevant literature. This approach allows us in the next section to define smoothing with sufficient generality that it can apply to these existing models. We note that in this paper we constrain our attention to *oblivious* graph behavior (i.e., the changing graph is fixed at the beginning of the execution), but that the definitions that follow generalize in a straightforward manner to capture adaptive models (i.e., the changing graph can adapt to behavior of the algorithm).

*Dynamic Graphs and Networks.*    Fix some node set $V$, where $n = |V|$. A *dynamic graph* $\mathcal{H}$, defined with respect to $V$, is a sequence $G_1, G_2, ...,$ where each $G_i = (V, E_i)$ is a graph defined over nodes $V$. If this is not an infinite sequence, then the *length* of $\mathcal{H}$ is $|\mathcal{H}|$, the number of graphs in the sequence. A *dynamic network*, defined with respect to $V$, is a pair, $(\mathcal{H}, C)$, where $\mathcal{H}$ is a dynamic graph, and $C$ is a *communication rules* function that maps *transmission patterns* to *receive patterns*. That is, the function takes as input a static graph and an assignment of messages to nodes, and returns an assignment of received messages to nodes. For example, in the classical radio network model $C$ would specify that nodes receive a message only if exactly one of their neighbors transmits, while in the $\mathcal{LOCAL}$ model $C$ would specify that all nodes receive all messages sent by their neighbors. Finally, an *algorithm* maps process definitions to nodes in $V$.

Given a dynamic network $(\mathcal{H}, C)$ and an algorithm $\mathcal{A}$, an execution of $\mathcal{A}$ in $(\mathcal{H}, C)$ proceeds as follows: for each round $r$, nodes use their process definition according to $\mathcal{A}$ to determine their transmission behavior, and the resulting receive behavior is determined by applying $C$ to $\mathcal{H}[r]$ and this transmission pattern.

*Dynamic Network Types.* When we think of a dynamic network model suitable for running executions of distributed algorithms, what we really mean is a combination of a description of how communication works, and a set of the different dynamic graphs we might encounter. We formalize this notion with the concept of the *dynamic network type*, which we define as a pair $(\mathcal{G}, C)$, where $\mathcal{G}$ is a set of dynamic graphs and $C$ is a communication rules function. For each $\mathcal{H} \in \mathcal{G}$, we say dynamic network type $(\mathcal{G}, C)$ contains the dynamic network $(\mathcal{H}, C)$.

When proving an upper bound result, we will typically show that the result holds when our algorithm is executed in any dynamic network contained within a given type. When proving a lower bound result, we will typically show that there exists a dynamic network contained within the relevant type for which the result holds. In this paper, we will define and analyze two existing dynamic network types: *(1-interval) connected networks* [7,9,11,12], in which the graph in each round is connected and $C$ describes reliable broadcast to neighbors in the graph, and *pairing networks* [4], in which the graph in each round is a matching and $C$ describes reliable message passing with each node's neighbor (if any).

## 3  Smoothing Dynamic Graphs

We now define a version of smoothed analysis that is relevant to dynamic graphs. To begin, we define the *edit distance* between two static graphs $G = (V, E)$ and $G' = (V, E')$ to be the minimum number of edge additions and removals needed to transform $G$ to $G'$. With this in mind, for a given $G$ and $k \in \{0, 1, ..., \binom{n}{2}\}$, we define the set:

$$editdist(G, k) = \{G' \mid \text{the edit distance between } G \text{ and } G' \text{ is no more than } k\}.$$

Finally, for a given set of dynamic graphs $\mathcal{G}$, we define the set:

$$allowed(\mathcal{G}) = \{G \mid \exists \mathcal{H} \in \mathcal{G} \text{ such that } G \in \mathcal{H}\}.$$

In other words, *allowed* describes all graphs that show up in the dynamic graphs contained in the set $\mathcal{G}$. Our notion of smoothing is always defined with respect to a dynamic graph set $\mathcal{G}$. Formally:

**Definition 1.** *Fix a set of dynamic graphs $\mathcal{G}$, a dynamic graph $\mathcal{H} \in \mathcal{G}$, and smoothing factor $k \in \{0, 1, ..., \binom{n}{2}\}$. To $k$-smooth a static graph $G \in \mathcal{H}$ (with* *respect to $\mathcal{G}$) is to replace $G$ with a graph $G'$ sampled uniformly from the set editdist$(G, k) \cap$ allowed$(\mathcal{G})$. To $k$-smooth the entire dynamic graph $\mathcal{H}$ (with respect to $\mathcal{G}$), is to replace $\mathcal{H}$ with the dynamic graph $\mathcal{H}'$ that results when we $k$-smooth each of its static graphs.*

We will also sometimes say that $G'$ (resp. $\mathcal{H}'$) is a *$k$-smoothed* version of $G$ (resp. $\mathcal{H}$), or simply a *$k$-smoothed* $G$ (resp. $\mathcal{H}$). We often omit the dynamic graph set $\mathcal{G}$ when it is clear in context. (Typically, $\mathcal{G}$ will be the set contained in a dynamic network type under consideration.)

*Discussion.* Our notion of $k$-smoothing transforms a graph by randomly adding or deleting $k$ edges. A key piece of our definition is that smoothing a graph with respect to a dynamic graph set cannot produce a graph not found in any members of that set. This restriction is particularly important for proving lower bounds on smoothed graphs, as we want to make sure that the lower bound results does not rely on a dynamic graph that could not otherwise appear. For example, if studying a process in a dynamic graph that is always connected, we do not want smoothing to disconnect the graph—an event that might trivialize some bounds.

# 4    Connected and Pairing Dynamic Network Types

We now define two dynamic network types: the *connected network type* [7,9,11, 12], and the *pairing network type* [4]. We study random walks (Section 6) and flooding (Section 5) in the context of the connected network type, whereas we study token aggregation (Section 7) in the context of the pairing type.

## 4.1    Connected Network

The *connected network type* [7,9,11,12] is defined as $(\mathcal{G}_{conn}, C_{conn})$, where $\mathcal{G}_{conn}$ contains every dynamic graph (defined with respect to our fixed node set $V$) in which every individual graph is connected, and where $C_{conn}$ describes reliable broadcast (i.e., a message sent by $u$ in rounds $r$ in an execution in graph $\mathcal{H}$ is received by every neighbor of $u$ in $\mathcal{H}[r]$).

*Properties of Smoothed Connected Networks.* For our upper bounds, we show that if certain edges are added to the graph through smoothing, then the algorithm makes enough progress on the smoothed graph. For our lower bounds, we show that if certain edges are not added to the graph, then the algorithm does not make much progress. The following lemmas bound the probabilities that these edges are added. The proofs roughly amount to showing that sampling uniformly from editdist$(G, k) \cap$ allowed$(\mathcal{G}_{conn})$ is similar to sampling from editdist$(G, k)$.

The first two lemmas are applicable when upper-bounding the performance of an algorithm on a smoothed dynamic graph. The first lemma states that the $k$-smoothed version of graph $G$ is fairly likely to include at least one edge from the set $S$ of helpful edges. The second lemma, conversely, says that certain critical edges that already exist in $G$ are very unlikely to be removed in the smoothed version.

**Lemma 1.** *There exists constant $c_1 > 0$ such that the following holds. Consider any graph $G \in allowed(\mathcal{G}_{conn})$. Consider also any nonempty set $S$ of potential edges and smoothing value $k \leq n/16$ with $k |S| \leq n^2/2$. Then with probability at least $c_1 k |S| /n^2$, the $k$-smoothed graph $G'$ of $G$ contains at least one edge from $S$.*

**Lemma 2.** *There exists constant $c_2 > 0$ such that the following holds. Consider any graph $G = (V, E) \in allowed(\mathcal{G}_{conn})$. Consider also any nonempty set $S \subseteq E$ of edges in the graph and smoothing value $k \leq n/16$. Then with probability at most $c_2 k |S| /n^2$, the $k$-smoothed graph $G'$ removes an edge from $S$.*

Our next lemma is applicable when lower-bounding an algorithm's performance on a dynamic graph. It says essentially that Lemma 1 is tight—it is not too likely to add any of the helpful edges from $S$.

**Lemma 3.** *There exists constant $c_3 > 0$ such that the following holds. Consider any graph $G = (V, E) \in allowed(\mathcal{G}_{conn})$. Consider also any set $S$ of edges and smoothing value $k \leq n/16$ such that $S \cap E = \emptyset$. Then with probability at most $c_3 k |S| /n^2$, the $k$-smoothed graph $G'$ of $G$ contains an edge from $S$.*

## 4.2 Pairing Network

The second type we study is the *pairing network type* [4]. This type is defined as $(\mathcal{G}_{pair}, C_{pair})$, where $\mathcal{G}_{pair}$ contains every dynamic graph (defined with respect to our fixed node set $V$) in which every individual graph is a (not necessarily complete) matching, and $C_{pair}$ reliable communicates messages between pairs of nodes connected in the given round. This network type is motivated by the current peer-to-peer network technologies implemented in smart devices. These low-level protocols usually depend on discovering nearby nodes and initiating one-on-one local interaction.

*Properties of Smoothed Pairing Networks.* In the following, when discussing a matching $G$, we partition nodes into one of two *types*: a node is *matched* if it is connected to another node by an edge in $G$, and it is otherwise *unmatched*. The following property concerns the probability that smoothing affects (i.e., adds or deletes at least one adjacent edge) a given node $u$ from a set $S$ of nodes of the same type. It notes that as the set $S$ containing $u$ grows, the *upper bound* on the probability that $u$ is affected decreases. The key insight behind this not necessarily intuitive statement is that this probability must be the same for *all* nodes in $S$ (due to their symmetry in the graph). Therefore, a given probability will generate more expected changes as $S$ grows, and therefore, to keep the expected changes below the $k$ threshold, this bound on this probability must decrease as $S$ grows.

**Lemma 4.** *Consider any graph $G = (V, E) \in allowed(\mathcal{G}_{pair})$ and constant $\delta > 1$. Let $S \subseteq V$ be a set of nodes in $G$ such that: (1) all nodes in $S$ are of the same type (matched or unmatched), and (2) $|S| \geq n/\delta$. Consider any node $u \in S$ and smoothing factor $k < n/(2 \cdot \delta)$. Let $G'$ be the result of $k$-smoothing $G$. The probability that $u$'s adjacency list is different in $G'$ as compared to $G$ is no more than $(2 \cdot \delta \cdot k)/n$.*

## 5    Flooding

Here we consider the performance of a basic flooding process in a connected dynamic network. In more detail, we assume a single *source* node starts with a message. In every round, every node that knows the message broadcasts the message to its neighbors. (Flooding can be trivially implemented in a connected network type due to reliable communication.) We consider the flooding process *complete* in the first round that every node has the message. Without smoothing, this problem clearly takes $\Omega(n)$ rounds in large diameter static graphs, so a natural alternative is to state bounds in terms of diameter. Unfortunately, there exist dynamic graphs (e.g., the spooling graph defined below) where the graph in each round is constant diameter, but flooding still requires $\Omega(n)$ rounds.

We show that this $\Omega(n)$ lower bound is somewhat fragile by proving a polynomial improvement with any smoothing. Specifically, we show an upper bound of $O(n^{2/3} \log(n)/k^{1/3})$ rounds, with high probability, with $k$-smoothing. We also exhibit a nearly matching lower bound by showing that the dynamic spooling graph requires $\Omega(n^{2/3}/k^{1/3})$ rounds with constant probability.

### 5.1    Lower Bound

We build our lower bound around the dynamic *spooling graph*, defined as follows. Label the nodes from 1 to $n$, where node 1 is the source. The spooling graph is a dynamic graph where in each round $r$, the network is the min $\{r, n-1\}$-spool graph. We define the *i-spool graph*, for $i \in [n-1]$ to be the graph consisting of: a star on nodes $\{1, \ldots, i\}$ centered at $i$ called the *left spool*, a star on nodes $\{i+1, \ldots, n\}$ centered on $i+1$ called the *right spool*, and an edge between the two centers $i$ and $i+1$. We call $i+1$ the *head* node.

With node 1 as the source node, it is straightforward to see that, in the absence of smoothing, flooding requires $n-1$ rounds to complete on the spooling network. (Every node in the left spool has the message but every node in the right spool does not. In each round, the head node receives the message then moves to the left spool.) We generalize this lower bound to smoothing. The main idea is that in order for every node to receive the message early, one of the early heads must be adjacent to a smoothed edge.

**Theorem 1.** *Consider the flooding process on a $k$-smoothed $n$-vertex spooling graph, with $k \le \sqrt{n}$ and sufficiently large $n$. With probability at least $1/2$, the flooding process does not complete before the $\Omega(n^{2/3}/k^{1/3})$-th round.*

### 5.2    An $O(n^{2/3} \log n/k^{1/3})$ Upper Bound for General Networks

Next, we show that flooding in *every* $k$-smoothed network will complete in $O(n^{2/3} \log n/k^{1/3})$ time, with high probability. When this result is combined with the $\Omega(n^{2/3}/k^{1/3})$ lower bound from above, this shows this analysis to be essentially tight for this problem under smoothing.

*Support Sequences.* The core idea is to show that every node in every network is supported by a structure in the dynamic graph such that if the message can be delivered to *anywhere* in this structure in time, it will subsequently propagate to the target. In the spooling network, this structure for a given target node $u$ consists simply of the nodes that will become the head in the rounds leading up to the relevant complexity deadline. The *support sequence* object defined below generalizes a similar notion to all graphs. It provides, in some sense, a fat target for the smoothed edges to hit in their quest to accelerate flooding.

**Definition 2.** *Fix two integers $t$ and $\ell$, $1 \leq \ell < t$, a dynamic graph $\mathcal{H} = G_1, \ldots, G_t$ with $G_i = (V, E_i)$ for all $i$, and a node $u \in V$. A $(t, \ell)$-support sequence for $u$ in $G$ is a sequence $S_0, S_1, S_2, \ldots, S_\ell$, such that the following properties hold: (1) For every $i \in [0, \ell]$: $S_i \subseteq V$. (2) $S_0 = \{u\}$. (3) For every $i \in [1, \ell]$: $S_{i-1} \subset S_i$ and $S_i \setminus S_{i-1} = \{v\}$, for some $v \in V$ such that $v$ is adjacent to at least one node of $S_{i-1}$ in $G_{t-i}$.*

Notice that the support structure is defined "backwards" with $S_0$ containing the target node $u$, and each subsequent step going one round back in time. We prove that every connected dynamic graph has such a support structure, because the graph is connected in every round.

**Lemma 5.** *Fix some dynamic graph $\mathcal{H} \in \mathcal{G}_{conn}$ on vertex set $V$, some node $u \in V$, and some rounds $t$ and $\ell$, where $1 \leq \ell < t$. There exists a $(t, \ell)$-support sequence for $u$ in $\mathcal{H}$.*

The following key lemma shows that over every period of $\Theta(n^{2/3}/k^{1/3})$ rounds of $k$-smoothed flooding, every node has a constant probability of receiving the message. Applying this lemma over $\Theta(\log n)$ consecutive time intervals with a Chernoff bound, we get our main theorem.

**Lemma 6.** *There exists constant $\alpha \geq 3$ such that the following holds. Fix a dynamic graph $\mathcal{H} \in \mathcal{G}_{conn}$ on vertex set $V$, any node $u \in V$, and a consecutive interval of $\alpha n^{2/3}/k^{1/3}$ rounds. For smoothing value $k \leq n/16$, node $u$ receives the flooded message in the $k$-smoothed version of $\mathcal{H}$ with probability at least $1/2$.*

**Theorem 2.** *For any dynamic graph $\mathcal{H} \in \mathcal{G}_{conn}$ and smoothing value $k \leq n/16$, flooding completes in $O(n^{2/3} \log n/k^{1/3})$ rounds on the $k$-smoothed version of $\mathcal{H}$ with high probability.*

# 6   Random Walks

As discussed in Section 1, random walks in dynamic graphs exhibit fundamentally different behavior from random walks in static graphs. Most notably, in dynamic graphs there can be pairs of nodes whose hitting time is exponential [2], even though in static (connected) graphs it is well-known that the maximum hitting time is at most $O(n^3)$ [13]. This is true even under obvious technical restrictions necessary to prevent infinite hitting times, such as requiring the graph to be connected at all times and to have self-loops at all nodes.

We show that this lower bound is extremely fragile. A straightforward argument shows that a small perturbation (1-smoothing) is enough to guarantee that in *any* dynamic graph, all hitting times are at most $O(n^3)$. Larger perturbations ($k$-smoothing) lead to $O(n^3/k)$ hitting times. We also prove a lower bound of $\Omega(n^{5/2}/\sqrt{k})$, using an example which is in fact a static graph (made dynamic by simply repeating it). In some sense, it is not surprising that the lower bound on random walks is fragile, as there exist algorithms for accomplishing the same goals (e.g., identifying a random sample) in dynamic graphs in polynomial time [2,15].

## 6.1   Preliminaries

We begin with some technical preliminaries. In a static graph, a random walk starting at $u \in V$ is a walk on $G$ where the next node is chosen uniformly at random from the set of neighbors on the current node (possibly including the current node itself if there is a self-loop). The *hitting time* $H(u, v)$ for $u, v \in V$ is the expected number of steps taken by a random walk starting at $u$ until it hits $v$ for the first time. Random walks are defined similarly in a dynamic graph $\mathcal{H} = G_1, G_2, \ldots$: at first the random walk starts at $u$, and if at the beginning of time step $t$ it is at a node $v_t$ then in step $t$ it moves to a neighbor of $v_t$ in $G_t$ chosen uniformly at random. Hitting times are defined in the same way as in the static case.

The definition of the hitting time in a smoothed dynamic graph is intuitive but slightly subtle. Given a dynamic graph $\mathcal{H}$ and vertices $u, v$, the *hitting time from $u$ to $v$ under $k$-smoothing*, denoted by $H_k(u, v)$, is the expected number of steps taken by a random walk starting at $u$ until first reaching $v$ in the (random) $k$-smoothed version $\mathcal{H}'$ of $\mathcal{H}$ (either with respect to $\mathcal{G}_{conn}$ or with respect to the set $\mathcal{G}_{all}$ of all dynamic graphs). Note that this expectation is now taken over two independent sources of randomness: the randomness of the random walk, and also the randomness of the smoothing (as defined in Section 3).

## 6.2   Upper Bounds

We first prove that even a tiny amount amount of smoothing is sufficient to guarantee polynomial hitting times even though without smoothing there is an exponential lower bound. Intuitively, this is because if we add a random edge at every time point, there is always some inverse polynomial probability of directly jumping to the target node. We also show that more smoothing decreases this bound linearly.

**Theorem 3.** *In any dynamic graph $\mathcal{H}$, for all vertices $u, v$ and value $k \leq n/16$, the hitting time $H_k(u, v)$ under $k$-smoothing (with respect to $\mathcal{G}_{all}$) is at most $O(n^3/k)$. This is also true for smoothing with respect to $\mathcal{G}_{conn}$ if $\mathcal{H} \in \mathcal{G}_{conn}$.*

A particularly interesting example is the *dynamic star*, which was used by Avin et al. [2] to prove an exponential lower bound. The dynamic star consists of

$n$ vertices $\{0, 1, \ldots, n-1\}$, where the center of the start at time $t$ is $t \mod (n-1)$ (note that node $n-1$ is never the center). Every node also has a self loop. Avin et al. [2] proved that the hitting time from node $n-2$ to node $n-1$ is at least $2^{n-2}$. It turns out that this lower bound is particularly fragile – not only does Theorem 3 imply that the hitting time is polynomial, it is actually a factor of $n$ better than the global upper bound due to the small degrees at the leaves.

**Theorem 4.** $H_k(u, v)$ *is at most* $O(n^2/k)$ *in the dynamic star for all* $k \leq n/16$ *and for all vertices* $u, v$ *(where smoothing is with respect to* $\mathcal{G}_{conn}$*).*

## 6.3 Lower Bounds

Since the dynamic star was the worst example for random walks in dynamic graphs without smoothing, Theorem 4 naturally leads to the question of whether the bound of $O(n^2/k)$ holds for all dynamic graphs in $\mathcal{G}_{conn}$, or whether the weaker bound of $O(n^3/k)$ from Theorem 3 is tight. We show that under smoothing, the dynamic star is in fact *not* the worst case: a lower bound of $\Omega(n^{5/2}/\sqrt{k})$ holds for the *lollipop graph*. The lollipop is a famous example of graph in which the hitting time is large: there are nodes $u$ and $v$ such that $H(u, v) = \Theta(n^3)$ (see, e.g., [13]). Here we will use it to prove a lower bound on the hitting time of dynamic graphs under smoothing:

**Theorem 5.** *There is a dynamic graph* $\mathcal{H} \in \mathcal{G}_{conn}$ *and nodes* $u, v$ *such that* $H_k(u, v) \geq \Omega(n^{5/2}/(\sqrt{k} \ln n))$ *for all* $k \leq n/16$ *(where smoothing is with respect to* $\mathcal{G}_{conn}$*).*

In the lollipop graph $L_n = (V, E)$ the vertex set is partitioned into two pieces $V_1$ and $V_2$ with $|V_1| = |V_2| = n/2$. The nodes in $V_1$ form a clique (i.e. there is an edge between every two nodes in $V_1$), while the nodes in $V_2$ form a path (i.e., there is a bijection $\pi : [n/2] \to V_2$ such that there is an edge between $\pi(i)$ and $\pi(i+1)$ for all $i \in [(n/2) - 1]$). There is also a single special node $v^* \in V_1$ which has an edge to the beginning of the $V_2$ path, i.e., there is also an edge $\{v^*, \pi(1)\}$. The dynamic graph $\mathcal{H}$ in Theorem 5 is the dynamic lollipop: $G_i = L_n$ for all $i \geq 1$. The starting point of the random walk $u$ is an arbitrary node in $V_1$, and the target node $v = \pi(n/2)$ is the last node on the path.

The intuition for the 1-smoothing case is relatively straightforward: if the random walk is on the path then every $\Theta(n)$ rounds it will follow one of the randomly added smoothed edges, which will (with probability $1/2$) lead it back to the clique. So in order to hit $v$, it has to spend less than $n$ time in the path. A standard analysis of the one-dimensional random walk then implies that it will only move $O(\sqrt{n})$ positions from where it started, so it needs to start in the final $O(\sqrt{n})$ nodes of the path. In each round, it will only see an edge from its current location to this final set of nodes with probability $O(1/n^{3/2})$, and will follow it with probability only $O(1/n)$ (since it will likely be in the clique). Hence the total hitting time is $\Omega(n^{5/2})$. This idea can be formalized and extended to $k$-smoothing.

If we do not insist on the dynamic graph being connected at all times, then in fact Theorem 3 is tight via a very simple example: a clique with a single disconnected node.

**Theorem 6.** *There is a dynamic graph $\mathcal{H}$ and vertices $u, v$ such that $H_k(u, v) \geq \Omega(n^3/k)$ for all $k \leq n$ where smoothing is with respect to $\mathcal{G}_{all}$.*

# 7    Aggregation

Here we consider the aggregation problem in the pairing dynamic network type. Notice, in our study of flooding and random walks we were analyzing the behavior of a specific, well-known distributed process. In this section, by contrast, we consider the behavior of arbitrary algorithms. In particular, we will show the pessimistic lower bound for the aggregation problem for 0-smoothed pairing graphs from [4], holds (within constant factors), even for relatively large amounts of smoothing. This problem, therefore, provides an example of where smoothing does not help much.

*The Aggregation Problem.*  The aggregation problem, first defined in [4], assumes each node $u \in V$ begins with a unique token $\sigma[u]$. The execution proceeds for a fixed length determined by the length of the dynamic graph. At the end of the execution, each node $u$ *uploads* a set (potentially empty) $\gamma[u]$ containing tokens. An *aggregation algorithm* must avoid both losses and duplications (as would be required if these tokens were actually aggregated in an accurate manner). Formally:

**Definition 3.** *An algorithm $\mathcal{A}$ is an* aggregation algorithm *if and only if at the end of every execution of $\mathcal{A}$ the following two properties hold:*
*(1) No Loss: $\bigcup_{u \in V} \gamma[u] = \bigcup_{u \in V} \{\sigma[u]\}$. (2) No Duplication: $\forall u, v \in V, u \neq v :$ $\gamma[u] \cap \gamma[v] = \emptyset$.*

To evaluate the performance of an aggregation algorithm we introduce the notion of *aggregation factor*. At at the end of an execution, the aggregation factor of an algorithm is the number of nodes that upload at least one token (i.e., $|\{u \in V : \gamma[u] \neq \emptyset\}|$). Because some networks (e.g., a static cliques) are more suitable for small aggregation factors than others (e.g., no edges in any round) we evaluate the competitive ratio of an algorithm's aggregation factor as compared to the offline optimal performance for the given network.

The worst possible performance, therefore, is $n$, which implies that the algorithm uploaded from $n$ times as many nodes as the offline optimal (note that $n$ is the maximum possible value for an aggregation factor). This is only possible when the algorithm achieves no aggregation and yet an offline algorithm could have aggregated all tokens to a single node. The best possible performance is a competitive ratio of 1, which occurs when the algorithm matches the offline optimal performance.

*Results Summary.*  In [4], the authors prove that no aggregation algorithm can guarantee better than a $\Omega(n)$ competitive ratio with a constant probability or better. In more detail:

**Theorem 7 (Adapted from [4]).** *For every aggregation algorithm $\mathcal{A}$, there exists a pairing graph $\mathcal{H}$ such that with probability at least $1/2$: $\mathcal{A}$'s aggregation factor is $\Omega(n)$ times worse than the offline optimal aggregation factor in $\mathcal{H}$.*

Our goal in the remainder of this section is to prove that this strong lower bound persists even after a significant amount of smoothing (i.e., $k = O(n/\log^2 n)$). We formalize this result below (note that the cited probability is with respect to the random bits of both the algorithm and the smoothing process):

**Theorem 8.** *For every aggregation algorithm $\mathcal{A}$ and smoothing factor $k \leq n/(32 \cdot \log^2 n)$, there exists a pairing graph $\mathcal{H}$ such that with probability at least $1/2$: $\mathcal{A}$'s aggregation factor is $\Omega(n)$ times worse than the offline optimal aggregation factor in a $k$-smoothed version of $\mathcal{H}$ (with respect to $\mathcal{G}_{pair}$).*

## 7.1 Lower Bound

Here we prove that for any smoothing factor $k \leq (cn)/\log^2 n$ (for some positive constant fraction $c$ we fix in the analysis), $k$-smoothing does not help aggregation by more than a constant factor as compared to $0$-smoothing. To do so, we begin by describing a probabilistic process for generating a hard pairing graph. We will later show that the graph produced by this process is likely to be hard for a given randomized algorithm. To prove our main theorem, we will conclude by applying the probabilistic method to show this result implies the existence of a hard graph for each algorithm.

*The $\alpha$-Stable Pairing Graph Process.* We define a specific process for generating a pairing graph (i.e., a graph in $allowed(\mathcal{G}_{pair})$). The process is parameterized by some constant integer $\alpha \geq 1$. In the following, assume the network size $n = 2\ell$ for some integer $\ell \geq 1$ that is also a power of $2$.[2] For the purposes of this construction, we label the $2\ell$ nodes in the network as $a_1, b_1, a_2, b_2, ..., a_\ell, b_\ell$. For the first $\alpha$ rounds, our process generates graphs with the edge set: $\{(a_i, b_i) : 1 \leq i \leq \ell\}$. After these rounds, the process generates $\ell$ bits, $q_1, q_2, ..., q_\ell$, with uniform randomness. It then defines a set $S$ of *selected nodes* by adding to $S$ the node $a_i$ for every $i$ such that $q_i = 0$, and adding $b_i$ for every $i$ such that $q_i = 1$. That is, for each of our $(a_i, b_i)$ pairs, the process randomly flips a coin to select a single element from the pair to add to $S$.

For all graphs that follow, the nodes *not in $S$* will be isolated in the graph (i.e., not be matched). We turn our attention to how the process adds edges between the nodes that are in $S$. To do so, it divides the graphs that follow into *phases*, each consisting of $\alpha$ consecutive rounds of the same graph. In the first phase, this graph is the one that results when the process pairs up the nodes in $S$ by adding an edge between each such pair (these are the only edges).

---

[2] We can deal with odd $n$ and/or $\ell$ not a power of $2$ by suffering only a constant factor cost to our final performance. For simplicity of presentation, we maintain these assumptions for now.

In the second phase, the process defines a set $S_2$ that contains exactly one node from each of the pairs from the first phase. It then pairs up the nodes in $S_2$ with edges as before. It also pairs up all nodes in $S \setminus S_2$ arbitrarily. Every graph in the second phase includes only these edges. In the third phase, the process defines a set $S_3$ containing exactly one node from each of the $S_2$ pairs from the previous pairs. It then once again pairs up the remaining nodes in $S$ arbitrarily. The process repeats this procedure until phase $t = \log_2 |S|$ at which point only a single node is in $S_t$, and we are done.

The total length of this dynamic graph is $\alpha(\log_2(|S|)+1)$. It is easy to verify that it satisfies the definition of the pairing dynamic network type.

*Performance of the Offline Optimal Aggregation Algorithm.* We now show that the even with lots of smoothing, a graph generated by the stable pairing graph process, parameterized with a sufficiently large $\alpha$, yields a good optimal solution (i.e., an aggregation factor of 1).

**Lemma 7.** *For any $k \leq n/32$, and any pairing graph $\mathcal{H}$ that might be generated by the $(\log n)$-stable pairing graph process, with high probability in $n$: the offline optimal aggregation algorithm achieves an aggregation factor of 1 in a $k$-smoothed version of $\mathcal{H}$.*

*Performance of an Arbitrary Distributed Aggregation Algorithm.* We now fix an arbitrary distributed aggregation algorithm and demonstrate that it cannot guarantee (with good probability) to achieve a non-trivial competitive ratio in all pairing graphs. In particular, we will show it has a constant probability of performing poorly in a graph generated by our above process.

**Lemma 8.** *Fix an online aggregation algorithm $\mathcal{A}$ and smoothing factor $k \leq n/(32 \cdot \log^2 n)$. Consider a $k$-smoothed version of a graph $\mathcal{H}$ generated by the $(\log n)$-stable pairing graph process. With probability greater than $1/2$ (over the smoothing, adversary, and algorithm's independent random choices): $\mathcal{A}$ has an aggregation factor in $\Omega(n)$ when executed in this graph.*

A final union bound combines the results from Lemmas 7 and 8 to get our final corollary. Applying the probabilistic method to the corollary yields the main theorem—Theorem 8.

**Corollary 1.** *Fix an aggregation algorithm $\mathcal{A}$ and smoothing factor $k \leq n/(32 \cdot \log^2 n)$. There is a method for probabilistically constructing a pairing graph $\mathcal{H}$, such that with probability greater than $1/2$ (over the smoothing, adversary, and algorithm's independent random choices): $\mathcal{A}$'s aggregation factor in a $k$-smoothed version of $\mathcal{H}$ is $\Omega(n)$ times larger than the offline optimal factor for this graph.*

# References

1. Augustine, J., Pandurangan, G., Robinson, P., Upfal, E.: Towards robust and efficient computation in dynamic peer-to-peer networks. In: Proceedings of the ACM-SIAM Symposium on Discrete Algorithms (2012)

2. Avin, C., Koucký, M., Lotker, Z.: How to explore a fast-changing world (cover time of a simple random walk on evolving graphs). In: Aceto, L., Damgård, I., Goldberg, L.A., Halldórsson, M.M., Ingólfsdóttir, A., Walukiewicz, I. (eds.) ICALP 2008, Part I. LNCS, vol. 5125, pp. 121–132. Springer, Heidelberg (2008)
3. Clementi, A., Silvestri, R., Trevisan, L.: Information spreading in dynamic graphs. In: Proceedings of the ACM Symposium on Principles of Distributed Computing (2012)
4. Cornejo, A., Gilbert, S., Newport, C.: Aggregation in dynamic networks. In: Proceedings of the ACM Symposium on Principles of Distributed Computing (2012)
5. Denysyuk, O., Rodrigues, L.: Random walks on evolving graphs with recurring topologies. In: Kuhn, F. (ed.) DISC 2014. LNCS, vol. 8784, pp. 333–345. Springer, Heidelberg (2014)
6. Dinitz, M., Fineman, J., Gilbert, S., Newport, C.: Smoothed analysis of dynamic networks. Full version http://people.cs.georgetown.edu/cnewport/pubs/SmoothingDynamicNetworks-Full.pdf
7. Dutta, C., Pandurangan, G., Rajaraman, R., Sun, Z., Viola, E.: On the complexity of information spreading in dynamic networks. In: Proceedings of the ACM-SIAM Symposium on Discrete Algorithms (2013)
8. Ghaffari, M., Lynch, N., Newport, C.: The cost of radio network broadcast for different models of unreliable links. In: Proceedings of the ACM Symposium on Principles of Distributed Computing (2013)
9. Haeupler, B., Karger, D.: Faster information dissemination in dynamic networks via network coding. In: Proceedings of the ACM Symposium on Principles of Distributed Computing (2011)
10. Kuhn, F., Oshman, R.: Dynamic networks: models and algorithms. ACM SIGACT News 42(1), 82–96 (2011)
11. Kuhn, F., Lynch, N., Oshman, R.: Distributed computation in dynamic networks. In: Proceedings of the ACM Symposium on Theory of Computing (2010)
12. Kuhn, F., Oshman, R., Moses, Y.: Coordinated consensus in dynamic networks. In: Proceedings of the ACM Symposium on Principles of Distributed Computing (2011)
13. Lovász, L.: Random walks on graphs: a survey. In: Miklós, D., Sós, V.T., Szőnyi, T. (eds.) Combinatorics, Paul Erdős is Eighty, vol. 2, pp. 1–46. János Bolyai Mathematical Society (1996)
14. Newport, C.: Lower bounds for structuring unreliable radio networks. In: Kuhn, F. (ed.) DISC 2014. LNCS, vol. 8784, pp. 318–332. Springer, Heidelberg (2014)
15. Das Sarma, A., Molla, A.R., Pandurangan, G.: Fast distributed computation in dynamic networks via random walks. In: Aguilera, M.K. (ed.) DISC 2012. LNCS, vol. 7611, pp. 136–150. Springer, Heidelberg (2012)
16. Spielman, D.A., Teng, S.: Smoothed analysis of algorithms: Why the simplex algorithm usually takes polynomial time. J. ACM 51(3), 385–463 (2004)
17. Spielman, D.A., Teng, S.: Smoothed analysis: an attempt to explain the behavior of algorithms in practice. Commun. ACM 52(10), 76–84 (2009)
18. Spielman, D.A., Teng, S.H.: Smoothed analysis: an attempt to explain the behavior of algorithms in practice. Communications of the ACM 52(10), 76–84 (2009)

# Fault Tolerant Reachability for Directed Graphs

Surender Baswana[1], Keerti Choudhary[1]([✉]), and Liam Roditty[2]

[1] Department of Computer Science and Engineering,
IIT Kanpur, Kanpur 208016, India
{sbaswana,keerti}@cse.iitk.ac.in

[2] Department of Computer Science, Bar Ilan University, 52900 Ramat Gan, Israel
liam.roditty@biu.ac.il

**Abstract.** Let $G = (V, E)$ be an $n$-vertices $m$-edges directed graph. Let $s \in V$ be any designated source vertex, and let $T$ be an arbitrary reachability tree rooted at $s$. We address the problem of finding a set of edges $\mathcal{E} \subseteq E \backslash T$ of minimum size such that on a failure of any vertex $w \in V$, the set of vertices reachable from $s$ in $T \cup \mathcal{E} \backslash \{w\}$ is the same as the set of vertices reachable from $s$ in $G \backslash \{w\}$. We obtain the following results:

- The optimal set $\mathcal{E}$ for any arbitrary reachability tree $T$ has at most $n - 1$ edges.
- There exists an $O(m \log n)$-time algorithm that computes the optimal set $\mathcal{E}$ for any given reachability tree $T$.

For the restricted case when the reachability tree $T$ is a Depth-First-Search (DFS) tree it is straightforward to bound the size of the optimal set $\mathcal{E}$ by $n - 1$ using semidominators with respect to DFS trees from the celebrated work of Lengauer and Tarjan [13]. Such a set $\mathcal{E}$ can be computed in $O(m)$ time using the algorithm of Buchsbaum et. al [4].

To bound the size of the optimal set in the general case we define semidominators with respect to arbitrary trees. We also present a simple $O(m \log n)$ time algorithm for computing such semidominators. As a byproduct, we get an alternative algorithm for computing dominators in $O(m \log n)$ time.

## 1 Introduction

Networks in most real life applications are prone to failures. Failures, though unpredictable, are transient due to some simultaneous repair process that is undertaken in the application. This motivates the research on designing fault tolerant structures for various graph problems.

We distinguish between two models for fault tolerance. In the *Pre-Design* fault-tolerant model the network is designed from scratch such that it will fulfill

---

This research was partially supported by Israel Science Foundation (ISF) and University Grants Commission (UGC) of India. The research of the second author was partially supported by Google India under the Google India PhD Fellowship Award.

© Springer-Verlag Berlin Heidelberg 2015
Y. Moses (Ed.): DISC 2015, LNCS 9363, pp. 528–543, 2015.
DOI: 10.1007/978-3-662-48653-5_35

certain robustness requirements that are known at the design phase. In the *Post-Design* fault-tolerant model the network already exists and it has to fulfill new robustness requirements. This model reflects the scenario in which the network is a physical network such as a road network or an electricity network. Such networks are rarely redesigned from scratch but new robustness requirements are introduced through the years.

In this paper we consider the fault tolerant reachability problem in the post-design fault-tolerant model. From theoretical perspective this model is more challenging as it is stronger than the pre-design model.

We now define the problem formally. Given a directed graph $G = (V, E)$ and a source vertex $s$, a subgraph $H$ is said to be a Fault Tolerant Reachability Subgraph (FTRS) if for any pair of vertices $v, w \in V$, $v$ is reachable from $s$ in $G \backslash \{w\}$ if and only if $v$ is reachable from $s$ in $H \backslash \{w\}$. We consider the following problem. We are given an arbitrary reachability tree $T$ of $s$ and we are required to find a smallest set $\mathcal{E} \subseteq E$ of edges which on addition to $T$ gives an FTRS. We show that for each tree $T$, the optimal set $\mathcal{E}$ is of size at most $n - 1$. We also present an algorithm that computes this optimal set in $O(m \log n)$ time.

Parter and Peleg [15] considered the question of finding a sparse subgraph of $G$ that preserves the distances from $s$ under a single vertex failure. They showed that if $G$ is an undirected unweighted graph then it has a subgraph $H$ with $O(n^{3/2})$ edges such that for every $v, x \in V$, it holds that the distance from $s$ to $v$ in $H \setminus \{x\}$ is the same as in $G \setminus \{x\}$. They also showed a lower bound of $\Omega(n^{3/2})$. Recently Parter [14] showed a bound of $O(n^{5/3})$ for the case of dual failure. She also showed that this result is tight. For the case of weighted graphs, Demetrescu et al. [8] established a lower bound of $\Omega(m)$ for single source fault tolerant shortest paths structure. Therefore, in light of these lower bounds, it makes sense to relax the problem requirements in order to obtain a graph $H$ of linear (or almost linear) size, as required by many real world applications.

Baswana and Khanna [1] showed that if one is willing to consider only undirected graphs and to settle for an approximation then there is a subgraph with $O(n \log n)$ edges that preserves the distances up to a multiplicative error of 3. Parter and Peleg [16] improved this result and obtained a subgraph with at most $3n$ edges.

Focusing on the reachability in directed graphs instead of approximation of shortest paths in undirected graphs, can be viewed as a different type of relaxation.

The fault tolerant reachability is closely related to the notion of *dominators*. Given a directed graph $G$ and a designated vertex $s$ we say that vertex $v$ dominates vertex $w$ if every path from $s$ to $w$ contains $v$. A vertex $v$ is said to be the immediate dominator of $w$ if (i) $v$ is a dominator of $w$, and (ii) every dominator of $w$ (other than $v$ itself) is also a dominator of $v$.

In a celebrated work [13], Lengauer and Tarjan show that dominators can be computed in $O(m\alpha(m, n))$ time, where $\alpha(m, n)$ is the inverse Ackermann function. Buchsbaum et. al [4] showed how to implement the algorithm of Lengauer and Tarjan in $O(m)$ time. For more details on the work of dominators, see

[4,11,12]. To the best of our knowledge, all non trivial previous results are based on an initialization phase in which a Depth-First-Search (DFS) tree is computed.

Given a DFS tree $T$ rooted at $s$ it is straightforward using the ideas of Lengauer and Tarjan [13] to find an FTRS. This is implicit in [13] and is based on the notion of semidominators for DFS trees. This solves the FTRS problem in the *weaker* model of pre-design fault tolerant in which the tree can be chosen at the network design phase and hence can be chosen to be a DFS tree.

Our main result is that given any arbitrary tree $T$, we can efficiently compute an optimal set $\mathcal{E}$ whose addition to $T$ gives an FTRS. This solves the FTRS problem in the more general model of post-design. In order to achieve this we define semidominators with respect to arbitrary reachability trees and not just DFS trees. We expect that this definition could be of independent interest. As a byproduct of our new definition of semidominators we obtain the first non-trivial algorithm for computing dominators that does not rely on a DFS tree computation. The algorithm, however, has a running time of $O(m \log n)$ which is slower than the state of the art for this problem by a logarithmic factor.

## 1.1    Related Work

Most of the previous work on fault tolerant structures is on all-pair shortest paths (APSP). Demetrescu, Thorup, Chowdhury and Ramachandran [8] designed an $O(n^2 \log n)$ size data structure that can report the distance from $u$ to $v$ avoiding $x$ for any $u, v, x \in V$ in $O(1)$ time. Bernstein and Karger [3] improved the preprocessing time of [8] to $O(mn \text{ polylog } n)$. Duan and Pettie [10] improved the result of [8] by designing a data structure of $O(n^2 \log n)$ size that can handle two vertex faults.

Another closely related problem is the replacement paths problem. In this problem we are given a source $s$ and a target $t$ and for each edge $e$ on the shortest path from $s$ to $t$ the algorithm computes the shortest path from $s$ to $t$ in the graph without $e$. Many variants of this problem were studied along the years. For a recent overview see [17] and reference therein.

The questions of finding graph spanners, approximate distance oracles and compact routing schemes that are resilient to $f$ vertex or edge failures were studied in [5,6,9].

## 1.2    Organization of the Paper

We describe notations and terminologies in Section 2. For sake of completeness we provide an overview of the FTRS for a DFS tree in Section 3. Here we also highlight the difficulty in extending the existing algorithm for DFS tree to arbitrary tree. In Section 4, we generalize the concept of semidominators to arbitrary tree. In Section 5, we show that for any arbitrary tree $T$, there exists an optimal set $\mathcal{E}$ of at most $n - 1$ edges whose addition to $T$ will make it an FTRS. Furthermore, if we are given the semidominators for all vertices in $T$, the set $\mathcal{E}$ of edges can be computed in $O(n)$ time. In Section 6, we provide a simple

$O(m \log n)$ time algorithm to compute semidominators. In Section 7, we show the computation of dominators from semidominators.

## 2   Preliminaries

Given a directed graph $G = (V, E)$ on $n = |V|$ vertices and $m = |E|$ edges, and a source vertex $s \in V$, the following notations will be used throughout the paper.

- $T$: Any arbitrary tree of $G$ rooted at $s$.
- $T(v)$: The subtree of $T$ rooted at a vertex $v$.
- $par(v)$: The parent of $v$ in $T$.
- LCA$(u, v)$: The Lowest Common Ancestor of $u$ and $v$ in tree $T$.
- PATH$(a, b)$: The tree path from $a$ to $b$ in $T$. Here $a$ is assumed to be an ancestor of $b$.
- OUT$(S)$: The set of all those vertices in $V \backslash S$ which have an incoming edge from some vertex in set $S$.
- $deg(S)$: The sum of the degrees of all vertices in the set $S$.
- SDOM$(v)$: Semidominator of $v$ w.r.t. tree $T$.
- $(\sigma, w)$: The sequence obtained by appending $w$ at the end of a sequence $\sigma$.
- $\langle P :: Q \rangle$: The path formed by concatenating paths $P$ and $Q$ in $G$. Here it is assumed that the last vertex of $P$ is the same as the first vertex of $Q$.

Let $\mathcal{P} : \langle v_1, v_2, \ldots, v_n \rangle$ be a sequence of the vertices $V$ defined by any preorder traversal of tree $T$. For notational convenience henceforth, a vertex will also be denoted by its preorder numbering. Thus, $u \leq v$ would imply that the preorder number of $u$ is less than that of $v$.

**Definition 1.** *A simple path $P = (u_0, u_1, \ldots, u_t = v)$ in $G$ is said to be a detour with respect to a given tree $T$ if $u_0$ is an ancestor of $v$ in $T$, and for $0 < i < t$, none of the $u_i$'s is an ancestor of $v$ in $T$.*

A detour from $u$ to $v$ can be seen as an alternate path to $v$ when some intermediate vertex on PATH$(u, v)$ fails. It follows from Definition 1 that an edge $(u, v) \in T$ is also a detour for vertex $v$. However, such a detour cannot be used to handle any failures. The next definition is important to characterize those detours that are important for fault tolerant.

**Definition 2.** *A detour to $v$ with respect to $T$ that emanates from the ancestor of $v$ with minimal preorder number is called a highest detour of $v$.*

We denote the highest detour of $v$ with HD$(v)$. In case that there is more than one highest detour we pick one arbitrarily.

# 3    DFS Tree Versus Arbitrary Tree

Lengauer and Tarjan [13] presented an algorithm for computing immediate dominators. As part of their work they defined semidominators over a DFS tree $T$. Their definition of semidominators can be reformulated as follows:

**Definition 3 (Semidominators in DFS Tree).** *Let $T$ be a DFS tree. For any vertex $v$ ($v \neq s$), the semidominator* SDOM($v$) *is defined to be the highest ancestor of $v$ from which there is a detour to $v$. In other words,* SDOM($v$) *is equal to the first vertex on* HD($v$).

It can be shown that a subgraph $H$ of $G$ that is composed of a reachability tree $T$ and the highest detours of all the vertices with respect to $T$ is an FTRS of $G$. For the case when $T$ is a DFS tree, Lengauer and Tarjan [13] gave an $O(m\alpha(m,n))$ time algorithm for computing such an FTRS with at most $2n - 1$ edges. In order to prove the $2n - 1$ bound they used a crucial property of DFS tree which in simple words can be re-stated as follows.

*Property 1.* If (SDOM($v$), $v$) is not an edge in $G$ then we can always find a highest detour HD($v$) for $v$ which can be represented as $\langle$HD($w$) :: PATH($w, y$) :: $(y, v)\rangle$, where $y$ is an in-neighbor of $v$ and $w$ is either equal to $y$ or an ancestor of $y$.

For the case when $T$ is an arbitrary tree, and not a DFS tree, Property 1 no longer holds. A simple example that illustrates the situation for general trees is shown in Figure 1. Thus it is not immediately clear whether we can obtain an FTRS by adding at most $n - 1$ edges to an arbitrary tree given by an adversary. In order to achieve our goal, we define semidominators for arbitrary trees in the next section.

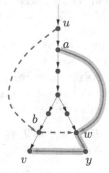

**Fig. 1.** The highlighted and dashed paths in the figure represent respectively the highest detours HD($v$) and HD($w$) for vertices $v$ and $w$. Detour HD($v$) cannot be expressed as $\langle$HD($w$) :: PATH($w, y$) :: $(y, v)\rangle$ because HD($w$) passes through an ancestor of $v$.

# 4    Semidominators with Respect to Arbitrary Trees

Given an arbitrary tree $T$, let $D$ be a detour from a vertex $u$ to a vertex $v$ with minimum number of non-tree edges. Let $(u_1, v_1)$ be the first edge in $D$ and let $(u_2, v_2), (u_3, v_3), \ldots, (u_k, v_k)$ be the sequence of non-tree edges in the order they appear in $D \setminus (u_1, v_1)$. Here $u_1 = u$ and $v_k = v$. Consider the edge $(u_i, v_i)$, where $1 < i \leq k$. Since the segment of $D$ from $v_{i-1}$ to $u_i$ is a path in $T$ it follows that $u_i \in T(v_{i-1})$. Moreover, $v_i \notin T(v_{i-1})$ as if $v_i \in T(v_{i-1})$ we can replace the segment of $D$ from $v_{i-1}$ to $v_i$ by $\text{PATH}(v_{i-1}, v_i)$, thereby reducing the number of non-tree edges.

Consider now only the vertices $(u, v_1, v_2, \ldots, v_k)$. From the above discussion it follows that these vertices satisfy the relation that $v_1 \in \text{OUT}(u)$, and for $1 < i \leq k$, $v_i \in \text{OUT}(T(v_{i-1}))$. This motivates us to define the notion of a valid sequence as follows.

**Definition 4 (Valid sequence).** *A sequence of vertices* $(u, v_1, v_2, \ldots, v_k = v)$ *is said to be a valid sequence with respect to tree* $T$ *if the following two conditions hold:*

*(i) $(u, v_1)$ is an edge in $G$.*
*(ii) for $1 < i \leq k$, $v_i \in \text{OUT}(T(v_{i-1}))$.*

Let $u$ and $v$ be any two vertices such that $u$ is an ancestor of $v$ in $T$. It follows from Definition 4 that if there exists a detour from $u$ to $v$ in $T$, then there exists a valid sequence from $u$ to $v$. However, the other direction is not always true, that is, a valid sequence from $u$ to $v$ in $T$ may not correspond to a detour in $T$. For example, consider the sequence $\sigma = (u, b, w, v)$ in Figure 1. This is a valid sequence but there is no detour from $u$ to $v$. The one to one correspondence between detours and valid sequences holds only when $T$ is a DFS tree.

We will now define semidominator with respect to arbitrary trees using valid sequence. In arbitrary trees, it will turn out that if there is a valid sequence from $\text{SDOM}(v)$ to $v$ and $\text{SDOM}(v) \neq par(v)$, then there are two vertex disjoint paths from $\text{SDOM}(v)$ to $v$. Our FTRS for any tree given tree $T$ will store these vertex disjoint paths in a compact manner.

**Definition 5.** *A vertex $u$ is semidominator of $v$ if (i) $u$ is an ancestor of $v$, (ii) there is a valid sequence from $u$ to $v$, and (iii) there is no other vertex on* $\text{PATH}(s, u)$ *which has a valid sequence to $v$.*

*Remark 1.* There is a detour from an ancestor $u$ of $v$ to $v$ in a DFS tree if and only if there is a valid sequence from $u$ to $v$. Hence in the case of DFS tree, Definition 5 degenerates to Definition 3.

The following lemma provides an alternative definition to semidominators. We shall use these two definitions interchangeably henceforth.

**Lemma 1.** *Let $u$ be a vertex with minimum preorder number such that there exists a valid sequence from $u$ to $v$. Then $u$ is the semidominator of $v$.*

**Proof.** To prove the lemma it suffices to show that $u$ must be an ancestor of $v$. Let us assume, towards a contradiction, that $u$ is not an ancestor of $v$. Thus, there is a vertex $w$ such that $w = \text{LCA}(u, v)$, $w \neq v$ and $w \neq u$. Let $(u = v_0, v_1, v_2, \ldots, v_k = v)$ be a valid sequence from $u$ to $v$. Let $w_1$ and $w_2$ be the children of $w$ such that $v_0 = u \in T(w_1)$ and $v_k = v \in T(w_2)$. Let $v_j$ be the first vertex of the sequence that doest not lie in $T(w_1)$. If $j = 1$, then the in-neighbor $v_0$ of $v_1$ lies in $T(w_1)$. If $j > 1$, then $v_j$ has an in-neighbor say $u_j$ that lies in $T(v_{j-1}) \subseteq T(w_1)$. Thus, $v_j \in \text{OUT}(T(w_1))$. The sequence $\sigma = (w, w_1, v_j, v_{j+1}, \ldots, v_k)$ is also a valid sequence that reaches $v$, and since $w < u$, we get a contradiction. $\qquad\square$

# 5   FTRS for any Arbitrary Tree

In this section we provide the construction of an optimal size FTRS containing any given arbitrary tree. Our starting point is the following lemma that will be used to show that in order to have two vertex disjoint paths from $\text{SDOM}(v)$ to $v$, for each $v$, we need to keep only one extra incoming edge per vertex.

**Lemma 2.** *Let $u, v, w \in V$ be three vertices such that $v \in \text{OUT}(T(w))$, $v \notin \text{OUT}(u)$, and $u$ is some common ancestor of $v$ and $w$. Let $H$ be a subgraph of $G$ containing tree $T$ and an edge $(y, v)$, where $y \in T(w)$. If $H$ contains two vertex disjoint paths from $u$ to $w$, then $H$ also contains two vertex disjoint paths from $u$ to $v$.*

**Proof.** Let us assume towards a contradiction that $H$ does not contain two vertex disjoint paths from $u$ to $v$. Then it follows from Menger's Theorem that there exists a vertex $x$ (other than $u$, $v$) such that every path from $u$ to $v$ in $H$ passes through $x$, therefore vertex $x$ is on $\text{PATH}(u, v)$. Let $P$ and $Q$ be two vertex disjoint paths from $u$ to $w$ in $H$ (see Figure 2). Since $w \neq x$, at least one out of these two paths, say $Q$, does not pass through $x$. Now $\langle Q :: \text{PATH}(w, y) :: (y, v) \rangle$ gives a path from $u$ to $v$ not passing though $x$. (Though this concatenated path may contain loops, but we can remove all these loops). Thus we get a contradiction. So $H$ must contain two vertex disjoint paths from $u$ to $v$. $\qquad\square$

We now show that a subgraph of $G$ containing a tree $T$ is an FTRS if it contains 2 vertex disjoint paths from $\text{SDOM}(v)$ to $v$, for each possible vertex $v$.

**Lemma 3.** *Any subgraph $H$ of $G$ satisfying the following conditions is an FTRS: (i) $H$ contains tree $T$, (ii) If $v$ is any vertex such that $\text{SDOM}(v) \neq par(v)$, then there exists two vertex disjoint paths from $\text{SDOM}(v)$ to $v$ in $H$.*

**Proof.** Consider the failure of an ancestor $x$ of a vertex $w$ in $T$. Suppose $w$ is reachable from $s$ in $G \setminus \{x\}$. Then there must exist a detour $D$ from $u$ to $v$, where $u$ and $v$ are respectively vertices lying above and below $x$ in $\text{PATH}(s, w)$. Now a detour from $u$ to $v$ implies that there exists a valid sequence from $u$ to $v$. So the semidominator of $v$ is either equal to $u$ or an ancestor of $u$. Since here $\text{SDOM}(v) \neq par(v)$, $H$ contains two vertex disjoint paths, say $P$ and $Q$ from $\text{SDOM}(v)$ to $v$. Without loss of generality we can assume that $x$ does not lie

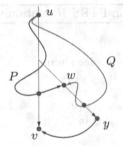

**Fig. 2.** Two vertex disjoint paths $P$ and $Q$ from $u$ to $w$.

in $P$. Thus $\langle \text{PATH}(s, \text{SDOM}(v)) :: P :: \text{PATH}(v, w) \rangle$ is a replacement path to $w$ (avoiding $x$) contained in subgraph $H$.                                                           □

For the rest of this section, let $\sigma(v)$ denote a valid sequence from $\text{SDOM}(v)$ to $v$ of minimum possible length. The following lemma will be used in the construction of an optimal size FTRS containing any arbitrary tree $T$.

**Lemma 4.** *Consider a vertex $v$ and its minimum length valid sequence $\sigma(v) = (u = v_0, \ldots, v_{k-1}, v_k = v)$. Let $w = v_{k-1}$ be the second last vertex in $\sigma(v)$. If $|\sigma(v)| > 2$, then $\text{SDOM}(w) = \text{SDOM}(v)$ and $|\sigma(w)| < |\sigma(v)|$.*

**Proof.** To prove this lemma we use the alternative definition of semidominators as given in Lemma 1. If $\text{SDOM}(w) < \text{SDOM}(v)$, then $(\sigma(w), v)$ will be a valid sequence for $v$ starting from a vertex whose preorder number is less than that of $\text{SDOM}(v)$. This is because $v \in \text{OUT}(T(w))$. Similarly, if $\text{SDOM}(v) < \text{SDOM}(w)$, then $\sigma(v) \setminus \{v\}$ will be a valid sequence for $w$ starting from a vertex whose preorder number is less than that of $\text{SDOM}(w)$. Thus $\text{SDOM}(w)$ must be equal to $\text{SDOM}(v)$. Now suppose $|\sigma(v)| \leq |\sigma(w)|$. Then $\sigma(v) \setminus \{v\}$ would be a valid sequence from $\text{SDOM}(w)$ to $w$ of length strictly less than $|\sigma(w)|$. Hence $|\sigma(w)|$ must be less than $|\sigma(v)|$.                                                           □

Let $L$ be the list of vertices in $G$ arranged in the non-decreasing order of length of $\sigma(v)$. The following theorem presents an algorithm for computing an FTRS of optimal size assuming that the minimum length valid sequences for all vertices is known.

**Theorem 1.** *Given any arbitrary reachability tree $T$ rooted at $s$, Algorithm 1 computes an optimal set $\mathcal{E}$ such that $T \cup \mathcal{E}$ is an FTRS. Moreover, the size of $\mathcal{E}$ is always bounded by $n - 1$.*

**Proof.** Note that $H$ already contains the tree $T$. So it follows from Lemma 3 that it is sufficient to prove that for any vertex $v$ if $\text{SDOM}(v) \neq par(v)$, then $H$ contains two vertex disjoint paths from $\text{SDOM}(v)$ to $v$. The proof is by induction on list $L$. Consider a vertex $v$ such that $\text{SDOM}(v) \neq par(v)$. If $(\text{SDOM}(v), v)$ is a forward edge, then the tree path from $\text{SDOM}(v)$ to $v$, and the edge $(\text{SDOM}(v), v)$ are two vertex disjoint paths from $\text{SDOM}(v)$ to $v$ in $H$. Thus let us consider the

---

**Algorithm 1.** Computing an FTRS $H$ containing an arbitrary tree $T$.

---

1  $H \leftarrow T$;
2  **foreach** $v \in L$ **do**
3      **if** $(\text{SDOM}(v), v)$ *is a forward edge* **then**
4         |   $H \leftarrow H \cup (\text{SDOM}(v), v)$;
5      **else if** $|\sigma(v)| > 2$ **then**
6         |   $w \leftarrow$ Second last vertex in $\sigma(v)$;
7         |   $y \leftarrow$ In-neighbor of $v$ lying in $T(w)$;
8         |   $H \leftarrow H \cup \{(y, v)\}$;
9      **end**
10  **end**

---

case when $|\sigma(v)| > 2$. Let $w$ be the second last vertex of $\sigma(v)$ and $y$ be an in-neighbor of $v$ lying in $T(w)$. So Lemma 4 implies that $\text{SDOM}(w) = \text{SDOM}(v)$, and $w$ precedes $v$ in list $L$.

We first consider the case when $\text{SDOM}(w) \neq par(w)$. Since $w$ will appear before $v$ in $L$, by induction hypothesis $H$ contains two vertex disjoint paths from $\text{SDOM}(w)$ to $w$. Now the edge $(y, v)$ lies in $H$, so Lemma 2 implies that $H$ contains two vertex disjoint paths from $\text{SDOM}(v)$ to $v$ also. Next let us consider the case when $\text{SDOM}(w) = par(w)$. Since $v$ lies outside $T(w)$ but in the subtree rooted at $par(w) = \text{SDOM}(v)$, we have that $\text{SDOM}(v) = \text{LCA}(w, v) = \text{LCA}(y, v)$. Thus in this case $\text{PATH}(\text{SDOM}(v), v)$ and $\text{PATH}(\text{SDOM}(v), y)::(y, v)$ form two vertex disjoint paths from $\text{SDOM}(v)$ to $v$. Hence, it can be seen that Algorithm 1 computes an FTRS containing tree $T$.

Note that we add an extra incoming edge to $v$ only if $\text{SDOM}(v) \neq par(v)$. In this case, there exist two vertex disjoint paths from $\text{SDOM}(v)$ to $v$ in $G$. So $v$ will be reachable from $s$ even after failure of $par(v)$. Thus any FTRS must keep an additional incoming edge to $v$ in this case. Hence the subgraph $H$ is indeed a minimum size FTRS containing tree $T$.     □

*Remark 2.* Given $\text{SDOM}(v)$ and a minimum length $\sigma(v)$ for each $v$, Algorithm 1 takes $O(n)$ time to compute optimal FTRS containing any given tree $T$.

In the following section, we present an $O(m \log n)$ time algorithm for computing $\text{SDOM}(v)$ and a minimum length $\sigma(v)$ for all $v$. This implies that given any tree $T$, we can compute an optimal FTRS containing $T$ in $O(m \log n)$ time.

# 6  Algorithm for Computing Semidominators and Valid Sequences

Our algorithm for computing semidominators is an iterative algorithm. It processes the vertices in the increasing order of the preorder numbering $\mathcal{P}$ of $T$. Let $v_i$ denote the vertex at the $i^{th}$ place in $\mathcal{P}$. During $i^{th}$ iteration, the algorithm computes the set $W_i$ consisting of all those vertices whose semidominator is $v_i$.

Consider a vertex $v_i$. Let $B$ denote the set of all those vertices $w$ for which there exists a valid sequence starting from $v_i$ and ending at $w$. The set $B$ can be computed as follows. We initialize $B$ as the out-neighbors of $v_i$. Next we add $\text{OUT}(T(w))$ to $B$ for each $w$ in $B$, and proceed recursively. By the alternative definition of semidominators as in Lemma 1 we have that $W_i = B \setminus (\cup_{j<i} W_j)$.

In order to design an efficient implementation of the algorithm outlined above, there are two requirements. The first requirement is that while computing valid sequences from $v_i$ we should not process those vertices whose semidominator have already been computed. For this purpose, we keep a flag variable *active/inactive* corresponding to each vertex $w$ in $G$. At any instant of time the active vertices are those vertices whose semidominator has not yet been computed. The second requirement is that given any vertex $w$ we should be able to compute the set of active nodes in $\text{OUT}(T(w))$ efficiently. In order to fulfill these requirements, we use a data structure $\mathcal{D}$ that supports the following two operations efficiently.

1. $\text{ACTIVEOUTNGHBRS}(\mathcal{D}, T(w))$: return the set of active nodes in $\text{OUT}(T(w))$.
2. $\text{MARKINACTIVE}(\mathcal{D}, S)$: mark the vertices in set $S$ as inactive. This is done by simply deleting from $\mathcal{D}$ the incoming edges to all vertices present in set $S$.

The data structure $\mathcal{D}$ is a suitably augmented segment tree formed on an Euler tour of the tree $T$. The data structure takes $O(deg(A) \log n))$ time to perform $\text{ACTIVEOUTNGHBRS}(\mathcal{D}, T(w))$ operation, where $A$ is the set of vertices reported. It takes $O(deg(S) \log n)$ time to perform $\text{MARKINACTIVE}(\mathcal{D}, S)$ operation. We provide the complete details of the data structure in Subsection 6.1.

Algorithm 2 gives the pseudo code for computing semidominators. It maintains a queue $\mathcal{Q}$ throughout the run of algorithm. The semidominator of the vertices is computed in the order they are enqueued. Initially all the vertices in $G$ except root are marked as active. A vertex is marked inactive as soon as it is enqueued in $\mathcal{Q}$. In the $i^{th}$ iteration the algorithm computes the set of all those vertices whose semidominator is $v_i$ as follows. First it computes the set $S$ of all the active out-neighbors of $v_i$. This set is enqueued and for each $w \in S$, $\sigma(w)$ is set as $(v_i, w)$. Next while $\mathcal{Q}$ is non empty, it removes the first vertex say $x$ from $\mathcal{Q}$. For each active node $w$ in $\text{OUT}(T(x))$, $\sigma(w)$ is assigned as $(\sigma(x), w)$ and $w$ is enqueued in $\mathcal{Q}$. This process is repeated until $\mathcal{Q}$ becomes empty. Vertex $v_i$ is assigned as semidominator of all the vertices enqueued in the $i^{th}$ iteration.

Figure 3 illustrates the execution of our algorithm. Figure 3(a) depicts the first iteration which is supposed to compute $W_1$. The vertices that are enqueued before the while loop are $\langle 2, 14 \rangle$. The execution of the while loop will place vertices 15 and 16 into the queue in this order. It can be visually inspected that these vertices constitute $W_1$. Similarly Figure 3(b) depicts the second iteration that is supposed to compute $W_2$. The vertices that are enqueued before entering the while loop are $\langle 3, 7, 12 \rangle$. The execution of the while loop will place vertices 5,10,4,8,11 into the queue in this order. It can be visually inspected that these vertices constitute $W_2$.

**Algorithm 2.** Computing semidominator and the corresponding valid sequence

```
 1  Q ← ∅;
 2  for i = 1 to n do
 3  │   S ← Set of active vertices lying in OUT(vᵢ);
 4  │   ENQUEUE(Q, S);
 5  │   MARKINACTIVE(D, S);
 6  │   foreach w ∈ S do σ(w) = (vᵢ, w);
 7  │   while (Q ≠ ∅) do
 8  │   │   x ← DEQUEUE(Q);
 9  │   │   SDOM(x) ← vᵢ;
10  │   │   S ← ACTIVEOUTNGHBRS(D, T(x));
11  │   │   ENQUEUE(Q, S);
12  │   │   MARKINACTIVE(D, S);
13  │   │   foreach w ∈ S do σ(w) = (σ(x), w);
14  │   end
15  end
```

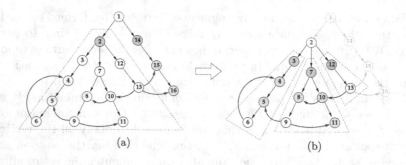

(a)                                    (b)

**Fig. 3.** The filled vertices in Figure (a) and (b) respectively constitute the sets $W_1$ and $W_2$. Figure (b) shows that all the vertices in $W_1$ are marked inactive in round 2.

For each vertex $u$, let $\sigma(u)$ denote a valid sequence from SDOM($u$) to $u$ of minimum possible length. Let $L$ be the list of vertices in $G$ arranged in the non-decreasing order of $|\sigma(u)|$. Then it can be proved by induction on $L$ that Algorithm 2 correctly computes (i) semidominator of $u$, and (ii) a minimum length valid sequence from SDOM($u$) to $u$, for each vertex $u$ in $G$.

We now analyze the time complexity of Algorithm 2. The total time taken by Step 3 in the algorithm is $O(m)$. The time taken by steps 5, 10, and 12 is $O(\log n)$ times the sum of degrees of vertices enqueued in $Q$. Since each vertex is enqueued at most once, the running time of the algorithm is $O(m \log n)$.

**Theorem 2.** *There exists an $O(m \log n)$ time algorithm that for any given graph with $n$ vertices and $m$ edges, and any given reachability tree $T$, computes the semidominator and a minimum length valid sequence for each vertex in $G$.*

From Theorems 1 and 2, we directly get the following result.

**Theorem 3.** *There exists an $O(m \log n)$ time algorithm that for any given graph $G$ with $n$ vertices and $m$ edges, and any given reachability tree $T$ rooted at source, computes an optimal set $\mathcal{E}$ such that $T \cup \mathcal{E}$ is an FTRS for $G$.*

## 6.1  Data Structure

Let $\mathcal{T}$ be a segment tree [2] whose leaf nodes from left to right correspond to the sequence $\langle v_1, ..., v_n \rangle$ (see Figure 4). Our data structure will be $\mathcal{T}$ whose nodes are suitably augmented as follows. Let $(u, v)$ be an edge in $G$. We store a copy of the edge as the ordered pair $(u, v)$ at all ancestors of $u$ (including itself) in tree $\mathcal{T}$. Thus each edge in $G$ is stored at $O(\log n)$ levels in $\mathcal{T}$. Let $\mathcal{E}(b)$ be the collection of edges stored at any node $b$ in $\mathcal{T}$. We keep the set $\mathcal{E}(b)$ sorted by the second endpoint of the edges in a doubly link list. For each edge $(u, v) \in E$, we also store pointer to all $\log n$ copies of it in $\mathcal{T}$. The size of the data structure is $O(m \log n)$ in the beginning.

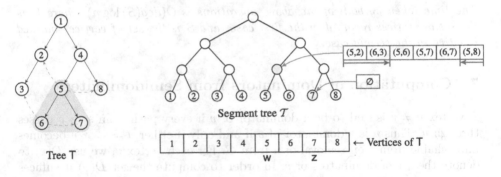

**Fig. 4.** Data Structure.

The operation MARKINACTIVE($\mathcal{D}, S$) involves deletion of incoming edges to all the vertices in set $S$. Since we store pointers to all $\log n$ copies of an edge, a single edge can be deleted from the data structure in $O(\log n)$ time. So the time taken by this operation is $O(deg(S) \log n)$.

We now show that $\mathcal{D}$ can perform the operation ACTIVEOUTNGH-BRS($\mathcal{D}, T(w)$) quite efficiently. Let $S_0$ be the set of active nodes in OUT($T(w)$). Note that the preorder numbering of the vertices in $T(w)$ will be a contiguous subsequence of $[1, .., n]$, and $w$ would be the vertex of minimum preorder number in $T(w)$. Let $z$ be the vertex with maximum preorder number in subtree $T(w)$ (This information can be precomputed in total $O(n)$ time for all vertices in the beginning). So $[w, .., z]$ denotes the set of vertices in $T(w)$.

Notice that any contiguous subsequence of $[1, .., n]$ can be expressed as disjoint union of at most $\log n$ subtrees in $\mathcal{T}$. Let $\tau_1, ..., \tau_\ell$ denote these subtrees for the subsequence $[w, .., z]$. For $i = 1$ to $\ell$, let $E_i$ denote the set of all those edges $(x, y)$ such that $x$ is a leaf node of $\tau_i$ and $y$ lies outside the set $[w, .., z]$. It can be observed that the desired set $S_0$ corresponds to the set of second-endpoints of all edges in the set $\cup_{i=1}^{\ell} E_i$. Let $b_1, ..., b_\ell$ respectively denote the roots of subtrees $\tau_1, ..., \tau_\ell$ in $\mathcal{T}$. Then set $E_i$ can be computed by scanning the list $\mathcal{E}(b_i)$ from beginning (and respectively end) till we encounter an edge $(u, v)$ with $v$ lying in range $[w, .., z]$. (See Figure 4). Thus the time taken by the operation ACTIVE-OUTNGHBRS$(\mathcal{D}, T(w))$ is bounded by $O(deg(S_0) + \log n)$, where $S_0$ is the set of vertices reported.

This data structure can be preprocessed in $O(m \log n)$ time as follows. First we compute set $\mathcal{E}(b)$ for each leaf node $b$ of $\mathcal{T}$. This takes $O(m)$ time. Now $\mathcal{E}(b)$ for an internal node $b$ can be computed by simply merging the lists $\mathcal{E}(b_1)$, $\mathcal{E}(b_2)$ where $b_1$ and $b_2$ are children of $b$. The space complexity of $\mathcal{D}$ is also $O(m \log n)$.

**Theorem 4.** *Given a graph G, it can be preprocessed in $O(m \log n)$ time to build a data structure of size $O(m \log n)$ to perform the following operations.*

1. ACTIVEOUTNGHBRS$(\mathcal{D}, T(w))$: *return the set of active nodes in* OUT$(T(w))$.
2. MARKINACTIVE$(\mathcal{D}, S)$: *mark the vertices in set S as inactive.*

*The time taken by both of the above operations is $O(deg(S) \log n)$ where $S$ is the set of vertices reported in the first case, and $S$ is the set of vertices marked inactive in the second case.*

# 7   Computation of Dominators from Semidominators

A vertex $u \neq v$ is said to be a dominator of $v$ if every path from $s$ to $v$ passes through $u$. Thus $u$ is a dominator of $v$ if and only if either $u = s$, or $v$ becomes unreachable from $s$ on removal of $u$ from $G$. For each vertex $v$, we use $D(v)$ to denote the set of dominators of $v$. In order to compute the set $D(v)$ it suffices to compute $idom(v)$ defined as follows.

**Definition 6 ([13]).** *Vertex $u$ is said to be immediate dominator of $v$, denoted by $u = idom(v)$, if $u$ is a dominator of $v$ and every other dominator of $v$ (other than vertex $u$ itself) is also a dominator of $u$.*

The algorithm for computing immediate dominators from semidominators is almost the same as for the restricted case when $T$ is a DFS tree. For the sake of completeness, we now provide this algorithm. The starting point is the concept of relative dominators defined as follows.

**Definition 7 ([4]).** *A vertex $w$ is said to be a relative dominator of $v$ if $w$ is a descendant of* SDOM$(v)$ *on* PATH$($SDOM$(v), v)$ *for which* SDOM$(w)$ *has the minimum preorder numbering.*

The following relationship between relative dominators, immediate dominators, and semidominators was shown by Buchbaum et al. [4] for DFS tree. We show that this relation holds even for any arbitrary tree as well.

**Lemma 5 ([4]).** *For any vertex $v$, if $\text{SDOM}(rdom(v)) = \text{SDOM}(v)$, then $idom(v) = \text{SDOM}(v)$, otherwise, $idom(v) = idom(rdom(v))$.*

**Proof.** Let $w$ be a relative dominator of $v$, and $u = idom(w)$. For the case when $w = v$, it is easy to see that $idom(v) = \text{SDOM}(v)$. Thus we consider the case $w \neq v$. In this case, in order to prove that $idom(v) = u$, we need to show that $u$ is a dominator of $v$ and there does not exists any other dominator of $v$ on $\text{PATH}(u, v)$.

We first show that $v$ is unreachable from $s$ in $G \setminus \{u\}$. Since $u = idom(w)$, we have that $w$ is unreachable from $s$ in $G \setminus \{u\}$. Assume towards a contradiction that there is a path from $s$ to $v$ in $G \setminus \{u\}$. Then there must exist a detour $D$ from $a$ to $b$ where $a$ is an ancestor of $u$ and $b$ is a descendant of $w$ belonging to $\text{PATH}(w, v)$. Since detour $D$ implies existence of a valid sequence from $a$ to $b$, it follows that $\text{SDOM}(b) \in \text{PATH}(s, a)$. This contradicts that $w$ is a relative dominator of $v$. Hence $v$ is unreachable from $s$ in $G \setminus \{u\}$. Thus $u$ is a dominator of $v$.

In order to show that $u$ is the immediate dominator of $v$, it suffices to show that there does not exist any vertex on $\text{PATH}(u, v) \setminus \{u\}$ whose removal disconnects $v$ from $s$. Assume towards a contradiction that there exists such a vertex $x$. Since there are two vertex disjoint paths from $\text{SDOM}(v)$ to $v$, so $x$ can not lie on $\text{PATH}(\text{SDOM}(v), v) \setminus \{\text{SDOM}(v), v\}$. Also note that $x$ can not lie on $\text{PATH}(u, w) \setminus \{u, w\}$ as there are two vertex disjoint paths from $idom(w)$ to $w$. Since $\text{SDOM}(v)$ is an ancestor of $w$, this contradicts the existence of $x$. □

Lemma 5 suggests that once we have computed relative dominators, the immediate dominators can be computed in $O(n)$ time by processing the vertices of $T$ in a top down manner. The task of computing relative dominators can be formulated as a data structure problem on a rooted tree as follows.

Each tree edge $(u, y)$ is assigned a weight equal to $\text{SDOM}(y)$. It can be seen that if $(a, w)$ is minimum weight edge on $\text{PATH}(\text{SDOM}(v), v)$, then $w$ is a relative dominator of $v$. So in order to compute relative dominators, all we need is to compute the least weight edge on any given path of tree $T$. This problem turns out to be an instance of *Bottleneck Edge Query* (BEQ) problem on trees with integral weights. Demaine et al. [7] recently presented the following optimal solution for this problem.

**Theorem 5 (Demaine et al. [7]).** *A tree on $n$ vertices and edge weights in the range $[1, n]$ can be preprocessed in $O(n)$ time to build a data structure of $O(n)$ size so that given any $u, v \in V$, the edge of smallest weight on $\text{PATH}(u, v)$ can be reported in $O(1)$ time.*

We process tree $T$ in a top down order to compute $idom(v)$ as follows. We first compute $rdom(v)$ in $O(1)$ time by performing BEQ query between $v$ and $\text{SDOM}(v)$. Using the data structure stated in Theorem 5, it takes $O(1)$ time. Let $w = rdom(v)$. If $w = v$, then we set $idom(v) \leftarrow \text{SDOM}(v)$. Otherwise, we set $idom(v) \leftarrow idom(w)$. Since we process the vertices in a top down fashion, $idom(w)$ has already been computed. Hence it takes $O(1)$ time to compute $idom(v)$. So it can be concluded that we can compute immediate dominators of all vertices in $O(n)$ time only if we know semidominators of all vertices.

# References

1. Baswana, S., Khanna, N.: Approximate shortest paths avoiding a failed vertex: Near optimal data structures for undirected unweighted graphs. Algorithmica **66**(1), 18–50 (2013)
2. Bentley, J.L.: Solutions to Klee's rectangle problems, Dept. of Comp. Sci., Carnegie-Mellon University, Pittsburgh, PA (1977) (unpublished manuscript)
3. Bernstein, A., Karger, D.: A nearly optimal oracle for avoiding failed vertices and edges. In: STOC 2009: Proceedings of the 41st Annual ACM Symposium on Theory of Computing, pp. 101–110. ACM, New York (2009)
4. Buchsbaum, A.L., Georgiadis, L., Kaplan, H., Rogers, A., Tarjan, R.E., Westbrook, J.: Linear-time algorithms for dominators and other path-evaluation problems. SIAM J. Comput. **38**(4), 1533–1573 (2008)
5. Chechik, S.: Fault-tolerant compact routing schemes for general graphs. Inf. Comput. **222**, 36–44 (2013)
6. Chechik, S., Langberg, M., Peleg, D., Roditty, L.: f-Sensitivity distance oracles and routing schemes. Algorithmica **63**(4), 861–882 (2012)
7. Demaine, E.D., Landau, G.M., Weimann, O.: On cartesian trees and range minimum queries. Algorithmica **68**(3), 610–625 (2014)
8. Demetrescu, C., Thorup, M., Chowdhury, R.A., Ramachandran, V.: Oracles for distances avoiding a failed node or link. SIAM J. Comput. **37**(5), 1299–1318 (2008)
9. Dinitz, M., Krauthgamer, R.: Fault-tolerant spanners: better and simpler. In: Gavoille, C., Fraigniaud, P. (eds.) Proceedings of the 30th Annual ACM Symposium on Principles of Distributed Computing, PODC 2011, San Jose, CA, USA, June 6–8, 2011, pp. 169–178. ACM (2011)
10. Duan, R., Pettie, S.: Dual-failure distance and connectivity oracles. In: SODA 2009: Proceedings of 19th Annual ACM -SIAM Symposium on Discrete Algorithms, Philadelphia, PA, USA, pp. 506–515. Society for Industrial and Applied Mathematics (2009)
11. Fraczak, W., Georgiadis, L., Miller, A., Tarjan, R.E.: Finding dominators via disjoint set union. J. Discrete Algorithms **23**, 2–20 (2013)
12. Georgiadis, L., Tarjan, R.E.: Dominators, directed bipolar orders, and independent spanning trees. In: Czumaj, A., Mehlhorn, K., Pitts, A., Wattenhofer, R. (eds.) ICALP 2012, Part I. LNCS, vol. 7391, pp. 375–386. Springer, Heidelberg (2012)
13. Lengauer, T., Tarjan, R.E.: A fast algorithm for finding dominators in a flowgraph. ACM Trans. Program. Lang. Syst. **1**(1), 121–141 (1979)
14. Parter, M.: Dual failure resilient BFS structure (2015). arXiv:1505.00692
15. Parter, M., Peleg, D.: Sparse fault-tolerant BFS trees. In: Bodlaender, H.L., Italiano, G.F. (eds.) ESA 2013. LNCS, vol. 8125, pp. 779–790. Springer, Heidelberg (2013)

16. Parter, M., Peleg, D.: Fault tolerant approximate BFS structures. In: Chekuri, C. (ed.) Proceedings of the Twenty-Fifth Annual ACM-SIAM Symposium on Discrete Algorithms, SODA 2014, Portland, Oregon, USA, January 5–7, 2014, pp. 1073–1092. SIAM (2014)
17. Williams, V.V.: Faster replacement paths. In: Randall, D. (ed.) Proceedings of the Twenty-Second Annual ACM-SIAM Symposium on Discrete Algorithms, SODA 2011, San Francisco, California, USA, January 23–25, 2011, pp. 1337–1346. SIAM (2011)

# Locally Optimal Load Balancing

Laurent Feuilloley[1,2], Juho Hirvonen[2], and Jukka Suomela[2]([✉])

[1] École Normale Supérieure de Cachan, Cachan, France
[2] Helsinki Institute for Information Technology HIIT,
Department of Computer Science, Aalto University, Espoo, Finland
jukka.suomela@aalto.fi

**Abstract.** This work studies distributed algorithms for *locally optimal load-balancing*: We are given a graph of maximum degree $\Delta$, and each node has up to $L$ units of load. The task is to distribute the load more evenly so that the loads of adjacent nodes differ by at most 1. If the graph is a path ($\Delta = 2$), it is easy to solve the *fractional* version of the problem in $O(L)$ communication rounds, independently of the number of nodes. We show that this is tight, and we show that it is possible to solve also the *discrete* version of the problem in $O(L)$ rounds in paths. For the general case ($\Delta > 2$), we show that fractional load balancing can be solved in $\mathrm{poly}(L, \Delta)$ rounds and discrete load balancing in $f(L, \Delta)$ rounds for some function $f$, independently of the number of nodes.

## 1  Introduction

In this work, we introduce the problem of *locally optimal load balancing*, and study it from the perspective of distributed algorithms. In this problem, we are given a graph $G = (V, E)$, and each node has up to $L$ units of load. The task is to distribute load more evenly so that the loads of adjacent nodes differ by at most 1:

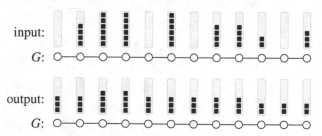

That is, we want to *smooth out* the load distribution, and find an *equilibrium* in which no edge can improve its load distribution by selfishly moving load between its endpoints.

---

See the full version of this work [10] for detailed proofs and additional illustrations.

© Springer-Verlag Berlin Heidelberg 2015
Y. Moses (Ed.): DISC 2015, LNCS 9363, pp. 544–558, 2015.
DOI: 10.1007/978-3-662-48653-5_36

A bit more formally, in the load balancing problem we are given an input vector $x\colon V \to \{0, 1, \ldots, L\}$, and the task is to find an output vector $y\colon V \to [0, L]$ and a flow $f\colon E \to \mathbb{R}$ so that for each node $v \in V$ we have

$$y(v) = x(v) + \sum_{(u,v)\in E} f(u, v), \tag{1}$$

and for each edge $(u, v) \in E$ we have

$$|y(u) - y(v)| \leq 1. \tag{2}$$

Here is an illustration of the input and a feasible solution in the special case that $G$ is a path:

x: 0  4  6  6  0  6  0  4  4  2  0  3

y: 3  3  4  4  3  3  3  3  3  2  2  2

f: 3  2  0  2  1  2  1  0  1  1  1

The problem comes in two natural flavours:

- *Discrete load balancing*: $y(v) \in \{0, 1, \ldots, L\}$, i.e., load units are indivisible.
- *Fractional load balancing*: $y(v) \in [0, L]$, i.e., load units can be divided.

## 1.1   Centralised Algorithms

Both discrete and fractional load balancing can be solved easily with the following algorithm: Start with $y \leftarrow x$ and $f \leftarrow 0$. Then repeatedly pick an *unhappy edge* $(u, v) \in E$ with $y(u) \geq y(v) + 2$, and move one unit of load from $u$ to $v$. This algorithm clearly converges, as the potential function $\sum_v y(v)^2$ decreases by at least 2 in each step.

## 1.2   Local Solutions and Local Algorithms

In the above centralised algorithm, we can think that each node $v$ has a pile of $y(v)$ tokens and we always move the topmost token. Then the height of a token decreases by at least one every time we move it; hence no individual token is moved more than $L$ times. This argument shows that there always exists a *local solution* in which the final position of a token is always within distance $L$ from its origin; that is, each token can stay in its radius-$L$ neighbourhood.

   In this work we are interested if the problem can be solved with a *local algorithm*: is it possible to solve the problem so that we can compute the flow $f(u, v)$ for each edge $(u, v) \in E$ based on only the information that is available within distance $T$ from $(u, v)$ in graph $G$, for some $T$. Equivalently, we want to know if there is a (deterministic) distributed algorithm in the usual LOCAL model [21] that solves the load balancing problem in $T$ *communication rounds*, or more succinctly, in *time $T$*.

We will assume that the input graph has a maximum degree of $\Delta$. We are interested in local algorithms with a running time of $T = T(L, \Delta)$ that may depend on the maximum load $L$ and maximum degree $\Delta$, but is independent of the number of nodes $n = |V|$. Such an algorithm could be used to solve load balancing even in infinitely large graphs, and it would be very easy to e.g. parallelise such algorithms, as each part of the output can be determined based on its local neighbourhood.

## 1.3  Smoothing with Moving Average

There is a special case that can be easily solved with a local algorithm in time $T = O(L)$: fractional load balancing in 2-regular graphs (cycles and infinite paths). We can simply calculate the moving average of the input loads with a window of size $\Theta(L)$. More concretely, each node gives a fraction $1/(2L + 1)$ of its input load to every node (including itself) in its radius-$L$ neighbourhood. This way the final loads of adjacent nodes differ by at most $L/(2L + 1) < 1/2$ units. The same strategy can be applied easily in, e.g., $d$-dimensional grids.

Among others, the present work seeks to answer the following questions:

– Is the running time of $O(L)$ optimal here, or could we solve it in time $o(L)$?
– Can we generalise this kind of smoothing algorithms to arbitrary graphs, and if so, what is the running time?
– Can we generalise this kind of smoothing algorithms to discrete load balancing?

## 1.4  Contributions

The contributions of this work are as follows. We start with a simple lower bound:

**Theorem 1.** *Load balancing requires $\Omega(L)$ rounds, even in the case of paths and cycles.*

Then we prove negative results for various algorithm families that have been used widely in the prior work. To this end, we define the following algorithm families:

– *Match-and-balance algorithms*: In each step, the algorithm finds a matching $M$ and balances the load (fully or partially) for each edge in $M$. More precisely, for each edge $(u, v) \in M$ with $y(u) > y(v)$, the algorithm increases the flow $f(u, v)$ by at most $(y(u) - y(v))/2$. For example, many natural distributed versions of the centralised algorithm from Section 1.1 are of match-and-balance type.
– *Careful algorithms*: In each round, for each edge $(u, v) \in E$, the algorithm increases or decreases $f(u, v)$ by at most $poly(L)$. All match-and-balance algorithms are also careful algorithms.

– *Oblivious algorithms*: The total amount of load moved from node $u$ to $v$ only depends on the initial load of $u$ and the distance between $u$ and $v$. For example, the moving average algorithm from Section 1.3 is oblivious.

We show that algorithms of any of these types cannot find a locally optimal load balancing efficiently (or at all):

**Theorem 2.** *Any match-and-balance algorithm takes $\Omega(L^2)$ rounds in the worst case, even in paths and cycles.*

**Theorem 3.** *Any careful algorithm takes $\Delta^{\Omega(L)}$ rounds in the worst case.*

**Theorem 4.** *There are no oblivious algorithms for infinite d-regular trees with $d \geq 3$.*

We then present the main contributions—local algorithms for load balancing. First, we show that we can circumvent the barrier of Theorem 2:

**Theorem 5.** *Discrete load balancing can be solved in time $O(L)$ in paths and cycles, with a deterministic local algorithm.*

**Corollary 1.** *The time complexity of both fractional and discrete load balancing in paths and cycles is $\Theta(L)$.*

Next we show that we can also circumvent the barriers of Theorem 3 and 4 for fractional load balancing—naturally, we have to design an algorithm that is neither oblivious nor careful:

**Theorem 6.** *Fractional load balancing can be solved in time $\mathrm{poly}(L, \Delta)$ in graphs of maximum degree $\Delta$ with a deterministic local algorithm.*

Finally, we show that discrete load balancing can be solved locally, i.e., in time that is independent of $n$:

**Theorem 7.** *Discrete load balancing can be solved in time $T(L, \Delta)$, for some function $T$, in graphs of maximum degree $\Delta$ with a deterministic local algorithm.*

Whether there is an *efficient* algorithm for discrete load balancing in the general case remains an open question.

## 2  Related Work

There is a vast body of literature related to problems that are superficially similar to locally optimal load balancing. However, in many cases the primary goal is something else—for example, achieving a near-optimal global solution—and the algorithms just happen to also find a locally optimal solution.

Most of the previous solutions are inefficient. In particular, we are not aware of any solution that comes close to $O(L)$ for discrete load balancing on paths, or close to $\mathrm{poly}(L, \Delta)$ for fractional load balancing in general graphs. In prior work, the inefficiency typically stems from at least one of the following factors:

1. *Inherently global problems*: A lot of prior work focuses on problems that are inherently global—for example, the task is to find a solution such that the difference between the minimum load and the maximum load is at most 1. It is easy to see that any algorithm for solving such problems takes $\Omega(n)$ rounds in the worst case.
2. *Natural but inefficient algorithms*: Many papers study various natural processes for doing load balancing. Many of these are of match-and-balance type, and virtually all of these are careful. Typically, the negative results of Theorems 2 and 3 apply.

In contrast, we study a problem that can be solved efficiently, and our algorithms demonstrate that it is indeed possible to break the barriers of Theorems 2 and 3. In what follows, we will discuss related work in more detail.

**Reducing a Global Potential with Local Rules.** There is a lot of literature on load balancing when the goal is to reduce a global potential function by iterating a local balancing rule. Examples of such potential functions are the difference between the maximum and the minimum load (*discrepancy*), the maximum load (*makespan*), and the quadratic difference to the average load.

Various models are considered: two classic models are the *diffusion model*, where vertices distribute their load to all their neighbours, and the *matching model*, where the load is exchanged only along the edges of a matching—for example a random matching or an edge colouring.

In the *continuous case*, where the loads are assumed to be infinitely divisible, the speed of convergence was analysed for simple schemes both in the diffusion model [23,25] and the matching model [6,13]. In both the speed of convergence is essentially captured by the spectral properties of the graph in question.

In the context of indivisible loads, known as the *discrete case*, similar problems were first studied for networks designed to balance the load quickly [22]. Different schemes for reducing the discrepancy in the discrete case were analysed, and the question of whether the speed of convergence in the continuous case could be matched remained open [1,12,13,20]. Recently Sauerwald and Sun [24] were able to prove convergence as fast as in the continous case, up to constant factors. Nevertheless, reducing discrepancy is a global problem and can take linear time in the worst case.

**Semi-matching Problem.** In the *semi-matching problem* the nodes of a graph are divided into clients and servers [15]. Each client has to be assigned to an adjacent server. The goal is to optimise the total waiting time of the clients. Czygrinow et al. [8] presented a distributed algorithm for finding a locally optimal semi-matching in time poly($\Delta$); this also implies a factor-2 approximation of globally optimal semi-matchings. The semi-matching problem is very similar to the locally optimal load balancing problem, especially when limited to the case of degree 2 clients, with the tokens being more "localised". Indeed, our linear lower bound can be adapted to prove a lower bound for locally optimal semi-matchings. However, to our knowledge, efficient semi-matching algorithms do not directly imply efficient load-balancing algorithms.

**Balls into Bins.** In the *d-choice process* each of $n$ balls goes in the least loaded of $d$ random bins. Dependency of the maximum load on the parameter $d$ is well known [3,17,26]. The choice of the bins can be modelled by a graph [18]; in one variant the bins are connected by edges and each ball does a local search until it finds a local minimum [5,7]. This process produces a locally optimal load balancing, but the model of computing is sequential (balls arrive one at a time).

**Sandpile Models and Chip-Firing Games.** Our stability condition is similar to what is used in *sandpile models* [4,9,16] and *chip-firing games* [2]. However, in these problems the goal is usually to describe final configurations for fixed, very simple algorithms that simulate a natural phenomenon.

**Filtering.** *Sliding window algorithms* for computing the *running average* or for *image filtering* are natural local algorithms. Averaging type algorithms, however, cannot guarantee an integral solution to load balancing problems. *Median filtering* does guarantee integral solutions for integral inputs; however, it does not preserve the total load.

**Games and Equilibriums.** The locally optimal load balancing problem can be seen as a problem of finding an equilibrium state, where no single load token can gain advantage by moving. We show that such an equilibrium can be found locally, that is, the decisions made in one part of the graph do not propagate too far. This is in contrast with problems such as finding *stable matchings*, where there is a local algorithm only for finding almost-stable matchings [11].

**Matchings.** Locally optimal load balancing is closely related to *bipartite maximal matching*: if the initial loads are $x(v) \in \{0, 2\}$, then it is easy to see that a solution can be found using a bipartite maximal matching algorithm. This is a problem that can be solved in time $O(\Delta)$ [14]. Showing a matching lower bounds is a major open question, and we do not expect that one can prove tight lower bounds for locally optimal load balancing as a function of $\Delta$ before we resolve the distributed time complexity of bipartite maximal matching.

In our algorithms for discrete load balancing, we will use the bipartite maximal matching [14] algorithm as a subroutine. For fractional load balancing, we use the *almost-maximal fractional matching algorithm* due to Khuller et al. [19] as a subroutine.

## 3   Negative Results

We will now prove the negative results of Theorems 1–4. For simplicity, we prove the statements for deterministic distributed algorithms; it is fairly straightforward to extend the results to randomised algorithms (e.g., consider the expected values of the outputs).

Recall that in Section 1 we defined the problem so that the output is bounded by $L$. However, we will not exploit this restriction in any of the lower-bound proofs. The negative results hold verbatim for a relaxed version of the problem in which the outputs can be any nonnegative real numbers. We only assume that the inputs are bounded by $L$.

## 3.1 Load Balancing on Paths and Cycles

We start with the unconditional lower bound that holds for any algorithm, for both fractional and discrete load balancing, and in the simplest possible case of paths or cycles.

**Theorem 1.** *Load balancing requires $\Omega(L)$ rounds, even in the case of paths and cycles.*

*Proof.* We will give the proof for the case of paths; the case of cycles is very similar. Consider a path $P$ with $n$ nodes, labelled with the numbers $1, 2, \ldots, n$ from left to right, for a sufficiently large $n$. Let $A$ be a load-balancing algorithm. For an input $x \colon V \to \{0, ..., L\}$, we write $A(x)$ for the output of $A$ on input $x$. Let $h = \lfloor L/2 \rfloor - 1$.

Consider the following constant inputs: $x_0 \colon v \mapsto 0$ and $x_L \colon v \mapsto L$. Let $y_0 = A(x_0)$ and $y_L = A(x_L)$. Clearly $y_0(v) = 0$ for all $v$ and $y_L(v) \geq L$ for at least one $v$. Hence we can find two nodes, $\ell$ and $r$, such that $y_0(\ell) = 0$, $y_L(r) \geq L$, and $|r - \ell| = L - 1$.

W.l.o.g., assume that $\ell < r$. Let $m = (r + \ell)/2$ be the midpoint between $\ell$ and $r$. Now define an input $x$ such that $x(i) = 0$ for $i \leq m$ and $x(i) = L$ otherwise. Note that the radius-$h$ neighbourhoods of $\ell$ are identical in $x_0$ and $x$. Similarly, the radius-$h$ neighbourhoods of $r$ are identical in $x_L$ and $x$.

Let $y = A(x)$. If $y(\ell) = y_0(\ell)$ and $y(r) = y_L(r)$, we have a contradiction: the distance between $\ell$ and $r$ is smaller than their load difference, and hence there has to be an unhappy edge between them. Therefore $y(\ell) \neq y_0(\ell)$ or $y(r) \neq y_L(r)$. In both cases, there is a node $v$ that changed its output between two instances, even though the inputs were identical up to distance $h$. Hence the running time of $A$ has to be at least $h + 1 = \Theta(L)$. $\qquad\square$

## 3.2 Match-and-Balance Algorithms

Recall that in each round, a match-and-balance algorithm finds some matching $M$, and then for each edge $(u, v) \in M$ with $y(u) > y(v)$, the algorithm increases the flow $f(u, v)$ by at most $(y(u) - y(v))/2$. Note that $M$ does not need to be a maximal matching, a maximum matching, or a random matching—the following lower bound holds regardless of how clever the algorithm tries to be in its selection of the matching $M$, and even if it gets the matchings in zero time from an oracle.

**Theorem 2.** *Any match-and-balance algorithm takes $\Omega(L^2)$ rounds in the worst case, even in paths and cycles.*

The basic idea of the proof is simple. Let $A$ be a match-and-balance algorithm.

1. We construct an instance in which $A$ has to move $\Omega(L^3)$ units of load in total.
2. We prove that $A$ can move only $O(L)$ units of load per round.

Hence we have a lower bound of $\Omega(L^2)$ for the running time of $A$.

We will again study the case of paths; the case of cycles is very similar. Let $P$ be a path with $2n + 1$ nodes, labelled with $-n, -n + 1, \ldots, n$ from left to right. We say that a load vector is *monotone* if $y(i) \geq y(j)$ for all $i \leq j$. The key feature of match-and-balance algorithms is that a monotone load vector remains monotone after each step.

**Lemma 1.** *Match-and-balance algorithms maintain a monotone load configuration on $P$.*

*Proof.* A simple case analysis, see the full version of this work [10]. $\qquad\Box$

In a monotone configuration, we can only move $O(L)$ units of load per round.

**Lemma 2.** *Any match-and-balance algorithm $A$ can move at most $L/2$ units of load in a single round on path $P$ with a monotone load configuration.*

*Proof.* Since $A$ maintains a monotone load configuration, the sum of the load differences over all edges is at most $L$. Therefore even if $M$ contains all edges with a non-zero load difference, the algorithm can move only at most $L/2$ units of load per round in total. $\qquad\Box$

*Proof (of Theorem 2).* We will consider the input vector $x$ where $x(i) = L$ for $i \leq 0$ and $x(i) = 0$ otherwise. The vector is monotone and hence it remains monotone throughout the execution of $A$. Consider the output of node 0. There are two cases:

1. The output of node 0 is at most $h = L/2$. Now for each $i = 0, 1, \ldots, h - 1$, we can observe that the load of node $-i$ has decreased by at least $h - i$ units, and by monotonicity, all of this load has been moved to the right. In particular, for each $i$ we have moved $h - i$ units of load from node $-i$ over at least $i + 1$ edges. The total amount of work done by the nonpositive nodes is at least the tetrahedral number $1 \cdot h + 2 \cdot (h - 1) + \ldots + h \cdot 1 = \Theta(h^3) = \Theta(L^3)$.
2. The output of node 0 is at least $h = L/2$. Now for each $i = 0, 1, \ldots, h - 1$, we can observe that the load of node $i$ has increased by at least $h - i$ units, and by monotonicity, all of this load has been moved from the left. The total amount of work done by the nonnegative nodes is at least $\Theta(L^3)$.

By Lemma 2, moving $\Theta(L^3)$ units of load takes $\Omega(L^2)$ rounds. $\qquad\Box$

### 3.3   Careful Algorithms

Recall that careful algorithms move $O(L)$ units of load per round—this includes, for example, all match-and-balance algorithms, as well as many other natural algorithms that simulate the physical process of collapsing piles of tokens.

**Theorem 3.** *Any careful algorithm takes $\Delta^{\Omega(L)}$ rounds in the worst case.*

*Proof.* Construct the input $(G, x)$ as follows: We have a tree $G_u$ rooted at $u$, a tree $G_v$ rooted at $v$, plus an edge $\{u, v\}$. Both trees are of depth $L/4$; each non-leaf node has $d - 1$ children. All nodes of $G_u$ have an input load of 0, and all nodes of $G_v$ have an input load of $L$.

Now consider any solution $(y, f)$. If $y(u) \geq L/4$, then all nodes of $G_u$ have a load of at least 1, and there are $d^{\Omega(L)}$ nodes in $G_u$. All of the load has to be moved across the edge $\{u, v\}$, and hence $f(v, u) = d^{\Omega(L)}$. Otherwise $y(u) < L/4$, and $y(v) < L/4 + 1$. In this case all nodes of $G_v$ have a load of at most $L - 1$, and again we can conclude that $f(v, u) = d^{\Omega(L)}$.

A careful algorithm starts with $y \leftarrow x$ and $f \leftarrow 0$ and changes each element of $f$ by at most $\text{poly}(L)$ in each round. Hence any careful algorithm has to spend $d^{\Omega(L)}$ for this instance.                                                                 $\square$

### 3.4   Oblivious Algorithms

Recall that in an oblivious algorithm, the total amount of load moved from node $u$ to $v$ only depends on the initial load of $u$ and the distance between $u$ and $v$. For example, the algorithm that computes the moving average in an infinite path is an oblivious algorithm. In the full version of this work [10] we show that such algorithms do not exist for infinite regular trees of a degree larger than 2:

**Theorem 4.** *There are no oblivious algorithms for infinite $d$-regular trees with $d \geq 3$.*

## 4   Discrete Load Balancing in Paths and Cycles

We will now prove the positive results. We first give an algorithm that exactly matches the lower bound of Theorem 1.

**Theorem 5.** *Discrete load balancing can be solved in time $O(L)$ in paths and cycles, with a deterministic local algorithm.*

**Infinite Directed Paths.** We will first show how to do load balancing in an *infinite path with a consistent orientation*. That is, each node $v$ has a degree of 2, and it can refer to its *left neighbour* $v - 1$ and *right neighbour* $v + 1$ in a globally consistent manner.

We will interpret the path with tokens as a 2-dimensional grid, indexed by $(v, i)$, where $v \in V$ is a node and $i \in \{1, \ldots, L\}$ is a possible location for a token. We say that $(v, i)$ is a *slot*. Initially, slot $(v, i)$ holds a *token* if $x(v) \geq i$. Our plan is to move the tokens around in the grid so that we maintain the following stability conditions.

**Definition 1.** *A token in slot* $(v, i)$ *is* $k$-*stable if* $i = 1$ *or there is a token in slot* $(v + k, i - 1)$. *A configuration is* $k$-*stable if all tokens are* $k$-*stable. For a set* $K$, *a configuration is* $K$-*stable if it is* $k$-*stable for all* $k \in K$.

We write $[\![a, b]\!] = \{a, a + 1, \ldots, b\}$. Initially, the configuration is 0-stable. If we can find a $[\![-1, 1]\!]$-stable configuration, we can construct a feasible solution to the load balancing problem by simply setting $y(v)$ to be equal to the number of tokens in slots $(v, \cdot)$.

However, we will now design an $O(L)$-time algorithm with a *stronger* stability condition: it will compute a $[\![-3, 3]\!]$-stable configuration. Informally, we smooth out the load distribution so that the slope of the load curve is at most $1/3$. This extra slack will be helpful when we eventually want to solve the problem in paths without consistent orientations.

This algorithm is based on the concept of *pushes*. For a node $v$ and integer $\ell$, define the $\ell$-diagonal of $v$ as the following list of slots:

$$S(v, \ell) = \big((v - \ell, 1), (v - 2\ell, 2), \ldots, (v - L\ell, L)\big)$$

In an $\ell$-push we redistribute the tokens in each $S(v, \ell)$: if there are $k$ tokens in $S(v, \ell)$, then we redistribute the tokens so that the first $k$ elements of $S(v, \ell)$ are occupied and the remaining $L - k$ elements are empty. In essence, we let the tokens slide along each diagonal so that they are piled on the bottom of each diagonal.

An $\ell$-push can be efficiently implemented in time $O(\ell L)$ with a distributed algorithm: for example, node $v$ is responsible for redistributing the tokens in slots $S(v, \ell)$, and we first use $O(\ell L)$ rounds so that each node $v$ can discover everything related to $S(v, \ell)$, and then another $O(\ell L)$ rounds so that node $v$ can inform the relevant nodes regarding how to move tokens in $S(v, \ell)$.

Clearly, after an $\ell$-push we will have an $\ell$-stable configuration. The non-trivial part is that $\ell$-pushes do not interfere with any stability that we have previously achieved.

**Lemma 3.** *For every choice of integers* $\ell$ *and* $k$, *if a configuration is* $k$-*stable, then it is still* $k$-*stable after an* $\ell$-*push.*

*Proof.* See the full version of this work [10].  □

Now we can easily find a $[\![-3, 3]\!]$-stable configuration in time $O(L)$: the algorithm simply does an $\ell$-push for each $\ell \in [\![-3, 3]\!]$, sequentially, in an arbitrary order. We will call this algorithm $A_1$.

*Remark 1.* It may be helpful to compare pushing with the lower-bound construction of Theorem 2: while a match-and-balance algorithm can only move $O(L)$ units of load per round in monotone configurations, an $O(1)$-push can move $\Omega(L^3)$ units of load per $O(L)$ rounds in certain monotone configurations.

**Finite Directed Paths and Cycles.** Algorithm $A_1$ finds a $[\![-3,3]\!]$-stable configuration in infinite directed paths in time $O(L)$. It is fairly straightforward to use $A_1$ to design an algorithm $A_2$ that works in finite directed paths and cycles and still finds a $[\![-3,3]\!]$-stable configuration in time $O(L)$. We give the technical details in the full version of this work [10].

**Undirected Paths and Cycles.** So far we have designed an algorithm $A_2$ that finds a $[\![-3,3]\!]$-stable configuration in paths and cycles with a globally consistent orientation. Now we show how to use it to design an algorithm $A_3$ that finds a $[\![-1,1]\!]$-stable configuration in paths and cycles without an orientation.

It can be shown that *some* form of local symmetry-breaking is needed. We will use the familiar *port-numbering model*: Each node $v$ has up to two communication ports, labelled with $(v,1)$ and $(v,2)$. The ports are identified with the endpoints of the edges; each edge joins a pair of ports. The port numbers at the endpoints of an edge do not need to match—for example, an edge $\{u,v\}$ may join $(u,1)$ to $(v,1)$ or $(u,1)$ to $(v,2)$.

In algorithm $A_2$, we construct a *virtual graph* $G'$ as follows: Each node $v$ splits itself in two virtual nodes, $v_1$ and $v_2$. The virtual nodes also have two ports. For each edge $e = \{u,v\}$, depending on the type of $e$ we connect the virtual nodes of $u$ and $v$ as follows:

- $e$ joins $(u,1)$ to $(v,1)$: connect $(u_1,1)$ to $(v_2,2)$ and $(u_2,2)$ to $(v_1,1)$,
- $e$ joins $(u,1)$ to $(v,2)$: connect $(u_1,1)$ to $(v_1,2)$ and $(u_2,2)$ to $(v_2,1)$,
- $e$ joins $(u,2)$ to $(v,1)$: connect $(u_1,2)$ to $(v_2,1)$ and $(u_2,1)$ to $(v_1,2)$,
- $e$ joins $(u,2)$ to $(v,2)$: connect $(u_1,2)$ to $(v_1,1)$ and $(u_2,1)$ to $(v_2,2)$.

If $G$ was a path with $n$ nodes, then $G'$ consists of two disjoint paths with $n$ nodes each. If $G$ was an $n$-cycle, then $G'$ consists of either one cycle with $2n$ nodes or two cycles with $n$ nodes each.

The key observation is that there is a *consistent* port numbering in $G$: port 1 of a virtual node is always connected to port 2 of an adjacent virtual node. We can now interpret the ports so that in each virtual node port 1 points "left" and port 2 points "right".

Each node first splits its input load arbitrarily between its virtual copies. Then we run algorithm $A_2$ to find a $[\![-3,3]\!]$-stable configuration in the virtual graph, and then map all tokens back to the original graph: the new load of $v$ is the sum of the new loads of $v_1$ and $v_2$.

Now we have a configuration where the maximum load difference between a pair of adjacent nodes is 2. However, the load is *approximately well-balanced*: a load difference of more than 2 implies a distance of at least 4. Therefore we can easily find a $[\![-1,1]\!]$-stable configuration in $O(1)$ time with local operations. For example, we can apply a match-and-balance algorithm: find a maximal matching $M$ of unhappy edges and move a token over each edge. Conveniently, all edges become happy, including those that were not in $M$. It is easy to find a maximal matching $M$ in $O(1)$ time, as this is in essence maximal matching in a bipartite graph of maximum degree 2: on one side we have the nodes that are "too low" and on the other side we have the nodes that are "too high" in comparison with their neighbours.

In summary, we can find a $[\![-1, 1]\!]$-stable configuration in any path or cycle in time $O(L)$, and therefore we can do discrete load balancing in any path or cycle in time $O(L)$.

## 5   Discrete Load Balancing in General Graphs

We will now show how to do discrete load balancing in graphs of maximum degree $\Delta$.

**Theorem 7.** *Discrete load balancing can be solved in time $T(L, \Delta)$, for some function $T$, in graphs of maximum degree $\Delta$ with a deterministic local algorithm.*

Again, we will imagine that each node $v$ has $L$ *slots*, labelled $(v, \cdot)$, and each token is placed in one of the slots. Initially slots $(v, 1), (v, 2), \ldots, (v, x(v))$ are occupied with tokens.

We define the *(downward) cone* $C(v, i)$ of slot $(v, i)$ as the set of slots $(u, j) \neq (v, i)$ such that $i - j \geq \mathrm{dist}(v, u)$. In the algorithm, if there is a token in $(v, i)$ and all slots of the cone $C(v, i)$ are full, then we say that the token is *stable*, and we *freeze* it, i.e. it will never be moved again.

In the algorithm we try to match the highest unfrozen tokens with the free slots in their cones. If they succeed then they move to these slots; otherwise they can be frozen.

We now give the pseudo-code of the algorithm in a centralised way, prove the correctness of the algorithm, and then show that it is actually a local algorithm. The algorithm proceeds as follows:

1. All stable tokens of the initial configuration are frozen.
2. For each $h = L, L - 1, \ldots, 1$:
   (a) Construct the virtual bipartite graph $F_h = (T \cup S, E)$, where $T$ consists of unfrozen tokens at level $h$, $S$ consists of all empty slots at levels below $h$, and there is an edge $\{t, s\}$ if $s \in S$ is an empty slot in the cone of token $t \in T$.
   (b) In $F_h$, find a maximal matching $M$.
   (c) For every unfrozen token $t$ at level $h$: if the token is matched with a slot $s$ in $M$, move the token to slot $s$, otherwise freeze it.
   (d) Collapse the tokens so that for each node $v$ that holds $k$ tokens, the tokens are in the slots $(v, 1), (v, 2), \ldots, (v, k)$.

First, remark that we maintain the invariant that at round $h$, all load in slots at height $h$ either moves down or is safely frozen. Indeed, if a token is not matched, then all slots in its cone will be full at the end of the loop, and if it is matched, it moves to a strictly lower level, thereafter the invariant is true for level $h$ and maintained for the levels above. At the end of the algorithm all the tokens are frozen, thus the configuration is stable.

We stated the algorithm in a centralised manner, but it is actually local: The vertices only need the knowledge of their radius-$L$ neighbourhood to find their neighbours in graph $F_h$. Graph $F_h$ has a maximum degree of $O(L\Delta^L)$. Therefore we can find a maximal matching in $F_h$ by simulating $O(L\Delta^L)$ rounds of the proposal algorithm [14] in the virtual graph $F_h$. The simulation has a multiplicative $O(L)$ overhead—adjacent nodes in $F_h$ are at distance $O(L)$ in graph $G$. Finally, we have $O(L)$ iterations, giving the overall complexity of $O(L^3\Delta^L)$.

# 6    Fractional Load Balancing in General Graphs

In fractional load balancing, we can use the same basic idea as what we had in the discrete case, but much faster:

**Theorem 6.** *Fractional load balancing can be solved in time* $\mathrm{poly}(L,\Delta)$ *in graphs of maximum degree* $\Delta$ *with a deterministic local algorithm.*

The key idea is that we can add $\epsilon$ units of slack, and find an *almost* maximal *fractional* matching, instead of a maximal integral matching. With the algorithm by Khuller et al. [19], this can be done in $O(\log\frac{1}{\epsilon}+\log\Delta)$ rounds, which gives us an exponential speedup over the $O(\Delta)$-round algorithm for maximal bipartite matching. We give the details of the algorithm in the full version of this work [10].

# 7    Conclusions

In this work, we have introduced the problem of finding a *locally optimal load balancing*, and studied its distributed time complexity. We have shown that the problem can be solved in a strictly local fashion, but to do it, one has to resort to algorithms that are very different from typical load-balancing strategies that are used in the literature. Among the key findings are:

- an $O(L)$-time algorithms for discrete load balancing in paths and cycles,
- a $\mathrm{poly}(L,\Delta)$-time algorithm for fractional load balancing in graphs of maximum degree $\Delta$.

The main open question is the distributed time complexity of the discrete load balancing problem. Our algorithm is local, but it has a running time exponential in $L$; the key question is whether $\mathrm{poly}(L,\Delta)$-time algorithms exist. We suspect that it is related to another long-standing open question—the distributed time complexity of bipartite maximal matching. Indeed, a $\mathrm{polylog}(\Delta)$-time algorithm for bipartite maximal matching would imply a $\mathrm{poly}(L,\Delta)$-time algorithm for discrete load balancing. We conjecture that such algorithms do not exist, but proving such lower bounds seems to be still beyond the reach of current techniques.

Another open question is the generalisation of the results from the LOCAL model to the CONGEST model [21]. In particular, the polynomial-time algorithm for fractional load balancing heavily abuses the unlimited bandwidth of the LOCAL model, but it seems that there are no major obstacles for designing an analogous algorithm that works efficiently in the CONGEST model.

**Acknowledgments.** We have discussed this problem and its variants over the years with numerous people, including, at least, Sebastian Brandt, Pierre Fraigniaud, Mika Göös, Petteri Kaski, Barbara Keller, Janne H. Korhonen, Juhana Laurinharju, Tuomo Lempiäinen, Christoph Lenzen, Joseph S. B. Mitchell, Pekka Orponen, Joel Rybicki, Thomas Sauerwald, Stefan Schmid, and Jara Uitto. Many thanks to all of you for your comments, and many thanks to the anonymous reviewers for their feedback on this work. Computer resources were provided by the Aalto University School of Science "Science-IT" project.

# References

1. Aiello, W., Awerbuch, B., Maggs, B., Rao, S.: Approximate load balancing on dynamic and asynchronous networks. In: Proc. 25th Annual ACM Symposium on Theory of Computing (STOC 1993), pp. 632–641. ACM Press (1993). doi:10.1145/167088.167250

2. Anderson, R., Lovász, L., Shor, P., Spencer, J., Tardos, E., Winograd, S.: Disks, balls, and walls: analysis of a combinatorial game. The American Mathematical Monthly **96**(6), 481–493 (1989). http://www.jstor.org/stable/2323970

3. Azar, Y., Broder, A.Z., Karlin, A.R., Upfal, E.: Balanced allocations. SIAM Journal on Computing **29**(1), 180–200 (1999). doi:10.1137/S0097539795288490

4. Bak, P., Tang, C., Wiesenfeld, K.: Self-organized criticality: An explanation of the $1/f$ noise. Physical Review Letters **59**(4), 381–384 (1987). doi:10.1103/PhysRevLett.59.381

5. Bogdan, P., Sauerwald, T., Stauffer, A., He, S.: Balls into bins via local search. In: Proc. 24th Annual ACM-SIAM Symposium on Discrete Algorithms (SODA 2013), pp. 16–34. SIAM (2013). doi:10.1137/1.9781611973105

6. Boyd, S., Ghosh, A., Prabhakar, B., Shah, D.: Randomized gossip algorithms. IEEE Transactions on Information Theory **52**(6), 2508–2530 (2006). doi:10.1109/TIT.2006.874516

7. Bringmann, K., Sauerwald, T., Stauffer, A., Sun, H.: Balls into bins via local search: cover time and maximum loads. In: Proc. 31st International Symposium on Theoretical Aspects of Computer Science (STACS 2014), pp. 187–198 (2014). doi:10.4230/LIPIcs.STACS.2014.187

8. Czygrinow, A., Hańćkowiak, M., Szymańska, E., Wawrzyniak, W.: Distributed 2-approximation algorithm for the semi-matching problem. In: Aguilera, M.K. (ed.) DISC 2012. LNCS, vol. 7611, pp. 210–222. Springer, Heidelberg (2012)

9. Dhar, D.: Theoretical studies of self-organized criticality. Physica A **369**(1), 29–70 (2006). doi:10.1016/j.physa.2006.04.004

10. Feuilloley, L., Hirvonen, J., Suomela, J.: Locally optimal load balancing (2015). http://arxiv.org/abs/1502.04511

11. Floréen, P., Kaski, P., Polishchuk, V., Suomela, J.: Almost stable matchings by truncating the Gale-Shapley algorithm. Algorithmica **58**(1), 102–118 (2010). doi:10.1007/s00453-009-9353-9. http://arxiv.org/abs/0812.4893

12. Ghosh, B., Leighton, F.T., Maggs, B., Muthukrishnan, S., Plaxton, C.G., Rajaraman, R., Richa, A.W., Tarjan, R.E., Zuckerman, D.: Tight analyses of two local load balancing algorithms. SIAM Journal on Computing **29**(1), 29–64 (1999)

13. Ghosh, B., Muthukrishnan, S.: Dynamic load balancing by random matchings. Journal of Computer and System Sciences **53**(3), 357–370 (1996). doi:10.1006/jcss.1996.0075

14. Hańćkowiak, M., Karoński, M., Panconesi, A.: On the distributed complexity of computing maximal matchings. In: Proc. 9th Annual ACM-SIAM Symposium on Discrete Algorithms (SODA 1998), pp. 219–225. SIAM (1998)

15. Harvey, N.J.A., Ladner, R.E., Lovász, L., Tamir, T.: Semi-matchings for bipartite graphs and load balancing. Journal of Algorithms **59**(1), 53–78 (2006). doi:10.1016/j.jalgor.2005.01.003

16. Kadanoff, L.P., Nagel, S.R., Wu, L., Zhou, S.M.: Scaling and universality in avalanches. Physical Review A **39**(12), 6524–6537 (1989). doi:10.1103/PhysRevA.39.6524

17. Karp, R.M., Luby, M., Meyer auf der Heide, F.: Efficient PRAM simulation on a distributed memory machine. Algorithmica **16**(4–5), 517–542 (1996). doi:10.1007/s004539900063

18. Kenthapadi, K., Panigrahy, R.: Balanced allocation on graphs. In: Proc. 17th Annual ACM-SIAM Symposium on Discrete Algorithm (SODA 2006), pp. 434–443. SIAM (2006). doi:10.1145/1109557.1109606. http://arxiv.org/abs/cs/0510086

19. Khuller, S., Vishkin, U., Young, N.: A primal-dual parallel approximation technique applied to weighted set and vertex covers. Journal of Algorithms **17**(2), 280–289 (1994). doi:10.1006/jagm.1994.1036

20. Muthukrishnan, S., Ghosh, B., Schultz, M.H.: First- and second-order diffusive methods for rapid, coarse, distributed load balancing. Theory of Computing Systems **31**(4), 331–354 (1998). doi:10.1007/s002240000092

21. Peleg, D.: Distributed Computing: A Locality-Sensitive Approach. SIAM Monographs on Discrete Mathematics and Applications. SIAM, Philadelphia (2000)

22. Peleg, D., Upfal, E.: The token distribution problem. SIAM Journal on Computing **18**(2), 229–243 (1989). doi:10.1137/0218015

23. Rabani, Y., Sinclair, A., Wanka, R.: Local divergence of Markov chains and the analysis of iterative load-balancing schemes. In: Proc. 39th Annual Symposium on Foundations of Computer Science (FOCS 1998), p. 694. IEEE (1998). doi:10.1109/SFCS.1998.743520

24. Sauerwald, T., Sun, H.: Tight bounds for randomized load balancing on arbitrary network topologies. In: Proc. 53rd Annual Symposium on Foundations of Computer Science (FOCS 2012), pp. 341–350. IEEE, October 2012. doi:10.1109/FOCS.2012.86

25. Sinclair, A., Jerrum, M.: Approximate counting, uniform generation and rapidly mixing Markov chains. Information and Computation **82**(1), 93–133 (1989). doi:10.1016/0890-5401(89)90067-9

26. Vöcking, B.: How asymmetry helps load balancing. Journal of the ACM **50**(4), 568–589 (2003). doi:10.1145/792538.792546

# Distributed Large Independent Sets in One Round on Bounded-Independence Graphs

Magnús M. Halldórsson and Christian Konrad[(⊠)]

ICE-TCS, School of Computer Science, Reykjavik University, Reykjavik, Iceland
{mmh,christiank}@ru.is

**Abstract.** We present a randomized one-round, single-bit messages, distributed algorithm for the maximum independent set problem in polynomially bounded-independence graphs with poly-logarithmic approximation factor. Bounded-independence graphs capture various models of wireless networks such as the unit disc graphs model and the quasi unit disc graphs model. For instance, on unit disc graphs, our achieved approximation ratio is $O((\frac{\log n}{\log \log n})^2)$.

A starting point of our work is an extension of Turán's bound for independent sets by Caro and Wei which states that every graph $G = (V, E)$ contains an independent set of size at least $\beta(G) := \sum_{v \in V} \frac{1}{\deg_G(v)+1}$, where $\deg_G(v)$ denotes the degree of $v$ in $G$. Alon and Spencer's proof of the Caro-Wei bound in [1] suggests a randomized distributed one-round algorithm that outputs an independent set of expected size equal to $\beta(G)$, using messages of sizes $O(\log n)$, where $n$ is the number of vertices of the input graph. To achieve our main result, we show that $\beta(G)$ gives poly-logarithmic approximation ratios for polynomially bounded-independence graphs. Then, for $O(1)$-claw free graphs (which include graphs of bounded-independence), we show that using a different algorithm, an independent set of expected size $\Theta(\beta(G))$ can be computed in one round using single bit messages, thus reducing the communication cost to an absolute minimum.

Last, in general graphs, $\beta(G)$ may only give an $\Omega(n)$-approximation. We show, however, that this is best possible for one-round algorithms: We show that each such distributed algorithm (possibly randomized) has an approximation ratio of $\Omega(n)$ on general graphs.

## 1 Introduction

**Something For Almost Nothing.** When designing approximation algorithms, the usual goal is to find desirable trade-offs between approximation guarantee and the resources required by the algorithm, such as computation time, memory consumption, the number of queries to the input, or, in the area of distributed computing, message size and the number of communication rounds. In past years, in various algorithmic disciplines, research has been carried out in order to determine the minimum amount of resources required to achieve non-trivial solutions.

Supported by Icelandic Research Fund grants 120032011 and 152679-051.

© Springer-Verlag Berlin Heidelberg 2015
Y. Moses (Ed.): DISC 2015, LNCS 9363, pp. 559–572, 2015.
DOI: 10.1007/978-3-662-48653-5_37

Often, it is asked how much effort it takes to obtain at least something from the given problem instance. Examples include property testing algorithms [18] that query a given instance only a few times in order to reason about whether the instance is close to having a certain property or it is far from having this property. In distributed computing, this phenomenon can be observed for example with regards to communication patterns and the total number of communication rounds. It has been shown that non-trivial computation is possible even when the communication pattern of nodes is restricted to beeps [4]. Moreover, research on so-called local algorithms [12,17] that employ only a few communication rounds has been carried out and highly non-trivial results have been obtained (e.g. even some NP-hard problems can be solved in only a constant number of communication rounds [2]).

In this paper, we ask whether non-trivial computation is possible if we grant a distributed algorithm only a single communication round. Specifically, we ask whether reasonable approximations to the maximum independent set problem can be computed in this harsh setting.

**Computational Model.** We consider a network of computational units of unbounded computational power $V$ modelled by a graph $G = (V, E)$. The graph $G$ constitutes the input graph of the problem. We assume that vertices have unique IDs. Initially, besides its ID, every node $v \in V$ also knows its degree $\deg_G(v)$. Communication occurs in simultaneous communication rounds along the edges $E$ of $G$. Then the runtime of a distributed algorithm is the total number of communication rounds. In this work, we mainly focus on algorithms that run in a single communication round. In the $\mathcal{LOCAL}$ model, algorithms may exchange messages of unbounded sizes. In the $\mathcal{CONGEST}$ model, message sizes are restricted to $O(\log n)$, where $n$ denotes the number of vertices of the input graph.

**Independent Sets.** An independent set $I$ in a graph $G = (V, E)$ is a subset of non-adjacent vertices. An independent set $I$ is maximal if it is inclusion-wise maximal, i.e., $I \cup \{v\}$ is not an independent set for any $v \in V \setminus I$. A maximum independent set is one of maximal size. The independence number of graph $G$ is the size of a maximum indendent set in $G$ and is denoted by $\alpha(G)$. Computing maximum independent sets is NP-hard on general graphs [10] and is even hard to approximate within factor $n^{1-\epsilon}$ for any $\epsilon > 0$ [21]. The independent set problem is one of the most studied problems in distributed computing, and we detail related work further below.

**Our Main Result.** Our main result concerns graphs of *polynomially bounded-independence*, a graph class that includes unit disc graphs and similar graph classes that are used for modelling wireless networks (for a precise definition see the next paragraph). We show that in the harsh setting of a single communication round, a poly-logarithmic approximation ratio can be achieved in polynomially bounded-independence graphs. Furthermore, we show that not only the number of communication rounds but also message sizes can be reduced to an absolute minimum, i.e., to single bit messages.

**Bounded-Independence Graphs.** Graphs of bounded-independence capture many intersection graphs of geometrical objects which in turn are used for modelling conflict graphs of wireless networks. Given a collection $X = \{X_1, \ldots, X_n\}$ of geometrical objects, the corresponding intersection graph is obtained by assigning $X$ as the vertices of the graph, and an edge is introduced between two vertices $X_i, X_j$ iff the objects $X_i$ and $X_j$ intersect. In the literature, conflict graphs of wireless networks are often modelled by unit disc graphs [7], the intersection graph of discs with equal radii, where the radius of the discs corresponds to the transmission range of the wireless transmitters. Unit disc graphs have many nice properties that allow for the design of efficient distributed algorithms, but the assumption of identical transmission radii for all wireless transmitters is often too restrictive. Consequently, the unit disc graphs model has been extended to more elaborate models such as quasi unit disc graphs [13] or general disc graphs. In a general disc graph, no restriction on the radii of the discs are imposed. Then, the parameter $\delta = r_{max}/r_{min}$ is introduced into the analysis of algorithms, where $r_{max}$ and $r_{min}$ denote the maximal and the minimal radius of a disc, respectively.

All graphs of the graph classes mentioned above are of bounded-independence, a property that restricts the size of a maximum independent set within the set of nodes at a given maximal distance from any node. The $r$-neighborhood of a node $v$ is the set of nodes at distance at most $r$ from $v$ (excluding $v$).

**Definition 1.** *A graph* $G = (V, E)$ *is of* bounded-independence *if there is a bounding function* $f(r)$ *so that for each node* $v \in V$, *the size of a maximum independent set in the* $r$-*neighborhood of* $v$ *is at most* $f(r), \forall r \geq 1$. *We say that* $G$ *is of* polynomially bounded-independence *if* $f(r)$ *is a polynomial.*

It is easily verified that unit disc graphs are of bounded-independence with respect to a bounding function in $O(r^2)$, and (general) disc graphs are of bounded-independence with respect to a bounding function in $O((r\delta)^2)$. Many important problems such as the maximal independent set problem, or the $(\Delta+1)$-coloring problem can be solved on bounded independence graphs by a distributed algorithm by Schneider and Wattenhofer that uses $O(\log^* n)$ communication rounds [19] which underlines the usefulness of this graph class for distributed computation.

**Turán's Bound and a One-Round Algorithm.** A starting point of our work is an extension of a celebrated theorem by Paul Turán. Turán showed that every graph $G = (V, E)$ contains an independent set of size at least $n/d$, where $d$ is the average degree of $G$. This result has been extended by Caro [3] and Wei [20] who showed that there is an independent set of size at least

$$\beta(G) := \sum_{v \in V} \frac{1}{\deg_G(v) + 1},$$

where $\deg_G(v)$ denotes the degree of vertex $v$ in $G$. An independent set of expected size $\beta(G)$ can be found by a simple linear time randomized algorithm that follows from an analysis of the Caro-Wei bound by Alon and Spencer in [1]. This algorithm works as follows: Every node $v$ chooses a random real value between 0 and 1 and adds itself to the independent set $I$ if none of its neighbors have chosen a larger real value than $v$. Then, the probability that a node $v$ is added to the independent set is $\frac{1}{\deg_G(v)+1}$, and, hence, by linearity of expectation, $\mathbb{E}|I| = \sum_{v \in V} \frac{1}{\deg_G(v)+1} = \beta(G)$.

This algorithm can also be implemented distributively in a single communication round. Instead of choosing a random real value, every node chooses a random value from a large enough ordered set (e.g. $\{1, 2, \ldots, n^3\}$ suffices) so that neighboring nodes choose different values with large enough probability. In order to be able to determine such a number, nodes require knowledge of $n$, i.e., the order of the input graph. Furthermore, communicating the chosen value to neighboring nodes requires messages of size $O(\log n)$. This algorithm fulfills, hence, the restrictions of the $\mathcal{CONGEST}$ model. In the following, we will refer to this algorithm as ALON-SPENCER-IS.

It is easy to see that in general graphs, an independent set of size $\beta(G)$ may be a factor $\Theta(n)$ smaller than the independence number $\alpha(G)$[1]. This raises the following questions:

1. Are there interesting graph classes for which $\beta(G)$ is a non-trivial approximation to the independence number $\alpha(G)$?
2. What are the minimum communication requirements for achieving the $\beta(G)$ bound?
3. Is there a one-round independent set algorithm with approximation factor $o(n)$ on general graphs?

**Our Results in Detail.** Concerning Question 1, we identify that in graphs of polynomially bounded-independence, an independent set of size $\beta(G)$ is a polylogarithmic approximation to a maximum independent set. For instance on unit disc graphs, an independent set of size $\beta(G)$ is an $O((\frac{\log n}{\log \log n})^2)$-approximation to a maximum independent set. Furthermore, we prove that our analysis is tight up to a constant factor on $d$-dimensional unit sphere graphs, for any constant integer $d$. We also show that on the more general class of $k$-claw free graphs[2], for $k \geq 3$, a similar result cannot be obtained. In the full version of this paper, we provide $k$-claw free graphs for which the Caro-Wei bound is not a polylogarithmic approximation to the independence number of the graph.

With regards to Question 2, we show that for the more general class of $O(1)$-claw free graphs, the communication requirements can be reduced to an absolute minimum at the price of losing a constant factor. We present a different and even simpler one-round algorithm that computes an independent set of

---

[1] Consider, for instance, the graph $G = (C \cup I, E_1 \cup E_2)$ with $|C| = |I| = n/2$. The edges $E_1$ turn $C$ into a clique. Furthermore, for every $u \in C$ and $v \in I$, the edge $(u, v)$ is included in $E_2$. Then, the size of a maximum independent set is $n/2$ while $\beta(G) \leq \frac{3}{2}$.

[2] A graph is $k$-claw free, if it does not contain the complete bipartite $K_{1,k}$ as an induced subgraph.

expected size $\Theta(\beta(G))$ using single bit messages, thus decreasing the message sizes from $O(\log n)$ to 1. This algorithm has the additional advantage that it does not require the knowledge of $n$ in advance. The latter property and the low communication requirements allow this algorithm to be implemented in wireless and radio networks. Note that our main result, a poly-logarithmic approximation one-round single bits messages algorithm for the maximum independent set problem in polynomially bounded-independence graphs, follows from the previous two results.

Last, we answer Question 3 in the negative. We provide a lower bound that shows that any possibly randomized one-round algorithm with error probability at most $1/n$ has approximation ratio $\Omega(n)$.

**Further Related Work.** As already mentioned, independent sets are among the most studied problems in distributed computing. However, most works consider the maximal independent set problem while we consider the maximum independent set problem in this paper. It is known that computing a maximal independent set requires $\Omega(\sqrt{\log n})$ communication rounds [12] in general graphs, and even on a ring, $\Omega(\log^* n)$ rounds are necessary [14,15]. Concerning approximations to the maximum independent set problem, a $(1+\epsilon)$-approximation can be computed in $O(\log^* n)$ rounds in planar graphs [5]. As in graphs of bounded-independence, a maximal independent set is a constant factor approximation to a maximum independent set, the previously mentioned $O(\log^* n)$ rounds algorithm of Schneider and Wattenhofer [19] gives a constant-factor approximation. Last, we note that the Caro-Wei bound and Turán bound have been previously used as quality guarantees for independent set approximation (e.g., [6]).

**Notations.** Throughout the paper, we use the following notations. Let $G = (V, E)$ be a graph. For a node $v \in V$, let $\Gamma_G(v)$ denotes the neighborhood of $v$ and $\deg_G(v) = |\Gamma_G(v)|$ its degree. The *d-neighborhood of* $v$, denoted $\Gamma_G^d(v)$, is the set of nodes of distance at most $d$ from $v$ excluding $v$, while the set of nodes at distance exactly $d$ from $v$ is denoted by $\Gamma_G^{(d)}(v)$. Let $\Gamma_G^d[v] := \Gamma_G^d(v) \cup \{v\}$ (and $\Gamma_G[v] = \Gamma_G(v) \cup \{v\}$). For a subset of vertices $U \subseteq V$, the graph $G|_U$ is the subgraph of $G$ induced by the vertices $U$.

**Outline.** First, in Section 2, we prove our main result that the Caro-Wei bound is a poly-logarithmic approximation to the independence number in polynomially bounded-independence graphs. An algorithm with single-bit messages achieving the Caro-Wei bound up to a constant factor for $O(1)$-claw free graphs is discussed in Section 3. Then, in Section 4, we show that on general graphs, any possibly randomized distributed one-round algorithm computes an independent set of size at most $O(1)$, while the graph has an independence number of $\Omega(n)$. Last, in Section 5 we show that our analysis of Section 2 is tight for $d$-dimensional unit sphere graphs.

**Full Version.** In the full version of this paper, we provide additional results. We show that in $O(1)$-claw-free graphs, $\beta(G)$ generally is not a poly-logarithmic approximation to $\alpha(G)$. Furthermore, we argue that running our algorithm from

Section 3 iteratively multiple times does not substantially improve the approximation ratio of the algorithm.

## 2    Poly-Logarithmic Approximation on Bounded-Independence Graphs

We show that in graphs of polynomially bounded-independence, an independent set of size $\beta(G)$ is a poly-logarithmic approximation of a maximum independent set.

We first show that in any graph $G = (V, E)$, for any node $v \in V$ and a large enough constant $C$, the sum of the inverted degrees in the $C\frac{\log n}{\log\log n}$-neighborhood of $v$ is $\Omega(1)$ (Lemma 1). The size of an independent set in such a $C\frac{\log n}{\log\log n}$-neighborhood in a bounded-independence graph is at most $f(C\frac{\log n}{\log\log n})$, by definition. Hence, within the $C\frac{\log n}{\log\log n}$-neighborhood of any node $v \in V$, the ratio between the size of a maximum independent set and the Caro-Wei bound is $O(f(\frac{\log n}{\log\log n}))$. Then, by decomposing the input graph $G$ into components of diameters at most $2C\frac{\log n}{\log\log n}$, we extend this result to hold for the entire graph (Theorem 1).

**Lemma 1.** *Let $G = (V, E)$ be an arbitrary graph with maximal degree $\Delta$. Let $m = \min\{\Delta, C\frac{\log n}{\log\log n}\}$, for a large enough constant $C$. Then:*

$$\sum_{u \in \Gamma_G^m[v]} \frac{1}{\deg_G(u)} = \Omega(1).$$

*Proof.* Let $v \in V$ be any node, and let $d_0 = \deg_G(v)$. For abbreviation, let $s_j = |\Gamma_G^{(j)}(v)|$ for $j \geq 1$. We set $s_0 = 1$ and we clearly have $s_1 = d_0$. Furthermore, let $d_i = \frac{1}{s_i}\sum_{u \in \Gamma_G^{(i)}(v)} \deg_G(u)$ be the average degree of the nodes in $\Gamma_G^{(i)}(v)$. Then, the inverted degree sum of the nodes in the $m$-neighborhood can be bounded as follows:

$$\sum_{u \in \Gamma_G^m[v]} \frac{1}{\deg_G(u)} = \frac{1}{d_0} + \sum_{j=1}^{m}\sum_{u \in \Gamma_G^{(j)}(v)} \frac{1}{\deg_G(u)} \geq \frac{1}{d_0} + \sum_{j=1}^{m}\sum_{u \in \Gamma_G^{(j)}(v)} \frac{1}{d_j}$$

$$= \frac{1}{s_1} + \frac{s_1}{d_1} + \sum_{j=2}^{m} \frac{s_j}{d_j}, \tag{1}$$

where the first inequality follows from the relationship between the harmonic mean and the arithmetic mean. For $i \geq 2$, consider a node $u \in \Gamma_G^{(i)}(v)$ of degree at least $d_i$. Then, $\Gamma_G(u) \subseteq \Gamma_G^{(i-1)}(v) \cup (\Gamma_G^{(i)}(v) \setminus \{u\}) \cup \Gamma_G^{(i+1)}(v)$. Hence, $\deg_G(u) \leq s_{i-1} + s_i - 1 + s_{i+1}$, and since $d_i \leq \deg_G(u)$, we also have $d_i \leq s_{i-1} + s_i + s_{i+1}$. Similarly, for $d_1$ we obtain the inequality $d_1 \leq s_1 + s_2$. Using this in Inequality 1, we obtain:

$$\sum_{u \in \Gamma_G^m[v]} \frac{1}{\deg_G(u)} \geq \frac{1}{s_1} + \frac{s_1}{d_1} + \sum_{j=2}^{m} \frac{s_j}{d_j} \geq \frac{1}{s_1} + \frac{s_1}{s_1+s_2} + \sum_{j=2}^{m} \frac{s_j}{s_{j-1}+s_j+s_{j+1}}. \quad (2)$$

Suppose that the sequence $(s_i)_{1 \leq i \leq m}$ is not strictly increasing. Let $j$ be the smallest index so that $s_j \leq s_{j-1}$. If $j = 2$, then the term $\frac{s_1}{s_1+s_2}$ of Inequality 2 can be bounded by $\frac{s_1}{s_1+s_2} \geq \frac{s_1}{s_1+s_1} = 1/2$, and thus, $\sum_{u \in \Gamma_G^m[v]} \frac{1}{\deg_G(u)} > \frac{1}{2} = \Omega(1)$. Suppose that $j > 2$. Then, since $j$ is the smallest index, we have $s_{j-2} < s_{j-1}$. Therefore, the addend with index $j-1$ of the sum in the right side in Inequality 2 can be bounded as follows:

$$\frac{s_{j-1}}{s_{j-2}+s_{j-1}+s_j} > \frac{s_{j-1}}{3 \cdot s_{j-1}} = 1/3,$$

which implies $\sum_{u \in \Gamma_G^m[v]} \frac{1}{\deg_G(u)} > \frac{1}{3} = \Omega(1)$. Assume now that the sequence $(s_i)_i$ is strictly increasing. We bound the right side of Inequality 2 as follows:

$$\sum_{u \in \Gamma_G^m[v]} \frac{1}{\deg_G(u)} \geq \frac{1}{s_1} + \frac{s_1}{s_1+s_2} + \sum_{j=2}^{m} \frac{s_j}{s_{j-1}+s_j+s_{j+1}}$$

$$\geq \frac{1}{s_1} + \frac{s_1}{s_1+s_2} + \sum_{j=2}^{m} \frac{s_j}{2 \cdot s_j+s_{j+1}}. \quad (3)$$

Let $J \subseteq \{2,\ldots,m\}$ be the subset of indices so that for each $j \in J : \frac{s_j}{2 \cdot s_j+s_{j+1}} \leq \frac{\log\log n}{\log n}$. This implies that we have $s_{j+1} \geq s_j \left( \frac{\log n}{\log\log n} - 2 \right)$, for $j \in J$. Since the sequence $(s_i)_i$ is strictly increasing, we can bound the size of the set $J$ as follows:

$$\left( \frac{\log n}{\log\log n} - 2 \right)^{|J|} \leq n,$$

and therefore $|J| = O(\frac{\log n}{\log\log n})$. We now set $m = C\frac{\log n}{\log\log n}$ for a large enough constant $C$ so that there are $\Theta(\frac{\log n}{\log\log n})$ indices $i$ with $i \notin J$ and $\frac{s_i}{2 \cdot s_i+s_{i+1}} \geq \frac{\log\log n}{\log n}$. Then, the addends in the right side of Inequality 3 that correspond to those indices $i \notin J$ sum up to a constant which proves part 1 of the result.

We derive now a bound on $m$ that depends on the maximal degree $\Delta$. To this end, we depart from Inequality 3. Notice that the bound on $\Delta$ implies $s_j \leq s_{j-1}\Delta$. Therefore, for any $j$, the addend in Inequality 3 that corresponds to $j$ is bounded as follows: $\frac{s_j}{2s_j s_{j-1}} \geq \frac{s_j}{2s_j+\Delta s_j} = \frac{1}{2+\Delta}$. Setting $m = \Theta(\Delta)$ implies that the right side of Inequality 3 sums up to a constant. $\square$

**Theorem 1.** *Let $G = (V,E)$ be of polynomially bounded-independence with maximal degree $\Delta$ and with bounding function $f$. Then:*

$$\alpha(G) = O\left( \beta(G) \cdot f(\min\{\Delta, \frac{\log n}{\log\log n}\}) \right).$$

*Proof.* Let $m = \min\{\Delta, C\frac{\log n}{\log\log n}\}$ where $C$ is the constant as in Lemma 1. Let $S$ be a maximal $2m$-independent set in $G$, i.e., a maximal set of vertices of mutual distance at least $2m$. Let $I^*$ denote a maximum independent set in $G$. Since $S$ is maximal, every vertex in $I^*$ is at a distance at most $2m$ from a vertex in $S$, and thus $|I^*| \le |S| \cdot f(2m)$. Since $S$ is $2m$-independent, the $m$-neighborhoods around nodes in $S$ are disjoint. Thus, using Lemma 1, we have

$$\beta(G) = \sum_{v\in V}\frac{1}{\deg_G(v)} \ge \sum_{s\in S}\sum_{v\in\Gamma_G^m(s)}\frac{1}{\deg_G(v)} = \Omega(|S|).$$

Thus,

$$\alpha(G) \le |S| \cdot f(2m) = O(\beta(G) \cdot f(2m)) = O(\beta(G)f(m)),$$

since $f$ is a polynomial function.                                              □

## 3   Distributed Algorithm with Single Bit Messages

In the previous section, we showed that an independent set of size $\beta(G)$ is a poly-logarithmic approximation on graphs of polynomially bounded-independence. The ALON-SPENCER-IS algorithm computes an independent set of expected size $\beta(G)$, and thus we obtain a one-round poly-logarithmic approximation algorithm for the maximum independent set problem on graphs of polynomially bounded-independence with message sizes $O(\log n)$. In this section, we improve on the message complexity of the previous algorithm. We propose an alternative algorithm that computes an independent set of expected size $\Theta(\beta(G))$ on $O(1)$-claw free graphs using single bit messages. As bounded-independence graphs are $(f(1) + 1)$-claw free and $f(1)$ is a constant, this algorithm also constitutes an improvement for bounded-independence graphs.

We will consider the one-round algorithm, Algorithm 1, which can be seen as a simplified version of the well-known distributed maximal independent set algorithm by Luby [16]. In each round of Luby's algorithm, nodes of a general graph $G = (V, E)$ are added to an initially empty independent set. One round consists of two phases: First, every node $v \in V$ pre-selects itself with probability $\Theta(\frac{1}{\deg_G(v)})$ as a candidate to join the independent set. Then, in the second phase, ties are broken among the pre-selected nodes so that nodes with larger degree are preferred. Finally, selected nodes and their neighbors are removed from $G$, and the round is completed. The algorithm terminates when $G$ is empty. In our version of the algorithm, a simplified method for breaking ties is used. Instead of preferring nodes with larger degree, we only add a pre-selected node to the independent set if none of its neighbors have been pre-selected. This method of breaking ties has been previously used, e.g., in [8,9,11].

We first derive a bound on the inverted degree sum of the neighborhood of an arbitrary node $v \in V$ in a $k$-claw free graph $G = (V, E)$.

**Lemma 2.** *Let $G = (V, E)$ be a $k$-claw free graph. Then for every $v \in V$,*

$$\sum_{u\in\Gamma_G(v)}\frac{1}{\deg_G(u)} \le k - 1 .$$

---

**Algorithm 1.** One-round independent set algorithm

---

**Require:** $G = (V, E)$ {Input graph}
1: $I \leftarrow \varnothing$ {the independent set to be computed}
2: $p_i \leftarrow \frac{1}{2 \deg(v)}$
3: $T_v \leftarrow \text{coin}(p_i)$ {Pre-selection step: If $T_v = true$ then $v$ is a candidate to join $I$}
4: **for all** $v \in V$ with $T_v = true$ **do**
5:    **if** $\bigvee_{u \in \Gamma_G(v)} T_u = false$ **then** {Check whether a neighbor of $v$ has been pre-selected}
6:       $I \leftarrow I \cup \{v\}$ {$v$ is selected into the IS}
7:    **end if**
8: **end for**

---

*Proof.* Let $v$ be a node and let $H_v = G|_{\Gamma_G(v)}$ be the subgraph induced by $v$'s neighbors. Observe that for $u \in V(H)$, $deg_G(u) \geq deg_H(u) + 1$. Since $G$ is $k$-claw free, $\alpha(H) \leq k - 1$. Thus, using the Caro-Wei bound, we get that

$$\sum_{u \in \Gamma_G(v)} \frac{1}{\deg_G(u)} \leq \sum_{u \in V(H)} \frac{1}{\deg_H(u) + 1} \leq \alpha(H) \leq k - 1 \ .$$

$\square$

**Theorem 2.** *Algorithm 1 is a randomized distributed one-round algorithm using single bit messages that finds independent sets with expected $\Theta(\beta(G))$ size on graphs $G$ with constant claw size. In particular, when $G$ is polynomially bounded-independence, it achieves an expected approximation ratio $O(f(\min\{\Delta, \frac{\log n}{\log \log n}\}))$.*

*Proof.* Let $v$ be any node in $G$. Algorithm 1 adds $v$ to the independent set if two independent events happen: $v$ is pre-selected in Line 3 of Algorithm 1 while none of its neighbors are pre-selected. Then, by the linearity of expectation,

$$\mathbb{E}|I| = \sum_{v \in V} \mathbb{P}[v \in I] = \sum_{v \in V} \mathbb{P}[v \text{ pre-selected}] \cdot \mathbb{P}[v \in I \mid v \text{ pre-selected}]$$

$$= \sum_{v \in V} \frac{1}{\deg_G(v)} \cdot \prod_{u \in \Gamma_G(v)} (1 - \frac{1}{\deg_G(u)}) =$$

$$= \sum_{v \in V} \frac{1}{\deg_G(v)} \cdot \Theta \left( e^{-\sum_{u \in \Gamma_G(v)} \frac{1}{\deg_G(u)}} \right) = \Theta(1) \cdot \beta(G) \ ,$$

applying Lemma 2 in the last equality. If $G$ is of bounded-independence with bounding function $f$, it is $(f(1) + 1)$-claw free, which is a constant. Applying Theorem 1 we obtain the approximation result. $\square$

*Implementing Algorithm 1 in Beep Models and Wireless Networks.* Algorithm 1 places minimal demands on the underlying model in which it is implemented. Initially, nodes only require the knowledge of their own degree (or of an estimate thereof), and, in particular, information about the network size is not needed. In many wireless networks, the degree of local congestion provides a good estimate for a node's degree, and congestion can often be inferred using carrier sensing techniques.

The communication structure of the algorithm naturally fits beep-like models and wireless networks. Pre-selected nodes send a signal to all their neighbors. Hence, models that only support radio broadcast rather than the transmission of individual messages to neighboring nodes are sufficient for implementing this step. With regards to the reception of signals from neighboring nodes, in Line 5 of the algorithm, nodes only have to be able to learn whether no neighboring node emitted a signal or whether at least one neighboring node emitted a signal. This type of information matches precisely what can be learned by a node in one round in the discrete beeping model as introduced in [4]. Also, in wireless networks, carrier sensing can yield information that is possibly weaker (a node that is within a short range did transmit) but sufficient for the operation of our algorithm.

## 4    Lower Bound for One-Round Algorithms on General Graphs

In this section, we prove that no distributed one-round algorithm can compute an independent set whose size exceeds the Caro-Wei bound by more than a constant. In particular, every possibly randomized distributed one-round algorithm on general graphs has an approximation factor of $\Omega(n)$, where $n$ is the number of vertices of the input graph.

Consider an arbitrary $d$-regular bipartite graph $H = (A, B, E)$ with $|A| + |B| = n'$. Let $G = (V, E)$ be the graph consisting of a $(d+1)$-clique and a copy of $H$ which is disjoint from the $(d+1)$-clique. Let $n = |V|$, and hence $n' = n - d - 1$. $G$ is clearly $d$-regular. Furthermore, since $H$ contains an independent set of size $n'/2$, the independence number of $G$ is $\alpha(G) = \frac{n-d-1}{2}$. We assume that each node has a unique label chosen from $\mathcal{U} = \{1, \ldots, m\}$, where $m \geq n$. Let $\mathcal{L}$ denote the set of all possible labellings.

In order to prove our lower bound, we exploit the fact that all nodes in $V$ have the same local *views*, i.e., in one round, all nodes can only learn the $d$ labels of their adjacent nodes. As all nodes run the same algorithm, clearly in average over all possible labellings $\mathcal{L}$, the probabilities for all nodes to end up in $I$ is equal. This fact is used in the following theorem:

**Theorem 3.** *Every possibly randomized one-round distributed algorithm for maximum independent set has an expected approximation factor of at least $\frac{(n-\Delta-1)(\Delta+1)}{2n}$, where $\Delta$ is the maximal degree of the input graph.*

*Proof.* Consider the $d$-regular graph $G = (V, E)$ as defined above. Then $\Delta = d$. Consider a possibly randomized one-round algorithm for maximum independent set. Then, as previously argued, for all $u, v \in V$, we have:

$$\mathbb{P}\left[u \in I\right] = \mathbb{P}\left[v \in I\right], \text{ and} \tag{4}$$

$$\mathbb{E}|I| = \sum_{u \in V} \mathbb{P}\left[u \in I\right], \tag{5}$$

where the probabilities are taken over all possible labellings $\mathcal{L}$ and the random coin flips of the algorithm. Let $p$ be the probability that a node ends up in $I$. Let $C$ denote the $(d+1)$-clique of $G$. Then, $p \cdot |C| = \mathbb{E}|I \cap C| \leq 1$, and hence, $p \leq \frac{1}{|C|} = \frac{1}{d+1}$. Therefore, $\mathbb{E}|I| \leq np = \frac{n}{d+1}$. Next, since $\alpha(G) = \frac{n-d-1}{2}$, the expected approximation ratio is at least $\frac{(n-d-1)(d+1)}{2n}$. $\qquad\square$

*Remark.* The graph $G$ of the previous construction is disconnected. This can be circumvented by removing arbitrary edges $u_1v_1, u_2v_2$, where $u_1v_1$ is contained in the $(d+1)$-clique and $u_2v_2$ is outside the $(d+1)$-clique, and reinserting edges $u_1u_2$ and $v_1v_2$. The resulting graph is connected and equally suits for proving the same lower bound.

## 5  Lower Bound for $d$-dimensional Unit Sphere Graphs

In this section, we show that the statement of Theorem 1, i.e., for any graph $G = (V, E)$ of polynomially bounded-independence with bounding function $f$ we have $\alpha(G) = O\left(\beta(G)f(\min\{\Delta, \frac{\log n}{\log \log n}\})\right)$, is tight for $d$-dimensional unit sphere graphs. As a consequence, the analysis of Algorithm 1 is also tight.

In the full version of this paper, we investigate on the performance of running multiple rounds of Algorithm 1. We show that a super-constant number of iterations is necessary in order to improve on the one-round bound performance by more than a constant factor.

A $d$-dimensional *unit sphere graph* $G = (S, E)$ is the intersection graph of $d$-dimensional unit spheres $S = \{s_1, \dots, s_n\}$ (all spheres have the same radius): Each sphere $s_i$ constitutes a vertex in $G$ and two spheres are adjacent iff they intersect. For $d = 1$, a unit sphere graph is a unit interval graph, and for $d = 2$, a unit sphere graph is a unit disc graph.

Let $d > 0$ be some fixed dimension. We will denote our hard instance graph with $H_k = (V_H, E_H)$ where $k$ is a parameter which we define later. We start our construction of $H_k$ with a *grid graph* $G_k = (V_G, E_G)$ that is parametrized by an integer $k \geq 1$. The vertex set of $G_k$ is defined as $V_G = \{v_x \mid x \in \{0, 1, \dots, k-1\}^d\}$. Let $v_x, v_y$ with $x, y \in \{0, \dots, k-1\}^d$ be two vertices of $V_G$. Then $v_x$ and $v_y$ are adjacent iff $|x - y| = 1$, where $|x| = \sum_{1 \leq i \leq d} |x_i|$.

The hard instance graph $H_k$ is obtained from $G_k$ as follows: For every vertex $v_x \in V_G$, a clique $C_x$ of size $s(|x|)$ is introduced in $H_k$, where $s(i) = d^i k^{di} \log^i n$. Suppose that $v_x$ and $v_y$ are adjacent nodes in $G_k$. Then all nodes of $C_x$ are connected to all nodes of $C_y$ in $H_k$, or, in other words, $C_x \cup C_y$ also forms a clique in $H_k$.

First, notice that the graph $H_k$ is in fact a $d$-dimensional unit sphere graph. Each vertex $v \in C_x \subseteq V_H$ with $x \in \{0, \dots, k-1\}^d$ corresponds to a sphere centered at position $x$ with radius $1/2$ (for convenience, in this construction

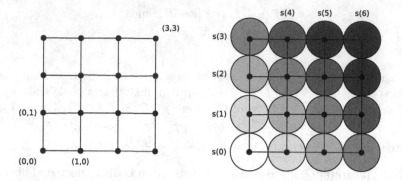

**Fig. 1.** Illustration of the two dimensional case: On the left, the grid graph $G_4$ is illustrated. On the right, the hard instance unit disc graph $H_4$ is shown. $H_4$ is obtained from $G_4$ by replacing each node at position $(i, j)$ with a clique of size $s(i + j)$.

we suppose that all spheres have the radius $1/2$ instead of $1$). An example is provided in Figure 1.

We state now that $H_k$ is of bounded-independence with respect to the bounding function $f(r) = (2r + 1)^d$.

**Lemma 3.** *The $d$-dimensional unit sphere graph $H_k$ is of bounded independence with respect to the bounding function $f(r) = (2r + 1)^d$.*

*Proof.* The size of an independent set in the $k$-neighborhood of a node $v \in C_x \subseteq V_H$ for some $x \in \{0, \ldots, k-1\}^d$ is the same as the size of an independent set of the node $v_x \in V_G$ in the corresponding grid graph. Therefore, the $r$-neighborhood of an arbitrary node $v_x \in V_G$ with $x \in \{0, \ldots, k-1\}^d$ is a subset of the nodes with indices $j \in \{x_1 - r, \ldots, x_1 + r\} \times \cdots \times \{x_d - r, \ldots, x_d + r\}$. Therefore, $|\{x_1 - r, \ldots, x_1 + r\} \times \cdots \times \{x_d - r, \ldots, x_d + r\}| = (2r + 1)^d$ is an upper bound on the size of an independent set in the $r$-neighborhood of $v$.  □

Next, we identify the correct value for $k$ so that graph $H_k$ has $O(n)$ vertices, and we show that $\beta(H_k) = O(1)$.

**Lemma 4.** *Consider graph $H_k = (V_H, E_H)$, and let $k = O(\frac{\log n}{d^2 \log \log n})$. Then: $|V_H| = O(n)$ and $\beta(H_k) = O(1)$.*

*Proof.* Denote by $n_i$ the number of cliques at distance $i$ from the clique with index $(0, \ldots, 0)$. Furthermore, denote by $V_i := \{v \in C_x : |x| = i\}$ the set of nodes at distance $i$ from the clique with index $(0, \ldots, 0)$.

First, note that by construction of $H_k$ we have $n_i \le n_{i+1} d$. This allows us to establish a relation between $|V_i|$ and $|V_{i+1}|$:

$$|V_i| = n_i \cdot s(i) \le n_{i+1} d \cdot (d^i k^{di} \log^i n) \le n_{i+1} (d^{i+1} k^{di} \log^i n) = \frac{|V_{i+1}|}{k^d \log n}.$$

Then, as $|V_H| = \sum_{i \in \{0,\ldots,d(k-1)\}} |V_i|$ and by the previous inequality, we obtain: $|V_H| = O(|V_{d(k-1)}|)$. Then, setting $k = \Theta(\frac{\log n}{d^2 \log \log n})$ proves the first part of the lemma:

$$|V_H| = O\left(|V_{d(k-1)}|\right) = O\left(d^{kd} k^{d^2 k} \log^{kd} n\right) = O(n).$$

Next, in order to prove that $\beta(H_k) = O(1)$, notice that $|V_i| \le n_i s(i)$. Moreover, the nodes of $V_i$ have a degree of at least $s(i+1)$, the size of a clique at distance $i+1$. Each node of the clique $C_{(k-1,\ldots,k-1)}$ clearly has a degree of at least $s(d(k-1))$. Thus, we have:

$$\sum_{v \in V_H} \frac{1}{\deg_{H_k}(v)} = \left(\sum_{i \in \{0,\ldots,d(k-1)-1\}} n_i \cdot \frac{s(i)}{s(i+1)}\right) + \frac{n_{d(k-1)} s_{d(k-1)}}{s_{d(k-1)}} \le$$

$$\left(\sum_{i \in \{0,\ldots,d(k-1)-1\}} k^d \cdot \frac{1}{dk^d \log n}\right) + 1 = \frac{k-1}{\log n} + 1 = O(1),$$

where we used the rough estimate $n_i \le k^d$. $\qquad\qquad\square$

Finally, we obtain the main theorem of this section on the performance of Algorithm 1.

**Theorem 4.** *Consider graph* $H_k = (V_H, E_H)$, *and let* $k = O(\frac{\log n}{d^2 \log \log n})$. *Then, Algorithm 1 computes an* $\Omega((\frac{\log n}{d^2 \log \log n})^d)$ *approximation to the maximum independent set problem on* $H_k$.

*Proof.* Lemma 4 yields that the graph $H$ has $O(n)$ vertices, and the inverted degree sum of $H$ is $O(1)$. As in Algorithm 1 the probability that a node ends up in the independent set is bounded from above by its inverted degree, Algorithm 1 computes an independent set of expected size $O(1)$. Since the graph $H$ contains an independent set of size $\Omega((\frac{\log n}{d^2 \log \log n})^d)$, the theorem follows. $\qquad\square$

# References

1. Alon, N., Spencer, J.H.: The probabilistic method. John Wiley & Sons (2004)
2. Barenboim, L.: On the locality of some NP-complete problems. In: Czumaj, A., Mehlhorn, K., Pitts, A., Wattenhofer, R. (eds.) ICALP 2012, Part II. LNCS, vol. 7392, pp. 403–415. Springer, Heidelberg (2012)
3. Caro, Y.: New results on the independence number. Tech. rep., Tel Aviv University (1979)
4. Cornejo, A., Kuhn, F.: Deploying wireless networks with beeps. In: Lynch, N.A., Shvartsman, A.A. (eds.) DISC 2010. LNCS, vol. 6343, pp. 148–162. Springer, Heidelberg (2010). http://dl.acm.org/citation.cfm?id=1888781.1888802
5. Czygrinow, A., Hańćkowiak, M., Wawrzyniak, W.: Fast distributed approximations in planar graphs. In: Taubenfeld, G. (ed.) DISC 2008. LNCS, vol. 5218, pp. 78–92. Springer, Heidelberg (2008)

6. Halldórsson, B.V., Halldórsson, M.M., Losievskaja, E., Szegedy, M.: Streaming algorithms for independent sets. In: Abramsky, S., Gavoille, C., Kirchner, C., Meyer auf der Heide, F., Spirakis, P.G. (eds.) ICALP 2010. LNCS, vol. 6198, pp. 641–652. Springer, Heidelberg (2010)
7. Halldórsson, M.M.: Wireless scheduling with power control. ACM Trans. Algorithms **9**(1), 7:1–7:20 (2012)
8. Halldórsson, M.M., Konrad, C.: Distributed algorithms for coloring interval graphs. In: Kuhn, F. (ed.) DISC 2014. LNCS, vol. 8784, pp. 454–468. Springer, Heidelberg (2014)
9. Halldórsson, M.M., Mitra, P.: Nearly optimal bounds for distributed wireless scheduling in the SINR model. In: Aceto, L., Henzinger, M., Sgall, J. (eds.) ICALP 2011, Part II. LNCS, vol. 6756, pp. 625–636. Springer, Heidelberg (2011). http://dl.acm.org/citation.cfm?id=2027223.2027287
10. Karp, R.M.: Reducibility among combinatorial problems. In: Miller, R.E., Thatcher, J.W. (eds.) Complexity of Computer Computations, pp. 85–103. Plenum Press (1972)
11. Kesselheim, T., Vöcking, B.: Distributed contention resolution in wireless networks. In: Lynch, N.A., Shvartsman, A.A. (eds.) DISC 2010. LNCS, vol. 6343, pp. 163–178. Springer, Heidelberg (2010). http://dl.acm.org/citation.cfm?id=1888781.1888803
12. Kuhn, F., Moscibroda, T., Wattenhofer, R.: What cannot be computed locally! In: Proceedings of the Twenty-third Annual ACM Symposium on Principles of Distributed Computing, PODC 2004, pp. 300–309. ACM, New York (2004)
13. Kuhn, F., Wattenhofer, R., Zollinger, A.: Ad-hoc networks beyond unit disk graphs. In: Proceedings of the 2003 Joint Workshop on Foundations of Mobile Computing, DIALM-POMC 2003, pp. 69–78. ACM, New York (2003)
14. Laurinharju, J., Suomela, J.: Brief announcement: Linial's lower bound made easy. In: Proceedings of the 2014 ACM Symposium on Principles of Distributed Computing, PODC 2014, pp. 377–378. ACM, New York (2014)
15. Linial, N.: Locality in distributed graph algorithms. SIAM J. Comput. **21**(1), 193–201 (1992)
16. Luby, M.: A simple parallel algorithm for the maximal independent set problem. In: Proceedings of the Seventeenth Annual ACM Symposium on Theory of Computing, STOC 1885, pp. 1–10. ACM, New York (1985)
17. Naor, M., Stockmeyer, L.: What can be computed locally? SIAM J. Comput. **24**(6), 1259–1277 (1995)
18. Rubinfeld, R.: Sublinear time algorithms. In: Proceedings of the International Congress of Mathematicians (2006)
19. Schneider, J., Wattenhofer, R.: An Optimal Maximal Independent Set Algorithm for Bounded-Independence Graphs. Distributed Computing **22**, March 2010
20. Wei, V.: A lower bound on the stability number of a simple graph. Tech. rep., Bell Laboratories (1981)
21. Zuckerman, D.: Linear degree extractors and the inapproximability of max clique and chromatic number. In: Proceedings of the Thirty-eighth Annual ACM Symposium on Theory of Computing, STOC 2006, pp. 681–690. ACM, New York (2006)

# Tight Bounds for MIS in Multichannel Radio Networks

Sebastian Daum$^{(\boxtimes)}$ and Fabian Kuhn

Department of Computer Science, University of Freiburg, Freiburg im
Breisgau, Germany
{sdaum,kuhn}@cs.uni-freiburg.de

**Abstract.** In [8] an algorithm has been presented that computes a
maximal independent set (MIS) within $O(\log^2 n/\mathcal{F} + \log n \operatorname{polyloglog} n)$
rounds in an $n$-node multichannel variant of the standard graph-based
radio network, with $\mathcal{F}$ communication channels. The model assumes that
there is no collision detection and it that the network is a polynomially
bounded independence graph (BIG), a natural combinatorial generalization of well-known geographic families. The upper bound of [8] is known
to be optimal up to the polyloglog $n$ factor.

In this paper, we adapt this algorithm and its analysis to improve the
result of [8] in two ways. Mainly, we get rid of the polyloglog $n$ factor in the runtime and we thus obtain an asymptotically optimal MIS
algorithm. In addition, our new analysis allows to generalize the class
of graphs from those with polynomially bounded local independence to
graphs with arbitrarily bounded local independence.

## 1 Introduction

In recent years there has been an increased interest in algorithms for *shared spectrum networks* [26]. Nowadays, most modern wireless communication networks
feature a multitude of communication frequencies [1, 2, 5][1]—and we can certainly
expect this trend to continue.

In the light of this development, in the present paper, we settle the question
of determining the *optimal* asymptotic time complexity of computing a maximal
independent set (MIS) in the multichannel variant of the classic radio network
(RN) model first introduced in [4,7]. The task of constructing an MIS is one of
the best studied problems in the area of large-scale wireless networks. On the
one hand this is due to MIS (together with coloring problems) being one of the
key problems to study the problem of symmetry breaking in large, decentralized
systems. On the other hand an MIS provides a simple local clustering of the
graph, which can be used as a building block for computing more enhanced
organization structures such as, e.g., a communication backbone based on a
connected dominating set [6,18,28]. This is specifically relevant in the context

---

[1] For example, the IEEE 802.11 WLAN standard provides a channel spectrum of up
to 200 (partially overlapping) channels and Bluetooth specifies 79 usable channels.

© Springer-Verlag Berlin Heidelberg 2015
Y. Moses (Ed.): DISC 2015, LNCS 9363, pp. 573–587, 2015.
DOI: 10.1007/978-3-662-48653-5_38

of wireless mobile ad hoc networks or sensor networks, in which devices cannot rely on already existing infrastructure to organize themselves.

**Related Work.** In [3,21] Alon et al. and Luby presented a simple randomized parallel algorithm to compute an MIS of a general graph. It is straightforward to a standard distributed message passing model and as a consequence, the algorithm soon became an archetype for many distributed MIS algorithms also in other—usually more limiting—settings. We assume here an extension to the RN model, for which an MIS algorithm with runtime $O(\log^2 n)$ has been presented in [22] for the class of unit disk graphs (UDGs)—and proven asymptotically optimal in [11]. While the UDG restriction is well-known and popular, a more general variant known as bounded independence graphs (BIGs), that contains UDGs, has become the focus of quite some research, e.g., [20,24,25]. In particular, [25] shows that an MIS and many related structures can be computed in $\Theta(\log^* n)$ rounds in such graphs if there are no collisions.

Much of the early algorithmic multichannel research has focused on networks with faults assuming a malicious adversary that can jam up to $t$ of the $\mathcal{F}$ available channels, e.g., [10,14–17,19,27]. In addition, for fault-free networks, in [23] a series of lower bound proofs were provided, which show that $\Omega(\log^2 n/\mathcal{F} + \log n)$ rounds are needed to solve any problem requiring communication. In [19] a new technique (*heralding*) to deal with congestion in multichannel RNs has been established to solve leader election in single-hop networks in $O(\log^2 n/\mathcal{F} + \log n)$ rounds. [12] and [8] extend this technique to solve the problems of computing an approximate minimum dominating set and an MIS, respectively.

**Contributions.** In RN models, in almost all cases a restriction to the underlying graph model is assumed. One of the most general ones are so-called $\alpha$-bounded independence graphs (BIGs), where $\alpha(r)$ is a function that limits the size of a *maximum* independent set in any $r$-neighborhood of the given graph. The algorithm from [8] solves the MIS problem in time $O(\log^2 n/\mathcal{F} + \log n(\log\log n)^d)$ in such graphs for which $\alpha$ is bounded by a polynomial of degree $d$. Here we get rid of the polyloglog factor and thus show how to close the gap to the lower bound from [23]. At the same time, we remove any restriction on $\alpha$. We do so by adjusting the algorithm from [8]—and though the change is relatively small, it leads to a significantly more involved analysis.

## 2 Preliminaries

Algorithm and analysis of this paper are based on [8] and its complete version [9]. Here we try to be as self-contained as possible. However, due to lack of space, proofs are omitted and we focus on motivating and explaining the algorithms and main ideas of the analysis. For a full, detailed version, we refer to [13].

**Radio Network Model.** We model the network as a graph $G = (V, E)$. $n := |V|$ or a polynomial upper bound on $n$ is known by all nodes. Nodes start out dormant and are awakened/activated by an adversary. While there is no access to a global clock, communication happens in synchronous time slots (rounds). The network comprises $\mathcal{F}$ communication channels. In each round each node can choose to operate on one channel, either by listening or broadcasting. A broadcasting node receives no message in that round, and its signal reaches all neighbors that operate on the same channel. A node $v$ listening can decode an incoming message iff in that round exactly one of its neighbors broadcasts on the same channel. If more neighbors broadcast, their signals collide at $v$ and $v$ receives nothing, unable to detect this collision.

**Notation.** In our algorithm all nodes move between a finite set of states: $\mathbb{W}$ – *waiting*, $\mathbb{D}$ – *decay*, $\mathbb{A}$ – *active*, $\mathbb{H}'$ – *herald candidate*, $\mathbb{H}$ – *herald*, $\mathbb{L}'$ – *leader candidate*, $\mathbb{L}$ – *leader*, $\mathbb{M}$ – *MIS node*, $\mathbb{E}$ – *eliminated/dominated*. We overload this notation to also indicate the set of nodes being in said state, e.g., $\mathbb{X} := \{v \in V : v \text{ is in state } \mathbb{X}\}$. Since nodes change their states, in case of ambiguity, we write $\mathbb{X}_r$ for the set of nodes in $\mathbb{X}$ in round $r$. State changes always happen between rounds. We define $V_{\mathrm{HF}} := \mathbb{A} \cup \mathbb{H}' \cup \mathbb{L}' \cup \mathbb{H} \cup \mathbb{L}$ as the nodes in the so-called herald filter (abbreviated throughout the paper by *HF*).

We use $N(v)$ to denote the neighbors of $v$ in $G$, while $N^k(v)$ denotes the set of nodes in distance at most $k$ from $v$, including $v$. For $S \subseteq V$ we write $N_S(u)$ or $N_S^k(u)$ to abbreviate $N(u) \cap S$ or $N^k(u) \cap S$ respectively. Also we let $N(S) := \bigcup_{v \in S} N(v)$. We call $v \in V$ *alone* or *lonely*, if $N_{V_{\mathrm{HF}} \cup \mathbb{M}}(u) = \emptyset$.

We say that an event $A$ happens *with high probability (w.h.p.)*, *with decent probability*, or *with constant probability (w.c.p.)*, if it happens with probability at least $1 - n^{-c}$, $1 - \log^{-c} n$, or $\Omega(1)$, respectively, where $c$ is an arbitrarily large chosen constant. By $x \gg y$ we denote that $x > cy$ for sufficiently large $c > 1$.

**Bounded Independence.** In addition to the communication characteristics of the network, we require the network graph to be a BIG [20,24]. A graph $G$ is called an $\alpha$-*BIG* with *independence function* $\alpha : \mathbb{N} \to \mathbb{N}$, if for every node $v$ no independent set $S$ of the subgraph induced by $N^d(v)$ exceeds cardinality $\alpha(d)$. Note that $\alpha$ does not depend on $n$ and thus for fixed $d$, $\alpha(d)$ is a constant. In [8], $\alpha$ is required to be a polynomial, whereas in this paper, we put no restrictions on $\alpha$. It can easily be verified that one can always upper bound the largest independent set of the subgraph induced by $N^d(v)$ by $\alpha(2)^d$ and thus $\alpha$ is upper bounded by some exponential function. For simplicity we define a constant $\alpha := \alpha(2)$ and assume that all nodes know the value of $\alpha$.

**Number of Channels.** We assume that $\mathcal{F} = \omega(1)$ as otherwise single channel algorithms achieve the same asymptotic bounds. For $\mathcal{F} = \omega(\log n)$ we only use $\Theta(\log n)$ channels since more channels do not lead to an additional asymptotic advantage. For ease of exposition we assume $\mathcal{F} = \Omega(\log \log n)$ and refer to [9] for an explanation of how to adapt to the case $\mathcal{F} = o(\log \log n)$.

**Maximal Independent Set.** An MIS is computed in time $T$ if the following properties hold w.h.p. for each round $r$ and node $v$ (waking up in round $r_v$):

(P1) $v$ declares itself as either *dominating* ($\in \mathbb{M}$) or *dominated* ($\in \mathbb{E}$) before round $r_v + T$ and this decision is permanent.

(P2) If $v$ is *dominated* in round $r$, then $N(v) \cap \mathbb{M}_r \neq \emptyset$.

(P3) If $v$ is *dominating* in round $r$, then $N(v) \cap \mathbb{M}_r = \emptyset$.

# 3    Algorithm Description

Detailed pseudo-code can be found in [13]. Here we only present pseudo-code for the core structure of our MIS algorithm (Algorithm 1).

---

**Algorithm 1** HeraldMIS—core structure

Input:   $\sigma_\oplus,\ \sigma_\ominus,\ \Delta_{max},\ \pi_\ell,\ \alpha,\ n,\ n_\mathcal{D} = \Theta(\mathcal{F}),\ n_\mathcal{A} = \Theta(\log\log n),\ n_\mathcal{R} = \Theta(\alpha(2)),$
  $\tau_W = \Theta(\log n),\ \tau_\mathbb{D} = \Theta(\log n/\mathcal{F}),\ \tau_{lonely} = \Theta(\log^2 n/\mathcal{F} + \log n),\ \tau_{rbg} = \Theta(\log n)$

States:   W—waiting, $\mathbb{D}$—decay, M—MIS node, E—eliminated
  A—active, L/L′—leader (candidate), $\mathbb{H}$/$\mathbb{H}'$—herald (candidate)

Channels:   $\mathcal{R}_1, \ldots, \mathcal{R}_{n_\mathcal{R}}$—report, $\mathcal{D}_1, \ldots, \mathcal{D}_{n_\mathcal{D}}$—decay,
  $\mathcal{A}_1, \ldots, \mathcal{A}_{n_\mathcal{A}}$—herald, $\mathcal{H}$—handshake, $\mathcal{G}$—red-blue game

1: $count \leftarrow 0$; $state \leftarrow W$; $\gamma \leftarrow \perp$; $lonely \leftarrow \perp$; $\gamma_{min} \leftarrow \log^{-24} n$
2: **while** $state \neq E$ **do**
3:   $count \leftarrow count + 1$
4:   $lonely \leftarrow lonely + 1$
5:   $\gamma \leftarrow \min\{\gamma \cdot \sigma_\oplus, 1/2\}$
6:   uniformly at random pick $q \in [0,1)$, $j \in \{1, \ldots, n_\mathcal{D}\}$ and $k \in \{1, \ldots, n_\mathcal{R}\}$
7:   **switch** $state$ **do**
8:     **case** W or $\mathbb{D}$: run DFILTER                ▷ stage 1—decay filter
9:     **case** A: run HERALDPROTOCOL                ▷ stage 2—herald filter
10:     **case** $\mathbb{H}'$ or L′: run HANDSHAKE
11:     **case** $\mathbb{H}$ or L: run REDBLUEGAME
12:     **case** M: run DOMINATOR                ▷ stage 3—MIS node
13:   **if** $lonely = \tau_{lonely}$ **then**
14:     $state \leftarrow M$
15: **endWhile**

---

**Theorem 1.** *Alg.* HERALDMIS *solves MIS within* $O(\log^2 n/\mathcal{F} + \log n)$ *rounds.*

First we summarize how the algorithm works, including results from [9]. The algorithm is divided into three stages, decay filter (states W and $\mathbb{D}$), herald filter (states A, L′, $\mathbb{H}'$, L and $\mathbb{H}$), and decided nodes (states M and E). Nodes move forward within those stages—possibly omitting the *HF*—but never backwards. The decay filter is a powerful tool that provides that over the full runtime of the algorithm the degree of the graph induced by nodes in the *HF* is in $O(\log^3 n)$. In short, nodes first only listen for a while (W), then they start broadcasting on one out of $\Theta(\mathcal{F})$ random channels with probability $p = 1/n$ ($\mathbb{D}$), doubling $p$ every $O(\log n/\mathcal{F})$ rounds. If a node broadcasts, it moves to the *HF* and if it receives a message it restarts in W. The decay filter is the same as in [9] and for a detailed description and analysis we refer to [9]. Eliminated nodes (E) know that they neighbor an MIS node and stop their protocol. MIS nodes (M) try to inform their neighborhood (eliminating them), but they also actively disrupt protocols in the *HF*, causing them to fail. Apart from this, there is no influence between nodes being in different stages.

In this paper we almost exclusively focus on the *HF*. It helps for understanding the algorithm to *only* think of the graph induced by nodes in the *HF*.

The *HF* is divided into three blocks, *active state/herald protocol* (A), *handshake protocol* (L′ and $\mathbb{H}'$) and *red-blue protocol* (L and $\mathbb{H}$). In the first block nodes try to contact surrounding nodes. If this happens, both nodes engage in a handshake, which can only succeed, if none of them neighbors any node in the MIS or the third block. Upon success, both nodes start a series of coin flipping games, with the purpose of ensuring that no two neighboring nodes that became leaders ($\mathbb{L}$) *simultaneously*, can join the MIS. The blocks that differ from the algorithm in [9] are the active state and the red-blue protocol, where the changes in the latter compensate the changes in the more complicated active state.

There are two ways for a node $v$ to join the MIS—either by waiting for a long time without hearing from anyone, or by successfully communicating with a node $u$, *teaming up* with it (as a leader-herald pair) and together passing through handshake and red-blue protocol. The farther a pair advances in these blocks, the closer its leader is to join the MIS. We now recap the behavior of a node $v$ in the *HF*, i.e., $v \in V_{\mathrm{HF}}$, pointing out changes to the original algorithm.

**Loneliness.** $v$ maintains a counter *lonely*, which is reset to zero whenever $v$ gets a message. If *lonely* ever exceeds $\tau_{lonely} = \Theta \left( \log^2 n / \mathcal{F} + \log n \right)$, then $v$ *assumes* that it is *alone/lonely* in the *HF* (i.e., $N_{V_{\mathrm{HF}} \cup \mathbb{M}}(v) = \emptyset$) and joins the MIS—w.h.p., this action is safe, i.e., should $v$ not be alone, then its neighbors are far from joining the MIS themselves and $v$ has enough time to eliminate them.[2]

**Activity.** Also, $v$ maintains an *activity* value $\gamma(v) \in [\gamma_{min}, 1/2]$, with the initial value $\gamma_{min} = \Omega(1/\operatorname{polylog} n)$. $\gamma(v)$ solely governs the behavior of $v$ in $\mathbb{A}$, yet all nodes in $V_{\mathrm{HF}}$ maintain this value. Nodes outside $V_{\mathrm{HF}}$ have zero activity. By default, in each round, $\gamma(v)$ increases by a (small) constant factor $\sigma_\oplus > 1$ such that after $\Theta(\log\log n)$ rounds it reaches the maximum value $1/2$. However, whenever $v$ hears from a *leader* or *herald*, then $v$ reduces $\gamma(v)$ by a (large) constant factor $\sigma_\ominus \gg \sigma_\oplus$. This is a change to the original algorithm, where $\gamma(v)$ could only increase, and the reason is as follows. Leaders are likely to become MIS nodes, and if they do they eliminate their neighbors anyway. For safety reasons a leader $l$ needs to wait $\Theta(\log n)$ rounds before it may join the MIS. During that time, if $l$'s neighbors keep high activity values, progress might be hindered in a $\delta' = O(\log\log n)$ neighborhood of $l$, which is why in [9] an $\alpha(\delta') = O(\operatorname{polyloglog} n)$ speed loss had to be accepted and also why the algorithm of [9] only works for polynomial $\alpha$. By also reducing $\gamma$, progress is guaranteed even in close proximity of a leader-herald pair and nodes can join the MIS in a much more pipelined fashion. At the same time, 'unjustified' activity value reductions only cause 'minor damage' that can be mitigated.

**Herald Protocol.** In the active state ($\mathbb{A}$), $v$ participates in the *herald protocol* with probability $\gamma(v)$, otherwise it tries to learn of nearby leaders, heralds or MIS nodes, by listening to one of *constantly* many *report channels* $\mathcal{R}_1, ..., \mathcal{R}_{n_\mathcal{R}}$, $n_\mathcal{R} \geq 3\alpha^2$. If $v$ participates in the herald protocol, then it chooses a channel $\mathcal{A}_i$ from $\mathcal{A}_1, ..., \mathcal{A}_{n_\mathcal{A}}$ with probability $2^{-i}$, listens on $\mathcal{A}_i$ with probability $\pi_\ell \leq 1/10$ or broadcasts its *ID* otherwise.[3] If $v$ listens, but receives nothing, nothing happens

---

[2] In [9] there existed some component called *loneliness support block*, operating on its own set of channels $\mathcal{S}_1, ..., \mathcal{S}_{n_S}$; this block and its channels have been removed.

[3] We want to note that $\pi_\ell$ is a constant parameter that we can choose arbitrarily.

and $v$ stays in $\mathbb{A}$. Should $v$ receive from some node $u$, then next round it engages with $u$ in the *handshake protocol* as a *herald candidate* ($\mathbb{H}'$), in the hope of moving forward to the *red-blue protocol* together with $u$. If $v$ chooses to broadcast, then it deterministically pursues the handshake as a *leader candidate* ($\mathbb{L}'$), hoping that some other node $u$ heard its message and joins in for the handshake.

**Handshake and Red-Blue Protocol.** For a detailed description and analysis, see [13] and [9]. In short, a node $h \in \mathbb{H}'$ that received a message in the herald protocol sends for two rounds on $\mathcal{H}$, then listens twice, and sends again for two rounds. A node $l \in \mathbb{L}'$ that was sending before acts reversely, i.e., it listens, sends and listens. Only nodes that receive *all* expected messages move forward to the red-blue protocol, otherwise return to $\mathbb{A}$. The handshake can only possibly be completed if a pair of exactly one broadcaster and one receiver participates.

The *red-blue protocol* is a repetition of $\tau_{rbg}/8 = \Theta(\log n)$ *red-blue games* of 8 rounds each. In odd rounds, both $l$ and $h$ of the leader-herald pair send a blocking signal on $\mathcal{H}$, causing nearby handshakes to fail. At the beginning of each game, the leader $l$ randomly picks blue or red. If it picks red, it sends a message on $\mathcal{G}$ in round 2 and it listens on $\mathcal{G}$ in round 4, for blue it acts reversely. In round 6, $l$ sends the index $k'$ of the meeting channel for the next red-blue game on a previously decided meeting channel $\mathcal{R}_k$.[4] In round 8 it listens on $\mathcal{R}_{k'}$. The herald $h$ on the other hand sends both in rounds 2 and 4. It listens in round 6 to update the meeting channel and in round 8 it sends on $\mathcal{R}_{k'}$.

By design of the handshake and the blocking signals in the red-blue protocol, $l$ can neighbor a leader or herald of a different pair *only* if that other node moved to the red-blue protocol simultaneously or with a 2-round shift. If $l$ has such a neighbor, at some point it will not hear its herald in round 2/4, when it listens. $l$ then aborts the protocol, notifies $h$ in round 6 and returns to $\mathbb{A}$. The messages sent by $l/h$ in round 6/8 also have the purpose of letting nearby listening active nodes reduce their activity values. An *isolated pair* on the other hand cannot be knocked out anymore[5] and after $\tau_{rbg} = \Theta(\log n)$ rounds the pair can assume that there is no other conflicting pair nearby and the leader joins the MIS.

The handshake did not change and red-blue games have been extended by 2 rounds—round 8 now gives heralds also the possibility to reach their neighbors.

**Summary of Changes.** Compared to the algorithm in [9], the following three things changed. The *loneliness support block* is not executed anymore, except for maintaining the counter *lonely*. Also, the threshold $\tau_{lonely}$ has been lowered to $\Theta\left(\log^2 n/\mathcal{F} + \log n\right)$ to reflect the new runtime of the algorithm. The main change is that nodes reduce their activity $\gamma$ if they hear from a leader or herald. The change in the red-blue game is an addition of 2 rounds: the 7th round is just a copy of rounds 1, 3 and 5; the 8th round gives the herald of the pair a possibility to notify nearby active nodes in order to reduce their activity values—so far only leaders and MIS nodes were able to reach out to their neighbors.

Note that while the algorithm itself has barely changed, the analysis needed to be extended significantly in order to achieve the optimal runtime.

---

[4] The very first meeting channel is fixed by $l$ during the handshake.

[5] Except by an MIS node, but that already implies progress.

# 4   Analysis

To prove that Algorithm 1 indeed solves MIS in the given time bounds, we take the following approach. In [9] it was proven that the graph, induced by nodes that passed the decay filter, has maximum degree $\Delta_{max} = O(\log^3 n)$. A node $u$ in the *HF* joins the MIS either if it assumes to be alone, or if it manages to create and maintain a leader-herald bond with a neighboring node for $\tau_{rbg} = \Theta(\log n)$ rounds. If $u$ in the *HF* stays alone, we are done; once $u$ has a neighbor in $V_{\text{HF}}$, then within radius $\delta := \delta_\alpha = \Theta(\log \log n)$ soon an isolated leader-herald pair is created that maintains its bond for $\tau_{rbg}$ rounds.[6] So far this is the same as in [9]. There, however, a stagnation of up to $\tau_{rbg}$ rounds might follow before the next isolated pair or MIS node is created in $N^\delta(u)$. Since up to $\alpha(\delta)$ nodes in $N^\delta(u)$ can join the MIS before $u$ or one of its neighbors joins itself, the runtime of the *HF* is $O(\tau_{rbg}\alpha(\delta))$, or $O(\log n \, \text{polyloglog} \, n)$ if $\alpha$ is polynomial.

Here, by decreasing activity levels of nodes neighboring leader-herald pairs, the stagnation that can be caused by leaders on their way to join the MIS lasts for no longer than $O(\log \log n)$ rounds in expectation. This allows the creation of isolated leader-herald pairs in $N^\delta(u)$ in a pipelined manner, reducing the expected runtime of the *HF* to $O(\alpha^\delta \log \log n)$. Unlike in [9], here we also can choose $\delta$ as an arbitrarily small value in $\Theta(\log \log n)$ without increasing the runtime by more than constant factors. Choosing $\delta < \log \log n / \log \alpha$ and a Chernoff argument bounds the runtime of the *HF* by $O(\log n)$ w.h.p.

In more detail, let $u$ be a node entering the *HF* in round $t_u$. For sake of contradiction assume that $u$ is undecided by time $t_u + \tau_{RT}$. If $u$ stays lonely, it joins the MIS eventually in $\tau_{lonely} \ll \tau_{RT}$ rounds. Note that for $u$ to move from being non-lonely to lonely, some node in $N^2(u)$ must have joined the MIS shortly before and eliminated all neighbors of $u$ in $V_{\text{HF}}$. This happens at most $\alpha^2$ times and thus $u$ spends at most $\alpha^2 \tau_{lonely} \ll \tau_{RT}$ rounds alone. Hence, assume that $u$ is not lonely, i.e., neighbors $u'$, and that no node in $N^2(u)$ joins the MIS. We show that then most of the time both $u$ and $u'$ have a high activity value $\gamma$.

The following argumentation motivates this. For $u$ to decrease $\gamma(u)$, it must neighbor a pair. Let us call isolated pairs (in which the leader does not neighbor another leader or herald) *good pairs* and the others *bad pairs*. Conditioning on the event of a pair being created, w.c.p. that pair is good. This is considered progress, as it guarantees one of two things: Within $O(\log n)$ rounds either the leader itself joins the MIS or a neighbor of this pair does. In the opposite case of bad pairs being created, in expectation these remain bad pairs only for a constant number of rounds. Moreover, w.h.p., there are $O(\log n)$ rounds *in total* in which bad pairs exist in $N^3(u)$ after $t_u$, also causing only $O(\log n)$ rounds of $u$ and $u'$ having their activity below $1/2$. Adjusting parameters we get that for some $\tau_{prog} = O(\tau_{lonely})$ and an arbitrarily small constant $\varepsilon$, for $(1 - \varepsilon)\tau_{prog}$ rounds in $[t_u, t_u + \tau_{prog}]$ the activity values of both $u$ and $u'$ are $1/2$.

Furthermore, all pairs, good and bad, inform their neighbors. By the definition of good pairs, its leaders are independent. With our choice of $\delta$ thus at most

---

[6] "Soon" indeed means in $O(1)$ rounds in expectation, as long as $\mathcal{F} = \Omega(\log \log n)$.

$O(\sqrt{\log n})$ good pairs exist in $N^\delta(u)$. We argue that the activity values of nodes neighboring a pair that has run the red-blue protocol for $\Omega(\log\log n)$ rounds (which almost surely holds for good pairs), are below $\gamma_{low} := \Theta(1/\operatorname{polylog} n)$ with some decent probability (i.e., $1 - \log^{\Omega(1)} n$). The total number of nodes in $N^\delta(u)$ becoming part of a good pair in $[t_u, t_u + \tau_{prog}]$ is $O(\sqrt{\log n})$ and hence $O(\sqrt{\log n}\Delta_{max})$ nodes neighbor good pairs in that time. A union bound and a Chernoff bound provide that the total amount of rounds in which any node $v$ in $N^\delta(u)$ neighboring a good pair has $\gamma(v) > \gamma_{low}$, is less than $\varepsilon\tau_{prog}$.

Together with the previous claim we get that in $(1 - 2\varepsilon)\tau_{prog}$ rounds in $[t_u, t_u + \tau_{prog}]$ both conditions are true: $\gamma(u) = \gamma(u') = 1/2$ and *all* good pairs in $N^\delta(u)$ "silenced" their neighbors—i.e., all their neighbors have activity below $\gamma_{low}$. Let us call a round with this property *promising for u*. Without going into detail, we can show that now within distance $\delta$ there exists a node $w$ with the property of being so-called $\eta$-fat, i.e., $w$'s neighborhood is at least roughly as active as that of any of its neighbors'. Fatness implies that w.c.p. two nodes $l$ and $h$ in $N^1(w)$ become a *good* leader-herald pair. As said before, such a pair reduces the activity values of its neighbors rather quickly, which causes the property of $\eta$-fatness to move away from $w$ to another node in $N^\delta(u)$ and we can repeat the argument. If a bad pair is created, then $\eta$-fatness might shortly fade, but is restored quickly, so we can almost omit this case. Again using Chernoff tail bounds, we show that at some point $u$ itself becomes $\eta$-fat and now the creation of an MIS node in $N^2(u)$ is inevitably.

We summarize again. Once an MIS node or good pair arises in constant distance from $u$, we are done. In an $\Omega\left(\log^2 n/\mathcal{F} + \log n\right)$ interval, $u$ is mostly in a promising state. W.c.p. every $O(1)$ rounds a node in $N^\delta(u)$ becomes part of a good pair or joins the MIS. In expectation, within $\Theta(\log\log n)$ rounds MIS nodes eliminate their neighbors and good pairs *silence* theirs. After any of those events happen, we measure the time until $u$ is in a promising state again. Using Chernoff over $O(\sqrt{\log n})$ such random variables results in needing at most $O(\log n)$ time, thus, by then $u$ must be covered.

## 4.1   Guarantees from the Decay Filter

Due to lack of space we refer to [9] and [13] for a more detailed description of what the decay filter accomplishes.[7] But we informally state the two main results. For each node $v$ the decay filter guarantees that over the runtime of $\Theta(\log^2 n/\mathcal{F} + \log n)$ rounds, (1) $v$ or one of its neighbors enters the *HF*, but (2) no more than $\Delta_{max} = O(\log^3 n)$ nodes in $N^1(v)$ do.

From now on we only look at the graph $G'$ induced by $V' := V_{\mathrm{HF}} \cup \mathbb{M}$, induced by non-eliminated nodes that made it past the decay filter. *All* notations are tied to this subgraph, though we omit this in our notations, i.e., $N(u)$ means the neighborhood of $u$ in $G'$. Instead, if we need to consider nodes from the states $\mathbb{W}$ and $\mathbb{D}$, then we explicitly say so and show this e.g. by writing $N_G(u)$.

---

[7] The underlying algorithm has been first used and analyzed in [11], in a slightly more restrictive graph model and in [8] it was shown that it also works in BIGs.

## 4.2   Definitions for the Herald Filter

Practically all parameters (including the above mentioned $\Delta_{max}$) depend in one way or another on the bound on independence, i.e., on $\alpha$, but in most cases those dependencies are captured in the hidden constants of those asymptotic bounds.

For our analysis of a node $u$ that enters the *HF*, we observe a specific $\delta = \Theta(\log \log n)$ neighborhood $N^\delta(u)$ of $u$. We set

$$\delta := \delta_\alpha := \frac{\log \log n}{2 \log \alpha} = \Theta(\log \log n), \tag{0}$$

i.e., $\alpha^\delta = (2^{\log \alpha})^{\frac{\log \log n}{2 \log \alpha}} = \sqrt{\log n}$. The choice of $\delta$ guarantees that any independent set in a $\delta$-neighborhood is of size at most $\sqrt{\log n}$.

Our main goal is to show quick progress in $N^\delta(u)$. Progress is clearly achieved if an MIS node arises, but due to the way a node can become an MIS node, we also consider the creation of an isolated leader-herald pair progress (more precisely, the *leader* of the pair needs to be isolated from other nodes in $\mathbb{L}$ or $\mathbb{H}$), as the leader will eventually join the MIS (or be knocked out permanently by a newly created MIS node).

**Definition 1.** *(Good Pair, Bad Pair) Consider a leader-herald pair $(l, h)$ in round $r$. We say $(l, h)$ is a good pair in round $r$ if none of the neighbors of $l$ (other than $h$) is (1) in state $\mathbb{L}$ or (2) in state $\mathbb{H}$ or (3) is a herald candidate in round 5 or 6 of its respective handshake. Otherwise $(l, h)$ is a bad pair.*

Note that the definition of a good/bad pair is independent of possibly neighboring MIS nodes. MIS nodes existing already for 4 rounds prevent the creation of leader-herald pairs in their neighborhood completely. If on the other hand a new MIS node appears next to a leader-herald pair (which is w.h.p. only possible through the loneliness route), then we have progress in a close neighborhood. Also, note that only the leader of the pair must be 'isolated'. There are two reasons for this: (1) only leaders join the MIS (2) by protocol design the *herald* of a pair can only receive messages from MIS nodes or its own leader—not by other leaders (not even in round 6) nor other heralds. This is due to the fact that any neighboring heralds act completely synchronously and a leader neighboring a non-paired herald is ahead by precisely 2 rounds.[8] Note also that bad pairs can become good, but not vice versa. This is because all leaders and heralds prevent the creation of further leaders/heralds in their neighborhood.

**Definition 2.** *(Activity Mass) For a node $u$ we define $\Gamma(u) := \sum_{v \in N^1(u)} \gamma(v)$. We call this the* activity sum *or* activity mass *of node $u$. Furthermore we let $\Gamma^\circ(u) := \Gamma(u) - \gamma(u) = \sum_{v \in N(u)} \gamma(v)$. In some cases we are only interested in the activity mass of active nodes and then we have $\Gamma_\mathbb{A}(u) := \sum_{v \in N^1_\mathbb{A}(u)} \gamma(v)$ and $\Gamma^\circ_\mathbb{A}(u)$ is defined analogously. Also*

$$\gamma_{min} := \log^{-24} n = \Theta(1/\operatorname{polylog} n),$$
$$\gamma_{low} := \sqrt{\gamma_{min}} = \log^{-12} n.$$

---

[8] Cf. Lemma 8.10 in [9] and the actions of nodes in rounds 6/8 of a red-blue game.

**Definition 3.** *(Fatness) We call a node $u$ $\hat{\eta}$-fat for some value $\hat{\eta} \in (0,1)$, if it holds that $\Gamma(u) \geq \hat{\eta} \cdot \max_{v \in N(u)}\{\Gamma(v)\}$.*

In simple words, in terms of activity mass, $u$ is (at least) in the same 'league' as its neighboring nodes. Using this we choose a specific fatness parameter $\eta < 1$:

$$\eta = \eta_\alpha := \alpha^{-8} \leq \alpha^{-2\frac{\log \Delta_{max}}{\log \log n}}$$

The choice of $\eta$ assures that a chain of activity sums $(\Gamma(v_i))_{i \geq 1}$ of nodes $v_i$ on a path $v_1, v_2, v_3, \ldots$ with $\Gamma(v_i) \geq \eta^{-1}\Gamma(v_{i-1})$ and $\Gamma(v_1) \geq 2$ has length at most $\delta$, because

$$(\eta^{-1})^\delta = (\alpha^{-8})^{-\frac{\log \log n}{2 \log \alpha}} \geq (2^{\log \alpha})^{2\frac{\log \Delta_{max}}{\log \log n}\frac{\log \log n}{2 \log \alpha}} = \Delta_{max} \overset{\gamma(u) \leq 1/2}{>} \max_{u \in V_{HF}} \Gamma(u).$$

The algorithm needs to know a few more parameters. $\sigma_\oplus$ and $\sigma_\ominus$ govern the changes in a node's activity level. The former is a small constant, greater than, but close to 1. In most rounds a node $u$ increases $\gamma(u)$ by $\sigma_\oplus$. $\sigma_\ominus$ is a much larger factor used for decreasing activity, large enough to undo many previous increments, but still in $O(1)$.

$$\sigma_\oplus := 2^{6/(1000\bar{m})} > 1$$
$$\sigma_\ominus := \sigma_\oplus^{20\bar{m}} = 2^{12/100} > 1$$

$\bar{m}$ is a large enough constant that depends on $n_\mathcal{R}$, but assuming that $n_\mathcal{R} \geq 3\alpha^2$, $\bar{m} \geq 2^{16}n_\mathcal{R}$ suffices. Since $\gamma_{min} = \log^{-24} n$, $167\bar{m} \log \log n = \Theta(\log \log n)$ consecutive increments raise a node's activity value to $1/2$. Analogously, $\Theta(\log \log n)$ decrements decrease it to its minimal value $\gamma_{min}$.

Also two time thresholds $\tau_{rbg} = \Theta(\log n)$ and $\tau_{lonely} = \Theta\left(\log^2 n / \mathcal{F} + \log n\right)$ are needed by the algorithm. $\tau_{rbg}$ is the number of rounds a node spends in the red-blue protocol. If a node $u \in V_{HF}$ does not receive a single message for $\tau_{lonely}$ consecutive rounds, $u$ deduces that it is alone or all its neighbors got eliminated, and joins the MIS. In our analysis we use further time thresholds $\tau_{notif} = \Theta(\log n)$, $\tau_{prog} = \Theta\left(\log^2 n / \mathcal{F} + \log n\right)$ and $\tau_{RT} = \Theta\left(\log^2 n / \mathcal{F} + \log n\right)$, for which the following inequality chain holds:

$$\tau_{RT} \gg \tau_{lonely} \gg \tau_{prog} \gg \tau_{rbg} \gg \tau_{notif}$$

$\tau_{notif}$ is the maximum time needed for an MIS node to notify, w.h.p., all its neighbors. If a node $u$ is not lonely, then, w.h.p., significant progress is achieved in less than $\tau_{prog}$ rounds; more precisely, an MIS node is created in $N^{O(1)}(u)$. W.h.p., $\tau_{RT}$ is the maximum time a node spends in the *HF* before it gets decided.

### 4.3   Candidate Election—Nodes in States $\mathbb{A}$ (and $\mathbb{L}'$)

In this section we want to establish a few facts about how nodes can transit from state $\mathbb{A}$ to state $\mathbb{L}'$ or $\mathbb{H}'$, respectively. Note that nodes can switch between states $\mathbb{A}$ and $\mathbb{L}'$ without communication, but to get towards any of the three states $\mathbb{H}'$, $\mathbb{L}$ and $\mathbb{H}$, communication is mandatory.

For some node $u$, *constant* $k$, round $r$ and an index $i \in \{1, \ldots, n_A\}$ we can show that with probability $1 - \Omega(\alpha^k \pi_\ell)$ no node in $N_{\mathbb{A}}^k(u)$ receives anything on any herald election channel $\mathcal{A}_i$. If we condition on certain events tied to index $i$, like knowing (by peeking at random bits of some nodes) that some nodes *do not* operate on $\mathcal{A}_i$, *do* operate on $\mathcal{A}_i$, *do* operate *and* broadcast or listen on $\mathcal{A}_i$, then the statement does still hold true for all other channels. I.e., regardless of conditioning on aforementioned events, with probability $1 - \Omega(\pi_\ell)$ no node in $N_{\mathbb{A}}^k(u)$ receives anything on any channel $\mathcal{A}_j \neq \mathcal{A}_i$. Thus, by choosing $\pi_\ell$ small, we can decrease the chances of herald creation.

For lack of space we refer to [13] for a proper lemma statement.

Under certain conditions the creation of herald candidates can be lower bounded. However, for our algorithm to work, we not only need to prove that they are created, but that this happens in *solitude*, i.e., in a close neighborhood no other herald candidates are created. The next lemma—an adaption of Lemma 8.8 from [9]—ensures this.

**Lemma 1.** *Let $t$ be a round in which for a node $u \in \mathbb{A}$ the following holds:*
- *there is no herald candidate in $N^2(u)$,*
- *all nodes $v \in N^2(u)$ that neighbor a herald or leader, have $\gamma(v) \leq \gamma_{low}$,*
- *all nodes in $N^2(u)$ neighboring MIS nodes are eliminated,*
- *$\Gamma(u) \geq 1$,*

*If in addition it holds that either*
*(a) $\Gamma(u) < 5\alpha$, $u$ is $\frac{1}{5\alpha}$-fat and $\gamma(u) = \frac{1}{2}$, or*
*(b) $\Gamma(u) \geq 5\alpha$ and $u$ is $\eta$-fat,*
*then by the end of round $t' \in [t, t+7]$, with probability $\Omega(\pi_\ell)$ either a node in $N^2(u)$ joins the MIS or a good pair $(l, h) \in (\mathbb{L} \cap N^1(u)) \times (\mathbb{H} \cap N^1(u))$ is created.*

Let us start with an intuition of this Lemma. The basic intention is to show that if $u$ is $\eta$-fat, then w.c.p. in constant many rounds a *good* leader-herald pair with both endpoints in $N^1(u)$ arises—for this $u$ itself does not have to have a high $\gamma$ value, i.e., $u$ does not need to be a likely part of the pair. The lemma lists many requirements. We show that shortly after a node $v$ moves to the *HF*, in distance $\delta = O(\log \log n)$ most of the time there exists a node $u$ that satisfies these conditions. We also show that if an isolated pair is created in $N^1(u)$, those requirements are again satisfied $O(\text{polyloglog } n)$ rounds later (in expectation) by another node $u'$ in this $\delta$-neighborhood of $v$.

We want to point out that in the neighborhood of a fat node $u$ with $\Gamma(u)$ at least one, w.c.p. "good things" happen (i.e., the creation of MIS nodes or good leader-herald pairs) within constant many rounds, *even if* there are herald candidates nearby or *even if* some nodes neighboring *bad* leaders/heralds have high $\gamma$ values. In other words, the first two requirements could be omitted. Instead we use other results to show that from those relaxed conditions one can get to the tighter ones listed here w.c.p. in constant many rounds. We argue in Subsection 4.4, that every time an isolated pair is created, the algorithm achieves progress, as it guarantees the creation of an MIS node nearby—even if this event is delayed by $O(\log n)$ rounds.

Therefore, Lemma 1 "promises" progress in the proximity of a fat node. However, we have no such statement for areas without fat nodes. Indeed an excessive creation of bad pairs in such areas can even cause problems for our argumentation. The next result, which is a key result within the whole analysis, implies that *if* a pair is created at all, then w.c.p. this pair is good. This allows us to proof later in Lemma 4 that nodes in the *HF* are practically always very active in the candidate election process—unless they already neighbor an MIS node or a good pair.

**Lemma 2.** *Let $r$ be a round in which node $u$ is in state $\mathbb{A}$ and $N_{\mathbb{A}}(u) \neq \emptyset$. Let $B^u$ be the event that at the end of round $r$, $u$ moves to state $\mathbb{H}'$ due to receiving a message from some node $v \in N_{\mathbb{A}}(u)$ on some channel $\mathcal{A}_{\bar{\lambda}}$. Further, let $D^u \subseteq B^u$ be the event that $B^u$ holds and in addition no other node $v' \in N^3(v) \backslash \{u\}$ receives any message on channel $\mathcal{A}_{\bar{\lambda}}$ in round $r$. It holds that*

$$\mathbf{P}(B^u) = \begin{cases} O\left(\pi_\ell \frac{\gamma(u)}{\Gamma_{\mathbb{A}}^{\circ}(u)}\right) & \Gamma_{\mathbb{A}}^{\circ}(u) > 2 \\ O\left(\pi_\ell \gamma(u) \Gamma_{\mathbb{A}}^{\circ}(u)\right) & \Gamma_{\mathbb{A}}^{\circ}(u) \leq 2 \end{cases},$$

$$\mathbf{P}(D^u) = \begin{cases} \Omega\left(\pi_\ell \frac{\gamma(u)}{\Gamma_{\mathbb{A}}^{\circ}(u)}\right) & \Gamma_{\mathbb{A}}^{\circ}(u) > 2 \\ \Omega\left(\pi_\ell \gamma(u) \Gamma_{\mathbb{A}}^{\circ}(u)\right) & \Gamma_{\mathbb{A}}^{\circ}(u) \leq 2 \end{cases}.$$

A simple corollary is—using the remarks in the beginning of Subsection 4.3— that if $u$ gets a message from $v$ and there are no leaders or heralds nearby, then w.c.p. $u$ and $v$ form a good leader-herald pair after 6 rounds.

### 4.4  Handshake & Red-Blue Protocol—States $\mathbb{L}'$, $\mathbb{H}'$, $\mathbb{L}$, $\mathbb{H}$

We next very shortly recap and summarize the effects of the so-called *Handshake* and *Red-Blue Game*, but for detailed information please see [9,13].

Foremost, the handshake cannot be passed by two nodes $l$ and $h$, if $l$ also reached another herald $h'$. But the handshake *also* guarantees, that if two leader-herald pairs neighbor each other during the red-blue protocol, i.e., one node from one pair neighbors a node of another pair, then both pairs conducted the handshake at the *same* time (or with an offset of 2 rounds).

The red-blue protocol grants that if a good pair $(l, h)$ is executing the protocol, then a new MIS node arises nearby within $\tau_{rbg} = \Theta(\log n)$ rounds (usually the leader $l$). On the other hand, any bad pair remains bad for only $O(1)$ rounds in expectation (note that good pairs can never turn bad).

### 4.5  Joining the MIS—Nodes in States $\mathbb{M}$ and $\mathbb{E}$

*Property 1 (P).* The set $\mathbb{M}$ is an independent set at all times.

This intuitive assumption is needed for some of the upcoming statements; it is clearly true at the beginning of the algorithm, when $\mathbb{M} = \emptyset$. Lemma 7 shows that if (P) is violated, then w.h.p. a contradiction occurs. The next lemma makes sure that nodes in $N(\mathbb{M})$ soon learn of their coverage.

**Lemma 3.** *Assume (P) holds. Let $v$ be a node that enters state $\mathbb{M}$ at time $t$. Let $w$ be a node in $N_G(v)$ that is awake at time $t' \geq t$ and, if $w \in \mathbb{L} \cup \mathbb{H}$, that it is at most in round $\frac{9}{10}\tau_{rbg}$ of its corresponding red-blue protocol. Then by time $t' + \tau_{notif} = t' + O(\log n)$, w.h.p., $w$ is in state $\mathbb{E}$.*[9]

## 4.6   Progress and Runtime

Lemma 8.13 of [9] shows that once a good leader-herald pair $(l, h)$ is created, its leader (or another node in $N^2(l)$) joins the MIS within $O(\log n)$ rounds. Also, within close proximity of *fat* nodes (which exist in any $\delta$-neighborhood of nodes in $V_{\mathbb{HF}}$) w.c.p. such solitary pairs are created every $O(1)$ rounds. In the algorithm of [9] it might happen that after a good pair $(l, h)$ is created $N^\delta(u)$, the only fat node in $N^\delta(u)$ is close to $(l, h)$. A good pair blocks the creation of other pairs around, so progress might be stalled until $l$ joins the MIS, eliminating its neighbors (and therefore their activity) and finally, forcing the local condition of fatness to move to a different area of the graph.

Here we changed the algorithm to take care of this potential stagnancy issue. We want the attribute of fatness to move away from a good pair $(l, h)$ long before $l$ joins the MIS. More precisely, another node not neighboring good pairs should become fat within $o(\log n)$ rounds. For this we require good pairs to reduce the activity levels of their neighborhoods. However, a leader-herald pair does not know whether it is good or bad before the $\tau_{rbg} = \Theta(\log n)$ red-blue games are over. The idea to deal with this difficulty is the following. Good pairs manage in expectation within $O(\log \log n)$ rounds to reduce their neighborhood's activity far enough such that most of the time those nodes can be considered inactive. Bad pairs, however, last for only $O(1)$ rounds in expectation, and are created rarely enough[10] for affected nodes to recover their lost activity quickly. In other words, the longer a node is a leader, the more likely it is indeed a good one.

Careful analysis allows to transform these observations into high probability results. In the following $\gamma(u, t)$ denotes the activity level of node $u$ in round $t$. Also, let $\varepsilon$ be a small constant—about 0.1 is sufficiently small for the proofs.

**Lemma 4.** *Let $t$ be a time at which a node $u \notin N^1(\mathbb{M})$ is in the HF. Then, w.h.p., one of following holds:*
*(a) Within $\tau_{prog} = O(\log^2 n/\mathcal{F} + \log n)$ rounds, $u \in N^1(\mathbb{M})$, or*
*(b) $|\{t' \in [t+1, t+\tau_{prog}] : \gamma(u, t') = 1/2\}| \geq (1 - \varepsilon)\tau_{prog}$.*

Next we upper bound the number of rounds in which *any* neighbors of good pairs within distance $\delta$ from $u$ manage to exceed the activity threshold $\gamma_{low}$.

**Definition 4.** *For a node $u$ and a round $r$ let $I(u, r)$ be the event that*
*− all nodes $x \in N^\delta(u)$, which neighbor an MIS node, are in state $\mathbb{E}$, and*
*− all nodes $x \in N^\delta(u)$, which neighbor a good herald $h$ or good leader $l$, $h, l \in (\mathbb{H} \cup \mathbb{L}) \setminus N(\mathbb{M})$, have $\gamma(x) \leq \gamma_{low} = \sqrt{\gamma_{min}} = \log^{-12} n$ and are neither bad leaders nor bad heralds.*

---

[9] Note that this lemma also considers nodes $w$ from the decay filter.
[10] Controlled by reducing the parameter $\pi_\ell$.

**Lemma 5.** *Assume (P) holds. Further, let $\bar{r}$ be a round in which node $u$ is in the HF and set $J := [\bar{r} + 1, \bar{r} + \tau_{prog}]$. Then, w.h.p., one of the following holds:*
- *Within $\tau_{prog} = O(\log n)$ rounds, there is an MIS node in $N^1(u)$, or*
- *$|\{r \in J : I(u, r) holds\}| \geq (1 - \varepsilon)\tau_{prog}$.*

**Lemma 6.** *Assume (P) holds. Let $t_u$ be a round in which some $u \notin N^1(\mathbb{M})$ has a neighbor $u' \notin N^1(\mathbb{M})$ in the HF. Then, w.h.p., within $\tau_{prog} = O(\log^2 n/\mathcal{F} + \log n)$ rounds a node in $N^1(\{u, u'\})$ joins the MIS.*

**Lemma 7.** *W.h.p., (P) is not violated throughout the runtime of the algorithm.*

Now we have everything at hand to prove Theorem 1.

*Proof Sketch (of Theorem 1).* As stated, the runtime of the decay filter is within $O\left(\log^2 n/\mathcal{F} + \log n\right)$, i.e., for each node $u$ in the decay filter, by that time a node $v \in N^1_G(u)$ enters the HF. Also, over the course of $O(\log^2 n)$ rounds, the maximum degree of the graph $G'$ induced by all nodes in $V_{\mathrm{HF}}$ is in $O(\log^3 n)$.

Let thus $u$ be a node that enters the HF. If it stays lonely for $\tau_{lonely} = \Theta\left(\log^2 n/\mathcal{F} + \log n\right)$ rounds, then $u$ joins the MIS and we are done. Hence assume that $u$ does hear from a neighboring node $u'$ in the HF before $\tau_{lonely}$ rounds have passed. We can now apply Lemma 6 to get an MIS node $v$ created within $\tau_{prog} = O\left(\log^2 n/\mathcal{F} + \log n\right)$ rounds. It either neighbors $u$, in which case within $\tau_{notif} = O(\log n)$ rounds $u$ is decided w.h.p., or it neighbors $u'$, which is also then eliminated in $\tau_{notif}$ rounds. That way $u$ can become lonely again. However, since an MIS node has been created in $N^2(u)$, this can happen at most $\alpha^2$ times. Thus, at most $\tau_{RT} = 2\alpha^2\tau_{lonely}$ rounds after $u$ entered the HF, $u$ is decided.

# References

1. 802.11, I.: Wireless LAN MAC and Physical Layer Specifications, March 2012
2. Alliance, Z.: Zigbee specification. ZigBee Document 053474r06 1 (2005)
3. Alon, N., Babai, L., Itai, A.: A Fast and Simple Randomized Parallel Algorithm for the Maximal Independent Set Problem. Journal of Algorithms (1986)
4. Bar-Yehuda, R., Goldreich, O., Itai, A.: On the Time-Complexity of Broadcast in Multi-Hop Radio Networks: An Exponential Gap Between Determinism and Randomization. Journal of Computer and System Sciences **45**(1), 104–126 (1992)
5. Bluetooth Consortium: Bluetooth Specification Version 4.2, December 2014
6. Censor-Hillel, K., Gilbert, S., Kuhn, F., Lynch, N., Newport, C.: Structuring unreliable radio networks. In: Proc. ACM Symp. on Principles of Distr. Comp. (PODC), pp. 79–88 (2011)
7. Chlamtac, I., Kutten, S.: On Broadcasting in Radio Networks–Problem Analysis and Protocol Design. IEEE Trans. on Communications **33**(12), 1240–1246 (1985)
8. Daum, S., Ghaffari, M., Gilbert, S., Kuhn, F., Newport, C.: Maximal independent sets in multichannel radio networks. In: Proc. ACM Symp. on Principles of Distr. Comp. (PODC) (2013)
9. Daum, S., Ghaffari, M., Gilbert, S., Kuhn, F., Newport, C.: Maximal Independent Sets in Multichannel Radio Networks. Tech. Rep. 275, U. of Freiburg, Dept. of Computer Science (2013)

10. Daum, S., Gilbert, S., Kuhn, F., Newport, C.: Leader election in shared spectrum networks. In: Proc. ACM Symp. on Principles of Distr. Comp. (PODC) (2012)
11. Daum, S., Kuhn, F., Newport, C.: Efficient symmetry breaking in multi-channel radio networks. In: Aguilera, M.K. (ed.) DISC 2012. LNCS, vol. 7611, pp. 238–252. Springer, Heidelberg (2012)
12. Daum, S., Kuhn, F., Newport, C.: Efficient Symmetry Breaking in Multi-Channel Radio Networks. Tech. Rep. 271, U. of Freiburg, Dept. of Computer Science (2012)
13. Daum, S., Kuhn, F.: Tight Bounds for MIS in Multichannel Radio Networks (2015). CoRR abs/1508.04390, http://arxiv.org/abs/1508.04390
14. Dolev, S., Gilbert, S., Guerraoui, R., Kuhn, F., Newport, C.: The wireless synchronization problem. In: Proc. ACM Symp. on Principles of Distr. Comp. (PODC), pp. 190–199 (2009)
15. Dolev, S., Gilbert, S., Khabbazian, M., Newport, C.: Leveraging channel diversity to gain efficiency and robustness for wireless broadcast. In: Peleg, D. (ed.) Distributed Computing. LNCS, vol. 6950, pp. 252–267. Springer, Heidelberg (2011)
16. Dolev, S., Gilbert, S., Guerraoui, R., Newport, C.: Gossiping in a multi-channel radio network: an oblivious approach to coping with malicious interference (extended abstract). In: Pelc, A. (ed.) DISC 2007. LNCS, vol. 4731, pp. 208–222. Springer, Heidelberg (2007)
17. Dolev, S., Gilbert, S., Guerraoui, R., Newport, C.: Secure communication over radio channels. In: Proc. ACM Symp. on Principles of Distr. Comp. (PODC) (2008)
18. Ephremides, A., Wieselthier, J.E., Baker, D.J.: A Design Concept for Reliable Mobile Radio Networks with Frequency Hopping Signaling. Proc. of the IEEE 75(56–73) (1987)
19. Gilbert, S., Guerraoui, R., Kowalski, D., Newport, C.: Interference-resilient information exchange. In: Proc. IEEE Conf. on Computer Communications (INFOCOM) (2009)
20. Kuhn, F., Moscibroda, T., Nieberg, T., Wattenhofer, R.: Fast deterministic distributed maximal independent set computation on growth-bounded graphs. In: Fraigniaud, P. (ed.) DISC 2005. LNCS, vol. 3724, pp. 273–287. Springer, Heidelberg (2005)
21. Luby, M.: A Simple Parallel Algorithm for the Maximal Independent Set Problem. SIAM Journal on Computing 15(4), 1036–1053 (1986)
22. Moscibroda, T., Wattenhofer, R.: Maximal independent sets in radio networks. In: Proc. ACM Symp. on Principles of Distr. Comp. (PODC), pp. 148–157 (2005)
23. Newport, C.: Radio network lower bounds made easy. In: Kuhn, F. (ed.) DISC 2014. LNCS, vol. 8784, pp. 258–272. Springer, Heidelberg (2014)
24. Schmid, S., Wattenhofer, R.: Algorithmic models for sensor networks. In: Proc. Workshop on Parallel and Distr. Real-Time Systmes (WPDRTS), pp. 1–11 (2006)
25. Schneider, J., Wattenhofer, R.: A log-star distributed maximal independent set algorithm for growth-bounded graphs. In: Proc. ACM Symp. on Principles of Distr. Comp. (PODC), pp. 35–44 (2008)
26. Sherman, M., Mody, A., Martinez, R., Rodriguez, C., Reddy, R.: IEEE Standards Supporting Cognitive Radio and Networks, Dynamic Spectrum Access, and Coexistence. IEEE Communications Magazine 46(7), 72–79 (2008)
27. Strasser, M., Pöpper, C., Capkun, S.: Efficient uncoordinated FHSS anti-jamming communication. In: Proc. ACM Symp. on Mobile Ad Hoc Networking and Computing (MOBIHOC) (2009)
28. Wan, P.J., Alzoubi, K.M., Frieder, O.: Distributed construction of connected dominating set in wireless Ad Hoc networks. In: Proc. IEEE Conf. on Computer Communications (INFOCOM) (2002)

# Nonuniform SINR+Voroni Diagrams Are Effectively Uniform

Erez Kantor[1]([✉]), Zvi Lotker[2,3], Merav Parter[4], and David Peleg[4]

[1] CSAIL, Massachusetts Institute of Technology, Cambridge, MA 01239, USA
erezk@csail.mit.edu
[2] Ben-Gurion University, Beersheba, Israel
[3] University Paris Diderot, Paris, France
[4] The Weizmann Institute of Science, Rehovot, Israel

**Abstract.** This paper concerns the behavior of an *SINR diagram* of wireless systems, composed of a set $S$ of $n$ stations embedded in $\mathbb{R}^d$, when restricted to the corresponding *Voronoi diagram* imposed on $S$. The diagram obtained by restricting the SINR zones to their corresponding Voronoi cells is referred to as hereafter as an *SINR+Voronoi diagram*.

While uniform SINR diagrams (where all stations transmit with the same power) are simple and nicely structured (e.g., the station reception zones are convex and "fat") [3], nonuniform SINR diagrams might be complex (e.g., the reception zones might be fractured and their boundaries might contain many singular points) [9]. In this paper, we establish the (perhaps surprising) fact that a nonuniform SINR+Voronoi diagram is topologically almost as nice as a uniform SINR diagram. In particular, it is convex and effectively (In the sense that its fatness measure does not depend on the number of stations $n$ but only on parameters typically bounded by a constant.) fat. This holds for every power assignment, every path-loss parameter $\alpha$ and every dimension $d \geq 1$. The convexity property also holds for every SINR threshold $\beta > 0$, and the effective fatness holds for any $\beta > 1$. These fundamental properties provide a theoretical justification to engineering practices basing zonal tessellations on the Voronoi diagram, and helps to explain the soundness and efficacy of such practices.

We also consider two algorithmic applications. The first concerns the *Power Control with Voronoi Diagram* (PCVD) problem, where given $n$ stations embedded in some polygon $\mathcal{P}$, it is required to find the power assignment that optimizes the SINR threshold of the transmission station $s_i$ for any given reception point $p \in \mathcal{P}$ in its Voronoi cell $\text{Vor}(s_i)$. The second application is approximate point location; we show that for

E.K is supported in a part by NSF Award Numbers CCF-1217506, CCF-AF-0937274, 0939370-CCF, and AFOSR Contract Numbers FA9550-14-1-0403 and FA9550-13-1-0042. Z.L is supported in part by the Ministry of Science Technology and Space, Israel, French-Israeli project MAIMONIDE 31768XL, the Israel Science Foundation (grant 1549/13) and the French-Israeli Laboratory FILOFOCS. M.P and D.P are supported in part by the Israel Science Foundation (grant 1549/13) and the I-CORE program of the Israel PBC and ISF (grant 4/11). M.P is also supported by Rothschild and Fulbright Fellowships.

© Springer-Verlag Berlin Heidelberg 2015
Y. Moses (Ed.): DISC 2015, LNCS 9363, pp. 588–601, 2015.
DOI: 10.1007/978-3-662-48653-5_39

SINR+Voronoi zones, this task can be solved considerably more efficiently than in the general non-uniform case.

# 1    Introduction

## 1.1    Background and Motivation

A common method for designing a cellular or wireless network in the plane is
by computing the Voronoi diagram of the base-stations, and making each base-
station responsible for its own Voronoi cell. This choice is natural, since it ensures
that the distance from every point $p$ in the plane to the station responsible for
it is minimal. Yet what affects the performance of a wireless network is not
just the distance. Rather, reception at a given point in a given time is governed
by a complex relationship between the reception point and the set of stations
that transmit at that time. This relationship is described schematically by the
SINR formula, which also dictates the reception zones around each transmitted
station. Hence the areas in the intersection between SINR reception regions and
their corresponding Voronoi cells deserve particular attention, and are the focus
of the current paper.

We consider the *Signal to Interference-plus-Noise Ratio (SINR)* model, where
given a set of stations $S = \{s_0, \ldots, s_{n-1}\}$ in $\mathbb{R}^d$ concurrently transmitting with
power assignment $\psi$, and background noise $N$, a receiver at point $p \in \mathbb{R}^d$ successfully receives a message from station $s_i$ if and only if $\mathrm{SINR}(s_i, p) \geq \beta$, where
$\mathrm{SINR}(s_i, p) = \frac{\psi_i \cdot \mathrm{dist}(s_i,p)^{-\alpha}}{\sum_{j \neq i} \psi_j \cdot \mathrm{dist}(s_j,p)^{-\alpha} + N}$ for constants $\beta \geq 1$ denoting the minimum
SINR required for a message to be successfully received, and $\alpha$ denoting the
path-loss parameter, and where dist() denotes Euclidean distance.

To model the reception zones we use the convenient representation of an
*SINR diagram*, introduced in [3], which partitions the plane into $n$ reception
zones, one per station, and a complementary zone where no station can be heard.
The topology and geometry of SINR diagrams was studied in [3] in the relatively
simple setting of *uniform power*, where all stations transmit with the same power
level. It was shown therein that uniform SINR diagrams are particularly simple:
the reception zone of each station is convex, fat and strictly contained inside the
corresponding Voronoi cell.

SINR diagrams in the general *nonuniform* setting (i.e., with arbitrary power
assignments) were studied in [9]. The topological features of general SINR diagrams turn out to be much more complicated than in the uniform case, even
for networks with a small number of stations. In particular, the reception zones
are not necessarily fat, convex or even connected, and their boundaries might
contain many singular points.

In this paper, we explore the behavior of the reception zones of SINR diagrams when restricted to Voronoi diagrams. The resulting diagram, referred to
as an *SINR+Voronoi* diagram, consists of $n$ reception zones, one per station,
obtained by the intersection of the SINR reception zones with their corresponding Voronoi cells. Studying SINR+Voronoi diagrams is motivated by the complexity of general nonuniform SINR zones and, perhaps more importantly, by the

abundant usage of hexagonal networks in practice; cellular networks are commonly designed as hexagonal networks, where each node serves as a base-station to which mobile users must connect to make or receive phone calls. A mobile user is normally connected to the nearest base-station, hence the base-stations divide the area among them, such that each base-station serves all users that are located inside its hexagonal grid cell (which is in fact its Voronoi cell). Due to the disk shape of the sensing range of the sensor devices, using a hexagonal tessellation topology is the most efficient way to cover the whole sensing area, and indeed many routing, location management and channel assignment protocols are based on it [6,12–15]. It is thus intriguing to ask whether the reception zones of *nonuniform* SINR diagrams enjoy some desirable properties (e.g., assume a convenient form) when restricted to their corresponding Voronoi cells.

In this paper, it is shown that the diagram obtained from a nonuniform SINR diagram by restricting its reception zones to their respective Voronoi cells (e.g., hexagonal cells in the grid) behaves almost as nice as a *uniform* SINR diagram: the resulting reception zones are *convex*, and their fatness measure depends only on parameters typically bounded by a constant, and in particular is independent of the number of stations in the network. For an illustration see the reception zone of station $s_0$ in Figure 1(a).

These fundamental properties provide a theoretical justification to engineering practices basing regional tessellations on the Voronoi diagram, and help to explain the soundness and efficacy of such practices.

To prove convexity, we extend the proof for the uniform setting of [3] to the nonuniform setting[1]. Apart from the theoretical interest, this result is of considerable practical significance, as obviously, having a convex reception zone inside each hexagonal cell may ease the development of protocols for various design and communication tasks such as scheduling, topology control and connectivity.

We note that convexity within a Voronoi cell is important also in the mobile setting, where no fixed tessellation can be assumed. For example, in the setting of Vehicular ad-hoc network (VANET) [17], the stations are mobile but each user is still mapped to the closest base-station. Hence, although the hexagonal tessellation is no longer preserved, the convexity within the (dynamic) Voronoi tessellation is still relevant (for an illustration, see Fig. 1(b)-(c)).

As an application for the convexity property, we consider the problem where one wishes to cover the entire area of a given bounded polygon $\mathcal{P}$ by using a base-station network embedded in $\mathcal{P}$. One natural way to do that is by assigning each base-station an area of coverage. Usually the base-station needs to cover the area of its Voronoi cell up to where it intersects with $\mathcal{P}$. Assuming the power with which each base-station transmits can be controlled, it is desirable to increase the SINR ratio as much as possible in order to increase the capacity of the cellular network. The problem of determining the transmission energy of

---

[1] Note that in the uniform setting too, convexity is guaranteed only inside the Voronoi cell, but since the entire reception zone is restricted to the Voronoi cell, this implies that the entire zone is convex. In contrast, in the nonuniform setting, the reception zone of a station with a high transmission energy might exceed its Voronoi cell.

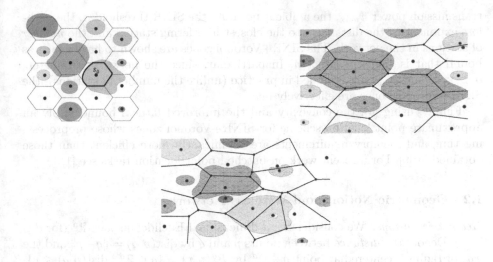

**Fig. 1.** The overlay of an SINR diagram of a nonuniform wireless network on the corresponding Voronoi diagram. (a) Hexagonal Voronoi cells; the intersection between the reception region of station $s_0$ and the Voronoi cell around it is highlighted in bold. (b) Slight random perturbation to a hexagonal network. (c) Random positions.

each base-station so as to maximize the capacity of the entire network is called the *Power Control Voronoi Diagram* (PCVD) problem. We show that although PCVD is a non-convex and non-discrete problem, it can be solved in a nearly optimal manner.

Our algorithm is especially useful in the mobile setting where the positions of base-stations change with time. This scenario can happen in sudden-onset disasters and ad-hoc vehicle networks, since in these cases, the network structure is not fixed and it is not clear how to divide the coverage areas between the base-stations. Although it is natural to use the Voronoi diagram, it is not clear how to assign the transmission energies in a way that guarantees a full coverage of the area of interest. The solution proposed in this paper for this problem has the advantage that it can adapted to a dynamic setting quite efficiently since it depends upon the Voronoi tessellation that can be maintained efficiently in a dynamic setting [5,8]. Exploiting the convexity property in Voronoi cells, we propose a discrete equivalent formulation of the PCVD problem. Specifically, we show that given the convexity guarantee, it is sufficient to insist on achieving the optimal threshold $\beta$ only on the vertex set of each Voronoi cell (where unbounded Voronoi cells are bounded by using a bounding polygon $\mathcal{P}$ that contains the entire coverage area). Computing a power assignment maximizing the coverage within Voronoi cells has been considered also in [16] from a game theoretic point of view; yet no analytic result has been known so far for this problem.

We then turn to consider the fatness property. In [9], it was shown that the fatness of nonuniform zone can be bounded by some function of the maximum transmission power $\psi_{max}$, the ambient noise $N$, the SINR threshold $\beta$, the path-loss exponent $\alpha$, the distance $\kappa$ to the closest interfering station and the *number of stations* in the network. The SINR+Voronoi zones are shown to have a fatness bound that is *independent* of $n$. In particular, since the network parameters $\alpha, \beta, \kappa, N$ and $\psi_{max}$ are bounded in practice (unlike the number of stations), the SINR+Voronoi zones are effectively fat.

Finally, using [4], the convexity and the improved fatness bound imply an approximate point location scheme for SINR+Voronoi zones whose preprocessing time and memory requirements are significantly more efficient than those obtained in [9]. For a recent work on batched point location tasks see [1].

## 1.2   Geometric Notions and Wireless Networks

*Geometric notions.* We consider the $d$-dimensional Euclidean space $\mathbb{R}^d$ (for $d \in \mathbb{Z}_{\geq 1}$). Denote the *distance* between points $p$ and $q$ by $\mathrm{dist}(p, q) = \|q - p\|$ and the *ball* of radius $r$ centered at point $p \in \mathbb{R}^d$ by $B^d(p, r) = \{q \in \mathbb{R}^d \mid \mathrm{dist}(p, q) \leq r\}$. Unless stated otherwise, we assume the 2-dimensional Euclidean plane, and omit $d$. The basic notions of open, closed, bounded, compact and connected sets of points are defined in the standard manner.

We use the term *zone* to describe a point set with some "niceness" properties. Unless stated otherwise, a zone refers to the union of an open connected set and some subset of its boundary. It may also refer to a single point or to the finite union of zones.

The point set $P$ is said to be *star-shaped* with respect to point $p \in P$ if the line segment $\overline{pq}$ is contained in $P$ for every point $q \in P$. In addition, $P$ is said to be *convex* if it is star-shaped with respect to any point $p \in P$, see [7].

For a bounded zone $Z \neq \emptyset$ and an internal $p \in Z$, denote the maximal and minimal diameters of $Z$ w.r.t. $p$ by $\delta(p, Z) = \sup\{r > 0 \mid Z \supseteq B(p, r)\}$ and $\Delta(p, Z) = \inf\{r > 0 \mid Z \subseteq B(p, r)\}$, and define the *fatness parameter* of $Z$ *with respect to* $p$ to be $\varphi(p, Z) = \Delta(p, Z)/\delta(p, Z)$. The zone $Z$ is said to be *fat* with respect to $p$ if $\varphi(p, Z)$ is bounded by some constant.

*Wireless networks and SINR Diagrams.* We consider a wireless network $\mathcal{A} = \langle d, S, \psi, N, \beta, \alpha \rangle$, where $d \in \mathbb{Z}_{\geq 1}$ is the dimension, $S = \{s_0, s_1, \ldots, s_{n-1}\}$ is a set of $n \geq 2$ *radio stations* embedded in the $d$-dimensional space, $\psi$ is an assignment of a positive real *transmitting power* $\psi_i$ to each station $s_i$, $N \geq 0$ is the *background noise*, $\beta \geq 0$ is a constant *reception threshold*, and $\alpha > 0$ is the *path-loss parameter*. The *signal to interference & noise ratio (SINR)* of $s_i$ at point $p$ is defined as

$$\mathrm{SINR}_{\mathcal{A}}(s_i, p) = \frac{\psi_i \cdot \mathrm{dist}(s_i, p)^{-\alpha}}{\sum_{j \neq i} \psi_j \cdot \mathrm{dist}(s_j, p)^{-\alpha} + N} . \tag{1}$$

Observe that $\mathrm{SINR}_{\mathcal{A}}(s_i, p)$ is always positive since the transmission powers and the distances of the stations from $p$ are always positive and the background noise is non-negative. In certain contexts, it may be more convenient to consider the reciprocal of the SINR function,

$$\text{SINR}_{\mathcal{A}}^{-1}(s_i, p) = \frac{1}{\psi_i} \left( \sum_{j \neq i} \psi_j \left( \frac{\text{dist}(s_i, p)}{\text{dist}(s_j, p)} \right)^{\alpha} + N \cdot \text{dist}(s_i, p)^{\alpha} \right). \quad (2)$$

When the network $\mathcal{A}$ is clear from the context, we may omit it and write simply $\text{SINR}(s_i, p)$. The fundamental rule of the SINR model is that the transmission of station $s_i$ is received correctly at point $p \notin S$ if and only if its signal to noise ratio at $p$ is not smaller than the reception threshold of the network, i.e., $\text{SINR}(s_i, p) \geq \beta$. In this case, we say that $s_i$ is *heard* at $p$. We refer to the set of points that hear station $s_i$ as the *reception zone* of $s_i$, defined as

$$\mathcal{H}_{\mathcal{A}}(s_i) = \{ p \in \mathbb{R}^d - S \mid \text{SINR}_{\mathcal{A}}(s_i, p) \geq \beta \} \cup \{ s_i \} .$$

(Note that $\text{SINR}(s_i, \cdot)$ is undefined at points in $S$ and in particular at $s_i$ itself, and that $\mathcal{H}_{\mathcal{A}}(s_i)$ is not is not necessarily connected or restricted to the Voroni cell $\text{VOR}(s_i)$). The *null zone* is the set of points that hear no station $s_i \in S$ (due to the background noise and interference), $\mathcal{H}_{\mathcal{A}}(\emptyset) = \{ p \in \mathbb{R}^d - S \mid \text{SINR}(s_i, p) < \beta, \forall s_i \in S \}$. An SINR diagram $\mathcal{H}(\mathcal{A}) = \{ \mathcal{H}_{\mathcal{A}}(s_i), \; 0 \leq i \leq n - 1 \} \cup \{ \mathcal{H}_{\mathcal{A}}(\emptyset) \}$ is a "reception map" partitioning the plane into the stations reception zones and the null zone. The following important technical lemma from [3] will be useful in our later arguments.

**Lemma 1.** *[3] Let $f : \mathbb{R}^d \to \mathbb{R}^d$ be a mapping consisting of rotation, translation, and scaling by a factor of $\sigma > 0$. Consider some network $\mathcal{A} = \langle d, S, \psi, N, \beta, \alpha \rangle$ and let $f(\mathcal{A}) = \langle d, f(S), \psi, N/\sigma^2, \beta, \alpha \rangle$, where $f(S) = \{ f(s_i) \mid s_i \in S \}$. Then $f$ preserves the signal to noise ratio, namely, for every station $s_i$ and for all points $p \notin S$, we have $\text{SINR}_{\mathcal{A}}(s_i, p) = \text{SINR}_{f(\mathcal{A})}(f(s_i), f(p))$.*

Avin et al. [3] discuss the relationships between an SINR diagram on a set of stations $S$ with *uniform* transmission powers and the corresponding *Voronoi diagram* on $S$. Specifically, it is shown that the $n$ reception zones $\mathcal{H}_{\mathcal{A}}(s_i)$ around each point $s_i$ are strictly contained in the corresponding Voronoi cells $\text{VOR}(s_i)$ where

$$\text{VOR}(s_i) = \{ p \in \mathbb{R}^d \mid \text{dist}(s_i, p) \leq \text{dist}(s_j, p) \text{ for any } j \neq i \} . \quad (3)$$

In contrast, the reception zone of a nonuniform SINR diagram is *not* necessarily contained within the Voronoi cell of the corresponding station (e.g., a strong station with high transmission energy may be successfully received in points outside its Voronoi cell). Kantor et al. [9] showed that nonuniform SINR diagrams are related to a *weighted* variant of Voronoi diagrams [2].

*SINR+Voronoi Diagrams.* Consider a wireless network $\mathcal{A} = \langle d, S, \bar{\psi}, N, \beta, \alpha \rangle$. Let $\text{VOR}(s_i)$ be the Voronoi cell of station $s_i$ (see Eq. (3)). Define $\mathcal{VH}_{\mathcal{A}}(s_i)$ be the reception zone of $s_i$ restricted to its Voronoi cell, where

$$\mathcal{VH}_{\mathcal{A}}(s_i) = \mathcal{H}_{\mathcal{A}}(s_i) \cap \text{VOR}(s_i) .$$

The SINR+Voronoi diagram consists of the $n$ Voronoi-restricted reception zones

$$\mathcal{VH} = \langle \mathcal{VH}_{\mathcal{A}}(s_0), \ldots, \mathcal{VH}_{\mathcal{A}}(s_{n-1}) \rangle .$$

## 2    Convexity of SINR+Voronoi Zones

Without loss of generality, throughout we fix a station $s_0$ and show the following (for an illustration see Fig. 2).

**Theorem 1.** *For every wireless network* $\mathcal{A} = \langle d, S, \psi, N \geq 0, \beta > 0, \alpha \rangle$, *The Voronoi-restricted reception zone* $\mathcal{VH}_{\mathcal{A}}(s_0)$ *is convex.*

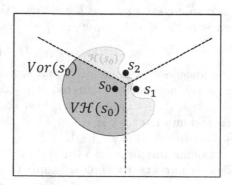

**Fig. 2.** The reception region of $s_0$ is non-convex but its part restricted to the Voronoi cell of $s_0$ is convex. The green area depicts $\mathcal{H}(s_0)$. The Voronoi-restricted reception zone $\mathcal{VH}(s_0)$ is the darker region.

### 2.1    Proof Outline

The following technical lemma from [11] plays a key role in our analysis. Denote the origin point by $q = (0,0)$, let $p_L = (1,0)$, $p_R = (-1,0)$ and define $\rho_i = \text{dist}^2(s_i, q)$, for every $i = 0, ..., n-1$.

**Lemma 2 ([11]).** *Let* $\mathcal{A}$ *be a noise-free network* $(N = 0)$ *and let* $q \notin S$. *Then*

$$\max\{\text{SINR}_{\mathcal{A}}^{-1}(s_0, p_L) \, , \, \text{SINR}_{\mathcal{A}}^{-1}(s_0, p_R)\} \geq \sum_{i=1}^{n-1} \frac{\psi_i}{\psi_0} \cdot \left(\frac{\rho_0 + 1}{\rho_i + 1}\right)^{\alpha/2} \, .$$

Our proof scheme for Lemma 1 is as follows. For simplicity, consider the two-dimensional case. Using [3], the proof naturally extends to any dimension $d \geq 2$. Consider pairs of reception points $p_1, p_2 \in \mathcal{VH}_{\mathcal{A}}(s_0)$. We classify such pairs into two types. The first type is where $s_0 \in \overline{p_1 p_2}$. This type is handled in Lemma 3, where it is shown that $\mathcal{VH}_{\mathcal{A}}(s_0)$ is *star-shaped* with respect to $s_0$. The complementary type, where $s_0 \notin \overline{p_1 p_2}$, is handled in two steps. First, in Lemma 4, we consider the simplified case where there is no background noise (i.e., $N = 0$) and use Lemma 2 to establish the claim. Finally, we consider the general noisy case where $N > 0$ and establish Theorem 1.

**Lemma 3.** $\mathcal{VH}_\mathcal{A}(s_0)$ *is star-shaped with respect to* $s_0$.

*Proof.* In fact, we prove a slightly stronger assertion. Consider some point $p \in$ VOR($s_0$). We show that SINR($s_0, q$) > SINR($s_0, p$) for all internal points $q$ in the segment $\overline{s_0\,p}$. By Lemma 1, we may assume without loss of generality that $s_0 = (0,0)$ and $p = (-1,0)$. Consider some station $s_i$, $i > 0$. Note that $s_i$ is outside the unit circle around $p$ (since $p$ is in VOR($s_0$)). Therefore, if $s_i$ is not located on the positive half of the horizontal axis, then it can be relocated to a new location $s_i'$ on the positive half of the horizontal axis by rotating it around $p$ so that dist($s_i', p$) = dist($s_i, p$) and dist($s_i', q$) $\leq$ dist($s_i, q$) for all points $q \in \overline{s_0\,p}$ (see Fig. 3). This process can be repeated with every station $s_i$, $i > 0$, until all interfering stations $s_i \neq s_0$ are located on the positive half of the horizontal axis without decreasing the interference at any point $q \in \overline{s_0\,p}$. Therefore it is sufficient to establish the assertion under the assumption that $s_i = (a_i, 0)$, where $a_i > 0$, for every $i > 0$. Let $q = (-x, 0)$ for some $x \in (0,1]$. To show that SINR($s_0, q$) > SINR($s_0, p$), we consider the reciprocal of the SINR function from Eq. (2) on $s_0$ and $q$, which in the defined setting assumes the form

$$f(x) = \mathrm{SINR}^{-1}(s_0, q) = \sum_{i=1}^{n-1} \left[ \frac{\psi_i}{\psi_0} \left( \frac{x}{a_i + x} \right)^\alpha \right] + \frac{x^\alpha}{\psi_0} \cdot N \, ,$$

and prove that $f(x) < f(1)$ for all $x \in (0,1)$. This follows since the derivative $\frac{df(x)}{dx} = \frac{\alpha x}{\psi_0} \cdot \left( \sum_{i=1}^{n} \frac{\psi_i \cdot a_i}{(a_i + x)^{(\alpha+1)}} + N \right)$ is positive for $x \in (0,1]$.　∎

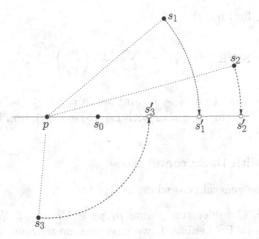

**Fig. 3.** Relocating stations. All stations are mapped to the positive $x$-axis, so that the SINR value at point $p$ with respect to the station $s_0$, is preserved.

## 2.2   Convexity without Background Noise

We now complete the proof for the noise free case where $N = 0$.

**Lemma 4.** *For every wireless network $\mathcal{A}_0 = \langle d, S, \bar{\psi}, N = 0, \beta, \alpha \rangle$, $\mathcal{VH}_{\mathcal{A}_0}(s_i)$ is convex for every $s_i \in S$.*

*Proof.* By Lemma 3, it remains to show that $\overline{p_1 p_2} \subseteq \mathcal{VH}_{\mathcal{A}_0}(s_0)$ for any pair of points $p_1, p_2 \in \mathcal{VH}_{\mathcal{A}_0}(s_0)$ such that $s_0 \notin \overline{p_1 p_2}$. Note that by the convexity of a Voronoi cell, $\overline{p_1 p_2} \subset \mathrm{VOR}(s_i)$. Thus, there is no station $s_i$ on this segment, concluding that the $\mathrm{SINR}_{\mathcal{A}_0}(s_0, p)$ function is continuous on the $\overline{p_1 p_2}$ segment. It remains to prove that $\overline{p_1 p_2} \subseteq \mathcal{H}_{\mathcal{A}_0}(s_0)$, i.e., that $\mathrm{SINR}_{\mathcal{A}_0}(s_0, q) \geq \beta$ for any $q \in \overline{p_1 p_2}$. We now show that for every $q \in \overline{p_1 p_2}$,

$$\mathrm{SINR}_{\mathcal{A}_0}(s_0, q) \geq \min\{\mathrm{SINR}_{\mathcal{A}_0}(s_0, p_1), \mathrm{SINR}_{\mathcal{A}_0}(s_0, p_2)\}.$$

Specifically, we show that the dual statement holds, namely, that

$$\mathrm{SINR}_{\mathcal{A}_0}^{-1}(s_0, q) \leq \max\left\{\mathrm{SINR}_{\mathcal{A}_0}^{-1}(s_0, p_1), \mathrm{SINR}_{\mathcal{A}_0}^{-1}(s_0, p_2)\right\}. \tag{4}$$

By Lemma 1 and by the continuity of the $\mathrm{SINR}_{\mathcal{A}}$ function in the segment $\overline{p_1 p_2}$, it is sufficient to consider the case where $p_1 = (-1, 0)$, $p_2 = (1, 0)$ and $q = (0, 0)$, the middle point between $p_1$ and $p_2$ on the segment. By applying Lemma 2, we have

$$\max\{\mathrm{SINR}_{\mathcal{A}_0}^{-1}(s_0, p_1) \,,\, \mathrm{SINR}_{\mathcal{A}_0}^{-1}(s_0, p_2)\} \geq \sum_{i=1}^{n-1} \frac{\psi_i}{\psi_0} \cdot \left(\frac{\rho_0 + 1}{\rho_i + 1}\right)^{\alpha/2}. \tag{5}$$

On the other hand, by Eq. (2),

$$\mathrm{SINR}_{\mathcal{A}_0}^{-1}(s_0, q) = \sum_{i=1}^{n-1} \frac{\psi_i}{\psi_0} \cdot \left(\frac{\rho_0}{\rho_i}\right)^{\alpha/2}. \tag{6}$$

As $q \in \mathrm{VOR}(s_0)$, we have that $\rho_i \geq \rho_0$ and hence $\rho_0/\rho_i \leq (\rho_0 + 1)/(\rho_i + 1)$ for every $i \in \{1, ..., n-1\}$. This, together with Eq. (5) and (6), implies Ineq. (4). $\blacksquare$

## 2.3   Convexity with Background Noise

We now consider the general case where $N \geq 0$.

*Proof (Theorem 1).* Consider two points $p_1, p_2 \in \mathcal{VH}_{\mathcal{A}}(s_0)$. We need to show that $\overline{p_1 p_2} \subseteq \mathcal{VH}_{\mathcal{A}}(s_0)$. By Lemma 1, we may assume without loss of generality that $p_1 = (-1, 0)$ and $p_2 = (1, 0)$. Let $d_N = \max\{\mathrm{dist}(s_0, p_1), \mathrm{dist}(s_0, p_2)\}$.

Let $\mathcal{A}^*$ be a noise-free $(n+1)$-station network obtained from $\mathcal{A}$ by replacing the background noise with a new station $s_N$ located in $(0, d_N)$ with transmission power $\psi_N = N \cdot (d_N^2 + 1)^{\alpha/2}$. That is, $\mathcal{A}^* = \langle d = 2, S^*, \bar{\psi}^*, N = 0, \beta, \alpha \rangle$, where $S^* = S \cup \{s_N\}$ and $\bar{\psi}^* = (\psi_0, ..., \psi_{n-1}, \psi_N)$. It is easy to verify that $\psi_N \cdot$

$\text{dist}(s_N, p_i)^{-\alpha} = N$ and $\psi_N \cdot \text{dist}(s_N, q)^{-\alpha} \geq N$, for every $q \in \overline{p_1 p_2}$. Thus, on the one hand,

$$\text{SINR}_{\mathcal{A}^*}(s_0, p_i) = \text{SINR}_{\mathcal{A}}(s_0, p_i), \text{ for } i \in \{1, 2\}, \tag{7}$$

and on the other hand, for all points $q \in \overline{p_1 p_2}$,

$$\text{SINR}_{\mathcal{A}}(s_0, q) \geq \text{SINR}_{\mathcal{A}^*}(s_0, q). \tag{8}$$

We now show that $p_1, p_2 \in \mathcal{VH}_{\mathcal{A}^*}(s_0)$. We first claim that $p_1, p_2 \in \text{VOR}^*(s_0)$ where $\text{VOR}^*$ is the Voronoi diagram of the set $S^*$. Since $p_1, p_2 \in \mathcal{VH}_{\mathcal{A}}(s_0)$, in particular $p_1, p_2 \in \text{VOR}(s_0)$. This implies that $\text{dist}(s_0, p_i) \leq \text{dist}(s_j, p_i)$, for every $i \in \{1, 2\}$ and $j \in \{1, ..., n-1\}$. In addition, $\text{dist}(s_N, p_i) > d_N \geq \text{dist}(s_0, p_i)$, implying that $p_1, p_2 \in \text{VOR}^*(s_0)$ as needed. It remains to show that $p_1, p_2 \in \mathcal{H}_{\mathcal{A}^*}(s_0)$. Since $p_1, p_2 \in \mathcal{H}_{\mathcal{A}}(s_0)$, $\text{SINR}_{\mathcal{A}}(s_0, p_i) \geq \beta$ for $i \in \{1, 2\}$. Thus, by Eq. (7), $\text{SINR}_{\mathcal{A}^*}(s_0, p_i) \geq \beta$ as well, and $p_1, p_2 \in \mathcal{H}_{\mathcal{A}^*}(s_0)$. Finally, since $p_1, p_2 \in \mathcal{VH}_{\mathcal{A}^*}(s_0)$ where $\mathcal{A}^*$ is a noise free network, by Lemma 4 it holds that $\text{SINR}_{\mathcal{A}^*}(s_0, q) \geq \beta$, for all points $q \in \overline{p_1 p_2}$. Thus, by Ineq. (8), also $\text{SINR}_{\mathcal{A}}(s_0, q) \geq \beta$, for all points $q \in \overline{p_1 p_2}$, are required. Theorem 1 follows.  ∎

## 3    Fatness of SINR+Voronoi Zones

In this section we develop a deeper understanding of the shape of SINR+Voronoi reception zones by analyzing their fatness. Consider a nonuniform power network $\mathcal{A} = \langle d, S, \bar{\Psi}, N, \beta, \alpha \rangle$ with positive background noise $N > 0$, where $S = \{s_0, ..., s_{n-1}\}$, and $\alpha \geq 0$ and $\beta > 1$ are constants[2].

We focus on $s_0$ and assume that its location is not shared by any other station (otherwise, $\mathcal{H}(s_0) = \{s_0\}$). Let $\kappa = \min_{s_i \in S \setminus \{s_0\}} \{\text{dist}(s_0, s_i)\}$ denote the distance between $s_0$ and the closest interfering station. The known fatness bounds for uniform and nonuniform reception zones are summarized as follows.

**Fact 2.** Let $\mathcal{A}$ be an $n$-station network.
(a) If $\mathcal{A}$ is uniform, then $\varphi(s_0, \mathcal{H}_{\mathcal{A}_u}(s_0)) = O(1)$.
(b) If $\mathcal{A}$ is nonuniform, then $\varphi(s_0, \mathcal{H}_{\mathcal{A}_{nu}}(s_0)) = O(\psi_{max}/\kappa \cdot \sqrt{n/N})$ for $\alpha = 2$.

We now show that in the SINR+Voronoi setting, the fatness of $\mathcal{VH}_{\mathcal{A}}(s_0)$ with respect to $s_0$, can be bounded as a function of $\psi_{max}$, $\kappa$, $\alpha$, $\beta$ and $N$, namely, it is independent of the number of stations $n$.

**Theorem 3**

$$\varphi(s_0, \mathcal{VH}(s_0)) \leq \frac{\sqrt[\alpha]{\beta} + 1}{\sqrt[\alpha]{\beta} - 1} \cdot \max\left\{1, \frac{3}{\kappa} \cdot \sqrt[\alpha]{\frac{\psi_0}{N \cdot \beta}} \cdot \max\{1, \sqrt[\alpha]{\beta} - 1\}\right\}.$$

In certain cases, tighter bounds can be obtained. In particular, we say that an SINR+Voronoi zone $\mathcal{VH}_{\mathcal{A}}(s_0)$ is *well-bounded* if the minimal enclosing ball of $\mathcal{VH}_{\mathcal{A}}(s_0)$ is fully contained in the Voronoi cell $\text{VOR}(s_0)$. Then we have:

---

[2] Note that the convexity proof presented in Section 2 holds for any $\beta \geq 0$.

**Lemma 5.** *If* $\mathcal{VH}_\mathcal{A}(s_0)$ *is a well-bounded zone, then* $\varphi(s_0, \mathcal{VH}_\mathcal{A}(s_0)) = O(1)$.

The proof of Thm. 3 is provided in the full version. Its overall structure is similar to that of Thm. 4.2 in [3], but requires delicate adaptations for the nonuniform setting. The radius $\Delta(s_0, \mathcal{VH}_\mathcal{A}(s_0))$ is easily bounded by considering the extreme case where $s_0$ is the solitary transmitting stations. Our main efforts went into bounding the small radius $\delta(s_0, \mathcal{VH}_\mathcal{A}(s_0))$ by a function independent of $n$. The proof consists of three main steps. First, we bound the fatness of SINR+Voronoi zones in a setting of two stations in a one-dimensional space. Then, we consider a special type of nonuniform power networks called *positive collinear* networks. Finally, the general case is reduced to the case of positive collinear networks.

## 4    Applications

In this section, we present two applications for the properties established in the previous sections. In Subsec. 4.1, we present an application for the convexity property and describe a new variant of the power control problem. In Subsec. 4.2, we exploit the convexity and the improved bound on the fatness of SINR+Voronoi zones to obtain an improved approximate point location scheme for SINR+Voronoi diagram.

### 4.1    The Power Control Voronoi Diagram (PCVD) Problem

In the standard power control problem for wireless networks, one is given a set of $n$ communication links $L = \{\ell_0, \ldots, \ell_{n-1}\}$, where each link $\ell_i$ represents a communication request from station $s_i$ to receiver $r_i$. The question is then to find an optimal power assignment for the stations, so as to make the reception threshold $\beta$ as high as possible and ease the decoding process. As it turns out, this problem can be solved elegantly using the Perron–Frobenius (PF) Theorem [18]. Essentially, since every station is required to satisfy a fixed number of receivers (in the standard formulation, there is actually one receiver per station), the system can be represented in a matrix form that has some useful properties.

We now consider a new variant of the problem in which every station has to satisfy a continuous *zone* rather than a fixed number of points. The motivation for this formulation is that it allows one to attain an optimal complete coverage of the reception map. We now define the problem formally.

In the *Power Control for Voronoi Diagram* (PCVD) problem, one is given a network of $n$ stations $S = \{s_0, \ldots, s_{n-1}\}$ embedded in some $d$-dimensional bounded polygon[3] $\mathcal{P}$ and the task is to find an optimal power assignment for the stations, so as to make the reception threshold $\beta$ as high as possible while still $\text{SINR}_\mathcal{A}(s_i, p) \geq \beta$ for every $s_i$ and every point $p \in \text{VOR}(s_i) \cap \mathcal{P}$.

Note that without the convexity property within $\mathcal{VH}_\mathcal{A}(s_i)$ zones, established in the previous section, it is unclear how to formulate this problem by using a *finite* set of inequalities. This is because each Voronoi cell consists of infinitely

---

[3] The role of $\mathcal{P}$ is to guarantee that all Voronoi cells restricted to $\mathcal{P}$ are bounded.

many reception points, each of which must satisfy an SINR constraint. Due to the convexity property, we can provide the following succinct representation of the problem. For every station $s_i \in S$, let $\mathcal{V}_i$ be the vertex set[4] of the bounded polytope $\mathrm{VOR}(s_i) \cap \mathcal{P}$. Let $m = \sum_{i=0}^{n-1} |\mathcal{V}_i|$. The optimization task consists of $m$ inequalities and $n + 1$ variables ($n$ variables corresponding to the power assignment and $\beta$). This yields the following formulation.

$$\text{maximize } \beta \text{ subject to:} \tag{9}$$
$$\mathrm{SINR}(s_i, p) \geq \beta \text{ for every } s_i \in S \text{ and } p \in \mathcal{V}_i \,.$$

We first claim that this is a correct formulation for the Power Control for Voronoi Diagram problem. Let $\beta^*$ be the optimum solution of Program (9). By the feasibility of this solution, $\mathrm{SINR}(s_i, p) \geq \beta^*$ for every $p \in \mathcal{V}_i$. Since the reception zone is convex within its Voronoi cell, we get that $\mathrm{SINR}(s_i, p) \geq \beta^*$ for every $p \in \mathrm{VOR}(s_i)$ (in particular, in the optimum $\beta$, the reception zone contains the Voronoi cell of the station).

To solve Program (9), note that for any fixed $\beta$, the inequalities are linear in the $n$ transmission power variables and hence the resulting set of $m$ linear inequalities is solvable in polynomial time. A nearly optimum power assignment can then be found by searching for the best $\beta$ via binary search up to some desired approximation.

## 4.2 The Closest Station Point Location Problem

In the *Closest Station Point Location Problem*, one is given a nonuniform power network $\mathcal{A}$ with $n$ transmitting stations, $S = \{s_0, \ldots, s_{n-1}\}$. Given a query point $p \in \mathbb{R}^2$, it is required to answer whether $s_p$ is heard at $p$, where $s_p$ is the closest station to $p$ (i.e., $p \in \mathrm{VOR}(s_p)$).

Since nonuniform SINR zones are non-convex and non-fat, the preprocessing time and memory required in the approximate point location scheme of [10] are polynomial but costly. In this section we show that one can solve approximate point location tasks for *nonuniform* networks with effectively the same bounds as obtained for *uniform* networks (where $\psi_{max}$ and $N$ are bounded by constants), as long as the query point $p$ belongs to the Voronoi cell of the station that should be heard at $p$. Hence Lemma 5.1 of [3] yields the following.

**Theorem 4.** *For every $n$-station nonuniform power network with SINR+ Voronoi reception zones $\langle \mathcal{VH}_{\mathcal{A}}(s_1), \ldots, \mathcal{VH}_{\mathcal{A}}(s_n) \rangle$, it is possible to construct, in preprocessing time $O((\psi_{\max}/(\kappa \cdot N))^{3/\alpha} \cdot n^2 \cdot \epsilon^{-1})$, a data structure DS requiring memory of size $O((\psi_{\max}/(\kappa \cdot N))^{3/\alpha} \cdot n \cdot \epsilon^{-1})$ that imposes a $(2n + 1)$-wise partition $\widetilde{\mathcal{VH}} = \langle \mathcal{VH}_{\mathcal{A}}^+(s_1), \ldots, \mathcal{VH}_{\mathcal{A}}^+(s_n), \mathcal{VH}_{\mathcal{A}}^?(s_1), \ldots, \mathcal{VH}_{\mathcal{A}}^?(s_n), \mathcal{VH}_{\mathcal{A}}^- \rangle$ of the Euclidean plane, such that for every $i \in \{0, \ldots, n-1\}$,*

*(a) $\mathcal{VH}_{\mathcal{A}}^+(s_i) \subseteq \mathcal{VH}_{\mathcal{A}}(s_i)$,*
*(b) $\mathcal{VH}_{\mathcal{A}}(s_i) \cap \mathcal{VH}_{\mathcal{A}}^- = \emptyset$,*

---

[4] Note that the $\mathcal{V}_i$ sets are not disjoint and hence vertices are counted multiple times

(c) $\mathcal{VH}_{\mathcal{A}}^?(s_i)$ *is bounded and its area is at most an $\epsilon$-fraction of the area of* $\mathcal{VH}_{\mathcal{A}}(s_i)$.

*Furthermore, given a query point $p$, it is possible to extract from* DS, *in time* $O(\log n)$, *the zone in* $\mathcal{VH}$ *to which $p$ belongs. Hence the closest station point location query can be answered with approximation ratio $\epsilon$ and query time* $O(\log(\psi_{max} \cdot n/(N \cdot \kappa)))$, *where $\kappa = \min_{i,j} \text{dist}(s_i, s_j)$.*

For comparison, the general point location scheme of [10] requires $O(n^{10}\psi_{max}^4/\epsilon^2)$ preprocessing time and $O(n^8\psi_{max}^4/\epsilon^2)$ memory bits.

## 5    Conclusion

The Voronoi diagram of the base stations is a natural model for wireless networks in the plane. In this paper we show that restricting nonuniform reception zones to their corresponding Voronoi regions yields zones that are (almost) as nice as uniform reception zones. The increasing demand for mobile and high performance networks has created a need to dynamically determine the power with which each base station should transmit in order to optimize the network capacity. A common approach is to assign each base station its own Voronoi cell. When the network is dynamic, the Voronoi cell is no longer fixed and one can no longer compute in advance the parameters required for optimal network performance. We consider the resulting fundamental Power Control for Voronoi Diagram (PCVD) problem. The convexity property guaranteed for SINR reception zones within Voronoi regions enables us to discretize the PCVD problem while maintaining optimality. In addition, we showed that point location queries for SINR+Voronoi zones can be answered with almost the same bounds as for the uniform case. We believe that this approach may pave the way for designing additional algorithms for dynamic mobile networks

## References

1. Aronov, B., Katz, M.J.: Batched point location in SINR diagrams via algebraic tools. In: Halldórsson, M.M., Iwama, K., Kobayashi, N., Speckmann, B. (eds.) ICALP 2015. LNCS, vol. 9134, pp. 65–77. Springer, Heidelberg (2015)
2. Aurenhammer, F., Edelsbrunner, H.: An optimal algorithm for constructing the weighted voronoi diagram in the plane. Pattern Recognition **17** (1984)
3. Avin, C., Emek, Y., Kantor, E., Lotker, Z., Peleg, D., Roditty, L.: SINR diagrams: Convexity and its applications in wireless networks. J. ACM **59**(4) (2012)
4. Avin, C., Lotker, Z., Pignolet, Y.-A.: On the power of uniform power: capacity of wireless networks with bounded resources. In: Fiat, A., Sanders, P. (eds.) ESA 2009. LNCS, vol. 5757, pp. 373–384. Springer, Heidelberg (2009)
5. Basch, J., Guibas, L.J., Hershberger, J.: Data structures for mobile data (1997)
6. Chen, B., Jamieson, K., Balakrishnan, H., Morris, R.: Span: An energy-efficient coordination algorithm for topology maintenance in ad hoc wireless networks. Wireless Networks **8**, 481–494 (2002)

7. de Berg, M., Cheong, O., van Kreveld, M., Overmars, M.: Computational Ge-ometry: Algorithms and Applications. Springer-Verlag (2008)
8. Guibas, L.J., Mitchell, J.S.B., Roos, T.: Voronoi diagrams of moving points in the plane. In: Schmidt, G., Berghammer, R. (eds.) Graph-Theoretic Concepts in Computer Science. LNCS, vol. 570, pp. 113–125. Springer, Springer (1992)
9. Kantor, E., Lotker, Z., Parter, M., Peleg, D.: The topology of wireless communication. In: Proc. STOC (2011)
10. Kantor, E., Lotker, Z., Parter, M., Peleg, D.: The topology of wireless communication (2011). http://arxiv.org/pdf/1103.4566v2.pdf
11. Kantor, E., Lotker, Z., Parter, M., Peleg, D.: The minimum principle of SINR: a useful discretization tool for wireless communication. In: Proc. FOCS (2015)
12. Kim, Y., Kim, J., Nam, H., An, S.: Hex-grid based routing protocol in wireless sensor networks. In: Computat. Sci. & Eng., pp. 683–688 (2012)
13. Nocetti, F.G., Stojmenovic, I., Zhang, J.: Addressing and routing in hexagonal networks with applications for tracking mobile users and connection rerouting in cellular networks. IEEE Trans. Par. & Distr. Syst. 13, 963–971 (2002)
14. Ping, L.R., Rogers, G., Zhou, S., Zic, J.: Topology control with hexagonal tessellation 2, 91–98 (2007)
15. Stojmenovic, I.: Honeycomb networks: Topological properties and communication algorithms. IEEE Trans. Par. & Distr. Syst. 8, 1036–1042 (1997)
16. Xu, X., Li, Y., Gao, R., Tao, X.: Joint voronoi diagram and game theory-based power control scheme for the hetnet small cell networks. EURASIP J. Wireless Comm. and Networking 2014, 213 (2014)
17. Yousefi, S., Mousavi, M.S., Fathy, M.: Vehicular adhoc networks (vanets): challenges and perspectives. In: IEEE ITS Telecomm., pp. 761–766 (2006)
18. Zander, J.: Performance of optimum transmitter power control in cellular radiosystems. IEEE Tr. Vehic. Technol. 41, 57–62 (1992)

# Stable Leader Election in Population Protocols Requires Linear Time

David Doty[1] and David Soloveichik[2][✉]

[1] University of California, Davis, Davis, CA, USA
doty@ucdavis.edu
[2] University of Texas at Austin, Austin, TX, USA
david.soloveichik@utexas.edu

**Abstract.** A population protocol *stably elects a leader* if, for all $n$, starting from an initial configuration with $n$ agents each in an identical state, with probability 1 it reaches a configuration **y** that is *correct* (exactly one agent is in a special leader state $\ell$) and *stable* (every configuration reachable from **y** also has a single agent in state $\ell$). We show that any population protocol that stably elects a leader requires $\Omega(n)$ expected "parallel time" — $\Omega(n^2)$ expected total pairwise interactions — to reach such a stable configuration. Our result also informs the understanding of the time complexity of chemical self-organization by showing an essential difficulty in generating exact quantities of molecular species quickly.

## 1 Introduction

*Background.* Population protocols (PPs) were introduced by Angluin, Aspnes, Diamadi, Fischer, and Peralta[2] as a model of distributed computing in which the agents have very little computational power and no control over their schedule of interaction with other agents. They also can be thought of as a special case of Petri nets/vector addition systems[15,16], which were introduced in the 1960s as a model of concurrent processing. In addition to being an appropriate model for electronic computing scenarios such as mobile sensor networks, they are a useful abstraction of "fast-mixing" physical systems such as animal populations[18], chemical reaction networks, and gene regulatory networks[7].

A PP is defined by a finite set $\Lambda$ of *states* that each agent may have, together with a *transition function* $\delta : \Lambda \times \Lambda \to \Lambda \times \Lambda$.[1] Given states $r_1, r_2, p_1, p_2 \in \Lambda$, if $\delta(r_1, r_2) = (p_1, p_2)$ (denoted $r_1, r_2 \to p_1, p_2$) and a pair of agents in respective states $r_1$ and $r_2$ interact, then their states become $p_1$ and $p_2$.[2] A *configuration*

---

D. Doty—Author was supported by NSF grants CCF-1219274 and CCF-1442454 and the Molecular Programming Project under NSF grant 1317694.

D. Soloveichik—Author was supported by an NIGMS Systems Biology Center grant P50 GM081879 and NSF grant CCF-1442454.

[1] Some work on PPs allows "non-deterministic" transitions, in which the transition function maps to subsets of $\Lambda \times \Lambda$. Our results are independent of whether the PP is deterministic or nondeterministic in this manner.

[2] In the most generic model, there is no restriction on which agents are permitted to interact. If one prefers to think of the agents as existing on nodes of a graph, then it is the complete graph $K_n$ for a population of $n$ agents.

© Springer-Verlag Berlin Heidelberg 2015
Y. Moses (Ed.): DISC 2015, LNCS 9363, pp. 602–616, 2015.
DOI: 10.1007/978-3-662-48653-5_40

of a PP is a vector $\mathbf{c} \in \mathbb{N}^\Lambda$ describing, for each state $s \in \Lambda$, the *count* $\mathbf{c}(s)$ of how many agents are in state $s$. Executing a transition $r_1, r_2 \to p_1, p_2$ alters the configuration by decrementing the counts of states $r_1$ and $r_2$ by 1 each and incrementing $p_1$ and $p_2$ by 1 each.[3]

Associated with a PP is a set of *valid initial configurations* that we expect the PP to be able to handle.[4] Agents interact in a pairwise manner and change state based on the transition function. The next pair of agents to interact is chosen uniformly at random among the $n$ agents. (An interaction may be a "null transition" $r_1, r_2 \to r_1, r_2$.) We count the expected number of *interactions* until some event occurs, and then define the "parallel time" until this event as the expected number of interactions divided by the number of agents $n$. This measure of time is based on the natural parallel model where each agent participates in a constant number of interactions in one unit of time, hence $\Theta(n)$ total interactions are expected per unit time [4]. In this paper all references to "time" refer to parallel time.

In order to define error-free computation in PPs, we rely on to the notion of *stable* computation [5]. The PP must get to a configuration that is correct[5] and "stable" in the sense that no subsequent sequence of transitions can take the PP to an incorrect configuration. Error-free computation must be correct in an "adversarial" schedule of transitions: we require that from every configuration reachable by *any* sequence of transitions from the initial configuration, it is possible to reach to a correct stable configuration. Since the configuration space is finite, requiring stability is equivalent to requiring, under the randomized model, that a correct stable configuration is reached with probability 1.[6]

A PP works "with a leader" if there is a special "leader" state $\ell$, and every valid initial configuration $\mathbf{i}$ satisfies $\mathbf{i}(\ell) = 1$. This is in contrast to a uniform initial configuration ($\mathbf{i}(x) = n$ for some state $x$ and $\mathbf{i}(y) = 0$ for all states $y \neq x$) or an initial configuration only encoding the input ($\mathbf{i}(x_i) = n_i$ for $i \in \{1, \ldots, k\}$ to represent any input $(n_1, n_2, \ldots, n_k) \in \mathbb{N}^k$). It is known that the predicates $\phi : \mathbb{N}^k \to \{0, 1\}$ stably computable by PPs are exactly the semilinear predicates, whether an initial leader is allowed or not [5]. Although the initial leader does not alter the class of computable predicates, it may allow faster computation. Specifically, the fastest known PPs to stably compute semilinear predicates

---

[3] Possibly some of $r_1, r_2, p_1, p_2$ are equal to each other, so the count of a state could change by 0, 1, or 2.

[4] The set of valid initial configurations for a "self-stabilizing" PP is $\mathbb{N}^\Lambda$, where leader election is provably impossible [6]. We don't require the PP to work if started in any possible configuration, but rather allow potentially "helpful" initial configurations as long as they don't already have small count states (see "$\alpha$-dense" below).

[5] What "correct" means depends on the task. For computing a predicate, for example, $\Lambda$ is partitioned into "yes" and "no" voters, and a "correct" configuration is one in which every state present has the correct vote.

[6] It is also equivalent to requiring that every *fair* sequence of transitions reaches a correct stable configuration, where "fair" means that every configuration infinitely often reachable is infinitely often reached [5].

without a leader take as long as $\Theta(n)$ to converge.[7] In contrast, with a leader, it is known that any semilinear predicate can be stably computed with expected convergence time $O(\log^5 n)$ [4]. Thus, in certain circumstances, the presence of a initial leader seems to give PPs more computational power (e.g., to converge quickly). Angluin, Aspnes, and Eisenstat [4] asked whether polylogarithmic time stable computation of semilinear predicates is possible without a leader; absent a positive answer, the presence of a leader appears to add power to the model.

*Statement of main result.* Motivated in part by the apparent speedup possible with an initial leader, we ask how quickly a leader may be elected from a configuration lacking one. We pose the problem as follows: design a PP $\mathcal{P}$ with two special states $x$ (the initial state) and $\ell$ (the leader state, which may or may not be identical to $x$) such that, for every $n \in \mathbb{N}$, from the initial configuration $\mathbf{i}_n$ defined as $\mathbf{i}_n(x) = n$ and $\mathbf{i}_n(y) = 0$ for all other states $y$, has the following property. For every configuration $\mathbf{c}$ reachable from $\mathbf{i}_n$, there is a configuration $\mathbf{y}$ reachable from $\mathbf{c}$ that *has a stable leader.* By this we mean that in all configurations $\mathbf{y}'$ reachable from $\mathbf{y}$ (including $\mathbf{y}$ itself), $\mathbf{y}'(\ell) = 1$.[8]

There is a simple $O(n)$ expected time PP for stable leader election, with (assuming $x \equiv \ell$) the single transition $\ell, \ell \to \ell, f$. Our main theorem shows that *every* PP that stably elects a leader requires time $\Omega(n)$ to reach a state with a stable leader; thus the previous PP is asymptotically optimal.

*Multiple leader states, multiple leaders, and other initial configurations.* A more general notion of leader election is to identify a subset $\Psi \subset \Lambda$ of states that are all considered leader states, and to require the PP to eventually reach a configuration $\mathbf{y}$ in which $\sum_{\ell \in \Psi} \mathbf{y}(\ell) = 1$, and this sum is 1 in every configuration reachable from $\mathbf{y}$. This corresponds more appropriately to how leader states actually coordinate computation in PPs: a leader agent must remember some state information in between transitions (hence it changes state while remaining the unique leader). Our techniques actually show this stronger result as well (as explained in Section 3.2). Further, our result implies that a PP cannot elect any fixed quantity of leaders (e.g. exactly 256) or variable quantity of leaders under a fixed bound (e.g. at most 256) in sublinear expected time.

In the simplest formulation of the task of leader election, we always start with $n$ agents in state $x$ (as described above). Can we capture more generally leader election from a configuration "without a pre-existing leader"? Intuitively, we want to exclude initial configurations with states present in small but non-zero

---

[7] See "Open questions" for the distinction between time to *converge* and time to *stabilize.* In this paper, the time lower bound we prove is on stabilization.

[8] Note that this problem abstracts away the idea that the leader might be *useful* for something (such as computing predicates quickly). In particular, if a certain PP requires an initial leader, and the correctness of the PP depends on the count of the leader never exceeding 1, prior to the conclusion of the leader election, the presence of multiple leaders may result in unintended transitions. However, our main result is a impossibility theorem, showing that even if the objective is simplified to stable leader election, without requiring the leader to be useful for any subsequent task, this *still* requires $\Omega(n)$ time.

count. We can exclude such initial configurations, but allow otherwise deliberately prepared starting conditions, using the notion of $\alpha$-dense configurations: any state present in the initial configuration has count $\geq \alpha n$. Our general negative result (Theorem 3.2) implies that even starting with best-case initial configurations, as long as, for some constant $\alpha > 0$, they are all $\alpha$-dense, sublinear time leader election is impossible. An open question relates to weakening the notion of $\alpha$-dense (see below).

*Why simple proofs fail.* It is tempting to believe that our negative result could follow by a simple argument based on reasoning about the last transition to change the count of the leader.[9] However, as the following example illustrates, reasoning about the last transition to change the count of the leader is insufficient if some transition can produce a new leader. Consider the following PP, with initial configuration $\mathbf{i}$ given by $\mathbf{i}(r) = n^{1/4}$, $\mathbf{i}(x) = n - n^{1/4}$, and transitions:

$$r, r \to \ell, k \qquad (1) \qquad\qquad x, k \to k, k \qquad (3)$$
$$r, k \to k, k \qquad (2) \qquad\qquad \ell, \ell \to \ell, k \qquad (4)$$

It can be shown (the analysis is presented in the full version of this paper) that this PP stably elects a leader in sublinear time $O(n^{1/2} \log n)$ from the above described non-$\alpha$-dense initial configuration. Intuitively, it takes expected time $\Theta(n^{1/2})$ for transition (1) to occur for the first time, producing a single leader. Transition (4) ensures that if transition (1) occurs more than once, the PP will eventually stabilize to a single leader. However, with high probability, transitions (2) and (3) consume all $r$ and $x$ in $O(\log n)$ time *before* (1) executes a second time. The probability is high enough that the overall expected time to reach a state with a stable leader is sublinear. Although the above example does not violate our theorem (since it relies on a non-dense initial configuration), it shows that any proof of the main result cannot be based solely on reasoning about the final transition. The proof must also effectively establish that configurations, such as the initial configuration of the above PP, cannot be reached with high probability in sublinear time.

*Chemical reaction networks.* The main result and proof are stated in the language of PPs; however, the result holds for more general systems that have PPs as a special case. The discrete, stochastic chemical reaction network (CRN) model has been extensively used in the natural sciences to model chemical kinetics in a well-mixed solution [14], and the model is also used prescriptively for specifying the behavior of synthetic chemical systems [10,17]. As an essential form of self-organization, biological cells seem able to precisely control the count of certain molecules (centriole number [11] is a well studied example). How chemical systems transform relatively uncontrolled initial conditions to precisely controlled amounts of desired species is still not well understood. Our negative result

---

[9] Indeed, if we start with more than one leader, and no transition rule can produce a new leader, then we can easily prove the impossibility of sublinear time leader election as follows. To quickly reduce from two leaders to one, the other agent's state must be numerous in the population. Thus, the same transition could occur again, leaving us with no leaders.

applied to CRNs[10] implies that generating with probability 1 an exact count of a certain species, whether 1 or 256, is *necessarily* slower ($\Omega(n)$ time) than, for example, destroying all molecules of the species (through the reaction $X \to \varnothing$), which takes $O(\log(n))$ time.

*Open questions.* An important open question concerns the contrast between *convergence* and *stabilization*. We say a PP electing a leader *converges* when it stops changing the count of the leader (if it is correct, this count should be 1), and we say it *stabilizes* when it first enters a configuration from which the count of the leader *cannot* change. In many PPs these two events coincide, but it is possible to converge strictly before stabilizing.[11] Our proof shows only that stabilization must take expected $\Omega(n)$ time. We leave as an open question whether there is a PP that stably elects a leader and converges in expected $o(n)$ time. Recall that there are PPs that work with a leader to stably compute semilinear predicates with convergence time $O(\log^5 n)$ [4]. Thus if stable leader election can converge in expected sublinear time, by coupling the two PPs it might be possible to achieve stable computation of arbitrary semilinear predicates with sublinear convergence time.

It is similarly open to determine the optimal stabilization time for computing semilinear predicates. The stably computing PPs converging in $O(\log^5 n)$ time [4] provably require expected time $\Omega(n)$ to stabilize, and it is unknown whether faster stabilization is possible even with an initial leader.

The open question of Angluin, Aspnes, and Eisenstat [4] asks whether their efficient high-probability simulation of a space-bounded Turing machine by a PP could remove the assumption of an initial leader. That simulation has some small probability $\epsilon > 0$ of failure, so if one could elect a leader with a small probability $\epsilon' > 0$ of error and subsequently use it to drive the simulation, by the union bound the total probability of error would be at most $\epsilon + \epsilon'$ (i.e., still close to 0). However, it remains an open question whether the necessary PP exists. Alistairh and Gelashvili [1] showed that relaxing the requirement of $O(1)$ states to $O(\log^3 n)$ states allows for a leader to be elected with high probability in expected time $O(\log^3 n)$.[12]

Our general negative result applies to $\alpha$-dense initial configurations. However, is sublinear time stable leader election possible from other kinds of initial configurations that satisfy our intuition of not having preexisting leaders? It is known, for example, that for each $0 < \varepsilon < 1$, an initial configuration with $\Theta(n)$ agents in one state and $\Theta(n^\varepsilon)$ in another state can elect a leader in expected time $O(\log^2 n)$ with high probability [4], although this protocol has a positive

---

[10] Our result holds for any CRN that obeys Theorem 4.3, the precise constraints of which are specified in [13] (those constraints automatically apply to all PPs).

[11] For example, consider the execution of the PP example above (1)–(4). Suppose (1) occurs just once, and then transition (2) occurs repeatedly and eliminates all $r$ from the population. In this case, convergence happened when (1) occurred, but the PP stabilized only when all $r$ was eliminated. Although in our example both convergence and stabilization occur in sublinear expected time, in general stabilization may occur with a substantial delay after convergence.

[12] Indeed, our proof technique fails if the number of states is not constant with respect to $n$.

probability of failure. Above we give an example PP that stably elects a leader (convergence and stabilization) in $O(n^{1/2} \log n)$ time starting from an initial configuration with $\Theta(n)$ agents in one state and $\Theta(n^{1/4})$ in another state. In general we want to better characterize the initial configurations for which sublinear time leader election is possible.

## 2 Preliminaries

If $\Lambda$ is a finite set (in this paper, of *states*), we write $\mathbb{N}^\Lambda$ to denote the set of functions $\mathbf{c} : \Lambda \to \mathbb{N}$. Equivalently, we view an element $\mathbf{c} \in \mathbb{N}^\Lambda$ as a vector of $|\Lambda|$ nonnegative integers, with each coordinate "labeled" by an element of $\Lambda$. Given $s \in \Lambda$ and $\mathbf{c} \in \mathbb{N}^\Lambda$, we refer to $\mathbf{c}(s)$ as the *count of $s$ in $\mathbf{c}$*. Let $\|\mathbf{c}\| = \|\mathbf{c}\|_1 = \sum_{s \in \Lambda} \mathbf{c}(s)$ denote the total number of agents. We write $\mathbf{c} \le \mathbf{c}'$ to denote that $\mathbf{c}(s) \le \mathbf{c}'(s)$ for all $s \in \Lambda$. Since we view vectors $\mathbf{c} \in \mathbb{N}^\Lambda$ equivalently as multisets of elements from $\Lambda$, if $\mathbf{c} \le \mathbf{c}'$ we say $\mathbf{c}$ is a *subset* of $\mathbf{c}'$. It is sometimes convenient to use multiset notation to denote vectors, e.g., $\{x, x, y\}$ and $\{2x, y\}$ both denote the vector $\mathbf{c}$ defined by $\mathbf{c}(x) = 2$, $\mathbf{c}(y) = 1$, and $\mathbf{c}(z) = 0$ for all $z \notin \{x, y\}$. Given $\mathbf{c}, \mathbf{c}' \in \mathbb{N}^\Lambda$, we define the vector component-wise operations of addition $\mathbf{c} + \mathbf{c}'$, subtraction $\mathbf{c} - \mathbf{c}'$, and scalar multiplication $m\mathbf{c}$ for $m \in \mathbb{N}$. For a set $\Delta \subset \Lambda$, we view a vector $\mathbf{c} \in \mathbb{N}^\Delta$ equivalently as a vector $\mathbf{c} \in \mathbb{N}^\Lambda$ by assuming $\mathbf{c}(s) = 0$ for all $s \in \Lambda \setminus \Delta$.

A *population protocol (PP)* is a pair $\mathcal{P} = (\Lambda, \delta)$,[13] where $\Lambda$ is a finite set of *states*, and $\delta : \Lambda \times \Lambda \to \Lambda \times \Lambda$ is the (symmetric) *transition function*. A *configuration* of a PP is a vector $\mathbf{c} \in \mathbb{N}^\Lambda$, with the interpretation that $\mathbf{c}(s)$ agents are in state $s$. By convention, the value $n \in \mathbb{Z}^+$ represents the total number of agents $\|\mathbf{c}\|$. A *transition* is a 4-tuple $\alpha = (r_1, r_2, p_1, p_2) \in \Lambda^4$, written $\alpha : r_1, r_2 \to p_1, p_2$, such that $\delta(r_1, r_2) = (p_1, p_2)$. This paper typically defines a PP by a list of transitions, with $\delta$ implicit (there is a null transition $\delta(r_1, r_2) = (r_1, r_2)$ if a different transition is not specified). If an agent in state $r_1$ interacts with an agent in state $r_2$, then they change states to $p_1$ and $p_2$.

More formally, given a configuration $\mathbf{c}$ and transition $\alpha : r_1, r_2 \to p_1, p_2$, we say that $\alpha$ is *applicable* to $\mathbf{c}$ if $\mathbf{c} \ge \{r_1, r_2\}$, i.e., $\mathbf{c}$ contains 2 agents, one in state $r_1$ and one in state $r_2$. If $\alpha$ is applicable to $\mathbf{c}$, then write $\alpha(\mathbf{c})$ to denote the configuration $\mathbf{c} - \{r_1, r_2\} + \{p_1, p_2\}$ (i.e., the configuration that results from applying $\alpha$ to $\mathbf{c}$); otherwise $\alpha(\mathbf{c})$ is undefined. A finite or infinite sequence of transitions $(\alpha_i)$ is a *transition sequence*. Given an initial configuration $\mathbf{c}_0$ and a transition sequence $(\alpha_i)$, the induced *execution sequence* (or *path*) is a finite or infinite sequence of configurations $(\mathbf{c}_0, \mathbf{c}_1, \dots)$ such that, for all $\mathbf{c}_i$ ($i \ge 1$), $\mathbf{c}_i = \alpha_{i-1}(\mathbf{c}_{i-1})$. If a finite execution sequence, with associated transition sequence $q$, starts with $\mathbf{c}$ and ends with $\mathbf{c}'$, we write $\mathbf{c} \Longrightarrow_q \mathbf{c}'$. We write $\mathbf{c} \Longrightarrow \mathbf{c}'$

---

[13] We give a slightly different formalism than that of [5] for population protocols. The main difference is that since we are not deciding a predicate, there is no notion of inputs being mapped to states or states being mapped to outputs. Another difference is that we assume (for the sake of brevity in some explanations, not because the difference is essential to the proof) the transition function is symmetric (so there is no notion of a "sender" and "receiver" agent as in [5]; the unordered pair of states completely determines the next pair of states).

if such a transition sequence exists (i.e., it is possible for the system to reach from $\mathbf{c}$ to $\mathbf{c}'$) and we say that $\mathbf{c}'$ is *reachable* from $\mathbf{c}$. If it is understood from context what is the initial configuration $\mathbf{i}$, then say $\mathbf{c}$ is simply *reachable* if $\mathbf{i} \Longrightarrow \mathbf{c}$. Note that this notation omits mention of $\mathcal{P}$; we always deal with a single PP at a time, so it is clear from context which PP is defining the transitions. If a transition $\alpha : r_1, r_2 \rightarrow p_1, p_2$ has the property that for $i \in \{1, 2\}$, $r_i \notin \{p_1, p_2\}$, or if $(r_1 = r_2$ and $(r_i \neq p_1$ or $r_i \neq p_2))$, then we say that $\alpha$ *consumes* $r_i$. In other words, applying $\alpha$ reduces the count of $r_i$. We similarly say that $\alpha$ *produces* $p_i$ if it increases the count of $p_i$.

We will find ourselves frequently dealing with infinite sequences of configurations.[14] The following lemma, used frequently in reasoning about population protocols, shows that we can always take a nondecreasing subsequence.

**Lemma 2.1 (Dickson's Lemma [12]).** *Any infinite sequence* $\mathbf{x}_0, \mathbf{x}_1, \ldots \in \mathbb{N}^k$ *has an infinite nondecreasing subsequence* $\mathbf{x}_{i_0} \leq \mathbf{x}_{i_1} \leq \ldots$, *where* $i_0 < i_1 < \ldots$.

In any configuration the next interaction is chosen by selecting a pair of agents uniformly at random and applying transition function $\delta$. To measure time we count the expected total number of interactions (including null), and divide by the number of agents $n$. (In the population protocols literature, this is often called "parallel time"; i.e. $n$ interactions among a population of $n$ agents corresponds to one unit of time). Let $\mathbf{c} \in \mathbb{N}^\Lambda$ and $C \subseteq \mathbb{N}^\Lambda$. Denote the probability that the PP reaches from $\mathbf{c}$ to some configuration $\mathbf{c}' \in C$ by $\Pr[\mathbf{c} \Longrightarrow C]$. If $\Pr[\mathbf{c} \Longrightarrow C] = 1$,[15] define the *expected time to reach from* $\mathbf{c}$ *to* $C$, denoted $\mathsf{T}[\mathbf{c} \Longrightarrow C]$, to be the expected number of interactions to reach from $\mathbf{c}$ to some $\mathbf{c}' \in C$, divided by the number of agents $n$.

## 3    Main Results

### 3.1    Impossibility of Sublinear Time Stable Leader Election

We consider the following *stable leader election* problem. Suppose that each PP $\mathcal{P} = (\Lambda, \delta)$ we consider has a specially designated state $\ell \in \Lambda$, which we call the *leader state*. Informally, the goal of stable leader election is to be guaranteed to reach a configuration with count 1 of $\ell$ (a leader has been "elected"), from which no transition sequence can change the count of $\ell$ (the leader is "stable"). We also assume there is a special initial state $x$ (it could be that $x \equiv \ell$ but it is not required), such that the only valid initial configurations $\mathbf{i}$ are of the form $\mathbf{i}(x) > 0$ and $\mathbf{i}(y) = 0$ for all states $y \in \Lambda \setminus \{x\}$. We write $\mathbf{i}_n$ to denote such an initial configuration with $\mathbf{i}_n(x) = n$.

**Definition 3.1.** *A configuration* $\mathbf{y}$ *is* stable *if, for all* $\mathbf{y}'$ *such that* $\mathbf{y} \Longrightarrow \mathbf{y}'$, $\mathbf{y}'(\ell) = \mathbf{y}(\ell)$ *(in other words, after reaching* $\mathbf{y}$, *the count of* $\ell$ *cannot change);* $\mathbf{y}$ *is said to have a* stable leader *if it is stable and* $\mathbf{y}(\ell) = 1$.

---

[14] In general these will not be *execution* sequences. Typically none of the configurations are reachable from any others because they are configurations with increasing numbers of agents.

[15] Since PP's have a finite reachable configuration space, this is equivalent to requiring that for all $\mathbf{x}$ reachable from $\mathbf{c}$, there is a $\mathbf{c}' \in C$ reachable from $\mathbf{x}$.

The following definition captures our notion of stable leader election. It requires the PP to be "guaranteed" eventually to reach a configuration with a stable leader.

**Definition 3.2.** *We say a PP elects a leader stably if, for all $n \in \mathbb{Z}^+$, for all $\mathbf{c}$ such that $\mathbf{i}_n \Longrightarrow \mathbf{c}$, there exists $\mathbf{y}$ with a stable leader such that $\mathbf{c} \Longrightarrow \mathbf{y}$.*

In other words, every reachable configuration can reach to a configuration with a stable leader. It is well-known [5] that the above definition is equivalent to requiring that the PP reaches a configuration with a stable leader with probability 1.

**Definition 3.3.** *Let $t : \mathbb{Z}^+ \to \mathbb{R}^+$, and let $Y$ be the set of all configurations with a stable leader. We say a PP elects a leader stably in time $t(n)$ if, for all $n \in \mathbb{Z}^+$, $\mathsf{T}[\mathbf{i}_n \Longrightarrow Y] \leq t(n)$.*

Our main theorem says that stable leader election requires at least linear time to stabilize:

**Theorem 3.1.** *If a PP stably elects a leader in time $t(n)$, then $t(n) = \Omega(n)$.*

Thus a PP that elects a leader in sublinear time cannot do so stably, i.e., it must have a positive probability of failure.

The high-level strategy to prove Theorem 3.1 is as follows. With high probability the PP initially goes from configuration $\mathbf{i}_n$ to configuration $\mathbf{x}_n$, such that in the sequence $(\mathbf{x}_n)$ for increasing population size $n$, every state count grows without bound as $n \to \infty$ (indeed $\Omega(n)$); this follows from Theorem 4.3. We then show that any such configuration must have an "$O(1)$-bottleneck transition" before reaching a configuration with a stable leader (informally this means that every transition sequence from $\mathbf{x}_n$ to a configuration $\mathbf{y}$ with a stable leader must have a transition in which both input states have count $O(1)$, depending on the PP but not on $n$). Since it takes expected time $\Omega(n)$ to execute a transition when both states have constant count, from any such configuration it requires linear time to stably elect a leader. Since one of these configurations is reached from the initial configuration with high probability, those configurations' contribution to the overall expected time dominates, showing that the expected time to stably elect a leader is linear.

## 3.2   More General Impossibility Result in Terms of Inapplicable Transitions and Dense Configurations

Rather than proving Theorem 3.1 using the notion of leader stability directly, we prove a more general result concerning the notion of a set of inapplicable transitions. The two generalizations are as follows. (1) A configuration $\mathbf{y}$ is stable by Definition 3.1 if no transition altering the count of $\ell$ is applicable in any configuration reachable from $\mathbf{y}$; Definition 3.4 generalizes this to an arbitrary subset $Q$ of transitions. (2) The valid initial configurations of Section 3.1 are those with $\mathbf{i}_n(x) = n$ and $\mathbf{i}_n(y) = 0$ for all $y \in \Lambda \setminus \{x\}$; Theorem 3.2 generalizes this to any set $I$ of configurations that are all "$\alpha$-dense" (defined below) for a fixed $\alpha > 0$ independent of $n$, with a weak sort of "closure under addition" property: namely, that for infinitely many $\mathbf{i}, \mathbf{i}' \in I$, we have $\mathbf{i} + \mathbf{i}' \in I$.

**Definition 3.4.** *Let $Q$ be a set of transitions. A configuration $\mathbf{y} \in \mathbb{N}^\Lambda$ is said to be $Q$-stable if no transition in $Q$ is applicable in any configuration reachable from $\mathbf{y}$.*

If we let $Q$ be the set of transitions that alter the count of the leader state $\ell$, then a $Q$-stable configuration $\mathbf{y}$ with $\mathbf{y}(\ell) = 1$ exactly corresponds to the property of having a stable leader.

Let $I \subseteq \mathbb{N}^\Lambda$ and $Q$ be a set of transitions. Let $Y$ be the set of $Q$-stable configurations reachable from some configuration in $I$. We say that a PP $\mathcal{P} = (\Lambda, \delta)$ $Q$-stabilizes from $I$ if, for any $\mathbf{i} \in I$, $\Pr[\mathbf{i} \Longrightarrow Y] = 1$.[16] If $I$ and $Q$ are understood from context, we say that $\mathcal{P}$ *stabilizes*. For a time bound $t(n)$, we say that $\mathcal{P}$ stabilizes in *expected time* $t(n)$ if, for all $\mathbf{i} \in I$ such that $\|\mathbf{i}\| = n$, $\mathsf{T}[\mathbf{i} \Longrightarrow Y] \leq t(n)$.

To prove our time lower bound, we show that a "slow" transition necessarily occurs, which means that the counts of the two states in the transition are "small" when it occurs. We will pick a particular nondecreasing infinite sequence $C$ of configurations and define "small" relative to it: the "small count" states are those whose counts are bounded in $C$ (denoted $\mathsf{bdd}(C)$ below).

**Definition 3.5.** *For an (infinite) set/sequence of configurations $C$, let $\mathsf{bdd}(C)$ be the set of states $\{\, s \in \Lambda \mid (\exists b \in \mathbb{N})(\forall \mathbf{c} \in C)\ \mathbf{c}(s) < b \,\}$. Let $\mathsf{unbdd}(C) = \Lambda \setminus \mathsf{bdd}(C)$.*

*Remark 3.1.* Note that if $C = (\mathbf{c}_m)$ is a nondecreasing sequence, then for all $k \in \mathbb{N}$, there is $\mathbf{c}_m$ such that for all $s \in \mathsf{unbdd}(\mathbf{c}_m)$, $\mathbf{c}_m(s) \geq k$. (Note that if $C$ is not nondecreasing, the conclusion can fail; e.g., $\mathbf{c}_m(s_1) = m, \mathbf{c}_m(s_2) = 0$ for $m$ even and $\mathbf{c}_m(s_1) = 0, \mathbf{c}_m(s_2) = m$ for $m$ odd.)

Let $0 < \alpha \leq 1$. We say that a configuration $\mathbf{c}$ is $\alpha$-*dense* if for all $s \in \Lambda$, $\mathbf{c}(s) > 0$ implies that $\mathbf{c}(s) \geq \alpha\|\mathbf{c}\|$, i.e., all states present in $\mathbf{c}$ occupy at least an $\alpha$ fraction of the total count of agents.

Theorem 3.1 is implied by the next theorem, which the rest of the paper is devoted to proving.

**Theorem 3.2.** *Let $\mathcal{P} = (\Lambda, \delta)$, let $Q$ be any subset of transitions of $\mathcal{P}$, let $\alpha > 0$, and let $I \subseteq \mathbb{N}^\Lambda$ be a set of $\alpha$-dense initial configurations such that, for infinitely many $\mathbf{i}, \mathbf{i}' \in I$, $\mathbf{i} + \mathbf{i}' \in I$. Let $Y$ be the set of $Q$-stable configurations reachable from $I$, and let $\Delta = \mathsf{bdd}(Y)$. Suppose $\mathcal{P}$ $Q$-stabilizes from $I$ in expected time $o(n)$. Then there are infinitely many $\mathbf{y} \in Y$ such that $\forall s \in \Delta$, $\mathbf{y}(s) = 0$.*

In other words, if some states have "small" count in all reachable stable configurations, then there is a reachable stable configuration in which those states have count 0. A PP $\mathcal{P}$ that stably elects a leader is a PP in which $Q$ is the set of transitions that alter the count of $\ell$, $I = \{\, \mathbf{i}_n \mid n \in \mathbb{N} \,\}$ (note all $\mathbf{i}_n$ are 1-dense), $Y$ is the set of configurations reachable from $I$ with a stable leader, and $\mathcal{P}$ $Q$-stabilizes from $I$. Hence by Theorem 3.2, if $\mathcal{P}$ stabilizes in expected time $o(n)$, there is a stable reachable $\mathbf{y}$ where $\mathbf{y}(\ell) = 0$, a contradiction. Thus Theorem 3.1 follows from Theorem 3.2.

---

[16] Recall that the condition $\Pr[\mathbf{i} \Longrightarrow Y] = 1$ is equivalent to $[(\forall \mathbf{c} \in \mathbb{N}^\Lambda)\ \mathbf{i} \Longrightarrow \mathbf{c}$ implies $(\exists \mathbf{y} \in Y)\ \mathbf{c} \Longrightarrow \mathbf{y}]$.

We can also use Theorem 3.2 to prove that stable leader election requires linear time under the more relaxed requirement that there is a set $\Psi \subset \Lambda$ of "leader states," and the goal of the PP is to reach a configuration $\mathbf{y}$ in which $\sum_{\ell \in \Psi} \mathbf{y}(\ell) = 1$ and stays 1 in any configuration reachable from $\mathbf{y}$. Choosing $Q$ as the set of transitions that alter that sum, Theorem 3.2 implies this form of stable leader election also requires $\Omega(n)$ expected time.

Throughout the rest of this paper, fix $\mathcal{P} = (\Lambda, \delta)$, $\alpha$, $I$, and $Q$ as in the statement of Theorem 3.2.

# 4   Technical Tools

## 4.1   Bottleneck Transitions Require Linear Time

This section proves a straightforward observation used in the proof of our main theorem. It states that, if to get from a configuration $\mathbf{x} \in \mathbb{N}^\Lambda$ to some configuration in a set $Y \subseteq \mathbb{N}^\Lambda$, it is necessary to execute a transition $r_1, r_2 \rightarrow p_1, p_2$ in which the counts of $r_1$ and $r_2$ are both at most some number $b$, then the expected time to reach from $\mathbf{x}$ to some configuration in $Y$ is $\Omega(n/b^2)$.

Let $b \in \mathbb{N}$. We say that transition $\alpha : r_1, r_2 \rightarrow p_1, p_2$ is a $b$-bottleneck for configuration $\mathbf{c}$ if $\mathbf{c}(r_1) \leq b$ and $\mathbf{c}(r_2) \leq b$.

**Observation 4.1.** *Let* $b \in \mathbb{N}$, $\mathbf{x} \in \mathbb{N}^\Lambda$, *and* $Y \subseteq \mathbb{N}^\Lambda$ *such that* $\Pr[\mathbf{x} \Longrightarrow Y] = 1$. *If every transition sequence taking* $\mathbf{x}$ *to a configuration* $\mathbf{y} \in Y$ *has a* $b$-*bottleneck, then* $\mathsf{T}[\mathbf{x} \Longrightarrow Y] \geq \frac{n-1}{2(b \cdot |\Lambda|)^2}$.

A proof of Observation 4.1 is given in the full version of this paper. Intuitively, it follows because if two states $r_1$ and $r_2$ have count at most $b$, where $b$ is a constant independent of $n$, then we expect to wait $\Omega(n)$ time before agents in states $r_1$ and $r_2$ interact.

**Corollary 4.2.** *Let* $\gamma > 0$, $b \in \mathbb{N}$, $\mathbf{c} \in \mathbb{N}^\Lambda$, *and* $X, Y \subseteq \mathbb{N}^\Lambda$ *such that* $\Pr[\mathbf{c} \Longrightarrow X] \geq \gamma$, $\Pr[\mathbf{c} \Longrightarrow Y] = 1$, *and every transition sequence from every* $\mathbf{x} \in X$ *to some* $\mathbf{y} \in Y$ *has a* $b$-*bottleneck. Then* $\mathsf{T}[\mathbf{c} \Longrightarrow Y] \geq \gamma \frac{n-1}{2(b \cdot |\Lambda|)^2}$.

## 4.2   Sublinear Time from Dense Configurations Implies Bottleneck Free Path from Configurations with Every State "Populous"

The following theorem, along with Corollary 4.2, fully captures the probability theory necessary to prove our main theorem.[17] Given it and Corollary 4.2, Theorem 3.2 is provable (through Lemma 4.1) using only combinatorial arguments about reachability between configurations.

---

[17] Theorem 4.3 was proven for a more general model called Chemical Reaction Networks (CRNs) that obey a certain technical condition [13]; as observed in that paper, the class of CRNs obeying that condition includes all PPs, so the theorem holds unconditionally for PPs. The theorem proved in [13] is more general than Theorem 4.3, but we have stated a corollary of it here. A similar statement is implicit in the proof sketch of Lemma 5 of a technical report on a variant model called "urn automata" that has PPs as a special case [3].

For ease of notation, we assume throughout this paper that all states in $\Lambda$ are *producible*, meaning they have positive count in some reachable configuration. Otherwise the following theorem applies only to states that are actually producible. Recall that for $\alpha > 0$, a configuration $\mathbf{c}$ is $\alpha$-*dense* if for all $s \in \Lambda$, $\mathbf{c}(s) > 0$ implies that $\mathbf{c}(s) \geq \alpha \|\mathbf{c}\|$. Say that $\mathbf{c} \in \mathbb{N}^\Lambda$ is *full* if $(\forall s \in \Lambda)\ \mathbf{c}(s) > 0$, i.e., every state is present. The following theorem states that with high probability, a PP will reach from an $\alpha$-dense configuration to a configuration in which all states are present (full) in "high" count ($\beta$-dense, for some $0 < \beta < \alpha$).

**Theorem 4.3 (adapted from [13]).** *Let* $\mathcal{P} = (\Lambda, \delta)$ *be a PP and* $\alpha > 0$. *Then there are constants* $\epsilon, \beta > 0$ *such that, letting ,* $X = \{\ \mathbf{x} \in \mathbb{N}^\Lambda \mid \mathbf{x}\ \text{is full and}$ $\beta$-*dense* $\}$, *for all* $\alpha$-*dense configurations* $\mathbf{i}$, $\Pr[\mathbf{i} \Longrightarrow X] \geq 1 - 2^{-\epsilon\|\mathbf{i}\|}$.

In [13], the theorem is stated for "sufficiently large" $\|\mathbf{i}\|$, but of course one can always choose $\epsilon$ to be small enough to make it true for all $\mathbf{i}$.

The following lemma reduces the problem of proving Theorem 3.2 to a combinatorial statement involving only reachability among configurations (and the lack of bottleneck transitions between them). In Section 5 we will prove Theorem 3.2 by showing that the existence of the configurations $\mathbf{x}_m$ and $\mathbf{y}_m$ and the transition sequence $p_m$ in the following lemma implies that we can reach a $Q$-stable configuration $\mathbf{v} \in \mathbb{N}^\Gamma$, where $\Gamma = \mathsf{unbdd}(Y)$ and $Y$ is the set of $Q$-stable configurations reachable from $I$.

**Lemma 4.1.** *Let* $\alpha > 0$. *Let* $\mathcal{P} = (\Lambda, \delta)$ *be a PP such that, for some set of transitions* $Q$ *and infinite set of* $\alpha$-*dense initial configurations* $I$, $\mathcal{P}$ *reaches a set of* $Q$-*stable configurations* $Y$ *in expected time* $o(n)$. *Then for all* $m \in \mathbb{N}$, *there is a configuration* $\mathbf{x}_m$ *reachable from some* $\mathbf{i} \in I$ *and transition sequence* $p_m$ *such that (1)* $\mathbf{x}_m(s) \geq m$ *for all* $s \in \Lambda$, *(2)* $\mathbf{x}_m \Longrightarrow_{p_m} \mathbf{y}_m$, *where* $\mathbf{y}_m \in Y$, *and (3)* $p_m$ *has no* $m$-*bottleneck transition.*

The proof of Lemma 4.1 is in the full version of this paper. Intuitively, the lemma follows from the fact that states $\mathbf{x}_m$ are reached with high probability by Theorem 4.3, and if no paths such as $p_m$ existed, then all paths from $\mathbf{x}_m$ to a stable configuration would have a bottleneck and require linear time. Since $\mathbf{x}_m$ is reached with high probability, this would imply the entire expected time is linear.

### 4.3    Transition Ordering Lemma

The following lemma was first proven (in the more general model of Chemical Reaction Networks) in [8]. Intuitively, the lemma states that a "fast" transition sequence (meaning one without a bottleneck transition) that decreases certain states from large counts to small counts must contain transitions of a certain restricted form. In particular the form is as follows: if $\Delta$ is the set of states whose counts decrease from large to small, then we can write the states in $\Delta$ in some order $d_1, d_2, \ldots, d_k$, such that for each $1 \leq i \leq k$, there is a transition $\alpha_i$ that consumes $d_i$, and every other state involved in $\alpha_i$ is either not in $\Delta$, or comes later in the ordering. These transitions will later be used to do controlled "surgery" on fast transition sequences, because they give a way to alter the count of $d_i$, by inserting or removing the transitions $\alpha_i$, knowing that this will not affect the counts of $d_1, \ldots, d_{i-1}$.

**Lemma 4.2 (Adapted from [8]).** *Let $b_1, b_2 \in \mathbb{N}$ such that $b_2 > |\Lambda| \cdot b_1$. Let $\mathbf{x}, \mathbf{y} \in \mathbb{N}^\Lambda$ such that $\mathbf{x} \Longrightarrow \mathbf{y}$ via transition sequence $q$ that does not contain a $b_2$-bottleneck. Define $\Delta = \{ d \in \Lambda \mid \mathbf{x}(d) \geq b_2 \text{ and } \mathbf{y}(d) \leq b_1 \}$. Then there is an order on $\Delta$, so that we may write $\Delta = \{d_1, d_2, \ldots, d_k\}$, such that, for all $i \in \{1, \ldots, k\}$, there is a transition $\alpha_i$ of the form $d_i, s_i \to o_i, o_i'$, such that $s_i, o_i, o_i' \notin \{d_1, \ldots, d_i\}$, and $\alpha_i$ occurs at least $(b_2 - |\Lambda| \cdot b_1)/|\Lambda|^2$ times in $q$.*

The intuition behind the proof is that the ordering is given (this is somewhat oversimplified) by the last time in $q$ the state's count drops below $b_2$. Each state in $\Delta$ must go from "large" count ($b_2$) to "small" count ($b_1$), so when a state $d_i$ is below count $b_2$, if a non-$b_2$-bottleneck transition $d_i, d_j \to \ldots$ occurs, then $d_j$ must exceed $b_2$. This, in turn, means that state $d_j$ cannot yet have dropped below count $b_2$ for the last time, so $d_j$ is later in the ordering. The full argument is more subtle (and uses a different ordering) because it must establish that the transition's *outputs* in $\Delta$ also come later in the ordering.

## 5    Proof of Theorem 3.2

By Lemma 4.1, there are sequences $(\mathbf{x}_m)$ and $(\mathbf{y}_m)$ of configurations, and a sequence $(p_m)$ of transition sequences, such that, for all $m$, (1) $\mathbf{x}_m(s) \geq m$ for all $s \in \Lambda$, and for some $\mathbf{i} \in I$, $\mathbf{i} \Longrightarrow \mathbf{x}_m$, (2) $\mathbf{y}_m$ is $Q$-stable, and (3) $\mathbf{x}_m \Longrightarrow_{p_m} \mathbf{y}_m$ and $p_m$ does not contain an $m$-bottleneck.

By Dickson's Lemma there is an infinite subsequence of $(\mathbf{x}_m)$ for which both $(\mathbf{x}_m)$ and $(\mathbf{y}_m)$ are nondecreasing. Without loss of generality, we take $(\mathbf{x}_m)$ and $(\mathbf{y}_m)$ to be these subsequences. Let $\Delta = \mathsf{bdd}(\mathbf{y}_m)$ and $\Gamma = \mathsf{unbdd}(\mathbf{y}_m)$.

To prove Theorem 3.2 we need to show that there are configurations in $Y$ (the set of $Q$-stable configurations reachable from $I$) that contain states only in $\Gamma$. Note that stability is closed downward: subsets of a $Q$-stable configuration are $Q$-stable. For any fixed $\mathbf{v}^\Gamma \in \mathbb{N}^\Gamma$, $\mathbf{v}^\Gamma \leq \mathbf{y}_m$ for sufficiently large $m$, by the definition of $\Gamma$ (the states that grow unboundedly in $\mathbf{y}_m$ as $m \to \infty$). Thus *any* state $\mathbf{v}^\Gamma \in \mathbb{N}^\Gamma$ is automatically $Q$-stable. This is why Claims 5.1, 5.2, and 5.3 of this proof center around reaching configurations that have count 0 of every state in $\Delta$.

Recall the path $\mathbf{x}_m \Longrightarrow_{p_m} \mathbf{y}_m$ from Lemma 4.1. Intuitively, Claim 5.1 below says that because this path is $m$-bottleneck free, Lemma 4.2 applies, and its transitions can appended to the path to consume all states in $\Delta$ from $\mathbf{y}_m$, resulting in a configuration $\mathbf{z}_m^\Gamma$ that contains only states in $\Gamma$. The "cost" of this manipulation is that, to ensure the appended transitions are applicable, we add extra agents in specific states corresponding to $\mathbf{e} \in \mathbb{N}^\Lambda$. Claim 5.1 is not sufficient to prove Theorem 3.2 because of this additional $\mathbf{e}$; the subsequent Claims 5.2 and 5.3 will give us the machinery to handle it. The full proofs of Claims 5.1, 5.2, and 5.3 are given in the full version of this paper, and we give examples and intuition to explain them here.

**Claim 5.1.** *There is* $\mathbf{e} \in \mathbb{N}^{\Lambda}$ *such that for all large enough* $m$, *there is* $\mathbf{z}_m^{\Gamma} \in \mathbb{N}^{\Gamma}$, *such that* $\mathbf{x}_m + \mathbf{e} \Longrightarrow \mathbf{z}_m^{\Gamma}$.

*Example.* We illustrate Claim 5.1 through an example. Define a PP by the transitions

$$
\begin{array}{lr}
b, a \to f, c & \text{(5)} \\
b, c \to f, a & \text{(6)} \\
a, c \to f, f & \text{(7)}
\end{array}
\qquad\qquad
\begin{array}{lr}
f, c \to f, b & \text{(8)} \\
f, b \to f, f & \text{(9)}
\end{array}
$$

For convenience, for state $s \in \Lambda$, let $s$ also denote the count of that state in the configuration considered. Let configuration $\mathbf{x}_m$ be where $f = 100$, $a = 100$, $b = 100$, $c = 100$. Suppose a transition sequence $p_m$ without an $m$-bottleneck ($m = 100$) takes the PP from $\mathbf{x}_m$ to $\mathbf{y}_m$, in which $a = 3$, $b = 2$, $c = 1$, and $f = 394$. Then in the language of Lemma 4.2, $\Delta = \{a, b, c\}$; these states go from "large" count in $\mathbf{x}_m$ to "small" count in $\mathbf{y}_m$.

Our strategy is to add interactions to $p_m$ in order to reach a configuration $\mathbf{z}_m^{\Gamma}$ with $a = b = c = 0$. There are two issues we must deal with. First, to get rid of $a$ we may try to add 3 instances of (5) at the end of $p_m$. However, there is only enough $b$ for 2 instances. To eliminate such dependency, in Claim 5.1, whenever we add a transition $b, a \to f, c$, we add an extra agent in state $b$ to $\mathbf{e}$. (In general if we consume $r_2$ by adding transition $r_1, r_2 \to p_1, p_2$, we add an extra agent in state $r_1$ to $\mathbf{e}$.) Second, we need to prevent circularity in consuming and producing states. Imagine trying to add more executions of (5) to get $a$ to 0 and more of (6) to get $c$ to 0; this will fail because these transitions conserve the quantity $a + c$. To drive each of these states to 0, we must find some ordering on them so that each can be driven to 0 using a transition that does not affect the count of any state previously driven to 0.

Lemma 4.2 gives us a way to eliminate such dependency systematically. In the example above, we can find the ordering $d_1 \equiv a$, $d_2 \equiv c$, and $d_3 \equiv b$, with respective transitions (5) to drive $a$ to 0 (3 executions), (8) to drive $c$ to 0 (4 executions: 1 to consume the 1 copy of $c$ in $\mathbf{y}_m$, and 3 more to consume the extra 3 copies that were produced by the 3 extra executions of (5)), and (9) to drive $b$ to 0 (6 executions: 2 to consume 2 copies of $b$ in $\mathbf{y}_m$, and 4 more to consume the extra 4 copies that were produced by the 4 extra executions of (8)).

Intuitively, Claim 5.2 below works toward generating the vector of states $\mathbf{e}$ that we needed for Claim 5.1. The vector $\mathbf{e}$ can be split into the $\Delta$ component and the $\Gamma$ component; we will handle the $\Gamma$ component later. The "cost" for Claim 5.2 is that the path must be taken "in the context" of additional agents in states captured by $\mathbf{p}$. Importantly, the net effect of the path preserves $\mathbf{p}$, which will give us a way to "interleave" Claims 5.1 and 5.2 as shown in Claim 5.3.

**Claim 5.2.** *For all* $\mathbf{e}^{\Delta} \in \mathbb{N}^{\Delta}$, *there is* $\mathbf{p} \in \mathbb{N}^{\Lambda}$, *such that for all large enough* $m$, *there is* $\mathbf{w}_m^{\Gamma} \in \mathbb{N}^{\Gamma}$, *such that* $\mathbf{p} + \mathbf{x}_m \Longrightarrow \mathbf{p} + \mathbf{w}_m^{\Gamma} + \mathbf{e}^{\Delta}$, *and* $\mathsf{unbdd}(\mathbf{w}_m^{\Gamma}) = \Gamma$.

*Example.* Recall the example above illustrating Claim 5.1. Claim 5.2 is more difficult than Claim 5.1 for two reasons. First, we need to be able to obtain any counts of states $a$, $b$, $c$ (ie $e^{\Delta}$) and not only $a = b = c = 0$. Second, we no longer have the freedom to add extra states as $e$ and consume them. Note that $p$ cannot fulfill the same role as $e$ because $p$ must be recovered at the end.

For instance suppose $e^{\Delta}$ is $a = 7$, $b = 2$, $c = 1$. Recall that $y_m$ has $a = 3$, $b = 2$, $c = 1$. How can we generate additional 4 copies of $a$? Note that all transitions preserve or decrease the sum $a + b + c$. Thus we cannot solely add interactions to $p_m$ to get to our desired $e^{\Delta}$. The key is that we can increase $a$ by removing existing interactions from $p_m$ that consumed it. Indeed, Lemma 4.2 helps us by giving a lower bound on the number of instances of transitions (5),(8),(9) that must have occurred in $p_m$. (Note that in Claim 5.1, we didn't need to use the fact that these transitions occurred in $p_m$. Now, we need to ensure that there are enough instances for us to remove.) In our case, we can remove 4 instances of interaction (5), which also decreases $c$ by 4. To compensate for this, we can remove 4 instances of interaction (8), which also decreases $b$ by 4. Finally, we remove 4 instances of interaction (9). The net result is that we reach the configuration $a = 7$, $b = 2$, $c = 1$, $f = 130$.

Note that unlike in Claim 5.1, we have more potential for circularity now because we cannot add the other input to a transition as $e$. For example, we can't use transition (7) to affect $c$ because it affects $a$ (which we have previously driven to the desired count). Luckily, the ordering given by Lemma 4.2 avoids any circularity because the other input and both of the outputs come later in the ordering.

Importantly, as we remove interactions from $p_m$, we could potentially drive the count of some state temporarily negative. Performing these interactions in the context of more agents ($p$) ensures that the path can be taken.

**Claim 5.3.** *For infinitely many* $i \in I$, *there is* $v^{\Gamma} \in \mathbb{N}^{\Gamma}$ *such that* $i \Longrightarrow v^{\Gamma}$.

Intuitively, Claim 5.3 follows by expressing $i = i_1 + i_2$ where $i_1 \Longrightarrow x_{m_1}$ and $i_2 \Longrightarrow x_{m_2}$, so $i \Longrightarrow x_{m_1} + x_{m_2}$. We then apply Claim 5.2 to $x_{m_2}$ (with $x_{m_1}$ playing the role of $p$) to get to a configuration with the correct $e$ for Claim 5.1, and then apply Claim 5.1 to remove all states in $\Delta$.

Finally, Theorem 3.2 is proven because $v^{\Gamma}$ is $Q$-stable and it contains zero count of states in $\Delta$. To see that $v^{\Gamma}$ is $Q$-stable recall that $v^{\Gamma} \leq y_{m'}$ for sufficiently large $m'$ since $\Gamma = \mathrm{unbdd}(y_m)$ and $v^{\Gamma}$ contains only states in $\Gamma$. Since stability is closed downward, and $y_{m'}$ is $Q$-stable, we have that $v^{\Gamma}$ is $Q$-stable as well.

**Acknowledgements.** The authors thank Anne Condon and Monir Hajiaghayi for several insightful discussions. We also thank the attendees of the 2014 Workshop on Programming Chemical Reaction Networks at the Banff International Research Station, where the first incursions were made into the solution of the problem of PP stable leader election.

# References

1. Alistarh, D., Gelashvili, R.: Polylogarithmic-time leader election in population protocols. In: Halldórsson, M.M., Iwama, K., Kobayashi, N., Speckmann, B. (eds.) ICALP 2015. LNCS, vol. 9135, pp. 479–491. Springer, Heidelberg (2015)
2. Angluin, D., Aspnes, J., Diamadi, Z., Fischer, M., Peralta, R.: Computation in networks of passively mobile finite-state sensors, Distributed Computing 18, 235–253 (2006). http://dx.doi.org/10.1007/s00446-005-0138-3, preliminary version appeared in PODC 2004
3. Angluin, D., Aspnes, J., Diamadi, Z., Fischer, M.J., Peralta, R.: Urn automata. Tech. Rep. YALEU/DCS/TR-1280, Yale University, November 2003
4. Angluin, D., Aspnes, J., Eisenstat, D.: Fast computation by population protocols with a leader. Distributed Computing 21(3), 183–199 (2008). Preliminary Version appeared in DISC 2006
5. Angluin, D., Aspnes, J., Eisenstat, D., Ruppert, E.: The computational power of population protocols. Distributed Computing 20(4), 279–304 (2007)
6. Angluin, D., Aspnes, J., Fischer, M.J., Jiang, H.: Self-stabilizing population protocols. In: Anderson, J.H., Prencipe, G., Wattenhofer, R. (eds.) OPODIS 2005. LNCS, vol. 3974, pp. 103–117. Springer, Heidelberg (2006)
7. Bower, J.M., Bolouri, H.: Computational modeling of genetic and biochemical networks. MIT press (2004)
8. Chen, H.-L., Cummings, R., Doty, D., Soloveichik, D.: Speed faults in computation by chemical reaction networks. In: Kuhn, F. (ed.) DISC 2014. LNCS, vol. 8784, pp. 16–30. Springer, Heidelberg (2014). http://dx.doi.org/10.1007/978-3-662-45174-8_2
9. Chen, H.L., Doty, D., Soloveichik, D.: Deterministic function computation with chemical reaction networks. Natural Computing 13(4), 517–534 (2014). Preliminary Version appeared in DISC 2012
10. Chen, Y.J., Dalchau, N., Srinivas, N., Phillips, A., Cardelli, L., Soloveichik, D., Seelig, G.: Programmable chemical controllers made from DNA. Nature Nanotechnology 8(10), 755–762 (2013)
11. Cunha-Ferreira, I., Bento, I., Bettencourt-Dias, M.: From zero to many: control of centriole number in development and disease. Traffic 10(5), 482–498 (2009)
12. Dickson, L.E.: Finiteness of the odd perfect and primitive abundant numbers with n distinct prime factors. American Journal of Mathematics 35(4), 413–422 (1913)
13. Doty, D.: Timing in chemical reaction networks. In: SODA 2014: Proceedings of the 25th Annual ACM-SIAM Symposium on Discrete Algorithms, pp. 772–784, January 2014
14. Gillespie, D.T.: Exact stochastic simulation of coupled chemical reactions. Journal of Physical Chemistry 81(25), 2340–2361 (1977)
15. Karp, R.M., Miller, R.E.: Parallel program schemata. Journal of Computer and System Sciences 3(2), 147–195 (1969)
16. Petri, C.A.: Communication with automata. Tech. rep, DTIC Document (1966)
17. Soloveichik, D., Seelig, G., Winfree, E.: DNA as a universal substrate for chemical kinetics. Proceedings of the National Academy of Sciences 107(12), 5393 (2010). Preliminary Version appeared in DNA 2008
18. Volterra, V.: Variazioni e fluttuazioni del numero dindividui in specie animali conviventi. Mem. Acad. Lincei Roma 2, 31–113 (1926)

# Hardware Transactions in Nonvolatile Memory

Hillel Avni[1], Eliezer Levy[1]([✉]), and Avi Mendelson[2]

[1] Huawei Technologies, European Research Center
{hillel.avni,eliezer.levy}@huawei.com
[2] Technion CS & EE Departments, Haifa, Israel
avi.mendelson@technion.ac.il

**Abstract.** Hardware transactional memory (HTM) implementations already provide a transactional abstraction at HW speed in multi-core systems. The imminent availability of mature byte-addressable, nonvolatile memory (NVM) will provide persistence at the speed of accessing main memory. This paper presents the notion of persistent HTM (PHTM), which combines HTM and NVM and features hardware-assisted, lock-free, full ACID transactions. For atomicity and isolation, PHTM is based on the current implementations of HTM. For durability, PHTM adds the algorithmic and minimal HW enhancements needed due to the incorporation of NVM. The paper compares the performance of an implementation of PHTM (that emulates NVM aspects) with other schemes that are based on HTM and STM. The results clearly indicate the advantage of PHTM in reads, as they are served directly from the cache without locking or versioning. In particular, PHTM is an order of magnitude faster than the best persistent STM on read-dominant workloads.

## 1 Introduction

In [10], Herlihy and Moss defined hardware transactional memory (HTM), as a way to leverage hardware cache coherency to execute atomic transactions in the cacheable shared memory of multicore chips. The basic idea was that each transaction is isolated in the local L1 cache of the core that executes it. The semantics of atomicity were borrowed from the database research [4]. However, database transactions, unlike HTM transactions, are persistent, i.e. once a transaction committed successfully, it is also backed up to stable storage.

As HTM lingered, much research was done on software transactional memory (STM) in order to obtain low overhead and scalable synchronization among memory transactions without hardware assistance. Intel's first HTM implementation reached the market in 2013. At the same time, STM was incorporated into the GCC compiler [3,12].

Latest developments in memory technology (such as phase change memory, STT-RAM, and memristors) introduce the possibility of NVM devices that are fast and byte-addressable as DRAM, more power-efficient than DRAM, yet nonvolatile and cheap as HDD. This paper proposes to provide HTM transactions

© Springer-Verlag Berlin Heidelberg 2015
Y. Moses (Ed.): DISC 2015, LNCS 9363, pp. 617–630, 2015.
DOI: 10.1007/978-3-662-48653-5_41

with fast persistent storage by using NVM instead of (or in addition to) DRAM while keeping the volatile cache hierarchy intact.

The remainder of this paper is organized as follows. We conclude the Introduction section by reviewing related work. Section 2 introduces the model and terminology of PHTM. Section 3 defines the PHTM implementation, and explains the correctness of PHTM. Section 4 evaluates PHTM performance, and Section 5 concludes and discusses future work.

## 1.1  Related Work

Coburn et al. [5] suggested NV-Heaps, a software transactional memory (STM) that works correctly with NVM. The basic idea follows DSTM [9], in which transactional objects are stored in NVM. A transactional object can be opened for writing, and then the STM transaction, T, copies it to an undo log, and locks it. T maintains a volatile read log and a non-volatile undo log for each transaction. If a system failure occurs, T is aborted and the undo log, which is persistent, is used to reverse the changes of T.

While NV-Heaps is object-based, the Mnemosyne STM [13], which was published at the same time, is word-based and is derived from TinySTM [8]. However, the ideas behind these algorithms, i.e. nonvolatile undo log and a volatile read log, are identical.

While correct and feasible, the software-based methods exhibit poor performance due to bookkeeping overhead and locking serialization. Thus, some database implementations [11, 14] use HTM for synchronization. However, these databases still use HDDs for persistence.

PMFS [7] uses NVM for storage of a file system and [6] uses NVM for persistence in an OLTP database. PMFS does use HTM, but only for very specific purposes of managing file system metadata.

This paper introduces the combination of NVM and HTM for the purpose of transaction processing. Our contribution is the presentation of a concrete implementation that provides full ACID semantics to transactions. We emulate this implementation and compare its performance to other approaches using STM, HTM, and NVM.

## 2  Persistent HTM

The imminent availability of mature Non-Volatile RAM (NVM) technology is bound to disrupt the way transactional systems are built. NVM devices are fast and byte-addressable as DRAM, more power-efficient than DRAM, yet non-volatile and cheap as HDD. Therefore, NVRAM will obliterate the traditional multi-tier memory hierarchy that is fundamental to the durability guarantees of ACID transactions. In this foreseen situation, maintaining invalid states in main memory can render a system crash unrecoverable. Therefore, a fresh and careful approach is required in the design of persistence and recovery after a crash (Restart) schemes that would harness the benefits of NVM. In the sequel, we use the following terms:

- **HTM:** A synchronization mechanism that commits transactions atomically, and maintains isolation. Once an HTM transaction T commits, all its newly modified data is in volatile cache.
- **An HTM transaction $T_k$:** A transaction executed by a processing core $P_k$.
- **NVM:** nonvolatile, byte addressable, writable memory.
- **Restart:** The task of a restart is to bring the data to a consistent state, removing effects of uncommitted transactions and applying the missing effects of the committed ones.

The hardware model investigated here includes unlimited NVM, many cores and no disk. All NVM is cacheable and caches are volatile and coherent. The system includes limited size DRAM. Finally, we use the term *Persistent HTM (PHTM)* to refer to the notion of existing HTM realizations, with the minimal necessary hardware and software adjustments needed for the incorporation of NVM. The PHTM system includes software and hardware.

## 2.1 Problem Definition

A difficulty arises when NVM persistency meets the growing number of cores on modern hardware. On the one hand, as data is in NVM, it is unnecessary to allocate another persistent storage for it, which reduces persistency overhead. On the other hand, as an address is written, the new value must be exposed atomically with a new consistent and persistent state. One alternative for guaranteeing this atomicity is by means of locks. With the ever growing number of cores, locking will introduce bottlenecks. A method to achieve atomicity without locking is HTM, but HTM cannot access physical memory. The problem is to close the gap between HTM and NVM and allow an application to maintain consistent and persistent states in NVM without locking and without duplicating the data.

## 2.2 Data Store Flow

The state of a data item $x$ (an addressable word), which is written by an HTM transaction T, is specified as follows (see Figure 1). Note that $x$ may be cached in the volatile cache or reside only in the NVM (just like any other addressable word):

1. **Private / Shared:** *Private* means $x$ is only in the L1 cache of one thread, and is not visible to other threads. When $x$ is *Shared*, the cache coherency makes its new value visible.
2. **Persistent / Volatile:** *Persistent* means that the last write of $x$ is in NVM, otherwise, the new value of $x$ is *Volatile* in cache and will disappear on a power failure.
3. **Logged / Clear:** When $x$ is *Logged*, a restart will recover $x$ from nonvolatile log. If $x$ is *Clear*, the restart will not touch $x$, since its log record has been finalized or its transaction aborted.

Notice that although Figure 1 illustrates the state machine of a single write in a PHTM transaction, the *Logged* state should be for the entire transaction. That is, turning all writes of a single transaction from clear to logged requires a single persistent write. In a PHTM commit, all writes are exposed by the HTM and are simultaneously logged. Each write must generate a persistent log record, but until a successful commit, the write is not logged in the sense that it will not be replayed by a restart process.

When the HTM transaction $T_k$ writes to a variable $x$, $x$ is marked as transactional in the L1 cache of $P_k$ and is private, i.e., exclusively in the cache of $P_k$. It is volatile, as it is only in cache, and clear, i.e. not logged, as the transaction is not yet committed. Upon an abort or a power failure, the volatile private value of $x$ will be discarded and it will revert to its previous shared and persistent value.

In the PHTM commit, the state of $x$ changes twice. It becomes shared, i.e. visible and at the same time it is also logged. Both changes must happen atomically in a successful commit. After a successful commit, the PHTM flushes the new value of $x$ transparently to NVM and clears $x$. If there is a system failure and restart when $x$ is logged, the recovery process uses the log record of $x$ to write the committed value of $x$ and then clears $x$.

It is important to observe that the log in NVM is not a typical sequential log. Instead, it holds unordered log records only for transactions that are either in-flight or are committed and their log records have not been recycled yet.

## 3  PHTM Implementation

If the L1 cache was nonvolatile, HTM would be persistent as is without any further modifications. A restart event could abort the in-flight transactions, and a committed HTM transaction, while in the cache, would be instantly persistent and not require any logging. However,

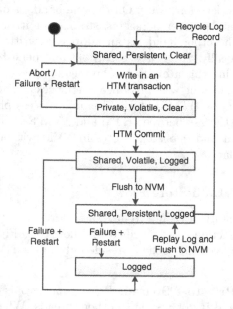

**Fig. 1.** State machine for a persistent transactional variable

due to hardware limitations, e.g. fast wear out and slow writes of NVM, the cache hierarchy will stay in volatile SRAM in the foreseeable future.

## 3.1 Hardware Ramifications

As shown in Figure 1, PHTM requires that the successful commit of the transaction $T_k$ will atomically set the persistent commit record of $T_k$. The $tx\_end\_log(T_k)$ instruction is added for this purpose. This instruction performs an HTM commit and sets the commit record of $T_k$. Figure 2 shows the layout of the persistent footprint of $T_k$ in NVM. It includes the logged indication which serves as the commit record of $T_k$. The $tx\_end\_log(T_k)$ writes the commit record in NVM, and in addition sets the status of the writes of $T_k$ to *Logged*.

PHTM requires that log records are flushed from cache to NVM by a live transaction without aborting itself. We call this process the *Finalization* of T. In T finalization, after $tx\_end\_log(T)$, flushing of the data written by T from cache to NVM must not abort ongoing concurrent transactions that read this value. Considering the HTM eager conflict resolution, these flushes must not generate any coherency request and for performance, they should not invalidate the data in the cache. Such operations are designated "transparent flushes" (TF) as they have no effect of the cache hierarchy and the HTM subsystem.

In summary, we define a new HW-related primitive called **Transparent flush (TF)** as follows: If $\alpha$ is a cached shared memory address, $TF(\alpha)$ will write $\alpha$ to physical shared memory, but will not invalidate it and will not affect cache coherency in any way. If $T_k$ reads $\alpha$ transactionally, and then $T_q$, where possibly $k \neq q$ executes $TF(\alpha)$, $T_k$ will not abort because of it. The ARM DC CVAC instruction to clean data cache by virtual address to point of coherency [1], and the cache line write back (CLWB) instruction from Intel future architecture [2] are examples in this direction.

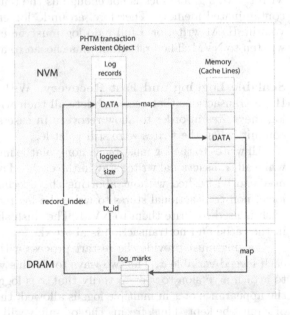

**Fig. 2.** PHTM System

## 3.2 Software Details

The API of PHTM is $tx\_start()$ and $tx\_end()$ as in a non-persistent, Intel HTM transaction. $tx\_start()$ is translated to starting an HTM transaction, while $tx\_end()$ is translated to flushing the transaction persistent structure, followed by a $tx\_end\_log(T)$ instruction, followed by flushing of the data itself. The machine store instructions are replaced by the preprocessor with the $tx\_write()$ function.

The log records and the size field that appear in the PHTM transaction persistent object (Figure 2) are flushed as part of the transaction, but **not** as part of the $tx\_end\_log(T_k)$ instruction. However, multiple writes to the same cache line will write to the same log record. Thus, as an optimization, the log records are flushed only once before commit to prevent multiple flushes of the same data.

In a system with NVM, it is assumed that the compiler will automatically replace the $tx\_end()$ with $tx\_finalization(T)$ (Algorithm 2), and the store instructions with $tx\_write$ (Algorithm 1). This type of preprocessing already exists for GCC STM support. In case a PHTM transaction gets aborted, all its writes (to volatile memory) are undone automatically, and the commit record is not set, so there is no overhead.

**Fallback.** The HTM follows a best effort policy, which means it does not supply a progress guarantee. As a result, after a certain number of aborts in the standard volatile HTM, the transaction must take a global lock and commit. However with NVM, a global lock is not enough as the tentative writes may have already contaminated memory. Therefore, an undo log entry must be created for every volatile HTM write, or a full redo log must be created before the first value is written to NVM. The first option was chosen to avoid read after write overhead.

**Scalable Logging and Fast Recovery.** With volatile cache and committed HTM transactions that accommodate all their writes in cache, it is necessary to log the writes in order to allow recovery in case a restart happened after HTM commit, when the writes were still volatile.

All writes to the log must reach non-volatile memory before an HTM commit, while all transactional writes stay in the cache. This implies that the log to NVM needs to be flushed without aborting the executing transaction. As the log is local, non-transactional stores to write the log records can be used, and later, a flush is used to write them to NVM. The flush should be a TF so the log stays in the cache and no transaction is aborted.

Logging must provide the restart process with the last committed value for each logged variable $x$. The two ways to do this with concurrent transactions is to attach a version to $x$ or to verify that $x$ is logged only once in the system. If the appearance of $x$ in multiple logs is allowed, then the latest version of the log of $x$ must be kept. Thus, freeing the log safely will require communication among the committed transactions, e.g. barriers. This communication is not scalable. On the other hand, not freeing the log will require unbounded memory and a longer time for recovery in restarts.

Instead, each address is allowed to appear at most in one log. To avoid instances of the same address in multiple logs, a volatile array of log marks is added in which each memory address is mapped to one mark. When a transaction is about to write $x$, it also marks $x$ as logged. Until $x$ is flushed, no other transaction can write it. The reason marks are used is to prevent a write to a variable that was already written by another transaction, but not yet flushed, so it is still logged. All other conflicts are handled directly by the HTM. The array of marks can be volatile, as in case of restart it is known that the logged addresses are unique, and that the restart and recovery process do not create any new log records. After restart, a new and empty array of marks can be allocated.

The writing of the marks is a part of a transaction, i.e. if $T_k$ writes $x$, it also marks $x$ and in committing, the writing and the marking will take effect simultaneously as they are both transactional writes, while at abort, they are both canceled. As long as the mark is set, the value of $x$, which appears in the log of $T_k$, cannot be changed. Therefore, after $x$ is secured in NVM and cleared, the mark is unset. It is important to emphasize that the transactional load instructions ignore the marks and execute in full speed, which is a key advantage of PHTM as Reads are processed in hardware speed.

**Write.** It is assumed there is a map function that extracts the index of the mark from the address. The map not only performs mapping of every address to a unique mark, but also maps all the addresses in the same cache line to the same mark. As cache flushing is in cacheline units, the log records and the marks are maintained in cacheline granularity.

---

**Algorithm 1.** PHTM Write Instrumentation

---

```
 1: function TX_WRITE(addr, val, T)       14:          T.size ← T.size + 1
 2:     id ← T.self_id                    15:          T.addr[rec_index] ← addr
 3:     m ← log_marks[map(addr)]          16:          T.data[rec_index] ← C_addr
 4:     ▷ C_addr is the cache line of addr 17:     else
 5:     if m.tx_id = T.self_id then       18:        ▷ C_addr is marked
 6:        ▷ T already accessed C_addr    19:          _xabort(MARKED)
 7:          rec_index ← m.rec_index      20:     end if
 8:     else                              21:   end if
 9:        if m.tx_id = null then         22:   ▷ log the writing
10:          ▷ C_addr is not marked       23:   T.data[rec_index][offset] = val
11:            m.tx_id ← id               24:   ▷ Perform the actual writing
12:            rec_index ← T.size         25:   addr ← val
13:            m.rec_index ← rec_index    26: end function
```

---

Algorithm 1 shows the implementation of $tx\_write$. It starts by locating the mark of the address (Line 3). If the mark was already marked by T (Line 6), T extracts the $record\_index$ from the mark (Line 7). Otherwise, if the mark is free (Line 10), T sets the mark to point to itself (Line 11). Next, T allocates a log entry (Lines 12 - 14), which is in the index currently pointed by the size field. T stores the index in the mark so later writes to the same line by T will use this index and increment the size field. Next, T stores the address in the log (Line 15) and since this is the first access to this cacheline, T stores the original content of this cacheline (Line 16). The restart will write full cache lines, and thus the original values of the unwritten parts of the lines need to be kept.

If the address is currently marked by another transaction, T explicitly aborts with the code MARKED (Line 19). When the abort handler sees the reason for the abort was MARKED, it will not count this as a conflict and will not fallback to locking. After acquiring the log mark, the value is written into the private, logged copy of the cache line (Line 24), and then it is written to actual memory (Line 25). Writing the marks is done in transactional mode, so they are added to the transaction size, and may cause size violation and aborts that do not occur in the standard HTM.

**Finalization.** In Algorithm 2, the code for *tx_finalize* is presented. This code replaces the HTM _xend instruction to commit persistent HTM transactions. Before committing the HTM transaction, the log, including its size (Line 3), and data (Lines 6 and 5 ) are flushed to NVM using TF. Then the PHTM commits using the new *tx_end_log*, and if the commit was successful it simultaneously sets the logged indication of T (Line 11). Next, all the cache lines that include data that was written during the transaction are flushed to NVM (Line 13). After flushing, the data is persistent, so the log is cleared by writing zero to the log indication and flushing it to NVM (Line 17). Only after clearing the log can the marks (line 22) be freed and the size of the log (Line 20) be reset.

---

**Algorithm 2.** PHTM Finalization

---

```
 1: function TX_FINALIZE(T)              13:        TF(T.addr[s])
 2:     ▷ Transparently flush the log    14:     end for
 3:     sz ← T.size                      15:     ▷ Clear log with regular flushes
 4:     for all s < sz do                16:     T.logged ← 0
 5:         TF(T.addr[s])                17:     Flush(T.logged)
 6:         TF(T.data[s])                18:
 7:     end for                          19:     T.size ← 0        ▷ Clear the marks
 8:     TF(T.size)                       20:     Flush(T.size)
 9:     ▷ HTM commit and log             21:     for all s < sz do
10:     tx_end_log(T.logged)             22:         marks[map(addr[s])] ← null
11:     ▷ Transparently flush data       23:     end for
12:     for all s < sz do                24: end function
```

---

## 3.3   Correctness and Liveness

The correctness and liveness of PHTM are derived from HTM with the necessary adjustments.

**Correctness.** When power is not interrupted the PHTM is operating exactly as HTM with the addition of each transaction maintaining private information about its writes and success. It is left to show that after a power failure in any point of the execution, the last committed write of an address is in NVM. If the last committed write is not logged than in Line 13 of Algorithm 2 it was already flushed to NVM. If it is is logged than it was marked in Line 3 of Algorithm 1 and it is the only logged write to the address, so the recovery process will set it in NVM. If the last write is not successfully committed then it is only in the local volatile cache of the transaction executor and it will vanish at power down.

**Liveness.** As a PHTM transaction includes an HTM transaction and HTM has no progress guarantees, PHTM has no progress guarantees either. However, an HTM transaction cannot delay another concurrent HTM transaction, while if a PHTM transaction stops before clearing its marks in Line 22 of Algorithm 2 it can stop a concurrent transaction from writing the marked address. The mark, which is a writer-writer lock, is set only from commit to the end the data flush. If a transaction $T_1$ committed but swapped out before clearing its write-set, it can lockout a concurrent writer $T_2$. To resolve this situation $T_2$ may clear $T_1$, as the data is already shared. This help involves communication among transactions so it is technically complicated and breaks the isolation among transactions. It may also require that the synchronization primitives used will be persistent.

## 4    Evaluation

In this section the performance of PHTM is evaluated using an RB-Tree data structure and a synthetic benchmark. The synthetic benchmark checks the overheads of PHTM and how it interacts with the size limitation of the HTM.

These tests were executed on an Intel Core i7-4770 3.4 GHz Haswell processor with 4 cores, each with 2 hyper threads. Each core has private L1 and L2 caches, whose sizes are 32 KB and 256 KB respectively. There is also an 8 MB L3 cache shared by all cores. Section 4.1 describes how the PHTM hardware was emulated, i.e. the NVM and the $tx\_end\_log$ instruction. Section 4.2 explains how a persistent STM for a fair comparison was emulated and in Section 4.3 some preliminary performance results are presented.

### 4.1    Hardware Emulation

Intels Haswell processors feature an HTM facility that is used the experiments. However, NVM and PHTM are still not realized in hardware so they are emulated for evaluation. We emulate the effects of power failure in PHTM by leaving the power on and zeroing only the volatile regions, i.e. the log marks. To emulate the $tx\_end\_log$, the commit record is written during the transaction. As this is part of the transaction, the HTM itself makes the commit record visible simultaneously with a successful commit. In TF emulation, only the NVM access time is emulated by inserting a 100 nanosecond delay according to the expected NVM performance. The interconnect traffic is not emulated, as this traffic is identical to the interconnect traffic in the solution compared to, i.e., the persistent STM.

## 4.2 Compared Algorithms

**PHTM.** is compared with standard **HTM**, with an emulation of a persistent software transactional memory (**PSTM**), and with standard **STM** without persistence. The STM is from GCC [3,12], but in the lowest optimization level. In order to provide a fair comparison of all 4 algorithms, compiler optimization, which can reduce the number of accesses, is avoided.

Analagous to PHTM, PSTM implements a redo log in persistent memory. The overhead of writes in PSTM is one flush of the log entry before commit and one flush of the data after commit, so it is comparable to PHTM. PSTM is based on Mnemosyne [13], but with few adjustments. A redo log and in-place writing was chosen to be implemented in order to avoid huge read after write penalties. PHTMs advantage over STM concerns the processor speed loads. For a fair comparison, the PSTM loads should be as fast as possible in order to challenge the PHTM.

The shortcomings of PSTM concern its STM nature, i.e. the overhead associated with instructions instrumentation, locking and versioning. The problems of PHTM concern its HTM origin, i.e. limited transaction size and sensitivity to contention.

## 4.3 Benchmarks

PHTM performance is evaluated without contention on a synthetic array benchmark. It is then tested on an RB-Tree to see its performance under contention. The algorithms checked include **HTM**, **PHTM**, **STM** and **PSTM**. In the graphs, the **HTM-CAP** and **PHTM-CAP** lines are added to count the number of HTM capacity aborts and the **HTM-CON** and **PHTM-CON** lines are added to count the number of conflict aborts in some of the graphs. Aborts are counted in operations per second that where aborted. A conflict abort is retried 20 times before taking a global lock, but a capacity abort is not retried and locks immediately, as a retry has low chance for success.

**Array Workloads.** In this workload all transactions have the same number of accesses in order to make their execution time comparable. The tests access a set of consecutive memory addresses, so the cache is filled with no fragmentation. Each accessed address is in a separate cache line.

*Read-Only:* First, the performance of PHTM on a read-only workload is observed. This is the best case for PHTM, as a PHTM load is in processor speed. In Figure 3a, every transaction performs 512 load instructions cyclically to various numbers of consecutive cache lines. It can be seen that as long as HTM capacity limit is avoided, PHTM and HTM perform the same and outperform STM and PSTM by an order of magnitude. The tests in Figure 3a execute on all

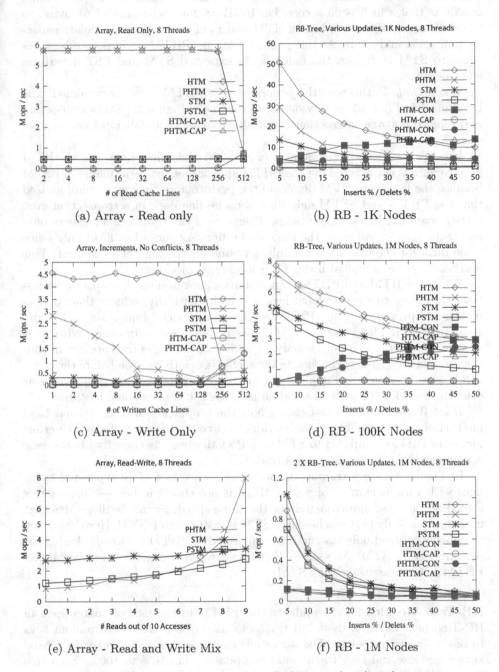

(a) Array - Read only

(b) RB - 1K Nodes

(c) Array - Write Only

(d) RB - 100K Nodes

(e) Array - Read and Write Mix

(f) RB - 1M Nodes

**Fig. 3.** Synthetic array and a red-black tree benchmarks

8 hardware threads. There is hyper threading and the cache size of each thread is half as that which is on a core, i.e. 16KB or 256 cache lines of 64 bytes, so when the access set size is 512 all HTM and PHTM transactions violate capacity limitation and abort. At this point, HTM and PHTM performance becomes equal to STM as it uses the fallback. As expected STM and PSTM perform equivalently.

*Write-Only:* In this test, the performance of PHTM writes is examined. The benchmark in Figure 3c is very similar to the one in Figure 3a. Every transaction performs 512 `store` instructions cyclically to various numbers of consecutive cache lines.

It is observed that as the number of accessed cache lines increases, the HTM performance is not affected but the PHTM approaches the performance of PSTM because the flushes to NVM dominate the performance. It must be emphasized that the PHTM and PSTM only flush a cache line once in a transaction even if they write the line multiple times. Therefore if the transaction accesses only one cache line, it will write the same cache line 512 times but flush only twice - one flush for the data after commit, and one for the log before commit. This overhead can be mitigated if the TF is made non-blocking.

When the HTM and PHTM transactions start reaching the capacity limitation, they execute with a global lock which dramatically reduces their performance and prevents scaling. PHTM reaches the capacity limitation well before standard HTM. This is because PHTM writes a log entry for every write, so it accesses a larger amount of memory. In addition, the log entries are not in continuous memory, so they can violate the cache associativity even before the cache is full. Note that in a real implementation non-transactional `store` instructions could be used for the log and avoid an increase the transactional footprint.

*Read-Write Mix:* This test checks how the proportion of transactional `load` instruction vs. the number of transactional `store` instructions affects the performance of PHTM compared to STM and PSTM when the capacity aborts issue is eliminated, i.e. in small transactions.

In Figure 3e, every transaction performs 10 accesses of 10 separated cache lines with various number of writes. HTM is not shown in because it performs a read and a write approximately in the same speed. Figure 3e illustrates that until the read-only part reaches 80%, STM is faster than PHTM. However, when the portion of read-only instructions reaches 90%, PHTM is already double the performance of STM. As seen in Figure 3a, when the portion reaches 100%, PHTM is 12 times faster than STM.

**RB-Tree Workloads.** To evaluate the PHTM in the face of contention, an RB-Tree benchmark is used. All transactions access a tree with random keys to insert, delete or lookup. The workloads executed run on 8 cores with a fixed keys-range size and vary the amount of updates from 10% to 100%. Each tree starts half full and the number of inserts equals the number of deletes to preserve the tree size.

The first set of tests is performed on a small 1K nodes tree. As seen in Figure 3b there are no capacity aborts in HTM and PHTM. Conflict aborts rise but the scalability is comparable to STM. In this test PHTM is about 6 times faster than PSTM. The second set of tests in Figure 3d is executed on a 1M tree, and we can see that capacity aborts are visible, but low. As a result, PHTM is only 40% faster than PSTM. Still the scalability is the same even though conflict aborts are high, which suggests STM also experiences similar aborts rate. To further increase the capacity challenge, we execute transactions that do the same operation on two 1M trees atomically. As seen in Figure 3f, the capacity aborts rises and PHTM performance drops to PSTM.

As expected, capacity limitation is the worst problem of HTM as it forces transactions to serialize, and the big obstacle to PHTM performance is capacity aborts which it inherits from HTM. In each of the performed tests PHTM keeps a constant difference from HTM (and PSTM from STM) throughout the contention levels. The difference is due to the portion of writes in the workload. The smaller the tree, less time is spent on traversing it, so the relative part of writing grows, and the persistent algorithm overhead increases.

## 5   Conclusion

Future generations of systems are expected to accommodate thousands of cores and petabytes of NVM. Lock based synchronization, as well as traditional log-based persistence will introduce unacceptable overhead in those systems. PHTM is a first step towards ACID transactions that avoid locking and provide persistence in a way that is specialized to NVM. Preliminary experiments show PHTM is 12x faster than its persistent STM counterpart on read-dominant workloads. When contention exists, it is still 6x faster, and when the capacity limit is hit, PHTM falls back to a software-based approach and then its performance equals the performance persistent STM. These performance advantages stem from the fact that PHTM avoids all locking in the reader path and its commit is instantaneously visible. PHTM presents a concept that should serve as a blueprint for possible realizations that would evolve with the availability of mature NVM technology. Once the HW model we used will be instantiated as a concrete system, further optimizations might be needed. Moreover, we expect that the current limitations of HTM technology will be alleviated and then the applicability of the PHTM scheme can be extended.

## References

1. ARM architecture reference manual for ARMv8-a architecture profile. https://silver.arm.com/download/ARM_and_AMBA_Architecture/AR150-DA-70000-r0p0-00bet6/DDI0487A_e_armv8_arm.pdf
2. Intel architecture instruction set extensions programming reference. https://software.intel.com/sites/default/files/managed/0d/53/319433-022.pdf
3. Tm support in the gnu compiler collection. http://gcc.gnu.org/wiki/TransactionalMemory

4. Bernstein, P.A., Hadzilacos, V., Goodman, N.: Concurrency Control and Recovery in Database Systems. Addison-Wesley Longman Publishing Co. Inc., Boston (1987)
5. Coburn, J., Caulfield, A.M., Akel, A., Grupp, L.M., Gupta, R.K., Jhala, R., Swanson, S.: NV-heaps: making persistent objects fast and safe with next-generation, non-volatile memories. In: Proceedings of the Sixteenth International Conference, ASPLOS XVI, pp. 105–118. ACM, New York (2011)
6. DeBrabant, J., Arulraj, J., Pavlo, A., Stonebraker, M., Zdonik, S., Dulloor, S.: A prolegomenon on oltp database systems for non-volatile memory. In: ADMS@VLDB (2014)
7. Dulloor, S.R., Kumar, S., Keshavamurthy, A., Lantz, P., Reddy, D., Sankaran, R., Jackson, J.: System software for persistent memory. In: Proceedings of the Ninth European Conference on Computer Systems, EuroSys 2014, pp. 15:1–15:15. ACM, New York (2014)
8. Felber, P., Fetzer, C., Riegel, T.: Dynamic performance tuning of word-based software transactional memory. In: PPoPP 2008: Proceedings of the 13th ACM SIGPLAN Symposium on Principles and Practice of Parallel Programming, pp. 237–246. ACM (2008)
9. Herlihy, M., Luchangco, V., Moir, M., Scherer III, W.N.: Software transactional memory for dynamic-sized data structures. In: Proceedings of the Twenty-Second Annual Symposium on Principles of Distributed Computing, PODC 2003, pp. 92–101. ACM, New York (2003)
10. Herlihy, M., Moss, J.E.B.: Transactional memory: architectural support for lock-free data structures. In: Proceedings of the 20th Annual International Symposium on Computer Architecture, ISCA 1993, pp. 289–300. ACM, New York (1993)
11. Leis, V., Kemper, A., Neumann, T.: Exploiting hardware transactional memory in main-memory databases. In: IEEE 30th International Conference on Data Engineering, Chicago, ICDE 2014, IL, USA, March 31–April 4, pp. 580–591 (2014)
12. Riegel, T.: Software Transactional Memory Building Blocks. Ph.D. thesis, Technische Universität Dresden, Dresden, 01062 Dresden, Germany (2013)
13. Volos, H., Tack, A.J., Swift, M.M.: Mnemosyne: Lightweight persistent memory. SIGPLAN Not. **47**(4), 91–104 (2011)
14. Wang, Z., Qian, H., Li, J., Chen, H.: Using restricted transactional memory to build a scalable in-memory database. In: Proceedings of the Ninth European Conference on Computer Systems, EuroSys 2014, pp. 26:1–26:15. ACM, New York (2014)

# Space-Optimal Counting in Population Protocols

Joffroy Beauquier[1], Janna Burman[1(✉)], Simon Clavière[2], and Devan Sohier[2]

[1] LRI - CNRS UMR-8623, Université Paris Sud, Orsay, France
{joffroy.beauquier,janna.burman}@lri.fr
[2] PRiSM - CNRS FRE-3709, Université de Versailles, Versailles, France
{simon.claviere,devan.sohier}@prism.uvsq.fr

**Abstract.** In this paper, we study the fundamental problem of *counting*, which consists in computing the size of a system. We consider the distributed communication model of *population protocols* of finite state, anonymous and asynchronous mobile devices (*agents*) communicating in pairs (according to a *fairness* condition). This work significantly improves the previous results known for counting in this model, in terms of (exact) space complexity. We present and prove correct the first space-optimal protocols solving the problem for two classical types of fairness, *global* and *weak*. Both protocols require no initialization of the counted agents.

The protocol designed for global fairness, surprisingly, uses only one bit of memory (two states) per counted agent. The protocol, functioning under weak fairness, requires the necessary $\log P$ bits ($P$ states, per counted agent) to be able to count up to $P$ agents. Interestingly, this protocol exploits the intriguing Gros sequence of natural numbers, which is also used in the solutions to the Chinese Rings and the Hanoi Towers puzzles.

## 1 Introduction

Counting is a fundamental task in computer science, as illustrated by numerous and important applications of this paradigm in many domains, like network traffic monitoring, database query optimization, or data mining. The context of this work is that of dynamic wireless ad-hoc networks. In this context, many efficient counting protocols have been proposed recently (e.g., [18, 23, 25, 27]).

More precisely, we consider large-scale ad-hoc networks of mobile sensors, in which cheap and tiny devices, with limited communication, memory and computation power, move around and cooperate for achieving some task. Such networks are of an unknown size, fundamentally asynchronous (no common clock), anonymous (no identifiers) and not permanently connected (due to communication

The extended version of this paper can be consulted in [8].

J. Beauquier—The work of this author was partially supported by the Israeli-French Maimonide research project.

J. Burman—The work of this author was partially supported by the Israeli-French Maimonide and the INS2I PEPS JCJC research projects.

© Springer-Verlag Berlin Heidelberg 2015
Y. Moses (Ed.): DISC 2015, LNCS 9363, pp. 631–646, 2015.
DOI: 10.1007/978-3-662-48653-5_42

limitation). The design of these networks is now focused on complex collections of heterogeneous devices that should be robust, adaptive and self-organizing, serving requests that vary with time. There are many reasons for these devices to fail: extreme external conditions of temperature or pressure, battery exhaustion, failures inherent to their cheap realization, etc. The ability to count them (e.g., for, possibly, replacing some) may be crucial for ensuring that the tasks are performed efficiently. In this work, we propose solutions to this problem, concerning especially the reliability and the size requirements of the memory of the network nodes.

To be able to analyze our solutions, we adopt a formal communication model that suits the considered networks. This is the model of *population protocols* (PP) [3]. In PP, mobile devices, called agents, are anonymous, undistinguishable and asynchronous. Each agent has a finite state, that evolves over the course of interactions. When two agents are sufficiently close one to the other, they interact, and the effect of the interaction is a change of their states. The mobility is modeled in a very general way, by a fairness assumption which is called *global fairness*. In addition to this original fairness of PP, we consider also a classical type of fairness for distributed computing, which we call here *weak*. While global fairness captures the randomization inherent to many real systems, weak fairness only ensures progress of system entities. In general, PP is well adapted to dynamic networks in which the topology changes (like in peer-to-peer networks), or to networks in which nodes move unpredictably (like in mobile sensor networks).

The objective of this paper is to make a step towards a better understanding of the possibilities and limitations of such networks, in studying the feasibility and the complexity of the fundamental task of counting the number of agents. The task of counting anonymous agents in PP has already been studied and several results are known. Basically, we improve these results in terms of exact space complexity. Moreover, the solutions we give are space optimal. Space is a crucial factor, since a low memory is a basic condition in large-scale and unreliable networks.

Current and previous studies on counting in PP consider various parameters of the model that affect attractivity, efficiency and feasibility of the solutions. We list and explain them below together with the related impossibility results:

- The first parameter is the nature of the *fairness*: global or weak. We consider both cases, as already explained above. See formal definitions in Sec. 2.
- The second parameter is the requirement of *initialization* of agent states. On one hand, efficient protocols for dynamic and unreliable networks should not require initialization. There are at least two reasons for that. First, the agents are cheap and prone to failures. So, it should be expected that some memory or communication errors happen. Second, in dynamic and unreliable environments, it should be possible to execute most of the tasks, and counting too, in a repetitive way. In both cases, re-initializing the network could be a real problem. Moreover, it is generally hard to know when such a

re-initialization should be done, as termination detection is generally difficult to obtain in such networks.

On the other hand, if no agent state can be initialized, it is impossible to realize counting in PP, under weak or global fairness. This can be proven by using a classical technique of network partitioning (see [9] and [8], Prop. 1).

Thus, to be able to solve the problem and still avoid initialization, all previous works, as well as the current one, assume the initialization of *only one* particular (and thus distinguishable) agent called the *base station* (BS).

– For defining the data structures used by finite-state agents in the solutions, all previous studies assume the existence of a known *upper bound $P$ on the number of (non-BS) agents*. The space complexity of the solution is then expressed as a function of the necessary number of states per agent with respect to $P$. This is justified in the case of weak fairness, since it has been proved in [9] that $P$ (or more) agents cannot be counted with strictly less than $P$ states per agent by deterministic protocols (considered here as well). However, in case of global fairness, we show that this assumption is not needed, by presenting a protocol using only two states per agent.

– Finally, population protocols may be *symmetric* or *asymmetric*. In symmetric protocols, two agents in an interaction (and thus in the corresponding transition) are indistinguishable if their states are identical. Thus, their states are identical also after the transition. In asymmetric protocols, two agents in an interaction can be always distinguished (e.g., there is always an initiator and a responder in the interaction). Our study considers the more difficult and general case of symmetric protocols. Such protocols can be deployed in networks with either symmetric or asymmetric communications.

**Most Related Work.** Before presenting the contributions, we summarize the previous results about counting in symmetric PP. For the reasons explained above, all these results assume a distinguishable agent BS and do not require any initialization of non-BS agents. Moreover, BS is considered to be a powerful device, so its resources are in general not concerned by the protocol design.

In [9], the authors present different solutions to counting in PP. In particular, they propose a symmetric protocol using $4P$ states per non-BS agent under weak fairness, and prove the above-mentioned lower bound of $P$ states. The authors of [18] improve the solution in [9] from $4P$ to $2P$ states, under weak fairness, and to $\frac{3}{2}P$ under global fairness. This latter result for global fairness is improved to $P$ in [7].

Note that an asymmetric population protocol can be transformed into a symmetric one using the transformer of [10]. However, this transformer requires global fairness and doubles the number of states per agent. This makes it inadequate for obtaining a space efficient symmetric solution from an asymmetric one (in terms of exact space complexity).

**Contributions.** For the first time, we present and prove correct two space-optimal symmetric population protocols solving the counting problem. One solves the problem under global fairness, and uses only one bit of memory (two states) per non-BS agent (Protocol 1, Sec. 3). It is shown that one agent state is not enough to solve the problem. The other protocol, designed for weak fairness, uses only the necessary $P$ states per non-BS agent (Protocol 2, Sec. 4). Both protocols do not assume any initialization of the counted agents, but the necessary initialization of BS. The protocol assuming weak fairness is *silent* (i.e., no state changes after convergence). However, we show that no silent space-optimal counting protocol exists in our framework under global fairness.

**Other Related Work.** Apart from the works already mentioned in the context of PP, there are many others related to counting in related models. Many, like [14, 23–25, 27], consider the synchronous model of dynamic graph. In this model, a computation proceeds by synchronous rounds and, for each round, an adversary chooses the links available for sending messages. Similarly to our case, in the cited works, all nodes execute the same code and have no information about the network (in most cases). In addition, all, except [23], assume anonymous nodes having no unique identifiers. However, in contrast with this work, all nodes have to be initialized, and authors are concerned with *asymptotic* complexity in terms of rounds, bits and messages. All, but [14], study counting. [14] studies a related problem of assigning (short) labels to nodes.

The problem of counting *approximatively* the number of nodes in a network, using probabilities, is known under the term of *size estimation*. A common approach to network size estimation is to use random walks [16,29] relying on a token traversing the network and collecting information from the visited agents. Another strategy is to use randomly generated numbers [22], and then exploit classical results on order statistics to infer the number of participants [6,31].

In the context of large scale peer-to-peer and dynamic networks in general, probabilistic and gossiping methods have also been proposed for estimating the size of the network [15,20,22,26,28].

Another problem related to counting is the *resource controller* problem, introduced in [1] and optimized in [13,21]. One of the main difference with our model is that the topological changes there can be delayed until permission has been granted by the *controller*.

To summarize, the most significant differences of the works mentioned in this section with the current work is that we consider a totally asynchronous model of finite state anonymous and non-initialized deterministic processes. Moreover, in the considered model, termination detection is difficult and in many cases impossible. This makes sequential composition of protocols challenging.

## 2    Model and Notations

As a basic model we use the model of *population protocols* of Angluin et al. [5] with some adaption as detailed below. In this model, a system consists of a collection $\mathcal{A}$ of pairwise interacting agents, also called a population. Each agent represents a finite state sensing and communicating mobile device. Among the agents, there may be a distinguishable agent called the *base station* (BS), which can be as powerful as needed, in contrast with the resource-limited non-BS agents. The non-BS agents are also called *mobile*, interchangeably. The size of the population is the number of mobile agents, denoted by $N$, and is unknown (a priori) to the agents.

A *(population) protocol* can be viewed as a *finite* transition system whose states are called *configurations*. A *configuration* is as a vector of (local) states of all the agents. Each agent has a state taken from a finite set, the same for all mobile agents, but generally different for BS.

In this transition system, every transition between two configurations is described by a *transition* between two agents happening during an interaction. That is, when two agents $x$, in state $p$, and $y$, in state $q$, interact (meet), they execute a transition $(p, q) \to (p', q')$. As a result, $x$ changes its state from $p$ to $p'$ and $y$ from $q$ to $q'$. If $p = p'$ and $q = q'$, the corresponding transition is said to be *null* (such transitions are specified by default), and non-null otherwise.[1] The transitions are *deterministic*, if for every pair of states $(p, q)$, there is exactly one $(p', q')$ such that $(p, q) \to (p', q')$. We consider only deterministic transitions and thus, only *deterministic protocols*. Transitions and protocols can be *symmetric* or *asymmetric*. Symmetric means that, if $(p, q) \to (p', q')$ is a possible transition, then $(q, p) \to (q', p')$ is also a possible transition. In particular, if $(p, p) \to (p', q')$ is symmetric, $p' = q'$. Asymmetric is the contrary of symmetric.

Let $C$ and $C'$ be configurations. Then, $C \to C'$ is a transition (between two configurations), if $C'$ can be obtained from $C$ by a single transition of two agents in an interaction. This means that $C$ contains two states $p$ and $q$ and $C'$ is obtained from $C$ by replacing $p$ and $q$ by $p'$ and $q'$ respectively, where $(p, q) \to (p', q')$ is a transition. If there is a sequence of configurations $C = C_0, C_1, \ldots, C_k = C'$, such that $C_i \to C_{i+1}$ for all $i, 0 \le i < k$, we say that $C'$ *is reachable* from $C$, denoted $C \xrightarrow{*} C'$.

An *execution* of a protocol is an infinite sequence of configurations $C_0, C_1, C_2, \ldots$ such that $C_0$ is the starting configuration and for each $i \ge 0$, $C_i \to C_{i+1}$.

An execution is said *weakly fair*, if every pair of agents in $\mathcal{A}$ interacts infinitely often. An execution is said *globally fair*, if for every two configurations $C$ and $C'$ such that $C \to C'$, if $C$ occurs infinitely often in the execution, then $C'$ also occurs infinitely often in the execution. This definition together with the finite state space assumption, implies that, if in an execution there is an infinitely often reachable configuration, then it is infinitely often reached [4]. Global fairness can be viewed as simulating randomized systems (without introducing randomization explicitly) [19].

A *problem* is defined by a predicate $\mathcal{D}$ on executions. A population protocol $\mathcal{PP}$ is said to *solve a problem* $\mathcal{D}$, if and only if every execution of $\mathcal{PP}$ satisfies the conditions defining $\mathcal{D}$. The problem of *counting* is defined by the following conditions: eventually, in any execution, there is at least one agent (BS, in our

---

[1] In practice, when interacting with BS, the computations can be done completely on the side of BS (i.e., the state of BS is not communicated to the mobile agent). The non-BS agent only updates its state with the resulting one. In interactions between two mobile agents, in the protocols described in this paper, the agents only have to be able to compare their states.

case) obtaining a value of $N$ in some variable and this value does not change. Note that the counting predicate is required to be satisfied only eventually (and forever after). When it happens, we say that the protocol has *converged*. We consider only *semi-uniform* protocols in the sense that the size of the population $N$ is not used by a protocol and all agents, except BS, are (a priori) indistinguishable and interact according to the same possible transitions [12,30]. A protocol is called *silent*, if in every execution, eventually, no agent state changes [11].

For simplicity, we do not present the rules of our protocols under the form of possible transitions, but under the equivalent form of a pseudo-code.

## 3   Space-Optimal Counting under Global Fairness

In this section, we present a space-optimal protocol (Protocol 1 below) solving the counting problem under global fairness. The protocol uses only one bit of memory, i.e., only two states per mobile (non-BS) agent.

It is easy to see that with only one state per mobile agent, counting is impossible. Indeed, in this case, BS cannot distinguish between populations of one or more mobile agents ([8], Prop. 2). In addition, a partition argument can be used to show why no silent (uniform) counting protocol exists with only two states per agent ([8], Prop. 3).

**Protocol 1 Description.** Each mobile agent $x$ has one bit $mark_x$, which is flipped at each interaction of $x$ with BS. Between any two mobile agents, there are only null transitions. BS maintains a variable $size\_total_{BS}$ that eventually and forever holds the size of the population $N$. In addition, it maintains an array $size_{BS}[2]$ of two elements, where $size_{BS}[0]$ holds an estimation for the number of mobile agents currently marked 0 (i.e., with $mark = 0$), and similarly, $size_{BS}[1]$ estimates the number of agents currently marked 1. Eventually, these estimations become correct forever and $size\_total_{BS}$ too, because the latter is computed at each transition as the sum of $size_{BS}[0]$ and $size_{BS}[1]$ (line 6). The protocol itself can be described in a simple way. Whenever an agent marked 0 interacts with BS, BS flips its mark (to 1), decrements the estimation of 0 marked agents, i.e., $size_{BS}[0]$ (if it is not 0), and increases the estimation of 1 marked agents, i.e., $size_{BS}[1]$ (similarly for an agent marked 1).

The idea behind this solution is to try to reach a configuration, using the force of global fairness, where all agents are marked similarly, let us say, by 0 (the proof of Theorem 1 shows that it occurs eventually). From such a configuration, there is always a *possible* segment of execution where each agent $x$ interacts with BS, exactly once. In each such interaction, the mark of $x$ is flipped, to "remember" that it has been "counted". By the end of such an execution segment, all agents are marked 1 (i.e., as "counted"). Moreover, both estimations of the number of agents marked 1 and 0 in $size_{BS}[1]$ and in $size_{BS}[0]$, respectively, are correct and stay correct from this moment on. Thus, the estimation of the size of the population (in $size\_total_{BS}$) becomes also correct.

---

**Protocol 1** Space-Optimal Counting under Global Fairness (one bit per agent)

**Variables at BS:**
$size_{BS}[2]$: array of two non-negative integers, initialized to 0
$size\_total_{BS}$: non-negative integer initialized to 0; eventually holds $N$
**Variable at a mobile agent $x$:**
$mark_x$: in $\{0,1\}$, initialized *arbitrarily*

1: **when** a mobile agent $x$ interacts with BS **do**
2:     **if** $size[mark_x] > 0$ **then**
3:       $size[mark_x] \leftarrow size[mark_x] - 1$
4:       $mark_x \leftarrow 1 - mark_x$
5:     $size[mark_x] \leftarrow size[mark_x] + 1$
6:     $size\_total_{BS} \leftarrow size_{BS}[0] + size_{BS}[1]$

---

**Correctness of Protocol 1.** Let us denote by $\#0(C)$, respectively $\#1(C)$, the number of agents marked 0 (i.e., with $mark = 0$), respectively 1, in a configuration $C$.

**Lemma 1.** *For every configuration $C$, $size_{BS}[0] \leq \#0(C)$ (resp. $size_{BS}[1] \leq \#1(C)$).*

*Proof.* First, let us prove the lemma for $size_{BS}[0]$. We prove by induction on the index $k \geq 0$ of a configuration in an execution $(C_0, C_1, C_2, \ldots, C_k, \ldots)$. At the starting configuration $C_0$, $k = 0$, the lemma holds because of the initialization of $size_{BS}[0]$ to 0. Let us assume that the lemma holds for $k = k'$ and prove it for $k = k' + 1$. Then, $size_{BS}[0] \leq \#0(C_{k'})$. From any configuration, and from $C_{k'}$ in particular, the only possible interaction $(BS, x)$ is of two types, either $x$ is marked 0 ($mark_x = 0$), or 1:

- If $x$ is marked 0, during the following transition, its mark is flipped to 1 (line 4) and thus $\#0(C_{k'+1}) = \#0(C_{k'}) - 1$. At line 5, $size_{BS}[0]$ is decremented too (if it is not 0), and this is the only line that changes $size_{BS}[0]$ in this transition (line 5 changes $size_{BS}[1]$). Thus, after this transition, in $C_{k'+1}$, $size_{BS}[0] \leq \#0(C_{k'+1})$.
- If, during an interaction $(BS, x)$ at $C_{k'}$, $x$ is marked 1, during the following transition, its mark is flipped to 0 (line 4) and thus $\#0(C_{k'+1}) = \#0(C_{k'}) + 1$. At line 5, $size_{BS}[0]$ is incremented too, and this is the only line that changes $size_{BS}[0]$ in this transition (line 5 changes $size_{BS}[1]$). Thus, after this transition, in $C_{k'+1}$, $size_{BS}[0] \leq \#0(C_{k'+1})$.

Thus, the lemma holds for $size_{BS}[0]$. As $size_{BS}[1]$ is managed exactly in the same (but symmetric) way as $size_{BS}[0]$, the lemma also holds for $size_{BS}[1]$. $\square$

As $size\_total_{BS}$ is always set to the sum of $size_{BS}[0]$ and $size_{BS}[1]$ (line 6), we have the following corollary.

**Corollary 1.** *In any configuration, $size\_total_{BS} \leq N$.*

Lemma 2 below is easily obtained by observing the pseudo-code.

**Lemma 2.** *The value of size_total$_{BS}$ never decreases.*

*Proof.* The value of size_total$_{BS}$ can decrease only by executing line 5, $size[mark_x] \leftarrow size[mark_x] - 1$. Whenever this line is executed in a transition, line 5 is executed in the same transition too. Due to line 4, in line 5, $size[1 - mark_x] \leftarrow size[1 - mark_x] + 1$. Thus, if line 5 is executed in some transition, size_total$_{BS}$ does not change. In all other cases, it can only increase.  □

**Theorem 1.** *Under global fairness, (symmetric) Protocol 1 solves the counting problem. Eventually, size_total$_{BS}$ = N and does not change anymore.*

*Proof.* To prove the theorem, we show below that, from any possible configuration, there is a reachable configuration $C^*$ s.t., in $C^*$, size_total$_{BS}$ = N. Then, by global fairness, such configuration is eventually reached. Finally, by corollary 1 and lemma 2, we have size_total$_{BS}$ = N in all subsequent configurations.

Now we show why $C^*$ is always reachable. Consider a configuration $C$. In $C$, let $size_{BS}[0] = x_0, size_{BS}[1] = x_1$, where $x_0, x_1$ are non-negative integers $\leq N$. By lemma 1, there are $0 \leq x_0', x_1' \leq N$ s.t. $\#0(C) = x_0 + x_0'$ and $\#1(C) = x_1 + x_1'$. Then, from $C$, there is the following possible execution (that reaches $C^*$). First, $x_1 + x_1'$ agents marked 1 interact with BS, each one exactly once. It is easy to verify, by the code of Protocol 1, that at the end of this segment of execution, $size_{BS}[0] = x_0 + x_1 + x_1', size_{BS}[1] = 0$ and $\#0(C) = x_0 + x_0' + x_1 + x_1' = N, \#1(C) = 0$ (all agents are marked 0). Now, $x_0 + x_1 + x_1'$ agents interact with BS (each one exactly once), what results in $size_{BS}[0] = 0, size_{BS}[1] = x_0 + x_1 + x_1'$ and $\#0(C) = x_0', \#1(C) = x_0 + x_1 + x_1'$. Finally, $x_0'$ agents marked 0 interact with BS, each one exactly once. Now, $size_{BS}[0] = 0, size_{BS}[1] = x_0 + x_0' + x_1 + x_1' = N$ and $\#0(C) = 0, \#1(C) = x_0 + x_0' + x_1 + x_1' = N$ (all agents are marked 1). In this configuration, size_total$_{BS}$ = N, and thus $C^*$ is reachable from (any configuration) $C$.  □

## 4 Space-Optimal Counting under Weak Fairness

In this section, we present a silent symmetric space-optimal protocol (Protocol 2 below) solving the counting problem under weak fairness (see Theorem 2 and Corollary 2). The protocol is correct starting from arbitrary states in mobile agents, but BS. It uses at most $P$ states per agent, which is *necessary* in the current conditions for solving counting in populations with at most $P$ mobile agents $(N \leq P)$ [9].

**Protocol 2 General Description.** In this protocol, BS eventually counts the mobile agents and stores the value in variable $n$. To realize this, BS successively attempts to guess the number of mobile agents in the population, starting from 1 and ending with $N$ (this guess is stored in $n$). For each guess $n < P$, BS tries to name (differently) mobile agents in state 0 (zero-state) interacting with BS (lines 3 and 9). That is, BS tries to assign to these agents distinct states from $\{1, \ldots, n\}$ (also called here names). State 0 has a special technical role. Whenever two agents with identical names (*homonyms*) interact, they change their state to

0 (line 12). Thus, this state indicates to BS that, either it has created homonyms before, or that homonyms (or, simply, agents in state 0) existed already in the population in the starting configuration.

Thus, zero-state mobile agents are named by BS. The names are given one by one following some finite sequence $U^*$ of names (line 9). For simplicity, in the presented protocol, this sequence is computed in advance and depends on $P$. However, for an optimized version, the required prefix of $U^*$, $U_N$, can be computed on the fly, during an execution (see Remark 1). Sequence $U^*$ guarantees that, if there are $N < P$ agents, whatever their starting states are, the naming succeeds. If no naming succeeds, BS concludes that there are more than $P - 1$ agents, that is $N = P$. Thus, the protocol actually realizes a (consecutive minimal) naming for any $N < P$ in order to realize finally a counting for any $N \le P$.

Another important property of $U^*$ is that, for every guess $n$, if all the terms of $U^*$, from the first to some $l_n^{th}$ term, have been used by BS to name interacting agents, then BS can conclude that the guess of $n$ is wrong. It is safe then to switch to the next guess $n + 1$ (line 8). In the sequel, we denote the prefix of $U^*$ of length $l_n$ by $U_n$ ($l_n = |U_n|$). Any term of $U_n$ is in $\{1, \dots, n\}$. Thus, if BS meets an agent in a state $> n$, it can conclude that it has never seen this agent before. Hence, it can safely deduce that $N > n$, and switch to the next guess $n + 1$ (lines 5 - 8).

As long as there are agents in state 0 or in a state $> n$, and $n < P$ (line 2), the base station continues renaming and counting, because all these agents will eventually interact with BS (by weak fairness). If there are homonyms, eventually they meet too and switch to state 0 (again, by fairness).

## Naming Sequence $U^*$ - The Gros Sequence

As a matter of fact, sequence $U^*$ is not unique. We choose and define one of the possible such sequences. We also prove the properties claimed about it above. To define the sequence $U^*$, we consider the infinite sequence $U_\infty$, whose left prefix $U_n$ is defined recursively by $U_n \equiv U_{n-1}, n, U_{n-1}$, where $U_1 \equiv 1$. Sequence $U^*$ is obtained for $n = P - 1$, i.e., $U^* \equiv U_{P-1} \equiv U_{P-2}, P - 1, U_{P-2}$. For example, the prefix $U_4$ of $U_\infty$ is: $1, 2, 1, 3, 1, 2, 1, 4, 1, 2, 1, 3, 1, 2, 1$.

Let $l_n \equiv |U_n|$. By construction of sequence $U_\infty$, $l_1 = 1$, and $l_{n+1} = 2l_n + 1$, which gives $l_n = 2^n - 1$. Then, using the recursive definition of $U_\infty$ we obtain that $\forall n, U_\infty(2^n) = n + 1$ and $\forall n, \forall 1 \le k < 2^n, U_\infty(2^n + k) = U_\infty(k)$.

*Remark 1.* Based on this alternative description, $U_\infty$, and $U^*$ in particular, can be defined iteratively. The $k^{th}$ term of $U_\infty$ is one plus the index of the least significant non-zero bit in the binary decomposition of $k$. Thus, BS does not need to store the whole sequence of names in advance. It can compute the next state to assign to a mobile agent based on a single integer variable. Such computation of the sequence does not depend on $P$, but on the number of the sequence terms which will be actually used. For this sequence, the number of terms used to name $n$ agents is at most $l_n = 2^n - 1$. In consequence, the number of interactions (before convergence) between BS and an agent in state 0 or $> n$ is at most $l_N$.

---

**Protocol 2** Space-Optimal Counting under Weak Fairness ($P$ states per agent)

---

**Variables at BS:**
   $n$: non-negative integer initialized to 0                   // guess of $N$
   $k$: non-negative integer initialized to 0     // pointer to the $k^{th}$ element of $U^*$
**Shortcuts at BS:**
   $U^*$: constant sequence of elements in $[1, \ldots, P-1]$ computed in advance
      by the recursion $U_1 \equiv 1, U^* \equiv U_{P-1} \equiv U_{P-2}, P-1, U_{P-2}$
   $U^*(k)$: returns the $k^{th}$ element of $U^*$
   $l_n = 2^n - 1 \ (\equiv |U_n|)$

 

**Variable at a mobile agent $x$:**
   $name_x$: non-negative integer in $[0, \ldots, P-1]$, initialized *arbitrarily*

 

1: **when** a mobile agent $x$ interacts with BS **do**
2:   **if** $n < P \wedge (name_x = 0 \vee name_x > n)$ **then**
3:     **if** $name_x = 0$ **then**
4:       $k \leftarrow k + 1$             // advance $k$ to point to the next element of $U^*$
5:     **else if** $name_x > n$ **then**
6:       $k \leftarrow l_n + 1$// because agent $x$ with a name $> n$ could not be seen before by
              BS, the population must be larger than $n$, and $k$ is updated accordingly
7:     **if** $k > l_n$ **then**
8:       $n \leftarrow n + 1$           // pointer $k$ indicates that the population is larger
9:       $name_x \leftarrow U^*(k)$       // set the name of $x$ to the the $k^{th}$ element of $U^*$
10: **when** two mobile agents $x$ and $y$ interact **do**
11:   **if** $name_x = name_y$ **then**
12:     $name_x \leftarrow name_y \leftarrow 0$           // set homonym states to 0

---

*Remark 2.* It appears that $U_\infty$ is known in the literature under the name of Gros sequence. This sequence can be found all over mathematics. It has remarkable properties with respect to the binary numeration, generating a Gray code. It encodes an Hamiltonian cycle on the edges of a $n$-dimensional cube. It is also the "greediest" square-free sequence (if one builds the sequence in choosing at each step the smallest integer that does not produce a square). Finally, the Gros sequence solves the Chinese Rings puzzle and, surprisingly, solved the Tower of Hanoi puzzle long before the latter was at all invented. For details refer to [2,17].

    One of the intuitions behind the use of the Gros sequence for counting is related to the Hamiltonian cycle property on a cube. Consider a multi-dimensional cube whose vertices are labeled by the multi-sets of $n$ names and edges connect vertices that differ by exactly one name. Whatever the initial names are (the agents can be arbitrarily initialized), the Gros sequence leads, by traveling along the Hamiltonian cycle it encodes, to the vertex where all names are distinct. In the corresponding configuration the counting can be performed.

    Now we give a more precise, but also more technical, explanation why, by using this particular sequence $U^*$, BS correctly counts $N \ (\leq P)$ agents. Consider the prefix $U_n = U_{n-1}, n, U_{n-1}$ of $U^*$. By assigning successively the numbers given by $U_n$, and in particular by the prefix $U_{n-1}$, BS can assign *distinct* names from $\{1, \ldots, n-1\}$ to *all* agents, only if $N \leq n-1$. If it is not the case ($N > n-1$), BS eventually detects it whenever it meets an agent $x$, either in state $> n-1$, or in state $0$ *after* the last name in $U_{n-1}$ has been assigned (i.e., homonyms still exist). Then, BS guesses that $N = n$, and continues naming with the subsequence $(n, U_{n-1})$. That is, it assigns state $n$ to agent $x$ which becomes unique, if effectively $N = n$. If this is the case, BS should successfully rename the remaining $n-1$ agents with $n-1$ states from $\{1, \ldots, n-1\}$, following, once again, the naming sequence defined by $U_{n-1}$. From now on, the procedure repeats for the sequence $U_{n+1} = U_n, n+1, U_n$. If the guess of $N = n$ was wrong, BS eventually detects it (at least, by the end of the prefix $U_n$), and switches to guess $n+1$. That is, it will continue naming according to $(n+1, U_n)$. This continues until the guess of BS is correct, or till all attempts have failed, meaning that $N = P$.

## Correctness of Protocol 2

In the proofs below, we consider a set $E$ of non-zero-states associated to a configuration $C$ s.t., for every $s \in E$, the number of mobile agents in state $s$ in $C$ is odd. This allows to focus only on the transitions involving BS, and not on transitions between homonyms, which will happen eventually and do not change the parity of the number of agents in any state. Moreover, for any $E, E' \subseteq \{1, \ldots, n\}$, we denote by $E \triangle E' \equiv E \cup E' - E \cap E'$ their symmetric difference. In particular, $E \triangle \{e\}$ ($e \in \{1, \ldots, n\}$) is $E \cup \{e\}$ if $e \notin E$, and $E - \{e\}$ if $e \in E$.

In Lemma 3 below, we prove that when the sequence $U^*$ is used by the protocol, it guarantees that, if $N < P$, $E$ evolves until $E = \{1, \ldots, N\}$, where all mobile agents have distinct names. Then, using Lemma 3 we obtain the main Theorem 2.

**Lemma 3.** *Let $E_0 \subset \{1, \ldots, n\}$ and $E_{k+1} = E_k \triangle \{U_\infty(k+1)\}$. There exists some $1 \leq j \leq 2^n - 1$ such that $E_j = \{1, \ldots, n\}$.*

*Proof.* Let $\mathcal{H}_n$ ($n \in \mathbb{N}$) be the induction hypothesis *"for any subset $E_0 \subset \{1, \ldots, n\}$ and such that $E_{k+1} = E_k \triangle \{U_\infty(k+1)\}$, there is $E_j = \{1, \ldots, n\}$ for some $1 \leq j \leq 2^n - 1$".*

Let us prove the basis for $n = 1$, i.e., for $\mathcal{H}_1$. As $U_\infty(1) = 1$, if $E_0 = \emptyset$, then $E_1 = \{1\}$ and $j = 1$. If $E_0 = \{1\}, j = 0$. Thus $\mathcal{H}_1$ is true.

Assume that, for $n \in \mathbb{N}$, $\mathcal{H}_n$ is true, and consider $E_0 \subset \{1, \ldots, n+1\}$.

First, consider the case where $n+1 \in E_0$. Set $E'_0 = E_0 - \{n+1\}$ and $E'_{k+1} = E'_k \triangle \{U_\infty(k+1)\}$. For all $k \leq 2^n - 1$, $E_k = E'_k \cup \{n+1\}$. According to $\mathcal{H}_n$, there exists $j$ such that $E'_j = \{1, \ldots, n\}$. Then, $E_j = E'_j \cup \{n+1\} = \{1, \ldots, n+1\}$.

Now consider $n+1 \notin E_0$. For all $k \leq 2^n - 1$, $U_\infty(k) \leq n$, and $n+1 \notin E_k$. Then, as $U_\infty(2^n) = n+1$, $E_{2^n} = E_{2^n-1} \cup \{n+1\}$. Set $E'_0 = E_{2^n-1}$ and $E'_{k+1} = E'_k \triangle \{U_\infty(k+1)\}$. For all $k \leq 2^n - 1$, $E_{2^n+k} = E'_k \cup \{n+1\}$. According to $\mathcal{H}_n$, there exists $j$ such that $E'_j = \{1, \ldots, n\}$. Then, $E_{2^n+j} = \{1, \ldots, n+1\}$. By induction, the lemma is true.                                            □

**Theorem 2.** *Protocol 2 solves the counting problem, under weak fairness, for up to $P$ mobile agents, each with $P$ states. Moreover, the protocol names up to $P - 1$ mobile agents with distinct names (for any $N < P$, the names are in $\{1, \ldots N\}$).*

*Proof.* Consider an execution $(C_0, C_1, C_2, \ldots)$ of the protocol. For every $i \geq 0$, let $E_i$ denote the set of states s.t., for every $s \in E_i$, the number of mobile agents in state $s$ in $C_i$ is odd. If $E_i = \{1, \ldots, N\}$, then all the agents have distinct states. Let $n_i$ and $k_i$ denote (respectively) the values of the variables $n$ and $k$ of BS in a configuration $C_i$.

Lemma 3 implies that, for any $N < P$, if $E_0 \subset \{1, \ldots, N\}$ and $E_{k+1} = E_k \triangle \{U^*(k+1)\}$, there exists some $1 \leq j \leq 2^N - 1$ ($l_N = 2^N - 1$) such that $E_j = \{1, \ldots, N\}$ ($|U^*| = 2^P - 1$).

If $n_i < N$, agents cannot all have distinct non-zero-states in $\{1, \ldots, n_i\}$. Consider a configuration where $n_i < N$. There are two cases (i) and (ii) concerning possible transitions with BS. In case (i), there are agents in state 0, or/and there are different agents in the same state (homonyms), that will eventually interact and change their states to 0 (line 12). In both sub-cases, a mobile agent in state 0 eventually meets BS; and in the corresponding transition, in line 4, $k$ increases. Once $k_j > l_{n_j}$ ($j > i$), $n_j$ is incremented (lines 7 - 8). In case (ii), there exists a mobile agent $x$ with $name_x > n_i$, what causes $n$ to increase too. Thus, eventually, $n_j = N$. We show now that the protocol converges to $n = N$ and not a larger value.

- First, assume that the case (ii) does not occur. Consider the first configuration ($C_i$) with $n_i = N$, and suppose $N < P$. Starting from this configuration, BS assigns states to agents following $U_N$. $E_i \in 2^{\{1, \ldots, N\}}$, $k_i > l_{N-1}$ (lines 7 - 8), and only the following transitions between $C_i$ and $C_{i+1}$ are possible:
  1. a transition between homonyms (lines 11 - 12), which results in $E_{i+1} = E_i$;
  2. a transition between BS and an agent in state 0 (lines 3, 4 and 9), which results in $E_{i+1} = E_i \triangle \{U^*(k_i)\}$.

  The number of non-zero homonyms in a given configuration is finite, and transitions of type 1 decrease this number, so that an infinite sequence of transitions of this type is impossible. Thus, while $E_i \neq \{1, \ldots, N\}$ (meaning that there are homonyms or agents in state 0), transitions of type 2 happen. These transitions also increment $k_i$. Let $i_1$, $i_2$, ... denote the indexes of transitions of type 2: $E_{i_{j+1}} = E_{i_j} \triangle \{U^*(k_j)\}$. Lemma 3 implies that there is some $j$ such that $E_{i_j} = \{1, \ldots, N\}$. At this point, all agents are in distinct states, and the protocol has converged with $n = N$, because $n$ increases only if the naming with $n$ states has failed, i.e., when $k > l_n$, (lines 7 - 8) and this impossible in the considered case.
- In case (ii), BS interacts with an agent $x$ with $name_x > n_i$. Agent $x$ has not been assigned before, since otherwise, it would have been given a state $\leq n_i$. The naming with $n_i - 1$ agents would have failed already, while this agent had no interaction. Thus, the execution up to step $i$ is undistinguishable from

an execution with at least $n_i$ agents, but with the agent currently meeting BS, there are at least $n_i + 1$ agents. Thus, $N \geq n_i + 1$. In any case, $n_i \leq N$. □

**Corollary 2.** *Protocol 2 is silent.*

*Proof.* By Theorem 2, for any $N < P$, the protocol finally names all mobile agents with distinct names in $\{1, \ldots N\}$, and thus the condition at line 2 stops being satisfied. Hence, in this case, eventually, no agent changes its state. In the remaining case of $N = P$, the condition at line 2 stops being satisfied when $n$ reaches and stays equal to $N$ (what happens, by Theorem 2). After that, no agent can change its state. □

## 5   Conclusion and Perspectives

In this paper, we presented two population protocols for counting, under two classical fairness assumptions. Under global fairness, we gave a protocol with only two states per agent and, under weak fairness, a protocol with $P$ states ($P$ being an upper bound on the size of the system). In terms of exact space complexity, both protocols are optimal in space and considerably improve the best solutions known up to now, presenting a totally different angle of attack.[2]

Using a memory of only one bit has certainly practical advantages in applications for large-scale networks connecting very simple artifacts. Moreover, the assumption of global fairness, necessary for the correctness of the corresponding protocol, is realized in practice. As described in [5], this is because in practice, a variety of parameters and events (like power-supply, local clock frequency or movement of nodes) affect the scheduling of a system in a random way, making the assumption of global fairness realistic.

The second protocol, under weak fairness, solves the challenge of counting up to $P$ with exactly $P$ states per agent. Nevertheless, due to the nature of the Gros sequence, its time complexity, in terms of non-null transitions or in terms of *(asynchronous) rounds*, is exponential (a round being a shortest fragment of execution where each agent interacts with each other). This is because, in the worst case, the number of non-null transitions (or rounds) till convergence depends on the number of times BS renames a mobile agent. This is $2^{P-1} - 1$ times, due to the length of the used Gros sequence ($|U^*| = 2^{P-1} - 1$; see Remark 1).

We conjecture that this complexity is necessary for the optimal memory space. Intuitively, starting from an arbitrary configuration with $P$ mobile agents, and with only $P$ available states, no protocol at BS can detect the lacking names (states) in the population, during a worst case execution. That is why, in this

---

[2] One may notice that the proposed protocols look more like centralized protocols than distributed ones. This comes from the nature of the problem and from the strong memory constraints. First, as without BS the problem is impossible, any solution has to use some sort of centralization; otherwise BS would not be necessary. Second, reducing the memory to the minimum, strongly limits the useful information that mobile agents can exchange to progress towards the solution.

case, BS cannot advance in naming (required for counting) faster than by following a sequence of at least $O(2^P)$ names. This length is necessary, because there exist $O(2^P)$ different starting configurations and from *any* such configuration, a sequence of at least $O(2^P)$ names is required (in the worst case), for BS to obtain a configuration with distinctly named mobile agents, and count them.

Studying formally the trade off between space and time complexities for counting algorithms in population protocols could be a valuable sequel to the present work. Considering existing counting protocols designed for weak fairness, we can identify the following tendency. With $\log P$ bits of memory per mobile agent, the space-optimal protocol that we present in this paper has an exponential complexity. An additional bit of memory allows to design protocols like in [18] with a logarithmic round complexity, while another additional bit allows to solve this problem in a constant number of rounds [9]. It will be interesting to study whether such drastic trade-offs are necessary.

For global fairness, much less studies about counting protocols and especially about their complexity analysis exist. This is certainly an additional interesting research direction.

Finally, another possible perspective concerns the space complexity of BS. One may imagine a system, where all agents including the distinguishable BS are resource-limited, motivating the study of the necessary space requirements for BS.

**Acknowledgments.** The authors would like to thank Jean-Paul Allouche and Jean Berstel for identifying the Gros sequence, and the anonymous reviewers for their thoughtful and helpful remarks.

# References

1. Afek, Y., Awerbuch, B., Plotkin, S.A., Saks, M.E.: Local management of a global resource in a communication network. In: Symposium on Foundations of Computer Science, pp. 347–357 (1987)
2. Allouche, J.-P., Shallit, J.O.: Automatic Sequences - Theory, Applications, Generalizations. Cambridge Univ. Press (2003). ISBN 978-0-521-82332-6
3. Angluin, D., Aspnes, J., Diamadi, Z., Fischer, M.J., Peralta, R.: Computation in networks of passively mobile finite-state sensors. Dist. Comp. **18**(4), 235–253 (2006)
4. Angluin, D., Aspnes, J., Eisenstat, D., Ruppert, E.: The computational power of population protocols. Dist. Comp. **20**(4), 279–304 (2007)
5. Angluin, D., Aspnes, J., Fischer, M.J., Jiang, H.: Self-stabilizing population protocols. ACM Trans. Auton. Adapt. Syst. **3**(4) (2008)
6. Baquero, C., Almeida, P.S., Menezes, R., Jesus, P.: Extrema propagation: Fast distributed estimation of sums and network sizes. IEEE Trans. Parallel Distrib. Syst. **23**(4), 668–675 (2012)
7. Beauquier, J., Burman, J., Clavière, S.: Comptage et nommage simples et efficaces dans les protocoles de populations symétriques. In: ALGOTEL 2014, pp. 1–4, June 2014

8. Beauquier, J., Burman, J., Clavière, S., Sohier, D.: Space-Optimal Counting in Population Protocols [Extended Version]. Technical report, LRI - CNRS, University Paris-Sud, June 2015
9. Beauquier, J., Clement, J., Messika, S., Rosaz, L., Rozoy, B.: Self-stabilizing counting in mobile sensor networks with a base station. In: Pelc, A. (ed.) DISC 2007. LNCS, vol. 4731, pp. 63–76. Springer, Heidelberg (2007)
10. Bournez, O., Chalopin, J., Cohen, J., Koegler, X.: Playing with population protocols. In: CSP, pp. 3–15 (2008)
11. Dolev, S., Gouda, M.G., Schneider, M.: Memory requirements for silent stabilization. Acta Inf. **36**(6), 447–462 (1999)
12. Dolev, S., Israeli, A., Moran, S.: Self-stabilization of dynamic systems assuming only read/write atomicity. Dist. Comp. **7**(1), 3–16 (1993)
13. Emek, Y., Korman, A.: New bounds for the controller problem. In: DISC, pp. 22–34 (2009)
14. Fraigniaud, P., Pelc, A., Peleg, D., Perennes, S.: Assigning labels in an unknown anonymous network with a leader. Dist. Comp. **14**(3), 163–183 (2001)
15. Ganesh, A.J., Kermarrec, A.-M., Le Merrer, E., Massoulié, L.: Peer counting and sampling in overlay networks based on random walks. Dist. Comp. **20**(4), 267–278 (2007)
16. Gkantsidis, C., Mihail, M., Saberi, A.: Random walks in peer-to-peer networks: Algorithms and evaluation. Perform. Eval. **63**(3), 241–263 (2006)
17. Hinz, A.M., Klavzar, S., Milutinovic, U., Petr, C.: The Tower of Hanoi - Myths and Maths. Birkhäuser Basel (2013). ISBN 3034802366, 9783034802369
18. Izumi, T., Kinpara, K., Izumi, T., Wada, K.: Space-efficient self-stabilizing counting population protocols on mobile sensor networks. Theor. Comput. Sci. **552**, 99–108 (2014)
19. Jiang, H.: Distributed Systems of Simple Interacting Agents. Ph.D thesis, Yale University (2007)
20. Kempe, D., Dobra, A., Gehrke, J.: Gossip-based computation of aggregate information. In: FOCS, pp. 482–491 (2003)
21. Korman, A., Kutten, S.: Controller and estimator for dynamic networks. Inf. Comput. **223**, 43–66 (2013)
22. Kostoulas, D., Psaltoulis, D., Gupta, I., Birman, K.P., Demers, A.J.: Active and passive techniques for group size estimation in large-scale and dynamic distributed systems. Journal of Systems and Software **80**(10), 1639–1658 (2007)
23. Kuhn, F., Lynch, N.A., Oshman, R.: Distributed computation in dynamic networks. In: STOC, pp. 513–522 (2010)
24. Di Luna, G.A., Baldoni, R., Bonomi, S., Chatzigiannakis, I.: Conscious and unconscious counting on anonymous dynamic networks. In: Chatterjee, M., Cao, J., Kothapalli, K., Rajsbaum, S. (eds.) ICDCN 2014. LNCS, vol. 8314, pp. 257–271. Springer, Heidelberg (2014)
25. Di Luna, G., Baldoni, R., Bonomi, S., Chatzigiannakis, I.: Counting in anonymous dynamic networks under worst-case adversary. In: ICDCS, pp. 338–347 (2014)
26. Le Merrer, E., Kermarrec, A.-M., Massoulié, L.: Peer to peer size estimation in large and dynamic networks: a comparative study. In: HPDC, pp. 7–17 (2006)
27. Michail, O., Chatzigiannakis, I., Spirakis, P.G.: Naming and counting in anonymous unknown dynamic networks. In: Higashino, T., Katayama, Y., Masuzawa, T., Potop-Butucaru, M., Yamashita, M. (eds.) SSS 2013. LNCS, vol. 8255, pp. 281–295. Springer, Heidelberg (2013)
28. Mosk-Aoyama, D., Shah, D.: Computing separable functions via gossip. In: PODC, pp. 113–122 (2006)

29. Ribeiro, B.F., Towsley, D.F.: Estimating and sampling graphs with multidimensional random walks. In: ACM SIGCOMM, pp. 390–403 (2010)
30. Tel, G.: Introduction to Distributed Algorithms, 2nd edn. Cambridge University Press (2000)
31. Varagnolo, D., Pillonetto, G., Schenato, L.: Distributed statistical estimation of the number of nodes in sensor networks. In: IEEE Conference on Decision and Control, CDC, pp. 1498–1503 (2010)

# Brief Announcement: On the Voting Time of the Deterministic Majority Process

Dominik Kaaser[1], Frederik Mallmann-Trenn[2,3], and Emanuele Natale[4]

[1] University of Salzburg
[2] École Normale Supérieure
[3] Simon Fraser University
[4] Sapienza Università di Roma

We study the *deterministic binary majority process* which is defined as follows. We are given a graph $G = (V, E)$ where each node has one out of two opinions. The process runs in discrete rounds where in every round each node computes and adopts the majority opinion among all of its neighbors.

It was proved independently by Goles and Olivos [2], and Poljak and Sůra [3] with the same potential function argument that the process always converges to a two-periodic state. Their proof was popularized in the *Puzzled* columns of Communications of the ACM [6]. Let the *convergence time* of a given graph, for a given initial opinion assignment, be the time it takes until the two-periodic state is reached. In this work we give bounds on the *voting time*, which is the maximum convergence time over all possible initial opinion assignments. Frischknecht et al. [1] note that the potential argument by Goles et al. [2,3,6] can be used to prove an $\mathcal{O}(|E|)$ upper bound on the voting time which is also shown to be tight.

Among its widespread applications, variants of the majority process have been used in the area of distributed community detection [4], where the voting time is essentially the convergence time of the proposed community-detection protocols. A lot of attention has been given to the two-periodic state to which the majority process converges to. However, besides the $\mathcal{O}(|E|)$ upper bound that follows from the result by Goles et al. [2,3,6], no further upper bound on the voting time that holds for any initial opinion assignment has been proved. Still, one can observe that in many graphs the voting time is much smaller than $\mathcal{O}(|E|)$, e.g., the voting time of the complete graph is one.

We show that computing whether the voting time is greater than a given number is NP-hard. Unlike many generalizations of the majority process, this is the first NP-hardness proof that does not require any additional mechanisms besides the bare majority rule of the deterministic binary majority process.

**Theorem 1.** *For a given simple graph $G$ and an integer $k$ computing whether there exists an initial opinion assignment for which the voting time of $G$ is at least $k$ is NP-complete.*

A module of a graph is a subset of vertices $S$ such that for each pair of nodes $u, v \in S$ it holds that $N(u) \setminus S = N(v) \setminus S$. By carefully exploiting the structure of the potential function by Goles et al. and leveraging the particular behavior that certain modules of the graph exhibit in the majority process, we are able to prove that the voting time of a graph can be bounded by that of a smaller

© Springer-Verlag Berlin Heidelberg 2015
Y. Moses (Ed.): DISC 2015, LNCS 9363, pp. 647–648, 2015.
DOI: 10.1007/978-3-662-48653-5

graph. This graph can be constructed in linear time by contracting suitable vertices. Thus, we obtain a new upper bound that asymptotically improves on the previous $\mathcal{O}(|E|)$ bound on graph classes characterized by a high number of modules that are either cliques or independent sets. Our bound relies on a well-known graph contraction technique, e.g., see the notion of *identical vertices* in [5]. Before we state our upper bound precisely, we need the following definitions.

**Definition 1.** *A set of nodes $S$ is called a family if and only if for all pairs of nodes $u, v \in S$ we have $N(u)\backslash\{v\} = N(v)\backslash\{u\}$. We say that a family $S$ is proper if $|S| > 1$. Given a graph $G = (V, E)$, its asymmetric graph $G^{\Delta} = (V^{\Delta}, E^{\Delta})$ is the sub-graph of $G$ induced by the subset $V^{\Delta} \subseteq V$ constructed by replacing every family of odd-degree non-adjacent nodes with one node and replacing any other proper family with two nodes.*

The set of families of a graph forms a partition of the nodes into equivalence classes. We prove that the voting time of the majority process is bounded by that of the graph $G^{\Delta}$, obtained by contracting its families into one or two nodes, as stated in the following theorem.

**Theorem 2.** *Given any initial opinion assignment on a graph $G = (V, E)$, the voting time of the majority process is at most*

$$1 + \min\{|E^{\Delta}| - |V_{odd}^{\Delta}|/2, |E^{\Delta}|/2 + |V_{even}^{\Delta}|/4 + 7/4 \cdot |V^{\Delta}|\} \ .$$

*Furthermore, this bound can be computed in $\mathcal{O}(|E|)$ time.*

For instance, for the convergence time of the Turán graph $T(n, r)$ we obtain an $\mathcal{O}(r^2)$ bound and for the convergence time of full $d$-ary trees we get an $\mathcal{O}(|V|/d)$ bound, compared to the previously best known bounds of $\mathcal{O}(n^2)$ and $\mathcal{O}(|V|)$, respectively, originating from the $\mathcal{O}(|E|)$ bounds.

# References

1. Frischknecht, S., Keller, B., Wattenhofer, R.: Convergence in (social) influence networks. In: Afek, Y. (ed.) DISC 2013. LNCS, vol. 8205, pp. 433–446. Springer, Heidelberg (2013)
2. Goles, E., Olivos, J.: Periodic behaviour of generalized threshold functions. Discrete Mathematics **30**(2), 187–189 (1980)
3. Poljak, S., Sůra, M.: On periodical behaviour in societies with symmetric influences. Combinatorica **3**(1), 119–121 (1983)
4. Raghavan, U., Albert, R., Kumara, S.: Near linear time algorithm to detect community structures in large-scale networks. Physical Review E **76**(3), 036106 (2007)
5. Sarıyüce, A., Saule, E., Kaya, K., Çatalyürek, U.: Shattering and compressing networks for betweenness centrality. In: Proc. SDM 2013, pp. 686–694 (2013)
6. Winkler, P.: Puzzled: Delightful Graph Theory. Comm. ACM **51**(8), 104 (2008)

# Brief Announcement:
# Rumor Spreading with Bounded In-Degree

Sebastian Daum, Fabian Kuhn, and Yannic Maus

Dept. of Comp. Science, University of Freiburg, Freiburg, Germany
daum.sebastian@gmail.com, {kuhn,yannic.maus}@cs.uni-freiburg.de

## 1 Introduction, Model and Motivation

Random gossip (**push** and **pull**) is one of the most studied protocols for disseminating information in a network, e.g., [1,3]. Classically, in each time unit, every node $u$ is allowed to contact a single random neighbor $v$. If $u$ knows the data (rumor) to be disseminated, node $v$ learns it (known as **push**) and if node $v$ knows the rumor, $u$ learns it (known as **pull**). While in the classic gossip model, each node is only allowed to contact a single neighbor in each time unit, each node can possibly be successfully contacted by and thus interact with many neighboring nodes. As an extreme case, consider the behavior of random **pull** in a star network where a single center node is connected to $n-1$ leaf nodes. In fact, all recent papers which study the time complexity of the random **push-pull** protocol critically rely on the fact that a node can be contacted by many nodes in a single round, e.g., [2]. However, in order to obtain applicable and scalable protocols, ideally, we would like to not only limit the number of interactions each node initiates, but also the number of interactions each node participates in.

We therefore study a weaker variant of the described random **pull** algorithm, which we call **rpull** (stands for restricted **pull**). In each round, every node can still initiate a connection to one uniformly random neighbor. However, if a single node receives several connection requests, only one of these connections is actually established. We consider two versions of how one of these incoming requests is selected. Assume that in a given round some informed node $v$ receives requests from a set of neighbors $R_v$. In the *adversarial* **rpull** protocol, an (adaptive) adversary picks some node $u \in R_v$ which will then learn the rumor, whereas in the *random* **rpull** protocol, we assume that a uniformly random node $u \in R_v$ learns the rumor (chosen independently for different nodes and rounds). While the choice of which neighbor a node (actively) contacts with a request is under the control of the protocol, it is not necessarily clear how one of the incoming requests in $R_v$ is chosen, e.g., it might be determined by the underlying network infrastructure in which case the adversarial model allows to study the worst-case behavior.

A full version of this paper can be found at *http://arxiv.org/abs/1506.00828*

© Springer-Verlag Berlin Heidelberg 2015
Y. Moses (Ed.): DISC 2015, LNCS 9363, pp. 649–650, 2015.
DOI: 10.1007/978-3-662-48653-5

## 2    Contributions

**Separation of Adversarial and Random Pull:** For trees we can show that both forms of **rpull** are asymptotically as fast as **pull** plus an additive term in the order of the degree of the node that initially has the rumor. On general graphs we show an exponential separation between adversarial and random **rpull**.

**Theorem 1.** *There is a graph such that for all source nodes, the random **rpull** protocol informs all nodes of the network in polylogarithmic time, w.h.p., whereas the adversarial **rpull** algorithm requires time $\tilde{\Omega}(\sqrt{n})$ to even succeed with a constant probability.*

**Comparison of Pull and RPull:** Let $\delta$ and $\Delta$ denote the smallest and largest degrees of a given graph $G$. In each round of **rpull**, in expectation, each informed node receives at most $\Delta/\delta$ requests. Hence, if an uninformed node $u$ sends a request to an informed node, $u$ should receive the rumor with probability at least $\Omega(\delta/\Delta)$. Consequently, intuitively, the slowdown of using random **rpull** instead of the usual **pull** protocol should not be more than roughly $O(\Delta/\delta)$.

**Theorem 2.** *For every given instance, if the **pull** algorithm informs all nodes in $\mathcal{T}$ rounds with probability $p$, the random **rpull** algorithm reaches all nodes in time $O\left(\mathcal{T} \cdot \frac{\Delta}{\delta} \cdot \log n\right)$ with probability $(1 - o(1))p$. The same result holds when comparing random **push-pull** with random **push-rpull**[1].*

While the statement is intuitive its proof turns out more involved. Formally, we prove a stronger statement and couple the random processes defined by **pull** and random **rpull** such that for every start configuration, w.h.p., the set of nodes informed after $O\left(\frac{\Delta}{\delta} \cdot \log n\right)$ rounds of random **rpull** is a superset of the set of nodes informed in a single **pull** round. We achieve this by coupling both processes with an intermediate process which is similar to **rpull** but removes dependencies between nodes which request from the same neighbor. Note that there is no coupling of **pull** and **rpull** in the classical sense, i.e., a coupling which does relinquish the *w.h.p.* term.

   Furthermore, we show that for such a round-by-round analysis, our bound is tight. That is, there are configurations where $\Omega\left(\frac{\Delta}{\delta} \log n\right)$ random **rpull** rounds are needed to simulate a single **pull** round, w.h.p..

## References

1. Demers, A., Greene, D., Hauser, C., Irish, W., Larson, J., Shenker, S., Sturgis, H., Swinehart, D., Terry, D.: Epidemic algorithms for replicated database management. In: Proc. Symp. on Principles of Dist. Comp. (PODC), pp. 1–12 (1987)
2. Giakkoupis, G.: Tight bounds for rumor spreading in graphs of a given conductance. In: Proc. Symp. on Theoretical Aspects of Comp. Sc. (STACS), pp. 57–68 (2011)
3. Karp, R., Schindelhauer, C., Shenker, S., Vöcking, B.: Randomized rumor spreading. In: Proc. Symp. on Foundations of Comp. Sc. (FOCS), pp. 565–574 (2000)

---

[1] By **push-rpull** we denote the combination of **rpull** with a simultaneous execution of the classic **push** protocol.

# Brief Announcement: On the Power of One Bit in Graph Exploration Without Backtracking

Artur Menc[1], Dominik Pająk[2], and Przemysław Uznański[3]*

[1] Wrocław University of Technology, Poland
[2] Computer Laboratory, University of Cambridge, UK
[3] Helsinki Institute for Information Technology HIIT,
Department of Computer Science, Aalto University, Finland

We consider a model of a deterministic $(\mathcal{M}_a, \mathcal{M}_w)$-agent with $\mathcal{M}_a$ bits of internal memory and $\mathcal{M}_w$ bits at each node of some graph $G$ that is able to visit vertices and traverse edges of $G$. The memory at each node is accesible only upon visiting to that node. The goal of the agent is to explore an anonymous and initially unknown $G$, i.e. visit all its $n$ nodes. We assume that there is no global labeling of nodes but we assume local port-labeling i.e., edges outgoing from each node of degree $d$ are uniquely labeled with numbers from 1 to $d$. The label of the port via which the agent entered to its current location is not a part of the input to our agent hence $\mathcal{M}_a + \mathcal{M}_w \geq \log_2 d$ as each deterministic algorithm needs at least $d$ different inputs to produce $d$ different outputs.

**Upper bound.** Exploration by a $(0, \log d)$-agent is possible by using procedure called ROTOR-ROUTER that works in pessimistic time $\Theta(mD)$ [1,4] in any graph with $m$ edges and diameter $D$. In ROTOR-ROUTER the agent upon consecutive visits to node $v$ is propagated to neighbors of $v$ in a round-robin fashion. Previous work on ROTOR-ROUTER [1,4] showed that this procedure exhibits the following regular structure. In subsequent phases, it traverses Eulerian cycles of subgraphs of directed symmetric version of $G$, where $i$-th phase starts with the $i$-th traversal of the arc associated with port 1 outgoing from the starting vertex. In each phase, ROTOR-ROUTER follows the same trajectory as in previous phases, with the exception that each so-called border vertex $v$ (a vertex whose set of outgoing arcs contains both traversed and not traversed arcs at the beginning of a given phase) is a root of a new exploration subphase. In an exploration subphase, some neighborhood of border vertex $v$ is explored, including all unvisited neighbors of $v$, potentially creating new border vertices.

*Algorithm overview.* In our algorithm ONE-BIT, the agent carries one bit of information (two states: $\alpha$-MODE and $\beta$-MODE), that is whether the last seen vertex was visited at most $\deg(v)$ times or not. Exploration subphase in one non-interrupted $\alpha$-MODE resembles an exploration subphase from ROTOR-ROUTER, that is starting each time from some border vertex $v$, and ending in the same

---

* Part of this work was done while D. Pająk was visiting P. Uznański at Aix-Marseille Université. Partially supported by the Labex Archimède and by the ANR project MACARON (ANR-13-JS02-0002)

Y. Moses (Ed.): DISC 2015, LNCS 9363, pp. 651–652, 2015.
DOI: 10.1007/978-3-662-48653-5

vertex $v$, while traversing only new arcs. Denote a sequence of vertices visited by $v_0 = v, v_1, \ldots, v_k = v$. When returning to $v$ for the $\deg(v)$-th time, the algorithm detects that every neighbor of $v$ was visited, and switches to $\beta$-MODE, where agent will follow the same sequence $v_0, v_1, \ldots, v_k$ traversing each arc for the second time. However, whenever in a $\beta$-MODE the agent detects that its current location is a new border vertex, let us call it $v_i$, then current $\beta$-MODE will be interrupted by a subsequent (recursive) phases of $\alpha$-MODE and $\beta$-MODE both starting and ending in $v_i$. Only after those two phases (and possible recursive ones), the agent will fall back to original $\beta$-MODE traversal and continue to $v_{i+1}$.

**Theorem 1.** *An $(1, \mathcal{O}(\log d))$-agent following algorithm* ONE-BIT *explores with return any graph in time $4m$, by traversing every edge twice in each direction. Moreover, after the exploration is completed, the memory state of the agent and of each node is equal to the initial state.*

**Lower bounds.** Exploration using a $(\infty, 0)$-agent corresponds to a well known problem of Universal Traversal Sequences. Exploration time in this model is lower bounded by $\Omega(n^{1.51})$ on the path [3] and by $\Omega(n^4)$ in general graphs [2]. We show lower bound for $(0, \infty)$-agent. The following theorem is an evidence that the ROTOR-ROUTER is the best strategy for oblivious agent with memory on nodes.

**Theorem 2.** *For any $(0, \infty)$-agent the worst-case exploration time of graph $G$ is at least $(n-1)^2$ if $G$ is a path and $\Omega(n^3)$ if $G$ can be an arbitrary graph.*

**Conclusions.** We showed that in the model with unknown inport having only one type of memory leads to pessimistic exploration time $\Omega(n^3)$. On the other hand $(1, \mathcal{O}(\log d))$-agent can explore in optimal time $4m$. Secondly we show that a single type of memory cannot guarantee that the agent will stop after completeing the task while our ONE-BIT algorithm for $(1, \mathcal{O}(\log d))$-agent has this property.

# References

1. Bampas, E., Gąsieniec, L., Hanusse, N., Ilcinkas, D., Klasing, R., Kosowski, A.: Euler tour lock-in problem in the rotor-router model. In: Keidar, I. (ed.) DISC 2009. LNCS, vol. 5805, pp. 423–435. Springer, Heidelberg (2009)
2. Borodin, A., Ruzzo, W.L., Tompat, M.: Lower bounds on the length of universal traversal sequences. JCSS **45**(2), 180–203 (1992)
3. Dai, H.K., Flannery, K.E.: Improved length lower bounds for reflecting sequences. In: Cai, J.-Y., Wong, C.K. (eds.) COCOON 1996. LNCS, vol. 1090, pp. 56–67. Springer, Heidelberg (1996)
4. Yanovski, V., Wagner, I.A., Bruckstein, A.M.: A distributed ant algorithm for efficiently patrolling a network. Algorithmica **37**(3), 165–186 (2003)

# Brief Announcement: Uniform Information Exchange in Multi-channel Wireless Ad Hoc Networks

Li Ning[1], Dongxiao Yu[2], Yong Zhang[1,2], Yuexuan Wang[2,3],
Francis C.M. Lau[2], and Shengzhong Feng[1]

[1] Shenzhen Institutes of Advanced Technology, Chinese Academy of Sciences, China
{li.ning,zhangyong,sz.feng}@siat.ac.cn
[2] Department of Computer Science, The University of Hong Kong, Hong Kong
{dxyu,fcmlau}@cs.hku.hk
[3] College of Computer Science and Technology, Zhejiang University, China
amywang@hku.hk

We consider a complete graph of $n$ nodes, any pair of which can communicate with each other directly through one of $\mathcal{F}$ available wireless channels. $n$ is not known to the nodes. Time is divided into synchronous rounds. In each round, a node can select at most one channel to listen to or transmit on. Transmission is successful if there is exactly one node transmitting on a channel (and one or more nodes listening). If two or more nodes transmit on the same channel, a collision occurs and their transmissions fail. Nodes can detect collisions, i.e., can distinguish collision from silence. We study distributed solutions to the *information exchange problem*: given initially $k$ nodes each holding a packet, the task is to disseminate these $k$ packets to all $n$ nodes as quickly as possible. We assume that multiple packets can be packed in a single message.

Recently, due to the advent of mobile devices that can operate on multiple channels, some attention has been given to studying the effect of multiple channels on improving communication [1–4]. However, all existing works require prior knowledge of $n$. In ad hoc networks, to make $n$ known to all the nodes in fact can be a tough task. Moreover, in ad hoc networks, the value of $n$ could change sporadically or even frequently due to nodes leaving and joining. Hence, there is practical need for designing *uniform* protocols that do not require any prior information about the network including $n$ and $k$. Not knowing the parameters $n$ or $k$ greatly increases the difficulty of designing fast algorithms, especially in the case where different nodes can operate on different channels, as it is hard to manage the transmission probabilities over the distributed set of nodes.

The details of this work can be found in [5].

This work is supported in part by NSFC of China (61402461, 61073174, 11171086, 61433012, U1435215), Shenzhen Funding Program for Fundamental Research (JCYJ20140509174140680), Natural Science Foundation of Hebei (A2013201218), and the HKU Small Project Fund.

© Springer-Verlag Berlin Heidelberg 2015
Y. Moses (Ed.): DISC 2015, LNCS 9363, pp. 653–654, 2015.
DOI: 10.1007/978-3-662-48653-5

## Uniform Information Exchange Protocol

Given $\mathcal{F}$ available channels, our protocol applies a very intuitive rule for the nodes to select a channel: in each round, a node selects one channel uniformly at random, and then transmits or listens on the selected channel. If a node listens and detects that the selected channel is *idle*, it doubles its transmission probability, or otherwise, it halves the probability. To achieve the desired efficiency in using the channels, the total transmission probability of all the nodes should be in a "safe range", $[\alpha_1 \cdot \mathcal{F}, \alpha_2 \cdot \mathcal{F}]$ with constants $\alpha_2 > \alpha_1 > 0$. Since the nodes distributedly and independently select their channels, the per-channel total transmission probability of nodes selecting a channel may vary substantially from channel to channel. This causes difficulties in analyzing whether the safe range is still guaranteed after an update (halving or doubling). In our protocol, the nodes selecting the same channel update their transmission probabilities consistently, and we show that whenever the total transmission probability of all the nodes falls outside the safe range, there are enough channels where the nodes would behave consistently to pull the total transmission probability back to be within the safe range. Our protocol also applies the technique of *indirection*: "if your message is received by another transmitter, then you need never to transmit again." With this in place, transmitting nodes become fewer and fewer as the protocol executes. When the number of transmitting nodes becomes rather small, using all $\mathcal{F} > 1$ channels is not beneficial, as it is harder for these nodes to meet each other over a randomly selected channel. In our solution, when there are only a few transmitting nodes remaining, they stop selecting a random channel but would operate on a pre-defined channel.

**Main Results.** The proposed protocol can accomplish the dissemination in $O(k/\mathcal{F} + \mathcal{F} \cdot \log n)$ rounds with high probability, assuming collision detection. This result is asymptotically optimal when $k$ is large ($k \geq \mathcal{F}^2 \cdot \log n$). Furthermore, our protocol can handle dynamic joining and leaving of nodes efficiently. After a node joining or leaving, the existing nodes will adapt quickly to a state of "safe range", in which the $\mathcal{F}$ channels will continue to be made full use of. Our protocol is probably the first known *uniform* protocol for information exchange.

## References

1. Daum, S., Ghaffari, M., Gilbert, S., Kuhn, F., Newport, C.C.: Maximal independent sets in multichannel radio networks. In: PODC 2013 (2013)
2. Halldórsson, M.M., Wang, Y., Yu, D.: Leveraging multiple channels in ad hoc networks. In: PODC 2015 (2015)
3. Wang, Y., Wang, Y., Yu, D., Yu, J., Lau, F.C.M.: Information exchange with collision detection on multiple channels. JOCO, 1–18 (2014)
4. Yu, D., Wang, Y., Yu, Y., Yu, J., Lau, F.C.M.: Speedup of information exchange using multiple channels in wireless ad hoc networks. In: INFOCOM 2015 (2015)
5. Ning, L., Yu, D., Zhang, Y., Wang, Y., Lau, F.C.M., Feng, S.: Uniform Information Exchange in Multi-channel Wireless Ad Hoc Networks. CoRR abs/1503.08570 (2015)

# Brief Announcement: Self-stabilizing Virtual Synchrony

Shlomi Dolev[1], Chryssis Georgiou[2], Ioannis Marcoullis[2], and Elad M. Schiller[3]

[1] Ben-Gurion University of the Negev, Israel
[2] University of Cyprus, Cyprus
[3] Chalmers University of Technology, Sweden

*Introduction.* Systems satisfying the Virtual Synchrony (VS) property provide message multicast and group membership services in which all system events, group membership changes, and incoming messages, are delivered in the same order. VS is an important abstraction, proven to be extremely useful when implemented over asynchronous, typically large-scale, message-passing distributed systems, as it simplifies the design of distributed applications, e.g., *State Machine Replication* (SMR). The VS property ensures that two or more processors that participate in two consecutive communicating groups should have delivered the same messages. Self-stabilizing systems can tolerate transient faults that drive the system to an unpredicted arbitrary configuration. Such systems automatically regain consistency from any such configuration, and then produce the desired system behavior ensuring it for a practically infinite number of successive steps, e.g., $2^{64}$ steps. We present the first, to our knowledge, *self-stabilizing virtual synchrony* algorithm.

*An Overview of Our Results.* We consider an asynchronous message passing system consisting of $n$ uniquely identified processors of which a minority may become inactive (crash). Any message that is sent infinitely often from one active processor to another active processor is eventually received. The communication links have known bounded capacity, and can emulate reliable FIFO communication channel protocols using existing self-stabilizing algorithms.

*Bounded labeling scheme for multiple writers.* We extend an existing self-stabilizing labeling scheme to support counter incrementing by multiple label creators (writers) rather than by a single writer. The *labels* are related to an integer counter allowing the system to stabilize. A 64-bit counter, for example, is considered to be practically infinite. There are two main challenges to achieve the result. Multiple writers can concurrently create labels. To overcome this issue, we include the writer identity to break symmetry and decide which label is the most recent one. In this way, the scheme ensures that every active processor $p_i$ eventually "cleans up" the system from obsolete labels of which $p_i$ appears to be the creator, but may be the result of the system's initial arbitrary state.

The second challenge is to overcome problems emerging from labels attributed to inactive processors that cannot clean-up their own labels. Note that there is no knowledge of these processors' inactivity. Consider an initial

© Springer-Verlag Berlin Heidelberg 2015
Y. Moses (Ed.): DISC 2015, LNCS 9363, pp. 655–656, 2015.
DOI: 10.1007/978-3-662-48653-5

system state including a cycle of labels $\ell_1 \prec \ell_2 \prec \ell_3 \prec \ell_1$, all of the same creator, say $p_x$, where $\prec$ is the label order relation. If $p_x$ is active, it will eventually learn about these labels and introduce a label greater than them all. But if $p_x$ is inactive, the system's asynchronous nature may present the three labels to some active processor $p_i$ in their order of precedence and force their adoption, indefinitely. We settle this issue by keeping a label history of proven sufficient label size. The algorithm is proved to be self-stabilizing and to provide a global maximal label.

*Practically infinite counter for multiple writers.* We extend the labeling scheme to handle *counters*, where a counter consists of a *label*, as used in the labeling scheme; an integer *sequence number*, ranging from 0 to $2^b$, say $b = 64$; and a processor *id*. The counter increment algorithm uses the same structures and procedures as the labeling algorithm, but now with counters instead of labels. The challenge for the counter algorithm is to make sure that when a label has an exhausted counter (i.e., one that has reached its maximum) the label is changed and a new label is chosen. The counter algorithm is proved to guarantee eventually monotonic counter increment by multiple writers given a minority of inactive processors. The counter increment algorithm can be used to obtain a self-stabilizing MWMR shared memory emulation.

*Self-stabilizing virtual synchrony.* Systems guaranteeing the VS property provide two main services: a membership service and a reliable multicast service. We provide these services in a coordinator-based solution, considering a single majority group in the system, the primary partition. The membership service provides the current group *view* of the recently live and connected group members. A view is composed of the view identifier obtained from the counter increment algorithm, and the group membership is provided by a failure detector (FD). The output of the coordinator's FD defines the set of view members; this helps to maintain a consistent membership among the group members, despite inaccuracies between the various FDs. The coordinator is also responsible for the consistency of the multicast mechanism within the group. To this end, it requests, collects and combines input from the group members, and then multicasts the updated information before initiating a new multicast round. Each participant keeps the last delivered message and the view identifier that delivered this message. This, together with the intersection property of majorities, and after taking care of some subtle issues, provides the VS property. As part of our VS solution, we also implement a virtually synchronous SMR algorithm. Every processor maintains a replica of the state machine and the last processed (composite) message. Starting from an arbitrary configuration, our algorithm eventually implements replicated automaton emulation that preserves VS. Full details can be found in [1].

# References

1. Dolev, S., Georgiou, C., Marcoullis, I., Schiller, E.M.: Self-stabilizing virtual synchrony. In: Pelc, A., Schwarzmann, A.A. (eds.) SSS 2015. LNCS, vol. 9212, pp. 248–264. Springer, Heidelberg (2015). (arXiv:1502.05183)

# Brief Announcement: Distributed Task Allocation in Ant Colonies

Anna Dornhaus[1], Nancy Lynch[2], Tsvetomira Radeva[2], and Hsin-Hao Su[3]

[1] University of Arizona
[2] Massachusetts Institute of Technology
[3] University of Michigan

A common problem in both distributed computing and insect biology is designing a model that accurately captures the behavior of a given distributed system or an ant colony, respectively. While the challenges involved in modeling computer systems and ant colonies are quite different from each other, a common approach is to explore multiple variations of different models and compare the results in terms of the simplicity of the model and the quality of the results. We consider the task allocation problem as a case study and explore multiple models inspired from both distributed computing and biological experiments. We compare the models with respect to their significance in understanding real ant behavior and also their technical relevance to distributed computing.

**Task Allocation:** In ant colonies, the task allocation problem is a distributed assignment of ants to tasks with the goal of satisfying the demands of all tasks. The first attempt at modeling the task allocation problem from a distributed computing perspective was in [2], where the authors show that the ants can solve the task allocation problem in $O(|T| \log |A|)$ rounds, where $A$ is the set of ants and $T$ is the set of tasks. Biologists have also modeled the ant task allocation process from a distributed perspective by designing various models [5,6] that try to match the actual ant behavior.

**Summary of Results:** We consider two families of models based on the type of input ants receive from the environment. In our first family of models, each ant learns from the environment (1) whether it is successful at the current task it is working on, and (2) a new task it can start working on if it is idle or unsuccessful at its old task. For (1), we consider a function that ensures the number of successful ants working on a given task is no more than the demand for the task. For (2), we consider different options, ranging from a uniformly random task to a task chosen based on the proportion of ants already working on it. We show that, depending on the choice of this function, the running time of the resulting task allocation process ranges from $O(\log |T|)$ to $O(|T| \log |A|)$ rounds, also proving a better time bound for the algorithm in [2].

The second family of models we consider captures the individual variation in the work units each ant provides to different tasks. Task allocation with individual variation is NP-hard; we provide a simple mechanism to *approximately*

This work is sponsored in part by NSF grants BIO-1455983, CCF-0939370, CCF-1217338, CNS-1318294 and AFOSR grant FA9550-13-1-0042.

© Springer-Verlag Berlin Heidelberg 2015
Y. Moses (Ed.): DISC 2015, LNCS 9363, pp. 657–658, 2015.
DOI: 10.1007/978-3-662-48653-5

satisfy the demands of each task (assuming this is possible). We show that after $O(|A|^{1-\epsilon})$ rounds, the ants converge to a solution that satisfies the demands with an $O(W|A|^{1/2+\epsilon})$ additive error, where $W$ is the ratio between the largest and the smallest number of work units provided by the ants. In each round, each ant switches to the current most promising task with some probability, and that probability diminishes in each subsequent round. The current most promising task for a given ant is the task with the largest deficit (the difference between the demand and the work provided already) weighted by the work units the ant is capable of providing for the task. The main technique in our analysis is derived from the multiplicative weight update method for solving linear programs [1,7] with modifications to accommodate the limited capabilities of ants. We conjecture that the above technique has potential applications outside the ant world; for example, task allocation among non-communicating agents with individual variation and a global view of task deficits.

**Contribution to Biology:** One goal of our analysis is to show that if task allocation is allowed to be approximate, it need not become significantly more difficult with larger colony sizes; this is supported by the fact that, in our results, the convergence time of the task allocation process depends only logarithmically, or does not depend at all, on $|A|$. This conclusion is not obvious from prior theory results (e.g. [2]), which contradicted the notion of empiricists that larger colonies perform better at task allocation [4].

Our results also provide a novel hypothesis for the existence of idle ants: we show that the task allocation process is faster when there are extra ants compared to the case where the number of ants is very close to the total sum of demands. While the existence of idle ants is supported by empirical evidence [3], biologists do not have an adequate explanation for this behavior. These general observations make our results broadly relevant for understanding the evolution of division of labor in biological systems.

# References

1. Arora, S., Hazan, E., Kale, S.: The multiplicative weights update method: a meta-algorithm and applications. Theory of Computing **8**(1), 121–164 (2012)
2. Cornejo, A., Dornhaus, A.R., Lynch, N.A., Nagpal, R.: Task allocation in ant colonies. In: Proc. 28th Symposium on Distributed Computing, pp. 46–60 (2014)
3. Dornhaus, A., Holley, J.-A., Pook, V.G., Worswick, G., Franks, N.R.: Why do not all workers work? colony size and workload during emigrations in the ant temnothorax albipennis. Behavioral Ecology and Sociobiology **63**(1):43–51, 2008.
4. Dornhaus, A., Powell, S., Bengston, S.: Group size and its effects on collective organization. Annual review of entomology **57**, 123–141 (2012)
5. Gordon, D.M., Goodwin, B.C., Trainor, L.E.H.: A parallel distributed model of the behaviour of ant colonies. Journal of Theoretical Biology **156**(3), 293–307 (1992)
6. Pacala, S.W., Gordon, D.M., Godfray, H.C.J.: Effects of social group size on information transfer and task allocation. Evol Ecol **10**(2), 127–165 (1996)
7. Young, N.E.: Randomized rounding without solving the linear program. In: Proc. 26th ACM-SIAM Symposium on Discrete Algorithms, pp. 170–178 (1995)

# Brief Announcement: A Concurrency-Optimal List-Based Set

Vincent Gramoli[1,2], Petr Kuznetsov[3], Srivatsan Ravi[4], and Di Shang[2]

[1] NICTA
[2] University of Sydney
vincent.gramoli@sydney.edu.au,dsha5693@uni.sydney.edu.au
[3] Télécom ParisTech
petr.kuznetsov@telecom-paristech.fr
[4] TU Berlin
srivatsan.ravi@tu-berlin.de

*Measuring concurrency.* Multicore applications require highly concurrent data structures. Yet, the very notion of concurrency is vaguely defined, to say the least. What is meant by a "highly concurrent" data structure implementing a given high-level object type? Generally speaking, one could compare the concurrency of algorithms by running a game where an adversary decides on the schedules of shared memory accesses from different processes. At the end of the game, the more schedules the algorithm would accept without hampering high-level correctness, the more concurrent it would be. The algorithm that accepts all correct schedules would then be considered *concurrency-optimal*.

*The lack of concurrency.* To illustrate the difficulty of optimizing concurrency, let us consider a highly concurrency-friendly data structures: the sorted linked list. Since updates on a list-based set affect only a small number of contiguous list nodes, most of them could, in principle, run concurrently without conflicts.

The Lazy Linked List [1] achieves high concurrency by holding locks on only two consecutive nodes when updating but suffers from an overly conservative post-locking validation scheme. More precisely, both insert($v$) and remove($v$) traverse the structure until they find a node whose value is larger or equal to $v$, at which point they acquire locks on two consecutive nodes. Only then the existence of the value $v$ is checked: if $v$ is found (resp. not found), then the insertion (resp., removal) releases the locks and returns without modifying the structure. To illustrate that this concurrency limitation may lead to poor scalability, consider Figure 1 that depicts the performance of a 100-element Lazy Linked List under a workload of 10% updates (insertions/removals) and 90% of contains on a 64-core machine. The list is comparatively small, hence all updates (even the failed insertions and removals) are likely to contend. We can see that when we increase the number of threads beyond 40, the performance drops significantly. This observation raises an interesting question: Does there exist a concurrency-optimal list-based set algorithm?

The author is supported by the Agence Nationale de la Recherche, ANR-14-CE35-0010-01, project DISCMAT.

Y. Moses (Ed.): DISC 2015, LNCS 9363, pp. 659–660, 2015.
DOI: 10.1007/978-3-662-48653-5

*Our contribution.* We answer this question in the affirmative. We propose the *Versioned List*, the first concurrency-optimal list-based set algorithm to date [2]. Its key feature is a *versioned try-lock*, a novel synchronization step inspired by transactional memory (TM). It allows us to implement a pre-locking validation: an update operation uses a CAS to set a versioned try-lock immediately after the validation of the node succeeds. In short, a lock is taken and schedules are rejected only if the data structure has to be modified under the effect of either a successful insertion or a successful removal. The versioned try-lock can be implemented using a

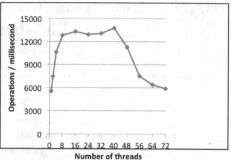

**Fig. 1.** The concurrency limitation of the Lazy Linked List based set leads to poor scalability as operations potentially contend on meta-data even when they do not modify the structure

StampedLock since Java 8 and a uint in C/C++. The Versioned List algorithm combines this new version try-lock with existing efficient mechanisms: the logical deletion technique of the Harris-Michael algorithm [3,4] and the wait-free traversal of the Lazy Linked List [1]. If acquiring the try-lock fails because of a version change, then the operation re-reads some nodes.

We show that the Versioned List algorithm implements a linearizable set and rejects a concurrent schedule only if otherwise the linearizability of the set type is violated. Our algorithm is thus provably concurrency-optimal: no other correct list-based set algorithm can accept more schedules. This observation unveils an interesting desirable data structure property by which concurrent operations conflict on metadata only when they "conflict" on data, for which we need to exploit the semantics of the high-level data type. Note that this property extends the formal definitions of DAP [5–7] that are all trivially ensured by classic linked list implementations simply because all their operations "access" the *head* node and, thus, are allowed to conflict on the metadata.

## References

1. Heller, S., Herlihy, M., Luchangco, V., Moir, M., Scherer III, W.N., Shavit, N.: A lazy concurrent list-based set algorithm. In: Anderson, J.H., Prencipe, G., Wattenhofer, R. (eds.) OPODIS 2005. LNCS, vol. 3974, pp. 3–16. Springer, Heidelberg (2006)
2. Gramoli, V., Kuznetsov, P., Ravi, S., Shang, D.: A concurrency-optimal list-based set. Technical Report 1502.01633, arXiv (2015)
3. Harris, T.L.: A Pragmatic implementation of non-blocking linked-lists. In: Welch, J.L. (ed.) DISC 2001. LNCS, vol. 2180, pp. 300–314. Springer, Heidelberg (2001)
4. Michael, M.M.: High performance dynamic lock-free hash tables and list-based sets. In: SPAA, pp. 73–82 (2002)
5. Attiya, H., Hillel, E., Milani, A.: Inherent limitations on disjoint-access parallel implementations of transactional memory. In: SPAA, pp. 69–78 (2009)
6. Guerraoui, R., Kapalka, M.: Principles of Transactional Memory. Synthesis Lectures on Distributed Computing Theory. Morgan & Claypool Publishers (2010)
7. Ellen, F., Fatourou, P., Kosmas, E., Milani, A., Travers, C.: Universal constructions that ensure disjoint-access parallelism and wait-freedom. In: PODC, pp. 115–124 (2012)

# Brief Announcement: HTM-Assisted Combining

Alex Kogan and Yossi Lev

Oracle Labs

## 1 Introduction

Transactional lock elision (TLE) [2] and flat combining (FC) [1] are two techniques aimed to improve performance of lock based programs. TLE uses hardware transactional memory (HTM) for *optimistic synchronization*, where critical sections' code is run concurrently using hardware transactions as long as their associated lock is not held; the lock is only acquired when a transaction fails to commit. FC, on the other hand, is effective when *many threads are trying to acquire the lock*; the thread holding the lock (denoted as *combiner*) executes operations on behalf of threads waiting for the lock. Along with improved cache locality, this approach allows optimizing a sequence of operations by either combining them together into a more compact operation, or by eliminating one operation with another. Therefore, while TLE is often beneficial for data structures whose operations rarely conflict (e.g., a binary tree), FC is more suitable for data structures with inherently conflicting operations (e.g., a stack or a queue).

This work introduces the *HTM-assisted Combining Framework* (HCF), that integrates the optimistic synchronization and combining approaches for a "best of both words" solution. We demonstrate that it is not sufficient to simply apply the FC algorithm if and when the lock is acquired by threads using TLE, as threads that are not waiting for the lock are still prevented from making any progress. HCF, on the other hand, attempts to combine operations using HTM, and thus allows multiple (combiner and non-combiner) threads to access the data structure concurrently. In particular, HCF allows multiple threads to concurrently combine different kind of operations, and hence is well suited for data structures with operations of different nature. For example, consider a priority queue, where we expect all RemoveMin operations to conflict with each other, while Insert operations can still run in parallel with all other operations. With HCF, we can use TLE for Insert operations while concurrently combining RemoveMin operations. Importantly, due to the use of HTM, this is achieved using a simple sequential implementation of the data structure protected by a global lock, without the need to reason about fine-grained synchronization. In particular, the choice of how many combiners to use and which operations to combine can only affect performance, not correctness.

## 2 Overview of HCF

**Algorithm Overview:** HCF assigns each operation Op to a publication array, PA(Op), that has at most one thread executing as a combiner for the operations

© Springer-Verlag Berlin Heidelberg 2015
Y. Moses (Ed.): DISC 2015, LNCS 9363, pp. 661–662, 2015.
DOI: 10.1007/978-3-662-48653-5

it stores. Using multiple publication arrays allows concurrent execution of operations that are unlikely to conflict with each other. In the following we briefly describe how operations are applied using HCF.

A thread T first tries to apply the operation Op using a hardware transaction (TX). If failed (perhaps multiple times), it announces the operation in PA(Op), and keeps trying to execute Op using a TX, while checking that the operation is not being helped by a combiner thread. If Op is still not completed after these attempts, T becomes the combiner for the operations in PA(Op), where it tries to execute a subset of them (including Op) using one ore more TXs. Finally, if T failed to apply Op using TXs in the combining phase, it acquires the data-structure lock and finishes the combining operation while holding the lock, without using HTM. Both combining phases (with or without HTM) allow any data-structure specific combining and elimination techniques that can reduce the contention on the main data structure, and help executing operations faster. Critically, like with TLE, any TX run by HCF respects the data structure's lock, testing that it is not held and aborting otherwise.

**Evaluation:** We evaluated HCF with a priority queue data structure, implemented as a skip-list, so we can efficiently combine $N$ RemoveMin operations by chopping off the first $N$ elements in the list. Experiments were done on an Intel Haswell (Core i7-4770) 4-core hyper-threaded machine (total of 8 hardware threads). HCF allows us to assign the RemoveMin and Insert operations to different publication arrays, so they can execute in parallel, while still restricting the parallelism (and enable combining) between operations of the same type. We used different number of TX trials in each phase for the two operation types, as multiple RemoveMin operations are much less likely to succeed in parallel, while Insert operations can enjoy from parallel execution. Furthermore, in the combining phases, all RemoveMin operations were combined into a single operation, but no combining or helping was applied for Insert operations. The throughput results confirm that when running only RemoveMin operations, FC significantly outperforms TLE, and when running only Insert operations, TLE has the upper hand. In both cases, our HCF variants provide competitive or better results to that of the winning strategy. The biggest advantage of HCF, however, is evident in the 50%-50% operation mix experiment. There, the variants that use different configurations of HCF for Insert and RemoveMin outperform all other mechanisms (including the naive solution that uses TLE and applies FC if and when a thread is acquiring the lock) by a large margin (e.g., by about 40% at 8 threads). This demonstrates one of the most important benefits of our algorithm: the ability to easily apply different combining policies in parallel for different operations executed on the same data structure.

## References

1. Hendler, D., Incze, I., Shavit, N., Tzafrir, M.: Flat combining and the synchronization-parallelism tradeoff. In: Proceedings of the ACM Symposium on Parallelism in Algorithms and Architectures (SPAA), pp. 355–364 (2010)
2. Rajwar, R., Goodman, J.R.: Speculative lock elision: enabling highly concurrent multithreaded execution. In: Proceedings of the 34th Annual ACM/IEEE International Symposium on Microarchitecture, pp. 294–305 (2001)

# Brief Announcement: Left-Right - A Concurrency Control Technique with Wait-Free Population Oblivious Reads

Pedro Ramalhete[1] and Andreia Correia[2]

[1] Cisco Systems,
pramalhe@gmail.com
[2] ConcurrencyFreaks
andreiacraveiroramalhete@gmail.com

We present a new concurrency control algorithm with Blocking Starvation-Free write operations and Wait-Free Population Oblivious read operations, which we named the Left-Right technique. This technique requires using two instances of a given resource, and can be used on any data structure, allowing concurrent access to it, similar to a Reader-Writer lock, but in a non-blocking manner for reads, and it does not need an automatic Garbage Collector (GC).

To allow concurrent read and write access to a data structure or object written for single threaded execution, a common approach is to use a Reader-Writer lock. Another alternative is Copy-On-Write (COW), which consists of replacing the instance by a copy of that instance with the applied modification. Peterson [3] has presented several solutions to the *Concurrent Reading While Writing* problem. One of them guarantees wait-free progress for both reads and writes, allowing Readers and Writer to access simultaneously *buff1* and *buff2* instances, which compromises memory reclamation.

The Left-Right is a concurrency control technique with two identical objects or data structures, that allows an unlimited number of threads (Readers) to access one instance in read-only mode, while a single thread (Writer) modifies the other instance. The Writer starts by working on the right-side instance (`rightInst`) while the Readers read the left-side instance (`leftInst`), and once the Writer completes the modification, the two instances are *switched* and new Readers will read from the `rightInst`. The Writer will wait for all the Readers still running on the `leftInst` instance to finish, and then repeat the modification on the `leftInst`, leaving both instances up-to-date. It us up to the Writer to ensure that Readers are always running on the data structure that is currently *not* being modified. The synchronization between Writers is achieved with an exclusive lock that is used to protect write-access (`writersMutex`).

The components ensuring a Writer performs in exclusivity are the following: a `leftRight` variable which is toggled by the Writer between LEFT and RIGHT, that indicates which instance the Readers should go into; a `versionIndex` variable, which is modified by the Writer, functioning like a *timestamp*; and a Reader's indicator [1], `readIndic`, for each Reader to *publish* the `versionIndex` it read. The `readIndic` is a data structure that allows Readers to publish their state through `arrive()` and `depart()`, and for the Writer to determine the presence

© Springer-Verlag Berlin Heidelberg 2015
Y. Moses (Ed.): DISC 2015, LNCS 9363, pp. 663–664, 2015.
DOI: 10.1007/978-3-662-48653-5

of ongoing Readers with `isEmpty()`. A simple implementation of the `readIndic` is to use two single atomic synchronized counters, one per `versionIndex`.

```
const int arrive(void) {
    int vi = _versionIndex.load();
    _readIndic[vi]->arrive();
    return vi;
}


void depart(const int vi) {
    _readIndic[vi]->depart();
}


void toggleVersionAndWait(void)
{
    int vi = _versionIndex.load();
    int p = vi & 0x1;
    int n = (vi+1) & 0x1;
    while(!_readIndic[n]->isEmpty())
    {
        this_thread::yield();
    }
    _versionIndex.store(n);
    while(!_readIndic[p]->isEmpty())
    {
        this_thread::yield();
    }
}
```

```
template<typename R, typename A>
R applyRead(A& arg1,
            function<R(T*,A)>& f) {
    const int vi = arrive();
    T* inst = _leftRight.load() == LEFT
        ? _leftInst : _rightInst;
    R ret = f(inst, arg1);
    depart(vi);
    return ret;
}


template<typename R, typename A>
R applyMut(A& arg1,
           function<R(T*,A)>& f) {
    lock_guard<mutex> m(_writersMutex);
    if (_leftRight.load() == LEFT) {
        f(_rightInst, arg1);
        _leftRight.store(RIGHT);
        toggleVersionAndWait();
        return f(_leftInst, arg1);
    } else {
        f(_leftInst, arg1);
        _leftRight.store(LEFT);
        toggleVersionAndWait();
        return f(_rightInst, arg1);
    }
}
```

As shown on the C++ code above, the Writer calling `applyMut()` will acquire the lock on `writersMutex` to guarantee mutual exclusivity between Writers, and proceed to modify the instance opposite to the one currently referenced by `leftRight`. Then, it toggles the `leftRight`, making the modification visible to new Readers. The final step is to modify the other instance, but first, it is necessary to guarantee that no Reader is accessing the intance, and this guarantee is provided by `toggleVersionAndWait()`. The method `applyRead()` shown above has no loops, and always executes in a constant number of steps, thus ensuring that read operations are wait-free population oblivious.

In summary, read operations can run concurrently with all operations, and will *never have to wait* for a Writer or for other Readers. Moreover, new Readers have no impact on the Writer's progress, making its progress starvation free relative to Readers. In addition, Writers will be starvation free if a starvation free `writersMutex` lock is used. We believe that due to its performance, low latency, and flexibility of usage, in practice, this technique can be used to wrap any data structure or object, as an alternative to other synchronization techniques, such as Reader-Writer locks, or COW with RCU [2] memory reclamation.

# References

1. Lev, Y., Luchangco, V., Olszewski, M.: Scalable reader-writer locks. In: Proceedings of the Twenty-First Annual Symposium on Parallelism in Algorithms and Architectures, pp. 101–110. ACM (2009)
2. McKenney, P.E., Walpole, J.: What is rcu, fundamentally? (2007)
3. Peterson, G.L.: Concurrent reading while writing. ACM Transactions on Programming Languages and Systems (TOPLAS) 5(1), 46–55 (1983)

# Brief Announcement: Tight Space Bounds for Memoryless Anonymous Consensus

Leqi Zhu

University of Toronto, Toronto, ON M5S 3G4, Canada
lezhu@cs.toronto.edu

**Introduction.** Tight $\Theta(n^2)$ bounds are known for the total step complexity of randomized algorithms for $n$-process consensus from registers [1]. However, there is a large gap between the best known space lower bound of $\Omega(\sqrt{n})$ registers [2] and the $\Theta(n)$ space complexity of the best existing algorithms. We prove matching upper and lower bounds of $n$ for the space complexity of nondeterministic solo-terminating consensus in a restricted computational model. Specifically, we consider an asynchronous system with $n$ anonymous processes, which communicate through an $m$-component multi-writer snapshot. Each process alternately performs SCAN and UPDATE. The location and value of each UPDATE can depend only on the result of the preceding SCAN by the same process. The only exception is the first UPDATE by each process, which can also depend on its input. We call algorithms designed for this model *memoryless*.

**Lower Bound.** Let $C$ be any configuration of an $n$-process memoryless anonymous consensus algorithm. A process is *free* in $C$ if it has already taken at least one step and is poised to perform a SCAN in $C$. Since processes are anonymous and memoryless, an adversary can cause any two free processes in $C$ to behave identically if they both see the same result on their next SCAN. We say $C$ is *solo v-deciding for free processes* if there is a solo execution by a free process starting from $C$ that decides $v$. We say $C$ is $(P, q)$-*bivalent* if $P$ is a set of processes covering distinct components and $q \notin P$ is a process covering a component such that $C\beta_P$ is solo $v$-deciding for free processes and $C\beta_q$ is solo $\bar{v}$-deciding for free processes, for some $v \in \{0, 1\}$, where $\beta_q$ is an UPDATE by $q$ and $\beta_P$ consists of one UPDATE by each process in $P$.

Given a $(Z \cup \{p\}, q)$-bivalent configuration $C$, consider the longest prefix $\alpha'$ of $q$'s solo terminating execution $\alpha$ from $C$ such that $C\alpha'\beta_{Z \cup \{p\}}$ is solo $v$-deciding for free processes. The next step $\delta$ by $q$ in $\alpha$ after $\alpha'$ must be an UPDATE to a component not covered by $Z \cup \{p\}$. Running $p$ from $C\alpha'\beta_P$ until it is about to perform an UPDATE yields a $(\{p\}, q)$-bivalent configuration $C'$. Since $C'$ is also $(\{q\}, p)$-bivalent, the same argument implies that there is an execution from $C'$ in which $q$ takes at least two steps, such that the resulting configuration $C''$ is $(\{q\}, p)$-bivalent and every process in $Z$ is free. Note that at least $|Z| + 2$ different components were updated in the execution from $C$ to $C''$ (via $\delta$ and $\beta_{Z \cup \{p\}}$).

I would like to thank my advisor, Dr. Faith Ellen, and David Solymosi. This work was supported by the Natural Sciences and Engineering Council of Canada.

Y. Moses (Ed.): DISC 2015, LNCS 9363, pp. 665–666, 2015.
DOI: 10.1007/978-3-662-48653-5

We show that, if $C$ is $(\{p\}, q)$-bivalent and $Z$ is a set of free processes in $C$, there is an execution $\gamma$ from $C$ in which $p$ and $q$ take at least two steps, such that $C\gamma$ is $(Z \cup \{p\}, q)$-bivalent. The proof is by induction on $|Z|$. The base case, when $Z = \emptyset$, holds by the previous paragraph. Fix any $Z' \subset Z$ with $|Z'| = |Z| - 1$. By induction, there is an execution $\gamma_1$ in which $p$ and $q$ take at least two steps, such that $C\gamma_1$ is $(Z' \cup \{p\}, q)$-bivalent. By the preceding paragraph, there is an execution $\gamma_2$ from $C\gamma_1$ in which at least $|Z'| + 2$ components have been updated and $p$ and $q$ have taken at least 2 steps, such that $C\gamma_1\gamma_2$ is $(\{p\}, q)$-bivalent and each process in $Z'$ is free in $C\gamma_1\gamma_2$. By induction, there is an execution $\gamma_3$ such that $C\gamma_1\gamma_2\gamma_3$ is $(Z' \cup \{p\}, q)$-bivalent. Among the components updated in $\gamma_2\gamma_3$, there is at least one component $j$ which is not covered by $Z' \cup \{p\}$ in $C\gamma_1\gamma_2\gamma_3$. Let $z' \in Z' \cup \{p, q\}$ be the last process to UPDATE component $j$ prior to $C\gamma_1\gamma_2\gamma_3$, and let $\sigma'$ be the SCAN by $z'$ before this UPDATE. Note that every process in $Z'$ is free immediately before $\sigma'$. Modifying the execution $\gamma_1\gamma_2\gamma_3$ to let the remaining free process in $Z - Z'$ perform its SCAN immediately after $\sigma'$ gives a $(Z \cup \{p\}, q)$-bivalent configuration.

To obtain the lower bound, construct a $(\{p\}, q)$-bivalent configuration having a set $Z$ of $n-2$ free processes. Apply the previous argument to get a $(Z \cup \{p\}, q)$-bivalent configuration. Running $q$ until it is about to UPDATE a component not covered by $Z \cup \{p\}$ gives a configuration with $n$ components covered. This proof method, which uses induction on the number of free processes to build larger coverings, seems applicable in the general case. In fact, we recently used this method to give a different, much simpler proof of the $\Omega(\sqrt{n})$ lower bound in [2].

**Upper Bound.** We describe an $n$-process memoryless anonymous obstruction-free consensus algorithm using an $n$-component multi-writer snapshot, matching the lower bound. The algorithm can also be made randomized wait-free by [3].

Intuitively, 0 and 1 are competing to complete *laps*. If $v$ gets a substantial lead on $\overline{v}$, then $v$ is decided. Initially, each component contains $(0, 0)$. If a process with input $x$ sees this initial state in a SCAN, it updates component 1 with $(\overline{x}, x)$. Otherwise, it determines the laps, $\ell_0$ and $\ell_1$, of 0 and 1 by finding the largest values in the first and second entries of the components returned by its SCAN. If some component is not $(\ell_0, \ell_1)$, then it updates the first such component with $(\ell_0, \ell_1)$. So, suppose all components are the same. If value $v$ is ahead of value $\overline{v}$ by at least 2 laps, for some $v \in \{0, 1\}$, then it decides $v$. If not, it increments the larger of $\ell_0$ and $\ell_1$ (breaking ties in favour of $\ell_0$) and updates component 1 with $(\ell_0, \ell_1)$. This is repeated until the process decides.

# References

1. Attiya, H., Censor, K.: Tight bounds for asynchronous randomized consensus. J. ACM **55**(5), 20 (2008)
2. Fich, F., Herlihy, M., Shavit, N.: On the space complexity of randomized synchronization. J. ACM **45**(5), 843–862 (1998)
3. Giakkoupis, G., Helmi, M., Higham, L., Woelfel, P.: An $O(\sqrt{n})$ space bound for obstruction-free leader election. In: Afek, Y. (ed.) DISC 2013. LNCS, vol. 8205, pp. 46–60. Springer, Heidelberg (2013)

# Brief Announcement: On the Uncontended Complexity of Anonymous Consensus

Claire Capdevielle[1], Colette Johnen[1], Petr Kuznetsov[2], and Alessia Milani[1]

[1] Univ. Bordeaux, LaBRI, UMR 5800, F-33400 Talence, France
[2] Télécom ParisTech

Consensus is one of the central distributed abstractions. By enabling a collection of processes to agree on one of the values they propose, consensus can be used to implement any generic replicated service in a consistent and fault-tolerant way. Therefore, complexity of consensus implementations has become one of the most important topics in the theory of distributed computing.

It is known that consensus cannot be solved in an asynchronous read-write shared memory system in a deterministic and fault-tolerant way. One way to circumvent this impossibility is to only guarantee progress (using reads and writes) in executions meeting certain conditions, e.g., in the absence of *contention*. Alternatively, a process is guaranteed to decide in the *wait-free* manner, but stronger (and more expensive) synchronization primitives, such as *compare-and-swap*, can be applied in the presence of contention.

We are interested in consensus algorithms in which a *propose* operation is allowed to apply primitives other than reads and writes on the base objects only in the presence of *interval contention*, i.e., when another *propose* operation is concurrently active. Such algorithms are called *interval-solo-fast*.

Ideally, interval-solo-fast algorithms should have an optimized behavior in *uncontended* executions. It appears therefore natural to explore the uncontended complexity of consensus algorithms: how many memory operations (reads and writes) can be performed and how many distinct memory locations can be accessed in the absence of interval contention?

In general, interval-solo-fast consensus can be solved with only *constant* uncontended complexity. We therefore restrict our study to *anonymous* consensus algorithms, i.e., algorithms not using process identifiers and, thus, programming all processes identically. Besides intellectual curiosity, practical reasons to study anonymous algorithms in the shared memory model are discussed in [GR07].

**Our results.** On the lower-bound side, we show that any anonymous interval-solo-fast consensus algorithm exhibits non-trivial uncontended complexity that depends on $n$, the number of processes, and $m$, where $m$ is the size of the set of input values that can be proposed. More precisely, we show that, in the worst case, a *propose* operation running *solo*, i.e., without any other process

Partially supported by the ANR project DISPLEXITY (ANR-11-BS02-014). This study has been carried out in the frame of the Investments for the future Programme IdEx Bordeaux- CPU (ANR-10-IDEX-03-02). The third author was supported by the Agence Nationale de la Recherche, under grant agreement N ANR-14-CE35-0010-01, project DISCMAT.

Y. Moses (Ed.): DISC 2015, LNCS 9363, pp. 667–668, 2015.
DOI: 10.1007/978-3-662-48653-5

invoking *propose*, must write to $\Omega(\min(\sqrt{n}, \log m / \log \log m))$ distinct memory locations. This metrics, called *solo-write complexity*, is upper-bounded by *step complexity* of the algorithm, i.e., the worst-case number of all primitives applied by an individual *propose* operation. In the special case of *input-oblivious* algorithms, where the sequence of memory locations written in a solo execution does not depend on the input value, we derive a stronger lower bound of $\Omega(\sqrt{n})$ on solo-write complexity. Our proof only requires the algorithm to ensure that operations terminate in solo executions, so the lower bounds also hold for *abortable* and *obstruction-free* consensus implementations.

On the positive side, we show that our lower bound is tight. Our matching consensus algorithm is based on our novel *value-splitter* abstraction, extending the classical *splitter* mechanism, interesting in its own right. Informally, a value-splitter exports a single operation *split* that takes a value in a value set $V$ as a parameter and returns a boolean response so that (1) if a *split* operation completes before any other *split* operation starts, then it returns *true*, and (2) all *split* operations that return *true* were invoked with the same parameter value.

Our consensus algorithm adapts the classical splitter-based algorithm [LMS03] to the new value-splitter abstraction. We have implemented an anonymous and input-oblivious value-splitter that exhibits $O(\sqrt{n})$ space and solo-write complexity. Also we have slightly modified the *weak conflict detector* proposed in [AE14], to implement a regular (not input-oblivious) value-splitter exhibiting space and step complexity of $O(\log m / \log \log m)$. These two value-splitter read-write implementations combined with our consensus algorithm provide the matching upper bound.

**Table 1.** Space and solo-write complexity for anonymous interval-solo-fast consensus

| Input-oblivious | Not input-oblivious | | |
|---|---|---|---|
| $\Omega(\sqrt{n})$ | $\Omega(\min(\sqrt{n}, \frac{\log m}{\log \log m}))$ | | |
| $O(\sqrt{n})$ | if $\sqrt{n} \leq \frac{\log m}{\log \log m}$, $O(\sqrt{n})$ | if $\sqrt{n} \geq \frac{\log m}{\log \log m}$, $O(\frac{\log m}{\log \log m})$ | [LMS03, AE14] |

Our results are summarized in Table 42 and detailed in [? ]. Overall, they imply the first nontrivial *tight* lower bound on the space complexity for consensus known so far. They also show that there is an inherent gap between anonymous and non-anonymous consensus algorithms.

# References

[AE14]  Aspnes, J., Ellen, F.: Tight bounds for adopt-commit objects. Theory of Computing Systems **55**(3), 451–474 (2014)

[CJKM]  Capdevielle, C., Johnen, C., Kuznetsov, P., Milani, A.: On the uncontended complexity of anonymous consensus. https://hal.archives-ouvertes.fr/hal-01180864/document

[GR07]  Guerraoui, R., Ruppert, E.: Anonymous and fault-tolerant shared-memory computing. Distributed Computing **20**(3), 165–177 (2007)

[LMS03]  Luchangco, V., Moir, M., Shavit, N.: On the uncontended complexity of consensus. In: Fich, F.E. (ed.) DISC 2003. LNCS, vol. 2848, pp. 45–59. Springer, Heidelberg (2003)

# Brief Announcement: Anonymous Obstruction-free $(n, k)$-Set Agreement with $n - k + 1$ Atomic Read/Write Registers

Zohir Bouzid[1], Michel Raynal[1,2], and Pierre Sutra[3]

[1] IRISA, Université de Rennes, 35042 Rennes, France
[2] Institut Universitaire de France
[3] University of Neuchâtel, Switzerland

**Abstract.** This paper presents an obstruction-free solution to the $(n, k)$-set agreement problem in an asynchronous anonymous read/write system using solely $(n - k + 1)$ registers. We then extend this algorithm into *(i)* a space-optimal solution for the repeated version of $(n, k)$-set agreement, and *(ii)* an $x$-obstruction-free solution using $(n - k + x)$ atomic registers (with $1 \leq x \leq k < n$).

## 1 Context and Motivation

Due to failures, concurrent processes have to deal not only with finite asynchrony, i.e., arbitrary process speed, but also with infinite asynchrony. In this context, mutex-based synchronization is useless, and pioneering works in *fault-tolerant* distributed computing have instead promoted the design of concurrent algorithms.

**A first challenge: multi-writer registers.** When processes communicate with *Single-Writer Multi-Reader* (SWMR) atomic registers, a concurrent algorithm usually associates each process to a register. If now processes communicate with *Multi-Writer Multi-Reader* (MWMR) atomic registers, as any process can write any register, the previous association is no longer granted for free. To still benefit from existing SWMR registers-based solutions, we can emulate SWMR registers on top of MWMR registers. In a system of $n$ processes, $n$ MWMR registers are needed for the simulation to be non-blocking [4]. Hence, if the underlying system provides less than $n$ MWMR registers, the simulation approach is irrelevant and novel techniques must be found.

**A second challenge: anonymity.** Some algorithms based on MWMR registers require processes to write control values that include their identities. On the contrary, in an *anonymous* system, processes have no identity, the same code, and the same initialization of their local variables. Hence, they are in a strong sense identical. In this context, the core question that interests us is the following: "Is it possible to solve a given problem with MWMR registers and anonymous processes, and if the answer is "yes", how many registers do we need ?"

**Consensus and $k$-set agreement.** This paper focuses on the $k$-set agreement problem in a system of $n$ processes. This problem introduced in [3], and denoted $(n, k)$-set agreement in the following, is a generalization of consensus, which corresponds to the case where $k = 1$. Assuming that each participating

© Springer-Verlag Berlin Heidelberg 2015
Y. Moses (Ed.): DISC 2015, LNCS 9363, pp. 669–670, 2015.
DOI: 10.1007/978-3-662-48653-5

process proposes a value, every non-faulty process must decide a value that was proposed by some process, and at most $k$ different values can be decided.

**Impossibility results and the case of obstruction-freedom.** When $k$ or more processes may fail, there is no deterministic wait-free read/write solution to $(n, k)$-set agreement [1]. To sidestep this impossibility, we consider a weak progress property, namely *obstruction-freedom*. For $(n, k)$-set agreement, this property states that a process decides only if it executes solo during a "long enough" period of time. The notion of $x$-obstruction-freedom [7] generalizes this idea to any group of at most $x$ processes.

## 2   Contributions of the Paper

This paper details an obstruction-free solution to the $(n, k)$-set agreement problem in an asynchronous anonymous read/write system where any number of processes may crash. Our algorithm makes use of $(n - k + 1)$ MWMR registers, i.e., exactly $n$ registers for consensus. In anonymous systems, $(n, k)$-set agreement requires $\Omega(\sqrt{\frac{n}{k} - 2})$ MWMR registers [6]. On another hand, the best obstruction-free $(n, k)$-set agreement algorithm known so far requires $2(n-k)+1$ registers [5]. Hence, our algorithm provides a gain of $(n - k)$ MWMR registers.

In the *repeated* version of the $(n, k)$-set agreement problem, processes participate in a sequence of $(n, k)$-set agreement instances. It was recently proved [6] that $(n - k + 1)$ atomic registers are necessary to solve repeated $(n, k)$-set agreement. This paper shows that a simple modification of our base construction solves *repeated* $(n, k)$-set agreement without additional atomic registers, being consequently optimal.

Our base algorithm, its extension to solve repeated $(n, k)$-set agreement, as well as an $x$-obstruction-free variation that uses $n - k + x$ MWMR registers are all detailed in our companion technical report [2].

## References

1. Borowsky, E., Gafni, E.: Generalized FLP impossibility result for $t$-resilient asynchronous computations. In: STOC 1993 (1993)
2. Bouzid, Z., Raynal, M., Sutra, P.: Anonymous Obstruction-free $(n, k)$-Set Agreement with $n - k + 1$ Atomic Read/Write Registers. RR 2027, Univerité de Rennes 1 (2015)
3. Chaudhuri, S.: More Choices Allow More Faults: Set Consensus Problems in Totally Asynchronous Systems. Information and Computation **105**, 132–158 (1993)
4. Delporte-Gallet, C., Fauconnier, H., Gafni, E., Lamport, L.: Adaptive register allocation with a linear number of registers. In: Afek, Y. (ed.) DISC 2013. LNCS, vol. 8205, pp. 269–283. Springer, Heidelberg (2013)
5. Delporte-Gallet, C., Fauconnier, H., Gafni, E., Rajsbaum, S.: Blackart: obstruction-free k-set agreement with |MWMR registers| < |proccesses|. In: Gramoli, V., Guerraoui, R. (eds.) NETYS 2013. LNCS, vol. 7853, pp. 28–41. Springer, Heidelberg (2013)
6. Delporte, C., Fauconnier, H., Kuznetsov, P., Ruppert, E.: On the space complexity of set agreement. In: PODC 2015 (2015)
7. Taubenfeld, G.: Contention-sensitive data structures and algorithms. In: Keidar, I. (ed.) DISC 2009. LNCS, vol. 5805, pp. 157–171. Springer, Heidelberg (2009)

# Brief Announcement: Faster Data Structures in Transactional Memory Using Three Paths

Trevor Brown

University of Toronto, Toronto, Ontario, Canada

With the introduction of Intel's restricted hardware transactional memory (HTM) in commodity hardware, the transactional memory abstraction has finally become practical to use. Transactional memory allows a programmer to easily implement safe concurrent code by specifying that certain blocks of code should be executed atomically. However, Intel's HTM implementation does not offer any progress guarantees. Even in a single threaded system, a transaction can repeatedly fail for complex reasons. Consequently, any code that uses HTM must also provide a non-transactional fallback path to be executed if a transaction fails. Since the primary goal of HTM is to simplify the task of writing concurrent code, a typical fallback path simply acquires a global lock, and then runs the same code as the transaction. This is essentially transactional lock elision (TLE). Changes made by a process on the fallback path are not atomic, so transactions that run concurrently with a process on the fallback path may see inconsistent state. Thus, at the beginning of each transaction, a process reads the state of the global lock and aborts the transaction if it is held.

Despite its widespread use, there are many problems with this fallback path. If transactions abort infrequently, then processes rarely execute on the fallback path. However, once one process begins executing on the fallback path, all concurrent transactions will abort, and processes on the fast path will cascade onto the fallback path. This has been called the *lemming effect*, from the myth that lemmings will leap from cliffs in large numbers.

One simple way to mitigate the lemming effect is to retry aborted transactions a few times, waiting between retries for the fallback path to become empty. For some common workloads (e.g., range queries and updates on an ordered set implemented with a binary search tree), some operation is nearly always on the fallback path, so concurrency is very limited and performance is poor. Thus, waiting for the fallback path to become empty is not always a good solution.

A more sophisticated solution is to design transactions so they can commit even if processes are executing on the fallback path. One way to do this is to start with a hand-crafted fallback path that uses fine-grained synchronization, and obtain a fast path by wrapping each operation in a transaction (and then optimizing the resulting sequential code). This technique was explored by Liu et al. [1]. To support concurrency between the two paths, the fast path must read and update the meta-data used by the fallback path to synchronize processes. Unfortunately, the overhead of manipulating meta-data on the fast path can eliminate much or all of the performance benefit of HTM.

This work was supported by NSERC. I thank my advisor Faith Ellen for her helpful comments on this work. Some experiments were performed while at Oracle Labs.

© Springer-Verlag Berlin Heidelberg 2015
Y. Moses (Ed.): DISC 2015, LNCS 9363, pp. 671–672, 2015.
DOI: 10.1007/978-3-662-48653-5

To overcome this, we introduce a novel approach for obtaining faster algorithms by using three execution paths: an HTM-based fast path, an HTM-based middle path and a non-transactional fallback path. Our approach eliminates the lemming effect without imposing any overhead on the fast path. Each operation

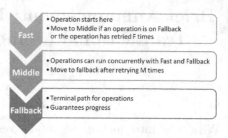

begins on the fast path, and moves to the middle path after it retries $F$ times. An operation on the middle path moves to the fallback path after retrying $M$ times on the middle path. The fast path does not manipulate any synchronization metadata used by the fallback path, so operations on the fast path and fallback path cannot run concurrently. Thus, whenever an operation is on the fallback path, all operations on the fast path move to the middle path. The middle path manipulates the synchronization meta-data used by the fallback path, so operations on the middle path and fallback path can run concurrently. Operations on the middle path can also run concurrently with operations on the fast path. The lemming effect does not occur, since an operation does not have to move to the fallback path simply because another operation is on the fallback path. Since processes on the fast path do not run concurrently with processes on the fallback path, the fallback path does not impose any overhead on the fast path.

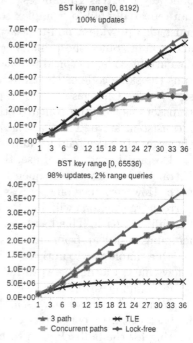

Experiments were performed on a 36-core Intel system, comparing the performance of a binary search tree with several two- and three-path algorithms, and different retry strategies, over a variety of workloads. In the 100%

update workload, the three-path algorithm matches the performance of TLE and significantly outperforms the other algorithms. In the workload with range queries, TLE succumbs to the lemming effect and performs very poorly. These results suggest that three-path algorithms can be used to obtain the full performance benefit of HTM while robustly avoiding the lemming effect.

## References

1. Liu, Y., Zhou, T., Spear, M.: Transactional acceleration of concurrent data structures. In: Proceedings of the 27th ACM on Symposium on Parallelism in Algorithms and Architectures, SPAA 2015, New York, NY, USA, pp. 244–253. ACM (2015)

# Brief Announcement: Space Bounds for Reliable Multi-Writer Data Store
## Inherent Cost of Read/Write Primitives

Gregory Chockler[1], Dan Dobre[2],
Alexander Shraer[3], and Alexander Spiegelman[4]

[1] Royal Holloway, University of London
Gregory.Chockler@rhul.ac.uk
[2] European Patent Office
dan@dobre.net
[3] Google, Inc.
shralex@google.com
[4] Technion
sashas@tx.technion.ac.il

## 1 Introduction

Reliable storage emulations from fault-prone components have established themselves as an algorithmic foundation of modern storage services and applications. Most existing reliable storage emulations are built from storage services supporting *custom-built* read-modify-write (RMW) primitives (e.g., [2]). Since such primitives are not typically available with pre-existing or off-the-shelf components (such as cloud storage services or network-attached disks), it is natural to ask if they are indeed essential for efficient storage emulations.

In this paper, we answer this question in the affirmative. We prove that the number of registers required to emulate a reliable multi-writer register for $k$ clients from a collection of multi-writer multi-reader (MWMR) atomic base registers hosted on crash-prone servers requires at least $kf$ registers where $f$ is the maximum number of tolerated server failures. We further show that this bound cannot be circumvented even in the failure-free runs where emulated register operations do not execute concurrently, which implies that no such algorithm can be adaptive to point contention.

Given the base registers are stored on servers, we also address the number of servers required to support the emulation under assumption that the number of registers per server is bounded by a known constant $m$. We show that the number of servers required to support $k$ clients exceeds the requisite $kf/m$ servers stipulated by our space bound by at least $f + 1$ additional servers.

Our bounds apply to any reliable implementations of a multi-writer register, which are at least *safe* [8], and *solo-terminating*. They complement and tighten the lower bounds of [1], and shed light onto inherent costs of the existing constructions of reliable services out of unreliable MWMR registers [4].

On a positive side, we show that Compare-and-Swap (CAS) primitives, which readily available with many popular cloud data stores (such as Amazon DynamoDB) can be used to emulate a reliable multi-writer atomic register with constant storage and adaptive time complexity.

This work was partially supported by Royal Society International Exchanges grant.

Y. Moses (Ed.): DISC 2015, LNCS 9363, pp. 673–674, 2015.
DOI: 10.1007/978-3-662-48653-5

# 2 Overview of the Results

We assume an asynchronous distributed system where clients coordinate by accessing shared objects stored on a collection of servers. Both clients and servers can fail by crashing. We study *space complexity* of storage services that mask the client and server failures by emulating a single reliable MWMR register. Our reliability requirement is $f$-*tolerance*, that is, the register must remain correct as long as at most $f$ servers and any number of clients crash.

**Lower Bounds** Below, we give statements of our space lower bounds for $f$-tolerant register emulations where the objects stored on servers are MWMR atomic wait-free registers. The proofs can be found in [5].

**Theorem 1.** *For any $k \geq 0$, $f \geq 0$, there is no $f$-tolerant algorithm emulating a multi-writer safe [8] solo-terminating register for $k$ clients that uses less than $kf$ base registers in all failure-free runs $r$ such that no two emulated register operations execute concurrently in $r$.*

**Theorem 2.** *For any $f > 0$, there is no $f$-tolerant algorithm that emulates a multi-writer safe solo-terminating register such that the number of registers used by the emulation is adaptive to point contention [3].*

**Theorem 3.** *For any $m > 0$, $\ell > 0$, and $f \geq 0$, there is no $f$-tolerant algorithm emulating a multi-writer safe solo-terminating register register for $k \geq \ell m$ clients using less than $\ell f + f + 1$ servers if each server can store at most $m$ registers.*

**Upper Bound** In [5], we show that a single CAS object per server is sufficient to implement an $f$-tolerant wait-free atomic MWMR register for any number of clients whose time complexity is adaptive to point contention. Our result is derived in a modular fashion by first obtaining the RMW primitive required by the multi-writer ABD emulation (MW-ABD) of [7] from a sinlge CAS, and then plugging the resulting primitive into MW-ABD.

# References

1. Aguilera, M., Englert, B., Gafni, E.: On using network attached disks as shared memory. In: PODC 2003 (2003)
2. Attiya, H., Bar-Noy, A., Dolev, D.: Sharing Memory Robustly in Message-Passing Systems. J. ACM **42**(1)
3. Attila, H., Fouren, A.: Algorithms Adapting to Point Contention. J. ACM **50**(4)
4. Basescu, C., Cachin, C., Eyal, I., Haas, R., Sorniotti, A., Vukolic, M., Zachevsky, I.: Robust data sharing with key-value stores. In: DSN 2012 (2012)
5. Chockler, G., Dobre, D., Shraer, A., Spiegelman, A.: Space Bounds for Reliable Multi-Writer Data Store: Inherent Cost of Read/Write Primitives (2015). https://pure.royalholloway.ac.uk/portal/files/25314522/main.pdf
6. Gafni, E., Lamport, L.: Disk Paxos. Distributed Computing **16**(1)
7. Gilbert, S., Lynch, N.A., Shvartsman, A.A.: Rambo: A Robust, Reconfigurable Atomic Memory Service for Dynamic Networks. Distributed Computing **23**(4)
8. Shao, C., Pierce, E., Welch, J.L.: Multi-writer consistency conditions for shared memory objects. In: Fich, F.E. (ed.) DISC 2003. LNCS, vol. 2848, pp. 106–120. Springer, Heidelberg (2003)

# DISC 2015 Special Poster Session List

1. The Entropy of a Distributed Computing Schedule.
   *Joffroy Beauquier, Blanchard Peva, Janna Burman and Rachid Guerraoui*

2. Local Approximation of Independent Sets and Coloring.
   *Marijke Bodlaender, Magnus M. Halldorsson and Christian Konrad*

3. Atomic Snapshots with Small Registers.
   *Tian Chen, Faith Ellen, Yuanhao Wei and Leqi Zhu*

4. Large Cuts with Local Algorithms on Triangle-Free Graphs.
   *Juho Hirvonen, Joel Rybicki, Stefan Schmid and Jukka Suomela*

5. Approximation of Distances and Shortest Paths in the Broadcast Congest Clique.
   *Stephan Holzer and Nathan Pinsker*

6. Adaptive Broadcast by Fault-Local Self-Stabilizing Spanning Tree Switching.
   *Sushanta Karmakar*

7. Fast MST Computation in Congested Clique with Near-Optimal Message Complexity.
   *Sriram V. Pemmaraju and Vivek B. Sardeshmukh*

8. On Liveness of Dynamic Storage with Infinitely Many Reconfigurations.
   *Alexander Spiegelman and Idit Keidar*

© Springer-Verlag Berlin Heidelberg 2015
Y. Moses (Ed.): DISC 2015, LNCS 9363, p. 675, 2015.
DOI: 10.1007/978-3-662-48653-5

# Author Index

Printed in the United States
By Bookmasters